THE
REVELATION
TO JOHN

*A Commentary on the
Greek Text of the Apocalypse*

STEPHEN S. SMALLEY

InterVarsity Press
Downers Grove, Illinois

InterVarsity Press, USA
P.O. Box 1400, Downers Grove, IL 60515-1426
Internet: www.ivpress.com
Email: mail@ivpress.com

InterVarsity Press®, USA, is the book-publishing division of InterVarsity Christian Fellowship/USA®, a student movement active on campus at hundreds of universities, colleges and schools of nursing in the United States of America, and a member movement of the International Fellowship of Evangelical Students. For information about local and regional activities, write Public Relations Dept., InterVarsity Christian Fellowship/USA, 6400 Schroeder Rd., P.O. Box 7895, Madison, WI 53707-7895, or visit the IVCF website at <www.intervarsity.org>.

Design: Cindy Kiple

Cover Images: Giraudon/Art Resource, NY

USA ISBN 0-8308-2800-1

Printed in Great Britain ∞

Library of Congress Cataloging-in-Publication Data

A catalog record for this book is available from the Library of Congress.

P	*18*	*17*	*16*	*15*	*14*	*13*	*12*	*11*	*10*	*9*	*8*	*7*	*6*	*5*	*4*	*3*	*2*	*1*
Y	*18*	*17*	*16*	*15*	*14*	*13*	*12*	*11*	*10*	*09*	*08*	*07*	*06*	*05*				

Contents

Foreword   ix
Abbreviations   xi
  1 *General*   xi
  2 *Ancient Writers*   xv
  3 *Dead Sea Scrolls*   xvi

Introduction   **1**
    The Text   1
  1 The Approach   2
  2 The Origin   2
  3 The Situation   3
  4 The Johannine Community and Its Literature   4
    A Further Aim   5
  5 The Character   6
    Revelation as Prophecy   7
  6 The Use of the Old Testament   8
  7 The Testimony   10
    Balance in John's Testimony   11
  8 The Symbolism   13
  9 The Interpretation   15
 10 The Relevance   16
    Christ   16
    Time   16
    Church   17
    World   17
    Power   18
    Resurrection   18
 11 The Structure   19
 12 The Drama   21

THE REVELATION TO JOHN

Prologue: The Oracle Is Disclosed (1.1–8)   **25**
Translation   25
Text   25
Literary Setting   26

Comment 27
  Superscription: The Revelation to John (1.1–3) 27
    Excursus: Angels in Revelation 28
  Salutation and Doxology (1.4–8) 31
Theology 38

Act 1
CREATION, AND SALVATION THROUGH
JUDGEMENT (1.9—11.19)

Scene 1: Seven Oracles (1.9—3.22) **43**
Translation 43
Text 45
Literary Setting 46
  The Oracles to the Seven Churches 47
Comment 49
  Vision of the Son of Man (1.9–18) 49
  The Commission to Write (1.19–20) 56
  Letters to the Seven Churches (2.1—3.22) 59
  Ephesus (2.1–7) 59
    The Nicolaitans 62
  Smyrna (2.8–11) 64
  Pergamum (2.12–17) 67
  Thyatira (2.18–29) 71
  Sardis (3.1–6) 80
  Philadelphia (3.7–13) 86
  Laodicea (3.14–22) 95
Theology 104

Interval: Adoration in Heaven's Court: God and
His Christ (4.1—5.14) **106**
Translation 106
Text 107
Literary Setting 109
  Excursus: Graeco-Roman Drama and Revelation 109
Comment 113
Theology 141

Scene 2: Seven Seals (6.1–17) **143**
Translation 143
Text 143
Literary Setting 145
Comment 146
  Seals 1–4: The Four Horsemen (6.1–8) 146
    The Four Riders 151
  Seal 5: The Cry of the Martyrs (6.9–11) 156
    Excursus: Vengeance in the Apocalypse 160
  Seal 6: The Great Earthquake (6.12–17) 166
Theology 173

Interval: The Church Protected (7.1–17) 174
Translation 174
Text 175
Literary Setting 177
Comment 178*
    Excursus: The Identity of the 144,000 (7.4–8) 184
    Excursus: The Theology of Power in Revelation 194
Theology 201

Scene 3: Seven Trumpets (8.1—9.21) 203
Translation 203
Text 204
Literary Setting 209
Comment 211
  Seal 7: Silence in Heaven (8.1) 211
  Prelude: Censing of the Saints (8.2–6) 213
  Trumpets 1–4: Portents of the End (8.7–12) 218
  The Eagle's Warning (8.13) 224
  Trumpet 5 (First Woe): Locusts (9.1–12) 225
  Trumpet 6 (Second Woe): Fiendish Cavalry (9.13–21) 235
Theology 244

Interval: God's Sovereignty (10.1—11.19) 246
Translation 246
Text 247
Literary Setting 253
  (A) Revelation 10.1–11 254
  (B) Revelation 11.1–13 254
  (C) Revelation 11.14 255
  (D) Revelation 11.15–19 255
Comment 256
  The Angel from Heaven (10.1–11) 256
  Measuring the Temple (11.1–2) 269
  The Two Witnesses (11.3–14) 275
  Trumpet 7 (Third Woe): Redemption through Conflict (11.15–19) 288
Theology 295

Act 2
SALVATION THROUGH JUDGEMENT, AND NEW CREATION (12.1—22.17)

Scene 4: Seven Signs (12.1—14.20) 299
Translation 299
Text 301
Literary Setting 310
Comment 312
  Sign 1: The Woman (12.1–2) 312
    The Sources beneath Revelation 12 312
  Sign 2: The Huge Dragon (12.3–6) 316

Sign 3: War in Heaven (12.7–9)   321
A Song of Praise in Heaven (12.10–12)   326
Sign 4: War on Earth (12.13–18)   329
Sign 5: The Beast from the Sea (13.1–10)   335
Sign 6: The Beast from the Earth (13.11–18)   344
A Vision of the Redeemed (14.1–5)   353
Sign 7: Angelic Judgement (14.6–20)   360
Theology   378

Interval: A New Exodus (15.1–8)   **380**
Translation   380
Text   380
Literary Setting   382
Comment   382
Prologue (15.1)   382
An Exodus Hymn (15.2–4)   383
The Angelic Commission (15.5–8)   389
Theology   393

Scene 5: Seven Bowls (16.1–21)   **395**
Translation   395
Text   396
Literary Setting   398
Comment   399
Prelude: The Angelic Mission (16.1)   399
Bowls 1–3: Natural Disasters of Judgement (16.2–4)   400
Judgement Doxologies (16.5–7)   402
Bowls 4–7: The Final Battle Heralded (16.8–21)   404
Theology   416

Interval: The Fall of Babylon (17.1—18.24)   **418**
Translation   418
Text   420
Literary Setting   424
Comment   426
Introduction (17.1–2)   426
Vision of the Woman and the Scarlet Beast (17.3–6)   428
The Interpretation of the Vision (17.7–18)   433
Lament over Babylon and a Call to Rejoice (18.1–20)   442
Babylon Destroyed (18.21–24)   461
Theology   466

Scene 6: Seven Visions (19.1—20.15)   **468**
Translation   468
Text   469
Literary Setting   474
Comment   476
Introduction: Rejoicing in Heaven (19.1–5)   476
Vision 1: The Marriage Feast of the Lamb (19.6–10)   480
Vision 2: The Warrior-Messiah (19.11–16)   487
Vision 3: Antichrist Destroyed (19.17–21)   496

Vision 4: Satan Bound (20.1–3) 500
   Excursus: The Millennium in Revelation 502
Vision 5: A Millennial Reign (20.4–6) 505
Vision 6: Satan Destroyed (20.7–10) 511
Vision 7: Final Judgement (20.11–15) 515
Theology 520

Interval: Prelude to the Final Scene (21.1) **522**
Translation 522
Text 522
Literary Setting 522
Comment 523
   The New Creation 523
Theology 525

Scene 7: Seven Prophecies (21.2—22.17) **526**
Translation 526
Text 527
Literary Setting 532
   Revelation 21.2–8 533
   Revelation 22.6–9 534
   Revelation 22.10–17 534
Comment 534
   Prophecy 1: New Covenant (21.2–4) 534
   Prophecy 2: New Life (21.5–8) 539
   Prophecy 3: New Jerusalem (21.9–21) 544
   Prophecy 4: New Temple (21.22–27) 556
   Prophecy 5: New Relationship (22.1–5) 561
   Prophecy 6: New Advent (22.6–9) 566
   Prophecy 7: New Testimony (22.10–17) 570
Theology 578

Epilogue: The Oracle Is Complete (22.18–21) **581**
Translation 581
Text 581
Literary Setting 582
Comment 582
Theology 586

Bibliography 589
Indexes
   Greek Terms 598
   Scriptural References and Ancient Sources 600
   Subjects 621
   Modern Authors 631

Foreword

My engagement with the literature in the New Testament which bears the name of John has, over the years, resulted in studies on the Fourth Gospel (1978/1998) and Letters (1984), and included an introduction to the Revelation (1994). Although, with Bishop John Robinson, I have always felt reluctant to write full-scale commentaries ('you have to say something about every word of the text'), I allowed myself to be persuaded by Professor Ralph Martin to undertake the Word Biblical Commentary on 1, 2, 3 John. Having become immersed in the stimulating world of the Apocalypse through *Thunder and Love* (a title chosen by Susan, my late wife), I then felt drawn inexorably towards the challenge of treating Revelation in depth, and happily responded to an invitation from SPCK to write the present volume.

The canvas of John's Apocalypse is in many ways unusual, and often baffling. But I have always found the work itself fascinating; and I believe that the significance of its testimony is relevant for every age. The commentary which follows is therefore offered as one contribution to the scholarly study of Revelation, as well as an attempt to unravel its secrets for the benefit of members of the Christian Church in our own day.

Given the fairly recent appearance of two major commentaries on the Greek text of Revelation, written by David Aune and Gregory Beale, justification for a third may seem to be lacking. Nevertheless, two features in my approach are, I believe, distinctive. One is my perception of the nature of John's community, which caused the publication of the Johannine corpus, beginning with Revelation, in the first place. The other is my sensitivity to the literary shape of the Apocalypse, which I view as a creative and coherent drama. The conclusions about Revelation, which I reached earlier, have also been broadly sustained in this commentary; and my conviction has been reinforced that John's drama must be read and interpreted with close reference to his Gospel and Letters.

Commentators on such a complex composition as Revelation inevitably enter into the labours of earlier scholars in this field; and I gladly acknowledge my debt to so many of them, and not least to Aune and Beale. Diane Jackson, my Secretary when I was Dean of Chester, initiated the electronic version of the manuscript with great skill and patience, and has remained a cheerful source of strength since. The first steps in committing this work to writing were taken in St Deiniol's Library, Hawarden, where the Staff have been consistently welcoming and helpful; and I am grateful to them all. Jovian and Evelyn, my son and daughter, have provided technical assistance, as well as moral support, in this undertaking; and my brother-in-law, John Paterson, has been dazzlingly sleuthful in tracing some of the more obscure bibliographical and textual references. I pay tribute also to the Editors at SPCK, and in particular Simon Kingston, the Head of Publishing, for their unfailing courtesy and wise advice, and to many friends in all parts of the world, including members of the Church of Melanesia in the Solomon Islands, for their constant interest in this project, and their encouraging desire to see it completed.

Professor Charles F. D. Moule, as Lady Margaret's Professor of Divinity in the University of Cambridge, was foremost among my theological teachers. Charlie's comprehensive learning and Christian humility have always been a great inspiration to me personally, and I continue to value highly the way in which he has shown us all that scholarship and faith can belong together. This commentary is dedicated to him now, as a modest token of unlimited esteem and warm affection.

Stephen Smalley
The Feast of the Ascension, 2004

Abbreviations

1 General

1 Apoc. Jas.	*The (First) Apocalypse of James*
1 Clem.	*1 Clement*
2 Clem.	*2 Clement*
2 Apoc. Bar.	*2 (Syriac) Apocalypse of Baruch*
3 Apoc. Bar.	*3 (Greek) Apocalypse of Baruch*
3 (Slavonic) Apoc. Bar.	*3 (Slavonic) Apocalypse of Baruch*
AB	Anchor Bible Series
ABRL	Anchor Bible Reference Library Series
Acts Andrew	*Acts of Andrew*
Acts Pil.	*Acts of Pilate*
Acts Thom.	*Acts of Thomas*
AG	*A Greek-English Lexicon of the New Testament and Other Early Christian Literature*, ed. W. F. Arndt and F. W. Gingrich. Chicago: University of Chicago Press; and Cambridge: Cambridge University Press, 1957
ANTC	Abingdon New Testament Commentaries Series
Ap. Jas.	*Apocryphon of James*
Apoc. Abr.	*Apocalypse of Abraham*
Apoc. Adam	*Apocalypse of Adam*
Apoc. Daniel	*Apocalypse of Daniel*
Apoc. Elijah	*Apocalypse of Elijah*
Apoc. Ezra	*Greek Apocalypse of Ezra*
Apoc. Paul	*Apocalypse of Paul*
Apoc. Peter (Akhm.)	*Apocalypse of Peter (Akhmimic)*
Apoc. Peter (Eth.)	*Apocalypse of Peter (Ethiopic)*
Apoc. Sed.	*Apocalypse of Sedrach*
Apoc. Zeph.	*Apocalypse of Zephaniah*
Asc. Isa.	*Martyrdom and Ascension of Isaiah*
Assum. Moses	*Assumption of Moses*
ATR	*Anglican Theological Review*
AV	Authorized Version
Barn.	*Epistle of Barnabas*
BDAG	*A Greek-English Lexicon of the New Testament and Other Early Christian Literature*, 3rd edn, ed. F. W. Danker. Chicago and London: Chicago University Press, 2000
BDF	F. Blass, A. Debrunner, R. W. Funk, *A Greek Grammar of the New Testament*. Chicago: University of Chicago Press; and Cambridge: Cambridge University Press, 1961

BETL	Bibliotheca Ephemeridum Theologicarum Lovaniensium
BGBE	Beiträge zur Geschichte der biblischen Exegese
BI	Biblical Interpretation Series
BJRL	*Bulletin of the John Rylands Library*
BNTC	Black's New Testament Commentary Series
BST	The Bible Speaks Today Series
BTDNT	*Theological Dictionary of the New Testament*, ed. G. Kittel and G. Friedrich, abr. G. W. Bromiley. Grand Rapids: Eerdmans; and Exeter: Paternoster Press, 1985
BZNW	Beihefte zur Zeitschrift für die neutestamentliche Wissenschaft
CB (NT)	Coniectanea Biblica (New Testament Series)
CBQ	*Catholic Biblical Quarterly*
CBS	Continuum Biblical Studies Series
col.	column
Did.	*Didache*
Diogn.	*Epistle to Diognetus*
EB	Expositor's Bible Series
ESV	English Standard Version
ESW	Ecumenical Studies in Worship Series, ed. J. G. Davies and R. George
et al.	*et alia/alios* ('and others')
ExpTim	*Expository Times*
FCC	Fortress Continental Commentaries Series
frag(s).	*fragment(s)*
Gospel Phil.	*Gospel of Philip*
Gospel Thom.	*Gospel of Thomas*
GT	*A Greek-English Lexicon of the New Testament* (Grimm), 4th edn, ed. J. H. Thayer. Edinburgh: T. and T. Clark, 1901
Hermas	Shepherd of Hermas
Mand.	*Mandates*
Sim.	*Similitudes*
Vis.	*Visions*
IBD	*The Illustrated Bible Dictionary*, 3 vols, ed. N. Hillyer. Leicester: Inter-Varsity Press, 1980
ICC	International Critical Commentary Series
IDB	*The Interpreter's Dictionary of the Bible*, 4 vols, ed. G. A. Buttrick. New York and Nashville: Abingdon Press, 1962
Int	*Interpretation*
INT	Interpretation Series: A Bible Commentary for Teaching and Preaching
IVPNTC	IVP New Testament Commentary Series
JBL	*Journal of Biblical Literature*
JCH	Jewish and Christian Heritage Series
Jos. As.	*Joseph and Aseneth*
JSNT	*Journal for the Study of the New Testament*
JSNTS	Journal for the Study of the New Testament Supplement Series
JSOT	*Journal for the Study of the Old Testament*
JSPS	Journal for the Study of the Pseudepigrapha Supplement Series

JTS (ns)	*Journal of Theological Studies* (new series)
Jub.	*Jubilees*
Lat.	Latin
LXX	Septuagint
M.	*Mishnah*
Mart. Pol.	*The Letter of the Smyrneans on The Martyrdom of St Polycarp*
Midr.	*Midrash(im)*
Midr. Rab.	*Midrash Rabbah*
MKNT	Meyer's Kommentar über das Neue Testament
MNTC	Moffatt New Testament Commentary Series
MT	Masoretic Text
NA	B. and K. Aland et al., *Novum Testamentum Graece* (Nestle-Aland), 27th, revised edn. Stuttgart: Deutsche Bibelgesellschaft, 1995
NCB	New Century Bible Series
NDT	*New Dictionary of Theology*, ed. S. B. Ferguson, D. F. Wright and J. I. Packer. Leicester and Downers Grove: Inter-Varsity Press, 1988
NEB	New English Bible
NHL	*The Nag Hammadi Library in English*, 4th edn, ed. J. M. Robinson. Leiden: E. J. Brill, 1996
NIBC (NT)	New International Biblical Commentary (New Testament Series)
NICNT	New International Commentary on the New Testament Series
NIDNTT	*New International Dictionary of New Testament Theology*, 3 vols, ed. C. Brown. Grand Rapids: Zondervan; and Exeter: Paternoster Press, 1975–78
NIGTC	New International Greek Testament Commentary Series
NIV	New International Version
NJB	New Jerusalem Bible
NovT	*Novum Testamentum*
NRSV	New Revised Standard Version
NTC	New Testament in Context Series
NTG	New Testament Guides Series
NTL	New Testament Library Series
NTM	New Testament Message Series
NTR	New Testament Readings Series
NTS	*New Testament Studies*
NTT	New Testament Theology Series
Odes Sol.	*Odes of Solomon*
OTP	*The Old Testament Pseudepigrapha*, 2 vols, ed. J. H. Charlesworth. ABRL. London: Darton, Longman and Todd, 1983 and 1985.
PC	Proclamation Commentaries Series
PG	J. Migne, *Patrologia Graeca*
PGL	*A Patristic Greek Lexicon*, ed. G. H. W. Lampe. Oxford: Clarendon Press, 1961
PL (Supp.)	J. Migne, *Patrologia Latina* (Supplement)
Ps. Clem. *Hom.*	Pseudo-Clementine *Homilies*
Ps. Clem. *Recog.*	Pseudo-Clementine *Recognitions*

Pss. Sol.	*Psalms of Solomon*
Quest. Barth.	*Questions of Bartholomew*
Quest. Ezra	*Questions of Ezra*
Readings	Readings: A New Biblical Commentary
REB	Revised English Bible
RSV	Revised Standard Version
RV	Revised Version
SB	H. L. Strack and P. Billerbeck, *Kommentar zum Neuen Testament aus Talmud und Midrash*, 4 vols. Munich: Oskar Beck, 1922–28
SBT	Studies in Biblical Theology Series
sc.	*scilicet* ('namely')
Sib. Or.	*Sibylline Oracles*
SJT	*Scottish Journal of Theology*
SNTSMS	Society for New Testament Studies Monograph Series
ST	Studies in Theology
T. 12 Patr.	*Testaments of the Twelve Patriarchs*
T. Ash.	*Testament of Asher*
T. Benj.	*Testament of Benjamin*
T. Dan	*Testament of Dan*
T. Jos.	*Testament of Joseph*
T. Jud.	*Testament of Judah*
T. Levi	*Testament of Levi*
T. Naph.	*Testament of Naphtali*
T. Reub.	*Testament of Reuben*
T. Sim.	*Testament of Simeon*
T. Zeb.	*Testament of Zebulon*
T. Abr. (A / B)	*Testament of Abraham (Recension A / B)*
T. Adam	*Testament of Adam*
T. Isaac	*Testament of Isaac*
T. Job	*Testament of Job*
T. Jos. (Arm.)	*Testament of Joseph (Armenian Version)*
T. Mos.	*Testament of Moses*
T. Sol.	*Testament of Solomon*
Talmud (Babylonian)	
(b.) Ḥag.	*Hagigah*
(b.) Sanh.	*Sanhedrin*
(b.) Shab.	*Shabbath*
Targ. (Pal.)	*Targum (Palestinian)*
Isa.	Isaiah
Neof. I	*Neofiti I*
Ps(s).	Psalm(s)
Ps.-Jon.	*Pseudo-Jonathan*
Zech.	Zechariah
TDNT	*Theological Dictionary of the New Testament*, 10 vols, ed. G. Kittel and G. Friedrich. Grand Rapids: Eerdmans, 1964–76
Theod.	Theodotion
ThZ	*Theologische Zeitschrift*
TNTC	Tyndale New Testament Commentaries Series
TPINTC	Trinity Press International New Testament Commentaries Series

TPL	The Preacher's Library
TR	Textus Receptus
TynB	*Tyndale Bulletin*
UBS	United Bible Societies
vg	Vulgate
v.l.	*varia lectio* ('variant reading')
WBC	Word Biblical Commentary Series
WUNT	Wissenschaftliche Untersuchungen zum Neuen Testament
ZNW	*Zeitschrift für die neutestamentliche Wissenschaft*

2 Ancient Writers

Andreas	Andreas (Andrew)
Comm. in Apoc.	*Commentarius in Apocalypsin* (Commentary on the Apocalypse)
Apollodorus	
Lib.	*The Library*
Clement Alex.	Clement of Alexandria
Paed.	*Paedagogos* (The Instructor)
Quis dives	*Quis dives salvetur?* (Who Is the Rich Man That Shall Be Saved?)
Strom.	*Stromateis* (Miscellanies)
Dio Cassius	
Hist. Rom.	*Historia Romana* (Roman History)
Eusebius	
HE	*Historia Ecclesiastica* (Ecclesiastical History)
Ignatius	
Eph.	*Letter to the Ephesians*
Magn.	*Letter to the Magnesians*
Philad.	*Letter to the Philadelphians*
Pol.	*Letter to Polycarp*
Rom.	*Letter to the Romans*
Smyrn.	*Letter to the Smyrneans*
Trall.	*Letter to the Trallians*
Irenaeus	
Adv. Haer.	*Adversus Haereses* (Against Heresies)
Josephus	
Ant.	*Antiquities of the Jews*
Bell. Jud.	*Bellum Judaicum* (The Jewish War)
Cont. Ap.	*Contra Apionem* (Against Apion)
Justin	
1 Apol.	*First Apology*
Dial.	*Dialogue (with Trypho)*
Juvenal	
Sat.	*Satyra* (Satires)
Origen	
Comm. in Joan.	*Commentarius in Evangelium Joannis* (Commentary on the Gospel of John)
De Princ.	*De Principiis* (On First Principles)
Ovid	
Metam.	*Metamorphoses* (Transformations)

Philo
    De Decal.   *De Decalogo* (On the Decalogue)
    De Leg. All.   *De Legum Allegoriae* (On the Allegorical Interpretation
                                  [of Genesis 2, 3])
    De Opif. Mund.   *De Opificio Mundi* (On the Creation of the World)
    De Praem.   *De Praemiis et Poenis* (On Rewards and Punishments)
    De Som.   *De Somniis* (On Dreams)
    De Spec. Leg.   *De Specialibus Legibus* (On the Special Laws)
    De Vit. Mos.   *De Vita Mosis* (On the Life of Moses)
    Quaest. in Exod.   *Quaestiones et Solutiones in Exodum* (Questions and Answers
                                    on Exodus)
    Quod Det.   *Quod Deterius Potiori Insidiari Soleat* (That the Worse Is
                                    Wont to Attack the Better)
Pliny (the Elder)
    Nat. Hist.   *Naturalis Historiae* (Natural History)
Pliny (the Younger)
    Ep.   *Epistulae* (Letters)
Polycarp
    Phil.   *Letter to the Philippians*
Seneca (the Elder)
    Cont.   *Controversiae* (Disputes)
Seneca
    Epist.   *Epistulae Morales* (Moral Epistles)
Suetonius
    Calig.   *Lives of the Caesars: Caligula*
    Dom.   *Domitian*
    Tiber.   *Tiberius*
Tacitus
    Ann.   *Annales* (Annals)
    Hist.   *Historiarum* (The Histories)
Theophilus   Theophilus of Antioch
    Ad Autol.   *Ad Autolychum* (To Autolychus)
Victorinus
    Comm. in Apoc.   *Commentarius in Apocalypsin* (Commentary on the Apocalypse)

3 Dead Sea Scrolls

CD (-A, -B)   *Damascus Document (-A, -B)*
1Q   Cave 1
1Q22 (1QDM)   *Dibrê Moshe (Words of Moses)*
1QH   *Hymns of Thanksgiving*
1QM   *War of the Sons of Light against the Sons of Darkness*
1QpHab   *Habakkuk Pesher*
1QS   *Community Rule*
4Q   Cave 4
4Q161 (4QpIsa^a^)   *Isaiah Pesher^a^*
4Q164 (4QpIsa^d^)   *Isaiah Pesher^d^*
4Q242 (4QPrNab ar) *Prayer of Nabonidus*
4Q280   *Curses against Melkiresha*
4Q418   *Instruction^d^*
4Q525 (4QBéat)   *Beatitudes*

4Q542 (4QTQahat ar)	*Testament of Qahat*
4QapocrMoses[a]	*Apocryphon of Moses[a]*
4QDibHam[a]	*Words of the Luminaries[a]*
4QpHos[b]	*Hosea Pesher[b]*
4QpNah	*Nahum Pesher*
4QpPs[a]	*Psalms Pesher[a]*
4QPs[f]	*Psalms[f]*
4QShirShabb	*Songs of Sabbath Sacrifice*
4QTanh	*Tanhûmîm*
4QTest	*Testimonia*
11Q	Cave 11
11QMelch	*Melchizedek*
11QT[a]	*Temple*

Introduction

This commentary attempts to provide a careful exegesis of the Greek text of John's Revelation, together with an interpretation which keeps in constant view the seer's basic flow of theological thought. A detailed introduction to the Apocalypse already exists in the form of my earlier work, *Thunder and Love* (1994); and the magisterial commentaries by Aune (1997–98) and Beale (1999) include exhaustive surveys of all the major critical and hermeneutical issues involved in the scholarly investigation of this document. With such material as a presupposition, the following introduction accordingly does no more than set out some preliminary considerations which are basic to any study of Revelation, including the nature of the Greek text itself. Reference will also be made to the overarching approach adopted in the commentary, and to my own convictions about the origin, purpose and composition of John's drama. Further support for these is provided in the comments themselves.

The Text

The exegesis in this commentary is based on the Greek text which appears in the 1995 impression of the 27th, revised edition of NA (B. and K. Aland et al., *Novum Testamentum Graece* [Nestle-Aland]). In the textual notes frequent reference is also made to the balanced and discerning textual criticism carried out by the Editorial Committee of the United Bible Societies (UBS) Greek New Testament, and published in Metzger, *Textual Commentary* (1975). In addition, the versions of the text and notes in the commentaries of Swete (1909), Beckwith (1919/1967) and Charles (1920) have been consulted, as well as the detailed examinations of the topic in Aune and Beale.

Five main *sources* of evidence exist in any quest to establish the originality of the Greek text of John's Revelation: six fragmentary papyri, possibly dating from the second century AD; eleven uncial MSS, fourth century or later; largely medieval minuscule MSS (293 in number); quotations by Greek and Latin Fathers, in works originating from the second to the sixth century and beyond; and translated versions in Latin, Armenian, Georgian, Coptic, Ethiopic and Syriac, certainly in existence from the fourth century onwards.

There are five major text *types* to be found in the textual scene of the Apocalypse: the best group of textual witnesses is neutral (notably the early uncials A and C); the next most valuable text tradition is represented by 𝔓47, the oldest witness to the text of Revelation, א and Origen (2351); the text of Andreas (Andrew) of Cappadocia in Caesarea, whose commentary on the Apocalypse was written between AD 563 and 614; the Byzantine text (designated throughout as Byz, meaning either the tradition as a whole, or MSS within it); and mixed texts, deriving from the types in Andreas and Byzantine. See Aune cxxxvi–clviii; for a slightly different assessment of the quality of the textual tradition in Revelation note Beale 70–71.

The sigla and abbreviations used in the textual notes of the present commentary are generally those which appear in the *apparatus criticus* of NA.

1 The Approach

The stance adopted in this commentary is literary and theological, rather than simply critical and historical. The analytical work of earlier commentators, such as Peake (1919) and Charles, cannot be discarded; but recent research on the Apocalypse, represented for instance in the work of John Court (*Revelation*, 1994; 'Reading the Book' 164–67) and of Alan Garrow (*Revelation*, 1997), in the 2001 collection of essays edited by Steve Moyise (*Studies in the Book of Revelation*), and in my own monograph, *Thunder and Love*, is rightly sensitive also to the literary nature of John's composition. The paragraphs which deal here with the Literary Setting and Theology of each section should therefore be regarded as of leading importance. For genre criticism of Revelation, given its amalgam of varied literary types, see further Court, *Revelation* 15–17. These forms include visions, epiphanies, auditions, discourses, dialogues and the use of formulae; see Aune lxxxii–lxxxiv.

In line with a such a narrative approach, the contents of Revelation are viewed in this commentary more from a synchronic than a diachronic perspective. That is to say, the Apocalypse is treated as a unity, and indeed as a coherent drama, even if it may be accepted that its author has drawn on earlier sources (as perhaps in Rev. 2—3; 7.1–8), and engaged in some light editing of the text (see 11.1–3; 17.9–11). I find it difficult to respond positively to the radical rearrangement of the material in Revelation proposed by Charles, or to the elaborate source-critical theories which he constructs in order to amend a 'depravation of the text' (see esp. 1, l–lxv); and the suggestion of Aune (esp. cxviii–cxxxiv) that the Apocalypse came to birth in two major stages ('first and second editions') appears to be equally unnecessary. See also the summary of critical analyses, reaching back to work dating from the seventeenth century, in Swete (xlix–l) and Beckwith (224–39). It has to be said that hypotheses of this kind are notoriously subjective, and indeed speculative, and that they are by no means essential to a proper understanding of the text. At the same time, I am happier to argue for the basic unity of the Apocalypse (Smalley, *Thunder and Love* 97–101; see also Swete li–liv).

2 The Origin

While it is important to keep an open mind on the question of the authorship of Revelation (so Beasley-Murray 36–37), the position adopted in this commentary is that the book is the work of John the apostle, who was also the beloved disciple (see Smalley, *Thunder and Love* 35–40). It has been frequently assumed (e.g. by Moffatt [317–20]; Beckwith [197–208]; Kiddle [xxxvi–xliii]; Rist [354–56]; Boring [8–12]; Roloff [8–12]) that the Apocalypse may be dated to the reign of the Emperor Domitian, the last representative of the Flavian house (AD 81–96), as a response to fierce persecution which took place during his reign. But this view has recently been challenged seriously, both because encouragement in the face of persecution may not be regarded as the single motive behind the composition of Revelation, and also on account of the insecurity surrounding the evidence for imperial oppression during the time of Domitian (cf. Thompson, *Book of Revelation* 95–197; Wilson, 'Domitianic Date' 587–605; Knight 21–28; Boxall, *Revelation* 86–104; Prigent 68–84). This leaves the way open to revive the alternative view, common among nineteenth-century scholars, that Revelation was written between AD 64, as a result of persecution under Nero, and AD 70, the fall of Jerusalem (see the summary of the research representing these two positions in Robinson, *Redating* 224–26).

As it happens, I believe that it is perfectly possible to locate the writing of Revelation in the reign of Vespasian (AD 69–79); and I have argued that the book emerged just before the fall of Jerusalem to Titus, Vespasian's son, in AD 70. See Smalley, *Thunder and Love* 40–50, esp. 49–50; cf. also on 13.4; 17.9–11. An early date for the Apocalypse means that it appeared *before* the Gospel of John (which I place in AD 80; see Smalley, *John* 90–93) and the Johannine Letters (AD 90; see Smalley, *1, 2, 3 John* xxxii; similarly Hengel, *Johannine Question* 51, who regards the old hypothesis that the central parts of Revelation were composed in the time after Nero as 'still worth considering'). I suggest that this conclusion fits the internal and external evidence for the dating of Revelation; it is also supported by the theological thrust of the drama itself. For the members of John's circle, the earthly Jerusalem and its Temple would have been a central holy place in which to encounter God, and also a spiritual centre of gravity. If Jerusalem were about to be destroyed, the vision in Rev. 21—22 of a stunning and emphatically *new* holy city, where God's people will dwell eternally in a close covenant relationship with him, would have provided exactly, and at the right moment, all the spiritual encouragement they needed (for the purpose of the Apocalypse see further below).

Throughout this commentary, the author of the Apocalypse and its prophet-seer will be described as 'John'. Although my own contention is that this name is synonymous with John the apostle, its use is not intended to foreclose discussion of the authorship issue.

3 The Situation

The Apocalypse was written essentially as a testimony to God's plan in Christ for his world, and to disclose by means of a series of visions the fulfilment of his salvific purposes, through his judgement, both in history and in eternity. Earlier commentators commonly held the view that this message was intended to encourage the congregations of Asia, and the Church in general, because its members were facing external persecution and oppression. The explanation by Beckwith (208–16) is typical.

In a time of crisis, the Church was entering a period of crucial conflict between the forces of evil, epitomized by Rome, and the forces of good, found in the vindicated Lord of the Church. To meet this situation, Beckwith argues, the writer exhorts his hearers to be steadfast in faith; and he fortifies their courage by 'revealing the ultimate destruction of the powers of evil, and the perfect consummation of the Christian hope in the establishment of the kingdom of God' (209). Kiddle (xxxvi–xliii) adopts a similar approach, when he identifies the Apocalypse as a call for endurance, amid a storm of opposition from Rome intensified by devotion to the imperial cult. The followers of Jesus in John's day, Kiddle maintains, needed to direct their faith and hope towards the worship of Christ, and not of Caesar, even if this involved martyrdom on the way (xli–xliii).

Such an understanding of the purpose of Revelation is less than adequate, since it makes a number of unwarranted assumptions. First, it presupposes that external persecution was the sole reason for the composition of the Apocalypse, and it will be suggested that this was not the case (see below). Second, this approach assumes a late, Domitianic date for the origin of Revelation, whereas it is possible to argue that the book came to birth much earlier (see above). Third, it is important in the course of interpreting the Apocalypse not to restrict the identity of 'Rome', or indeed 'Babylon'. John sees both of these in general, not civic or imperial, terms; for they are representative concepts, and images which stand for unrighteous opposition to God in any society or system at any time (see on 12.3–4; 13.1–18; 17.1–6; et al.).

It is true that Revelation appeared in an age of conflict, and of imperial opposition to the Christian Church. The persecution and martyrdom of believers during the reign of

Nero (AD 54–68), and the cruelty of Domitian himself during the reign of Vespasian (AD 69–79), even before he became Emperor (according to Suetonius *Dom.* 9—10, esp. 10.1), probably formed a backcloth to John's witness (see on 2.13; 6.9–11; 13.4; et al.), and determined to some extent the hopeful and supportive nature of his testimony. Nevertheless, external opposition to Christianity derived from Judaism, as well as the Roman state (see on 2.9; 3.9; also Sweet 28–31); and it is in any case likely that the problems which directly confronted the churches of John's time, and shaped the contents of Revelation, arose from *within* his community, and not merely from beyond it. To the character of that community we now turn.

4 The Johannine Community and Its Literature

The relationship between the New Testament documents that bear the name of John (Revelation, Gospel, Letters) is a topic of continuing scholarly interest. There are obvious similarities between the language and thought of the Fourth Gospel and 1, 2, 3 John; and, although this is often disputed (as by Charles 1, xxix–l; Roloff 11–12), it is also possible to argue that sufficient subtle but clear affinities exist between John's Gospel and the Apocalypse as to suggest that both documents came from the same Christian circle, if not from the same hand (see Smalley, 'John's Revelation' 549–71; also Fiorenza, *Book of Revelation* 85–113). Given such a premise, the further conclusion may be drawn that Revelation antedated the Gospel, and was composed by John the apostle himself (cf. Robinson, *Redating* 221–53).

In addition, I would say that the history of John's community, gathered in some way around the prophet-seer, is reflected in the Johannine corpus as a whole. The character of the group, that is to say, may be traced from Revelation to 3 John. For John's 'community' see further Culpepper and Black, *Exploring the Gospel of John* 21–144. To my mind, the collection of essays edited by Richard Bauckham, *Gospels for All Christians* (1998), arguing that the Gospels were intended for a *general* early Christian readership, does not disprove the existence of a Johannine community. The Letters of John, for example, were clearly addressed in the first place to the situation and needs of a specific group of people, and even mention individuals within it (cf. 3 John 1, 9, 12).

That situation, embracing the community as a totality, may most easily be defined by looking afresh at the balanced teaching of John's Gospel, and investigating first of all the character of the readers for whom it was intended. Asia Minor in the first century AD included a world which was immensely varied in its cultural, political, philosophical and religious background. In terms of religion, the traditions of Judaism and Hellenism were basic to Asian society (cf. Brown, *Introduction* 55–96). The spiritual hinterland of the congregations within the Johannine circle was clearly equally diverse, being both Jewish and Greek in character. As a result, I take it that three groups of believers belonged to the congregations, headed by Ephesus (see on Rev. 1.11), which were initially addressed in the Johannine corpus. On the one hand there were Jewish Christians, who had come out of the synagogue and professed their commitment to Jesus, but still felt a loyalty to Judaism. This section of the community, nurtured in a monotheistic faith, may have found it difficult to accept that Jesus was Messiah, and indeed *divine*; and all the more might this be true if they were under pressure from unbelieving Jews in dispersion, and tempted to slip back into Judaism by denying that Jesus is the Christ. At the same time, these members of the community would have given an exalted place to the Jewish Law; and their stance in general would have much in common with the Ebionites.

On the other hand there were Hellenistic Christians, including probably Jewish Christians of Grecian derivation, who had emerged from a pagan background but remained influenced by the dualist, pre-gnostic beliefs of Hellenistic systems of salvation which were later categorized as 'docetic'. Such individuals within the circle would have been ready to believe that Jesus was from God; but they might well have been less at ease with the notion that Jesus was fully *human*. The third group to be postulated consists of those believers whose understanding of Jesus was more balanced. They favoured neither the view of the former Jewish adherents, that Jesus was just a man, nor that of the ex-pagans, that he was simply God-like. They saw their Lord as *both*.

My thesis suggests that these three groups of believers found it increasingly uncomfortable to exist together in the same community. In particular, the christological differences between the 'Judaic' and 'Hellenistic' parties might well have caused friction, and a desire for independence. If the author of John's Gospel initially intended to address the volatile scene within his own community, and the needs of those within it whose faith was real but inadequate, this would account for the doctrinal equilibrium in his teaching about the person of Christ. The writer is not only recounting the gospel about Jesus but also relating it directly to the belief and behaviour of his followers. For the sake of the Jewish Christians, John demonstrates that Jesus is not merely human but also divine. For the benefit of the adherents from a Greek background, the evangelist emphasizes the truth that Jesus is not only one with God, but also one with his Church. As such, he can be the 'Saviour of the world' (John 4.42; cf. 1 John 4.14). In a divisive and potentially disintegrating situation, John appeals for calm: for a love commanded, and a unity desired, by Jesus himself (John 13.34–35; 15.12, 17; 17.11, 21–23). The balance which is so marked in the Christology of the Fourth Evangelist is equally apparent in the Revelation and Letters of John.

Given this understanding of the purpose of the Fourth Gospel, the developing story of life within the Johannine community may be detected in its early stages from the witness of Revelation, and in its closing period from the scenes reflected in the Letters of John. The congregations of Asia, as we know from the oracles to the seven churches in Rev. 2—3, contained members who came from mixed backgrounds, both Jewish and Gentile. The message of Christ to them, handed on through the angels and the prophet-seer, concerned the need for right belief and steadfast courage; it was also related to the moral demand for acceptable 'works' (2.2, 5; 3.1–2; cf. 9.20; 14.13; 20.12–13; et al.). Such a challenge would have evoked a response from both the Jewish and Greek membership of John's community.

The evidence of John's Gospel just reviewed suggests that this challenge was being resisted, and that an appeal for love and unity was required. The contents of John's Letters imply a progressive polarization of theological and ethical opinion. Those with a 'low' Christology had moved further towards an Ebionitic stance, while those whose estimation of Christ's person was 'high' had become more clearly inclined towards a gnostic-docetic position. Secession was taking place, with 'many deceivers' from both parties leaving the community (2 John 7). The attitude of Diotrephes (3 John 9–10) shows that the situation has been turned on its head, and that what was later known as orthodoxy was being treated as heterodox, and the reverse. The teaching of the Johannine corpus, therefore, does not seem to have solved the problems which beset John's immediate community, even if it includes theological and practical truths which are fundamental to the Christian scheme, and relevant to every age. For this section see further Smalley, *Thunder and Love* 119–37; also *John* 181–85; *1,2,3 John* xxii–xxxii. For a different, but related, interpretation of the life of the Johannine circle see Brown, *Community*, esp. 25–164.

A Further Aim

It has been suggested that incipient theological and practical problems, which were being experienced by John's own community, formed a background to the composition of Revelation. They also appear to have shaped its theology, and in particular its balanced Christology. The development and outcome of these internal difficulties may be plotted from John's Apocalypse, through his Gospel and to the Letters. Meanwhile, it may be detected from the material in all parts of Revelation that another major problem, causing further tensions, already existed in the Johannine circle: the lure of spiritual idolatry. The tendency towards falsehood of all kinds, and the inclination to worship the beast rather than God, is closely related to the doctrinal error which existed within John's community, and to the pressure from outside it to compromise with the truth, and behave wrongly.

Sweet (27–35) sees this as determinative for John's message, which he defines as an answer to the idolatry and materialism of pagan society in the first-century Mediterranean world, over which the 'baleful influence of deified Rome' brooded ominously (34). Preparing the Church for the final crisis, Sweet maintains, the writer of the Apocalypse accordingly makes the practical demand of moral separation from the world, undergirding his plea for believers to remain faithful even to death (11.8) with the theological truth of the uniqueness and sufficiency of Christ (Sweet 34–35). Beale (28–33) adopts a similar position, but rightly regards the focus of Revelation as an exhortation for believers to bear faithful witness to Jesus in the middle of a 'compromising, idolatrous *church* and world' (33, italics mine).

The seer's chief concern is to present a drama about God's salvation through his judgement to a community which was *itself* infected with falsehood. The members of John's circle were inclined to inadequate belief, notably about the person of Jesus, and therefore to wrong conduct. The temptation to compromise with the truth, and use power unjustly, would be increased by the fact that these adherents were surrounded by a pagan society which encouraged people to eat food which had been sacrificed to idols (Rev. 2.6, 14–15, 20) and dominated by an imperial rule which absolutized its own power and prosperity (cf. Bauckham, *Theology* 35–39). The prophet-seer therefore warns his readers about the dangers of idolatry in any form: social, political, ecclesiastical or economic. In a passage of striking imagery (the destruction of Babylon, Rev. 17—18), for example, he demonstrates the inevitable downfall of human arrogance. By contrast, and by means of a testimony which is relevant to any Christian group in any age, John urges his congregations to worship God, rather than the beast, and to reject the wiles of Satan by following the exalted Lamb (14.1). See further on 9.20; 19.20; 20.10; 21.8; 22.15, 18–19.

5 The Character

In terms of its literary genre, Revelation stands on its own. While there are points of contact with the epistles in the New Testament (see on 1.4; 22.21), it is clearly much more than a letter. Equally, although the Apocalypse is addressed to a situation, and in the first place to a community, which is historical (Chapters 2—3), and even if it takes seriously God's activity on earth as well as in heaven (6.1–17; et al.), this document cannot be regarded simply as a historical record. Revelation is sufficiently in touch with history to indicate that it is not a piece of narrative fiction; but its theological content and presentation, however deconstructed, show that ultimately the drama belongs to another world altogether. Similarly, although the work contains a strongly prophetic dimension (see below), it should not be understood merely as predictive prophecy, in which the author explains what is to happen in the future alone. Revelation certainly includes visions of the next world, and of the nature of the new Jerusalem; but it is also firmly related to this age, and challenges believers about their responsibilities in the present.

Revelation, then, is not fiction; but neither is it just a letter, solely history, or predictive prophecy alone. As the first word in the opening verse (1.1) makes clear, it is an apocalypse: 'A revelation (ἀποκάλυψις, *apokalypsis*) from Jesus Christ, which God gave him, to make known to his servants what must swiftly take place'. Apocalyptic may be broadly defined as a literary medium, which enables its audience to understand divine truths which have hitherto remained hidden and secret. Writing of this kind can be found in the Old Testament (notably in Ezekiel and Daniel, both of which have influenced the composition of Revelation), in the apocryphal and pseudepigraphical literature of Judaism (e.g. *1, 2, 3 Enoch*), in the Qumran scrolls (such as 1QS, 1QM and 1QH), and in the New Testament (cf. Mark 13 par., as well as the Apocalypse itself). It is evident that the roots of the apocalyptic material which emerges in John's Revelation lie firmly embedded in Judaism, even if the writer has used his sources to produce a distinctive composition which in the end is clearly (Jewish-)Christian. For a study of apocalyptic in Judaism and early Christianity see Rowland, *Open Heaven*, esp. the description of the genre at 9–72.

But even the designation of Revelation as an 'apocalypse' is, by itself, inadequate. To be sure, it exhibits many characteristics of Judaeo-Christian apocalyptic, such as the use of vivid metaphorical language and the appearance of dangerous animals (lion, dragon, beast), together with numerical speculation (666; 144,000). Revelation also shares with its apocalyptic antecedents the characteristic features of dualism, with its contrast between the present world and the age to come (21.1); of pessimism about a society which is hostile and wicked (9.20–21); and of determinism, meaning that God's plan of judgement and salvation for his creation, once set in motion, cannot be interrupted (11.14).

Nevertheless, two particular and important traditions within the apocalyptic literature of Judaism are missing in John's Apocalypse. The first is pseudonymity, whereby great figures from the past (Adam, Enoch, Moses, Baruch, Ezra) are enlisted as fictitious authors who will compensate for the decline of independent prophetic authority in the later period of Israel's history. By contrast, 'John' is named as a witness to the testimony of this book, and as its scribe (1.1, 4, 9–10; 22.8–9); but God, revealed in the exalted Christ and by the Spirit, is clearly the chief author of its message (1.1, 4–7, 10–13; 2.1; 14.13; 19.9; 21.5; 22.6–7, 10, 17; et al.).

The second apocalyptic tradition which is virtually absent from Revelation is the interpretation of visions. In Jewish apocalypses mysteries concealed in heaven, determining the future destiny of humanity, are regularly disclosed in visions, and an angelic figure is needed to explain them (cf. Dan. 7.15–27; 4 Ezra 10.29–59; *1 Enoch* 27.1–5; et al.). In John's Apocalypse visionary accounts are central to his dramatic presentation, and expressions of 'seeing' and 'hearing' are frequent (1.12; 4.1; 5.1; 7.1; 13.1; 18.1; 19.6; 21.1; et al.). But the seer is rarely puzzled by these disclosures, and the inherited pattern of an obscure vision followed by its interpretation is almost completely missing from this book. The exceptions are 7.13–17 and 17.7–18 (q.v.); but even there the author seems to be using a literary technique to gain the attention of his audience, rather than offering through the angel a clear explanation of the imagery involved. For this section see Roloff 3–7.

Revelation as Prophecy

So far it has not seemed possible to identify the literary genre of Revelation with precision; and even the description of the work as traditional 'apocalyptic' has been found inadequate. It is therefore necessary to widen the scope of this investigation by drawing in the subject of prophecy. This book is referred to in the text precisely as one of 'prophecy' (προφητεία, *prophēteia*); see 1.3; 22.7, 10, 18–19. John writes, in his own name, to declare divine knowledge which is not secret and arcane, but open and clear. The 'oracles' of Rev. 2—3, each of which includes an exhortation to respond to the commands of the Spirit (2.7; et al.), and the seven 'prophecies' of 21.2—22.17, with their declarations about new life in the new creation, are prophetic and oracular in character. John is proclaiming God's word of judgement and salvation to his people in relation to their present, as much as their future, existence.

In this way, John stands in the line of Old Testament prophets; and in the Apocalypse there seems to be at times a conscious attempt to make this connection clear. Rev. 1.1, for example, echoes the typical opening words of Hebrew prophecy (cf. Isa. 1.1 LXX; Amos 1.1; see also Amos 3.7 LXX). At Rev. 10.8–11 John receives a direct prophetic call, which in content resembles the vocation of Jeremiah (Jer. 1.10), and in character echoes the summoning of Ezekiel (Ezek. 2.8—3.3). When the writer claims that he was 'in the Spirit (on the Lord's Day)' (Rev. 1.10; 4.2), and that he was 'carried away in spirit' (17.3; 21.10), this probably refers not so much to a state of ecstatic trance, typical of any seer, as to motivation by the Spirit to declare, in the style of a Jewish prophet, God's testimony to his own.

In Revelation, then, John the Divine appears as a prophet. He bears witness to divine 'words of prophecy' (1.3), and shares immediately in the 'spirit of prophecy' (19.10). He does not dwell on the past, nor is he preoccupied solely with the future. The seer announces God's salvific, historical activity in Christ (5.9–10; et al.), the ultimate establishment of his sovereign rule (19.6), and the possibility for every believer of an unbroken covenant relationship with him in eternity (21.1—22.5). But while it may be said that the author of the Apocalypse is an inheritor of the prophetic tradition within Judaism, he cannot be regarded as simply another Old Testament prophet, or even as being closer to the Hebrew, rather than the New Testament, style of prophecy (against Hill, 'Prophecy and Prophets in the Revelation' 410). John mediates the revelation of Jesus Christ to his community, and he shares in its prophetic life (Rev. 22.9). To that extent he is a *Christian* prophet: that is to say, a prophet of Christ. He rereads, and restates, the Old Testament disclosure in the light of the Christ event (Feuillet, *Apocalypse* 65); and he does so creatively. From this perspective, John records 'what is taking place now, and what is about to happen later on' (Rev. 1.19), as well as challenging and encouraging his own community, and the Church belonging to any age.

John exhibits, then, a double identity. He is a seer, who clearly participates in an unveiling, and writes in the mode of an apocalyptist. The curtain is raised on the final scene of humanity's story, which conveys 'pictorially and in symbol, the conviction of the ultimate victory of God' (Moule, *Birth* 150). But John is also a prophet of Christ, who portrays graphically the word of God's saving judgement to the churches of his own day. Such diversity, prophetic and apocalyptic, combines the discrete audience of Hebrew prophecy (God's own people) with the universal appeal inherent in the literature of the apocalyptists (cf. Vielhauer, 'Apocalyptic' 590).

Revelation may be identified, therefore, as apocalyptic deepened by prophetic insight, and also as prophecy intensified by apocalyptic vision. John is not simply a seer, but a *prophet-seer*; and this term will be frequently used to describe him in this commentary. As prophet, he reaches backwards, and into the present and future, in order to interpret God's word to his own circle and to the world beyond; but he does so with the ability of a seer to perceive and uncover the end of salvation's drama. He brings heaven and eternity within the grasp of believers, on earth and in time, who may be struggling to maintain and commend their faith in Jesus. For this section see Smalley, *Thunder and Love* 23–34, esp. 30–31.

6 The Use of the Old Testament

The composition of the Apocalypse is clearly indebted to the Jewish-Christian background of its author, and to the Old Testament itself. John lived in a Graeco-Roman society, knew about proto-gnostic ideas and magical texts, both Jewish and Graeco-Roman, and was presumably familiar with the mainstream thought and literature of the classical world. See further Barrett, 'Gnosis' 125–37, esp. 134–35; Aune 453–54 (on Rev. 7.2). But the influence exerted by Judaism is paramount and the atmosphere of the Old Testament is pervasive.

Revelation contains more references to the Old Testament than any other document in the New Testament, even if these parallels are often allusive. The prophet-seer draws on many books in the Old Testament, including the Pentateuch, Judges, Proverbs, Song of Solomon and Job. But his thought is more often shaped by the major prophets and by the Psalms. Thus, John frequently uses Daniel (and, in particular, chapter 7), as well as echoing regularly the prophecies of Ezekiel and Isaiah. The Old Testament plays such a major part in the Apocalypse, it may be concluded, that a proper understanding of its use is necessary for an adequate interpretation of the drama in its entirety. See Swete cxxxix–clii; also Beale 77.

Swete (cliv–clv) believes that John depended mainly on the LXX version when alluding to the Old Testament; although Charles (1, lxvi–lxxxvi), noting that the writer often departs from the wording of the LXX, claims that the prophet-seer kept more closely to the Hebrew text. According to Beale (78), it is more likely that John draws on Semitic (including Qumranic) *as well as* Greek sources, and frequently modifies them both. Beale (78–79) also points out the 'non-formal' character of John's use of Old Testament Scripture, and his preference for allusion (clear, probable, possible) over direct quotation. Many of these reminiscences are merged into one picture (cf. 1.12–20; 4.1–11; 13.1–8). Whether John used these allusive and evocative combinations consciously (so Caird 25–26), or otherwise, remains a matter for discussion; but a mixture of 'conscious intention and unconscious activity' in these mosaics is always a possibility (Beale 79).

The prophet-seer uses the Old Testament in a variety of ways; see Beale 86–96.

(a) At times he takes over Old Testament contexts or sequences as models on which to base his creative compositions (e.g. broad patterns from Dan. 2 and 7 may be traced in Rev. 1; 4—5; 13; and 17).

(b) John develops Old Testament themes, such as those involved in the imagery of the earthquake and the messianic holy war (cf. Bauckham, *Climax of Prophecy* 199–237).

(c) He also uses intertextual analogies, whereby familiar people, places and events in Judaism are brought over and applied to a new historical situation. Examples are: the 'ancient serpent' of 12.9 (cf. Gen. 3.1–15); horsemen (Rev. 6.1–8) and plagues (8.6–9.19; 16.1–21) as agents of divine judgement (Zech. 1 and 6; Exod. 8–12); the tribulation of God's people, with persecutors symbolized as beasts (Rev. 11—13, 17 = Dan. 7); idolatrous teaching typified by Balaam (Rev. 2.14; Num. 25; 31.16) and Jezebel (Rev. 2.20–23; 1 Kings 16.31); and the idea of divine protection expressed in the 'sealing' of the saints (Rev. 7.2–8; Ezek. 9). These Old Testament markers are handled with freedom, but retain their continuity with earlier associations.

Beale (91–96) also refers in this connection to John's apocalyptic tendency to apply to the world what the Old Testament relates in the first place to Israel (cf. Exod. 19.6 and Rev. 1.6; 5.10); to his use of indirect fulfilment (Dan. 2.28–29, 45 and Rev. 1.1, where Daniel's vision of the defeat of cosmic evil in the distant future is perceived by the seer as inaugurated in his own day); and to the practice of inversion (e.g. Isa. 45.14; et al. and Rev. 3.9, where the expectation that Gentiles will recognize Israel as God's chosen people is reversed, so that Jewish persecutors are made to submit to the true Israel).

The place of the Old Testament in the formation of John's thought in Revelation is accordingly that of a servant and guide. It does not merely aid the gospel, as in an academic exercise (so Lindars, 'Old Testament in the New' 59–66, esp. 66); it also leads the way to further contemplation of the Christ-event, and to a deeper comprehension of the redemptive history to which it is the key. In that sense, the Old and New Testaments interpret each other (Beale 97). For this section see further Glasson, *Moses*; Beale, *Use of the Old Testament* 13–128; Paulien, 'Criteria and the Assessment' 113–29; Prigent 13–17; Boxall, *Revelation* 42–46; Mathewson, *New Heaven* 216–36.

7 The Testimony

Controlling John's testimony throughout the Apocalypse is his underlying perception that God's salvation comes to his creation *through* judgement. The thunder and love of God belong together, just as they did in the apostle himself. In the New Testament, the term 'salvation' (σωτηρία, *sōtēria*; the cognate verb is σώζω, *sōzō*, 'to save') can mean material deliverance from danger and fear (as in Acts 27.34) or, more significantly, the spiritual and eternal healing which God in Christ gives to the believer (cf. Rom. 10.10; et al.).

The noun 'salvation' occurs only three times in Revelation, during ascriptions of praise to God as the one who dispenses wholeness through the Lamb (7.10; 12.10; 19.1), while the verb is not used at all. However, the *idea* of divine healing is present every-where in the drama; and, as in John's Gospel, it is often expressed by the idea of eternal 'life' (Rev. 2.10; 11.11; et al.; cf. John 3.16; 17.3; et al.). God makes accessible to the believer, and to the Church as a whole, the water, the tree and the light of life (Rev. 21.6; 22.1–5); and, by his grace, the names of the faithful are written in the book of life (3.5; 20.15; 21.27). Closely related to the concept of salvation in the Apocalypse is the notion of 'redemption', where Jesus is the new Moses achieving a new Exodus (see 5.9; 14.3–4, using the verb ἀγοράζω, *agorazō*, 'ransom, redeem'; also 15.2–4).

The seer perceives that salvation, in this sense, is achieved through the judgement of God. Divine judgement, God's justice or righteousness, speaks of his verdict on account-able human error; it represents God's reaction to people and nations who fall short of his moral standards (in Revelation, see 15.3–4; 16.5, 7; 19.2; cf. 19.11, the righteousness of Christ). The biblical concept of judgement has a forensic background (cf. 1 Cor. 4.1–5); and in Revelation, as in the Fourth Gospel, it operates locally in the present, as well as universally in the future. The members of the Johannine churches in Asia are warned that they need to repent of their sinful belief and idolatrous conduct, and that otherwise judgement will follow immediately (Rev. 2.14–16, 20–24; 3.3, 19); but the stark and dramatic vision of discrimination in 20.11–15 is both future and general in its reference.

The theological pattern of salvation through judgement is consistent throughout Revelation. War breaks out in heaven, before the Devil is toppled from power and God's sovereignty is established (12.7–10). The saints are victorious in the end, but only because of the blood of the Lamb (12.11). The thrones of judgement are set, before the faithful are brought to life, and Satan, Death and Hades are thrown into the lake of fire (20.4–15). The white throne of judgement is ultimately replaced by the life-giving throne of God and the Lamb (20.11–15; 22.1). Elisabeth Fiorenza (*Book of Revelation* 46–56, esp. 55) has shown that the theme of judgement in the Apocalypse is formally related to the notion of community, and developed in the visions of cosmic plagues which lead up to the final disclosures about the new world (21.1). She rightly maintains that John's judge-ment motif always comes to a climax with the announcement of coming salvation for the community of the world (see the judgement hymn of 11.15–18, which is followed in verse 19 by a vision of the covenant ark). See also on John's eschatology, below.

Such a testimony (1.2; 22.16) includes a positive understanding of judgement, and its related concept of 'wrath' (6.16–17; 11.18; et al.). God's justice is real, and its purpose is serious; but his judgement is ultimately an expression of his love. Deliverance and glory and power belong to God, the prophet-seer hears the heavenly crowd crying, *because* his judgements are fair and just (19.1–2). The divine decisions taken against those who oppose God lead to the vindication of those who remain true to him (6.9–10). The dead are judged, as in a courtroom (20.12); but the Holy One judges in righteousness, so that the conquerors may reign with Christ eternally (11.18; 16.5–7; 20.4), even if those who wish are permitted to remain outside the gates of the new Jerusalem (21.27; 22.15). Divine judgement, through the Lamb (19.11), is thus transposed from a future terror into a present encouragement. This balance in the teaching of Revelation is highlighted in the headings given in this commentary to the two main Acts of John's drama: 'Creation, and Salvation through Judgement'; followed by 'Salvation through Judgement, and New Creation'.

Balance in John's Testimony

Attention has already been drawn to the symmetry in the Christology of the Apocalypse; and it has been suggested that this balance – Jesus is one with the Father and with humanity – may be related to the teaching about the person of Christ in John's Gospel, and ultimately to the purpose of the Johannine corpus as a whole (see above, 4–6; also Smalley, 'John's Revelation' 549–71, esp. 550–68). Such equilibrium is characteristic of John's testimony throughout Revelation; and it stems from his distinctive *cosmology*. For the thought of the prophet-seer in Revelation, like that of the fourth evangelist, consistently brings together the material and the spiritual. Since the Word became flesh (John 1.14), the physical and historical dimension has been invaded by the metaphysical in such a way that matter can become the carrier of spirit. In Jesus, heaven and earth have been conjoined (John 1.51). In his Gospel, as a result, John thinks and operates on two levels at once; and this produces an allusive quality in his teaching, which often includes irony. See Smalley, *Thunder and Love* 58–63.

This two-dimensional view of the world may also be found in Revelation. The author of the Apocalypse constantly thinks and writes on two levels at once, and the marked presence of angels in the drama makes the connection evident (see on 1.1). So the faithful in the seven churches of Asia (Rev. 2—3) belong at the same time to earth *and* heaven, and in each case it is the 'angel' of the local community who is addressed (2.1; et al.). The symbolic visions and prophecies which form the content of the book, like Babylon and Jerusalem themselves, carry throughout a double reference; indeed, their immediate and historical application makes possible an interpretation beyond history. This typically Johannine two-level way of thinking is specially marked in the intervals between the scenes (see on Rev. 4—5; 7; 10—11; 15; 17—18; 21.1). The ethical *dualism* which belongs to Revelation echoes the balance in its theology. Good and evil, the Church and the world, Christ and Satan are locked into a combat which involves suffering; but the victorious outcome of the struggle is predictable and, indeed, known in advance (19.11—20.14; et al.). See further on 6.12; 10.1–3; 11.8, 19. Cf. Collins, *Apocalypse* xii–xvii; 'Book of Revelation' 384–414, esp. 390–403.

The balance between the earthly and the heavenly is typical of John's *Christology*. The Jesus of the Apocalypse is the one who was crucified in history, but is now exalted and alive in eternity (1.18); he is first and last, but active in the life of the Church (1.8, 17; 2.8–17); he is the Lion who is also the Lamb (5.5–6), the messianic Lord of earth as well as heaven (12.9–10) and the glorified Christ who dispatches his angel to the angels of the local churches with a testimony for them (22.16). Significantly for the purpose of Revelation (see above), the prophet-seer also ascribes to Jesus, in the opening vision of 1.12–20, the attributes of God himself. Both God and Jesus are confessed as Alpha and Omega (1.8; 22.13). Christ, like the Father himself, is seen in the Apocalypse as the mediator of creation, redemption and the final kingdom (3.14; 5.5–14; 19.11–16), and the kingdom of the world is described as becoming jointly 'the sovereign realm of our Lord and his Messiah' (11.15).

At the same time, the exalted Christ who is one with God is also human. He appears as 'a son of man figure', although clothed in the vesture of majesty (1.13). He keeps close to the congregations of Asia, and promises to come to them soon (2.16; 3.11; 22.12, 20), while sharing with God himself the eternal throne of sovereignty (22.3). The high Christology of Revelation, which includes a perception of the unity between Jesus and God (1.8, 17; et al.), delineates this drama as inescapably Christian in character (against Charles [1920], who believes that the seer rewrote Jewish apocalyptic sources, using his own diction; see e.g. *idem* 1, 191–203, on 7.1–8; cf. also Rowland, *Open Heaven* 193–267; Guthrie, *Relevance* 16–17).

The *pneumatology* of Revelation is similarly balanced. John's teaching in this area seems to prepare the way for the fourth evangelist's view of the person and ministry of the Spirit. Although the Spirit's character in the Apocalypse appears to be less than fully personal (1.4; 4.5; 5.6), and is not identified as the Paraclete (John 14.16, 26; et al.), he *is* understood as a person who may be distinguished from both the Father and the Son (Rev. 1.4–6; 22.17), as well as identified with them (3.1). The words of Christ are accordingly described as the speech of the Spirit (2.1, 7; et al.). The prophet-seer also develops the personal nature of the Spirit's being in a sophisticated manner by representing him as responsive to the divine will (14.13; 22.12, 17); see Bruce, 'Spirit' 342–44.

Second, while there is no concept in Revelation of the Spirit indwelling the Church and its members (contrast, for instance, John 14.17; 1 John 3.24; et al.), the Spirit is closely related to the prophet-seer himself (Rev. 1.10; 4.2; 21.10; et al.). Third, even if clear elements in the ministry of the Spirit, such as teaching, witness, renewal and leading into the truth (cf. John 3.5; 14.26; 15.26; 16.13; et al.), are not present in the Apocalypse, the Spirit nevertheless bears witness to what is to come (Rev. 1.10–11, 19; 4.1–2; 22.6; et al.), judges (5.6), and acts as the Spirit of prophecy who testifies through the witnesses of Jesus (cf. esp. on 19.10; also 11.3–10; 22.6). For this section see further Smalley, 'Paraclete' 292–96.

Above all, John's presentation of the activity of the Spirit in Revelation, as in the Fourth Gospel, links together heaven and earth. For the seer perceives that the Spirit is at work in both dimensions, and that he brings them together. Thus, John receives his visions on Patmos 'in the Spirit' (1.9–10; et al.); in ecstasy he is taken up from earth to heaven (4.1–2); and in Spirit he sees the new Jerusalem coming *down* from God in heaven (21.10). This balanced view is not out of line with the doctrine of the Spirit in the Pauline corpus and other parts of the New Testament (cf. Swete, *Holy Spirit*, esp. 272–78). But, in my judgement, its careful symmetry is designed, as part of the theological perspective in Revelation, to address the circumstantial needs and problems which were being experienced by the immediate audience of the drama (see above).

Symmetry of this kind also belongs to the *eschatology* of Revelation. John draws together the present and the future, the temporal and the eternal; and he constantly views eternity in and through time. The centre of salvation lies in the Christ-event, and in him time is divided anew. Thereafter, the Christian Church looks forward to a final and decisive appearing of the exalted Messiah, and to life in the new Jerusalem (see on Rev. 21.2); but, at the same time, the saints look back to that moment when history was invaded in a new way by that which is supra-historical.

In the scheme of the Revelation, this means that thematic theology is more important than chronology (cf. Fiorenza, *Book of Revelation* 46–56). The eschatological climax of the Apocalypse is not at the end of time, or at the end of the book; for, although a final judgement is envisaged (Rev. 20.7–15), in one sense the end never comes (see on

22.20). The centre of the ages lies in the past (Chapters 4—5), even if the sovereignty of God in Christ has still to be acknowledged (5.13–14). The achievement of God's plan for his world, and the subjugation of secular rebellion, forms the story of Rev. 6—22; but meanwhile John never says *when* the end will come, and finality itself appears to be elusive (see on 6.17; et al.). In the writer's understanding of salvation, the past, the present and the future are all important, and his eschatology never loses contact with reality (see Topham, 'Dimensions of the New Jerusalem' 417–19, esp. 417). His testimony is for the Asian community *and* for the Church universal. For John, the apocalypse of the future is already in progress; and a new and eternal quality of living is offered through the Lamb in the present. Such an eschatological perspective is distinctive, and provides a specially creative setting for the drama which unfolds within it.

A final theological concept in Revelation, which again manifests a typically Johannine balance, is that of the Church. The *ecclesiology* of the prophet-seer is predominantly corporate, and he mostly portrays the Church as a unity, or local churches as collective groups. The occasional individual is brought on to the earthly stage, such as Antipas the witness (Rev. 2.13), or John himself (1.1). But usually the Church as a whole is in view, whether it is criticized, praised, divided, opposed or attacked. Notably in Rev. 2—3, its members are together: working, confessing, enduring, conquering, worshipping and listening. If togetherness is a mark of the Church on earth, the same is manifestly true of the Church triumphant in Revelation. Some individual, supernatural dramatis personae are introduced, including God himself (4.2–3), the Lamb (5.6), an elder (7.13), an identifiable angel (8.3), Michael and the dragon (12.7), and two separate beasts (13.1, 11). Yet the company of the new Israel in its totality is at the centre of the dramatic action which takes place in heaven. Together, its members worship and receive healing through judgement (21.3–4; et al.). Even the heavenly roll-call (7.4–8) is by tribes, not by personal names; the vision in the remainder of that scene is of a great and innumerable multitude (7.9–10); and the woman who flees to the wilderness is not an individual, but a collective, ecclesial figure (12.1–6; see esp. on 12.1). The covenant theme, which is a feature of the new life in the new Jerusalem, similarly speaks of a close relationship between God and his *people*, who are sealed as authentic members of the new Israel (7.2–3; 10.1–7; 21.2—22.5).

The ecclesiological sector of John's theology evinces the same coherence as that which belongs to the others so far reviewed. The Church of God and of the Lamb in Revelation is both militant on earth and triumphant in heaven. Once more there is a double polarity, as John moves his audience from the material to the spiritual levels, and back again. So the martyred and resurrected prophets, by heavenly command, go up to heaven from the great city in a cloud (11.7–12); the messianic head of the Church is born on earth, but 'snatched away' in exaltation up to God in heaven (12.5); the glorified Lamb stands with the company of the redeemed on Mount Zion itself (14.1); an angel in midheaven proclaims the eternal gospel to those who live on earth (14.6); the redeemed community in Christ is not totally separated from the society of this world, since the new Jerusalem comes down out of heaven from God (21.1–2); and through it all the Church, on earth and in heaven, worships its Lord even as it waits for him (1.5–7; 3.3; 4.11; 7.14–17; 11.16–18; 15.3–4; 22.20–21). For this section see further Smalley, 'Johannine Community' 98–99. For the interpretation of John's theology as a whole see Smalley, *Thunder and Love* 147–57.

8 The Symbolism

The Apocalypse is rich in its use of symbols, and is indeed one of the most figurative compositions in the whole of the New Testament. The prophet-seer draws heavily on this literary form, which was a normative part of the apparatus of Jewish and Christian apocalyptic literature, to help him disclose truths about the present and the future to the members of his audience, and offer them encouragement in the face of spiritual, doctrinal and political insecurity. Most, if not all, of these symbols would have been familiar to John's hearers, even if the significance of some of them – notably in numerical form – may not be immediately apparent to a present-day readership (see on 13.18; 14.1; et al.).

The symbols in Revelation are typically Johannine in character, in that they bring together the levels of matter and spirit (see above). As with any part of the drama of the Apocalypse, John's symbolism must be read in the light of both dimensions, physical and spiritual, temporal and eternal. Thus, for example, the seven angels are commanded from the *heavenly* tent to pour out their bowls of wrath upon the *earth* (15.5—16.1). Similarly, the apparently material elements of thunder and fire, of water and light, and the earthly instruments of sickle and sword, of thrones and incense, have a double, spiritual significance, both judgemental and salvific, to which in each case they point.

A number of principles must be applied, if the symbolism of Revelation is to be interpreted properly, and the total message of this book rightly understood.

(a) The history of the interpretation of the Apocalypse has been marked by a sharp division between those who have treated the work and its imagery literally, and those whose perception of the drama is entirely metaphorical, and therefore spiritual. Associated with the literal approach is the reception of Revelation in the early Church, and the fact that the book remained a 'disputed' part of the scriptural canon until at least the fourth century AD (cf. Boring 2–5; Roloff 14–15). In my view, it is impossible to take the symbolism of the Apocalypse literally, and to do so is to misread John totally. At the same time, I would suggest that it is equally misguided to attempt an interpretation of John's symbolism in absolutely 'spiritual' terms, without any reference to the physical realities which are their counterpart; for the one level consistently points to the other, and informs it (see above).

(b) John's eschatology, it has been noted above, embraces the present as well as the future. As a result his symbolism, and Revelation as a whole, cannot be understood as referring solely to what will take place in the future or at the end. The trumpets herald judgement here, as well as hereafter (8.2–6); the gates of the heavenly city stand open now, to welcome believers who have washed their robes already, or will do so in time to come (22.14); and the throne of God's sovereignty is established in this world, as well as in the next (4.2–3; 20.11; 22.1).

(c) When the prophet-seer's apocalyptic imagery draws on the background of the Old Testament, it is reasonable to begin with its use in Judaism in order to interpret it. Earthquakes, for example, are a repeated biblical symbol for the dissolution of a rebellious society at the self-manifestation of God (as at Isa. 29.6; Zech. 14.5). Revelation continues that symbolism (Rev. 6.12; 8.5; 11.13; 16.18; et al.). But many of John's other pictures, including those drawn from the Old Testament – such as temple, altar and incense – have been given a new meaning, precisely because the seer is now using them in a Christian context (see on 5.8; 6.9; 8.3–4; 21.22; et al.).

(d) Details involved in the symbolism of the Apocalypse are not always germane to the central idea which is being expressed. For example, the christological significance of the Lamb in heaven, slaughtered but victorious (5.6), is at that moment in the throne-vision more important than the exact relevance and meaning of the scroll which Christ takes, and is alone able to open (5.7–10). John paints his dramatic canvas more as an impressionist, with broad strokes, than as a creator of photographic detail.

(e) In any search for the meaning of John's apocalyptic symbolism, coherence is crucial. It will not do to concentrate on one image at the expense of others, or to link one symbolic depiction, such as that of the beast or Babylon, with a figure or society belonging to a particular period of history. This was the practice of some medieval commentators, but it remains a faulty exegetical procedure (cf. Guthrie, *Relevance* 31).

(f) The final interpretative principle relates to the double polarity of the symbolism in Revelation, noted above. It is that the meaning of John's symbols is always greater than the symbols themselves (Cf. Ellul, *Apocalypse* 33–35). This suggestion involves a further theological principle, concerning the difference between a symbol and a sacrament (on this point see further Smalley, *John* 234–38). In the Christian scheme, a *symbol* is a depiction, usually of a material object or element, which is used to evoke a spiritual reality. A *sacrament*, in contrast, actually conveys, through the physical instruments involved, what is spiritual and indeed divine. Like the fourth evangelist, accordingly, John the Divine does not stop with the symbolic. He introduces a truly sacramental dimension to his theology and thought since, throughout the vision of the Apocalypse, the seer perceives that matter is the potential carrier of spirit.

It will be for John the evangelist to develop this teaching later. Meanwhile the John of Revelation understands already, in his visions as in his symbolism, that the concept of human salvation through divine judgement is not only pictured but also made real. The destruction of Babylon (Rev. 17—18), for instance, is not simply an evocation of God's wrath in response to rebellious humanity; it also demonstrates what actually takes place in society whenever systemic evil and idolatry prevail. The light which shines eternally in the holy city, through the glory of God and in response to faith (21.23–24), also tangibly breaks through the darkness of this world at the present time. As with all John's imagery, such symbols make it possible for the believer to discern and encounter the reality of divine judgement and love, and to experience the ultimate reality of God himself in Christ (21.3–4; cf. Ellul, *Apocalypse* 35; also, for this section, Smalley, *Thunder and Love* 157–60).

9 The Interpretation

Previous scholarly comment on the meaning and message of the Apocalypse has tended to concentrate on the eschatological scope of the work, and notably on the nature of the millennium, the reign of one thousand years mentioned in Rev. 20 (q.v.). Interpretations have ranged from the literalism of such early Fathers as Justin Martyr (*Dial.* 81) and Irenaeus (*Adv. Haer.* 5.34.2–35.2), through the spiritualizing, allegorical methods of Origen (*De Princ.* 2.11.2–3) and Andreas (*Comm. in Apoc.* 60–63; as in *PG* 106, 407–15, esp. 410), to a method of understanding Revelation which, as in many contemporary studies, takes proper account of the situation of John himself, as well as of the events which will anticipate and finally bring about a future consummation.

Earlier expositions of the Revelation have given rise to four main approaches to its interpretation. It will be clear from the Introduction so far, and from the exegesis which follows (note particularly the treatment of the millennium passage at 20.1–10), that the interpretative approach adopted in this commentary is neither *preterist* (a first-century AD, contemporary-historical, view; cf. Farrar, 'The Beast' 321–51, esp. 335 [the Nero-story is the 'key' to Revelation]), nor *historicist* (the work describes the movements in Christian history as they have been fulfilled up to the time of the individual commentator; cf. Bengel 186–89), nor *futurist* (Revelation discloses what has yet to take place in the purposes of God; cf. Milligan, *Lectures* 126–60, esp. 156–60). For these three views, all of which include fine variations, see Beale 44–48. For a survey of the range of possibilities still open to the interpreter of the Apocalypse see further Court, *Myth and History* 1–19.

I follow Beale (48–49) in adopting a view which may be best described as *modified idealist*. Revelation is a symbolic portrayal of the timeless conflict between the forces of good and evil, God and Satan. But this involves a final consummation in judgement and salvation, even if that finality is not depicted in terms which are precisely chronological. In the Apocalypse, salvation history is seen to be under the sovereignty of God and the risen Lamb, who guide the events narrated 'until they finally issue in the last judgment and the definitive establishment of (God's) kingdom' (Beale 48). For a similar stance see the commentaries by Hendriksen (1962), Caird (1984), Hughes (1990), Sweet (1990), Wilcock (1991) and Knight (1999).

10 The Relevance

There is a place, in such a study as this, for considering the relevance of the book of Revelation to the Christian life and thought of our own day. How may John's testimony be applied to the spiritual needs and practical problems of the contemporary Church, and of the world in which it is placed? That this is a proper enquiry is supported by the fact that the author of the Apocalypse composes his drama against two backcloths. He speaks first to the situation of the Johannine community itself, with its internal doctrinal and ethical problems, and its external pressures. But John the Divine's vision also embraces a cosmic dimension, since the Spirit speaks through him to the churches *in* time, and to the people of God *throughout* time, and into eternity. This disclosure has a reference which is both universal and timeless (1.1–2).

The possible applications of John's message are numerous, as are the interpretations of its teaching. On the basis of the commentary which follows, I will offer just six topics for consideration, all of which are theologically interrelated.

Christ

The Apocalypse demonstrates the need for the Christian Church and its members to adopt a Christology which is balanced. The person of Christ in Revelation, as in other parts of the Johannine corpus, is poised between the earthly and the exalted, the human and the divine. Such symmetry enables the living and exalted Jesus to become the Saviour of the world (1.4–7; cf. John 4.42; 1 John 4.14). It also shapes the purpose of the Apocalypse, which was written in part to address the problems of belief and behaviour within John's own circle. Inadequate christological understanding, which was not confined to the Johannine congregations in Asia (cf. 1 Cor. 1.10–25; et al.), brought about tensions, and provoked an idolatrous tendency to compromise with pagan society (see on Rev. 2.14–15; et al.). Nevertheless, John's plea for balance, from Revelation to 3 John, was not heeded; and secession, followed by the disintegration of the community, followed.

The story of John's churches provides a warning for the Christian Church of today. Whenever, in the history of the Church, the balance of its christological teaching has been upset, doctrinal and practical errors have resulted. A living, worshipping and morally affirmative community of believers needs to take serious account of the apocalyptist's plea for equilibrium in understanding the person of Jesus. The same is true if the Church of God is to make any worthwhile contribution to ecumenical progress or world mission. See further Robinson, 'What Future for a Unique Christ?' 9–17.

Time

The balance which is characteristic of the Christology of the Apocalypse extends to its eschatology. The visions of the prophet-seer relate not just to the future but also to the realities of the present; and Revelation speaks of the need to take seriously all the tenses of salvation: past, present and future. The kingdom of God, and the King of the kingdom, come in *now*, as well as at the end of the age (1.3; 2.16; 22.12–13; et al.); and such an eschatological promise includes its own challenge, to submit to the divine sovereignty in time, as well as in eternity. Because the apocalypse is always in progress, moreover, the Church and its members cannot escape from the responsibilities of the present, into a purely 'spiritual' realm of the future. Unlike the dualist separations between this world and the next, typical of gnostic thought, Revelation presented John's community with a call to live and work in the present, and not simply to anticipate the future. Repentance and faith were essential in first-century Asia Minor, just as they are for Christians at any time (2.5; 3.10–11; 9.21; 22.14–15; et al.). The risen Christ stands at the door of the Church on earth (3.20), as well as being enthroned within the gates of the heavenly Jerusalem (22.1).

Such teaching requires a willingness for the saints in any age to be faithful in meeting their obligations towards both Church and society, in national and international terms. Because John's eschatological testimony embraces the present as well as the future, moreover, it holds out both the individual and collective hope of renewal and transformation, in this world as well as in the next (see on 21.1). The pressing demand now is for the Church to share this new dimension of being with others, and to work for urban and rural renaissance in the society which surrounds it. Transfiguration of this kind, it needs to be added, includes within it the dynamic need to be *continually* transfigured.

Church

Attention has already been drawn to the strongly corporate nature of John's teaching in Revelation about the Church, as about salvation itself (see above). However, despite this sense of collective belonging within the Christian body, the prophet-seer was actually addressing churches with divisive problems, and a situation of incipient disunity and disintegration. In contrast, John's vision of the Church triumphant is of a circle which is truly united, characterized by healing rather than disparity. The Lord God is the light of those who belong to the new Jerusalem, and its members will reign *together* for ever (22.1–5). The seer understands that the consummation of God's purposes for the salvation of his people will be achieved when humanity exists eternally in covenant community with him (21.2–26). See further on the cubic shape of the holy city at 21.16.

The conflict on earth between good and evil, whatever form that struggle takes, will always produce difficulty and suffering. Nevertheless, John's Revelation shows that ultimately the establishment of God's sovereignty, and the perfection of his people, will be the triumphant outcome. That consummation may be anticipated even now. There is no need to wait until entry into the holy city becomes a reality for the process of ecumenism to begin. It may seem that the political unity of the world remains an elusive dream. But there is no reason why the unity of the Church in the present should not become its token and guarantee.

World

John's cosmology in Revelation includes a double polarity which is typical of his theology in general. The drama of the Apocalypse is enacted on two levels at once, the heavenly and the earthly; and such a perspective leads the prophet-seer to take a positive view of creation. With a sacramentalism which is truly Johannine (see above), the writer is able to affirm the value of this world, as well as the next, and to acknowledge the relationship between them. As a result, it is possible to investigate what *on earth* the book is all about, in addition to probing its spiritual significance (cf. Caird, 'Deciphering the Book of Revelation' 13–15). In John's balanced vision, the old order becomes the new; and in the new world, which receives its focus in the new Jerusalem, God dwells with his people in close, covenant relationship (see on 21.1–7). But the connection between heaven and earth remains, and God in Christ is seen to be at work in both.

Two major, practical implications arise from the seer's distinctive understanding of the world. First, as in the Fourth Gospel, the writer seems to be inviting his audience to celebrate life, and to *enjoy* God's new creation. According to the Judaeo-Christian scheme, God's creation is good: indeed, very good (Gen. 1.31). It is only spoilt by humanity's attitude towards it, and our treatment of it. In place of this, John's teaching in Revelation asserts positively that the world and its heavenly counterpart are to be properly affirmed, and underscores the point by using messianic banquet imagery (Rev. 3.20; 7.16–17; 19.9; 22.17; et al.). The second application of John's cosmology relates to ecological issues. If the world is good, and rightly to be enjoyed, then it is to be respected. The Church in our own day has a responsibility to give an overt lead in the task of preserving and conserving nature, and of protecting creation from the selfish ravages of those who would abuse it. Christians, as well as others, are called to be friendly towards the earth (see further Sweet 2–5).

Power

The material in the Apocalypse carries obvious sociological implications, but includes as well a clearly political reference (cf. Thompson, *Book of Revelation*, esp. 171–210). Essays in the theology of power had been written before Revelation, notably in the prophecy of Daniel. But the Apocalypse was the first attempt to present a theodicy of salvation through judgement to a Christian audience (see Robinson, 'Interpreting' 56–64, esp. 58–61). John writes in the light of the definitive advent of God in Christ, as a result of which all power, in heaven and on earth, has been given to the Lamb who is victorious over Satan and his angels (Rev. 5.12; 12.7–12). One task of the prophet-seer is to address a situation of unbelief and persecution, death and destruction, in which that truth appears to have no relevance; and his attempt to do so was prompted by the problems of inadequate belief and conduct, and political oppression, which were being experienced by his own community (see above).

John's answer is twofold. First, the distress will not continue for ever, since God's victorious power will ultimately prevail, and the Church will be delivered (12.12; 20.1–15). Second, all power is derived, either from God or from the forces of evil (1.8; 13.2); and this means that its human use may be for purposes which are good or ill. As a result the members of the Church, and of society itself, are challenged to use the power they receive properly: with both justice and love (see on 19.1–16). See further the excursus on 194–95.

Resurrection

The final contemporary application of the message of Revelation concerns John's teaching about life beyond death. The drama of the Apocalypse is shot through with the reality of hope, both individual and corporate. At one level, John assures the members of his congregations that, if they endure faithfully, they will survive external antagonisms and internal conflicts. Evidently this happened. Even if the Johannine circle, as such, eventually disappeared, Ignatius was still able, in the early years of the second century AD, to address the churches of Asia, including Ephesus, as flourishing groups (Swete xcvii). But the testimony of hope in Revelation is ultimately more inclusive than this. It holds out to every believer the serious expectation of resurrection and the promise of God's final victory in Christ over evil and death. Now, and always, God may dwell with his people and they with him (21.3).

There is accordingly a universal reference in Revelation. The theme of a divine judgement which is salvific is addressed to the whole Church, and to every society in every age. By the light of the glory of God and of the Lamb the nations walk (21.24), and the therapeutic leaves of the tree of life are intended indiscriminately for the whole world (22.2). This need not imply that everyone will respond to the invitation to receive God's eternally new life. To enter the new Jerusalem it is still necessary to keep the covenant and to be holy (7.9–14; 22.11–15); and part of John's intention is to show his hearers that right conduct, flowing from adequate faith, is enabled by the Lamb himself, who is one with the Father as well as with his Church. Nevertheless, John's vision of the new life which God offers to the world through his Son is in the end inclusive rather than exclusive. All who wish may come to him, just as he comes to his believing community (21.2–4).

Such a hope can bring encouragement to the Church of the present, as it must have done to the community of faith in John's day. Light from the heavenly city shines on our own darknesses: personal, communal, international. The book of Revelation as a whole is a standing reminder that life is stronger than death, that hope cannot be conquered by despair, and that eventually the kingdom of this world will become the kingdom of our Lord and of his Messiah, and that he will reign for ever and ever (11.15). For this section see further Smalley, *Thunder and Love* 173–80.

11 The Structure

No scholarly consensus exists about the structural analysis of Revelation, and the many theories which have been advanced are often complex in character (see further Aune xc–cv; Beale 108–51). Moreover, while a narrative approach to the book is entirely legitimate, it cannot be detached from the theology and interpretation of the Apocalypse; and this inevitably opens the way to further variations. In this connection, a broad distinction may be drawn between commentators, such as Charles, who understand John's sevenfold visions (seals, trumpets, bowls) in a strictly chronological sense, and those who follow Victorinus of Pettau, who died *c.* AD 304, in finding in this material a pattern of recapitulation. That is to say, the recurring cycles in Revelation are interpreted as descriptions of the same situation of judgement and salvation, perceived from differing eschatological viewpoints (cf. Boxall, *Revelation* 9–12). Modern commentaries usually adopt some form of the theory of recapitulation (Mounce 31); and my own view is that the content of Revelation, rather than being chronologically ordered, is theologically and thematically conceived (cf. Fiorenza, *Book of Revelation* 163).

Establishing the exact sequence of the material in the Apocalypse, then, is difficult and ultimately unimportant. It is more crucial to perceive the timeless truth about God's salvific purposes for his creation, now and in the future, which forms the heart of John's testimony. Nevertheless, there is progress in Revelation; but it is a development which moves the audience to 'a fuller experience of the divine plan for final victory rather than a progress that ticks off the minutes on an eschatological clock' (Mounce 33). The movement of the drama is spiral, not linear. The numbered plagues intensify the depth of the judgement to come, rather than making it happen (see on 6.17); the trumpets announce that divine retribution has arrived, but instead of human repentance (9.21) a heavenly hymn of praise ushers in a vision of the ark of the covenant (11.19); the bowls express a final outpouring of God's wrath, and yet Babylon remains to be destroyed (Chapters 17—18). The whole action points towards the end of history, the conquest of wrongdoing, and a consummation of God's eternal will for the faithful (Chapters

19—22). But, in the Apocalypse at least, that end never arrives (22.20). See further on
John's eschatology, above; also Milligan 367–74, on the new Jerusalem (21.9—22.5)
as a vision of God dwelling in a covenant relationship with his people in the past, present
and future.

In view of the distinctive nature of John's teaching in Revelation, therefore, it
is preferable to attempt an analysis of the structure of the book in literary terms alone;
although the theological content of John's themes may still be allowed to emerge in that
way. Using such an approach, commentators have reached varied conclusions. Kiddle
(xxvii–xxxiii), for instance, regards the Apocalypse as a creative, poetic work, which
follows no logical plan, but impresses on its readers the reality of impending
judgement. Others have discovered in Revelation patterns which are liturgical in
character, and claim that these have influenced the form of the book. See e.g. the work
of Stanley, 'Carmenque Christo' 173–91; Delling, 'Zum gottesdienstlichen Stil' 107–
137; Läuchli, 'Gottesdienststruktur' 359–78; Shepherd, *Paschal Liturgy*, esp. 77–97;
O'Rourke, 'Hymns' 399–409; Vanni, 'Liturgical Dialogue' 348–72; Barker, *The
Revelation* 373–88; Filho, 'Apocalypse of John' 213–34. For a study which is sensitive
to the shaping of the Apocalypse by symbolic figures and colours, and to the reception of the work in art, see Prévost, *How to Read the Apocalypse*, esp. 25–41.

The suggestion that the book of Revelation reflects elements of (Greek) drama is not
new. Note the work of Dansk, *Drama of the Apocalypse*; Brewer, 'Influence of Greek
Drama' 74–92; and Bowman, 'The Revelation' 436–53. But until the publication of
Michael Wilcock's commentary (1975/1989; see esp. 15–18), and my own monograph,
Thunder and Love (see esp. 103–10), scholars have seemed reluctant to explore the idea
that the Apocalypse *in toto* has been arranged as a sustained and carefully constructed
dramatic presentation. It appears to me that Revelation lends itself naturally to such an
interpretation, and that to approach the work in terms of its dramatic structure throws
floods of light on John's central testimony. Furthermore, I see no conflict between the
reception of John's genuine visions on Patmos, and the artistic awareness and creative
skill with which he has committed them to writing later. See further below, and on
1.9–11.

For a full treatment of the dramatic features which control the composition of the
Apocalypse see Smalley, *Thunder and Love* 105–107. These include the involvement
of the audience in the action; the progress of the narrative in spiral, rather than linear,
form; the use of intervals between the main acts; the inclusion of colour in the backcloth; and the forensic setting of the entire play. This is made up of two major acts, which
announce the central theological themes of Revelation; these are introduced by a prologue, and concluded by an epilogue. The resulting structure of the apocalyptic drama,
with its marked sevenfold patterning, is set out below.

12 The Drama

The Revelation to John

Prologue: The Oracle Is Disclosed (1.1–8)
   Superscription: The Revelation to John (1.1–3)
   Salutation and Doxology (1.4–8)

Act 1: Creation, and Salvation through Judgement (1.9—11.19)

Scene 1: Seven Oracles (1.9–3.22)
   Vision of the Son of Man (1.9–18)
   The Commission to Write (1.19–20)
   Letters to the Seven Churches (2.1—3.22)
      Ephesus (2.1–7)
      Smyrna (2.8–11)
      Pergamum (2.12–17)
      Thyatira (2.18–29)
      Sardis (3.1–6)
      Philadelphia (3.7–13)
      Laodicea (3.14–22)

Interval: Adoration in Heaven's Court: God and His Christ (4.1—5.14)

Scene 2: Seven Seals (6.1–17)
   Seals 1–4: The Four Horsemen (6.1–8)
   Seal 5: The Cry of the Martyrs (6.9–11)
   Seal 6: The Great Earthquake (6.12–17)

Interval: The Church Protected (7.1–17)

Scene 3: Seven Trumpets (8.1—9.21)
   Seal 7: Silence in Heaven (8.1)
   Prelude: Censing of the Saints (8.2–6)
   Trumpets 1–4: Portents of the End (8.7–12)
   The Eagle's Warning (8.13)
   Trumpet 5 (First Woe): Locusts (9.1–12)
   Trumpet 6 (Second Woe): Fiendish Cavalry (9.13–21)

Interval: God's Sovereignty (10.1—11.19)
   The Angel from Heaven (10.1–11)
   Measuring the Temple (11.1–2)
   The Two Witnesses (11.3–14)
   Trumpet 7 (Third Woe): Redemption through Conflict (11.15–19)

The Revelation to John (*cont'd*)

Act 2: Salvation through Judgement, and New Creation (12.1—22.17)

Scene 4: Seven Signs (12.1—14.20)
   Sign 1: The Woman (12.1–2)
   Sign 2: The Huge Dragon (12.3–6)
   Sign 3: War in Heaven (12.7–9)
      A Song of Praise in Heaven (12.10–12)
   Sign 4: War on Earth (12.13–18)
   Sign 5: The Beast from the Sea (13.1–10)
   Sign 6: The Beast from the Earth (13.11–18)
      A Vision of the Redeemed (14.1–5)
   Sign 7: Angelic Judgement (14.6–20)

Interval: A New Exodus (15.1–8)
   Prologue (15.1)
   An Exodus Hymn (15.2–4)
   The Angelic Commission (15.5–8)

Scene 5: Seven Bowls (16.1–21)
   Prelude: The Angelic Mission (16.1)
   Bowls 1–3: Natural Disasters of Judgement (16.2–4)
   Judgement Doxologies (16.5–7)
   Bowls 4–7: The Final Battle Heralded (16.8–21)

Interval: The Fall of Babylon (17.1—18.24)
   Introduction (17.1–2)
   Vision of the Woman and the Scarlet Beast (17.3–6)
   The Interpretation of the Vision (17.7–18)
   Lament over Babylon and a Call to Rejoice (18.1–20)
   Babylon Destroyed (18.21–24)

Scene 6: Seven Visions (19.1—20.15)
   Introduction: Rejoicing in Heaven (19.1–5)
   Vision 1: The Marriage Feast of the Lamb (19.6–10)
   Vision 2: The Warrior-Messiah (19.11–16)
   Vision 3: Antichrist Destroyed (19.17–21)
   Vision 4: Satan Bound (20.1–3)
   Vision 5: A Millennial Reign (20.4–6)
   Vision 6: Satan Destroyed (20.7–10)
   Vision 7: Final Judgement (20.11–15)

Interval: Prelude to the Final Scene (21.1)
   The New Creation

Scene 7: Seven Prophecies (21.2—22.17)
   Prophecy 1: New Covenant (21.2–4)
   Prophecy 2: New Life (21.5–8)
   Prophecy 3: New Jerusalem (21.9–21)
   Prophecy 4: New Temple (21.22–27)
   Prophecy 5: New Relationship (22.1–5)
   Prophecy 6: New Advent (22.6–9)
   Prophecy 7: New Testimony (22.10–17)

Epilogue: The Oracle Is Complete (22.18–21)

THE REVELATION TO JOHN

The Oracle Is Disclosed
(1.1–8)

Translation

1 [1]A revelation from Jesus Christ, which God gave him, to make known to his servants what must swiftly take place; and he disclosed it by sending his angel to his servant John, [2]who bore witness to everything that he perceived: the word of God, and the testimony of Jesus Christ. [3]Happy is the reader, and those who listen to the words of the prophecy and adhere to what is written in it; for the moment is approaching.

[4]John, to the seven churches which are in Asia: grace and peace to you from the one who is, and who was, and who is coming; and from the seven spirits who are in front of his throne, [5]and from Jesus Christ, the faithful witness, the firstborn from the dead and the prince of temporal rulers.

To him who loves us, and has released us[a] from our sins by his blood, [6]and has appointed us as a royal house, priests to his God and Father, to him be glory and might for ever and ever.[b] Amen.

> [7]Look! He is coming with the clouds,
>> and every eye will see him, including those who stabbed him;
>> and all the families on earth will lament on his account.
> So be it. Amen.
> [8]'I am the Alpha and the Omega',[c] says the Lord God,
>> 'who is, and who was, and who is coming: the Omnipotent.'

Text

[a] The major MSS (including 𝔓18 ℵ[c] A C Andreas it[h] syr[ph, h] arm Primasius) read λύσαντι ἡμᾶς ἐκ (*lysanti hēmas ek*, 'has released us from', as in the translation; while others (especially ℵ*) omit ἡμᾶς (*hēmas*, 'us'). But the context demands the inclusion of the object of Christ's redemption, even if it is implied by the use of ἡμᾶς (*hēmas*, 'us') earlier in the sentence. For λύσαντι (*lysanti*, 'released') a few witnesses (e.g. 025 1006 Byz it[gig] vg cop[bo] eth) have λούσαντι (*lousanti*, 'washed'). Swete (7–8) points out that the concept of 'release' from sin is biblical (Job 42.9, LXX; cf. Rev. 20.7), but admits that 'cleansing' from iniquity in this passage makes good sense, and presents a more usual metaphor (so Ps. 51.2; Isa. 1.16; 1 Cor. 6.11; Heb. 10.22; Rev. 7.14, q.v.). However, the alternative reading rests on inferior authority, and should be rejected. In any case 'redemption' (through judgement) is a leading theological theme in this part of the Apocalypse, and indeed throughout the book.

[b] In the phrase εἰς τοὺς αἰῶνας τῶν αἰώνων (*eis tous aiōnas tōn aiōnōn*, 'for ever and ever', lit. 'to the ages of the ages'), as in ℵ C vg syr[ph,h] arm eth, et al., some MSS (including 𝔓18 A 046 cop[bo]) omit τῶν αἰώνων (*tōn aiōnōn*, 'and ever'); and one MS (2344) omits εἰς τοὺς αἰῶνας, *eis tous aiōnas*, 'for ever'. The simple doxological formula, 'for ever' (cf. Rom. 16.27), is likely to be more original here, and expanded (under liturgical influence) later.

^c 'Alpha and Omega' is read by ℵ^c A C 025 it^h arm eth, et al. But a few witnesses (such as ℵ⋆ vg) add ἀρχὴ καὶ τέλος (*archē kai telos*, 'the beginning and the end'). If the longer text were original, however, it is difficult to account for the shorter. The variant must be a copyist's expansion, influenced by 21.6 (q.v.).

Literary Setting

The first section of the book of Revelation (1.1–8) introduces a literary and theological composition which contains a strong, overarching and dramatic structure. This consists of a prologue, two main acts with their leading themes, and an epilogue:

Prologue: The Oracle Is Disclosed (Rev. 1.1–8)
Act 1: Creation, and Salvation through Judgement (1.9—11.19)
Act 2: Salvation through Judgement, and New Creation (12.1—22.17)
Epilogue: The Oracle Is Complete (22.18–21)

For the unity and structure of the Apocalypse see Smalley, *Thunder and Love* 97–110, esp. 105. Michaels (26) notes the repeated use of ἐν πνεύματι (*en pneumati*, 'in the Spirit') in Revelation, which in his view creates four main sections in the book: 1.9—3.22; 4.1—16.21; 17.1—21.8; 21.9—22.15. These divisions are preceded by an introduction (1.1–8), and followed by a conclusion (22.16–21). I would argue that the unity of the Apocalypse is dramatically structured, and tighter than Michaels allows.

The Prologue itself falls into two parts: the superscription (1.1–3) and the address (verses 4–8). The opening verses (1–3) set out the origin of John's revelation, its content and the effect on those who proclaim and receive its teaching. The address (verses 4–8) includes John's greeting to the seven churches making up the Johannine community in Asia Minor (on this community see Smalley, *Thunder and Love* 57–73, 134–37; also *idem*, 'Johannine Community' 95–104; *idem, John* 181–85).

In the first verse (4) of the address, the writer adopts an epistolary form common in the New Testament: the name of the author, a reference to the recipient(s), and a benediction followed by a doxology (as in 1 Cor. 1.1–3; Eph. 1.1–2; cf. 2 John 1–3). There is a sense, therefore, in which the whole of Revelation, from 1.4 to its close, is an epistle (so Charles 1, 8). Letters were well-established forms of instruction in Greek literature before the Christian era (Finkenrath, 'ἐπιστολή' 246–49, esp. 246); and the New Testament epistles are descendants of this means of teaching. The didactic content of Revelation seems to be cast in a similarly epistolary form. So John refers to 'reading aloud' (presumably during worship; cf. Rom. 16.16; Col. 4.16) the 'prophecy' which follows; and he speaks of attention being given to it by the congregation (Rev. 1.3). Seven letters also appear in Rev. 2 and 3; and the epilogue reads like the conclusion of an actual epistle (22.18–21; see also 22.6–17).

Moreover, as with all the New Testament letters, the Apocalypse is addressed to a living and contemporary church situation: to deal with particular community problems, as well as to encourage its audience in the face of persecution (see 4–6). But Revelation is *more than a letter*: it is also an apocalypse and a prophecy. The writer is a Christian prophet, as well as a seer who uses Jewish apocalyptic sources and forms (Smalley, *Thunder and Love* 28–31). So this book manifests features in line with the literary genres of apocalyptic and visionary prophecy known to us from elsewhere, including the Old Testament (ibid. 102); and John can move in eight verses from addressing his immediate congregations in Asia (Rev. 1.3–4) to an announcement of the future coming of Christ (verse 7) and a reminder that God is the universal and sovereign power controlling the entire drama of salvation, the living and eternal source and goal of human history (verse 8).

The literary form of the Apocalypse, then, established in microcosm during the brief recitation of the prologue, is epistolary; but it is also apocalyptic and prophetic. The work as a whole has a dramatic and unified structure (note, at the outset, the careful symmetry of the benediction and doxology in Rev. 1.4–6), with a persistent narrative storyline which relates initially to John's own, historical community in Asia towards the end of the first century AD. Yet the storyline can be deconstructed, and the audience can become any listeners at any time. For the writer's message has a spiritual and doctrinal and practical dimension, which is ultimately universal and eternal in its significance.

Kirby, 'Rhetorical Situations' 197–207, uses rhetorical criticism, as a useful hermeneutical tool, to interpret the first three chapters of the Apocalypse. Rev. 1—3, he suggests, contains three rhetorical situations: Christ addresses John (Rev. 1); Christ addresses the seven churches (2—3); and John, as the rhetor, addresses his audience in the work as a whole (Kirby, 'Rhetorical Situations' 197).

Comment

Superscription: The Revelation to John (1.1–3)

1.1 The word ἀποκάλυψις (*apocalypsis*, 'apocalypse') is used anarthrously, without an article: *a* revelation, not *the* apocalypse. Apocalyptic literature, within and beyond the Bible, may be generally described as 'symbolic writing which is designed to unveil, for the benefit of its readers, divine truths which hitherto have remained hidden and secret' (see Smalley, *Thunder and Love* 24–28, esp. 24). John's revelation, expressed in this generic form, is being handed on to a particular community at a special moment in history; but it is perhaps understood as part of God's ongoing self-disclosure: *a* revelation, one of a number, the origin of which is to be found in God himself, rather than *the* definitive vision, which is never repeated.

The genitive in Ἰησοῦ Χριστοῦ (*Jēsou Christou*, 'of Jesus Christ') is subjective. The revelation is mediated to John *from* the Son, as the Father gave it to him. In the Fourth Gospel, Jesus the Son speaks only what he has heard from God the Father (John 8.26–29; 14.10). The Word of God utters the words of God (John 12.49–50). So here, the risen Christ declares to his followers what the Father has made known to him (cf. Beasley-Murray 50–51).

The exalted title, 'Jesus Christ', is found in Revelation only here, and at 1.2 and 5. Otherwise John uses 'Jesus' alone, nine times (as at Rev. 1.9 [*bis*]; 12.17); 'Lord Jesus' twice (22.20; 22.21, v.l.); and '(the) Lord' once (14.13; but cf. 11.8, '*their* Lord').

The intention of the visionary disclosure is to communicate with 'his servants'. These are the Christian prophets, of whom John is one, inheritors of the prophetic role extant in the Old Testament period (cf. Amos 3.7, using 'his servants the prophets'; Rev. 10.7; 11.18; 22.6). They are to be made aware of what 'must' (δεῖ, *dei*), take place swiftly (cf. Dan. 2.28 LXX). This phrase indicates the sure accomplishment of God's purposes, rather than a 'hasty consummation' of history (Charles 1, 6). For John's eschatology in this passage, see the theological comment below.

The subject of 'he disclosed (the revelation)' is Jesus himself, who made it known (ἐσήμανεν, *esēmanen*) to his servant John. The word translated 'made known' in this text (from the verb σημαίνειν, *sēmainein*) is characteristically Johannine (cf. John 12.33; 18.32). It derives from the root σημεῖον (*sēmeion*, 'a sign'), which is the fourth evangelist's term to describe the miracles of Jesus, the *significance* of which he is concerned to explain. So, in this setting, ἐσήμανεν (*esēmanen*) means more than 'he indicated'; it has the force of 'signifying', or (as in the translation) 'disclosing' deep truths. The seer will inevitably and consistently interpret the truth he receives symbolically; and this should warn the reader against an interpretation of Revelation which is literal and (although anchored in history) purely historical.

The revelation comes to 'John', the faithful 'servant' (δοῦλος, *doulos*, lit. 'slave') of the Lord (cf. Rev. 1.4, 9; 22.8), who is otherwise unidentified. The view adopted in this commentary is that the author thus named is John the apostle, the beloved disciple (see above, 2–3; also Smalley, *Thunder and Love* 37–50). The vision is mediated through the mission of an 'angel'. For angels in Revelation see the excursus, below. A chain of disclosure is apparent in the opening of the Apocalypse, as at 10.1–10 (q.v.): from God to Jesus, through his angel to the prophet John, and through the seer to God's servants. In this verse the angel is described as 'his' angel (ἀγγέλου αὐτοῦ, *angelou autou*): this means a mediator intimately associated with the risen Christ, and easily able therefore to communicate the vision from him to John (see also 22.16).

Excursus: Angels in Revelation

In the drama of the Apocalypse angels play an important part (the term ἄγγελος, *angelos*, is used 67 times in Revelation). In the Bible generally, angels act as messengers of God, who move between heaven and earth, and connect them (the root meaning of the Greek word for 'angel' is precisely 'messenger', or 'envoy'). These figures are in touch with physical reality, and are sometimes mistaken for human beings (as in Gen. 18.1–16; Luke 24.4–7); but angels also transcend this world, and are closely related to God (cf. Gen. 22.11–18). According to the New Testament, angels are subordinate to Jesus in the chain of being (Heb. 1.3–14); but they took part in the giving of the Law at Sinai (Gal. 3.19), show an interest in human beings (1 Cor. 4.9), and carry souls to Paradise (Luke 16.22). However, Satan also has his angels (Matt. 25.41; 2 Cor. 12.7; Rev. 12.7–9).

In Revelation, Jesus is the supreme 'messenger' of God (as in Gal. 4.14), drawing together in himself the material and the spiritual. Carrell, *Jesus and the Angels*, esp. 226–30, argues that Christ in the Apocalypse is presented as an explicitly angelomorphic figure. But ultimately he is more than an angel, in the sense of a created, non-divine heavenly being. The Lamb Christology of the drama generally shows that he is ontologically divine (ibid. 226); and this supports the view adopted in this commentary, that the prophet-seer's view of the person of Jesus is consistently high.

A significant background to the ministry of angels in Scripture is to be found in the Old Testament, where two kinds of heavenly being are designated.

(a) There are angels who are members of Yahweh's court, and are there to serve and praise him (Job 1.6; Isa. 6.2–3). The divine assembly also includes, especially in post-exilic writing, other heavenly beings who are not always called angels. They witness the creation of the world (Job 38.6–7, Heb. 'sons of God'); appear in warlike contexts (Josh. 5.13–15, 'a man'); and mediate death (Ps. 78.49, 'destroying angels') or revelation (Ezek. 40.3, 'a man'; Zech. 2.1–5, 'the angel'). Cherubim, with human and animal characteristics (Ezek. 1.5–14), and seraphim, with six wings (Isa. 6.2), are particular kinds of angelic being (see on the four living creatures in the throne-vision of Rev. 4.6–8; et al.).

(b) Distinguished from other angels is 'the angel of Yahweh (the Lord)', who is virtually a hypostatic representation of Yahweh and whose task is chiefly to help his people (Exod. 14.19, 'the angel of God' and the Israelite army; Exod. 23.20–23, 'my angel' leading the people of Israel to the promised land) or individuals (2 Kings 1.3–4, 'the angel of the Lord' and Elijah). The later literature of Judaism differentiates between the angels of the presence, who are able to keep the Sabbath, and the angels of service (see further on Rev. 7.1).

Messengers of God in the Exodus tradition can also be described as angels of death and destruction (Exod. 4.24; 12.12). 'Angels of punishment' often appear in Jewish apocalyptic writing (*1 Enoch* 53.3 [the angels of plague, co-operating with Satan, are contrasted with the angel of peace], et al.); and, although it is not specified whether they are good or bad, the implication is that they are demonic in nature. According to *1 Enoch* 20.2, the archangel Uriel exercises authority over the evil underworld.

Angels have special roles to play in the Apocalypse.

(a) They share in the worship of heaven around the throne of God (Rev. 5.11; 7.11) and take their place in the hierarchy of the heavenly temple, from whence they emerge with judgemental trumpets (8.2), incense (8.3–5) and libation bowls (16.1). The angelic elders and living creatures (see on 4.4, 6) in the throne room participate in the liturgy (4.8–11; 5.9–10; 11.16; 19.4); and the four cherubim are the heavenly prototypes of the two cherubim flanking the mercy-seat in the holy of holies in the earthly temple (Exod. 25.18–22; cf. Bauckham, *Theology* 33).

(b) Angels in the Apocalypse also mediate revelation and interpret visions (1.1; 10.1–10; 14.6–11; 17.1, 7–18), as well as being agents of God by implementing divine and saving judgement (7.1–3; 8.2–3; 9.1, 13; 11.15; 12.7–12; 14.15–20; 15.1, 6–7; 18.1–2; 19.17–18; 20.1–3). The 'strong angel' of 5.2 and 10.1 (q.v.) speaks for the divine council in proclaiming redemptive justice. For the satanic 'angel of the pit' in the Apocalypse see 9.11; for 'angels of destruction' see on 9.14–15.

(c) The identity of the 'angels of the seven churches' (1.20; see 2.1; et al.) constitutes an interesting problem in Revelation. These angels, addressed in each of the oracles to the seven churches in Rev. 2—3, are best interpreted as the heavenly counterparts of the Johannine communities in Asia; they are the spirituality of the earthly congregations, considered as single entities, rather than angelic beings in the strict sense. Cf. Wink, *Powers* 69–86, esp. 70; see also further on Rev. 1.20.

(d) The term ἀρχάγγελος (*archangelos*, 'chief angel' [BDAG 137*a*] or 'archangel') does not appear in Revelation, and only occurs in the New Testament at 1 Thess. 4.16 and Jude 9. But the concept of a leading angel can be found in the itemizing of the seven angels of the Apocalypse from 8.2, 7 ('the first') to 11.15; and the angels with the trumpets in that section are probably to be identified with archangels (see on 8.2). The only names given to archangels in the New Testament are Gabriel (Luke 1.19) and Michael (Rev. 12.7). In the text from Revelation Michael is not in fact identified as an 'angel'; but he has his own host of angels, and must therefore be an archangel.

(e) From Rev. 7.1–3 (q.v.) onwards, the progress of John's drama is marked by a series of angelophanies. These occur in two distinctive literary forms, which have few parallels in the apocalyptic literature of Judaism or Christianity beyond Revelation; and this suggests that they are the creation of the author himself, rather than being inherited and redacted from another source.

1 The first form is angelic *action*, which appears four times (7.1; 8.2; 15.1; 20.1–3). Its structure is fourfold: introductory phrase ('[after this] I saw'); the object of the vision (angel[s]) is stated; the action by or to the angel(s) is described; and an abrupt change of subject is introduced (7.2; 8.3; 15.2; 20.4). The seer appears in these angelic manifestations as an observer, who does not interact with the heavenly messenger (contrast 22.8–10).

2 The second form is angelic *speech*, and this occurs nine times (7.2–3; 10.1–7; 14.6–20 [six angelophanies; but the angel of 14.17 does not speak, and only acts later]; 18.1–3; 19.17–18). The literary pattern of this form is similar to the first at the start, but then differs markedly: introductory formula ('and I saw'); the object

of the vision (another angel) is recorded; the angel moves to the centre of the action; the angel 'cries aloud'; and the angel makes a brief statement (except in 10.3), which is crucial to the action. A mixed form of angelic action and speech is present at 14.14–20, a passage which twice includes the introduction of a second angel, who gives a command to the first (cf. 7.2). Only at 7.2–3 is angelic action (7.1) immediately followed by speech. For the literary form of angelophanies in the Apocalypse see Aune 434–35.

On 'angel' see Bietenhard, 'ἄγγελλος', esp. (for Revelation) 103. For angels in the Apocalypse generally see Carrell, *Jesus and the Angels* 20–23; and for their biblical portrayal see Williams, *Case for Angels, passim.*

2   John moves from announcing the origin of his apocalypse to a description of its content. The writer himself is a decisive link in the chain of revelation, mediating God's word through Christ and his angel to the Church ('his servants', verse 1: see Boring 64–67). But although the world is not mentioned explicitly in the chain, and the (prophetic) community of faith becomes the immediate recipient of the disclosure, John's message is also relevant to those outside the Church. Indeed, they appear later as the enemies of God (cf. Rev. 12.7–17; 18.1–24; et al.), and therefore as opponents of the Johannine circle. The prophetic testimony (ὅς ἐμαρτύρησεν, *hos emartyrēsen*, 'he [John] bore witness') is inevitably directed in the end to society as well as to the Church (cf. Rev. 1.9; 6.9; 12.17; 22.20; et al.). The verb ἐμαρτύρησεν (*emartyrēsen*, 'bore witness') is an epistolary aorist; since, from the viewpoint of the readers of this book, the testimony had been given earlier.

The concept of 'witness', which appears frequently in Revelation, provides a further and important link between this book and John's Gospel. In both documents the drama is played out in a court room. The fourth evangelist presents Jesus as a defendant to whom testimony is given by a series of witnesses, including the Paraclete. In the end the true identity of Jesus is revealed, as one with God and one with humanity, and the defendant ironically becomes the judge. John wishes his readers to make their own decision about Christ's person and to 'see' who he really is (John 20.31). As Caird (17–18) points out, the forensic setting of Revelation is even more realistic. Jesus was on trial before Pilate, the Roman governor: and the adherents of John's community may have to appear before a Roman judge, and certainly will do so if they are martyred. Their earthly Christian witness, however, will be evidence heard in the court of heaven, presided over by a God whose discrimination is true and just (Rev. 19.2). It therefore needs to be faithful (11.18).

John bore witness to 'the word of God, and the testimony of Jesus Christ'. These two phrases are used later in the Apocalypse (at 1.9; 6.9; 20.4) with reference to the Christian revelation in its totality: the message *from* God, to which testimony is given *by* Jesus the Christ (τὴν μαρτυρίαν Ἰησοῦ Χριστοῦ, *tēn martyrian Jēsou Christou*, 'the witness of Jesus Christ'; as in this verse, and verse 1, Ἰησοῦ Χριστοῦ, *Jēsou Christou*, 'Jesus Christ', is a subjective genitive). But here the expressions are governed by the following words, ὅσα εἶδεν (*hosa eiden*, 'everything that he perceived'), and therefore relate to the subject matter of the document before us. John's role in Rev. 1.1–2 echoes that of the beloved disciple, who bears testimony to the tradition about Jesus, in John 21.24; it also reflects that of the witnesses to the word of life at 1 John 1.1–4.

3   The superscription concludes with a stanza of four lines, containing an invocation of happiness on the (liturgical) reader of the prophecy and its audience. This double blessing is the first of seven beatitudes in Revelation (see 14.13; 16.15; 19.9; 20.6; 22.7,

14; and cf. Luke 11.28). For the relationship between the sayings of the exalted Jesus in the Apocalypse and the tradition of the words of Jesus in primitive Christianity see Aune 264–65. The use of the blessing here forms an emphatic inclusion with 22.7 ('happy is the one who adheres to the words of the prophecy of this book'), in the closing chapter. Those who 'listen' to the prophecy are identified with its 'adherents'; in the Greek, the verbs ἀκούοντες (*akouontes*, lit. 'hearing') and τηροῦντες (*tērountes*, lit. 'keeping') occur close together. In other words, the author assumes that hearing the prophetic witness will issue in a response of faith and obedience. The blessings of salvation are not automatic, but involve active participation in their outworking (cf. Beasley-Murray 52, who links the beatitudes of the Apocalypse with those in the sermon on the mount [e.g. Matt. 5.3], which also announce the happiness of 'those who look to God for redemption'). See further DeSilva, 'Honor Discourse' 105–107, who sees the seven makarisms as part of John's programme to outline for members of the Johannine churches 'the path to honor before God's court' (106).

All the more is this last point true, the writer continues, 'for the moment is approaching'. The Greek for 'moment' is καιρός (*kairos*, lit. 'time'). In the New Testament καιρός (*kairos*) normally refers to one, critical and divinely ordained moment in the line of history (χρόνος, *chronos*, 'period of time') as a whole. So far as the Christian concept of time is concerned, the decisive 'moment' (καιρός, *kairos*) dawned with the coming of Jesus, in whom 'time' (χρόνος, *chronos*) is divided anew. Because of his advent, an hour of fulfilment has arrived, the rule of God has broken in, and we are summoned to a reaction of repentance and faith (see Mark 1.15).

In the present verse, John reminds his readers that all time is now therefore critical, and that the present as well as the future, and those who live in them, stand under the 'judgement' (κρίσις, *krisis*) of God. The 'moment' is 'approaching'; but it is always pressing in (cf. 1 Pet. 4.7). So the Johannine Christians must respond to the reported vision with obedience, and indeed love; they should let the light of the last day fall on the issues of *their* day (cf. Beasley-Murray 53).

On καιρός (*kairos*, 'time') see further AG 395–96; Hahn, 'καιρός'; Delling, 'καιρός'.

Salutation and Doxology (1.4–8)

4   John, otherwise unidentified since he was known to his community, now addresses directly the churches in his circle. On the apostolic authorship of Revelation see Smalley, *Thunder and Love* 35–50; also above, 2–3. There are seven congregations, listed in verse 11; and they are situated in Roman proconsular Asia, on the west coast of Asia Minor. The number seven may be exact; but knowing the Johannine predilection for 'sevens' (there are seven signs in John's Gospel, for example, and seven scenes and seven visions in the Apocalypse; see further Smalley, *Thunder and Love* 66, 100–101), it may also suggest completeness. Seven is a sacred number, used also in the Old Testament and rabbinic literature as the symbol of perfection. Philo takes it up from Greek philosophical speculation (cf. *De Opif. Mund.* 89–106; *De Decal.* 96–105). The article by Schmitz and Brown, 'ἑπτά', esp. 691–92, proposes that the book of Revelation as a whole consists of seven visions, each consisting of seven items, and that these visions correspond to the seven days of the creation saga in Gen. 1.

If 'seven' connotes completeness in this context, the heptad of churches enumerated here may be representative of the churches in the area (so Beasley-Murray 53). However, John salutes these congregations, and writes to them, as a unit ('the seven', ταῖς [*bis*] ἑπτά, *tais hepta*); and in my judgement he is addressing them as *his* community, made up as it is of seven member-churches (against Caird 14–15).

Moreover, the teaching of the prophet-seer is presented in epistolary form. The Apocalypse as a whole, and not simply the opening section (Rev. 1.4—3.22), is addressed to a living community, with problems and possibilities of its own. This particular group of readers, the members of John's church, must therefore be kept in view throughout the interpretation of the book of Revelation, if it is to be understood correctly. The vision speaks to every age; but it was first set down for one generation.

Continuing the epistolary style of writing (see above, 26–27), John bestows on his audience a blessing of 'grace and peace'. This is typically Pauline (e.g. 1 Cor. 1.3; Swete 5); although in 2 John 3 we have the benediction, 'grace, mercy and peace'. The prayer for 'grace' (χάρις, *charis*) is a Christian variation of the normal Hellenistic greeting, χαῖρε (*chaire*, 'welcome'): and this is combined with the customary Hebrew salutation of 'peace' (שלום, *shālôm*). So Mounce 45. This association brings together the two backgrounds which seem to have existed in the Johannine community, Greek and Jewish, and speaks to them both (see above, 4–5). Theologically, it also links a characteristic gift of the new age with a representative blessing of the old (cf. Num. 6.26; see Beasley-Murray 54). Grace is God's love in action; peace on earth should be the result.

The grace and peace invoked stem from a triune source. The benediction comes first from 'the one who is, and who was, and who is coming'. This is a description of God which paraphrases the divine name as it is found in Exod. 3.14–15 ('I am who I am: the God of Abraham, Isaac and Jacob'). A community under threat from christological tensions within it, and religious persecution beyond, needs to be assured that its life and the very course of history itself are under the sovereign control of an eternal God (he 'is'), whose presence embraces all time: past and future, as well as present.

Part of John's literary technique in Revelation is to place words and phrases in numerical sequences (cf. the 'fours' at Rev. 5.9, 13; et al.). It is obvious that numbers have a symbolic importance for this writer (see on 'seven', earlier in this verse). Three is the number of the divine (verse 8) or a parody of the divine (Rev. 17.8); and so here the description of God's eternity, as in verse 8, is threefold ('is, was, is coming'). On numbers generally in the Apocalypse see Resseguie, *Revelation Unsealed* 10–12, 48–69; cf. also Pope, 'Number', esp. 563–66.

There are grammatical problems in the Greek expression, ἀπὸ ὁ ὢν καὶ ὁ ἦν καὶ ὁ ἐρχόμενος (*apo ho ōn kai ho ēn kai ho erchomenos*, 'from the one who is, and who was, and who is coming').

(a) The description of God is the nominative, whereas the preposition ἀπό (*apo*, 'from') is normally followed by the genitive. However, Beckwith suggests that John is treating the divine name as an indeclinable noun, appropriate to the unchangeable majesty of God (424). That the writer is not ignorant of the Greek language is apparent from the fact that the second ἀπό (*apo*) in this verse *is* followed by a genitive plural: ἀπὸ τῶν ἑπτὰ πνευμάτων (*apo tōn hepta pneumatōn*, 'from the seven spirits').

(b) The finite verb ἦν (*ēn*, 'was') is used in two parallel clauses which are participial: ὁ ὢν (*ho ōn*, 'who is') and ὁ ἐρχόμενος (*ho erchomenos*, '[the one] who is coming'). But there is no past participle for the verb 'to be' in Greek; and Charles (1, 10) believes that at this point John is in any case thinking Hebraically, since the Greek phrase ὁ ὢν καὶ ἦν (*ho ōn kai ēn*, lit. 'the one who is and was') exactly reproduces the Hebrew הַהֹוֶה וְהָיָה (*hahoveh v^ehāyāh*, lit. 'the one who is, and he was'). The writer uses (one) 'who is coming', rather than 'who is to be', as being more suited to the eschatology of his apocalypse (see Rev. 1.7; 2.5; et al.).

The grace and peace, for which John prays on behalf of his churches, derive secondly from 'the seven spirits who are (the verb is implied in the Greek) in front of his (God's) throne'. The 'seven spirits' are sometimes understood as the seven (arch)angels of the

Presence, familiar in Jewish angelology. *1 Enoch* 20.1–8 lists these as Uriel (or Suruel), Raphael, Raguel, Michael, Saraqa'el, Gabriel and (v.l.) Remiel (cf. Tobit 12.15; 2 Esdras 4.1; Dan. 10.13; note also Rev. 8.2). Cf. *OTP* 1, 23–24; Swete 5. Similarly, in the *Targum of Pseudo-Jonathan* on Gen. 11.7, the Lord speaks to 'the seventy (*sic*) angels (corresponding to the 'seventy nations', verse 8) which stand before him'; cf. Bowker, *Targums* 182. But, although John's background is fundamentally Jewish as well as Christian, such an allusion to a group of angelic beings seems incoherent and unnecessary in the present context (see Mounce 69). Equally, it is unlikely that the seer's thought in this verse is coloured by the seven planets of pagan mythology and politics (against Caird 15; cf. Peake, *Revelation* 210–11; Beasley-Murray 55).

We are on more secure ground if we seek to interpret this expression in the light of parallel usages in the Apocalypse itself. At Rev. 3.1, for example, John writes to the angel of the church in Sardis with words from the one having 'the seven spirits of God, even the seven stars'. The initial addresses at the head of each of the letters to the churches in Asia (Rev. 2—3) include a designation of the exalted Christ which echoes the theology of an opening section of the Apocalypse (Rev. 1.12–16). So in Rev. 1.16 the victorious Son of man (verse 13) holds 'seven stars' in his right hand; and in 1.20 this 'mystery' (τὸ μυστήριον, *to mystērion*) is interpreted as meaning 'the angels of the seven churches'. However, the passage Rev. 1.12–16 contains no reference to the 'seven *spirits* (of God)'; even if it is possible to identify 'spirits' with 'angels' at Rev. 3.1, by taking καί (*kai*, 'and') before τοὺς ἑπτὰ ἀστέρας (*tous hepta asteras*, 'the seven stars') as epexegetic (of 'the spirits'), rather than as conjunctive (cf. Mounce 47; see below, 80–81).

The references to 'the seven spirits of God' (as in 3.1, τοῦ θεοῦ, *tou theou*, 'of God', is added) at Rev. 4.5 and 5.6, in the throne room vision, provide us with firmer evidence. In Rev. 4.5 the spirits are equated with the 'seven torches of fire' burning in front of God's throne; and at 5.6 the 'seven eyes' of the Lamb are identified as the 'seven spirits of God' which are sent out on a mission to the whole world. This imagery picks up Zech. 4.2*b*, 10*b*, where 'seven lamps' are described as the (seven) 'eyes of the Lord, ranging throughout the whole earth'. The LXX of Zech. 4.2*b* includes the term λύχνοι (*lychnoi*, '[little] lamps'), which is the diminutive of the word used for 'lamps' (λαμπάδες, *lampades*) in Rev. 4.5.

An earlier commentator on the Apocalypse, the third-century Bishop of Pettau, Victorinus, interpreted the allusion to the 'seven spirits' in the present text (Rev. 1.4*b*) in the light of the Septuagintal version of Isa. 11.2, where the prophet enumerates the spiritual qualities which will rest on the Davidic prince of peace in the coming kingdom. (See *PL* (Supp.) 1, 103 cols 1–2.) 'The spirit of the Lord will rest upon him', we learn, and the MT then specifies his gifts (in three couplets of two) as sixfold: wisdom and understanding, counsel and strength, knowledge and the fear of God. The LXX interrupts the poetry and parallelism by adding a seventh gift: that of 'godliness' (εὐσέβεια, *eusebeia*). The resulting Christian, and indeed trinitarian, application of the Isaiah text has proved a popular way of interpreting Rev. 1.4*b* ever since; so Morris 48–49, esp. 49. However, F. F. Bruce, for one, thinks that John's dependence on the LXX text, and his application of it in this way, is 'unlikely in the Apocalypse', and indeed 'improbable' (Bruce, 'Spirit' 333–37, esp. 334, 336).

Nevertheless, putting the evidence together, it makes sense to understand the 'spirits' in verse 4 (even without an Isaianic background to the text) as a reference to the Spirit of God, manifested in his completeness (= sevenfold, where 'seven' is the number of perfection; it is unlikely that the writer has been influenced in his choice of this numeral by the fact that later he addresses seven churches in Asia [cf. Sweet 65]). The one Spirit is thus symbolized by the two elements from Zechariah's fifth vision: the seven torches (Rev. 4.5) and the seven eyes (5.6). The reality symbolized becomes one with the symbols (Beckwith 424–27, esp. 426; Bruce, 'Spirit' 336).

Such an interpretation may be supported in two further directions.

(a) The spirits in this passage appear with the Father (verse 4*a*) and the Son (verse 5), as the source of grace and peace. The co-ordination is presumably deliberate. John's blessing has a threefold divine origin: from God as Father, Spirit and Son.

(b) That unusual order is determined by the appearance of the members of the Godhead in the vision of Rev. 4 and 5. *God* is seated on a throne (4.2–3), which is a mark of his heavenly and eternal kingship and power (cf. 4.5; 7.9; et al.); before the throne can be seen the seven *spirits* (4.5); and the *Lamb* comes to the throne to take the scroll from the hand of God (5.6–7).

On this section see further, and similarly, Sweet 61–65; Smalley, 'Paraclete' 292–93, 298–99 n. 18; also Peake, *Revelation* 210–12. On the Spirit of God in Johannine thought see also Thompson, *The God* 145–88.

5 The formula of blessing is completed by a reference to its third source: Jesus, the Christ, who initially received and disclosed the vision. John uses the title of exaltation, 'Jesus Christ', for the third and last time in this book. Jesus is referred to first as 'the faithful witness'. The Greek of this, and of the other two descriptions of Jesus in this verse, is in the nominative, although ἀπό (*apo*, 'from') normally takes the genitive (as in the last phrase of verse 4, and Ἰησοῦ Χριστοῦ, *Jēsou Christou*, 'Jesus Christ', here). In verse 4 we noticed the same grammatical anomaly in John's allusion to God (q.v.); but there it was suggested that the seer was thinking theologically of God's ever-present nature. In this context, and several others in the Apocalypse which include similar solecisms (e.g. Rev. 2.13; 3.12; 14.12; 20.2), the writer appears to be using a Hebraism. In the indirect cases a noun in Hebrew is uninflected; and John may accordingly on these occasions be treating the Greek as without inflection, so that he places the nominative ὁ μάρτυς (*ho martys*, 'the witness') in apposition to the genitive Ἰησοῦ Χριστοῦ (*Jēsou Christou*, 'Jesus Christ'). So Charles 1, 13–14; cf. Swete 6–7.

The threefold description of Jesus begins by referring to him as a 'witness' (μάρτυς, *martys*). Only here and at 3.14 (q.v.) is Jesus described in this way. The expression 'faithful witness' is used of Antipas at Rev. 2.13 (cf. 3.14). It appropriately picks up Ps. 89.37 and Isa. 55.4, which both refer to David, the Messianic model, as a (lasting) witness. Jesus the Messiah was obediently faithful to his Father's will and salvific plan, throughout his ministry and in his passion; he is now and for all time the supreme martyr (μάρτυς, *martys*, 'witness', gives us the English word 'martyr'), whose death and exaltation brings life to all believers and whose testimony authenticates the revelation given to John. The role of Jesus as 'witness', that is to say, is exercised both in history and beyond it (cf. Rev. 22.20, where the exalted Jesus testifies to the truths disclosed in the Apocalypse). Nevertheless, in John's Gospel it is the historical Jesus who testifies (using the verb μαρτυρεῖν, *martyrein*, 'to bear witness') to the truth which he has received from God (cf. John 3.32; 5.31; 8.18; 18.37; et al.). See further on Rev. 3.14.

John refers to Jesus, secondly, as 'the firstborn from the dead, the prince of temporal rulers'. In Judaism the Messiah was traditionally 'the firstborn', as in Ps. 89.27 (a passage which the author appears to have in mind here): 'I will make him the firstborn, the highest of earthly kings'. The firstborn son in a Jewish family enjoyed a privileged position, and eventually became its head. In this Psalm, the firstborn belongs to God (his 'Father', verse 26), and is the highest of all the kings of the earth, just as Yahweh is supreme above all beings, including those of heaven.

This translates easily into Christian and Johannine thought. Jesus came from God, to be the way to him and to return to him (cf. John 13.1–3; 14.6). By his death and resurrection he is crowned with messianic power; exalted at God's right hand, he exercises sovereign rule over earthly potentates, including Roman emperors, and 'pioneers the path of resurrection to glory' (Beasley-Murray 57). For πρωτότοκος (*prōtotokos*, 'firstborn') see Col. 1.15; also Bartels, 'πρωτότοκος'. The term, ἄρχων (*archōn*, 'prince' or 'ruler') in the New Testament is used of Christ only here. Cf. Rev. 19.16; Phil. 2.11; also Bietenhard, 'ἀρχή'; Delling, 'ἀρχων'.

Some commentators suggest that the threefold description of Jesus in this verse – 'witness', 'firstborn', 'prince' – relates to his work in the past (his ministry), present (bringing resurrection life to the Church) and future (when he is disclosed as 'the prince of rulers'). Cf. Beasley-Murray 56. Swete, in similar vein, believes that the titles correspond to the tripartite intention of the Apocalypse, which is at once a divine testimony, a revelation of the risen Lord and 'a forecast of the issues of history' (Swete 7). However, there is no need to stretch the threefold nature of this identification of Jesus, particularly as the second and third references, given their Old Testament background and context, belong closely together. Indeed, the final phrase ('the prince of temporal rulers') is almost epexegetic of the second ('the firstborn from the dead'). *Because* Jesus has been raised from death, he *is* the prince of earthly rulers. Moreover, the eschatology of Revelation is so balanced that it is difficult, if not impossible, to force this threefold description of Christ into a chronological timescale. Jesus is Lord over the earth and its inhabitants *now*, as well as coming in future glory (cf. the representation of God's eternity in 1.4b; also 3.20; 22.13). John's blessing derives from an exalted and messianic prince, from whose cross flow eternally healing and power for all the nations (cf. Rev. 17.14; 22.2).

The beatitude in 1.4 and 5 is followed by a threefold doxology (cf. Rom. 11.33–36). For the textual variant of λύσαντι (*lysanti*, 'released') see above, 25. The seer has spoken of Jesus last because he appears third in order in the vision of Rev. 4 and 5 (see above, 34), and because this apocalypse is christologically centred. A spontaneous ascription of praise to the living Lord Jesus therefore arises naturally. The obedient martyr-witness has acted in love; the prince has been crucified; his actions spell our release from the captivity brought about by sin. R. E. Brown (*Introduction* 780–81) finds baptismal language in the doxology (cf. 1 Pet. 1.2, 19; 2.9).

It will not be long before John introduces Jesus as the Lamb of God (5.6). Perhaps anticipating this designation, he ascribes glory to one whose sacrifice harks back to the lambs of Passover in the Old Testament (as in Exod. 12), but makes possible a new exodus and a lasting deliverance from sin in a way which transcends Jewish rituals decisively (cf. Heb. 10.11–18).

John reminds us that the love of Jesus, shown in his passion at one moment in history, is continuous. So he uses the present tense in the participle ἀγαπῶντι (*agapōnti*, lit. [to the one] 'loving'). John's revelation is, above all, a triumphant disclosure of God's love, expressed through his judgement (cf. Smalley, *Thunder and Love* 147–49).

Second, Jesus has 'released us from our sins'. The concept of emancipation from the power of sin through the death (αἷμα, *haima*, lit. 'blood') of Jesus is Johannine; although it features more in the Apocalypse and the Letters of John than in the Fourth Gospel (so Rev. 5.9–10; 7.14; 12.11; 1 John 1.7; 2.2; 4.9–10). In the Gospel revelation is a dominant theological category, rather than redemption (but see John 1.29, 36; 10.11–18). Cf. Smalley, *John* 255–56. The Greek terms for 'sin', like the Hebrew, are varied. The most common is the one used here, ἁμαρτία (*hamartia*). In both the Old Testament and the New, 'sin' describes 'every departure from the way of righteousness, both human and divine' (AG 42). In 1 John ἁμαρτία (*hamartia*, 'sin') is defined as both 'lawlessness' (ἀνομία, *anomia*, 3.4) and 'wrongdoing' (ἀδικία, *adikia*, 5.17). The background to the image of 'redemption' from sin, to describe Christ's salvation, is that of the slave-market: involving in both cases what Morris (*Cross* 358) calls 'loosening a bond at cost'. See further Procksch, 'λύτρον'.

The 'blood' of Jesus occupies an important place in New Testament thought, and must be interpreted especially against the background of the cultic observances on the Day of Atonement (Lev. 16; but cf. also Exod. 12; 30.10). Here John, in line with other New Testament writers, is saying that Jesus, in perfect, loving obedience to the Father's will, offered the true and lasting sacrifice for sin (cf. Rom. 3.25; Heb. 9.11–14). For 'blood', as including the thought of *life* more than death (so Lev. 17.11), see Smalley, *1, 2, 3 John* 25; also Behm, 'αἷμα'. Jesus is glorified because he has 'set us free from sin by giving himself, his life, for us' (Boring 77); although, unlike Paul, John nowhere explains the connection between the two events.

6   The first part of this verse is parenthetical; but it is an integral part of the threefold doxology in progress. Through the cross, John says thirdly, Jesus has appointed his followers as a 'royal house'. The use here of a finite verb, ἐποίησεν ἡμᾶς (*epoiēsen hēmas*), 'he has appointed us'), instead of the participial form of the verbs which occur in the preceding, parallel clause, ἀγαπῶντι (*agapōnti*, lit. 'loving') and λύσαντι (*lysanti*, lit. 'loosing'), may be a Hebraism (so Charles 1, 14–15).

The word translated 'royal house' ([ἐποίησεν ἡμᾶς] βασιλείαν, [*epoiēsen hēmas*] *basileian*, lit. '[he made us] a kingdom') echoes the thought of Israel as 'a kingdom of priests and a holy nation' (Exod. 19.5–6, LXX has βασίλειον ἱεράτευμα, *basileion hierateuma*, 'kingdom of priests' or 'royal priesthood'; cf. Isa. 61.6). This is the first of several occasions when John uses Old Testament images of Israel to describe the Christian Church. The first believers saw themselves as members of the new and true Israel: the inheritors in full of the spiritual blessings which were foreshadowed in the life of God's people following the Exodus from Egypt. The 'royal house', to which the followers of Christ are appointed, speaks of 'rule' as well as 'realm' (Sweet 66). Christians, like their Lord, are able to conquer the spiritual opposition exercised in the world (1 John 5.5). In that position, as priests, they both serve God and help to mediate his judgement and salvation to the world.

Mounce (50) interprets the 'royal house' as corporate, and its 'priestly' members as individual. But βασιλείαν (*basileian*, 'royal house') and ἱερεῖς (*hiereis*, 'priests') are in apposition; for the priesthood belongs to the totality of the Church and not to its individual members (as in 1 Pet. 2.9; cf. Rev. 2.26–27; 5.10; 20.4–6; 21.22—22.5). For a study of the communal dimension to the seer's ecclesiology see Smalley, 'Johannine Community' 95–104, esp. 98–99.

John refers to the God 'and Father' (καὶ πατρὶ αὐτοῦ, *kai patri autou*) of Jesus Christ. The phrase as a whole is an indication of the seer's balanced Christology. Jesus is one with the Father, and also one with the priesthood of believers who serve him (cf. John 10.30).

The doxology closes with an ascription of eternal 'glory and might' (κράτος, *kratos*, lit. 'power') to Christ, followed by a liturgical 'Amen'. Cf. Rev. 4.11; 7.12; et al.; also 1 Chron. 29.11; *Did.* 8.2; 10.5. For 'might' see on Rev. 5.13.

In the Bible, 'glory' (δόξα, *doxa*) is a property belonging to God, the essence of his nature as recognized by his responsive creation. The term is used frequently in Revelation (17 times) and John's Gospel (18 times), but not at all in the Johannine Letters. In the sense of God's powerful majesty (as in Rev. 19.1), the notion of δόξα (*doxa*, 'glory') is inherited from the Old Testament (using כָּבוֹד, *kābôd*; cf. Ps. 108.1, 5). Against this background, John the Divine can speak of 'the glory of God' (Rev. 15.8); while the fourth evangelist applies the concept to Christ (John 12.41; 17.22). Ultimately, the eschatological 'glory' is revealed from heaven, as a means of transfiguring the created world (Rev. 21.10–11).

In the doxology of this verse, 'glory', in the sense of 'honour', is ascribed to the exalted Christ, as the Son of the Father. But this is a spiritual quality, which in the end can only be acknowledged because it derives from the being of the Godhead itself. See further Aalen, 'Glory' 44–48; also Johnston, '*Ecce Homo!*' 125–38, esp. 133–36, who draws attention to the humiliation as well as the splendour belonging to the Johannine portrait of Jesus. That irony, we may add, is endemic to the theology and Christology of the Revelation.

The benediction and doxology together in verses 4–6 reveal much about the Christian Church as a whole, and the Johannine community in particular, to which the Apocalypse is given. But they also speak encouragingly to a beleaguered circle, threatened within and without, about the Lord from whom the revelation comes: a crucified and exalted Saviour, reigning in glory, to whom is committed all heavenly and earthly power for the purposes of salvation through judgement (cf. Rev. 11.17; Phil. 2.10–11). See Milligan 7–8.

7   John has been supporting the members of his churches by enabling them to glimpse behind Caesar's throne the superior power and authority of the Lord's Messiah (Caird 18). Now, he suddenly switches from present possibilities to future reality. The temporal rulers in the Roman Empire do not recognize God's sovereignty in Christ at the moment; but eventually this will be disclosed universally.

John's vision of Christ's parousia is future, but it embraces the past and the present. The faithful witness who died is risen and alive (verse 5). The one who shares the problems and persecutions of the seer and those gathered around him (verse 9) is also to come with the clouds (cf. verse 8).

To describe that advent, the author introduces an adapted *testimonium* ('testimony') from Zech. 12.10. 'Testimonies' make up quotations from the Old Testament which were used in the early Church to support the apostolic claim that Jewish prophecies about the coming Messiah and the end-time had been fulfilled in Jesus of Nazareth. John combines the *testimonium* from Zech. 12 with an apocalyptic phrase from Dan. 7.13. Thus: 'Look! He is coming with the clouds (Daniel), and every eye will see him, including those who stabbed him; and all the tribes on earth will lament on his account (Zechariah)'.

There are allusions to the Zechariah text at Matt. 24.30 and John 19.37; but while Revelation and Matthew both have the conflation with Dan. 7.13, Revelation and John use the non-Septuagintal ἐξεκέντησαν (*exekentēsan*, 'stabbed'; Zech. 12.10 LXX has κατωρχήσαντο, *katōrchēsanto*, 'mocked'). It is quite possible that the text behind Matthew once contained this same distinctive verb, translated 'stabbed', and that all three writers were drawing in common on a piece of early passion apologetic which at first accounted for the death of Jesus by crucifixion, and later became generalized as a reference to his coming in judgement. In their appeal to primitive exegetical tradition the Apocalypse and Fourth Gospel thus exhibit once again a striking, if subtle, affinity. See Smalley, *Thunder and Love* 63–64; also Lindars, *Apologetic* 251–59, esp. 257.

Christ comes *with* (μετά, *meta*) the clouds, not *on* them: as in Matt. 24.30 (using ἐπί, *epi*, 'upon') and Mark 13.26/Luke 21.27 (ἐν νεφέλαις/νεφέλῃ, *en nephelais/nephelē[i]*, 'in [a] cloud[s]' [with great power and glory]'). These are heavenly clouds of glory, associated in Hebrew thought with the divine presence (Exod. 13.21; Acts 1.9), such as those which emanate from the realm of God in Rev. 10.1; 11.12 (cf. 14.14–16, where the Son of man is seated on a white cloud).

The victorious advent of the exalted Messiah is perpetually imminent. For he is 'coming soon' (cf. Rev. 3.11; 22.7, 12, 20); and that arrival will be known to everyone: both those within the Church and the enemies of God outside it. The audience of the apocalypse, John states parenthetically, will include those who 'stabbed' him (ἐξεκέντησαν, *exekentēsan*). This could be an allusion to the soldier's spear-thrust, recorded after the crucifixion at John 19.34 (using ἔνυξεν, *enyxen*, 'he pierced'). If so, the following sentence indicates that the final reference is much wider: 'all the families on earth will lament on his account'. The tribes, or ethnic groupings, in all the world, not just in Israel, will respond to this advent (cf. Zech. 12.12; Matt. 24.30). Those who have opposed Christ and his Church will become aware of the implications of their actions and reactions (cf. Mounce 51). They will 'lament' (κόψονται, *kopsontai*), not for themselves but 'on his account': because of all the suffering he has undergone. Whether repentance will follow, John does not say; only that sorrow will be one outcome of the divine judgement which is arriving.

The prophet-seer seals that emphatic and solemn announcement with a double affirmation: 'so be it', spoken in Greek and Hebrew (ναί, ἀμήν, *nai, amēn*, lit. 'yes', 'amen'). The two forms appear in this context to be used synonymously; but note the differing meanings of ἀμήν (*amēn*, 'amen') in Revelation highlighted by Charles (1, 19–20). The use of the two languages in the subscription would be entirely appropriate for John's readers who belonged to a Jewish, as well as Hellenistic, background.

8   God himself now speaks, as he does directly in the Apocalypse only here, and at 21.3–8 (but see 16.1, 17). After the threefold benediction, and tripartite doxology, both structured with a literary sensitivity, the Prologue to the drama of Revelation ends by bringing its audience back to the originating being of God (see verse 1).

The voice of God declares that he is 'Alpha and Omega', which are the first and last letters of the Greek alphabet, corresponding to the Hebrew א (*aleph*) and ת (*tau*). Cf. Isa. 44.6. At Rev. 21.6 this expression is expanded by the parallel phrase, 'the beginning and the end' (ἡ ἀρχὴ καὶ τὸ τέλος, *hē archē kai to telos*), which carries the same implications as 'first and last'. At Rev. 22.13 (q.v.) all three descriptions ('Alpha and Omega, first and last, beginning and end') are applied to Jesus himself; and this may have influenced the textual variation in the Greek of this verse, noted above (26).

John is saying that God is in control of his world, and of all the human activity within it; he is the eternal origin and goal of history in its entirety. The eternity of God is underlined by the following descriptive phrase, 'who is, and who was, and who is coming'. This is repeated from verse 4 (q.v.), and forms an inclusion at the end of the address with its opening. The advent theme of verse 7, centred in the returning Christ, is picked up here once again, and set within the total context of the judgement and salvation brought by the living Godhead.

Two attributes of God are specified in this text: he is 'Lord', and 'the Almighty'. Κύριος (*kyrios*, 'Lord') is frequently used in the New Testament to refer to Jesus (so Luke 22.61; John 20.28; Acts 2.47; Phil. 2.11; 1 Pet. 1.3; et al.); and this usage occurs also in Revelation (e.g. 17.14; 22.21). But in the Apocalypse 'Lord' is more usually ascribed to God (as here, and at 4.11; 11.4; et al.). The title ὁ παντοκράτωρ (*ho pantokratōr*, 'the Almighty'), ascribed here to God, is also found in secular Greek (AG 613) and Jewish literature (e.g. *Sib. Or. frag.* 1.7–8). It appears nine times in Revelation (1.8; 4.8; 11.17; 15.3; 16.7, 14; 19.6, 15; 21.22) and only once in the New Testament outside it (2 Cor. 6.18, in a quotation). God's word to his people through John's Apocalypse assures them of his eternal power, as well as his abiding sovereignty. He is the universal ruler. The drama ahead will show us that power worked out inevitably in justice and love; we shall see God's sovereignty displayed in sacrifice.

Theology

In the Prologue to the Apocalypse John uses the same dramatic technique evident from his Gospel. (See Smalley, *John*, 135–39). First, he introduces the main theological themes, with their distinctive content, as these will be explicated in the body of the play: his doctrines of God, Christ, the world, time, Spirit and Church. These are highlighted by the presence in Rev. 1.1–8 of key concepts, such as revelation (apocalypse) itself, word of God, witness, prophecy, imminence, seven churches, eternity, seven spirits, martyrdom, resurrection, kingship, love, redemption, blood, Church, priesthood, glory, advent, judgement, repentance, power and sovereignty.

As in the Gospel, John also brings on to the stage in this opening section the main characters of his drama. Inevitably these belong more to the heavenly, than to the earthly, realm, given the apocalyptic as well as narrative character of this work. So the eternal Godhead is represented, as Father, Son and Spirit. Nevertheless, an 'angel' connects heaven and earth in this passage (1.1), and mediates the revelation to John, the servant of Christ, in a historical setting. The literary form of the vision is intended to be read aloud in the context of liturgical, community worship (verse 3); John addresses the seven Asian churches directly (verse 4); we hear of the death and resurrection of Jesus in time, and of his victory over temporal rulers (verse 5); the writer describes the nature and ministry of the Church in the world (verse 6), and we are told of the reaction to Christ's advent by all the families 'on earth' (verse 7). Moreover, eternity presses in on time (verse 3); and God is Lord of all time, including the present (verses 4 and 8).

But, as once more in John's Gospel, the central character of the drama dominates the scene; and in a few verses we learn much about Jesus the Messiah which will be filled out later, as the apocalypse unfolds. So, for example, Jesus is described in his historical and suprahistorical roles of witness, firstborn from the dead, and prince of rulers; he also appears as loving Redeemer, head of the Church and vindicated Lord.

All theology, by definition, runs back to an eternal and universally sovereign *God*; and that is ultimately John's starting point. It is God the Father who gives the revelation to God the Son, who mediates it to the angel, who hands it on to the seer, who shares it with his community (verses 1–2). But the apocalypse has a *christological* centre. What happens will take place soon through the actions of the Christ. John's understanding of the person of Jesus, moreover, is elevated but balanced. He is presented three times in this section with the exalted title 'Jesus Christ' (verses 1, 2 and 5). He is risen and ruling and victorious (verses 5, 7), one to whom glory and sovereignty are due (verse 6). Yet Jesus the prince is also the salvific Redeemer, whose blood was shed; he is the living Lord who first became a martyr-witness (verses 5–6).

The same balance colours the distinctive theological outlook of John's Revelation as a whole. This equilibrium stems from the conviction that, to use the subsequent formulation of the Fourth Gospel, 'the Word became flesh' (John 1.14). As a result, John understands that heaven and earth, the material and the spiritual, have become uniquely and finally conjoined; in answer to faith, matter can now be the carrier of spirit, and the blessings of eternity may be experienced in time (John 1.51). In the Apocalypse as in the Gospel of John, the author therefore thinks and writes on two levels at once; for, albeit from a Christian perspective, he shares with pre-Christian apocalyptists the Jewish (and not Platonic) idea that in heaven there exists a transcript of earthly reality, both good and bad.

The seer's *cosmology* in the Prologue, then, is such that (as we have seen already) he moves easily between the heavenly and the earthly, and back again. The same perspective is apparent in his *pneumatology*, where the 'seven spirits' before the throne of God (verse 4) eventually make contact with earth in its totality (5.6); and this is true also of John's *ecclesiology*, since the priestly ministry of Christ's 'royal house' is exercised as a service to God, but anchored in the reality of daily living (verse 6).

Overarching John's theological interpretation in these opening verses, and the drama of the Apocalypse as a whole, is the special nature of his balanced *eschatology*. For the seer draws together the present and the future, the temporal and the eternal. To him the coming of Christ and his complete rule are always imminent (verses 1, 3), and the day of the Lord is always at hand (22.7, 12; cf. Mark 1.15). The apocalypse of the future has already begun; and Jesus is present even now in the experience and activity of the Johannine congregations (1.3, 6), as well as promising to return at the end (verse 7).

The stance taken in this commentary is that the balance in John's theology, and particularly in his Christology, was influenced by the problems and needs of his circle. Its members needed reassurance not only that God in Christ and by the Spirit was in control of Rome, as of the world, but also that Jesus was one with the Father *and* one with his Church (cf. John 10.30; 14.28; 16.28). John's Apocalypse would give the adherents of his circle confidence to face increasing persecution from the empire. It would also provide a spiritual basis for that confidence by recalling the Johannine Christians to adequate christological belief, and therefore to right behaviour. In this way the stability of a community, incipiently troubled from within and without, might be ensured.

Act 1

CREATION, AND SALVATION THROUGH JUDGEMENT
(1.9—11.19)

SCENE 1
Seven Oracles
(1.9—3.22)

Translation

[9]I John, your brother and fellow-partner in Jesus, in the conflict and sovereignty and steadfastness, found myself on the island called Patmos on account of God's word and the witness of Jesus. [10]On the Lord's Day I found myself in the Spirit, and heard behind me a loud, trumpet-like voice [11]saying, 'Write your vision in a book, and send it to the seven churches: to Ephesus and to Smyrna, and to Pergamum and Thyatira and Sardis, and to Philadelphia and Laodicea.'

[12]So I turned round to see whose voice it was speaking to me and, on turning, I saw seven gold lampstands, [13]and among the lampstands was a son of man figure, dressed in a long robe and wearing a gold sash across his chest. [14]His head of hair was white as white wool – like snow; and his eyes flamed like fire. [15]His feet were like fine bronze, glowing[a] as in a furnace, and his voice sounded like the roar of many waters. [16]In his right hand he held seven stars, and from his mouth projected a sharp, two-edged sword; and his face was like the sun, shining with all its power.

[17]And when I saw him, I fell down at his feet as though dead. But he laid his right hand on me, saying, 'Do not be afraid. I am the first and the last, [18]the living one who was dead; but look, here I am alive for ever and ever, holding the keys to Death and Hades! [19]So write down what you have seen, even what is taking place now, and what is about to happen later on. [20]Here is the secret of the seven stars which you saw in my right hand, and the seven golden lampstands: the seven stars are the angels of the seven churches, and the seven lampstands are the seven churches themselves.

2 [1]'To the angel of the church in Ephesus, write: These are the words of the one holding the seven stars in his right hand, who is walking among the seven golden lampstands. [2]I know what you are doing, your effort[b] and steadfastness; and that you cannot tolerate evildoers, and have put to the test those styling themselves apostles, although they are not, and have found them to be liars. [3]You certainly possess steadfastness: you have endured for my sake, and without flagging. [4]But I have this against you, that you have given up your initial love. [5]So recall how far you have fallen; think again, and act as you did at first. Otherwise, unless you repent, I will visit you and remove your lampstand from its place. [6]However, you have this in your favour: that you hate, as much as I do, the practices of the Nicolaitans. [7]Let anyone with an ear listen to what the Spirit is saying to the churches. I will allow the conqueror to eat from the tree of life which is in God's paradise.

[8]'And to the angel of the church in Smyrna, write: This is the message of the first and the last, who was dead and has come to life. [9]I know about your conflict and poverty (although you are rich!), and about the slander of those claiming to be Jews when they are not: who belong, indeed, to the synagogue of Satan. [10]Do not be at all[c] afraid of what you are about to suffer. But beware! The devil is on the point of throwing some of you into prison, to put you to the test; and you will be persecuted[d] for ten days. Keep faith, even to death, and I will give you the reward of life. [11]Let anyone with an ear listen to what the Spirit is saying to the churches. The conqueror will not in any way be harmed by the second death.

[12]'Then write to the angel of the church in Pergamum: So speaks the one who has the sharp, two-edged sword. [13]I know where you are living, that is, where Satan has his throne. Yet you are holding fast to my cause; and you have not broken trust with me, even[e] in the time[f] of my faithful Antipas, my witness, who was put to death in that place of yours where Satan lives. [14]But I have a few criticisms to make of you: for example, some of you there are adhering to the teaching of Balaam, who instructed Balak how to place a stumbling block in the path of the people of Israel, so that they would eat food offered to idols, and practise fornication. [15]Similarly, you also have among you some who are maintaining the teaching of the Nicolaitans. [16]So think again; otherwise I will visit you soon, and make war against them with the sword of my mouth. [17]Let anyone with an ear listen to what the Spirit is saying to the churches. I will give to the conqueror a share of the hidden manna; and I will also hand over a white stone, and written on the stone will be a new name, known only to the recipient.

[18]'Next, write to the angel of the church in Thyatira: These are the words of God's Son, whose eyes flame with fire, and whose feet are like fine bronze. [19]I know what you have done: your love and faith, and ministry and steadfastness; and I am aware that your recent activities outweigh your earlier ones. [20]But I have this against you: that you put up with Jezebel, the woman[g] who describes herself as a prophetess, and is instructing my servants and misleading them into practising fornication and eating meat offered to idols. [21]And I have given her time for repentance; but she refuses to think again about her fornication. [22]So look! I am throwing her into a sickbed,[h] and bringing great pain on those who are committing adultery with her, unless they repent of what she is doing;[i] [23]and I will strike her children dead. Then all the churches will realize that I am the searcher of minds and hearts, and will give to each of you the deserts of your conduct.[j] [24]But this is my advice to the rest of you in Thyatira, those who do not accept this teaching, who have no knowledge of what they term, "the deep things of Satan". I am laying on you no further burden; [25]only hold fast to what you have until I come. [26]And to the conqueror, that is the one who takes my works to heart until the end, I will give authority over the nations – [27]to smash them with an iron staff, as when earthenware jars are broken – [28]just as I have received authority from my Father. To that person I will also give the morning star. [29]Let anyone with an ear listen to what the Spirit is saying to the churches.

3 [1]'And to the angel of the church in Sardis, write: So speaks the one who holds the seven spirits of God, even the seven stars. I know what you are doing: you have a reputation for being alive, but in fact you are dead. [2]Be vigilant! Establish what is left, and on the point of dying; for I have not found anything you do[k] to be complete in the eyes of my God. [3]So bear in mind what you have received and heard; pay attention to it, and repent. But if you are not vigilant, I will arrive like a thief; and you will not know at what hour I will come upon you. [4]Yet you still have a few people left in Sardis who have not stained their clothing; and they will walk beside me in white, as they deserve. [5]The conqueror will be similarly[l] clothed in white robes; and I will never erase that person's name from the book of life, but will openly acknowledge the name before my Father, and in the presence of his angels. [6]Let anyone with an ear listen to what the Spirit is saying to the churches.

[7]'Then write to the angel of the church in Philadelphia: This is the message of the holy one, the true one – he who holds the key of David, who opens and no one will close, who shuts and no one opens. [8]I know what you are doing. Look, I have placed in front of you an open door, which no one is able to close. For, although you have little strength, you have remained loyal to my word, and have not repudiated my name. [9]See, I am handing over those from the synagogue of Satan, who style themselves Jews (they are not Jews, only liars), and I will make them come and prostrate themselves at your feet, and they will learn that I have loved you. [10]For you have faithfully kept my call to endurance; and I will keep you safe from the time of ordeal which is about to erupt over the whole world, to test the inhabitants of the earth. [11]I am coming soon; hold fast to what you have, so that no one can deprive you of

your crown. [12]I will make the conqueror a pillar in the temple of my God, never to leave it; and I will write on that person the name of my God, and the name of the city of my God – the new Jerusalem – which descends out of heaven from my God, and my own new name. [13]Let anyone with an ear listen to what the Spirit is saying to the churches.

[14]'Finally, write to the angel of the church in Laodicea: The words of the Amen, the faithful and true witness, the origin of God's creation. [15]I know what you are doing: that you are neither cold nor hot. Would that you were either cold or hot! [16]But, because you are lukewarm, neither hot nor cold, I am on the point of vomiting you out of my mouth. [17]For you are claiming, "I am rich, I have made my fortune, and I have all I need"; not realizing that you are a pitiful wretch, poor, blind and naked. [18]So I advise you to purchase from me gold refined in the fire, that you may become rich, white robes to wrap around you, to keep the shame of your nakedness from being visible, and salve to anoint your eyes, so that you can see. [19]I punish and discipline those whom I love; so be in earnest, and repent. [20]See, I am standing at the door and knocking; if anyone hears my voice and opens the door I will enter, and share a meal with that person. [21]I will give to the conqueror a place beside me on my throne, just as I have conquered, and sat down beside my Father on his throne. [22]Let anyone with an ear listen to what the Spirit is saying to the churches.'

Text

[a] AG (738) describes πεπυρωμένης (*pepyrōmenēs*, 'glowing', lit. 'having glowed'), read by A C Primasius, as one of the 'linguistic peculiarities' of Revelation. As it stands, the word is certainly used ungrammatically; and this difficulty suggests its originality. The version πεπυρωμένοι (*pepyrōmenoi*, plural), with 025 046 Tyconius, et al., is no better. Following Charles (1, 29), we assume that John intended to write πεπυρωμένῳ (*pepyrōmenō[i]*), dative of the past participle, agreeing with χαλκολιβάνῳ, *chalkolibanō[i]*, 'fine bronze', since κάμινος, *kaminos*, 'furnace', is feminine; cf. Swete 17–18), as in ℵ vg syr[ph,h] eth Irenaeus[lat], and that all the variants here are corrections.

[b] Some MSS (including ℵ cop[sa,bo] arm eth) add σου (*sou*, 'your') to κόπον (*kopon*, 'effort'), as read by A C 025 syr[ph] vg Jerome, et al.; and co[bo mss] have the plural κόπους σου (*kopous sou*, 'your efforts'). The additions and replacements are probably influenced by the surrounding syntax; and the text is in any case governed by the context. The 'works' of the Ephesians (τὰ ἔργα σου, *ta erga sou*, 'your efforts') are specified as two in particular: 'effort and steadfastness'; and they are both qualified by the *one* possessive, σου (*sou*, 'your').

[c] Instead of the grammatically correct μή (*mē*, 'not'), read by A C 046 and some versions, several MSS and versions (including ℵ 025 1006 1611 vg) have μηδέν (*mēden*, emphatic, 'not at all'). Despite the weighty attestation to the emphatic negative, it is possibly a later expansion; although as such it fits the mood of the passage admirably. A subsequent contraction from μηδέν (*mēden*, 'in no way') to μή (*mē*, 'not') is less probable. Metzger (*Textual Commentary* 731), however, thinks it unlikely that copyists would have introduced a grammatical difficulty.

[d] For ἕξετε (*hexete*, 'you will have [persecution]'), future indicative, as read by ℵ C 2053 vg co, et al., some witnesses (including A 025 1611[1854,2344] Primasius) have ἔχητε (*echēte*, '[that] you may have; present subjunctive). Probably a copyist was conforming to the mood of the preceding verb, πειρασθῆτε (*peirasthēte*, lit., 'that you may be tested'). So Beckwith 455; against Swete (32), who regards the second subjunctive in ἔχητε (*echēte*, '[that] you may have') as authentic, indicating a further disclosure of Satan's plans. Swete (32) takes ἕξετε (*hexete*, 'you will have') as the correction.

[e] Some MSS (ℵ 025 046 it[dem], et al.) omit καί (*kai*, 'even') after τὴν πίστιν μου (*tēn pistin mou*, lit. 'my faith' or 'faith in me'). But the exegesis of the context demands the inclusion

of the word. Generally, John is saying, those in Pergamum have remained faithful to Christ, *even* at such critical moments as the martyrdom of Antipas.

[f] After ἐν ταῖς ἡμέραις (*en tais hēmerais*, lit. 'in the days'), as in A C 2053, et al., some witnesses, including most miniscules, add αἷς (*hais*, lit. 'which' = 'of'), or ἐν αἷς (*en hais*, 'in which' = 'of'). But these seem to be later insertions, designed to ease the construction of the sentence.

[g] A 046 Byz Cyprian Primasius, and other witnesses, add σου (*sou*, 'your') after τὴν γυναῖκα (*tēn gynaika*, 'the woman'); and A has the full version, τὴν γυναῖκα τὴν σου (*tēn gynaika tēn sou*, 'that woman of yours'). But the insertions were evidently made by copyists, influenced by the fourfold occurrence of σου (*sou*, 'your') in the preceding sentences (Beckwith 471).

[h] The term κλίνην (*klinēn*, 'bed' or 'couch') is unusual, although it is attested by the majority of MSS (including ℵ C 025). The variations φυλακήν (*phylakēn*, 'prison'), κλίβανον (*klibanon*, 'furnace') and ἀσθένιαν (*asthenian*, 'sickness') are scribal conjectures, attempting to interpret the nature of the threatened punishment (cf. Mounce 88 n. 21).

[i] The major witnesses read ἐκ τῶν ἔργων αὐτῆς (*ek tōn ergōn autēs*, lit. 'from her works' = 'what she is doing'). The phrase is omitted altogether by cop[bo mss]; and 2432 oddly has ἔργου αὐτοῦ, *ergou autou*, 'his work'). A textual contender is ἔργων αὐτῶν (*ergōn autōn*, 'their works'), as in A, et al. But the first version ('her works') is correct: the fornication and adultery for which repentance is required stem initially from Jezebel ('her fornication', verse 21), not from the deceived faithful.

[j] The reading τὰ ἔργα ὑμῶν (*ta erga hymōn*, lit. 'your works' = 'conduct') is followed by the majority of MSS (including ℵ[c] A C 025 1 eth Andrew). One witness (ℵ*) omits the phrase completely; and 2432 has ἡμῶν (*hēmōn*, 'our [works]'). Other variants are (ἔργων) αὐτῶν (*[ergōn] autōn*, 'their [works]'), as in 1626 2058 arm; and (ἔργων) αὐτοῦ (*[ergōn] autou*, 'his [works]'), read by 046 it[ar,haf] vg[cl] cop[sa,bo] Cyprian Ambrosiaster. These departures are logical, but clearly the work of copyists.

[k] Instead of σου τὰ ἔργα (*sou ta erga*, lit. 'the works of you' = 'anything you do'), as in ℵ 025 046 Arethas, et al., some witnesses (A C 1[mg] arm) have the anarthrous σου ἔργα (*sou erga*, 'your works'). The phrase σου τὰ ἔργα (*sou ta erga*, 'the works of you') is characteristic of John's literary style (cf. Rev. 2.2, 19; 3.1, 8, 15); and it makes good sense in the present passage. But, on the principle that in textual criticism the more difficult reading is likely to be the original, τά (*ta*, 'the') should probably be omitted from this verse.

[l] For οὕτως (*houtōs*, 'thus' or 'so' = 'similarly'), which appears in ℵ C vg arm eth Primasius, et al. (A has οὕτω, *houtō*, a variant of οὕτως, *houtōs*, with the same meaning), some witnesses (such as ℵ[c] 025 046 Andrew) read (ὁ νικῶν) οὗτος (*[ho nikōn] houtos*, lit. 'this one' = 'he [the conqueror]'). But 'similarly' in this context makes good sense, alongside the promise in verse 4; and its use has a parallel at Rev. 11.5.

Literary Setting

The first scene in Act 1 of Revelation is introduced by a dramatic section (1.9–20) describing the origin and setting of the apocalyptic vision which is to follow (Rev. 2—22). These verses also bring the audience closer to the seven churches in Asia which are soon to be addressed directly; and, indeed, they are named individually (verse 11). John's epistolary style, evident from the start of the address (1.4), is continued here and to the end of chapter 3; and it surfaces again at the close of the Revelation (22.8–21).

But, as we have seen (above, 26–27), this work is much more than a letter. So the apocalyptic and prophetic elements of the drama predominate in the body of Revelation
(4—22.7), and they emerge already in this opening section.

Revelation is rich in its use of symbols, and John draws heavily on this literary form
to communicate his message. This need not surprise us, given that the seer is writing
an apocalypse, and that symbolism was a normative part of Jewish and Christian
apocalyptic literature. (On symbolism in the Revelation and Gospel of John see Smalley,
Thunder and Love 157–60).

In 1.9–20 we discover immediately a cluster of symbols (lampstands, stars, a sword,
keys), and a number of similes which possess a symbolic character ([like] trumpet, wool,
fire, bronze, waters, sun). These symbols, as in the Apocalypse generally, join together
with literary sensitivity the physical and spiritual dimensions; and they embrace the present,
as well as the future. So the trumpet-like voice of the exalted Son of man addresses John
on the sabbath in Patmos (verse 10); the risen Christ among the lampstands places his
right hand on the prostrate seer (verse 17); and the stars, held by the heavenly Jesus, are
the 'angelic' leaders of the seven local churches (verse 20). Similarly, the two-edged sword
of divine judgement borne by the Son of man speaks of discrimination exercised
imminently among the Asian churches, as well as of judgement to come at the end (verse
16; cf. 2.12, 16; 19.15, 21); and the 'keys' of Death and Hades represent the Messiah's
authority over their domain in this life, as well as the next (verse 18; cf. 3.7; 9.1; 20.1).

Symbols such as the ones which appear in this passage, or elsewhere in Revelation,
cannot and should not, of course, be interpreted literally. By definition, symbols point
to a reality which is greater than themselves; they are pictures, usually incorporating
a material element or object, which are used to represent and evoke a spiritual reality.
To this extent John's symbols, in the Fourth Gospel as well as Revelation, include a
sacramental dimension: *conveying*, through the material instruments involved, what is
spiritual and indeed divine. The sword of divine judgement (verse 16) is more than a
picture. It is a harsh reminder of the war which will break out in reality between the
Godhead and its enemies: in the churches (2.16), or among the nations (19.15). In the
same way, the downfall of Babylon, described in Rev. 18, is not simply an evocation of
God's wrath in answer to the rebellion of humanity; it also demonstrates what actually
takes place in any parallel situation. John the evangelist develops this teaching in his
Gospel. Meanwhile John the Divine perceives already, in his symbols as well as in
his visions, that the concept of human salvation through God's judgement is not only
pictured but also made real. (See further Smalley, *Thunder and Love* 160; Smalley, *John*
234–38; Ellul, *Apocalypse* 33–35.)

The Oracles to the Seven Churches

The place of Rev. 2 and 3 in the Apocalypse as a whole has given rise to scholarly debate,
particularly in terms of the unity of this document. It can be argued, for example, that
the seven epistles (which are perhaps better termed 'oracles') in these two chapters stand
somewhat alone, since they appear to be concerned not with the last days, but
with existing conditions in certain of the churches in Asia Minor. So Beckwith 217.
Similarly, Charles (1, 37–47) argues that the seven letters were actual communications,
sent to their respective churches before Revelation was written. He goes on to maintain that subsequently, in the reign of Domitian, when Christianity and Caesarism came
into conflict, these missives were edited (to include Rev. 3.10 and new material at the
close of each letter), and incorporated into Revelation as a means of addressing the new
crisis precipitated by the Emperor. The main evidence adduced by Charles (see 43–44)
rests on the assumption that the eschatology of the Apocalypse as a whole implies an
eventual universal martyrdom; whereas (except at Rev. 3.10) the letters embody the more

primitive expectation that the Church would survive until the second advent, even if local persecution took place. Furthermore, if Rev. 2 and 3 are removed from the Apocalypse, in the view of some scholars, no major dislocation of the text occurs, and chapter 4 then follows chapter 1 logically. So Ramsay, *Letters* 37, who regards Rev. 2.1—3.22 as a non-Jewish passage, fitted by John into an extant apocalyptic work of Jewish origin and plan, because the letter form had by then established itself as 'the most characteristic expression of the Christian mind' (35; see 35–49).

The argument that the eschatological perspective in the seven oracles differs from that to be found elsewhere in Revelation cannot be upheld if the nature of John's eschatology is taken seriously (see above, 12–13). John's theology of time is such that the present is joined to the future, and the eternal is discovered through the temporal; and this is true of Rev. 2 and 3, as of the Apocalypse in its totality.

Again, Ramsey's view that the presence of Rev. 2 and 3 disturbs the continuity of chapters 1 and 4 is undermined if the relationship between the seven letters and the material in Rev. 1 is examined carefully. First, the headings to each letter relate deliberately and theologically to the description of the Son of man in the vision of Rev. 1.12–20. Cf. Rev. 2.1 and 1.12–13, 16, 20 (with seven stars and golden lampstands); 2.8 and 1.17–18 (first and last, and living); 2.12 and 1.16 (with the sharp sword); 2.18 and 1.14–15 (eyes like fire, feet like bronze); 3.1 and 1.(4–5), 16, 20 (with seven spirits and stars); 3.7 and 1.18 (with the key[s]); 3.14 and 1.17 (beginning = first). (However, Charles [1, 44–46] regards these and the epistolary endings as secondary additions.)

Second, a continuity exists between Rev. 2 and 3 and the remainder of the book, in terms of the themes of the oracles. Thus Sweet, for example 52–54, finds the subjects of assurance and endurance in Rev. 4.1—8.1 to echo the thought of the letters to Smyrna and Philadelphia (which are in any case close in thought to one another; see Kiddle 48); those of idolatry and witness in Rev. 8.2—14.20 to pick up the contents of the letters to Pergamum and Laodicea; and the epistles to Thyatira and Laodicea to contain ideas which are developed in 15.1—22.5. Whether or not Sweet's analysis is accepted in detail, sufficient has been said to claim that in general terms there is a definite community of theology and thought between the letters to the seven churches in Rev. 2 and 3 and the teaching of John in the rest of the Apocalypse. To my mind, such a conclusion undergirds the structural and theological unity of the drama in Revelation, for which I would argue. Beale ('Hearing Formula' 167–80) believes that a significant role of the seven letters in Rev. 2 and 3, especially in their repeated conclusions, is 'to anticipate the symbolic communication of chapters 4–21' (167), rather than to describe the condition of first-century churches, and thus of the Church at any time before the final tribulation. However, these two roles are not necessarily incompatible.

The seven oracles themselves follow a regular literary pattern, which may be set out as follows:

Salutation
Description of Christ (recapitulating Rev. 1)
Disclosure (using 'I know')
Assessment (good or bad)
Action (human) or reaction (divine)
Encouragement (usually)
Final promise (to the conqueror)
Closing formula ('anyone with an ear').

In the first three oracles (2.1–17), the repeated closing formula precedes the final promise.

Beale, 'Hearing Formula' 171, noting that this structure does not conform to the typical epistolary formula, refers to the letters instead as 'prophetic messages'. Kirby, 'Rhetorical

Situations' 197–207, has analysed Rev. 2—3 in terms of rhetoric; on the 'letter' genre itself see Aune 124–30. For the nature and importance of the number seven, in Revelation and the Fourth Gospel, see above, 31; also Boring 31–32; Aune 114–15. On the composition of the seven oracles in general see further Aune, 'Form and Function' 182–204, esp. 203–204. Aune regards these writings as public proclamations, rather than letters as such. In his view, John adopts on each occasion the form of a Roman imperial edict, to emphasize that Christ, rather than the Emperor, is King. Note also Aune 117–32.

The story of the community around the beloved disciple in the first Christian century, as well as of the Church in society at any time, is about to begin.

Comment

Vision of the Son of Man (1.9–18)

1.9 The writer resumes from verse 4 the epistolary form of his address to the churches; and he identifies himself again, for the third time, as John (see on verse 1). This designation is required by the context, since the speaker at the close of the preceding ecstatic words (verses 7–8) is God. But the literary style here ('I John') is also characteristic of Jewish prophets when relating their visions to others; cf. Dan. 8.1 (using ἐγὼ Δανιήλ, *egō Daniēl*, 'I Daniel'); also Isa. 6.1; *1 Enoch* 12.3; 2 Esdras 2.33; and note Rev. 22.8.

John is beginning to narrate a vision which he has received through the risen Christ from God (verse 1); and that is his authority for the loving, as well as judgemental, message to follow. He uses the title '(your) brother' (ὁ ἀδελφὸς ὑμῶν, *ho adelphos humōn*), because of its official associations; in Acts 15.23, for example, it is used to describe apostles and elders; cf. 2 Pet. 3.15, where Paul is referred to as a 'brother'. But the term 'brother' also helps to establish a community of interest between John and the fellow-members of his churches. Even if their faith, and especially their view of the person of Christ, was inadequate, the seer remains a brother Christian among like-minded believers. The word ἀδελφοί (*adelphoi*, 'brothers [and sisters]') is regularly used in the New Testament to describe the followers of Jesus as a body (cf. Matt. 28.10; Rom. 1.13; 1 Cor. 1.10; Heb. 3.1; Jas. 1.2; et al.).

The fellowship between John and the adherents of his circle is emphasized by the qualifying words which follow. He is 'fellow-partner' as well as a 'brother'. There is no article (ὁ, *ho*, 'the') before συγκοινωνός (*synkoinōnos*, 'fellow-partner'), as there is before ἀδελφός (*adelphos*, 'brother'). The term συγκοινωνός (*synkoinōnos*, 'fellow-partner') has its root in the word κοινωνία (*koinōnia*, 'partnership' or 'fellowship'), and echoes Paul's language. Cf. Rom. 11.17; 1 Cor. 9.23; Phil. 1.7 (using συγκοινωνός, *synkoinōnos*, 'fellow-partner'); also 2 Cor. 6.14; Philem. 6 (using κονωνία, *koinōnia*, 'partnership') et al. But see also the usage of this diction elsewhere in the New Testament, for example at 1 Pet. 4.13; 5.1; 1 John 1.3 (*bis*); and note Rev. 18.4. Partnership and suffering are often associated in early Christian thought (so 2 Cor. 1.7; Phil. 3.10; et al.).

John shares as a brother and fellow-partner 'in Jesus', with the members of his circle, 'in the persecution and sovereignty and steadfastness'. The construction ἐν Ἰησοῦ (*en Jēsou*, 'in Jesus') is reminiscent of Paul's favourite formula, ἐν Χριστῷ (*en Christō[i]*, 'in Christ'), as in 1 Cor. 5.17; and this similarity has probably produced the manuscript variations at this point. So one witness (A) has the exact expression, 'in Christ' (ἐν Χριστῷ, *en Christō[i]*) here, instead of 'in Jesus' (ἐν Ἰησοῦ, *en Jēsou*). The sense of both forms is identical, and indicates the intimate relationship with Jesus experienced by the believer (cf. further Smalley, 'Christ-Christian Relationship' 95–100, esp. 97). To be in unison with Christ, according to both Paul and John, is to have eternal life.

In the text before us, ἐν Ἰησοῦ (*en Jēsou*, 'in Jesus') governs the whole of the preceding phrase in the Greek: ὁ ἀδελφὸς ὑμῶν καὶ συγκοινωνὸς ἐν τῇ θλίψει καὶ βασιλείᾳ καὶ ὑπομονῇ (*ho adelphos hymōn kai synkoinōnos en tē[i] thlipsei kai basileia[i] kai hypomonē[i]*, 'your brother and fellow-partner [in Jesus] in the persecution and sovereignty and steadfastness'); note the repeated ἐν (*en*, 'in'). John is in fellowship with the Jesus who suffered and rose from death, and he therefore shares in partnership with all those who belong to Christ. As a fellow-believer, the writer participates with his community in any persecution, from Rome or from the Jews, which is to come; although θλῖψις (*thlipsis*) can mean 'tribulation', as well as 'persecution', in the sense of enduring the suffering which may accompany faithful Christian witness (cf. John 16.33; Acts 14.22; 2 Tim. 3.12). The term may also include a reference to the time of intense suffering which is associated with the arrival of the millennial kingdom (Mounce 54); cf. Rev. 20.1–15.

With 'conflict' (see also on 2.9–10) John links 'sovereignty' and 'steadfastness'. The sequence is deliberate and significant. Christian believers who are called to suffer, as Jesus did, also share in the sovereignty of their Lord and reign with him (Rev. 1.6; 2 Tim. 2.12; cf. Acts 14.22). As a result, they will receive the steadfastness and patience which are his gift, and become conquerors (cf. Rev. 2.26–29; 5.10; 20.4–6). The Greek at this point associates 'steadfastness' very closely with 'in Jesus': ὑπομονῇ ἐν Ἰησοῦ (*hypomonē[i] en Jēsou*, lit. 'steadfastness in Jesus'). The patient endurance in suffering, shared with others who are in fellowship with Christ, is also enabled by him.

There is no need to restrict the reference of βασιλεία (*basileia*, 'sovereignty') here to a 'coming period of messianic blessedness' (Mounce 54), for John's eschatology throughout this statement is characteristically balanced. Persecution may overtake the faithful Christian at any time; believers participate now, as well as in the future, in Christ's sovereign rule over the world; and steadfastness is a constant demand from the Church, and his gift to it. For ὑπομονή (*hypomonē*, 'steadfastness'), as a virtue belonging to Jesus and required from his followers, cf. 2 Thess. 3.5; Col. 1.11; et al.

John 'found himself' (the aorist indicative middle ἐγενόμην, *egenomēn*) on Patmos island. The verb, from γίνομαι (*ginomai*, lit. 'become', or 'come to be'), is forceful, and suits the dramatic character of this ecstatic scene. Patmos, on which John evidently received his vision, is a fairly small island in the Aegean, about 40 miles west of Miletus and 65 miles south-west of Ephesus. It is first mentioned by Thucydides, *Peloponnesian War* 3.33.3, and later by Strabo, *Geography* 10.5.13, and Pliny (the Elder), *Natural History* 4.12.23. By the time of John the island seems to have been well inhabited and an established centre for the cults of Artemis and Apollo. See Aune 76–77.

John's exile to Patmos was presumably the result of his Christian testimony ('on account of God's word and the witness of Jesus') and an attempt by the Roman authorities to prevent the further growth of the Church in Asia. But the assumption that John was banished from Ephesus, and underwent a penal sentence on Patmos (harsh, according to Ramsay, *Letters* 82–86, esp. 85), is not based on secure evidence; and this has resulted in considerable scholarly debate and speculation. The earliest witness is Clement of Alexandria (*Quis dives* 42), who says of John the apostle that, 'on the death of the tyrant, he removed (μετῆλθεν, *metēlthen*, which may also be translated "went across" or "returned") from the island of Patmos to Ephesus'. See Eusebius, *HE* 3.23.1–19, where Eusebius identifies the 'tyrant' as the Emperor Domitian (cf. 23.1); but, against the late dating of Revelation which such an identification implies, see Wilson, 'Domitianic Date' 587–605, esp. 605, who places the Apocalypse in AD 64–65 or 68–69.

The inference is that John was separated from his Asian churches because of judicial condemnation; and this certainly became part of the early tradition about John (see Swete clxxvii–viii). Victorinus, for example, commenting on Rev. 10.11 (*Comm. in Apoc.* 10.3; *PL* col. 143), refers to John being 'condemned to the quarries' (*in metallo damnatus*) on

Patmos (by Domitian): and this strongly implies that the apostle had to undergo the punishment of hard labour.

Caird (21–23) suggests that John was exiled by the Asian proconsul to an island within his jurisdiction, applying the ruling of *relegatio ad insulam* ('relegation to an island'), which existed at the time. So Tertullian describes John's sentence: '*Ioannes . . . in insulam relegatur*' ('John was banished to an island'; *De Praescript. Haer.* 36), adding that he was first immersed in boiling oil without harm. There are still questions to be asked about this line of conjecture, however, as Hemer reminds us (Hemer, *Letters* 27–29): in particular, whether Patmos was actually in the province of Asia. But on balance, the explanation that John's exile took place within Asian jurisdiction, from Jewish and Roman opponents, and that it involved hard labour but not life imprisonment, seems a reasonable interpretation of the evidence before us, and fits easily into the situation described in Rev. 1.9. See further Peake, *Revelation* 214–18. For a discussion of the effect of the writer's surroundings, in captivity, on his vivid imagery see Hemer, *Letters* 29–30.

John's imprisonment was 'on account of God's word and the witness of Jesus': that is, because he, as the leader of a strong Christian community, was preaching the gospel openly in Asia. It does not mean that the apostle went to Patmos to evangelize or to receive his apocalypse. Apart from the situation outlined above, John always uses διά (*dia*, 'on account of') to introduce cause, not purpose (cf. Rev. 2.3; 4.11; et al.). The genitive in τὴν μαρτυρίαν Ἰησοῦ (*tēn martyrian Jēsou*, 'the witness of Jesus') is subjective. The message John proclaimed derived from God, and is authenticated by Jesus. See on Rev. 1.2.

10 The vision was granted to John 'on the Lord's Day' (ἐν τῇ κυριακῇ, *en tē[i] kyriakē[i]*). Before the Common Era, the first day of each month was called 'Emperor's (Sebaste-) Day' in Asia Minor (Hemer, *Letters* 31, 223). From this practice it became natural for the early Christian Church to name the first day of each week (Sunday) the 'Lord's Day', because this was the day of the resurrection of Jesus, when his followers met together for worship. Charles (1, 23) thinks that the designation was prompted, in apocalyptic circles, by the hostile attitude to the Roman empire adopted by Christianity. For later testimony to the use of 'Lord's Day' as a synonym for Sunday see *Did.* 14.1; Ignatius, *Magn.* 9.1 (distinguishing the 'Lord's Day' from the sabbath, which illustrates the double threat to the Church in Asia: Jewish, as well as Roman); Eusebius, *HE* 4.26.2. See also Acts 20.7; 1 Cor. 11.20. This is the first place where the 'Lord's Day' is mentioned in Christian literature.

John 'found himself in the Spirit' on this occasion. The verb ἐγενόμην (*egenomēn*, lit. 'was' or 'came to be') is used in the same forceful way as in the previous verse, to underscore the trance-like state of the seer at this point (cf. Rev. 4.2). We should certainly understand ἐν πνεύματι (*en pneumati*, 'in the Spirit') here to mean 'in the (Holy) Spirit (of God)'; cf. 1.4. A parallel use of the phrase, in a non-ecstatic context, is the description of believers as being normally 'in Spirit' (ἐν πνεύματι, *en pneumati*), rather than ἐν σαρκί (*en sarki*, 'in flesh', like the worldly), since the Spirit of God dwells in them (Rom. 8.9). Cf. Acts 22.17; and the reverse process (Peter 'came to himself') at Acts 12.11. Wilcock (42) notes the balance between 'in Patmos' (verse 9) and 'in Spirit' here. On earth we suffer; but spiritually we can triumph.

The diction in the second part of this verse follows closely the text of Ezek. 3.12: 'Then the spirit lifted me up, and I heard behind me a loud, trumpet-like voice'. There is probably no symbolic significance in John's reference to the voice coming from 'behind' him (ὀπίσω μου, *opisō mou*, 'behind me'; lxx κατόπισθέν μου, *katopisthen mou*, 'behind me'). It is simply an appropriate – if dramatic – way of describing a voice which comes unexpectedly from an unseen person (Beckwith 436). Given that Jesus speaks next, the voice obviously belongs to him. It is 'loud' and 'trumpet like' (φωνὴν μεγάλην ὡς σάλπιγγος, *phonēn megalēn hōs salpingos*): that is to say, the voice is clear, as well as great in volume. For 'hearing a (loud) voice', as a medium of John's revelation, see on 4.1.

On John's use, here and in the Apocalypse generally, of ὡς (*hōs*) and ὅμοιος (*homoios*), both meaning 'as', or 'like', see Charles 1, 35–37. He regards both the particle and the adjective as equivalent in construction and meaning throughout Revelation (1, 37); note esp. Rev. 1.13 and 14.14.

11 John is instructed to write down his vision. Like most New Testament writers, including the fourth evangelist, the seer uses βλέπειν (*blepein*, 'to see') not ὁρᾶν (*horan*, 'to see'), in the present tense (cf. John 1.29; 9.19; et al.; note also 2 John 8). John is to 'write' what he 'sees' (ὅ βλέπεις, *ho blepeis*) in a book. The verb suggests spiritual perception, as in a vision, rather than physical sight by itself. This is very Johannine in its theological, as well as literary, character (so John 12.35–41; 20.29; et al.). The command of Jesus to John is connected by the participle λεγούσης (*legousēs*, 'saying'), which agrees with the dependent genitive σάλπιγγος (*salpingos*, 'trumpet'), and not with the earlier noun φωνή (*phonē*, 'voice'). Cf. the similar commands to write in Tobit 12.20; 2 Esdras 12.37. See also on verse 19.

The Apocalypse is to be sent to the 'seven churches' in Asia (see on Rev. 1.4; for the needs of these communities, both Jewish and Hellenistic in background, cf. further Smalley, *Thunder and Love* 125–32). The churches are listed as they appear in a rough geographical circle on the western coast of Asia Minor, beginning with the leading congregation at Ephesus. The road leads from there northwards to Smyrna and Pergamum, and winds southwards through Thyatira, Sardis and Philadelphia to Laodicea, and back to Ephesus. The churches are addressed in this order in Rev. 2—3.

Ramsay (*Letters* 185–96, esp. 191–93; cf. Hemer, *Letters* 25–26) argues that the province of Asia at this time was divided into seven postal districts, each having as its point of origin one of the seven cities mentioned here. These were centres not only for communication but also for judicial administration, with Ephesus as the leading administrative headquarters. This view makes sense of John's address to these seven communities as part of a strategically placed group, particularly if their message is seen to have a wider application to the Church of Christ as a whole (cf. Rev. 2.7, 11; et al.). It is also appropriate to the situation of the Church in the first century if, by now, the centre of the Christian world had shifted from Palestine to Asia, and Ephesus had succeeded Jerusalem in its spiritual responsibility for the world (see Beasley-Murray 65–66). The Asian background to the literature in the New Testament associated with the names of John and Paul is evidence by itself for the occurrence of this shift.

However, I would still like to propose that it was these seven churches alone which initially made up the Johannine community, and that they existed where they did precisely because they were well placed as centres for the communication of the gospel in terms of both mission and growth.

12 John 'turned round' in response to the voice. The verb ἐπέστρεψα (*epestrepsa*, 'I turned [round]'), which is repeated in the form of an aorist participle in the second half of the verse (ἐπιστρέψας, *epistrepsas*, 'on turning', lit. 'having turned [round]'), is dramatically descriptive. Cf. Mary Magdalene, in the garden of resurrection, 'turning round' (ἐστράφη, *estraphē*, lit. 'she turned') to see the risen Jesus (John 20.14).

The reference to John 'seeing a voice' becomes less odd in character if we accept the argument of James Charlesworth ('Jewish Roots of Christology' 19–41), based on his examination of the use of 'the voice' in Jewish and Christian apocalyptic literature, that 'the voice' in Rev. 1.12 is intended as the designation of a heavenly creature or divine being. The seer, that is, encounters not a disembodied voice, but a being who is visible.

If Charlesworth is right, moreover, it means that the author of Revelation presents us at the outset of his apocalypse with a vision of the exalted Son of God, who is also like a Son of man (verse 13), which parallels exactly the description of his nature provided by the fourth evangelist in John 1: he is pre-existent, but also incarnate (see 1.14). Both Johns are indebted to the development of the hypostatic Wisdom (Sophia) concept, familiar to us from early Judaism (cf. Wis. 7.22—11.1): where Wisdom has a distinct personality and real substance, and can be addressed as a heavenly or human being. But while John the Divine 'remits' his hypostatic figure in Christian terms (Charlesworth, 'Jewish Roots of Christology' 40), and employs the notion of 'voice', John the evangelist uses the *Logos* concept (close to wisdom) in the presentation of his Christology. See further Smalley, *Thunder and Love* 61.

Like his prophetic predecessors, John 'hears' the voice (of God), as well as 'seeing' it (Rev. 1.10, 12); cf. Ezek. 1.1, 28. Each time the seer describes himself in Revelation as being 'in Spirit' (ἐν πνεύματι, *en pneumati*), the prophetic activities of seeing and hearing are mentioned in fairly close proximity (Rev. 1.10–12; 4.2; 5.1–2, 11; 17.3, 6; 18.4; 21.10, 1–3; 22.8 [*bis*]).

Having turned round, John sees not only (by implication) the 'voice' – that is, the glorified Son – but also, as part of his christological vision, 'seven golden lampstands (or menorahs)'. The imagery used here is interpreted in verse 20 of this chapter (q.v.): the 'lampstands' are the (seven) Asian churches and the 'stars' in the right hand of the risen Lord (verse 16) are the 'angels' of those churches. The idea of lampstands as a symbol for churches stems from Zechariah's vision of Israel as a seven-branched candelabra (Zech. 4.2–11, which was one of the readings for the Jewish Festival of Lights, or Dedication [Hanukkah]). But whereas in the Old Testament the picture of the people of God (God among his people) is that of one lampstand, with seven lamps on it, the congregations in this passage are symbolized as seven individual lampstands, gathered round the voice. Each church represents the Johannine circle in its totality (see on verse 11) and the reality of the Christian community as a whole (cf. 1 Cor. 1.1, 'the church *of* God *in* Corinth'); together they make up the new Israel of God (cf. Beasley-Murray 66). See further on 11.3–4.

13   Among the seven churches (lampstands), as their head, the prophet sees 'a son of man figure'. The expression ὅμοιον υἱὸν ἀνθρώπου (*homoion huion anthrōpou*, lit. '[one] like a son of man') is anarthrous; and the lack of a definite article suggests very strongly that John is not using 'son of man' as a title of Jesus, as he does (for example) in John's Gospel (cf. John 1.51; et al.; see further Smalley, 'Johannine Son of Man').

Nevertheless, the description of the exalted Christ as 'a son of man figure' is drawn from the same background in Daniel 7, where 'one like a son of man' is representative of Israel ('the saints of the Most High'), and suffers with God's people (verse 25), as well as being vindicated before the throne of the Ancient One (verses 13–14; cf. Ps. 80.17). Here are the materials for the fourth evangelist's presentation of Jesus as Son of man, honoured after undergoing humiliation for his Church. They also provide the theological underpinning for the introduction of the 'Son of man' figure in this verse, even if the expression on this occasion is used in a nontitular way, and the emphasis is on the glory of Jesus, rather than on his humility.

John's Christology in the present passage, that is to say, is consistently high. The Son of man figure seems to merge with God. He is a celestial visitor, who appears in clothing and with personal characteristics which point to his divine status (verses 13–16); and he speaks of his pre-existence and sovereign exaltation (verses 17–18). Eventually, we are left in no doubt that he is the risen and glorified Lord Christ, the eschatological judge (1.16, 18) who also 'possesses the glory of heaven' and 'shares the likeness of God himself' (Beasley-Murray 66; cf. Mounce 57; see also Dunn, *Christology* 91–92). Carrell, *Jesus and the Angels* 129–74, maintains that the form of Jesus in the Christophany of 1.13–16 is more akin to an angelophany than a theophany. Christ is clothed in all the attributes of a glorious angel; but he is still divine, because his angelomorphic appearance is only temporary (Carrell, *Jesus and the Angels* 174). See also Rev. 14.14, which is the only other allusion in the New Testament to Dan. 7.13, apart from Rev. 1.7, outside the four Gospels.

A catena of Old Testament allusions underlies the description of Christ in this and the following verses (14–16). He is generally portrayed in language which is drawn from Dan. 7.9 (referring to the Ancient of Days) and 10.5–6 (the angel). The 'long robe' and 'golden sash' across the chest in this verse pick up the list of sacred vestments worn by the Jewish high priest, according to Exod. 28.4; 29.5; and 39.29 (Caird 25); although such clothing was worn generally by people of status, and the details of the priestly sash, or 'belt' (Exod. 39.29, made of 'fine twisted linen, and embroidered with needlework') are missing. See Morris 53–54. The word ποδήρης (*podērēs*, 'long robe') is a *hapax legomenon* in the New Testament.

The fact that the 'golden sash' is worn high across the chest of Christ (πρὸς τοῖς μαστοῖς, *pros tois mastois*, lit. 'around the breast'), rather than around his waist, leads Beasley-Murray (67) into a theological flight of fancy. The lower position, he claims, is reminiscent of a workman, who has tucked his robe into the belt while labouring; whereas the ascended Lord has completed *his* task. But this is to read more into the text than it can bear. The ungrammatical χρυσᾶν (*chrysan*), for χρυσῆν (*chrysēn*, 'gold') may simply be a colloquialism (so Swete 16; cf. BDF 25–26).

14–15 John now describes the personal appearance of the exalted figure: his hair, eyes, feet and voice. The phrase 'his head of hair' (ἡ . . . κεφαλὴ αὐτοῦ καὶ αἱ τρίχες, *hē . . . kephalē autou kai hai triches*) should properly be translated, 'his head, that is, his hair', giving epexegetical or explanatory force to the word καί (*kai*, 'that is'). See AG 393; BDF 228. The Chief of Days is said in Dan. 7.9 to have clothing 'white as snow' and hair (on his head) 'like pure wool'; cf. *1 Enoch* 46.1. The author of Revelation adapts this description slightly, and refers it completely to the hair of Christ ('white as white wool-like snow'); this indicates once again the exalted nature of John's Christology. The whiteness of Christ's hair denotes wisdom and degree (cf. Prov. 16.31; Wis. 4.8–9), not pre-existence (so Andreas, *Comm. in Apoc.* 7, ad loc.; *PG* 106, 227–30).

The eyes of the son of man figure, in John's vision, 'flamed like fire'; cf. Dan 10.6. This characteristic recurs in the letter to Thyatira (Rev. 2.18), and in the appearance of the messianic victor at 19.12. The image suggests discriminating insight, as well as sovereignty over the Church and the world.

To the writer, the 'feet' of Christ were 'like bronze, glowing as in a furnace' (verse 15). The etymology of the Greek word χαλκολιβάνῳ (*chalkolibanō[i]*, 'bronze') is uncertain, and its use (here and at 2.18) is confined to Revelation. Swete (17) concludes that the term refers to a 'mixed metal of great brilliance'. The expression as a whole depends on the description of the feet of the living creatures in Ezek. 1.7 (LXX); but see again Dan. 10.6. It speaks of the 'strength and stability' of Jesus (Mounce 59). For the textual and linguistic difficulties involved in the phrase ἐν καμίνῳ πεπυρωμένης (*en kaminō[i] pepyrōmenēs*, '[bronze] glowing as in a furnace') see above, 45. The translation used here provides a clear and acceptable meaning.

The voice of the exalted Christ sounded to the prophet-seer 'like the roar of many waters'. This image is used, once more, of the voice of God in the Old Testament (Ezek.

43.2); and the same symbolism is used by John to describe the 'voice from heaven' in Rev. 14.2, and the 'voice of a great multitude' of the redeemed at 19.6. It connotes the 'awe-inspiring power and majesty' of God (Beasley-Murray 67).

16 The writer adds loosely to his description of the exalted Christ a further three clauses (cf. the construction in verses 14–15). The first is a reminder of divine beneficence; in the second God's discrimination is predominant; and the third creates a typically Johannine theological pattern of salvation *through* judgement.

The Son of man holds in his 'right' hand (symbolizing power, as well as protection) the 'seven stars'. These are later (verse 20) identified as the 'angels of the seven churches', just as the 'lampstands' are described as the 'seven churches' themselves (see verses 12–13). The churches of Asia, representing the Church at large, are thus closely related to Christ. He is in the midst of them (among the menorahs, verse 13); but he also sustains their spiritual life, and protects them carefully (cf. Beckwith 440). For the 'stars' see Dan. 12.3; also *1 Enoch* 104.2.

Despite upholding the Church on earth, God in Christ also speaks to it a word of judgement. From the mouth of the risen Lord comes a 'sharp, two-edged sword' (ῥομφαία δίστομος ὀξεῖα, *hromphaia distomos oxeia*). The word for 'sword' here (ῥομφαία, *hromphaia*) means a large and broad weapon, as used by barbaric peoples, notably the Thracians (AG 744); see also Rev. 2.12, 16; 6.8; 19.15, 21. The term for a more conventional 'sword' or sabre is μάχαιρα (*machaira*), which occurs in Rev. 6.4; 13:10, 14, and elsewhere in the New Testament. God's judgement is directed against his people when they lack repentance (Rev. 2.16), and against the world when it opposes the Lord (6.8; 19.15; cf. the similar imagery of destruction at Isa. 11.4).

However, there is a resolution of the tension between the judgement and salvation described in the first two clauses. The 'face' of the risen Christ appears as 'the sun shining with all its power' (a condensed expression, meaning 'the sun when it shines'). Ὄψις (*opsis*, 'face') appears in the New Testament only here and at John 11.44; but cf. John 7.24. The dazzling splendour of divinity, seen in the face of the glorified Son of man, is a portrayal of the light embodied in the Word made flesh, as John the evangelist was later to proclaim. Eternal life may be found in Jesus the Christ, and that life is the light of all people (John 1.3). Through the darkness of spiritual opposition, the light shines in judgement and without being extinguished. But for those who believe, and enter the light, salvation through judgement becomes possible (John 3.17–21; cf. 8.12; 12.35–36; 1 John 1.5–7; Rev. 18.21–24; 21.23–24; 22.5). The Lord's countenance shone with a sun-like quality which was powerful and undimmed (cf. *2 Enoch* 1.5; Judg. 5.31*b*). The apostle John may well have had in mind at this point the glory of God seen in the transfiguration of Christ Jesus during his ministry (cf. Matt. 17.1–2).

17–18 The drama of this apocalyptic scene is already intense. Now the main characters interact, with movement as well as speech; and the dramatic tension increases. Falling to the ground under the powerful influence of supernatural disclosures is a typical feature of visionary passages in the Bible (cf. Ezek. 1.8; Dan. 8.17; Matt. 17.6; Acts 9.4; see also *1 Enoch* 14.14). As this scene is symbolic, as well as dramatic, there is no difficulty in John's statement that the Lord lays upon the seer his 'right hand', which has just been described as holding 'seven stars' (verse 16). The hand which sustains the world and the churches also gives life to individual believers (cf. Swete 19). Again, as in verse 16, we hear that it is the 'right' hand of Christ which is laid on John: the side of power, as well as protection; and the entire action at this point is a gesture of blessing, as well as of commissioning.

Another point of contact with the transfiguration narrative in Matthew is evident here; for the Matthean account includes a reference to the transfigured Christ 'touching' the disciples (Matt. 17.7). Swete (19) connects the command to be unafraid, followed by the announcement, 'I am (ἐγώ εἰμι, *egō eimi* [the first and the last]')', with the walking on the water scene in Mark 6.50 par. ('it is I, do not be afraid'), q.v. But Beckwith (441) points out that the analogy is not exact; for in the miracle narrative 'I am' *precedes* μὴ φοβεῖσθε (*mē phobeisthe*, 'do not fear').

The expression, ἐγώ εἰμι (*egō eimi*, 'I am'), has in any case a Johannine ring about it, familiar to us from the Fourth Gospel (cf. John 6.35; 8.12; et al.). The whole phrase, 'I am the first and the last', runs back to Isa. 44.6 (cf. 48.12), where it refers to the divine existence from eternity to eternity. God is the creator, the origin and goal of all life. That a description of the Father (see also and esp. Rev. 1.8) should be applied to the exalted Son (as in verse 14) is a further example of John's high Christology in this section of the Apocalypse.

The title 'first and last' is expanded epexegetically to include the phrase 'the living one'. This translation assumes that καί (*kai*) is explicative, meaning, 'that is/also'. However, Charles (1, 31) connects 'the living one' (ὁ ζῶν, *ho zōn*) with the words which follow, on the grounds that the phrase, 'I am first and last', is complete in itself. 'The living one' is a further title of God to be found in the Old Testament (cf. Josh. 3.10; Ps. 84.2; Hos. 1.10; et al.), which is also freely used in the New Testament (Matt. 26.63; Acts 14.15; Rom. 9.26; Heb. 3.12; 1 Pet. 1.23; et al.). Once more, a title applied to God is now applied to his Christ.

That Jesus has 'life in himself' is a constant theme in the Johannine literature (John 5.26; cf. Rev. 22.1; 1 John 5.11–13). Indeed, John's Gospel was evidently written so that its believing audience might have 'life in the name' of Jesus the Christ and Son of God (John 20.31). He is Life in an absolute sense (John 14.6) and the source of all created life (John 1.1–4; Col. 1.16; Heb. 1.2; cf. Hughes 28). Paradoxically, the life-giver experienced death on the cross; but this action became, through resurrection, the means of eternal life for the followers of the world's Saviour (John 10.11–18; 1 Cor. 15.20–22; 1 John 4.7–14). In contrast to the 'dead (or inanimate) gods of paganism' (Mounce 61; cf. Ps. 115.4–7), Jesus the Christ is 'alive for ever and ever' (εἰς τοὺς αἰῶνας τῶν αἰώνων, *eis tous aionas tōn aiōnōn*, lit. 'to the ages of the ages'). Not merely has he risen from the dead; his life is continuing, and he also dispenses life to the believer unendingly (cf. 1 Pet. 1.3). For ἐγενόμην (νεκρός) (*egenomēn [nekros]*, 'I was/became [dead]'), see verse 9.

The living one holds 'the keys to Death and Hades', the possession of which implies power and control over these realms (cf. Matt. 16.19; Rev. 3.7; 9.1; 20.1). This sentence is closely associated with the two preceding clauses, and sets out the basis and evidence of Christ's authority over death and its outcome (cf. Beckwith 441).

The Greek ᾅδης (*ha[i]dēs*, 'Hades') equates to the Hebrew שְׁאוֹל (*šᵉʾôl*, 'Sheol'). Hades and death are regularly linked in the Apocalypse (Rev. 6.8, where the reference seems more personal; 20.13–14, local). Hades represents the dwelling of departed spirits, and is to be distinguished from Gehenna, the place of torment (Matt. 5.22, 29, 30). According to rabbinic teaching, God alone exercises supremacy over Death and Hades (*Targ. Ps.-Jon.* on Deut. 28.12; (*b.*) *Sanh.* 113*a*). Here the risen Christ is significantly revealed as sharing this authority: not only potentially, which may be the implication of John 5.25–29, but actually, and from the moment of his exaltation (ἔχω, *echō*, present, 'I have' or 'I hold'). For the contraction κλεῖς (*kleis*, 'keys') = κλεῖδας, see BDF 47(3).

The Commission to Write (1.19–20)

19   This verse is closely related to the preceding one through the particle οὖν (*oun*, 'so' or 'therefore'). The basis of the message which John is to communicate to the churches of Asia (in the first place) is to be found in the eternal Lord of death and life, whose commands and promises assure the faithful of the triumph of his kingdom over the powers of death and evil (cf. Beckwith 442). The instruction to write is recapitulated from verse 11, and made specific.

Charles (1, 33; see also Boring 84) takes the remainder of the verse ('[write down] what you have seen, what is taking place now and what is about to happen later on') as a 'rough' description of the contents of the Apocalypse. Thus ἃ εἶδες (*ha eides*, 'what you have seen') refers to the vision of the triumphant Son of man just narrated; καὶ ἃ εἰσίν (*kai ha eisin*, 'even what is taking place now') means the present condition of the Asian churches, about to be declared; and καὶ ἃ μέλλει γενέσθαι μετὰ ταῦτα (*kai ha mellei genesthai meta tauta*, 'and what is about to happen later on') embraces the visions in Revelation from chapter 4 onwards, with their insistently future tense. (Similarly, but cautiously, Swete 21.) For (ἃ) μέλλει (γενέσθαι), (*ha*) *mellei* (*genesthai*), lit. '(the things which are) about (to happen)', with a present rather than an imperfect infinitive, see BDF 356. For μετὰ ταῦτα (*meta tauta*, 'later on', lit. 'after these things') see Rev. 4.1; 9.12; John 13.7.

However, John's eschatology is essentially balanced; for him the present includes the future, and the future runs back to God's salvific activity in the past. (See Smalley, *Thunder and Love* 62–63, 174–76.) So, while 'what has been seen' includes the previous vision (verses 12–16), it can also refer to all that the seer will recount in the Apocalypse as a whole (the verb εἶδες, *eides*, 'seen', is an aorist: it is in the past tense, but it has a present meaning). Similarly, 'what is taking place now' may be associated with the situation in the seven churches. But this was already known to the seer, without a vision; the important spiritual disclosure was to be located in the word of the risen Christ to those communities, and through them to the Church for all time. The same is true eschatologically of the subsequent events ('what is about to happen later on') which John is commanded to set down. It is true that Rev. 4—22 looks towards the future of the Church and of the world (note 4.1). But these future disclosures point to eternal truths which are perpetually relevant. Such is the case, for example, with Rev. 4 and 5 (the court of heaven), which reveal the essential and immediate nature of God and of the Lamb; with Rev. 17 and 18, which narrate the destruction of the harlot and the fall of Babylon, as symbols of the abiding conflict between the world and the Church, transcended by the victory of Christ; and with Rev. 21 and 22, where the promise of life beyond death can be interpreted in terms of a present, as well as an eschatological, possession for every believer.

It is therefore important to regard the scope of this verse as wide ranging. John is commanded to write down in Ephesus the vision he received on Patmos (cf. Smalley, *Thunder and Love* 137): that is to say (the first καὶ, *kai*, 'even', is epexegetic or explanatory), he is to describe God's saving activity through his exalted Christ, in the Church and in the world, as this is relevant for today, and for all the days to come.

Kirby ('Rhetorical Situations' 199) suggests that the command to write down the vision here (as in 1.11) directly involves John himself as rhetor; whereas in chapters 2 and 3 Jesus dictates the letters.

20 The Greek of this verse is irregular, and does not depend on the command in verse 19 to 'write (down)', γράψον (*grapson*). First, τὸ μυστήριον (*to mystērion*, 'the mystery' or 'secret') is a rare absolute accusative (but cf. Acts 26.3; Rom. 8.3; 12.1; 1 Tim. 2.6); and τὰς ἑπτὰ λυχνίας (*tas hepta lychnias*, 'the seven lampstands') is also in the accusative, rather than in the genitive expected after 'the mystery'. See further Charles 1, 33; BDF 291(1).

The symbols of the stars and the lampstands, which appeared in the preceding vision (Rev. 1.12–16, q.v.), are now interpreted. Together, they form a 'secret' (τὸ μυστήριον, *to mystērion*) which needs explanation, and which is disclosed here to special (believing) individuals. Cf. Dan 2.47; Rev. 17.7. For the 'seven lampstands', representing the

Johannine community, and beyond that the Church in its universality, see on verse 12. The 'seven stars', which have been perceived in (ἐπί, *epi*, lit. 'upon') the Son of man's right hand (denoting power and protection; see verse 16), are understood as the 'angels' of the seven churches. (For 'seven', see on verses 12, 16.)

There has been much scholarly debate about the meaning of this phrase. At its simplest, it could refer to the 'guardian angels' of the Asian congregations (cf. Dan. 10.13–14, 20–21, where nations are described as having protective angel-patrons; and Matt. 18.10, which speaks of the guardian angels of children). The difficulty with this exegesis is that the seer is clearly writing, in the letters to the churches and in the Apocalypse as a whole, to living (Johannine) church communities, and beyond them to the Church at large (note the mention of individuals at Rev. 2.13, 24; 3.20; et al.). He is not writing in the first place to angels (cf. Charles 1, 34–35).

Since ἄγγελος (*angelos*) means 'messenger', and the word is used in the Old Testament in relation to human as well as heavenly intermediaries (e.g. Gen. 19.1–23; Judg. 13.6; Zech. 4.1–6), it could be argued that the 'angels' in this context are the responsible leaders of the churches around John the apostle, authorized by the congregations themselves (cf. SB 3, 790–92). Nevertheless, as we have just seen, the seven letters of Rev. 2 and 3 are addressed to Asian communities as a whole, and not first to their presiding officers. Moreover the term 'angel' in Revelation, beyond Chapters 1–3 (59 times), is regularly used in association with heavenly – not human – beings.

Swete (22), followed by Beasley-Murray (60), discovers a useful parallel in the Persian *fravashis* of Zoroastrianism. These are heavenly counterparts of earthly communities, in this case the Johannine churches. The seer writes to congregations in Asia, whose failures are typically human. But their distinctive character emerges from the truth that, like John himself, they are Christian: 'in Jesus' (Rev. 1.9, q.v.). So they become fellow-partners in Christ with all that has to be endured; and John deliberately addresses their 'angels', to remind them of the spiritual dimension to their daily life and witness. For the Church of God is located in heaven, as well as in this world; and its *angels* draw together the spiritual and material spheres in typically Johannine fashion (cf. John 1.51).

Beasley-Murray (70) also points out that the seven planets were 'a common symbol in the ancient world for sovereignty'. In this way the 'stars' could symbolize the political power wielded by the Roman Emperors. John develops this thought by representing the stars as being in the possession of the exalted Christ, not of the Caesars. The symbolism of 'the stars which are the angels of the churches' now becomes clear: sovereignty over the universe belongs not to Rome, or to any political authority which seeks to oppose God, but to the Lord of the Church himself. This theological concept is central to the drama of the Apocalypse as a whole; it will also provide its audience with encouragement in the face of persecution from without, and incipient doctrinal tensions within. See further on this passage Beasley-Murray 68–70; Caird 24–25. For the relationship between 'stars' and 'angels' see Ramsay, *Letters* 62–73; note also *1 Enoch* 86.1–3.

The angels of the churches are represented by stars, while 'the seven lampstands are the seven churches themselves', giving both light and life. The stars are reminders of the spiritual character of God's Church, and the lamps of its material embodiment (cf. Swete 22). The direct repetition ἑπτά (*hepta*, 'seven [lights]'), ἑπτά (*hepta*, 'seven [churches]') reinforces attractively John's predilection for this (perfect) number.

Kirby ('Rhetorical Situations' 199) argues that the vision of Rev. 1.10–20 establishes the writer's ethos as a prophet; and he claims that rhetorically it would be important for John to do this at the outset of his work. Kirby also maintains that the prophet-seer (which is the writer's real identity, we may add) arouses the emotions of his audience by instilling in its members a sense of the numinous in the presence of the triumphant, messianic

Son of man; and that he capitalizes on his readers' familiarity with visions in the Old Testament texts (here, notably Ezek. 1; Dan. 10; and Zech. 4) and the awe which they in turn would inspire.

Letters to the Seven Churches (2.1—3.22)

As we move into the next section of the first scene of Act 1, and hear the solemn words spoken to John's Asian communities, the manner of address becomes more specific. In the first chapter, the revelation of Jesus Christ is mediated through John the Divine, his servant, to the seven churches collectively (1.1–11). In Rev. 2 and 3 the individual congregations each receive a letter; and now the exalted Son of man himself is the speaker. He knows these churches, their weaknesses and their strengths; and he relates to them in differing ways, which correspond to the revelation of his divine, multi-faceted character already understood from the vision in Chapter 1 (cf. Maurice 32–34).

The tension between faith and works in these two chapters is complemented by the overarching theological theme of salvation through judgement.

Ephesus (2.1–7)

2.1   The first letter, or prophetic oracle, is sent to the congregation at Ephesus. According to tradition, John the apostle was closely associated with that city; and there is no reason to doubt that the literature in the Johannine corpus originated from there. See Smalley, *Thunder and Love* 137; Smalley, *John* 186. As the leading church in John's Asian community, therefore, Ephesus is appropriately saluted first (as in 1.11, q.v.).

Ephesus itself was situated on an Aegean gulf, near the mouth of the river Cayster. It was an important city, built on a grand scale; and it formed part (but not the capital) of the Roman province of Asia when that was organized in 133 BC. It was a major commercial centre, standing as it did at the convergence of three popular trade routes. By the New Testament period, Ephesus had grown to a population of more than a quarter of a million.

The city was politically and religiously, as well as commercially, significant. Rome granted Ephesus self-governing status; and it was a place of assize, where justice was dispensed by the governor. Ephesus was also famous for its marketplace and massive theatre. Built on the western slope of Mount Pion, the theatre overlooked the harbour, now silted up; and it could accommodate an audience of about 25,000 people. It is possible that performances in this building influenced the dramatic character of John's writing, in the Apocalypse as in the Gospel.

The religious life of Ephesus was vibrant, and marked by imperial worship. A shrine and great altar were set up to Caesar Augustus in the earlier years of his reign (30 BC–AD 14); and provincial temples of the imperial religion were built under Nero, Hadrian and Severus. Related, in cultic terms, but more dominant in the city, was the religious following of Artemis (Latin, Diana), the goddess of the whole Province (cf. Acts 19.23–35, esp. 35). Originally a fertility figure, under Greek cultural influence Artemis became the focus of an influential religious system. Her temple, magnificently rebuilt after a great fire in 356 BC, was four times the size of the Parthenon in Athens. Pliny the elder (*Nat. Hist.* 36.95–97) tells us that this temple took 120 years to build; it was 425 feet long and 225 feet wide. There were 127 columns, 60 feet in height, each constructed by a different king; 36 of these columns, Pliny says, were carved with reliefs. On Ephesus see Ramsay, *Letters* 210–36.

The Christian gospel was brought to Ephesus by Paul (cf. Acts 16.6; 18.19–20, when he left Priscilla and Aquila in the city; 19.8–10, when he spent two years of missionary activity there); and his work was carried on by Timothy (1 Tim. 1.3). But John the apostle seems by tradition most closely associated with Ephesus, and to have established the Christian Church there most firmly (cf. Eusebius, *HE* 3.23.1–4, et al.).

The oracle to Ephesus is addressed to 'the angel of the church'; and this is a regular introductory formula in the seven letters. Christ speaks to the spirit of the church: namely, to the church in its spiritual, as well as earthly, expression (see on 1.20). John is commanded to 'write' (γράψον, *grapson*) the letters in a way that recalls the injunction to 'write' at 1.19. However the reference is now specific.

The remaining words in verse 1 relate directly to 1.20 (q.v.), but also recapitulate one relevant aspect of the glorified Christ described at 1.16 (see also verses 12–13). For the unity of Rev. 1–3 see above, 47–49.

The exalted Son of man 'holds the seven stars (= angels) in his right hand' and 'walks among the seven golden lampstands'. That is to say, Jesus as Lord controls and protects the churches, including Ephesus, and is watchfully present among them. Evidently the Ephesian Christians needed the help of the risen Christ, as he related to them, in this way. They had 'given up' their 'initial love', and needed to think again about their ethical behaviour.

There is an important equilibrium in the estimate of Christ's person at this point; and it persists in the salutations to the other six Johannine churches in Rev. 2 and 3. The risen Lord *can* assist the struggling congregations in Asia around John, precisely because he is in touch with both heaven and earth. Christ's right hand, which holds the stars, has already touched the prophet-seer himself (1.17*b*); just as the exalted figure of the Son of man, before whom John prostrates himself, also calmly 'walks' among the congregations on earth. The insistent balance in John's Christology throughout these two chapters, and elsewhere in Revelation, may be related to growing problems of theology and consequent ethical praxis within the Johannine community, where heterodox groups from Jewish and Hellenistic backgrounds were placing too much emphasis on either the humanity or the divinity of Christ (cf. Acts 19.10; see above, 4–6; also Smalley, *Thunder and Love* 125–32).

The expression τάδε λέγει (*tade legei*, 'these are the words', lit. 'thus says'), here and at 2.8, 12, 18; 3.1, 7, 14, regularly appears in the LXX to introduce the message of a prophet (cf. Isa. 56.1; Jer. 4.27; Amos 1.6; et al.).

2–3   Five of the seven letters in these two chapters begin with the phrase Οἶδα τὰ ἔργα σου (*oida ta erga sou*, 'I know what you are doing', lit. 'I know your works'). At Rev. 2.9 the Lord *knows about* the 'affliction and poverty' of the Smyrneans; at 2.13 the one with the sharp, two-edged sword *knows* where those in Pergamum 'are living, that is, where Satan has his throne'.

The one who walks among the lampstands 'knows' his people and their actions (cf. John 2.24, Jesus 'knew all people'). As it stands, the words are neutral; they can refer to achievement or failure (cf. Rev. 2.3, 4; 3.8, 15). In a book written to clarify and strengthen *faith*, the emphasis on *works* is noteworthy (cf. Beasley-Murray 73–74). Faith is demonstrated by action; and this accounts for the New Testament demand for works in the believer which are worthy of faith (cf. Eph. 2.8–10; Jas. 2.18–26). The triad, actions – effort – steadfastness, appears to be traditional (cf. 1 Thess. 1.3 = faith – love – hope; 2 Thess. 1.3–4). But in this passage two particular expressions of activity on the part of the Ephesian Christians are spoken of with approval: 'effort' in maintaining a true faith, particularly in christological terms; and 'steadfastness' through Christ, in the face of testing from persecution without and tensions within. 'Effort' and 'steadfastness' thus explain the nature of the 'works' to which the Lord refers.

The recipients of this oracle are now commended for being intolerant of 'evildoers' and critical of false 'apostles'. The reference is to one group, not two. The evildoers are pseudo-apostles. Their character will be defined later, in terms of the sect of the Nicolaitans (verse 6, q.v.); and further commendation and also condemnation will be announced before that point is reached.

Those 'styling themselves apostles', who had been discerned as 'liars', seem to be itinerant false teachers, who placed themselves about the local elders (Swete 25; cf. 1 Cor. 12.28; 15.7; Eph. 4.11, referring to [a wider group of] ideal apostles). All those who claimed to exercise an 'orthodox', apostolic ministry in the primitive church needed the process of discrimination to be applied to their doctrinal stance. In the case of the Johannine community the special concern, as here, related to christological balance (see above, 4–6; cf. also 1 John 4.1, 'prove the spirits, to see whether [or not] they derive from God'). Paul similarly dismissed as 'super-apostles' those who claimed authority in the Church, but did not perform the 'signs of a true apostle' (2 Cor. 12.11–12; cf. 11.13; Acts 20.29–30). Evidently, according to Ignatius, the Ephesian community regularly closed its ears to harmful teaching of the kind alluded to here (*Eph.* 6.2; 9.1).

In verse 3, John underscores Christ's approval of the steadfast and unceasing endurance manifested by the church at Ephesus. In all, seven marks of faithfulness are mentioned in verses 2 and 3; although one (ὑπομονή, *hupomonē*, 'steadfastness') is repeated. Of these the fourth, doctrinal faithfulness, appears to be the most significant; and this characteristic is taken up again at verse 6. Cf. Milligan 45.

The conjunction καὶ ὑπομονὴν ἔχεις, καὶ ἐβάστασας . . . καὶ οὐ κεκοπίακες (*kai hupomonēn echeis, kai ebastasas . . . kai ou kekopiakes*, 'and you have steadfastness, and you have endured . . . and you have not flagged'), with its repeated καί (*kai*, 'and'), is a stylistic feature in the Apocalypse (e.g. 5.7; 7.13–14; 8.7). The perfect οὐ κεκοπίακες (*ou kekopiakes*, 'you have not flagged') points to a condition which still existed when the endurance (ἐβάστασας, *ebastasas*, 'you have endured') was at an end (Swete 26).

4 Despite the commendations, disapproval follows. The Ephesian Christians had 'given up' their 'initial love'. Perhaps zeal for doctrinal truth had caused mutual love in the community to become diminished. More particularly, this feature in its life may well have been brought about by the theological tensions over the nature of Christ's person which were already beginning to develop: with some emphasizing the divinity of Jesus at the expense of his humanity, and others taking the opposite stance. In view of verse 6 (q.v.), the former group seems at this time to have become more prominent at Ephesus.

Charles (1, 51) sees a parallel between ἔχω κατὰ σοῦ (*echō kata sou*, 'I have [this] against you') and Matt. 5.23, ὁ ἀδελφός σου ἔχει τι κατὰ σοῦ (*ho adelphos sou echei ti kata sou*, 'your brother has something against you'); cf. Mark 11.25. The verb found here in the form ἀφῆκας (*aphēkas*, 'you have given up') is frequently used in the Fourth Gospel (John 4.3; 10.12; 16.28), in the sense of 'leave' (but see John 20.23 = 'forgive').

5 The Ephesian community is summoned to think again, and to return to the situation of warm mutual love and loving activity from which it has departed (see on verse 4).

Repentance, recollection, can lead to healing in relationships (as with the prodigal son, Luke 15.17–18). In this case, however, the church at Ephesus needs not only loving attitudes but also love in action. See 1 John 3.11–18, esp. 18, which contains a similar exhortation in a parallel, Johannine situation. For the love command in that passage see Smalley, *1, 2, 3 John* 181–99. The scope of the love which the risen Christ commends here (for God and for others) is unlimited; but, in the first instance, it relates to the needs of the Johannine community itself.

The sequence, μνημόνευε, μετανόησον, ποίησον (*mnēmoneue, metanoēson, poiēson*, 're-call', 'think again', 'act') could represent 'the three stages in the history of conversion', with the present imperative mood of the first injunction (the others are aorist) perhaps suggesting the constant need for spiritual recollection. (So Swete 27.) But all *three* commands, in the life of the Christian and of the Church, require an obedient response which is constant.

Without repentance, the Ephesian congregation is liable to immediate judgement. God's discrimination, in his creation as in his Church, becomes the perpetual means of his redemption. (See Smalley, *Thunder and Love* 147—49.) But his judgement is real; and it is present (as here), as well as future. The present tense of ἔρχομαι (*erchomai*, lit. 'I am coming') emphasizes this immediacy. Christ is speaking about his parousia now, not at the end.

Without a change of heart, leading to loving conduct, the community is in danger of extinction. Lack of love leads to spiritual death, individually and corporately. So the congregation is enjoined to return to its former ways of harmony and love (in matters of doctrine), or risk 'the removal of the lampstand from its place' (cf. Kiddle 24). The picture is of each λυχνία (*lychnia*, 'lampstand'), on which the lamps were hung, being independent, rather than forming part of a fixed candelabrum (cf. Rev. 1.12–13, 20; 2.1). So, any one lampstand (= church) can be removed at will. Evidently this warning was heeded at first; for later Ignatius can describe the church at Ephesus as 'worthy of all felicitation' and, more importantly in view of the present situation, 'righteous in nature, according to faith and love in Christ' (*Eph.* Prologue; 1.1).

The words εἰ δὲ μή (*ei de mē*, lit. 'but if not') are equivalent to the phrase, later in the verse, ἐὰν μὴ μετανοήσῃς (*ean mē metanoēsē[i]s*, 'unless you repent').

6   The harsh criticism of the Ephesian congregation, voiced in verses 4 and 5, is now modified; and the false teaching which it had pleasingly resisted (verses 2 and 3) becomes at last identified. The ἀλλά (*alla*, 'but' or 'however'), which introduces this verse with its affirmation, balances the ἀλλά in the negative criticism of verse 4. The phrase ἀλλὰ τοῦτο ἔχεις (*alla touto echeis*, lit. 'but you have this') is elliptical; it needs to be completed, as in our translation, by such an expression as 'in your favour'.

The language here is strong: hatred, both human and divine, is in view. In the Old Testament the Lord is said to hate wrongdoing, evil and falsity (Isa. 61.8; Zech. 8.17), as well as loving justice (Isa. 61.8); while wrath as well as love are said to be characteristic of Jesus Christ (Mark 3.5; Rev. 6.16–17; John 15.9, 12). The balance of divine discrimination and mercy, of salvation *through* judgement, is a theological feature of the Apocalypse (cf. Rev. 20.4–15; 21.22—22.5). Here the concerned 'hatred' is directed against doctrinal error, which is evidently anathema to the Godhead, as to the Ephesians.

The Nicolaitans

What, then, were 'the practices of the Nicolaitans'? This group, the name of which means literally 'conquerors of the people, the laity' (= Balaam?), is mentioned again in the letter to Pergamum (Rev. 2.15); and other descriptions of false teaching and erroneous behaviour in the messages to Pergamum (2.13–14) and Thyatira (2.20, 24) may be relevant to the discussion of this question. We can therefore consider these texts together.

Debate about the nature of the Nicolaitan sect has been extensive (see Fiorenza, *Book of Revelation* 114–32, esp. 115–17; also Hemer, 'Nicolaitan'); and information about it can only be inferred from the Apocalypse itself. In the present context of Rev. 2.1–7, we hear of itinerant false apostles who came from outside the community, and whose teaching needed to be tested (verse 2; cf. *Did.* 11). It is a reasonable assumption, in view of the mention of the sect shortly afterwards, that these false teachers belonged to the Nicolaitan group. At Pergamum, however, Nicolaitans seem to have been actual *members* of the community (Rev. 2.15); and they are named immediately after an allusion to those who are 'adhering to the teaching of Balaam' (verse 14). Probably this teaching was also, therefore, Nicolaitan in character.

It is likely that 'the teaching of Balaam' is a reference to an incident in Num. 25.1–2 (cf. 31.16), where Balaam is regarded as responsible for Israel's harlotry with Moabite women, who in turn encouraged the Hebrews to attend their sacrifices, and to 'eat and bow down to their gods' (Num. 25.2). Balaam, in that case, is seen as 'the father of religious syncretism' (Caird 39); and this clearly relates to the heretical situation in the Johannine community, which is in view at this point in Revelation.

Thus the Balaam saga is more about idolatry, than immorality; so that in Num. 31.16 Balaam's counsel is said to have resulted in 'treacherous' action against the Lord. When therefore we hear, in Rev. 2.14, of church members following Balaam, who taught Balaak to put a stumbling-block in the path of the Israelites, 'so that they would eat food offered to idols, and practise fornication', this is probably a description of those at Pergamum who were guilty of religious infidelity, more than sexual licence. The verb πορνεύω (*porneuō*, 'commit fornication') is used scripturally in both senses (cf. Rev. 18.3). Similarly, when Christians in the church at Thyatira are castigated for 'putting up with Jezebel', who was in the same way teaching believers to practise fornication and eat meat offered to idols (2.20), we are presumably yet again in the presence of those who were Nicolaitan in outlook: devotees more of false doctrine than immoral behaviour. However, theology and praxis cannot be separated; for erroneous belief leads to wrong behaviour. The false apostles troubling the church at Ephesus, and Nicolaitan associates of the communities of Pergamum and Thyatira, were capable of both. They followed false teaching (Rev. 2.2, 14–15, 20); but they were also prepared to transgress the chief commands of the Jerusalem Council specified in Acts 15.29 (cf. Charles 1, 53).

Patristic witness to the Nicolaitan error, based on the relevant texts in the Apocalypse, rather than on independent information, suggests that this libertine and heretically inclined sect was pre-gnostic in character (cf. also Rev. 2.24). In this case, John's circle included those from a Greek background whose Christology could easily have become unbalanced, and whose understanding of Jesus as divine rather than human might well have introduced tensions to the community at large. Other errors, and their resulting problems, will become apparent; but the Nicolaitan deviation is at the outset an important aspect of the life and history of John's congregation. See further on Rev. 2.9; 3.9; et al. For the testimony of the Fathers to the gnostic character of Nicolaitanism see Smalley, *Thunder and Love* 88; on the whole subject of the Nicolaitans see ibid., 87–89, and the literature there cited.

7   The letter to Ephesus ends with a summons to obedient attention, reminiscent of similar prophetic calls in the Old Testament which use the phrase, 'hear the word of the Lord' (e.g. Isa. 1.10; Jer. 2.4; Hos. 4.1; Amos 7.16). The same formula occurs in each of the seven letters, three times near the end, and four times at the end. (See above, 48.) Christ invites the Ephesian audience not merely to 'listen' to what is being said to the churches, but also to act upon the message. The prophetic form at this point echoes words of the historical Jesus as recorded in the synoptic Gospels, but not in John (cf. Mark 4.9; Matt. 11.15; Luke 14.35).

In this verse there occurs the first explicit reference in the Apocalypse to the Spirit (but cf. 1.4, 10). The writer does not distinguish between the exalted Christ and the work of the Spirit (cf. Boring 89). The revelation comes from God through Jesus Christ, and is mediated to John by his angel (1.1). Now the voice of Christ in victory is heard, as the Spirit speaks to the churches. He speaks continuously (λέγει, *legei*, 'is saying' is in the present tense) to the 'churches'. In the first place, the word is directed towards the seven churches of Asia, including Ephesus. But, as with Revelation in general, the scope of the message is far reaching. Christ addresses the Church as a whole, and for all time. However, the corporate reference of 'churches' does not exclude the responsibility which the individual carries to respond to the divine command. So ὁ ἔχων οὖς (*ho echōn ous*, 'anyone who has an ear') is in the singular. On the Spirit in Revelation and John's Gospel see Smalley, 'Paraclete'.

The 'conqueror' is given 'permission' (NRSV) to eat from the tree of life. In τῷ νικῶντι (*tō[i] nikōnti*, lit. 'to the one who is conquering') there may be an allusion to the *Nico*laitans (see Rev. 2.6, 15). But νικᾷν (*nika[i]n*, 'to conquer') is a characteristically Johannine term; and it is used frequently in Revelation (cf. 2.11, 17, 26; 3.5; 5.5; 12.11; 17.14; 21.7; et al.; also John 16.33; 1 John 2.13–14; 4.4; 5.4–5). This is not surprising, in view of the fact that the Apocalypse records and predicts 'victories won by Christ and the Church' (Swete 29). John sees Christian faith in the light of spiritual conquest: victory over doctrinal error and imperial persecution (note 1 John 5.4, 'this is the victory which has overcome the world: our faith'). The present participle, νικῶντι (*nikōnti*, lit. 'the one who is conquering'), suggests the timeless demand for victory on the part of the believer. The linguistic construction of the final promise in each of the seven letters, or oracles, differs slightly; but each affirmation contains in some form the anticipation of eternal life.

The conquering one is allowed, now as well as in the future and at the end, to 'eat from the tree of life which is in God's paradise'. The imagery here clearly recalls the scenes of Eden and the Fall in Gen. 2—3, with their mention of 'the tree of life' in the middle of the garden (2.9; 3.22; paradise lost), and the heavenly city at the end of Revelation (21—22), where 'the tree of life' with its therapeutic leaves may be found (22.2; paradise regained). See also Prov. 3.18 (wisdom is a 'tree of life' to those who lay hold of her). In apocalyptic thought, the tree of life represents for the righteous a reward after judgement (*1 Enoch* 24.4—25.7; *T. Levi* 18.10–14; cf. Mounce 72). See further on 22.2.

Access to life afforded to humankind at the time of creation was interrupted by sin (Gen. 3.22–24), but restored through Christ, the second Adam (Rom. 5.12–21; 6.23). As part of the new creation, the redeemed will share eternal life in all its fulness. The old order becomes the new; and the new order ('paradise') is God himself, dwelling in close relationship with his people (Rev. 21.3–4). The symbol of 'eating' from the life-giving tree emphasizes this promised intimacy. As with any meal or (messianic) banquet, table fellowship denotes friendship and mutual trust (cf. Exod. 12.21–27, the Passover; Judg. 16.23–25, the Philistine feast given when Samson was captured; Isa. 25.6–8, the eschatological banquet; 1 Cor. 11.23–26, the Lord's Supper; see also 1QSa 2.17–21; Luke 14.12–24).

The term παράδεισος, *paradeisos*, 'paradise') is used in the LXX for 'garden' at Gen. 2.8, 15; et al.; and for a 'walled park' at Eccles. 2.5; Song of Sol. 4.13(12); et al. It is a Persian loan-word (*pairidaiza*), meaning a 'walling round' (Beasley-Murray 79–80).

Smyrna (2.8–11)

8   The second oracle is addressed through the spirit of the church (for 'angel', see on 1.20 and 2.1) to the congregation at Smyrna. This is the only complete city of the seven mentioned in Rev. 2—3 which still exists (modern Izmir). Lying about 35 miles north of Ephesus, on the south-east shore of an Aegean gulf, Smyrna had a good harbour, which afforded protection in times of war; and the city was conveniently placed at the start of a profitable trade route to the east.

Smyrna was originally founded as a Greek colony, more than a thousand years before Christ; but that ancient city was soon captured by Ionian Greeks, and colonized in turn. Ionian Smyrna was great, and its dominion extensive; but eventually the city gave way to the increasing power of the Lydian kingdom. About 600 BC the old city was captured and destroyed by Alyattes. In 290 BC Hellenic Smyrna was rebuilt by Antigonus, and then Lysimachus, about two miles away from the old city. It was beautiful, and famous for its large theatre, stadium and library. Some contemporary coins defined Smyrna's rank as 'first of Asia in beauty and size' (Ramsay, *Letters* 255). Mount Pagus towered 500 feet over the harbour; and a road curved around it 'like a necklace on the statue of a goddess' (Mounce 73; the simile comes from Aristides). Temples, to Cybele and Zeus, were built at either end of the road.

Smyrna enjoyed a close relationship with Rome and the imperial cult. It became the first city in the ancient world to erect a temple in honour of *Dea Roma* ('The Goddess Rome'); and Tacitus records that in 23 BC Smyrna was granted permission – over ten other rival cities in Asia – to build a temple to the emperor Tiberius (*Annals* 4.55–56). The fact that Smyrna was so loyal to Rome, and contained a large Jewish population which was actively hostile towards the Church, meant that it was difficult to survive as a Christian in the city; and martyrdoms for the faith were common (see on verse 9). A Christian community was probably founded at Smyrna during Paul's third missionary journey, while he was living in Ephesus (see Acts 19.26). We know from the letter of Ignatius to Smyrna, written in the early years of the second century AD, that at the time the community there was well established and organized (cf. Ignatius, *Smyrn.* 12.1–2). On Smyrna see further Ramsay, *Letters* 251–67.

At the beginning of the majority of the seven letters in Rev. 2—3, the exalted Lord is identified in terms which deliberately echo some part of his appearance in the initial vision of 1.12–18. Usually the description is appropriate to the situation of the community which is being addressed. So here Smyrna, which was already experiencing persecution (cf. verse 9), as well as internal doctrinal tensions, is given a 'message' from 'the first and the last, who was dead and has come to life'. God the Son, who shares in the Father's creation, is sovereign and everlasting (cf. 1.17); and he is victorious over death. Thus faithfulness on the part of the Smyrnean community, in matters of belief and behaviour, will be rewarded with eternal life. For ἔζησεν (*ezēsen*, aorist, 'has come to life [again]') see AG 336. 1β.

9   The congregation at Smyrna is known to have been experiencing 'conflict' (θλίψιν, *thlipsin*); cf. Rev. 1.9. This stemmed in part from the hostile world of imperial power in which the Christian Church was called to maintain a faithful witness. But it also resulted from the environment of conflicting religious pluralism, both Jewish and pagan, which surrounded the congregation at Smyrna, together with the expression of that conflict in its own life (see above, 4–6; cf. also Boring 91). These believers were also subject to 'poverty' (τὴν πτωχείαν, *tēn ptōcheian*). This means real deprivation, not just being poor: for which the Greek is πένης (*penēs*). The poverty of the Johannine churches, even in a city as prosperous as Smyrna, is noteworthy. Swete (31) suggests that this could be due partly to the fact that the Christian converts, here and elsewhere, were drawn chiefly from the poorer strata of society (cf. 1 Cor. 1.26–29; Jas. 2.1–4), and in part to the demands literally made upon them by their faith (2 Cor. 8.1–5; Heb. 10.34).

There follows a paradox. Poor in material terms the church in Smyrna may be, but they are rich *spiritually*; and those riches cannot be taken away from them. The believers are 'rich towards God' (Luke 12.21; cf. 1 Tim. 6.17–19; Jas. 2.5). Such wealth characterized the church in Smyrna, but was patently lacking among the Laodiceans (Rev. 3.17–18).

The remaining part of this verse throws considerable light on the nature of the Johannine churches of Asia. Whereas John's circle included members who were at home in a Greek, pre-gnostic environment (see on the 'Nicolaitans', 2.6; also 2.15), it also embraced those from a Jewish background, some of whom were 'slandering' the

Smyrnean believers. This is a reference to Jews who have forfeited their name, and membership of God's people, by stirring up hostility against the Christians: much as Jewish resentment against Jesus encouraged Pilate to condemn him to death (John 19.14–16*a*; cf. Sweet 85). They should have formed the 'synagogue of the Lord' (cf. Num. 16.3; 20.4, LXX); but now they have become instruments of the Accuser, 'a synagogue (συναγωγή, *synagōgē*, lit. "congregation") of Satan'. Cf. also 3.9.

Clearly, this is a description of a local situation: what was actually happening in Smyrna (and Philadelphia; cf. 3.9). Jealous of the success of Christians in evangelizing God-fearers and even other Jews, these bitter opponents of Christianity were inciting attack on the churches from the Roman imperial powers. *The Letter of the Smyrneans on The Martyrdom of St Polycarp* (*c.* AD 150) shows the length to which the Jews of that time could go in prosecuting their hatred of Christianity. When Bishop Polycarp of Smyrna confessed that he was a believer, 'the Jews living in Smyrna' joined with heathens in expressions of 'uncontrollable anger' (12.2), before helping to gather wood with which to burn the saint alive (13.1).

Presumably these Jews belonged to local synagogues, and were expressing their antagonism towards former Jews who now followed Christ. But it is not impossible that some of them may themselves have been members of John's community, and have come out of it under pressure from their fellow-Jews. Perhaps finding it difficult to accept the tenets of their newly found faith, and in particular the claim that Jesus was divine, they may have reverted to Judaism. In that case it is easy to see how hostility on their part, towards their former centre of allegiance, would have been all the more fierce. See Smalley, *Thunder and Love* 125–26.

10   The faithful are exhorted not be 'at all' (μηδέν, *mēden*, is emphatic) afraid of the suffering which lies ahead. More sinister than poverty and slander (verse 9), imprisonment, persecution and even death can be anticipated. Rome is seen as the embodiment of opposition to God, and the exercise of imperial persecution as the work of the devil who is behind the 'synagogue of Satan' (verse 9). The 'devil' is called 'the accuser' of Christians at Rev. 12.10 and 'the Satan' at 12.9; 20.2 (cf. 2.13). His purpose is to cause the imprisonment of 'some' members of the Johannine community (ἐξ ὑμῶν, *ex humōn*, 'some of you', is a partitive genitive used as an object; cf. Matt. 23.34; 2 John 4; also [used as the subject] Rev. 11.9; John 16.17). In this way the commitment of the whole body will be 'put to the test' (cf. Luke 22.31). It was firmly believed in primitive Christianity that the Jewish and pagan enemies of the Church were prompted by Satan. Cf. *Mart. Pol.* 2.4; also Swete 32.

The phrase καὶ ἕξετε θλῖψιν ἡμερῶν δέκα (*kai hexete thlipsin hēmerōn deka*, lit. 'and you will have persecution for ten days') forms a separate sentence if the reading ἕξετε (*hexete*, 'you will have') is followed. But if the alternative version, ἔχητε (*echēte*, 'that you may have') be allowed, then the words are governed by the subject ὁ διάβολος (*ho diabolos*, 'the devil'). See above, 45. If the faithful do not yield to their affliction immediately, the devil will prolong the persecution (cf. Swete 32).

The genitive in ἡμερῶν δεκα (*hēmerōn deka*, lit. 'during ten days') is temporal. The number 'ten' is possibly a reflection of Dan. 1.14 (Daniel and his companions, on a special diet, are 'tested for ten days'); cf. Gen. 24.55; Num. 14.22; Job 19.3. However, it is more likely that the numeral is chosen because it represents a period which includes real suffering, but is itself restricted; and the limit is known to God (cf. 2 Cor. 4.17–18). For the use of 'ten' in the Apocalypse see Beckwith 254.

The members of the church in Smyrna are urged to 'keep faith' in all their troubles, both internal and external. The adjective πιστός (*pistos*) means '(being) trustworthy', rather than 'believing' in the sense of keeping *the right* faith. Nevertheless, in view of the incipient christological problems in the Johannine community, the latter sense cannot be excluded completely. Those who remain loyal in the face of adversity are promised 'the reward of life'. Meanwhile, faith is to be kept 'even to death' (ἄχρι θανάτου, *achri thanatou*); for martyrdom is in view as a constant possibility. The conjunctions ἄχρι (*achri*, 'until', 'to' or 'even to') and μέχρι (*mechri*) are identical; but ἄχρι (*achrî*) is used regularly in Revelation (11 times), while μέχρι (*mechri*) does not appear at all.

The 'crown' or 'reward' (στέφανον, *stephanon*) which is to be received by the faithful is probably an allusion to the garland, or laurel wreath, given to the victor at the games: for which Smyrna was famous. Cf. 2 Tim. 2.5; 1 Cor. 9.24–25; 1 Pet. 5.4. Ramsay (*Letters* 256–57, 275) believes that the writer may have had in mind the garlands worn in the service of the pagan temples in Smyrna, or the circle of buildings and towers which 'crowned' the fairest city in Asia (cf. Swete 33; also the literature cited in Ramsay, *Letters* 443). Beasley-Murray (82–83) argues that the symbol may have in view the representations, applied in the ancient world to divine beings as well as mortals, of a crown of light around the head: to indicate glory. In this case 'the reward of life' means being 'crowned with glory in the life of the age to come' (83). See further Aune 172–75.

The καί (*kai*, 'and') which introduces this promise is consecutive. 'Keep faith . . . and (*so*) I will give you the reward of life'. In the phrase τὸν στέφανον τῆς ζωῆς (*ton stephanon tēs zōēs*, 'the reward of life'), τῆς ζωῆς (*tēs zōēs*, 'of life') is epexegetic: the reward consists of eternal life in Christ. The promise is equivalent in essence to that in 2.7, at the close of the letter to Ephesus; although there the symbolism involves the 'tree' of life.

11   For the introductory formula in this verse, 'let anyone with an ear listen to what the Spirit is saying to the churches', see on 2.7. Action, as well as attention, is required from the Johannine churches.

The one who conquers is promised deliverance from harm 'by the second death'. The conqueror will not *in any way* be harmed (the double negative, οὐ μή, *ou mē*, is strong) by death. The concept of the 'second death' occurs again in Rev. 20.6, 14; 21.8, where it is defined as 'the lake of fire' (see below, 510). The idea is to some extent anticipated in Dan. 12.2 (cf. John 5.28–29). See also, more exactly, Philo, *De Praem.* 12.70, which speaks of 'two kinds of death'. But the expression appears frequently in the Targums, and was probably familiar currency in Judaism, where a distinction is made between the physical death which everyone suffers and the fate of those who experience judgement in the world to come (a *second* death; cf. SB 3, 830–31).

The Christians at Smyrna in this context are presented with a challenge, as well as an encouragement. They face a period of testing, during which some may well be martyred for their witness to the risen Lord. The ones who conquer will not be 'harmed by death', because they will receive the 'reward of life'. But the choice remains, even if the second death in the end has no power over those who share in the first resurrection (20.6, q.v.). See Mounce 77. As with the oracle addressed to Philadelphia, the living Christ speaks to Smyrna in entirely positive terms.

Pergamum (2.12–17)

12   The next oracle, or letter, is addressed to the Johannine congregation in the Mysian capital city of Pergamum, which (continuing the progress of the Asian circle of churches) stands 40 miles or so north of Smyrna, and about 10 miles inland from the Aegean Sea. Its name in Greek (*Pergamon*) means 'citadel'; and it stood on a hill one thousand feet in height, commanding the surrounding valley of the Caicus. Piny describes Pergamum as *longeque clarissimum Asiae*, '(and) by far the most distinguished (city) of Asia' (*Nat. Hist.* 5.33 [126]).

Pergamum rose to prominence in the third century BC, when it became the capital of the Attalids, and a centre of Hellenic culture. A large library existed in the city, and parchment (the word derives from the Greek περγαμηνή [*pergamēnē*]) was, according to legend, invented there. When Attalus III, the last king of Pergamum, died in 133 BC, he bequeathed his realm to Rome; and the city accordingly became the seat of government of the Roman province of Asia (see Caird 37).

On the upper terrace of the citadel was to be found a cluster of sacred and royal buildings. The most notable of these was the gigantic altar erected, as a platform 800 feet above the city, to Zeus; this probably commemorated the victory of Attalus I over the Galatians. Apart from Zeus, Pergamum was a centre of worship for three other important religious cults of the period: Athene, the patron goddess; Dionysus; and Asclepios (Σωτήρ, *Sōtēr*, 'Saviour'), the god of healing, whose shrine is described by Charles (1, 60) as being the 'Lourdes of the Province of Asia' at that time. Galen, the famous physician of the ancient world, came from Pergamum and studied there.

The Johannine community in Pergamum is likely to have come into conflict with the imperial cult, for which the city was the official seat in Asia. Pergamum was, for example, the first Asian city permitted to construct a shrine dedicated to the worship of a living ruler. The Emperor Augustus allowed this to take place in 29 BC, when a temple was built, as Tacitus informs us, to 'the divine Augustus and to the city of Rome' (*Annals* 4.37); but see also on Smyrna above, 64–65.

The dominance of the Roman Empire and its pagan cults in Pergamum accounts for the contents of the opening section in this letter. The exalted Christ speaks as the one 'who has the sharp, two-edged sword' (cf. 1.16, where the sword comes, as in a word of judgement, from his mouth). In a provincial capital where the proconsul wields the *ius gladii* ('right of the sword'), or the power to execute at will, the sovereign Christ with the double-edged sword 'would remind the threatened congregation that ultimate power over life and death belongs to God' (Mounce 79). But the Johannine balance is constant. For the believer, if not for God's enemies, judgement becomes the means of eternal life (see verse 17).

For the opening formula in this verse see on 1.20; 2.1.

13   The oracle acknowledges that the Christians at Pergamum live (permanently) in a place 'where Satan has his throne'. This phrase could allude to the existence of altars of Zeus or Asclepios in the citadel. (The serpent, the symbol of Asclepius, was everywhere to be seen in Pergamum.) But, more probably, it is a reference to the prominence of Pergamum as the cult centre of emperor worship in Asia. The city had become Satan's residence ('where he lives'; see later in this verse), and indeed his 'throne'. Swete (34) points out that θρόνος (*thronos*, 'throne') in the New Testament is always a chair of state or seat of office, whether of a judge (Matt. 19.28) or a king (Luke 1.32, 52), or of God or Christ (Matt. 5.34; 25.31; cf. Rev. 4.2–11; 7.9–12; 19.5; 20.11–12; 21.3–5; et al.). Now, at Pergamum, Satan is enthroned and holds his court. Rome is seen as the centre of Satan's activity (although not strictly his personification) in the west (cf. Rev. 13.2; 16.10); while Pergamum is perceived as his seat of state in the east (Mounce 79).

Despite the pagan environment in which the Johannine community at Pergamum existed, and in the face of opposition from within and without (see verses 14–15), there had been no lessening of Christian zeal ('you are holding fast to my name') and no denial of the Christian faith (or 'breaking faith' with the exalted Lord). The 'name' (ὄνομα, *onoma*) of Jesus is the summation of his being and character; and Paul claims that his exalted status will in the end be made clear when he is confessed universally as the *Lord* Jesus Christ (Phil. 2.4–11, esp. 11). According to Acts 4.10–12, Peter claimed that the 'name' of Jesus Christ of Nazareth was responsible for the healing of the lame man at the Beautiful

Gate (Acts 3.6–7) and that the same 'name' is uniquely salvific. To that name the Pergamene church had remained steadfast.

Equally, its members had not denied their faith in Christ. In the phrase τὴν πίστιν μου (*tēn pistin mou*, 'faith in me'), μου (*mou*, lit. 'of me') is probably to be construed in the first place as an objective genitive: 'you have not (or did not) deny your faith in me' (= 'you have not broken faith with me', as in the translation). But the genitive may also be taken as subjective: 'you have not denied my (the Christian) faith'; in which case the risen Christ may be commending the congregation at Pergamum for maintaining a balanced faith in his person as both human and divine (see Smalley, *Thunder and Love* 60–62, 152).

Nevertheless, the use of the aorist tense in ἠρνήσω (*ērnēsō*, lit. 'you did not deny'), even if it has a present reference, suggests one particular moment in the past. The context makes it clear that the occasion in question was the martyrdom of Antipas: you did not break faith with me *even* (καί, *kai*; see the textual notes above, 45–46) in the days of Antipas. The name Antipas (Ἀντιπᾶς) is a contraction of Antipatros (Ἀντιπάτρος), which occurs often in Josephus (e.g. *Ant.* 14.10). Nothing is otherwise known of him; although the Menologia say that Antipas was slain under Domitian, and the Martyrologia claim that he was cast into a heated brazen bull (see Bengel, *Gnomon* 209). He seems to have been the only contemporary martyr at Pergamum (contrast Smyrna); and he need not necessarily have been a member of that congregation. Eusebius (*HE* 4.15.48) mentions later martyrs at Pergamum: 'Carpus and Papylus and a woman, Agathonice, who were perfected gloriously after very many magnificent confessions.'

Charles (1, 62) regards ὁ μάρτυς μου (*ho martys mou*, 'my witness') as a solecism which is really a Hebraism. The same is presumably true of ὁ πιστός μου (*ho pistos mou*, 'my faithful (one)'. Antipas was a 'witness', put to death 'in that place of yours' (παρά, *para*, lit. 'beside' or 'near', is emphatic). In due course the term 'witness' (μάρτυς, *martys*) came to be applied to those whose testimony to Christ resulted in their death (martyrdom); but the technical sense of that word had not been established by the end of the first century AD. Cf. Morris 66. The repeated reference to the residence (and rule) of Satan at Pergamum ('where Satan lives') may indicate that the powers of evil exercise constant sway in the citadel, and need to be perpetually challenged. See on verse 13a.

14–15 Disapproval follows commendation. For the exegesis of these verses, and an explanation of the pre-gnostic teaching to which reference is made in them, see on 2.6. Cf. also, in the message to the community at Thyatira, 2.20–24.

The Pergamene church has withstood the dangers threatening it from Rome and the imperial cult outside; but it has at the same time allowed false doctrine to arise from within, and to win adherence from some of its members. By ὀλίγα (*oliga*, 'a few things'), only one chief error is meant; although it is spoken of generically. The use of ἐκεῖ (*ekei*, '[you have some] there') in verse 14 is parallel to παρ' ὑμῖν (*par' hymin*, 'in that place of yours') in verse 13: that is, in Pergamum.

Charles (1, 63–64) argues that verse 15 is an explanation of verse 14, and also picks up 2.6. Verse 15 begins with οὕτως (*houtōs*, 'similarly') and ends with ὁμοίως (*homoiōs*, 'also'). But the connection is different in each case. For οὕτως (*houtōs*, 'similarly') is linked to the statement in the previous verse (14) about those who follow the teaching of Balaam (note the use of ἔχεις, *echeis*, 'you have', in both verses); whereas ὁμοίως ('also') refers back to the situation in Ephesus (2.6). Then καὶ σύ (*kai su*, 'you also') in verse 15 belongs with ὁμοίως (*homoiōs*, 'also' or 'likewise'), hidden in the translation, and is reinforced by it. The meaning is thus: 'similarly, you also (likewise, as well as the church at Ephesus, the members of which are pursued by false teachers) have some who are maintaining the teaching of the Nicolaitans'. At Pergamum, unlike Ephesus, some members of the Johannine community had actually adopted these heterodox views and practices.

In this case, according to Charles (1, 63–64), the Balaamites (adherents of 'the teaching of Balaam') are the equivalent of the Nicolaitans. This passage in the letter to the Pergamene congregation throws light, as a result, on the background and nature of the Johannine community, as Hellenistic and not only Jewish. See further the oracle to Thyatira.

16   The Pergamene Christians as a body are summoned to active repentance. But it is for those in particular who have embraced the incipiently heretical stance of the Balaamites and Nicolaitans to think again. 'Otherwise' (the elliptical εἰ δὲ μή, *ei de mē*; cf. 2.5), an immediate parousia of the exalted Christ will ensue, and war will be made 'against them' (μετ᾽ αὐτῶν, *met᾽ autōn*, not 'against you'; but cf. κατὰ σοῦ, *kata sou*, 'against you', in verse 14).

The eschatology of the Apocalypse is balanced. The Christ, who comes in swift judgement ('soon') to the church at Pergamum, stands above time and dwells in eternity. But he comes to his own as Saviour and Judge in the present (cf. 2.5; 3.20), as well as at the end (19.11—20.3; see also 22.12–13).

The nature of the judgement to be exercised by the glorified Christ against the Pergamenes is not specified, although there is a possible parallel to be discovered at 2.22–23, the discrimination promised against 'Jezebel' (q.v.). For the symbol of the 'sword (of my mouth)' see on 1.16; 2.12; 19.15, 21. Just as Balaam was put to death by the sword for advising the Midianites to lure the people of Israel into sexual sin at Peor (Num. 31.8, 16), so the Balaamites (Nicolaitans) will die by the sword of the Spirit if they continue in their error (cf. Kiddle 34). The construction, πολεμήσω μετ᾽ αὐτῶν (*polemēsō met᾽ autōn*, 'I will make war against them'), is regarded by Charles (1, 65) as a Hebraism. It is confined to Revelation (cf. 12.7; 13.4; 17.14); and the verb itself ('to make war') is found outside the Apocalypse only at Jas. 4.2. Sweet (88) connects the letter to Pergamum with Rev. 8.1—14.20, where (as here) the themes of idolatry and witness are prominent. The links with Rev. 13 are certainly strong.

17   For the opening formula of this verse see on 2.7 and 11.

The closing section of this oracle raises two intriguing questions: the nature of the 'hidden manna' and of the 'white stone' with its secret inscription, which are to be given to 'the conqueror' (cf. 2.7).

The identity of the manna is fairly straightforward. After the Exodus, a pot of manna was stored up in the ark as a memorial (Exod. 16.32–34; cf. Heb. 9.4). According to Hebrew tradition, when the temple was destroyed Jeremiah (2 Maccabees 2.4–8, esp. 7) or an angel (*2 Baruch* 6.5–9) rescued the ark and its sacred objects. These were hidden in the earth, to be preserved until the messianic age, when they would be restored. Such an allusion would have been of special relevance to a Jewish-Christian audience, which would have readily found in it a comforting promise. Proper faith in the Messiah, coupled with right behaviour, were to be rewarded by blessings: such as feeding on manna in the messianic kingdom (cf. Beckwith 460–61).

The genitive, τοῦ μάννα τοῦ κεκρυμμένου (*tou manna tou kekrummenou*, 'the hidden manna'), is partitive (hence, 'a *share* of the manna'); and this is the only use of the construction in the New Testament with a verb of giving.

The reference to the inscribed 'white stone' is more problematic; and various interpretations have been suggested by commentators (see Hemer, *Letters* 96–103). Hemer himself (96) lists seven possible meanings: a jewel in Old Testament or Jewish tradition (cf. *2 Baruch* 6.7); the casting vote of acquittal (cf. Ovid, *Metam.* 15.41–42); a token (*tessera*) of recognition (see Livy 39.30.4–5); an amulet with a divine name (so Charles 1, 66–67); a token of gladiatorial discharge (cf. Ovid, *Tristia* 4.8.23–24); a process of Asclepian initiation (cf. Aristides, *Apology* 10); and a writing material with a significant form or colour (see Ramsay, *Letters* 304–305).

Of these suggestions, the one which seems most readily to fit the context is the *tessera*: a token of admittance, membership or recognition. Those who survive the dangers threatening the church, at Pergamum and elsewhere (problems of wrong belief and erroneous praxis; cf. Rev. 2.13–15), and who 'repent' (verse 16), are promised both the joys of the messianic kingdom and the assurance of a close relationship with Jesus himself.

The stone given to the overcomers is said to have a 'new name' (ὄνομα καινόν, *onoma kainon*) written upon it. If this 'stone' be regarded as some kind of magic amulet, or charm, the name in question could be that of Christ, who speaks of his own 'new name' (τὸ ὄνομά μου τὸ καινόν, *to onoma mou to kainon*, 'my new name') at Rev. 3.12. As the secret knowledge of a god's name in pagan religion was thought to have warded off evil, so now the name of Christ, given to the believer and inscribed on stone, might bestow on his followers a talismanic power against every assailant, such as the false teachers and wrongdoers at Pergamum mentioned at Rev. 2.14 (cf. also 22.15; cf. Beckwith 461–62).

But it is difficult to know in what sense the name of Christ in this passage can be described as 'secret'. The reference to the name of Christ being 'unknown', at Rev. 19.12, is not a parallel; for there the secret name of Christ is known to himself alone (so Hemer, *Letters* 102–103). It is therefore more reasonable to understand the new 'name' as that given to the *Christian*, symbolizing entrance to new life and new status (cf. Isa. 62.2; 65.15; 2 Cor. 5.17).

Taken with the interpretation of the earlier part of verse 17 offered above, the meaning of the text as a whole then becomes clear. The faithful at Pergamum, who maintain truth against error, are marked out for a special growing relationship with their triumphant Lord. They are promised, now and in eternity, a new character, a new protection and a new happiness. The 'white' (λευκήν, *leukēn*) colour of the inscribed stone will then symbolize the triumph of the victor's faith. The word ψῆφος (*psēphos*, 'stone') is rare in biblical Greek, and appears only three times in the New Testament (twice here and at Acts 26.10, where it means a contrary 'vote').

Charles (1, 67 n. 1) regards the 'new character' promised to the conqueror as a difficulty in the way of this exegesis. For the new character of the victors, in his view, has already been established by their faithfulness. However, the promise is eschatological; and it alludes in any case to the growth and perfecting of a relationship which is transfigured, and needs continually to *be* transformed. (So Hemer, *Letters* 103; cf. also 2 Cor. 3.18; 1 Cor. 13.9–12).

As with the 'manna' in this verse, so with the 'stone', we have further evidence here to confirm the likelihood that the Johannine congregations of Asia contained members who came from mixed backgrounds, Hellenistic as well as Hebraic, and that both are in mind in this letter.

Thyatira (2.18–29)

18 Hemer (*Letters* 106) describes the message to Thyatira as the 'longest and most difficult' of the seven letters, addressed to the 'least known, least important and least remarkable' of the Asian cities. Its history is unrecorded, and we lack archaeological evidence to uncover its past (cf. Mounce 84).

Thyatira itself (the original site was named Teuthrania; cf. Strabo, *Geography* 12.3.22), now the modern town of Akhisar, lay on the overland route between Pergamum and Sardis, just across the Mysian border. The city was situated on the south bank of the Lycus, in a long valley connecting the rivers Hermus and Caicus. An important road also ran along this valley, on the direct route between Constantinople and Smyrna.

Thyatira was founded by Seleucus I, as a military outpost guarding one of the approaches to his empire. But there were no natural fortifications; and, as Ramsay points out (*Letters* 323), it is one of those cities whose situation 'exposes (it) to destruction by every conqueror, and yet compels (its) restoration after every siege and sack'.

In 190 BC the city of Thyatira fell to the Romans; it was first annexed to the Pergamene kingdom, and then became part of the Province of Asia. Under Roman rule, and with the establishment of peace and greater stability, the city grew and prospered as a marketing and manufacturing centre. It was in a favourable position for communication and trade; and inscriptions from first-century coins mention a wide range of Thyatiran trade guilds. Ramsay (*Letters* 324–25) lists ten of them: wool-workers, linen-workers, makers of outer garments, dyers, leather-workers, tanners, potters, bakers, slave-dealers and bronze-smiths. Cf. Acts 16.14–15, where Luke refers to the conversion of Lydia, a dealer in purple cloth from the city of Thyatira.

The religion of Thyatira, like the history of the city itself, is obscure, although the coinage of the period gives us some useful information. The divine guardian of the city was the conquering hero Tyrimnos, who may have originated from Macedonia, and is usually depicted on horseback with a battle-axe over his shoulder. Tyrimnos was related by nature to the protecting deity of Thyatira, who was also known as Propolis, because his temple was to be found 'in front of the city'; Propator, as the divine ancestor of the city and its leading families; and Helios (Apollo), the sun-god. See further Ramsay, *Letters* 319–20. The religion of this city was evidently syncretistic.

For the opening formula in this verse, and the meaning of τῷ ἀγγέλῳ (*tō[i] angelō[i]*, 'to the angel'), see on 1.20; 2.1.

The risen Christ speaks through John to the church at Thyatira, and describes himself (uniquely in Revelation; but see 1.6, and note the implication of 2.18; 3.5; et al.) as 'God's Son' (ὁ υἱὸς τοῦ θεοῦ, *ho huios tou theou*). See further Michel and Marshall, 'Son'. This title suggests a special relationship between Jesus and the Father, familiar to us from the Johannine Gospel and Letters (cf. John 10.30; 1 John 5.6–13; et al.). Its use in this context may be due to the quotation from Ps. 2.8–9 at Rev. 2.26–27, and be prompted by the proximate verse 7 of Ps. 2, 'the Lord said to me, "you are my Son"'. But in any case, the description of Jesus serves to create a strong contrast between the local divinity, the cult of Apollo Tyrimnos, and Jesus the true Messiah. The true Son of God is not Tyrimnos or the Roman emperor, the self-proclaimed sons of Zeus, but Jesus himself.

For the description of the Son's eyes and feet, typically picking up the appearance of the exalted Christ in the vision of Rev. 1.12–16, see on 1.14–15. The blazing eyes enable Jesus to see through the misguided beliefs of the Thyatiran community, encapsulated in their tolerance of Jezebel and of Satanic practices; while the burnished feet speak of Christ's strength and judgement (cf. 2.26–27).

Duff ('I Will Give to Each of You' 116–33, esp. 133) believes that the oracle to the church at Thyatira is intended to sharpen the contrast between John and his opponent 'Jezebel', who may have dabbled in magic (see also on verses 20–23). The introduction to the letter, in this verse, therefore heightens the theme of judgement on false teaching within the Johannine community by associating the punishment which follows (verses 22–23) directly with the flashing eyes of God's Son himself. The powerful-eyed divinity, according to Duff, is presented in the guise of the 'evil-eyed' Hekate, who exacts appropriate vengeance (see also on verse 27). So the deserts of their misguided conduct are handed out to the heterodox followers of the prophetess (verse 23).

If this be allowed, it must be stated that the judgement in question is balanced, here as elsewhere in Revelation, by the salvific work of God's Son (see verse 28); and also that the allusions to the practices of witchcraft in this passage (through the goddess Hekate), if they exist, have been adapted and transposed from Graeco-Roman tradition so as to describe the activities of a Son who receives authority from his Father (verse 28), and who is therefore truly from God. Cf. Aune ('Apocalypse', esp. 484–94), who finds allusions to magic elsewhere in this work (e.g. at Rev. 1.8 [cf. 1.17; 2.8; 21.6; 22.13], the exalted Son of man is 'the first and the last'; 1.18, he holds the 'keys to Hades'; and 2.16 [cf. 3.11; 22.7, 12, 20], he is 'visiting soon').

19 The exalted Christ speaks to the Johannine community at Thyatira in a way which directly echoes the address to the Ephesians (Rev. 2.2), and to the remaining three churches of Asia Minor (Rev. 3.1, 8, 15). He 'knows' the practical expression of Christianity which is to be found in these circles ('what you have done'). The 'works' (ἔργα, *erga*) of the Thyatirans are specified as 'love and faith, and ministry and steadfastness'. (The use of σου [*sou*, 'your'], at the conclusion of the fourfold list of qualities, indicates that these nouns are to be understood as a group, expanding the content of σου τὰ ἔργα [*sou ta erga*, lit. 'your works']). The first two characteristics speak of the motivation for Christian praxis: 'love', which naturally comes first in a Johannine context (cf. John 15.12; 1 Tim. 1.14), and 'faith', which implies not only continuing trust and faithfulness, but also *right* faith (including a balanced Christology; cf. Rev. 2.13; 13.10). The second pair of qualities identify the results which follow from love and faith: 'ministry' (διακονία, *diakonia*) for God, and to others in the community (cf. Rom. 15.25; 2 Cor. 9.1), and 'steadfastness', particularly in the face of both internal conflict and external opposition; cf. Mark 13.13. (See Mounce 85–86; Morris 70.)

However, despite the parallel in the opening address between the messages to Thyatira and Ephesus, there are differences in the state of the two communities. Four qualities characterize the church at Thyatira, whereas only two ('effort' and 'steadfastness') are mentioned in the Ephesian correspondence. Moreover, while the Christians at Ephesus had evidently given up their original love, for God and for others (Rev. 2.4), the expression of love in practice at Thyatira has increased ('your recent activities outweigh your earlier ones'). Swete (42) suggests that the more generous praise at this point is a prelude to the blame which will follow.

20–21 The risen Jesus criticizes the community at Thyatira for its tolerance of false teaching. Uniquely, in the seven messages, an individual is named as being responsible for this practice. (See on Rev. 2.5 and 2.14–15, where the reference to wrong belief and behaviour is general.) The only other person named in the seven letters is Antipas (2.13); but he is praised (for his faithfulness), rather than being condemned.

The Thyatirans are accused (the Greek means lit. 'I have [this] against you') of putting up with 'that woman'. For ἀφεῖς (*apheis*, 'put up with', lit. 'leave alone') see John 12.7. For the textual variant τὴν γυναῖκα σου (*tēn gynaika sou*, 'your woman') see above, 46. The self-styled prophetess is nicknamed 'Jezebel', after the idolatrous Queen of Israel, wife of Ahab, whose fate at the hands of Jehu was prophesied by Elijah (cf. 1 Kings 16.31; 21.23; 2 Kings 9.30–37). Michaels (78–79) points out that the power exercised by such a person must be viewed in the light of three facts: in primitive Christianity women prophesied freely (cf. Acts 21.9); in contemporary Roman and Oriental cults in Asia Minor women often played major roles as priestesses (cf. Frend, *Rise of Christianity* 200); and the prophetesses Priscilla and Maximilla were prominent leaders of the Montanist movement in the same geographical area during the later part of the second century AD (cf. Eusebius, *HE* 5.14).

The precise identity of this prophetess is unknown. However, she was clearly using her persuasive influence to encourage Johannine believers to compromise with the pagan society in which they lived: by indulging in sexual licence and by sharing common meals dedicated to pagan deities. Pressure to behave in this way would be strong in a city like Thyatira; its economic life was dominated by trade guilds, and participation in pagan religious rites was essential for membership of them (Mounce 86). The teaching in question was seductive, but probably informal; it may have been associated with Nicolaitanism (see Rev. 2.6, 15), and to that extent have been gnostic in character (see also on verse 24). This points again to the mixed nature of John's audience: Greek, as well as Jewish. It is John's role to play Elijah to this woman's Jezebel (Caird 45).

At Pergamum antinomianism was practised by 'some' (Rev. 2.14); while at Thyatira it seems to have been aggressively promoted, and therefore widespread as well as deeply ingrained (notice the reference in verse 23 to Christ searching 'minds and hearts'). Charles (1, 70) regards ἡ λέγουσα ἑαυτὴν προφῆτιν (*hē legousa heautēn prophētin*, 'who describes herself as a prophetess') as a Hebraism. The same is true, in his view, of the next phrase, καὶ διδάσκει καὶ πλανᾷ (*kai didaskei kai plana[i]*, lit. 'and teaches and misleads'), where the participle λέγουσα (*legousa*, lit. 'saying') has been resolved into two finite verbs. The verb πλανάω (*planaō*, 'deceive') is used elsewhere in the Apocalypse only of Satan and his agents: the beast (Rev. 13.14) and Babylon (18.23). See Sweet 94.

Jezebel is misleading the members of the church in Thyatira into 'practising fornication and eating meat offered to idols'. See on Rev. 2.14*b*. The community is thereby encouraged to contravene the directive of the Jerusalem Council (Acts 15.29), which laid on believers 'no further burden' than four essentials: including abstinence from what has been sacrificed to idols and from fornication. The order of the words here is the reverse of that in 2.14. Pagan feasting often led to sexual proclivity; but the mention of 'fornication' first in this context may suggest that immorality was the main objective of the prophetess (so Charles 1, 71).

The Jezebel-like leader no doubt shared in the Nicolaitan error (see above, 62–63). But she need not have been part of the Johannine community in Thyatira. She was using her position in any case, in opposition to John, to mislead its members; and she had been given time (perhaps by John) for repentance from 'her fornication'. Whereas the reference to fornication in verse 20 is undoubtedly literal, as with 'eating meat offered to idols', the meaning of 'fornication' here is figurative. Jezebel was unwilling to think again about her unfaithful association with the pagan society around her. The idea of religious infidelity as harlotry is familiar to us from the Old Testament (Hos. 2.2–13; 9.1; cf. Exod. 34.15; Judg. 2.17; Ezek. 16.23–43; et al.). The refusal of the false prophetess to repent is to have dire punitive consequences (verses 22–23).

22   The period allowed for repentance has expired, and judgement follows: Jezebel is to be thrown on to a 'sickbed', and her adulterous associates are to be brought into 'great pain'. Ἰδού (*idou*, 'so look', lit. 'behold') is minatory (NRSV translates 'beware'). The force of βάλλω (*ballō*, 'I am throwing') is futurist present (Mounce 88 n. 17). The action of the exalted Christ is imminent; so the present tense of the verb in the Greek is more likely to be correct than the future βαλῶ (*balō*, 'I will throw'), as read by א^c P 38 Tert, et al. cf. Rev. 2.5. So Swete 44, against Bengel 213. The action of 'throwing' suggests prostration rather than violence (Swete, ibid.); for the 'bed' in question is one of sickness (instead of a bed of adultery), rather than a funeral bier (Hort 30) or the 'dining couch' of trade-guild feasts (Ramsay, *Letters* 351–52); cf. Ps. 41.3 LXX. The explanatory scribal conjectures (see above, 46) indicate the difficulties felt about the use of the fairly rare term κλίνη (*klinē*, 'bed', only here in the Apocalypse, and eight times elsewhere in the New Testament). Sickness as a punishment for sin was an accepted connection in the first century AD (cf. John 9.1–3; 1 Cor. 11.27–30).

Those who 'are committing adultery' alongside Jezebel are being brought into 'great pain'. The present participle (τοὺς μοιχεύοντας ([*tous*] *moicheuontas*, '[those who are] committing adultery') is intensive: the pagan vices, into which members of John's church were being led by the false teaching of the prophetess, are being practised while the divine judgement is about to descend. For μοιχεύω (*moicheuō*, 'commit adultery') see on verse 21. The use of the verb is semi-figurative (AG 528). The beguiled companions of Jezebel were certainly guilty of spiritual infidelity to Christ; but a literal meaning of the verb may be included in his condemnation of their activity.

The 'great pain', into which they are being thrown, balances the 'sickness' brought upon Jezebel. For θλῖψις (*thlipsis*, 'pain' or 'pressure') see Rev. 1.9; 2.9, 10; 7.14; also Mark 13.19, 24. The sense is once again semi-figurative. The associates of the false prophetess will perhaps literally experience pain and suffering; but they will also figuratively undergo tribulation or affliction.

But there is still hope for the dupes of Jezebel. Judgement will follow, 'unless they repent of what she is doing'. No time is left for the prophetess, yet there can be for her adherents if they think again (the literal meaning of the verb translated 'repent'). Nevertheless, their repentance concerns *her* deeds, not their own: (μετανοήσωσιν) ἐκ τῶν ἔργων αὐτῆς ([*metanoēsōsin*] *ek tōn ergōn autēs*, lit. '[repent] from her works'). This slightly awkward construction has caused some inevitable textual variations (see above, 46). But πορνεία (*porneia*, 'fornication') and μοιχεία (*moicheia*, 'adultery') are clearly the works of Jezebel, not those of the faithful Christian. If that contrast is pressed, the meaning of the text becomes clearer: the right-thinking and correctly behaving members themselves of the troubled community at Thyatira are being summoned to repent *on behalf of* Jezebel's activity, which has nothing to do with their own practices. Then judgement on the church might be averted. Cf. Rev. 2.16 (q.v.), which could imply a similarly vicarious repentance by the faithful at Pergamum, in order to deflect 'war' against the Nicolaitans; see also on 2.24.

For the future indicative (μετανοήσωσιν, *metanoēsōsin*, lit. 'they will repent') after ἐὰν μή (*ean mē*, 'unless') see BDF 373 (2).

23 The promised judgement continues, and becomes more severe. The 'children' of the prophetess will be 'struck dead'. Beckwith (467) takes τὰ τέκνα αὐτῆς (*ta tekna autēs*, 'her children') literally, and argues that the death of the woman's children adds to her punishment. But the death of Jezebel's children is best understood as the third expression of judgement against the false prophetess and her antinomian followers: sickness – pain – death. John uses typically prophetic language to express the thought that the entire group of Jezebel's adherents will be destroyed: those who share the sin of their spiritual mother ('are committing adultery with her', verse 22), and those who embrace her misguided teaching ('her children'). Cf. Beasley-Murray 91–92. Beale (260–61) thinks that the allusion here to 'the woman' and 'her children' evokes the language of the 'elect lady and her offspring' in 2 John 1 (q.v.), where a community and its individual members are in view. But the reference in 2 John is entirely corporate, whereas the self-styled prophetess who is like Jezebel in this oracle is clearly an individual, albeit unknown. See further Smalley, *1, 2, 3 John* 318–19.

The phrase ἀποκτενῶ ἐν θανάτῳ (*apoktenō en thanato[i]*) literally translates 'I will kill in/with death'. It is a Hebraism meaning, 'utterly to slay by pestilence' (cf. Ezek. 33.27; Rev. 6.8). There may be a reference here to the slaughter of Ahab's 70 sons in 2 Kings 10.1–11; although, as Beckwith (467–68) points out, that event is not associated with vengeance on Jezebel. He finds a better parallel, in terms of both cause and motive, with the death of the child of David and Bathsheba (2 Sam. 12.14).

As a result of Christ's judgement, all the Johannine churches, and not just members of the Thyatiran community, will realize that he is 'the searcher of minds and hearts' (ὁ ἐραυνῶν νεφροὺς καὶ καρδίας, *ho eraunōn nephrous kai kardias*). The word νεφροί (*nephroi*) means literally the 'kidneys', and is used metaphorically in Judaeo-Christian thought of the mind and will (Cf. Ps. 7.9; only here in the New Testament). The 'heart' (καρδία, *kardia*, Heb. לֵב, לֵבָב, *lēḇ, lēḇāḇ*) designates the spiritual, emotional and rational centre of human life as a totality (cf. Deut. 6.6; Ps. 22.26). See Sorg, 'καρδία'.

In this part of the verse the principle of divine judgement, as expressed by the prophet Jeremiah, is being quoted. See Jer. 17.10, 'I the Lord test the mind and search the heart, to give to all according to their ways, according to the fruit of their doings' (cf. Matt. 16.27; Rom. 2.6). However, God's inevitable judgement on the 'conduct' of the antinomians is righteous (cf. Jer. 11.20, 'you, O Lord of hosts, judge righteously, you test the heart and the mind . . .'), and never separated from his love (cf. verse 28*b*; Isa. 35.4; Rev. 19.1–2; John 3.16–21; 12.47–50; 1 John 4.16–21).

Williams ('Touch of God') draws attention to the way in which, throughout these seven letters, the tone 'swings disconcertingly between vitriol and a language of haunting authority' (113). So here God's Son, whose eyes flame like fire and whose feet are like fine bronze, throws Jezebel into a sickbed, brings great pain on her fellow-adulterers and strikes her children dead. The searcher of minds and hearts deals out to the misguided the just consequences of their actions. We need, Williams claims, to realize that the power of the Living One is dangerous, and that we 'would know less of it without the fractured and disturbed languages of people like John the Divine, and their contemporary equivalents' (116). If Williams is right, we should read the Apocalypse as a literary whole in the light of the 'two scripts' (112) which he discovers in the seven oracles.

24–25   Advice is now given to 'the rest' of those in Thyatira, who do not accept Jezebel's teaching. This could be a reference to the Johannine community as such, from which the prophetess and her heretical circle had separated. In that case the Jezebel 'sect' would be attempting to win over to its antinomian ways converts from John's church. See on verse 22*b*; also Michaels 80.

The contrast between the groups around John and Jezebel is heightened as the verse proceeds. Not only do the Johannine Christians, noted for their love, faith, ministry and steadfastness (verse 19), reject the teaching of the prophetess; they also have no knowledge of what the secessionists call 'the deep things of Satan' (τὰ βαθέα τοῦ σατανᾶ, *ta bathea tou satana*). The writer is probably using the genitive 'of Satan' in an ironic, rather than literal, sense (as in Rev. 2.9, with reference to those Jews who claim to belong to God's 'synagogue', but who in reality form part of the 'synagogue of Satan', cf. 3.9). The Nicolaitans at Thyatira, led by their false prophetess, thought that they were familiar with the 'deep things of *God*' (see 1 Cor. 2.10); but in reality they possessed a knowledge of *satanic* truth.

The gnostic character of this group, over against the Johannine community, is clear. A later gnostic teacher, Carpocrates (*c*. AD 130–50), held that the whole range of human experience must be traversed by the soul; and this involves a knowledge of diabolical, as well as divine, mysteries (Peake, *Revelation* 246–47). Such knowledge, in gnostic terms, freed initiates from the bonds of the world, and assured them of ultimate salvation. Because they were free, they could live easily in a pagan society (so Rev. 2.13–15; cf. verse 20), adopting either an ascetic or a liberated way of life. The libertine lifestyle of the gnostic, as we know from the Fathers, manifested itself primarily in the practice of immorality, and eating food which had been sacrificed to idols: precisely as in the case of heterodox believers at Thyatira and Pergamum.

The claim to know the 'deep things' of religion may have provided Jezebel and her Nicolaitan group with their justification for ethical licence. They regarded themselves as spiritually mature, and able to discern more readily the truth as they saw it. In this connection, the prophetess may even have appealed to Paul's reference (in 1 Cor. 2.9–10) to revelation by the Spirit, and to the Spirit searching 'the deep things of God' (τὰ βάθη τοῦ θεοῦ, *ta bathē tou theou*). So Michaels 80.

On this passage see further Smalley, *Thunder and Love* 88–89. Cf. also Schlier, 'βάθος', esp. 517; Rudolph, *Gnosis* 252–72; Fiorenza, *Book of Revelation* 116–17, and the literature there cited. For a possible, additional allusion in this verse to Ophitism, an early gnostic cult which often claimed deep knowledge of a divine being, note Smalley, *Thunder and Love* 94 n. 95. On gnosticism generally see ibid. 84–89; also Frend, *Rise of Christianity* 195–205.

The risen Jesus wishes to lay upon those in Thyatira, who have not been led astray, no further responsibility than 'holding fast' to what they have. (For the use of the verb βάλλω [*ballō*, 'place' or 'throw'] see on verse 22.) It may be that the apostolic decree (Acts 15.28–29) is in mind at this point; although, apart from the use of βάρος (*baros*, 'burden'), the Greek is different. If an allusion is intended, it is not in negative terms (abstinence) but positive (holding fast). The Johannine believers are not to be led astray, but to maintain their faith: that is to say, they are to adopt a balanced view of the person of Christ, and so to behave in an appropriately Christian and not idolatrous manner.

They are to do so, moreover, until the parousia. The very fact that the advent of Jesus in the future can be contemplated by this assembly with joy and hope, rather than fear, suggests again that Jezebel and her company, with their unbalanced gnostic Christology and libertine praxis, were a threatening but separate group. See on verse 24; for the eschatology of this verse see on 2.16.

For ὃ ἔχετε κρατήσατε (*ho echete kratēsate*, 'hold fast to what you have') see Rev. 3.11. The aorist imperative κρατήσατε (*kratēsate*, 'hold fast') is not ingressive (expressing the start of conduct which contrasts with previous behaviour, as in Jas. 4.9), but a strict command as such ('complexive–terminative', BDF 337 [i]). The tense of ἥξω (*hēxō*, 'I come'), with ἄχρι (*achri*, 'until') is either future indicative or (so Charles 1, 74) aorist subjunctive; cf. Rev. 7.3; 15.8.

26–27 Each of the seven letters contains a promise to the 'conqueror'. But in this passage we come near to a definition of those who conquer. Not only do they maintain the traditions of ('orthodox') belief and behaviour held by the Christian Church (verse 25); they also 'take to heart', and observe, the works of Christ 'until the end'. The καί (*kai*) introducing ὁ τηρῶν (*ho tērōn*, 'the one who takes to heart') is therefore explanatory, meaning 'that is'.

As Beasley-Murray (93) rightly says, the works of Christ are to be reflected in the life of the Christian. The words and works of Jesus, expounded after the resurrection by the Spirit, are the believer's model and inspiration for existence (cf. John 16.12–15), and lead to even greater works than those performed in love by the Christ (John 14.10–12; 15.12–13). Such works are to be practised 'until the end' (ἄχρι τέλους, *achri telous*): whether that be at the final advent of Christ or at the conqueror's death.

In verses 26b–27 John paraphrases Ps. 2.8–9. This Psalm was interpreted messianically from the first century BC. (Note *Pss. Sol.* 17.23–24, where the son of David, as ruler of Israel, is promised the authority to 'smash the arrogance of sinners like a potter's jar, to shatter all their substance with an iron rod'.) It is a characteristic feature of Jewish eschatology, carried over into Christian thought, that the followers of the Messiah would share in his final rule (Matt. 19.28; 1 Cor. 6.3; Rev. 5.10). See Mounce 90.

The conqueror is promised a Christ-like authority (cf. verse 28) 'over the nations' (ἐπὶ τῶν ἐθνῶν, *epi tōn ethnōn*), which here stand for all that is opposed to God. For the (unusually negative) term '(all) the nations' see Rev. 11.2, 18; 15.3–4; 20.3, 8; et al. In Christ, vindication is possible from imperial harassment externally, and internally from satanic influences (notably present in Jezebel). The full exegesis of this promise needs to be considered in relation to the next verse.

In the Greek of the quotation from Ps. 2.8, we have a resumption in the dative pronoun (δώσω) αὐτῷ (*[dōsō] autō[i]*, '[I will give] to that one') of the nominative at the beginning of verse 26, ὁ νικῶν (*ho nikōn*, 'the conqueror'). Charles (1, 75) notes that in Revelation ἐξουσία (*exousia*, 'authority') without the article, as here, implies limited authority (cf. 6.8; 9.3); but with the article, full authority is meant (cf. 13.12; 16.9). The fourth evangelist does not use the article with ἐξουσία (*exousia*, 'authority') at all; and the word does not occur in the Johannine Letters. In this passage, human authority is bound to be subservient to divine power.

Christ promises that the conqueror will have authority over the nations, 'to smash them with an iron staff, as when earthenware jars are broken'. What does this mean? The prediction is problematic in terms of both language and meaning. In the first place, attention needs to be given to the verb translated here as 'to smash'. John's quotation of Ps. 2.9 uses the Greek ποιμανεῖ (*poimanei*). The LXX similarly renders the Hebrew for 'you shall break (them with a rod of iron)' in this verse as ποιμανεῖς (*poimaneis*); and the verb ποιμαίνω (*poimainō*) can mean either 'shepherd' or 'rule'. It is therefore possible that John is following the LXX at this point, and that he intended ποιμαίνω (*poimainō*) to have one of these two meanings in the present context. 'Shepherding', or 'ruling', would then bear the sense of warding off attacks with a shepherd's iron staff, or inflicting punishment (so Swete 46–47; Mounce 90).

However, it is unusual for John the divine to follow the LXX version in his quotations from the Old Testament. Unlike the fourth evangelist, he normally makes his own translation from the Masoretic Text. So it is more likely that the author of Revelation was writing independently of the LXX, and that he made a similar mistake as the LXX translator in so doing. For there is ambiguity in the Hebrew. The verb stem רָעַע (*rā'a'*), used in the MT of Ps. 2.9, means 'smash', or 'destroy'; whereas the parallel form רָעָה (*rā'â*), which underlies the LXX text, signifies 'shepherd', or 'tend'. Possibly John, who knew Hebrew better than Greek, thought that the Greek equivalent, ποιμαίνω (*poimainō*), also carried these two meanings, whereas it does not. In any case, the context demands the translation 'to smash (the nations)', which is exactly balanced by συντρίβεται (*syntribetai*, '[as when earthenware jars are] broken'), later in the verse (against Hemer, *Letters* 124–25). Cf. Mic. 5.5; Jer. 6.3; see also on Rev. 7.17; 12.5; 19.15. See further Poole, *Synopsis* cols 1706–707; Charles 1, 75–76; Caird 45–46 (Charles and Caird agree that the correct meaning is 'to smash').

What, then, is the theological significance of this promise? When will authority be given by Christ, to the conquerors, to 'smash the nations with an iron staff'? At the conclusion of all the other letters to the Johannine churches of Asia, the conqueror is promised a spiritual gift which is to be realized in the life beyond death: permission to eat from the tree of life in paradise (2.7); freedom from the second death (2.11); the hidden manna, and a new name on the white stone (2.17); entry into the realm and book of life (3.5); participation in the eternal temple of God (3.12); and a share in Christ's heavenly reign (3.21). It is likely, therefore that the promise in the present verse should be similarly construed (cf. also verse 28*b*).

The Psalmist looked forward to the messianic age, when all opposition to God's sovereignty would be overcome (Ps. 2.8–9). John's vision is to see this hope as being achieved in the life and death and exaltation of Jesus the Messiah, and as being shared by all his faithful followers, who truly believe and 'take his works to heart until the end'. It is therefore at 'the end' – the end of the world, or at the death of the believer – that the promise will take effect. Resistance to God, typified by the Roman *imperium*, will then be finally overcome, and the saints in Christ will ultimately be vindicated, as he is glorified.

The Church in the new Jerusalem will know that the power of the risen Christ is final and all-embracing (cf. Rev. 22.14–15). His judgement, inseparable from his love, is complete.

Caird (46) interprets the 'iron staff' with which the nations are smashed as 'the death of (God's) Son and the martyrdom of his saints'; cf. 1 John 5.4 (faith is the victory which 'conquers the world'). The reference to breaking 'earthenware jars' (τὰ σκεύη τὰ κεραμικά, *ta skeuē ta keramika*) at the end of this verse is also derived from Ps. 2.9. The familiar idea of the potter smashing a rejected vessel is developed in Jer. 18.1–11. Hemer (*Letters* 125) points out the aptness of the allusion in view of the known existence of a guild of potters in Thyatira. The old order is broken up; but this is followed by the reconstruction of a new order in Christ, the head of the glorified community of the Church (cf. Swete 47).

28   The first part of this verse belongs with verse 27. The Son gives authority over the nations to the conqueror, but his authority in turn is God-given: ὡς κἀγὼ εἴληφα παρὰ τοῦ πατρός μου (*hōs kagō eilēpha para tou patros mou*, lit. 'just as I also have received [it] from my Father'). The words recall Ps. 2.7; cf. Acts 2.33. See also verse 26. In the Apocalypse, Jesus is closely related to the Father (cf. Rev. 1.8, 17–18; 22.3–4). But he is also presented as a Son to a Father (here, and at 3.2, 12); and his ultimate authority is conferred by God. In the end, he is *mediator*: between God and his Church, and between heaven and earth; and he is also united with both. John's Christology, for the sake of his community's needs, is consistently balanced. See above, 4–5. Cf. Smalley, *Thunder and Love* 164.

The conqueror is also promised 'the morning star'. Only in this letter do we hear of a double promise to the one who prevails (see the repeated δώσω [*dōsō*, 'I will give'] here, and at verse 26). The symbol of the 'morning star' is introduced in this verse, without a particular context by which it may be explained. Several suggestions have been offered (see the survey in Mounce 90); but none seems entirely satisfactory. The 'morning star' is actually Venus, the symbol of victory. But it is reasonable to link this expression here to Rev. 22.16, where Jesus describes himself as 'the bright morning star'. Believing conquerors are those who share Christ's authority over pagan opposition, and who also participate in the messianic status of the risen Christ himself, while entering into his eternal life. If the angels of the seven churches of John can be described as 'stars' (cf. Rev. 1.20), and the exalted Christ appears as one who holds the seven stars in his right hand (1.16, 20; 2.1; 3.1), then the head of the Church may aptly be regarded as the brightest star, whose coming ushers in the dawning of the new age (cf. 2 Pet. 1.19; also Isa. 14.12; *Sib. Or.* 5.512–14). See Swete 47–48; also Milligan 56; Charles 1, 77; Beasley-Murray 93–94; Morris 74; Hughes 52–53; Aune 212–13.

Sweet (97) and Hemer (*Letters* 125) connect this symbol with the 'star' and 'sceptre' mentioned as emblems of messianic authority in the prophecy of Balaam at Num. 24.17. If the opposition to Christ at Thyatira were an expression of Nicolaitanism, which is equated at Pergamum with the teaching of Balaam (cf. Rev. 2.14–15), it would be appropriate to introduce at this point a reminiscence of words attributed to Balaam. As Hemer (125) also says, if Balaam's name stood for an accepted type of antinomianism, 'there would be the more point in citing his words as unwilling testimony to the sovereignty of Christ'. Even so, the symbol of the 'morning star' in this passage may still be considered as primarily a reference to the glorified Christ himself, the final possession of the conquering and faithful believer.

29   For the repeated formula, which urges the Johannine community to listen to the voice of the Spirit, and to respond to his words (cf. Matt. 7.24–25), see on Rev. 2.7,

11, 17. The use generally in this proclamation of the masculine singular substantive participle, ὁ ἔχων (*ho echōn*, lit., 'the one having'), is not intended to be exclusive. It embraces all members of John's church, male and female, who can understand the Spirit's testimony and act upon it.

Sardis (3.1–6)

3.1 The city of Sardis was situated 50 or so miles east of Ephesus, on a northern outcrop of Mount Tmolus overlooking the fertile plain of the river Hermus. Its virtually impregnable acropolis, constructed on a spur of the mountain, consisted of perpendicular rock walls, easily eroded, rising on three sides 1500 feet above the valley; and this provided a natural citadel. As Sardis developed in its early days, a lower city was built on the banks of the river Pactolus, a southern tributary of the Hermus. Hence the plural form of the name Sardis: Σάρδεις (*Sardeis*).

Once the capital of the ancient Lydian kingdom, Sardis was at its most powerful under Croesus, in the sixth century BC. The city fell to Cyrus in 546 BC, and became the seat of Persian government in Asia Minor. Later, Sardis formed part of the kingdom of the Seleucids (218 BC); then it came under Pergamene control, and was subject finally (in 133 BC) to Rome. In AD 17 the city suffered a disastrous earthquake, although the considerable generosity of the Emperor Tiberius enabled it to be rebuilt (cf. Tacitus, *Ann.* 2.47). In AD 26 Sardis competed with ten other Asian cities for the distinction of constructing an imperial temple, although eventually Smyrna won that privilege (Tacitus, *Ann.* 4, 55–56). See further Mounce 92.

At its height, Sardis was a famous and wealthy city. In the time of Croesus, in the sixth century BC, gold was mined from the Pactolus; and it was in the city that gold and silver coins were first struck, and the art of dyeing wool was first discovered. But by the Roman period decline had set in; and Ramsay (*Letters* 354–68) describes Sardis in the New Testament period as 'the city of death'. Hemer (*Letters* 134) considers Ramsay's judgement as overdrawn; but the reference to 'death' in the letter to Sardis at Rev. 3.2 may well allude as much to a city of past glory as to an ailing church.

Hemer (*Letters* 134–40) also draws attention to the likelihood that both Jewish and Hellenistic influences on the city of Sardis can be detected in the first century AD. The possibility of a Jewish presence in a Greek city is problematic (but see on Rev. 3.4; also Aune 218–19); the existence of paganism is undoubted. For example, excavations in the lower city have uncovered a large temple (160 by 300 feet), built in the period of Antiochus III on the sixth-century BC foundations of another temple, founded by Croesus. The later temple was destroyed in 499 BC and reconstructed, but never finished. It was dedicated to Cybele, a local goddess, who can be identified with the Greek Artemis. She was reputed to have the power of restoring the dead to life. If the Johannine community at Sardis were subject to such mixed pressures, both Jewish and Hellenistic, this points once more to the nature of John's church, and provides a basis for its putatively troubled, doctrinal (christological) situation. See above, 4–6.

1 For the opening phrase, 'to the *angel* of the church in Sardis', see on Rev. 2.1. This community receives the strongest condemnation from the exalted Christ of any of the Johannine churches. Its troubles may well have stemmed from its sheltered and wealthy existence. To prepare the way for the hard words to follow (after the usual formula, τάδε λέγει [*tade legei*, 'so speaks']), the Lordship of Christ is asserted in the strongest possible way: he 'holds the seven spirits of God, even the seven stars'. The spirits and the stars, the Spirit and the angels, are agents of God's revelation; and they dispense the judgement, as well as the love, of the Almighty. Both are 'held' (ὁ ἔχων, *ho echōn*, lit. 'the one who holds') by Christ, and are under his jurisdiction, for a ministry of correction taking place among his followers (cf. Wall 80).

For the 'seven spirits' and the 'stars' see on Rev. 1.4; 5.6; 1.16, 20; 2.1; 3.1. As before, John makes a deliberate and qualitative connection between this manifestation of the risen Christ and his appearance in the vision of chapter 1 (see esp. verse 16). In the phrase, τὰ ἑπτὰ πνεύματα τοῦ θεοῦ καὶ τοὺς ἑπτὰ ἀστέρας (*ta hepta pneumata tou theou kai tous hepta asteras*, 'the seven spirits of God, even the seven stars'), the καί (*kai*) is epexegetic, meaning 'even', or 'namely'. The seven spirits of God (= the Spirit) are a divine reality, whereas the seven stars are a symbol of that reality (Aune 219).

A paradox follows. The Sardians have a reputation (ὄνομα, *onoma*, lit. 'name') for being spiritually alive, but in fact their actions show them to be spiritually 'dead' (νεκρός, *nekros*). The καί (*kai*) linking the two parts of this statement is adversative, meaning 'but', or 'however'. So serious is the state of the disciples that the normal pattern in the seven letters of preceding condemnation with commendation (e.g. Rev. 2.13–14) is abandoned. The oracle is one of judgement, and the threat of names being erased from the book of life (3.5) is imminent.

2–3 The summons to 'be vigilant' in the face of the impending judgement introduces a further four imperatives in this letter: 'establish', 'bear in mind', 'pay attention' and 'repent' (see further on this verse and verse 3). For the construction γίνου γρηγορῶν (*ginou grēgorōn*, lit. 'become vigilant') see Rev. 16.10, καὶ ἐγένετο ἡ βασιλεία αὐτοῦ ἐσκοτωμένη (*kai egeneto hē basileia autou eskotōmenē*, lit. 'and its kingdom became darkness'). The present participle, γρηγορῶν (*grēgorōn*, 'vigilant'), implies continuity: 'be *constantly* vigilant'. The verb γρηγορέω (*grēgoreō*, 'to be vigilant'), which is not used in John's Gospel, is found three times in Revelation: here, in verse 3 and at 16.15. Cf. also Matt. 24.42 = Mark 13.35.

Ramsey (*Letters* 376–79) believes that John's allusion here to the Sardian need for vigilance (see also verse 3*b*) was deliberate, and that it was suggested by the two occasions in the past history of the city when the acropolis fell into enemy hands through over-confidence and lack of vigilance on the part of its defenders: in the time of Croesus in the sixth century BC, and in 218 BC, when Antiochus the Great captured Sardis. Note the account of the capture of the seemingly impregnable citadel of Sardis by Cyrus in Herodotus 1.76–84. See further Charles 1, 79; Morris 74–75; Aune 219–20; also Hemer, 'Sardis Letter', esp. 94 (the complex of traditions relating to Croesus 'had become proverbial').

The Sardians are urged to 'establish what is left, and on the point of dying'. The metaphor is shifted; and instead of the community as a whole being represented as 'dead' (verse 1), some of its members are now characterized as being weak and 'on the point of dying'. This implies a divine command: that the few in the congregation who are true believers, and balanced in their view of the person of Christ, should care for those who are not (see verse 4; cf. Ezek. 34.4).

The phrase '(establish) what is left', in the Greek ([στήρισον] τὰ λοιπά, [*stērison*] *ta loipa*), is in the neuter plural. But this need not mean that τὰ λοιπά (*ta loipa*, lit. 'the remaining things') must be construed in an entirely impersonal sense (cf. Heb. 7.7; BDF 138.1). The expression refers in the first place to the spiritually ailing Christian community at Sardis; but it no doubt includes the city of the past itself (cf. Swete 49). The call to establish a new life, in the midst of paganism without and indifference within, is addressed generally. In ἃ ἔμελλον (ἀποθανεῖν) (*ha emellon [apothanein]*, lit. 'the things which are about to [die]') we have an epistolary imperfect.

The church at Sardis is outwardly alive (verse 1); but its apparent prosperity disguises its mediocre and indeed moribund spiritual condition. For the most part it could therefore be regarded as free from the problems which troubled the Johannine circle as a whole. It lacks the enthusiasm even to promote christological heterodoxy, and it is 'too innocuous to be worth persecuting' (Caird 48).

The glorified Christ has not found 'anything (the Sardians) do' complete. Here, and at verse 1, the vernacular possessive σου (τὰ ἔργα) (*sou [ta erga]*, lit. 'your [works]') throws the emphasis on the noun: lit. 'the *works* you do' (as in verse 1). This is a reference to the community as a whole: its spiritual life and activity are incomplete, and half-hearted. The church lacks love, faith, ministry and steadfastness (see Rev. 2.19).

The word πεπληρωμένα (*peplērōmena*, 'complete') is used again, in another form, at Rev. 6.11; it appears more frequently in the Fourth Gospel (John 3.29; 16.24; 17.13; et al.), and twice in the Johannine Letters (1 John 1.4; 2 John 12). It is possible that the term, associated with πλήρωμα (*plērōma*, 'fulness'), contains gnostic overtones; but if so these have been used and Christianized for the sake of John's audience (see Smalley, *John* 54–61). Cf. the call to 'perfection' enunciated at Matt. 5.48; 19.21; note also 1QS 2.2; 8.20; 9.2; et al. (the perfection of complete obedience to the Torah).

The phrase ἐνώπιον τοῦ θεοῦ (*enōpion tou theou*, 'in the eyes of God', lit. 'before God'), sometimes in the form ἐνώπιον τοῦ κυρίου (*enōpion tou kyriou*, 'before the Lord'), is an Old Testament formula which is used eight times in Revelation (3.2; 8.2, 4; 9.13; 11.4, 16; 12.10; 16.19; see also Rev. 3.5; 7.15; 15.4). In the Apocalypse the expression is mostly used in a local sense, meaning 'in the presence of God'; but once it has a cultic reference, signifying the worship of the nations 'before God' in his temple (15.4). In the present verse, 'in the eyes of God' is used figuratively, and means (uniquely in Revelation) 'in the knowledge, or opinion, of God'. The addition of μου (*mou*, 'my') to 'God' ([ἐνώπιον] τοῦ θεοῦ μου, *[enōpion] tou theou mou*, '[in the eyes of] my God') occurs in the Apocalypse only here and at 3.12 (four times). The expression 'my God' is used elsewhere in the New Testament, attributed to Jesus, solely at John 20.17 (Jesus says to Mary, 'I am ascending to my God') and Mark 15.34 par. (the cry of dereliction from the cross). But note '*our* God' (ἡμῶν, *hēmōn*, s.v.l.) at Rev. 12.10. Cf. Aune 220–21.

The series of imperatives continues in verse 3. Already (verse 2) the members of the community at Sardis have been exhorted to be 'vigilant' and to 'establish what is left'. Now, on this basis (οὖν, *oun*, 'so'), they are charged to 'bear in mind', 'pay attention' and 'repent'. The command to 'bear in mind (what you have received and heard)' is a present imperative: μνημόνυε (*mnēmonue*, lit. 'remember'). The recollection of the Sardians is to be constant. They are to remember the Christian kerygma, the good news of life through God's love in Christ, the Saviour of the world (cf. John 3.16; 1 John 4.7–9; John 4.42; 1 John 4.14; see also Acts 20.31; 2 Tim. 1.13–14). There is an important change of tense between 'received' and 'heard'. The first, εἴληφας (*eilēphas*, 'received') is in the perfect; the second, ἤκουσας (*ēkousas*, 'heard') is aorist. The faith of the Sardians came by 'hearing' the gospel at a particular moment in time (aorist); but on that occasion they received the faith as an ongoing trust (perfect). Cf. Swete 50; Mounce 94.

The word πῶς (*pōs*) normally means 'how', indicating manner. But here it is connected with the verb τήρει (*tērei*, 'pay attention to'), which requires an object (= 'it', namely, the gospel); and this suggests that πῶς (*pōs*) should be translated here as 'what' (Beckwith 474). The Sardians are to 'pay attention' to their faith (lit. 'keep' it), and to 'repent'. Once again the tenses of the verbs differ. The present imperative τήρει (*tērei*, 'pay attention') implies continuous action; while the aorist μετανόησον (*metanoēson*, 'repent') presupposes a single act. The verb μετανόησον (*metanoēson*) means literally 'to change the mind'. The church at Sardis needs a new beginning.

If the Sardian community is not vigilant, the oracle continues, Christ will unexpectedly ('like a thief') arrive in judgement. The conjunction οὖν (*oun*, 'but') at the beginning of the sentence is resumptive. It looks back to the leading command in verse 2 to 'be vigilant', to which the succeeding imperatives ('establish', 'bear in mind', 'pay attention' and 'repent') are subordinate (cf. Swete 50).

The description of Christ's arrival as 'thief'-like clearly alludes to the dominical parable of the burglar at night (Matt. 24.43–44 = Luke 12.39–40; cf. the advent of the day of the Lord, referred to at 1 Thess. 5.2; 2 Pet. 3.10). In the teaching of Jesus, the parable seems to refer to the parousia, his coming at the end of time (against Dodd, *Parables* 167–71); and this is evidently the interpretation put upon its use by Paul and the writer of 2 Peter. Some commentators (e.g. Charles 1, 81; cf. Kiddle 46) assume that a similar reference is intended in the present verse.

But there are two arguments against this understanding. First, the final advent of Christ cannot be said to depend on the vigilance of the church at Sardis. Second, similar commands to repent, in the face of an alternative coming of Christ, are issued to the communities at Ephesus (Rev. 2.5, q.v.) and Pergamum (2.16, q.v.). In both cases the reference is to an imminent and historical advent of the Lord in judgement ('I will visit you and remove your lampstand from its place'; 'I will visit you soon'); although it is unwise to speculate about the form such a judicial arrival might take. In these contexts, language traditionally associated with the parousia of Christ at the end has been adapted to his more immediate and historical coming to specific communities for judgement. Similarly, the church at Laodicea is later urged to repent (Rev. 3.19); and this command is immediately followed by the assertion that the risen Lord is already at the door, promising present table-fellowship (3.20). See Beasley-Murray 96–97.

It seems likely, therefore, that here we should understand the arrival of Christ 'like a thief' to mean his imminent and historical coming to the Sardian community for purposes of judgement. However, John's eschatology – in Revelation, as in other parts of the Johannine corpus – is always balanced. For him, the present points forward to the future, and the future includes the present. All 'appearances' of Christ are therefore part of his ongoing parousia: in time, and at the end of time. (See further Smalley, *Thunder and Love* 62–63.) In the same way, the promise of table-fellowship with the Laodiceans (Rev. 3.20) is proleptic of the messianic feast (cf. Rev. 21.3–7; 22.1–5, 17; note Isa. 25.6–10*a*).

The parenthetical saying at Rev. 16.15, q.v. ('look, I am coming like a thief') should be interpreted in the same way as at 3.3, since again it refers to Christ's imminent advent to his Church. Because that text seems to interrupt the context in which it occurs, Charles (1, 80, hesitantly) 'restores' it to what he believes was its original position: before 3.3*c*. But this is arbitrary, and produces unnecessary repetition if the move is made. See further, against this source-critical analysis, Hemer, *Letters* 145–46; also on 16.15.

However, the arrival of Christ will occur, and, whenever it takes place, the Sardians will without vigilance be taken by surprise. They will not 'know' (γνῷς, *gnō[i]s*) at what hour' the Lord will 'come upon' (ἐπί, *epi*, 'upon', is forceful) them. The subjunctive γνῷς (*gnō[i]s*, 'know'), after οὐ μή (*ou mē*, an emphatic double negative, 'not [at all]'), is normative in the Apocalypse. See BDF 365. The accusative ποίαν ὥραν (*poian hōran*, '[at] what hour') is rare, and denotes an exact point in time. CF. BDF 161(3).

The use of the second person singular in the Greek of this verse, and generally in the seven letters to the churches in Asia, is direct and intensive. The community as a whole is being addressed; but individual members within it cannot escape the need for urgent action and spiritual renewal.

4 The harsh tone of the letter to Sardis is softened at this point. It is recognized that a few members of the community have not been influenced by the surrounding pagan society, so as to fall away from the true faith and behave wrongly. At Pergamum some have failed (Rev. 2.14), and at Thyatira many have put up with Jezebel (2.24). But in Sardis the majority have become heterodox or apathetic, or both.

An exception is provided by the 'few people' (ὀλίγα ὀνόματα, *oliga onomata*, lit. 'few names') left, 'who have not stained their clothing'. For the use of ὄνομα (*onoma*, 'name') as the equivalent of 'person' see Rev. 11.13; Acts 1.15; also Num. 1.2, 20; also Swete 51. The verb ἔχεις (*echeis*, 'you have') is singular, referring to the 'angel' of the church being addressed, as distinct from the collective group within the congregation which is being faithful.

The allusion to '(stained) clothing' would be instantly appreciated in Sardis, where the manufacture and dyeing of woollen goods was a leading occupation (Mounce 95). 'Clothing' in this context is a metaphor for the moral, as well as spiritual, condition of an individual (see also Rev. 7.13–14; 22.14). So the absence of staining implies ethical purity on the part of the minority in Sardis: members of the church who have not aligned themselves with the prevailing standards belonging to the pagan city. Note the reverse situation in Zech. 3.1–5, where the dirty garments of the high priest (verse 3) denote the sins of both priest and people, while their removal (verse 4) symbolizes cleansing from guilt. Aune (222) compares the similar imagery used in *1 Apoc. Jas.* 28.16–17, from the Nag Hammadi Library (Robinson, *Nag Hammadi* 263).

The deserving few are promised that they will 'walk' beside the exalted Christ; and this denotes a close relationship to him. The use of the verb περιπατεῖν (*peripatein*, 'to walk') in this context is possibly influenced by the references in the Old Testament to Enoch (Gen. 5.22) and Noah (Gen. 6.9) 'walking' (by implication intimately) with God; and note the command to Abraham (Gen. 17.1) to do the same. But in the New Testament, 'walking' often becomes a synonym for Christian discipleship (as in John 12.35; Rom. 6.4; 2 Cor. 5.7; 1 John 1.6–7; 2.6; 2 John 4; et al.) To 'walk worthily of the Lord', therefore, is the equivalent of 'behaving' as a true disciple of Christ (so Eph. 4.1; 1 Thess. 2.12; Polycarp, *Phil.* 5.1). See also Rev. 14.4, where the vision of the redeemed (who are 'undefiled'), 'following the Lamb wherever he goes', similarly uses the language of discipleship.

The faithful will be dressed in 'white robes'. The adjective ἐν λευκοῖς (*en leukois*, lit. '[in] white') is plural; and this points to the garments with which the disciples of Jesus are to be clothed (cf. τὰ ἱμάτια αὐτῶν, *ta himatia autōn*, 'their clothing', earlier in the verse). More than one interpretation of the colour 'white' is possible.

(a) Michaelis, 'λευκός' 249–50, argues that in Revelation white clothes point to membership of the heavenly world. They are a divine gift, and express the supernatural glory of the righteous. Similarly Swete (51–52) reminds us that white apparel in the Bible is associated with festivity (Eccl. 9.8), victory (2 Macc. 11.8), purity (Rev. 7.9–10, 14) and the heavenly state (Rev. 19.11; et al.); and he claims that all these associations meet in this verse.

(b) Ramsay (*Letters* 386–88) finds a parallel between the white robes of the faithful and the white toga worn by Roman citizens at a triumph (cf. Col. 2.15; 2 Cor. 2.14). This view makes particular sense in the present setting. The vision of the white-clad attendants of the victorious Christ, walking in his triumphal procession, contrasts positively and challengingly with the situation of defeat and defection which characterized the city and church of Sardis. Interestingly, Tertullian (*Scorpiace* 12) interprets Rev. 7.14 also in terms of a Roman triumph. See further Hemer, *Letters* 146–47.

(c) It is possible that all these evocations are present in this verse. But the predominant thought associated with the white robes of the believing minority at Sardis must be that of spiritual purity, and therefore of victorious morality. We may note that white garments are associated with priests in the ancient world, and with their people on holy occasions (Josephus, *Ant.* 327, 331; cf. Exod. 28.4; Lev. 16.4); with heavenly messengers (Mark 16.5 par.; John 20.12; Acts 1.10; *T. Levi* 8.2); with martyrdom (Rev. 6.11; and cf. the similarly attired white-robed 'army of martyrs' *[candidatus exercitus martyrum]*), mentioned in the Te Deum; with God himself (Dan. 7.9; cf. Ps. 104.2); and with Jesus at his transfiguration (Mark 9.3 par.).

The faithful in this section of John's community, then, are marked out by their loyalty to Christ, in the face of pressures to compromise and become disloyal. The clothing of these adherents remains unstained indeed: their faith in Jesus is adequate, and as a result their behaviour is ethical. Their heavenly, resurrection reward is well deserved (cf. Rev. 6.11). See also on verse 5.

The true Christians at Sardis are described as 'deserving' to walk with their Lord (ἄξιοί εἰσιν, *axioi eisin*, lit. 'they are worthy'). Elsewhere in the Apocalypse ἄξιος is used only of God or of Christ (e.g. Rev. 4.11; 5.12). But similar applications to the Christian can be found elsewhere in the New Testament (e.g. Eph. 4.1; Col. 1.10) and in early Christian literature (so Ignatius, *Eph.* 4.1; *Magn.* 12.1).

5 Three promises are given to those who survive victoriously. The conqueror, like the faithful minority at Sardis, is first assured of being clothed 'in white robes'. For οὕτως (*houtōs*, 'similarly') see above, 69. The thought and promise are repeated from verse 4, and stated in more general terms. For '(in) *white* (robes)' ([ἐν ἱματίοις λευκοῖς, *[en himatiois] leukois*) see on verse 4. White robes are referred to in the Apocalypse seven times, using the Greek words ἱμάτιον (*himation*, 'garment', Rev. 3.5, 18; 4.4); στολή (*stolē*, '[long, flowing] robe', 6.11; 7.9, 13); and βύσσινος (*byssinos*, 'fine linen', 19.14). With one exception (Rev. 3.18, where the Laodiceans are advised to purchase 'white robes' to hide the shame of their nakedness), the immediate context is supernatural: the white clothing belongs to martyrs awaiting vindication, elders in the heavenly throne room, the triumphant multitude before the Lamb, and the armies of heaven who follow the warrior Messiah. It is reasonable to conclude, therefore, that the white garments mentioned in this verse (as in verse 4) represent attire belonging to those who are with Christ in the heavenly dimension. They are the clothing of the faithful in the resurrection life (cf. Charles 1, 82; also 2 Cor. 5.1, 4; *1 Enoch* 62.16; *2 Enoch* 22.8). As they are made white by the blood of the Lamb (Rev. 7.13–14), the image is an appropriate expression for justification by faith (so Mounce 96). For the use of colours in Revelation, including white, see Smalley, *Thunder and Love* 106–107.

The second promise is that the victor's name will never be 'erased from the book of life'. The idea of a book of the living as a divine register of the faithful is widespread in ancient Israelite and Jewish literature (Exod. 32.32–33; Ps. 69.28; Dan. 12.1; 1QM 12.1–2; cf. Isa. 4.3); and it also appears in the New Testament and in early Christian writings (Luke 10.20; Heb. 12.33; Hermas, *Sim.* 2.9 [where the plural, 'books', is used]). In Revelation, the phrase 'book of life' (distinguished from a 'book of deeds' in 20.12, q.v.) occurs six times, and in two forms. (a) As ἡ βίβλος τῆς ζωῆς (*hē biblos tēs zōēs*, 'the book of life'), here and at 20.15, v.l.; (b) in the parallel expression, using the diminutive, τὸ βιβλίον τῆς ζωῆς (*to biblion tēs zōēs*, 'the book of life'), at 13.8, v.l.; 17.8; 20.12; 21.27, v.l. The textual variants suggest that John used these two forms interchangeably.

The primary setting for the use of this motif of the 'book of life' is judicial: God sits on his throne of judgement, surrounded by heavenly courtiers (Dan. 7.9–10; Rev. 20.12–15; *1 Enoch* 47.3; 90.20), and is given records for the purpose of dispensing justice. The metaphor stems originally from the royal courts of the ancient Near East (cf. Ezra 4.15; Esth. 6.1); although the concept itself runs back to Sumerian and Akkadian literature (so Aune 223). The traditional form of the statement about being 'erased from the book of life' can be seen from the close parallel between this verse and *Odes Sol.* 9.11.

To be 'erased', or 'blotted out' (ἐξαλείψω, *exaleipsō*, the tense is future) of the book of the living meant initially 'to die' (as in Exod. 32.32–33); but the idea came to mean 'erasure' or 'disenfranchisement' from a register of citizenship (cf. *1 Enoch* 108.3). In the classical world, the name of a person condemned to death was first erased from the roll of citizens. See Dio Chrysostom, *Orations* 31.84: Xenophon, *Hellenica* 2.3.51, where Critias strikes the name of Theramenes from the list of citizens (ἐξαλείφω ἐκ τοῦ καταλόγου, *exaleiphō ek tou katalogou*, 'I strike off [this man] from the roll'), before he is condemned to death.

Caird (49–50) finds in this text John's belief in a 'conditional predestination'. The names in the book of the living, following the divine initiative, have been there since the foundation of the world (Rev. 17.8); and these belong to citizens of heaven (21.27). The right to appear in this roll cannot be earned; but it may be forfeited. Nevertheless, John is being positive at this point. The names of spiritual conquerors, at Sardis as elsewhere, will never disappear from the book of life; their glorious life will endure (cf. Hendriksen 74).

The final promise to the victors in Christ is open acknowledgement before the Father in the presence of his angels. For 'angels' (ἀγγέλων, *angelōn*) see on 1.1; 7.1; et al. The verb ὁμολογήσω (*homologēsō*, 'I will openly acknowledge', or 'confess') is found only here in the Apocalypse. The sentence is strongly reminiscent of the saying of Jesus in the Q passage at Luke 12.8 = Matt. 10.32, especially in the Lucan version (which includes a reference to 'God's angels'). See also *2 Clem.* 3.2. On earth the followers of Christ are liable to be persecuted and despised; but beyond earth, and in the heavenly court, they will be openly vindicated (cf. Milligan 58). The eschatological mood of this verse is predominantly future: the conquerors are told, for their encouragement, what *will* happen to them after this life. But John's eschatology is markedly balanced; and the wide-ranging spiritual inheritance of which he speaks could as well have reference to present, post-conversion, blessings.

The author idiomatically uses ὁμολογεῖν (*homologein*, 'to acknowledge openly') with the accusative of the person here (as in *2 Clem.* 3.2), rather than the Aramaism ἐν (*en*, 'in') with the dative, as in the Q parallel (ἐν αὐτῷ, *en autō[i]*, lit. 'in him'). See BDF 220.2. Aune (227) suggests that if John is dependent on a less Semitic version of the saying of Jesus in this context, he may have inherited the logion from oral tradition. The writer has also substituted τὸ ὄνομα αὐτοῦ (*to onoma autou*, 'the name', lit. 'his name') for αὐτόν (*auton*, 'him') in this sentence, to be consistent with the use of τὸ ὄνομα αὐτοῦ (*to onoma autou*) in the preceding promise.

6   For the literary formula in this verse, see on Rev. 2.7.

Philadelphia (3.7–13)

7   The city of Philadelphia (modern Aleshehir), situated less than 30 miles south-east of Sardis, lies at the eastern end of a broad valley leading down to the Aegean Sea near Smyrna. It is built on high ground to the south of the river Cogamis, which is a tributary of the Hermus. Philadelphia's strategic location, at the crossing-point of trade routes leading to the regions of Phrygia, Lydia and Mysia, caused it to be a commercially important city. Its economy was based on industry and agriculture. (See further Mounce 98.)

When Antiochus IV was defeated at Magnesia in 190 BC the region of Lydia, in which Philadelphia is situated, came under the control of the Pergamenes. There is some doubt about the identity of the city's founder: whether it was Eumenes II, king of Pergamum, or his younger brother Attalus II Philadelphus (159–138 BC). The name 'Philadelphia' harks back to the title of Attalus ('Philadelphus', meaning 'brotherly love'), and is a reminder of the close and loyal relationship which existed between Attalus and Eumenes. Given the confusion over the founder of Philadelphia, it is difficult to be certain about the date of its establishment; but the city (no doubt built on the site of an earlier community) seems to have originated between 189 BC, when the region came under the rule of Eumenes, and the death of Attalus in 138 BC. See further Hemer, *Letters* 153–56.

Ramsay (*Letters* 391–400, esp. 391–92) describes Philadelphia as a 'missionary city', because its development under Pergamene control was intended to promote Hellenistic culture in the region. According to Ramsay this aim was successful, since by AD 17 Greek had replaced the Lydian tongue as the only language spoken in the country. However, Hemer (*Letters* 154) regards this view as overstated, in that it underestimates the military importance of Philadelphia.

In AD 17 the city (with 11 others around it) suffered a devastating and levelling earthquake, which affected the contemporary world as the most catastrophic disaster in living memory. Tacitus (*Ann.* 2.47.3–4) claims that Sardis was the worst hit; but he adds that Philadelphia (also close to the volcanic district) was excused the payment of tribute for five years because of the damage to it. An early and important witness to the problems which beset the Philadelphians at the time of the great earthquake and subsequently is Strabo (*Geography* 12.8.18; 13.4.10), who speaks of insecure walls in the city, and buildings being planned with a view to the occurrence of earthquakes, to which Philadelphia is 'ever subject' (σεισμῶν πλήρης, *seismōn plērēs*, lit. 'full of earthquakes').

Strabo elsewhere refers to the generosity of the Emperor Tiberius in providing relief for the Philadelphians (13.4.8; cf. Dio Cassius 57.17.8), as a result of which the city was renamed Neocaesarea. Hemer (*Letters* 157) notes that the effect of this catastrophe is reflected in the coins of the period less than might be expected; but that may be because no coins were struck in the reign of Tiberius (cf. Ramsay, *Letters* 397, 407). It is probable that this oracle to Philadelphia was written with the aftermath of the earthquake still in mind (see e.g. on Rev. 3.12).

Philadelphia is situated in a vine-growing area; and not surprisingly its chief pagan cult was the worship of Dionysus, the god of wine. Between AD 211 and 217 a provincial temple to the imperial cult was built, and in AD 214 Philadelphia was given the title Neokoros, 'warden of the temple' (see Mounce 99). Some members of the Johannine community would have come out of this Greek background; but others may have been of Jewish extraction. See on Rev. 3.9. So when Ignatius of Antioch, on his way to martyrdom in Rome (about AD 110), stayed at Philadelphia, he discovered the presence of a Judaizing influence on the Christian church in the city (*Philad.* 6.1). That is to say, John is addressing in this letter a congregation subject to both Jewish and Hellenistic influence (see above, 3–6; also Smalley, *Thunder and Love* 67–69, 121–37).

Eusebius (*HE* 5.17.3–4) refers to Ammia of Philadelphia, who was a prophetess in the Montanist tradition. *The Letter of the Smyrneans on The Martyrdom of St Polycarp* (19.1) tells us that 11 Christians from Philadelphia were martyred with Bishop Polycarp of Smyrna.

The proclamation to Philadelphia has many parallels with that to Smyrna. Both are designed to encourage the faithful in the face of problems within the church and outside it; and they cover much of the same ground. The two communities are also the only ones in the Asiatic group of seven to receive unqualified praise from Christ. See further Kiddle 48–49.

For the opening literary formula in verse 7 see on Rev. 2.1. So far John has introduced each letter by making a literary connection between the appearance of the risen

Christ as he speaks to the Asian communities and the vision of the exalted Son of man in Rev. 1. The same victorious Lord who walks among the seven gold lampstands (1.12–13, 20) also addresses the churches of Christ on earth. We may notice once more John's balanced cosmology.

However, although further connections with Rev. 1 could have been made, through the Son's apparel and appearance (his robe, sash, hair, voice and face, verses 13–16), the speaker uses other sources to identify himself as the holy and true Messiah who guards the entrance to God's kingdom. For the phrase 'holy and true', see Rev. 6.10. There it appears during a prayer to God offered by the martyrs, in the form ὁ ἅγιος καὶ ἀληθινός (*ho hagios kai alēthinos*, 'the holy and true'). Here the substantive adjectives are placed side by side, without the conjunction: ὁ ἅγιος, ὁ ἀληθινός (*ho hagios ho alēthinos*, 'the holy one, the true one'). The two terms, 'holy' and 'true', occur conjoined in Revelation only at 3.7 and 6.10; and they do not appear elsewhere together, in early Jewish or Christian literature, as divine characteristics.

The description 'holy' (ἅγιος, *hagios*) is not used of Jesus in the Apocalypse other than at 3.7, although the epithet is often used in the plural (ἅγιοι, *hagioi*, lit. 'holy ones') to refer to the 'saints' of God (e.g. 5.8; 13.7). In other parts of the New Testament, the substantive adjective ὁ ἅγιος (*ho hagios*, 'the holy one') is occasionally used to describe Jesus. See Mark 1.24; John 6.69; Acts 3.14; cf. Hab. 3.3; *1 Clem.* 23.5; Justin, *Dial.* 116.1; Clement Alex., *Paed.* 1.7; also Luke 1.35; 1 John 2.20.

The term ὁ ἀληθινός (*ho alēthinos*, 'the true one') is used in the New Testament only at 1 John 5.20, first of God and then of Jesus (cf. Smalley, *1, 2, 3 John* 306–307): 'The Son of God has . . . given us insight to know him who is the truth (τὸν ἀληθινόν, *ton alēthinon*), and we are in him who is the truth (ἐν τῷ ἀληθινῷ, *en to[i] alēthino[i]*), in his Son Jesus Christ'. In other places, ἀληθινός occurs adjectivally as a characteristic of the Father or the Son (cf. John 7.28; 1 Thess. 1.9; 1 John 5.20c; Rev. 3.14); and three times it qualifies descriptions of Jesus (the Word) as the '(true) light' (John 1.9; 1 John 2.8), or the '(true) vine' (John 15.1). The cognate term ἀληθής (*alēthēs*, 'true') sometimes appears as a designation of Jesus (cf. Mark 12.14; John 7.18); and at John 14.6 Jesus is referred to absolutely as 'the truth' (ἡ ἀλήθεια, *hē alētheia*).

The exalted Christ addresses the community at Philadelphia in his role as 'the holy one, the true one'. He is the embodiment of absolute sanctity and truth, in striking contrast to the heterodox members of the congregation (of Jewish background, or Hellenistic), whose faith and practice were incomplete and false. He alone, moreover, 'holds the key of David'. The risen Lord, that is to say, possesses the key to the messianic kingdom, in heaven or on earth; he thereby controls access or otherwise to that realm, and so to God's eternal life (see above, and on verse 9).

The reference to 'the key of David' (τὴν κλεῖν Δαυίδ, *tēn klein David*) clearly alludes to Isa. 22.20–22, where it is said of Hezekiah's faithful steward, Eliakim son of Hilkiah, that he will be vested with the symbols of authority and power: robe, sash and 'the key of the house of David'. With that key in his possession, moreover, 'he will open, and no one will shut; he will shut, and no one will open' (verse 22). Cf. 2 Kings 18.18 = Isa. 36.3; Matt. 16.19; note also *Targ. (Pal.)* Isa. 22.22, where the sense is somewhat different ('I will place the key of the sanctuary house and the government of David's house in his hand'). See Aune 235. The mention of David in the present verse reminds the Johannine community of the prophetic hopes belonging to the people of Israel, which have now been fulfilled in the exaltation of the Christ (cf. Swete 54).

Δαυίδ (*David*, 'David') is indeclinable, but assumes here the form of an objective genitive. Christ has the key *to* the kingdom of God, the true Israel, since he has all authority in heaven, on earth and in Hades (cf. Matt. 28.18; Rev. 1.18, q.v.). The literary structure of the final section of this verse is chiastic: open/close, shut/open (ABBA).

Note also the triplet in 'he holds the key, he opens, he shuts' (cf. Resseguie, *Revelation Unsealed* 49–50), and the poetic form of the introduction to Christ's 'message'.

8   The exalted Christ, who holds the keys of absolute authority and power, also knows what the Philadelphians are 'doing' (οἶδά σου τὰ ἔργα, *oida sou ta erga*, lit. 'I know your works'), as well as what they are believing. For the phrase, 'I know what you are doing', see Rev. 2.2, 19; 3.1, 15. Elsewhere in the seven letters, Christ is said to 'know' supernaturally the precise actions and status of the Johannine Christians (so Rev. 2.3, 9, 13). Similar divine perception is attributed to Jesus in the Fourth Gospel (e.g. John 1.48; 2.25; 6.64; 21.17).

The following sentence is a parenthesis, since the precise 'deeds' of the Philadelphians are specified later in this verse. Meanwhile, an 'open door' has been placed in front of them. The metaphor of an open door or gate is used in the New Testament in two senses. (a) To denote an opportunity for effective evangelism (cf. 1 Cor. 16.9; 2 Cor. 2.12; Col. 4.3). (b) To mean admittance to the messianic kingdom of life (cf. John 10.7, 9; Acts 14.27; Rev. 3.20).

Ramsay (*Letters* 404) adopts the former sense, and regards the 'open door' as a Pauline metaphor for evangelism, which passed into common usage in the primitive Church. He claims, therefore, that it means here 'a good opportunity for missionary work' (ibid.; similarly Swete 54; Caird 51; cf. Hendriksen 75, who seems to adopt both senses). But there is no doubt that the second meaning of this text is to be preferred. First, a reference to evangelistic activity, as a major challenge to the Philadelphian Christians, would be out of place in this parenthetical statement, standing as it does between two parts of a sentence commending the steadfastness of the community in the past. Second, the preaching of the gospel, as such, does not feature elsewhere in the seven oracles, or indeed in the whole of Revelation. Third, the promise to the members of the church at Philadelphia that, as a reward for their true and balanced faith, they will inherit the kingdom, entirely fits the present context and connects with the theological thrust of the previous verse. Christ has placed in front of (δέδωκα, *dedōka*, lit. '[I have] given [to]') this congregation an open door to the realms of eternal life; and, as they remain faithful to him, no one is able to deny them access. See further Beckwith 480.

The use of αὐτήν (*autēn*, lit. 'it') is a pleonasm, since it repeats the relative ἥν (*hēn*, 'which'), earlier in the phrase. This is a Semitic idiom, common in the New Testament (cf. BDF 297). The repetition is hidden in the translation. For the figurative use of θύρα (*thyra*, 'door') in early Christian literature see *PGL* 658.

After the parenthesis, a clause beginning with ὅτι (*hoti*, 'for', or 'because') explains the actions of the Philadelphian community, and the basis on which the exalted Christ has placed an open door into the kingdom before this church. 'You have little strength' is collective, and may be a literal reference to the size of the congregation. Strabo tells us that few people lived in the city of Philadelphia itself, after the devastating earthquake of AD 17, but rather spent their lives as farmers in the country (*Geography* 13.4.10; cf. 12.8.18). Yet, despite its limited strength, the community has largely kept the faith.

There follows an antithesis. Positively, the church at Philadelphia has 'remained loyal' to Christ's word; and negatively, it has 'not repudiated' his name (cf. Rev. 2.13.) The fact that the verbs here are in the aorist tense (ἐτήρησας/οὐκ ἠρνήσω, *etērēsas/ouk ērnēsō*, lit. 'you have kept/you did not deny') may suggest that a particular past occasion is in mind.

The Greek for 'you have remained loyal to my word' is ἐτήρησάς μου τὸν λόγον (*etērēsas mou ton logon*, lit. 'you have kept my word'). That phrase is repeated at 3.10 (q.v.), and used with a plural object (λόγους, *logous*, 'words') at Rev. 22.7, 9 (cf. John 8.51–52; 15.20; 17.6; 1 John 2.5). A parallel phrase, with the same meaning, appears at Rev. 12.17 and 14.12: 'those who keep the commands of God' (τῶν τηρούντων/οἱ τηροῦντες τὰς ἐντολὰς τοῦ θεοῦ, *tōn tērountōn/hoi tērountes tas entolas tou theou*); cf. 1 John 2.3–5, where 'word' and 'command' are also used interchangeably. Loyalty to Christ's word, in this context, therefore implies obedience to his commandments, of which the first is love (John 15.12; 1 John 3.23). Cf. Aune 237.

Obedience to the commands of Christ includes, conversely, not repudiating his name. Denying the 'name' of Jesus amounts to a rejection of the Christian faith (cf. Matt. 10.33; Acts 4.12; 2 Tim. 2.12; Justin, *1 Apol.* 31.6). Such repudiation is possible through both speech and action (2 Pet. 2.1; Titus 1.16; *1 Clem.* 3.4). Repudiating the name of Christ may also imply a misunderstanding of the nature of his person; and we know this to have been characteristic of some members of the Johannine community. See 1 John 2.22, and the comment on that verse in Smalley, *1, 2, 3 John* 110–15. For ὄνομα (*onoma*, 'name') see Bietenhard and Bruce, 'Name', esp. 652–55; cf. also on verse 12.

Because the Philadelphians have kept faith with Christ, and not repudiated him, they are promised divine affirmation and protection in return (see verses 9–10). Cf. Hendriksen 75.

9 The Lord's response to the faithfulness of the Philadelphian believers (verse 8) is now expressed. Those from 'the assembly of Satan' are to be 'handed over', and they will 'prostrate themselves' at the feet of the Christians.

As at Smyrna (Rev. 2.9), there seems to have existed in Philadelphia a deep rift between the church and the Jewish community. Those of Jewish descent claimed to be the legitimate people of God, but the adherents of the Christian congregation believed that the *Church* was the true Israel. As Paul says, 'a person is a Jew who is one inwardly, and genuine circumcision is a matter of the heart' (Rom. 2.29; cf. the contrast in verse 28). So the Jewish nation, which had not accepted that Jesus is Messiah, no longer qualified for membership of God's Israel (Gal. 6.16); and those belonging to the local community who styled themselves Jews were, by that very means, proving themselves to be 'liars'. In their fierce opposition to the gospel of Christ they had turned themselves into the 'assembly of Satan'. For this expression see on Rev. 2.9; cf. also 2 Cor. 11.14–15; Rev. 12.10; Ignatius, *Philad.* 6.1–2, where the Bishop testifies to the dire presence of Judaizers in the city.

Some of these opponents may have been former members of the Philadelphian believing community (cf. the situation at Smyrna), who had been forced out of it under coercion from their fellow-Jews. Their antagonism towards the church, in that case, is likely to have been all the more intense (see on 2.9). For the putatively generalized anti-Judaism in this passage, as at 2.9 (and in the Fourth Gospel: e.g. John 8.44; 9.22, 34; 12.42; 16.2), see van Henten, 'Anti-Judaism in Revelation?', esp. 123–25.

The syntax in the opening section of this verse is awkwardly elliptical, and an object needs to be supplied in the initial clause: 'I am handing over (those [αὐτούς, *autous*]) from the assembly of Satan'. The sentence as a whole then balances the later declaration, 'I will make them (αὐτούς, *autous*) come . . .'. Both parts of the verse are introduced in the Greek by the injunction ἰδού (*idou*, 'see'), although the second command is hidden in our translation. The verb διδῶ (*didō*, 'I am handing over', lit. 'I give') replaces the earlier and fuller form δίδωμι (*didōmi*, 'I give'). See Charles 1, 88, who regards the subsequent τῶν λεγόντων . . . καὶ οὐκ εἰσίν (*tōn legontōn . . . kai ouk eisin*, lit. 'saying . . . and they are not') as an 'unmistakable Hebraism' (ibid.).

In what sense will the members of the assembly of Satan, falsely self-designated 'Jews', be 'handed over', so as to become totally subject to the church at Philadelphia? This could mean either that they will become converted to the Christian faith or that eschatological prophecy will be fulfilled, and they will finally recognize the Christian Church to be the true Israel of God. The former meaning fits the exegesis of the 'open door' in verse 8 as an opportunity for mission; but we have already argued that such an understanding is unlikely (see 89). An eschatological interpretation is therefore preferable. Isaiah's post-exilic vision is to be realized. In the end, all who despised God's people will 'bow down' at their feet (Isa. 60.14); the nations will offer their wealth to Israel, come submissively in chains to the people of God, and acknowledge Yahweh as supreme (Isa. 45.14; cf. 49.23; Zech. 8.20–23). There is a grim reversal here. What the Jews originally expected from the Gentiles, 'they themselves will be forced to render' to the Church (Mounce 102); in this case obedience will be given to a community consisting of Gentile, as well as Jewish, Christians. However, for that to happen a 'conversion' of some kind must first have taken place.

The reference to 'prostration' (προσκυνήσουσιν, *proskynēsousin*, lit. 'they shall worship') is non-religious, and implies no more than a traditional, oriental gesture of homage. In the sentence, 'I will make them come (and prostrate themselves at your feet)' (ποιήσω αὐτοὺς ἵνα ἥξουσιν . . . , *poiēsō autous hina hēxousin* . . .), the infinitive belonging to an accusative and infinitive construction has been replaced by ἵνα (*hina*, lit. 'that') and a finite verb. See BDF 408. The verb προσκυνεῖν (*proskynein*, 'to prostrate' or 'to worship') is used 24 times in Revelation, mostly in association with the worship of God and the Lamb (e.g. Rev. 4.10; 5.14; cf. 22.3), or with the cult of the Beast (e.g. 13.4, 8; 19.20; 20.4; cf. 9.20).

The verse concludes with a ringing endorsement of the faith belonging to the Philadelphian congregation. The exalted Christ promises them that the Jewish nation 'will learn that I have loved (ἠγάπησα, *ēgapēsa*) you' (cf. Isa. 43.4, possibly). The Lord's love in this context may include the thought of election (so Aune 238); but it also speaks of God's affection for his people, and in the Apocalypse that is never separated from his judgement. The pronoun ἐγώ (*ego*, 'I') is emphatic: 'I, the Messiah'. The verb ἀγαπᾶν (*agapan*, 'to love') occurs three times in Revelation: once referring to self-preservation ('clinging to life', Rev. 12.11) and twice to the sacrificial love of Christ for his servants (1.5; 3.9; cf. John 13.1). But see also 20.9.

10   Christ keeps his people because they keep his word (verse 8) and his call to endurance. The encouragements for Philadelphia, as for Smyrna, are intended for all the faithful, and stem from divine love (verse 9). Cf. Wilcock 55.

For the phrase, 'you have faithfully kept my call to endurance' (ἐτήρησας τὸν λόγον [τῆς ὑπομονῆς μου], *etērēsas ton logon [tēs hypomonēs mou]*), see on verse 8. The verb τηρεῖν (*tērein*, 'to keep') is used twice in this verse, in close proximity and with two different senses (an example of paronomasia; see BDF 488.1). First it means 'obey' (as in verse 8), and second it means 'preserve'. But since there is an obvious play on words in the Greek, the translation uses 'kept/keep (you safe)' in both places.

The Philadelphians have faithfully obeyed Christ's 'call to endurance', in the face of impending disturbances within the community and outside it. The Greek τὸν λόγον τῆς ὑπομονῆς μου (*ton logon tēs hypomonēs mou*) means literally, 'the word of my patience/endurance'. The term ὁ λόγος (*ho logos*, 'the word') is used in Revelation 18 times, sometimes as the equivalent of 'gospel' (e.g. Rev. 12.11). For the phrase ὁ λόγος τοῦ θεοῦ (*ho logos tou theou*, 'the word [or message] from God') see Rev. 1.2, 9; 6.9; 20.4.

The risen Christ promises in return to 'keep safe', in the sense of 'continue to preserve', the Philadelphian community (cf. John 17.15, for a similar meaning). See *Odes Sol.* 9.6. 'The time of ordeal' (τῆς ὥρας τοῦ πειρασμοῦ, *tēs hōras tou peirasmou*, lit. 'the hour of testing'), which is about to erupt over the whole world, refers to all the trials which were expected by the primitive Church to precede the return of Christ (cf. Matt. 24.15–31; Mark 13.5–27). The use of the definitive article, ἡ ὥρα (*hē hōra*, 'the time'), may suggest that a particular event is in mind, familiar to the audience being addressed.

The idea of this 'ordeal' was inherited and transposed from early Judaism, in which it was anticipated that a period of intense distress and suffering would immediately pre- cede the eschatological victory of God (Dan. 12.1; *T. Mos.* 8.1; *2 Apoc. Bar.* 27.1–15; *Did.* 16.5; cf. Aune 239). This 'time of ordeal' can also be characterized as 'the pangs of childbirth' (Isa. 26.16–19; Hos. 13.13; Mic. 4.9–10; cf. Mark 13.8). In John's eschato- logy, the 'testing' of the faithful may be understood as taking many forms (see the series of 'woes' in Rev. 6; 8.7—9.21). These can occur at any moment in history, not just one; and together they are proleptic of the final establishment of God's victorious sovereignty. See further on 7.14.

The time of ordeal, or testing, is about to erupt 'over the whole world' (ἐπὶ τῆς οἰκουμένης ὅλης, *epi tēs oikoumenēs holēs*): that is to say, it will affect all humanity, and not simply the physical earth (see the next sentence; so Beckwith 483). The noun πειρασμός (*peirasmos*, lit. 'testing') appears only here in the Apocalypse (the cognate verb is used here and at Rev. 2.2, 10). 'Testing', in this context, means discrimination, not temptation: it implies the process of determining the true character of a situation or a society through careful scrutiny.

The final sentence in this verse parallels the preceding clause, and repeats its content and thought. The time of ordeal will 'test the inhabitants of the earth'. The phrase, 'the inhabitants of the earth' (τοὺς κατοικοῦντας ἐπὶ τῆς γῆς, *tous katoikountas epi tēs gēs*) is used nine times in Revelation (3.10; 6.10; 8.13; 11.10 [*bis*]; 13.8, 14 [*bis*]; 17.8), and three times in a varied form (13.12; 14.6; 17.2). In each case the expression is a tech- nical term, which refers negatively to unbelievers who are subject to divine judgement because they persecute the people of God, and practise idolatry. See further on 11.10. 'Earth-dwellers' often appear in early Jewish literature, in the context of the universal judgement of the nations of the world (so *1 Enoch* 37.2, 5; 48.5; *2 Apoc. Bar.* 48.32; et al.).

The fact that God's people will be 'kept safe from the time of ordeal' cannot mean that they will escape it physically. The 'testing' process will affect the whole living world, but the faithful will not be hurt by it spiritually. For once, it is the opponents of God who will be 'tested' in judgement, not the Christian Church: the loyalty of which, by this very means, will be clearly demonstrated. Christ is speaking here to one particular believing community in the first century AD. But there is no reason why his promise, and the context of universal judgement and parousia in which it is set, cannot be pro- jected on to a more general canvas in time and space.

11 To the Philadelphian community, Christ is 'coming soon'. The present tense is vivid (Morris 79). The congregation has just been reminded dramatically of the (final?) judgement which is to overtake the nations in the (distant?) future. Now, the risen Lord announces his imminent advent: here to encourage the faithful, elsewhere in the Apocalypse to warn the godless. The balanced eschatology is typically Johannine. The exalted Christ will come in glory at the end; but he also comes to his churches, for judgement and salvation, now (cf. Rev. 2.5, 16; 22.7, 12, 20*a*). For the thought of Christ's parousia by itself, when it is not necessarily associated with his immediate arrival, see Rev. 1.7; 2.25; 16.15; 22.20*b*.

The Philadelphians are urged to 'hold fast' to their present faith and spiritual inheritance, in the face of coming difficulties, lest they be deprived of their possessed 'crown' (see Rev. 2.10, where the promise to the faithful of the 'crown of life' is stated positively; cf. also 1 Cor. 9.25). The athletic metaphor is appropriate in this letter, since Philadelphia was noted for its games and festivals (Mounce 104; Hemer, *Letters* 165). The community's encouragement in this exercise is the prospect of Christ's near advent. John does not resolve the tension between the opening of this proclamation, which assures the faithful that no one but the risen Lord can open and close the door to the kingdom (3.7–8), and this final exhortation, which suggests that the powers of evil could lead the Christian community away from its status in Christ. Wall (85) finds a resolution in the biblical concept of covenant. This is always a partnership, with both unconditional and conditional aspects attached to it: 'a relationship entered into by God's love through the church's response of faith, but then maintained by divine love through the church's faithfulness to the Lord' (ibid.). See 1 John 2.28—3.10; 3.16–24; 5.16–20; also John 17.12–13.

12 The speaker turns, as at the end of each address, to the individual members of the Philadelphian community. The Greek at the start of this verse is abrupt: ὁ νικῶν, ποιήσω αὐτόν, *ho nikōn, poiēsō auton*, lit. 'the conqueror, I will make him'). But, as Swete (57) says, it 'adds to the movement of the sentence'. Ὁ νικῶν (*ho nikōn*, 'the conqueror') is unrelated grammatically to the remainder of the sentence.

To the one who faithfully keeps Christ's 'call to endurance' (verse 10), and therefore qualifies as 'a conqueror', is given the promise of becoming a 'pillar' (στῦλον, *stylon*) in the temple of God. This metaphor suggests 'stability and permanence' (Mounce 104), and is found in other parts of the New Testament. So James, Cephas and John are described as 'acknowledged pillars' of the Christian community (Gal. 2.9); and the Church of the living God is itself categorized as 'the pillar and bulwark of the truth' in 1 Tim. 3.15; cf. *1 Clem*. 5.2. The idea of permanence is intensified in the emphatic clause which follows: ἔξω οὐ μὴ ἐξέλθῃ ἔτι (*exō ou mē exelthē[i] eti*, 'never to leave it' [the temple], lit. 'he [the conqueror] will never again go out, outside'). For those used to fleeing from the city into the countryside, because of the constant threat of earthquakes, the promise of a lasting existence in the new Jerusalem would have been very appealing.

Walker, *Holy City* 263–64, finds in this part of the verse possible support for the apostolic authorship of John's Apocalypse. The writer speaks with authority as one who, once privileged to have been in Jerusalem and now away from it, does not wish his audience to 'feel underprivileged through their distance from Jerusalem' (263). All the treasures of the holy city will eventually come to *them* (ibid.).

'The temple', in this context, does not refer to the Jewish Temple or the Christian Church, the new Israel, but to the heavenly temple, the dwelling-place of God with his eschatological people (cf. *1 Enoch* 90.28–29). See Aune 241. However, ultimately God himself is the temple (Rev. 21.22); and if the conquerors have become 'pillars' in this temple, they have become eternally united with him (cf. Charles 1, 91). Christ speaks of the temple of '*my* God' (ἐν τῷ ναῷ τοῦ θεοῦ μου, *en tō[i] naō[i] tou theou mou*); and the expression 'my God' is used in the Apocalypse only in this verse (four times) and at 3.2 (q.v.). The addition of the personal pronoun emphasizes the intimate relationship which exists between the Son and the Father (even if they are not presented as such), as well as between the Godhead and the Church (cf. Rev. 1.1, 17–18; 2.8; et al.). For John's balanced Christology, in Revelation and the Fourth Gospel, see Smalley, *Thunder and Love* 60–62, 129–31, 152.

Several sources are possible for the imagery of the 'pillar' in God's temple. Kiddle (53–54) refers to the practice of the imperial cultic priest, who at the end of his period of office erected his statue in the temple, and inscribed on it his name. But a sculpture is hardly synonymous with a pillar; and Hemer (*Letters* 166) points out that there is no evidence for this precise custom, and also that no provincial temple of the imperial cult existed in Philadelphia until about AD 213. Other sources for the metaphor could be the two pillars in the temple of Solomon, which carried the personal names of Jachin and Boaz (1 Kings 7.15–22, esp. 21), or the ceremonial 'king's pillar' in Solomon's temple (2 Kings 11.14; 23.3). See Aune 241–42.

However, the most likely background to the use of this imagery is the oracle of Isa. 22.15–25, to which allusion has already been made in verse 7. In the Isaianic passage, Eliakim is informed that he will not only carry the key of the house of David, but that he will also become 'like a peg in a secure place . . . a throne of honour to his ancestral house' (Isa. 22.23). Nevertheless, the prediction is that, in the end, the peg will give way, and the house will fall (verse 25). By contrast, the faithful at Philadelphia, who were well aware of the possibility through earthquakes of crumbling edifices, are promised that they will become not pegs in a wall, but sturdy pillars in God's temple, at one with him through Christ for ever. Cf. Beasley-Murray 101–102.

The exalted Jesus promises to write on the conqueror 'the name of my God'. It is not clear from the Greek whether the 'name' is to be written on the 'pillar', or on the 'overcomer'; for ἐπ'αὐτόν (*ep auton*) can refer to either. But since the conqueror has already been identified with the temple pillar, and therefore permanently with the name of God (his personal nature; see on verse 8) himself, we are probably correct to translate ἐπ'αὐτόν (*ep auton*) here as 'on that person'. For 'my God' see on verse 12*a*. Not only do the faithful belong inescapably to God. They are also, second, closely related to the name of God's city, the new Jerusalem, 'which descends out of heaven from (my) God'. The language here recalls Ezek. 48.35 (cf. Isa. 60.14; 1 Macc. 14.26–49; Rev. 3.9). For 'new Jerusalem', as a symbol for the intimate covenant fellowship which God shares with his people in the new creation, see further on 21.2.

In Ezek. 48.35 'the name of the city' (of the new Jerusalem) is called 'the Lord is there'; for God has established his temple in its midst, and his glory will reside there for ever (note Ezek. 48.10). The thought in this verse is repeated at Rev. 21.2, where John introduces a vision of the divine city and temple at the end-time, and pictures God dwelling in a close relationship with his people, through Christ, for all eternity (21.3–4, 10–11). It also connects with the concept of 'sealing' the faithful, for spiritual protection and preservation, in 7.2–9, which in turn is reflected in the vision of the new Jerusalem at 21.12 (q.v.). Note also the concept of faithful conquerors, persevering through an ordeal and then being rewarded with the presence of God and of Christ, at Rev. 7.14–17 (q.v.). As Beale (294) points out, the identification of believers with the 'temple' (the divine presence) in the present verse, is the gathering up of the process which begins with Christ unlocking the doors of the 'invisible sanctuary of salvation' in 3.7–8.

Walker, *Holy City* 241–42, finds it significant that the first reference to 'Jerusalem' and its 'temple' in Revelation should appear in a context where John distinguishes sharply between Christians (Jewish or Gentile) and non-Christian Jews, and where the author also claims (3.9) that the latter will have to acknowledge the vindication of the former. Walker concludes that these verses 'have a polemical ring to them' (242), and argues that this note persists when the vision of the new Jerusalem is presented at the end (Rev. 21—22).

The city of the new Jerusalem, as at 21.2, 'descends out of heaven'. John's cosmology, like his Christology and eschatology, is balanced. The drama of the Apocalypse, as of John's Gospel, is played out on two levels at once; for, in the Word made flesh, heaven and earth are finally and fully drawn together. God's holy city is in touch with the material world, the theatre of his salvific purposes in Christ; but the faithful also 'ascend' to the heavenly sanctuary, to dwell with the Lord for ever (cf. Rev. 21.2, 22–26). So the 'city', like the 'temple', is used by John as a symbol for the presence of God, and for the potential which the believer has to abide in him, through Jesus, for ever.

The term πόλις (*polis*, 'city') is used here for the first time in Revelation. The image of the heavenly city, here and elsewhere in the Apocalypse, notably in Rev. 21 and 22, is significant (cf. Rev. 11.2; 20.9; 21.2, 10, 14–16, 18–19, 21, 23; 22.14, 19). Cities are creations of people, not of God, with whom gardens are more naturally associated (cf. the garden of Eden, in Gen. 2 and 3). But the city which provides the setting for the Church triumphant is no ordinary city; see further on Rev. 21.15–17, where the measurements of the new Jerusalem are given.

The exalted Lord promises the conqueror identification with the name (or nature) of his God, and of the city (or presence) of his Father. The overcomer is also promised, third, association with Christ's 'own new name'. The appearance of these promises in a triplet, each section of which uses the term ὄνομα (*onoma*, 'name'), is characteristic of John's style in the Apocalypse (cf. verse 7; also Resseguie, *Revelation Unsealed* 49–50). It is one name that is in view, with three characters: God, the covenant and Christ. See Ramsay, *Letters* 412.

By Christ's 'new name' (note the emphatic placing of the adjective: τὸ ὄνομά μου τὸ καινόν, *to onoma mou to kainon*, lit. 'my name, the new') cannot be meant a familiar primitive title of Jesus, such as 'Lord' or 'Son of God'. In that case, as Swete (58) points out, the Johannine ascription of Λόγος (*Logos*, 'Word') might well have been in mind. Cf. Rev. 19.12–13. At 3.12 the 'new name' of Christ is mentioned in parallel with the 'name' of God (his nature and purposes; see verse 8); and this is probably the ultimate significance of the hidden name of God's Messiah at 19.12 (q.v.) But Christ's name in this context also symbolizes the fuller revelation, of his being and salvific judgement, which awaits the final parousia (cf. 2.17). The victorious Christ and the conquering Christian will both appear in a new light, and with a new character (cf. Swete 58). Note Col. 3.4; 1 John 3.2; also Ignatius, *Philad.* 5. But those blessings are immediate, since the eschatological reference in this verse need not apply simply to the distant future. Cf. Smalley, *Thunder and Love* 150–52, 174–76.

Ramsay (*Letters* 409–12) reminds us that Philadelphia, alone among the seven cities, replaced its name with a name derived from the imperial religion: Neocaesarea, to honour Tiberius for his help with rebuilding the city after the great earthquake; and he finds a reference to this fact in the (new) names of verse 12. (Later, Philadelphia adopted the further name of Flavia, the family name of Vespasian.) But the allusion, if present, hardly adds to the interpretation and understanding of this verse (cf. Mounce 105).

13 For the exhortation see on Rev. 2.7. The proclamation to Philadelphia is for all seven of the churches in Asia, and ultimately for the whole Church of God.

Laodicea (3.14–22)

14 The city of Laodicea (modern Eskihisar, 'the old fortress') was founded by Antiochus II (261–246 BC), who named it after his wife Laodice. It was situated in the Lycus valley, in south-west Phrygia, at the junction of two important trade routes (according to Ramsay, *Letters* 416, Laodicea was a 'knot on the road-system'). One route led east from Ephesus and the Aegean, along the river Maeander to the Anatolian plateau; the other went south from Pergamum, the provincial capital, to the Mediterranean at Attaleia. Along the southern route lay in order five of the seven cities addressed in Rev. 2—3: Pergamum, Thyatira, Sardis, Philadelphia and Laodicea itself. Close by were located the cities of Hierapolis, to the north (cf. Col. 4.13), and Colossae, to the south (cf. Col. 1.2). Laodicea was built on a high plateau, about two miles south of the river Lycus. The city is mentioned in the New Testament on four occasions (Col. 2.1; 4.13, 15, 16). See further Hemer, *Letters* 178–82.

Laodicea was a wealthy city; and in the time of the Roman Empire, indeed, it was financially the wealthiest in Phrygia. Strabo (*Geography* 12.16) claims that the fertility of its territory and the prosperity of some of its citizens made the city great. He adds that the surrounding countryside produced excellent sheep, and that the Laodiceans derived splendid revenue from the soft, raven-black wool of their flocks, used in their flourishing textile industry. Banking, related to the city's commercial and agricultural prosperity, was a feature of life in Laodicea. We also know from Tacitus (*Ann.* 14.27.1) that, after a serious earthquake in AD 607, the city was rebuilt from its own wealth, and without financial assistance from Rome.

The city of Laodicea was also famous for its medical school, which was related to the nearby temple and cult of Mēn Carus, 13 miles away. Mēn was an ancient and local god of healing, who was later identified with Asclepios. Ramsay (*Letters* 419) points out that the Laodicean school of physicians followed the teaching of Herophilos (330–250 BC) who, believing that compound diseases require compound medicines, created strange systems of heterogeneous mixtures: including ointment for the ears, and an eye-salve made from powder mixed with oil.

It is likely that Laodicea had a large Jewish population (Ramsay, *Letters* 420–22), and this possibly included an important body of citizens. But, in the view of Hemer (*Letters* 182), the evidence is 'mostly indirect and inferential'. See ibid. 182–84.

Laodicea suffered from a lack of natural resources, especially water. This had to be brought to the city from springs near Denizli, six miles to the south, through a system of stone pipes. This aqueduct could easily become isolated, particularly in the dry season when the river Lycus might evaporate; and the city would then be left in a parlous state. For this section see Mounce 106–108.

For the opening literary formula in verse 14 see on Rev. 2.1, et al. Since this is the last letter in the septet of oracles to the churches in Asia, the translation of the introductory word καί (*kai*, lit. 'and') can bear the meaning 'finally'. The words in this message are spoken by the risen Christ, to whom are now applied three leading and interlocking christological titles. As in the previous letter, there is unusually no direct connection with the vision of the exalted Son of man in Rev. 1.12–18 (see on Rev. 2.1; cf. 2.8, 12, 18; 3.1). The titles in question are: (a) the Amen; (b) the faithful and true witness; (c) the origin of God's creation.

(a) The titular, as opposed to liturgical, use of 'Amen' is unusual, and occurs only here in the New Testament. Note the inclusion of the article, ὁ (*ho*, 'the'). It is most unlikely, therefore, that the term has been drawn in at this point to serve as an appropriate liturgical conclusion to the seven letters. Theologically, and more significantly, it probably recapitulates Isa. 65.16, which speaks of the need to bless and swear by 'the God of faithfulness' (NRSV), or the 'God of Amen', as in vg.; cf. Isa. 25.1. The LXX rendering is τὸν θεὸν τὸν ἀληθινόν (*ton theon ton alēthinon*, lit. 'the true God'; this translation rests on a different vocalizing of the Hebrew, from אָמוּן ['*ēmûn*, 'faithfulness'] to אֹמֶן ['*ōmen*, 'truth']). That such a description, 'Amen', only otherwise associated with God, should be applied to Jesus, is an indication of John's high (if balanced) Christology.

   In the Old Testament and Judaism אָמֵן (Greek ἀμήν, *amēn*, 'amen') means that which is 'sure and valid' (H. Schlier, 'ἀμήν' 336); it involves the acknowledgement of a word which is valid, and the validity of which is binding (ibid. 335). So, in this context, Jesus Christ is regarded as guaranteeing the truth of his message, just as God's sure character stands behind his word (Beasley-Murray 104).

(b) The significance of the 'Amen' title is further explicated by the phrase in apposition to it, 'the faithful and true witness' (ὁ μάρτυς ὁ πιστὸς καὶ ἀληθινός, *ho martys ho pistos kai alēthinos*; as we have seen from the LXX rendering of Isa. 65.16, and depending on the vocalization adopted, the Hebrew אמן ['*mn*, 'amen'] can mean both 'faithful' and 'true'). There is a close parallel to this description at Rev. 1.5 (q.v.), where Jesus Christ is referred to as ὁ μάρτυς ὁ πιστός (*ho martys ho pistos*, 'the faithful witness'). Only here and at 1.5 is the term 'witness' used of Jesus in the New Testament (but cf. Rom. 1.9, 'God is my witness'); see also Rev. 22.20, where the exalted Jesus speaks as the one who 'testifies to these truths' (ὁ μαρτυρῶν ταῦτα, *ho martyrōn tauta*). The testimony of Jesus takes place on earth *and* in heaven: he faithfully completes his earthly ministry and passion; *and*, as the supreme martyr for all time, he gives credence to the true witness of John the Divine. See further on Rev. 1.5.

Aune (255–56) finds in this phrase of verse 14 ('the faithful and true witness') an allusion to Ps. 89.37 (LXX 88.37), where the moon is described as 'an enduring witness in the skies' (cf. Job 16.19). For the combination, 'faithful and true', see Rev. 19.11 (of the Messiah); 21.5 and 22.6 (of John's prophetic message); 3 Macc. 2.11 (of God); cf. also Rev. 2.13 (of the faithful witness, Antipas).

(c) In the third description of the exalted Lord in this verse, Christ is denoted as 'the origin of God's creation' (ἡ ἀρχὴ τῆς κτίσεως τοῦ θεοῦ, *hē archē tēs ktiseōs tou theou*, lit. 'the beginning of the creation of God'). This account of Jesus is strongly reminiscent of Col. 1.15 (cf. 1.18), where Paul speaks of Christ as 'the firstborn (πρωτότοκος, *prōtotokos*) of all creation'. If Rev. 3.14 depends in any way on Col. 1.15, this may be due to the probability that the churches of Laodicea and Colossae exchanged letters (see Col. 4.16). It also supports the likelihood that there was some affinity between the Pauline and Johannine churches, and therefore between John and Paul theologically (cf. Smalley, 'Christ-Christian Relationship').

Verse 14 uses the term ἀρχή (*archē*, lit. 'beginning') of the exalted Christ; and in Col. 1.18 this is equated with πρωτότοκος, *prōtotokos*, 'firstborn') as in Col. 1.15 (cf. Rev. 1.5). The word ἀρχή (*archē*) can mean 'beginning' in a temporal or causal sense. In the Prologue to John's Gospel, the meaning is in the first place temporal: the Word was 'in the beginning with God' (John 1.1–2; cf. Prov. 8.22 LXX, of Wisdom). In early Christianity the term ἀρχή (*archē*) was similarly used as a title for Christ (cf. Justin, *Dial.* 61.1; 62.4). But already the temporal understanding is complemented by the causal. Cf. Theophilus, *Ad Autol.* 2.10 (*PG* 6, cols 1063–64), Jesus is the beginning, because he 'leads and rules' everything; also Clement Alex., *Strom.* 7.1; Origen, *Comm. in Joan.* 1.19; *PGL* 235 a–b. This understanding is in line with the thought of John 1, and indeed of Col. 1, where the Word shares pre-existently in creation (John 1.3–4), and Christ is the origin and destiny of all things (Col. 1.16–17). It may be concluded that while ἀρχή (*archē*) in Rev. 3.14 refers in the temporal sense to Christ's pre-existence (he is the 'beginning'), it goes on to include the notion of the Son sharing in the Father's creative handiwork (he is the 'origin' of God's creation). This is the justification for our translation. The expression 'beginning and end' (ἡ ἀρχὴ καὶ τὸ τέλος, *hē archē kai to telos*) is used of God in Rev. 21.6 (q.v.), and applied to the exalted Christ at 22.13 (cf. 1.8, 17).

Silberman ('Farewell') argues that all three titles of the exalted Christ in this passage reflect Jewish speculation on Prov. 8.22, 30 (14.5, 25) and Gen. 1.1, and that they are well known Old Testament epithets of wisdom. He is followed by Trudinger ('O AMHN'), who nevertheless does not agree with Silberman's conclusion that Revelation was originally a Semitic document (279). On this verse see further Aune 254–57. For the Old Testament setting of Christ's titles, as used in verse 14, cf. Beale 297–301; also Beale, 'Background of Rev 3.14'. He notes the influence of Isa. 43.10–12 and 65.15–16.

The titles themselves, as in the other six letters of Rev. 2—3, are related to the remainder of the message to Laodicea, and therefore to the life of the community. This church needed new life and power, and was spiritually at a lower ebb than any of the other Asian congregations. Even in the moribund circle at Sardis there was a faithful remnant. But no such group remains here; and there is no commendation, as there is with varying measure in all the other proclamations.

The Laodicean Christians are lukewarm, and they need to be spiritually renewed (verses 15–17). The Amen, the faithful and true witness, wants them to become zealous and committed (verses 18–20). Otherwise, judgement will follow (verse 16*b*). But if there is repentance (verse 19), discrimination can lead to salvation (a perpetual Johannine theme), and the conquerors will receive a reward and become part of Christ's new creation (verse 21). The exalted Christ stands at the door, waiting for a faithful response (verse 20). See Beale 301–302.

15–16   For the sentence, 'I know what you are doing' (τὰ ἔργα, *ta erga*, lit. 'your works') see on Rev. 2.2, 19; 3.1, 8. Such an introduction to the body of the letter is by now familiar. As Jesus in the Fourth Gospel 'knows' about people, and their consciences (cf. John 2.24–25; 4.29; et al.), so the exalted Christ sees into the hearts of the Johannine adherents and discerns their consequent behaviour.

In the case of the Laodicean community, Christ 'knows' that its members are neither cold nor hot (οὔτε ψυχρὸς εἶ οὔτε ζεστός, *oute psychros ei oute zestos*), but 'lukewarm' (χλιαρός, *chliaros*). As a result, he is on the point of 'vomiting' them out of his mouth. The three pairs, 'cold and hot', which appear in semi-chiasmic form (AB/AB/BA), are figures of speech corresponding to attitudes of hostility and friendliness towards the risen Lord. In the wisdom literature of the Old Testament the images of 'cold' and 'hot' relate to personal restraint or lack of self-control respectively (cf. Prov. 17.27; 15.18). Here the imagery is apparently indicative of the spiritual temperature of the Laodiceans: they were neither 'against' Christ nor 'for' him; and the precise expression of their lukewarmness is detailed in verses 17 and 18.

The metaphorical language in this passage has often been attributed to the local situation. Six miles north of Laodicea, across the Lycus, was the city of Hierapolis, famous for its hot springs. The mineral-laden water from these flowed across the plateau, becoming nauseously lukewarm, and cascaded over the cliff right opposite Laodicea. So Swete 60–61.

However, Rudwick and Green, 'Lukewarmness', have argued that the adjectives in these two verses, 'cold', 'hot' and 'lukewarm', are not to be interpreted in terms of the spiritual temperature of the Laodicean Christians. In their view, the contrast is rather between the hot, medicinal waters of the city of Hierapolis to the north and the cold, pure waters of Colossae to the south. So the community at Laodicea was 'totally ineffective' (178). It was distasteful to the Lord, because it was providing neither healing for the spiritually sick (hot) nor refreshment for the spiritually weary (cold). In other words, this congregation is being chastised for the barrenness of its works, rather than for the nature of its commitment: although it has to be said that the two (praxis and faith) are inextricably related. One advantage of this exegesis is that it overcomes the obvious problem involved in Christ seeming to prefer a church to be 'cold' rather than 'lukewarm': 'would that (ὄφελον, *ophelon*) you were either cold or hot!' For ὄφελον (*ophelon*, 'would that') in a wish see BDF 359 (1).

The imagery of Christ being on the point of 'vomiting' the lukewarm Laodiceans out of his mouth (μέλλω σε ἐμέσαι ἐκ τοῦ στόματός μου, *mellō se emesai ek tou stomatos mou*, lit. 'I am about to vomit [or spit] you out of my mouth') is vivid, and evokes the emetic effect of drinking lukewarm water. To soften the expression, the MS 2329 reads ἐλέγχω σε ἐκ (*elenchō se ek*, 'I refute you out of . . .'). But the meaning is the same, since 'vomiting' implies rejection. Despite the threatened judgement, repentance is still possible (verses 18–20). As ever, condemnation can lead to commendation (see verse 21). On verses 15–16 see further Hemer, *Letters* 186–91.

17   The real state of the Laodiceans is now explained in detail. The material wealth of the city is well known (see above, 95–96). But this community was claiming to be spiritually rich as well. The members of John's congregation wrongly thought they possessed real affluence of all kinds, because they had amassed a fortune and become self-sufficient. The repeated use of the first person pronoun, 'I', underlines the arrogance of the assumption by individual believers. Their complacency is reminiscent of the rich farmer in the parable of Jesus (Luke 12.16–21). The claim, 'I am rich, I have made my fortune', also reminds us of Ephraim's exclamation, 'I am rich, I have gained wealth for myself', in Hos. 12.8; to this outburst the prophet replies, 'Ephraim has given bitter offence, so his Lord will pay him back for his insults' (verse 14).

The situation of the Laodiceans is in fact deeply ironic. Those who thought that they had all they needed are shown to be spiritually bankrupt. *They* (the pronoun in the Greek, σύ, *sy*, lit. 'you', is emphatic) have collectively become a 'pitiful wretch'. This expression translates two Greek adjectives, ταλαίπωρος (*talaipōros*, 'wretched') and ἐλεεινός (*eleeinos*, 'pitiful'). The former is used in the New Testament only here and at Rom. 7.24.

Three further adjectives are used to describe the condition of this church. The Laodicean community is also said to be 'poor, blind and naked' (πτωχὸς καὶ τυφλὸς καὶ γυμνός, *ptōchos kai typhlos kai gymnos*, lit. 'poor and blind and naked'). One article (ὁ, *ho*, lit. 'the'), hidden in the translation, governs all five epithets; and this demonstrates that five aspects of the same condition are being presented here. The final three adjectives almost certainly contain allusions to the city's local scene (cf. verse 18). Despite its financial wealth, it is 'poor'; despite its medical school and famous eye-salve, it is 'blind'; and, in the face of its flourishing textile industry, it is 'naked' (cf. Beasley-Murray 106; also above, 95–96).

18   The ironic tone of verse 17 is continued in this verse. Grammatically the two verses belong together, although they are separated in the translation. The force of the language is as follows: *because* (ὅτι, *hoti*) you say . . . (17), therefore (not in the Greek) I advise you . . .' (18). The self-satisfied Laodiceans are advised to obtain important spiritual resources for precisely those areas in which they assume no need exists (Mounce 111). The purchases are to be made specifically from the risen Christ (παρ' ἐμοῦ, *par' emou*, 'from me'), who alone can provide them. First, they are encouraged to buy 'gold refined in the fire': that is to say, they need spiritual wealth, which has been tested in the fire of the refiner and found to be trustworthy, as opposed to their financial and complacent state of well-being. For the idea of purity being attained by removing dross see Ps. 66.10; Isa. 1.25. The same image is used at 1 Pet. 1.7 (q.v.) to depict the genuineness of faith. Clearly the language of these injunctions is metaphorical. The thought is therefore paradoxical, for only in a figurative sense can the poor buy gold. Cf. Isa. 55.1–2 ('you that have no money, come, buy and eat'); also, for the use of ἀγοράζειν (*agorazein*, 'to purchase') in this metaphorical manner, see Matt. 25.9–10.

Second, the Laodiceans are exhorted to purchase 'white robes' to wrap around them and to protect them from spiritual nakedness. For 'white robes' see on Rev. 3.4–5. Only here in the Apocalypse are such garments referred to in a natural sense; although the context is still figurative, and the robes symbolize righteousness (as in Rev. 4.4; et al.). The white colouring of the garments in question can be contrasted with the black fabrics manufactured by the Laodiceans in their prosperous textile industry (see above, 95; so Swete 62, against Mounce 111). Nakedness in biblical thought is symbolic of judgement and humiliation (Isa. 20.1–4; cf. 2 Sam. 10.4; Mark 15.20; John 19.23–24); while the reception of fine clothing is a mark of vindication and honour (cf. Gen. 41.42; Esth. 6.6–11).

The third purchase enjoined upon this community is salve for the anointing of their eyes, for they are spiritually blind. Once again the local situation is reflected in this reference to eye-salve. The famous school of medicine at Laodicea, where the ophthalmologist Alexander Philalethes practised (Strabo, *Geography* 12.8.20), exported a powder which was extensively used to make ointment for the eyes (see further Ramsay, *Letters* 419, 429; Hemer, *Letters* 196–99). The Greek word κολλ(ο)ύριον (*koll[o]yrion*, 'salve', Latin *collyrium*) is the diminutive of κολλούρα (*kolloura*), which perhaps means a roll or loaf of bread. The 'Phrygian' powder seems to have been applied to the eyes as a 'doughy paste' (so Mounce 111 n. 33). Horace (*Satires* 1.5.30–31) speaks of putting black ointment (*collyrium*) on his 'sore eyes' during a journey to Brundisium.

The negative connotations of the last three adjectives in verse 17*b* ('poor, blind and naked') are balanced in the present verse by three positive exhortations, although the order of the second and third commands, in relation to the epithets in verse 17, is reversed. Each exhortation, giving the reasons for the 'purchase' of a gift from Christ, is set out in a purpose clause, using ἵνα (*hina*, 'that') with the subjunctive. The Laodicean Christians are to buy genuine wealth (gold) to become truly rich, white robes to cover their humiliation with honour, and salve to regain their spiritual perception.

The symbolic significance of the substantives (gold, garments and eye-salve) need not be pressed (so Beckwith 491). The overall meaning is that great spiritual inadequacy in this community is to be redressed by gifts from God through Christ. However, the reference to spiritual perception is characteristically Johannine, since the language of seeing (as of hearing) in John's corpus is very important. The writer wants his audience to 'see' who Jesus really is, and to respond to his true identity as being both one with God *and* one with us (cf. Rev. 1.11; 22.4; John 9.39; 20.29; 1 John 3.2; also Rev. 22.17, 18; John 5.24; 8.47; 1 John 1.1, 3).

19   The tone of this oracle now changes abruptly. The risen Christ assures the Laodicean church that the severe rebuke which he has just administered stems from his love. The intention is to summon the believers as a whole (verse 19) and individually (verse 20) to repentance and renewed faith.

The first clause ('I punish and discipline those whom I love') is loosely drawn from Prov. 3.12, which is quoted almost verbatim from the LXX in Heb. 12.6 (cf. *Pss. Sol.* 10.2; *1 Clem.* 56.4). Here the 'Lord' of Prov. 3.12 is understood to be the exalted Christ, and the proverb is made his own. It is introduced by the emphatic pronoun, ἐγώ (*egō*, 'I'). The theme of 'educative discipline' (Aune 260) is common in wisdom literature, where the need to chasten one's children out of care for them (Prov. 13.24; et al.; Philo, *Quod Det.* 145[39]) is applied to the relationship between God and his people (Prov. 3.11–12; cf. Deut. 8.5; Job 5.17–18; Ps. 94.12–13; *Pss. Sol.* 10.1–3; 14.1; Philo, *Quod Det.* 146[40]).

The use of the verb φιλῶ (*philō*, 'I love') in this text is remarkable. There is probably no great difference in meaning between this word and the other verb in the New Testament meaning 'to love' (ἀγαπᾶν, *agapan*), which is used in the LXX of Prov. 3.12, quoted here. But elsewhere in Revelation (see 1.5; 3.9) the verb used of Christ's love for people is precisely ἀγαπᾶν (*agapan*); and the same verb is employed in the LXX and the New Testament (except at John 16.27) of God's love for us. (However, at John 11.3, 36 and 20.2, φιλεῖν [*philein*, 'to love'] is used of the affection of Jesus for Lazarus and the beloved disciple.) Charles (1, 99) regards the use of what he calls the exceptional and 'emotional' verb φιλεῖν (*philein*, 'to love') in this context as a 'touching and unexpected manifestation of love to those who deserve it least' among the seven Asiatic congregations (ibid.). But this may be reading too much into the Greek language at this point.

The conjunction ἐάν (*ean*, lit. 'if') has been left untranslated. Its sense in the present text approaches that of ὅταν (*hotan*, 'whenever'); see AG 210. The two verbs ἐλέγχω καὶ παιδεύω (*elenchō kai paideuō*, 'I punish and discipline') represent two stages in the one process. The negative aspects of the believers' chastisement are balanced by the positive intention of educative discipline on the part of Christ. For ἐλέγχειν (*elenchein*, 'to punish' or 'to convict') see John 3.20; 8.46; 16.8; cf. also Eph. 5.13; 2 Tim. 4.2. Note Büchsel, 'ἐλέγχω' 474, who states that the verb means 'to convict of sin', and that it includes the idea of 'summoning to repentance'. The choice of the verb παιδεύω (*paideuō*, 'I discipline') is probably influenced by its appearance in the LXX of Prov. 3.11, the verse which precedes the one alluded to in this passage (so Swete 63). For the meaning of this verb in the New Testament see further Bertram, 'παιδεύω, κτλ' 619–25, esp. 623 (in Rev. 3.19 it includes the thought of 'rousing' or 'stirring').

The Laodicean community is urged, in view of Christ's warning, to 'be in earnest, and repent'. Its lukewarm spiritual character is to be replaced by a genuine enthusiasm for the faith (ζήλευε, *zēleue*, 'be in earnest'); and its members are to 'think again' about their present condition, and actively renew the character and moral praxis of their Christian lives. (The literal meaning of μετανόησον [*metanoēson*, 'repent'] is to 'change the mind'; cf. Rev. 2.5; 3.3).

The threat of judgement on the community and the summons to repentance are inseparable from Christ's love. They are followed (verse 20) by the promise of immediate table-fellowship. The balanced theme of salvation through judgement, here and in all parts of the Johannine corpus, is characteristic and constant.

20 This verse, addressed now to the individual believers who belong to the church at Laodicea, opens with a metaphorical epiphany motif (Aune 260). We hear the voice of a friend (verse 19), who stands at the threshold of people's lives, seeking admittance. The vision is intense, as it is brought before John's very eyes (Morris 83); note the commanding ἰδού (*idou*, 'see'), which introduces the manifestation. The tenses of the verbs in this sentence are significant. Jesus is 'standing' (ἕστηκα, *hestēka*, perfect, lit. 'I have stood') at the door; and this suggests that he has been there for some time. Meanwhile he 'knocks' (κρούω, *krouō*, present, 'I am knocking'); and this implies a repeated and gentle request for entry (against Caird 57, who speaks of an 'imperious hammering' on the door). Cf. Song of Sol. 5.2.

The risen Lord is pictured in this scene in an attitude of unexpected and vulnerable condescension (cf. Mounce 113). With those who had in their self-sufficiency excluded him from their fellowship, Christ waits for a personal relationship to be restored. Theologically, the presentation is in line with the prophetic view in Judaism of a God who seeks friendship with his wayward people, and holds out his hands to them continually in love despite their recalcitrance. Cf. Isa. 65.1–2; Hos. 2.16–23; 11.7–9; 1 Pet. 2.4–10.

A conditional clause follows, using ἐάν (*ean*, 'if') with the subjunctive. There is no certainty that a response to the voice will be made. We have heard the 'voice' (φωνή, *phonē*) of Jesus already in the Apocalypse, in the vision of the Son of man in glory at the very beginning of this scene (1.10, 12, 15). There, his powerful voice sounded like the roar of many waters. Here, by contrast, the voice of Christ is intimate, pleading and personal. Cf. John 10.3, 16; 18. 37*b*.

If the call of Christ is heeded, entrance will be made and close table-fellowship will follow (cf. John 14.23; 6.53–56). At this moment Jesus seems to be the guest rather than the host (contrast Luke 12.36–37). For 'entering a house', see Mark 9.28; also Acts 11.3. To share a common meal in the Middle East, then as now, is a sign of intimacy and trust. The meal suggested by the verb δειπνήσω (*deipnēsō*, 'I will share a meal') is the δεῖπνον (*deipnon*, 'meal' or 'supper'), which was the main repast at the end of the day, and a principal occasion for hospitality. As such, it was a leisurely and not a hurried affair (cf. John 14.23). See Swete 64; Morris 83.

Three main interpretations of this dramatic scene, where the exalted Jesus enters through the open door and shares a meal, are possible.

(a) The reference may be eschatological, and speak of the return of Christ, either imminently (note 'I am standing at the door'; cf. Mounce 113) or in the future. So Swete 63–64; Beckwith 491; Kiddle 60; against Beasley-Murray 107. Cf. Charles 1, 101.

This accords with the eschatological atmosphere of the following verse (21), where the conqueror is promised a place beside the exalted Christ on his final throne of triumph. It also echoes fairly directly the parable of Luke 12.35–38, in which the faithful are depicted as 'opening the door' to their master, returning from the wedding banquet, 'as soon as he comes and knocks' (verse 36). However, if the scope of verse 20 is eschatological, the parousia of Jesus in question is likely to be immediate, rather than distantly future (note the tenses of the verbs translated as 'I am standing' and 'knocking'; see above, 101), although John's eschatology is consistently balanced, and the present advent of Christ to his Church always anticipates his final return in glory (see on 22.7, 12); cf. also Rev. 2.5, 16; 3.3).

(b) Alternatively, this verse may be linked with verse 19, and construed in association with the call to repentance issued there. That summons to think again, in other words, is implemented when the audience individually responds to the invitation to 'open the door'; and it provides the motivation for such a reaction. So Beasley-Murray 107; Mounce 113–14, Beale 308–309. If this interpretation be followed, the primary reference of the verse is both present and personal, not future and eschatological. Nevertheless, in Johannine thought, the one need not exclude the other.

(c) In either case, allusions to the eucharist may be present (cf. Swete 64; and esp. Caird 58: John here uses language 'resonant with eucharistic associations to describe a coming of the Lord' which is intimate and personal). The common meal in Judaeo-Christian thought, like the 'banquet', was symbolic of the intimacy to be enjoyed in the future messianic kingdom (cf. *1 Enoch* 62.14: Isa. 25.6; 55.1–3; Luke 22.30; Matt. 26.29; Rev. 19.9). See further Link, 'Blessing, et al.' 210. The eucharistic setting of this verse may also be suggested by the use of the verb δειπνέω (*deipneō*, lit. 'eat', 'dine'). The same verb, and its cognate noun (δεῖπνον, *deipnon*, 'meal' or 'supper'), appears elsewhere in the New Testament in the context of the Last Supper (Luke 22.20; John 13.2, 4: 21.20) and of the Lord's Supper (1 Cor. 11.20, 21, 25). Cf. John 6.35, 52–58; Rev. 19.17. Beasley-Murray (107) argues that the similarity of thought and language here, to that which is used in connection with the Lord's Supper, is due 'less to direct reminiscence of the Supper than to the event to which the Supper itself looks forward' (see Mark 14.25; Luke 22.28–30). Nevertheless, it is hard to exclude from the exegesis of this verse all reference to the eucharist, even if John's theology is ultimately more concerned with the sacramental, than with the sacraments themselves. See Smalley, *John* 232–38, esp. 235–37; *Thunder and Love* 58–60.

The primary thought in this verse is of the restoration of fellowship in the present between the exalted Christ and the Laodicean believers (Wall 87). But it is possible that all the other allusions and associations, to which attention has been drawn, are present as well; and we have already noticed the way in which John's eschatology, like his theology generally, overlaps. There *is* a reference to the appearance of Christ, in the present as well as in the future; personal response to the attendant Lord *is* undertaken as a result of his demand for repentance; and eucharistic resonances *do* surround the promise that present fellowship is an anticipation of eternal blessedness.

21   The risen Christ has issued promises to 'the conqueror' (here ὁ νικῶν, *ho nikōn*) towards the end of each preceding oracle. Now the title is explained with reference to the Lord's own conquest, and in terms of possible Christian martyrdom.

Jesus is victorious because, in his cross and exaltation, he has overcome sin and death. His conquest is also the Father's. As a result the saints and martyrs, who have themselves been faithful even to death, are able to share in that double victory. They can participate with God in Christ in his sovereign rule (his 'throne').

Swete (64) points out that the parallelism is not exact, since the rewards of victory are not the same in the case of Christ and the disciples. The martyrs, Swete argues, share *Christ's* rule, while the Lord participates in the *Father's* throne. However, this is to divide untheologically the person and work of the Son from the being of the Father, with whom he is one. The kingly rule shared by the martyrs is exercised by the Godhead as a whole: including the Spirit.

In verse 20 (q.v.) the coming of Christ is in the immediate present. He invites the believer to share his life with him now. By contrast, the promise in this verse relates emphatically to the future. The faithful martyrs, in Laodicea and elsewhere, are promised that they will in the end become part of Christ's triumphant kingdom. In both contexts the language is highly symbolic. Cf. Beasley-Murray 107.

The promise to the conqueror here relates in the first place to the millennial kingdom. Its fulfilment is enacted in the seer's vision at Rev. 20.4–6, where the martyrs are seated on thrones of judgement, and rule with Christ for a thousand years. Cf. Matt. 19.28 = Luke 22.30; also *1 Enoch* 45.3 (of the Elect One); 108.12 (of those who love God); Mark 10.40; 2 Tim. 2.11–12. But the reign of the saints and martyrs is not limited to the millennium. That future period of time anticipates the possibilities of the everlasting kingdom of God, when the faithful will reign with him for ever and ever (Rev. 22.5). Cf. Charles 1, 102.

Charles 1, 101 regards this verse as 'wholly eschatological'. But while the reference is clearly to the future (see above), what takes place in eternity cannot be completely detached from Christian faith and praxis, on the part of the Laodicean community, in the present. For John's balanced eschatology see further Smalley, *Thunder and Love* 150–52.

The use of ὁ νικῶν . . . αὐτῷ (*ho nikōn . . . autō[i]*, lit. 'the one who conquers . . . to that one [I will give]') is a Hebraism. So is the use of δώσω (*dōsō*, 'I will give'), followed by the (aorist) infinitive καθίσαι (*kathisai*, 'to sit'). See 2.7.

For ὡς κἀγὼ ἐνίκησα (*hōs kagō enikēsa*, 'just as I have conquered') see John 16.33 (ἐγὼ νενίκηκα τὸν κόσμον, *egō nenikēka ton kosmon*, 'I have conquered the world'); also 1 John 5.4. In the present verse, ἐνίκησα (*enikēsa*, 'I have conquered') is a historical aorist, looking back to Christ's victory as past and complete. At John 16.33, the verb νενίκηκα (*nenikēka*, 'I have conquered'), in the perfect tense, regards that victory as continuing in its effects. See Swete 64. The verb ἐκάθισα (*ekathisa*, 'I sat down') is another historical aorist. Christ's conquest was accomplished by the resurrection, while his heavenly session (he 'sat down beside [his] Father on his throne') followed at the moment of the ascension (cf. Eph. 1.20; Heb. 1.3; 12.2).

The seventh letter draws to its close with a crowning promise. Such is the love of the Son of man (verse 19) that the faithful are now able to share fully in the life and victory and authority of God himself. Throughout the apocalyptic visions which follow, the nature of the divine victory becomes clear. In the ongoing struggle between good and evil, no other victory is needed than that which is won by the cross of Christ, 'faithfully proclaimed to the world in the . . . witness of his Church' (Caird 58).

22 For the seventh and last time we hear the exhortation to 'listen to what the Spirit is saying to the churches'. The messages to the seven Johannine churches of Asia were addressed to historical Christian communities in the first century AD. But they provide challenge and encouragement to the universal Church for all time. For the literary formula itself, in this verse, see on 2.7.

Theology

This first complete scene in Act 1 of the drama of Revelation is introduced by the vision of 1.9–20. Theologically, the section contains a typically Johannine balance between what takes place in heaven (1.9–20), and what is acted out on earth (Rev. 2—3, the oracles to the seven churches of Asia). But the opening vision includes historical references to Patmos and the local Johannine communities; just as the seven messages issue from the risen Christ, who is described in terms which recapitulate his divine appearance in Chapter 1. Such balance was suited to the christological needs of John's congregations (see above, 4–6).

Evidently the prophet-seer knows personally all seven Asian churches in his circle. He cares for them because of their strengths, and despite their weaknesses. Thus, some communities are affirmed in their faith, while others are rebuked for their lack of appropriate belief and behaviour (see below). The members of this group are not addressed individually, although particular individuals are occasionally in view (as at Rev. 2.13, 15). The exalted Lord speaks rather to John's adherents as those who belong to witnessing communities, which sometimes produce martyrs (cf. 2.13; 3.21); and, through them, he challenges and encourages the Church eschatologically, as well as for all time.

Four major theological themes run through this scene (cf. Boring 91–97).

(a) *Judgement*, and the consequent need for repentance. All the churches except Smyrna and Philadelphia are summoned to think again. Some (Ephesus, Thyatira, Philadelphia) are commended for the way they have behaved in situations of crisis; others (Pergamum, Sardis, Laodicea) are reproved for their inadequate faith and feeble Christian praxis. Without constant repentance, judgement follows (2.5, 16, 21–23; 3.3, 19).

(b) *Love*, which is the counterpart of judgement, and indeed the eventual means of humanity's salvation. The church at Ephesus is reminded of its former love (2.4–5), and the Thyatiran community is praised for its growing spiritual fruit of love, as well as for its faith (2.19). In both cases the love in question is expressed in action: through 'works' (2.5) and 'ministry' (2.19); and that is a standing demand for Christian living.

(c) *Conflict*. This is a rich theological theme (see on 1.9 and 2.9). The Church, and not merely the Johannine circle, is called to witness faithfully to Jesus Christ in the midst of a hostile world of imperial harassment. In the seven oracles it is anticipated that this hostility will develop into a fierce persecution (2.10; 3.10; cf. 7.14). This will point forward to the end; but it has already begun (note 1.9).

John's community is also placed in an environment of conflicting religious pluralism: under attack from the Jewish synagogue (2.9; 3.9), and likely to be seduced by distorted pagan beliefs (2.6, 15). As a result, further spiritual conflict exists within the congregations themselves, the members of which are divided in their theological, and especially christological, opinions (see above, 4–5).

These conflicts, apparent on earth, reflect a deeper conflict between good and evil which is being waged in heaven. The forces of evil, in the *persona* of the Satan, are at work in the synagogues of Asia (2.9; 3.9) and in the exercise of Roman authority (2.10, 13). More positively, the power of God is effective, and the Spirit speaks, in the Asian congregations (2.7, 23; 3.8; et al.). The cosmic battle between God and Satan is being experienced already in the life of the Johannine community. It will be projected on to a larger screen, and with an eternal perspective, from Chapter 4 onwards; but it is presupposed in the immediate messages to the seven churches in Rev. 2—3. See further Boring 91–92.

(d) The need for *steadfastness* stems from the situation of conflict. The Greek word translated 'steadfastness' is ὑπομονή (*hypomonē*) meaning 'standing one's ground', especially in tribulation or conflict (so Matt. 10.22 = 24.13 = Mark 13.13). The term implies an active stance of remaining firm, enduring patiently, for the sake of Christ's name (cf. Rev. 2.3, 13; 3.8) rather than resigning passively. It includes what Fiorenza calls 'consistent resistance' to the oppressive power of Rome (*Book of Revelation* 4). The Asian congregations of Ephesus, Thyatira and Philadelphia are commended for demonstrating this quality in their Christian life and witness (2.2, 3, 19; 3.10). But spiritual steadfastness can be costly. At Pergamum, holding fast to the cause of Christ resulted in the martyrdom of Antipas.

Thompson (86–87) groups the seven churches of Asia into three pairs (with one congregation remaining by itself), according to their Christian response. Smyrna and Philadelphia are praised without qualification; Sardis and Laodicea are both assessed negatively; while Pergamum and Thyatira can be placed somewhere between those two contrasting pairs, in that they are made up of members who are both worthy *and* ready to compromise their faith. Ephesus stands apart, since it receives almost unqualified praise (note the qualification in 2.4, the community had 'given up' its 'initial love'). Cf. also Sweet 44–45, who sees connections between the messages to the seven churches, and links their themes (especially in the case of the first four) to the material in the remainder of the apocalyptic drama.

The central concerns of the letters as a body are complacency and compromise, and the need to repent (Sweet 45). Together, the oracles provide a serious warning, relevant to the contemporary Church, about the dangers of ceasing to love (Ephesus), fear of conflict (Smyrna), doctrinal compromise (Pergamum), ethical compromise (Thyatira), spiritual lifelessness (Sardis), the failure to remain steadfast (Philadelphia) and lukewarmness (Laodicea). See Mounce 115.

But the exalted Lord also speaks to the angels of the churches where Christian faith and good practice are to be found with commendation and encouragement. Moreover, the seven letters contain more than moral instruction. There is a theological undergirding to them (see also above, 47). The Lord of the Church is sovereign (cf. Rev. 1.17–18). Through a balanced faith in him, as one with God and one with humanity, ethical behaviour (not always characteristic of the Asian communities) becomes possible.

The theme of divine sovereignty and Christian responsibility appears at the end of this scene, in the closing words of the address to the Laodiceans (3.21, q.v.); and it anticipates the next section of the Apocalypse. God is sovereign, and rules from the throne. Here is an evocation of the vision of the throne room in Chapter 4. Christ shares that throne, after his death and exaltation, with God in the present. Rev. 5, with its powerful imagery, will explicate this teaching. Christian believers are meanwhile called to the responsibility of sharing the sovereign relationship of the Father and the Son through spiritual death and resurrection in Jesus, and if need be through martyrdom. Cf. Boring 97.

INTERVAL
Adoration in Heaven's Court:
God and His Christ
(4.1—5.14)

Translation

4 ¹After this I looked, and there in heaven a door was standing open! And the voice, which I had previously heard speaking^a to me in trumpet tones, said,^b 'Come up here, and I will reveal to you what must take place later on.' ²At once, I found myself in the Spirit; and there, in heaven, was standing a throne with someone seated on it! ³And the seated figure is like jasper stone and carnelian in appearance; and encircling the throne is a rainbow, bright as beryl. ⁴All round the throne are twenty-four other thrones; and on these sit twenty-four elders, robed in white garments, with gold crowns on their heads. ⁵Coming from the throne are flashes of lightning, and roarings and peals of thunder; and in front of the throne burn seven blazing torches, which are the seven spirits of God. ⁶Also in front of the throne there appears to be a sea of glass, transparent as crystal.

At the heart of the throne, and around it, are four living creatures, with eyes all over, front and back: ⁷the first living creature is like a lion, the second like an ox, the third has a human face,^c and the fourth is like an eagle in flight. ⁸These four living creatures, each with six wings, have eyes all over, around and underneath. Day and night they do not cease to chant,

> 'Holy, holy, holy,
> the Lord God, the Omnipotent,
> who was, and is, and is to come.'

⁹And whenever the living creatures offer glory and reverence and thankfulness to the one who is seated on the throne, and lives eternally, ¹⁰the twenty-four elders prostrate themselves before the one who is sitting on the throne, worshipping him who is alive for ever and ever. They lay their crowns before the throne, crying,

> ¹¹'You are worthy, our Lord and God,
> to receive glory and reverence and power;
> for you created everything:
> through your will all things existed,^d and were created.'

5 ¹Then I saw on the right palm of the one seated on the throne a scroll, with writing inside and on the back,^e securely sealed with seven seals. ²Again, I saw a strong angel proclaiming in a loud voice, 'Who is worthy to open the scroll, and break its seals?' ³But no one, either in heaven or on earth or underneath the earth, was fit to open the scroll, or to look inside it. ⁴So I was weeping^f greatly, because no one could be found who was fit to open the scroll, or to look inside it. ⁵Then one of the elders said to me, 'Do not weep; see, the Lion from the tribe of Judah, the Root of David, has conquered, so that he can open the scroll with its seven seals.'

⁶Then I noticed a Lamb standing between the throne, with its four living creatures, and the elders. He appeared to have been slaughtered; but he had seven horns and seven eyes: which are the seven^g spirits of God sent out into all the earth. ⁷He went and took the scroll

from the right hand of the one who was sitting on the throne. [8]As he took the scroll, the four living creatures and the twenty-four elders prostrated themselves before the Lamb. Each held a harp, and golden bowls full of incense: these[h] are the prayers of God's people. [9]They chanted a new song,

> 'You deserve to take the scroll, and to break its seals:
> because you were slaughtered and with your life-blood
>   you ransomed for God[i] saints
>   from every tribe and language, people and nation.
> [10]You have made them a royal house and priests for our God,
> and they will reign[j] on earth.'

[11]As I looked, I heard the voice of many angels surrounding the throne, and the living creatures and the elders; they numbered myriads upon myriads, and thousands upon thousands, [12]singing loudly,

> 'The Lamb who was slaughtered deserves to receive
>   power and riches, wisdom and strength, and
>   reverence and glory and blessing.'

[13]Then I heard the whole creation, in heaven and on earth, and underneath the earth and in the sea, and[k] everything in them, crying,

> Blessing and reverence, and glory and might,
> be to the one who is seated on the throne,
> and to the Lamb,
> for ever and ever.'

[14]'Amen', replied the four living creatures; and the elders prostrated themselves, and worshipped.

Text

[a] The genitive participle λαλούσης (*lalousēs*, 'speaking') should be in the accusative, to agree with the relative pronoun ἣν (*hēn*, 'which'), referring to ἡ φωνή (*hē phonē*, 'the voice'). Later scribes accordingly changed it to the accusative λαλοῦσαν (*lalousan*, 'speaking'; so ℵ Byz it[gig] Primasius Ambrose, et al.). Others (e.g. 2329) alter the case of the participle to the nominative (λαλοῦσα, *lalousa*, 'speaking'), apparently to make it agree with the nominative φωνή (*phonē*, 'voice'). Other MSS replace the verb λαλέω (*laleō*, 'speak') with the parallel verb, λέγω (*legō*, 'say', or 'speak') in all three cases. See Exod. 19.16–19 LXX; and Beale 318. Clearly the genitive participle, being the more difficult grammatically, is the original reading.

[b] The participle λέγων (*legōn*, lit. 'saying'), as read by ℵ* A 0169 Byz, et al., is masculine nominative. But it should be feminine, in agreement with the antecedent φωνή (*phonē*, 'voice'). Some MSS (e.g. ℵ[a] P), as a result, change the case to the feminine λέγουσα (*legousa*, 'saying'). However, the form λέγων (*legōn*, 'saying'), if not grammatically appropriate, must be the original reading.

[c] In the phrase τὸ πρόσωπον ὡς ἀνθρώπου (*to prosōpon hōs anthrōpou*, lit. 'the face as of a man') some witnesses (including 046 1611[c]) omit τό (*to*, 'the'). But this is obviously 'a thoughtful correction introduced by copyists' (Metzger, *Textual Commentary* 735). The genitive ἀνθρώπου (*anthrōpou*, 'of a man'), attested by A it[gig] vg syr[p] cop[sa] Irenaeus[lat], et al., is replaced in 025 1611* syr[h], et al. by the nominative ἄνθρωπος (*anthrōpos*, 'a man'). The strong external support for the reading using the genitive, together with transcriptional probability, suggests that it is original. The singular reading ὡς ὅμοιον ἀνθρώπῳ

(*hōs homoion anthrōpō[i]*, lit. 'as like a man'), in א, is accounted for by assimilation to the descriptions of the other three creatures in the surrounding context.

[d] An apparent problem is suggested by the Greek of the statement, καὶ διὰ τὸ θέλημά σου ἦσαν καὶ ἐκτίσθησαν (*kai dia to thelēma sou ēsan kai ektisthēsan*, '[and] through your will [all things] existed, and were created'): namely, that there was existence before God's creation. Accordingly, some MSS (e.g. 1854 sa) read εἰσίν (*eisin*, 'they are') for ἦσαν (*ēsan*, lit. 'they were'); while a few others, including 046, insert οὐκ (*ouk*, 'not') before ἦσαν (*ēsan*,'[they] existed'). These are obvious attempts to deal with a theological difficulty, and are to be regarded as secondary. Swete (75) deems the latter to be 'an ingenious correction'.

[e] The reading ἔσωθεν καὶ ὄπισθεν (*esōthen kai opisthen*, 'inside and on the back') is supported by A 2329 syr^{h} Origen$^{1/4}$ Cyprian, et al. There is also strong support for the variant ἔσωθεν καὶ ἔξωθεν (*esōthen kai exōthen*, 'inside and outside'), particularly from the versions and patristic witnesses (e.g. 025 046 it^{gig} vg syr^{p} cop^{bo} arm Hippolytus Hilary Oecumenius). It is likely that the text as it stands is original. After the Church began to use codices for its sacred books, the terminology suited to writing on scrolls, where the contents could overflow on to the *verso* of the papyrus, seemed inappropriate; and the copyists therefore substituted ἔξωθεν (*exōthen*, 'outside'), implying the other side of a codex page, for ὄπισθεν (*opisthen*, 'on the back'). A few MSS (א cop^{sa} Origen$^{2/4}$) read ἔμπροσθεν καὶ ὄπισθεν (*emprosthen kai opisthen*, 'in front and on the back'); but this version seems to be influenced by a later desire to conform to the text of Ezek. 2.10 LXX.

[f] Some MSS (including vg Primasius) add ἐγώ (*egō*, 'I') after καί (*kai*, 'and'). Evidently this was a later attempt by copyists to identify the subject of the otherwise ambiguous form ἔκλαιον (*eklaion*, '[I was, or they were] weeping'). A lacks verse 4 in its totality. Presumably in this case the scribe moved directly from βλέπειν αὐτό (*blepein auto*, 'to look inside it') at the end of verse 3 to the same words at the conclusion of verse 4.

[g] The evidence for the inclusion of ἑπτά (*hepta*, 'seven') before πνεύματα (*pneumata*, 'spirits') is strong (including 𝔓24 א 046 it^{gig} syr^{ph} cop^{sa,bo} arm Hippolytus). But this is fairly evenly balanced against the evidence for its omission (AP^{vid} 1611 vg eth Irenaeus^{arm}, et al.). In transcription, the word may have been accidentally omitted through confusion with the two uses of 'seven' earlier in the verse; and equally ἑπτά (*hepta*, 'seven') may have been inserted by scribes to conform to the phraseology of Rev. 1.4; 3.1; 4.5. Although Metzger (*Textual Commentary* 735–36) remains open, it seems likely that the numeral was part of the original text, since the formula as a whole is an established element in John's theology of the Spirit (see on 1.4).

[h] The relative pronoun αἵ (*hai*, 'these') refers to θυμιαμάτων (*thymiamatōn*, 'incense'), the genitive plural of a neuter noun, rather than to φιάλας (*phialas*, 'bowls'), the accusative plural of a feminine noun. The feminine case of αἵ (*hai*, 'these') has presumably been governed by the following feminine word προσευχαί (*proseuchai*, 'prayers'). As a result, some witnesses (including א 046 1006) have changed the pronoun to the neuter ἅ (*ha*, 'these').

[i] The evidence for the reading τῷ θεῷ (*tō[i] theō[i]*, 'for God') is slight (A eth); but this version of the text best accounts for the origin of the others (Metzger, *Textual Commentary* 736). Some scribes wished to make clear the object of Christ's ransom in this section of the hymn, and therefore introduced ἡμᾶς (*hēmas*, 'us') either before the expression τῷ θεῷ (*tō[i] theō[i]*, 'for God'), as in 94, 2344, et al., or after it (א 046 1611, et al.). Others (1 2065* Cyprian, et al.) replaced the words τῷ θεῷ (*tō[i] theō[i]*, 'for God') with ἡμᾶς (*hēmas*, 'us'). These later emendations then clashed with the well-attested use of αὐτούς

(*autous*, 'them') in verse 10 (א A 1611* latt sy[ph,hmg], et al.), which in turn caused some witnesses (including it[gig] vg[cl] sa Primasius) to accept the replacement personal pronoun ἡμᾶς (*hēmas*, 'us').

[j] The third personal plural future form, βασιλεύσουσιν (*basileusousin*, 'they will reign'), is well attested (א 025 1 94 it[gig] vg syr[ph] cop[sa,bo] arm, et al.), and is entirely suited to the context. Two other variations are no doubt secondary: (a) the present tense βασιλεύουσιν (*basileuousin*, 'they reign'), supported by A 046 1006 1611 syr[h], et al.; and (b) the first person plural future form βασιλεύσομεν (*basileusomen*, 'we shall reign'; 2432, et al.), arising from the use of ἡμᾶς (*hēmas*, 'us') in some readings of verse 9.

[k] The simple text using καί (*kai*, 'and') is attested by א 1611* 2020, et al. Other versions seem to be later attempts to supply a verb for the relative clause, with or without an additional relative pronoun, after θαλάσσης (*thalassēs*, 'sea'). These are: (a) ἐστίν, καί (*estin, kai*, 'is, and'), read by A 1006 1611[c] 1854 2344 Arethas, et al. (b) ἅ ἐστιν, καί (*ha estin, kai*, 'which [neuter plural] are, and'), supported by 025 046 1 2073, et al., followed by TR. (c) ὅσα ἐστίν, καί (*hosa estin, kai*, 'all who [neuter plural] are, and'), as in 1828 2053, et al.

Literary Setting

The two chapters, Rev. 4—5, together provide the first interval in the first Act of John's drama. (For the dramatic character of Revelation see further, below.) The intervals which occur between each of the seven major scenes of the Apocalypse emphasize the careful and dramatic structuring of the work as a whole (see the analysis above, 19—22; see also Smalley, *Thunder and Love* 106). These intervals frequently contain, as here, a hymnic response to the vision which has just been unfolded; and they are used by the writer, chorus-like (but see below), to reflect upon and to recapitulate the scenes immediately preceding and following them. So the present interval looks back to the life of the people of God on earth, described in the messages to the seven churches of Asia (Rev. 2—3), by setting out the theological perspective given to this life by the Church in eternity. The first interval also enunciates the doctrinal agenda for the drama of Revelation, by including an exalted vision of God (Rev. 4) and the Lamb (Chapter 5).

Stanley ('Carmenque Christo' 173—91) believes that the hymns in Rev. 5, and the references there to Jesus as the sacrificed Lamb, were used by the communities within the Johannine sphere of influence during the celebration of the eucharist (ibid. 182—83). Similarly, Läuchli ('Gottesdienststruktur') argues for a eucharistic sequence in the hymnic material of Revelation; while Shepherd (*Paschal Liturgy*, esp. 77—97) claims that the five parts of the paschal vigil are directly reflected in the structure of the Apocalypse as a whole. While eucharistic parallels may be discovered in the movement of Revelation, they are by no means obvious; and, if they are identified, this could well be the result of reading back into the text the liturgies of a later period (as Shepherd, ibid. 79, admits). But, in any case, to perceive the eucharist as a major framework of reference within which to interpret Revelation is to work on altogether too narrow a canvas. Johannine theology is sacramental in a broad sense, and is never preoccupied with the rites of baptism or eucharist as such (see Smalley, *John* 234—38). Such an understanding is applicable to the drama of the Apocalypse in its totality.

Excursus: Graeco-Roman Drama and Revelation

Scholars have identified Revelation as a dramatic work by discovering links between the Apocalypse and Graeco-Roman drama. Benson (*Apocalypse* 4—6, 14—41, esp. 37—41), for example, regards the hymns in Revelation as occupying the place of the chorus in Greek plays. Similarly Brewer ('Influence of Greek Drama'), followed by Bowman ('The Revelation'), maintains that the literary construction of Revelation is directly affected by the patterns of Graeco-Roman drama, notably so far as the use of the chorus is concerned (see the plays of Aeschylus, Sophocles and Euripides, Plautus and Terence). Cf. Kitto, *Greek Tragedy* 85–93, 257–63; Beare, *Roman Stage*, esp. 45–69, 91–112, et passim. Bowman ('The Revelation' 445–46) also finds links between the angelic interventions in the Apocalypse and the descending and ascending gods of Greek tragedy. He further suggests that the furniture for John's cosmic drama in the Apocalypse, especially evident in Rev. 4—5 (sanctuary, great throne, twenty-four thrones and elders, altar of sacrifice), reflects the arrangement of the theatre from the third century BC onwards (as at Ephesus) with which his readers would have been familiar (stage, backdrop, side-scenes, altar). See ibid. 448–50.

As in the Gospel (cf. Smalley, *John* 141–42), so in Revelation, Greek drama may well have been one element in the writer's dramatic inspiration. Unlike the Gospel, however, there is in Revelation very little sustained dialogue such as is characteristic of Greek drama. Equally, although the hymns are used to some extent as a medium of interpretation in the Apocalypse, they do not permit the kind of discussion on the action by the chorus which is found in Greek plays (see Guthrie, *Relevance* 24).

With the consummate skill of an artist, John structures his material in the Revelation so as to advance his central, christological subject in a series of dramatic disclosures towards a climax. This 'spiralling' technique can also be found in John's Gospel (Smalley, *John* 147–48), and in 1 John (cf. Lieu, *Johannine Epistles* 22–23). So at each stage of the Apocalypse, including this one, we learn something fresh about Jesus himself. He is the exalted Son of man (Rev. 1), who is also involved in the life of local churches (2—3). He is the Lion, and also the sacrificial Lamb of God (4—5).

Rev. 4—5 together create what Beasley-Murray (108) calls a 'fulcrum' in Revelation. In relation to Chapters 1—3 they provide a fuller understanding of the Christ who is seen in glory during the vision of Rev. 1, and who walks among the lampstands of the seven Johannine churches of Asia in Rev. 2—3. In relation to the rest of the book (Rev. 6—22), they initiate a series of messianic judgements in the form of seven seals, which follow immediately (6.1–17; 8.1–5), and which lead to the final advent of Christ and the descent of the city of God to earth (21—22).

But Chapters 4 and 5 also form by themselves a self-contained scene in the drama, revealing the grounds for assurance that God's sovereign purposes of grace for the universe will be achieved, whatever the problems besetting the Church in the world: either persecution outside, or theological tensions within. Universal adoration and praise inevitably follow. Cf. Beasley-Murray 108.

All the intervals in the drama contain a double reference: a contrast, which for John is usually a complement. Here the duality is that of earth and heaven (see the non-complementary contrasts in Rev. 10.1—11.19, truth and error; and in 17.1—18.24, the Church and the world). In Rev. 4.1–2a there is a definite movement from the material to the spiritual realm, from earth to heaven. A door is standing open in heaven, and the prophet-seer on Patmos is invited to pass through it, to see what happens in that dimension. As a result, John is better able to understand the work of God on earth. Charles (1, 102–103) points out that the atmosphere changes dramatically at this moment. Restlessness, problems, imperfection and fear give place to perfect assurance and peace.

The literary form of Rev. 4—5 is a throne-vision report. The setting is the heavenly throne room, where a door stands open. John is invited to ascend to heaven (Rev. 4.1b), and to receive the revelation of 'what must take place later on'. What follows is a first-hand report on the action from the prophet-seer, not simply a description of the throne room and its occupants (as in *T. Levi* 3.4–9; *3 Enoch* 28.7–10; 35.1–6). The only first-personal, autobiographical reports of ecstatic heavenly ascent in early Christianity (or, indeed, in early Judaism) are to be found here and in 2 Cor. 12.1–10 (where the narrator is presumably the apostle Paul himself; for further links between John and Paul see Smalley, 'Christ-Christian Relationship'). Cf. further Aune 276–78.

This throne-vision begins, then, with the ascent to heaven of the seer, although this movement is not always a feature of such visions. Heavenly ascent is part of the Jewish tradition of Merkavah ('chariot') mysticism, which becomes developed in later rabbinic teaching and literature (see Scholem, *Jewish Gnosticism* 9–13). Cf. 2 Kings 2.1–12 (the ascent of Elijah, note verse 11); also 1 Kings 22.19–22 = 2 Chron. 18.18–21. Note also Isa. 6.1–13, where the prophet's vision of the Lord does not involve an ascent to heaven, and temple and heavenly throne room seem to merge. On Merkavah mysticism see further Aune 278–79; also Rowland, *Open Heaven* 218–27, esp. (for Rev. 4) 222–27.

At the centre of the vision in Rev. 4 and 5 stands the throne, a symbol of sovereign authority, with God seated upon it. Around him appear twenty-four elders and four living creatures (Rev 4.6–9, 10–11), singing his praises in adoration. This scene is typical of the ancient 'divine council' concept, found in Israelite and middle-eastern thought generally, where God is enthroned in the middle of his heavenly court, surrounded by various angelic beings and lesser deities, with differing functions, who act as courtiers. Cf. Job 15.8; Ps. 89.6–7; Jer. 23.18. The members of this divine assembly are described as 'gods', 'sons of God', 'sons of the gods', 'sons of the Most High' or 'holy ones' (Exod. 15.11; Ps. 29.1, NRSV 'heavenly beings'; Job 1.6; Ps. 82.1, 6; Deut. 33.2–3). In the Old Testament prophets are at times represented as taking part in the heavenly council, listening to its deliberations, and then declaring God's word on earth (cf. Jer. 23.18, 22; Amos 3.7).

John's report of his vision of God in Rev. 4 is dramatically intense. It is continued and explicated in Chapter 5 (note the repeated verb εἶδον [*eidon*, 'I looked/saw'] at 4.1 and 5.1). The creation by God (Rev. 4) is balanced by his redemption in Christ (5). Aune (329–30) notes the similarity between the dramatic sequence in Rev. 5 and *Odes Sol.* 23.5–22, where the enemies of God are conquered, and a letter is eventually unsealed by a 'wheel'. The wheel is a feature of Merkavah mysticism, as we know from the throne-vision of Ezek. 1. There the moving wheel is associated with four living creatures; and these figures also appear in the vision of Rev. 4—5, which clearly looks back to the Ezekiel text. Both scenes are dominated by a sovereign and victorious heavenly figure: the Lamb in Rev. 5 and the Son of Truth in *Odes Sol.* 23. Only they can open a heavenly document and reveal its significance.

However, there are differences in the two narrations. For example, the drama in Rev. 5 is set in heaven, while the context of *Odes Sol.* 23 is earthly; the Lamb unseals the scroll in Revelation, but the wheel opens the letter (or 'large volume', verse 21) in *Odes Sol.* 23; the sealed scroll in Rev. 5 represents the sovereign will of God as this is worked out in the future of humanity, whereas the large volume in *Odes Sol.* 23 is the Son of Truth himself; the enemies of God are conquered in *Odes Sol.* 23 (see verses 13–15, 19–20), but that conquest is delayed in the Apocalypse until Rev. 6.1—8.1.

A large part of the scene in Rev. 5 is taken up with a performance of the heavenly liturgy. Two hymns of praise are sung: verses 2, 9–10 and 12; these are followed by a doxology in verse 13, and an 'amen' in verse 14. John uses the literary technique of *aporia* (break, or difficulty) in the first hymn, whereby a question is asked in verse 2 ('who is worthy to open the scroll, and break its seals?'), and the answer is delayed until verse 9 ('you [the Lamb] deserve to take the scroll, and to break its seals'). See further below, 135.

The dominant figure in Rev. 5 is the Lamb, who receives honour and adoration from the living creatures and the elders. This scene has been interpreted in the past in differing ways. Some scholars see the depiction of the Lamb in this chapter as an *enthronement* (so Sweet 121–27); and a background for this view has traditionally been discovered in Near Eastern mythology (cf. Aune 332–35). But the author of Revelation need not have been influenced by non-Jewish enthronement patterns, since coronation accounts are already present in the Old Testament (solely at 1 Kings 1.32–48 and 2 Kings 11.12[–20]). See further de Vaux, *Ancient Israel* 102–107. However, there is no reason at all to describe the proceedings in Rev. 5 in terms of an enthronement. No description of an actual enthronement occurs in this chapter, nor is there any reference to the insignia which are conferred upon a monarch on such occasions.

A second and more promising interpretation of the action surrounding the Lamb in Rev. 5 views his appearance as a *commission*. Müller ('Die himmlische Ratsversammlung') has demonstrated that the commissioning of a person in response to a question is a traditional motif in heavenly council scenes, both in Hebrew and ancient Near Eastern texts. So in the divine assemblies described in 1 Kings 22.1–38 and Isa. 6.1–13, questions are asked in order to identify an individual who might serve as God's messenger. In 1 Kings 22.20 Yahweh asks the court, 'Who will entice Ahab?'; and at Isa. 6.8 the Lord says, 'Whom shall I send?' See esp. Müller, 'Die himmlische Ratsversammlung' 260–61. Such accounts of commissioning seem to form an appropriate backcloth to the scene in Rev. 5, where the strong angel asks the assembly, 'Who is worthy to open the scroll?' (verse 2).

While commissioning may form part of the dramatic process envisioned in Rev. 5, Aune (336–38) argues that *investiture* is a better way to understand what happens in the heavenly court. He bases this claim on an analysis of the text of Rev. 5 as an adaptation of Dan. 7.9–14 (for the links between Rev. 5 and Dan. 7 see below, 126) and Ezek. 1—2, and on the association between the vision in the Apocalypse and investiture features in other visions of the heavenly court, especially in 1 Kings 22 and Isa. 6. In Dan. 7 one like a Son of man is not enthroned, but *invested* with dominion and glory and kingship by the Ancient One (verses 13–14): and from this action stems the Son's authenticated ability to participate in the judgemental and salvific purposes of God (verses 26–27).

'Investiture' refers to the act of establishing someone in executive office; and that is precisely what happens in the drama of Rev. 5, which is clearly played out against the background of Dan. 7. The Lamb is the only one who is worthy to open the sealed scroll (Dan. 7 mentions open books [verse 10], but not an apocalyptic scroll). But as soon as he receives the scroll from the right hand of God (Rev. 5.7) the hymnic chorus breaks out (verses 9–10, 11–12, 13, 14), and he is given 'power and riches, wisdom and strength, and reverence and glory and blessing'. With such authorization the Lamb can share in God's sovereign plan for humanity of salvation through judgement (articulated in Rev. 6—22). See further Beale 366–69; and, on this section as a whole, cf. Aune 332–38.

So the scene in the interval unit Rev. 4—5 presents Christ, in the form of a Lamb, being commissioned for divine service. But more precisely he is invested with authority to act with grace in the human situation. In the vision of the exalted Son of man in Rev. 1.12–20, the majesty and power of the ascended Lord are in focus; here the chief thought is the outcome of his redemptive death (Beckwith 263).

The verb sequences in Rev. 4 and 5 are a mixture of past (imperfect), present and future tenses (see the Comment, below). The use of the imperfect and present tenses helps to make the action vivid and immediate, and to switch the audience into the progress of the drama. The future tense (as in Rev. 4.9–10) implies that the events in question have not yet occurred (Aune 276).

Comment

4.1   John links the vision in Rev. 4—5 to the action of the first scene by using the conjunctive phrase, μετὰ ταῦτα (*meta tauta*, lit. 'after these things'). The apocalypse of the heavenly throne room and its assembled court is introduced by the phrase, εἶδον, καὶ ἰδού, *eidon, kai idou*, lit. 'I saw, and behold' (cf. Rev. 7.1, 9; 15.5; 18.1; Dan. 8.2–3 LXX). The prophet-seer constantly 'sees' the truths of God unveiled. For the form καὶ εἶδον, καὶ ἰδού, *kai eidon, kai idou*, lit. 'then I saw, and behold', see Rev. 6.2, 5, 8; 14.1, 14; 19.11 (cf. LXX Ezek. 1.4, 15; Dan. 10.5). The particle ἰδού (*idou*, 'behold') by itself is used to herald the visions here, and at Rev. 4.2; 12.3; et al.

Verbs of hearing are frequently used in the Apocalypse to describe John's visions; and on three occasions 'hearing' and 'seeing' are associated (see 5.11; 8.13; 22.8). Often the writer 'hears a (loud) voice' (ἤκουσα φωνὴν [μεγάλην], *ekousa phōnēn [megalēn]*, 'I heard a [loud] voice'), as at Rev. 9.13; 10.4, 8; 12.10; 14.2, 13; 16.1; 18.4; 19.1, 6; 21.3. In John's Gospel verbs of seeing and hearing are also important (cf. John 4.42; 20.29); but there they are used in the context of the need for faith in Jesus as the Messiah. See Smalley, *John* 175–76.

The prophet sees in heaven a door, 'standing open' (cf. Rev. 3.20). The Greek is the passive perfect participle, ἠνεῳγμένη (*ēneō[i]gmenē*, lit. 'was opened'). This implies a divine action: God himself opens the door in heaven for the seer. Such a sight was natural for a visionary (see 3 Macc. 6.18; *1 Enoch* 14.15; *T. Levi* 5.1; although these references do not include the mention of a 'door' as such). The 'keys to Death and Hades' specified at Rev. 1.18 (q.v.) imply that a door leads into the underworld (cf. 20.13–15). So here, entrance to the heavenly dimension is represented as being made through a door (see further Aune 280–82). John's cosmology implies a three-tiered universe; and his down-to-earth 'door' imagery, associated with the realms 'above and below', is a reminder of his constant balance in the Apocalypse between the material and the spiritual. See Smalley, *Thunder and Love* 58–60.

The term οὐρανός (*ouranos*, 'heaven') itself is used in the singular throughout Revelation, except at 12.12 (q.v.), a text which may be influenced by Isa. 44.23. John's perception of a single heaven contrasts with the common understanding in antiquity of a plurality of heavens: seven or more (cf. Mounce 118 n. 3; see Rist 401 for references in Judaic literature). Heaven is the realm of space and the Spirit; it is the dwelling-place of God and his Christ. See further Thompson 88–90.

The prophet-seer hears a voice, which initially spoke to him 'in trumpet tones', summoning him to heaven. This is a reference to the 'trumpet-like voice' of the Son of man, who spoke to John during the vision at Rev. 1.10–11. Note the christological associations of the same voice in 1.12, q.v.; the Son's voice also sounds 'like the roar of many waters' (1.15). There is no distinction between the speakers, that is to say, in the passage 1.9–20; as here, the voice heard throughout is that of the exalted Christ (so Beckwith 436; Beasley-Murray 111–12). Thus the force of ἡ φωνὴ ἡ πρώτη (*hē phōnē hē prōtē*, lit. 'the first voice') is not chronological (first, rather than second), but sequential (the same voice, 'previously heard').

John is invited, as part of this vision, to ascend to heaven, where Christ promises to reveal to him 'what must take place later on'. There is nothing inconsistent in this invitation, where the risen Lord becomes the agent of a disclosure of which he is part. The central figure of Chapter 5, Christ himself, can summon John to heaven and reveal himself to the seer precisely because he is to play a key role in God's salvific plans for the future of his creation. In any case, if John's pictures appear to break the bounds of consistency, that is because they are intended to kindle the imagination and elicit faith (cf. Beasley-Murray 112).

The apocalypse to John (δείξω σοι, *deixō soi*, lit. 'I will show you') involves what must take place 'later on' (μετὰ ταῦτα, *meta tauta*, lit. 'after these things'). In 1.19 (q.v.) Christ commands the seer to write down what is about to happen 'later on' (μετὰ ταῦτα, *meta tauta*). Now he is to be shown those happenings more closely. For ἃ δεῖ γενέσθαι (*ha dei genesthai*, 'what must take place') see Rev. 1.1; also Dan. 2.29, 45 LXX.

The revelation of 'what is to happen later on' does not mean that everything after the heavenly council depicted in Rev. 4—5 (recorded in 6—22) must be viewed as a prediction of what is to happen chronologically in the future. John does not think in purely linear terms. His eschatology, as we have seen (12–13, 16–17), is balanced; from a heavenly perspective past, present and future belong together. So the visions of 'what must take place later on' will include historical events, which are judged in the light of the end; but God's eternal and saving purposes in Christ for his world also give meaning to what has happened in the past (cf. 12.1–6), and what always will come about in the present (cf. 1.19; 2—3). John consistently interweaves heaven and earth. 'What must take place' refers, finally, not so much to *events* as to the coming of Jesus, in time and in eternity, and to the relationships with him and with each other which stem from that advent. Cf. further Sweet 115; Boring 100–101; Mounce 118–19.

2   There is an immediate response when the voice of the exalted Christ (verse 1) is heard. John 'at once' (εὐθέως, *eutheōs*) found himself in the Spirit. Charles (1, 109–11) finds a difficulty in the expression, as it implies a fresh state of ecstasy; whereas the prophet-seer has evidently been in a spiritual trance since 1.10 (q.v.), where the same phrase in the Greek occurs: ἐγενόμην ἐν πνεύματι (*egenomēn en pneumati*, 'I found myself in the Spirit'). But John has not necessarily returned to a non-ecstatic state of existence in between. The situation described at 4.1, with a door standing open in heaven and the invitation to ascend issued by the voice of the exalted Christ, is part of the same vision-ary experience. In this verse, therefore, we are presented with an intensification of the seer's ecstasy, rather than another form of it. (Cf. Ezek. 11.1, 5, where the prophet is first carried away, and then receives the Lord's Spirit in order to prophesy.) Moffatt (376) notes that 'a fresh wave of ecstasy catches up the seer'. For a similar approach see Swete 67; Sweet 115; Mounce 119.

For the verb ἐγενόμην (*egenomēn*, 'found', lit. 'became') see on Rev. 1.10. John the seer is also a prophet (1.3); so that being 'in the (Lord's) Spirit' (not his own) is a mode suited to the spiritual revelation which he is about to receive (cf. 1 Kings 22.19; Amos 3.7). The prophet's actual ascent to heaven is not described, since it is to be understood in a spiritual sense, and is part of a vision. For similar 'visionary trips to paradise' (Mounce 119 n. 6) see *Odes Sol.* (e.g. 36.1, 'I rested on the Spirit of the Lord, and she raised me up to heaven [or on high]'). There is no reason to interpret this movement corporately as a symbol of the Church's physical rapture before the tribulation (so Beale 319; cf. Rev. 20.4–6, q.v.). For 'heaven' (οὐρανός, *ouranos*) see on verse 1.

The demonstrative particle ἰδού (*idou*, lit. 'behold') is used 26 times in the Apoca-lypse, as a dramatic way of calling attention to noteworthy scenes and figures within them. Cf. previously Rev. 1.7, 18; 2.10, 22; 3.8, 9 (*bis*), 20; 4.1. As the prophet-seer enters heaven, he encounters at once a 'throne (θρόνος, *thronos*) with someone seated on it'. To heighten the tension in this section of the drama, John does not immediately disclose the identity of the throne's occupant; although this quickly becomes apparent. We have heard before in Revelation of God's throne, used as a symbol of his sover-eignty (cf. 1.4; 3.21); but now the throne itself appears in a blaze of heavenly glory.

There are 17 references to God's throne in Rev. 4—5, out of 38 occurrences of the term in Chapters 4—22. The fact that the seer speaks so often of the throne of God, in this pivotal scene in his drama, underlies the divine control which in his view is exercised over the world's affairs: including its suffering. God's power is apparent in heaven, and manifest on earth. Such a claim is affirmed in the next four scenes of the Apocalypse (Scenes 2–5) by the fact that all the judgements of God in Rev. 6—16 issue from his throne (cf. 6.16; 8.3–5; 16.17).

The universal sovereignty of God which is symbolized by his throne is enhanced by its central location on the stage of heaven. In John's supernatural cosmology the elders and living creatures (together with the Lamb and the angels, in Chapter 5) surround the throne in a circle (see Hendriksen 83–85). In this way they discover their significance (see below). So also humanity is judged on the basis of its response to God's sovereign rule (6.16–17). To this extent, the scene in Rev. 4—5 is not so much a description of heaven, as of 'the entire universe from the aspect of heaven' (Hendriksen 84). On this section see further Beale 320.

For the imperfect ἔκειτο (*ekeito*, '[a throne] was standing') see John 19.29 (2.6; 21.9). The word καθήμενος (*kathēmenos*, lit. 'sitting') is a participle, which functions as a finite verb ('seated'). The phrase καθήμενος ἐπί (*kathēmenos epi*, 'seated on') in Revelation is normally used with the accusative, as here (P has the genitive) and at 6.2; 11.16; but sometimes it occurs with the dative (as in 4.9 [א A]; 7.10), and occasionally with the genitive (4.10; 5.1, 7; 6.16). See Charles 1, 112–13. God's posture on the throne ('*seated* on it') reinforces the thought of his sovereign control.

3 The 'seated figure' is evidently God (see verse 2). John does not attempt to describe the divine appearance in anthropomorphic terms. Rather, he suggests the Lord's splendour and brilliance by using the analogy of precious stones: jasper, carnelian and beryl. Clearly the seer is indebted to the Old Testament in this context, and especially to the theophanic description of Yahweh (partly in human terms) at Ezek. 1.26–28. But other Old Testament allusions can be associated with this passage: namely, Exod. 24.10; 28.17–20; Ezek. 9.2 (LXX); 10.1 (LXX); and 28.13. All three stones to which reference is made in this verse are mentioned in Exod. 28. 17, 20 (a description of the breast piece of the high priest's ephod) and Ezek. 28.13 (in the lament over the king of Tyre); and this implies that the influence on John of those texts is here particularly strong. In classical literature cf. Plato, *Phaedo* 110 E.

Beale (320–21) points out that the stones in 4.3 anticipate the fuller list of precious stones in Rev. 21.11, 18–21, where the glory of God is revealed throughout the new creation, and not only in heaven. Moreover, 'jasper' is the first stone to be mentioned in Chapter 21 (verses 11 and 18), and is there (at verse 11) linked explicitly with divine glory. The fact that the 'jasper stone' (λίθῳ ἰάσπιδι, *lithō[i] jaspidi*) is placed first in the list belonging to the present verse, therefore, intensifies the sense of God's glory which is being evoked. It is not necessary to associate each of the three gems mentioned here with particular qualities. Together they symbolize God's sovereign glory and majesty, and the unapproachable light in which he dwells (cf. Ps. 104.1–2; 1 Tim. 6.16).

The jasper stone may have been translucent rock crystal; carnelian (sardis) is red, and emerald green. In this case, the three precious stones contain the principal colours of the rainbow, which is described as 'encircling' (κυκλόθεν, *kyklothen*, lit. 'all around') God's throne (cf. Knight 59; for 'throne' see on verse 2). The bright rainbow is a reminder of the glory of God, as in Ezek. 1.28, where the appearance of the likeness of the glory of the Lord is compared to 'the bow in a cloud on a rainy day' (cf. *Midr. Rab.* Num. 14.3, citing Ezek. 1.28; also *Midr. Rab.* Gen. 35.3).

But the rainbow is also a sign of the covenant between God and his people made with Noah after the flood (Gen. 9.8–17), when God's saving love is extended to his creation through his judgement upon it. The theological rhythm of salvation through judgement is typically Johannine (see Smalley, *Thunder and Love* 147–49; note also the outline on

116   *Interval: Adoration in Heaven's Court (4.1—5.14)*

108–110). The scene is set for the visions which follow: God's activity of discrimination will be consistently tempered by his mercy. Judgement is real; but it is ultimately an expression of divine love, and designed to lead to the wholeness of humanity. Salvation and glory and power belong to God, John hears the heavenly multitude crying, *because* his judgements are true and just (Rev. 19.1–2; cf. 11.18).

4 John sees twenty-four other thrones all round God's throne (for which, see on verse 2). A more conventional arrangement of the heavenly court is found in 1 Kings 22.19, where Micaiah sees the Lord sitting on his throne, with the heavenly host standing to his right and left. Here, the 'twenty-four other thrones' are placed 'all around' (κυκλόθεν, *kyklothen*, as in verse 3) God's seat. For the use of κυκλόθεν (*kyklothen*), in this sense of 'encircling', see 3 Kgdms 5.4; 4 Macc. 5.1. For the placing of thrones near God's throne of judgement see Dan. 7.9–10. For the idea of one or more thrones located, with their angelic leaders, in a series of heavens see *Asc. Isa.* 7.13–37; 8.9; 10.1–31; et al. The term 'thrones' is also used as a metaphor for members of the angelic host (Col. 1.16; *T. Levi* 3.8; *Asc. Isa.* 7.27), and as a synonym for the heavenly reward of the righteous (*1 Enoch* 108.12).

Twenty-four 'elders' (πρεσβυτέρους, *presbyterous*) are seated on the (twenty-four) 'other thrones'. The number twenty-four is used nowhere else in apocalyptic literature; and, indeed, no other early Jewish or early Christian composition includes a vision of God presiding over a heavenly court, surrounded by this number of elders. Aune (288) therefore concludes that John himself may well have created the 'twenty-four elders' for this scene; although he acknowledges that other features of the throne room setting in Rev. 4—5 have been drawn from Old Testament and apocalyptic traditions (ibid.). See the references to angelic councils in Job 1.6; 2.1; Ps. 89.7; Dan. 7.9–10; *1 Enoch* 47.2–3; 60.2. Cf. also Bornkamm, 'πρέσβυς, κτλ' 668–70.

There have been many and varied attempts to identify the twenty-four elders in these two chapters (4—5) of the Apocalypse; and some of the explanations overlap (see the surveys in Charles 1, 129–33; Aune 288–91; cf. also Beale 322). The most serious contenders may be mentioned.

1 They have been identified as the heavenly counterparts of the leaders of the twenty-four priestly courses of the second-temple period (cf. 1 Chron. 23.6[7–24]; 24.7–18); although, except for bearing incense representing the prayers of God's people (Rev. 5.8; cf. 4.10), the elders do not exercise priestly functions.
2 They represent saints of the Old Testament.
3 A popular interpretation is to regard the two sets of twelve elders (although John does not introduce this division) as patriarchs and apostles, representing together the saints of the Church as a whole: Israel old and new (cf. Brown, *Introduction* 786). However, the scene in Rev. 4—5 is less ecclesial, than courtly.
4 A more likely explanation, and a variant of the last, is to regard the elders as angelic members of the heavenly court: divine representatives of the body of the faithful, all of whom are priests (Rev. 1.6). See Charles 1, 133. This is in line with the biblical tradition which suggests that every human being has a 'guardian angel' (cf. Tobit 5.1–22; Acts 12.15; also Matt. 18.10). Angels and human beings are in any case related in biblical and Johannine thought (see on Rev. 1.20); and John typically conjoins, in a context such as this, the spiritual and the material.
5 The elders have also been identified as individual Christians who have sealed their faith through martyrdom; or
6 as figures from astral mythology, such as the twenty-four star-gods of the zodiac.

See further Swete 69; Moffatt 378–79; Beckwith 498–99; Kiddle 84–85; Beasley-Murray 113–14; Mounce 121–22.

It is apparent from this review of possible interpretations that the basic background underlying the concept of the twenty-four 'elders', here and elsewhere in the Apocalypse, is to be located in early Judaism, probably reaching back to even earlier, oriental (Babylonian) sources (so Beckwith 498). However, Beasley-Murray (114 n. 1) rejects the theory that the twenty-four elders derive from Babylonian astrological religious thought through Judaic apocalyptic. In his view, there is no evidence at all of an 'angelic order of twenty-four in heaven' in Jewish apocalypticism.

'Elders' often appear in the Old Testament, on two occasions forming a group in the presence of the Lord (Exod. 24.9–10; Isa. 24.23 LXX, using [ἐνώπιον τῶν] πρεσβυτέρων, [*enōpion tōn] presbyterōn*, lit. '[before the] elders'); and these passages may have influenced John's composition at this point. In ancient Israel, the term 'elder' designated authority exercised by leaders in social, civic and national groupings (cf. Judg. 11.5–11; Ruth 4.2– 4; Exod. 18.12, 'elders of Israel'; et al.). In the community of Qumran, elders were given a place of dignity after the priests (1QS 6.8; CD 9.4). Those who held religious or political authority in early Judaism were generally known as 'elders' (cf. 1 Macc. 1.26; 11.23; 1 Esdras 6.5, 8 ['elders of the Jews']; Judith 6.16; Mark 8.31 par.; Acts 4.5, 8, 23).

In the early Church the term πρεσβύτερος (*presbyteros*, 'presbyter' or 'elder') is often used of those fulfilling a leadership role within Christian ministry (Acts 14.23; 20.17; 1 Tim. 5.17, 19; Jas. 5.14; 1 Pet. 5.1; *Did.* 15.1–2; *2 Clem.* 17.3, 5; Ignatius, *Magn.* 2.1; 7.1; *Trall.* 3.1; 7.2). However, the twenty-four elders in the throne room scene of Rev. 4—5 do not act primarily as presbyteral ministers or priests in this sense (but see above, 116). Against this view see Brown, *Introduction* 805, who argues that the use of 'elders' in verse 4 suggests a period reflected in Titus and 1 Tim., when bishops, presbyters and deacons have been installed, without replacing apostles, prophets and teachers.

More important than the identity and background of the twenty-four elders in Revelation, we may conclude, is their *function*. As divine representatives of the faithful, their chief task is to participate fully in the worship of God. In the scene of Rev. 4—5, their role in this respect is presented as central; although elsewhere in the Apocalypse it is more peripheral (7.11, 13; 11.16–18; 14.3; 19.4). For the acts of worship they are robed in 'white garments' and wear 'gold crowns' on their heads (see below). In worship the elders prostrate themselves before God (4.10; 5.14; 11.16; 19.4), and lay their gold crowns before his throne (4.10). They share the worship of heaven closely with the four living creatures (4.8–10), joined either by the angels (5.11–14; 7.11–12) or the voice of a great multitude (19.1–8). In the liturgical action of Rev. 19, the elders respond to the worship offered with the words, 'Amen. Hallelujah!' (verse 4). They sing hymns of praise to God, either on their own (4.10–11; 11.16–18), or with the living creatures (5.9–10); and they each hold a harp and 'bowls full of incense' (5.8) which are described as 'the prayers of God's people' (ibid.). In the vision of Rev. 20.4 (q.v.), John sees thrones, and judgement given to those who are seated on them. If this includes a reference to the twenty-four elders, then their function (only here, in the Apocalypse) is also judicial (cf. Matt. 19.28). See further Aune 288.

Various explanations have been advanced to explain John's choice of the actual number 'twenty-four', in association with the elders and their matching thrones.

1 It is the sum of two sets of twelve elders, together representing the old Israel (the twelve tribes) and the new. But the author of the Apocalypse himself nowhere suggests this division, which is in any case artificial, and not known in the New Testament (see above, 116).
2 It coincides with the number of hours in a day; and this would be an appropriate association for those who engage in worship continuously (cf. *T. Adam* 1.1—2.12, listing the forms of prayer appropriate to creation during twenty-four hours). But can

the liturgy of eternity be measured in time? (See, however, the time reference in heaven at Rev. 8.1, 'silence for about half an hour').

3 The number stems from the traditional, rabbinic view that the Hebrew Old Testament contains the work of twenty-four canonical writers (cf. Beale 322).

4 The number corresponds to the totality of symbols for the universe (cf. Aune 292).

5 It reflects the number of lictors (twenty-four) who accompanied the Emperor Domitian (see Dio Cassius, *Hist. Rom.* 67.4.3). But this presupposes a Domitianic dating for the Apocalypse, and in our view this is unacceptable (see above, 2–3).

None of these attempts to explain the precise number of elders present at verse 4 is entirely satisfactory, and some are frankly strained. Beckwith (498) believes that the author has derived the number from 'some representation current in popular tradition, but not elsewhere recorded'; yet the term '(twenty-four) elders' in this context (here πρεσβυτέρους, *presbyterous*) is used without an article, and this implies a reference which would *not* be commonly understood and appreciated. No doubt we have in this passage part of John's own dramatic symbolism, the origin of which was known to him alone. See further Charles 1, 128–33; Aune 287–92; Beale 322–26.

There are three accusatives in the Greek of this verse, with apparently no verb to govern them: θρόνους (*thronous*, 'thrones', *bis*), πρεσβυτέρους (*presbyterous*, 'elders') and στεφάνους (*stephanous*, 'crowns'). It is possible that they are governed by the verb εἶδον (*eidon*, 'I looked', or 'I saw') in verse 1; but Charles (1, 116) regards this explanation as 'wholly unsatisfactory'. Perhaps this is a further example of John's immediate and dramatic, if strictly ungrammatical, style.

The elders are 'robed in white garments, with gold crowns on their heads'. Their white robes represent, figuratively, the clothing of the faithful in the resurrection life. They denote spiritual purity and righteousness, together with victorious morality. For 'white garments' see on Rev. 3.4; cf. also 3.5, 18; 6.11; 7.9, 13, 14.

The 'gold crowns' of the elders symbolize the royal nature of the vindicated faithful; and this is an authoritative character which they share with their Lord and derive from him (see Rev. 1.6; 5.10; 17.14; 19.16; also 1 Pet. 2.9).

The elders resemble angels through their white attire, but are distinguished from the angels by their human form and gold crowns (Knight 60). In this way they connect the heavenly and the human worlds. As in Rev. 1.9—3.22, the representatives of the faithful are pictured in angelic form to remind the members of John's churches that one dimension of their existence and experience is already heavenly. This will act as an encouragement for their endurance, and as an inspiration for their liturgy (1.3, 9; cf. 4.10). See further on 'angels' at 1.20; cf. also Beale 323.

Suetonius, *Domitian* 4.4, records that this Roman emperor presided at competitions in the stadium wearing a purple toga, and 'upon his head a golden crown, with figures of Jupiter, Juno and Minerva'; and that he was surrounded by priests similarly attired: except that 'their crowns bore his image as well'. But such a practice occurred too late to have influenced John's composition in this scene. More cogently, at Rev. 14.14 the exalted Son of man is described as wearing a 'gold crown' (στέφανον χρυσοῦν, *stephanon chrysoun*) on his head. Once more, the faithful inherit their royalty from their risen Lord.

5 From God's throne dramatically issue the apocalyptic phenomena of lightning and thunder. 'Roarings' (φωναί, *phōnai*, lit. 'voices') and 'peals (of thunder)' (βρονταί, *brontai*, lit. 'thunders') are virtually synonymous. Cf. the combination, 'voice of thunder' (φωνὴ βροντῆς, *phōnē brontēs*), at Rev. 6.1; 14.2; 19.6 (pl.). In the Apocalypse lightning and thunder (together with earthquake), at the conclusion of each series of judgements, herald the manifestation of God's glory (8.1–5; 11.15–19; 16.17–18). With the exception of 8.5, the order of the portents in these contexts is the same as in 4.5 (cf. Bengel 219).

The lightning and thunder in this passage recall the theophany on Mount Sinai to Moses and the people, which according to Exod. 19.16–25 was introduced by thunder and lightning (verse 16); cf. Ezek. 1.13; Heb. 12.18–21. In Hebrew poetry, the thunderstorm is a common symbol for the power as well as the glory of the Lord. That power is disclosed in judgement (1 Sam. 2.10, 'the Most High will thunder in heaven, the Lord will judge the ends of the earth'), and at times for the purposes of salvation through judgement (Job 37.1–13; Ps. 18.7–24; cf. *1 Enoch* 59.1). Such a typically Johannine theological pattern is perhaps picked up in the present verse (5), suggesting that the God of the old creation and of the new acts again for healing as well as with discrimination. Cf. Beasley-Murray 115. We may also discover here the motif, clearly discernible in the Fourth Gospel, of Jesus as the new Moses who makes possible the new Exodus (cf. Smalley, *John* 271–72).

'Seven blazing torches' burn before (ἐνώπιον, *enōpion*, 'in front of') the throne of God; and these are identified with the 'seven spirits of God'. The 'blazing torches' (λαμπάδες πυρός, *lampades pyros*, lit. 'torches of fire') may hark back to Ezek. 1.13 ('torches moving among the living creatures'); cf. *2 Baruch* 21.6, where countless holy beings, 'who are flame and fire', stand around the throne. The imagery implies fulness (picked up by the use of the perfect number seven, which is influenced by the reference to the 'seven spirits of God' in the next part of the sentence); but it also suggests intensity and energy. Fire and flame were associated in the primitive mind with divinity, and were regarded with awe as an expression of divine holiness and purity (so Moffatt 379). For the association between fire and crystal, as in verse 6 (also 15.2), see Exod. 24.9–10, 17; Ezek. 1.22, 27; cf. (more closely) *1 Enoch* 14.9–10.

For the 'seven spirits of God', as the equivalent of the Spirit of God manifested in his completeness, see on Rev. 1.4; cf. also verse 2. John's identification of the 'seven blazing torches' as the 'seven spirits of God' is a natural one; for torches were among the cherubim (Ezek. 1.13), even as the sevenfold Spirit of God is present and at work among the churches (Rev. 1.4; 3.1; 5.6; et al.). Cf. Beasley-Murray 115.

So far, in this dramatic throne room scene, the overpowering presence of God the transcendent Creator, and of his Spirit, has been evident to the faithful conquerors. We still await the appearance of the third person of the Godhead (see Chapter 5).

6 The background to what appears to be a 'sea of glass, transparent as crystal', also and awesomely visible before God's throne, is uncertain. One possibility is Ezek. 1.22, where the prophet sees 'something like a dome, shining like crystal', spread out above the heads of the living creatures. Aune (296) compares the enormous bronze basin of water, mounted on twelve bronze oxen, in Solomon's temple (1 Kings 7.23–26; cf. 2 Kings 25.13).

It is more probable that the crystalline sea of glass before the throne recollects the 'waters that were above the dome (or firmament)', which are in turn distinguished from the 'waters below' in the creation narrative (Gen. 1.7). See Ps. 104.3; 148.4, where God's presence is described as appearing 'on the waters'; cf. also Job 28.25; 37.18; *T. Levi* 2.7; *2 Enoch* 3.3 (Enoch, in the first heaven, sees 'a vast ocean, much bigger than the earthly ocean').

John's theology differs from this cosmology, and from the mythology about water in ancient religions (cf. Caird 65–68). What we are given in this verse is not a sea, but what *appears* to be a 'sea of glass, transparent as crystal'. Its very transparency, according to Moffatt (379), suggests the ether, 'clear and calm, shimmering and motionless'. The image also evokes God's holiness and ultimate distance from his creatures (see the hymn in Rev. 4.8).

In the Apocalypse, the 'sea' is frequently referred to as a part of God's natural creation (5.13; 7.1–3; 8.8–9; et al.; but note 13.1, where the beast rises out of the sea). In three contexts, however, the allusion is figurative: here, at 15.2 (*bis*) and at 21.1 (q.v.). In the passage 15.1–4 the 'sea of glass' is mentioned again, mixed with the fire of judgement. This time the conquerors stand beside it and sing the song of Moses and of the Lamb (15.3–4), as did the Israelites at the Sea of Reeds (cf. Exod. 15.1–18). In other words, another Exodus is about to take place, accompanied by judgemental plagues similar to those which occurred in Egypt. Once more, John is describing waters of holiness, which symbolize fiery judgement against *un*holiness, or opposition to God in any form. Small wonder, then, that in the vision of the new heaven and earth in Rev. 21.1 the sea has disappeared. There is no enmity against the Lord in the new Jerusalem, and he dwells among his people as their God (21.2–4). See further Kiddle 88–90; Beasley-Murray 116.

John sees, in his vision of heaven, four 'living creatures' (τέσσερα ζῷα, *tessera zō[i]a*), who are associated in some way with God's throne. These four beings are reminiscent of the living creatures mentioned in the visions of God at Ezek. 1.5–28. However, there are variations. In Ezekiel, each of the creatures has four faces (1.6, 10), and four wings instead of six (1.6; see Rev. 4.8); moreover, in the Old Testament passage it is the rims of the wheels with which the creatures are aligned (Ezek. 1.18) that are 'full of eyes', and not their bodies (as in Rev. 4.6). The living creatures of the Apocalypse also recall the seraphs of Isaiah's vision in the temple (Isa. 6.2–3), each with *six* wings (verse 2), who lead the praises of God by reciting the trisagion (see Rev. 4.8).

It seems that John has blended and transformed the images of his sources (Mounce 124). Not surprisingly, as a result, the identity of the living creatures (as of the twenty-four elders) has given rise to differing interpretations (see the history in Charles 1, 119–23). They are called cherubim in Ezek. 10.15, 20, and therefore appear to belong to an angelic order (the cherubim are associated with two other orders of angels, guarding the throne of glory, in *1 Enoch* 71.7). Cherubim appear scripturally in connection with the account of the Fall (Gen. 3.24); the ark (Exod. 25.18); the temple (1 Kings 6.23); and the divine name, 'you who are enthroned upon the cherubim' (Ps. 80.1; et al.). See Swete 71.

We conclude that the 'living creatures' of Rev. 4 belong to an exalted order of heavenly, angelic beings (so Beckwith 501; against Swete 71 and Wall 94–95, who both identify them with the best in the animate creation; but see the clear reference to the creation at Rev. 5.13). They are the immediate guardians of the divine presence; and, with other angels (5.11), they lead the heavenly company in the adoring worship of God (4.8–11; 5.8–14). But they need not be out of touch with the Church on earth. It is most unlikely that the four living creatures are to be identified with either the four constellations of stars (cf. Charles 1, 123), or the four principal signs of the zodiac (cf. Mounce 124 n. 26).

The position of the living creatures in relation to God's throne is not easy to establish. They are 'at the heart' of it, ἐν μέσῳ τοῦ θρόνου (*en mesō[i] tou thronou*, lit. 'in the midst of the throne', from Ezek. 1.5 LXX), and 'around' it, κύκλῳ (adv.) τοῦ θρόνου (*kuklō[i] tou thronou*, 'around the throne'). The repetition of 'the throne' may suggest that an editorial hand has been at work (so Charles 1, 118–19).

The creatures do not *support* the throne, as in Ezek. 1.22, 26, but *surround* it. (In *1 Enoch* 40.2 the four angels stand *on* the four wings of the Lord of the Spirits; and, according to *2 Apoc. Bar.* 51.11, those who are saved will be shown the majesty of the 'living beings *under* [or lower than] the throne', as well as 'all the hosts of the angels'). The living creatures of Rev. 4.6 are indeed 'at the heart (or in the middle) of the throne, and around it'. They prostrate themselves in worship (5.8, [14]), and are free to move independently (15.7). We need not press the figurative details. John is disclosing a throne-vision in the Spirit, and speaking of angelic beings. It is apparent that they are closely associated with God's being (hence the translation, 'at the *heart* of the throne'), even as they lead his praise and worship before him.

The creatures have 'eyes all over, front and back'. This phrase alludes to Ezek. 1.18; 10.12, where the wheels beside the living creatures are said to be 'full of eyes all around'. The Hebrew word for 'wheels' (אופנים, *ôpanním*) was used in later Jewish literature to mean a member of the angelic orders (*1 Enoch* 71.7; *3 Enoch* 1.8; 7.1; 25.5–6; et al.). Once more, the associations in this context of Revelation are angelic. The term 'eyes', as it happens, can also be used as a metaphor for 'stars' (Plutarch, *Moralia, Dinner of the Seven Wise Men* 161 F, 'through all these eyes of hers [Justice], God watches in every direction the deeds that are done . . . on land and on the sea'; cf. Charles 1, 123). See further Aune 297–98.

For the living creatures to be 'full of eyes' all around (cf. verse 8) suggests that they are alert and knowledgeable. 'Nothing escapes their notice' (Mounce 124).

7 Each of the living creatures (cherubim) in the vision of Ezek. 1, to which John is apparently indebted in this scene, possessed four faces (1.6, 10): a lion on the right, an ox on the left, an eagle behind and a man in front. Only one of the creatures in the throne room of Rev. 4 has a face; the others present the forms of a lion, an ox and an eagle in flight. The order of the lists also differs slightly: the human face is mentioned third by John and first by Ezekiel.

John is still describing angelic beings at this point (see on verse 6), and is not alluding to the personification of divine immanence in nature (so Swete 71). Attempts have regularly been made to interpret the appearance of the living creatures symbolically. Hendriksen, for example (87), sees them as representing strength (lion), service (ox), intelligence (man) and swiftness (eagle), and notes that these are characteristics regularly attributed to angels (Ps. 103.20; Heb. 1.14 and Ps. 103.21; cf. Luke 12.8 and 15.10; Dan. 9.21; et al.). Irenaeus, writing towards the end of the second century AD (*c.* 170), equates the living creatures – although without reference to Revelation – to the four Gospels and their writers; and he does so by placing the Gospels in a most unusual order: lion (John), ox (Luke), man (Matthew) and flying eagle (Mark). See Irenaeus, *Adv. Haer.* 3.11.8. But this is a relatively late, and entirely fanciful, view.

Such interpretations are speculative and unnecessary. The 'living creatures' described in this verse are angelic beings, with a life and identity of their own; and we need not be more precise than this. Although they belong to the orders of angels, however (and here John moves on his description of these beings from the previous verse), the living creatures are still in touch with God's creation, and can represent it; just as the twenty-four elders of Rev. 4.4 (q.v.) are angelic members of the heavenly court, representing the body of the faithful in the Church. Indeed, the four recognizable living creatures are eventually associated with the outworking of God's judgement in his creation (Rev. 6.1–7; 15.7–8). Cf. Sweet 120.

Here is a further example of John's balanced cosmology. Since the Word became flesh (John 1.14), heaven and earth remain indissolubly conjoined. What takes place in the courtroom of heaven has relevance for John's church on earth.

The Greek of verse 7 is sparse in verbs, and in each description of the four living creatures the present tense of the verb 'to be' is supplied. The only verb occurs in the sentence, 'the third (creature) has (ἔχων, *echōn*, lit. "having") a human face'. The use of the participle, instead of a finite form of the verb, is a Hebraic and Aramaic idiom (Charles 1, 124).

8 Each of the four living creatures (see verses 6–7), like the seraphim of Isa. 6.2, has six wings. In view of the nature and content of the chant later in this verse, it appears

that Isa. 6.1–3 is primarily in the writer's mind at this point. But the (four-)winged creatures of Ezek. 1 (see verse 6) cannot be far away. John draws on more than one source
to construe his theophany (Knight 61); and presumably wider influences from the
ancient Near East in any case lie behind the symbolism of both prophets (Aune 301).

The 'wings' of the living creatures suggest swiftness to carry out the will of God
(Mounce 125). Cf. Ps. 18.10, where God is pictured as coming 'swiftly upon the wings
of the wind'. In Ezek. 10.16 God is described as being carried on his chariot-throne by
the cherubim, who 'lifted up their wings to rise up from the earth'.

The Greek of the opening part of this verse is awkward. The phrase καὶ τὰ τέσσερα
ζῷα (*kai ta tessera zō[i]a*, lit. 'and the four living creatures') stands by itself, and needs to
be complemented. The ζῷα (*zō[i]a*, 'living creatures') can be taken as the subject of the
verb γέμουσιν (*gemousin*, lit. 'are full [of eyes]'), which stands apart; or the verb ἦν (*ēn*,
'were'; the singular form is governed by the neuter plural of the subject) can be supplied
with ἔχων (*echōn*, 'having'; on which see verse 7). The form ἓν καθ᾽ ἕν . . . ἀνά (*hen kath
hen . . . ana*, lit. 'one by one . . . each') is an emphatic distributive; cf. BDF 248.1.

For the 'eyes' of the creatures see on verse 6, where there is a parallel description.
But this time the creatures are said to have 'eyes all over, around and underneath'
(κυκλόθεν καὶ ἔσωθεν, *kyklothen kai esōthen*, lit. 'around and inside'). The probable meaning of this difficult picture can be derived from Ezek. 10.12, where the wings as well
as the bodies of the cherubim (living creatures) are said to be 'full of eyes all around' (cf.
Ezek. 1.18; *3 Enoch* 25.6). Here, then, the eyes of the creatures are positioned *all round*
the body, and *underneath* (on the underside of) the wings. This is a more satisfactory
explanation than that which connects κυκλόθεν (*kyklothen*, 'around') with the previous
clause, and adopts the reading (from 046), καὶ ἔξωθεν καὶ ἔσωθεν (*kai exōthen kai esōthen*,
lit. 'and outside and inside'). Taken literally, to have 'eyes within' remains a difficult
concept. See Swete 72; Mounce 125 n. 33.

As in verse 6, the 'eyes' of the angelic beings (and again, we need not press the
symbolic details of this throne-vision) imply alertness: they exhibit, on God's account
and in respect of his creation, all-seeing intelligence (Beckwith 502), intellectual pene-
tration (Hendriksen 87) and wakefulness (Sweet 120).

The four angelic beings lead the faithful, belonging to the Church in heaven and
on earth, in a 'ceaseless tribute of praise' (Swete 72). Cf. *1 Enoch* 39.12 ('those who do
not slumber' bless God, using the trisagion); 71.7. Swete needlessly refers to this as the
activity of *nature* alone, under the hand of God (ibid.; see also on verse 6). But ceaseless
adoration features regularly in apocalyptic descriptions of heaven (note also *T. Levi* 3.8;
2 Enoch 21.1); and we have already argued that the 'living creatures' are angelic, and not
simply natural, figures (see above, 120). It might be claimed, against this interpretation,
that the worship of this chant is offered 'day and night' (ἡμέρας καὶ νυκτός, *hēmeras kai
nyktos*): divisions of time which belong to a material, rather than spiritual, setting. However, John's vision of heaven is never detached from earth (see on verse 1); and time
references, within John's description of eternity, occur elsewhere in the Apocalypse (see
8.1). As always, the Johannine eschatology is balanced. 'Day and night' is a hendiadys,
meaning 'ceaselessly'.

The chanted trisagion (a Greek form; Latin *sanctus*, or *tersanctus*), 'holy, holy, holy',
is based on Isaiah's description of the worship of the Seraphim in the temple (6.3 LXX).
See further Aune 302–307. But John adapts his source freely. He inserts ὁ θεός (*ho theos*,
'God') after κύριος (*kyrios*, 'Lord'); he changes σαβαώθ (*sabaōth*, 'of hosts', lit. 'sabaoth')
into ὁ παντοκράτωρ (*ho pantokratōr*, the 'Omnipotent'); he removes Isaiah's πλήρης πᾶσα
ἡ γῆ τῆς δόξης αὐτοῦ (*plērēs pasa hē gē tēs doxēs autou*, 'the whole earth is full of his glory'),
as being inappropriate in an act of praise which is offered in heaven (see above); and he
adds ὁ ἦν καὶ ὁ ὢν καὶ ὁ ἐρχόμενος (*ho ēn kai ho ōn kai ho erchomenos*, '[the one] who was,

and is, and is to come') from Rev. 1.4, 8 (q.v.; but note the variant order here, 'who was, and is', rather than 'who is, and who was').

The praise of the living creatures is directed to the attributes of God which are central to John's vision here, and throughout the Apocalypse: his holiness, power and eternity (cf. Mounce 125). God is holy (whole), and therefore ultimately separate from his creation and created beings; although, in his love, he is willing to be in relationship with them. By implication, humanity is incomplete and *un*holy.

Walker, 'Origin' 132–33, believes that the threefold form 'holy, holy, holy', here and in the underlying text at Isa. 6.3, was originally a single ascription, 'holy' (קָדוֹשׁ, qādôš), to which the MT has added, as a pious 'improvement' (133), a double ascription with the force of 'exceeding holy' (see 1 Sam. 2.3; Eccles. 7.24). So the trisagion of Isa. 6.3/Rev. 4.8, in Walker's view, is in origin a conflate reading, meaning 'holy, exceeding(ly) holy'.

The holy one is also 'the Lord, the Omnipotent' (for the formula see LXX Amos 4.13; Hos. 12.5; Nahum 3.5; Zech. 10.3; Mal. 2.16; et al.). For 'Lord' see Rev. 1.8; also Foerster and Quell, 'κύριος, et al.' 1086–95. For the title παντοκράτωρ (*pantokratōr*, 'Omnipotent' or 'Almighty'), used only in Revelation apart from 2 Cor. 6.18, see on Rev. 1.8. The description suggests God's absolute power in and over his creation; and divine sovereignty is clearly in view in the vision of Rev. 4. But his omnipotence always exists in tension with his love for humanity, and the proper expression of human free will. God's power would in any case be understood as a means of encouragement and strength for those facing persecution from outside John's circle, and doctrinal conflict from within the churches (cf. Matt. 10.28; John 16.33).

God is also eternal, in his holiness and his omnipotence (cf. Exod. 3.14–15). These divine qualities exist, as he does, beyond time. God's steadfast and abiding character embraces past, present and future; he acts in time and draws time and eternity together. (See the parallel reference to Jesus, as the same 'yesterday, today and for ever', in Heb. 13.8.) The eternity of God is referred to again twice in the verses which follow (9–10).

The worship of this passage is monotheistic in content, and makes no reference to the exalted Christ. The liturgy becomes binitarian in Rev. 5, once the sovereignty of Christ has been established (Knight 61). Moreover, what began as a heavenly vision, a dramatic tableau unveiled to the seer step by step, now becomes 'a scene of active worship and proclamation' (Michaels 92) in which we can participate. Note the use of verbs in the present tense, from verses 5 to 8. With John, we enter heaven to see and hear what we now understand to be a ceaseless round of immediate, liturgical adoration; and this embraces the worship of the saints on earth.

9–10 The twenty-four elders (see on verse 4) join the living creatures (see on verses 6–8) in this activity of worshipping God; and such an association is constant in the Apocalypse (cf. Rev. 5.8, 14; 7.11; 14.3; 19.4). The verbs in these two verses are in the future tense, which may imply that the joint adoration in this context will not take place until God's power is established on earth. Beckwith (503) notes that the future indicative with ὅταν (*hotan*, lit. 'when') is rare, but rightly claims that it should be taken here with a frequentative force, similar to the Hebrew imperfect: '*whenever* the living creatures offer glory . . . the elders prostrate themselves'. So also Swete 73. The actions are understood as simultaneous; although Beckwith classes this construction as 'among the writer's grammatical errors' (503).

The angelic creatures offer to the ever-living God, seated on the throne (see on verses 2–3), 'glory and reverence and thankfulness'. The phrase δόξα καὶ τιμή (*doxa kai timē*, 'glory and honour, or reverence') is drawn from the LXX of Ps. 8.5; 28(29).1; 95(96).7. It is linked in the New Testament with ἀφθαρσία (*aphtharsia*, 'immortality', Rom. 2.7), ἔπαινος (*epainos*, 'praise', 1 Pet. 1.7), δύναμις (*dynamis*, 'power', Rev. 4.11) and ἰσχύς (*ischys*, 'strength', Rev. 5.12). 'Glory' and 'reverence', in this doxology, speak of the spontaneous acknowledgement of God's inherent and supreme nature and authority; while 'thankfulness' denotes a human response to God's gifts in creation and redemption (cf. Swete 73; Moffatt 381; Beckwith 503). He is glorious and to be revered; and that is the incentive for our thankful reaction to his being and activity. For δόξα (*doxa*, 'glory') and τιμή (*timē*, 'reverence' or 'honour') see further Aalen, 'Glory, Honour'; cf. also on Rev. 1.6. For εὐχαριστία (*eucharistia*, 'thankfulness') see Conzelmann, 'εὐχαριστία, κτλ', esp. 411–15; also Esser, 'εὐχαριστία', esp. 819.

Praise is offered by the angelic beings to the one who 'lives eternally' (τῷ ζῶντι εἰς τοὺς αἰῶνας τῶν αἰώνων, *tō[i] zōnti eis tous aiōnas tōn aiōnōn*); see on verse 8*b*. This expands the earlier description, in verse 2, of someone (God) seated on a throne. The closest verbal parallels in the Greek Old Testament to this phraseology are to be found in Dan. 4.34 (Theod.); 12.7 LXX; and these texts appear to have influenced the style of the prophet-seer in this passage, supplementing the framework from Dan. 7 which lies behind the scene in Rev. 4—5 (cf. Beale 333). See 112, 126.

The description in verse 10 of the God who receives praise and reverence, as one who 'sits on the throne and is alive for ever and ever', is repeated almost exactly in the Greek from verse 9*b*. A Danielic background is once more in evidence. In Dan. 4.34 and 12.7 the affirmation of God's eternity contrasts with the temporary rule of evil monarchs, whose power has been abrogated because they have claimed to be divine (as with Nebuchadnezzar, Dan. 4.30–33), or have persecuted the people of God (Antiochus Epiphanes and others, Dan. 11.30–35; 12.7). See Beale 334. So here, all opposition to God is by implication condemned, as is all compromise with those who falsely claim divine power for themselves (note verse 11; cf. also Rev. 2.13, 20, et al.). God's eternal reign is supreme; and this is an encouragement for the faithful in John's church, or any other, who are experiencing conflict of any kind. They are promised vindication in the end, if they endure (cf. Dan. 12.1–3, 12); although at present they may be 'no match for their oppressors' (Beale 334).

The angelic beings, leading the adoration of heaven, and the elders who represent the glorified Church, praise God for his being and creation (cf. Milligan 74–75). The twenty-four elders prostrate themselves before the throne (πεσοῦνται, *pesountai*, lit. 'they will fall down'; for the future tense see above), which is a proper response to the majesty of God; to worship him (προσκυνήσουσιν, *proskynēsousin*, lit. 'they will worship') is a suitable acknowledgement of his eternal being (cf. Mounce 126). Such a posture (of worship) can be interpreted simply as a mark of respect (cf. Matt. 8.2, a leper 'knelt' [προσεκύνει, *prosekynei*, lit. 'was kneeling'] before Jesus). But here the word 'worship' evokes the custom, common in the East, of prostrating oneself before a deity in abject homage (see Charles 1, 133).

The elders 'lay their crowns before the throne', before they sing the praises of God. (For λέγοντες, *legontes*, 'crying', lit. 'saying', see on 5.9). They acknowledge that their authority (see verse 4) is delegated, and to be returned to their sovereign Lord, who is alone worthy of universal glory and honour (verse 9). There is a human parallel in Tacitus, who records (*Ann.* 15.29) that Tiridates, after the usual sacrifice of victims, 'lifted the diadem (the emblem of his royalty) from his head, and placed it at the feet of the image' of the Emperor Nero.

11 The adoration of the elders, unlike that of the living creatures, is direct and personal. It begins, '*you* are worthy' (ἄξιος εἶ, *axios ei*), in consensus language which has a political ring; and note the use of 'our' (Lord and God), ἡμῶν, *hēmōn*, with the emphatic personal pronoun σύ (*su*, 'you') before ἔκτισας (*ektisas*, 'you created') in line 3, and the use of σου (*sou*, 'your') in line 4 (but see 5.9–10). It also differs from the earlier ascription of praise (verse 8) by referring to the divine work of creation (11*b*), rather than to the attributes of God.

Suetonius (*Dom.* 13) speaks denigratingly of the Emperor Domitian (AD 81–96) in terms which reflect by inversion the first line of this hymn. The emperor, he says, delighted to hear the people in the amphitheatre shout on his feast day, 'Good fortune attend our Lord!' (*Domino feliciter!*). With no less arrogance, Suetonius continues, Domitian dictated a circular letter which began, 'Our Master and our God bids that this be done' (*Dominus et deus noster hoc fieri iubet*). In contrast to the cult of emperor worship which was introduced by Domitian, and writing much earlier than this emperor's reign, John makes it clear that, for the Christian, God the Creator alone is 'worthy' of worship (= worth-ship). The claims of all other pseudo-gods are blasphemous. On 'Lord and God' (ὁ κύριος καὶ ὁ θεός, *ho kyrios kai ho theos*), here, see on verse 8*b*.

God is worthy, the elders cry, 'to receive glory and reverence and power' (cf. 5.12–13). On 'glory and reverence' see on verse 9*a*. The triplet in this context is completed by the addition of 'power' (δύναμις, *dynamis*). That sovereign power is especially evident in God's creation, which is celebrated in the remaining lines of the hymn. For 'power' (δύναμις, *dynamis*) cf. Betz, 'δύναμις', esp. 604; see also on 7.10, 12.

God 'created everything' (ἔκτισας τὰ πάντα, *ektisas ta panta*). John's readers from a Hebraic background would find no difficulty with such a statement. Those with gnostic tendencies, whose origin was Hellenistic, needed to be reminded that God has never stood apart from his creation, but is always deeply involved in it. As Creator, he is responsible for every part of the universe.

Moreover, creation is solely the result of God's will (cf. Dan. 4.35). The Greek construction of this point is unusual, not to say difficult. First there is an ambiguity in the preposition διά (*dia*), which means literally '*because of* (your will)'. This, in turn, denotes either the operating cause or the intention of creation ('for the sake of your will'; Beasley-Murray 119). Both meanings appear to be present. Creation came about by the operation of God's will; but the universe came into being through him precisely so that his holy purposes for humanity could be accomplished. His is the ultimate and gracious power, in creation and salvation.

Through God's will, the hymn continues, 'they (all things) existed, and were created' (ἦσαν καὶ ἐκτίσθησαν, *ēsan kai ektisthēsan*). For the MSS variations which attempt to deal with the apparent claim that existence preceded creation see the textual notes above (108).

Despite the difference in the tenses (ἦσαν, *ēsan*, is imperfect, and ἐκτίσθησαν, *ektisthēsan*, aorist), both verbs are in the past tense; and this means that they may be treated as a hendiadys (cf. Caird 68), emphasizing that God is the universal Creator. But if the variation in the verbs themselves, as well as their tenses, can be allowed to carry weight, then it is more likely that the meaning is, 'everything existed first in the eternal mind and will of God (imperfect), and then at an appointed time, through his will, came into being (aorist)'. So Hughes 76; Mounce 127. Beale (335) argues that the first verb refers to the ongoing preservation of the created order, and the second to the beginning of creation itself; and that the order was pastorally motivated, to 'encourage God's people to recognize that everything which happens to them throughout history is part of God's creation purposes' (ibid.). But this exegesis appears to stretch the limits of the text too far; even if encouragement for John's community, on the basis of God's sovereignty in creation, is the special theme of this particular hymn.

Charles (1, 127) finds it hard to reconcile the conception that the offering of praise to God by the living creatures is continuous and unbroken (verse 8), with the fact that spontaneous worship breaks out at intervals: here, and through part of Rev. 5. But, as

Charles himself (ibid.) admits, it is on occasions of great crisis in the Apocalypse that worship and thanksgiving are called forth (Rev. 5.8, 13–14; 11.16; 19.4; see also 5.9–10). In any case, we may add, spontaneous acts of praise such as these are not necessarily interruptions of an ongoing and ceaseless liturgy, but rather intense expressions of it from time to time, and for particular reasons.

John has unfolded for his audience, in the circle of the seven Asian churches and beyond, a vision of the holy God in his transcendence and sovereignty. He is eternal, and worthy to be adored: to receive glory and reverence, and thankfulness and power. But he is also active in the world, which he created. This affirmation underlies Rev. 4, but also the whole of the Apocalypse itself. The world is God's world. By design it is good; and over it, and its history, he is Lord. The only proper response to this dramatic disclosure, among the saints belonging to the Church in heaven and on earth, is awe and obeisance.

So far, in this throne room scene, no specifically Christian theological context has been included. We have been made aware that all things have been created according to the divine will, and specifically to serve God's immutable purposes. Such a belief is an encouragement for all those, in the first century AD and at any moment, who face conflict and suffering. The question then remains: how are the purposes of God to be fulfilled, in a way that will affect – creatively and redemptively – Church and society on earth? John's answer will be provided in the next section of the throne room vision.

5.1   The second part of John's vision is, in some ways, a continuation of the first. Although the prophet-seer has been viewing the heavenly court and its worship through-out Chapter 4, he has not been mentioned in person since 4.2. In this verse he reappears, standing next to (or near) the throne (see verses 2, 4, 6, et al.). The throne itself, with the one seated on it, provides a further connection with the previous chapter (note 4.2, 9, 10, et al.), throughout which the sovereign God has been pictured in awesome splendour (cf. Beckwith 504). But now the disclosure moves on, and we hear of a securely sealed scroll. This symbolizes God's salvific plan, to assert his sovereignty over a rebellious world, and to achieve his loving purposes in creation through the victory of the Lamb. The angelic chorus of praise which heralds that conquest forms the major theme of Rev. 5.

But the revelation of the Victor himself is delayed until verse 6; and this heightens the dramatic intensity of the scene. The focus of attention is at last brought to bear on the action of the Lamb, and its significance for the world and for God's kingdom (Beasley-Murray 120).

Beale (337) argues that Rev. 4.1—5.1 follows a structural outline identical to that in Dan. 7.9–28 and Ezek. 1—2. However, in Rev. 5.2–14 the Danielic outline is followed, rather than that of Ezek 1—2, and in this section the allusions to Dan. 7 are more numer-ous than those to Ezek. 1—2. Nevertheless, as Bauckham (*Theology* 81) shows, through-out Rev. 4—10, chapters which are connected by the 'strong angel' of 5.2 and 10.1 (q.v.), John is closely following the inaugural prophetic vision of Ezek. 1.1—3.11. Allusions to this passage move from Rev. 5.1, the scroll in God's right hand, to its opening by the Lamb (5.7—8.1); the scroll is then taken by the strong angel from heaven to earth (10.1–2), and given to the prophet-seer to eat (10.8–10). This chain of revelation, from God to the prophet John, corresponds exactly to the movement in 1.1 (q.v.); see Bauckham, *Theology* 81–82.

John sees (καὶ εἶδον, *kai eidon*, 'then I saw') the one seated on the throne (on that circumlocution for God, and on 'the throne' itself, see on 4.2). This is the first occur-rence in the Apocalypse of the phrase καὶ εἶδον (*kai eidon*, lit. 'and I saw'), where it is used 32 times. It functions to introduce a new vision narrative (Rev. 8.2; et al.); to lead into a scene within a continuing vision narrative (as here, 5.1; also 6.1; et al.); and to draw attention to an important figure or action in a continuing vision narrative (5.2; et al.). Cf. also μετὰ ταῦτα εἶδον (*meta tauta eidon*, lit. 'after this I saw') at 4.1. See Aune 338.

The imagery of the scroll in the hand of God is derived from Ezek. 2.9–10. The 'right' hand of God is an anthropomorphism representing his strength. The scroll appears to be resting 'on' (ἐπί, *epi*) the open palm of God, so that it is visible to the seer, rather than being held 'in' (ἐν, *en*) it (so Charles 1, 136; Swete 75; against Beckwith 504). But cf. Rev. 20.1, where the angel holds the key to the bottomless pit and a great chain 'in' (ἐπί, *epi*) his hand (some MSS, including ℵ, there read ἐν [*en*, 'in'] for ἐπί [*epi*, lit. 'upon']).

The nature of the scroll itself, sealed and with writing inside and on the back, is problematic. The Greek word is βιβλίον (*biblion*, lit. 'small book'). The diminutive force has disappeared in New Testament usage; and the term, when meaning a volume as such, is equivalent to βίβλος (*biblos*, 'book'). See John 20.30; 21.25. Note the diminutive form at Rev. 10.2 (the angel held in his hand a 'small scroll', lit. 'small book', using βιβλαρίδιον, *biblaridion*).

It is probably right to describe the document in this passage as a 'scroll', rather than a book. It is easier to seal a scroll with seven seals, than it is to do the same with a codex. The scroll can then be seen as a prophecy about the future, which needed to be sealed from human sight until the time of fulfilment (cf. Dan. 8.26; 12.9). But it is more likely that the scroll here should be interpreted as 'some form of legal document' relating to the destiny of humanity: either a doubly inscribed contract deed or a testament (Beasley-Murray 120). Cf. Ps. 139.16; *1 Enoch* 47.3; 81.1–2.

Roller ('Das Buch', esp. 102–107) provides a full account of the doubly written contract, which was known in antiquity all over the Middle East, and used for every kind of legal transaction. It goes back to the early Babylonian custom of writing a deed on a clay tablet, wrapping it round with more clay, and stating the nature of the contract on the outside. The ancient Egyptians used papyrus and parchment, instead of clay, for their contracts; and, in this case, the sealed document would be preserved in an earthenware jar (as with the deed of purchase described in Jer. 32.9–15; cf. Roller 101–102). The Romans introduced wax sheets for such contracts, especially, from the time of Nero, in relation to the rights of the military.

This kind of doubly inscribed deed might well have been in mind when John refers to the scroll on God's right palm. It is a contract which guarantees the promise of God's kingdom and salvation for all believers. However, an alterative understanding, popular since the time of Theodor Zahn, views the scroll as a testament or will. Zahn (*Introduction* 3, 393–96) argues that the document with seven seals is 'the symbol of the promise and assurance by God' to his Church of the future kingdom (394). The contents of God's covenant will await realization, and it is the returning Christ who will 'open the testament of God and execute it' (ibid. 395). Theologically this is Johannine, and indeed biblical. God has promised new life to his creation, and Christ is the one who, in time and in eternity, eventually brings this about.

There are, however, two main objections to the interpretation of this scroll as a will or testament. First, such a document is not normally executed until all the contents have been disclosed; whereas in Rev. 6—8 God's judgements, as the seals are opened, become progressively apparent. But the same difficulty is involved if the scroll is explained as a doubly written contract; and, in any case, 'a symbol does not have to fit at all points' (Beasley-Murray 122). Second, Roller points out that a testament never possessed the form of a doubly inscribed document ('Das Buch' 106). But the characterization of the scroll in Rev. 5.1 as having 'writing inside and on the back' derives from Ezek. 2.9–10, where the scroll is unsealed, and is presumably, therefore, not a doubly written testament as such.

Beasley-Murray (122) accordingly questions whether John has modified Ezekiel's document to make it a contract-deed, or alternatively changed Ezekiel's prophecy of overflowing judgements (cf. Ezek. 3.1—7.27) into a testament of the kingdom preceded by judgements (cf. Rev. 21—22; 6—20). In truth, however, both interpretations (deed or testament) are close together. As a contract or a will, the scroll symbolizes the gift of God's covenant promises to his followers, through the life and death and exaltation of Jesus the Christ. These will be enacted in broad outline in the remainder of the Apocalypse, Rev. 6—22.

The covenant motif in this scene, and in what follows in the Apocalypse, is predominant (cf. Rev. 11.19; although that is the single occurrence in the Johannine corpus of the widely used biblical term, διαθήκη [*diathēkē*, 'covenant']). God's purposes for his world – to assert his sovereignty over wrongdoing, and realize in love his plan of salvation – are expressed in terms of a personal relationship between himself and his people, finally and fully achieved in Christ. In that covenant, God is bound by solemn oath to perform what he has promised; but the human response to those promises must be one of faith (cf. Heb. 8.6–7; 1 John 3.23). See further Beale 340–42. On 'covenant' see Guhrt, 'διαθήκη'.

The contents of the scroll will be revealed as the visionary section of the Apocalypse is unfolded. They include God's judgement (e.g. Rev. 6.12–17; 8.6—9.6; 18.1–24), but also, through his judgement, his salvation and joy (cf. Rev. 12.7–12; 21.1—22.21). The scroll contains the divine plan for the future of creation, but also for its present existence (for this balance in John's eschatology see Smalley, *Thunder and Love* 62–63). Note, for example, the temporal perspective in the description of the fall of Babylon in Rev. 18, and the eternal dimension attaching to the vision of the heavenly Jerusalem in Rev. 21—22. It needs to be emphasized that the order of the events to be related by the prophet-seer cannot be regarded as chronological. God's purposes are ultimately perceived from a viewpoint which is beyond time, and therefore outside a chronological framework.

The scroll is an episthograph, for it has writing 'inside and on the back', as with the book given to the prophet at Ezek. 2.10. Cf. Pliny, *Ep.* 3.5; his uncle wrote many volumes, some of which were 'written on both sides' (using the adjective *opisthographus*) in a very small character. That the scroll has writing on both sides indicates the 'extensive and comprehensive' nature of God's decrees (Mounce 130). The process of writing on the reverse side of a papyrus scroll, where the fibres are placed vertically, would be more difficult than using the front side (where the fibres run horizontally).

The scroll is also 'securely sealed with seven seals'. According to Stauffer (*Christ and the Caesars* 182–83) a legal Roman will had to be sealed by witnesses at least seven times, and Augustus as well as Vespasian left such testaments for their successors. But the use of 'seven' in this context is undoubtedly influenced by John's predilection for the number and its symbolism (see on Rev. 1.4). The verb translated '*securely* sealed' (κατεσφραγισμένον, *katesphragismenon*) is emphatic: the scroll is not just sealed, but inexorably so. The imagery may suggest that the purposes of God cannot be thwarted or violated. The verb 'to seal' by itself is σφραγίζειν (*sphragizein*). The compound form is found only here in the New Testament.

For the 'scroll' see further Aune 338–46. For 'seal' see further on 6.1.

2   The heavenly vision continues, with καὶ εἶδον (*kai eidon*, lit. 'and I saw') repeated from verse 1 (q.v.). In this case the conjunction καί (*kai*, lit. 'and') can bear the force of the translation, 'then'. For the 'angel' of John's vision see on 1.1; also 7.1–3. For angels in Revelation see 28–30. The angel in this verse is described as 'strong' (ἰσχυρόν, *ischyron*);

and such a figure is mentioned again at Rev. 10.1(–3); 18.21. This angel plays a key role in the apocalyptic drama of Revelation, and points forward especially to the heavenly being who comes to earth at 10.1(q.v.); cf. also verse 1. In Chapter 10 an essential stage in John's prophetic mission and message is reached; and for that scene the earlier part of the play has been a necessary preparation. See Bauckham, *Theology* 82.

The strength of the angel in verse 2 is significant; and so is the fact that he 'proclaims' (κηρύσσοντα, *kēryssonta*; the verb also means 'to announce' or 'preach') his message, rather than simply speaking it, 'in a *loud* voice' (ἐν φωνῇ μεγάλῃ, *en phōnē[i] megalē[i]*; see also [10.3]; 14.7, 9, 15). John's account at this point is evidently marked by dramatic force. The proclamation of the angel is of supreme importance, and his voice also needs to reach the outer bounds of the universe: as far as heaven, earth and underneath the earth (so verse 3, q.v.). Charles (1, 139) regards κηρύσσοντα ἐν (*kēryssonta en*, 'proclaiming in [a loud voice]') as a Hebraism.

There is a firm Old Testament background to this section of the heavenly courtroom scene. The angelic questioner of Rev. 5.2 echoes to some extent the reference to the heavenly spokesperson in Dan. 4, who is sent 'in strength' from the Lord. Cf. Dan. 4.13–14 (LXX and Theod.); 4.23 (LXX). These two figures carry out a similar function. The angel in Daniel (4) speaks for the heavenly council, and issues a decree of judgement on King Nebuchadnezzar, which is to be followed by restoration. In Revelation (5) the angel is also the spokesperson for the divine council, and proclaims to the universe God's decree of judgement and redemption. See Beale 338; cf. also Müller, 'Die himmlische Ratsversammlung'.

The imagery of sealed and opened books (or scrolls) in association with the end-time, present in the second half of this verse ('Who is worthy to open the scroll, and break its seals?'), also derives from the Old Testament: but solely from Daniel. Cf. Dan. 7.10 (Theod.), βίβλοι ἠνεῴχθησαν (*bibloi ēneō[i]chthēsan*, 'the books were opened'), and Rev. 5.2*b*, ἀνοῖξαι τὸ βιβλίον (*annoixai to biblion*, 'to open the scroll'). Note also the connection between the future breaking of the scroll's seals mentioned in the present context (λῦσαι τὰς σφραγῖδας αὐτοῦ, *lysai tas sphragidas autou*, lit. 'to break its seals') and the 'unsealing' at the end-time referred to in Dan. 12.8 (LXX, using λύσις, *lysis*, 'unloosing') and Dan. 12.9 (Theod.). Cf. also, more distantly, Dan. 8.26 ('seal up the vision') and Isa. 29.18 ('the deaf shall hear the words of a scroll'); also Dan. 12.4.

The angel asks who is 'worthy' (ἄξιος, *axios*) to perform the task of unsealing the scroll. The worthiness in question has more to do with morality and authority than with physical strength. The need is for a being whose 'rank and office give him before God worthiness to perform this supreme service in regard to the divine decrees' (Beckwith 507). But worthiness and ability seem to be identical in this context, so that the verb ἐδύνατο (*edynato*, 'was fit' or 'able [to open the scroll]') is used as a parallel in verse 3. Perhaps a combination of physical strength, moral quality and legal authority is in mind (note 4.11). So Thompson 94. Cf. Matt. 3.11 (John the Baptist in relation to Jesus), where οὐ ἱκανός (*ou hikanos*, lit. 'not able') is identical with the οὐκ ἄξιος (*ouk axios*, 'not worthy') of John 1.27.

The order of the actions in the angel's question, where the scroll is to be opened before its seals are broken, may appear odd. But, as Beale (338) points out, the central issue is the authority in question to take possession of the scroll. Hence 5.9, 'you deserve to take the scroll, and to break its seals'. The scroll is opened (possessed) in Rev. 5, but not unsealed until the following chapter (6) and 8.1. Charles (1, 139) takes λῦσαι (*lysai*, 'to break [its seals]') as defining more precisely the preceding verb, ἀνοῖξαι (*anoixai*, 'to open'). But this seems to miss the point.

For the scroll and its (seven) seals see on verse l.

3–4   No one in the universe is found who is able to open the scroll and examine its material. Humanity by itself is morally incompetent, since it falls short of God's righteous standards (note John 2.24–25; cf. Rom. 3.9–10). See Hughes 78. Only one who is like the Father can fulfil his demands and his salvific purposes. The 'opening' of the scroll and the exhibition of its contents signifies the disclosure of those purposes; but it also includes their fulfilment (Beckwith 508). God's Messiah alone can demonstrate how God's will for his creation will be carried out to its consummation.

The threefold division of the universe into heaven, earth and 'underneath the earth', runs back also to the Old Testament; although there it is expressed differently. See Exod. 20.4 (heaven above, the earth beneath, the water under the earth); cf. Exod. 20.11; Ps. 146.6. By the time of the New Testament the third division has become synonymous with Hades. Cf. Phil. 2.10; also Rom. 10.6–7. For the fourfold division of creation, including the sea, note Rev. 5.13. For a two-level division of the cosmos into heaven and earth/sea, elsewhere in Revelation, cf. 10.5; 12.12; 14.6; 21.1. Note also the cosmology of 10.6: heaven, earth and sea.

The prophet-seer weeps unrestrainedly because of the situation presented in verse 3, which is repeated almost exactly in verse 4. The verb ἔκλαιον (*eklaion*, 'I was weeping') is in the imperfect tense, denoting a continuous action in the past. It is almost as if we come across John, to discover that his great grief has long been in progress. For the seer, time can be measured even in eternity (see on 8.1). Aune (349) thinks that this dramatic episode may have been influenced by Isa. 29.11.

The prophet weeps not only because no worthy being has yet been found to open the scroll and look inside it but also because it seems as if the promised disclosure of 4.1 will not now take place. For weeping as an apocalyptic motif see 2 Esdras 5.13; *1 Enoch* 90.41 (uncontrollable tears); *2 Enoch* 1.3; *3 Apoc. Bar* 1.1; *Asc. Isa.* 2.10.

5   One of the elders speaks to the prophet-seer. For 'elders' (πρεσβύτεροι, *presbyteroi*) see on 4.4. There is no necessary symbolism in the choice of an elder as a spokesman. It is an element of the Apocalyptist's dramatic art that he brings variety into his narrative by introducing different agents to keep the action moving. Cf. 6.1 (a living creature); 8.13 (an eagle); 11.15 (an angel); 16.1 (a voice); et al. So Beckwith 508.

The elder restrains John's tears by speaking to him about the Christ of God (λέγει, *legei*, lit. 'he says', is in the present tense, the immediacy of which in the Greek helps to switch the audience into the action). Christ is described by using two familiar messianic titles.

(a)   'The Lion from the tribe of Judah'. This martial description is taken from Gen. 49.9–10, where it refers to the Messiah's sovereign power. In 2 Esdras 11.37; 12.31 the anointed one is also represented as a lion.

(b)   The other title applied to the Christ is 'the Root of David' (that is, a branch from David's root). This derives from Isa. 11.1, 10 (cf. 2 Esdras 12.31–32 [where the titles 'lion' and 'offspring', or 'branch', are conjoined]; Sir. 47.22; Rev. 22.16; also Jer. 23.5).

The prophecy in Isa. 11.1–10 speaks of the ideal king who was to rise from the family of Jesse, the father of David, to be a signal to the nations. In *Pss. Sol.* 17 this prophecy is adapted by the author to describe the militant Lord Messiah driving out the unrighteous Gentiles (cf. verses 21–25), and establishing God's reign, with Israel as the leading nation (cf. verses 26–34, 44–46). See Caird 74. The words of the elder to John in the present context might have indicated that these messianic expectations were about to be fulfilled, through Christ as warrior and king.

But, in this verse and the next, there is a profound theological shift, as the drama in heaven unfolds with movement and intensity, and as its implications for God's world become more apparent. First, the Lion is perceived as a Lamb (verse 6, q.v.). Before that, second, it is reported that the Messiah 'has conquered' (ἐνίκησεν, *enikēsen*; the aorist tense denotes a completed action in the past which has ongoing effects). Sweet (128) suggests that νικᾶν (*nikan*, 'to conquer') can bear a forensic and athletic, as well as military, sense.

The nature of the conquest becomes evident later in this scene, where we hear of the ransom of God's saints through the death of the Lamb (5.9). In this way evil and death, and all that is opposed to God, are conquered (although the writer does not explain the process), and the victory of believers becomes possible in Christ. See 3.21, where that conquest has already been mentioned; also 2.7; 12.11; 15.2. The Jewish understanding and appearance of the Messiah are retained in the Apocalypse; but they are transposed into a totally Christian conception. As the revealer and agent of God's saving will, Jesus the Christ acts as Messiah for all God's people, both Jewish and Christian (cf. Beckwith 509).

Jesus is one with God and one with us (verses 6 and 7). For John's balanced Christology, suited to his audience, see further on Rev. 1.12; see also Smalley, *Thunder and Love* 60, 152. The consequence is that he can open 'the scroll with its seven seals' (for which, see on verse 1). He alone qualifies for this task; he is the only one who is 'worthy' (ἄξιος, *axios*, as in verse 2; see also the use of the same term in verse 9) to open the sealed scroll, and thus carry out God's salvific purposes. This vision takes place in heaven, and the seer is given an eternal perspective on the progress of God's creation. But what he hears and sees in the throne room has to do as much with what has already happened, in the death and resurrection of the Messiah of God, as with the future which will be revealed in the remainder of the Apocalypse (6—22).

The verb ἀνοῖξαι (*anoixai*, 'to open') qualifies ἐνίκησεν (*enikēsen*, 'has conquered'); and the infinitive expresses result. The meaning is therefore, as in the translation, 'the Lion/the Root has conquered, *so that* he can open the scroll'. The Greek, meaning lit. 'has conquered to open', is elliptical. For the concept of an open, unsealed document see also Rev. 22.10 (q.v.), where the angel forbids John to seal up the words of the prophecy in the Apocalypse, because the time is near. By then the history of the world and of the Church has been unveiled; and the command is that the record of this in Revelation should remain equally transparent and unsealed.

6 Hearing and sight are close together in John's Revelation, as in his Gospel (e.g. Rev. 1.10, 12; 7.4, 9; John 12.45, 47; 20.14, 16). In the Gospel, both concepts, particularly 'seeing', are close to the notion of believing (cf. John 6.36; 14.9–10; 20.8, 29; see Smalley, *John* 175–76). Sweet (125) argues that in the Apocalypse what is heard, the 'voice', represents the inner reality (spirit); while what is seen, the 'appearance', represents the outward reality (flesh). But it is more accurate to say that the author of Revelation uses what is seen to *interpret* what is heard (as in 22.8, where 'hearing' and 'seeing' are twice conjoined). So, in the context of Rev. 5, John *hears* about a Lion and Davidic Root, associated in the Old Testament with military deliverance; but now *he sees* a Lamb, who makes deliverance from sin possible through his sacrificial death (cf. Caird 73). For καὶ εἶδον (*kai eidon*, 'then I noticed', lit. 'and I saw') see on verse 1.

Here is a powerful 'rebirth of images' (Caird 73). The advent of Jesus the Christ, in his person as in his work, means that the 'Lion' of Judaism must be understood as the 'Lamb' of the new covenant. The juxtaposition of these contrasting images expresses John's Judaeo-Christian 'reinterpretation of current Jewish eschatological hopes' (Baukham, *Climax of Prophecy* 214).

The term ἀρνίον (*arnion*, 'lamb') is used consistently in Revelation (29 times; see also John 21.15) instead of ἀμνός (*amnos*, 'lamb'), the word used of Christ in John 1.29, 36 (also 1 Pet. 1.19). The diminutive force of ἀρνίον (*arnion*, 'lamb') need not be pressed (Beckwith 509). The sacrificial background to John's image of the 'lamb', running back to Isa. 53.7, is clearly present in this verse (the Lamb has been 'slaughtered', verse 6*b*), and probably includes the theme of the paschal lamb, which also underlies the passion narrative in the Fourth Gospel (cf. Mounce 132). However, the character of the Lamb throughout the Apocalypse (except at 13.11, which refers to the beast) is exalted. Christ in Revelation is the victorious Lamb, who overcomes the forces of evil, and whose death removes sin; although his conquest has been achieved through earthly suffering, and his blood has actually been shed (7.14). He is Lord and King (17.14), a figure of wrath as well as of triumph (6.16); he is Ruler, in addition to Redeemer.

For ἀρνίον (*arnion*, 'Lamb') see further Jeremias, 'ἀρνίον'. For the possible links between the Lamb in Revelation and John's Gospel see Smalley, *Thunder and Love* 61–62.

The position of the Lamb in relation to the throne, the creatures and the elders, is obscure, although geographical precision need not be sought in a visionary description. It could mean that the Lamb was standing in the middle of the living creatures and elders (at the 'centre of the throne', as in Rev. 7.17); although 5.7 appears to militate against this interpretation. More probably ἐν μέσῳ . . . ἐν μέσῳ (*en mesō[i] . . . en mesō[i]*, lit. 'in the middle . . . in the middle') should be taken as a Hebraism, giving the sense in the translation: the Lamb was standing (victoriously) between the living creatures encircling the throne and the outer circle of twenty-four elders (for which see on 4.2 and 4.6). Cf. Charles 1, 140. But see Knight, 'Enthroned Christ', who points out that only one throne of God is mentioned in the Apocalypse, and that it is shared by the Father and the Lamb (cf. 3.21; 22.3). Knight therefore argues that the present verse (5.6) should also be interpreted to mean that the Lamb is in the midst of the throne, with God, and that the living creatures and the elders surround them both. This results in a high Christology (Knight, ibid. 46–50). The Lamb in verse 6 is carefully distinguished from the throne-creatures, and from the elders who rank above the angels. But he is 'so intimately asso-ciated with God that it is difficult to believe he is not God' (Knight, ibid. 47). Similarly Hannah, 'Divine Throne', who sees the living creatures as a constituent part of the throne, with the Lamb among them; see esp. ibid. 541–42.

The Lamb 'appeared to have been slaughtered'. The verb ἐσφαγμένον (*esphagmenon*, 'slaughtered', lit. 'having been slain') is in the perfect tense, as is the participle ἑστηκός (*hestēkos*, 'standing', lit. 'having taken his stand'), earlier in the verse. The use of the perfect in the Greek indicates the ongoing effect of the Lamb's completed sacrificial death. The phrase 'slaughtered Lamb' is used again at Rev. 5.12 and 13.8.

The fact that the Lamb 'appeared' to have been slain (ὡς ἐσφαγμένον, *hōs esphagmenon*, lit. 'as slaughtered') does not mean that the death of Christ was unreal; rather, this language expresses the fact that, although the Lamb has been crucified, he is now alive. The cross was an event in history; but it was followed by resurrection (cf. Aune 353). The verb σφάζειν (*sphazein*, 'to slaughter') occurs in the New Testament (apart from 1 John 3.12) only in Revelation, where it is used four times (5.6, 9, 12; 13.8) to describe the death of Christ. At Rev. 13.3 the Greek phrase ὡς ἐσφαγμένην εἰς θάνατον (*hōs esphagmenēn eis thanaton*, lit. 'as slaughtered to death') is used of one of the beast's heads; and this may be a deliberate parody of the reference to the Lamb's death in the present verse.

The Greek at this point uses a simple participle. The prophet-seer noticed a Lamb ἔχων (*echōn*, lit. 'having') seven horns and seven eyes. The translation includes an adversative 'but (he had)', to emphasize the Lamb's resurrection after crucifixion.

The Lamb with 'seven horns' is an idea familiar to us from the Jewish apocalyptic tradition. Cf. *1 Enoch* 90.9, 37–38. In *T. Jos.* 19.8 a lamb (in the presence of 'something like a lion') conquers and destroys the enemies of Israel; although this text seems to have been rewritten by a Christian editor. The 'horn' (κέρας, *keras*) is an Old Testament symbol for power or strength (cf. Dan. 7.7, 20; 8.3, 5); and this is the meaning of the image in the Apocalypse (so 12.3; 13.1, 11; 17.3, 7, 12, 16). Only in this verse, however, is the symbol used in connection with the power of the Lamb. Elsewhere in Revelation it refers to the delegated strength of God's opponents. Barker (*The Revelation* 130–33) associates the 'seven horns' of the Lamb, etymologically and theologically, with shining (divine) light, since the Hebrew term 'shine' ('ray') is the same as the Hebrew word for horn (קֶרֶן, *qeren*). Cf. 1QH 7.11; 2 Cor. 3.12–18. She also regards this detail, together with the 'seven eyes' which follow, as indicative of the Lamb's apotheosis after being in God's presence (similarly Moses in Exod. 34.29; *1 Enoch* 89.36). On 'the sacrificed Lamb' of Rev. 5 in general see further Barker, *The Revelation* 129–43.

It is probably true that we lack certain evidence to show that the Lamb was an established symbol of the messianic conqueror in pre-Christian Judaism (Bauckham, *Climax of Prophecy* 183–84; cf. Aune 353–54). Nevertheless, John's rebirth of images in this passage is such that the nature of divine power, seen in the conquering Messiah (the Lion), must be understood and interpreted in the light of God's sacrificial love revealed in Jesus the Christ (the Lamb). This salvific event lies at the heart of God's purposes for his world, and its effects are eternal. Cf. Boring 109–10, who makes too sharp a distinction between the victorious and piacular roles of Christ in the present context.

The Lamb has 'seven' horns, denoting his perfect and irresistible might, and 'seven' eyes, which represent 'that completeness of vision which leads to perfect knowledge' (Mounce 133). On John's predilection for seven, as the perfect number, see on 1.4; also Smalley, *John* 135. The background to the 'seven eyes' can be found in Zech. 4.10 (the seven eyes of the Lord, ranging through the whole earth). This composite image, not to be taken with any kind of literalism, is John's own creation, although the elements he uses are traditional.

The eyes are further identified as 'the seven spirits of God sent out into all the earth'. For the 'seven spirits of God', as the equivalent of the Spirit of God, see on 1.4; also 3.1; 4.5. The Spirit has been described so far in Revelation as being with God, 'in front of the throne'. Now, and as a result of the exaltation of the Lamb, the Spirit-Paraclete is sent out into God's world, to be at work in and through the Church in the present and final stages of human history. Jesus is one with God, and in him all the fulness of God was pleased to dwell (Col. 1.19); he is also one with his post-resurrection Spirit. For the 'seven spirits' see further Smalley, 'Paraclete' 292–93; also Bruce, 'Spirit' 333–37.

In the Greek of the last clause in this verse, ἀπεσταλμένοι (*apestalmenoi*, 'sent out') agrees in gender with ὀφθαλμούς (*ophthalmous*, 'eyes', masculine); but in the end it is the πνεύματα (*pneumata*, 'spirits', neuter) which are sent out.

7   The movement in this verse is swift and dramatic. The Lamb, close to God and one with him, deservedly takes the scroll (τὸ βιβλίον, *to biblion*, 'the scroll', is understood rather than being mentioned) from the Father's right hand. This harmony between the nature and will of God and of his Christ is further explicated in John's Gospel (cf. John 10.30; 16.28; 17.1–11; et al.). See further Smalley, *John* 238–48, esp. 238–40. It provides the means of effecting God's salvific purposes for his creation, through the death and exaltation of his Son. That plan, reaching into time and eternity, is about to be revealed and executed. Cf. Kiddle 102. For the imagery here see on 5.1; see also Rev. 4.2.

John combines in this verse the aorist tense (ἦλθεν, *ēlthen*, 'he went') with the perfect (εἴληφεν, *eilēphen*, '[he] took'); for a similar conjoining see Rev. 3.3; 8.3, 5; 19.3–4; et al. Charles (1, 143–44) regards the combination as a Semitism, and points out that it is not found in the Fourth Gospel. The use of the perfect tense may suggest a sequential and realistic action: 'first the Lamb went, and now he has taken' (cf. Dan. 7.13–14). Alternatively, the perfect could point to the abiding results of the Lamb's action. See Swete 79.

8   The adoration of the Lamb is now described. It is offered first by the living creatures and the elders, in association with the Church on earth (verses 8–10); next by hosts of angels (11–12); and finally by the whole of creation (13). For the figure of the Lamb see on verse 6.

As the Lamb receives the scroll (see Rev. 5.1, 7), the living creatures (4.6–8) and the twenty-four elders (4.4) prostrate themselves in worship before him, recognizing his ability to carry out God's plan of salvation. The symbolism is as much descriptive (the death of Jesus on the cross occurs in history) as determinative (when the Lamb breaks the seals, 6.1 onwards, earthly events follow). See 4.1; cf. also Caird 76.

For the act of prostration (lit. 'the elders fell down') see (1.17); 4.10; 5.14; 7.11; 11.16; 19.4. The worship of God in Revelation, and of the Lamb in this scene, includes 'falling down' before the Godhead (the verb in each case is πίπτειν, *piptein,* 'to fall down', used in association with προσκυνεῖν, *proskynein,* 'to worship'). In the throne room scene at this point it is curious that the verb προσκυνεῖν (*proskynein,* 'to worship') itself is not employed; the creatures and elders simply 'prostrated themselves' before the Lamb, although presumably by now he occupied the throne with God. But see verse 14.

The Lamb's investiture, and the acceptance of his Lordship, takes place in the three doxologies which follow. See above, 111–12; also Hendriksen 91–93; Aune 332–38, esp. 336–38.

The Greek makes it clear, as the translation does not, that it is the twenty-four elders, and not the living creatures, who hold the harps and bowls. For the construction ἔχοντες ἕκαστος (*echontes hekastos* 'each held', lit. 'each having') includes a masculine plural participle, which refers to the antecedent οἱ εἴκοσι τέσσαρες πρεσβύτεροι (*hoi eikosi tessares presbyteroi,* 'the twenty-four elders', masculine) and not to τὰ τέσσερα ζῷα (*ta tessera zō[i]a,* 'the four living creatures', neuter plural). The role of the elders in this case may reflect the situation of the twenty-four orders of Levites who, according to 1 Chron. 25.1–31, were 'trained in singing to the Lord' (verse 7), and prophesied 'with lyres, harps and cymbals' (verses 1, 6). See Rev. 4.4; also Beale 357.

Each elder holds 'a harp, and golden bowls full of incense'. The term κιθάρα (*kithara,* 'harp' or 'kithara') is used in the Apocalypse three times (5.8; 14.2; 15.2), and elsewhere in the New Testament only at 1 Cor. 14.7 (but see the cognates in Rev. 14.2 and 18.22). John does not claim that the elders sang to their own musical accompaniment, but this idea is implied both here and at Rev. 14.2; 15.2. In such a situation it would be difficult, but not impossible, to play the harp while holding an incense bowl (cf. Aune 355–56). The harp, which has strings of unequal length, is a developed form of the lyre, with its equally long strings.

There is a close association in the Old Testament and early Jewish literature between hymns, or sacred songs of praise, and their accompaniment by stringed instruments. See 1 Chron. 16.42; 2 Chron. 9.11; Ps. 43.4; 81.2; 98.5; 150.3–4; 1 Macc. 4.54; 13.51; *T. Job* 14.1–3. Cf. Thompson 95–96.

The elders also hold 'golden bowls (φιάλας, *phialas*) full of incense'. The term φιάλη (*phialē,* 'bowl') occurs 12 times in Revelation (5.8; 15.7; 16.1, 2, 3, 4, 8, 10, 12, 17; 17.1; 21.9), and nowhere else in the New Testament. It refers to a flat, shallow bowl or cup used in cultic rituals as a utensil for drinking or pouring out libations (cf. Exod. 25.29; 37.16; Josephus, *Ant.* 3.143; 'two cups [φιάλαι, *phialai*] of gold filled with incense' were placed with the loaves of the presence in the tabernacle). The gold colour of the bowls, mentioned here, serves to enhance their use for liturgical purposes.

In the present context the 'bowls' are filled with incense, and are used positively and beneficially. Elsewhere in the Apocalypse, however, the φιάλαι (*phialai,* 'bowls') are described as containing God's wrath, and are employed to inflict punishments on the earth and its inhabitants (Aune 356).

The religious use of cultic 'bowls', such as the ones mentioned in this verse, is found in Greek religion (so Diodorus [Siculus] 4.49.8. 'The Argonauts . . . paid their vows to the great gods, and dedicated in the sacred precincts the bowls (τὰς φιάλας, *tas phialas*) which are preserved there even to this day'). But it is highly likely that the immediate background to this symbol is to be found in Judaism, where angelic beings preside as priests over the heavenly worship of God, rather than in Graeco-Roman cultic practice (cf. Job. 1.6; Isa. 6.2–3; see further Bietenhard, 'ἄγγελος' 101). The harps and incense bowls held by the twenty-four elders during this act of worship suggests their angelic status (Aune 358).

A parenthesis follows: the incense stands for 'the prayers of God's people'. Incense was a normal part of Jewish ritual (cf. Deut. 33.10). The feminine plural relative pronoun αἵ (εἰσιν) (*hai [eisin]*, lit. 'which [are]') refers to the incense and not to the bowls, although θυμίαμα (*thymiama*, 'incense') is neuter. The gender of the pronoun is determined by attraction to the feminine προσευχαί (*proseuchai*, 'prayers'); for the neuter variant ἅ (*ha*, 'which') see the textual note on verse 8.

In Rev. 8.3–4 incense and 'the prayers of all God's people' are similarly associated. But there the two are distinguished (incense is offered *with* the prayers), whereas here the 'incense' is understood as a metaphor for the 'prayers' of God's people. That image derives from Ps. 141.2 ('let my prayer be counted as incense before you'). Cf. also Justin, *Dial.* 118.2; Origen, *Contra Celsum* 8.17, on Rev. 5.8). The only other use of θυμίαμα (*thymiama*, 'incense') in the Apocalypse, in a different context, is at 18.13.

The word ἅγιοι (*hagioi*, translated 'God's people', lit. 'holy ones'), in this verse, refers to Christians who worship God; it describes their relationship to God, and not their sanctity (Aune 359). See the use of the term elsewhere in Revelation (11.18; 13.7, 10; 14.12; et al.), and in the New Testament and early Christian literature (Acts 9.13, 32, 41; 26.10; Rom. 8.27; 1 Cor. 6.1–2; Eph. 1.15; Heb. 6.10; Jude 3; Ignatius, *Smyrn.* 1.2; Justin, *Dial.* 139.4; et al.). Note also Ps. 34.9, where the Israelite faithful are called 'holy ones', and admonished to 'fear the Lord'; Dan. 7.21–22; 8.24.

Moreover, the offering of 'the prayers of God's people' is a liturgical activity which can evidently take place in any part of the Christian Church: in heaven, or on earth. Once more, John's cosmology is balanced, and draws together both the spiritual and the material.

The elders, angelic beings who represent the body of the faithful (see on 4.4), assist in presenting the prayers of God's people. The idea of angels acting as intermediaries, and helping to present the prayers of God's people to him, is typical of later Hebraic thought (cf. Tobit 12.15; *3 (Greek/Slavonic) Apoc. Bar.* 11.4, where Michael the Archangel 'descends' to the fifth heaven to receive the prayers of the people). The developing emphasis in Jewish thought on God's transcendence made it appropriate to introduce such intermediaries; the twenty-four elders occupy this role in the Apocalypse. (See further Mounce 135.)

9–10 The last hymn of praise to be heard in this heavenly court scene had been offered to God the Lord, as Creator (4.11). Now, as a mark of the Lamb's investiture (see above, 112), the four living creatures and twenty-four elders chant a paean of praise to him as Redeemer. This recognizes his authority to mediate between God and his Church as Saviour ('you deserve to take the scroll'), and is a response to the action of receiving the scroll from the one sitting on the throne (verse 7; on the 'scroll' see verse 1). It also confirms the answer to the question in 5.2. Given his divine and human nature, the Lamb alone is capable of bringing about God's salvific purposes for his creation. For a trinitarian version of heavenly worship offered to Jesus, the Holy Spirit and God himself, see *Asc. Isa.* 9.27–42.

The elders, in association with the Church below, accordingly break out in a hymn of praise. They chanted (ᾄδουσιν, a[i]dousin, lit. 'they sing', is a historic present tense) 'a *new* song' (ᾠδὴν καινήν, ō[i]dēn kainēn), because the Lamb is the mediator of a new covenant. Their song is new in quality, and not simply in origin (so Ps. 33.3; Isa. 42.10; et al.). Its newness speaks also of God's new creation through the Lamb, in which the redeemed of the Lord are new creatures for whom the new life has come (2 Cor. 5.17), who hear Christ's new name as citizens of the new Jerusalem (Rev. 2.17; 21.1–2), and who rejoice to hear the Creator say that he is making all things new (21.5). See Hughes 81–82. This expression, 'new song', occurs in Revelation only here and at 14.3; and in both contexts harps are mentioned.

The song is introduced by the verb, hidden in the translation, λέγοντες (legontes, lit. 'saying'). Interestingly, although the Apocalypse implies that music is a significant feature of the life of the Church in heaven (but not, according to Rev. 2—3, a characteristic of the churches of Asia), music as such is not mentioned at all in Revelation, and many of the hymns are *said*, rather than being sung (as at 4.10–11, q.v.; 7.11–12; in the present context the elders appear to speak *as well as* to sing). However, the chanting of songs, like the playing of musical instruments (14.2; et al.), is clearly heard in heaven from time to time (cf. 14.3; 15.3; note 4.8, 'ceaselessly'). See Smalley, *Thunder and Love* 115 n. 86.

The Lamb deserves 'to take the scroll, and to break its seals'. See on 5.2. The adjective ἄξιος (axios, 'worthy') introduces three hymns in Revelation, all within the throne room scene of Chapters 4 and 5. The first (4.11) uses ἄξιος εἶ (axios ei, 'you are worthy'), in the second person singular, to lead into a hymn of praise to God. The second (here) uses the same form to introduce a hymn to the Lamb; while the third (5.12), at the start of a second hymn to the Lamb, has the phrase ἄξιόν ἐστιν (axion estin, 'he is worthy'), in the third person. For hymns offered to Christ in heaven see *Ap. Jas.* 14.29–31; 15.17–22 (in *NHL* 36). The Lamb is worthy to take and open the scroll (see on 5.1–2) because he is one with God and with us, and his death can therefore become the means of life and redemption for all people. This thought is explicated in the remainder of verse 9.

The Christology and soteriology of this hymn (verses 9b–10) are remarkably high. The Lamb is honoured for his divine person (see verse 7), and for his work of redemption on behalf of humanity: its cost ('you were slaughtered'), its scope (a universal ransom) and its outcome (believers become 'a royal house and priests for our God'). See Moffatt 386. The saving nature of Christ's work stems from the unique character of his divine-human person (against Swete 81). The slightly dramatic verb ἐσφάγης (esphagēs, 'you were slaughtered') is used to describe the sacrificial death of Christ only in Revelation (5.6 q.v., 9, 12; 13.8). The background is evidently to be found in Isa. 53.7 LXX, where the Servant of God is described as being led to the slaughter 'like a lamb' (ὡς πρόβατον ἐπὶ σφαγὴν ἤχθη, hōs probaton epi sphagēn ēchthē); cf. Rev. 6.9; 18.24, describing the martyrdom of the saints.

The verb in this context is technical. Normally, in the New Testament, ἀγοράζειν (agorazein) means simply 'to buy'. But Paul uses the term to refer to the effects of the death of Christ, and in so doing evokes the language of the market-place, where slaves were 'ransomed' or 'redeemed' at a price (so 1 Cor. 6.20; 7.23; for the compound form, using ἐξαγοράζειν [exagorazein, 'to buy back'], see Gal. 3.13; 4.5). Cf. Fee, *First Corinthians* 264–65. Apart from the Pauline use of this soteriological image, it is found in the New Testament only in the Apocalypse (here, and at 14.3, 4) and in 2 Peter (2.1).

In the present context, the worshippers declare that the Lamb has paid the price for ransoming those enslaved by sin with his 'life-blood' (ἐν τῷ αἵματί σου, en tō[i] haimati sou, lit. 'in his blood'), where ἐν (en, 'with' or 'in') denotes the price paid, as in 1.5, q.v.; cf. Acts 20.28; 1 Pet. 1.18–19. See Swete 81. For 'blood', as the seat of life in biblical thought, see on 1.5; cf. further Laubach, 'Blood'. The verb ἠγόρασας (*ēgorasas*, 'you ransomed') is not accompanied by an exactly determined object; hence 'saints' is supplied in the translation (see above, 107). People in general, and believers in particular, were purchased by the blood of the Lamb, by his sacrificial death, 'for God'. That is, they were destined to serve him; as a result of which sanctification and eternal life become possible (cf. Rom. 6.22).

The scope of Christ's ransom is indicated in the remaining words of verse 9: 'saints from every tribe and language, people and nation'. For the polysyndetic phraseology see Dan. 3.4, 7; 5.19; 6.25; 7.14. In these Danielic passages *three* ethnic units ('peoples, nations and languages') are mentioned, in contexts where a universal audience is in view; although the LXX version of Dan. 3.4 mentions *four* such units ('nations and lands, peoples and tongues'). Similarly, a fourfold (polysyndetic) phrase is used in 4 Ezra 3.7 to describe the descendants of Adam: 'nations and tribes, peoples and clans'; cf. 4 Ezra 3.16. See the shorter lists in Isa. 66.18; Zech. 8.22; *Pss. Sol.* 17.29.

Similar lists of three or, more often, four ethnic groups occur in six other passages in Revelation (7.9; 10.11; 11.9; 13.7; 14.6; 17.15); these are always in polysyndetic form, but usually in a different order. See Aune 362.

There is probably not much difference in meaning to be discovered between the actual Greek terms used in the list of ethnic groups which appears in this verse (ἐκ πάσης φυλῆς καὶ γλώσσης καὶ λαοῦ καὶ ἔθνους, *ek pasēs phylēs kai glōssēs kai laou kai ethnous*, 'from every tribe and language, people and nation'); although 'people and nation' might imply a broader grouping than 'tribe and language'. Josephus (*Ant.* 7.356–57) accordingly uses 'people', 'nation' and 'tribe' as synonyms for Israel, or parts of it. In any case, the terms speak together of universality. The challenging good news of the death and exaltation of the Lamb, and of his redeeming sacrifice, is addressed to the whole of God's creation (cf. John 21.4–11; 1 Tim. 2.3–4; 1 John 2.2). Swete (81) attempts unnecessarily to limit the wide scope of Christian salvation implied in this section of Revelation.

The presentation of the sacrifice of Christ in this hymn appears to be untypically Johannine, since its character is objective, and indeed Pauline (see above, on John's 'ransom' imagery). In the Fourth Gospel, at least, the interpretation of the death of Jesus leans in a subjective, exemplarist direction, even if it is not wholly exemplarist in character. Cf. Smalley, *John* 255–56. However, as Knight (65) points out, John (unlike Paul, we may add) does not say *how* the Lamb's death achieves its stated effect; only *that* this has happened.

The new song which is being chanted in the heavenly court clearly refers in the end to the redeemed. Christian believers have been given a new status: they have been created 'a royal house and priests for our God', in order to 'reign on earth' (verse 10). For the phrase 'royal house (or kingdom) and priests' see Exod. 19.6; see also on 1.6. What was promised to the Israelites at Sinai is fulfilled in the establishment of the Church through the death of Christ (Mounce 136).

Two spiritual privileges are envisaged for the redeemed. They are to be a 'royal house' (βασιλείαν, *basileian*, lit. 'kingdom') and 'priests' (ἱερεῖς, *hiereis*) for God. The word ἱερεῖς (*hiereis*, 'priests') may be construed as either a nominative or an accusative plural. Here it is clearly an accusative, reinforcing the dual nature of the status of the redeemed, as in 1.6. In both cases the mode is active: as a royal house they reign, and as priests they serve. To be a Christian 'is to be both king and priest, but with a sovereignty and priesthood derived from Christ, as his were derived from God' (Caird 77). Note the use of this hymnic motif again in Rev. 20.6; cf. also 1 Pet. 2.9.

The ransomed, it is promised, will 'reign on earth'. The idea of the powerless faithful acquiring power under the dominion of God, and thus sharing in his reign, is an apocalyptic theme which appears in Dan. 7.18, 27, and subsequently in early Christian texts. Cf. Matt. 19.28 = Luke 22.30; 1 Cor. 6.2; *Gospel Thom.* 2; *Acts Thom.* 136–37; also 1QM 12.15. The same theme can be found in Rev. 20.6 (the priestly saints of God will reign on earth for a thousand years), and at 22.5 (God's servants will reign for ever).

The translation opts for the future tense, βασιλεύσουσιν (*basileusousin*, 'they will reign'); see above, 107. But the sense remains unchanged, whichever MS reading is adopted. Eschatologically, and in apocalyptic terms, the present points towards the future, and the end-time includes the present (cf. Smalley, *Thunder and Love* 150–52). Equally, if the reign of the saints takes place in the future, it must be a future following immediately on Christ's redeeming work, and the appointment of the ransomed as kings and priests (cf. Caird 77).

The royal priests 'will reign *on earth*'. The prophet-seer recognizes that God's salvific plan will be expressed in his whole creation, and not just (so Rev. 4—5) in heaven. The Church militant, as well as triumphant, already worships the Lamb; and it will continue to do so, with its members as kings and priests, eternally. See Rom. 5.17.

11–12 The worship of the Lamb in heaven, and this by implication echoes that of the Church on earth (cf. Rev. 4.11; 5.6, 10), continues. But at this point it becomes manifestly universal, since John hears as part of his vision 'the voice of many angels' who surround the throne of God, as well as the voices of the creatures and elders. The membership of the redeemed has already been evinced as potentially world-wide (verse 9); and their praise is now extended to include representatives of all creation, divine and human.

For the formula καὶ εἶδον (*kai eidon*, 'as I looked', lit. 'and I saw') see 5.1, 6; 10.1; et al. For the relationship between sight and hearing, in the Apocalypse and John's Gospel, see on 4.1; 5.6. For 'angels' see on 1.1, 20; 3.5; 5.2; 7.1; et al. Unusually, the throne-vision of Rev. 4—5 has not so far involved the appearance of angels (plural; one 'strong angel' is introduced at 5.2), unlike similar apocalyptic heavenly court scenes (so 1 Kings 22.19; Dan. 7.10; *1 Enoch* 47.3). Their absence is fully compensated for here by the inclusion of 'many' angels: indeed, myriads and thousands of them. Cf. Aune 363. Angels encircling God's throne are mentioned again at 7.11; note also the ministry of the Angel of God, Iaoel, in *Apoc. Abr.* (9.1–4; 10.3–4; et al.). For the 'throne', as a symbol of God's sovereignty, see on 4.2. For the 'living creatures' and 'elders' see 4.6–8; 4.4.

The sentence, 'they numbered myriads upon myriads (or ten thousands upon ten thousands), and thousands upon thousands' (καὶ ἦν ὁ ἀριθμὸς αὐτῶν μυριάδες μυριάδων καὶ χιλιάδες χιλιάδων, *kai ēn ho arithmos autōn myriades myriadōn kai chiliades chiliadōn*, lit. 'and the number of them was . . .'), is parenthetical, and refers to the angels, and not to the other beings around the throne who have just been identified. The description, μυριάδες μυριάδων καὶ χιλιάδες χιλιάδων (*myriades myriadōn kai chiliades chiliadōn*, lit. 'myriads of myriads and thousands of thousands'), denoting a countless multitude, is taken from Dan. 7.10, q.v.

Both the LXX and Theod. versions of that text have the order χίλιαι . . . μύριαι (*chiliai . . . myriai*, 'thousands . . . ten thousands'); although the arrangement in this verse is found also in *1 Clem.* 34.6. Cf. also Num. 10.36; *1 Enoch* 14.22; 40.1; 60.1; 71.8. Beale (364) finds in this passage further evidence of the way in which the seer's composition of Rev. 5.2–10 has been influenced by Dan. 7.

The hymn in verse 12, chanted by the assembled heavenly company, is introduced by the nominative participle λέγοντες (*legontes*, lit. 'saying'). This is loosely added, as if the subject of the verb, in the nominative, had preceded it; but it has not (Beckwith 513). The masculine plural form of the participle, rather than the feminine singular, to agree with φωνήν (*phōnēn*, 'voice'), or the feminine plural, in harmony with μυριάδες . . . χιλιάδες (*myriades . . . chiliades*, 'myriads . . . thousands'), may well have resulted from attraction to the masculine noun of multitude, ὁ ἀριθμός (*ho arithmos*, lit. 'the number'); for the crowds of angels are in focus at this stage of the scene (cf. Beale 365). The chorus chants 'loudly' (φωνῇ μεγάλῃ, *phonē[i] megalē[i]*, lit. 'with a loud voice'), as befits such widespread and inclusive worship and praise.

The slaughtered Lamb, they say, 'deserves to receive power and riches, wisdom and strength, and reverence and glory and blessing'. For 'slaughtered' (ἐσφαγμένον, *esphagmenon*) see on verses 6 and 9. The literal meaning of ἄξιόν ἐστιν τὸ ἀρνίον (*axion estin to arnion*) is 'worthy is the Lamb'. (For 'Lamb' see on verse 6.) The term ἄξιος (*axios*, 'worthy') is directly linked to the previous uses of the word in Rev. 5 (verses 2, 4 and 9); although Aune (364) attempts to drive a wedge between them. See on 5.9. Because of the unity between the nature and will of God and of his Son, the Father's saving purposes for his creation can be effected in the Messiah (see on verse 7). Such teaching is reinforced in the present hymn. Because Jesus is one with God and one with humanity, he can 'receive' (λαβεῖν, *labein*, lit. 'take') the qualities usually reserved for God alone, just as he 'took' the scroll of salvation itself (verse 7). The reception of such gifts is part of the Lamb's investiture. See further 1 Chron. 29.11–12; Dan. 2.37; Matt. 11.27; 28.18; for similar doxologies offered to Christ cf. *1 Clem.* 65 (also 64); *Mart. Pol.* 21.

Seven qualities are ascribed to Christ the Lamb; five of them are also gifts which God can bestow on earthly (Israelite) kings. See Aune 365–66.

(a) Two of these, 'power' (δύναμις, *dynamis*) and 'strength' (ἰσχύς, *ischys*), are synonymous. This attribute is frequently used in the Old Testament to help delineate the nature of God's kingship (Exod. 15.13; 1 Chron. 16.27–28; Ps. 62.11; Isa. 45.24), and occasionally as the characteristic of a king (1 Sam. 2.10; cf. Ps. 28.8). Elsewhere in the Apocalypse, and again in hymnic passages, δύναμις (*dynamis*, 'power') is used four more times of God, but never of the Lamb/Christ (4.11; 7.12; 11.17; 19.1); and ἰσχύς (*ischys*, 'strength') is used only of God (7.12). For 'power' in Revelation see further on 7.12.

(b) 'Riches' (πλοῦτος, *ploutos*, otherwise 'wealth') can be associated with kingship in Revelation (18.17); but wealth is never attributed to God as King in the Old Testament. Only here in the Apocalypse are 'riches' ascribed to the Godhead.

(c) 'Wisdom' (σοφία, *sophia*) appears in one other hymnic setting of Revelation as a prerogative of God (7.12). In Hebrew thought it is often regarded as an appropriate gift for kings to receive from God (cf. 1 Kings 5.12, of Solomon; et al.).

(d) 'Reverence' (τιμή, *timē*) denotes the 'worth' ascribed to a person, and the respect accorded especially to someone of exalted status (cf. Schneider, 'τιμή, τιμάω'). Reverence is therefore the prerogative of gods, as of kings, and indeed of God himself (e.g. Isa. 29.13). The term is used elsewhere in the Apocalypse of God twice (4.11; 7.12), and once of both God and the Lamb (5.13).

The remaining two qualities in the septet are essentially those which should be attributed to the Godhead.

(e) 'Glory' (δόξα, *doxa*) occurs elsewhere in Revelation as an ascription to God (4.11; 7.12; 19.1), and it is used once of God and the Lamb together (5.13). See Aalen, 'Glory, Honour', 44–48. The attributes 'reverence' and 'glory' are often paired in the LXX (e.g. 2 Chron. 32.33; Ps. 28.1; Job 40.10; 1 Macc. 14.21; et al.; cf. *1 Enoch* 50.1; 99.1), and in the New Testament and early Christian literature (so Rev. 21.26; also 1 Tim. 1.17; Heb. 2.9; 2 Pet. 1.17; *1 Clem.* 61.1–2).

(f) 'Blessing' (εὐλογία, *eulogia*) occurs three times in the Apocalypse, as a predicate of the Lamb (here), or of God (in the doxologies of 5.13; 7.12). Like δόξα (*doxa*, 'glory') above, and εὐχαριστία (*eucharistia*, 'thankfulness') in 4.9, the word expresses what is offered to Christ on the part of humanity, in distinction from itself. That distinction is made clear in 1 Chron. 29.10–13 (Beckwith 513) which, together with Dan. 2.20, may well stand behind the combination of attributes cited in this hymn (cf. Beale 364). See also Job 37.22–24; 40.10.

13   As elsewhere in Revelation, this major scene ends with a liturgical outpouring of worship (cf. 7.15–17; 11.16–18). The concluding paean of praise in the heavenly throne room is offered by the whole cosmos (πᾶν κτίσμα, *pan ktisma*, lit. 'every created being'). This cannot exclude participation by the company of the angels, whose chants of worship have just been heard in verses 11–12, but who are nevertheless not mentioned in the antiphonal response to the hymn at verse 14 (against Beckwith 514). The entire assembly offers adoration, because the Lamb is identified as the worthy recipient of the scroll (verse 7), and can therefore act as the agent of God's salvation. The resulting doxology includes the Father, as well as the Son (see below).

This scene of cosmic acclamation points towards the events of the end-time, and the gathering up of all life in Christ (cf. Eph. 1.10). But if universal praise is in mind at this point in Revelation it must include, as then, adoration on the part of those who are at present God's opponents (Beale 365). This is a further example of John's balanced eschatology, between the events of the present and those of the future. Cf. Phil. 2.10–11; Col 1.20; and note the judgement promised in Rev. 14.7–11 on those who currently worship the beast, rather than God (also *1 Enoch* 46.5–6).

The seer 'heard' (ἤκουσα, *ēkousa*) the whole of creation joining in the worship of the Godhead; and this picks up in a literary fashion the use of the same verb in the same form at verse 11 (q.v.), where hearing and sight are associated. The fourfold division of creation into heaven, earth, underground and sea, echoes verse 3, q.v.; although 'in the sea' (ἐπὶ τῆς θαλάσσης, *epi tēs thalassēs*, lit. 'upon the sea') is added. In this formula, and in the inclusion of the expression 'everything in them' (superfluous after πᾶν κτίσμα, *pan ktisma*, 'the whole creation'), the author may have been influenced by Ps. 146.6 and Song of 3 Ch. [= Song of Three Children/Jews], esp. verses 35–59; see also Exod. 20.11 and Neh. 9.6, where God is praised as King and Creator. The total situation being described is metaphorical, since it is not literally possible for every created being to sing or 'cry' such a doxology as this.

Three of the eternal prerogatives ascribed to the Godhead in the present hymn ('blessing', 'reverence' and 'glory') are repeated from verse 12, q.v., albeit in a different order (for further variations of order in such lists see 1.6; 4.9, 11; 7.12). To the collection is added κράτος (*kratos*, 'might'); see 1.6. This word is used in the LXX of human strength (Deut. 8.17; Job 21.23), but more usually with reference to the power of God (Job 12.16, where the term is linked to ἰσχύς [*ischys*, 'strength']; Ps. 61.13 = 62.11; et al.). In the Old Testament, and generally in the New Testament, the term κράτος (*kratos*, 'might'), as applied to God and Christ, seems to denote more particularly the outer aspect of the divine strength (hence the translation 'might'). Cf. 1 Tim. 6.16; 1 Pet. 4.11; 5.11. See Michaelis, 'κράτος, κτλ', 905–10, esp. 908; also Braumann, 'κράτος', 717–18.

This universal and cosmic praise is offered eternally ('for ever and ever'), both to God ('the one who is seated on the throne'; see on 4.2) and to the Lamb (see on 5.6). Until now the worship taking place in the throne room in Rev. 4—5 has been ascribed either to God (4.8, 11) or to his Christ (5.9–10, 12). The unique relationship between the Father and the Son, however, has been explicit throughout (note the closeness of the Lamb to the throne, 5.6–7). Now it is clear that they are joined together explicitly as objects of Christian worship; and this is a further important indication of John's high Christology in Revelation. Throughout the seer's visions, from now on, God and the Lamb will appear together as equals sharing the same throne. They are disclosed as objects of fear or worship and as key players in the drama which is being enacted. Note Rev. 6.16; 7.9, 10, 17; 14.4; 21.22–23; 22.1, 3. The Lamb of the throne-vision is no longer simply an image of the Jewish Messiah; he has become evidently 'the divine and sovereign Christ of Christian theology' (Michaels 98; see ibid. 97–98 for this section).

14   The final doxology is uttered in a narrative setting, since it calls forth an antiphonal response from the four living creatures and the elders (for which see 4.4, 6). The whole act of worship may reflect the liturgy of the Johannine community at the time. The heavenly beings (ζῷα, *zō[i]a*), who pronounced the first doxology in this throne room scene (4.8), now close the cosmic hymn of praise with a solemn and confirmatory ἀμήν (*amēn*, 'amen'): 'so be it'. The elders remain silent, but worship by 'prostrating themselves' (ἔπεσαν καὶ προσεκύνησαν, *epesan kai prosekynēsan*, '[they] prostrated themselves, and worshipped'). For this posture see on 4.10; see also 7.11; 11.16; 19.4.

'Amen' is used in the Apocalypse in four different but complementary ways.

(a)   As a confirmatory response to another speaker (here, and at Rev. 22.20).
(b)   As an affirmation in an act of (doxological) praise (1.6–7; 7.12 [only in this text does 'amen' appear at the beginning and the end of the doxology]; 19.4).
(c)   As the conclusion of a prayer (22.21, according to some witnesses).
(d)   As a title of Jesus (3.14, q.v.).

The double 'amen' (ἀμήν, *amēn*) characteristically introduces the words of Jesus in John's Gospel (John 1.51; et al.); by itself, it is also used by Paul and others in the New Testament as a liturgical formula at the end of prayers (Rom. 1.25; et al.). See further for this section Charles 1, 151–52.

Theology

The predominant theological theme in the throne-vision of Rev. 4—5 is that of divine sovereignty. The sovereign God of creation (4) is the reigning Lord of judgement and redemption (5), who accomplishes his will through the crucified and risen Christ. God's sovereignty in creation is the basis for his sovereign activity in salvation through judgement.

This motif picks up the motif of divine sovereignty and human responsibility which emerges at the conclusion of Rev. 3 (verse 21, q.v.); and it discovers its theological background in the Old Testament (Dan. 7, combined with Isa. 6 and Ezek. 1—2). God and the Lamb are thus central to this throne room scene; even if God is neither named nor described, except by allusion (4.3), and remains passive throughout, while the Lamb acts but does not speak. See Moffatt 375; Beasley-Murray 108; Beale 366–69; Aune 373.

In the scheme of Revelation, theology is more important than chronology. The eschatological climax of the Apocalypse is not at the end of time, or at the end of the book. There *is* a consummation devoutly to be wished; but the fulcrum of Revelation is to be found precisely in this interval scene of Rev. 4.1—5.14, and not in the parousia and descent of the heavenly city in Rev. 21—22. The crucified and risen Lamb has already made redemption possible, and he has ascended his Father's throne. The centre of the ages lies in the past, and the sovereignty of God in Christ has already been acknowledged by the heavenly host (in the hymns of 4.11 and 5.9–13). However, its acceptance by the whole of creation, promised in Rev. 5.13–14, still lies in the future. The achievement of that acclamation, and the consequent subjugation of earth's rebellion, is the story of Rev. 6—22. See Beasley-Murray 25—26; Smalley, *Thunder and Love* 151.

Caird (60–61) reminds us that the complex symbols in this section of John's vision (open door, throne, jewels, elders, lightning and thunder, torches, living creatures, scroll, angels, Lion, Lamb, et al.) are the pictorial counterpart of earthly realities; and theologically they may be either determinative or descriptive. John understands that some heavenly events take place because God has determined that their equivalents should shortly occur on earth, such as divine judgement on human opposition to his rule (note the fall of Babylon in Rev. 18). But other activities happen in heaven because earthly actions have brought them about (see what follows the breaking of the seals in Rev. 6—8).

Rev. 4 and 5 together constitute a dramatic and theologically powerful introduction to the next scene of Act 1 (6.1–17), and to the remainder of the action in the Apocalypse. God's eschatological plan for humanity and the universe has been initiated and is about to be fully disclosed. The drama has already taken place on earth (Rev. 2–3), in heaven (4—5), or both (1). But throughout, and from now on, the reference is balanced. For in Christ, the Word made flesh, the material and the spiritual are fully and finally brought together.

The same is true of the worship of heaven depicted in the throne-vision of Rev. 4—5. Heaven and earth are drawn close together in the Christ-event and the subsequent exaltation of the Lamb; and this truth is vividly symbolized by the twenty-four elders and the four living creatures. Now the ceaseless adoration of the saints in heaven and in eternity is wrapped together with the worship of the conquering faithful in the Church on earth and in time. The one is cheered by the other.

All this would be intensely relevant for John's churches in Asia during the first century AD, as they faced doctrinal conflict within the community, and persecution from Roman imperialism outside it. The severity of that oppression in the later part of the first Christian century, particularly under Domitian, has been questioned recently (cf. Slater, 'Social Setting'; Boxall, *Revelation* 98–104). Given an alternative external setting, it might be that the Johannine community needed encouragement instead (or as well) to resist the pressures from indigenous pagans to conform to traditional social practices in Roman Asia, to become morally lax, and to compromise with the imperial cult (cf. Rev. 2.13–16, 20–25; et al.). The theological teaching in this apocalyptic scene would have accordingly strengthened Christian faithfulness and resolve at the time; it is similarly germane to the life of the Christian Church today, as the Church confronts situations that may be equally serious.

SCENE 2
Seven Seals
(6.1–17)

Translation

6 ¹Then I watched, as the Lamb broke the first of the seven seals; and I heard one of the four living creatures call out in a thunderous voice,ᵃ 'Come!'ᵇ ²And, as I watched,ᶜ there was a white horse! Its rider held a bow. He was given a crown; and he rode out as a conqueror, intent on further conquest.ᵈ

³When he broke the second seal, I heard the second living creature call out, 'Come!' ⁴And out came another horse, this time fiery red. Its rider was allowed to remove peace from the earth,ᵉ so that people would slaughter one another; and he was given a powerful sword.

⁵When the Lamb broke the third seal, I heard the third living creature call out, 'Come!' And there, as I watched, was a black horse! Its rider held in his hand a pair of scales. ⁶And I heard what sounded like a voice from among the four living creatures saying, 'A choenix of wheat for a day's pay, and a day's pay for three choenixes of barley; but do not spoil the oil and the wine!'

⁷When he broke the fourth seal, I heard the voice of the fourth living creature call out, 'Come!' ⁸And there, as I watched, was a pale-coloured horse! Itsᶠ rider's name was Death,ᵍ and Hades accompanied him; and they were given authority over a quarter of the earth, to kill by sword and famine, by pestilence and by the wild animals of the earth.

⁹When the Lamb broke the fifth seal, I saw underneath the altar the souls of those who had been slaughtered because of God's word, and because of the witness which they had maintained. ¹⁰And they cried out with a loud voice, 'Sovereign Lord, holy and true, how long will it be before you administer justice, and avenge our deaths caused by the inhabitants of the earth?' ¹¹Each of them was then given a white garment; and they were told to be patient for a little longer, until the number of their servant-companions, that is their colleagues, who were about to be killed as they had been, was complete.ʰ

¹²Then I watched while he broke the sixth seal, and a massive earthquakeⁱ occurred; the sun turned black as haircloth, the whole moon became like blood, ¹³and the stars of the sky fell to the earth like late fruit dropping from a fig tree when it is battered by a strong wind. ¹⁴The sky was split like a scroll that is rolled up, and every mountain and island was removed from its place. ¹⁵Then earthly kings, the courtiers and military leaders, the rich and the powerful and everyone, slave or free, hid themselves in the caves and among the mountainous rocks, ¹⁶calling to the mountains and the crags, 'Fall down on us, and hide us from the sight of the one who is seated on the throne, and from the wrath of the Lamb! ¹⁷For the critical day of theirʲ judgement has arrived, and who is able to stand firm in it?'

Text

ᵃ The nominative φωνή (*phōnē*, 'voice'), as read by A C 046 Byz, et al., is likely to be original, in view of its harshness following ὡς (*hōs*, lit. 'as'), and its position after the genitive λέγοντος (*legontos*, lit. 'saying'). The MS variations φωνῇ (*phōnē[i]*, lit. 'with a voice', dative), offered by 2329, et al. (cf. Swete 85), φωνῆς (*phōnēs*, lit. 'of a voice', genitive), as in 025, et al., and φωνὴν (*phōnēn*, 'voice', accusative), read by ℵ, et al., all appear to be attempted corrections. The genitive φωνῆς (*phōnēs*, 'voice') seems to be a grammatical alteration, since the case following ὡς (*hōs*, 'as') is normally the same as that preceding it, which in this instance is genitive.

b The command ἔρχου (*erchou*, 'Come!'), by itself, is well attested (A C 025 1006 1611 vg cop[sa,bo], et al.). Some witnesses, including ℵ 046 it[gig] eth, et al., add καὶ ἴδε (*kai ide*, 'and see') or (so 296 2049 TR) καὶ βλέπε (*kai blepe*, 'and behold'). But these later additions assume that the verb 'come' is addressed to the prophet-seer (cf. 4.1), whereas the injunction applies to the first apocalyptic horse. The reading ὅτι ἔρχομαι (*hoti erchomai*, 'I come'), as in arm, is due to 'freedom in translation' (Metzger, *Textual Commentary* 737). For the same variations, by similar witnesses, see 6.3, 5 and 7.

c The inclusion of the words καὶ εἶδον (*kai eidon*, lit. 'and I looked') is firmly supported by ℵ (A C have ἴδον, *idon*, 'I looked') 025 1 1006 1611 it[gig] vg syr[h] cop[bo] arm, et al. The phrase does not appear in 046 and several minuscules, most of which add καὶ ἴδε (*kai ide*, 'and see') in verse 1 (q.v.). The omission may be accidental; but it is more likely to have been deliberate on the part of copyists who had included καὶ ἴδε (*kai ide*, 'and see') at the end of verse 1, and therefore considered καὶ εἶδον (*kai eidon*, 'as I watched') to be repetitious here. The readings εἶδον (*eidon*, 'I watched') in cop[sa], and καὶ ἤκουσα καὶ εἶδον (*kai ēkousa kai eidon*, 'I heard and I saw') in syr[ph], are again due to free translation (Metzger, *Textual Commentary* 737). See the similar MS differences at 6.5 and 8.

d The variation in ℵ, et al., καὶ ἐνίκησεν (*kai enikēsen*, 'and he conquered', using the aorist indicative), instead of the well-attested καὶ ἵνα νικήσῃ (*kai hina nikēsē[i]*, 'intent on conquest', lit. 'and that he might conquer', using the aorist subjunctive of purpose), can be discounted. The thought of intention, rather than completion, suits the mood and theology of the passage (see below). But see Rev. 5.5.

e The reading ἐκ τῆς γῆς (*ek tēs gēs*, lit. 'out of the earth') is strongly supported by MS evidence (ℵ* C 025 046 1006 1611[1611,1854] it[gig,61] vg arm, et al.), and is likely to be original. The replacement of ἐκ (*ek*, 'from') by ἐπί (*epi*, 'upon', 1611[2344]) or by ἀπό (*apo*, 'away from', 1 1828 2053 TR) is likely to be the result of later, stylistic alteration. Some MSS (including A 2081 Andreas) omit the preposition ἐκ (*ek*, 'from'); but this must be a transcriptional error.

f The reading ἐπάνω αὐτοῦ (*epanō autou*, lit. 'on it'), supported by ℵ A 046 Victorinus it[gig] (*in illo*), et al., is probably original. The appearance of the preposition ἐπάνω (*epanō*, 'on'), by itself (C 025 1611 Andreas vg, et al.), presumably involves an accidental omission of the pronoun. The version ἐπ᾿ αὐτόν (*ep auton*, 'upon it'), as in 1854, et al., must be an assimilation to that expression as it is used in 6.2, 4 and 5.

g The definite article ὁ (*ho*, 'the') with θάνατος (*thanatos*, 'Death') is attested by 025 Andreas Byz 2351, et al., but omitted by ℵ C, et al. (ὁ ἀθάνατος, *ho athanatos*, 'immortal', as in A, is an error). The inclusion of the article is likely to be original. It balances the use of ὁ (*ho*, 'the') with the associated name ᾅδης (*ha[i]dēs*, 'Hades'); and it is line with the characteristic appearance of the definite article with proper names, used predicatively, in Revelation (cf. 8.11; 12.9; 19.13; 20.2).

h The form πληρωθῶσιν (*plērōthōsin*, lit. 'should be completed'), in the aorist subjunctive passive, is read by A C 1611[2344] it[gig,61] vg syr[ph,h] arm. Other witnesses (including ℵ 025 046 1006 1611[1854]) have πληρώσωσιν (*plērōsōsin*, 'should complete', aorist subjunctive active). The latter is likely to be a transcriptional error, especially as no object is in view in the context; and, despite using the rare, intransitive sense of the verb πληροῦν (*plēroun*, 'to complete'), the former is probably original. The indicatives in two other variations, πληρώσουσιν (*plērōsousin*, lit. 'they will complete'), read by 1611[1611,2329] 2065, et al., and πληρώσονται (*plērōsontai*, lit. 'they will complete [for themselves]', middle), as in 296 2049 Arethas TR, are apparently secondary.

[i] The Greek version καὶ σεισμός (*kai seismos*, lit. 'and an earthquake') is well attested (א C 025 046 1 1006 it[gig,61] vg syr[ph,h] arm eth Primasius, et al.), and likely to be original. Some witnesses (including A 296 2066) add ἰδού (*idou*, 'behold!') before σεισμός (*seismos*, 'earthquake'); but, although typical of the style of apocalyptic (see 6.2, 5, 8), this reading is not strongly supported. It is also more probable that the exclamation would have been added to the text, rather then dropped from it. The omission of καὶ . . . ἐγένετο (*kai . . . egeneto*, lit. 'and . . . there came') in cop[sa ms] is accidental, and a case of homoeoteleuton.

[j] The reading αὐτῶν (*autōn*, 'their'), referring to God and the Lamb, is strongly supported by א C 1611 1854 2053 it[gig,61] vg syr[ph,h], et al. The variant αὐτοῦ (*autou*, 'his'), referring simply to Christ, is less well attested (A 025 046 cop[sa,bo] arm eth, et al.), and seems to be an explanatory correction. It avoids the ambiguity of the plural pronoun, and it connects with the reference to the Lamb in verse 16. If αὐτῶν (*autōn*, 'their') be accepted as original, however, there is still an exegetical case to be made for preferring the singular reading (so Aune 386; and see below, ad loc.)

Literary Setting

The vision of Jesus, as the risen and vindicated Son of man, given to John in Rev. 1, provides the spiritual basis and direct authority for the disclosures which follow in the Apocalypse. These begin with the oracles to the seven local Asian churches in the Johannine community (1.9—3.22), in a section which speaks of faith and works in the daily life of the Christian and of the Church.

The following chapters (Rev. 4—5) are, as we have seen (above 110, 141–42), pivotal to the dramatic action of the book as a whole. They present us with the leading themes of creation through the holy God, and redemption through the invested Lamb (cf. the evocation of Genesis and Exodus throughout Revelation; see Sweet 6). On this basis, Chapter 6 begins to unfold the notion of God's righteous judgement on unfaithfulness of any kind in the world, together with the ideal establishment within it of his divine will. (Note the way in which the great earthquake and its aftermath, in 6.12–17, is offset by the cry of the martyred faithful in verses 9–11.) So the scroll's seven *seals*, forming the first metaphor of judgement, begin to be broken (6.1–17; 8.1); and the four *riders* (or horsemen) of the Apocalypse are introduced (6.1–8). With their appearance, the dramatic action of the book begins (Smalley, *Thunder and Love* 76).

The pervading theme of *judgement* in this scene, dramatically presented by the opening of the seals, is interwoven in equally theatrical terms with the motif of *power*. Thus the breaking of the first four seals leads in each case to the advent of one of the four riders, who are associated with separate but related causes. These indicate the consequences of misusing power, and the sorrow brought on the world when it rejects the cause of Christ: military power (conquest), political power (warfare), economic power (famine) and negative power (death). See below, esp. on verse 1. On all four occasions, one of the 'living creatures' issues an invitation for the riders to appear, with the peremptory summons, 'Come!'

The scene in Rev. 6 is structurally related to the vision of the Lamb in Chapter 5 in the same way as the oracles of Rev. 2—3 arise out of the vision of the exalted Son of man in Chapter 1. The divine agent is first depicted in person; then he appears in actions appropriate to the initial disclosure. The Lamb of Rev. 5 breaks the seals of the scroll

(6.1–8). At no point during the fracturing of the seals, either here or at 8.1, do we hear that the scroll is opened, or that anyone reads from it. In each case, however, the action which follows undoubtedly corresponds to that part of the contents of the scroll. The prophet-seer discovers the prophesied event itself immediately acted out in his vision; and, in this way, the account of what is to happen (now and in the future) is narrated with powerful and dramatic force. See Beckwith 515.

As Mounce (139) points out, the scroll itself cannot be opened until all seven seals are removed. To that extent the sovereign purposes of God, in judgement and love, symbolized by the scroll (see on 5.1), cannot be implemented until the seventh seal is broken (8.1) and the seven trumpets are heard. Nevertheless, as each seal is broken we are at once introduced to a series of preliminary judgements (see also above). These represent historical movements and forces through which the judicial and salvific purposes of God can be carried out before the end.

The seven seals of Revelation divide into two groups of four (6.1–8) and three (6.9, 12; 8.1). This literary pattern is repeated in the symbols of the trumpets (8.6–12; 9.1, 13; 11.15) and (less clearly) of the bowls (16.1–8; 16.10, 12, 17).

The narrative *form* of John's vision in Rev. 6 evinces points of contact with similar scenes in Zechariah (see below). But the *content* corresponds very closely to the eschatological discourse of Jesus in Luke 21.9–36 par., even if this comparability need not imply John's literary dependence on Luke (against Charles 1, 158). In the Lucan version Jesus speaks of the advent of wars, insurrections, national uprisings, earthquakes, famines, plagues, signs from heaven and persecution. These portents are all encompassed and played out within the six seals of Rev. 6, where they herald the consummation (as in Luke 21 par.). In Jewish thought the age to come, the 'day of the Lord', is understood as being introduced by a time of unprecedented woe. Cf. Isa. 13.6–22; Ezek. 30.2–19; Joel 1.15—2.11; Zech. 14.1–5; also Mark 13.7–8 ('this is but the begining of birthpangs . . . the end is still to come'). See further Charles 1, 153–61; Mounce 140.

In this scene, as in Rev. 4—5, the seer is still in *heaven*. But the events following the breaking of each seal (except the fifth, verses 9–11, which is specifically located; see below on 'underneath the altar' in verse 9) take place on *earth*, and affect humanity. They are 'not a kind of symbolical tableau pictured on the heavens' (Beckwith 516). In the same way the four riders, who appear in response to the command of the living creatures, represent the same number of *earthly* causes (see below).

Comment

Seals 1–4: The Four Horsemen (6.1–8)

6.1   The Lamb opens all seven of the scroll's seals (cf. 5.1); for he alone is qualified to do so (cf. 5.5, 9), and thus to set in train events which will ultimately bring about the consummation of human history. For the number seven see on 1.4. For 'seal' (σφραγίς, *sphragis*), see on 5.1. The general context of Rev. 5.1—8.1 is apocalyptic, and indeed heavenly; and the gradually opening scroll in Rev. 6 and 8.1, which has been sealed against unauthorized scrutiny, enfolds God's purposes of judgement and love. Nevertheless, the term 'seal' in the present chapter (verses 1, 3, 5, 7, 9, 12), as in 5.1, 2, 5, 9; 8.1, carries a literal sense (in 7.2; 9.4, q.v., the associations are more individual). The use of a seal, as a mark of authenticity and authority, or as a means of witnessing a legal document, would have been familiar to Jews as to Romans (cf. Dan. 12.4, 9; also Rev. 22.10).

The situation and language here are highly symbolic; and the figure of the Lamb himself (for which see on 5.6) is clearly anthropomorphized. Despite the translation, only in this instance is the Lamb specified as the subject of the verb ἤνοιξεν (ēnoixen, 'he broke', lit. 'he opened'); in the remaining six occurrences of this verb (6.3, 5, 7, 9, 12; 8.1), τὸ ἀρνίον (to arnion, 'the Lamb') is assumed. For the phrase καὶ εἶδον (kai eidon, 'then I watched', lit. 'and I saw') see on 5.1; cf. also 4.1. The use of μίαν ἐκ (mian ek, 'the first of') is probably a Hebraism (so Charles 1, 161). The partitive use of ἐκ (ek, lit. 'out of') is common in the Apocalypse (see Rev. 6.1b; 7.5–8; et al.). For the complete expression καὶ εἶδον ὅτε (kai eidon hote, 'then I watched as', lit. 'and I saw when'), with the aorist verb ἤνοιξεν (ēnoixen, 'broke'), see BDF 382 (a 'vulgar' use of ὅτε [hote, 'as'], in the narration of the past, to mean 'when').

The prophet 'hears' (ἤκουσα, ēkousa, 'I heard') as well as 'sees' the action of his vision. For this Johannine combination, implying spiritual audition and perception, see on Rev. 4.1 (1.10, 12); cf. also 5.11; 8.13; 22.8 (bis). For ἑνὸς ἐκ (henos ek, 'one of') see the paragraph above. For the four 'living creatures' see on 4.6. They belong to an exalted order of heavenly, angelic beings; and they are close in some ways to the twenty-four 'elders' of Rev. 4.4, et al., who are divine members of the heavenly court, representing the body of the priestly faithful.

The four cherubim in succession summon the four riders. For the MS evidence which suggests that the command to appear is addressed instead to John see the textual notes above, 144. Swete (85) mistakenly relates the injunction 'Come!' to Christ; but, despite the apparent parallels at 22.17 and 20, and the attempt by some exegetes to identify the first horseman with the Messiah (see below), the context naturally demands otherwise. This is the first occasion in the Apocalypse when angelic beings give orders to other supernatural creatures, suggesting an implicit hierarchical order (see 7.2–3; 14.15, 18; and note Zech. 2.3–5). Cf. Aune 392–93.

For the injunction to 'come', now addressed to demons, see *T. Sol.* 1.9, 11; 3.1. (The verb ἔρχεσθαι, erchesthai, can mean either 'come' or 'go', depending on the context.) The phrase 'in a thunderous voice' (ὡς φωνὴ βροντῆς, hōs phōnē brontēs, lit. 'a voice as of thunder') is used in this scene only to call the first rider. Elsewhere in Revelation 'thunder' is a metaphor describing an unusually loud voice (see 14.2; 19.6; cf. also [4.5; 5.2]; *3 Apoc. Bar.* 11.3; 14.1–2). God's voice is often described in the Old Testament as thunderous (1 Sam. 7.10; Job 37.2–5; Ps. 29.3–9; Isa. 29.6; Amos 1.2); and note the association of thunder with the theophanies which occurred at the time of the Exodus (Exod. 9.23–34, et al.).

2 This verse introduces the first of the four apocalyptic riders in Revelation (see also 6.4, 5, 8). He holds a bow, wears a crown, and is 'intent on further conquest'. The imagery of the coloured horses and their cavaliers stems from Zechariah. In Zech. 1.8–17 we have a vision of a rider on a red horse, with red, sorrel and white horses (and their riders?) behind him (verse 8). The motif of coloured horses (red, black, white, dappled grey) appears again at Zech. 6.1–8; but this time the horses are drawing chariots. However, characteristically, John has modified his Old Testament sources. In Zechariah the colours seem to have no particular significance; whereas in the context of Rev. 6 they reflect the character of the rider, and symbolize specific causes. In Zechariah the steeds (and their cavaliers) are the 'four winds of heaven' (6.5), sent out to patrol the earth (1.10; 6.7); while in the present passage their appearance (from where, we are not told) releases disasters on the earth.

See Stauffer, *Christ and the Caesars* 184–85, who refers to the race in four colours which formed part of the imperial games in the Roman period, but which became in one instance an 'apocalyptic death-race', involving anti-Caesar on a red horse (184). Ovid, *Metam.* 8.24–37, alludes to the legendary figure of Minos, mounted on a white horse, and carrying a javelin as well as bow and arrows.

To describe his vision, John borrows from Zechariah the symbol of the horses and their colours; but, instead of yoking the horses to chariots, he places on them four riders who become the focus of interest in this scene (cf. Swete 85–86). Together, they represent the same number of *causes*: conquest (military power), war (political power), famine (economic power) and death (the power of negation). This depiction of the horsemen, in its totality, expresses in broad and symbolic terms the misfortune and sorrow precipitated by sinful humanity when it rejects the cause of Christ, the ultimate Victor and true King, and arrogates to itself power of both a physical and intellectual kind (cf. Smalley, *Thunder and Love* 76).

John is dealing here with the (right and) wrong *use of power*. Cf. Ellul, *Apocalypse* 147–56, who regards the four riders as the 'four chief components of history' (150). Milligan 88–97, esp. 90, points out, in relation to the breaking of the first four seals, that because the unrighteous have rejected the offers of the Prince of peace, and are at enmity with the only one who makes human solidarity possible, they are also at war among themselves (note verses 4, 6, 8).

It might appear that the outcome of breaking the first four seals of the scroll, together with the advent of the four apocalyptic horsemen, is entirely negative. The throne room scene of Rev. 4—5 presumably promised more than age-old disasters, human wickedness and the wrong use of power. But John has already reminded us that Jesus won the right to open the scroll (5.5) through the sacrifice of the cross (5.9). The salvific purposes of God, in time and in eternity, are achieved through the death of Christ who is the Lamb; and his kingship has its source in complete humiliation, which ended in triumphant exaltation (cf. John 12.31–32). As the powers of evil became agents of divine victory, therefore, so human wickedness can be turned eventually to the service of God's saving plan. 'Because Christ reigns from the cross, even when the four horsemen ride out on their destructive missions, they do so as emissaries of his redemptive love' (Caird 83; see 82–83).

For καὶ εἶδον (*kai eidon*, lit. 'and I saw'), see on 5.1; and cf. verse 1. The characteristic phrase, (καὶ) εἶδον, καὶ ἰδού (*[kai] eidon, kai idou*, lit. '[and] I saw, and behold') occurs seven times in the Apocalypse; see 6.2, 5, 8; 7.9; 14.1, 14; 19.11. The identity of the rider on the white horse, who now appears on the stage, and the meaning of this symbol, have given rise to much exegetical discussion.

Two major interpretations have been offered: personal and Christian, or impersonal and general.

(a) *Personal* 1 An explanation which runs back to Irenaeus (*AH* 4.21.3) associates the rider on a white horse in this context – simply, it has to be said through the phrase ἐξῆλθεν νικῶν καὶ ἵνα νικήσῃ (*exēlthen nikōn kai hina nikēsē[i]*, lit. 'he went forth conquering, and to conquer') – with Christ himself. (In the Greek of this syntactically difficult sentence, the sense of which is nonetheless clear, the introduction of καί [*kai*, 'and'] is ascensive, giving the meaning suggested by the translation, 'conquering, to conquer even more'. See AG 394 II.2.)

This is a view popular among older commentators (e.g. Milligan 88–90). It rests largely on the link between this passage and Rev. 19.11, where there occurs the phrase καὶ ἰδοὺ ἵππος λευκὸς, καὶ ὁ καθήμενος ἐπ' αὐτόν (*kai idou hippos leukos, kai ho kathēmenos ep' auton*, lit. 'and behold, a white horse, and the one seated on it'), repeated verbatim from 6.2. In Rev. 19.11–16 (q.v.) the white horse and its rider, mentioned at verse 11, clearly symbolize Christ. The cavalier is clothed in a robe dipped in blood (verse 13), he is called 'The Word of God' (verse 13), he conquers the nations with God's wrath (verse 15), and he is named as 'King of kings and Lord of lords' (verse 16).

So in the present verse (6.2) it could be argued that the colour of the horse (white) is an image of divine righteousness and purity; that the 'bow' (τόξον, *toxon*, only here in the New Testament) which the rider holds represents an instrument of war, used by the victor to scatter the rebellious nations like stubble (Isa. 41.2); that the crown (στέφανος, *stephanos*) which he receives is a sign of messianic royalty; and that his activity of conquest speaks of the triumphant progress of the gospel (cf. 5.5, using ἐνίκησεν [*enikēsen*, 'has conquered'] of Christ). There is a possible parallel between the last idea (conquest, as spreading the good news of Christ) and Mark 13.10, where the universal proclamation of the gospel is said to precede the end, and the eschatological signs of distress which will usher it in (cf. Matt. 24.14). Note Milligan 89; see further and similarly Hendriksen 93–96; also Ellul, *Apocalypse* 147–48. Sweet (138) sees the rider as the representative of Christ's 'faithful witnesses'.

However, there are difficulties in the way of this exegesis. First, on close examination the two riders of Rev. 6 and 19 have little in common, other than that they are mounted on white horses. In 6.2 the cavalier wears a victor's wreath and holds a bow (by implication, with arrows); in 19.11–16 he is described as wearing on his head many 'diadems' (διαδήματα, *diadēmata*, verse 12; not στέφανος, *stephanos*, 'a crown', as in 6.2), and as being armed with a sharp sword coming from his mouth (verse 15). The setting of 6.2 is that of conquest and victory, while in 19.11–16 the context is one of righteous retribution (cf. Mounce 142).

Second, this explanation conjoins the person of Christ and the proclamation of the gospel with an impersonal series of calamities which result inevitably from human sinfulness (war, famine and death). It makes more sense if the cause signified by the first horseman is in line with the other three. See Boring 123, who points out that the theologian-artist Albrecht Dürer, in a woodcut crafted in 1497/98, correctly saw that the first apocalyptic rider of Rev. 6 (on the right of the picture) belongs to the same series as the rest.

A third problem created by interpreting the first horseman as Christ is the awkwardness involved in the fact that the Lamb breaks the seals of the scroll (6.1, et al.), while at the same time being the first rider to appear when the initial seal is opened (so Aune 393–94). Finally, the use of the aorist passive ἐδόθη (*edothē*, lit. 'there was given' [to him a crown]) in Rev. 6.2 (see also verses 4 and 8) constitutes an anomaly if Christ is in view at this point. For although the word is sometimes associated in the Apocalypse with God's gracious and redemptive purposes (as in Rev. 6.11; 12.14; 19.8), it is more frequently applied to evil powers which are given divine permission 'to carry out their nefarious work' (Caird 81). See its occurrence in Rev. 9.1, 3, 5, in association with the denizens of the abyss; 13.5, 7 (the monster) and 13.14, 15 (the false prophet). It is most unlikely, in this case, that the expression would be used here in connection with Jesus.

2 A variation of the personal interpretation of the first apocalyptic horseman is to see him as the Antichrist, who appears in Revelation in different guises, making war on the faithful (cf. 11.7; 13.7), and who acts as an agent of woes in the period of eschatological judgement (see 1 John 2.18).

So Rissi, 'Rider', esp. 415–16. Michaels (100–101) also favours this view; but in the end he identifies the rider of the white horse in 6.2 as 'false prophecy' (101).

Such a solution to the problem, however, appears to be strained. Moreover, as with the personal equation of the first rider with Christ, the inclusion of Antichrist here breaks the sequence of otherwise impersonal causes which are mentioned during this scene in Rev. 6. It must therefore be rejected. See Poirier, 'First Rider', who agrees that this figure is not to be identified with the Antichrist. In Poirier's estimate, he is instead cast in the drama as heaven's avenger, 'with a wholly positive role in God's plan' (261).

(b) *General* The major alternative interpretation of the white horse and its first apocalyptic rider is to discover in this image a symbol of military conquest, possibly satanic in character. This fits comfortably with the general, impersonal identification of the series of four riders as *causes*: dire expressions of the sinfulness of human beings, who are in need of Christ's redemption, and candidates for his salvific work.

The appearance of the images of the 'bow' and the 'crown' in this verse accords with such an explanation. In the Old Testament the bow is a symbol of military power (Ps. 46.9; Isa. 21.15; Jer. 50.42; Hos. 2.18). The crown symbolized victory (note Rev. 2.10–11; 4.4; cf. Isa. 22.21 LXX; Zech. 6.9–14; also Josephus, *Ant.* 3.172; 17.197). See Thompson 101. This interpretation of the rider on the white horse as a militaristic figure is espoused by a majority of modern commentators. Cf. Maurice 83–84; Swete 86; Moffatt 389; Beckwith 517–19; Charles 1, 163–64; Beasley-Murray 131–32 (he represents 'an overwhelming power in warfare', 131); Morris 101–102; Hughes 84–85.

Beale 375–78, esp. 377, regards the first rider as a representative of satanic forces which attempt to deceive and oppress believers, paralleled by the beasts later in the Apocalypse (12.3–4; 7–9; 13.1–18; et al.). This makes sense of the horseman's appearance on a *white* horse. Elsewhere in Revelation 'white' symbolizes the abiding righteousness of Christ and the saints (as in 3.4–5; cf. 1.14; 3.18; 4.4; 6.11; 7.9, 13–14; 19.14; see also 20.11). So, in the present context, the colour white may refer to 'the forces of evil as they try to appear righteous and thus deceive by imitating Christ' (Beale 377). Cf. 2 Cor. 11.13–15; and see the reverse of the parody in Rev. 19.11–16; note also 13.1–8; 17.17. On John's use of colours in Revelation see Smalley, *Thunder and Love* 106–107.

A particular version of the general interpretation of the first rider, as the representative of military power and conquest, locates the origin of this imagery in the Parthian kingdom. Parthia was situated on the eastern border of the Roman Empire, and was never subdued by the Romans. Indeed, the Roman armies were defeated in the Tigris valley by the Parthian General Vologeses in AD 62; and this invasion may be in mind here (see also, possibly, Rev. 9.13–16; 16.12).

Those who find a reference to the threat to Rome from Parthia, in this verse, point especially to the fact that the crowned conqueror holds a *bow*. The bow was not a Roman, but a Parthian, weapon; and the Parthians were the only mounted archers, in the first century AD, who typically rode white horses. So, according to Boring (122), the picture of conquering Parthians in verse 2 heralds the end of Roman imperialism (to be replaced by God's rightful sovereignty, 11.15–19), and forms an *inclusio* with the closing scene of this section describing eschatological woes: the description of the fall of Babylon, at 17.1—18.24. For the Parthian identification at this point see also Ramsay, *Letters* 58–59; Kiddle 113–14; Fiorenza 63. Even if the conquest of Rome by Parthia is in mind here, however, it simply functions as a focus of the broader and more important reference in this verse to the cause of 'military conquest in general' (Mounce 142; see further on this section Aune 393–95).

The Four Riders

We may summarize our interpretation of the first apocalyptic rider in 6.2, and relate it to the series of four horsemen in 6.1–8.

(a) The four cavaliers represent causes: the manifestation of truths connected with Christ's kingdom, inasfar as his standards judge the world (cf. Milligan 89). In the case of the first rider, lust for power and the search for world domination ('a conqueror, intent on further conquest') are condemned (Hughes 85).

(b) Those causes (military power, war, famine and death) are expressions of God's eschatological judgements, anticipating the end; and the riders themselves are seen as (possibly satanic) agents in this process. Together, the horsemen portray the discrimination of God against human arrogance and rebellion of any kind, exemplified particularly in Rome's opposition to the Church (cf. Boring 122). When power is wrongly used, negative consequences inevitably follow; but God can use these results as part of his judicial (and salvific) activity.

(c) The agents of destruction in this passage, like the causes they symbolize, are ultimately under the hand of God. In the end, and at the end, his power in Christ is sovereign (cf. 4.8, 11; 5.9–10, 13; 6.10; et al.). Hence the use of ἐδόθη (*edothē*, lit. 'there was given'), implying God's permission to act, in 6.2, 4, 8 (see above). Cf. Caird 81. For the passive of divine activity, used 22 times in the Apocalypse, see on 9.3; cf. also (in the plural) 8.2; 12.14.

3–4   The second seal is broken, and another living creature issues a command for a further cavalier to appear. For the language and imagery of verse 3 see on verse 2.

'Another horse, this time fiery red' enters (verse 4). For the horse and its rider see on 6.2. The author of this vision omits the characteristic phrase, εἶδον, καὶ ἰδού (*eidon, kai idou*, lit. 'I saw, and behold'), which is used to herald the appearance of the other three horses and their riders in Rev. 6.1–8, and substitutes the verb ἐξῆλθεν (*exēlthen*, lit. 'he came out'). As with all four cavaliers and their steeds, their origin is not specified.

The use of the adjective ἄλλος (*allos*, 'another'), to qualify ἵππος (*hippos*, 'horse'), need not imply that this horse and the remaining steeds, with their riders, belong to a discrete group, separated from the first horse mentioned in verse 2. All four belong to a coherent sequence; so that 'another', in this context, is merely a synonym for 'second' (see above). The colour of the second horse, 'fiery red' (πυρρός, *pyrros*), speaks of the blood which results from the slaughter involved in warfare.

The second rider is 'allowed' (ἐδόθη, *edothē* [lit. 'was given', sc. 'the authority'], for which see on verse 2) to 'remove peace from the earth'. For peace, in the sense of the harmony and wholeness which are desirable for the world and its society, see Beck and Brown, 'Peace', esp. 781–82. As in the case of all the horsemen, the reference to the action following the advent of the rider (here strife, instead of peace) is symbolic, and does not allude to any particular historical event (so Beckwith 519). However, the disappearance of the *Pax Romana*, and its replacement by anarchic violence, is an obvious example of the catastrophic effects of human wrongdoing and warmongering. See also Boring 122.

The verb σφάζειν (*sphazein*, 'to slaughter'), used in relation to people rather than animals, includes overtones of savagery. Cf. AG 803, s.v. σφάζω; also Michel, 'σφάζω, κτλ' 934–35, esp. 935. See further on 6.9. The phrase ἵνα σφάξουσιν (*hina sphaxousin*, lit. 'that they would slaughter') is governed by ἐδόθη (*edothē*, 'there was given'), in parallel with λαβεῖν (*labein*, lit. 'to take [peace]'). For the use of ἵνα (*hina*, 'that') with the future indicative, rather than with the more usual subjunctive, see Burton, *Syntax* 90 (211); also BDF 369 (2). This purpose clause is introduced by the combination καὶ ἵνα (*kai hina*, lit. 'and that'; in the translation, 'so that'). See Rev. 6.2; 13.17. For the reverse conjunction, ἵνα καί (*hina kai*, lit. 'that also'), see 13.15; John 7.3; 11.37; et al.

The rider in verse 4 is also 'given a powerful sword'. This is the second appearance of ἐδόθη (*edothē*, 'there was given') in this verse; see above, and on 6.2, 8. The sense of divine permission is still in view, although possibly not as strongly as in verses 4*a* and 8. Here, and at verse 2, the first meaning, while still symbolic, has to do with objects received (crown, sword).

The 'powerful sword' (μάχαιρα μεγάλη, *machaira megalē*, lit. 'great sword') is a symbol of the authority already given to the second horseman to 'remove peace from the earth'. This literary device of reversing the expected sequence of events, so that in this instance slaughter is mentioned before the instrument which brings it about has been received, frequently occurs in the Apocalypse (cf. 3.3, 17; 10.4, 9; 20.4–5, 12–13; 22.14). The first seal (verses 1–2), with its theme of conquest, suggests invasion from outside; whereas the second, involving mutual slaughter, may well refer to internecine strife (cf. the theme of removing restraint and precipitating lawlessness in 2 Thess. 2.6–12; see also Zech. 14.13–14). So Mounce 143.

'Bearing the sword' is a metaphor used by Paul in Rom. 13.4 to denote the power of the ruling authorities to execute God's wrath on the wrongdoer. As a weapon, the sword was regularly used by ancient cavalry in warfare (Aune 396). Roman emperors carried swords as an emblem of their office. See Dio Cassius, *Hist. Rom.* 42.27.2; Tacitus, *Hist.* 3.68 (Vitellius offers his 'dagger', *pugionem*, to the consul, and intends to deposit the 'imperial insignia', *insignia imperii*, in the Temple of Concord); Suetonius, *Galba* 11 (also a 'dagger'); cf. Plutarch *Lives: Anthony* 3.172 (the military leader habitually appeared in public wearing a 'large sword'). See also Isa. 27.1; Jer. 32.24; Ezek. 21.14. In Ezek. 21.1–17; 38.21; *1 Enoch* 88.2, a divine agent gives a sword to evil beings so that they may slay one another.

The gift of a sword to the second apocalyptic rider, then, suggests the power and authority to wage war with which he was for the time being entrusted by God. The first horseman 'rode out' (ἐξῆλθεν, *exēlthen*); but nothing indicates that the second rider completed his mission. That mission, symbolized by the red colouring of the rider's horse, would have been swiftly appreciated by John's audience. Revelation was written at a time of anarchy and civil disorder. During the year AD 68–69, just before the prophet-seer composed his apocalyptic work in AD 70 (see above, 2–3; cf. also Smalley, *Thunder and Love* 40–49), Rome had been ruled by four Emperors (Nero, Galba, Otho and Vitellius); and Vespasian himself came to the throne on 1 July 69. Between the reigns of Nero and Vespasian the three temporary leaders, who were not universally recognized, were manifestly rebellious caretakers. Such a setting provides the obvious backcloth to the Johannine vision in this passage of universal discord and self-destruction, echoing rebellion against God.

5–6 For the first part of verse 5 see on verse 2.

The decree to be executed by the third horse and its rider again involves suffering. For καὶ εἶδον (*kai eidon*, lit. 'and I saw') see on 5.1. The colour of the third steed is black, which here (verse 5) symbolizes famine and consequent death (see verse 6). Black is associated in antiquity, in the Middle Ages and since with darkness, the underworld and negation. In the present context 'black' also alludes to the vision of Zech. 6.2–6, where a team of black horses pulls the second chariot. For the combination of 'hearing' and 'seeing' note verse 1.

The third cavalier holds in his hand a 'pair of scales' (ζυγόν, *zygon*). Balance scales feature from time to time in the Old Testament, occasionally to highlight the bad practice of engineering false weights (e.g. Prov. 11.1; 20.23; Hos. 12.7; Amos 8.5; Mic. 6.11; but see the references to the honest or regular use of scales in Prov. 16.11; Isa. 40.12; 46.6). In the current situation of impending famine, the symbol of a pair of scales implies the need to ration food, and especially bread (verse 6). The metaphorical use of *scales* (or dealing out bread by weight), to denote famine, also occurs in the Old Testament (see Lev. 26.26; 2 Kings 7.1; Ezek. 4.10, 16). However, balances are normally used to measure weight, whereas in this passage the emphasis is on (great) cost by volume (Beckwith 520; Aune 396). The apparent inconsistency is best explained by the reminder that John is transmitting here a vision, not a record book.

The seer hears 'what sounded like a voice (ὡς φωνήν, *hōs phōnēn*, lit. "as a voice")' from among the four living creatures'. For hearing, associated with sight, in this vision see on verse 1; see also verse 5. The use of ὡς (*hōs*, lit. 'as'), to suggest mystery, is a characteristic of John's style in the Apocalypse (cf. 4.6; 8.1; [14.3]; 19.1, 6). See Charles 1, 35–36. The origin of the voice is not specified. Clearly it derives from the heavenly presence; but, if we are meant to understand that the living creatures (plural) are speaking, the Greek would then presumably have ἐκ (*ek*, 'from'), rather than ἐν μέσῳ (*en mesō[i]*, lit. 'in the middle of'). So Beckwith 520. It may be concluded that this is the voice of God, or of the Lamb, or both; see Rev. 5.13. For the 'four living creatures' see on 4.6–8 (also verse 1). They can be understood as heavenly, angelic beings.

What follows may be construed as a slogan in the market-place. The conditions of iniquity and injustice in society lead to violence; for, with famine and vastly inflated prices for food, only the rich can afford plentiful supplies of wheat, barley, oil and wine. 'The scales of the third horseman measure the economic structures of a fallen world, where poor persons are deprived of food, and where the earth's poor have need for God's bounty' (Wall 110).

The voice fixes a maximum price, in a time of famine, for basic provisions; but, even so, the cost is exorbitant. The δηνάριον (*dēnarion*, 'day's pay', lit. 'denarius'), the currency unit in the Roman Empire, was the daily wage of people who worked (see Matt. 20.2). A 'choenix' (χοῖνιξ, *choinix*) was a container in the Hellenistic world measuring just under two pints, roughly equivalent to a quart. The Hebrew measure was 60–70 pints (cf. Ezek. 45.10–11 lxx). A choenix of wheat constituted a person's daily consumption, according to Herodotus (7.187) when estimating the amount of food eaten by the army of Xerxes, although his precise calculation may not be entirely accurate. Barley was cheaper than wheat in New Testament times, probably – as indicated here – three times less expensive; and it was therefore largely the food of the poor. See 2 Kings 7.18 (Swete 88).

The famine depicted in this context is thus represented as severe, even if also limited. Information provided by Cicero (*Verrine Orations* 3.81.188–89; see also Josephus, *Ant.* 14.28) suggests that the purchasing power of the denarius was up to 16 times greater than that envisaged here, where a day's wage can purchase only two pints of wheat (but more barley): sufficient for a person's immediate needs, and no more. Cf. Mark 13.8 par.

The 'oil and wine' which must be protected are, along with the grain, staple products and not luxuries; see Deut. 7.13. However, the deeper roots of the olive tree and the vine means that they can in any case survive more easily when the corn fails (Sweet 140). '(Olive) oil' (ἔλαιον, *elaion*) is mentioned in Revelation only here and at 18.13. Elsewhere in the Apocalypse 'wine' (οἶνος, *oinos*) is a symbol of divine wrath (14.10; 16.19; 19.15) or sexual passion (14.8; 17.2; 18.3).

This proclamation as a whole, then, seeks to prevent further human poverty and suffering by restricting price rises on basic foodstuffs, and by forbidding the destruction of the people's liquid supplies. Divine judgement on human economic injustice needs to be respected.

Is the situation of John's vision historically based? Some scholars find in the reference to 'spoiling the wine' an allusion to the edict of the Emperor Domitian, issued between AD 90 and 93, which decreed that no new vineyards should be planted, and that others should be destroyed, in order to devote the land to grain; so Kiddle 117 (tentatively); Hemer, *Letters* 158. See Suetonius, *Dom.* 7.2; 14.2. But there are several objections to this proposal.

(a) Domitian did not persist with his policy (Suetonius, *Dom.* 7.2).
(b) There is no clear evidence that the Domitianic vine edict was promulgated because of a famine, and in any case it does not explain the presence of the 'oil' which is to be protected.
(c) Famines occurred frequently in the Roman Empire, and were also a regular feature of Jewish apocalyptic expectation (Isa. 14.30; Ezek. 6.11–12; Mark 13.8 par.; 2 Esdras 16.18–34).

It is therefore difficult to associate the famine mentioned in this verse with any specific historical event (so Beckwith 522; Charles 1, 167–68; Aune 400); and the Vespasianic dating given to Revelation in this commentary (AD 70) certainly rules out any reference here to the edict of Domitian (around AD 92).

It is just possible that the limited famine presupposed in verse 6 can be linked to historical events which took place during the reign of Nero, AD 54–68 (Charles 1, 167). See Tacitus, *Ann.* 15.5 (famine caused by locusts); 15.18 (Nero proving that the supply of corn was not a matter for anxiety); Suetonius, *Nero* 45.1 (Nero, during a period of famine, turning the high cost of grain to his profit); cf. Josephus, *Ant.* 20.9.2 (priests starving in the time of Ananias, the high priest). Equally, in the reign of Vespasian himself (AD 69–79), although admittedly towards the end of it, a famine occurred in Prusa, with a consequent riot against the supposedly grain-hoarding rich, including the emperor (see Dio Chrysostom, *Discourses* 46.5–14). But these points of contact are strained. It is more likely that John's vision at this point is entirely general, and not specific. It evokes the recurring affliction of famine, and sees it as an abiding judgement of God on human injustice and its resulting effect of disparity and hardship.

For the verb ἀδικεῖν (*adikein*, 'to spoil' or 'to harm'), in the phrase μὴ ἀδικήσῃς (*mē adikēsē[i]s*, 'do not spoil'), see 2.11; also Isa. 10.20 LXX; Rev. 7.2–3; 9.4, 10, 19; 11.5 (*bis*). The command not to 'spoil the oil and the wine' is addressed directly to the third horseman, as the second person singular aorist subjunctive of the verb makes clear. The aorist is one of prohibition, implying that no devastation has yet taken place. Black ('Some Greek Words' 143–44, esp. 144) proposes that, in this verse, μὴ ἀδικήσῃς (*mē adikēsē[i]s*, 'do not spoil') means, 'do not (fraudulently) withhold the oil and the wine', with the possible intention of obtaining an exorbitant price (144). This would be in line with the occasional, but by no means frequent, use of ἀδικεῖν (*adikein*) and its cognates in the LXX to translate the Hebrew term עָשַׁק, *'ašaq*, meaning 'to oppress, defraud', as in Deut. 24.14.

7–8   For the formula in verse 7, introducing the fraction of the fourth seal, see on verse 1; see also verses 3 and 5. There are slight verbal variations. Verses 3, 5 and 7 are almost identical, implying without specifying that the one opening the seals is the Lamb; except that in the present context the 'voice' of the living creature is explicitly mentioned. In verse 1, the formula καὶ εἶδον (*kai eidon*, 'then I watched') is used; 'the Lamb' appears; he breaks 'the first of the seven seals', and not simply a seal; the prophet-seer hears 'one of the four living creatures' crying out, and not just a creature; and the cry is described as being uttered in a 'voice like thunder', ὡς φωνὴ βροντῆς (*hōs phōnē brontēs*, lit. 'as a voice of thunder').

Dramatically, the fourth horse and its rider appear on the scene. As in verses 2 and 5 (but not 4), the literary phrase καὶ εἶδον, καὶ ἰδού (*kai eidon, kai idou*, lit. 'and I watched, and behold!') is used; see on 6.2.

The horse in this context is 'pale-coloured'. The adjective χλωρός (*chlōros*), when used of plants or vegetation, means 'green' or 'light green'. So LXX Gen. 1.30; Ezek. 17.24; also Mark 6.39. At Gen. 2.5 LXX and Rev. 9.4, πᾶν χλωρόν (*pan chlōron*, lit. 'everything green') denotes 'every plant'. But this word can also be applied to the colour of persons who are sick or dead, in contrast to their usual colour when healthy (Hippocrates, *Prognostic* 2); and it can also qualify the reaction of fear (Homer, *Iliad* 7.479; *Odyssey* 11.43, ἐμὲ δὲ χλωρὸν δέος ᾕρει, *eme de chlōron deos hē[i]rei*, 'pale fear seized me'). See AG 890–91. The pale colour of the horse in this verse picks up the description of the fourth team of horses in Zech. 6.3, 6 (NRSV 'dappled grey'). It is also an appropriate hue to be allied with a rider whose mission is to herald God's judgement in death.

Unlike the other cavaliers, the fourth horseman is given a name: 'Death'. John's use of θάνατος (*thanatos*, 'death') at this point is apparently ambiguous, since the LXX frequently translates the Hebrew term דֶּבֶר, *deber*, meaning 'pestilence', as θάνατος (*thanatos*, 'death'). This is true at Lev. 26.25 and Ezek. 14.19–21, two contexts which (according to Beale 382) provide the model for Rev. 6.1–8, containing as it does a direct allusion to the passage from Ezekiel in this verse (four acts of divine judgement [sword, famine, wild animals and pestilence] will be sent upon Jerusalem). Elsewhere in Revelation John uses θάνατος (*thanatos*, 'death') to mean 'pestilence' (2.23, possibly; 18.8, certainly); and this reinforces the likelihood that the name 'Death' in the present passage includes, and indeed presupposes, the thought of pestilent disease, as in verse 8*b*. So Bengel 227; Beasley-Murray 133–34; Court, *Myth and History* 64.

Death in verse 8 is accompanied by Hades (ὁ ᾅδης ἠκολούθει μετ᾽ αὐτοῦ, *ho ha[i]dēs ēkolouthei met' autou*, lit. 'Hades was following after him'). In Revelation Death is personified four times (1.18; 6.8; 20.13, 14), and on each occasion the reference is associated with a personified Hades; although in 1.18 (q.v.) the genitives τοῦ θανάτου καὶ τοῦ ᾅδου (*tou thanatou kai tou ha[i]dou*, 'of Death and Hades') are probably objective, referring more to place than to person (cf. Aune 401). The fact that 'Death' always precedes 'Hades' in the four passages cited suggests that the former controls the latter. 'Death' is a person, while 'Hades' is his kingdom (ibid.).

'Hades' is the region of the imprisoned dead. In Greek mythology the god Hades personifies the underworld (Homer, *Iliad* 15.188). In classical Greek Hades always appears as a person (Homer, *Iliad* 23.244); whereas in Hellenistic Greek Hades can also be represented in spatial terms (Josephus, *Ant.* 6.332). In the LXX 'death' and 'Hades' are combined, as virtual synonyms, to describe the abode of the dead. See Ps. 48(49). 15–16; Prov. 2.18; Song of Sol. 8.6; Job 33.22; cf. also *Pss. Sol.* 16.2; 4 Ezra 8.53.

In the present scene Hades is depicted as 'accompanying' Death. This must mean that Hades follows behind Death, rather than being seated on the same horse, or on another; for that would undermine the strong symbolism of the four apocalyptic horsemen themselves (Beasley-Murray 134). Hades in this vision follows on foot, 'grimly gathering in the victims of pestilence' (ibid.).

The fourth rider releases pestilence, leading to death. But his actions also encapsulate those of the first three horsemen (symbolizing militaristic conquest, strife and famine), all of which can result in death. The seer now announces that authority is given to Death and Hades to kill not only through warfare ('sword'), famine and pestilence (see on verse 8*a*), but also by the activity of earthly 'wild animals'. The word for 'sword' (ῥομφαία, *hromphaia*) means a large and broad, barbaric weapon, easily capable of killing people; it is also to be distinguished from the more conventional, if 'powerful', implement of destruction (μάχαιρα, *machaira*, 'sword') mentioned above at 6.4. See further on 1.16.

This fourfold pattern of calamities is a direct allusion to Ezek. 14.21 (see above), although it is presented here in a slightly different order. Cf. the similar patterns at Lev. 26.14–33 and Deut. 32.23–26. There may be a logical sequence intended in the four judgements of Rev. 6.1–8, since war tends to produce famine, disease, multiplying wild beasts and death; cf. Bauckham 1293. But more important in this passage is the thought of devilish antagonism, opposed to God and aimed at the communities of faith and unbelief (Beale 383). The Old Testament formulas about the judgement of literal warfare 'have been expanded by John to include woes of spiritual warfare' (ibid.).

The four living creatures (verses 1, 3, 5, 6, 7) offer the praise of believing members in the Church throughout the whole of creation. At the same time, the judgements of God brought about by the four woes of the apocalyptic horsemen symbolize and effect the suffering of the whole world, which is already in progress and will continue until the end. The riders form a discrete group. They represent all the ways by which death, and at the same time God's victorious purposes for his creation despite human misery, can be brought about. For the powers of evil and death become, through the salvific death and resurrection of Christ, God's agents for the furtherance of his kingdom. That Death and Hades, like their other three colleagues, are subject to the sovereignty of God in his Messiah is clear from the use of ἐδόθη (*edothē*, lit. 'it was given') in verse 8 (see also on 6.2; also verse 4). Their 'authority' (ἐξουσία, *exousia*) is delegated, and ultimately belongs to God himself.

Death and Hades are given the right to deal destruction, in four ways, 'over a quarter of the earth' (ἐπὶ τὸ τέταρτον τῆς γῆς, *epi to tetarton tēs gēs*). This might imply that the four ways of death specified in verse 8, and in 6.1–8, are each to be allowed to take effect in one quarter of the creation. But a more plausible interpretation takes this phrase to mean more specifically that one quarter of the human race is to be destroyed. This sounds like an unbelievably major disaster. But there is no indication that a single, catastrophic event is in mind; and John probably intends us to understand, in any case, that the deaths undergone by individual human beings are too often, and unnecessarily, self-inflicted by war and famine, and similar evils (see Wilcock 72; Bauckham [1293] notices the escalation of judgement which is implied between this scene and the 'woes' of Rev. 8.13—9.12, where a *third* of creation is affected).

The first group of seal-openings has now been completed. It describes the position of the first-century Roman Empire, outwardly conquering, but inwardly full of unrest and mortality. There are parallels here, perhaps, with the Johannine communities of the day, the members of which were subject to their own tensions, both social and doctrinal (see above, 4–6). These elements repeat themselves in history, and are among the forces released by God's discrimination in order to anticipate Christ's final advent, and the disclosure of the ultimate secrets of the sealed scroll. Cf. Swete 89; Morris 105.

The unsealed message of the four apocalyptic horsemen, then, insists that opposition to God in any form brings its own judgement, including conflict with others. This leads to death, now and in the future, as well as at the end; even if, through that process of divine appraisal, God can bring to his people and to his world both healing and life. That is, in fact, the witness of the drama of the Apocalypse in its entirety.

Seal 5: The Cry of the Martyrs (6.9–11)

9 With the breaking of the fifth seal (for which, see on 6.1, 3, 5 and 7), we move into the second section of Act 1 Scene 2 of Revelation. The action of unsealing described in this instance, unlike the previous four fractions, does not precipitate an angelic decree of woe, issuing from the throne room, but rather a human response to suffering of every variety. The Church, in its persecuted state, comes into view; and in this vision (verse

10) the martyrs cry out for their own judgement and justice. That vengeful theme is present in the Old Testament (e.g. Gen. 4.10, of Abel); and it is common in Jewish apocalyptic writing (cf. *1 Enoch* 47.1–4). It is also attested in the Gospels; note esp. Matt. 23.29–36. For the points of contact between Rev. 6 and the eschatological discourse of Jesus in the Synoptics see below, 166; for the motif of vindictiveness in the Apocalypse see below, 160–64.

Beale (390) argues that the reference to 'those who had been slaughtered' (τῶν ἐσφαγμένων, *tōn esphagmenōn*) in this verse (9) is inclusive: that not only Old Testament saints might be in view, but also believers who are members of the Christian Church, whether or not they have been literally martyred. He bases this identification on the occurrence of the term 'conquerer' in Rev. 2—3 (see 2.26–29, et al.), which describes those who overcome sin and compromise, as well as those who are executed for their faith (similarly, it may be added, Rev. 12.11; 15.2; 21.7; note also Rom. 12.21; 1 John 2.13–14; 5.5), and on the figurative use of sacrificial martyr language in the New Testament to refer to believers generally (cf. Matt. 10.38–39; Rom. 12.1–2; Phil. 2.17; et al.). However, the primary, and possibly precise, reference in this context appears to be to Christian martyrs as such, who have at any time been persecuted for testifying to the redemptive person and work of Jesus (against Milligan 98–102). They had died in the face of opposition (the term 'slaughtered' is dramatic and final), like Christ himself (5.6, 9), 'because of God's word, and because of the witness which they had maintained' (διὰ τὸν λόγον τοῦ θεοῦ καὶ διὰ τὴν μαρτυρίαν, *dia ton logon tou theou kai dia tēn martyrian*). This could have been a result of the Neronian persecution in AD 64. For the phraseology and its meaning, in this setting, see further on 1.2, 9. Now, 'under the altar', the martyrs cry for vengeance. For σφάζω (*sphazō*, 'slaughter') see Michel, 'σφάζω, κτλ'.

Nevertheless, Blount ('Reading Revelation' 409–10) rightly draws attention to the double use of διά (*dia*, 'because of', lit. 'through') at this point. This preposition is used frequently in the Apocalypse with the accusative to denote cause or reason; so 1.9; 6.9 (*bis*); 7.15; 12.11 (*bis*), 12; 17.7; 18.8, 10, 15; 20.4 (*bis*). The linguistic expressions at Rev. 1.9; 6.9; 12.11 and 20.4 are clearly related (cf. 1.2). See Aune clxxvii–viii; AG 180. The causal connection is evident in the present context. It is *because* of their witness to the Lordship of Jesus Christ that believers have suffered. Testifying to their faith, in active resistance to Rome, brings about their physical end, which in turn leads to the coming of God's kingdom. Blount ('Reading Revelation' 409) concludes that witnessing, not dying, is the prominent activity in Rev. 6.9–11. At the same time, as he admits (410), while Christian witness is the cause of the death of confessors, their martyrdom is the result. Trites, 'Μάρτυς' 72–80, oddly thinks that the reference in verse 9 is to the testimony of *Christ* to God (1.9, q.v.), which the martyrs had received, and for which they had been prepared to die (ibid. 75).

The seer perceives 'underneath the altar the souls' of the martyrs. The term ἡ ψυχή (*hē psychē*, 'the soul'), here in the plural, refers to 'the seat and center of the inner life' of a person, 'in its many and varied aspects' (AG 901). The ability of John to *see* a disembodied spirit presents no problem to a visionary.

If this scene is being enacted in heaven (but see below), the possibility of believers entering the presence of God immediately after death, which the situation implies, is in line with New Testament, and indeed Johannine, theology generally (cf. John 14.2–3; 17.24; 2 Cor. 5.1, 8; Phil. 1.23; 1 Thess. 4.14, 17). The normal Old Testament view of the dead departing to the underworld (Sheol, or Hades; see on verse 8), as in Ps. 16.10; 55.15 (so also Luke 16.23, Lazarus in Hades), presupposes a three-tiered view of the cosmos; and this pattern features elsewhere in Revelation (see 5.3, [13]; 14.7). For 'the home of the righteous', as an alternative heavenly location of the dead, see *1 Enoch* 39.1–8. Cf. L. L. Thompson 103–104.

The exact character of the 'altar' (θυσιαστήριον, *thysiastērion*; from the verb θυσιάζειν, *thysiazein*, 'to sacrifice') in this setting is open to discussion. The Greek term is used eight times in Revelation (6.9; 8.3 [*bis*]; 8.5; 9.13; 11.1; 14.18; 16.7). It occurs frequently in the LXX, with reference to the altar of burnt offering (Lev. 8.28), the altar of incense (Exod. 30.27), or altars in general (Ps. 43[42].4). In the New Testament θυσιαστήριον (*thysiastērion*, 'altar') is used primarily to describe the altar of burnt offering in the Temple at Jerusalem (so Matt. 23.18–20; Luke 11.51; 1 Cor. 10.18; Heb. 7.13; cf. *1 Clem.* 41.2), and occasionally with reference to altars in a broad sense (Rom. 11.3; Jas. 2.21). In the Apocalypse alone, the word is apparently used of the heavenly altar (but not at 11.1; see also Heb. 13.10); and, uniquely in the New Testament, it occurs in Revelation to mean specifically the altar of incense (four times: 8.3 [*bis*]; 8.5; 9.13). In addition, John employs the term figuratively as a synonym for 'sanctuary' (14.18).

Here (verse 9), as in Rev. 11.1 and 16.7, the altar in question seems to be that of the burnt offering (against Beale 391, who identifies it with the golden altar of incense in Rev. 8.3–5; 9.13; et al.). If this is so, it becomes easier to interpret the location of the souls of the martyred, which are said to be 'underneath' (ὑποκάτω, *hypokatō*) the altar. In the Levitical cult some of the blood of the victim, which in Judaic thought contained its 'life' (ψυχή, *psychē*; see Lev. 17.11), was poured out at the *foot* of the altar (Lev. 4.7). In the same way it may be understood at this point that the life ('soul') of the Christian martyrs, whose blood is poured out as a libation to God (Phil. 2.17; 2 Tim. 4.6), has been laid for safe-keeping at the base of the altar of burnt offering in heaven (cf. 4 Macc. 6.29). See further on Rev. 11.1; cf. also Charles 1, 172–74; Swete 90; Beckwith 524–25.

All this assumes that John's vision is of a heavenly altar as such; and this would be consistent with the other occurrences of the term θυσιαστήριον (*thysiastērion*, 'altar') in the Apocalypse, except Rev. 11.1. See also the same concept in Irenaeus, *Adv. Haer.* 4.18.6; Hermas, *Mand.* 10.3.2–3; *Sim.* 8.2.5 (the heavenly altar as a place of discrimination). The idea of an altar in the heavenly temple appears to be Jewish in origin (cf. *Shab.* 152[b], 'R. Eliezer said, The souls of the righteous are hidden under the Throne of Glory'); cf. further Charles 1, 173–74. Equally, the idea of heaven as the temple of God is common in the thought of Judaism (Hab. 2.20; cf. Ps. 18.6; *T. Levi* 18.6. See Mounce 146).

However, John's Christology in the complete vision of Rev. 6 needs to be taken seriously. It is true that the throne room scene of Chapters 4 and 5 takes place in heaven, and that the praises and actions of the Lamb emanate from there. But the consequences flowing from the unsealing of the scroll of God's purposes (see on 5.1; 6.1), here and in 8.1, are felt *on earth*. The cry in the present context (verses 9–11) is for God to avenge those believers who have suffered at the hands of his worldly opponents, including Rome, and who have met persecution and death for the sake of Christ as a result.

Moreover, the preposition ὑποκάτω (*hypokatō*, 'underneath'), in the sentence, 'I saw underneath the altar the souls of those who had been slaughtered', is emphatic, as in 5.3, 13: where the phrase 'underneath the earth' is distinguished from 'on earth' or 'in heaven'. Would John have used such forceful language if, following Lev. 4.7, he was simply referring to the existence of souls 'at the *base*' of the altar? Could he not have described their position as being 'in front of' (ἐνώπιον, *enōpion*) the altar, as earlier he had seen what appeared 'in front of', or 'before', God's throne (4.5–6)? The seer's choice of diction at this point reinforces the suggestion that the souls of the martyred, crying for vengeance 'underneath the altar', were not initially in heaven at all, but far 'below' it, on earth: on the same territory which has just been affected by the disasters of the first four seals. See Michaels 106; Charles 1, 172–74, esp. 173.

It is likely, therefore, that the initial reference in this section is to the altar in the Temple at Jerusalem (the article with the noun, ὑποκάτω τοῦ θυσιαστηρίου, *hypokatō tou thysiastēriou*, 'underneath *the* altar', suggests a particular and identifiable cultic object); and if the date for the composition of the Apocalypse adopted in this commentary of mid-AD 70 can be accepted, the Temple would still be standing (see Smalley, *Thunder and Love* 48–50). The Christian martyrs sacrificed their lives on earth, and at a moment in history; and there is a sense in which that libation is recorded in the holy city itself, 'underneath the altar'. John's vision of heavenly worship and activity is in any case clearly modelled on the Jerusalem Temple , since it was supremely the place of God's presence. So Walker, *Holy City* 243; cf. Mounce 395.

But the heavenly altar is not far away from the earthly; indeed, the two begin to merge in this verse. Such a fusion of the earthly and heavenly is typical of John's cosmology and theology (Smalley, *John* 234–38). On the one hand, the altar in Jerusalem reaches towards its heavenly counterpart, just as in the liturgy of Orthodox Christianity the angelic saints crowd into an earthly worship which is focused on the altar. At the same time, the altar in heaven is a reflection of its original in time and space. Those martyred for their faith in Jesus, whose death is seen as an offering to God, were 'slaughtered' on earth. But this sacrifice was in reality made in eternity, where the souls of the martyrs are now offered on the heavenly altar (so Charles 1, 174).

10   The Christian martyrs cry out 'with a loud voice'. The verb κράζειν (*krazein*, 'to cry out' or 'to call out') in this context may have juridical overtones (Aune 406), since those concerned are pleading for divine justice to be meted out. Their cries are dramatic and intense, as they speak in 'a loud voice' (φωνῇ μεγάλῃ, *phōnē[i] megalē[i]*, lit. 'with a loud voice'). The scene echoes the earlier call of the living creature (verse 1), commanding in a voice of thunder the first horseman to appear, and act with his colleagues as an agent of God's justice. For the phrase here see Rev. 1.10; 5.2, 12; 7.2, 10; 8.13; 10.3; 11.12, 15; 12.10; 14.7, 9, 15, 18; 19.1, 17; 21.3.

The term δεσπότης (*despotēs*, 'Sovereign Lord', lit. 'lord' or 'master') occurs in Revelation only at this point. Generally it is used as a designation for those in authority, especially owners of slaves (cf. 1 Tim. 6.1–2; Titus 2.9; 1 Pet. 2.18; *T. Job* 7.9); in 2 Tim. 2.21 and *T. Jos.* 3.2 it describes householders. The word is frequently used to refer to God in the LXX (e.g. Gen. 15.8; Josh. 5.14; Job 5.8; Prov. 17.2; Isa. 3.1; Jer. 15.11; Jonah 4.3), as well as in early Jewish and Christian literature (cf. *Life of Adam and Eve* 19.2; *T. Abr. [A]* 1.7; 4.6; *T. Job* 38.1; Luke 2.29; Acts 4.24; *Apoc. Ezra* 2.23; 4.5, et passim). In the Greek New Testament the term is applied to Jesus only twice (2 Pet. 2.1; Jude 4). It is possible, but unlikely, that the invocation ὁ δεσπότης (*ho despotēs*, 'Sovereign Lord', using the Greek nominative for the vocative) in the present context is addressed to Christ. However, in view of the predominant use of the term in association with God in biblical literature and elsewhere (see above), and the reference in the preceding verse to the word of God, to which the martyrs had faithfully testified, it is natural to construe the title here in relation to the Father, rather than in the first place to the Son (but see below). As such, the term emphasizes the reigning power of God (hence the translation), and implies his authority to act with justice.

The God of regal power is invoked as one who is 'holy and true' (ὁ ἅγιος καὶ ἀληθινός, *ho hagios kai alēthinos*). Those adjectives, in the asyndetic form 'the holy one, the true one', are used as titles of Christ in 3.7, on which see further. The two epithets, 'holy' and 'true', appear together in the Apocalypse only here and at 3.7; and they do not occur conjoined elsewhere in early Jewish or Christian literature as divine titles (but note 3.14, Jesus as the 'faithful and true' witness). The title 'the holy one' (ὁ ἅγιος, *ho hagios*), by itself, frequently describes God in the LXX, often in the phrase 'the Holy One of Israel' (e.g. 2 Kings 19.22; Job 6.10; Ps. 70(71).22; 88(89).19(18); Isa. 1.4; 10.20; 17.7; et al.; Jer. 3.16; Ezek. 39.7; Hab. 1.12). Ὁ ἀληθινός (*ho alēthinos*, lit. 'the true one') is used elsewhere in the New Testament only at 1 John 5.20, first of God and then of Jesus. The author of the Apocalypse uses only this form of the cognates for 'true', never ἀληθής (*alēthēs*, 'true') or ἀλήθεια (*alētheia*, 'truth'). 'True' is used in the Old Testament at times to distinguish Yahweh from other gods who are false (2 Chron. 15.3; Ps. 86.15; Jer. 10.10; see also John 17.3; 1 John 5.20; *1 Clem.* 43.6; *Diogn.* 8.9), or in the sense that he does not lie (Jer. 42.5; Rom. 3.4). For the meaning of the words 'holy and true', as applied to God in this verse (10), see further Seebass and Brown, 'ἅγιος' ('holy'); Thiselton, 'Truth'. The petition is offered to a God who is apart from all evil, and true to the ideals of justice and holiness (cf. Beckwith 526).

For the theme of justice and vengeance in this prayer see the excursus below. The verb ἐκδικεῖν (*ekdikein*, 'to avenge' or 'to procure justice') appears in Revelation only here and at 19.2 (q.v.), where vengeance for the blood of the martyrs, invoked during this scene, seems to have taken place. In 19.2, as in this verse, the preposition ἐκ (*ek*, lit.'from' or 'out of'), already in the verb, is repeated.

The use of the term 'blood' (τὸ αἷμα, *to haima*), as a synonym for the 'death(s)' of the faithful, is rare in Revelation (see 16.6; 17.6; 18.24; 19.2); and only in this setting and 19.2 does it refer to the blood of martyrs which requires vindication. For 'blood crying out for vengeance' see further Gen. 4.10 (the blood of Abel); 2 Macc. 8.3; 2 Esdras 15.8; *Sib. Or.* 3.311–13; also Ezek. 3.20; *1 Enoch* 47.4. For the expression 'the inhabitants of the earth' (τῶν κατοικούντων ἐπὶ τῆς γῆς, *tōn katoikountōn epi tēs gēs*) see on 3.10; see also 8.13; 11.10 (*bis*); 13.8, 14 (*bis*); 17.8. As here, it always means the world in its hostility to God's Messiah.

The phraseology of the martyrs' cry in verse 10 reads like a dramatization of the rhetorical questions posed by Jesus at the conclusion of the parable of the widow and the unjust judge (Luke 18.1–8; esp. verse 7, 'Will not God grant justice [using ποιήσῃ τὴν ἐκδίκησιν, *poiēsē[i] tēn ekdikēsin*] to his chosen ones who cry to him day and night? Will he delay long in helping them?'). See Aune 407. The formula, 'how long?', in the setting of prayers offered to God by those who are impatient for recompense to take place in the face of injustice, is a feature of Jewish literature (cf. Ps. 13.1–2; 74.9–11; 79.5–10; 89.46; Isa. 6.11; Jer. 47.6; Hab. 1.2; Zech. 1.12; 4 Ezra 4.33–37; similarly, in a social context, 1 Macc. 6.22).

Excursus: Vengeance in the Apocalypse

The cry for vengeance in the prayer of the martyrs recorded at Rev. 6.10 needs to be studied as part of the backcloth of violent imagery and apparent vindictiveness which colours the drama of the Apocalypse as a whole. When the sealed scroll is opened by the Lamb, the devastating consequences of misused and satanic power – warfare, famine, pestilence and death – are unleashed upon the earth and its inhabitants (5.1; 6.1–8). Believers are killed because of their faithful testimony to God's word (6.9–11); and everyone from royalty to serfdom flees to escape the divine wrath to come, heralded by cosmic disasters (6.12–17). The trumpets of the seven angels release hail and fire, blood and universal disorder (8.8–12). Desperate woes are predicted (8.13), which include plague, torture and unbearable suffering (9.1–21). The opponents of God, who worship the beast, are tormented endlessly in the very presence of the Lamb and the holy angels (14.9–11). An angel of judgement swings his sickle, and blood flows outside the city for two hundred miles (14.17–20). Seven bowls of God's wrath are poured out on the earth, causing widespread physical agony (16.1–21); Babylon, a vivid, symbolic encapsulation of worldly resistance to divine authority, falls dramatically amid vindictive cries of acclamation (18.1–24); and, in the final battle against God and Christ, vultures are gorged with the flesh of commanders and soldiers alike (16.14; 19.17–21). See Boring 112–13.

The imagery of violence, destruction and suffering in John's apocalyptic visions generally, and such a prayer for vengeance as the one contained in Rev. 6.10, raise crucial questions for this work in its totality, and indeed for Christian theology itself. Can the God of love be also a vengeful Lord who allows, and seems to dispense, suffering and death? The issue needs to be addressed. Some writers, who find this ambivalence intolerable, permit themselves to wonder if Revelation can be regarded as a Christian document at all, since it does not seem to be in line with the teaching of the New Testament. So very clearly Dodd, *Apostolic Preaching* 40–41; see also Charles, who treats Revelation at times (and at 6.10) as if it belongs entirely to the genre of Jewish apocalyptic literature (Charles 1, 176); cf. Rowland, *Open Heaven* 193–247; Guthrie, *Relevance* 16; on the Christian character of John's thought in the Apocalypse see Smalley, *Thunder and Love* 162–64.

Some commentators on the plea for justice itself, recorded at Rev. 6.10, regard it as pre-Christian in tone, and compare it unfavourably with the prayers of Jesus on the cross (Luke 23.34, v.l.) and of Stephen at his stoning (Acts 7.60), both of whom asked that their executioners should be forgiven (cf. Beckwith 526; Kiddle 119; Sweet 141; cf. also Michaels 107; Knight 69). The prayer of the martyrs certainly appears at first sight to conflict with the command to love found in John's Gospel, and elsewhere in the New Testament (John 15.12; 1 John 4.11–12; Rom. 13.8; Eph. 5.2; 1 Pet. 1.22; et al.); and it is true that there is no love command in Revelation. At the same time, we need to recall the presence of curses, as well as blessings, in the New Testament (e.g. Matt. 25.41; Acts 13.10–11; 1 Cor. 16.22; Gal. 1.8–9; also Rev. 22.18–19). Nevertheless, real theological problems are raised by Rev 6.10, and the vengeful and vindictive character which seems to belong to the drama of the Apocalypse as a whole; and the following comments are offered as an attempt to resolve them. (On the other side see Moyise, 'Lion', esp. 182–84.)

(a) The prayer for vengeance in Rev. 6.10 has precedents in the Old Testament, notably in the Psalms (e.g. Ps. 7.6–9; 58.3–11; 79.5–7; 109.7–20; 112.8; 119.154–58). Aune (407) rightly points out that such psalms should not be generally termed 'imprecatory', since calls for retribution appear in varied types of psalm, and none is completely imprecatory in character. The desire for divine vengeance often occurs in other Old Testament contexts as well (cf. 2 Sam. 3.28–29; 2 Chron. 24.22; Jcr. 15.15; Amos 7.16–17; et al.), particularly when the wicked appear to prosper while the righteous are persecuted (e.g. Neh. 4.4–5; Ps. 73.2–20). The theme of vengeance as part of God's just character ('it is mine, says the Lord') belongs to both Testaments (cf. Jer. 5.9; Hos. 4.9; Nahum 1.2; Rom. 12.19; Heb. 10.30). For 'cursing' and its effects see Ps. 59.12–13; 109.17; et al.

In these contexts, however, the wish for retribution is not simply an expression of personal antagonism towards other people, or an opportunity to curse them gratuitously. It is rather a protest of righteousness against iniquity (cf. Beckwith 526), a demand for God to act justly, and for wrong to be replaced by right. The cause of justice has been called in question, and the character and reputation of Yahweh seem to be at stake. See Caird (85), who points out that in the prayer of Rev. 6.10 John is using the legal language of public justice, and not that of private revenge. The point at issue is not the reaction of the saints to their persecutors, but the need for the validity of their faith to be attested. It is also important, in the setting of Rev. 6.10, to notice that the cry of the martyrs for God to avenge their deaths is *preceded* by a call for the administration of divine justice. A direct line may be drawn from all these appeals for judgement to the cleansing of the Temple by Jesus recorded in John 2.13–22 par. (note the reference at John 2.17, quoting Ps. 69.9, to 'zeal' for

God's house). He acts in this situation with an anger which is not personal, but God-centred, and therefore holy.

(b) Related to this point is the necessity, in the Christian scheme, to affirm the sovereignty of God. He remains the Lord of his kingdom, and his power is exercised in the saving ministry of the exalted Lamb (Rev. 4.11; 5.9–13; 19.6–8). His judgements are true and just (19.1–2); and there is accordingly a place for God's supreme justice to be established, in the face of deliberate human error and antagonism and injustice. The difference between the human and divine understanding of right and wrong, for the sake of the survival of the world, needs to be clarified (cf. John 16.8; 3.16), since the ancient prophetic call for justice to roll down like waters and righteousness to flow constantly like a stream (Amos 5.24) has nowhere been countermanded in the New Testament.

Hays, *Moral Vision* 169–85, sees Revelation as above all else 'a political resistance document' for those demanding justice (170, 183). He argues that the book is a critique of the political order, and of the unjust use of wealth and power by Rome (similarly Fiorenza 124). The boundaries between the Church and an unjust society are sharply drawn and absolute; and, within this system, the enemy is portrayed directly as demonic, to be opposed if not hated (Hays, *Moral Vision* 182). This is certainly one valid setting within which to understand and interpret the apparent vindictiveness of the Apocalypse, as in the description of the fall of Babylon in chapter 18 (q.v.).

(c) To this discussion the situation of the apostle John himself, and of his community, provides an instructive background. If the prophet-seer set out his apocalyptic visions after his return from exile in Patmos, in AD 70, he would be writing with the experience of previous and impending oppression from Rome very much in mind. The persecution of Nero in the past, and that from Domitian to come, together with the imminent fall of Jerusalem, and the rage John felt as a result of his own captivity, might well have coloured the tone of the Apocalypse, with its thunderous contrast between light and darkness, and good and evil, and its theme, so relevant to the apostle's personal experience, of salvation *through* judgement. His own suffering, moreover, would have been reflected in that of the Johannine circle, which was undergoing harassment and persecution from imperial forces and some Jewish opponents, as well as living with internal divisions, both doctrinal and practical, among its own members. A community which feels pushed to the edges of society and its own endurance will more easily express sentiments of resentment, and even revenge (Boring 114). See further on this section Smalley, *Thunder and Love*, esp. 68–69.

In Rev. 6.10 itself the suffering and endurance of the saints (cf. Rev. 13.10; 14.12) are placed in a cosmic, and not just community, context; and they refer to the present, as well as to the future. To that extent, the prayer of the persecuted martyrs becomes eschatological. It echoes the petitions in the Lord's Prayer, 'your kingdom come; rescue us from the evil one' (Matt. 6.10, 13 par.), and the invitation for the exalted Lord himself to come into the world with justice as well as love (Rev. 22.20; cf. 1 Cor. 16.22). Cf. Michaels 108.

(d) The violence and vengeance which pervade the language and symbolism of the Apocalypse were not entirely devised by its author. For his apocalyptic disclosures, with their contemporary and future reference, John has entered into earlier traditions, even if he has then adapted them for his own theological purposes. For example, the background to much of the imagery in Revelation is to be discovered in ancient Near Eastern combat myth, with its typical narrative pattern of a primordial battle between order and chaos. This is frequently presented as a struggle between two divine beings and their allies, in which the antagonist is depicted as a monster or dragon. Versions of this myth influenced Israelite-Jewish traditions at various stages (see Job 26; Ps. 74.12–17, Yahweh's conquest of Rahab and Leviathan at the creation, which reflects a Canaanite model). The final conflict, before the creator emerges as the victor, and order and fertility are established in the cosmos, usually includes scenes of havoc and violence. We hear many echoes of these mythical patterns in the Apocalypse; see esp. on Rev. 12. See further Collins, *Combat Myth*; Boring 114; Aune 667–74, who examines in addition the possible Greek, Egyptian and gnostic sources of combat mythology.

The author of the Revelation, as we have already seen, is deeply influenced by the imagery and language of the Old Testament and related Jewish literature. The source of John's thought and its expression is Scripture, and not merely personal bitterness directed against his persecutors. In general, he uses the biblical language of theophany, describing the awesome presence and activity of God, rather than his punishment of rebellious humanity (so Rev. 11.19; 19.1–4, against the background of Judg. 5.4–5; 1 Kings 19.11–13; Ps. 29.3–9; Ezek. 38.22; Joel 3.16–17; et al.). Equally, the violence and retribution which belong to the visions of the seals, trumpets and bowls in Rev. 6—19 derive from an Old Testament background. The Exodus motif provides a way of describing God's reaction to those who oppose his kingdom, so that hail and blood and plagues (Rev. 8.7–8; 15.5–8) become judgements on the Roman Pharaoh and Egypt of John's own day. The prophetic woes directed against Babylon, as the enemy of God's people (e.g. Isa. 13.19; 21.9; Jer. 51.6–14; cf. the stark vindictiveness, for whatever reason, of Ps. 137.8–9), are transposed into the eschatological woes to be inflicted on those who oppress the Church in the first Christian century (Rev. 14.8; 16.19; 18.1–24). Messianic woes are in any case a standard element in Jewish apocalyptic, as the new age is ushered in with a period of intense suffering (cf. *2 Apoc. Bar.* 26.1—30.5; Mark 13.7–8; see also on Rev. 3.10). For John's use of the terminology of God's 'wrath', in the context of vengeance in Revelation, see further on 6.16–17.

(e) The Apocalypse is rich in its use of symbols to represent realities, both physical and spiritual; and this kind of symbolism was a normative part of Jewish and Christian apocalyptic literature. Earthquakes, for example, are a repeated biblical symbol for the dissolution of a rebellious world at the self-manifestation of God (as at Isa. 29.6 and Zech. 14.5). Revelation continues that symbolism (see on 6.12). But, like the violent and vengeful imagery of hail and fire and blood (8.7), and locusts looking like horses equipped for battle (9.7), they are pictures. Like the 'sword' of 1.16; 2.12, 16; 19.15, which speaks of Christ's word of judgement (cf. Heb. 4.12), they are metaphors of discrimination. They convey the reality of divine opposition to evil and injustice, but they are not to be taken literally. See further Smalley, *Thunder and Love* 157–60.

Boring (116–17) regards John's imagery in Revelation, portraying violent judgement from God on his enemies, as confessional. It is 'insider language of the confessing community expressing praise and gratitude for salvation' (116). In the same way, the language of the plague narratives in Exodus, which is one of the biblical sources underlying the symbolism of Revelation, is confessional material, glorifying God's deliverance of Israel (Exod. 15.1–18) rather than making statements about the fate of the Egyptians (cf. Rev. 15. 2–4, another 'song of Moses'; 19.1–8). See also Ps. 91.1–8.

(f) John's theology and purpose in the composition of Revelation relate to the issue of vengeance in the book. He was writing for a divided community, troubled by imperial and Jewish oppression from outside, and doctrinal and ethical problems

within (see on the oracles in Rev. 2—3; also Smalley, *Thunder and Love* 132–34).
Through the Spirit (1.10) the prophet-seer discloses a vision of time and eternity,
of earth and heaven, in which the sovereign Lord unfolds his purposes for the world
of salvation through judgement. The God of movement and thunder is also a God
of love. He cares for his creation and his creatures (cf. John 3.16); and, as a result,
John's apocalyptic drama ends with the promised hope of God dwelling with his
people in an atmosphere of new life and tenderness (21.1–4). God's love is sealed
by the death and triumph of the Lamb (5.9–10, 11–13; cf. 1 John 3.16; 4.14–16),
on the basis of which the writer commends and commands love for each other
(Rev. 2.19; 2.2–5).

The Apocalypse accordingly stems from the exalted Son of man (1.12–16), who
in his love releases believers from their sins, and who is the firstborn from the dead
(1.5). Pivotal to the remaining action of Revelation is the throne room scene of
Chapters 4 and 5 (q.v.), and the worship offered there to God and to the Lamb. The
disclosures in Rev. 6—22 derive from that setting, and from the divine authority
and authorization symbolized by the sealed and subsequently opened scroll (5.1).
This represents God's kingdom of true judgement and love, triumphing ultimately
over human injustice and hatred and wrongdoing. The theological affirmation that
God's severity is balanced in this way by his kindness has consistent scriptural
warrant (so e.g. Gen. 9.5–6; Isa. 54.5–8; Hos. 6.6; Rom. 11.22).

John writes from this side of the resurrection, and as a (Jewish-)Christian. In Christ
a new age has dawned, even if its consummation has yet to be reached. The vengeance
and violence in the Apocalypse, both human and divine, need to be construed in this
light. Through the person and work of the risen Christ are revealed the victory of God
and of righteousness, and the assurance that self-sacrifice, mercy and the redemptive
power of love will always overcome the cruel, self-destructive power of evil. Here is a
call for the endurance and faith and obedience of the saints (13.10; 14.12), for justice
(11.16–19), and for a love which leads to life (22.1–2).

11   Each martyred saint is given a 'white garment', and this symbolic gesture appears
to be an immediate but provisional response to the petition for justice made by the persecuted in verse 10. Their cry has been heard, but their request has not yet been granted
(Beasley-Murray 136); see the final divine judgement given at 18.20; 19.2. The subject
of the actions in this verse is not entirely clear. Who is the one dispensing white garments and urging patience? The cry of the saints is addressed to the 'Sovereign Lord'
(verse 10), and God may well be answering their prayers. Equally, the Lamb presides in
this scene (chapter 6), as the one who opens the seals (6.1) and sets in motion on earth
the purposes of God for history and the history of salvation disclosed in heaven (Rev.
4—5). The details of this vision need not be pressed. A prayer for judgement has been
offered (see on verse 10), and therefore divine help and mercy follow.

Some commentators understand the 'white garment' (στολὴ λευκή, *stolē leukē*), given
to the martyrs, as a reference to the spiritual body which can be assumed by persecuted
saints before the end of the age as a mark of honour. So Charles 1, 176, 184–88; Caird
85–86. Apocalyptic writers certainly use the image of robes to describe the resurrection
bodies of the righteous (cf. *1 Enoch* 62.15–16; *2 Enoch* 22.8; *Asc. Isa.* 4.16–17; 8.14; 9.9–
11). But the garments in these contexts are nowhere described as 'white'; and in the
Christian scheme believers receive their heavenly forms only at the final resurrection.
So 1 Cor. 15.12–49; Phil. 3.20–21; although an intermediate state of being may be
implied in Paul's teaching at 2 Cor. 5.1–5 (so Martin, *2 Corinthians* 105–106); cf. also 1
Thess. 4.14 (Greek).

Elsewhere in the Apocalypse, moreover, white garments symbolize purity; and this is how the imagery should be interpreted in the present passage. See further on 3.4–5 (the conquerors will be arrayed in white); also 3.18, where the 'white robes' to be purchased by the Laodiceans cannot mean 'glorified bodies'; 7.9, 13–14 (the redeemed before the throne are robed in white); and cf. 22.14, v.l. The metaphor of white garments in this verse, as in 3.4–5, stands for the spiritual purity which derives from faithfulness in a time of imperial testing (cf. 4 Ezra 2.39–48, alluding to Rev. 6.11; and 7.9). The gift of a white garment is a heavenly recognition of the righteousness of the saints, who by this action are declared innocent. In answer to their petition, the persecuting inhabitants of the earth (verse 10) are shown by contrast to be opponents of God and his people, and therefore worthy of judgement. The verb ἐδόθη (*edothē*, 'was given') is an aorist passive of divine activity. It is used elsewhere in Rev. 6 of God's agents of destruction: the horsemen who are given divine authority to act (see verses 2, 4, 8).

The second part of verse 10 continues the divine response, now in verbal form, to the cry for vengeance from the martyrs articulated in verse 10. The saints are 'told to be patient for a little longer, until the number (of the martyrs) was complete'. The use of ἵνα (*hina*, 'that') with the future form of the verb, ἀναπαύσονται (*anapausontai*, 'they should be patient', lit. 'they should rest'), carries in this context the force of an active command, rather than a cause or a consequence. It follows from the direct address being given; and note the possible parallel at 14.13 (q.v.). For death as the 'rest' of the righteous see Wis. 4.7; Sir. 47.23 (of Solomon); 4 Ezra 7.88–101. For the idea of a predetermined number of God's people, clothed in white, being 'completed' see 2 Esdras 2.38–41; also *2 Apoc. Bar.* 23.4–7; *Mart. Pol.* 14, where Polycarp gives thanks for receiving 'a portion among the number of martyrs'. For the gnostic parallels see Aune 412–13. The verb πληροῦν (*plēroun*) is problematic, and carries several meanings; but in the passive, as here, the sense is 'to have the number made complete'. For the theme of the vindication of the saints after suffering see *1 Enoch* 47.1–4; 4 Ezra 4.33–37; *1 Clem.* 2.7; 59.2. For the use of apocalyptic traditions in this verse, and in the section Rev. 6.9–11, see Bauckham, *Climax of Prophecy* 48–56.

John does not say what is expected to happen when the period of patient waiting is over, and the number of the martyrs is complete; but, in answer to the prayer of verse 10, a positive response of divine judgement and vindication is implied (cf. Rev. 14.7, 12–13; also *1 Enoch* 97.3–5; 104.2–3). Such an assurance, that God and good will eventually triumph over evil, is the basis for persevering Christian faith and witness (Rev. 1.9; 5.9–10). The Greek phrase καὶ οἱ σύνδουλοι αὐτῶν καὶ οἱ ἀδελφοὶ αὐτῶν (*kai hoi syndouloi autōn kai hoi adelphoi autōn*, lit. 'their fellow-servants and their brothers'), using different plural nouns with the repeated conjunction καί (*kai*, 'and'), may imply that two distinct groups of martyrs are in view at this point. However, it is more likely that the second καί (*kai*, 'and') is epexegetic, giving the meaning in the translation: 'their fellow-servants, *that is* their colleagues'. In this case the same people are being described, but in varied terms (so Beckwith 527; Aune 411). The martyrs resting in patience will be joined by other victims of imperial persecution. They are united in their service of the same Lord (verse 10), and in their membership of the same Christian community (see on 1.9: John is their 'brother and fellow-partner').

The term ὁ σύνδουλος (*ho syndoulos*, 'fellow-servant', or 'fellow-slave') appears three times in the Apocalypse (here in the plural, and at 19.10; 22.9 in the singular), on each occasion as a title of honour (cf. Col. 1.7; 4.7; Ignatius, *Eph.* 2.1; *Philad.* 4; et al.). The word in this verse translated from the Greek as 'colleagues', is οἱ ἀδελφοί (*hoi adelphoi*), which is often used in the New Testament of believers in their relationship with each other (cf. Acts 6.3; Rom. 8.29; 1 Tim. 6.2; for texts in Revelation see 1.9; 12.10; 19.10; 22.9; in the last two instances the description is associated with 'fellow-servant'; note also Ignatius, *Eph.* 10.3; *Smyrn.* 12.1; et al.). In the present context, as elsewhere in the Apocalypse, the title ἀδελφός (*adelphos*, lit. 'brother') must be inclusive, since the Johannine community obviously included women (see Brown, *Community* 183–98); and this firm supposition is supported by the fact that the plural form, ἀδελφοί (*adelphoi*, lit. 'brothers'), when used of the literal sibling relationship, can mean 'brothers and sisters' (AG 15*b*). Charles (1, 177) regards the repeated αὐτῶν (*autōn*, 'their') in this sentence ('their fellow-servants', 'their colleagues') as an 'unconscious Hebraism'.

The 'number' (the word is implicit in the Greek, and supplied in the translation; see above) of the martyrs to be killed has yet to be completed. It is possible that there is a reference here to the recent persecution under the Emperor Nero in AD 64, and proleptically to the imperial harassment which was to develop in the period of Domitian (AD 81–96). The verb ἀποκτέννεσθαι (*apoktennesthai*, 'to be killed') can be taken figuratively as well as literally (cf. 6.9, using σφάζω, *sphazō*, 'slaughter'); although both here and in verse 9 the reference is predominantly to literal death in martyrdom (but see the metaphorical use of verbs of killing at Rom. 8.36). As with the decrees of suffering associated with the opening of the first four seals (Rev. 6.1–8), the martyrdom of the saints and the completion of their number are part of a plan which is in accordance with God's will (expressed in the throne-vision of Rev. 4—5), and therefore characteristic of his purposes of love, as well as judgement. See Beale 394.

Seal 6: The Great Earthquake (6.12–17)

12–14   The remainder of Chapter 6 discloses dramatically the divine response to the plea for justice and vengeance articulated by the martyrs in verse 10. In verse 11, God's unspecified intervention in the future is promised, but not yet realized. Now, beginning with verses 12–14, the action unfolds. Massive cosmic upheaval is to take place, affecting the whole of creation, including secular society as well as the Church. In this way, God's sovereignty will be established, opposition to him will be removed, and the faith of his persecuted servants will be vindicated.

The judgement scene in these verses draws heavily on standard apocalyptic imagery which is used in the Old Testament to describe the dissolution of the universe. See especially Isa. 34.4 LXX, which corresponds closely to the Greek of Rev. 6.13–14*a* (stars falling as fruit from a fig tree, and the sky split like a rolled-up scroll). Cf. also Isa. 13.10–13; 24.1–6, 17–23; Ezek. 32.6–8; Hos. 10.8; Joel 2.10, 30–31; 3.15–16; Hab. 3.6–11; and, less directly, Ps. 68.7–8; Jer. 4.23–28; Amos 8.8–9. In the same tradition note further 4 Ezra 5.4–8 (7.39–40); *T. Mos.* 10.3–6. The biblical texts behind this passage in Revelation are also evident in the composition of the eschatological discourse at Mark 13.24–25 (= Matt. 24.29), which in an early form may have influenced John's portrayal of events at the end; cf. also Acts 2.19–20 (= Joel 2.30–31). Common to all these passages are several varied metaphors of judgement, found also in Rev. 6.12–14: the shaking of the earth or mountains; the darkening of the sun and moon; the displacement of the stars and the splitting of the heavens; and the outpouring of blood.

For the breaking of the sixth seal by the Lamb, at the outset of verse 12, and the expression καὶ εἶδον (*kai eidon*, 'then I watched', lit. 'and I saw'), see on 6.1 (also 4.1; 5.1; 6.5, 8). The expression σεισμὸς μέγας (*seismos megas*), translated as 'a massive earthquake', could mean that a 'great shaking' occurred, as in the 'shaking of the heavens and earth and the nations' at Hag. 2.6–7, 21–22 (so Aune 413). But in the biblical tradition earthquakes as such are frequently the harbingers of Yahweh's advent (see Exod. 19.18; Isa. 24.18–20; 29.6; Joel 2.10; 3.16; Mic. 1.4; Nahum 1.5); and that is most likely to be the significance here.

The next three statements in verses 12 and 13, concerning the sun, the moon and the stars, involve the same literary pattern: an announcement of what happened, with an aorist verb in the Greek, followed by a simile using ὡς (*hōs*, 'as', 'like'). The notion of the Day of God's judgement on the world, as an event which is accompanied by the darkening or destruction of the sun, moon and stars, frequently appears in the Old Testament and Jewish literature. See Isa. 13.9–10; Ezek. 32.7–8; Joel 2.10, 31; Amos 8.9; Zeph. 1.15; also *T. Levi* 4.1; 4 Ezra 7.39; *Sib. Or.* 5.346–85; in the New Testament and beyond cf. Mark 13.24–25 par.; Acts 2.20; 2 Pet. 3.10; *Barn.* 15.5. Eclipses of the sun and moon often feature as prodigies in classical literature (see Aune 413). Presumably the cosmic activities portrayed in these verses (and verse 14), following the fraction of the sixth seal, are coterminous.

The likening of the blackened sun to 'haircloth' (σάκκος τρίχινος, *sakkos trichinos*, lit. 'sackcloth of hair'), in verse 12, includes a possible allusion to Isa. 50.3 ('I clothe the heavens with blackness, and make sackcloth their covering'). Haircloth is the vesture of mourning. The reference to the moon becoming (red) 'like blood' (verse 12), together with the description earlier of the sun turning black, directly echoes Joel 2.31. The blood-like colour of the moon in this eschatological scene perhaps suggests the reddish appearance of the moon in an eclipse (Beckwith 529). Only here and at *T. Mos.* 10.5, in lists of portents such as the ones we are considering, is the qualifying adjective 'whole' added to 'moon': 'the whole (full) moon (ἡ σελήνη ὅλη, *hē selēnē holē*) became like blood' (see verses 4–5 for parallels to Rev. 6.12–14). This need not, however, imply the literary dependence of John on *The Testament of Moses* (against Charles 1, 180), particularly as the wording of *T. Mos.* 10.5 is not especially close to Rev. 6.12.

The vivid imagery, in verse 13, of the stars falling like ripe figs from a wind-battered fig tree, is drawn from Isa. 34.4; although in that passage (LXX) it is the leaves of the tree which fall, rather than the fruit. Isa. 34.4 lies behind both verses 13 and 14; but the order of the disturbances is inverted, since in the Isaianic text the rolling up of the heavens precedes the falling of the late fruit. The word ὄλυνθος (*olynthos*) means a 'late, or summer, fig' (AG 568*a*). Swete (93), however, interprets this imagery to mean the shedding of green, unripe figs, which appear in the winter and in many cases drop off from the tree in the spring (similarly Mounce 151; Aune 415). Cf. Mark 13.28. Falling stars appear in three other contexts of the Apocalypse (8.10; 9.1; 12.4). In Judaic thought meteors, or darkened stars, are not necessarily associated with the dissolution of the cosmos; they can also be an omen in need of interpretation (4 Ezra 5.5), or an anticipation of God's judgement (Ezek. 32.7; Joel 2.10; 3.15; *Sib. Or.* 8.190, 341; cf. Mark 13.25 par.). Cf. Aune 415. The motif of the fallen star can also be used for the descent of Satan and his associated powers of evil (Jude 13; *1 Enoch* 86.1, 3; 88.1–3; 90.24; *T. Sol.* 20.16; *Apoc. Elijah* 4.11; cf. Luke 10.18).

A further consequence of the sixth seal being broken, affecting both heaven and earth, is described in verse 14: the sky was split, and every mountain and island was removed. The verb ἀποχωρίζω (*apochōrizō*) here means literally 'separate' (AG 101*b*). In this case the sky is separated into two halves, each of which is then rolled up like a scroll (cf. 5.1); so Swete 93; Beale 396. The background to this image is to be found directly in Isa. 34.4, where the Lord's judgement causes the skies to be rolled up 'like a scroll'; cf. Heb. 1.12. However, some commentators translate the passive form ἀπεχωρίσθη (*apechōristhē*) as 'vanished' (as in NRSV, REB), or 'disappeared' (NJB). So Beckwith 529 ('removal to another place'); Aune 415 ('disappeared from sight'). In this version of the portent, the sky is compared to a scroll being rolled up so that its contents are no longer to be seen; cf. *Sib. Or.* 3.80–84; 8.232–34, 412–13; also *Apoc. Peter* (*Eth.*) 5, elaborated by Macarius Magnes, *Apocritica* 4.7 (Hennecke, *Apocrypha* 2, 671). Nevertheless, the splitting of the heavens is a regular biblical image used to introduce a disclosure of God, although not always in judgement (cf. Exod. 19.16–20; 2 Sam. 22.10; Ps. 18.9; Isa. 64.1; Ezek. 1.1; Mark 1.10 = Matt. 3.16; John 1.51; Acts 7.56); and that appears to be the primary sense of the heavenly phenomenon in the context of this verse.

The second part of verse 14 continues to itemize the effects of the seal-breaking in verse 12, but links directly with the 'massive earthquake' mentioned in that verse. Mountains and islands, on land and in the sea, are consequently 'removed' from their places. The verb κινέω (*kineō*) means 'remove' or 'move away', more than 'shake' (against Aune 415–16). Mountains and islands, together with coastlands, are expected to represent stability in creation; and when they do not, and are in the process of removal, a theophany accompanied by divine judgement is heralded (so also Rev. 20.11; cf. Judg. 5.5; Ps. 18.7; Isa. 54.10; Jer. 4.23–26; Ezek. 26.18; Mic. 1.4; Hab. 3.6; Zeph. 2.11; Zech. 14.4 [the splitting of the Mount of Olives]; et al.). See also the impossibility of moving mountains suggested at Job 14.18; Ps. 125.1–2; Matt. 17.20; 1 Cor. 13.2. On ancient prodigies, and the plagues of Revelation, see Aune 416–19.

Two general questions are raised by verses 12–14, and indeed by the remainder of Chapter 6 (verses 15–17); and they are related. First, are the events flowing from the breaking of the sixth seal (verses 12–17) to be taken in a literal or figurative sense? If the final judgement is in view at this point (but see below), it could be argued that the sense of these portents is literal and material; for the dissolution of the cosmos, inasfar as it is describable, will presumably include similar occurrences (see 2 Pet. 3.10: when the Day of the Lord arrives, 'the heavens will pass away with a loud noise, and the elements will be dissolved with fire'). But it is much more likely that John is writing figuratively here, as in the earlier part of Chapter 6, where the opening of the first five seals leads in each case to a spiritual vision of the need for human justice, to be established by the divine. Moreover, the eschatological texts Mark 13.24–25 = Matt. 24.29 and Acts 2.20, which may have influenced the composition of this passage, like the Old Testament passages on which they depend (see above), are similarly figurative. The cosmic happenings portrayed in verses 12–14, therefore, are metaphors of God's judgement on the powers of evil which oppose his justice and goodness, and on the individuals who support those systems.

Second, does the scene unfolded in Rev. 6.12–14(17) delineate the final judgement of God at the end of the world, or is it a representation of the temporal tribulations which will precede it? Beale (398–99) argues strongly that this passage 'depicts figuratively the inauguration of the last judgment' itself (398). In support of this view, he claims (*inter alia*) that various phrases in 6.12–14 are used later in the Apocalypse to describe the final judgement (with verse 12 cf. 11.13 and 16.18–19; with verse 14 cf. 16.20, which belongs in Beale's view to the consummation scene of 16.17–21, and see 20.11; with verse 17 ['the critical day has arrived'] cf. 11.18 and 19.17–18). Furthermore, whereas the sun, moon and stars are destroyed in their totality, according to 6.12–13, in 8.12 only a third of these luminaries are affected in what is clearly a temporal affliction (cf. also 8.10; 9.1; 12.4).

But, as Charles (1, 183) suggests, the writer of Revelation 6.12–17 knows that the end is not yet, and that there is more to follow. As in the synoptic parallels cited above, the portents of the earthquake, sun, moon, stars and sky, mountains and islands, point towards the parousia, without necessarily introducing it historically. Similarly, the kingdom evidently arrives at 11.15–19, after the sounding of the seventh trumpet, yet heavenly signs, reflected on earth, follow in Chapter 12; and the outpouring of the seventh bowl (16.17–21) repeats the form of the sixth seal-fraction, but this is succeeded by a description of the splendour of Babylon, and indeed its eventual downfall (17—18). Three times we are brought to the edge of the end-time, without the Day of the Lord actually arriving. As Beasley-Murray (138) says, John depicts the last times 'from different vantage points'. This is entirely characteristic of the eschatology of the Apocalypse, as of the Fourth Gospel. In Johannine thought the present and the future, the temporal and the eternal, are brought together; and the end is always pressing in. The eschatological climax of Revelation is not at the end of time, or at the end of the book; for the consummation vision of Chapters 21 and 22 stems from the Christ-event celebrated in Chapters 4 and 5 (see above, 110–11). The apocalypse is therefore in progress from the outset of the drama; and on the way the audience is allowed to glimpse heaven from earth, eternity from time, the end from the beginning and back again. God in Christ comes in now, with judgement and love (cf. Isa. 35.4), as well as at the last day; and the one points to the other (for this characteristic tension in Johannine eschatology, signified by the 'hour' which is both present and future, see John 5.25; et al.). This is the eschatological framework within which to interpret and understand this section of the Apocalypse; for in it the parousia is anticipated, but in one sense experienced already. See further Smalley, *Thunder and Love* 62–63, 150–52.

15–16 God's purposes for his creation, symbolized by the effect of opening the sixth seal (verse 12), are far reaching. His corrective judgement releases devastating cosmic disorders in the heavens and on earth (verses 12–14), and it is universal in its personal consequences (verses 15–17). See also Rev. 13.16; 14.6–7; 19.18. All humanity is affected by divine justice, and no one can escape (cf. *2 Apoc. Bar.* 70.2–10). For the reaction of terror in the face of God's eschatological judgement, as in verses 15–17 (also following an earthquake), see Rev. 11.13. Cf. further Kiddle 124–26.

Seven groups of people are specified in verse 15 (cf. similar lists at 13.16; 19.18). John's predilection for the number seven is a feature of his writing (see on 1.4). This is an all-embracing description of the world's population, especially in its final reference to 'everyone, slave or free'. But the emphasis in the earlier part of the list is on those members of society whose status would normally cause them to feel secure; whereas in this situation they are as much at risk as anyone else (cf. Mounce 152). 'Earthly kings' (οἱ βασιλεῖς τῆς γῆς, *hoi basileis tēs gēs*) are mentioned first, as those in ultimate positions of authority and government, and leaders of the people, whether royal or not (GT 98*a*; cf. Isa. 24.21 LXX; Rev. 17.2, 18; 18.3, 9). The 'courtiers' (οἱ μεγιστάνες, *hoi megistanes*) come next in rank. Swete (94) identifies this class as civil officials, notably persecuting proconsuls; Charles (1, 183) regards them as Parthian princes. At Rev. 18.23 it is said that Rome's merchants had become the 'magnates' (μεγιστάνες, *megistanes*) of the earth. The 'military leaders' (οἱ χιλίαρχοι, *hoi chiliarchoi*) are high-ranking generals, specifically at this period of Roman history those occupying the role of a *tribunus militum*, the commander of a cohort of about six hundred soldiers. 'The kings and rulers and the exalted', functioning as the enemies of God, appear often in the *Similitudes of Enoch* (e.g. *1 Enoch* 38.5; 55.4; 62.3, 9; 63.1, 12; 67.8, 12). Those who are 'rich' (οἱ πλούσιοι, *hoi plousioi*) are so wealthy they do not need to work for a living; while the 'powerful' (οἱ ἰσχυροί, *hoi ischyroi*) are the élite of the land (2 Kings 24.15 LXX). A 'slave' (δοῦλος, *doulos*) is a servant in thrall to a master, in contrast to a 'free' person (ἐλεύθερος, *eleutheros*), who is born free (freeman) rather than being a liberated slave (freedman). On this section see L. L. Thompson 106.

John's dramatic description of humanity fleeing in terror from the effects of God's judgement, in verse 15*b*, is picked up in the Greek of verse 16 (using τοῖς ὄρεσιν καὶ ταῖς πέτραις, *tois oresin kai tais petrais* ['the mountains and the crags, or rocks'], and κρύψατε, *krypsate* ['hide']). It echoes the prophetic portrayal of the final Day of the Lord as a time when people will seek refuge in rocks and caves, to escape the discrimination of the Lord (so Isa. 2.10, 19–21). The terrified appeal in verse 16, for 'the mountains and the crags' (cf. 'the mountainous rocks' of verse 15*b*) to 'fall down' on the fugitives, may have been influenced by Hos. 10.8 ('they will say to the mountains, Cover us, and to the hills, Fall on us' [LXX Πέσατε ἐφ' ἡμᾶς, *pesate eph'hēmas*]); although in Rev. 6.16 the order of the verbs is reversed. According to Luke 23.30, Jesus applied this text (with the order of the verbs again reversed) to the impending fall of Jerusalem. 'Hiding' in guilt from the presence of the Lord is a biblical motif from the beginning of time (Gen. 3.8). Being buried by an earthquake, and under falling rocks, is better than facing divine judgement (cf. Nahum 1.5–6). But, in the light of God's correction, there is nowhere to hide. L. L. Thompson (106) finds in the eschatological implications of this passage, and in the human reaction to God's justice, the collapse of urban living (see Jer. 4.29) and the humbling of the rich and powerful (Isa. 2.17).

Representative human figures, fleeing from the onset of divine displeasure, plead to be hidden 'from the sight of the one who is seated on the throne'. For the characteristic circumlocution 'the one seated on the throne', meaning God, see on 4.2–3, 9–10; 5.1; et al. The 'sight' (πρόσωπον, *prosōpon*, lit. 'face', here in the genitive) of the Lord is an anthropomorphic image evoking his presence. The same figure of speech is used in the Old Testament to refer to the sight or presence of people (as in Gen. 44.23; et al.), and frequently in relation to the person and presence of Yahweh, who sometimes 'hides' his face from his people (e.g. Ezek. 39.24, 29); see Gen. 4.14; Exod. 33.20; Num. 6.25; Ps. 27.8; Isa. 54.8; Jer. 21.10; et al.). In the New Testament this image is seldom used of God (but see 1 Cor. 13.12; 2 Thess. 1.9, 'the face of the Lord', quoting Isa. 2.19 LXX; similarly 1 Pet. 3.12, quoting Ps. 33.17 LXX), and rarely of Jesus (Luke 7.27; 9.51–53; 10.1). The phrase as it stands in verse 16 ('the sight of the one who is seated on the throne') is unique in the Apocalypse; but πρόσωπον (*prosōpon*, lit. 'face') occurs twice elsewhere in Revelation to denote the presence of God (20.11) and of Jesus (22.4).

Once the sixth seal has been broken, and cosmic disturbances ensue, the world's population is fearful not only of God himself but also of 'the wrath of the Lamb' (verse 16*b*). The term ἡ ὀργή (*hē orgē*, 'wrath', 'anger') appears in the Apocalypse six times (6.16, 17; 11.18; 14.10; 16.19; 19.15). The specific phrase, 'the wrath of God' (in the genitival form τῆς ὀργῆς τοῦ θεοῦ, *tēs orgēs tou theou*), is used only at 19.15; although 'wrath' (using ὀργή, *orgē*) is attributed to God indirectly in three other texts (11.18; 14.10; 16.19). The subject of 'the day of their wrath' in verse 17 (q.v.) is uncertain, but seems to include both the Father and the Son. The expression 'the wrath of the Lamb' (in the form τῆς ὀργῆς τοῦ ἀρνίου, *tēs orgēs tou arniou*) appears only here (verse 16) in Revelation. A parallel Greek word for 'wrath', with virtually the same meaning in the LXX and the New Testament, is θυμός (*thymos*), which is used in Revelation in association with God (14.10, 19; 15.1; et al.), but can also characterize the devil (12.12) and even Babylon (14.8; 18.3).

There is debate about the significance of divine wrath in the New Testament. Dodd (*Romans* 20–24), commenting on Rom. 1.18, sees the concept of God's anger in the history of religion as the impersonal process of cause and effect: 'sin is the cause, disaster the effect' (ibid. 23). To attribute to God the passion of anger, Dodd argues, would accordingly be 'irrational' (24). Dodd is followed by Hanson (*Wrath of the Lamb*), who considers divine wrath to be the impersonal consequence of sin, worked out in history and disclosed at the parousia. In Hanson's view, this understanding is also to be found in John's Gospel which, like Revelation, connects wrath with the cross of Christ (ibid. 159–80, esp. 178–79; see further Smalley, *Thunder and Love* 63). However, 'wrath' in the Revelation and the New Testament generally is seen as a direct activity of God himself, realized in the present (Rom. 1.18; 3.5; Rev. 11.18) as much as in the future (Col. 3.6; 1 Thess. 1.10; Rev. 19.15); it may be described as the personal expression of God's holy and righteous character, when confronted by the deliberate evil and injustice of humanity, rather than simply an impersonal force or mechanism. However, the personal nature of that divine reaction needs to be carefully interpreted. The fact that in the New Testament ὀργή (*orgē*, 'anger', 'wrath') can be closely linked with such terms as ἐκδίκησις (*ekdikēsis*, 'vengeance', '[just] punishment', as in Luke 21.22–23) and δικαιοκρισία (*dikaiokrisia*, 'righteous judgement', as in Rom. 2.5) rules out the notion that God's wrath is an unbridled explosion of anger. 'The stress is more on the effects than on the emotion' (Stählin, 'Human and Divine Wrath in the NT' 722).

The eschatological dimension to the wrath of God in the Apocalypse unfolds on a massive scale. As well as divine anger being apparent, especially in future judgement (Rev. 19.15, where the 'winepress of the fury [θυμός, *thymos*] of the wrath [ὀργή, *orgē*] of God the Almighty' is unleashed on the nations), Revelation also speaks of the anger (ὠργίσθησαν, *ōrgisthēsan*, 'they raged') of the nations (11.18), and the fury (ὠργίσθη, *ōrgisthē*, 'he raged') of the devil, symbolizing the powers opposed to God's justice (12.17). The drama of Revelation can be understood in terms of two wraths, locked in conflict; although from this side of the resurrection we know the outcome. God's justice will introduce the final judgement, when God honours those who fear his name (20.6); but those who destroy the earth will themselves be brought to destruction (as in verse 16; see also 11.18). See Hahn, 'Anger, Wrath' 111.

There is also a constructive side to God's wrath, as the title of this Act, 'Creation, and Salvation through Judgement', suggests. Whenever the term ὀργή (*orgē*, 'wrath', 'anger') appears in Revelation, a creative, positive implication is predicated. The cry for the mountains to protect the world's population from God's wrath (6.15–17) heralds the protective 'sealing' of God's servants (7.1–17); the anger of God vented on the raging nations (11.18) is followed by a reward for the conquering saints who fear his name (11.18; 12.7–12); the announcement that God's wrath will be poured out on those who are allied with unjust resistance to the Church (14.9–11) introduces a call for the endurance of the saints, and a benediction on those who die in the Lord (14.12–13; cf. 15.2–4); the cup of God's furious wrath drunk by Babylon (16.19–21) and the winepress of wrathful fury trodden out by the Word of God (19.11–16) anticipate a vision of the new heaven and new earth, marked by peaceful reconciliation between God and his people, and healing among the nations (20–22). The cross of Christ *is* the judgement of this world; and God's wrath *is* the retributive expression of his righteousness in the face of evil and injustice. But through that wrath, that judgement, comes a world which is transformed. On this section see further Smalley, *Thunder and Love* 149; also Hahn, 'Anger, Wrath' 105–13; Stählin, 'Human and Divine Wrath in the NT' 722–26.

The dramatic expression in verse 16*b*, 'the wrath of the Lamb', is a hapax legomenon in Revelation. It also appears to be a contradiction in terms, particularly as only once in the Gospels is the term 'wrath' applied to Jesus (Mark 3.5); and, as a result, some commentators regard the phrase as a redaction (cf. Charles 1, 182–83; Aune 420). But the Lamb (ἀρνίον, *arnion*, as here) of the throne-vision in Chapter 5 is messianic, as well as sacrificial (see on 5.6). Christ in the Apocalypse is not a passive figure, but one who is exalted and conquering. He is Lion (5.5), Lord and King (17.14); he is a figure of wrath, as well as triumph. For Messiah as the eschatological judge see on verse 17; cf. also John 5.22, 27; Acts 10.42; Rom. 2.16; 1 Cor. 4.5; 2 Thess. 2.8. In the present context, the Lamb's role in judgement derives from his equality and partnership with the Father (5.13); and this is in line with John's high Christology in the Apocalypse. God and the Lamb share the praises of creation, and act together in judgement and love. When they do so, it seems that no one is able to stand firm (verse 17). Cf. Michaels 110.

17 That is the question. Before it is posed, the advent of the day of judgement is proclaimed. The use of the article ἡ (*hē*, 'the') and the qualifying adjective μεγάλη (*megalē*, 'critical', lit. 'great'), with the noun ἡμέρα (*hēmera*, 'day'), suggests that the writer is referring here to a specific, eschatological event known to his audience and expected by its members. John is speaking of the end-time, when a new age dawns and the process of God's positive judgement, already in process, reaches its point of consummation (cf. 1 Cor. 4.5). The Day of the Lord, as such, features elsewhere in the Apocalypse; see 16.14, where the Greek (in the genitival form τῆς ἡμέρας τῆς μεγάλης τοῦ θεοῦ, *tēs hēmeras tēs megalēs tou theou*, 'the great day of God') is very close to the language of this verse; cf. the related concepts at Rev. 11.18; 19.17–19; 20.7–10.

The judgemental Day of the Lord also forms part of the eschatological expectation of the prophets in the Old Testament (see esp. Zeph. 1.14–18, where the LXX of verse 14, ἐγγὺς ἡ ἡμέρα κυρίου ἡ μεγάλη [*engys hē hēmera kyriou hē megalē*, 'the great day of the Lord is near'] is similar to the thought of Rev. 6.17; cf. also Isa. 2.11–12; Lam. 2.21–22 ['the day of the anger of the Lord' has occurred]; Ezek. 7.19; 13.5; Joel 2.11, 31; Amos 5.18–20; Zeph. 2.2; Mal. 4.5; et al.). For the background to this anticipation of God's advent in judgement, as found in Jewish literature, see *1 Enoch* 10.6, 12; 62.3—63.12; 104.5; et al. For the phrase 'the Day of the Lord', and its parallels, cf. further *2 Enoch (J)* 18.6; *Pss. Sol.* 15.12; *Jub.* 24.30; *Apoc. Zeph.* 12.6. In the *Life of Adam and Eve (Apoc.)* 13.3; 37.5 'that great day' is a time of resurrection as well as judgement.

In his use of the judicial motif of the coming 'Day' of the Lord, and its literary equivalents, the writer of Revelation has inherited, and helped to shape, an earlier Christian tradition present in the New Testament. For 'the day of the Lord (Jesus)' see 1 Cor. 5.5; 1 Thess. 5.2; 2 Thess. 2.2–3; 2 Pet. 3.10; et al.; cf. *Barn.* 7.9 (they will see him 'on that day' [τῇ ἡμέρᾳ, *tē(i) hēmera(i)*]). See also Rom. 2.5 ('the day of wrath'); 2 Pet. 3.12 ('the day of God', uniquely); Phil. 1.10; 2.16 ('the day of Christ'); 1 Pet. 2.12 (Greek, 'the day of visitation'); 2 Pet. 3.7; 1 John 4.17 ('the day of judgement', as in *2 Clem.* 16.3; 17.6); Jude 6 ('the great day'). As in Rev. 6.17, God and his Christ share the final judgement; so Rom. 14.10 ('the judgement seat of God', v.l.) and 2 Cor. 5.10 ('the judgement seat of Christ'). In John's Gospel 'the last day' symbolizes resurrection (6.39–40, 44, 54; 11.24), more than judgement (12.48); contrast *Did.* 16.3, where 'the last days' usher in falsehood and lawlessness (cf. *Barn.* 12.9).

For the textual problem associated with the reading αὐτῶν (*autōn*, 'their [judgement]') see the notes above, 145. The singular αὐτοῦ (*autou*, 'his', referring to the Lamb) certainly connects with 'the wrath of the Lamb' mentioned in the previous verse. But that reading is probably secondary, and introduced to clarify the ambiguity of the plural. However, there is no real ambivalence. The Father and the Son share in judgement, as in love, in the Apocalypse (see above, and on verse 16); and it is God's justice above all which is in view on earth and in heaven throughout chapter 6, even if the Lamb who unseals the scroll is the agent of its process. The dénouement of this scene involves a final day of wrathful and corrective judgement, acted out by God in Christ, from which no evil or evildoer can escape. For ὀργή (*orgē*, 'judgement', lit. 'wrath') see on verse 16. The verb σταθῆναι (*stathēnai*, lit. 'to stand', the aorist infinitive passive of ἵστημι [*histēmi*, 'stand']), in this context, means '(who is able) to stand firm, upright (in the day of judgement?)' (so AG 383a), rather than '(who is able) to withstand, or stand against (that day?)' (so Aune 423). The question is not rhetorical; no one who opposes God's standards of truth and justice can stand fast in his presence, or in that of the Lamb. For similar interrogatory expressions of fear in the face of impending divine judgement see, for example, 1 Sam. 6.20; Ps. 76.7; Jer. 50.44; Joel 2.11; Nahum 1.6; Mal. 3.2. For the situation of reaction to God's impending wrath, depicted in verses 16 and 17, see *Sib. Or.* 3.556–61.

Beckwith (530) and Charles (1, 183) regard the statement and question in verse 17 as a misunderstanding not on the part of the writer, but of the wicked, who believe that the time of the last judgement has actually arrived. But it could equally well be John's own commentary on the scene (Beale 401). In any case, verse 17 is a continuation of the cosmic events described in verses 12–14, and the response to them given in verses 15–16; and we have seen above that this section contains powerful images of eschatological judgement which need to be taken seriously, but not literally. Verses

15–17 enshrine, at any point in history and the history of salvation, the inevitable reaction of the unjust in the light of true, critical justice. Moreover, we have already noticed (above, 168–69) that the writer of the Apocalypse, here as elsewhere, gives his audience glimpses of the end, and notice of events which point to it, without yet reaching the climax of history. One such glimpse is afforded in this section, and markedly in verse 17. See further Moffatt 394–96.

Theology

Theologically, the events and responses of this scene in Rev. 6, and beyond, flow from the throne-vision narrated in Rev. 4—5. The figurative and dramatic link is provided by the unsealing of the scroll by the Lamb in verses 1, 3, 5, 7, 9 and 12. In 5.1 the sealed 'scroll' signifies the purposes of God, in judgement and love, for his creation; and, given the divine and exalted nature of his person, which he shares with the Father (5.13), the messianic Lamb alone is qualified to open the document (5.5, 9). In so doing, the four apocalyptic horsemen 'leave a trail of death and destruction across the panorama of history' (Mounce 153), and cosmic events, heralding the end, are unleashed.

Despite this depiction of eschatological disaster, the originating vision of Chapters 4 and 5 means that God's sovereignty is paramount (as in 4.8–11). In the face of human evil and injustice, symbolized by the causes of military power, war, famine and death (6.1–8), all creation and its historical progress remain under the sovereign control of God and his Messiah. Rome may oppose God and his people, and persecute the saints; and the imperial authorities may become as a result the representatives of any resistance to that which is good. But God is the reigning Lord Almighty (6.10; see 4.8; 11.17; 19.6; et al.), and he will eventually vindicate himself by upholding the cause of the righteous martyrs (6.9–11). Meanwhile, God acts in judgement against all injustice and wrong. Cosmic order is essential to the harmonious existence of the world; but, when humanity resists God's moral law, the elements dissolve and the end is foreshadowed (6.12–16; cf. 2 Pet. 3.10–12). Nevertheless, God is at work in his world (Rev. 4.1), and he will bring it to its consummation in his time (6.17; cf. 2 Pet. 3.13).

The scene in this chapter, as a whole, points to the end; but the end is not yet (verse 17 notwithstanding). John's theology in Revelation, like his eschatology and cosmology, is balanced. He moves the dramatic action from time to eternity, and back again; so that his audience is able to glimpse the future from the present, and to view time in the light of eternity (see Smalley, *Thunder and Love* 150–52). As in the Fourth Gospel, moreover, heaven and earth are drawn together (Smalley, *John* 137–39, 276–82). The setting of the drama of the Apocalypse so far has varied between heaven (1.9–20; 4–5) and earth (1.1–8; 2–3; 6.1–17); see also 7.1–17. But in Christ, matter becomes the carrier of spirit (John 1.14); and from now on the cataclysmic happenings discernible in the created world (6.12–17) must be understood from the perspective of an entirely new order of existence (21.1—22.21).

The question in verse 17, 'Who is able to stand firm (in the day of judgement)?', in one sense cannot be answered (see on 6.17, above). The perpetrators of injustice and wrongdoing are unable to stand their ground in the presence of divine discrimination. But another reply is possible. God's judgement, mediated through the death and exaltation of Jesus Christ (Rev. 1.4–7, 17–18; 5.9–10; 6.16–17), cannot be separated from his love (1.5; 22.21; cf. Ps. 33.5). His steadfast mercy is a further dimension of his righteousness. The heavenly vision of Rev. 21—22, and its promise of God dwelling eternally with his people in security, is not far away. Meanwhile, a more immediate and glorious vision, of the protective sealing of the servants of God, is about to be enacted in Chapter 7.

The Church Protected
(7.1–17)

Translation

7 [1]Next I saw four[a] angels standing at the four[a] quarters of the earth, restraining the four[a] earthly winds, so as to prevent any wind from blowing on land or sea, or against any tree.[b] [2]Then I saw another angel, ascending from the east,[c] bearing the seal of the living God; and he cried aloud to the four angels who were permitted to despoil the land and sea,[3] saying, 'Do not lay waste either the land or the sea or the forests, until we have put the seal on the foreheads of the servants of our God.' [4]Then I heard how many received the seal: one hundred and forty-four thousand, from every tribe of the people of Israel, were sealed.[d]

[5]Twelve thousand from Judah's tribe were marked with the signet;
twelve thousand from Reuben's tribe;
twelve thousand from Gad's[e] tribe;
[6]twelve thousand from Asher's[e] tribe;
twelve thousand from Naphtali's tribe;
twelve thousand from Manasseh's[e] tribe;
[7]twelve thousand from Simeon's[e] tribe;
twelve thousand from Levi's tribe;
twelve thousand from Issachar's tribe;
[8]twelve thousand from Zebulun's tribe;
twelve thousand from Joseph's tribe;
and twelve thousand from Benjamin's tribe received the seal.

[9]After this I watched, and there[f] was a vast multitude! It was impossible for anyone to count how many were present; they came from every nation, race, people and language group. They stood[g] in front of the throne, and before the Lamb, dressed[h] in white robes, with palm branches[i] in their hands; [10]and they cry out[j] with a loud voice saying,

'Deliverance belongs to our God, who is seated on the throne,
and to the Lamb!'[k]

[11]And all the angels had been standing in a circle round the throne, and round the elders and the four living creatures; and they fell prostrate before the throne, and worshipped God [12]singing,

'So be it! Blessing and glory and wisdom,
thankfulness and reverence, and power and might,
be to our God for ever and ever! Amen.'[l]

[13]Then one of the elders addressed me saying, 'These people, dressed in white robes: who are they, and where did they come from?' [14]I replied, 'My[m] lord, you know that.' And he said to me, 'These are the ones who have survived the great ordeal; they have washed[n] their robes, and whitened them by the blood of the Lamb. [15]That is why they remain in front of God's throne, and serve him as ministers day and night in his sanctuary; and the one who is seated on the throne[o] will protect them. [16]They will never be hungry or thirsty again; and

neither sun nor burning heat will ever strike them. [17]For the Lamb at the heart of the throne will shepherd them, and will lead them to springs of living water; and God will wipe away every tear from[p] their eyes.'

Text

[a] Instead of τέσσαρας (*tessaras*, 'four'), as read by the major witnesses at the three appearances of the number in verse 1, the variant τέσσαρες (*tessares*, 'four') is attested by A, et al. (first and third time), and by 025 (second time). Despite the evidence, the accusative ending -ες (*-es*) is likely to be an earlier form, as used in Doric dialects (Aune 426). 'Four' in Greek is the only cardinal number with a separate accusative case.

[b] The version μήτε ἐπὶ πᾶν δένδρον (*mēte epi pan dendron*, lit. 'nor on any tree') is firmly supported by ℵ 1611[1854,2344] Andreas syr[ph], et al. Some MSS, including C 046 cop[sa] vg, have μήτε ἐπί τι δένδρον (*mēte epi ti dendron*, lit. 'nor on any tree'); but this is probably a secondary correction by a copyist, since the author of the Apocalypse always uses τις (*tis*, 'any') as a substantive, and not adjectivally. The variant μήτε ἐπὶ δένδρου (*mēte epi dendrou*, lit. 'nor on a tree'), as shown in A 1611[2329], is a similar error, particularly given that ἐπί (*epi*, 'on') with the genitive, as in this alternative, usually suggests the idea of position without movement; whereas, in 7.1, the winds are prevented from 'blowing against any tree'.

[c] The phrase ἀπὸ ἀνατολῆς (singular) ἡλίου (*apo anatolēs hēliou*, lit 'from the rising of the sun', meaning 'from the east') appears in that form in the major witnesses (ℵ C 025 046). Other MSS (including A Andreas cop[sa,bo] sy[ph]) have the plural version, ἀπὸ ἀνατολῶν (*apo anatolōn*, lit. 'from the risings [of the sun]'). The expression ἀπὸ ἀνατολῶν (*apo anatolōn*) is regularly used in the LXX to mean 'from the east' (e.g. Gen. 11.2; cf. Matt. 2.1; the singular form occurs in the LXX only once, at Num. 3.38); and it is likely that the plural MS variant in this verse is influenced by the Septuagintal usage and is therefore secondary.

[d] Despite being redundant (which is the reason for its omission by 94) and a solecism (see below, ad loc.), the nominative form ἐσφραγισμένοι (*esphragismenoi*, 'were sealed') is well attested, and doubtless the original reading. The variants ἐσφραγισμένων (*esphragismenōn*, 'were sealed', genitive plural, as in 2351 Andreas i, echoing the same case earlier in the verse) and ἐσφραγισμένοις (*esphragismenois*, 'were sealed', dative plural, as in Andreas f[2031,2056]) are clearly inferior. There are similar MS variations attested at verse 8.

[e] There are MS variants in the names of the tribes listed in verses 5–7. In verse 5 some witnesses (including 1611[1854] pc) read Δάν (*Dan*, 'Dan'), rather than Γάδ (*Gad*, 'Gad'); in verse 6 the reference to the tribe of Asher is omitted by 2351, et al., and bo has Δάν (*Dan*, 'Dan') instead of Μανασσῆ (*Manassē*, 'Manasseh'); while in verse 7 ℵ omits the presence of the tribe of Simeon in the list. The order and content of the list of tribes recorded in Rev. 7 is John's own, and does not correspond exactly to any listing of the people of Israel in the Old Testament. For the variations see the comments on 7.4–8 below, ad loc.

[f] The reading καὶ ἰδού (*kai idou*, lit. 'and behold') is likely to be original. Some witnesses (including A syr[ph] cop Methodius) omit the introductory formula altogether; while others (such as C 1611[1611]) omit ἰδού (*idou*, 'behold!'). The variations are probably the result of correction or error on the part of copyists.

[g] The reading ἑστῶτες (*hestōtes*, '[they] stood') is strongly supported (ℵ A 1611[2344] Andreas, et al.). Several MSS (including 1006 1611[1611] 2351 Byz) have ἑστῶτας (*hestōtas*,

'stood', with the accusative plural of the participle). This reflects scribal attempts to adjust the grammar of verse 9, which seems to demand the use of the accusative plural after εἶδον, καὶ ἰδοὺ ὄχλος πολύς (*eidon, kai idou ochlos polys*, 'I watched, and there was a vast multitude!'). But the nominative plural adjectival participle, ἑστῶτες (*hestōtes*, 'stood'), is correct and therefore orginal in this context. John treats ὄχλος (*ochlos*, 'crowd', 'multitude') as a collective noun which can be modified by a plural participle (cf. Rev. 9.18; 13.3–4; 19.1; John 12.12). The nominative case of the participle here agrees with ὄχλος (*ochlos*, 'multitude'). That noun is in the nominative, rather than the accusative of the object after εἶδον (*eidon*, lit. 'I saw'), because καὶ ἰδού (*kai idou*, lit. 'and behold'), an expression normally followed by the nominative, intervenes (as in Rev. 4.1, 2; 6.2, 5, 8; 12.3; 14.1, 14; 19.11). Other MSS (such as C Andreas c l) read ἑστώτων (*hestōtōn*, 'stood', genitive plural), which is an obvious assimilation to the three preceding uses of the genitive plural (Aune 429).

[h] For the accusative plural perfect passive participle, περιβεβλημένους (*peribeblēmenous*, 'dressed', 'clothed'), as read by ℵ* A C, et al., some witnesses (including ℵᶜ 025 Andreas) have the nominative form περιβεβλημένοι (*peribeblēmenoi*, 'dressed'). The accusative version, which is well supported, arises because the author has taken the participle as the object of the verb εἶδον (*eidon*, lit. 'I saw'). However, the phrase καὶ ἰδοὺ ὄχλος πολύς (*kai idou ochlos polys*, 'and there was a vast multitude') appears in between; and that construction is normally followed by the nominative (see the preceding note). The variation is doubtless a secondary correction.

[i] The reading φοίνικες (*phoinikes*, 'palm branches'), with the noun in the nominative plural, is attested by ℵᶜ A C 025 Andreas, et al. An alternative version, with φοίνικας (*phoinikas*, 'palm branches') in the accusative plural, is provided by other witnesses (ℵ* 2351 Byz, et al.). This variation is a correction, designed to bring the accusative case of φοίνιξ (*phoinix*, 'palm tree', or 'palm branch') into line with the preceding participial phrase, περιβεβλημένους στολὰς λευκάς (*peribeblēmenous stolas leukas*, 'dressed in white robes'). The accusative plural form of that phrase seems to be governed by the verb εἶδον (*eidon*, lit. 'I saw'), at the beginning of verse 9, after which all that the seer perceives can be regarded as the object of the vision. The original text, καὶ φοίνικες (*kai phoinikes*, lit. 'and palm branches'), is nevertheless in the nominative case because it follows καὶ ἰδού (*kai idou*, lit. 'and behold'; see notes [g] and [h], above), or just possibly because it appears at the start of a new clause. The grammar of this verse is evidently inconsistent.

[j] There are several variants of the reading κράζουσιν (*krazousin*, lit. 'they cry [out]', using the historic present tense), which appears in ℵ C 1611¹⁶¹¹, et al. The present tense κράζουσι (*krazousi*, 'they cry out'), without the final moveable ν (*n*, n), is supported by A Andreas Byz, et al. Some MSS (including it^gig cop^sa arm vg Cyprian Primasius) have the imperfect form of the verb, ἔκραζον (*ekrazon*, 'they were crying out'). This is no doubt a secondary correction, intended to overcome the perceived problem of using a present tense in the course of a scene otherwise narrated mostly in the past. The same is true of the aorist form ἔκραξαν (*ekraxan*, 'they cried out'), as witnessed by 1611²³²⁹ cop^sa mss. The final variation is the occurrence in some MSS (such as 1 cop^sa mss,bo Byz TR) of the participial form of the verb, in the present tense, κράζοντες (*krazontes*, 'crying out'), which again appears to be a later attempt to improve the syntax of this verse. Because of its very difficulty, and its superior attestation, the use of the historic present (κράζουσιν, *krazousin*, 'they cry out') at this point is likely to be original. It is in John's style to describe his visions with immediacy, and so to heighten the vibrancy of his drama. See further below, ad loc.

ᵏ Only ℵ⋆ adds the doxology at the end of this ascription, εἰς τοὺς αἰῶνας τῶν αἰώνων· ἀμήν (*eis tous aiōnas tōn aiōnōn, amēn*, lit. 'to the ages of ages, amen'); but this is clearly a scribal interpolation, copied from Rev. 7.12*b* (q.v.).

ˡ Some witnesses (such as C Andreas d 2019 Primasius) omit the concluding ἀμήν (*amēn*, 'amen'). But, although this could easily be a later liturgical addition, the overwhelming MS support for the inclusion of this word (ℵ A 025 046 1006 it^{gig,61} vg syr^{ph,h} cop^{sa,bo} arm eth, et al.) makes it clear that this is the original reading (so Metzger, *Textual Commentary* 740).

ᵐ Several MSS (including A 1 it^{a, gig} vg cop^{bo} Cyprian Primasius Beatus) omit μου (*mou*, 'my') after κύριέ (*kyrie*, 'lord'). These witnesses have possibly construed the address to the elder as a courtesy title, where κύριος (*kyrios*) means little more than 'sir', and therefore does not require the pronoun 'my' (see John 20.15; see also the comment on verse 14, below).

ⁿ The reading ἔπλυναν (*eplynan*, 'they have washed', aorist) is original. The variant ἐπλάτυναν (*eplatynan*, 'they enlarged'; cf. Matt. 23.5), as in 1611^{1854,2329} Byz, is clearly an error on the part of copyists, and does not make sense in the context. Mounce (165) suggests as an alternative that the image of washing garments in blood seemed unacceptable to the scribes.

ᵒ Instead of τοῦ θρόνου (*tou thronou*, '[on] the throne', with the genitive), as in ℵ A Andreas, some witnesses (including 025 1611^{1854} 2351 Byz) have the reading τῷ θρόνῳ (*tō[i] thronō[i]*, '[on] the throne', dative). The former version is probably original. But, like the second, it does not follow the usual grammar of the Greek construction translated as 'the one who is seated on the throne', since the case of ὁ θρόνος (*ho thronos*, 'the throne') after ἐπί (*epi*, 'on') normally agrees with the case of καθήμενος (*kathēmenos*, 'seated'). See further on Rev. 4.2; also 4.9 (dative); 5.1 (genitive) et al.; against 7.15; 21.5.

ᵖ For ἐκ (τῶν ὀφθαλμῶν αὐτῶν) (*ek [tōn ophthalmōn autōn]*), 'out of, from [their eyes]'), some MSS (such as ℵ 1611^{1854} 28 2351) read ἀπό (*apo*, 'from'). The variant may be the result of assimilation to the LXX of Isa. 25.8 (using ἀπό [*apo*, 'from']), which is alluded to at this point in verse 17. See Rev. 21.4, where another version of Isa. 25.8 LXX (with ἐκ [*ek*, 'from']) appears.

Literary Setting

Six seals of the scroll of destiny have been opened (6.1–17), and the seventh is still to come (8.1). The Day of the Lord has been anticipated (6.17), but not described; and the audience of this apocalypse now awaits the end-time. However, with characteristically skilful literary and dramatic craftsmanship, John interrupts the action with an interval (note the same structural pattern at 8.6—11.15, describing the sounding of the seven trumpets). He creatively interprets his traditions in order to let us glimpse, not the breaking of the seventh seal and the consummation of salvation history, which is not fully revealed even then, but the sealing of God's servants (note the Johannine play on words; cf. Sweet 146).

Instead of the end we are shown the Church, protected by God and the Lamb. The interval in Chapter 7 is not a digression in the narrative action, but an opportunity to build up the suspense before the scroll is finally opened. In the course of this interlude, John presents us with a vision of the nature of the Christian community on earth and in heaven, and the divine activity of assurance and salvation within it. Such an understanding would have provided the Johannine circle itself, surrounded in the first century AD by persecution, opposition and division, with the encouragement it needed to believe and behave rightly, and the strength required of its members to withstand evil and triumph over it. See Boring 127–28.

In Rev. 7, as so often in the drama of the Apocalypse, heaven and earth intersect. In the first section of the chapter (verses 1–8), introduced by the familiar literary formula, 'next I saw' (verse 1), John offers his audience a view of the Church on earth (where Chapter 6 ended, and at the four corners of which the four angels are now standing [7.1]). Although John's theology throughout Revelation is Jewish-Christian, and the remainder of Chapter 7 interprets verses 1–8 from a clearly Christian vantage point, dominated by God and the Lamb (verses 9–12, 15–17), there is nothing distinctively Christian discernible in the thought of this sub-division. Three actions take place within the vision of 7.1–8.

(a) Four angels restrain the four winds (verse 1).
(b) Another angel, bearing God's seal, urges restraint until the marking of the faithful has been completed (verses 2–3).
(c) A roll-call of the sealed, their number and descent, is heard but not seen by John (verses 4–8). Between verses 3 and 4 there is a break in what Aune (434) calls 'narrative logic', in that the sealing action is anticipated, but not described (see the comment on verse 4, below).

The second part of Rev. 7 (verses 9–17), introduced by a literary phrase similar to that in verse 1 ('after this I watched'), is set in heaven (where God's throne is placed, as in the heavenly court of Rev. 4—5 [7.9–12], and the heavenly sanctuary can be found [7.15]). The prophet-seer now discloses a vision of the Church at worship in the eternal presence of God, which balances the earthly setting of 7.1–8; and in so doing he provides a commentary on the nature of the Church, presented in 7.1–8, from a heavenly perspective. This scene falls into two sections: the liturgy offered by the multitude, including the angels, which surrounds the throne of God (verses 9–12); and the voluntary interpretation of that worship by an elder (verses 13–17). Another aporia occurs between verses 8 and 9 (as between 7.3–4), in that no account is given of the great ordeal against which the faithful have been protectively sealed (7.4–8), and out of which the Church triumphant has been delivered (7.14).

The angelophanies in 7.1–3, and further on in the Apocalypse, exhibit a distinctive literary form. See 28–30, and below, ad loc.

Comment

7.1 Although Rev. 7 forms an interval in the unfolding process of salvation history, completed in one sense by the breaking of the seventh seal at 8.1, this chapter begins by introducing a new and important division of the sixth seal (Charles 1, 203). Cosmic disasters have been unleashed by the opening of the sixth seal (6.12–17), and more plagues are to come (7.1–3). Meanwhile, the Church is to receive protection from the consequences of evil (verse 3). For the conjunctive phrase, μετὰ τοῦτο εἶδον (*meta touto eidon*, 'next I saw', lit. 'after this I saw'), and the importance of perception in the Apocalypse, see on 4.1. The same narrative formula is used at 7.9; 15.5; 18.1; but in the present context there is a stylistic modification, since John uses the neuter singular of the demonstrative pronoun τοῦτο (*touto*, 'this'), rather than, as elsewhere in Revelation, the plural form ταῦτα (*tauta*, 'these things'). A change of subject is indicated, and a new unit of text is introduced (Aune 450).

John sees 'four angels'. For 'angels' in the Apocalypse, and the literary form of the angelophanies in 7.1–3, see the excursus, 28–30. Here we have an example of angelic action, including four structural parts: the introductory formula, μετὰ τοῦτο εἶδον (*meta touto eidon*, 'next I saw'); the object of John's vision, τέσσαρας ἀγγέλους (*tessaras angelous*, 'four angels'); a description of the restraining action performed by the angels, holding back the 'four earthly winds' (τέσσαρας ἀνέμους τῆς γῆς, *tessaras anemous tēs gēs*); and an abrupt change of subject (the appearance of a second angel, 7.2).

The number of angelic beings in verse 1 seems to be determined by the four-quartered shape of the earth presupposed in this cosmic scheme (see below). The four angels of the winds, like the angels of fire (14.18) and water (16.5; cf. John 5.4 in some texts), perhaps belong to the lesser orders of angelic beings, who serve the works of nature. Cf. *1 Enoch* 60.11–22; 65.8; *Jub.* 2.2, where the angels of service are listed, against *Jub.* 2.17–22, where the angels of the presence are described as being able to keep the sabbath; also Heb. 1.7, quoting Ps. 104.4 (angels as servants).

The four angels are seen to be 'standing at the four quarters of the earth'. When the verb ἵστημι (*histēmi*, 'stand') is used in Revelation with ἐπί (*epi*, 'at', lit. '[up]on'), the preposition is normally followed, as here, by the accusative (so 3.20; 8.3 v.l.; 11.11; 12.18; 14.1; 15.2). The notion of the earth as square in shape, capable of being divided into the 'four quarters' (γωνίας, *gōnias*, 'quarters', lit. 'corners') of the compass, is a familiar concept in the cosmology of the ancient world, and perhaps Babylonian in origin (cf. Job 37.3; Isa. 11.12 [LXX the four 'wings', πτερύγων, *pterygōn*, of the earth], similarly Ezek. 7.2; Jer. 49.36; note Jer. 25.16). See also Rev. 20.8 (Satan will deceive the nations 'at the four corners of the earth' [ἐν ταῖς τέσσαρσιν γωνίαις τῆς γῆς, *en tais tessarsin gōniais tēs gēs*]); and 21.16, where the heavenly Jerusalem is described as cubiform ('the city is laid out as a square' [τετράγωνος, *tetragōnos*]). However, Mounce (155) thinks that the square or rectangular shape of the earth in this context need not be pressed, and that the expression in Isa. 11.12 (gathering the dispersed of Judah from 'the four corners of the earth') had much the same meaning for the prophet as it has for us today. The seer's perspective on this scene is heavenly, deriving from the dimension represented in Rev. 4—6; and as a result he can see the whole of the world at one glance. But the action in 7.1–8 is still located on earth.

The angels are described as 'restraining the four earthly winds'. Beale (406–408) argues strongly that the four 'winds of the earth' (τοὺς τέσσαρας ἀνέμους τῆς γῆς, *tous tessaras anemous tēs gēs*) should be identified as the four cavaliers of 6.1–8, since in Zech. 6.1–8, which lies behind Rev. 6.1–8, four horsemen are described as the 'four winds of heaven' (verse 5). In this interpretation Beale is following Kiddle (131–32); Caird (94); Beasley-Murray (142); Wilcock (79); et al. According to Beale (ibid.), the background from Zechariah would naturally still be in John's mind at this point; moreover, the indentification of the winds with the riders of Zech. 6 explains how believers can be protected spiritually from the disasters introduced by the four horsemen (Rev. 6.1–8), and takes us back to a period before their arrival.

However, this reading of the text is too specific, and difficult to support.

(a) In Jewish thought the four winds of heaven represented in any case the whole of the known world, and included all winds. Cf. Jer. 49.36; Ezek. 37.9; Dan. 7.2; 8.8; Zech. 2.6 (using the expression, 'the four winds of heaven', as in Zech. 6.5); *1 Enoch* 18.2 (the four winds 'bear' the earth); *4 Ezra* 13.5; *Life of Adam and Eve (Apocalypse)* 38.3; Mark 13.27 = Matt. 24.31. God is in control of the winds, bringing them out from their storerooms (Ps. 135.7; Jer. 51.16; et al.; cf. *1 Enoch* 18.1; *2 Enoch [J]* 40.10).

(b) The interpretation of the passage from Zech. 6, in Beale's exegesis, is strained. Admittedly the Hebrew is difficult; but, even if verse 5 be translated '(the chariots *are*) the four winds of heaven going out' (so NRSV), rather than 'these are going forth *to* the four winds of heaven' (RSV), differentiating the chariots (horses) from the winds (so Mounce 155 n. 3), the reference is not at any time directly to the horses (as winds), and still less (except by extensive implication) to their riders. In Zechariah's vision it is four *chariots* (6.1) which come out from between two mountains. Furthermore, according to Rev. 7.1, John sees four angels restraining four *earthly* winds, and not four 'winds of heaven', as in Zech. 6.5; although Beale (406) attempts to account for this major shift by claiming that the heavenly agents in view are accomplishing earthly havoc.

(c) Beale (ibid.) makes much of the chronology which he discerns in this passage, and in its theological antecedents at Rev. 6.1–8. Accordingly, he believes that the sealing of the faithful in 7.2–8 precedes the events of 6.1–8. (For Charles [1, 194–95], the order is reversed.) But John is presenting us with an eschatological *vision* in Rev. 6—7, as throughout, in which strict chronology is inappropriate. The drama of the Apocalypse unfolds the history of the Church and the world from varied aspects of time and eternity (see on 6.17); and, as a result, there is no need to fit the disclosures of 7.1–3 into a rigid, temporal timetable.

The four winds of Rev. 7.1, therefore, are best identified as the manifestation of God's activity of (saving) judgement (as in Jer. 49.36; *1 Enoch* 76.1–14 [the twelve winds of blessing and pestilence]). Winds as the general agents of divine judgement form a constant Old Testament image; see, e.g., Ps. 18.10; 104.3–4; Isa. 40.7, 24; Jer. 23.19; Ezek. 5.12 (Michaels [111] thinks that this passage, with its reference to the unfaithful being 'scattered to every wind', has directly influenced Rev. 7.1); Hos. 13.15–16 (the hot east wind, as 'a blast from the Lord', drying up the fountains and springs); Zech. 9.14. The winds in the present verse (Rev. 7.1) are to be restrained in order to prevent yet more disaster; and this points to their demonic and evil character, in opposition to the being of God (cf. the agents of divine judgement in 6.2–8). Moreover, the discrimination apparent in 7.1–3 is universal in nature: four angels at all quarters of the earth restrain four winds (see Milligan 114–15; Hughes 93). For the number four as an indication of universality see Rev. 4.6, 8; 6.1; 7.4; 9.13–14; 20.8; et al. For winds as angels or spirits see *Jub.* 2.2; *1 Enoch* 69.22; Heb. 1.7.

The winds must be restrained to ensure that no further judgemental activity, such as that which has been inaugurated in Chapter 6, should take place for the time being. For similar delaying tactics before 'judgement and destruction', on the part of angels, see *1 Enoch* 66.1–2; cf. also *2 Apoc. Bar.* 6.4–9; *Quest. Barth.* 4.31–34. The Greek translated in this verse as 'to prevent any wind from blowing' is ἵνα μὴ πνέη ἄνεμος (*hina mē pneē[i] anemos*), which is a negative clause of purpose with the present subjunctive, and could be construed to mean that no wind should be allowed to *carry on* blowing. In this case, the sense may be that the winds of pestilence have already begun to rise. They are not to blow 'on land or sea, or against any tree', a grouping which by metonymy probably stands for the world and its inhabitants (Beale 407); cf. verse 3. Trees are interpreted as people in the targums of Isa. 2.13; 14.8; and 61.3, and in any case have personal characteristics as they appear in those Hebrew texts.

The action represented in verse 1*b* need not be construed literally. Nevertheless it is true that the nature of middle-eastern terrain is semi-arid so that, when it is subjected to devastating winds and storms, this makes life all the more precarious for those who live in it. In such a situation, trees are particularly vulnerable, as the winds (of God) blow against them. The Greek at this point moves from ἐπί (*epi*, 'on') with the genitive (τῆς γῆς . . . τῆς θαλάσσης, *tēs gēs . . . tēs thalassēs*, 'land . . . sea'), to the same preposition with the accusative, ἐπὶ πᾶν δένδρον (*epi pan dendron*, 'against any tree'); and the change suggests movement ('against'), rather than location ('on'). See the textual note, above.

The eschatological disasters which the winds of divine judgement are called to restrain are revealed later in the Apocalypse. They include devastation (7.2–3); hunger, thirst and scorching heat (7.16); drought and sorrow (7.17); conflagration (8.7); plagues (8.8–11); darkness (8.12) and locusts (9.3–11). Cf. Ezek. 14.21. The 'winds' of judgement are not mentioned again in Revelation; and this fact supports the position of commentators like Beasley-Murray (141), who would argue that the source of Rev. 7.1–8 was originally a Jewish apocalyptic prophecy, which John has taken over and reapplied for his own Christian purposes. See below, esp. on verses 3 and 4.

2–3 A second angel appears on the scene. The literary form of this angelophany is that of angelic speech (see above, 29–30 and 178), which exhibits five structural features: an introductory formula, καὶ εἶδον (*kai eidon*, lit. 'and I saw'), for which see on 5.1; cf. also 5.2; 6.1; et al.; the object of the vision, ἄλλον ἄγγελον (*allon angelon*, 'another angel'); the ascent of the angel from the east; the loud cry of the angel to the other four angels (see verse 1); and the command of the angel to refrain from judgemental destruction, until the sealing of God's servants has taken place (verse 3). Only at this point in Revelation is the stylistic formation of angelic action (7.1) immediately followed by angelic speech (7.2–3).

For the phrase, 'ascending from the east' (the Greek ἀπὸ ἀνατολῆς ἡλίου, *apo anatolēs hēliou*, means literally 'from the rising of the sun'), see the textual note on verse 2, above. The eastern origin of this angel may be simply a picturesque detail (Mounce 156); but in a symbolic work like the Apocalypse such an understanding is very doubtful. It is more probable that 'the east' indicates here a promise of blessing, since benediction in the thought of Judaism is at times associated with the east, especially in relation to a theophany (cf. Gen. 2.8 [Eden]; Ezek. 43.2–4 [the glory of the God of Israel coming from the east]; Matt. 2.1 [magi from the east come to pay homage to Jesus]; *Sib. Or.* 3.652 [a King sent from the sun]; see also *1 Enoch* 61.1–13 [the measurement of Eden]; Ignatius, *Rom.* 2.2 [the Bishop of Syria fetched from the sun's rising]).

Beale (408) questions this interpretation, on the grounds that elsewhere in Revelation 'evil powers' are represented as coming from the east: the angels bound at the Euphrates (9.14) and the kings who travel across that river when it has been dried up (16.12). However, those are the only two such references in the Apocalypse; and the evil nature of the angelic and royal beings in question needs to be established (see further on 9.14–15; and 16.12). If we accept that evil as well as good originates from the east in this drama, an element of parody may be involved: the angel who protects the servants of God mocks the forces of evil by ascending from the same underworld (cf. Beale, ibid. 408); and this is consistent with the technique of parody used elsewhere in the book (e.g. the worship of the conquering beast, mimicking the triumphant worship of heaven, at 13.4–14). In any case, it is clear from the remainder of Chapter 7 that the angel from the east is the carrier of salvation and blessing, since he bears 'the seal of the living God'.

The term σφραγίς (*sphragis*, 'seal', or 'signet') occurs 12 times between Rev. 5.1 and 8.1, and acts as a literary keyword in this section (see further on 5.1). In this verse, as in 9.4, the associations are personal and individual: God's saints are marked and protected with his seal (7.4—8). Elsewhere, the image is more literal: the scroll carries seals of authorization, and they are broken only when the divine purposes of love through judgement are ready to be revealed (see further on 6.1). But the meaning is essentially the same. The 'seal' is not described further in this context; although by implication it is an object, such as a signet ring, which can be used to make a clay or wax impression (hence the translation of verse 5). Such an instrument would be used by oriental rulers to authenticate and preserve official documents. For the language of sealing in Jewish and Graeco-Roman magic see Aune 453–54, who notes (*inter alia*) *T. Sol.* 1.6–7, where Solomon receives from the Lord God through Michael a magical ring which gives him power over the demons (cf. its bizarre effects in *T. Sol.* 1.8–13). Similarly *Acts Andrew* 27.

For sealing in the New Testament generally, with its baptismal associations, see Smalley, 'Seal, Sealing'.

The immediate background to the concept of the angel bearing God's seal, and using it to mark the servants of God (verses 3–8), is to be found in Ezek. 9. There the Lord commands the angelic 'man clothed in linen' to mark the foreheads of the faithful Israelites, and he instructs other angels not to spare those who are unsealed (Ezek. 9.4–6). In Ezek. 9.4, 6 the Hebrew word for 'mark' is תו (*taw*), the full spelling of the last letter of the Hebrew alphabet, which at the time of Ezekiel was written in the form of a cross (+ or X). Any suggestion that this may be a typological prophecy of the seal in Rev. 7.1–8, referring to the death of Christ, should be firmly discounted.

The purpose of the marking in Ezek. 9 is to protect the righteous remnant of Israel from the four coming deadly acts of judgement, which are to be carried out by the Babylonians (Ezek. 14.12–23; note especially verse 21). See verse 1; also Gen. 4.15 (Cain); 4 Ezra 2.38; 6.5; CD (B) 19.12 (quoting Ezek. 9.4); *Pss. Sol.* 15.6, 9. That the divine protection offered to the true people of God is to be understood here in a primarily physical sense is affirmed by the fact that a similar marking, with blood, takes place at the time of the Exodus (Exod.12.7–28), to preserve the faithful Hebrews from the final judgemental plague. Beale (409) thinks that the passage in Exod. 12 may stand behind both Ezek. 9 and Rev. 7.

But spiritual protection need not be excluded from these Old Testament texts; and this is certainly the first meaning of the eschatological imagery of sealing in Rev. 7. Those who belong to the true Church of God (cf. 2.13) have the assurance of divine protection (as in 9.4); and this enables them to respond with faithfulness at all times to the suffering which they are called upon to endure, however that may be inflicted. Their trials become the means of conquest and strengthened belief (cf. 6.1–8 and 9–11). Such teaching would have afforded great encouragement to those, like the Johannine Christians, who were currently experiencing opposition from outside the community of the Church and personal conflict from within it. By contrast, the response of those who resist the love of God in situations of extreme difficulty can become increasingly unrepentant (9.19–21). The 'seal of the living God' in Rev. 7.2–3 is thus essentially salvific: those who are marked by it share fully in the healing through judgement which comes from the Christ of God. Note 14.1–4, where it emerges for the first time that the seal is equivalent to the names of the Lamb and his Father (verse 1), written on the foreheads of the redeemed (verses 3–4); cf. 3.12; 22.4. See further on verse 3; also Beale 409–10.

In the phrase, 'the seal of the living God', the noun σφραγῖδα (*sphragida*, 'seal', in the accusative) is anarthrous because it appears in this context for the first time. The only other occurrence of the concept of God's seal in Revelation is at 9.4 (q.v.), where the anaphoric article is used. Just as the eschatological sealing of the faithful against destruction seems to have been an accepted idea in the literature of Judaism, so in the Old Testament and elsewhere it was understood anthropomorphically that Yahweh, as every king, had his own seal (Aune 453). See Job 9.7; 37.7 (Heb. uncertain); Sir. 17.22; *T. Mos.* 12.9; et al. The signet ring of God is also used as a metaphor for the king of Israel (Jer. 22.24; Hag. 2.23).

The description of God as 'living' (Heb. אלהים חיים, *'ĕlohīm ḥayyīm*; Greek θεὸς ζῶν, *theos zōn*, 'living God') is frequent in Jewish and early Christian tradition. See Deut. 5.26; Josh. 3.10; 2 Kings 19.4, 16; Esth. 6.13 LXX; Ps. 84.2 (LXX 83.3); Isa. 37.4, 17; Jer. 23.36; Dan. 6.20, 26; *1 Enoch* 5.1; *T. Abr. (A)* 17.11; John 6.69, v.l.; Acts 14.15; Rom. 9.26; 1 Thess. 1.9; *2 Clem.* 20.2; Hermas, *Vis.* 2.3.2; *Sim.* 6.2.2; et al. The title is particularly appropriate when God is said to intervene on behalf of his people, and is often used to contrast Yahweh as the true and eternal Lord with other false and lifeless gods. See further Thompson, *The God* 57–100, esp. 73–77, who points out (76) that in

John's Gospel the expression 'living God' is replaced by 'living Father' (as in John 6.57). 'Living God' occurs in Revelation only at 7.2. In this verse the protective activity of God towards the faithful and his true and eternal nature opposed by the agents of evil on earth are especially evident. He is the *living* God: life-giving, and therefore sovereign.

The angel 'cries aloud' (see 6.10; 7.10; et al.) to the other four angels. They have already been mentioned in verse 1 (q.v.); hence the use of the article τοῖς (*tois*, '[to] the'). Only here and at 14.18 in the Apocalypse are angels said to give commands to other angels (but see 16.1); and this may imply an angelic hierarchy. In the phrase οἷς ἐδόθη αὐτοῖς (*hois edothē autois*, lit. 'to whom was given to them'), the pronoun αὐτοῖς (*autois*, 'them') is resumptive and redundant; it may be a Hebraism. The aorist passive of the verb ἐδόθη (*edothē*, lit. 'it was given') is a further example of divine permission in the Apocalypse; see on 6.2; and 9.3. The authority for the task of these angels derives from God himself. They were permitted eventually to 'despoil the land and the sea'. The verb ἀδικῆσαι (*adikēsai*, 'to despoil', aorist infinitive) means initially 'to act in an unjust manner, do wrong'; but it comes to signify, as in this passage, 'to cause damage, injure' (BDAG 20*a*). See Rev. 2.11; 6.6; 7.3; 9.4, 10, 19; 11.5 (*bis*); 22.11. For 'the land and the sea', this time without the inhabitants of the earth ('trees'), as in verses 1 and 3, see on verse 1.

For the command that no demonic forces should be allowed immediately to 'lay waste' the land, sea or forests (verse 3), see on verses 1 and 2. For the delaying tactics involved in this judgemental action see on verse 1. The timing is tense and dramatic. The angels are to wait until the divine 'seal' (for which see on verse 2) has been placed on the foreheads of God's servants (for this description see Rev. 1.1; 2.20; 19.2, 5; 22.3, 6). In the present context the verb 'to seal', in the first person plural aorist form σφραγίσωμεν (*sphragisōmen*, lit. 'we have sealed'), is used for the first time in the Apocalypse (cf. also 7.4 [*bis*], 5, 8; 10.4; 20.3; 22.10). It is not immediately apparent why the plural form of the verb is used in this context, since only one angel is speaking; but, as the seal of the living God is being carried by that heavenly messenger (verse 2), it may be implied that the salvific activity of the Father himself is included.

The verb σφραγίζειν (*sphragizein*, 'to seal') includes the ideas of authentication and ownership, as well as protection (BDAG 980*a*). The saints whose faith enables them to endure adversity and overcome the forces of evil (see 6.17) are marked out as true followers of God in Christ, and as those who belong to him. This understanding emerges clearly in verse 3, where the ones to be sealed are described as 'the servants (δούλους [*doulous*, lit. "slaves"]) of our God'. In the ancient world slaves were commonly branded or tattooed, often on the forehead, as a mark of ownership. See Aune 456–59; also Schneider, 'métōpon'.

The likelihood that the notion of sealing in this passage means 'possession', as well as 'protection', is confirmed by the evidence of Rev. 14.1; and 22.3–4. In both contexts the divine seal is identified as the 'name' of the Lamb and his Father, written on the 'foreheads' of the redeemed (ἐπὶ τῶν μετώπων αὐτῶν, *epi tōn metōpōn autōn*, lit. 'on their foreheads', as here). Cf. 2.17; 2 Tim. 2.19; also Rev. 13.17; 14.9–11, where the 'mark' (using χάραγμα, *charagma*, 'a mark [that is engraved]') of the beast on the foreheads of his followers is ironically associated with his 'name'. In Rev. 14.1 those who are marked as belonging to the Godhead number 144,000, as in 7.4 (q.v.); while in 22.3–4 they are described as 'servants' of God, using the term δοῦλος (*doulos*, 'slave' or 'servant'), as in 7.3. For the similar idea of sealing as a mark of divine ownership, as well as protection, see *Apoc. Elijah* 1.9–10; 5.4–6. For the equation of the 'seal' of the Son of God with his 'name' see Hermas, *Sim.* 9.16–17; for the motif of God's name, revealed to believers by Jesus as a means of protection, see John 17.6–26. In John 6.27 the Father 'sets his seal' (ἐσφράγισεν, *esphragisen*, 'he has sealed') on the Son as a mark of consecration: for he bears the divine name (John 5.43; 10.25). See further on Rev. 2.13, 17; 14.1.

Beale (411–12) points out that divine sealing and naming are together designations of membership of God's covenant community, through which the redeemed are empowered to carry out the role of witness intended for the true Israel (Isa. 42.6–7; et al.; cf. Sweet 147). The covenant background to the conjoining of 'seal' and 'name' in the Apocalypse (7.2–8; 14.1; 22.4), Beale notes, is to be found essentially in Exod. 28. In Exod. 28.11–21 the names of the twelve tribes of Israel are written on precious stones, like signets, to determine that their members belong to the covenant community; see Rev. 21.19–20, where most of those jewels are listed. The named stones correspond to the 'seal' (σφραγίς, *sphragis*) worn on the shoulders of the high priest (Exod. 28.11 LXX), and to the signet placed on Aaron's forehead (28.36–38). Both represent Israel, and enable the faithful and their worship to be 'consecrated to the Lord' (28.36; cf. 36.13 LXX), as well as being set apart from the judgement which defilement provokes. Similarly, in Rev. 7.2–3 God's sealing protects his people from the wrath of the Lamb (6.17), identifies them as his own possession, and enables them to fulfil their redeemed membership of the covenant community by entering the heavenly sanctuary and ministering before the throne of love (7.13–17).

It is possible that the 'sealing' terminology in 7.2–3 may be associated with the affirming and protective work of the Spirit in the believer, as elsewhere in the New Testament (e.g. 2 Cor. 1.22; Eph. 1.13; 4.30). If so, such an understanding is not explicitly developed by John in this passage. Baptismal associations, which may be detected in the Pauline texts just cited, are even harder to uncover in Rev. 7 (against Knight 71), since there is no clear mention of the Holy Spirit, and no reference to chrism (so Ford 116).

Those who are to be sealed are described as 'the servants of *our* (ἡμῶν, *hēmōn*, plural) God'. An angel speaks to other angels in verse 3; and they are linked to the saints in a bond of 'common service' (Swete 97). All are serving the same God. The servants (slaves) in this context are to be identified with the 'one hundred and forty-four thousand' of Rev. 7.4–8; see further on verse 4.

4   John 'heard' (ἤκουσα, *ēkousa*) how many received the seal (see verses 2–3); cf. 9.16. The next section (verses 4–8) is not strictly part of the vision of 7.1–3. The prophet-seer does not *see* the 144,000 until 14.1–5, nor is the actual 'sealing' of God's servants narrated at this point; although the perfect tense of the verbs of sealing in 7.4, 5 and 8 may imply the action, which is apparently completed by 9.4. In 7.4–8 we have the literary device of an audition. John *hears* a list of the servants who were sealed, and this explains how he knew the number without seeing the process. In the vision of Rev. 5.5–6 John hears about the Lion of Judah and sees the slaughtered Lamb; in the parallel at this point he hears the number of the sealed and (verse 9) sees a vast multitude.

Excursus: The Identity of the 144,000 (7.4–8)

This is one of the most intriguing issues confronting any student of Revelation. Who are the 144,000 servants represented in Rev. 7.3–8 as being 'sealed', and what relation do they bear to the 'vast multitude' at worship described in the remainder of the chapter (verses 9–17)? The MS variations in the transcription of the number 144,000 itself probably reflect some uncertainty about its meaning.

Aune (440) lists five constraints which, in his view, must govern any interpretation of 7.1–8.

(a)   According to verse 4b, those who are sealed are part of a larger group. They are 'from every tribe of the people of Israel' (ἐκ πάσης φυλῆς υἱῶν Ἰσραήλ, *ek pasēs phylēs huiōn Israēl*); and in that Greek phrase ἐκ (*ek*, lit. 'out of') with the genitive must be partitive.

As Caird (96) notes, the 12,000 members of each tribe referred to in verses 5–8 can only signify a portion of the whole group. See also the allusion to the vision of Ezek. 9.4, which occurs in Rev. 7.2; for in the Old Testament passage only *some* of Jerusalem's inhabitants are marked with a protective cross. However, the numbers here, as regularly in the Apocalypse, are symbolic rather than literal (see below); just as 'Israel' itself cannot be taken in a literal sense, since the twelve tribes as such did not exist in the first century AD (despite Josephus, *Ant.* 11.133–34). Moreover, John equates this community of the faithful with the same number in 14.1–5 (q.v.); and this cannot be limited to Jewish Christians, or a section of the Church, but must represent the totality of the redeemed (14.3). As Boring (129) points out, the key argument for identifying the 144,000 with the Church as a whole, in any case, is the primitive theological view of the Christian community as the continuation of Israel (cf. Matt. 10.5–6; 19.28; Luke 1.68–79; John 1.47; 5.43–47; Acts 26.14–23; Rom. 9–11; Jas. 1.1; 1 Pet. 2.9–10; et al.).

(b) There appear to be striking differences between the two groups described in Rev. 7.4–8 and 9–17. The first is specifically enumerated, while the second is 'impossible to count'; the former is drawn from the twelve tribes of the people of Israel, and the latter from a universal company; the 144,000 are located on earth, but the vast multitude worships in heaven; and the company in verses 4–8 seems to be in need of protection from imminent judgement, whereas the members of the innumerable crowd have 'survived the great ordeal'. Some of these alleged variations are more apparent than real. We have already seen that the Israelite and universal origins of the Christian community are not incompatible; and it is certainly true that the two companies of Rev. 7 are viewed first from an earthly and then from a heavenly perspective, in line with characteristic Johannine eschatology (see on 6.17). Equally, God's eternal purposes of judgement and love press into his creation continuously; so that the future is constantly depicted in Revelation from a present vantage point, and the current history of salvation is always understood in the light of the end. God's judgement is perpetually imminent, and his compassion readily shown at all times. See further Smalley, *Thunder and Love* 149–52.

We may return to the question of the numbering in Rev. 7.4–8. The enumeration 144,000 is clearly not intended by John to be taken literally; and it should be understood as part of the symbolism which is typical of his visionary drama as a whole. As Boring (130) reminds us, 'one thousand' is in any case used biblically to mean 'a very large number' (cf. Exod. 20.6; Num. 10.36; Deut. 7.9; 1 Sam. 18.7; Ps. 84.10; Dan. 7.10); so that, precisely as in Rev. 7.9 (the 'vast multitude which it was impossible for anyone to count'), the crowd of 144,000 is meant to convey the impression of an endless throng 'beyond all reckoning' (Boring ibid.). Moreover, the number 144,000 involves completeness, since 144 is the multiple of 12×12; and this picks up the expectation of later Judaism that at the eschaton God would assemble the full complement of the spiritual Israel (note *Pss. Sol.* 17.26–46; 2 Esdras 13.39–50; *2 Apoc. Bar.* 78–87, esp. 85.1–15; Matt. 19.28 = Luke 22.29–30; and cf. the measurements of the holy city, including a wall of 144 cubits, at Rev. 21.17). The numbering in this passage affirms that the eschatological hopes of Israel are realized in the Christian Church.

(c) Aune's third constraint relates to the reappearance of the 144,000 at Rev. 14.1–5, and whether that company is to be identified with the community listed in 7.4–8. My own view is that the two groups should be equated (see on 14.1), and that both represent the Church in its fulness (so Charles 1, 201).

(d) The passage in Rev. 7.4–8 may derive from an original Jewish source, which John has adapted for his own Christian purposes (see on verse 1). Nevertheless, these verses still need to be interpreted in the light of their present literary context, as Aune claims; and that is undoubtedly true.

(e) The sealing of the faithful protects them from the wrath of God coming on the world (9.4), but not from suffering inflicted by the ungodly. However, this is not a problem. As Aune says, eschatological tribulation was an expected part of first-century Christian experience (Mark 13.9–20 par.; *Did.* 16.5); and, as we have already seen, God's protection of the faithful does not exempt them from pain and even martyrdom, but enables them to become victorious through their endurance of evil (cf. Rev. 2.13, 19; 6.9–11; 7.14–17). Moreover, the protection afforded to the sealed in Rev. 9.4, referring back to 7.3–8, suggests that all Christians are included in this action, rather than an exclusive number.

Sufficient evidence has been marshalled so far to indicate that there are no major constraints in the way of interpreting both groups in Rev. 7, the 144,000 and the 'vast multitude' of verses 9–17, as in essence identical. They are representatives equally of the Christian community in its completeness (so Beckwith 534–37, esp. 535; Hendriksen 110–11; Hughes 94–95). The 144,000 are not to be regarded as the faithful, Christian remnant of Israel (against Peake, *Revelation* 276–80, esp. 278; cf. Beale 416–23); nor as a last generation of believers, at the end of the age, who are to be protected from earthly destruction (against Mounce 154; Aune 443); nor as a special group of martyrs, preserved from physical harm until they can witness effectively (against Kiddle 132–37; Caird 94–98). These interpretations are too exclusive.

There is one further identification, however, that is worthy of consideration. Bauckham (1294; cf. *idem, Climax of Prophecy* 215–29) argues that the 144,000 in Rev. 7.4–8 are martyrs, making up the messianic army of the remnant tribes of Israel, who are expected to fight the war against God's enemies in the last days. In support of this reading, Bauckham puts forward the following evidence (see esp. *Climax of Prophecy* 219–20; also Beale 422).

(a) A census in the Old Testament, such as the one in Rev. 7.5–8, was always used to assess the military strength of the nation (e.g. Num. 1.2–16; in 1.20–43 the men are numbered by tribes [LXX ἐκ τῆς φυλῆς, *ek tēs phylēs*, lit. 'from the tribe of', as similarly in Rev. 7]).

(b) Those so enumerated were males of military age (cf. the male virgins among the 144,000 in Rev. 14.1–5; note verse 4).

(c) The military census of Num. 1 lies behind 1QM (the 'War Scroll'), which contains the hope of the Qumran community that an imminent messianic war will usher in the conquest of a land of promise (cf. 1QM 2.2–3; 5.1–2; et al.).

(d) There are occasional references in the Old Testament to the expected return at the end-time of the ten tribes, and this included the hope that they would take part in a final war to defeat God's enemies (Isa. 11.14; also Isa. 14.2; Mic. 5.6–9; *Sib. Or.* 2.170–76).

It may be that military evocations are not far from the census of Rev. 7.5–8; but they are by no means obvious, and they do not in any case exhaust the theology of Rev. 7 in its entirety. The 144,000 of Rev. 7.4–8 and 14.1–5, like the saints elsewhere in Revelation, are worshippers more than soldiers. Moreover, they are not presented as martyrs in either context (contrast 6.9–11); and the remnant terminology which may be attached to the listing of the 144,000 may simply be carried over from the Old Testament (Beale 423).

Conclusion. The solution to the identity of the 144,000 which does least violence to the text, and accords with the theology of the remainder of Rev. 7, is to see this group as an inclusive symbol of all followers of Christ: the Christian Church in its totality, made up (like the Johannine circle itself) of those from a Jewish as well as Hellenistic background, and balanced by the faithful multitude who appear later in the chapter. The only difference between the two communities of John's vision is that the first is presented from an earthly viewpoint (as in Rev. 2—3; 6), and the second from the perspective of heaven (as in Rev. 5). One is militant and the other triumphant.

This thesis can be supported further by the following considerations (see also Milligan 116–23).

(a) Nowhere else in the Apocalypse is any distinction drawn between Jewish and Gentile Christians. In Rev. 2—3, Christ walks among every part of the seven Asiatic churches, which were made up (as we have seen) of both former Jewish *and* former Gentile members. The sealed scroll of Rev. 5.1—8.1 contains the judgemental and salvific purposes of God for his whole world and his entire Church. 'The struggle, the preservation, and the victory belong equally to all' (Milligan 117). The praises of God which ring through the drama of Revelation, and culminate in the vision of the holy city of the new Jerusalem (Rev. 21—22), are offered by all the saints of God, whatever their ethnic and religious background; and they all wear the same whitened robes (3.4, 5, 18; 6.11; 7.9, 13).

(b) The Church of Rev. 7.1–8 may be understood as the new Israel of God (see above). As with other Jewish nomenclature which he uses in Revelation (altar, tabernacle, temple, Mount Zion, Jerusalem), the prophet-seer in this passage is no doubt heightening and spiritualizing the term 'Israel'. John is aware of the Judaic roots of the Christian Church, and affirms them. But he also knows that, since the coming of Christ, 'Israel' embodies an idea which is deeper than the national associations of the word, and embraces the totality of the redeemed (cf. 12.10–12; also, in Paul, Rom. 9.6; Gal. 6.16). Even the use of tribal terminology in Rev. 7.4–8 need not imply exclusivity in terms of Jewish origins; since 'tribe' (φυλή, *phylē*) appears elsewhere in Revelation in contexts which are clearly universal in character (see 1.7; 21.12, the names of 'the twelve tribes of the Israelites' are inscribed on the gates of the new Jerusalem).

(c) The order and enumeration of the 144,000, sealed 'from every tribe of the people of Israel' (7.4), differs from any other biblical equivalent. There may be circumstantial reasons for this (see on verses 5–8, below); and, in fact, the Old Testament listings themselves do not agree with each other. But it is not impossible that John has also been influenced in his version by Christian, rather than Judaic, considerations; since he is now referring to the *new* Israel, the true and complete Church of God (cf. Milligan 118–19). Thus Judah, the fourth son of Jacob, may head the list (7.5) because this was the tribe to which Jesus belonged (Rev. 5.5; Heb. 7.14; cf. Gen. 49.10). The tribe of Dan is probably omitted because of its associations with Satan and idolatry (see Rev. 12.9; also Judg. 18.30; 1 Kings 12.29; *T. Dan* 5.5–6; and see the textual notes, above). Levi (Rev. 7.7) may have been inserted, rather than standing apart, because in Christ all believers are priests (1.6; cf. 1 Pet. 2.9); and Ephraim may have been replaced by Joseph (Rev. 7.8) because of its enmity towards Judah, the tribe from which Jesus was born (Luke 3.33; cf. Isa. 11.13; Hos. 5.9–15).

(d) John's visions include an ironic parodying of the sealing of God's servants (7.3), in that the followers of the satanic beast also receive his 'mark' (equated with his 'name', 13.17) on their foreheads (13.16, 17; 14.9; 16.2; 20.4; see above; and note similarly the divine name on the foreheads of the 144,000 at 14.1). This mark is imprinted on *all* the worshippers of the demonic image, without discrimination; and it is a reasonable inference that the 'seal of the living God' (7.2) similarly protects inclusively the followers of Jesus.

(e) If the servants of God who are sealed in 7.1–8 include only the faithful remnant of Israel, or a select group of Christian martyrs, or a particular circle of the faithful specially protected by God from divine plagues and human persecution just before the end-time (so Aune 443), it follows that the remaining members of the Church of Christ are *not* sealed and protected; and on no other occasion in Revelation does such a marking take place. Admittedly, the remainder of Chapter 7 reveals a universal community of the redeemed, the members of which together have 'survived the great ordeal' (verse 14). But, since sealing is a symbol of preservation from worldly disaster which may occur at any time, it is logical to suppose that all members of the Christian Church, and not just a chosen few, should at one time or another receive that blessing on earth.

(f) The proposal that the 144,000 are a symbol of the whole company of the Christian faithful, at any time and in any place, who are able to overcome suffering and persecution in this world (7.1–3) and share the victory of the saints in the next (7.9–17), receives confirmation from two inclusive expressions in this passage. The first is the action of the four angels in verse 1 (q.v.), who are shown to be 'restraining the four earthly winds'. Those demonic tempests are universal, and not particular, in nature; they affect potentially all creation, not just a part of it, and all Christians, not simply a privileged group of believers. Second, the language of verse 3 (q.v.) is broad in character and meaning. Those who are to be sealed are designated 'servants of God'; and, elsewhere in Revelation (see 1.1; 2.20; 19.2, 5; 22.3, 6), the term δοῦλος (*doulos*, lit. 'slave') is a designation for Christian believers in general (cf. also 1 Cor. 7.22; Col. 4.12; 1 Pet. 2.16; Jude 1; et al.). The whole Church of God is present in Rev. 7.1–8, as in the remainder of the chapter (see on verses 9–17).

5–8 There are conspicuous variations between the census in these verses and similar lists in the Old Testament (notably at Gen. 35.22*b*–26 [reproduced in *Jub.* 33.22]; 46.8–27; 49.2–28; Exod. 1.2–4; Num. 1.5–15; 13.4–14; Deut. 33.1–25). If John is drawing on a Jewish source at this point, and modifying it for his Christian purposes (see above, 185–86), this may have determined the order in which he places the twelve tribes of Israel. For example, Judah may well be mentioned first, rather than fourth, in Rev. 7.5, because it is the tribe from which the Messiah descended (Heb. 7.14; so Swete 98; Charles 1, 194; Beasley-Murray 143); see also above, 187. But equally, Judah is placed first in the Old Testament when the tribes are listed in geographical order, starting from the south and moving northwards, as at Num. 34.19–28; Josh. 21.4–7; 1 Chron. 12.23–37; and Judah can also take the lead in the military order of the groupings (Num. 2.3; 7.12; 10.14). Interestingly, the members of the Qumran community associated themselves explicitly with the house of Judah (cf. CD 4.6–12).

We conclude that there is no one reason for the tribal order in Rev. 7.5–8. John's arrangement seems to have been suggested partly by the sequence in which the patriarchs were born (Reuben, as the firstborn son of Jacob, normally heads the tribal lists, and therefore appears in the second place at verse 5), and partly by the geographical situation of the tribes (Swete 98). But, as we have already seen, Christian theology may also have influenced the listings in verses 5–8; and the position adopted in this commentary maintains that in any case John's vision in Rev. 7.1–8 is of the *new* Israel, the servants of God who belong to the Christian Church on earth, and who in that context are protected from the coming judgement and are able to inherit the blessings of salvation. The author of this passage is accordingly not concerned about exact tribal symmetry; neither does this exist in his biblical sources.

For the omission of Dan from the list of tribes at verses 5–8 see above, 187. The exclusion of Ephraim, and the inclusion of Manasseh (verse 6) and Joseph (verse 8), is a unique form, without satisfactory explanation. (Peake [*Revelation* 280] claims that the missing tribe Δάν [*Dan*, 'Dan'] was inadvertently copied as Μάν [*Man*, 'Man'], and then understood as an abbreviation for Manasseh; but this solution is without foundation, and will not serve [so Mounce 159].) Occasionally the tribe of Joseph is omitted from the census-lists of the Old Testament and replaced (as in Num. 1.5–15 and 13.2–14) by Ephraim and Manasseh, both of whom were sons of Joseph. Since Joseph is present in the list at Rev. 7.8, it is accordingly odd that either of his sons should be named, and that it should then be Manasseh; particularly since, in the census at Num. 13.11, Manasseh and Joseph are deliberately paired.

Mounce (160) concludes that Manasseh was included, once Dan (for whatever reason) had been omitted, to bring the number of the tribes back to twelve. Milligan (119) thinks that the omission of Ephraim was on account of its enmity with the messianic tribe of Judah (see above). Bauckham, *Climax of Prophecy* 221–22, points to Ezek. 37.15–23, a prophecy of the reunion of the twelve tribes in the messianic kingdom. There (verses 16, 19), the name of Joseph is glossed with references to Ephraim (his 'stick' and 'hand') in a way which might suggest that they are tribal equivalents (Bauckham, *Climax of Prophecy* 222). See also Num. 1.32, where the descendants of Joseph are specified as 'the descendants of Ephraim'. In *Barn.* 13.4–6, confusingly, Ephraim (the younger son of Joseph) is represented as a 'type' (τύπος, *typos*) of the people of the future (that is to say, Christianity); while Manasseh remains the inferior symbol of Judaism, unblessed by Jacob. None of this evidence helps us conclusively and in detail to account for the Johannine version of the twelve tribes of Israel in Rev. 7.5–8; but doubtless exact listing was not a major concern for the writer of the Apocalypse.

The tribe of Levi is included in John's roster (verse 7). Levi is sometimes omitted from Old Testament lists of the Israelite tribes, because that priestly grouping was without a traditional allocation of land. Its place was taken by passing over Joseph, and substituting his sons Ephraim and Manasseh (Aune 463). Bauckham (*Climax of Prophecy* 210–37) interprets the Apocalypse as a Christian war scroll, and the vision of the 144,000 and the innumerable multitude in Rev. 7.2–14 as that of a messianic army (Bauckham, *Climax of Prophecy* 215–29). In such a context he regards the listing of Levi (Rev. 7.7), among the twelve tribes, as possibly out of place in a military roll-call (Bauckham, *Climax of Prophecy* 222). But Rev. 7.4–8 does not have that primary character (see above). Admittedly Levi has a warlike appearance in the literature of Qumran (see 1QM 1.2; 4.2); although even in the War Scroll the chief task of the twelve Levites, one for each tribe, is described as maintaining the appointed religious offices (1QM 2.2). However, it is significant that Levi is always omitted from the military listings in the Old Testament (Num. 1.49; 2.33; 26.1–51; cf. 1 Chron. 21.6), and numbered separately in censuses when they are non-military (Num. 3.14–39; 26.57–62). Once more, the inclusion of the tribe of Levi at Rev. 7.7 may have nothing to do with a strictly Jewish, or indeed military, outlook on the twelve tribes of Israel. It may as well be ascribed to John's theological understanding of the twelve tribes as part of the true Israel of God, and is perhaps influenced by a Christian understanding of its priestly membership (see above).

A literary inclusion occurs at the beginning and end of the list of the tribes of Israel in verses 5–8, in that the verb ἐσφραγισμένοι (*esphragismenoi*, '[they] were marked with the signet' or 'received the seal', lit. 'they were sealed') is repeated at the start of verse 5, after Judah, and at the close of verse 8, after Benjamin. See the similar resonance in verse 4, *a* and *b*.

9   At this point a sudden and dramatic scene-change takes place. John's vision has disclosed the Church of God on earth, with its faithful members so sealed that they may endure and conquer the suffering and divine judgement coming upon the world at any time (see verses 1–8). Swiftly, the action moves to heaven, where the prophet now sees the same assembly from an ongoing and indeed eternal perspective (verses 9–17). A 'vast multitude' (ὄχλος πολύς, *ochlos polys*, lit. 'large crowd'; see 19.1, 6) comes into view, 'impossible for anyone to count' (verse 9); for its size is difficult to comprehend as that of the 144,000 listed in verses 4–8. The angels, living creatures and elders of the throne-vision in Rev. 4—5 are now accompanied in eternity by the redeemed of all time.

The heavenly Church of God stands in the line of his people Israel, and derives from a particular religious background in Judaism (see on the 144,000, and verses 2–8). But its redeemed adherents are clearly Christians, followers of the messianic Lamb (see verse 14). They belong to a universal company, and inherit the blessing of Abraham; therefore they are numberless as the stars (Gen. 15.5–6; 16.10; cf. Gal. 3.6–7; so Beasley-Murray 144). This promise or its fulfilment is frequently repeated, in varied forms, by both biblical and extra-biblical writers; see (e.g.) Exod. 32.13; Deut. 10.22; 1 Kings 3.8; Neh. 9.23; Isa. 10.22 = Rom. 9.27; Sir. 44.21; *Jub.* 13.20; 18.15; *T. Abr. [A]* 1.5; Heb. 11.12. For the unified understanding of the two groups in Rev. 7 (as the whole body of the Church, seen in different stages of its experience) see further Swete 98–99; also Beckwith 532–41, esp. 540; against Aune 466.

The believers in view in Rev. 7.9–17 are not just martyrs (Caird, Bauckham); nor do they simply make up the Church of the last generation, at the end-time (Mounce, Aune; see above). John may have had acutely in mind his own community, the members of which as he wrote were undergoing what may have seemed to them like unbearable pressure, imminently ushering in the ultimate eschatological consummation: namely, oppression and persecution from outside the Johannine circle, and disintegration within it (note the reference to Antichrist coming at the 'final hour' in 1 John 2.18; see further Smalley, *Thunder and Love* 121–37). But the vision in Rev. 7 is intended to provide encouragement for the servants of God (verse 3) in his Church at any time and all time, including the last days. Through Jesus the Lamb, slain and exalted (verses 14–17), all his followers can and will survive the greatest ordeals (verse 14, q.v.; the reference here need not be exclusively to martyrdom [so Aune 474]).

For the phrase μετὰ ταῦτα εἶδον, καὶ ἰδού (*meta tauta eidon, kai idou*, lit. 'after these things I saw, and behold') see on 4.1, where it is reproduced exactly. See also 6.2, 5, 8; 14.1. In 7.4 John 'heard' the number of the sealed; now he 'sees' a vast multitude. For the importance of seeing and hearing in Johannine thought, implying spiritual perception and audition, see on 4.1; 6.1; also 1.10, 12; 5.11; 8.13; 22.8; and cf. Smalley, *John* 175–76; Thompson, *The God* 105–17. The innumerable multitude which John saw in his vision seems to be starkly contrasted with the precisely measured extent of the 144,000, earlier in the chapter (verses 4–8, q.v.; and see above, 184–88). But this need not suggest that these two assemblies are to be as sharply distinguished. The seer is now the witness of a Church and kingdom which are not only universal in character but also heavenly in dimension (cf. Beckwith 543–44). A rough census of the Church militant is just about conceivable; however, such a count of the Church triumphant, spanning every Christian believer from all ages and to the end of the ages, must be regarded as impossible. Aune's comment (466–67) that the enormous size of the group described in verse 9 is striking, because the number of Christians living towards the end of the first century AD cannot have been very large, therefore misses the point.

In the Greek of the opening phrase in verse 9, the case of the ὄχλος πολύς (*ochlos polys*, 'vast multitude') seen by John is nominative; but, as the object of his vision, it should be accusative. However, the use of the nominative with the particle ἰδού (*idou*, lit. 'behold!') is not unknown in Revelation (see 4.1, 2; 6.2, 5, 8; 14.14). The pronoun αὐτόν (*auton*, 'it' [the multitude]) is resumptive, and strictly redundant (see the textual note on verse 9, above). The Greek means literally, 'I saw a vast multitude, which to count it (αὐτόν, *auton*) no one was able', where this pronoun modifies the relative pronoun ὅν (*hon*, 'which') and helps to define the antecedent πολύς (*polys*, 'vast', or 'great [in number]'). It may be regarded as a Semitism (Aune 428).

The multitude is comprehensive, representing 'every nation, race, people and language group'. This expression is used with variations elsewhere in Revelation (5.9, q.v.; 10.11; 11.9; 13.7; 14.6; 17.15), but each time in a different order. It originates from Daniel (see 3.4, 7, 96 [LXX]; 5.19 [Theod.]; 6.25 [LXX 26]; 7.14 [Theod.]; also Judith 3.8); although the Danielic groupings are cited in threes, rather than (as here, and in other contexts of the Apocalypse) in fours. The Christian Church is international in character, and includes not only those from every race (ἐκ παντὸς . . . φυλῶν, *ek pantos . . . phylōn*, lit 'from every tribe'), picking up the listing in Rev. 7.4–8, but also those with every possible background: national, social, political and cultural. They are now united by a common language (γλωσσῶν, *glōssōn*, lit. 'tongues'; cf. Thompson 108).

In the phrase, ἐκ παντὸς ἔθνους (*ek pantos ethnous*, 'from every nation'), the substantive ἔθνους (*ethnous*, 'nation', genitive singular) is anarthrous; and therefore the modifying adjective παντός (*pantos*) means 'every' (distributive), rather than 'all' (collective). That sense extends to the three nouns, in the genitive plural, which follow. The mixture of the singular and plural nouns in this part of verse 9, following the singular παντός (*pantos*, 'every'), is discordant. The vast multitude, in the seer's vision, 'stood in front of the throne, and before the Lamb'. This exact phraseology occurs only here in Revelation; but note the combination of 'throne', as a circumlocution for God, and 'Lamb' in verse 10; also 5.13; 6.16; 22.1, 3. On 'throne' see 4.2; for 'Lamb' see on 5.6. The plural adjectival participle ἑστῶτες (*hestōtes*, 'stood') is in the nominative case because it modifies ὄχλος πολύς (*ochlos polys*, 'vast multitude'); and that noun phrase is nominative, rather than accusative, after εἶδον (*eidon*, 'I watched', lit. 'saw'), since it appears with ἰδού (*idou*, lit. 'behold!'), a demonstrative particle usually followed by the nominative (as in 4.1, 2; 6.2, 5, 8; 12.3; et al.). The author also treats 'vast multitude' (ὄχλος πολύς, *ochlos polys*) as a collective noun, which may be used with the plural verb form ἑστῶτες (*hestōtes*, lit. 'they were standing'); note similarly 8.9; 9.18; 13.3–4; 18.4; 19.1; also John 12.12.

The redeemed are described as being 'dressed in white robes, with palm branches in their hands'. For the grammar of the phrase, περιβεβλημένους στολὰς λευκάς (*peribeblēmenous stolas leukas*, 'dressed in white robes'), see the textual note on verse 9, above. The plural form of the participle results from taking ὄχλος (*ochlos*, 'multitude'), earlier in the verse, as a collective noun (see above); so also the plural verb κράζουσιν (*krazousin*, 'they cry out') in verse 10. White robes in the Apocalypse symbolize purity, and thereby worthiness for admittance to eternal life (see on 3.4–5; 4.4; 6.11; 7.13–14). In the context of Rev. 7.9–17, a scene describing the worship of the Church in eternity, the metaphor of white garments also stands for the victory of faith (as in the case of the martyrs, 6.11), and possibly extends to the righteousness of Christ (Mounce 162). The colour white is associated in the Apocalypse with the exalted Son of man, whose head of hair appears to be intensely white (1.14), and with God, who sits in judgement on a large white throne (20.11). In Judaeo-Christian thought, white is also the characteristic colour of robes worn by supernatural figures, including the Godhead (see Dan. 7.9; 2 Macc. 11.8; *1 Enoch* 14.20; *T. Levi* 8.2; Mark 9.3 par. [the white clothes of the transfigured Jesus]; John 20.12; Acts 1.10).

The redeemed members of the Church in heaven carry 'palm branches (φοίνικες, *phoinikes*) in their hands'; and this seems to be a further image of victory. Palm fronds symbolized victory throughout the ancient world of the Mediterranean, and in Judaism accompany scenes of conquest and festive joy (see 1 Macc. 13.36–37, 51; 2 Macc. 10.7; 14.4). At the triumphal entry into Jerusalem, in the fourth evangelist's account (John 12.13), the crowds received Jesus with branches of palm trees; they did not, as in

Mark 11.8 par., cut down branches from the trees, and spread them on the road. John's version of this incident, at one level, clearly signifies that the palm branches are a sign of homage to a victorious leader (so Beasley-Murray, 209–10).

However, in Rev. 7.9 (and 15–17), as in John 12.13, allusions to *Succoth*, the Jewish Feast of Tabernacles, or Booths, may also be present. (The refrain chanted with variations by the onlookers at the triumphal entry, 'Hosanna! Blessed is the one who comes in the name of the Lord!', according to all four Gospels, derives from Ps. 118 [note verses 26–27]; and this Hallel Psalm formed part of the Tabernacles liturgy, as well as being sung at Passover and Dedication.)

The Feast of Booths was the most important of all the festivals in Judaism. It occurred at the crown of the year, when the harvest was complete; it celebrated the presence and protection of Yahweh during the Exodus wanderings, and anticipated the consummation of the messianic age (note the eschatological background to the Feast in Zech. 14; see esp. verses 4, 16–19). During this festival sheaves were carried around the Jerusalem Temple and into it. The sheaf, known as the לולב (*lulab*, lit. 'palm branch'), combined palm, myrtle and willow branches, in accordance with the provision of Lev. 23.40 (cf. Neh. 8.15). Ulfgard, *Feast and Future* 148–58, concludes from a detailed study that the vision of the redeemed multitude in Rev. 7.9–17 has been deeply influenced by the ritualism and eschatological significance of *Succoth*, with its background in the Exodus. See also Mazzaferri, *Genre* 259–383. Sweet (151–52) acknowledges the evocations of Tabernacles in this passage, but thinks there is a closer model in the palm branches carried at the Feast of Dedication, when the liturgy of the Feast of Booths was used to celebrate the cleansing of the Temple from the sacrilege of Antiochus Epiphanes (1 Macc. 4.54–59; 13.51; 2 Macc. 10.6–7). In the view of Sweet (152), the heavenly scene depicted in Rev. 7.9–17 is a celebration of the defeat of the kingdom of the beast (cf. 12.7–12), with its own 'desolating sacrilege' (Dan. 11.31; Mark 13.14; et al.). On the possible linkage between Rev. 7.9–17 and the Feast of Booths see further Aune 448–50, 468–70; also Milligan 124–26.

We may conclude that the worshipping and joyful multitude, in Rev. 7.9 and beyond, consists of those who are purified by the blood of the Lamb (see 7.14), and can therefore be victorious over suffering and evil. This is the character of the Church triumphant throughout eternity; and its victors glimpsed at this moment in John's drama, clutching their branches of palm, are celebrants of the victory of the kingdom of God itself. This meaning is developed in the hymns which follow at 7.10, 12, 15–17.

10   This verse records the first of two hymns of praise, sung by the victorious believers in the immediate presence of God and the Lamb. The spiritual excitement of the citizens of heaven is already apparent in their liturgy. They 'cry out with a loud voice'. For the plural form κράζουσιν (*krazousin*, 'they cry out') see on verse 9. The seer uses the historic present tense of the verb to heighten the dramatic tension, and to bring the audience into the action. The 'loud voice' suits the intensity of the worship offered in this transcendent and triumphant situation. It matches the similar tones of the angel from the east in verse 2 (q.v.); see also the cry of the martyrs at 6.10. In John's Gospel the verb κράζω (*krazō*, 'cry [out]') is used to introduce sayings of Jesus which involve a crucial disclosure (as at 7.28, 37; 12.44).

In the New Testament, the term σωτηρία (*sōtēria*, usually translated as 'salvation', or 'healing') often appears in contexts which relate to the physical or spiritual life and wholeness of the believer, present or future (as at Luke 1.69, 71, 77; 19.9 [the word does not occur in Mark or Matthew]; John 4.22; Acts 4.12; Rom. 1.16; Eph. 1.13; 1 Thess. 5.8–9; Heb. 1.14; 2.3; 1 Pet. 2.2; et al.). In these passages the notion of rescue from sin and judgement is also present. The verb σώζειν (*sōzein*, 'to save') is not used in Revelation;

nor is the noun σωτήρ (*sōtēr*, 'Saviour'), which can be found in the Johannine corpus only at John 4.42 and 1 John 4.14.

This language is introduced here for the first time in the Apocalypse, where it is associated with the eschatological triumph of God's kingdom, anticipating the final victory of his sovereignty. See Rev. 12.10; 19.1, the only other texts in this work where, again in a liturgical setting, σωτηρία (*sōtēria*, 'salvation' or 'deliverance') appears. See the background in Ps. 3.8 (LXX 3.9); Jonah 2.10 LXX. In the setting of Rev. 7.10, the term σωτηρία (*sōtēria*) therefore carries the primary sense of 'deliverance', or 'victory'. Charles (1, 326) regards it as a semantic Hebraism, based on the use of יְשׁוּעָה (*yᵉšûʿâ*) with that meaning in the Old Testament; cf. Exod. 14.13, 30; 2 Chron. 20.17, and see BDAG 986*b*. But the word must also include the notion of protection and preservation, since this is the theme of the chapter, and also the significance of the 'sealing' of the faithful in 7.1–8. Those who acknowledge the rule of God through his Christ belong to the company of the redeemed in heaven. They have successfully resisted the forces of evil which, on earth, have attempted to undermine their faith and tested their faithfulness (cf. 19.1–2); accordingly they wear 'white robes' (verses 9, 14), which symbolize purity achieved through preservation and perseverance.

In this spontaneous hymn of praise, then, the spiritual conquerors not only give thanks for their own victory (see verse 9) but also testify to the source of that victory in the deliverance and kingdom and power (verse 12) of the living God himself and of the Lamb. For the concept of redemptive deliverance in verse 9 see further Schneider, 'σώζω, σωτηρία', esp. 216.

The expression, ἡ σωτηρία τῷ θεῷ ἡμῶν (*hē sōtēria tō[i] theō[i] hēmōn*, 'deliverance belongs to our God'), may be a Hebraism (cf. *Pss. Sol.* 10.8; 12.6). Equally, it can be taken as a dative of possession (see the similar occurrence of the possessive genitive at 12.10; 19.1). The writer uses the same construction, with the dative, in other doxologies (see Rev. 1.5*b*–6; 4.9; 5.13; 7.12).

The phrase, 'deliverance belongs to our God', may also pick up the 'hosanna' of Ps. 118.25 (MT), which in turn has associations with the Feast of Booths (see on verse 9). For the plural ἡμῶν (*hēmōn*, 'our God') see verse 3. The whole host of heaven is engaging in this act of supernatural worship: not only the angelic beings of Rev. 4—6 and 7.2, but also the Church of God (universal and triumphant) in its entirety. As such, they are in tune with the blessed company of all faithful people, sealed by God, on earth (7.1–8). This form, 'our God', appears on eight other occasions in Revelation (4.11; 5.10; 7.12; 12.10 [*bis*]; 19.1, 5, 6). For the joint address to God seated on the throne (for which see 4.2; 5.1) and to the Lamb (see 5.6), see verse 9; also 5.13. Cf. 6.16; 22.1, 3, for the same pairing.

11–12 For the company of 'angels' (πάντες οἱ ἄγγελοι, *pantes hoi angeloi*, 'all the angels') see on 5.11; 7.2; also 28–30. The air is thick with angels in Revelation. These 'stand in a circle' around the throne of God (see verse 10), and around the two other groups of heavenly beings mentioned in the throne-vision of Rev. 4—5: the elders (see on 4.4) and the four living creatures (4.6–8; cf. 5.11). In verse 9 the 'vast multitude' of the Church in heaven is described as standing 'in front of the throne', so presumably its members encircle God himself, the Lamb and the angelic orders of being; although diagrams are not an endemic part of visions. The verb εἰστήκεισαν (*heistēkeisan*, 'they had been standing', pluperfect) applies only to the angels. The elders are referred to as seated in 4.4; and the posture of the four cherubim is nowhere described. But the angels in Revelation either fly (7.2; 10.1; 14.6; 20.1) or stand (as here; 7.1; 10.5; 19.17). They never sit down; and this suggests an awareness of the Jewish tradition that angels had no knees, and were as a result unable to be seated (so Aune 471).

The picture of heavenly beings falling prostrate before the throne of God recalls the scene in the throne room (4.10, q.v.; 5.14). But there, as in 11.16, the action is limited to the twenty-four elders (see also 5.8, elders and living creatures before the Lamb; 19.4, elders and cherubim before God). At this point (verse 11), in the presence of the elders and living creatures, it is the myriads of angels alone who engage in adoring worship. They respond to the victorious cry of the saintly host (verses 9–10) by offering to God 'prostrated' (ἐπὶ τὰ πρόσωπα αὐτῶν, *epi ta prosōpa autōn*, lit. 'on their faces') their own sevenfold doxology of praise (cf. Mounce 163).

The angels 'sing' (λέγοντες, *legontes*, lit. 'saying'), verse 12. For this translation, and for the place of music in heaven according to the Apocalypse, see on 5.9. The angelic hymn is prefaced by a liturgical ἀμήν (*amēn*, 'Amen'). This may be taken as a response to the chant of the victors in verse 10 (Aune 471); and it therefore appears in the translation with the literal meaning of the Hebrew equivalent אָמֵן (*'āmēn*), 'So be it!' The song of the angels concludes with a further 'Amen', this time as an affirmative response to their own offering of worship (but see the textual note on verse 12, above). See further on 5.14; also Rev. 1.6, 7, 18 (v.l.); 19.4; 22.20, 21 (v.l.). In the oracle to the church at Laodicea (3.14, q.v.) the word is used as a title of Jesus.

The ascription of praise in verse 12 seems to be addressed in the first place to God himself (for 'our God' see on verse 3; also verse 10). But it is not impossible that the Lamb is included in this act of worship, even if he is not explicitly mentioned (note his presence at verses 9, 10, 14, 17); so Mounce 163. Six of the seven qualities ascribed to (the) God(head) here are directed towards the Lamb at 5.12; but there they appear in a different order. In this verse εὐχαριστία (*eucharistia*, 'thankfulness') appears, since this is an appropriate response to the divine gift of victorious salvation, just as τιμή (*timē*, 'reverence') is a proper acknowledgement of God's salvific being before the Church and the world. If God alone is the object of the angels' praise, then the reference to his 'wisdom' (σοφία, *sophia*) is unique in Revelation (but see Luke 11.49; 1 Cor. 1.24; Eph. 3.10; et al.); this attribute is ascribed to the Lamb at 5.12. See further on 4.9; 5.12.

The inclusion of the article before all seven Greek nouns in this hymn, as with ἡ εὐλογία (*hē eulogia*, lit. '*the* blessing' or '*the* praise'), heightens their significance. The angels attribute special as well as eternal blessing and glory and wisdom, and thankfulness and reverence and power and might to their God. 'Power' (δύναμις, *dynamis*) and 'might' (ἰσχύς, *ischys*) are virtually synonymous (see further on 5.12); although Mounce (163) regards the former as God's ability to act, and the latter as his redemptive presence in the events of history.

Excursus: The Theology of Power in Revelation

The source and use of power is a key political issue in Revelation; and there is a sense in which the book is chiefly concerned with this question. The four causes which are unveiled as a result of the opening of the first four seals in 6.1–8, for example, are concerned essentially with the wrong and right use of power (see further on 6.2).

John writes the Apocalypse in the light of the definitive Christ-event, yet the world of his day is seen to lie in the grip of the forces of evil, and the Church is its victim. All power can be ascribed, as in 7.12, to God and the Lamb; yet unbelief and oppression continue, and the dragon is able to delegate his power and throne and great authority to the beast (13.2).

The seer's answer to this problem is to be discovered partly in Rev. 7. The conflict is limited (so 12.7–12): God's victorious power will ultimately prevail, and the Church which has been sealed and protected on earth will be delivered in eternity (7.4–17; see also Chapter 20). But meanwhile the nature of power has been transformed by the death and resurrection of Christ. As the slaughtered Lamb (5.9; 13.8), Jesus has been identified with the powerless. Yet through his crucifixion has come exaltation, and through divine judgement love has prevailed. So the slain Messiah deserves to receive power (5.11). He delivers the condemnation of God on the forces which are opposed to his righteousness and freedom; at the same time, he is crowned as the sovereign King of kings and Lord of lords (19.11–16), and gives life to every believer (19.14; 20.5–6). See further 520–21, on the theology of Rev. 19—20; also Boxall, *Revelation* 129–33.

John is clear that all power is derived, and that all just power belongs ultimately to God (4.11; 7.12; 11.16; 12.10; 15.3–4; 19.1–2). This means that, in the Church as in society, earthly power needs to be exercised with a justice and a love which echo the Father's own. Such teaching would have provided natural encouragement, as well as a challenge, to the Johannine community in AD 70. See further Smalley, *Thunder and Love* 178–79.

13–14 A dramatic dialogue, rare in the visions of Revelation, ensues. An elder anticipates the enquiry which the seer is about to make, and in so doing takes on the familiar apocalyptic role of the interpreting and mediating angel (see on 1.1). The question-and-answer format is common in prophetic literature, as the means of explaining a vision. Cf. Jer. 1.11–13; Ezek. 40—48; Dan. 7—12; Zech. 1—6; *1 Enoch* 21.5–10 (Uriel speaks to Enoch); 4 Ezra 4.1–11 (Uriel and Ezra); et al. The visionary and forensic setting of Dan. 7.9–18, with its myriads of angelic beings attending the throne of God, and its use of the question-and-answer technique, is very close to this scene in literary form; except that in the Danielic passage the narrator asks an attendant to interpret the meaning of the vision (7.16), whereas here the interrogation is assigned to the elder (cf. Aune 472). For 'elder' see verse 11, and on 4.4.

The Greek word εἷς (*heis*, 'one [of the elders]') can be construed as an ordinal number, meaning 'one', rather than two or more (so Rev. 17.12; 18.8; 21.21; et al.). But it is better understood as an indefinite pronoun, corresponding to the pronoun τὶς (*tis*, 'a certain [one]'); and it is so used with the partitive genitive elsewhere in the Apocalypse (e.g. 5.5; 17.1; 21.9). In the phrase, καὶ ἀπεκρίθη (*kai apekrithē*, 'then [one] addressed [me]'; lit. 'and answered'), no question is implied to which a response is now given (Beckwith 544). The construction reflects instead the use of the Hebrew verb עָנָה (*'ānâ*), which means 'begin to speak'; and it introduces here an enquiry prompted by what has already been described in verses 9–10 (similarly Isa. 14.10 lxx; Zech. 1.10 lxx; 2 Macc. 15.14; Matt. 12.38; Mark 10.51; Luke 14.3; John 2.18; 5.7; Acts 5.8; see also BDAG 114*a*). The idiom, καὶ ἀπεκρίθη . . . λέγων (*kai apekrithē . . . legōn*, lit. 'and he answered . . . saying'), is a Semitism which occurs only here in the Apocalypse. For the parallel use of the finite verb with a pleonastic participle see Ezek. 9.11 lxx; Dan. 3.16 (Theod.); John 1.26; *1 Enoch* 22.7, 9; *T. Job* 23.6.

The question addressed by the elder to John seeks information about the identity and spiritual descent of the vast multitude of the faithful witnessed in verse 9. For the description of the members of the Christian Church, as 'dressed in white robes', see on verse 9. In Revelation the seer never asks about the meaning of the symbols in his visions; and, in line with this characteristic feature, the question is therefore posed by the angelic being. The enquiries are answered by him, in reverse order, at verse 14; and in verses 15–17 he continues to enlarge on the present experience and future state of the protected redeemed.

The seer's reply to the question of the elder, as the dialogue continues, deflects the necessity for him to provide the answer. 'My lord' (κύριέ μου, *kyrie mou*), in verse 14, is a courtesy title used by John to address an angelic being. It is equivalent to 'Sir' (so NRSV), but also implies an element of reverence; hence the translation. Cf. the appearance of κύριος (*kyrios*, 'sir') in addresses to angelic messengers at lxx Gen. 19.2; Dan. 10.16;

Zech. 1.9; et al. For the response to a question, 'My lord, you know (that)', see Ezek. 37.3 ('O Lord God, you know'). Here the elder is an angel of revelation and interpretation; and this accounts for the emphatic σύ (*su*, 'you [know]') in John's response. The use of the perfect in the verb εἴρηκα (*eirēka*, 'I replied'; the Greek means lit. 'and I said to him'), alongside the aorist εἶπεν (*eipen*, 'he said'), suggests that the perfect tense earlier in the verse functions as an aorist. Such a linguistic feature does not occur in the Fourth Gospel. The faithful are identified as 'the ones who have survived the great ordeal'. The phrase οὗτοί εἰσιν (*houtoi eisin*, 'these are') introduces a 'demonstrative explanation' (Aune 472), which is a stylistic feature of Jewish apocalypses (cf. *1 Enoch* 22.6–7, 8–9; 23.3–4; et al.).

The definite article used in the anaphoric phrase 'the great ordeal' ([ἐκ] τῆς θλίψεως τῆς μεγάλης, *[ek] tēs thlipseōs tēs megalēs*, lit. '[out of, from] *the* great ordeal'; cf. 2.22) seems to imply a spiritual victory achieved by believers at a future, climactic moment in the history of salvation. In both Judaic and Christian thought there exists the anticipation that the ultimate revelation of God's rule will be preceded by 'a time of anguish' (Dan. 12.1, Heb. עת צרה, *'ēt ṣārā*). Cf. also 1QM 1.11–12; 15.1; *T. Mos.* 8.1; *Jub.* 23.11–21; 4 Ezra 13.16–19; *2 Apoc. Bar.* 27.1–15; Matt. 24.21 (using θλῖψις μεγάλη, *thlipsis megalē*, 'great suffering'); Mark 13.7–19; 1 Cor. 7.26. See further Rev. 3.21, and on 3.10 ('the time of ordeal which is about to erupt over the whole world'). In Hermas, *Vis.* 2.2.7–8 (based on Rev. 3.10; 7.14) the concept of woes associated with a final judgemental ordeal has become part of traditional eschatological expectation.

However, John's eschatology in Revelation is dynamic, and not linear. In the light of the Christ-event he perceives the future eschaton from the present, and narrates the events of history from the perspective of eternity. In the vision of verses 13–14, therefore, the seer is not simply declaring that the sealed faithful will survive the great ordeal which is to take place at the end of time, and before the return of Christ (against Beasley-Murray 147; Mounce 164). Nor should we take the present participle ἐρχόμενοι (*erchomenoi*, lit. 'coming') as an imperfect participle, meaning that the 'ordeal' is taking place at the moment of John's narration, and that Christian martyrs are currently arriving from the scene of the great tribulation (against Charles 1, 213). In the first place, the phrase οἱ ἐρχόμενοι (*hoi erchomenoi*, lit. 'those coming') should be translated in the past tense, in harmony with the two following main verbs in the aorist, ἔπλυναν (*eplynan*, 'have washed') and ἐλεύκαναν (*eleukanan*, 'whitened'). Moreover, the ecclesial vision of Rev. 7.9–17 refers to a company of the faithful which includes martyrs, but embraces *all* believers (see on verse 9).

We conclude that the 'great ordeal' survived by the redeemed does not occur exclusively at the end of history. The time of judgement has already been set in motion in John's day, and may overtake believers as well as unbelievers (cf. 2.22) at any time, until the end of time. It is a present reality, and not only a future certainty, which can assume the form of persecution (2.2–3), famine (6.5–6), imprisonment (2.10) and even death (2.13; 6.9). See 1.9; 2.9–10, 22; and the series of eschatological woes at 6; 8.7–9.21. Note similarly John 16.33; Acts 14.22; Rom. 5.3; 2 Tim. 3.12; Hermas, *Vis.* 2.3.1 (Hermas has already 'great tribulations' of his own). In the present context, accordingly, the future 'great ordeal' at the eschaton, which all the faithful survive, should be interpreted as a continuation of what has already begun (cf. Beale 435).

In the setting of Daniel's tribulation, the saints were persecuted because of their covenant loyalty to God (Dan. 11.29–35); whereas those who stood firm survived (11.32). The same theme emerges in Rev. 7, where those who refuse to compromise their loyalty to Christ, despite problems within the community and opposition from outside it, are eventually honoured as conquerors (see verse 14*b*; also 2.17; et al.). See further on this topic Beale 433–35; on θλῖψις (*thlipsis*, 'ordeal, tribulation, affliction') cf. also Schlier, 'θλῖψις'.

With an arresting and dramatic rebirth of images, the elder claims that the faithful have 'washed their robes, and whitened them by the blood of the Lamb'. Both verbs are in the aorist, indicating past expressions on earth of faith in God, and of commitment to Christ, which have continuing implications. For the figure of the Lamb see verses 9–10, and on 5.6. The clash of colours, in the figurative description of robes being washed in red blood to make them white, is a skilful and artistic touch by which the author intensifies the celebration and theology of redemption in this scene. For the exuberant use of colours in the Apocalypse see Smalley, *Thunder and Love* 106–107.

The phrase 'they have washed their robes' (ἔπλυναν τὰς στολὰς αὐτῶν, *eplynan tas stolas autōn*) has a close parallel in the Greek of Rev. 22.14 (s.v.l.), where a blessing is invoked on those who 'wash (present tense) their robes' (q.v.). In both contexts there may be an allusion to Exod. 19.10, 14; although in the Exodus passage the consecrated people wash their clothes in preparation for meeting the Lord on Sinai, and there is no reference to atonement. There is also a possible echo here of the lustration of clothes, for purposes of purification, demanded in Judaism after blood has been shed (Num. 31.19–20, 24; cf. 19.19, sprinkling and washing clothes after touching the dead), which in the Qumran community was one of the required actions following victory in the eschatological war (1QM 14.2–3; cf. Bauckham, *Climax of Prophecy* 226–27). But the most likely background to this symbol is to be discovered in Dan. 11.35 (cf. 12.10). In the setting of a 'time of anguish' (Dan. 12.1) the wise, who have been victims of suffering, are there described as being 'refined, purified and cleansed (Heb. made white)'. This text picks up the 'whitening' of the robes of the faithful mentioned in the next part of the sentence; and, more importantly, the scene in Rev. 7 resonates exactly with the thought and symbolism of the Danielic passage.

The garments of the redeemed in heaven are said to have been 'whitened' or 'made white' (ἐλεύκαναν, *eleukanan*) by (ἐν, *en*, lit. 'in') the blood of the Lamb. This thought may reflect the promise in the poem of Isa. 1, quoted at *1 Clem.* 8.4, that the scarlet sins of God's covenant people will become white as snow or wool (verse 18; cf. Zech. 3.4). There is no sacramental dimension to the theology of Rev. 7.13–14, and therefore no allusion here to baptism (against Knight 73). The clean, white robes of the faithful in 7.14 denote, as elsewhere in the Apocalypse, a purity which has manifested itself through an enduring faith in the redemptive death ('blood') of the Lamb; see 3.4, 5, 18 (where white robes and refined gold appear to be equated); 6.11. Jesus himself is similarly portrayed in 19.13 (q.v.) as wearing a robe 'dipped in blood'; although that context may not include sacrificial overtones. The dominant thought in the present pasage, then, concerns the purity, perseverance and protection of the saints of all ages, whose trust in the cross of Christ, and conquest of evil, have led to a victorious salvation through him (cf. 6.9–11; 12.11). For 'white robes' see further on 7.9, 13; also 19.14.

The exact phrase 'the blood of the Lamb' (ἐν τῷ αἵματι τοῦ ἀρνίου, *en tō[i] haimati tou arniou*) appears elsewhere in Revelation only at 12.11 (q.v., using διά, *dia*, lit. 'through'), although the blood of Christ or the Lamb is mentioned less precisely at 1.5 (where, according to most MSS, John uses a different metaphor for redemption); 5.9; 19.13 (q.v.). In the New Testament generally, the expressions 'blood of Jesus' (e.g. Heb. 10.19) and 'blood of Christ' (Eph. 2.13), and even 'blood of Christ, like that of a lamb' (1 Pet. 1.19), denote the atoning death of Jesus Christ. This language stems from the Jewish cultic practice of sacrifice, as a means of receiving forgiveness of sins (cf. Lev. 4; 5); and it incorporates the belief that blood is the seat of *life* (so Lev. 17.11; see also Heb. 9.22). In the Old Testament sacrificial blood not only removes sin but also purifies the penitent (Exod. 29.10–21); and this concept becomes, as in Rev. 7.14, an important image with which to interpret the idea of purifying atonement (cf. Heb. 9.14; 1 John 1.7). Cleansing from sin, represented as dirt (see Isa. 64.6), is a regular biblical metaphor (so Lev. 16.30; Num. 8.21; Ps. 51.2; Jer. 33.8; Ezek. 37.23; Sir. 23.10; Acts 15.9; 2 Cor. 7.1; Heb. 9.13; Jas. 4.8; 2 Pet. 1.9; 1 John 1.9; et al.). The Jerusalem Targum of Gen. 49.11 refers to washing garments 'dipped', or 'rolled', in blood (cf. Rev. 19.13; also Isa. 63.1–6).

Beale (438) points out that the picture in Rev. 7.14 of the saints 'whitening their robes in the blood of the Lamb' may contain an ambiguity, and imply that their endurance through suffering is deliberately modelled on Christ's, and therefore involves martyr-dom (cf. Boring 131; Bauckham 1294). However, the 'blood' (suffering, death), to which allusion is made in this context, is that of Christ, and not his followers (as in 1.5; 5.9; 12.11; against Bauckham, *Climax of Prophecy* 228–29); and the emphasis is entirely on the 'cleansing effects of his death on their behalf' (Beale 438). When the death of the faithful is described in the Apocalypse, the seer speaks about 'the blood of the saints' (6.10; 16.6; 17.6; 18.24; 19.2). We conclude, with Beale, that the scene presented in Rev. 7.13–14 encompasses the entire company of the redeemed, from all times and all places (as in verse 9), including those who have died for their faith, and not simply a select group of martyrs (so also Charles 1, 214; Beasley-Murray 145; cf. Milligan 131; against Caird 101–103; Boring 131–32; Aune 474–75; Bauckham 1294). See Rev. 22.14–15, where *all* those who 'wash their robes' have a right to enter the heavenly city, in contrast to *all* unbelievers, who are excluded; cf. also 21.7–8.

15–17   These three verses form a poetic stanza, with three lines in each strophe (NA includes the last three lines of verse 14 as an additional strophe). They depict the eternal blessings of God shared inclusively by the redeemed: the totality of the faithful from every age. For the scene in Rev. 7.9–17 enacts neither God's protection of Christians in this life (against Wilcock 83), which is the point of verses 1–8, nor the reward of believers at the climax of history (against Beasley-Murray 140, 145). Instead, it portrays the process of those whose commitment to Jesus, in his death and exaltation, has led them to persevere in faith against opposition on earth, and so to enter the very presence of God in heaven, and begin to enjoy a spiritual reward. The shift to the future tense at the end of verse 15, and in verses 16–17, is not significant; for in visionary experience time and space are present, but transcended by an eternal perspective (see also on 8.1). Once the faithful have been robed in white, and remain in front of God's throne (verse 15), everlasting benedictions are theirs without delay (cf. Mounce 165).

The poetic statement of verses 15–17 is introduced with the words διὰ τοῦτο (*dia touto*, 'that is why', lit. 'through this'). *Because* the protected saints have persevered, and by faith in the atoning work of Christ have survived the ordeals which Christians must expect (verses 13–14), they are entitled to enter the presence of God and of the Lamb. For 'God's throne', as the seat of his sovereign authority, see on 4.2; and for the expression 'in front of the throne' (ἐνώπιον τοῦ θρόνου, *enōpion tou thronou*) see 4.6. In the divine presence the redeemed serve God 'as ministers' day and night. The basic meaning of the verb λατρεύουσιν (*latreuousin*) is 'serve', in the sense of carrying out cultic religious duties (BDAG 587*b*); cf. LXX Lev. 18.21; Num. 16.9; *1 Enoch* 10.21; et al. The word is used of the prophetess Anna, who 'served' in the temple continuously, night and day, with fasting and prayer (Luke 2.37). By extension the term can carry overtones of 'worship', as possibly in the present heavenly context, and certainly at Phil. 3.3; et al. But the setting of Rev. 7.15, with its reference to the 'sanctuary' (temple), demands the natural translation of the verb as 'to serve as ministers'. Cf. similarly 22.3, which is the only other context in the Apocalypse where this word appears.

However, as in Rev. 22.3–5, the service in question is no longer the cultic ritual carried out by the Levitical priesthood. It concerns rather the spiritual worship of adoration and reverence offered by the servants of God. Such service is presented 'day and night' (ἡμέρας καὶ νυκτός, *hēmeras kai nyktos*), which simply means 'ceaselessly'; cf. the unending worship of the living creatures described in the same way at 4.8. The conquest of the righteous over evil and injustice means that they can participate in the continuous ministry of worshipping the Godhead (3.12), as members of a spiritual priesthood (1.6; 5.10). For the hendiadys 'day and night', or the reverse, used as a metaphor for 'endless' (worship) see Acts 26.7 (the twelve tribes 'worship night and day'). This figure is occasionally used in biblical references to continual prayer, or religious observance generally (so Neh. 1.6; Ps. 1.2; Judith 11.17; Luke 18.7; 1 Thess. 3.10; 2 Tim. 1.3). There is obviously no conflict between this verse ('day and night') and Rev. 21.25 ('no night' in heaven).

The saints serve God ceaselessly as ministers in his 'sanctuary' (ἐν τῷ ναῷ αὐτοῦ, *en tō[i] naō[i] autou*, lit. 'in his temple'). In Jewish literature the temple in heaven is regarded as the location of God's throne (*T. Levi* 5.1; 18.6–7), and the holy of holies as the divine dwelling-place (*T. Levi* 3.4–6). The heavenly temple is mentioned 11 times in Revelation (3.12, q.v.; 7.15; 11.19; 14.15, 17; 15.5, 6, 8 (*bis*); 16.1, 17). The concept is symbolic, not literal; and this becomes clear when the temple is ultimately identified with the presence of the Godhead (21.22; cf. 22.3). Such an interpretation also emerges in the last sentence of Rev. 7.15, where the one seated on the throne is said to 'protect' (σκηνώσει, *skēnōsei*, lit. 'he will tabernacle over') his people; cf. John 1.14. This imagery continues the theme of the Festival of Booths present in verse 9 (q.v.), where – as throughout Rev. 7 – the theological notion of protection is much in evidence; see also the imagery of 'sealing' in 7.1–8.

The promise that God will spread his tent over the faithful also recalls his preservation of Israel in the wilderness, with his presence in the tabernacle (Exod. 33.7–11; Num. 9.15–17; et al.), in the pillar of cloud and of fire (Exod. 13.21–22), and in the radiance of his Shekinah glory (Exod. 40.34–38; Deut. 5.24; cf. 2 Chron. 7.1–3). The preposition ἐπί (*epi*, 'over', lit. 'on'), in the phrase ἐπ' αὐτούς (*ep' autous*, lit. 'over them'), reinforces the belief that the Lord's immediate presence will shelter his own from all harm (cf. Isa. 4.5–6). The saints in glory can rejoice that God has protected them in their earthly spiritual journey, and now enables them to enjoy his uninterrupted presence peacefully in eternity.

Beale (440–41) has shown that the Old Testament background to the temple imagery in this passage is primarily to be located in Ezek. 37.26–28 (LXX), with its allusions to God's 'sanctuary' and 'tabernacle' being present in the midst of his people. This link is confirmed by the parallel in Rev. 21.3, where Ezek. 37.27 is quoted more fully, and followed at 21.4, 6 by the same allusions to Ezek. 37 as those found in 7.16–17. In both contexts the existence of a vast multitude of the redeemed is perceived as the fulfilment of a prophecy about Israel's latter-day restoration, which has now taken place in the Christian Church, the new Israel of God (cf. Beale 440). See also Zech. 2.10–11 (God dwelling with his people); 14.11 (Jerusalem abiding in security); 14.16–21 (Gentiles believing in the Lord, and celebrating the Feast of Tabernacles in the house of the Lord). For 'temple' in Revelation see further Walker, *Holy City* 243–48; for 'the one who is seated on the throne' see on 4.2; also 7.15a.

Verse 16 derives from Isa. 49.10, and is the most extensive allusion to an Old Testament passage in Revelation. The salvation and total well-being of the people of God are painted in colours and tones derived from the promises made by the prophet to the Israelite exiles returning from Babylon (Fiorenza 68). However, the translation is independent of the LXX. For example, ἔτι (*eti*, 'again', 'further') is inserted twice in the first line; and, in the second and third lines, the order of καῦμα (*kauma*, 'burning heat') and ἥλιος (*hēlios*, 'sun') is inverted. The promise of deliverance from hunger and thirst would be readily embraced by those who lived in a land where both were constant threats

(Mounce 166). But this points also to the satisfaction of a spiritual need, which is achieved in the presence and sight of God; for he is the fountain of life (Ps. 36.8–9; *1 Enoch* 48.1), and through his Son he leads the faithful to springs of living water (7.17; cf. 21.6; 22.1, 17). Note the theme of freedom from spiritual hunger and thirst at John 4.14; 6.35; 7.37–38; and cf. Matt. 5.6.

Equally, the redeemed are protected by the presence of God from all pain; they will never be struck either by the scorching sun or by burning heat. This exegesis takes καῦμα (*kauma*, 'burning heat') in the sense of the verbal equivalent in the LXX of Isa. 49.10, ὁ καύσων (*ho kausōn*, lit. 'that which consumes by heat'); in both contexts the reference may be to a searing east wind. The noun is used again at Rev. 16.9 where, contrastingly, 'fierce heat' (καῦμα μέγα, *kauma mega*) scorches those afflicted by the outpouring of the fourth bowl. The aorist tense of πέσῃ (*pesē[i]*, 'strike', lit. 'fall on') has a future rather than past implication, governed by the use of the future tense in the two verbs of the preceding sentence. The construction οὐδὲ μή (*oude mē*, lit. 'nor any'), with the aorist subjunctive, introduces a reinforced negative: neither sun nor heat will *ever* hurt believers.

The extensive allusion to Isa. 49.10 is interrupted (see again the last sentence of verse 17), for a reference to the role of the Lamb to be included (see on verses 9–10, 14). Several themes in verse 17 are reflected in Rev. 14.1–5, where the Lamb stands on Mount Zion (verse 1); the throne is set (verse 3); and the faithful follow the Lamb wherever he leads (verse 4). In the present verse Christ is described as being 'at the heart' (ἀνὰ μέσον, *ana meson*, lit 'in the middle') of God's throne. This position corresponds to that mentioned in verse 10, where God and the Lamb receive joint praise from the vast multitude of the redeemed for the salvific work of deliverance. John's Christology in this passage, as elsewhere in Revelation, is very high (see on 5.13). Jesus is one with God (1.12, q.v.); he has died to redeem humanity (5.9); and by his cross and resurrection he has conquered sin and mortality (1.5, 17–18). So now he is in a place of exaltation and equality at God's right hand (7.17), authorized to set in motion the divine purposes of salvation (5.5, 7–10), and able to receive the same adoration as the Father (5.11–14; 7.10). Verse 17 makes the unity of God and the Lamb explicit, by declaring that they share the same throne; see also 21.22–23; 22.1, 3.

The Lamb, the elder continues, will 'shepherd' the faithful. In the Old Testament the imagery of 'shepherding the flock' is often used to describe the relationship between a leader (especially a king) and his people; see 2 Sam. 7.7 (of David); Isa. 44.28 (Cyrus); Jer. 3.15 (Israel's leaders); Ezek. 34.23–24, which may lie behind Rev. 7.17 (David); Nahum 3.18 (Assyrian leaders); Mic. 5.4 (the coming ruler, interpreted messianically in Matt. 2.6). God himself as the shepherd of Israel is an equally common biblical metaphor, notably in the Old Testament (cf. Ps. 23.1–3; 80.1–2; Isa. 40.11; Jer. 31.10; Ezek. 34.11–22; et al.; also Matt. 18.12–14 = Luke 15.4–7).

In the New Testament Jesus is described as (the good) 'shepherd' with some regularity (so esp. John 10.1–16; also Matt. 15.24; Heb. 13.20; 1 Pet. 2.25; 5.4; cf. *1 Clem.* 16.1; et al.). Similarly, the image of believers as the flock of God or Christ, shepherded by leaders, is a familiar concept in early Christian writing (e.g. Mark 14.27 = Matt. 26.31; Acts 20.28; 1 Pet. 5.2; *1 Clem.* 44.3). See further Jeremias, 'poimēn'. The verb ποιμαίνειν (*poimainein*, 'to shepherd') occurs four times in Revelation, apart from 7.17. In the present verse the term carries overtones of great caring, explicated in the next sentence; in the other contexts (2.27, q.v.; 12.5; 19.15) it means 'rule'. The Fourth Gospel uses the noun ποιμήν (*poimēn*, 'shepherd') in association with Jesus, as at John 10.11, rather than the verb 'to shepherd'.

The shepherding ministry of the Lamb includes leading his own to 'springs of living water'. The allusion to Isa. 49.10 (in verse 16) is resumed after a brief interruption.

As God guides the exiles, freed from Babylon, to fountains of water, so the Lamb will lead the redeemed to 'springs of the waters of life' (which literally translates this part of verse 17). This symbol refers to water that is continuously flowing, rather than being static. The rendering of ὁδηγήσει (*hodēgēsei*) as 'he will lead', rather then 'he will guide', suggests the pivotal role of the Lamb in this action. On the basis of his passion and exaltation Jesus goes at the head of the faithful, the context suggests, in order to lead them to life-giving waters (see also the deliverance from thirst promised in verse 16). Fresh water-springs in a dry land quench the thirst of a shepherd and his flock; and, in the same way, the spiritual longings of humanity will ultimately be satisfied by the eternal presence of God (cf. Mounce 167).

The inverted syntax of the Greek expression ζωῆς πηγὰς ὑδάτων (*zōēs pēgas hydatōn*, lit. 'of life springs of waters') emphasizes the theme of life in this passage (note the usual order at 21.6); and this justifies the translation of the phrase by Swete (105) as 'Life's water-springs'. For this concept in the Old Testament see Neh. 9.20; Ps. 23.2; Isa. 58.11; Zech. 14.8; et al.; 'fountain of the water of life' is also used as a metaphor for Yahweh at Jer. 2.13 LXX. The Greek phrasing in Rev. 7.17 is similar to the Hebrew of 1QM 8.16, speaking of the elect: 'Thou, O my God, set in my mouth . . . a fountain of waters (חיים מבוע מים, *mabbūaʿ mayim ḥayyim*) unfailing'. The 'springs of living water' in verse 17 become in the final vision of Rev. 22.1 'a river of the water of life', flowing through the heavenly city from the joint throne of God and the Lamb; cf. also 21.6; 22.17. The Apocalypse and Gospel of John are closely associated in their common use of this imagery (cf. John 4.14; 6.35; 7.37–38; see also on verse 16).

The final sentence of this strophe, promising that God will 'wipe away every tear' from the eyes of the faithful, alludes directly to Isa. 25.8; cf. also Jer. 31.16 LXX and Rev. 21.4. In the Isaianic context the end of mourning results from the abolition of death (Isa. 25.7 LXX; Heb. verse 8). John probably implies the same cause in Rev. 7.17, but does not state it explicitly until 21.4 (q.v.). In both places it may be understood that Christ's conquest of death, in his cross and exaltation, results in victorious life for the believer, and the end of pain and sorrow. The tears in question must be those of grief, rather than relief (against Mounce 167). The hope of Israel's restoration is fulfilled in the salvation of Christ's followers, who have come through the ordeal of suffering on his account, and are now delivered from death and mourning to enjoy eternally God's life-giving presence. Cf. Beale 443.

Theology

In the interval during John's apocalyptic drama, provided by Chapter 7, it has been possible for the audience to stand back and catch a vision of the unfolding and saving purposes of God. These have been released by the Lamb, who breaks the seals of the scroll which plays such a crucial part in the throne-vision of Rev. 4—5 (and see 6). From the sovereign kingdom of God flow judgement on human error and injustice (6.1–17; 8.2—20.15), but also the assurance of divine love and protection. We are shown the sealing of the Christian Church on earth (7.1–8), and then the joy of the vast multitude in heaven. This is made up of those believers who, at any point in history and beyond, remain true to their faith in God and his supreme authority, use power correctly (see above, on verse 12), and readily survive suffering for the sake of Christ. They share accordingly the promises of eternal life and happiness in the divine presence, amid hymns of adoration and praise. As such, they are the successors of the children of Israel, and have entered their own Promised Land; this theology is especially evident in verses 9, 15–17.

Central to the salvific action of this scene is the figure of the Lamb, who shares the throne of God's sovereignty (verses 9–10), receives with him the worship and liturgy of the faithful (10) and shepherds believers, leading them to participate in the eternal source of divine life (17). He is one with God and one with his people; and through his death and resurrection (verse 14) he can therefore achieve the Father's plan of salvation (cf 5.9–11). The Christology of this chapter, as in the Apocalypse generally, is very high. The community around John, divided over its estimate of the person of Christ, needed such a balanced theology. Similarly, the adherents of the Johannine circle would have valued the encouragement which this vision provides of belonging to a Church which, both in time and in eternity, shares the divine blessings of protection and fulness of life.

Those blessings are more than simply physical gifts. But they *include* material qualities. Throughout Revelation, final salvation does not relate to spiritual reality alone; it means, as in the Fourth Gospel, the restoration first of complete human well-being, and the abolition of dehumanizing, suffering and injustice (see Smalley, *John* 232–38). The vision of the Church on earth and in heaven, in this chapter, is the answer to the outcry of those who seek righteousness in place of the destruction of their lives (cf. 6.9–10; see also Fiorenza 69). John's Apocalypse is relevant to God's world and his Church in time, as well as in eternity (Smalley, *Thunder and Love* 149–52). Above all, its message (not least in Chapter 7) enshrines and enacts the truth that God's justice and power, like his love, will in the end prevail (cf. Wall 121).

SCENE 3
Seven Trumpets
(8.1—9.21)

Translation

8 [1]And when[a] the Lamb broke the seventh seal, silence reigned in heaven for what seemed to be half an hour. [2]Next, I saw seven trumpets being given to the seven angels who were standing in God's presence. [3]Then another angel, holding a golden censer, moved to stand at[b] the altar; and he was given a vast quantity of incense to offer,[c] on the golden altar in front of the throne, simultaneously with the prayers of all the saints. [4]The smoke of the incense rose from the angel's hand to God's presence, with his people's prayers. [5]Then the angel took the censer, filled it with some burning coals from the altar, and hurled them down to the earth; this was followed by [d]peals of thunder, roarings, flashes of lightning[d] and an earthquake.

[6]The seven angels who held the seven trumpets now made ready to blow[e] them. [7]The first[f] sounded, and there followed hail and fire, mixed with blood, and these were hurled down to the earth; and one-third of the land was consumed by fire, together with one-third of the forests and every blade of green grass. [8]The second angel then blew his trumpet, and what looked like a huge mountain, blazing with fire,[g] was hurled into the sea. A third part of the waters turned into blood; [9]a third of the living creatures in the sea died; and a third of the ships were destroyed.[h] [10]And the third angel sounded, after which a great star, burning like a torch, dropped from the sky and fell on a third of the rivers and on the fresh-water springs. [11]The star's name is Apsinth;[i] and a third of all waters became bitter as wormwood,[j] so that people died in large numbers from drinking the poisoned water.

[12]Next, the fourth angel sounded his trumpet, and a third of the sun, moon and stars were forcefully struck, with the result that one-third of their illumination was obscured; a third of daylight was not visible, and similarly with night-time. [13]In my vision I heard an eagle,[k] calling aloud as it flew in midheaven, 'Disaster, disaster, disaster for the earth's inhabitants,[l] because of the remaining trumpet-blasts which the three angels are about to sound!'

9 [1]When the fifth angel sounded, I saw a star which had dropped from the sky on to the earth; and the star-angel was given the key of the shaft leading to the bottomless pit. [2]He opened the shaft of the bottomless pit; and from the shaft poured out smoke which looked like smoke from a great furnace, and the sun and the atmosphere were darkened[m] by the smoke from the shaft. [3]Out of the smoke, locusts spread over the earth; and they[n] were granted power similar to the authority wielded over the land by scorpions. [4]However, they were told[o] not to harm[p] any field, or green growth or tree on the earth, but only[q] those people who do not wear God's seal on their foreheads.[r] [5]Such they were permitted simply to torment, not to kill, for five months; and their torture was to be like the anguish produced by a scorpion when it stings someone.

[6]And at that time people will search for death,
     but not be able to find[s] it;
   they will long to die,
     but death will elude[t] them.

[7]These locusts looked like[u] horses armoured for battle. On their heads they wore what seemed to be wreaths with the appearance of gold;[v] their faces were like those of human

beings, [8]their hair was feminine in character, and their teeth were similar to those of lions. [9]Their chests resembled iron breastplates, and the whirring of their wings sounded like war-chariots with teams of horses charging into battle. [10]They have tails like[w] those of scorpions, with stings in them; and in their tails lies the ability to hurt people for five months. [11]They have over them, as leader, the angel of the bottomless pit: his Hebrew name is Abaddon, but in Greek he is called Apollyon. [12]The first disaster[x] has taken place; look, two more have still to occur, later![y]

[13]Then[y] the sixth angel sounded his trumpet; and I heard a single voice coming from the four[z] corners of the golden altar which stands in God's presence, [14]announcing[aa] to the sixth angel with the trumpet, 'Set free the four angels which are chained up at the great river, the Euphrates.' [15]So the four angels, who had been in readiness for this very hour and day and month and year, were released to destroy one-third of the human race. [16]And I learned how many belonged to their squadrons of cavalry: they numbered two hundred million.[bb]

[17]This is how the horses and their riders appeared in my vision: they wore breastplates which were in colour fiery-red, hyacinth-blue and sulphur-yellow. The horses' heads were like those of lions, and from their mouths were issuing fire, smoke and brimstone. [18]It was as a result of these three plagues, the fire, smoke and brimstone proceeding from their mouths, that one-third of the human race was destroyed.[cc] [19]For the power of the horses lies in their mouths, and also in their tails; since their tails have[dd] heads like serpents, and through them they inflict injury.

[20]The remainder of the human race, which had escaped death from these plagues, did not[ee] renounce their own handiwork; so they did not stop worshipping[ff] demons, the idols fashioned from gold and silver, brass, stone and wood, which cannot see or hear or move. [21]Nor did they give up their murdering, their magic arts,[gg] their immorality or their thefts.

Text

[a] The conjunction ὅταν (*hotan*, 'when', 'whenever') is attested in this form by A C 1006 1611, et al. There is stronger MS support for the equivalent ὅτε (*hote*, 'when'), as read by ℵ 025 052 TR; but this variation could well be the result of assimilation to the six uses of ὅτε (*hote*, 'when'), with the indicative verb ἤνοιξεν (*ēnoixen*, 'broke', 'opened'), in Rev. 6.1, 3, 5, 7, 9, 12. So Metzger, *Textual Commentary* 740.

[b] For ἐπὶ τοῦ θυσιαστηρίου (*epi tou thysiastēriou*, 'at the altar', with the genitive), which appears in ℵ C Byz, et al., some MSS (including A 025 1006 Andreas; see also Charles 2, 284) have the accusative form ἐπὶ τὸ θυσιατήριον (*epi to thysiastērion*, 'on the altar'). The genitival version is likely to be original; for although the preposition ἐπί (*epi*) takes both the accusative and the genitive cases, the meaning with the genitive ('at', or 'beside', rather than '[up]on') suits the context of verse 3, where the angel moves to stand 'at' the altar, and not 'on' it. The variant in the accusative may have been influenced by the (appropriate) use of that form later in the verse.

[c] In the purpose clause, 'to offer with the prayers of all the saints', ἵνα (*hina*, lit. 'in order that') is followed in the major witnesses (e.g. ℵ A C 598 1773) by the future indicative δώσει (*dōsei*, lit. 'he will give'). Other MSS (such as 052 2351 Andreas Byz) have the aorist δώσῃ (*dōsē[i]*, lit. 'he should give'); and 1006 Oecumenius[2053] reads δῶ (*dō[i]*), a second aorist with the same meaning. A consecutive clause in the Greek would normally take the subjunctive, and the two variants are clearly corrections to accord with that rule. But that the indicative version is the *lectio originalis* is confirmed by the constant use of the future indicative with ἵνα (*hina*, 'that') in Revelation (cf. 2.10; 3.9 (*bis*); 6.4, 11; 8.3 [here]; 9.4, 5, 20; 13.12; 14.13; 22.14). The best extant MS witness to the text of Revelation (A) uses the future indicative 16 times in clauses of purpose (cf. Aune 486).

^d The order of the phenomena which are described, following the angel's action, presents a problem in the MS attestation. The sequence βρονταὶ καὶ φωναὶ καὶ ἀστραπαί (*brontai kai phōnai kai astrapai*, lit. 'thunders and voices and lightnings') is present in ℵ 025 046 1006 1611 Byz latt syr^{ph} cop, et al. However, 1006 has 'thunders and lightnings'; A 052, et al. read 'thunders and lightnings and voices'; while 1611¹⁸⁵⁴ Oecumenius²⁰⁵³ Andreas TR, et al. support 'voices and thunders and lightnings'. There are close parallels at Rev. 4.5; 11.19; and 16.18, all of which follow the order, 'lightnings and voices and thunders'; and this is a logical sequence, since lightning normally precedes thunder. But no textual witness to this verse agrees with that order; and the weight of the MS evidence in favour of the first reading, followed in the translation, together with the difficulty involved in mentioning thunder before lightning, suggests very strongly that this is original.

^e For σαλπίσωσιν (*salpisōsin*, 'they should blow', aorist subjunctive), which appears in ℵ A 025 046 1006 1611¹⁸⁵⁴, some witnesses (including 1611²³²⁹) have σαλπίσουσιν (*salpisousin*, lit. 'they will blow', future indicative). The latter version is a correction, arising from the phonetic proximity of the vowels ω (*ō*) and ου (*ou*), and the influence of a tendency in the Apocalypse to use the future indicative with ἵνα (*hina*, 'that') in consecutive clauses. See note ^c, above.

^f Some MSS (1611²³²⁹ TR) introduce ἄγγελος (*angelos*, 'angel') after πρῶτος (*prōtos*, 'first'). This is clearly a later addition to the text; and, in view of the 'seven angels' mentioned in verse 6, it is unnecessary. It was doubtless motivated by the fact that in all the references to the other six angels with trumpets, in Rev. 8.8—11.15, the noun ἄγγελος (*angelos*, 'angel') is included with their enumeration.

^g The qualifying description of the huge mountain as 'blazing with fire' (πυρὶ καιόμενον, *pyri kaiomenon*) is strongly attested by major MSS (including ℵ A 025 052 1006 1611 Andreas vg syr^h cop^{sa,bo} arm Primasius). A few witnesses (e.g. 046 Byz Cassiodorus) omit πυρί (*pyri*, 'with fire'); but this is a secondary reading, which assumes that 'fire' does not need to be specified in the context of blazing or burning. In 8.10 'burning' appears without the use of fire; but they occur together at 21.8 (q.v.).

^h The third person plural second aorist passive, διεφθάρησαν (*diephtharēsan*, 'were destroyed'), has strong external support from ℵ A 046 1611 Andreas, et al. Some MSS (including 1773 2351 Byz TR) have at this point the third person singular second aorist passive, διεφθάρη (*diephtharē*, 'was destroyed'). This latter variation must be a move to correct the grammar of this passage, and to use a singular form of the verb with the singular substantive τὸ τρίτον (*to triton*, 'the third'). But the writer understands the noun 'third' here as collective, and therefore congruent with the use of a plural form of the verb 'to destroy' (so Rev. 7.9; 9.18; 13.3–4; 18.4; 19.1, 6). In view of the MS evidence, together with the internal support offered by the fact that it accords with the broad sense of the context, and represents the *lectio difficilior*, we may conclude that the plural form of the verb in this part of verse 9 is original.

ⁱ The article ὁ (*ho*, 'the') appears before Ἄψινθος (*Apsinthos*, 'Apsinth', 'Wormwood') in A 025 1773 Byz, et al., but is omitted by ℵ 052 Oecumenius²⁰⁵³ Andreas TR. The omission is a correction since, strictly speaking, 'wormwood' is a noun which is on its way to becoming a proper name; and, since it is unfamiliar to John's audience, it should have been used without the article. For similar corrections see Rev. 6.8; 12.9. At 9.11; 19.13, 16 the noun-names are in any case anarthrous. Some witnesses (including ℵ* 1611²³⁴⁴ Beatus) provide the acceptable variant spelling, Ἀψίνθιον (*Apsinthion*, 'Apsinth').

^j Instead of the preposition εἰς (*eis*, 'into'), in the accusative expression εἰς ἄψινθον (*eis apsinthon*, lit. 'into wormwood'), some MSS (including 1611²³²⁹ 2322 2351 Byz it^h syr^{ph}

Primasius) read the adverb ὡς (*hōs*, 'like', 'as'). Both words appear to make sense in the context. But the writer is saying that the waters *became* 'bitter as wormwood', and not that they *resembled* the herb. In this instance, therefore, εἰς (*eis*, 'into') is clearly original.

k In place of ἀετοῦ (*aetou*, 'eagle'), which is strongly supported by ℵ A 046 and most minuscules, 025 Andreas arm TR, et al. have ἀγγέλου (*angelou*, 'angel'). This may have been an accidental substitution; but it is more likely to have been deliberate, since the function ascribed here to an eagle seems more appropriate to an angel (see 14.6, where an angel 'flies in midheaven'). So Metzger, *Textual Commentary* 741. Swete (113) points out that had the Apocalyptist written ἀγγέλου (*angelou*, 'angel'), ἄλλου (*allou*, 'another') would probably have taken the place of ἑνός (*henos*, 'an', lit. 'one'). The two readings are conflated in 42 Byz Primasius as ἀγγέλου ὡς ἀετοῦ (*angelou hōs aetou*, 'angel as an eagle').

l For the accusative τοὺς κατοικοῦντας (*tous katoikountas*, lit. 'those dwelling'), as read by ℵ 1611[1611,1854] Oecumenius[2053] 2351 Byz, some witnesses (such as A 1611[2329] Andreas; and see Charles 2, 286) prefer the dative form τοῖς κατοικοῦσιν (*tois katoikousin*, lit. 'to those dwelling'). The variant is a correction, since οὐαί (*ouai*, 'disaster', lit. 'woe') with the accusative is rare in Revelation (only elsewhere at 12.12), and the exclamation is normally followed by the dative of the person or object involved (so Matt. 18.7; Mark 13.17; Luke 6.24; 1 Cor. 9.16; Jude 11). But note the use of the nominative at Rev. 18.10, 16, 19.

m The Attic form of the aorist passive verb, ἐσκοτώθη (*eskotōthē*, lit. 'was darkened'), is well attested (A 0207 1006, et al.); but ℵ 2351, et al. have the Hellenistic version of the same verb, with the same meaning, ἐσκοτίσθη (*eskotisthē*). See the parallel choice at 16.10. It seems that the Hellenistic variant is a later emendation (but note the same form at 8.12).

n Instead of the strongly attested feminine dative plural αὐταῖς (*autais*, lit. 'to them'), a few witnesses (ℵ 046 1611[2329]) have the masculine dative plural, with the same meaning, αὐτοῖς (*autois*). Since the pronoun modifies the feminine noun, ἀκρίδες (*akrides*, 'locusts'), it might be argued that the feminine version of the pronoun is a correction to bring the syntax into line. But its wide MS support must mean that αὐταῖς (*autais*, 'to them', feminine) is the original reading. Aune (485) suggests that the masculine variant may have originated as an attempt to construe the locust-demons as male warriors.

o The Hellenistic form of the verb ἐρρέθη (*errethē*, lit. 'it was told, commanded'), with the short epsilon ε (*e*) in the middle, is original. It is replaced in some MSS (including 046 1611[1854] 1862) by the Attic form, with the same meaning, ἐρρήθη (*errēthē*). But this is evidently the later work of copyists.

p In place of the future indicative of the verb, in the phrase ἵνα μὴ ἀδικήσουσιν (*hina mē adikēsousin*, lit. 'that they will not harm'), as read by A 025 1611[2329] 2351, the major variant (in ℵ 0207 Andreas Byz) has the aorist subjunctive verbal form, ἀδικήσωσιν (*adikēsōsin*, 'they should not harm'). This is a subsequent correction of the original, designed to make the grammar conform to the normal rule: which is that, in consecutive clauses using ἵνα (*hina*, 'that'), the mood of the verb is aorist and not future. But this is a regular stylistic feature in the Apocalypse; see the textual notes c and e, above.

q The word μόνους (*monous*, 'only'), present in the translation, is implied in the Greek text, and included by TR, et al. It is omitted by ℵ A 025 046.

r The reading ἐπὶ τῶν μετώπων (*epi tōn metōpōn*, lit. 'on the foreheads') is attested by ℵ A 025 1611[1854,2050], et al. The variant τῶν μετώπων αὐτῶν (*tōn metōpōn autōn*, 'their foreheads'), present in 1006 1611[1611,2329], et al., is a later attempt to complete the sense of the text by adding the necessary possessive pronoun 'their' (as in the translation).

Despite the plural subject ἀνθρώπους (*anthrōpous*, 'people', lit. 'men'), 0207 reads τοῦ μετώπου αὐτοῦ (*tou metōpou autou*, 'his forehead', singular); while 2351 has the curious mixture of plural and singular, τῶν μετώπων αὐτοῦ (*tōn metōpōn autou*, lit. 'his foreheads').

ˢ The reading εὕρωσιν (*heurōsin*, 'they should find [death]', second aorist) is well attested (it occurs in A C 025 1006[1006,1841] 1611[1854,2344], et al.; see also Charles 2, 290); it is also grammatical, since οὐ μή (*ou mē*, lit. 'not at all', 'by no means', intensive) normally takes the aorist tense. However, the variant εὑρήσουσιν (*heurēsousin*, 'they will find', future), as in ℵ 0207 94 2019, et al., could well be original, as it is the *lectio difficilior*. This construction, of οὐ μή (*ou mē*, 'not at all') with the future, is rare in the New Testament; and in Revelation it appears elsewhere only at 3.5 and 18.14. The future form may have been influenced by the surrounding verbs, also in the future, ζητήσουσιν (*zētēsousin*, 'they will search') and ἐπιθυμήσουσιν (*epithymēsousin*, 'they will long'). See also 3.3.

ᵗ In the original and well-attested reading, the verb φεύγει (*pheugei*, lit. 'flees') is in the present tense. But, as the preceding three verbs in the future make clear, the sense of the action in this passage is entirely prospective; hence the translation, '*will* elude'. The variant φεύξεται (*pheuxetai*, lit. 'will flee'), in 1611[1854,2329] 2351 Byz lat cop[bo], is an obvious scribal correction, designed to bring the tense of the verb into line with its future meaning.

ᵘ The adjective ὅμοια (*homoia*, 'like', neuter plural), present in 0207 Oecumenius[2053] Andreas, Byz lat, et al., is replaced by ὅμοιοι (*homoioi*, 'like', masculine plural) in ℵ 792 1611[2344] Primasius (*similes*, 'like') Tyc³ (*similes*) it[gig] (*similis*), et al. The first reading is grammatically correct, since the neuter nominative plural then agrees with the preceding neuter, τὰ ὁμοιώματα (*ta homoiōmata*, 'the likeness'). The masculine plural in the variation may represent a copyist's error; but equally, since it is a difficult reading, it could be original.

ᵛ There is strong support for the reading ὅμοιοι χρυσῷ (*homoioi chrysō[i]*, lit. 'like gold'); so ℵ A 025 1006 1611 2053 it[gig] vg syr[ph,h] cop[bo vid] arm eth, et al. Moreover, the dative singular form of a noun, with the plural of ὅμοιος (*homoios*, 'like'), is characteristic of John's literary style in Revelation (cf. 1.15; 2.18; 13.11; et al.). In this verse, the rare plural version χρυσοῖ (*chrysoi*, 'gold') is less well attested (046 0207 cop[sa], et al.), and represents an inferior text. In 2351 χρυσοῖ ὅμοιοι χρυσῷ (*chrysoi homoioi chrysō[i]*, lit. 'golden like gold') is an odd conflation (Metzger, *Textual Commentary* 741).

ʷ For ὁμοίας (*homoias*, 'like', accusative plural, agreeing with οὐράς, *ouras*, 'tails'), as read by 025 046 1006[1841] 1611 Andreas Byz, et al., some witnesses (including ℵ A 94 792 1006[1006]) have ὁμοίοις (*homoiois*, 'like', dative plural). The dative form of the variant is grammatically difficult; but even so this reading is probably inferior, and may be the result of assimilation to the following noun in the dative, σκορπίοις (*skorpiois*, 'scorpions'). For ὅμοιος (*homoios*, 'like') with the dative in Revelation see 13.11; cf. also note ᵛ, above.

ˣ In the phrase, ἡ οὐαὶ ἡ μία (*hē ouai hē mia*, 'the first disaster', lit. 'the woe the one'), attested by the major MSS Andreas Byz, some witnesses (e.g. 𝔓47 ℵ¹) omit the first definite article, ἡ (*hē*, 'the'), and others (including ℵ* cop[sa]) simply read οὐαὶ μία (*ouai mia*, lit. 'first woe'). The later omission of the article(s) in both variants was doubtless caused by the fact that elsewhere in the New Testament, and in the LXX, οὐαί (*ouai*, 'woe') is never articular. However, in the Apocalypse the feminine article *is* used with the term 'disaster' (as here; see also 11.14 [*bis*]).

ʸ The formula μετὰ ταῦτα (*meta tauta*, 'later', lit. 'after these things') is normally found at the beginning of a sentence or clause (as in Rev. 4.1*a*; 7.9; 15.5; 18.1; et al.);

and elsewhere in the Apocalypse it occurs at the end of a sentence only at 1.19 and 4.1*b*. As a result, many witnesses (including 046 0207 1006 2351 syr^ph) place the phrase at the start of verse 13. To smooth the connection, some MSS either move the introductory καί (*kai*, 'then', lit. 'and') so that it precedes μετὰ ταῦτα (*meta tauta*, 'later', lit. 'after these things'), as with 046, or omit the conjunction altogether (so 𝔓47 ℵ 61 69 2058 2344 syr^ph cop^sa,bo). The text adopted in the translation is, however, well supported (A 025 1611 lat vg syr^h Tyc^1,3 Andreas Arethas, et al.); it also accords with the writer's way of introducing angels which have been referred to previously (so 8.1–2, 8, 10, 12; 9.1). See Metzger, *Textual Commentary* 741.

z The fact that the voice came from the 'four' (τεσσάρων, *tessarōn*) corners of the altar is specified by 025 046 1006 1611^1854 vg syr^ph Cyprian Primasius Andreas Arethas Byz, et al. The number of the corners is omitted in external evidence which is fairly evenly balanced (𝔓47 ℵ^1 A 0207 1611^1611,2344 it^gig syr^h cop^sa,bo Oecumenius^2053, et al.; and see Charles 2, 293). 'Four' might have been added as a contrast to the 'single' voice mentioned immediately beforehand, and in parallel with the 'four' angels of verse 14; equally, the numeral might have been accidentally omitted in transcription because of its similarity to the following word, κεράτων (*keratōn*, 'corners'). So Metzger, *Textual Commentary* 742. NA includes τεσσάρων (*tessarōn*, 'four') in the Greek text, but places it in brackets.

aa The participle 'announcing' (lit. 'saying') has the masculine singular accusative form λέγοντα (*legonta*, 'saying') in ℵ* A 149 1611^2344 it^gig Cyprian Tyc Primasius, et al. But since it modifies the feminine singular accusative of the noun 'voice' (φωνήν, *phōnēn*), the participle should also have the feminine singular form, with the same meaning, λέγουσαν (*legousan*); and this is the subsequent correction found in 𝔓47 0207 1611 Oecumenius^2053 Andreas, et al. The variant λέγοντος (*legontos*, 'saying', genitive), present in 046 2351 Byz, et al., must be a scribal error. For the grammatical feature of a feminine noun being modified by a masculine participle or adjective elsewhere in Revelation, see 4.1; 11.4, 15.

bb The Greek form of the number 'two hundred million', δισμυριάδες μυριάδων (*dismyriades myriadōn*, lit. 'twice ten thousands of ten thousands'), is unusual; since δισμυριάς (*dismyrias*, 'a double myriad') occurs only here in the New Testament. This version is attested by A 1611^2344 2351 Andreas Origen it^gig vg Cyprian, et al. Because of its unfamiliarity, the reading is difficult and likely to be original; and, not surprisingly, it has given rise to a number of later variants. These include δύο μυριάδων μυριάδας (*duo myriadōn myriadas*, lit. 'two myriads of myriads'), as read by ℵ, where the accusative μυριάδας (*myriadas*, 'myriads') is presumably used because 'myriads' has been taken as the object of the following verb, ἤκουσα (*ēkousa*, 'I learned', lit. 'I heard'); and δύο μυριάδες μυριάδων (*duo myriades myriadōn*, 'two myriads of myriads'), as witnessed by 𝔓47 cop^bo, et al.

cc The third person plural of the aorist passive verb ἀπεκτάνθησαν (*apektanthēsan*, 'were destroyed', lit. 'were killed') is strongly attested by ℵ A C Andreas Byz, and must be original despite the awkward grammar involved. This is an example of a construction which follows the sense of the context, since τὸ τρίτον (*to triton*, 'one-third [of the human race]', singular) is construed by the writer as a collective noun requiring a plural verb form. It is corrected by 𝔓47 2019 2078 2436 to the singular aorist, ἀπεκτάνθη (*apektanthē*, 'it was destroyed'). See the similar variation in 8.9; and note ^h, above.

dd The nominative feminine plural participle ἔχουσαι (*echousai*, 'they have', lit. 'having') acts as a finite verb in this clause; and, in Revelation, participles formed from ἔχω (*echō*, 'have') are often used in this way (see 1.16; 4.7; 9.17; 10.2; 12.2; 19.12; 21.12, 14;

for participles treated as finite verbs in the Apocalypse cf. similarly 4.2; 10.8; 14.1). This is clearly the original reading. Corrections are to be found in several MSS of Andreas (to the finite verb ἔχουσι, *echousi*, 'they have'); and also in ℵ* 025 181 598 2019 (the equivalent of A and C) 2059, et al. (to the dative plural of the participle, ἔχουσαις, *echousais* ['having'], as modifying the preceding dative ταῖς οὐραῖς [*tais ourais*, 'tails'], which then creates a parenthesis made up of the intervening words; see further on 9.19).

ᵉᵉ The conjunction οὐδέ (*oude*, strictly 'neither', 'nor'; also 'and not') is difficult to construe without a correlative clause ('nor . . .'). This caused several witnesses (including C 1006 1611^1854 2351 Byz arm, et al.) to substitute οὐ (*ou*, 'not'); or (so 2329, et al.) the reading became καὶ οὐ (*kai ou*, 'and not'). The version οὐδέ (*oude*, 'and not'), as in 𝔓47 ℵ 046 69 1778 2020, et al., is doubtless original. Some MSS (such as A 025 1 1611 Andreas) have the related version, οὔτε (*oute*, 'neither', 'nor'); but this may well be the result of assimilation to the correlative construction, with οὔτε . . . οὔτε (*oute . . . oute*, lit. 'nor . . . nor'), later in the verse. So Metzger, *Textual Commentary* 742.

ᶠᶠ Instead of προσκυνήσουσιν (*proskynēsousin*, lit. 'they will worship', future indicative), as strongly attested by 𝔓47 ℵ A C MSS of Andreas Byz, some witnesses have the variant προσκυνήσωσι (*proskynēsōsi*, 'that they should worship', aorist subjunctive). The future indicative, rather than the strictly grammatical aorist subjunctive mood, is regularly used in purpose clauses with ἵνα (*hina*, 'that') throughout Revelation. This must therefore be the original form, with the aorist as a later attempt to correct the Greek grammar. See notes ᶜ, ᵉ and ᴾ, above.

ᵍᵍ The word φαρμάκων (*pharmakōn*, 'magic arts', 'sorcery') occurs nowhere else in the New Testament. This fact, combined with the strength of external MS support it receives from 𝔓47 ℵ 1006 1611, et al., makes it probable that we have here the *lectio originalis*. Furthermore, copyists would be more likely (with A 025 046 2351 Andreas) to change the form to the more technical φαρμακ(ε)ιῶν (*pharmak[e]iōn*, 'magic', as in Rev. 18.23; cf. Gal. 5.20), than the reverse.

Literary Setting

The third scene of the first Act of Revelation begins with the breaking of the scroll's seventh seal by the Lamb (8.1). At this point, John's vision resumes the description of the opening of the seals, and the results of that activity in the case of the first six, presented in the second scene (6.1–17). The close, retrospective link is signified by the use of καί (*kai*, 'and') at the very beginning of verse 1. In between, an interval has occurred (7.1–17), in which the security and the salvation of the Church on earth and in heaven have been strikingly depicted. It is part of the seer's literary craftsmanship to delay, in this manner, the final disclosure in a sevenfold sequence *through* the interlude to the next scene. The same process is evident in the seven trumpet-soundings of the present scene (8.6—9.19), and later in the action (11.15–18). By using this dramatic technique, the writer encourages his audience to recall the historical and theological implications of what has already been unfolded, before the revelation is purposefully moved forward; and, equally, the overall structure of the drama is tightened and controlled. Together, the sixth and seventh seals (6.12–17; 8.1) are the logical climax of the series; they provide an answer to the request of the saints for justice (6.9–10), by unfolding God's final purposes of saving righteousness (7.1—9.21).

The series of trumpet-plagues in Rev. 8—9 is introduced by a prelude (8.2–6). As with the preparation for the seven seals in 4.1—5.14, and for the seven bowls in 15.1–8, the setting here is presumably the temple in heaven, although this is not specified until

11.19. The scenery of the prelude fluctuates between royalty and ritual (note 8.3; so Moffatt 402). It is framed by the reference to the seven angels with trumpets in verses 2 and 6, and contains two central actions: an offering of incense by the angel upwards to God (verses 3–4), and the angelic hurling of burning coals downwards to the earth (verse 5).

The trumpets sounded by the angels in 8.7—11.15 form a group of seven. For the importance of that number in Revelation (as in the Fourth Gospel) see on 1.4; the Apocalypse is structured in seven main scenes; and it features heptads of seals, trumpets, bowls, visions and prophecies. The visions of the first four trumpet-blasts and their effects (Rev. 8.7–12) are described briefly, and are similar in character. An angel sounds; a plague erupts (hail, fire and blood; burning mountain; falling star; cosmic darkness); and dire consequences follow. The remaining three trumpets (9.1, 13; 11.15) also have a similarly coherent literary framework; although the plagues emanating from trumpets five and six (a different falling star; angelic destruction) are replaced in the final trumpet-call by the positive reaction of the saints, who praise God for his judgement and great power (11.15–18). These final three trumpets are associated with the three 'disasters' (woes) of 8.13, which are said to be imminent (note the portents which follow the opening of the temple in heaven [11.19], once the song of the faithful has been concluded). The narrative pattern in the Apocalypse of a heptad, divided into a homogeneous framework of four sections plus three, is repeated in the symbols of the seals (6.1–8, also described succinctly; and 6.9, 12; 8.1), and – less clearly – of the bowls (16.1–8; and 16.10, 12, 17).

Aune (497) points out that the material in this section and 11.15–18 forms a carefully defined textual unit, in which the trumpets are used as a structuring device (the same might be said of the heptads of seals and bowls). The metaphor of sounding trumpets as a means of heralding eschatological, divine judgement is logical; since in ancient warfare the trumpet was the instrument used to deploy successive units of soldiers to attack enemy forces. See the similar structural device, this time of three trumpets, present in the apocalyptic text *Apoc. Zeph.* 9–12. Aune (496) also notes the vividness and artistry belonging to the seer's description of the locusts in 9.7–11.

The first verse of this scene, 8.1, has a key role to play in the literary and dramatic, as well as theological, composition of the present section of John's Revelation (see further on verse 1, below). In some ways the verse stands on its own, and marks a pause in the action of the drama. The silence in heaven allows the audience to reflect on the unfolding of God's salvific purposes for his creation, both in time and in eternity; and the intensity of the moment is heightened by the total absence of any sound (Mounce 171). But verse 1 also looks back, through the interval of Chapter 7, to the eschatological events detailed in Chapter 6. At the same time, it takes us forward, to the trumpet-portents of Chapters 8 and 9, and beyond that again. For the end of the world, which has been expected at the time of the breaking of the seventh seal, does not occur. As at 6.12–17 (q.v.), we are brought to the edge of the consummation, and then told more about it (Kiddle 144). The final woes are yet to come; and even then it is not entirely clear when they all take place (see on 11.14).

This ambiguity is deliberate, and controlled by John's theology as well as by his dramatic skill. The seer's audience is constantly invited to glimpse the future from the present, and the reverse. For him, the kingdom of God is always breaking in; and time and eternity, like earth and heaven, are constantly drawn together (cf. Smalley, *Thunder and Love* 150–52, 174–76). The apocalypse is in progress from the outset, and the transfiguration of history has already begun (Robinson, 'Interpreting' 61–64, esp. 61). So it is that, in the course of the unveilings belonging to Revelation, our attention is made to focus on the historical and is simultaneously directed to its spiritual and eschatological backcloth. In that process, the silence of 8.1 builds up the dramatic suspense in the scene which follows. There is more to come; and that discovery is now awaited with breathless anticipation.

Comment

Seal 7: Silence in Heaven (8.1)

8.1   The action of breaking the seventh seal is clearly undertaken by the Lamb, as in the case of the first six seals (6.1–12); although this is implied, rather than stated, in the Greek (hence the translation). For the figure of the Lamb, and for the 'seals', see on 5.6; 5.1; also 6.1. The portents of 6.1—7.17 are best understood as providing an outline of the eschatological contents of the scroll, which symbolizes God's saving purposes for his world. The contents themselves are more fully described, once all seven seals have been opened, in the remainder of the drama of the Apocalypse, 8.2—22.5 (cf. Aune 507). For the place of 8.1 in this scheme of judgement and salvation see above, 210.

When the first six seals were opened, the prophet-seer either 'saw' a vision (6.9, 12), or 'heard' a voice (6.3), or both (6.1, 5–6, 7–8); cf. Michaels 116. In 8.1 there is neither sight nor sound, but only silence in heaven. As at 7.1–3 (see Charles 1, 223), this retards the action; and here it allows for reflection before the worship of the saints is offered to God. The silence itself is dramatic in character, and offsets vividly the sound of the trumpets to follow (8.6–12), and the noise of the portents described in verse 5 (see Brown, *Introduction* 788). In general, we may notice, Revelation is a very noisy book! (Cf. Boxall, *Revelation* 5.) The silence seems to last through the angelic activity of verses 2–4, but cannot remain as the setting of verse 5 (against Mounce 170).

The significance of the heavenly silence, for 'what seemed half an hour' in duration, may be interpreted in six possible ways.

(a) Victorinus (Bishop of Pettau, who died *c.* 304), the first commentator on Revelation, described it as symbolizing the 'beginning of eternal rest' (*initium quietis aeternae*). But, as Swete (107) points out, this understanding is exegetically irrelevant, as silence is not characteristic of heavenly rest. Moreover, much audible activity, in heaven and on earth, follows almost immediately.

(b) Charles (1, 223–24) famously regards the silence as a means whereby God can hear the prayers of all the suffering saints on earth (verses 3–4); and he quotes in support the Babylonian Talmudic tractate *Ḥag.* 12*b*, which speaks of the angels of service being silent by day so that the praises of Israel may be heard in heaven. See similarly Caird 106–107; Beasley-Murray 150–51; Bauckham, *Climax of Prophecy* 70–83, esp. 70–71; Walker, *Holy City* 243; et al. However, quite apart from the fact that there is no evidence that martyrs alone are in view in this section of the Apocalypse (see on 7.9–17), nothing in the text of 8.1–4 suggests that noise would prevent God from hearing the prayers of his people (cf. Aune 507).

(c) Some commentators (e.g. Sweet 159; Beale 448; cf. Wilcock 84) find in the imagery of 8.1 the promise of an eschatological return to the silence which preceded the first creation in Gen. 1, according to 4 Ezra 6.39; 7.30; *2 Apoc. Bar.* 3.7. But such an interpretation does not belong naturally to the context of this verse, from which the thought of primordial silence is apparently absent: except, possibly, in terms of the new creation replacing the old (so 7.14–17; cf. Beale 449; see also [d], below).

(d) Silence is associated in Old Testament and Judaic thought with judgement (although the Greek word σιγή [*sigē*, 'silence'] itself is rarely used in the LXX). Thus idolators, and persecutors of God's people, abide in the judgemental silence of Sheol (Ps. 115.17; 31.7; cf. 1 Sam. 2.9–10). Israel and Babylon are silent on account of God's judgement against them (Isa. 47.5; Lam. 2.10; Ezek. 27.32 Heb.; Amos 8.2–3). Similarly, when Alexander defeated his enemies, 'the earth became quiet before him' (1 Macc. 1.3). More germane to the 'silence' of Rev. 8.1 are Old Testament texts which speak of stillness and silent awe as the response to divine judgement issuing from the heavenly temple (cf. Hab. 2.20; Zech. 2.13; see also Isa. 23.2; 41.1–5). Old Testament and Jewish tradition also associate silence with both the defeat of the Egyptians and the redemption of Israel at the Sea of Reeds (Exod. 14.14; 15.1–18; Wis. 18.14, 'gentle silence enveloped all things'). In Wis. 18.21 the prayer and propitiatory incense of Moses, offered for the protection of God's people, seem to be equated (see Rev. 8.3–4); while in Wis. 19.3–21 the themes of Exodus, and deliverance as a new creation, predominate (note 19.6; cf. also Wis. 11.17–18). See further Beale 446–50.

The motifs of silence, judgement and new creation certainly belong to the present scene in Revelation (8.1—9.21), as do evocations of the Exodus and its accompanying plagues (see below); and the Old Testament material cited here may well be part of the dramatic backcloth to Rev. 8.1. Certainly the silence cannot be understood as 'emptiness' (so Beale 447). But nor is it necessarily purely judgemental in its significance. John's theology in the Apocalypse never allows God's activity of judgement to be separated from his work of salvific love; and if the thought of new creation arises from the silence of 8.1, this balance becomes apparent as a result. It has already informed the soteriology of Chapter 7, and it characterizes very strongly the effects of sounding the seventh trumpet (11.15–18).

(e) Silence in the Old Testament is also mentioned as the prelude to a divine manifestation. See Job 4.16–21 ('there was silence, then I heard a voice'); Hab. 3.16 ('I wait quietly for the day of calamity'); Zeph. 1.7 ('be silent before the Lord God, for the day of the Lord is at hand'); Zech. 2.13 ('be silent, all people, before the Lord; for he has roused himself from his holy dwelling'); cf. also Ezek. 1.28—2.1; 3.15–16. This is a 'silence of awesome expectation' (Hughes 101; cf. Mounce 170). Again, such symbolism may help to define the silence of Rev. 8.1; although, as Swete (107) notices, the apocalyptic silence here takes place in heaven, and not on earth.

(f) The last two suggestions about the interpretation of the silence in 8.1, (d) and (e), are of assistance in this hermeneutical task. But the most likely explanation, and the most natural, is to be derived from the setting of 8.1–5; and it is reached by taking seriously the leading context of worship in this passage (see esp. verses 3–4). In both Jewish and Greek tradition (and to that diversity both John and his audience would have been sensitive), silence in God's presence is necessary as a preparation for prayer, or for the performance of the temple liturgy. See Ps. 62.1; Hab. 2.20; Zech. 2.13; *T. Adam* 1.12; Homer, *Iliad* 9.171; Thucydides 6.32.1; et seq. Ignatius sees silence as being characteristic of the bishop, who is the didactic and liturgical representative of God (*Eph.* 6.1; *Philad.* 1.1); the bishop's ministry therefore reflects divine silence. See further Aune 507–508.

The heavenly silence, according to the stage direction of verse 1, 'reigned for what seemed half an hour'. The Greek is ἐγένετο (*egeneto*), which literally means 'happened' or 'took place'. The duration of the silence, 'about half an hour', is a brilliant example of the balance in John's eschatology, in which time and eternity, matter and spirit, constantly intersect (see Smalley, *Thunder and Love* 62–63, 150–52, 167 n. 43). Strictly speaking, eternity cannot be temporally measured; but, in an apocalyptic vision such as this, logic has no firm place. The whole description, half an hour's silence, symbolizes an interlude of some length, in preparation for the worship of God (see above). There is a close verbal parallel in Dan. 4.19 Theod., where Daniel stands distressed 'for about one hour' (ὡσεὶ ὥραν μίαν, *hōsei hōran mian*), after hearing a dream foretelling the death of Nebuchadnezzar. Milligan (135) relates the image to the eschatological 'hours' which strike in the Fourth Gospel (John 2.4; 4.23; 12.27), so that the 'half-hour' in Rev. 8.1 represents an interruption of the process of judgement. For analogies in Revelation see 18.10, 17, 19 (the judgement of Babylon takes place 'in one hour', μιᾷ ὥρᾳ, *mia[i] hōra[i]*); and note the discriminatory silence which follows at 18.22–23.

Prelude: Censing of the Saints (8.2–6)

2 This verse appears to interrupt the scene of worship and judgement which begins in verse 1, and continues at verses 3–5. It belongs with the inclusion represented by verse 6 (q.v.), and may form part of a process of redaction (so Charles 1, 221–23). At the same time, the placing of verse 2 before verses 3–5 allows verses 2–5 to act as a parenthetical transition, which both concludes the series of seals and introduces the trumpets (Beale 454). As at 5.1 (q.v.) and 6.1, John's vision begins with the familiar literary formula, 'next (lit. and) I saw' (καὶ εἶδον, *kai eidon*).

John sees heptads of angels and trumpets. For the importance of the number 'seven' in Johannine thought see on 1.4; also verse 1. The use of the anaphoric article τούς (*tous*, 'the'), before ἑπτὰ ἀγγέλους (*hepta angelous*, 'seven angels'), could mean that the writer is referring back to the (seven) angels who are introduced as a group anarthrously at 1.20 (q.v.), and mentioned individually and with the definite article after that (2.1, 8, 12, 18; 3.1, 5, 7, 14). Some would argue accordingly that the angels of 8.2 can be associated with the guardian angels of the seven churches (Beale 454), and even with the seven spirits of God in Rev. 1.4; 3.1; 4.5; 5.6 (Aune 509). However, this is the first time in the Apocalypse that the phrase '*the* seven angels' as such has occurred; and it is therefore most likely that John is referring here to a new company, but one that is well known to his audience (they reappear in Rev. 15—17). This is confirmed by the attached relative clause, which describes the (presumably familiar) role of these angels as that of 'standing in God's presence' (see below).

In this case, the seven angels of verse 2 are to be identified with the seven archangels who frequent the apocalyptic literature of Second Temple Judaism. See (e.g.) Tobit 12.15; *1 Enoch* 20.1–7 (8), where they are named as Uriel, Raphael, Raguel, Michael, Sariel, Gabriel (and Remiel); 40; 54.6; 71.8–9; *T. Levi* 3.5; 8.2; *3 Enoch* 17.1–3; cf. also 4Q403 (4QShirShabb^d) 1.23; 4 Q404 (4QShirShabb^e) *frag.* 1.1; *frag.* 2.2–10 (where the angels are called the 'seven chief princes'); *Jub.* 2.2, 18 ('angels of the presence', without enumeration); 1QH 14.13 ('angels of the face'). In biblical and Jewish tradition, angels act as God's agents of judgement, notably at the time of the Exodus (cf. Rev. 8.7–12, et passim); see Exod. 12.12–13, 23–27; Ps. 78.47–51; *Jub.* 49.2; et al.

Archangels occupy a special place in the hierarchy of heavenly beings, and may therefore be described (8.2) as 'standing in God's presence'. The stative verb ἑστήκασιν (*hestēkasin*, 'were standing', lit. 'they have stood', perfect tense) is used in a durative, rather than consecutive, sense; hence the translation '(they) were standing' rather than 'stood'. This is the only occasion in Revelation where a third person plural perfect is used with the older form of the ending: -ασι(ν), *-asi(n)*, rather than -αν (*-an*); contrast 18.3; 19.3; 21.6.

Charles (1, 225) interprets the notion of 'standing' in this verse to mean 'attendance', and therefore 'service'. Even if this thought should be included in the context, the heavenly figures with the trumpets in this section of the Apocalypse are archangels, and therefore by definition angels of the presence. They do not belong to the lesser orders of angelic beings, the angels of *service* as such, who in the thought of Judaism serve God through the works of nature. See 28–29, above. The emphasis on the posture of the angels in 8.2, as 'standing' in God's presence, may be influenced by the Jewish tradition that angels had no knees and were therefore unable to sit down (cf. Ezek. 1.7; and see on Rev. 7.11). It was also a common view in Judaism that no one is allowed to be seated in God's presence (cf. *3 Enoch* 16.1–5; 4Q405 [4QShirShabb[f]] *frag.* 20 col. 2.2). See Aune 509. For the expression ἐνώπιον τοῦ θεοῦ (*enōpion tou theou*, 'in God's presence', lit. 'before God'), as a means of conceptualizing the immediate existence of God, see Rev. 3.2; 8.4; 9.13; 11.16; 12.10; 15.4 ('before you'); 16.19. See also the parallel, 'before the throne', at 1.4; 4.5, 6, 10; 7.9, 11, 15 ('before the throne of God'); 8.3; 14.3; 20.12. Note also Luke 1.19, Gabriel 'standing in God's presence'. In the Old Testament the phrase 'before God', or 'before the Lord', is often the equivalent of 'before the ark' (as at Lev. 16.1–2; 1 Sam. 10.25; 2 Sam. 6.2–21; 2 Kings 16.14; et al.).

The seven (arch)angels were given 'seven trumpets' (ἑπτὰ σάλπιγγες, *hepta salpinges*). When they first appear, the angels are not holding trumpets. Receiving them implies 'momentous announcements' to come (Beckwith 551). In the Old Testament, and the literature of Judaism, trumpet-blasts are mentioned in various settings. Close to the present context, seven trumpets were used in the ritual destruction of Jericho (Josh. 6.1–27 [note verse 4]); and, in the War Scroll of the Qumran documents, seven Levites carry seven rams' horns (the equivalent of trumpets) into the eschatological conflict (1QM 7.14). Elsewhere, trumpets are used in similarly military situations. They provide an alarm (e.g. Ezek. 33.3–6); signal an attack (Judg. 7.8–22); represent a cry for help (Num. 10.9–10); summon a retreat (2 Sam. 18.16); and herald a victory (Ps. 47.[1–]5). Trumpets also appear in the announcement of good news (*Pss. Sol.* 11.1); as part of a theophany (Exod. 19.13–19); in scenes of religious ritual, including the anointing of kings (Joel 2.15; 1 Kings 1.34); and in eschatological events (1QM 2.16—3.11). They are accordingly, depending on the circumstances, the cause of terror or joy, or reverent anticipation. In Jewish apocalyptic imagery, trumpets suggest the salvation (Isa. 27.13; Zech. 9.14–15) and judgement (Isa. 58.1; Joel 2.1–2; Zeph. 1.14–16; 4 Ezra 6.23; *Sib. Or.* 4.171–78; *Apoc. Abr.* 31.1; *Apoc. Zeph.* 12.1; et al.) which are associated with the end-time. The trumpets of archangels are rarely mentioned in the literature of Second Temple Judaism; but see the reference to Gabriel's trumpet in *Quest. Ezra (B)* 11. See further on this section Aune 510–11.

In the New Testament generally, trumpets are traditionally the heralds of the parousia and judgement of Christ, and the beginning of the end (so Matt. 24.31 [but not in the synoptic parallels]; 1 Cor. 15.52; cf. *Did.* 16.6). In Revelation, 'trumpet' is used as a simile at 1.10 (a 'trumpet-like voice') and 4.1 (the 'trumpet-tones' of the voice). Eschatological trumpets, as symbols of divine judgement, appear for the first time in the present verse (8.2), and in the Apocalypse are confined to this scene (Chapters 8—9) and 11.15–18. Their sounding releases calamities on the physical universe (8.7–12), plagues on unrepentant humanity (9.1–21), and the triumphant proclamation of God's sovereignty over the world (11.15–19). They do not, as elsewhere in Christian literature, herald specifically the return of Jesus; although the blast of the seventh trumpet at 11.15 in one sense marks the end. In John's thought, however, the consummation is always imminent (see on 6.17 and 8.1).

3–4 The continuous process in the Apocalypse of unfolding the end-time is interrupted by the action of incense-offering (verses 3–5). This prelude to the seven trumpet-plagues is a dramatic scene similar in character to the vision of the twenty-four elders, with golden incense-bowls, used earlier in the play to introduce the opening of the seven seals (Rev. 5.8–10). The priestly function of censing here is undertaken by 'another angel'; and this vague description distinguishes the heavenly being in verse 3 from the seven angels with the trumpets of verse 2, who initiate the next series of eschatological events. The angel in question could be an angel of the presence (see Isa. 63.9; *Jub.* 1.27–29), but cannot possibly be Christ himself (as suggested by Hendriksen 117; Beale 454). Quite apart from any other consideration, the central character in Revelation, identified as the Lamb in verse 1, would never be assigned such an indefinite title (so Mounce 174). The angelophany of verses 2–5 is an example of the literary form of angelic action (see on 7.1; and, for the variety of heavenly agents in the Apocalypse, cf. above, 28–30).

The censing angel moves to stand 'at the altar' (ἐπὶ τοῦ θυσιαστηρίου, *epi tou thysiastēriou*); for ἐπί (*epi*, 'at') see the textual note, above. This altar has been identified with the brazen altar of burnt-offering, in the outer court of the sanctuary of the Temple, referred to at 6.9 (q.v.) and 8.5, and then distinguished from the golden altar of incense, within the Tabernacle, mentioned in the later part of the present verse (8.3). So Milligan 136–38; Beckwith (552–53) understands the altars of Rev. (5.8); 8.3, 5; 9.13; 14.18; 16.7 (cf. 11.1) as identical places of incense, rather than sacrifice. But, as Charles (1, 227) points out, there is no clear evidence in either Jewish or Christian apocalyptic literature for the existence of two altars in heaven (see further *idem*, 226–30; cf. also Aune 511); and the best way of interpreting the character of the (golden) altar which features in this scene (8.3*a*, 3*b*, 5) is to understand it as combining aspects of both the incense altar and the altar of burnt-sacrifice in the Jerusalem Temple (Beale 455; against Mounce 174).

Despite the link with the altar of 6.9 (see 6.10), however, there is no reason to associate the censing in this scene with the suffering of Christian martyrs alone (Beale, ibid.). The prayers of *all* the saints are offered on the altar (8.3*b*). They may include a request for divine vengeance from the Christian martyrs, as in 6.10 (q.v.); but they cannot be confined to this mode of intercession (so Aune 512–13). They are petitions for judgement on sin and injustice in general (hence the trumpet-plagues of 8.6—9.19); and, given the sacrificial evocations of this scene, they may also be an expression of self-offering and praise on the part of the faithful (see also 15.2–4; 19.6–8; cf. Boring 133).

The angel in verse 3 holds 'a golden censer' (λιβανωτὸν χρυσοῦν, *libanōton chrysoun*). The word λιβανωτός (*libanōtos*, 'censer') occurs in the New Testament only here and at verse 5; cf. 1 Chron. 9.29 LXX; 3 Macc. 5.2 LXX (the only uses of this noun in the Septuagint); *Mart. Pol.* 15.2. The cognate term λίβανος (*libanos*) means 'frankincense', which is the resinous gum obtained from an Arabian tree, and used for medicinal and sacral purposes (BDAG 594*b*); so Matt. 2.11; Rev. 18.13. Because in the present context John describes the censer (λιβανωτός, *libanōtos*) as 'golden', he must be referring to a ladle-shaped container, rather than the substance it holds. His usual word for 'incense' itself is θυμίαμα (*thymiama*), as in verse 3*b*; see also Rev. 5.8; 8.4; 18.13 (the only other uses of the noun in the Apocalypse); Luke 1.10–11. The censers of the Tabernacle were made of brass (Exod. 27.3), while those of Solomon's Temple were crafted in pure gold (1 Kings 7.50).

The angel was given a 'vast quantity' of incense to offer, corresponding no doubt to the 'vast multitude' of the saints (7.9; see 8.3*b*, 'all the saints') on whose behalf it is to be presented. The use of the aorist passive, in the phrase ἐδόθη αὐτῷ (*edothē autō[i]*, 'he was given', lit. 'there was given to him'), obscures the source of the incense which is provided. This is probably a passive of divine activity (as in 6.2 [q.v.], 4, 8, 11; 7.2; et al.), and therefore a circumlocution for the name of God (cf. Aune 512). In the throne-vision of *Apoc. Paul* 44, which evidently reflects the thought and imagery of John's Apocalypse, incense ('the smoke of a good odour') rises up beside the altar of the throne of God; cf. also *T. Levi* 8.10.

The burning of incense in cultic contexts is frequently mentioned in the Old Testament, often in association with sacrifice (e.g. Lev. 2.1; Num. 16.6–7; Exod. 30.7–10 [the 'regular incense offering', each morning and evening], 34–37). Incense and prayer, as in Rev. 8.3, belong together at Ps. 66.13–15; 141.2; Isa. 60.6; see also Ezra 9.5–15; Dan. 9.21; similarly Luke 1.9–11. In the present verse, and in verse 4, the incense is not used as a metaphor for prayer itself (as it is in 5.8, q.v.; against Mounce 174). Rather, burning incense and the prayers of all the saints are mingled on the altar *together*. For 'saints' (ἅγιοι, *hagioi*) see on 5.8. This exegesis depends on construing the expression ταῖς προσευχαῖς (*tais proseuchais*, 'with the prayers') as a temporal dative, meaning that the incense and the prayers of believers are connected, and offered simultaneously (so rightly Moule, *Idiom Book* 43–44); hence the translation. The parallel dative phraseology in verse 4 (q.v.) should be interpreted in the same way.

Alternatively, but less probably, the phrase may be understood as a dative of association (the incense and prayers ascend to God's throne together, yet without being closely associated; so apparently NRSV); as a dative of reference (the incense is the means by which the prayers are brought before God; Caird 107); or as a dative of advantage (the incense functions as a complement to the prayers of the saints, to make them more pleasing to God (Beckwith 553; Charles 1, 230; Aune 512). The last interpretation grazes the edge of a piacular, or atoning, interpretation of the incense-offering. However, while angels act as mediators in Jewish apocalyptic (cf. *T. Levi* 3.5–6; see also Num. 16.46–47; Dan. 9.20–23; 10.12–14; Sir. 45.16; Wis. 18.21), they do not occupy this role in the theology of Revelation, or indeed of the New Testament generally.

Altar and throne are conjoined in this vision. The prayers are offered, at the same time as the incense, on 'the golden altar in front of the throne'. The expression 'in front of the throne' (ἐνώπιον τοῦ θρόνου, *enōpion tou thronou*) is parallel to the phrase 'to God's presence' (ἐνώπιον τοῦ θεοῦ, *enōpion tou theou*, lit. 'before God') in verse 4; similarly 'the golden altar which stands in God's presence (before God)' at 9.13 (q.v.). See Num. 16.40, where incense is offered 'before the Lord'. These are circumlocutions, replacing a direct reference to God himself. For 'throne', as a symbol of God's absolute sovereignty, see on 4.2; and see the expression 'before the throne' at 4.10. Aune (512) suggests that the 'throne' may be a way of referring to the ark of the Lord; since the ark of the covenant was not far from the altar of incense in the Temple, and seems to have functioned as Yahweh's throne. Ps. 132.1–9, it may be added, is relevant; for there God is invited to go to a resting place in his house: 'you, and the ark of your might' (verse 8).

The imagery of verse 3 is recalled in verse 4. Prayer, incense and sacrifice are once more related (cf. Eph. 5.2), as the smoke of censing and the cries of God's people ascend jointly from the angelic hand (a natural picture, which includes a dramatic stage direction) to the divine presence. During the incense-offering of Israelite worship, coals from the altar would be placed on the firepan, and incense sprinkled on top of the burning embers (cf. verse 5); so e.g. Lev. 16.11–13. There are close links between the scene in Rev. 8.3–4 and *Life of Adam and Eve (Apocalypse)* 33.4. The definite article which introduces the censing angel in verse 4, τοῦ ἀγγέλου (*tou angelou*, lit. '[the hand] of the angel'), is anaphoric, and refers back to the 'other' angel of verse 3 (see also verse 5). This heavenly messenger could be Michael; see *3 Apoc. Bar.* 11.3–4 (Michael descending to receive the prayers of the people); *Apoc. Paul* 43 (Michael standing in God's presence, and praying for the human race).

5 The scene becomes one of judgement, as the offering of incense is followed by an assurance that the prayers of the saints will meet with a divine response. The smoke of incense has risen upwards (even in heaven!) from the angel's hand to God's presence; now the burning coals (without the incense), taken in the censer from the altar, are hurled downwards to the earth. Patterns of ascent and descent are an important part of the literary structure of the Apocalypse, as of the Fourth Gospel. For the angel, the censer and the altar see on verse 3. Fire falling from heaven is a regular symbol of divine judgement in biblical literature (cf. Gen. 19.24; Exod. 19.18; 2 Kings 1.10, 12, 14; Job 1.16; Ps. 11.6; 18.8; Luke 9.54; Heb. 12.29; according to Rev. 1.14; 2.18 the eyes of the exalted Son of man 'flame like fire'). The situation in this episode is reminiscent of Ezek. 10.2, when the prophet sees in his vision burning coals, taken from between the cherubim, scattered over Jerusalem as a mark of God's discrimination. See also Isa. 6.6 (fire taken from the altar by one of the seraphs).

The descent of burning coals from the heavenly altar, combined with the disturbances to nature signalled at the end of verse 5, therefore heralds the visitation of God to his world in judgement and his wrathful reaction to all evil and oppression (see on 6.16–17; and note the similar tokens given with the seventh trumpet-blast [11.19], and the emptying of the seventh bowl of wrath [16.18]; see also Ezek. 1.13). This divine and critical advent is symbolized by the portents which occur on earth, as each of the seven trumpets sounds in the remainder of this scene (8.6—9.19 and also 11.15–19). But these are signs of the end, which both embrace it and point towards it. They do not announce the final judgement (against Beale 457–58), even if they share in its character (see on 6.17; 8.1; and 214, above). In Revelation, the apocalypse is always in progress.

The verb εἴληφεν (*eilēphen*, 'took') is an aoristic perfect (Beckwith 554), which might suggest that the angel had laid aside the censer and now takes it up again; hence Aune's translation (481, 515), 'the angel *received* the censer'. But it is equally likely that this is a pleonasm, and that the word 'took' is simply used to introduce the action of filling the firepan (see the similar use of λαμβάνειν [*lambanein*, 'to take'] at John 19.23). In the phrase, ἐγέμισεν αὐτὸν ἐκ τοῦ πυρὸς τοῦ θυσιαστηρίου (*egemisen auton ek tou pyros tou thysiastēriou*, lit. 'he filled it from the fire of the altar'), the words ἐκ τοῦ πυρός (*ek tou pyros*, lit. 'from the fire') could be construed as a genitive of content. In this case the preposition ἐκ (*ek*, 'from') becomes redundant, and the meaning is 'he filled it with fire'. See a similar genitival form, without the preposition, at John 2.7 ('fill the jars with water'). In the context, however, πῦρ (*pyr*, 'fire') must include the notion of a combustible material (such as coal), which is added to the censer to make the flagration possible (cf. Lev. 10.1 LXX). It is therefore better to understand the genitive in the phrase ἐκ τοῦ πυρός (*ek tou pyros*) as partitive, while functioning as a dative, and to supply an indefinite relative pronoun (cf. John 3.25; also Rev. 2.7; 5.7; et al.). The meaning is then clearer, and takes the preposition ἐκ (*ek*) seriously: the angel filled the censer with '*some* (of the) burning coals (fire) from the altar', as in the translation. See Aune 516–17.

The hurling of the censer, or coals (or both; the Greek is ambiguous), to earth is accompanied by the eruption of cosmic portents. Similar groups can be found at 4.5; 11.19; 16.18. For the order of the phenomena see the textual note, above (205); of the four series, thunder precedes lightning in the present verse (5) alone. The narrative function of the four passages differs to some extent. In 8.5 the disturbances anticipate divine judgement; in 4.5 and 11.19 they are part of a theophany, in which God's sovereign power is disclosed; and in 16.18(–21) they effect the destruction which results from the pouring of the seventh bowl. Each time 'roarings' (φωναί, *phōnai*) are heard. These are distinguished from the sound of thunder; and, in these contexts at least, they may allude to the natural 'roar' of a storm (so BDAG 1071*b*; also Beckwith 554). In 8.13 the word is used for the trumpet-blasts of the angels.

An 'earthquake' (σεισμός, *seismos*) features, as one of the eschatological portents, here and at 11.19; 16.18 (see also 6.12; 11.13). Seismic disturbances have varied significance in theological contexts.

(a) Earthquakes can either anticipate divine judgement, as in 8.5, or (more usually) effect it (16.18–21; cf. also 2 Sam. 22.8; Isa. 24.18–20; Hag. 2.6–7, 21; Heb. 12.26; *Sib. Or.* 3.675–93).

(b) They symbolize the advent of God or his agent (Judg. 5.4; 1 Kings 19.11–12; Ps. 114.7–8; Ezek. 38.19–23; Matt. 28.2).

(c) An earthquake can also be associated with an event, or the promise of an event, which has great significance (Mark 13.8 par., a sign preceding the end; Matt. 27.51–54, cosmic disturbance at the death of Jesus). In the Old Testament, earthquakes are associated with the Exodus tradition (Ps. 77.18; 114.1–8; Hab. 3.6); although seismic phenomena are not mentioned specifically at the time of the Exodus itself. They also form a notable part of the Sinai theophany and its tradition (Exod. 19.18; cf. Ps. 68.8; Isa. 64.1, 3). Both traditions are linked with an earthquake at 4 Ezra 3.17–19.

The earthquake in Rev. 8.5 therefore heralds the coming of God in judgement; and this continual process is illustrated in the scenes which follow. It is an important symbol in Revelation, and not a conventional apocalyptic image. Earthquakes in John's visions explore a range of conceptual associations drawn from the Judaic tradition, and tighten the drama and structure of his composition. See Bauckham, *Climax of Prophecy* 199–209, esp. 202–209. Cf. also Hillyer, 'Shake', esp. 557–58; Aune 517–18.

6   This verse picks up the language and thought of verse 2 (q.v.), and resumes the dramatic action which has been delayed by the censing scene in verses 3–5. The eschatological acts which follow from the sounding of the seven trumpets, about to be blown, express the continous process of divine discrimination. They also point towards the consummation of salvation history in Christ. For the construction of ἵνα (*hina*, 'that') with the subjunctive σαλπίσωσιν (*salpisōsin*, lit. 'they should blow'), instead of an infinitive, see Rev. 6.11; 9.4; et al.

Trumpets 1–4: Portents of the End (8.7–12)

7   The trumpet-calls which follow seem to echo the earlier scene of unsealing the scroll. The seven trumpets divide into two groups of four (8.7–12) and three (9.1–19; 11.15–19), as with the preceding sequence of seven seals in 6.1–8; and 6.9–17; 8.1. The four horsemen in the seal-series of Chapter 6 uncover dark causes which are effected on earth; and the first four trumpets in Chapter 8 herald divine judgement on the world of nature. In both groups, the seals and the trumpets, the fifth and sixth unveilings are separated from the seventh by an intercalation (7.1–17; and 10.1—11.14).

Nevertheless, the trumpet-judgements in 8.7–15 do not follow the seal-judgements of 6.1—8.1 in chronological order; although the teaching of this section of the Apocalypse is in any case more important than its chronology (Efird 69). Nor is there a mere recapitulation of the seal-fracturings in the trumpet-calls (against Hughes 105; cf. Boring 135). First, although the trumpets (like the seals) describe proleptically the tribulations of the end-time, they do so from a different perspective. While the first four seals depict the critical and inevitable results of human wrongdoing, the trumpets disclose God's active participation in judging the world's opposition to him. Second, in the trumpet sequence the plague-judgements are more severe in their effects, and more cosmic in their scope, than is the case with the seal-judgements. The first four plagues are supernatural in character, and two of the last three are explicitly demonic (cf. Sweet 162). There are closer parallels between the series of trumpets and the later septet of bowls (15.1—16.21); see the table in Aune 498.

Although believers must be caught up in the results of the first four disasters, they are protected from the demonic activity which follows (see 9.4, 20–21). It is clear that the disasters ushered in by the trumpets, sounded by the angels, initially affect the *world* more than the Church. The trumpets, like the seals, unveil the character of that unjust society. They reveal the world as it is, and as God sees it, rather than as he intends it to be (contrast Rev. 21—22). The trumpet-blasts are warnings of impending danger (cf. the warning issued to the people, by the sentinel blowing his trumpet, in Ezek. 33.3–6). These calls should lead to a change of heart, but this is not the case (8.13). As the intensity of the judgement increases, so does the fierceness with which the need for repentance is rejected by humanity (9.20–21; 16.9, 11, 21). But the end and the final judgement are not yet. One-third only of the earth is affected by the plagues (8.7, 9, 10, 11, 12); and the trumpets of judgement end with the joy of salvation (11.15–18). After the seventh trumpet, heavenly worship takes place; and this is similar to the praise offered before God and the Lamb in the throne-vision of Chapter 5 (see verses 9–14).

For the marked parallels between this scene and the Exodus narrative in the Old Testament see below; cf. also Beale 465–67. On this section in general see further Beasley-Murray 152–56; Mounce 176–77.

Verse 7 begins with a trumpet-call from the first angel (see the textual note on this verse, above). For the seven angels and their trumpets see on verse 2. With the sounding of this trumpet, the second major series of divine judgements in the drama of Revelation begins. As an immediate response, 'hail and fire, mixed with blood' are hurled down to the earth. The downward movement of the portents which are associated with the first three trumpet-blasts and the fifth is striking. After the seventh (11.15–19), by contrast, the descent motif is balanced by that of ascent, as worship takes place in God's heavenly temple.

The first five trumpets, beginning with 8.7, are broadly patterned according to five of the plagues inflicted on the Egyptians before the Exodus (cf. Beale 465). In this verse, the Old Testament background is to be found in the seventh Egyptian plague of Exod. 9.22–25, where Moses stretches out his hand to heaven, and God sends 'thunder and hail and fire' down on the earth (9.23). See also Ezek. 38.22; Wis. 16.19, 22; and the eschatological, destructive rain of 'fire and blood' mentioned in *Sib. Or.* 5.377–80. One difference between the passages in Exodus and Revelation lies in the agents of destruction. In Exod. 9.13–35 most damage is caused by the hail (see verses 23–25); whereas in Rev. 8.7 the *fire* is responsible for extensive conflagration. This fire is a symbol of divine judgement (see on verse 5). Beale (474–81) argues that the fire in the first three trumpet-calls is an image of famine; and he connects it through the scales, fire and famine of Ezek. 5 (see verses 1–4, 12) with the deprivation signalled in Rev. 6.5–6 (the third seal). See also the link between famine and fire in Rev. 18.8.

The reference to 'blood', mixed with the hail and fire, may be an allusion to the first Egyptian plague, where the river Nile turns to blood (Exod. 7.14–25); similarly with the waters turning to blood in verse 8. So Sweet 163; Swete (110) suggests that the seer's phenomenon of blood-red rain may have been influenced by the fact that, in the Mediterranean, the air can become filled with particles of red sand from the Sahara. But John's consistent use of Old Testament and Judaic sources, and his deliberate indebtedness to the Exodus narrative in this scene, makes it much more likely that the Egyptian plagues are in mind at this point (cf. Mounce 178 n. 10). A further Jewish background may be located in Joel 2.30–31 (cf. Acts 2.19–20), where the prophet speaks of 'blood and fire' (Joel 2.30) as portents of the last days. In Rev. 8.7 the image of hail and fire, mixed with blood, is presumably also informed by the fiery-red colour of catastrophic storms before they break. The description of these judgements being 'hurled down to the earth' (ἐβλήθη εἰς τὴν γῆν, *eblēthē eis tēn gēn*) is similar to the action portrayed in verse 5 (the angel hurling the censer of burning coals 'down to the earth'). But the agents are different, as are the judgements involved. Here, the Greek verb ἐβλήθη (*eblēthē*, lit. 'was thrown'), in the aorist passive, is a collective singular.

The effect of the storm on the natural world, in this trumpet-judgement, is devastating. One-third of the land and its vegetable life is consumed by fire. An obvious backcloth to this situation is to be found in Zech. 13.8–9, where the prophet declares that two-thirds of the people of the land are to perish, and one-third will survive the fire of refinement. See also Ezek. 5.12 (one-third of Jerusalem will die of pestilence or famine, one-third will perish by the sword, and one-third will be scattered to every wind). Beale (474) notes that *Sib. Or.* 3.539–44 reflects on this text in Ezekiel, and adds to the forthcoming eschatological disasters drought, a 'lack of sowing and ploughing' (line 542), and 'much lamented fire on the earth' (line 543). This confirms Beale's claim that the burning fire of Rev. 8.7 is a metaphorical portrayal of judgement by famine.

John uses the expression 'one-third' (τὸ τρίτον, *to triton*, with the genitive) insistently in this passage (12 times between verses 7 and 12; cf. also 9.15, 18; 12.4). The fraction cannot be taken literally. It rather indicates that God's judgement is not yet final. This visitation is an admonition: signs in the heavens will precede the end (Luke 21.25–26), and repentance is demanded in the meantime (see Rev. 9.20–21). The repeated κατεκάη (*katekaē*, 'consumed by fire', lit. 'burned [up]') lends to verse 7 'the aura of a prophetic oracle' (Mounce 178 n. 11). The form of that verb is the equivalent of κατεκαύθη (*katekauthē*, with the same meaning); cf. 1 Cor. 3.15; 2 Pet. 3.10 (in A, et al.).

In the present context γῆ (*gē*) means 'land (or soil)', as opposed to the sea (verses 8–9) or inland waters (verses 10–11). The 'forests' (δένδρα, *dendra*, lit. 'trees') probably include fruit trees (olive, fig, vine), on which the inhabitants of Palestine and Asia Minor depended so heavily for their livelihood (cf. Matt. 7.17–19; Jude 12). 'Every blade of green grass' (πᾶς χόρτος χλωρός, *pas chortos chlōros*, lit. 'all green grass') should be broadened in meaning to embrace 'all vegetation' (Swete 111); cf. Mark 6.39. The contrast between *all* grass, and *one-third* of land and trees, may indicate nothing more than a desire for literary variation; cf. 'people in large numbers', verse 11 (so Sweet 163). The eschatological portents listed in verse 7, and indeed those which follow the next three trumpets, affect humanity as well as nature. In such an apocalyptic vision as this, the burning of the forests and every blade of grass is not at variance with the command not to harm the fields and trees, issued at 9.4 after the fifth trumpet has been blown.

8–9 The second trumpet-call continues the theme of judgement which marks the first. The initial plague scorched one-third of the land, and the next causes the destruction of a third of the sea. A huge mountain, 'blazing with fire' (πυρὶ καιόμενον, *pyri kaiomenon*), is hurled downwards into the waters. The descent motif reappears, as the phrase ἐβλήθη εἰς τὴν θάλασσαν (*eblēthē eis tēn thalassan*, 'was hurled into the sea'), in verse 8, balances an almost identical expression in the Greek of verse 7, with reference to hail and fire, mixed with blood, being 'hurled down to the earth' (ἐβλήθη εἰς τὴν γῆν, *eblēthē eis tēn gēn*). Fire is mentioned in each of the first three trumpet-plagues: a violent storm sets the earth ablaze (verse 7); a fiery mountain is thrown into the sea (verse 8); and a burning star is dropped on the rivers and springs. These pictures may pick up the action of the angel hurling incandescent coals to the earth in verse 5 (Mounce 180); but the situations are in any case different (see on verse 7).

Some commentators locate the background to the image of the blazing mass in the literal volcanic activity which took place in the Mediterranean world of the first century, such as the major eruption of Mount Vesuvius in August AD 79 (Swete 111; cf. Mounce 179; Aune 519–20). But the date of Revelation adopted in this commentary is AD 70; and, in any case, the typical source of John's material at this point is much more likely to be found in Jewish apocalyptic. In *1 Enoch* 18.13, for example, during the hero's portentous tour of Sheol, earth and heaven, there is an allusion in the judgement of the fallen angels to stars which looked like 'great, burning mountains'; cf. also *1 Enoch* 21.3–7; 108.3–6; *Sib. Or.* 5.512–31. Beale (475–76) suggests, interestingly and plausibly, that the blazing mountain in verse 8 is a metaphorical reference to a kingdom which is judged. See on 6.14; also 14.1; 17.9; 21.10 (mountains as the territory of rulers); and cf. 1.14; 3.18; 8.7; 13.13; 14.10, 18; et al. (fire in the Apocalypse as a symbol of judgement).

In Rev. 18.21 a mighty angel throws a stone of judgement (18.20) into the sea, and this denotes the fall of Babylon (18.21–24). All these elements (mountain, fire and stone) are brought together in the further background of Jer. 51, where stone and burning mountain become metaphors for Babylon undergoing judgement (see esp. verses 25–26, 63–64; and the presence of a sounding trumpet at verse 27). This evidence reinforces Beale's conclusion (476) that in Rev. 8.8. the blazing mountain hurled into the sea represents the judgement of a wicked kingdom, in this case Babylon (= Rome). A visionary experience, such as the one described by the seer in Rev. 8.8–9 (and elsewhere), is likely to gather ideas and images from a variety of sources, and transpose them creatively into a 'totally new figure' (Mounce 179).

The descent into the sea of what looked like a huge mountain, blazing with fire (the non-literal object, and not the agent, of God's judgement), results in phenomena which are devastatingly, but not completely, destructive; and they recall the portents in verse 7 (q.v.). The καί (*kai*, 'and') at this point, hidden in the translation, is consecutive. Further eschatological judgement is depicted as taking place. A third part of the waters turned into blood, so that some of the living creatures in the sea died (for the thrice-repeated τὸ τρίτον [*to triton*, 'the third'], in verses 8–9, see on verse 7). This portent alludes directly to Exod. 7.20–24, the first Egyptian plague, in which the river Nile (rather than the sea itself, however) became blood, the marine life died and the water became undrinkable; in this way, the Exodus motif in the present passage is recapitulated (see verse 7). Now, as then, the trumpet-plagues provide a warning of divine judgement to come.

Beale (477) discovers in the three catastrophes of verses 8–9, together with the image of fire in verse 8*a*, a further allusion to severe famine conditions. In his view, the pollution of the sea waters, the consequent death of sea life and the destruction of sea vessels, denote a partial but serious hindrance to maritime commerce, and a grave limitation of formerly rich economic resources. This anticipates the description in 18.11–19 of the total destruction of 'Babylon, the great city'. The seer predicts that, like Rome or any other focus of injustice and opposition to the goodness of God, the former centre of commercial prosperity will in the future experience divine wrath and purgative discrimination.

In verse 9, τὰ ἔχοντα (*ta echonta*, lit. 'those having [life]') is a solecism. That participial expression is in the nominative, in apposition to τῶν κτισμάτων (*tōn ktismatōn*, 'the creatures'); whereas it should be in the genitive, as modifying the same noun. The verb διεφθάρησαν (*diephtharēsan*, 'destroyed') is a third person plural second aorist passive, although its subject is the singular substantive τὸ τρίτον (*to triton*, 'the third'). However, the writer construes 'third' as a collective noun, which can take a plural verb form; see similarly Rev. 7.9; 9.18; 13.3–4; 18.4; 19.1.

10–11   The sounding of the trumpet by the third angel releases from the sky a 'great star, burning like a torch'; and, as a result of this action, the inland rivers and springs are contaminated, and people die in large numbers (see also 6.12–13). The image of fresh water being polluted continues the Exodus theme, and the eschatological warning inherent in the plagues, which runs right through this section (8.7—9.11). As in verse 8 (q.v.) the first Egyptian plague, in which the Nile turns to blood (Exod. 7.14–24), stands in the background to verses 10 and 11 (note Exod. 7.20; and see 7.19, where 'rivers, canals, ponds and pools of water' are affected; cf. also Ps. 78.44). The picture of a burning star, falling from heaven, may have been inspired by the notion of a meteorite (as an omen of destruction) catching fire as it plunges through the earth's atmosphere (Mounce 180). Like the blood-red, violent storm of verse 7, and the huge, blazing mountain of verse 8, the star is a symbol of divine visitation and impending crisis. Parallels with Persian eschatology (Moffatt 405; Beckwith 557) are difficult to establish; cf. Charles 1, 235.

Beale (478–79) understands the fire of verse 10 (a great star, 'burning like a torch') as a further metaphor of famine (see also on verses 7–9). He notes that elsewhere in the Apocalypse stars act as angelic beings (cf. 1.19); angels stand for people and kingdoms; while fire symbolizes divine judgement (see on verse 8). So here, in Beale's view, John is depicting the judgement of a (fallen) angel who represents a sinful community: such as Babylon (as in verse 8). See Isa. 24.21; also *1 Enoch* 18.13, 15; 21.3 (stars like burning mountains); 86–88 (the punishment of the fallen stars). If verse 10 alludes to Isa. 14.12–15, the identification of the falling star as Babylon's representative angel becomes more convincing (Beale 479; see also Caird 115; Sweet 163–64); for in that Isaianic passage the judgement of the ruler of Babylon and his nation occurs because its guardian angel ('the Day Star') has fallen from heaven ('the mount of assembly, above the stars', verse 13) down to the depths of Sheol. See also *Sib. Or.* 5.158–59. The star in Rev. 8.10, like the star-angel of 9.11, we may conclude, is an aspect of Satan, rather than the Satan himself (for that identification see Luke 10.18; cf. also Rev. 12.1–12); so Sweet 164. John presents us in this scene as a whole with a vision of the final judgement which the unjust and wrongdoers, represented by their angelic star, experience at any point in time, and up to the brink of eternity.

That only 'the third' (τὸ τρίτον, *to triton*) of the waters are included in the action, here and at verse 11, involves the concept of a crisis which is delayed in order to allow time for repentance (see on verses 7–9). In verses 8–9 a triplet of 'thirds' appears; in verses 7 and 10–11 the triplet is interrupted, probably for reasons of literary variation, by an inclusive 'all' or 'many'; and in verse 12 the triplet becomes a quintuplet (except that the fourth and fifth members are consecutive extensions of the first three). In verse 10b the burning star falling 'on' (ἐπί, *epi*) the rivers and fresh springs must mean that the luminary *affected* the inland waters (Aune 521). By implication from verse 11, a third of these rivers and springs were polluted (see above). Springs in the ancient world were associated with supernatural spirits, and even demons (Moffatt 405). For the Greek expression πηγὰς τῶν ὑδάτων (*pēgas tōn hydatōn*, 'fresh-water springs', lit. 'springs of waters') see the virtual parallels at Rev. 7.17; 21.6. But in those contexts the symbol of water is modified by the idea of spiritual 'life', as a gift bestowed in answer to Christian faithfulness. In 8.10 the waters are those of suffering and death (see verse 11), representing the spiritual deprivation caused by opposition to God in any form.

The falling star is called 'Apsinth' (verse 11). The plant ἄψινθος (*apsinthos*, 'apsinth') belongs to the genus *Artemisia*. It is proverbially bitter to the taste, and produces a dark green oil which can be used medicinally to kill intestinal worms; hence the translation 'wormwood' (as in NRSV, et al.). So BDAG 161b. The name is given to the falling star of verse 10 because of its effect on the waters, making them taste bitter. Although apsinth itself is not poisonous, water contaminated by the herb can lead to death if drunk over a long period (Beale 479). As well as recalling the Exodus plague of polluted waters (Exod. 7.14–24), the judgement scene in Rev. 8.10–11 derives from Jer. 9.15; 23.15 (the Lord will feed faithless Israel 'with wormwood', and give the people 'poisonous water to drink'). This pollution came about because the religious leaders contaminated the nation with their idolatrous Baal-worship (Jer. 9.13–14); so, in John's vision, God will bring the bitterness of suffering on those outside the covenant, and on those within who do not take its demands seriously (see also trumpets four and five). Once more, famine may be included in this act of discrimination (cf. Rev. 8.7–9); so Beale (479), appealing to Jer. 8.13–14, 19.

As with the first two plagues, human beings as well as nature are affected by divine judgement: 'people died in large numbers from drinking the poisoned water'. This is the reverse of the miracle at Marah, where Moses threw a piece of wood into the bitter water, and the water became sweet (Exod. 15.25). The seer's language in this passage of the Apocalypse is manifestly figurative. Apart from the texts from Jeremiah already cited, 'wormwood' regularly appears elsewhere in the Old Testament as a metaphor of bitterness, and the severe affliction which stems from the wrath of God. See Deut. 29.17–18 (in association with idolatry); Prov. 5.3–4; Lam. 3.15, 19; Amos 5.7; 6.12; cf. Hos. 10.4. Note also the symbolic reference to 'bitterness', meaning judgement, at Rev. 10.10 (using the same verb, πικραίνω [*pikrainō*, 'to make bitter'], as in 8.11). In 4 Ezra 6.22–24 trumpet-blasts, as throughout Rev. 8, introduce a judgement including famine, and affecting 'the springs of the fountains' (verse 24; cf. *Apoc. Abr.* 31.1–8; Zech. 9.14, where trumpets announce an eschatological fire which destroys the ungodly).

The scope of the judgement following the third trumpet-blast is limited: only a third of the waters are harmed, and a further chance of forgiveness is allowed (see on τὸ τρίτον [*to triton*, 'the third'] in verses 7–10). John's allusion to people dying 'in large numbers' (πολλοί, *polloi*, lit. 'many') may be regarded as a stylistic variation (see above, on verse 7). Contrast *Sib. Or.* 4.171–77, which refers to a trumpet-call heralding a total crisis, embracing the whole earth, the entire human race, all cities and rivers, and the sea. The preposition ἐκ (*ek*, 'from'), in the phrase ἐκ τῶν ὑδάτων (*ek tōn hydatōn*, lit. 'from the waters') may be construed causally: people died 'on account of the water', since it had been poisoned. The same is true of the following ὅτι (*hoti*, 'because [the water had been poisoned]'). The subject of ἐπικράνθησαν (*epikranthēsan*, lit. 'they became bitter'), the third person plural aorist passive verb in the final subordinate clause, is τῶν ὑδάτων (*tōn hydatōn*, lit. 'of the waters'). This is carried over from the preceding clause, so that, strictly speaking, the subject of the verb is unexpressed. The use of third person plural verbs without a directly expressed subject is a common grammatical feature in Revelation (cf. 7.11; 9.15; 16.9; et al.).

12 The fourth trumpet-plague continues the theme of divine judgement associated with the first three (see on verses 7–11), and involves the interruption of cosmic illumination. But once again the discrimination is partial, and opportunities for saving judgement are evidently still available (for τὸ τρίτον, *to triton*, 'the third', see above). Understanding the first half of the verse in parallel with the earlier plagues suggests that, as a result of the sun, moon and stars being forcefully struck, their light was lowered by one-third. Possibly the writer is thinking of these luminaries as torches, which can gradually burn out; alternatively John may be thinking of an eclipse, when the light of heavenly planets is partially obscured (see Amos 8.9; Aune 522). The Greek word ἐπλήγη (*eplēgē*) is from the verb πλήσσω (*plēssō*), which means not merely 'to strike', but (intensively) 'to strike with force'. The term occurs only here in the New Testament; in the LXX of Exod. 9.31–32 it is used of the destructive effect of the hail on crops (cf. also Ps. 101.5 LXX). The source of the blow to the sun, moon and stars is not disclosed, and literal detail is in any case unimportant in this apocalyptic scene. But, as throughout verse 12, the action of darkness is clearly caused by God. At every stage of the trumpet sequence he holds the final authority, even over eschatological disasters (Knight 76).

By contrast, the last two phrases of verse 12, 'a third of daylight (ἡ ἡμέρα, *hē hēmera*, lit. "the day") was not visible (μὴ φάνῃ, *mē phanē*, lit. "did not shine"), and similarly with night-time (ἡ νύξ, *hē nyx*, lit. "the night")', suggest a total absence of light for a third part of both day and night. Absolute darkness of this kind would be dramatic, and far more terrifying than a partial eclipse (Mounce 181; against Aune 522). It recalls the Exodus theme, which runs through this passage. In the ninth Egyptian plague dense darkness spread over the land for three days, so that people (other than the Israelites) could neither move nor see each other (Exod. 10.21–23). The plagues of the Exodus included judgement on false gods (Exod. 12.12); and God's opposition to unfaithfulness in the form of the wrong use of imperial power, or compromise with it, may be in mind at Rev. 8.12. See also, and similarly, Ezek. 32.7–8.

The writer of Wisdom (first century BC–AD) reflects on the plague narratives of Exodus, and sees them (and darkness in particular) as theological images of judgement on the Egyptians, because of their idolatry and oppression of God's people (cf. Wis. 15.1—16.29; 17.1–21; 18.3–4). In the same way, John probably sees the plague of darkness in the present verse as a symbol of divine reaction to idolatry in any form, and to the suffering inflicted by Rome on the saints (cf. Beale 482). But this judgement could also be directed at unfaithfulness and error within the community, as well as beyond it. The figurative language of 8.12 is echoed in 12.1–4 (q.v.), where satanic deception again includes members of the covenant community (verse 4) as well as angels in heaven (12.9). Cf. Beale 482–83. The plague of darkness in Rev. 8.12 is closely paralleled at 6.12–13, where cosmic disturbance similarly introduces judgement on falsehood and wrong-doing of every kind.

A further background to the phenomenon of cosmic darkness which follows the fourth trumpet-call (verse 12) may be located in the Creation narrative of Genesis 1, where it is said that God created the sun, moon and stars in the dome of the sky on the *fourth* day (verses 14–19, esp. 16); cf. Aune 523. If so, John may intend the diminishment of light in the universe not simply to represent a warning judgement on sinful humanity, but also to act as a precursor of the heavenly light and life which will be a reward for the faithful in the *new* creation; for at the end the sun and moon disappear, and the light of the eternal city is to be found in God himself and in the Lamb (so Rev. 21.22—22.5). However, darkness is a regular symbol of judgement and destruction in the Old Testament and in the literature of Qumran. See Isa. 13.10 = Mark 13.24 (the sun, moon and stars will not give their light); Joel. 2.1–2; and Amos 5.18 (the day of the Lord is a day of darkness); 1QM 13.5–6 (the lot of Belial and his wicked followers is darkness, but the lot of God is everlasting light); et al. In the New Testament darkness is also associated with demonic power. See 2 Cor. 6.14–15 (light and darkness are placed in parallel with Christ and Belial[r]); also Matt. 8.12; Col. 1.13; (2.13–15). In Johannine thought and theology beyond the Apocalypse the contrast between darkness and light, as an image for the difference between death and life, is a characteristic feature (cf. John 1.4–5; 8.12; 9.4–5; 11.9–10; 12.35–36; 13.30; et al.; 1 John 1.5–7; 2.8–11).

The Eagle's Warning (8.13)

13 In Rev. 8.12 the darkness of the fourth plague provides the transition from divine warnings to demonic woes, as in this verse (Mounce 182). The flight of the eagle provides a brief interlude before the sounding of the last three trumpets, just as there is an interval (somewhat longer) between the sixth and seventh trumpet-calls (see also on 8.1). For καὶ εἶδον (*kai eidon*, 'in my vision', lit. 'and I saw') see on 5.1. The vision is accompanied by a voice. 'Seeing' and 'hearing', often linked together, are important theological concepts in the Apocalypse (cf. Rev. 4.1; 5.11; 6.1; et al.), as elsewhere in the Johannine corpus. For 'sight', related to 'faith', in the Gospel of John see Smalley, *John* 175–76. Strictly speaking, the seer does not 'hear' the eagle flying in midheaven; what he 'hears' is the subsequent human voice of the bird, speaking on behalf of God.

The word ἀετός (*aetos*) means 'eagle', as a symbol of swiftness and strength; in other contexts (such as Matt. 24.28 = Luke 17.37) it refers to the predatory vulture (cf. Rev. 19.17–18, the angel calling to the birds that fly in midheaven to gather for the great supper of God). See also the fourth living creature, like an eagle in flight, at 4.7; also 12.14 (the woman is given the wings of the great eagle). In the phrase ἑνὸς ἀετοῦ (*henos aetou*, 'an eagle', lit. 'one eagle'), in verse 13, ἑνός (*henos*, 'one'), the genitive singular from εἷς (*heis*, 'one'), functions as an indefinite article (cf. 9.13; 18.21; 19.17). The eagle was regarded in classical thought as the messenger of Zeus (Aune 523). A speaking eagle appears as part of a vision at 4 Ezra 11.7–9; and in *2 Apoc. Bar.* 77.17–26 an eagle is sent to the exiled Israelites in Babylon with a letter containing the author's prophecy. For angels with the appearance of eagles see *3 Enoch* (2.1); 26.3; 44.5. For '(in) midheaven' ([ἐν] μεσουρανήματι, *[en] mesouranēmati*) see also 14.6; 19.17. The verb μεσουρανεῖν (*mesouranein*) means 'to be at the zenith (of the sun)' (BDAG 635*b*).

The eagle is heard 'calling aloud' (λέγοντος φωνῇ μεγάλῃ (*legontos phōnē[i] megalē[i]*, lit. 'speaking with a loud voice'; cf. 5.12; 14.7, 9; et al.) to the earth as it flies. God's messenger announces a series of three disasters which are to fall on the world's inhabitants. The eagle does not effect the judgements, since these are again introduced by angelic trumpet-calls (9.1, 13; 11.15); but because the creature is hovering in midair, and crying out with a loud voice, everyone can see and hear the warnings of judgemental woe to come. For reference to the eagle as an image of destruction in the Old Testament see Deut. 28.49; Jer. 48.40; Lam. 4.19; Ezek. 17.3; Hab. 1.8; et al.

In Rev. 18.10, 16, 19 the exclamation 'woe' is repeated twice for literary emphasis. Here the triplet corresponds to the remaining three trumpets; although the third woe is not specifically related to the final sounding (see on 11.14; cf. also 9.12; 12.12). The plagues which they herald (more positively at 11.15–19) affect people themselves, and not just (as with the first four) the *sources* of human life. They fall on 'the earth's inhabitants' (τοὺς κατοικοῦντας ἐπὶ τῆς γῆς, *tous katoikountas epi tēs gēs*, lit. 'those living on the earth'); and this implies that the divine judgements will afflict those in opposition to God, rather than believers. In 6.10 (q.v.) this phrase has such a technical sense; see also 3.10; 11.10 (*bis*); 13.8, 14 (*bis*); 17.8. Ethical disorder seems to produce cosmic disorder. In contrast, the sealed saints are protected from the imminent plague of locusts (9.4).

The word 'disaster' (οὐαί, *ouai*, lit. 'woe') is rarely used with the accusative in Greek literature, and in Revelation only here and at 12.12 (see also the textual notes on verse 13). The term derives from the Hebrew interjections אוֹי (*'ôy*) and הוֹי (*'hôy*), meaning 'woe' (as in 1 Kings 13.30; Isa. 3.9; Jer. 22.13; and frequently in the prophets). In the LXX the term occurs 73 times (e.g. Num. 21.29; Judith 16.17; Prov. 23.29; Ezek. 7.26; Zeph. 2.5). In the sentence '(disaster) because of the remaining trumpet-blasts', the preposition ἐκ (*ek*, lit. 'from'), with the genitive, has a causal force (hence 'because', in the translation); similarly verse 11. For the (remaining) 'trumpets' and 'angels' in verse 13 see on 8.2, 6. This verse has allowed us to hold our breaths, in dramatic anticipation of the further apocalyptic disclosures and signs of the end which are about to be made.

Trumpet 5 (First Woe): Locusts (9.1–12)

9.1 The vision of coming judgements continues with an angelic sounding of the fifth trumpet. John does not see a star actually falling from heaven, but witnesses the effects of its descent; the verb 'had dropped' (πεπτωκότα, *peptōkota*, lit. 'had fallen') is in form a perfect active participle, modifying ἀστέρα (*astera*, 'star'). For καὶ εἶδον (*kai eidon*, 'and I saw') see verse 13, and on 5.1. It was an accepted element of Judaic cosmology that stars were living beings, who possessed a conscious personal nature (Beckwith 560). See Judg. 5.20; Job 38.6–7; Dan. 8.10. Elsewhere in Jewish literature falling stars can symbolize evil angelic beings or demons (cf. *1 Enoch* 18.15–16; 21.6; 86.3; 88.1, 3; 90.24; *T. Sol.* 20.14–17; also Jude 13), and occasionally Satan himself (*1 Enoch* 86.1; *Apoc. Elijah* 4.11–12; Luke 10.18; see also Rev. 12.9; and on 6.13; 8.10–11). Here (9.1) the fallen star has a more positive character, representing not the angel of the abyss (9.11, q.v.) or Satan (12.9), but an angelic messenger of God, sent to earth as an agent of divine judgement (see verses 3–11). Note the parallel with *Sib. Or.* 5.155–61; and the similar figure at Rev. 20.1.

That the 'star dropped from the sky' is a supernatural being becomes clear from the remainder of this verse, and the next. The abrupt movement from the form of a star to that of a person is characteristic of the seer's literary style (cf. 1.16–17; 17.9–10; 20.12). The star-angel was given a key to the entrance of the bottomless pit. The use of the definite article twice, in the phrase τοῦ φρέατος τῆς ἀβύσσου (*tou phreatos tēs abyssou*, lit. 'of *the* shaft of *the* abyss'), shows that the concept of the 'bottomless pit (abyss)', and its opening, would be well-known to John's readers. The Greek word ἄβυσσος (*abyssos*, 'abyss') means literally 'without depth'; and in ancient mythology it refers to an infinite, subterranean region. In the lxx the term usually translates the Hebrew תְּהוֹם(*tᵉhôm*, 'deep sea', 'gulf'), as in Gen.1.2; Job 28.14; 36.16 (cf. Sir. 1.3; 16.18); and occasionally the word means 'underground waters', or 'the deep hollows of the earth' (so Deut. 8.7; Ps. 71.20; *1 Enoch* 17.7–8; *T. Levi* 3.9; *Pss. Sol.* 17.19; *Jub.* 2.2, 16). The idea of a 'bottomless pit' is sometimes used to represent the underworld, meaning the dwelling-place of the dead (Ps. 71.20; 88.6; [lxx 87.7]; *Jos. As.* 15.12; Rom. 10.7), and the location of imprisoned demons (*1 Enoch* 18–21 [see 21.7 Greek]; *Jub.* 10.7 [Greek fragment]; Luke 8.31). See further Charles 1, 240–42.

In Revelation the image of the 'abyss' appears seven times: here, and at 9.2, 11; 11.7; 17.8; 20.1, 3. In Rev. 9.1–11 the bottomless pit is the abode of locust-demons; the beast rises from the abyss in 11.7; and 17.8; and it is the dwelling-place of the angel of the pit, Abaddon or Apollyon (9.11), and of Satan (20.1–3). In Rev. 9.1–11 and 20.1–3 a cosmology on three levels is presupposed. In this verse (9.1) an angel-star descends from heaven to earth (balancing the movement of the eagle flying in midheaven, 8.13), and is given the key to the entrance of the abyss. A similar cosmic arrangement is implied at 20.1–3. In the throne-vision of Rev. 5 the three regions of heaven, earth and underneath the earth are mentioned, without using the term 'abyss' (verse 3); similarly, the four realms of heaven, earth, underneath the earth and the sea appear at 5.13. The three-decker universe features elsewhere in the Apocalypse in terms of heaven, earth and sea (10.6, q.v.; 12.12; 14.7; 21.1). In Johannine theology, heaven and earth are consistently conjoined through Christ (cf. John 1.51).

The term φρέαρ (*phrear*, 'shaft') occurs in the Apocalypse only in 9.1 and 2 (four times), where it stands for an opening leading to the depths of the nether world. In John 4.11–12 it means a 'well', the vertical shaft used to convey a supply of water (cf. Luke 14.5). These are the only appearances of the word in the New Testament. In Rev. 20.1 a descending angel holds in his hand a 'key' (κλείς, *kleis*, as in 9.1) to the bottomless pit. In the present verse the angelic messenger is given (by God) the key to the *shaft* of the abyss; and, by implication, this entrance can be locked or unlocked (see verse 2). For keys as a symbol of divine authority in the Apocalypse, in association with the exalted Son of man, see 1.18; 3.7. For καὶ ἐδόθη αὐτῷ (*kai edothē autō*, lit. 'and [the key] was given to him [the star-angel]'), as a passive of divine permission, see on 6.2–8; 7.2; 13.5; et al.; see also the passive verbs in 9.3–5.

2   For the imagery of the first sentence see verse 1. The shaft to the underworld, the location of demons, is represented as a locked door, to which God alone has the key (Aune 526–27). The star-angel is here delegated with divine authority, to unlock the entrance to the bottomless pit. As long as the shaft is sealed, it is implied, earth-dwellers are protected from the demonic powers below (see also verse 4); for the abyss is the place of chaos and destruction, harbouring forces of darkness and death (cf. *1 Enoch* 108.3–6). The pit is also a place of tormenting fires (ibid.; also *1 Enoch* 18.11; 21.7). When the 'subterranean smokestack' (Wall 128) is opened, therefore, clouds of smoke pour out; and agents of terror are released through the shaft to wreak their havoc on the earth.

The dense smoke, as from 'a great furnace' (ὡς καπνὸς καμίνου μεγάλης, *hōs kapnos kaminou megalēs*, lit. 'as the smoke of a great furnace'), rises up from the abyss. This scene recalls the description of God's descent on Mount Sinai (Exod. 19.16–24), when the mountain was wrapped in smoke because of the theophany, and (verse 18) the smoke went up 'like the smoke of a kiln' (LXX ὡς καπνὸς καμίνου, *hōs kapnos kaminou*). As the smoke ascends from the shaft (the upward movement balances the pattern of descent in verse 1), it obscures the sun and darkens the atmosphere. The noun ὁ ἀήρ (*ho aēr*, 'the atmosphere', lit. 'air') is probably used in a neutral sense, with its obvious meaning. It should not be connected with the 'ruler of the power of the air' (τοῦ ἀέρος, *tou aeros*) at Eph. 2.2 (so Mounce 186 n. 10).

The episode of the fifth trumpet-call has an Old Testament parallel in the eighth Egyptian plague of locusts (Exod. 10.1–20), the dense swarm of which blackened the landscape (verse 15). But its elaboration in this scene of Revelation (9.1–11) owes more to the description of the locust-judgement in the prophecy of Joel (Beasley-Murray 159). The plague of locusts, according to Joel 2.10, causes the sun, moon and stars to be darkened; and these heavenly portents, together with blood and fire and smoke, are signs of judgement, and heralds of the coming day of the Lord (2.30–31; 3.15; cf. Isa. 13.10; Mark 13.24–25).

In Rev. 8.12 the light from the sun, moon and stars was diminished as a result of God's direct action. Here, the sun and the atmosphere become overcast because of the smoke pouring out of the bottomless pit; although, like the attacking locusts themselves (verses 3–6), the demonic realm remains under the ultimate authority of the Lord. There is no need to interpret the fire and the darkness in this scene in sophisticated terms, such as the cumulative power of evil (Caird 119) or the pervasive influence of Satan in society (Hughes 109). Both elements are straightforward symbols of divine judgement on human wrongdoing, as with the 'darkness' of 6.12; and 8.12; although it is true that, throughout the Johannine corpus, darkness is also a metaphor for spiritual blindness (e.g. Rev. 21.25; John 1.5; 1 John 2.11). Verse 2 demonstrates that the divine judgement, which was previously limited to the demonic region, is now being extended to the earthly realm (Beale 494).

Verbs of 'darkening' are used only three times in Revelation (8.12; 9.2; 16.10). In the present context ἐσκοτώθη (*eskotōthē*, '[was] darkened', v.l.) is in the singular, because the verb agrees (as it would normally) with the number of the first subject (ὁ ἥλιος, *ho hēlios*, 'the sun') which follows.

3   The dense smoke from the shaft resolves itself into a swarm of locusts, which are further described in verses 7–11 (cf. Moffatt 406). These are clearly demonic in character since, like the beast itself, they arise from the infernal abyss (see 11.7; 17.8); and their leader is the angel of the bottomless pit itself (9.11). Behind this scene stand the judgemental plague traditions associated with the Exodus (see on verse 2). Note Exod. 10.1–20 (the eighth plague of locusts); Joel 1.2—2.11; also Ps. 78.46; 105.34–35; Amos 4.9; *Jub.* 48.5; Wis. 16.9; 17.3–21 (darkness over idolaters). Locusts are also mentioned in eschatological contexts which have no direct connection with the Exodus plagues (cf. *3 Apoc. Bar.* 16.3; *Sib. Or.* 5.454; Hermas, *Vis.* 4.1.6). In other Old Testament texts the locust is a symbol of destruction (Deut. 28.42; 1 Kings 8.37).

Here, the locusts 'spread over the earth' (ἐξῆλθον ἀκρίδες εἰς τὴν γῆν, *exēlthon akrides eis tēn gēn*, lit. 'came locusts on the earth'). The phraseology is reminiscent of the eighth Egyptian plague, where a dense swarm of locusts 'covered the surface of the whole land' so that it became black (Exod. 10.14–15). The desert locust, a migratory phase of the grasshopper (BDAG 39*a*), often and even today provides the poor with food (cf. the apparent diet of John the Baptist, according to Mark 1.6). Together, locusts invade cultivated terrain in search of food. They travel in columns several feet deep, and up to four miles in length, stripping the earth of all its vegetation. So, according to Exod. 10.(12), 15, the plague-locusts 'ate all the plants in the land', and nothing green was left. In the present context, however, as the following verses (4–6) indicate, their mission of judgement is to harm *people*, rather than to destroy the creation.

The locusts in the fifth trumpet-plague are given a scorpionlike power to torment earth-dwellers. For καὶ ἐδόθη αὐτοῖς ἐξουσία (*kai edothē autois exousia*, 'they were granted power') see on verse 1 (also 6.2; et al.). The verb in the passive, ἐδόθη (*edothē*, lit. 'there was given [to them]'), is a circumlocution which avoids using the direct name of God. It shows that the authority and power of the locusts is derived from the Lord of the universe (so also 2 Chron. 7.13), and that, as in the Exodus, he is in sovereign control of the critical progress of history and its outworking. The activity which emanates from the sounding of the trumpets is that of saving judgement; and it is ultimately divine (similarly verses 1 and 2).

The scorpion, a species of vermin (an arachnid, four to five inches long), was common in southern latitudes, and much feared because of its sting. This is administered by the end of its tail; and the effect of the poison which it secretes brings about torment, more than death (see verses 5–6). The hostility of scorpions to human beings becomes in the New Testament a symbol of the forces of spiritual evil (Luke 10.19; cf. Sir. 39.29–30). The locusts in the present trumpet-plague are granted such 'power' as is possessed by these creatures: not just 'over the land' but also over its inhabitants. Their consequent and redoubled 'authority' is not a quality which demands respect, but the ability to induce demonic fear, and indeed to terrorize. Beale (495) suggests that a further background to this passage in Revelation may be located in the concept of a 'demoralizing enemy', surrounded by smoke, at Isa. 14.29–31.

4–5   The plague of demonic locusts contributes to the seer's vision a further eschatological image of advancing judgement, which may overtake the unfaithful at any time. Their terrifying duty is to attack those who are not protected by God's love. The introductory καί (*kai*, lit. 'and') in verse 4 has an adversative force. The locusts could have destroyed the earth (which is mentioned twice in verse 3), but they were forbidden to do so; hence the translation, 'however'. The source of the injunction is not specified; but it is clearly divine. The verbal construction, καὶ ἐρρέθη αὐτοῖς (*kai errethē autois*, 'however, they were told', lit. 'and it was told to them') is another example of the passive voice being used as a circumlocution for the name of God or his angelic agent (see on verse 3; also 6.1–8). As with the release of the locusts (the star-angel was given the key of the shaft, verse 1), their enabling (they were granted power, verse 3) and their restriction (they were to torment, but not allowed to kill, verse 5), the limitation of the plague to the human and not the natural environment in this verse (4) indicates that the demonic activity in progress is under the sovereign control of God, and that its power is derived from him. Throughout the Apocalypse he remains 'the Lord God, the Almighty' (4.8; 11.17; 15.3; 16.7; 21.22). See Mounce 187.

For the future form of the verb, in the phrase ἵνα μὴ ἀδικήσουσιν (*hina mē adikēsousin*, 'not to harm', lit. 'that they will not harm'), see the textual note on verse 4, above. In the present context, the future construction after ἵνα (*hina*, 'that') acts as a subjunctive with the force of an imperative. As opposed to the effect of the Egyptian plague, where the plants and the trees of the land were completely destroyed (Exod. 10.15; cf. Joel 2.3), the locusts in this scene are instructed not to act as they naturally would. They must not harm any 'field' (χόρτον, *chorton*, lit. 'grass'), 'green growth' (χλωρόν, *chlōron*, lit. '[light] green [of plants]'; cf. the combination 'green grass' at 8.7; also Mark 6.39) or 'tree' (δένδρον, *dendron*) on the earth. The language is close to the description of the consequences of the first trumpet-plague listed at 8.7, q.v.; in an apocalyptic vision such as this, there is no necessary conflict between the parched grass of that plague and the green fields of 9.4. Aune (528–59) notices the verbal parallels between this verse and 7.2–3.

The demonic force of the locust-plague is to be directed towards those who do not believe. The faithful will escape, because they are 'sealed' by God, and protected by him in order to bear testimony to their Christian commitment. God is indeed Lord of this situation! As the children of Israel were protected from the plagues which devastated the unfaithful Egyptians (Exod. 11.7; Wis. 18.1; et al.), so the new Israel of God in Christ will be preserved from the torments which emerge from the nefarious pit (Mounce 187; cf. Ezek 9.3–8; *Pss. Sol.* 15.4–9). For the concept of the 'seal', and 'sealing', in Revelation see 7.1–8, esp. on verse 3. Sweet (168–69) finds a connection between 9.1–4 and the words attributed to Jesus in Luke 10.18–19 (after the fall of Satan from heaven the saints have been given power to tread on scorpions, and will come to no harm).

The locusts were given permission to torment, but not to kill, the unrighteous (verse 5); for such have not been sealed by God. For the passive of divine authority and activity see on verse 4. A second limitation is imposed on the harmful activity of the demonic creatures: the torment they inflict is to last for 'five months'. Various explanations of this period of time have been offered. It could refer to the life-cycle of the locust, which lasts for five months (Charles 1, 243); alternatively, it may correspond to the warm, dry season (spring to summer) during which the dangerous possibility of an invasion by locusts is immediately present (Beckwith 562). However, John's visions are typically symbolic, rather than literal; and, as with the locusts themselves, the period of five months in this context should therefore be interpreted figuratively. Aune (530) notes that the numeral 'five' is frequently used in biblical texts as a round number, meaning 'a few' (e.g. Lev. 26.8; Judg. 18.2; John 6.9 par.; Acts 20.6; 1 Cor. 14.19). So here, as in verse 10, the number probably indicates that the period of chastisement is to be limited (similarly Hemer, 'πέντε' 690); although the fact that, during the five months, the locust-plague is continuous, and not (as would normally be the case) intermittent, suggests its severity. The restriction is part of the divine plan, to allow time for repentance (as in verse 4; cf. verses 20–21).

The anguish caused by the locusts is again associated with the sting of a scorpion (see on verse 4). In Jewish literature the scorpion's sting is mentioned in a literal sense (Deut. 8.15); but more often the meaning is figurative and psychological (1 Kings 12.11, 14; Sir. 26.7). See the reference to spiritual torture, using the same language and once more in the context of the Exodus, at Wis. 11.9, 12; 16.1–6; 19.4; cf. also Wis. 2.24—3.6; Deut. 28.25–29 (so Beale 497–98). Here (verse 5) the 'tormenting' (using the verb βασανίζω, *basanizō*) by the scorpionlike locusts and the anguished 'torture' (the cognate noun βασανισμός, *basanismos*) they provide is clearly psychological in character; and the spiritual effects of the testing are developed in the following verse (6). The notion of 'torment' (or 'torture'), in the setting of eschatological tribulation, has a similarly figurative connotation elsewhere in Revelation (see 11.10; 14.10–11; 18.7–15; 20.10, where the Greek terminology of verse 5 reappears).

6   The fifth trumpet-call produces a plague of demonic locusts, whose scorpionlike stings cause anguish for the opponents of God's goodness (verses 1–5). The dramatic description of one form of the judgement which may be involved in the end-time, at any time, has so far been full of images; and this style will be resumed in verses 7–11, which detail the appearance of the locusts themselves. Verse 6, in between, is an aporia; for it suddenly switches the attention of the audience to the people who are affected by the crisis and the psychological consequences which the terrorizing has upon them. Aune (482, 531) notices that the literary form of this verse is poetic, since it consists of two parallel couplets (Psalmic in character), each containing an antithesis ('they will search/they will not find'; 'they will long to die/death will elude them'). Verse 6 is also marked by the use of three verbs in the future indicative: ζητήσουσιν (*zētēsousin*, 'they will search'); οὐ μὴ εὑρήσουσιν (*ou mē heurēsousin*, 'they will not find'; the double negative in the Greek is emphatic); and ἐπιθυμήσουσιν (*epithymēsousin*, lit. 'they will wish'). The only other verbs in the future tense in this scene are the two subjunctives at 9.4 and 5. On the use of the verb φεύγει (*pheugei*, lit. 'flees'), in the present tense but with a prophetic future force, in line with the three preceding verbs, see the textual note on verse 6, above. These literary and grammatical features suggest to Aune (531) that the present verse is a digression, or a redaction created for a second edition of Revelation.

The desire for death in place of a life of torment is common in the thought of Judaism. See 1 Kings 19.1–4; Job 3.1–26; 7.14–16; Ps. 55.4–8; Jer. 8.3; Jonah 4.3, 8; cf. Luke 23.27–30; also *Sib. Or.* 2.307–308; 8.353. The last two texts seem to depend on Rev. 9.6, applying it to the punishment of the wicked at the end. Note also *Apoc. Elijah* 2.5, 32 (suffering preceding the appearance of the Antichrist), and *Apoc. Daniel* 12.4–5 (the desire for death brought about by demonic forces in league with the Antichrist). See further Beale 498–99. The fifth trumpet-call is designed to challenge the persecutors of the saints, and those who are tempted to compromise with them, to realize that idolatry and syncretism are without hope, and to bring the rebels back to faith. It could also provide a warning to those within John's community whose understanding of Christian teaching is inadequate, and whose ethical behaviour is therefore unworthy, that God's saving judgement is always breaking into the life of the Church. See further Smalley, *Thunder and Love* 128–32. By contrast, true followers of Jesus experience peace, rather than torment (Phil. 4.7); and, rather than fearing death, they are able to embrace it willingly as a way of entering the presence of their risen Lord (Phil. 1.23).

7 The following paragraph describes in heightened form the appearance of the locusts themselves (verses 7–10), and the demonic character of their leader (verse 11). The seer's difficulty in expressing the exact details of his vision is evident from his repeated use in this section of the words ὅμοιος or ὡς (*homoios* or *hōs*, 'like', 'as') and ὁμοίωμα (*homoiōma*, 'likeness'). The graphic portrayal of the creatures, in verses 7–9, is derived from Joel 1–2; but the embellishments are John's own. In Joel's prophecy a plague of locusts devastates the land of Israel; and, as in Rev. 9.1, a trumpet-call heralds their advent (Joel 2.1; the sound of the trumpet also concludes the judgement at Joel 2.15). Joel's depiction of the attack finds its own background in the locust-plague which occurs in the narrative of the Exodus of the Israelites from Egypt (Exod. 10); and John accordingly supplements his allusions to the Egyptian plagues in verses 3–5 (q.v.) with further material here from Joel. In the Exodus saga the plague of locusts was a judgement on the hard-heartedness of the Egyptians, rather than a challenge to repentance (see Exod. 10.1–2, 20); but in the present passage of Revelation (9.20–21), as in Joel (2.12–14, 18–32), the possibility of salvific repentance after the judgement is to some extent in view.

The locusts described in this section are large, terrifying and destructive. Their onslaught, according to Joel, who may be describing either actual locusts, or an army which possesses their characteristics, leads to severe famine (Joel 1.5–12 [note verses 10–11], 16–20; 2.25), and causes psychological anguish to those who are harmed (Joel 2.6; cf. Rev. 9.5–6). Beale (500–501) points out that, whereas literal famine is not envisaged in the present verses of the Apocalypse (contrast 8.7–11), since the locusts are instructed not to harm the earth's vegetation (9.4), spiritual emptiness may be a part of John's imagery. Just as the actual famine conditions belonging to the first four plagues point to the judgement which is to come upon sinners because of their inward deprivation, so at the fifth trumpet-call the eschatological punishments of the locusts 'cause and reveal to the wicked the hunger and emptiness of their hearts' (Beale 500). Note the similar spiritualization of famine at Amos 8.11–14; cf. also *3 Apoc. Bar.* 16.3.

These locusts 'looked like horses armoured (ἡτοιμασμένοις, *hētoimasmenois*, lit. 'made ready') for battle; see also verse 9. There is an Old Testament background to the analogy between locusts and horses; see Jer. 51.27 ('horses like bristling locusts'); Joel 2.4–5 (the locusts 'have the appearance of horses', and charge like military 'war-horses'); Judg. 6.5; Nahum 3.15–17 (the destruction carried out by an invading army [on horseback] is compared to that of a 'thick' plague of locusts); cf. *T. Moses* 3.1 (the enemy cavalry will 'overrun' the land of Israel [like locusts]; the Exodus events are in the background here [see 1.4; 2.1; 3.11]); et al. The exaggerated likeness between locusts and horses perhaps accounts for the words for 'locust' in German (*Heupferd*, lit. 'hay-horse') and Italian (*cavalletta*, 'little horse'). So Mounce 189. That the horse-like locusts in verse 7 are prepared for battle could mean that they are keenly ready to inflict judgemental punishment on the unrighteous; equally, this statement may be a reference to their protective armour, mentioned at verse 9. Similarly, it is not entirely clear whether horses form one metaphor for the locusts, followed by others, or whether all the images in verses 7–10 are aspects of one (horse) metaphor. Verses 17–19 seem to suggest the latter (Beale 500); but, in any case, the overall meaning is the same.

On the heads of the locusts were what appeared to be 'wreaths (στέφανοι, *stephanoi*, lit. "crowns") like gold'. The demonic creatures emerge from the shaft to the underworld as locusts (verse 3); they are then presented in theriomorphic language (they look like warhorses, verse 7); and here they are described in anthropomorphic terms (they are wearing golden wreaths, and their faces seem to be human). See Aune 532. The symbolism of the golden 'wreaths' (as worn by victors at the Roman games) is explained in verse 9: the locusts possessed the power to carry through their mission to a triumphant conclusion (cf. Mounce 189). These are not the literal crowns worn in the Apocalypse by heavenly and divine beings (4.4; 12.1; 14.14; however, see 6.2), but the marks of a fearful dominion over humanity, which is allowed by God and delegated by Satan. It is most unlikely that the semblance of crowns in this context refers to the 'yellow greenish colour' of the locusts' *breasts* (Charles 1, 244), since the 'wreaths' in question appear precisely on the *heads* of the demonic creatures.

The locust-horses have apparently human faces, as in Joel 2.5, 7; the locusts of that vision seem like war-horses, but behave 'like a powerful army' (2.5) of warriors and soldiers (verse 7). The combination of the bestial and the human in these figures bestows on them a character which is unnatural, and potentially cruel, and an authority which is supernatural, and actually demonic (cf. Charles 1, 244–45).

8 In this verse the imagery used to describe the locusts from the bottomless pit continues to be anthropomorphic (their hair was 'feminine in character', ὡς τρίχας γυναικῶν, *hōs trichas gynaikōn*, lit. 'as the hair of women'), and then reverts to being theriomorphic (their teeth were 'similar to those of lions', ὡς λεόντων, *hōs leontōn*, lit. 'as of lions'). That the appearance of the 'hair' covering the locusts was female presumably means that it was long, as was natural for first-century women (cf. 1 Cor. 11.15). The figure may also include the thought of dishevelment, as in various Old Testament contexts (see Lev. 10.6 [a sign of mourning]; 13.45 [an indication of uncleanness]; Num. 5.18 [part of the sacrificial ritual for women accused of adultery]); cf. *T. Sol.* 13.1 (a female demon with untidy hair); *Apoc. Zeph.* 4.4 (ugly angels with 'loose' hair, like that of women); 6.8. (Satan's hair 'spread out like women's'). See further Aune 532. Some commentators have suggested that the feminine character of the creatures' hair in this verse alludes to the long antennae of the locust tribe, or to the streaming hair of Parthian warriors (Swete 118). Both proposals are unlikely. The two organs of sensation which protrude from the head of the locust are relatively short; and the irrational Roman fear of Parthian invaders was not shared by Palestinian Jewish-Christians (cf. Mounce 189; Aune 891–94). It is more probable that the point of contact is the hair on the bodies and legs of locusts, which in flight would 'emphasize the speed with which they carry forth their mission' (Mounce 189–90). Although long hair worn by men was sometimes regarded by the Greeks as a sign of effeminacy, for Jewish males it could be rather a symbol of vitality (Judg. 16.13–22 [Samson]; 2 Sam. 14.25–26 [Absalom]).

'Teeth like lions' is an almost proverbial expression for a fatally destructive force; see Job 4.10–11; Sir. 21.1–3. Here the terminology is drawn from Joel 1.6, where the invading army is depicted as having the teeth of lions and 'the fangs of a lioness'; cf. also Ps. 57.4; 58.6. In verse 8 the leonine character of the locusts' teeth underscores the fierceness of the threat posed by the demonic creatures. But, rather than following through the natural implications of this simile (they would tear people apart), John's vision attributes the terrifying pain they inflict to their scorpionlike stings (verse 10; cf. verses 5–6).

9   The persecuting locusts have 'chests' (θώρακας, *thōrakas*, lit. 'thoraxes') resembling 'iron breastplates' (θώρακας σιδηροῦς, *thōrakas sidērous*, lit. 'thoraxes of iron'). The locusts have already been described as looking like 'horses armoured for battle' (see also verse 9*b*). So the reference of 'thoraxes of iron' in this verse is primarily to the scaly and impenetrable exterior of these creatures, but might well include the thought of armour: a protective covering for the chest ('breastplate'), worn by warhorses in combat (BDAG 463*b*, 464*a*, *b*). According to 1 Sam. 17.5 (LXX), Goliath appeared in just such a coat of scale armour. For the imagery in this verse see Nahum 3.17 (Targum). Job 39.19–25 (MT and LXX) describes a warhorse responding to the sound of the trumpet; it goes into battle, clothed in terror and perfect armour, leaping 'like the locust'.

The imagery in the second part of verse 9 (the whirring of the locust wings in flight 'sounded like war-chariots with teams of horses charging into battle') derives from Joel 2.4–9, which lies behind the whole section Rev. 9.7–10. In Joel 2.4–5 threatening locusts, like a marauding army, charge into the fray like warhorses, 'with the rumbling of chariots'. Beale (501–502) also discovers in this passage echoes of Jer. 51.14, 27 (the Lord will 'fill you with troops like a swarm of locusts'; and preparations for war include bringing up 'horses like bristling locusts'). The setting of these verses from Jeremiah is the announcement of coming vindication for Israel against idolatrous Babylon (cf. 51.10, 17–18); and this context provides a significant backcloth to the activity of saving judgement evident in the present scene, as elsewhere in Revelation.

The awkward phrase ἁρμάτων ἵππων πολλῶν (*harmatōn hippōn pollōn*, lit. '[the sound] of war-chariots of many horses') contains two juxtaposed nouns in the genitive plural. The word ἵππων (*hippōn*, 'horses') may be construed as a genitive of association (usually it occurs with μετά, *meta*, 'with'), so that the expression means 'many war-chariots with horses'. Alternatively, both plural genitives can be taken as depending on the preceding noun φωνή (*phonē*, 'sound', 'voice'), giving the meaning 'the sound of war-chariots, of many horses'. Our translation, 'war-chariots with teams of horses', attempts to combine these two possible renderings.

10   The grotesque and vivid apocalyptic portrait of the locusts continues to be developed, now resuming the references to their scorpionlike nature from verses 3 and 5 (q.v.). However, the frightening aspect of the locusts is less important to the seer than their power to effect judgement. For this purpose, they have 'tails like those of scorpions, with stings in them'. The sting of the scorpion is administered through its tail (see on verse 3); but this is the first time in the present passage that the word 'tail' (οὐρά, *oura*) is used (twice in verse 10). Elsewhere in Revelation the noun occurs with reference to the serpent-like tails of the horses (9.19, *bis*; but that is not a real parallel), and to the tail of the dragon (12.4). The sudden use of the present tense to introduce this verse (ἔχουσιν, *echousin*, 'they have'), after verbs which predominantly feature the past tense in 9.1–9 (but see on verse 6), adds to the immediacy of the vision, and helps to switch the audience into the action (cf. 7.14–15; 22.2; et al.).

The picture of locusts 'with tails like scorpions' may suggest that the tails themselves are like scorpions (Charles 1, 245; cf. 9.19); but more probably it means that their tails are 'like the tails of scorpions' (cf. 13.11). The term κέντρον (*kentron*) normally means the 'sting' of an animal, as here (in 1 Cor. 15.55–56 = Hos. 13.14 it becomes a metaphor for 'the sting of death'). See also Acts 26.14 (9.4 v.l.), where the noun means a 'goad'. The judgemental activity of the scorpionlike locusts is concerned with torment, rather than death (see verse 5), and is designed to bring the unjust to repentance (verses 20–21). For the background to this scene in the Exodus narrative, and for the significance of 'five' months, as a round number for a limited period of judgement, see on verses 3, 5. Beale (502) notes a further possible source in Jer. 8.16–18, where images of a judgement which causes anguish (combining the sound of devouring warhorses, and serpents who bite) connote discrimination against idolaters (with Rev. 9.4, 20, cf. Jer. 8.19). See also 1 John 2.18–26; 4.1–3 (the forces of a demonic Antichrist work through the deception introduced by false teachers in the Church).

The locust-plague of Rev. 9.1–10(11) may be interpreted as the situation of eschatological crisis which results from general opposition to divine values, rather than an end-time event as such (so Hendriksen 121–22; Wilcock 97–98). Even if John's visions have as their primary focus 'the ultimate conflict of God and Satan that brings history to its close' (Mounce 191), it remains true that judgement of a salvific nature comes upon an unbelieving world at any time, right up to the consummation and into eternity.

11   The advancing army of locusts has 'the angel of the bottomless pit' as its leader. The present tense of the verb, ἔχουσιν (*echousin*, 'they have'), continues the sense of immediacy in the action introduced by the use of the same verb in verse 10 (q.v.). The appearance of the term βασιλεύς (*basileus*, lit. 'king') for 'leader' is surprising; particularly as, according to Prov. 30.27, 'locusts have no king (LXX ἀβασίλευτόν ἐστιν ἡ ἀκρίς, *abasileuton estin hē akris*, lit. "the locust is kingless"), yet all of them march in rank'. The connotation of this title needs to be understood in the light of the identity of the 'angel of the abyss', mentioned here. The context is demonic: a being from the underworld leads an army of tormenting creatures who have been brought out from the bottomless pit (verse 3; for 'abyss' see on verse 1). This angel is not, therefore, the messenger of God who unlocks the abyss (verse 1), nor such a figure as the archangel Uriel, whose name means 'fire of God', and whose authority extends over Tartarus (*1 Enoch* 20.2). We have here, rather, an angel of punishment, and the leader of opposition to God.

The use of the article with 'angel' (τὸν ἄγγελον, *ton angelon*, 'the angel') suggests that the supernatural being is familiar to John's readers; and this could imply that the reference is (albeit allusively) to Satan, the 'prince' (ἄρχων, *archōn*) of demons (cf. *T. Sol.* 2.9; Mark 3.22 par.; against Mounce 191). In line with this argument, Satan (Beliar) is designated specifically as 'the king of this world' at *Asc. Isa.* 4.2; cf. 4Q280 1.2 (a demonic opponent of God is named as Melkiresha, 'my king is evil'). However, when Satan is mentioned in other contexts of Revelation (2.9, 13, 24; 3.9; 12.9; 20.2, 7) he is carefully named; so it may be more accurate to interpret the angel of the abyss in verse 11 as a demonic leader *like* the Satan. In line with this suggestion, it is significant that the parallel demonic figures of the dragon and the beast, who are both leaders of evil forces, are represented as wearing royal diadems (12.3; 13.1; see the 'golden wreaths', on the heads of the locusts, at verse 7). See also on the falling star of 8.10.

The identification of the angel as a satanic figure is further supported by the LXX version of the prophetic vision in Amos 7.1 (not in the MT), where an invading army of locusts is captained by 'one caterpillar (locust), king Gog'. This connects with the Gog and Magog sequence in Ezek. 38–39, which is developed at Rev. 20.8 (q.v.), where Satan is precisely the leader of Gog and Magog, the eschatological figures of opposition to God's people. Cf. Beale 503. Note also the 'angels of punishment', which are presumably satanic, in 1 *Enoch* 53.3; 62.11; et al.; and the 'angel of death' and 'destroying angel' of the Exodus tradition (Exod. 4.24; 12.12, 23).

The angel of the bottomless pit is called by the Hebrew name 'Abaddon'. The adverb Ἐβραϊστί (*Hebraisti*, 'in Hebrew') appears in the Apocalypse only here and at 16.16; elsewhere in the New Testament it occurs only in the Fourth Gospel (John 5.2; 19.13, 17, 20; 20.6). The construction, ὄνομα αὐτῷ . . . Ἀβαδδών (*onoma autō[i]* . . . *Abaddōn*, lit. 'the name to him [is] Abaddon'), is also found at 6.8 (cf. also John 1.6; 18.10). In contrast, the form in the next part of verse 11, ὄνομα ἔχει Ἀπολλύων (*onoma echei Apollyōn*, lit. 'he has the name Apollyon'), where a proper name stands in apposition to the noun ὄνομα (*onoma*, 'name'), occurs only here in Revelation. The order of the Greek words in that sentence (in literal translation 'name he has') is also unusual; elsewhere the order is more logically reversed (see 13.17; 14.1; 19.12, 16; 21.14, 'has the name').

This is the only occasion in Revelation where the 'angel of the bottomless pit' and the name 'Abaddon' are featured. In Jewish thought, 'Abaddon' (אֲבַדּוֹן, *'ăbaddōn*) is a Hebrew term for the place of death and destruction (Job 31.12); it is also a poetic parallel for Sheol (Job 26.6; Prov. 15.11), for death (Job 28.22), for the grave (Ps. 88.11) and for the abyss (4Q DibHamᵃ [*frags.* 1–2] col. 7.8). In the LXX the Hebrew word 'Abaddon' can be translated as ἀπώλεια (*apōleia*, 'destruction'); see Ps. 87.12; Prov. 15.11. In the New Testament the eschatological figure of the Antichrist is described as 'the son of destruction' (2 Thess. 2.3); and in John 17.12 this expression is applied to Judas Iscariot. In Job 26.6 and 28.22 Abaddon is personified as the place of destruction; and, given the theme of devastation following the fifth trumpet-call, this may well be one source for the imagery in Rev. 9.11. 'The Destroyer', Abaddon, is a satanic angel-figure who, as the ruling prince of the underworld, leads his army of demonic creatures into a judgemental attack on unrighteousness. See further Jeremias, 'Abaddōn'.

The Greek name of the angel of the pit is given as 'Apollyon'. John translates the Hebrew for the sake of the mixed, Jewish-Hellenistic audience in his community. See also 16.16, and regularly in the Fourth Gospel (John 1.41; 4.25; et al.). 'Apollyon' derives from the Greek verb ἀπολλύναι (*apollynai*, 'to destroy'), and again means 'Destroyer'. There is an etymological connection between this verb and the name of the Greek sun-god Apollo, of whom the locust was one symbol (BDAG 116*b*). John may be introducing at this point a derogatory reference to the Emperor Nero, whose patron deity was Apollo, and hinting at his suspected role in the destruction of Rome in AD 64, shortly before the Apocalypse was written. (See Bell, 'Date' 98–99.) If so, it would be a deeply ironic touch on the seer's part to suggest that the destructive host of hell has as its king this – or any – emperor of Rome (Beasley-Murray 162–63).

The name-formula in this verse explicates the destructive effect of the plague of locusts (as in 6.8; and 8.11). Both designations given to the satanic leader-figure here, Abaddon and Apollyon, express his ability, under God, to bring about judgement on the unrighteous through demonic forces. Cf. Beale 503.

12   This verse, containing the voice of the narrator, provides a transition from the fifth trumpet-sounding to the final two. For the term 'disaster' (οὐαί, *ouai*, lit. 'woe') see 8.13;

see also on 11.14. The word normally functions as an interjection; and its use as a substantive (so verse 12) is, apart from Revelation, very rare (but see LXX Ezek. 2.10; 7.26; cf. Aune 536). The writer puts ἡ οὐαὶ ἡ μία (*hē ouai hē mia*, 'the first disaster') in the feminine, despite the occurrence later in the verse of a third person singular verb (ἔρχεται, *erchetai*, lit. 'comes'), which would normally follow *neuter* nouns (such as 'disasters') in the plural.

The three 'woes' in this scene of the Apocalypse, and at 11.14, appear chiefly as a structuring device, running alongside the last three trumpet-plagues, but not corresponding exactly to them. For the nature of the third disaster see on 11.14. But, like the seals of 6.1–17; 8.1, and the plagues themselves, the woes are not to be interpreted as symbols of single historical events, which occur in a strict chronological order. The disasters refer to judgemental calamities which come upon rebellious humanity at any time and in any place; and this is a challenge as much to members of the Christian Church as to those who reject its Lord. Although there is a firmly historical background to Revelation, in the Church and the world of the first Christian century, John is relating at this stage of the drama a series of visions. 'The first disaster has taken place' therefore means simply that the vision containing it has been unveiled; and this is confirmed in the second part of this verse by the introductory ἰδού (*idou*, 'look!'), and the concluding μετὰ ταῦτα (*meta tauta*, 'later', lit. 'after these things'), which are formulas belonging to non-historical sequences within the prophet-seer's visions (see 4.1; et al.). As throughout Revelation, if there is a concern with chronology in this verse it relates to John's apocalypses, and not to any historical order represented within them. So it is (verse 11*b*) that two more visions of disaster 'have still to occur, later' (for which see 9.13–19; 11.14). Cf. Hendriksen 116; Beale 505.

Trumpet 6 (Second Woe): Fiendish Cavalry (9.13–21)

13–14   The sixth angelic trumpet-call is accompanied by the sound of a commanding voice, heard by the seer; and this begins a description of the action to follow. For 'hearing' in Johannine thought, often associated with sight and understanding, see on 4.1; et al.; also 8.13. The identity of the 'single voice' (φωνὴν μίαν, *phōnēn mian*, lit. 'one voice') is not immediately clear. Presumably the voice does not belong to God, since it issues from an altar in his presence, although such an association is not impossible. It could be the voice of the Lamb (with God), as in the announcement at 6.6 (q.v.). Equally, the voice could be that of the angel-priest who, in 8.3–5, presents the prayers of the saints to God on the golden altar, or even the prayers themselves (so Mounce 193). There is doubtless a connection between the sixth trumpet-plague and the altar-prayer for vindication on the part of the martyred faithful in 6.9–10 (cf. Beale 505–506). To some extent, moreover, the trumpet-sequence is a response to the intercessions of *all* the saints, since it is their prayers which introduce this part of the unfolding eschatological drama (see 8.3–4). If we have in verse 13 the united plea of the Church for God's intervention in an unjust world, it could also account for the 'single' nature of the voice as heard by John.

It seems best, however, to interpret this voice generally as one of divine authorization, since it is God's powerful and judgemental activity in his creation which is the subject of this scene in Revelation, and the ultimate purpose of the trumpet-blasts themselves (see the divine passives in 9.1, 3, et al.). To this extent, the voice is similar in character to that of the eagle in 8.13. But whereas in the earlier context the eagle, as God's messenger, announces impending disasters in response to human rebellion, here the divine voice *initiates* the remaining woes.

The voice issues (there is no verb in the Greek) from the 'four corners' of the golden altar in God's presence. For a similar personification see 16.7. Rather than stemming literally from the 'corners' (κεράτων, *keratōn*, lit. 'horns') of the altar, the voice is heard coming from its midst (understanding the Greek as ἐκ [μέσου] τῶν τεσσάρων κεράτων, *ek [mesou] tōn tessarōn keratōn*, 'from [the midst of] the four corners', as in Matt.13.49). Cf. Mounce 193 n. 2. For the inclusion of 'four', in the Greek of this sentence, see the textual note on verse 13, above. 'Four' implies completeness, and 'horns' denote (animal) power. Beale (506), following Kiddle (161), suggests that the four horns of the altar in this passage therefore refer to God's complete power in answering the prayers of the saints: the unrighteous are being judged in the trumpet-plagues (cf. 14.18). For an incense altar with horns see Exod. 30.2, 10; for the altar with four horns in the tabernacle see Exod. 27.2. The corners of an altar in the Old Testament are sometimes represented as offering protection (cf. 1 Kings 1.50–51; 2.28–29). The 'golden altar' here corresponds to the altar of incense in 8.3 (q.v.), and combines aspects of both the incense altar and the altar of burnt-sacrifice in the Temple at Jerusalem. That it is said to 'stand in God's presence' (ἐνώπιον τοῦ θεοῦ, *enōpion tou theou*, lit. 'before God') indicates that the divine retribution to follow belongs to him, and not to any other authority. See the parallel expression, 'before the throne', at 8.3. For the eight uses of the term θυσιαστήριον (*thysiastērion*, 'altar') in Revelation see on 6.9.

For the first time in this sequence, an angel is involved (verse 14) in the action which follows a trumpet-call. The nominative phrase, ὁ ἔχων (*ho echōn*, lit. 'the one having [the trumpet]'), has as its antecedent the dative τῷ ἕκτῳ ἀγγέλῳ (*tō[i] hektō[i] angelō[i]*, 'to the sixth angel'). The nominative may be used because 'the one having' is understood as an angelic title; but it is more likely that John is construing 'the angel with (lit. having) the trumpet' as a parenthesis, referring back to the nominative 'sixth angel' at 9.13.

The voice from the golden altar (verse 13) commands the release of other angels, who are held back at the eastern border of the empire. As Mounce (192–93) points out, the severity of the plagues recorded in this scene increases as each trumpet sounds, and the consequences of the judgements unleashed become more intense and devastating. The progression moves from destructive portents in the heavens and earth (8.7–12), to the demonic locusts who swarm out from the netherworld with their terrifying commission of tormenting the unfaithful (9.1–11). Now fiendish cavalry, two hundred million in number and horrific in appearance, are poised to inflict lethal damage on an unbelieving society (verses 15–19).

For this to happen, the 'four angels which are chained up at the great river' are to be set free. The identity of these angels is not immediately apparent; but the context suggests that they are evil in character. First, they release considerable destruction (verses 15–19). This is akin to the anguish brought about by the locusts (9.4–6); but now death is involved (verse 18), and not just torture. Second, the antithetical use here of the verbs λῦσον (*lyson*, 'set free', 'unbind') and δεδεμένους (*dedemenous*, 'chained up', 'bound') puts these beings on a level with bad angels who have been restrained until a predetermined moment of demonic action. A similarly satanic 'serpent', locked in the pit for a thousand years, appears at 20.2–3; cf. also Tobit 3.17; 8.3. The nature of the 'binding' in this passage is not explicated.

The phrase τοὺς τέσσαρας ἀγγέλους (*tous tessaras angelous*, 'the four angels') includes a definite article; and this marks out the angels as figures which are in some way familiar to John's audience. It could be, therefore, that they are to be associated with the *four* angels who are introduced anarthrously at 7.1, as those who restrain the four earthly winds. So Kiddle 161–63. This parallel is possibly supported by the fact that, in the present section, the numeral 'four' bears no relation to the number of the horses or the plagues in the account which follows (verses 16, 18). However, as Charles (1, 223, 250) indicates, the only common element between these two sets of angels is their number. Otherwise, their place, condition and function differ. The angels of 7.1 are located at the four quarters of the earth, whereas here they are at the river Euphrates; the earlier group is standing, while in this verse they are chained up; and although the figures which appear at the start of Rev. 7 restrain the potentially damaging winds of the earth, in 9.14 they release destruction. Moreover, as we have seen, the supernatural beings of 7.1 are 'good' angels of service, and agents of God's activity in nature (cf. 9.1); and to that extent they differ in character from the 'bad' angels of destruction in this passage. Nevertheless, there is an entirely probable link to be found between Rev. 7.1 and 9.14; and it is to be found not in the two sets of angels, but in the four demonic *winds* of the former text and the four evil angels of the latter. The four angels of 7.1 hold back the four agents of divine judgement, whose nature is essentially opposed to God (cf. 6.2–8); and they are therefore restrained to prevent yet more disaster (see further on 7.1). There is no indication until the present scene that those winds have been released; but now this happens, and the judgement they bring is experienced by humanity (9.18–21). The delay is caused by the need in between to seal the servants of God, so that they cannot be harmed by the effect of the angelic winds (7.3–8; cf. 9.4). See also Beale 507.

A further background to the appearance of 'the four angels' in verse 14 may be located in the Jewish apocalyptic tradition which features four destructive powers, such as winds or spirits, issuing from the four corners of the earth; see Dan. 7.2; Zech. 6.5–8; *2 Apoc. Bar.* 6.4 (so Beckwith 566–67). Otherwise, no groups of four angels of punishment are found in this tradition. The four angel-winds here are in charge of an immeasurable horde of demonic horsemen, who charge across the pagan world spreading terror and death. They correspond to the leader of the locusts at 9.11; and, like him, 'they seem to disappear into the demonic forces they release' (Mounce 194).

The river Euphrates (verse 14*b*) deserves the description 'great', since it is nearly 2,000 miles long, and is the longest river in western Asia. It flowed at the eastern edge of the Roman Empire, down to the Persian Gulf, and marked the boundary between Israel and her main enemies. In the Old Testament there is a strong prophetic tradition which maintains that an army will appear from beyond the Euphrates ('the north'), to bring God's judgement on his sinful people. In Isa. 8.5–8, for example, the invading armies from Assyria are represented as the flood waters of the great River, which overflow its banks and sweep on into Judah. Even closer to the imagery of Rev. 9.14 is the portrayal in Jer. 46 of the coming judgement on Egypt. In that description an invading army of horsemen from the north, more numerous than locusts and wearing coats of mail, stands by the river Euphrates (see esp. verses 2, 4, 18–24). Cf. also Isa. 14.31; Jer. 10.22; Ezek. 39.2; Joel 2. 1–11, 20–25; et al. At the time when John was writing, the Parthian threat from the north, beyond the Euphrates, was associated with such a tradition in Judaism (see also *1 Enoch* 56.5–8, where the invasion is instigated by angels); cf. Caird 122. However, in this metaphorical passage the seer is recounting a vision, and not detailing a military exercise.

Beale (507) notes that the reference to the river Euphrates in verse 14 anticipates the battle of the sixth bowl in 16.12–16 (the 'great River' features in verse 12); indeed, the sixth trumpet and the sixth bowl seem to depict the same event from different viewpoints (cf. 9.19). The fact that the four angel-winds in the present verse are chained up, ready for action (verse 15), at the river Euphrates and not (as in 7.1) at the four corners of the earth, is not necessarily a mixing of metaphors (Beale, ibid.). John is providing a theological focus for his narrative. God's judgement, like his sovereignty, is universal and eternal; but it is discovered historically at particular moments, and it derives from exact and human circumstances. See also on verse 15.

15 The torment of the first woe is followed by widespread killing in the second. The four angel-winds, chained up at the river Euphrates until this moment (see on verse 14), are now 'released' to destroy one-third of the human race. The passive form of the verb here, ἐλύθησαν (*elythēsan*, 'they were released'), possibly draws attention to the role of the angels as agents of the divine will (Aune 537); they are set free on the authority of God, rather than of the sixth angel who was originally commanded to unchain them. These agents 'had been in readiness' for the action to follow; and the perfect tense of the verb, ἡτοιμασμένοι (*hētoimasmenoi*, lit. 'had been prepared', 'had been made ready'), intensifies the notion that the angel-winds were poised to attack at a particular moment in history (cf. Matt. 25.34, 41).

They were in readiness for this 'very hour and day and month and year'. In apocalyptic thought, the exact time for every event is fixed in advance by God (cf. *1 Enoch* 92.2, 'the Holy and Great One has designated [specific] days for all things'); and the use of a single article in this sentence, governing the four nouns (hour, day, month, year), highlights the double truth that God is responsible not only for this judgement but also for its precise timing (see also on verse 14). The ascensive chronological order, from 'hour' to 'year', is probably without significance in this context; although see Num. 1.1; Hag. 1.15; Zech. 1.7. Cf. Swete 122.

The angel-winds are released in order to destroy (ἵνα ἀποκτείνωσιν, *hina apokteinōsin*, lit., 'that they should destroy') a third of the human race. For the verb, meaning literally 'to kill', see on verse 18. When the fourth seal is broken, a fourth part of humanity was put to death (6.8); now, a third are to be destroyed by the fiendish cavalry (verse 18; but note 8.11, '*many* died' from the poisoned water). This is a divine judgement on a corrupt civilization: those who are elsewhere in the Apocalypse called 'the earth's inhabitants' (cf. 6.10; 8.13, q.v.). It is carried out by angels of punishment, who are under God's sovereign control; see *1 Enoch* 56.1–4; 66.1; *3 Enoch* 32.1; et al. Such theology – God as almighty – is central to the thought of this scene (cf. 9.1–3; et al.; also 1.8; et al.). According to 9.4, the devastating results of the fifth trumpet-blast will not affect the faithful, who are protected by the divine seal (cf. 7.3). There is no specific reference to the sparing of believers in the present context; but see verses 20–21.

16   There is an abrupt transition from verse 15 to this verse; and the four angel-winds, charged with their deadly task, are not mentioned again. Only the phrase in verse 15, 'to destroy one-third of the human race', which is picked up in verse 18, appears to connect the angels with the horses that now appear. Against Aune (538), however, there seems to be sufficient reason to regard the angel-winds of 9.14–15 as instigators (not necessarily leaders) of the demonic cavalry they unleash, and to interpret the sixth trumpet-plague as to some extent a parallel to the fifth.

(a)   The action of the sixth angel (verse 15) reflects that of the fifth (verses 1–2). But there is a progression. Whereas both angels release devastation, the sixth angel brings it about directly. Also, while the fifth angel unlocks the shaft leading to the bottomless pit, from which emerges a swarm of tormenting locusts, the sixth unchains the winds of the earth, with their commission to kill.

(b)   The Greek expression, 'squadrons of cavalry' (τῶν στρατευμάτων τοῦ ἱππικοῦ, *tōn strateumatōn tou hippikou*, lit. '[the number] of *the* troops of the cavalry') is articular; as with '*the* four angels' in verse 15. This suggests that John's audience will recognize the identity of both groups. Clearly, the riders in verses 16–19 are demonic creatures, rather than members of a literal army; and their obvious association in this context is with the previous set of supernatural beings. The angels, with their power over evil spiritual forces, are now portrayed as an innumerable multitude of soldiers on horseback, with a mandate to kill by means of these forces (Beale 509).

(c)   The connection between this plague and the last is strengthened by the similarity in the descriptions of the invading armies. The horses (= angel-winds), brought on for judgement by the sixth angel, evoke the appearance of the locusts in the reference to their breastplates, heads and tails (see below). Indeed, the locusts 'looked like horses' (verse 7; cf. verse 9). See also the horses in 6.1–8.

The number of the fiendish riders is put at 'two hundred million' (δισμυριάδες μυριάδων, *dismyriades myriadōn*, lit. 'double myriads of myriads', or 'twice ten thousands times ten thousands'). As part of the seer's imagery in this vision, the enumeration cannot be analysed or taken literally; and to that extent the translation 'two hundred million' is mathematically inaccurate. The calculation is broad, and symbolizes 'an indefinite number of incalculable immensity' (BDAG 252*a*) Cf. Ps. 67.18 LXX; also Rev. 5.11, drawing on Dan. 7.10. The sovereignty of God is universal, and his judgements on unrighteousness are all-embracing.

The last sentence in this verse, lit. 'I heard their number (ἀριθμόν, *arithmon*)', is parenthetical, and refers back to the 'number' (ὁ ἀριθμός, *ho arithmos*) of the cavalry mentioned earlier. The writer feels the need to provide authority for quoting a figure, although the calculation remains a part of his apocalyptic vision. Cf. similarly 7.4.

17–18   The 'squadrons of cavalry' (verse 16) are now described. John has 'heard' about the plague following the sixth trumpet-call (verses 13–16), and this is explained further in what he 'sees' (verses 17–19). For καὶ (οὕτως) εἶδον (*kai [houtōs] eidon*, lit. 'and [thus] I saw') see on 5.1. For the relation between vision and audition in the Apocalypse see on 4.1. This is the only occasion in Revelation when the prophet-seer mentions that a 'vision' (ὅρασις, *horasis*) is the medium of what is being disclosed to him (contrast Dan. 7.1–2, 7, 13; 8.2, 15; et al.). Apart from this verse, the sole use of that Greek term in the Johannine literature is at Rev. 4.3 (*bis*), where it refers to the appearance of what is seen. Here the writer is drawing attention to the symbolic nature of the account which is to follow.

The description of the devilish horses and their riders in verses 17–19 affords a parallel to the appearance of the demonic locusts in verses 3–10 (see also on verse 16). It is possible that, in the present verse, both horses and horsemen (regarded as one figure) are to be understood as wearing 'breastplates'. So Beckwith 568; Beale 510; also Moffatt 409, who points out that, in the Persian cavalry, horses as well as men were clad in 'bright plate'. Cf. the horse-like locusts of 9.9, whose chests 'resembled iron breastplates'. But more probably the armour in this picture belongs to the riders alone (so Mounce 196; also the translation of verse 17 in NJB). Their breastplates were red, blue and yellow, in correlation with the fire, smoke and brimstone (sulphur) issuing from the mouths of the horses (verse 17*b*). It is not immediately apparent whether the breastplates were mixed in colour (fiery- red, hyacinth-blue and sulphur-yellow), or whether each armour-plating was of a single hue (red or blue or yellow). However, the general impression would be the same. Swete (123) notes that the adjective πύρινος (*pyrinos*), as applied here to the breastplates, strictly means 'of fire'; whereas πυρρός (*pyrros*), as in 6.4 and 12.3, signifies 'flame-coloured' (red). He therefore concludes that the defensive armour of the warriors consisted of fire; but this interpretation seems to be needlessly literal. For John's use of colours in the Apocalypse see Smalley, *Thunder and Love* 106–107. The term ὑακίνθινους (*hyakinthinous*, 'hyacinth-coloured', i.e. dark blue), verse 17, is found only here in the New Testament; but see the use of a cognate at Rev. 21.20.

The riders in this scene play no active part in the execution of the plague. This is carried out by the horses themselves; and their description in verses 17–19 is even more grotesque than that of the locusts earlier in Chapter 9 (verses 7–10). They seem to be made up of three creatures; for they have the body of a horse, the head of a lion and tails with heads like serpents (cf. Aune 539, who notes that the appearance of the Chimaera, in Greek and Roman mythology, is very similar). Fire-breathing monsters were more common in Graeco-Roman literature than in the thought of Judaism. See Moffatt 409. Nevertheless, the source of John's imagery at this point is likely to be the Old Testament. In Job 41, for example, the sea monster Leviathan breathes out 'flaming torches and sparks of fire', and from its nostrils comes 'smoke, as from a boiling pot and burning rushes' (verses 19–21). The lions' heads of the horses recall the fierceness of the lion-like teeth of the locusts in the previous vision (9.8); and, like the lethal power of the horses' tails (verse 19), these symbols represent a destructiveness which is judgemental. See also Hab. 1.7–8 (the invasive Chaldeans are 'dread and fearsome', and their horses are 'swifter than leopards, and more menacing than wolves'); Wis. 11.18 (God could have plagued the Egyptians with 'unknown beasts full of rage', breathing out fire and smoke).

The 'fire, smoke and brimstone' which issue from the mouths of the horses in this passage indicate the demonic origin of these creatures, as well as their ability to destroy. The deadly character of this authority is underlined by John's repetition, from his description earlier in verse 17, of the 'fire' (πῦρ, *pyr*) and 'brimstone = sulphur' (θεῖον, *theion*) which appeared to clothe the horses. Elsewhere in Revelation that phrase is used with reference to the final judgement on all who bear the mark of the beast (14.10; cf. 21.8), and on the devil (20.10) and his followers (19.20). The judgement anticipated in the present context shares the same quality of divine discrimination, but is an expression of its incursion into human history at any moment in time.

In the Old Testament, the combination of fire and brimstone, sometimes with smoke, speaks of a fatal judgement (cf. Deut. 29.23; Isa. 34.9–10; Ezek. 38.22; also 2 Sam. 22.9; Ps. 18.8). In what is probably the leading background to the thought of verses 17 and 18, the overthrow of Sodom and Gomorrah in Gen. 19.24, 28 (cf. Jude 7), the exact triplet 'fire, smoke and brimstone' occurs uniquely; although in the LXX the order differs (sulphur, fire, smoke), and the term for 'smoke' is ἀτμίς (*atmis*), rather than καπνός (*kapnos*); cf. also Rev. 9.2. For judgement in the Apocalypse, associated with that which comes from the mouth, see verses 18–19; also 1.16; 2.12, 16; 3.16; 11.5; 19.15, 21.

The 'fire, smoke and brimstone' proceeding from the mouths of the demonic horses (for which see on verse 17) are identified in verse 18 with three separate plagues (cf. Lev. 26.21–26; Deut. 29.22–23). The repetition of the threefold phrase, albeit with a minor stylistic variation, emphasizes the seriousness of the divine judgement which is impending. The plagues result in the destruction of a third of the human race (cf. 8.7–10; 'one-third of mankind' is also the number of survivors, not victims, specified at *Sib. Or.* 3.544). The first disaster had brought torment (9.5); the second introduces death. But, as before, not everyone is affected; and this is a measure designed to allow for the possibility of repentance (cf. verses 20–21; also 9.4–6). The verb ἀποκτείνω (*apokteinō*, 'destroy', lit. 'kill') is used elsewhere in the Apocalypse with reference to literal and physical death (e.g. 2.13, 23; 6.11; 9.5; 11.5, 13; 13.10, 15; 19.21). But the context here seems to demand that the 'destruction' of humanity, which may include illness and deprivation, should be construed as that which is not only physical but also spiritual (so Beale 511–12). There is a possible figurative parallel at 6.8.

Aune (540) draws attention to an inclusion in the Greek of verses 17b–18a, with the repetition of the phrase ἐκ τῶν στομάτων αὐτῶν (*ek tōn stomatōn autōn*, 'from their mouths'). The passage as a whole, 'from their mouths/issuing/fire and smoke and brimstone/(one-third of the human race was destroyed)/from the fire and smoke and brimstone/proceeding/from their mouths', then becomes chiastic in structure (A B C [D] C′ B′ A′).

19 This verse explains the way in which the 'three plagues' of verse 18 are carried out by the horses (angel-winds) of 9.14–17. The creatures possess a 'power' (ἐξουσία, *exousia*, also 'authority') to kill, which lies in their mouths (verses 18–19). But, like the locusts (verse 3), they also wield the ability to 'inflict injury' on human beings (see verse 4, where the same verb, ἀδικεῖν [*adikein*, 'to hurt' or 'to harm'] is used); and this power is in their tails. The Greek in the second part of verse 19 is difficult to construe, and we should not press the literal details in such an apocalyptic vision as this. However, the meaning is probably as suggested in the translation: not that the horses have tails like snakes, with heads (so Mounce 197; also NRSV), but that 'their tails have heads (ἔχουσαι κεφαλάς, *echousai kephalas*), like serpents'. In any case, the picture reinforces the demonic nature of these creatures. They carry the authority to torment (see on verse 5), as well as to destroy; and this power relates to spiritual, as well as physical, suffering and death (cf. 12.15–16; also 2.11; 7.3; 9.4). As in 9.4, the harm involved cannot ultimately affect the genuine saint, who wears God's seal (7.3–8). For the metaphorical associations of serpents and scorpions in Judaism see Beale 515–16.

Various sources can be suggested for the derivation of the imagery describing these monstrous figures, with their serpent-headed tails. These include the Parthian custom of binding horses' tails to give them a snake-like appearance; the giants, with legs in the form of serpents, sculpted in the relief of the great altar of Zeus at Pergamum; and the so-called Amphisbaena, a mythical figure with a serpent's head at both ends, and which moved in either direction. See Beckwith 569, who (followed by Aune 541) also notes a close parallel in the Chimaera, a fire-spouting Greek monster who was part-lion and part-serpent in nature (see on verse 17). But a more immediate and natural background is to be found once more in the Old Testament. Thus Caird (122–23) links this vision with Ezekiel's prophecy of the unexpected invasion of Israel by Gog (Ezek. 38–39), an attack which symbolized the immense reserves of the powers of evil, from which there can be no security except in the final victory of God (cf. Ezek. 38.7–16). In the same way, John is here pointing out dramatically that the invasion of devilish cavalry is needed because the Roman world 'has tried to find security in that which is not God' (Caird 123; see also Mounce 197).

Beale (513–15) proposes that, in contrast to the fifth trumpet, the sixth includes deception, as well as death. The smoke and its consequent darkness (9.17–18) are images of the punishment which follows deception (see 8.12; 9.2–3), while fire is metaphorical for lethal judgement (see 9.18). The deception in view, according to Beale (513), manifests itself in part through false teachers who maintain the legitimacy for believers of some forms of idolatry (cf. 2.6, 14–15, 20–21; also the harm of deception seen as a judgement in Ps. 115.8; Isa. 63.17–19; Rom. 1.18–27; 2 Thess. 2.9–12; et al.). The theme of deception in the sixth trumpet-plague is further implied, in Beale's argument (ibid.), by the parallels between it and the sixth bowl (16.12–14), the background to which can be located in the Exodus narrative (see also 17.8, 17; 20.8).

The vision as a whole, in 9.13–19, speaks of the eschatological judgement of God on an unbelieving world, which can break into its history at any point, and in all possible human contexts.

20–21 These verses might be understood as a conclusion to the sequence of six plagues narrated so far in this scene. But the use of the verb ἀποκτείνω (*apokteinō*, 'kill') in verse 20, repeated from verse 18, suggests that this paragraph is a finale to the slaughter inflicted by the fiendish cavalry in the sixth trumpet-plague alone (cf. Aune 541). The fact that 'the remainder of the human race' (οἱ λοιποὶ τῶν ἀνθρώπων, *hoi loipoi tōn anthrōpōn*, lit. 'the rest of men') escaped death from the plagues of 9.13–19 implies that even those who 'survived' (which is the REB translation) were affected in some way by the suffering which took place. The sixth plague is an escalation of the fifth, in that death (both physical and spiritual) is involved, and not merely anguish (see on verses 18–19; also 9.5–6).

The survivors 'did not renounce (μετενόησαν, metenoēsan, lit. "they did not repent of") their own handiwork'. The introduction of the thought of renunciation (or repentance), here and in verse 21 (where the same Greek verb is used), appears to be unexpected. This suggestion is reinforced by the fact that nowhere in the trumpet sequence is the purpose of the plagues directly specified: either as a divine judgement on earlier wrongdoing, or as the means of encouraging a change of heart (so Aune 541). However, the intention of the metaphorical portents is clearly that of eschatological judgement; and the possibility of repentance is implied by the limitation of that discrimination (see on 8.7–12; 9.4–6, 10, 15, 18–19). It is true, nonetheless, that in the present verses and at 16.9, 11 (the only other occurrences of the verb μετανοεῖν, metanoein, 'to repent', in the Apocalypse outside the seven oracles of Rev. 2—3), the recorded human response to God's judgement is a *lack* of penitence and renunciation. In verses 20–21 the theme of repentance once again reflects the Exodus narrative (Exod. 7.13, 22, et al.). There, similarly, a change of heart by the Pharaoh never becomes a possibility; although this is in line with characteristic Hebraic theology, which often considers the result as if it were the cause (e.g. Isa. 6.9–10 = John 12.39–40). See Aune 541.

The terminology of repentance is used eight times in the letters to the seven churches (2.5 [*bis*], 16, 21 [*bis*], 22; 3.3, 19); and, apart from 2.22, the setting is one of a positive exhortation by the risen Christ for the members of those congregations to think again about their commitment and faithfulness. The chief problem in the Johannine community, from which repentance was needed, seems to have been that of compromise with the surrounding pagan culture, and in particular idolatry (see esp. 2.20–23). Beale (520) therefore suggests that the motif of renunciation (repentance) in 9.20–21 is linked to that in Rev. 2—3 in terms of those who, in the Church and beyond, compromise with an idolatrous society and who, like Jezebel's adherents (2.22–23), refuse to renounce their false syncretism. The warning to the indecisive is that demonic and destructive forces 'stand behind the idols that they are tempted to worship' (Beale, ibid.). See also on deception and idolatry in verses 17–19; and for that theme in the setting of the Exodus narrative see also Heb. 3.7–19.

In the second part of verse 20, and in verse 21, the seer provides us with a list of those malpractices which the faithless did not, and usually do not, renounce. The first, not surprisingly, is idolatry itself, which is described as 'their own handiwork' (ἐκ τῶν ἔργων τῶν χειρῶν αὐτῶν, ek tōn ergōn tōn cheirōn autōn, lit. '[they did not repent] of the works of their hands'). This is a typically Semitic phrase, used in the Old Testament and elsewhere with reference to idols as lifeless, handmade objects of worship. See esp. Ps. 115.4 = Ps. 135.15 ('their idols are silver and gold, the work of human hands'); also Deut. 4.28; 2 Chron. 34.25; Isa. 2.8; Jer. 32.30; Mic. 5.13; Acts 7.41 (with reference to the golden calf); et al. The phrase 'the work(s) of their hands' occurs less pejoratively in the literature of Judaism as a synonym for the actions of people (e.g. Job 1.10; Ps. 90.17; Isa. 65.22; *Pss. Sol.* 16.9), or for the creative activity of God (Ps. 92.4; Isa. 64.8; *Life of Adam and Eve [Apocalypse]* 33.5).

The unfaithful survivors of the latest plague are represented as refusing to renounce their handiwork, with the result that they 'did not stop worshipping demons'. The ἵνα (hina, 'that') clause in the Greek has a consecutive force; hence the translation. They 'did not renounce', so 'they did not stop'. Before the material nature of the idols is further described, a warning is given about their spiritual character. Idol-worship involves allegiance to demonic forces, which have just been symbolized by the eschatological creatures of verses 16–19. 'Demons' and 'idols' are not differentiated in this text (against Charles 1, 254). On the contrary, the conjunction καί (kai, 'and') which occurs between the two nouns is epexegetic, giving the sense 'demons, *that is* idols'. Precisely, the powers of darkness use idolatry to keep people, deceived and in darkness, under their thrall (cf. Beale 519). Equally, that which is not of God, if worshipped, becomes a demonic power (Sweet 173); cf. 13.3.

The word δαιμόνιον (*daimonion*, 'demon') is found in the Apocalypse only here and at 16.14; 18.2. It is a diminutive of the Greek term, with the same meaning, δαίμων (*daimōn*); and this form appears in the New Testament only at Matt. 8.31. The link between demons and idols is frequently made by Jewish writers (cf. Deut. 32.17 LXX; Ps. 95.5 LXX; *Jub.* 11.4; *1 Enoch* 99.6–7); and the assumption is clearly expressed in Old Testament thought (as at Deut. 32.16–17; cf. Wis. 15.15) that demon-like idols were worshipped as gods by the rebellious people of Israel. Paul claims in 1 Cor. 10.20 that pagans sacrifice to demons, and not to God.

The list of materials from which the idols were made ('gold and silver, brass, stone and wood') closely echoes Dan. 5.4; see also Dan. 2.31–35; 5.23; Wis. 15.9; 2 Macc. 2.2; Acts 17.29; 4Q242 (4QPrNab ar) *frags.* 1–3, 6–8. When idolatry is condemned in Judaism, the specification of various inanimate substances involved in their construction serves to emphasize the absurdity of worshipping objects which were supposed to be living. See Ps. 115.4–7; 135.15–17; Hab. 2.18–19; 3 Macc. 4.16; et al. In Revelation, idolatry as a general vice is denounced only here and at 22.15; although allusion is made elsewhere to particular forms of the pagan habit, such as eating meat offered to idols (2.14, 20) and the universal worship of the dragon-beast or his image (13.4, 14–15; 14.9, 11; 16.2; 19.20; 20.4). For antagonism to idolatry in other parts of the New Testament see 1 Cor. 10.14, 19; Gal. 5.19–20; Col. 3.5; 1 Pet. 4.3.

The description of the idols in verse 20, as composed of inanimate materials, continues with a further exposition of their lifeless and uncommunicative nature: 'they cannot see or hear or move' (similarly Wis. 15.15–17; *Sib. Or.* 5.77–85). In Hebraic thought, idolaters reflect the inertness of the objects they worship, and become spiritually inactive (cf. Ps. 115.8; 135.18; Isa. 6.9–10). The same thought may well be present in Rev. 9.20–21. The faithless have been deceived, and led into idolatrous behaviour. The hardening influence of the demons has caused them also to become spiritually inactive. They have neither renounced their idolatry nor heeded the warnings of impending judgement by the God they have rejected; and this is so, despite the fate of their companions in idol-worship. Cf. Beale 519.

The motif of impenitence, on the part of a humanity which is inclined to paganism, continues (verse 21) with the completion of a catalogue of wrongdoing begun in verse 20. In addition to idolatry, those who do not wear God's seal on their foreheads (9.4) refuse to give up murdering, magic arts, immorality or thieving. For the verb οὐ μετενόησαν (*ou metenoēsan*, lit. 'they did not repent') see on verse 20. Three of the four vices mentioned here (murder, immorality and theft), in that order, are prohibited in the sixth, seventh and eighth commandments of the Decalogue (Exod. 20.13–15 = Deut. 5.17–19); and this context has probably influenced the composition of verse 21. It is important to notice that the sin of idolatry heads the list of Ten Commandments (Exod. 20.4–5 = Deut. 5.8–9); and, both there and in the present context, the three errors specified may be taken as expressions of that fundamental wrongdoing against God (see verse 20). Such practices are involved in idolatrous worship, or can become acts of idolatry in themselves. Faithlessness of this kind, in fact, produces wrong behaviour of all kinds (cf. Wis. 14.27, 'the worship of idols is the beginning and cause and end of every evil'; Rom. 1.20–32).

Significantly, all four sins mentioned in verse 21 (murder, magic arts, immorality and thieving) are at different times connected with idolatry elsewhere in biblical literature. See 2 Kings 9.22; Isa. 47.9–48.5; Jer. 7.5–11; Hos. 3.1–4.2; Mic. 5.12–15; Wis. 12.3–6; Acts 15.20; Rom. 1.24–29; Gal. 5.19–20; Eph. 5.5; Col. 3.5; and note further Beale 519–20. Idolaters, murderers, sorcerers and fornicators are listed at Rev. 21.8 as sharing the second death; and at 22.15 those four groups of people are among those who are excluded from the new Jerusalem. The three vices of murder, immorality and theft in verse 21 are mentioned together at Mark 7.21; cf. also Luke 18.20; Rom. 13.9.

For 'murdering' (φόνος, *phonos*, lit. 'murder', 'killing') see the related term φονεύς (*phoneus*, 'murderer') at Rev. 21.8; 22.15. The noun φάρμακον (*pharmakon*, here translated as 'magic art') occurs in the New Testament only at Rev. 9.21; but see the cognates at Rev. 18.23; 21.8; 22.15. It can signify poison, or (as in verse 21) a drug used as a controlling medium; and this is the equivalent of a magic potion (see BDAG 1050*a*). The 'magic arts' referred to here are clearly nearer to sorcery than to witchcraft. The practice of magic was widespread in the ancient world, notably in Egypt and Asia Minor (cf. Moffatt 410). In the Apocalypse, magic (sorcery) is cited as the means by which Babylon deceives all the nations (18.23); and in 22.15 (cf. 21.8) those who indulge in magic arts are mentioned with the immoral, the killers, the idolaters and the liars, as having no right to enter the heavenly city. The word πορνεία (*porneia*, 'immorality') is a generic term for varying kinds of unsanctioned sexual intercourse (BDAG 854*a*). The warnings of divine judgement on sin, vividly depicted in this scene, are evidently not heeded by those who persist in idolatrous unbelief.

Theology

In the scene just concluded, the opening verse (8.1), with its mention of the opening of the final seal and silence in heaven, stands almost on its own. Yet there is an important theological, as well as structural, connection between this text, the visions of judgement and security which have already been disclosed in 6.1—7.17, and the trumpet-calls which are to follow (8.2—9.21). The breaking of the seventh seal should signify the consummation of God's plan for his creation (see on 5.1); but there is more to come. The last seal looks back to the first six, with their attendant expressions of divine judgement. But, although with the opening of all seven seals the eschaton begins to break in, the end is not yet; and more critical sequences, beginning with the seven trumpets, have yet to be revealed. John's apocalyptic drama causes us to participate in what appears to be an endless end of the world, and to wait for a conclusion which never fully arrives (cf. Barr, 'Waiting for the End', esp. 112). See further on 22.20. Meanwhile, the sealing of the saints and the depiction of the Church triumphant, in Rev. 7.1–17, remind us that God's judgements are the means by which he achieves his salvific purposes of love.

There is a contrast between the series of trumpets and the preceding heptad of seals. As Beasley-Murray (155) points out, the trumpets end in joy. Unlike the seal-judgements, the trumpets balance discrimination with the salvation of the new age; so that the scene following the delayed sounding of the seventh trumpet (11.15) is similar to the throne-vision of Rev. 5, and includes a virtual coronation of God and the Lamb (11.15–18). The strong typology of the Exodus narrative, which consciously underlies the trumpet-judgements in 8.7—9.19 and the opening of the heavenly temple at 11.19, is an appropriate theological backcloth both to the plagues themselves and to the deliverance which accompanies them. These acts of God are models for John, since the prophet-seer now universalizes them, and places them in a cosmic setting. The Pharaoh oppressing Israel is replaced by an imperial ruler who persecutes the world; and the conflict becomes a struggle between the forces of the underworld and the Lord of heaven. Historically, victory over the rebellious Egyptians was followed by entry into the Promised Land; the seventh trumpet-blast, in the vision of the next scene, is now succeeded by access to the kingdom of God (see also 15.2–8). Cf. Beasley-Murray 155–56.

The theme of judgement in Rev. 8—9 is strong. However (against Beale 517–18), the trumpet-plagues are not simply demonstrations of God's justice, which indicate the need for spiritual reform on the part of the unsealed, without being intended to bring about a change of heart. Human repentance is admittedly not stated explicitly as a reason for God's judgemental activity following the sounding of the seven trumpets; nevertheless, it is present in this heptad more than in the sequences of the seals or the bowls (but see 6.8). The limitation of the effects of the trumpet-calls suggests accordingly that divine restraint is in place in order to allow for the possibility of repentance, so ending the necessity for further punishment brought on by continuing impenitence. See esp. on 9.4–6, 20–21; and contrast the hardness of heart evident at 16.8–9, 10–11, 21. John's vision here includes a salutary warning for the unfaithful, as well as a reminder (in 9.4) to the saints that God's love and protection are ongoing.

The theology of the visions which are unveiled in Rev. 9.1–21 reinforces the positive, and by intention salvific, nature of the judgement-plagues by defining further the extent of the sovereignty which is exercised by God and the Lamb. It becomes clear in this scene, as also in the rest of the Apocalypse, that ultimately divine power controls the universe, including the realm of Satan. The authority of the demonic forces is derived, and will be finally removed from them (9.1–6, 13–15; cf. also 12.7–12; and see on 5.6). Cf. Kiddle 154–55.

Here is a basis of hope and encouragement for those Christians, in John's community and elsewhere, who are beleaguered. Whether the pressures upon them are brought about by Roman persecution, opposition from fellow-Jews, or divisions within their own circle caused by ethical compromise and doctrinal error (see above, 4–6), the saints can be reassured that God's purposes of love for his world are steadfast. False belief and behaviour, symbolized in this passage by idol-worship, must eventually be challenged and denounced; and it is apparent that idolatry is a modern, and not merely an ancient, phenomenon (Hughes 115; cf. Rist 437). Moreover, as the seer points out, the disasters unleashed by the forces of evil cannot in the end harm those who wear God's seal on their foreheads (9.4); despite universal chaos and unfaithfulness, they will be sustained (7.16–17). See further Beale 493.

The eschatology of the scene in Rev. 8—9, finally, cannot be interpreted in a linear fashion. As in all parts of this drama, time and eternity are drawn together; the present is viewed in the light of the end, just as eternity gathers up the circumstances of time. See Smalley, *Thunder and Love* 150–52, 174–76. The apocalypse is already and constantly in progress; and that is why, in Revelation, theology is more important than chronology (Fiorenza, *Book of Revelation* 35–56). The trumpets, like the seals and the bowls and similar images, do not refer to specific and consecutive events in time which can be identified, but to principles of right and wrong, divine goodness and human evil, which operate throughout the history of the world and its society. This interpretation is supported by the universal scope of John's imagery, in this passage and beyond. See further Milligan 153–54; Hendriksen 41–43.

INTERVAL
God's Sovereignty
(10.1—11.19)

Translation

10 ¹Then I saw another[a] strong angel descending from heaven, wrapped around in a cloud, with a halo above his head;[b] his face was like the sun, and his legs seemed to be fiery pillars. ²He also held in his hand a small scroll,[c] which had been opened. He placed his right foot on the sea, with his left foot on the land. ³And he cried out with a loud voice, like a roaring lion; and when he shouted, the seven claps of thunder made themselves heard. ⁴I was about to write down what[d] the seven thunderclaps had said, when I heard a heavenly voice saying, 'Seal up the message of the seven[e] thunderclaps, and do not consider writing it down!'

⁵Then the angel I had seen standing between the sea and the dry land raised his right[f] hand to heaven, ⁶and swore by[g] the one who lives eternally, and who created the heaven and the earth, the sea and everything in them,[h] 'There will be no more time of waiting; ⁷when the moment arrives for the seventh angel to sound his trumpet, then the hidden purpose of God, which he proclaimed to his[i] servants[j] the prophets,[j] will be fulfilled.'[k]

⁸Then the heavenly voice,[l] which I had heard, was again speaking[m] to me and saying,[n] 'Go and take the scroll[o] which lies open in the hand of the angel standing between the sea and the dry land.' ⁹So I went to the angel, and asked him to give[p] me the small scroll.[q] He said to me, 'Take it, and eat it; and although it will become bitter in your stomach, it will be sweet as honey to your taste.' ¹⁰So I took the small scroll[r] out of the angel's hand, and ate it; and to my taste it was sweet as honey, but when I had swallowed it my stomach became bitter. ¹¹Then I was told,[s] 'You must prophesy once more against peoples, nations, language groups and rulers.'

11 ¹Then I was given a measuring rod, resembling a staff; and I was instructed,[t] 'Get up, and measure the temple of God, including the altar area, and count the worshippers within it. ²But exclude the outer[u] court of the temple from your calculations, because it has been handed over to the Gentiles; and they will trample the holy city underfoot for forty-two months.

³'And I will permit my two witnesses to prophesy for those twelve hundred and sixty days, wearing[v] sackcloth.' ⁴These are the two olive trees and the two lampstands, in attendance on[w] the Lord of the earth. ⁵If anyone tries to harm these two, fire pours from their mouths and utterly destroys their enemies; since anyone who wishes[x] to harm them must be killed in this way. ⁶These two have the authority[y] to lock up the heavens, so that no rain can fall during the period of their prophecy; they also have power over the waters, to turn them into blood, and to afflict the land with every kind of plague as often as[z] they wish.[aa]

⁷But when they have completed their testimony, the beast ascending[bb] from the bottomless pit is going to make war on them, in order to conquer and kill them. ⁸And their dead bodies[cc] will lie in the square of the great city, which is called prophetically 'Sodom' and 'Egypt', where also their Lord was crucified. ⁹For three and a half days some of the peoples and races, and language groups and nations gaze at the dead bodies, and refuse to allow them burial; ¹⁰while the earth's inhabitants rejoice over them, and celebrate by exchanging gifts, because these two prophets had tormented the people of the world.

[11]And after the[dd] three and a half days a breath of life from God came into them,[ee] so that they stood up on their feet; and great terror struck those who saw them. [12]Then they heard[ff] a loud, heavenly voice saying[gg] to them, 'Come up here!' They ascended to heaven in a cloud, in full view of their enemies. [13]At that very moment there was a violent earthquake, so that a tenth of the city collapsed; seven thousand people were killed in the earthquake, and the survivors became filled with terror, and offered homage to the God of heaven.

[14]The second woe has taken place; look, the third disaster will occur soon!

[15]Then the seventh angel sounded his trumpet, and loud voices could be heard in heaven, saying,[hh]

> 'The kingdom of the world has become the sovereign realm of our Lord
> and his Messiah, who will reign for ever and ever.'

[16]Then the[ii] twenty-four elders,[jj] seated on their thrones in God's presence, prostrated themselves and worshipped God, [17]singing,

> 'We thank you, the Lord God Almighty,
>   you were, and you are;[kk]
> now you have assumed your full authority,
> and entered upon your reign.
> [18]The nations became enraged, but now your wrath has come,
> and the moment for judging the dead,
> for rewarding your servants the prophets and the saints,
> and those who revere[ll] your name,
> both the insignificant and the mighty,[mm]
> and for destroying completely those who ruin the earth.'

[19]Then God's heavenly[nn] temple was opened, and the ark of his[oo] covenant was visible within his sanctuary; and there followed flashes of lightning and roarings, and peals of thunder and an earthquake, and a heavy hailstorm.

Text

[a] The reading ἄλλον ἄγγελον (*allon angelon*, 'another [strong] angel') is well attested by A C Andreas Primasius Beatus, et al. Some MSS, including 025 046 1006[911] Byz Victorinus, omit ἄλλον (*allon*, 'another'); but this is an obvious correction, based on the perception by copyists that no previous angel has been mentioned in this passage (cf. 14.6). However, see 5.2; and further on verse 1, below.

[b] Instead of ἐπὶ τῆς κεφαλῆς (*epi tēs kephalēs*, lit. 'on the head'), as witnessed by 𝔓47 ℵ Andreas Byz, et al., some MSS (such as A C Byz) replace the genitives with the accusative phrase ἐπὶ τὴν κεφαλήν (*epi tēn kephalēn*), which has the same meaning. It is difficult to determine which reading is original, since the evidence is balanced, and the writer of the Apocalypse uses ἐπί (*epi*, 'on') with both the genitive (cf. 12.1) and the accusative (19.12), although more often with the accusative.

[c] The form βιβλαρίδιον (*biblaridion*, 'small scroll') appears in ℵ A C[2] 025 1 2351, et al. Some MSS (including C★ 1006 1611[1611 2344] Andreas) have the form, with the same meaning, βιβλιδάριον (*biblidarion*), which also occurs as a variant in verses 9 and 10. The use of βιβλίον (*biblion*, 'scroll'), as in 𝔓47 Byz it[gig], et al., may be influenced by the choice of that term in verse 8 (v.l.). Aune (549) argues that βιβλαρίδιον (*biblaridion*, 'small scroll') is a true diminutive, and that on morphological grounds it is the original reading here. See also BDAG 176*a*.

[d] The external evidence for reading ὅτε (*hote*, lit. 'when') is impressive, and includes A C 025 046 1006 1611[1854] 2053 vg syr[ph,h] arm. The variant ὅσα (*hosa*, '[the words] which')

occurs in 𝔓47 ℵ it^gig cop^sa,bo Primasius Beatus, et al. But this is probably an interpretative rewriting of the text, involving a 'modification' for purposes of exegesis (so Metzger, *Textual Commentary* 743). 'What' (= 'that which') appears in the translation of this verse, because the temporal adverb 'when' has disappeared in an attempt to express the sense of the Greek euphoniously.

^e The numeral 'seven' (ἑπτά, *hepta*) is omitted by 𝔓47, presumably as a later emendation designed to eliminate a reference to 'seven thunderclaps' (ἑπτὰ βρονταί, *hepta brontai*, lit. 'seven thunders') twice in the same verse (see also verse 3).

^f The words τὴν δεξιάν (*tēn dexian*, lit. 'the right [hand]') are included by ℵ C 025 Byz it^gig Primasius Beatus, et al.; they are missing from A Andreas vg syr^ph, et al. The later omission may have been caused by the reality that in Judaism the use of the uplifted right hand for oath-taking is extremely rare. See the comment on 10.5.

^g The use of the preposition ἐν (*en*, lit. 'on'), in this context, is difficult. Its absence is well attested (𝔓47 ℵ★ ℵ¹ 046 2351 Byz, et al.); and it is easier to account for its inclusion than its omission. Without ἐν (*en*, 'in'), the expression could mean that the angel swore *to* 'the one who lives eternally'; and the addition of the preposition helps to remove that ambiguity. Alternatively, it is not easy to explain the omission of the word, except as an error. Aune (550) therefore concludes that the strength of the MS evidence in favour of the omission of ἐν (*en*, 'in'), combined with the fact that this version is the *lectio difficilior*, suggests that the preposition was not part of the original text of verse 6. However, it is accepted by NA (651).

^h The expression καὶ τὴν θάλασσαν καὶ τὰ ἐν αὐτῇ (*kai tēn thalassan kai ta en autē[i]*, lit. 'and the sea and everything in it') is attested by 𝔓47 C 025 1006 1611^1854 vg cop^bo, et al.); but it is omitted by ℵ★ A 1611 it^gig syr^ph cop^sa, et al. Its absence is probably accidental, arising from the similarity of the three phrases in the sequence. The weight of the external evidence favours the originality of the words, which also form an appropriate part of the formal introduction to the angelic oath (cf. Metzger, *Textual Commentary* 743).

^i The emphatic form of the pronoun, ἑαυτοῦ (*heautou*, 'his'), is srongly supported by 𝔓47 ℵ A C 025 2053, et al. The weaker, but more usual, form αὐτοῦ (*autou*, 'his'), as read by 046 and a majority of minuscules, is clearly secondary.

^j TR and a few minuscules alter the accusatives δούλους (*doulous*, 'servants') and προφήτας (*prophētas*, 'prophets') to the dative case, which more commonly follows the verb εὐαγγελίζειν (*euangelizein*, 'to disclose', lit. 'announce good news'). This is clearly an inferior reading; however, see on verse 7. Some MSS (including 𝔓47 ℵ 2321 cop^sa) add καί (*kai*, 'and') after δούλους (*doulous*, 'servants'); but this variant is not strongly supported, and might have been inserted by copyists who were unfamiliar with the Old Testament stereotypical phrase, '[God's] servants the prophets' (Jer. 7.25; Amos 3.7; et al.). Nevertheless, as Aune (551) points out, the καί (*kai*, 'and') here may be epexegetical. In that case, the phrase could mean 'his servants, *that is* the prophets', which conforms to the style elsewhere of the writer of Revelation (see 1.2; 2.27; 12.2; 15.2; 18.13 [*bis*]; 19.16; et al.; cf. John 1.16). Note Aune cxcv.

^k Instead of ἐτελέσθη (*etelesthē*, lit. 'has been fulfilled', aorist indicative passive), as read by ℵ A C 025 1006 1611^2329, et al., some witnesses (including 1611^1854 2351 Andreas syr^h) have the aorist subjunctive passive, τελεσθῇ (*telesthē[i]*, 'may have been fulfilled'). The first version is original. Later scribes assumed that this sentence was governed by the conjunction ὅταν (*hotan*, 'when', 'whenever', which is followed by the subjunctive) in the previous phrase; whereas it is a main clause.

¹ As Aune (551) points out, the syntax of this sentence is rough (see further the comment on verse 8, below). The main problem is caused by the fact that the noun ἡ φωνή (*hē phōnē*, 'the voice') is in the nominative case, but is syntactically unrelated either to the following relative pronoun ἥν (*hēn*, 'which'), in the accusative, or to the subsequent clauses. The nominative form of 'voice' is clearly original, in view of its difficulty. Later copyists attempted to straighten out the syntax by replacing the nominative with the accusative, and rearranging the order of the words. Thus some MSS (such as 104 2091 Primasius vg) have the obviously secondary reading, καὶ ἤκουσα φωνήν (*kai ēchousa phōnēn*, 'and I heard a voice').

ᵐ The original reading is λαλοῦσαν (*lalousan*, 'speaking'), where the feminine accusative participle modifies the preceding relative pronoun ἥν (*hēn*, 'which'). See the preceding textual note. A few witnesses (2351 Byz) alter the accusative to the nominative, λαλοῦσα (*lalousa*), with the same meaning, to agree with the nominative form φωνή (*phōnē*, 'voice').

ⁿ See the two preceding textual notes. The participial form λέγουσαν (*legousan*, 'saying'), using the accusative by attraction to the earlier λαλοῦσαν (*lalousan*, 'speaking'), is original. 2351 Byz again correct to the nominative λέγουσα (*legousa*), with the same meaning, in proper agreement with the nominative form of φωνή (*phōnē*, 'voice').

ᵒ A number of synonyms for '(small) scroll' appear in the text and variations in Rev. 10. See the textual note on verse 2. Here, the form βιβλίον (*biblion*) is strongly attested (A C 1006 1611¹⁶¹¹·¹⁸⁵⁴ Oecumenius²⁰⁵³ latt), and is doubtless original (see also 5.1–9; et al.). The word is a faded diminutive of βίβλος (*biblos*, 'book'). Some MSS (including א 025 2351) read βιβλαρίδιον (*biblaridion*, 'small scroll'), as in verse 2; while others (Andreas Byz) have βιβλιδάριον (*biblidarion*), with the same meaning. See also verses 9 and 10.

ᵖ The reading δοῦναι (*dounai*, 'to give'), which uses the aorist infinitive, is strongly attested (so 𝔓47 א A C 046 1006, et al.), and clearly original. Some MSS (including Oecumenius²⁰⁵³ Andreas) have the second aorist imperative, δός (*dos*, 'give'). But this is to understand λέγων (*legōn*, lit. 'saying') here as the participle of a verb of command; whereas λέγειν (*legein*, lit. 'to speak') is used in the present context as a verb of asking (hence the translation). Against this view see BDAG 589*b*.

�q The form βιβλαρίδιον (*biblaridion*, 'small scroll') is well attested (Aᶜ C 025 2351, et al.), and probably original. Secondary textual variations, similar to those in verse 8 (q.v.), appear in several witnesses. See Aune 552.

ʳ See the previous note. Because of the variation between βιβλαρίδιον (*biblaridion*, 'small scroll') in verses 2 and 9 and βιβλίον (*biblion*, 'scroll') in verse 8, it is difficult to determine the original reading in verse 10. The MS evidence for βιβλαρίδιον (*biblaridion*, 'small scroll') is strong (A C 025 2351 TR, et al.), against βιβλίον (*biblion*, 'scroll') in א 046 1611¹⁸⁵⁴ lat, et al. The form βιβλιδάριον (*biblidarion*, 'small scroll') has support mostly from minuscules, among them 1006 1611 2053; also Andreas. Metzger, *Textual Commentary* 743–44, favours the version βιβλαρίδιον (*biblaridion*, 'small scroll'), both on the basis of the weight of external evidence, and also because the reading in 𝔓47 (βιβλίδιον, *biblidion*) seems to support that form of the term which is used variously in this passage.

ˢ The reading λέγουσιν (*legousin*, lit. 'they say') is attested by א A 1006 1611²³²⁹, et al. The plural form of the present tense is difficult, since no plural subject exists in the immediate context. The grammar is therefore corrected by later witnesses (such as 1611¹⁸⁵⁴ Andreas it syrᶜᵒᵖˢᵃ·ᵇᵒ) to the singular λέγει (*legei*, 'he says'). Impersonal plurals can be found elsewhere in the Apocalypse (cf. 2.24; 12.6; 16.15; 18.14); in 10.11 it could be used as a circumlocution for the name of God. Following Aune (548, 553), I translate λέγουσίν μοι (legousin moi, lit. 'they say to me') as a passive construction, 'I was told'.

ᵗ The masculine singular present participle λέγων (legōn, lit. 'saying') has no obvious antecedent, since the subject of the aorist passive phrase ἐδόθη μοι (edothē moi, 'I was given', lit. 'it was given to me') is not specified. To make sense of this awkward construction, later interpolations were made. Thus א²046 1611¹⁸⁵⁴,²³²⁹ 2351 Beatus Victorinus, et al. insert before λέγων (legōn, 'saying'), 'and the angel stood' (καὶ εἱστήκει ὁ ἄγγελος, kai heistēkei ho angelos; Latin et stabat angelus); while some texts of Andreas, at the same place, read καὶ ἐλέχθη μοι (kai elechthē moi, lit. 'it was told to me').

ᵘ The reading ἔξωθεν (exōthen, 'outer', lit. 'outside') has strong MS support, including 𝔓47 א¹ A 025 046 1006 1611¹⁶¹¹,¹⁸⁵⁴ Andreas vg syrʰ copˢᵃ,ᵇᵒ, and is to be preferred. Copyists who expected the αὐλή (aulē, 'court') in this context to be the inner courtyard of the temple, especially in the light of verse 1, were no doubt puzzled by the expression τὴν αὐλὴν τὴν ἔξωθεν (tēn aulēn tēn exōthen), meaning 'the outer court'. Some witnesses (such as א* 1611²³²⁹ syrᵖʰ Victorinus Byz) therefore alter the adverb to ἔσωθεν (esōthen, 'within'). Cf. Metzger, Textual Commentary 744.

ᵛ The reading περιβεβλημένοι (peribeblēmenoi, 'wearing', 'clothed', in the nominative), present in C 2053 Andreas Hippolytus Byz, constitutes a grammatical difficulty, since the participle modifies 'my two witnesses' (τοῖς δυσὶν μάρτυσίν μου, tois dysin martysin mou); and this is a noun group in the dative. Undoubtedly the nominative form of the participle, being the lectio difficilior, is original; in which case it must be construed as agreeing with the subject – logically nominative plural – of the verb προφητεύσουσιν (prophēteusousin, lit. 'they will prophesy'). The scribal correction of the solecism to the accusative form of the participle, περιβεβλημένους (peribeblēmenous, 'clothed'), to agree with σάκκους (sakkous, 'sackcloth'), is strongly supported by א* A 025 046 1611²³²⁹, et al. (cf. Charles 2, 300); but it is clearly secondary.

ʷ Two textual variations are to be found at this point in the Greek of verse 4.

(a) Although the reading is strongly supported, some MSS (including א 1611¹⁶¹¹,²³²⁹ 2351) omit the relative pronoun αἱ (hai) before ἐνώπιον (enōpion, lit. 'before'). This is a later, but unsuccessful, attempt to soften the incongruence between the pronoun in the feminine and the following participle, ἑστῶτες (hestōtes, lit. 'standing'), which is in the masculine. See the next part of this note.

(b) This incongruence, which is an obvious grammatical error, caused some copyists (as shown by א² 1006 1611¹⁸⁵⁴ Andreas) later to change the masculine participle into the feminine form, with the same meaning, ἑστῶσαι (hestōsai).

ˣ The aorist subjunctive form, after εἰ (ei, 'if'), of the verb θελήσῃ (thelēsē[i], lit. 'should wish'), as attested by א A, is original. The secondary version, θελήσει (thelēsei, lit. 'will wish', third person singular future indicative), appears in 𝔓47 1006 2351, et al. This is the result of confusion, since the Greek ending ῃ (ē[i]) is the equivalent of ει (ei). Some witnesses (among them C 2053 Andreas Primasius Byz) replace the aorist subjunctive with the present indicative, θέλει (thelei, 'wishes'); but this appears to be a secondary attempt to align the form of the verb with the present tense of the same verb, as it is used in the first part of verse 5. At that point (verse 5a) some MSS, such as 𝔓47, make a similar alteration in reverse, bringing the present tense into line with what is taken in verse 5b to be a future indicative.

ʸ Some MSS (including א Andreas Byz Hippolytus) omit the article τήν (tēn, 'the') before ἐξουσίαν (exousian, 'authority'). It is included by 𝔓47 A C 025 1611 2053 2351, et al. The noun ἐξουσία (exousia, 'authority'), when followed by an infinitive, is rarely used in Revelation with the article (but see 6.8; 9.10; 13.5). Nevertheless, in the present text it is easier to account for the accidental omission of the article than to explain its insertion. Aune (580) points out that this is one of a number of occasions when 𝔓47 and ℵ disagree on a reading, with the former preserving the *lectio originalis*.

ᶻ The MS evidence in Revelation for the use of the particles ἐάν (*ean*) and ἄν (*an*), both of which mean 'if', or 'whenever', is divided. In the present text, used with ὁσάκις (*hosakis*) to mean 'whenever', or 'as often as', ἐάν (*ean*) is read by 𝔓47 ℵ A Andreas Byz; whereas C 2053 2351, et al., have ἄν (*an*). On the showing of the external evidence, the former is likely to be original.

ᵃᵃ In place of the aorist subjunctive θελήσωσιν (*thelēsōsin*, lit. 'they [might have] wished'), as read by ℵ A Andreas Byz, et al., some witnesses have the present subjunctive form of the verb, θέλωσιν (*thelōsin*, 'they [might] wish'). The replacement is no doubt a secondary contraction. C has the future indicative θελήσουσιν (*thelēsousin*, 'they will wish'); but this is an impossible reading, as ἐάν (*ean*, 'if', 'when') is never used in Revelation with the future indicative, but always with the present or aorist subjunctive.

ᵇᵇ The reading τὸ ἀναβαῖνον (*to anabainon*, 'ascending'), agreeing with the neuter noun τὸ θηρίον (*to thērion*, 'the beast'), is well attested (C Andreas Byz 2351), and original. The variant, τὸ ἀναβαίνων (*to anabainōn*), with the same meaning but with the participle in the masculine, appears in A 2060 2286, et al. This irregular and secondary version has probably resulted from a confusion on the part of copyists between the letters o (*o*) and ω (*ō*) in the Greek alphabet.

ᶜᶜ In some leading MSS (including 𝔓47 ℵ 1611[1854,2329] Andreas lat syr) the plural form of the noun, τὰ πτώματα (*ta ptōmata*, 'the bodies'), replaces the singular τὸ πτῶμα (*to ptōma*, lit. 'the [dead] body'), as read by A C 1006 2351 Byz Tyconius, et al. The plural reading appears to be a secondary attempt at grammatical accuracy; although the singular version of the noun 'dead body' must be understood in this context as distributive, and therefore plural by implication.

ᵈᵈ The phrase μετὰ τὰς τρεῖς ἡμέρας (*meta tas treis hēmeras*, 'after the three days') is found in that form according to A C 2053 Byz, et al.; and this must be the original reading. Some witnesses, including ℵ 025 1611[1854,2344], omit the article τάς (*tas*, 'the'). But the article is anaphoric, referring back to the phrase 'three and a half days' in verse 9, where no article is used; and this literary usage is characteristic of John's style.

ᵉᵉ Four variants in the Greek are discernible at this point.

(a) There is support from A 1006 1611[1854,2329] 2351 Tyconius for the reading ἐν αὐτοῖς (*en autois*, lit. 'on them'); so also NA 653.
(b) Some MSS, including C 025 2053, have the simple version αὐτοῖς (*autois*, 'them').
(c) 𝔓47 ℵ Byz, et al. witness to the form εἰς αὐτούς (*eis autous*, 'into them').
(d) Some texts of Andreas read ἐπ' αὐτούς (*ep'autous*, 'upon them').

Variant (a) is difficult, and therefore likely to be original, since in the LXX and the New Testament generally the verb εἰσέρχεσθαι (*eiserchesthai*, 'to enter, come into') is regularly used with the preposition εἰς (*eis*, 'into'). In that case, 11.11 is the only occasion in the Apocalypse where ἐν (*en*, 'on', 'in') is used as the stylistic equivalent of εἰς (*eis*, 'in', 'into'). The other variants are secondary. Reading (b) is probably the result of haplography, given that the preceding word in the sentence ends in -εν (*-en*). The variation represented by (c) appears to be a correction of (a), in an attempt to make the construction grammatically more normal. The same is true of the final variant, (d), which merely employs the preposition ἐπί (*epi*, 'on', 'upon'), instead of εἰς (*eis*, 'into'). See further Aune 581.

ff The third person plural aorist indicative, ἤκουσαν (*ēkousan*, 'they heard') is read by ℵ* A C 025 2053 vg syr^ph TR, et al. Some witnesses, including 𝔓47 ℵ^c 046 Andreas Byz syr^h cop^bo arm 2351, replaced this with the first person singular aorist, ἤκουσα (*ēkousa*, 'I heard'). The plural form is clearly original. John uses the singular, often with εἶδον (*eidon*, 'I saw'), regularly throughout Revelation (e.g. 4.1; 6.1; 8.13); but interestingly this characteristic terminology does not appear in 11.1–13. As a result, copyists corrected the plural to the singular; and this is a more likely substitution than the reverse.

gg Instead of the genitive form φωνῆς μεγάλης . . . λεγούσης (*phōnēs megalēs . . . legousēs*, 'a loud voice saying'), as attested by 𝔓47 ℵ C Andreas, et al., the accusative version, with the same meaning, φωνὴν μεγάλην . . . λέγουσαν (*phōnēn megalēn . . . legousan*), appears in A 1611^1611,2329 2053 2351 Byz (cf. Charles 1, 290; 2, 304). The MS evidence is reasonably balanced, and it is not easy to determine the original reading here. Normally the verb ἀκούειν (*akouein*, 'to hear') is used in the Apocalypse with the genitive of the person speaking (as in 6.1, 3, 5, et al.), and the accusative of what is heard (as in 1.3; 7.4; et al.). However, when φωνή (*phōnē*, 'voice') is the object of the verb ἀκούειν (*akouein*, 'to hear'), as in the present context, it sometimes appears in the genitive (so 3.20; et al.), but more often in the accusative (1.10; 5.11; 6.6, 7; et al.). It is therefore possible that, in verse 12, the original genitival form of this phrase has been altered into the accusative. See further Aune 582.

hh The grammatically difficult masculine plural of the participle λέγοντες (*legontes*, 'saying') is attested by A 2053 2351 Byz. The feminine form with the same meaning, λέγουσαι (*legousai*), appears in 𝔓47 ℵ C 051 1006^1006,1841 MSS of 1611 Andreas. The feminine variant is strongly supported; but it must be a secondary scribal alteration, designed to make the participle agree with its feminine antecedent, φωναὶ μεγάλαι (*phōnai megalai*, 'loud voices').

ii The definite article οἱ (*hoi*, 'the'), before εἴκοσι (*eikosi*, 'twenty'), is present in C 1006 1611 2062 Andreas Byz, et al. It is omitted by ℵ* A, et al. The omission is clearly a scribal error. The seer's first use of the expression 'twenty-four elders', in 4.4 (q.v.), occurs without an article; but thereafter, in line with the style of Revelation, the article with 'elders' (referring back to their original mention) is consistently used (see 4.10; 5.5, 6, 11, 14, et al.).

jj The article οἱ (*hoi*, 'the'), preceding ἐνώπιον (*enōpion*, lit. 'before'), appears in 025 2351 194 2019, et al.; but it is omitted by 𝔓47 A 046 1006 Andreas. Once more, the omission has resulted from a subsequent scribal error; for, in the Apocalypse, the definite article is regularly repeated (as here) before an attributive when it follows an arthrous noun (cf. 1.4; 2.24; 5.5; et al.).

kk A few MSS, including 051 1006^1006,1841 Beatus, insert after ὁ ἦν (*ho ēn*, lit. 'the one who was') the phrase καὶ ὁ ἐρχόμενος (*kai ho erchomenos*, lit. 'and the coming one'). But this is obviously a later addition, influenced by the occurrence of the threefold ascription of praise in Rev. 1.4, 8 and 4.8.

ll The phrase, καὶ τοῖς ἁγίοις καὶ τοῖς φοβουμένοις (*kai tois hagiois kai tois phoboumenois*, 'and the saints, and those who revere [your name]'), using the dative case, is found in 2053 Andreas Byz, et al. In some MSS (including 𝔓47 A 2351; cf. Charles 1, 295) it appears in the irregular accusative form. Grammatically, the datives are correct, because those to be rewarded, including 'your servants, the prophets' (τοῖς δούλοις σου τοῖς προφήταις, *tois doulois sou tois prophētais*), are the indirect object of the verb δοῦναι (*dounai*, 'to give'). The secondary accusatives result from understanding 'the saints, and those who revere [your name]' as being in apposition to the phrase (in the dative) 'your servants, the prophets'.

[mm] The reading τοὺς μικροὺς καὶ τοὺς μεγάλους (*tous mikrous kai tous megalous*, 'the insignificant and the mighty') is found in $\mathfrak{P}$47 $\aleph^*$ A C 2351, et al. In some witnesses (including $\aleph^c$ 025 046 2053 Andreas Byz) the phrase appears (with the same meaning) in the dative, τοῖς μικροῖς καὶ τοῖς μεγάλοις (*tois mikrois kai tois megalois*). The accusative form is strongly supported and, after the preceding datives, more difficult; it is therefore (with Metzger, *Textual Commentary* 745) to be preferred. The accusatives can be understood as being in apposition to the earlier phrase, in the dative, 'your servants, the prophets'. See also the preceding textual note.

[nn] There is strong external evidence (from A C 1006[1006,1841] 1611[2329] 2351 Victorinus it[gig,h] cop[bo] arm eth, et al.) for including the definite article ὁ (*ho*, 'the') before the preposition ἐν (*en*, 'in') as part of the phrase, ὁ ἐν τῷ οὐρανῷ (*ho en tō[i] ouranō[i]*, lit. 'in the heaven'). Other witnesses (such as $\mathfrak{P}$47 $\aleph$ 025 046 051 Andreas Byz) omit the article. This may have been a grammatical correction; alternatively, the omission could be the result of 'transcriptional oversight' (Metzger, *Textual Commentary* 745). The presence of the article (repeated with an attributive, following an arthrous noun) is supported by superior MSS attestation, and conforms to the literary style of Revelation (see 11.16); it is therefore to be regarded as original.

[oo] The expression, ἡ κιβωτὸς τῆς διαθήκης αὐτοῦ (*hē kibōtos tēs diathēkēs autou*, 'the ark of his covenant'), is clearly original. Some witnesses (including $\mathfrak{P}$47 Byz) replace the personal pronoun αὐτοῦ (*autou*, 'his') with the more descriptive τοῦ κυρίου (*tou kyriou*, 'of the Lord'); and others again (chiefly $\aleph$) correct that reading to τοῦ θεοῦ (*tou theou*, 'of God'). These secondary forms are derived from the familiar Old Testament phraseology, 'the ark of the covenant of the Lord/of God' (e.g. Num. 14.44; Deut. 10.8; Judg. 20.27).

Literary Setting

The section Rev. 10.1—11.19, in its totality, constitutes the third interval in the drama of the Apocalypse, placed as it is between the final scene of Act 1 and the opening scene of Act 2. Just as Chapter 7 forms an interlude between the sixth and seventh seals, so 10.1—11.13 provides an interval between the sixth and seventh trumpets (for the unit 11.14–19, see below). As Rev. 7 views the Church from the perspective of both earth and heaven, so Rev. 10—11 describe the saints of God in the light of their double commitment to both prophecy and martyrdom (cf. Boring 139). Equally the present passage, like Chapter 7, should not be regarded as an interruption during a chronological sequence of events. The caesura is rather a literary device, used by John to unfold further the role and destiny of the Christian community before and during the end-time (Mounce 199).

Two episodes delay the sounding of the seventh trumpet: 10.1–11 (the angel from heaven) and 11.1–13 (the measuring of the Temple and the two prophetic witnesses). Aune (555) claims that, although these sections are juxtaposed, they are linked 'only superficially'. Nevertheless, there are literary and theological features in Rev. 10.1—11.13 which hold the two passages together; indeed, it is possible to argue for the dramatic unity of the interval as a whole.

(a) There is nothing to suggest that there is an aporia between 10.11 and 11.1, or that a new unit of material is being introduced. The location (on earth) is the same; and the subject of the action is still the seer, who continues to play an active rather than a passive part in the scene.

(b) In both 10.8–10 and 11.1–2 the prophet-seer performs a prophetic action. Indeed, the motif of prophecy is strong in both Rev. 10 and 11; and it draws them together.

Elsewhere in the Apocalypse, diction related to this theme occurs only sporadically, whereas in this part of the drama there is a concentration of 'prophecy' cognates. Thus, the verb προφητεύειν (*prophēteuein*, 'to prophesy') occurs in 10.11; 11.3 (and only there in Revelation); the noun προφήτης (*prophētēs*, 'prophet') appears in 10.7; 11.10; and the noun προφητεία (*prophēteia*, 'prophecy') is used in 11.6.

(c) There is one very close linguistic association between the sections. In Rev. 10.11 the seer is bidden to prophesy against 'peoples, nations, language groups and rulers'; while in 11.9, where the Greek terminology is almost identical, 'peoples and races, and language groups and nations' gaze in hostility at the dead prophets.

(d) The reference to the sounding of the trumpet by the seventh angel in 10.7 looks forward directly to the trumpet-blast and its consequences in 11.15–19; and the phrase 'your servants, the prophets' in the hymn at 11.18 repeats an expression recorded in the angelic announcement of 10.7.

(e) There is a literary and theological inclusion which unites the sub-divisions in 11.1–19. In 11.1 John is commanded to measure the earthly (if figurative) Temple; while in 11.19 the manifestly heavenly sanctuary is opened (cf. Michaels 146–47). Cf. Giblin, 'Revelation 11.1–13' 434–36; and see further the comments below.

(A) Revelation 10.1–11

The scene in Rev. 10.1–11, with its allusion to the 'strong angel' (verse 1) and the 'scroll' (verses 2, 8–10), recapitulates the throne-vision of 5.1–14. It consists of four sub-units: (a) the descent of the strong angel (10.1–3*a*); (b) the seven thunders (verses 3*b*–4); (c) the angel's oath (verses 5–7); (d) the commission to prophesy (verses 8–11).

(B) Revelation 11.1–13

The section Rev. 11.1–13 is 'a coherent literary unit' (Aune 585), with two subdivisions: verses 1–2 (measuring the Temple) and 3–13 (the two witnesses). For the complexities of composition and thought, in the passage as a whole, see below. Some commentators find two originally separate sources behind verses 1–2 and 3–13. For example, Charles (1, 270–73) thinks that 11.1–13 consists of two independent Jewish fragments, both written before AD 70, which have been combined by the author with some Christian adaptation (note in particular verse 8); cf. also Beasley-Murray 37–38. In contrast, Beckwith (584–88) shows that, even if John has here made use of an unknown apocalyptic source, and reinterpreted it for his own theological purposes, there are good grounds for treating the resulting passage as a single oracle. Note also the close connection between the two segments represented by the repeated enumeration ('forty-two months') in 11.2 and 11.3.

Aune (585–56) considers that the brief pericope 11.1–2 is 'obviously fragmentary' (ibid. 585).

(a) It does not cohere with the preceding text, 10.11, since the speaker behind the instruction to measure the Temple is not directly related to 'those' who require the seer to prophesy. But, as we shall see, the voices in both cases can be identified as divine.

(b) The command to describe the Temple is not specified as being carried out (contrast 1.8–9, 9–10). However, the measurement is implied; and note elsewhere in the Apocalypse (esp. in the oracles of 2—3) divine injunctions to repentance and faithfulness which are fulfilled only by implication (2.5, 10; 3.3, 20; et al.).

(c) The location of 11.1–2, in Aune's view, is ambiguous, and not necessarily the same as the earthly setting belonging to Chapter 10. Nevertheless, it will be suggested in due course that the context of both Rev. 10.1–11 and 11.1–13 is essentially this worldly, even if an other-worldly backcloth is also in view.

(d) The implication of 11.1–2 is that it refers to a period before the destruction of the Temple in AD 70, whereas Revelation was finally composed after that date. In my own view, by contrast, this work was written *in* AD 70, just before the fall of Jerusalem, even if some editing of it took place later. See above, 2–3. Nothing so far, therefore, compels us to support the claim that the character of the text Rev. 11.1–2 is 'fragmentary'.

The literary composition of Rev. 11.3–13 may be understood as comprising three sub-divisions: the mission and authority of the two witnesses (11.3–6); their death (verses 7–10); their victory (verses 11–12), followed by the judgement of their enemies (verse 13*a*) and the conversion of the survivors (13*b*). Cf. Aune 586–87. Aune (585–86) also points out that Rev. 11.1–2 features five verbs in the past tense; whereas 11.3–13 is dominated first by verbs in the future tense (verses 3–10) and then by past tense verbal forms (verses 11–13). He also regards the entire section 11.1–13 not as the report of a vision which John saw, even if it has been presented in a visionary style, but as a prophetic narrative.

(C) Revelation 11.14

This verse, with its mention of three disasters, is pivotal. It looks back to 9.12, where it is recorded that the first disaster (following the fifth trumpet-sounding) has taken place, and that two more have still to occur (the second is described in 9.13–19). In the present context (verse 14), it is announced that the second woe has occurred; and one more is promised in the future (see below). In this way, 11.14 functions as a means of drawing together structurally the material in this part of the Apocalypse. Additionally, it forms an inclusion with 11.19, which is also pivotal (see later).

(D) Revelation 11.15–19

This section is the conclusion of the sequence of trumpet-soundings, and structurally it looks back to 8.1—9.21 (Act 1 Scene 3), where the first six trumpet-angels are heard. The blast of the seventh trumpet, unlike the others, is not followed by a seventh set of plagues. Instead, it introduces much more positively a brief throne-vision; and, like Chapter 10, this connects, in form and content, with the heavenly scene of worship in Rev. 4—5. As a result, the character of these verses (11.14–19) is distinctive.

Within the text unit there are two sub-divisions.

(a) *Verses 15–18*. This sub-division consists of a responsory hymn in two parts, the second of which is introduced with a description of the posture of the elders (verse 16). The hymn has parallels with other liturgical outbursts in Revelation; but, especially in its eschatology, the stanza is also unique. For the poetic arrangement of its strophes see the translation. Hymns or liturgical poetry are used by the seer at or near the end of several major literary and dramatic divisions in the Apocalypse: the Prologue and two Scenes out of seven (1.5–8; 16.5–7; 22.17); and five Intervals out of six (5.9–14; 7.15–17; 11.15–18; 15.3–4; 18.21–24). Liturgical forms are an important feature in the composition of Revelation; but liturgy cannot be regarded as a controlling element in its overall structure (against Shepherd, *Paschal Liturgy*, and Vanni, *La struttura letteraria*). The work as a whole should be regarded as a drama. See Smalley, *Thunder and Love* 97–110, esp. 102–10.

(b) *Verse 19*. The concluding verse in this section is pivotal, and forms accordingly an inclusion with verse 14 (see above). It may be regarded as the conclusion to 11.14(15)–18 (Beckwith 274–75, 606), or as the introduction to 12.1–17 (Aune 661–62). More significantly, however, the literary structure of verse 19 should be understood as both. The heavenly manifestations are a response to the outcome of the seventh trumpet, and even to the total action of the interval (Rev. 10—11). But they also lead into the next scene, and provide a theological as well as structural interlocking between Chapters 10—11 and 12–15 (see below). My analysis of the Apocalypse as a drama places 11.19 with Rev. 10—11, where it initially belongs; but the verse also stands with the material which follows in Scene 4, and the subsequent interval (Rev. 12—15). For the possible structural significance of the formulaic reference to a thunderstorm and earthquake, in verse 19*b*, see further the comment below.

The literary composition of Rev. 10.1—11.19, like the thought and theology of this section, is complex. But it is also coherent, and demonstrates once more the craftsmanship and dramatic skill of the author, as this is evident throughout Revelation.

Comment

The Angel from Heaven (10.1–11)

10.1 In the opening vision of this interlude, the writer sees 'another strong angel descending from heaven'. For the apocalyptic expression καὶ εἶδον (*kai eidon*, lit. 'and I saw') see on 5.1; cf. also 9.1; et al. Here is a further example of the ascent/descent patterning in Revelation, and indeed in the Fourth Gospel, which pervades John's cosmology, and draws heaven and earth together. From Rev. 4.1 until now, John has seen the visions unfold from his position in heaven (Mounce 201), even if his images have described events in time as well as eternity. But at this point he is back on earth, even if he is in touch with spiritual disclosures. The angel of light comes *down* from heaven, from God; and it is from heaven that a voice is heard (verses 4, 8). His mission to a Church undergoing internal problems and external pressures is therefore crucial at this moment in Christian history, and relevant to its life at any time.

Beasley-Murray (168–69) thinks that John's position changes during the interval. In Chapter 10 he receives the scroll from the angel as a prophet on Patmos (note 1.3, and the commission to prophesy in 10.8–11); whereas in Chapter 11 the standpoint of the seer is the same as that in the first vision of Chapter 7, before the tribulation of the end-time. However, this interpretation is unnecessarily complicated, and overlooks the truth that the visions of the Apocalypse are mostly general in their presentation, and free from the detail and constraints of time and chronology. In the present scene, John is simply on *earth*, rather than in heaven.

For angels in the Apocalypse see above, 28–30. In verse 1 John sees ἄλλον ἄγγελον ἰσχυρόν (*allon angelon ischyron*, 'another strong angel'). Mounce (201) interprets this phrase as the equivalent of 'another angel, a mighty (strong) one' (cf. 'another horse, a red one' at 6.4). But, as he says, this does not mean 'another' angel in the sequence of trumpet-angels (8.7—9.13). There are three 'strong angels' in Revelation, and they appear at 5.2; 10.1; and 18.21. The angel of 18.21 has the individual function of carrying out a prophetic action, and he does not cry out with a loud voice. Alternatively, there seems to be a close connection between the strong angel of 10.1 and the first strong angelic being of 5.2. Both make a proclamation in a loud voice (5.2; 10.3), and both are associated with a scroll of destiny: sealed in 5.2, but open here (verse 2). The angels of 10.1 and 5.2, then, appear to be related, even if they are not identical. We have already noticed that there are links between the visions here and in Rev. 5, and this is the first of them. It suggests that the content of the revelation to be given will be similar.

Nevertheless, we are presented here with *another*, and seemingly different, angel; for example, the majestic description of the present figure in 10.1–2 has no parallel in 5.2.

Bauckham (1295*a*) believes that the awe-inspiring angel of 10.1 is the most important in Revelation, because the scroll in this chapter contains the primary content of John's prophetic revelation, and he is thus the one who transmits to John the apocalypse he has received from God through Christ (1.1; 22.16). See also Bauckham, *Climax of Prophecy* 253–57.

Beale (522–26) goes further, and argues convincingly that this figure is christological, if not divine, in character. Unlike other angels in Revelation, the strong being of 10.1 is given attributes which are assigned only to God in the Old Testament, or to God or Christ in the Apocalypse.

(a) The divine aura of this angel is indicated first by the fact that he is 'wrapped around in a cloud'. In biblical literature it is God or the Son of man alone who come in heaven or to earth with clouds. See e.g. Exod. 19.9–18; 24.15–18; Lev. 16.2; Num. 10.11–12; Neh. 9.12 (God dwells in a 'pillar of cloud'); Ps. 18.11; Jer. 4.13; Dan. 7.13; Matt. 17.5; Mark 13.26; Acts 1.9; 1 Cor. 10.1–2; in Revelation, note 1.7; 11.12; 14.14–16. Dan. 7.13–14 lies behind Rev. 1, where the one 'coming with the clouds' (verse 7) is later identified as 'a son of man figure' (verse 13), and assigned attributes of the divine Ancient of Days.

(b) Second, the divine evocations of the strong angel in 10.1 are enhanced by the reference to the 'halo (ἡ ἶρις, *hē iris*, otherwise "circle of light", or "rainbow") above his head'. An obvious background to this feature is to be found in Ezek. 1.26–28, where the splendour of the Lord is described as 'the bow in a cloud on a rainy day' (verse 28). As Beale (523) points out, the allusion to this passage in Ezekiel is appropriate, as well as likely, because it also underlies the portrait of the Danielic Son of man in Rev. 1.13–16, and because the pattern of the vision in Ezek. 1—3 is followed later in Rev. 10, where a heavenly being holds a scroll which is taken and eaten by a prophet. It is also significant that the only other reference to an ἶρις (*iris*, there 'rainbow') in Revelation, and indeed in the New Testament, is at 4.3, where a circle of light is said to surround the throne of God. It appears that the repetition of this noun in 10.1, now with an article (in 4.3 it is anarthrous), is a deliberate attempt on the part of the author to associate this strong angel with the Deity.

(c) Finally, the concluding two sentences in 10.1 underline the divine associations of the angelic figure in this verse. 'His face was like the sun' (τὸ πρόσωπον αὐτοῦ ὡς ὁ ἥλιος, *to prosopon autou hōs ho hēlios*) is an almost identical recollection of the Greek phrase describing the exalted Christ in Rev. 1.16, ἡ ὄψις αὐτοῦ ὡς ὁ ἥλιος (*hē opsis autou hōs ho hēlios*, 'his face was like the sun'). This simile also reproduces exactly the description in the Greek of the transfigured Jesus at Matt. 17.2. However, Bauckham (*Climax of Prophecy* 253 and n. 17) disputes the link between 10.1 and 1.16, on the grounds that in 1.16 a distinction exists by the addition of the phrase '(the sun) shining with all its power', and that faces shining like the sun are a common feature in portraits of heavenly beings (e.g. Matt. 13.43; 2 Enoch 1.5; T. Abr. [A] 12.5).

The comparison of the 'legs' (οἱ πόδες, *hoi podes*, lit. 'feet') of the angel to 'fiery pillars' provides a further connection between the portrait of this heavenly being and that of the risen Son of man in Rev. 1; for in 1.15 Christ's feet are likened to 'fine bronze, glowing as in a furnace' (cf. Dan. 10.6). However, there is a slight change in wording between the clause in 1.15 and the last phrase of 10.1, since the strong angel in the present verse has legs which 'seemed to be fiery pillars' (as legs are more easily likened to pillars than feet, the angel's 'feet' here can be understood by metonymy as 'legs'). Beale (524) suggests that this alteration is deliberate, in order to evoke the presence of Yahweh with the Israelites in the wilderness, where God appeared in 'a pillar of cloud and a pillar of fire' in order to guide (Exod. 13.21–22) and protect (Exod. 14.19, 24; cf. Num. 14.13–14;

et al.) his people. The themes of God's protection and covenant faithfulness are strongly present in the Apocalypse, not least in Chapters 7 and 11—17; cf. also 10.6–7.

All this leads Beale (525) to conclude that the strong angel of Rev. 10.1 is the divine angel of the Lord, comparable to the angel of the Exodus (Exod. 12.29), and to the divine angel who appears in Judges and elsewhere as God's prophetic mediator (Judg. 6.22; 1 Chron. 21.18; et al.). Beale is on more controversial ground when he goes on (ibid.) to claim that the angelic figure of 10.1 should also 'be identified with Christ himself'. The scene at the opening of Rev. 10 is certainly theophanic, and there is a real sense in which Jesus is the supreme 'angel' of the Apocalypse (see above, 28). Note also that both the Lamb of Rev. 5.5 and the angel of 10.3 are likened to a lion. But, despite 14.14 (where the Son of man is surrounded by 'other angels'), the term ἄγγελος (*angelos*, 'angel') is never used directly of Jesus Christ in Revelation, and is reserved for lesser heavenly beings (so Swete 126; Beckwith 580; cf. Hendriksen 123–24). Furthermore, this messenger is acting as a mediator between the Godhead and the prophet-seer, helping to disclose the divine plan to him and to the saints; and it is difficult to see how this function, and indeed the oath-taking in 10.6–7, could be appropriately undertaken by Christ himself.

We are exegetically on much safer ground if we conclude that the strong angel of 10.1 is the heavenly representative of Jesus, who possesses the characteristics of Christ (a possibility which Beale [526] acknowledges). In that case, the strong angel could be Michael, who represents Christ at 12.7–9 (q.v.); although Charles (1, 258–59) and Beasley-Murray (170) propose as a likely candidate Gabriel, whose name means '*strong man of God*' and relates to the Hebrew word גִּבּוֹר (*gibbōr*, 'strong', 'mighty'). The angel is 'strong', not so much physically (although notice his size, as depicted in verse 2) as spiritually. He is a powerful, key figure in the unfolding of God's apocalypse.

2   The strong angel held in his hand 'a small scroll, which had been opened'. The term for 'scroll' is βιβλαρίδιον (*biblaridion*), which should be translated 'small scroll'; for it is a diminutive of βιβλάριον (*biblarion*, 'small scroll'), which is itself a diminutive of βιβλίον (*biblion*, 'scroll', 'book'). For the Greek terminology see the textual note on verse 2, above. It is not immediately apparent how this scroll should be identified. Some commentators regard it as a general image for the word of God (so Hendriksen 125). But its character in this context, and in relation to the 'scroll' (using the Greek noun βιβλίον, *biblion*) which features in the throne-vision of Rev. 5 (see verses 1, 2, 3, 4, 5, 8, 9), suggests a more specific interpretation.

There are admittedly variations between the scrolls of Rev. 5.1 (q.v.) and 10.2 (also 8, 9, 10). Instead of the Greek term βιβλίον (*biblion*), which is used for 'scroll' in Chapter 5, the diminutive form βιβλαρίδιον (*biblaridion*, 'small scroll'), without a definite article (referring back to an earlier scroll), appears in Chapter 10; in 5.1 the scroll lies sealed on the right palm of God, whereas in 10.2 it is open and held by the strong angel; in Chapter 5 the Lamb takes the scroll (verse 7), but at 10.8–10 it is taken by the prophet-seer; and while heavenly praise follows the taking of the scroll in 5.8–10, the scene in Chapter 10 takes place on earth, and does not include worship. Such considerations, together with the assumption that the contents of the scroll in Rev. 5 refer only to the events of 6.1—8.5, have led some scholars to conclude that the scroll in Chapter 10 contains only the contents of Rev. 11.1–13. So Mounce 202–203; cf. Charles 1, 260, 269. Milligan (164) claims that the scroll of Rev. 5 contains 'the whole counsel of God' for his purposes in the world and in the Church, but that the document in Chapter 10 is limited to the Church alone. A smaller scroll would accordingly be 'sufficient for its tidings' (ibid.).

Nevertheless, the similarities between the two scrolls in Rev. 5 and 10 are striking, and indicate a close connection between them (see further Beale 527–30, 530–32): both scrolls are (eventually) opened; both are held by divine or angelic figures, who are lion-like; both have a clear background in Ezek. 2.9–10, where 'a hand' holding an open scroll is extended to the prophet; a further Old Testament source for both passages can be located in the end-time prophecy of Dan. 12 (note esp. verses 1–4); both scrolls have links with a strong angel who cries aloud, and with an eternal God (5.13; 10.6); in both visions a scroll is taken from the hand of a heavenly being, and the resulting prophetic commission uses similar language (note 4.1; 10.8); and both scrolls concern the destiny of a universal range of human beings (cf. 5.9; 10.11). Moreover, there is an important theological connection between Chapters 5 and 10 in terms of the chain of revelation which takes place within them. As Bauckham shows (*Theology* 81–82), the scroll in God's hand (5.1) is opened by the Lamb (5.7 — 8.1); the same scroll is then taken by the strong angel from heaven to earth (10.1–2), and given to the prophet-seer to eat (10.8–10). This movement corresponds exactly to that recorded in Rev. 1.1.

In view of these firm associations, it is reasonable to propose that the scroll of Rev. 10.2 should be interpreted in the light of the same symbol in Chapter 5. So also Mazzaferri, *Genre* 265–79; Wall 135–36; Bauckham, *Climax of Prophecy* 243–57; Michaels 133–34; Bauckham 1295*a*; against Mounce 202. The scroll of 5.1 (and 2–9) contains the divine plan for the future of creation, and also for its present existence (see the comment on 5.1). God's purposes for his world, to assert his sovereignty over wrongdoing and achieve in love his salvific will, are to be expressed in a covenant relationship between himself and his people, finally and fully realized in Christ. The contents of the scroll in Rev. 5 can only be disclosed when the seventh seal has been broken (8.1); and, despite glimpses on the way, they have not been fully revealed in the preceding scenes (6.1 — 9.21). But by 10.2 we learn that the scroll 'had been opened'; and, once it has been ingested by John, its purport can become clear.

However, the scrolls of Rev. 5.1 and 10.2 are not absolutely identical. For a start, the document in 10.2 is not as large: it is a 'small scroll' (βιβλαρίδιον, *biblaridion*), rather than a 'scroll' (βιβλίον, *biblion*). Its size relates to the need for John to swallow it (10.10). But the imagery also implies that a new focus and depth are being given at this stage to God's plan and purposes of salvation, inaugurated by the death and resurrection of the Lamb. He has received the scroll from God and opened it (6.1); and the perfect participle ἠνεῳγμένον (*ēneō[i]gmenon*, '[which] had been opened'), in 10.2, suggests a decisive and completed action; in other words, the scroll will remain in that condition. This represents the Lamb's assumption of authority over the Father's eschatological and cosmic purposes, which through the Son will now run their course (cf. Beale 527–28).

In one sense the apocalypse began to roll from that pivotal moment in the throne room (5.8); and it is followed by an unfolding of the scroll's summarized contents, although not in historical or chronological order, in Chapters 6 — 22. All that has happened before 10.1–2, then, is a preparation for this clearer and more complete revelation, introduced by the key figure of the strong angel in 10.1 (cf. Bauckham, *Theology* 82). Caird (126) sees the small scroll of 10.2 as a new version of the purposes of God contained in the larger scroll of 5.1, but now presented from the point of view of their achievement through the saints. Cf. Fiorenza, *Book of Revelation* 54, who regards the smaller document as 'the prophetic interpretation of the situation of the Christian community'; also Wall 136.

For a book which originates in heaven, but is destined for use on earth, see Hermas, *Vis.* 2.1, 4 (using βιβλαρίδιον [*biblaridion*, 'small book'] and βιβλίδιον [*biblidion*, 'small document'] as synonyms for βιβλίον [*biblion*, 'book']). The present participle ἔχων (*echōn*, lit. 'having'), at the outset of verse 2, acts as a finite verb (hence the translation, 'he held'), and may thus reflect Semitic style (Beale 529); see also 1.16; 14.14; et al. Apparently the strong angel was holding the small scroll in his left hand, since in verse 5 he raises his right hand to heaven for the oath.

The angel placed 'his right foot on the sea, with (δέ, *de*, lit. 'but', is adversative) his left foot on the land'. This description is the first indication that the 'strong' heavenly messenger is not only spiritually powerful (see on verse 1) but also physically gigantic (however, note in 10.1 the reference to his legs being like 'fiery pillars'). The idea of a figure capable of bestriding the ocean and the earth may have been inspired by the familiar bronze sculpture of the Colossos of Rhodes. This was erected *c.* 280 BC by Chares of Lindos, and stood on a promontory of the island, overlooking the harbour (see Aune 556–57). Cf. Shakespeare, *Julius Caesar* Act 1 Scene 2, where Cassius says of Caesar:

> Why, man, he doth bestride the narrow world
> Like a Colossus, and we petty men
> Walk under his huge legs and peep about
> To find ourselves dishonourable graves.

The stance of the angelic colossus symbolizes his universal authority, and therefore the inclusive scope of the gospel content of the scroll which he carries. The expression 'sea and land', or its equivalent, is used in the Old Testament to denote the creation of God in its totality (e.g. Exod. 20.11; Job 11.9; Ps. 146.6; Prov. 8.29; Isa. 42.10; Jonah 1.9), and especially the territory over which Adam, Noah and the ideal Davidic king were to have dominion (Gen.1.26; 9.2; Ps. 72.8; Zech. 9.10). Cf. Beale 529. The angel's authority over the sea and the land is also a reflection of God's ultimate conquest of evil; since the dragon, who personifies opposition to the goodness of God, stands on the '(sand of) the sea' (12.18) and brings up the beasts from the sea (13.1) and from the earth (13.11). Swete (127) suggests, less than convincingly, that the strong angel of 10.1–2 places his right foot on the sea 'as if to defy its instability'. But Swete (ibid.) also points out correctly that the sea is ever present in John's mind (5.13; 7.1, 3; 8.8–9; 15.2; et al.), and that the thought of a strong angel treating the Aegean as solid ground would have been attractive to one who had been exiled on Patmos.

The 'feet' (sing. πόδα, *poda*) of the strong angel in 10.2 are a reminder of his fiery 'legs' (using πόδες, *podes*, lit. 'feet') in verse 1 (q.v.), and therefore of the kind of authority which he is to exercise, for the image of fire elsewhere in the Apocalypse (1.14; 8.5; 18.8; et al.) is a metaphor of divine judgement. Mounce (203) notes that the dramatic appearance of this powerful heavenly figure contrasts markedly with the tableau of human rebellion, idolatry and immorality, which is presented in the immediately preceding scene (9.20–21).

3–4 The loud voice of the strong angel, who begins to announce God's will for his creation (cf. 5.2), suits his colossal size. The voice sounds 'like a roaring lion'; and this is an image which connotes the cosmic authority of the angel, as one who holds the gospel scroll. The allusions in the literature of Judaism which are in the picture also help to emphasize the divine attributes of the heavenly being who speaks, and who appears to be the special representative of Christ (see on verse 1). In 4 Ezra 11.37; 12.31–32, for example, the lion 'aroused out of the forest, roaring' is identified as the Messiah. The clear reference to Amos 3.7 at Rev. 10.7 (q.v.) makes it possible that the lion-like voice of God, described in Amos 3.8 ('The lion has roared; who will not fear? The Lord God has spoken; who can but prophesy?'), lies behind the present verse (10.3). The voice of Yahweh is further likened to that of a lion in Isa. 31.4; Hos. 11.10; cf. also Joel 3.16; Amos 1.2. In any case, the angel is about to deliver what is clearly a message from God (Roloff 124).

Mounce (203 and n. 17) suggests that, since the onomatopoeic Greek verb μυκάομαι (*mykaomai*, 'roar', found only here in the New Testament) is normally used for the lowing of oxen, its appearance in verse 3 implies that the angel's voice 'had a deep resonance' which would command the attention of his wide audience. See also Charles 1, 261; Swete 127, who reminds us that in the Apocalypse most events take place 'on a great scale'. Equally, supernatural beings in Revelation usually speak with loud voices (6.1; 11.15; 14.15, 18; et al.). In the phrase ὥσπερ λέων μυκᾶται (*hōsper leōn mykatai*, lit. 'as a lion roars'), the adverb ὥσπερ (*hōsper*, 'as', 'like') is found only here in Revelation. Elsewhere the word ὡς (*hōs*, 'as') is used in this sense (cf. verse 1, *bis*).

The loud voice of the strong angel appears initially to have been inarticulate; but this is not true of the seven claps of thunder which, in a dramatic response, 'made themselves heard' following his shout (see also the command not to record the message of the thunders in verse 4). There is considerable debate about the meaning of the seven thunderclaps. This is not immediately clear; although broadly speaking the seer is employing in 10.3–4 a metaphor to represent the declarations of a heavenly being or beings (cf. 6.1; 19.6–8; also John 12.28–29); so Beale 533. The use of the article with the noun, αἱ ἑπτὰ βρονταί (*hai hepta brontai*, 'the seven claps of thunder' [lit. '*the* seven thunders']), may suggest that these have been mentioned previously in Revelation; whereas the seven thunders appear only here in the drama. Alternatively, the 'seven claps of thunder' may be an apocalyptic cliché, familiar to John's audience, but otherwise unknown. This is the view of Sweet (178) who believes that, like the other heptads in Revelation, the thunderclaps are coined by the writer from traditional materials. For a similar anaphoric use of the article with a noun, used in Revelation without a retrospective reference, see 9.1; 11.3, 19; 16.14; et al. Thunder, like fire, is associated in the Apocalypse with judgement (cf. 4.5; 6.1; 8.5; 11.19; 16.18); and the characteristically Johannine number seven (see on 1.4) may be interpreted as a confirmation that the judgement to come is divine (Hughes 116). See also the use of thunder in the Old Testament as a symbol of God's judgement (Exod. 9.23–24; 1 Sam. 7.10; Ps. 77.17–18; Isa. 29.6; et al.).

Charles (1, 261–62) finds an analogy between the seven claps of thunder and the heavenly visions received by Paul, which were not to be disclosed to the churches (2 Cor. 4.12); however, this understanding is strongly disputed by Roloff (124), who points out that the thunders do not represent such a personal encounter, but rather God's will for the whole world. Mounce (204), following Kiddle (169–70), argues that the seven thunders, like the seals and trumpets, form another series of warning plagues; but these are not recorded as taking place, because the lack of repentance on the part of humanity (9.20–21) rendered them unnecessary. While there is no need to identify the thunders directly as a series of plagues, the prohibition in verse 4 (q.v.) probably does relate to the time allowed for repentance.

Most commentators (e.g. Aune 559) see a plausible link between the sevenfold sound of thunderclaps in verse 3 and Ps. 29, where (uniquely for the Old Testament) there are seven references to God's manifestation in judgemental thunder (verses 3, 4 [*bis*], 5, 7, 8, 9). If this Psalm is the chief, and presumably well-known, background to the image in Rev. 10.3–4, it would account for the presence of the article with the noun βρονταί (*brontai*, lit. 'thunders'). Cf. 13.10. However, note also the four sevenfold plagues in Lev. 26.14–39 (esp. verses 18, 21, 24, 28); and also the seven watches of Elijah's servant on Mount Carmel before the ensuing storm of judgement (1 Kings 18.43–45).

The divine message communicated by the seven thunderclaps is heard, and presumably understood, by John; but he is prevented from writing it down (verse 4). That he wished to do so may indicate that, throughout his visionary experience, the seer had been recording the heavenly disclosures which had been made to him (note the command to write in 1.11, 19); cf. Beale 533–34. The 'heavenly voice' (φωνὴν ἐκ τοῦ οὐρανοῦ, *phōnēn ek tou ouranou*, lit. 'voice from heaven') cannot be that of the Christ-like strong angel of 10.1–3, because that heavenly being is on earth (verse 2). The source of the voice implies that the one who speaks does so with authority (cf. 4 Ezra 6.17);

and it is reasonable to suppose therefore that the voice is divine, and that it belongs either to God, or to Christ, or both (cf. 4.1; 14.13; 18.4). The 'voices' of the strong angel (verse 3*a*), the seven thunders (verse 3*b*) and the speaker from heaven (verse 4), where the noun φωνή (*phōnē*, 'voice') is used in each case, are obviously related, even if they are not identical. Together, as so often in the Johannine literature, these voices cause heaven and earth to be conjoined.

The voice from heaven prohibits any record of the message of the seven thunder-claps (ἃ ἐλάλησαν αἱ ἑπτὰ βρονταί, *ha elalēsan hai hepta brontai*, lit. 'what the seven thunders have said'); this is a phrase in the Greek which is repeated almost exactly from the opening sentence of verse 4. The prohibition is expressed twice, and with consider-able emphasis: first positively ('seal up') and then by inversion negatively ('do not write it down'). This is an example of two events being placed in reverse order, since writing would normally precede the sealing of a scroll (see on 5.1; for this literary technique see similarly Rev. 3.3; 6.4; 10.9; et al.). The verb σφραγίζειν (*sphragizein*, 'to seal') seems inappropriate in this context, in that nothing has been written down so far in the scene which *could* be sealed up. However, the meaning of the command is more probably, 'keep the message secret by not writing it down' (cf. Aune 562).

The reason for this secrecy is not immediately apparent. Hughes (116) rightly points out that if John is forbidden to pass on or write down the message of the seven thunders, this means that it is also hidden from us. But he then goes on to propose that the words of the thunderclaps, which are never specified, might be enacted in the events which are subsequently recorded in the Apocalypse. This is an unlikely interpretation, since it stands in direct contradiction to the demand for the message to be concealed, and the implied obedient response from the seer, in 10.4. Equally questionable is the view of Moffatt (412), that John introduces the voice from heaven to justify his omis-sion of a seven-thunder source, or set of visions, circulating in contemporary prophetic circles (see verse 7). As Mounce (204) says, it is difficult in this case to understand why the thunders should have been mentioned at all. Swete (128) is also less than convinc-ing when he claims, with evident desperation, that the seer at this stage was conscious of having passed through experiences which he could not recall or express, and he interpreted this as the equivalent of a prohibition to put the vision on paper.

A more plausible explanation is offered by Caird (126–27), who suggests that the 'seal-ing' represents God's gracious offer to an unrepentant humanity (9.20–21). The Lord 'cuts short the time' (see Mark 13.20), and cancels the judgement symbolized by the thunderclaps; in this way, the advance of human self-destruction is halted, and some can be saved. Nevertheless, the seven bowls of judgement are yet to be unveiled in Revela-tion (16.1—17.1); cf. Beasley-Murray 172. Furthermore, in apocalyptic literature, and especially Daniel, the metaphor of sealing ('secret words') refers to the *delay* of future eschatological events, rather than to their cancellation (so Dan. 12.4–9, which lies behind Rev. 10.5–7). Cf. Beale 534. Beale himself (535–36) adopts an interpretative stance similar to that of Mounce (see above). He argues that the seven thunderclaps represent a further series of sevenfold judgements, which 'for some unknown reason' (Beale 535) is not revealed; for Mounce (204) the reason is a lack of human repentance, which precipitates the end. Beale (535) sees the thunders as designating 'some judgement' *preceding* the final judgement.

The clearest, and to my mind most convincing, interpretation is offered by Bauckham (*Climax of Prophecy* 259–61), who reminds us that the image of sealing in this passage is used to contrast the thunders, which are sealed and do not become part of John's prophetic revelation, and the scroll (verse 2), which has been unsealed so that it may become the content of the seer's remaining disclosures. The incident of the seven thunderclaps, therefore, makes clear that 'there are to be no more warning judgements, but *instead* there is to be what the scroll will reveal' (ibid. 260). The process of judgement, in Johannine theology generally, and certainly in the Apocalypse, is ongoing (see Smalley, *Thunder and Love* 150–52). We have already discovered in Revelation the end as imminent, but not realized (6.17; 8.1–5; et al.). So now, the rumbling thunders point towards the dénouement of the drama, and share in its character; but they do not precipitate it (against Caird; Mounce; Beale). The announcement of God's purposes of judgement and love for his creation (as contained in the small scroll) is to continue, both in history and in John's Revelation; and the time for these to be gathered up in Christ is always imminent, but also relentlessly future (despite the promise in verse 6 [q.v.] that there will be 'no more time of waiting').

5–6a   The record of John's vision is resumed from verses 1–2. Note the use of the verb εἶδον (*eidon*, lit. 'I saw'), frequent in the visionary material of the Apocalypse (4.1; 5.1; 6.1; et al.), in both verses 1 and 5. For the (strong) angel, standing between the sea and the dry land, see on verse 1. The heavenly being dramatically 'raised his right hand to heaven', and therefore in the direction of God, whose abode is heavenly (Isa. 57.15), to swear that the time of waiting will be no more (verses 6b–7). This is the only mention in Revelation of oath-taking.

Lifting hands in the Old Testament is a gesture used by people for a variety of purposes, since the Hebrew phrase נשׂא יד (*nāśāʾ yād*, 'lift up the hand') is not necessarily synonymous with swearing an oath. For example, raised hands can accompany prayer (Ps. 28.2), or blessing (Lev. 9.22). The gesture almost never appears as an element in human oath-taking (but see Abram's speech to the king of Sodom in Gen. 14.22–23 LXX). God is occasionally described in the LXX (but not in MT) as raising his hand to swear to his people (Ezek. 20.6; 36.7; 44.12; cf. [Yahweh raising his hand against the enemies of Israel] 1QM 15.13; 18.1, 3). In Deut. 32.40 LXX God lifts his *right* hand to heaven to make an oath; and only there and in the present verse (Rev. 10.5), in biblical literature, is oath-taking said to involve a specifically dextral movement. The immediate background to 10.5, however, is Dan. 12.7; but in that judgemental passage an angel elevates *both* hands, right and left, and swears by God that there *will* be some delay before the end (contrast verse 6b).

The angelic oath is sanctioned by two important theological references to the nature of God. First, the angel swears by the one who lives 'eternally' (εἰς τοὺς αἰῶνας τῶν αἰώνων, *eis tous aiōnas tōn aiōnōn*, lit. 'to the ages of the ages'). For the formula, regular in the Apocalypse, see also 1.18; 4.9–10; (7.2); 15.7. The assertion of God's sovereign eternity would have been an encouragement to those in John's community who were undergoing difficulty and oppression, or who were faced with the future possibility of martyrdom for their faith. The phrase 'the one who lives eternally' constitutes a circumlocution for the name of God.

But his identity is apparent from the second divine epithet which is used to confirm the angel's oath. God also 'created the heaven and the earth, the sea, and everything in them'. For this cultic expression, in liturgical texts, see Exod. 20.11; Neh. 9.6; Ps. 146.5–6; *T. Job* 2.4; *Sib. Or.* 3.20–23; Acts 4.24; and for the simpler, possibly Canaanite, form 'maker of heaven and earth' see Gen. 14.19, 22 = Judith 13.18; 1 Esdras 6.13. The formula as we have it in Rev. 10.6 implies a two-level cosmology: heaven on the one hand and earth and sea on the other. But if the 'sea' is also understood as the chaotic waters under the earth (Gen. 1.2; Deut. 5.8), the cosmic arrangement becomes threefold, as in Rev. 12.12; 14.7; 21.1 (cf. 5.13). See Aune 565–66. God's sovereignty over time extends to his creation in its entirety (the standard phrase καὶ τὰ ἐν αὐτῷ [*kai ta en autō(i)*, lit. 'and everything in it'], or its equivalent, is repeated three times in verse 6, although this is hidden in the translation). To speak of God in this way emphasizes his power to accomplish his purposes of salvation through judgement. His kingship and knowledge are universal; and therefore the end of history, like its origin, must be subject to his merciful control (cf. Mounce 206).

6b–7   The strong angel now begins his announcement about the culmination of salvation history. The conjunction ὅτι (*hoti*, lit. 'that'), which introduces the prophetic oath, is the object of the verb ὤμοσεν (*ōmosen*, 'he swore'). It acts as a pair of quotation marks, and is therefore omitted in the translation; this is the only such construction (after a verb of swearing) in Revelation. For similar syntax see Mark 14.71 par. The promise that 'there will be no more time of waiting' translates the Greek, χρόνος οὐκέτι ἔσται (*chronos ouketi estai*, lit. 'there will be no more time'). This cannot mean that an era of timelessness is about to begin, as Cullmann, *Christ and Time* 49–50, 62, rightly maintains (although such an interpretation is implied by the AV rendering, 'there should be time no longer'; similarly Milligan 158–59; Barker, *The Revelation* 185–86). The reference to the 'days' to come, when the seventh angel will sound his trumpet (verse 7), makes that thought impossible.

The word χρόνος (*chronos*, lit. 'time') is accordingly taken by several commentators as a synonym for 'delay' (so e.g. Charles 1, 263; Caird 128; Wilcock 101–102; Roloff 125; Mounce 205–206; also BDAG 1092b). Aune (568) correctly argues that 'delay' is strictly an inappropriate concept in this context, since it assumes that eschatological events have been postponed; and there is no hint of this in the Apocalypse (although, it should be added, time for repentance is built into its outline; so 6.8; 9.7–12, 20–21). Aune (548, 568, following Swete 129) therefore prefers the translation of χρόνος (*chronos*) as 'interval of time'; similarly the translation above, 'no more time of waiting' (cf. 6.11, 'longer time'; 20.3, 'short time'). The angel is saying that time is up, and that the events of the end are about to be set in motion. This can be so, even if in one sense the apocalypse of God's purposes, rolling from the beginning of time, always stretch into eternity. See further on verse 7.

The background to the angelic oath in verses 6–7 is to be found in the prophecy of Dan. 11.29—12.13, which concerns the suffering and persecution of God's people at the end-time (note Dan. 11.40, 'at the time of the end'), the destruction of the enemy, the establishment of God's kingdom and the reign of his saints. These events presage the consummation of history; and in Daniel there *is* an element of delay. For the angelic figure of Dan. 12.7 announces that everything will be 'accomplished' (LXX συντελεσθήσεται, *syntelesthēsetai*, lit. 'it will be completed') after an interval of 'a time, two times and half a time'. These ideas are picked up in Rev. 10.6–7, where it is prophesied that God's purposes are to be 'fulfilled' (ἐτελέσθη, *etelesthē*, lit. 'it will be completed', using the same root verb as in Dan. 12.7), and that a period of time will usher in the final stage of salvation history (see also Rev. 11.3; 12.6, 14; 13.5).

The situation in Rev. 10, however, develops the eschatology of Dan. 12, not least because there appears now to be greater urgency ('no more time of waiting', see on 6b). Moreover, according to Beale (540), Rev. 10.7 begins the seer's description of the way in which the Danielic prophecy will be completed, and the timing of that accomplishment; and these are amplified in Chapter 11. When the seventh angel blows his trumpet, 'the prophecy of Dan. 11.29—12.13 will be fulfilled and . . . God's purposes in history will be completed' (ibid.). Nevertheless, while it is true that Dan. 11—12 provides an immediate backcloth to the scene in Rev. 10.6–7, and beyond, there seems to be no reason to restrict the notion of the fulfilment of prophecy here to the passage in Daniel alone. The Apocalypse unfolds the future gathering up of God's plans of judgement and love for his whole creation; and these form the completion of his promises, through the Law and the prophets, as they are revealed throughout the Old Testament.

The introductory ἀλλά (*alla*, lit. 'but') of verse 7, hidden in the translation, represents a strong contrast. There will be no more waiting-time, *but rather* the final trumpet-blast will be heard. The phrase, ἐν ταῖς ἡμέραις τῆς φωνῆς τοῦ ἑβδόμου ἀγγέλου (*en tais hēmerais tēs phōnēs tou hebdomou angelou*, lit. 'in the days of the voice of the seventh angel'), is taken by Charles (1, 263–66) to mean a brief stage of trial, coinciding with the appearance of the Antichrist, immediately before the consummation of history. But it seems more in keeping with the sense of this passage to argue that the seventh trumpet signifies not a period of tribulation but the end of history itself, whenever that is to occur (see further on 11.14–15). Cf. Beckwith (582–83), followed by Beale (540).

The Greek, ὅταν μέλλῃ σαλπίζειν (*hotan mellē[i] salpizein*, lit. 'when he is about to sound'), could imply that the 'mystery' (verse 7b) will be completed *before* the angel sounds his trumpet (so NIV, 'when the seventh angel is about to sound his trumpet, the mystery of God will be accomplished'). But μέλλω (*mellō*, 'I am about to'), with the infinitive, can express divine determination (so Rev. 1.19; 6.11), or have the sense of a straight-forward future indicative (Beale 541). The meaning of the text in verse 7 is that the hidden purpose of God for his world will be fulfilled 'when the moment arrives for the seventh angel to sound his trumpet', as in the translation (cf. also REB). The only occurrence else-where in the New Testament of the construction ὅταν μέλλῃ (*hotan mellē[i]*, lit. 'when he is about to') with an infinitive is at Mark 13.4 = Luke 21.7.

The phrase, 'the hidden purpose of God' (τὸ μυστήριον τοῦ θεοῦ, *to mystērion tou theou*, lit. 'the mystery of God', using a subjective genitive) includes the technical Greek term μυστήριον (*mystērion*, 'hidden purpose', lit. 'mystery'). Paul uses exactly that expression as a description of Christ himself (Col. 2.2). As Mounce (207) reminds us, the idea of mystery was an important element in apocalyptic thought; for a mystery denoted a secret which was 'preserved in heaven and revealed to the enraptured apocalyptist' (ibid). See *1 Enoch* 40.2; 46.2; 71.3–4. The use of the word 'mystery' in the New Testament always includes an eschatological dimension, often referring to God's salvific purposes in Christ for his creation, hidden for a time but now made fully manifest (Rom. 16.25–26; 1 Cor. 2.7; also Rom. 11.25; 1 Cor. 15.51; 2 Thess. 2.7; et al.). This colouring is present when the term is used at Rev. 10.7, which is the only place in the Apocalypse where μυστήριον (*mystērion*, 'mystery') is used in precisely this way (cf. also 1.20; 17.5, 7). The word does not otherwise appear in the Johannine corpus.

In the present context (Rev. 10.7), the seer is speaking of the totality of God's saving plan as revealed in the consummation of human history (Swete 130; Mounce 207). It is a 'mystery', not because it is unknown but precisely because, otherwise secret, it has been disclosed by God (note the balance in the translation between 'hidden' and 'proclaimed'). His purposes, contained in the small scroll of verses 2, 8–10, have been made possible through the sacrificial death of the Lamb (5.9–10), and will be brought to completion in the coming kingdom of God (11.15). Beale (541–46) relates the content of the pur-pose of God in verse 7 to the cry for the vindication of the saints at 6.11. In response to the prayers of the saints, Beale (542) argues, and when the death of those believers destined for martyrdom has taken place, the final judgement can begin. While there may be a connection between the 'waiting' of 10.6b–7 and the question 'how long?' in 6.10–11, there is no need to limit the scope of the divine plans envisaged in Chapters 10—11 to the achievement of martyrdom. For 'mystery' in the New Testament see fur-ther Smalley, 'Mystery'; Bornkamm, '*mystērion*'.

The 'hidden purpose' of God will be 'fulfilled' at the sounding of the seventh trumpet. The verb ἐτελέσθη (*etelesthē*, 'fulfilled') is aorist passive. But it is proleptic, and carries a clearly future, anticipatory meaning with reference to God's activity at the end of time; hence the translation, '(the purpose) *will* be fulfilled'. God announced his purposes of salvation, in essence, to 'his servants the prophets'. This is the first use of the designation προφήτης (*prophētēs*, 'prophet') in the Apocalypse. Although 'prophets' are mostly Christian in Revelation (see 11.10, 18; 16.6; 18.20, 24; 22.6, 9), the reference in the present context must include Old Testament prophets, and perhaps 'prophecy' in general. For the expression 'his servants the prophets' see 11.18; also Amos 3.7; 1QpHab 2.8–10; 7.1–5 (both Qumranic passages use '[the words of] his servants, the prophets'). The conception is Deuteronomic (2 Kings 9.7; Jer. 7.25; et al.). The verb εὐηγγέλισεν (*euēngelisen*, 'proclaimed', lit. 'announced the good news') is found in the active voice only here and at 14.6 in the New Testament (cf. BDAG 402a). The choice of word is appropriate in the present context of the divine purposes of salvation.

8 The final scenes of the drama, with the triumph of God and goodness over evil, are about to begin; although these portray an eternal process, rather than a temporal sequence. The purposes of God, declared in principle in 10.1–7, are contained in the 'scroll' of verse 2 (see also on the 'thunders' in verses 3–4; and on verses 6b–7). To that small scroll, and to its more detailed contents, John now returns. At this point the seer enters into his visionary drama more fully than anywhere else in the Apocalypse (Thompson 123).

For the 'heavenly (divine) voice', which John hears for the second time, see on verse 4. The language of verse 8 looks back to the visionary situation of Rev. 10.1–7. It is the same 'voice'; for the articular form, ἡ φωνή (*hē phēnē*, '*the* voice'), refers back to the anarthrous appearance of the noun in verse 4 ('*a* voice'). Similarly, the voice from heaven speaks 'again' (πάλιν, *palin*); and this retrospective adverb introduces a contrast between what is not revealed in the 'seven thunderclaps' of verses 3–4, and what is disclosed in the opened scroll of this verse, and in the remainder of Revelation (cf. Beale 550). For the participles λαλοῦσαν (*lalousan*, 'speaking') and λέγουσαν (*legousan*, 'saying') see the textual notes on verse 8. The use of participles as finite verbs (the equivalent of 'the voice spoke to me and said'), as in 1.16; 4.2; 6.2; et al., emphasizes in this context the active, and no longer passive, role which John is about to play in the drama (cf. verse 4). So he is commanded to 'take' the scroll and 'eat it' (verses 8–10), as a part of his prophetic commission.

For the 'scroll which lies open in the hand of the angel' see on verse 2. The use of βιβλίον (*biblion*, 'scroll', or 'book') here, rather than βιβλαρίδιον (*biblaridion*, 'small scroll'), as in verses 2, 9, 10, suggests that the two words are more or less interchangeable (see on verse 2). The view taken in this commentary is that the '(small) scroll' of Rev. 10 is to be identified with the scroll of Rev. 5, even if its focus has now become sharper (see above; against Aune 571). The scroll of 5.1 (and 2–9) contains the divine purpose and plan for the future of God's world in Christ; but its contents cannot be disclosed until the seventh seal has been broken (8.1). In 10.2 it is said that the scroll 'had been opened' once and for all; the perfect participle, ἠνεῳγμένον (*ēneō[i]gmenon*, lit. 'opened'), which is used in verse 8 as in verse 2, implies a completed action which cannot be reversed. In verse 8, therefore, we are made aware that a more complete revelation of the 'hidden purpose of God' (verse 7), introduced by the 'strong angel' (verse 1), is about to be disclosed. For the first time, the scroll will unveil the true nature of the events of the end-time, and the way in which they will contribute to the final coming of God's kingdom (cf. Bauckham 1295b). As always, however, John's eschatology brings together the temporal and the eternal.

Beale (544–45) detects theological irony in the scroll-content of both Rev. 10 and Rev. 5. The victory of the Lamb has been achieved despite his apparent defeat by the kingdom of evil (5.9–13; cf. 6.16–17); while, through faithful witness before Christ, the suffering and martyrdom of the saints caused by the same powers of evil lead to resurrection and conquest (5.9–10; cf. 2.10–11; 7.14).

The angel is described, for the third time in this scene, as 'standing between the sea and the dry land' (see on verse 2; also verse 5). This repetition is not simply a rhetorical device (against Mounce 208). It is more positively a further reminder that the strong angel of Rev. 10, as the representative of Christ (see above), exercises sovereignty over all the earth; just as the Lamb's possession of the open scroll is symbolic of his worthiness to carry out the Father's universal purposes of judgement and salvation (5.2–9; cf. Beale 548; and note the matching language of Rev. 5.7–8 and 10.8).

9–10 These two verses are close together in literary form and theological content. The prophetic incident involving the scroll is first outlined in speech (verse 9), and then performed in dramatic action (verse 10). For the 'angel' and the 'small scroll' in this narrative unit see on verses 1, 2, 8. Still on earth, the seer obeys the command of the heavenly voice to 'take the scroll which lies open in the hand of the angel' (verse 8; cf. verse 2), and asks the angel to give him the small scroll. The angel repeats the injunction to take the scroll, but adds the invitation to 'eat it'; and this symbolic activity, with its consequences, is then described (verse 10).

The background to this scene is to be found in the prophetic commissioning of Ezek. 2.8—3.3, where Ezekiel is told to open his mouth and eat a scroll (2.8). Aune (572) compares the words of institution used by Jesus at the Last Supper, 'take and eat' (Matt. 26.26; cf. Mark 14.22; *Jos. As.* 16.15–16); but the setting in verses 9–10 is prophetic, and not remotely eucharistic. That John 'takes' the scroll suggests his appropriation of God's revelation, rather than his passive reception of it (also verse 8; cf. Mounce 208–209). More importantly, this action reinforces his divine and prophetic commission, which he has already received earlier in the drama (1.10–11; 4.1–2). Finally, the seer's possession of an open book connects with the Lamb's reception of the scroll (sealed, but imminently to be opened) in the throne-vision of 5.1–8. There, the imagery speaks of Christ's worthiness and ability to carry out God's purpose of judgement and salvation through his death and exaltation; in Rev. 10.9–10 John's similar action denotes his participation in the salvific authority of Jesus, as a result of which he shares in the inheritance and kingdom of the saints (Beale 548–49). Swete (130) picks up the allusion to Rev. 5 in this passage when he maintains that, by taking the scroll, John is demonstrating his fitness for the prophetic mission ahead of him (so 5.5).

The scroll which John receives contains the scheme of salvation history, which he is to declare (see above). This will be summarized in 11.1–13 (q.v.), and disclosed more broadly in the remainder of the Apocalypse. Cf. Bauckham 1295*b*. The seer needs to ingest the contents of the small scroll, in order to make its contents his own before communicating them to others. As with Ezekiel (3.3), the scroll becomes 'sweet as honey' (γλυκὺ ὡς μέλι, *glyky hōs meli*) to his taste (the Greek is lit. 'in [the] mouth'). The metaphor is used in the Old Testament to describe the saving and joyful effect which God's word has in leading those who listen to it (cf. Ps. 19.7–10; 119.97–104; Jer. 15.16; note also Prov. 16.24; 4Q418 *frag.* 9.16). Beale (550) believes that the sweet taste of the scroll represents the 'life-sustaining attribute of God's word, which empowers the prophet to carry out his task (Deut. 8.3)'.

But the angel also promises that the small scroll will become 'bitter' (πικρανεῖ, *pikranei*; the word in verses 9 and 10 also appears at 8.11, and only in these three places in Revelation) in the prophet's stomach; and this thought is not present in the Ezekiel parallel. The inversion in verse 9, whereby the bitterness of the digestion is mentioned *before* the sweetness of eating the scroll, is typical of the writer's style in the Apocalypse (cf. 3.3; 5.5; et al.), although the order bitter–sweet is reversed, to sweet–bitter, in verse 10. Ezekiel's commission was to warn rebellious and unrepentant Israel of the impending judgement of God which must follow unrighteousness and repeated opposition to him (Ezek. 3.16–21). That divine discrimination, balancing the sweetness of God's word, is symbolized by the words of 'lamentation and mourning and woe' written on the scroll he received (Ezek. 2.10). Similarly, John has a message for the Church of his day. Before the final triumph (sweetness), believers will pass through a great ordeal of suffering (7.14; bitterness). But the prophetic witness, which the seer is compelled to deliver (verse 11), also has a universal reference (Court, *Revelation* 49). God's saving offer of life and love is available for all; but it cannot be separated from his judgement on evil, and his triumph over it. Thunder and love belong together throughout the Apocalypse, and indeed in John's own experience; for to be a messenger of the gospel involves an existential embracing of both its bitterness and its sweetness (Roloff 126; cf. also Beasley-Murray 175).

11   The introduction to this verse, καὶ λέγουσίν μοι (*kai legousin moi*, lit. 'and they say to me'), is awkward; for it is not clear who is speaking. If the voice were that from heaven (verses 4, 8), or the angel's voice (verse 9), a singular form of the verb (rather than the third person plural) would presumably have been used at this point (see the textual note on verse 11). The plural could possibly indicate that both voices are speaking together; but it is more likely that the plural verb here is indefinite, with a meaning equivalent to the passive, 'it was said' (hence the translation, 'I was told'). In any case the source of the voice is divine.

The seer is told, 'You must prophesy once more' (δεῖ σε πάλιν προφητεῦσαι, *dei se palin prophēteusai*, lit. 'it is necessary for you to prophesy again'). The command involves a divine compulsion to proclaim God's word, as experienced by other prophets and evangelists in Jewish and Christian history: John 'must' prophesy (cf. Jer. 4.19; Amos 3.8; *Sib. Or.* 3.162–64; 1 Cor. 9.16–17; et al.). The adverb πάλιν (*palin*, 'once more') suggests that the seer's prophetic commissioning is the renewal of a task which has already been undertaken (see 1.10–11; 4.1–2; and on 10.10; cf. also Aune 573).

John's message of judgement and salvation (see verses 8–10) is to be directed 'against' (ἐπί, *epi*) a universal audience. The preposition ἐπί (*epi*) with the dative could mean 'about' or 'concerning' people, in a neutral sense (cf. 22.16, 'this testimony *for* the churches'). But in this context the word is used to reflect the characteristically negative, apocalyptic attitude towards the rebellious nations of the world adopted by the prophets of the Old Testament (cf. Jer. 25.13; LXX Jer. 32.30; Ezek. 4.7; 13.17; 25.2; et al.); see also Matt. 10.18 par.; Acts 9.15; *1 Clem.* 5.7. This interpretation is confirmed both by the negative content of the scroll described in Ezek. 2.9–10, which lies behind the imagery in this passage, and also by the judgemental as well as salvific nature of the remaining scenes in Revelation, to which the small scroll of 10.2, 8–10 points forward. See also Beale 554–55.

The prophet-seer is commanded to prophesy against 'peoples, nations, language groups and rulers'. A fourfold, polysyndetic list of ethnic units occurs seven times in the Apocalypse (5.9; 7.9; 10.11; 11.9; 13.7; 14.6; 17.15), on each occasion in a different order. See the background in Dan. 3.4, 7 LXX, where a threefold group of 'peoples, nations and languages', at the sound of a trumpet (cf. Rev. 10.7; 11.15), is instructed to fall down and worship the statue of Nebuchadnezzar. The fourfold formula of Rev. 10.11 appears in a closely related version at 5.9 and 7.9 (q.v.), to describe positively people throughout the world who have been redeemed by the Lamb. But here, and in the remainder of the Apocalypse, it is used negatively (see above, on the use of ἐπί [*epi*] with the dative, translated 'against', to introduce the formula), with reference to judgement on wrongdoers. Furthermore, the term φυλή (*phylē*, 'tribe', or 'race') in 5.9; 7.9 is replaced in 10.11 by 'rulers' (βασιλεῖς, *basileis*, lit. 'kings'). The change may suggest that God's word expressed through the prophets takes precedence over all human authority, however exalted (so Mounce 211). More probably, it anticipates the 'rulers' ('kings of the earth') in the visions to follow, who are to be judged (16.12, 14; 17.1–2, 9–18; 18.3, 9; 19.18–19). The fourfold formula in any case makes clear that the divine message of saving judgement, delivered through the prophet-seer, relates to everyone without distinction. The only difference is whether they are marked by the beast, or sealed by God.

Just as the 'small scroll' of Chapter 10 contains a proclamation of judgement and salvation which is universal in scope (verses 7, 11), so its prophecy is not just about what is to happen in the future. John's eschatology is consistently balanced between time and eternity; and in the Apocalypse, as here, he is concerned with the interpretation of God's word, and the ethical response to it, in the *present*, as well as in the future. See the use of προφητεία (*prophēteia*, 'prophecy') at 1.3; 22.7–10, 18–19. The prophecy of the seer in Revelation also relates to compromisers within the Church (2.6, 15, 20–23; 22.18–19), and not only to unbelievers outside it. Cf. Beale 555.

From now on, the language of the Apocalypse will become even more dramatic and mysterious, as John describes in visionary form and in sharper focus the events of the coming end-time (Rev. 11.1–13; and beyond). But the end itself is not yet (see on 6.17; 8.1; et al.), even following the sounding of the final trumpet (10.7; 11.14–15, q.v.). After the interval of 10.1—11.19, the seer will describe the heavenly city, and the consummation of salvation history (21—22). But, in between (12—20), he will hand on an apocalypse of the active processes within human society, and the nature of the supernatural powers which are at work behind its façade. Heaven and earth, time and eternity, belong together in Revelation.

Measuring the Temple (11.1–2)

11.1–2   The first part of Chapter 11 (verses 1–13) summarizes the contents of the 'small scroll' of Chapter 10. The focus is broadly on God's final purposes of judgement and love for his creation (see 10.8–10), and specifically on the fate of the witnessing Church during the period of the end-time, whenever that may occur. Between the two visions which occur after the sounding of the sixth trumpet, and before the seventh (9.13—11.15), John inserts (11.1–2) a brief but theologically important reference to the measuring of the Temple. It is possible that this segment, like 11.1–13 itself, derives from a separate source (so e.g. Beckwith 584–88; Charles 1, 270–73; Roloff 128–30). But John uses his original materials creatively and with great freedom; and it is more important to understand his resulting message than to reconstruct its derivation (cf. Mounce 212; despite Aune 594–96). For the literary unity of the interval section 10.1—11.13 see above, 253–54.

As throughout the Apocalypse, the language of the seer in 11.1–2 (and in this passage generally) is symbolic. Even if the Jerusalem Temple is in mind as the setting for these two verses, its literal existence is less important than its figurative significance. Equally, however, the interpretation of John's apocalyptic message at this point is not well served by understanding his symbolism in an unrestrained manner, which borders on allegory; so Kiddle (174–88), who claims that in 11.1–13 the 'temple' is the Christian Church; the 'two witnesses' are that part of the believing community which must suffer martyrdom; and the 'holy city' represents the city of civilization which is 'utterly alien to the will of God' (ibid. 185).

Given that the significance of 11.1–2 is symbolic, the imagery of this section has been understood by modern commentators along three main lines.

(a) First, the temple, altar and worshippers are taken to refer to the Jewish remnant, and the outer court and holy city to Israel as a whole, given up to the Gentiles in punishment for its sins (so Beckwith 588–90).
(b) Second, the protective measuring of the temple, altar and worshippers are regarded as symbolizing the preservation of believers, while the invasion of the outer court

and holy city represent the rejection and punishment of unbelieving Judaism (Swete 132–33). It is true that the literature of Second Temple Judaism often interprets the destruction of Jerusalem and its Temple as a punishment for Israel's disobedience (cf. *Apoc. Abr.* 27.5–7; *2 Apoc. Bar.* 1.3–4; *4 Baruch* 4.7–8; *Sib. Or.* 3.272–79; *T. Levi* 10.3; et al.).

(c) A popular exegesis of Rev. 11.1–2 views the temple, together with the altar and worshippers, as the Christian community of believers. This interpretation is based on the regular use, in the New Testament and early Christian literature, of 'temple' as a metaphor for the Church of Christ. See e.g. 1 Cor. 3.16–17; 2 Cor. 6.16; Eph. 2.19–22; 1 Pet. 2.5; Ignatius, *Eph.* 9.1; *Barn.* 4.11; *2 Clem.* 9.3. The outer court of the temple and the holy city are then understood as the 'outer life' of the Church, the members of which are exposed to suffering and death brought about by the enemies of God (so Boring 143; Hughes 120–21; Sweet 182; Bauckham, *Climax of Prophecy* 272; Mounce 213; et al.). Hendriksen (127–28) sees the temple ('sanctuary of God') as the true Church, and the 'court outside' as the realm of compromising and nominal Christendom, upon which the world tramples. This view of the temple and outer court as representing the Church from two different perspectives, internal and external, regularly includes the interpretation of the metaphor of 'measuring' in these two verses as meaning protection. But this preservation is seen not only, or not primarily, as protection against physical suffering and death; rather, it concerns security (sealing) from spiritual danger, and the ultimate salvation of the faithful (Hendriksen 127; Caird 132; Boring 143–44; Sweet 182; Mounce 213–14). Beale (557–71) interestingly interprets all five images of 11.1–2 (temple, altar, worshippers, outer court and holy city) as metaphors for the different but complementary aspects of the Christian community, the new people of God (cf. esp. ibid. 570–71; and see further below).

For the interpretative issues in this section see Aune, 593–98, esp. 597–98. Aune's own view (598) is not far from the approach adopted by the majority of commentators, with the exception of Beale, cited in (c) above. Aune emphasizes the salvation and protection which are available for faithful worshippers at the centre (the temple of God and its altar), inasfar as they have been measured and so divinely protected (cf. 12.6, 14, where the wilderness has the same function as a place of refuge). To this extent, the worshippers in the temple are analogous to the 144,000 saints, whom God has sealed, in the vision at 7.1–8; and this is a connection already made by Swete (133). Alternatively, Aune argues, danger and destruction lie at the periphery (the outer court and the holy city); and in that hostile environment God's faithful remnant can find protection from his enemies. But this safety is physical, and not merely spiritual; it includes escape from eschatological warfare and the plagues which punish wicked humanity, and 'the survival of God's chosen people at the end of days' (ibid. 598).

All these ideas, and those mentioned in (c), above, are reasonable theological inferences from the imagery of Rev. 11.1–2. The temple, worshippers and altar of verse 1 must signify the Christian community and its faithful members; just as the concept of 'measuring' symbolizes the preservation of the servants of God who have been sealed from danger of every kind. The outer court and holy city then represent the Church in its vulnerability. Its adherents, the Johannine circle included, remain subject to physical oppression from imperial and Jewish sources, and to the possibility of martyrdom (2.13; 6.10–11; 20.4). But the dangers surrounding the faithful extend to the realm of spirituality: the temptation to compromise with the world and to adopt its ethical standards (2.14–15; et al.); the struggle to maintain a balanced belief, especially about the nature of the person of Jesus (see on 11.3); and the ultimate enticement from the powers of evil to worship the beast, and reject the Godhead altogether (13.4–9; 18.1–24; 19.17–21).

The introductory καί (*kai*, 'then', lit. 'and') in verse 1, with no further introductory vision formula (as in 10.1), links 11.1–2 (and 1–13) directly with 10.8–11. The active participation of the seer in the action of this vision continues from 10.8. Now he is 'given a measuring rod, resembling a staff', and instructed to measure the temple (note the intensity of the imperative which introduces the command: ἔγειρε, *egeire*, 'get up'). The 'reed of measurement' (κάλαμος, *kalamos*) is an image which derives from Ezek. 40.3 LXX (see below). The term appears elsewhere in Revelation only at 21.15–16; cf. Luke 7.24; Mark 15.19 par. In 3 John 13 it is used for the 'reed pen' with which the elder had no desire to write to his readers (see Smalley, *1, 2, 3 John* 363). The instrument in question here would be a bamboo-like cane, grown in the Jordan valley, and sufficiently slender ('like a staff', ὅμοιος ῥάβδῳ, *homoios rhabdō[i]*) to be used for measuring. The 'staff-like rod' appears as an emblem of authority in both Jewish and Classical ceremony (Thompson 124); cf. Ps. 2.9; *Pss. Sol.* 17.23–26; *Sib. Or.* 8.248; also Rev. 2.27; 12.5; BDAG 902*b*.

The source of the rod 'given' to John, the means of his movement to the temple, and the execution of the command to measure, are not stated. Nor is the identity of the speaker who issues the instruction to measure the temple (for the vague λέγων, *legōn*, lit. 'saying', see the textual note on verse 1); although the subject of the voice and the giver of the staff are presumably both divine in character (see also on 10.11). Bengel (249) thinks that the speech is more conveniently attributed, by metonymy, to the rod itself! But see 9.13; 16.7 (the altar speaks).

The measuring which is enjoined in this scene has the character of a symbolic prophetic action, as described in the Old Testament (see e.g. 1 Kings 22.11; Isa. 8.1–4; Jer. 27.2—28.16; Ezek. 24.3–13; also Acts 21.11). 'Measuring' in the Old Testament can be a metaphor for destruction (cf. 2 Sam. 8.2; Isa. 34.11; Lam. 2.8; Amos 7.7–9; et al.). But it can also be a symbol of preservation (Ezek. 40.1–6; 42.20; Zech. 2.1–5; although in the Zechariah text there are too many people to be protected within the walls of Jerusalem, so that the Lord himself [verse 5] acts as a preserving wall around his people). Clearly the positive thought of preservation, and of sealing (cf. Rev. 7.1–17), is present in the measuring action of 11.1–2 (see above).

The background to this passage is Ezek. 40—42 itself, where the measuring of the eschatological temple provides a detailed description of the future temple (Aune 604). The common theme which connects the apocalyptic and prophetic texts of Ezekiel and Revelation is precisely that of measurement and protection. This image also marks out the boundary between the holy and the profane; and, in the context of Rev. 11.1, it limits the essence of holiness to that which exists within John's measurements: the membership of the Christian Church (cf. Thompson 124). In Rev. 11.1–2 it is the seer who is commanded to undertake the activity of measurement; in Ezek. 40.3, as in Rev. 21.15, the measuring reed is used by an angelic figure.

It is the 'temple of God' which is to be measured by John. The phrase, τὸν ναὸν τοῦ θεοῦ (*ton naon tou theou*, 'the temple of God'), occurs elsewhere in the Apocalypse, with the nominative of the noun, only at 11.19; although 3.12 has 'temple of *my* God'. In 11.19 the sanctuary is described as 'heavenly', whereas in the present context the reference is to the Temple in Jerusalem; and if Revelation were written in the middle of AD 70, which is the position adopted in this commentary, that Temple would still be standing. The background to the measuring of the temple in 11.1–2, as we have seen, is to be found in the visionary building of Ezek. 40—42; and this included two courts, an oblong inner section (Ezek. 40.28–37) and a square outer area (Ezek. 40.17–23). The construction in Ezekiel is modelled on the Temple of Solomon, which also had two courts, inner and outer (1 Kings 6.36; 7.9–12). The Herodian Temple of John's day, the building of which started in 19 BC, similarly consisted of an inner complex and a large, mainly commercial, area outside; the precinct within the high wall contained the holy of holies, the holy place and the three courts of the priests, Israelites and women.

This broadly twofold arrangement underlies the imagery of verses 1 and 2. The seer is instructed to measure the 'temple' (ναός, *naos*), meaning the inner precinct as a whole, but to exclude its 'outer court' (τὴν αὐλὴν τὴν ἔξωθεν τοῦ ναοῦ, *tēn aulēn tēn exōthen tou naou*, lit. 'the court outside the temple', verse 2). The outer forecourt of the Herodian Temple was surrounded by covered porticoes, open on the inside and closed on the outside, each of which had rows of columns. The portico on the eastern side of the Temple mount was known as Solomon's Porch (John 10.23; Acts 3.11; 5.12). The outer esplanade of the Temple was later called the court of the Gentiles, and was used extensively for purposes of trading (cf. Mark 11.15–17 par., using τὸ ἱερόν, *to hieron*, for 'temple', since this term included the outer court). See also 11QTemple (19) cols 38.1—40.15.

It has already been suggested (see above) that the 'temple' in 11.1–2 symbolizes the holy, sealed people of God, and that the 'outer court' represents the Church in its subjection to the powers of evil (note also, later in verse 2, the idea of this court being 'handed over to the Gentiles'). That these forces of unrighteousness included both Jewish and Roman enemies of Christianity would have been of immediate relevance to the Johannine community, members of which came from Hellenistic (Gentile) as well as Judaic backgrounds. Beale (562) identifies the temple with membership of the Church of Christ, among whom God dwells on earth; but he interprets the 'outer court' in a positive light as a reference to God's true people, among whom Gentiles are now included (Eph. 2.14), suffering for their witness (Beale 560–61). For 'temple' and 'outer court' see further Aune 605–606; also Millard and McKelvey, 'Temple'.

John's prophetic commission to measure the temple includes the 'altar' (τὸ θυσιαστήριον, *to thysiastērion*). Some interpreters take this to be a reference to the altar of incense, as in 8.3, 5; 9.13 (so Mounce 214; Bauckham 1295*b*). However, the altar in question in this passage is much more likely to be that of burnt offering (so 6.9; 14.18; 16.7). The altar of incense was located by itself in the holy place; whereas the altar of offering was to be found in the court of the priests, surrounded (as here) by worshippers in the courts of the Israelites and women (cf. Swete 132; Beckwith 590). The context precludes the possibility that John is being invited to measure the size of the altar, as a cultic object, by itself. As with the temple, 'measuring the altar' suggests the definition of an *area* (as in the translation), such as an altar room, with nearby worshippers in attendance.

Beale (563) understands the altar as 'the place of sacrifice' (a translation of the term allowed by AG 367*a*), which in this setting would describe the people of God as a suffering covenant community. In line with 6.9–10, the close proximity of believers to the altar implies that they are priests as well as worshippers, who have 'brought themselves to be sacrificed on the altar of the gospel', to which they have been called to testify (Beale 563). There is a certainly a close connection between the 'altar area' of this verse (11.1) and the altar of offering in the scene of the martyrs in 6.9–11 (see on verse 9). Being a faithful witness, John is saying prophetically, involves sacrifice and suffering. But, in liturgy as in life, believers are protected by God's gracious sealing, and enabled to worship him with thanksgiving (11.15–16), so that eventually they find their reward in the Almighty (11.18), who accepts their prayers (8.3–4). Measuring the temple and its altar area has to do with preservation, not perfection (against Hughes 120).

The verb μετρεῖν (*metrein*) can mean 'count', as well as 'measure'; so it can be used, as in verse 1, with reference to the limits of the temple and the altar, as well as to the number of worshippers. Those who, in this vision, worship at the temple altar belong to a community which is susceptible to harm, and gladly offers itself in sacrifice for the sake of Christ. In the phrase of Beale (570), their sacrificial living is the way believers worship. In the phrase, 'count the worshippers within it', ἐν αὐτῷ (*en autō[i]*, lit. 'in it') may allude to the temple, or the altar (construing ἐν, *en*, as 'near'; so BDAG 326*b*, and see John 8.20; Luke 13.4), or both.

The temple, altar and worshippers in the vision of Rev. 11.1, as in 6.9, resonate between the sanctuary on earth and the temple of God in heaven, just as in 11.19 the heavenly temple is not far away from the earthly. Indeed, the two places of offering merge; and this fusion of the material and the spiritual is typical of John's cosmology and theology (see further on 6.9). In John 2.19–21 the Temple of Judaism is identified with the body of Jesus, the head of the new Israel; for Christian believers, as 'temples' of God and the Spirit, cf. also 1 Cor. 6.19; 2 Cor. 6.16; Eph. 2.21; et al.

The instruction to the seer in verse 2*a*, 'exclude (the outer court) from your calculations' (ἔκβαλε ἔξωθεν, *ekbale exōthen*, lit. 'cast it outside'), must be construed figuratively to mean 'do not measure it' (μὴ αὐτὴν μετρήσῃς, *mē autēn metrēsē[i]s*), as in the Greek of the following repeated and emphatic command. The expression ἐκβάλλειν ἔξω (*ekballein exō*, lit. 'to throw outside') is normally used of *people* who are excluded, or expelled (as in John 9.34–35; 12.31; cf. Luke 4.29; Acts 7.58). But 'excluding the outer court' in this passage denotes precisely an injunction to refrain from 'measuring', or protecting, the unfaithful people (the 'Gentiles') to whom the court has been handed over (cf. Luke 13.28; see also below). For 'the outer court of the temple' see on verse 1. It is taken here to represent the Church of God in its subjection to the enemies of goodness and truth. The sealing of the saints ensures their inheritance of eternal life; but it does not guarantee their protection from physical suffering, or even martyrdom, at any time and up to the end-time. Cf. Bauckham 1295*b*.

The relationship between the two closely connected clauses in verse 2*b*, beginning with ὅτι (*hoti*, 'because' or 'for') and καί (*kai*, 'and'), is not immediately clear. The most logical way of construing the sentence is to take the Greek as it stands (see the translation). The subject of the aorist verb of divine permission, ἐδόθη (*edothē*, 'it has been handed over', lit. 'it was given'), is the (outer) temple-court, τὴν αὐλήν (*tēn aulēn*, 'the court'). The following future clause is then consecutive: 'exclude the court from your measurement, because it has been given over by God to the Gentiles, as a consequence of which they will trample over the holy city' (cf. verse 3). So Charles 1, 278; cf Aune 607–608, who prefers to take καί (*kai*, 'and') with the future indicative as a coordinate clause equivalent to an infinitive. This then forms the subject of the verb ἐδόθη (*edothē*, 'it was permitted'), and gives the literal sense, 'to conquer the holy city was permitted to the Gentiles' (similarly Beckwith 599).

The 'holy city' refers to Jerusalem itself, as in LXX Isa. 66.20; Joel 4.17 ('the holy city Jerusalem'); cf. Isa. 52.1. See also verse 8. In Second Temple Judaism, 'the holy city' is frequently used as a description of Jerusalem (see Dan. [Theod.] 9.24; 1 Macc. 2.7; 2 Macc. 14.15; 3 Macc. 6.5; Sir. 36.18; et al.; also Neh. 11.1; Isa. 48.2; 11QTemple [= 11Q19] 47.14–18; Matt. 4.5; 27.53). Beale (568–71) thinks that this image most probably evokes some aspect of the heavenly Jerusalem, as in Rev. 3.12; 21.2, 10, part of which is identified with believers living on earth (cf. also 20.9). The holy city is therefore the persecuted, true people of God, among whom he is present (Beale 568, 571; similarly Mounce 215).

It is true that, in the Apocalypse, the concept of the 'city', and in particular the 'holy city', relates to the heavenly Jerusalem; and this is certainly the case in the vision of the new Jerusalem at Rev. 21—22; see esp. 22.19. But in the present context, where the setting of the vision is earthly (see on verses 1–2*a*), the 'holy city' must initially be a description of the Jewish spiritual centre of gravity in Palestine. Believers oppressed by the enemies of God in that place of worship, with its Temple, and in that locus of faith which is the very dwelling-place of God (Ps. 76.2; Sir. 36.18), would be at their most sensitive and vulnerable (see above, on the 'outer court'). The holy city trampled by the Gentiles is especially, but not only, where the witnesses lie dead in the streets of the 'great city' (verse 8; see Bauckham, *Theology* 127). It is also the place where the suffering faithful are acutely aware of the pain and anguish inflicted by the unfaithful. Nevertheless, as Walker (*Holy City* 248–59, esp. 258–59) argues, the earthly Jerusalem in the Apocalypse points to the heavenly city, and gives way to it. For ultimately the new Jerusalem, revealed from heaven, is where God's sovereignty is finally acknowledged; it is therefore of eternal and abiding importance (cf. 22.14, 19). Cf. also Bauckham, *Climax of Prophecy* 272–73.

Meanwhile the idea of Jerusalem, the holy city and its witnessing inhabitants, being trampled underfoot by hostile Gentiles (τοῖς ἔθνεσιν, *tois ethnesin*, lit. 'by the nations') is closely paralleled in Luke 21.24 (Jerusalem will be 'trampled on by the Gentiles' until the times of the Gentiles are fulfilled). Like Rev. 11.2, this text from Luke alludes to LXX Zech. 12.3 (not MT), where it is prophesied that Jerusalem will be made 'a stone trampled by all the Gentiles'. The Greek verb πατεῖν (*patein*, lit. 'to tread heavily with feet, with the implication of destructive intent'; so BDAG 786*a*), and more usually its intensive cognate καταπατεῖν (*katapatein*, 'to trample under foot'), appears at times in the literature of Judaism with reference to the conquest and even destruction of Jerusalem, and the profanation of its Temple (e.g. LXX Isa. 63.18; Dan. 8.13; 1 Macc. 4.60; 3 Macc. 2.18; *Pss. Sol.* 2.2; 8.12; *2 Apoc. Baruch* 67.2; cf. 4QpNah *frags.* 3 + 4 col. 1.3).

In the context of the present passage (Rev. 11.2), the concept of 'trampling' may include once-for-all destruction; but its main sense is that of the enemies of God 'keeping in subjection', or 'oppressing', the saints of God for an indefinite period of time. That figurative interval is specified as 'forty-two months' (or three and a half years; so also 13.5), which in Revelation also appears under the designations 1,260 days (11.3; 12.6; where the months in view are solar units of 30 days each), and 'a time, and times and half a time' (12.14). The background to all three temporal descriptions is to be located in Dan. 8.9–14, which refers to the period of Jewish suffering under the Syrian despotic ruler Antiochus Epiphanes in 167–164 BC. But see also Dan. 7.25; 12.7, where the divinely limited period of tribulation for the saints is said to be precisely 'a time, two times (or "times") and half a time'; and in early Judaism that formula seems to have been understood as the equivalent of 'three and a half years' (Dan. 4.32; et al.; cf. Aune 609). In all these contexts, the time-reference becomes a symbol for a restricted period of time during which evil would be allowed to triumph (Mounce 215). But this does not last. In Daniel the sanctuary, trampled underfoot, is reconsecrated (8.14). In the Apocalypse the Christian Church, attacked and profaned by the beast (11.7), but protected by God (11.1), will eventually and as a result of faithful witness emerge triumphant (11.15–18; 12.10–12). See Matt. 16.18–19.

It may be relevant that almost three and a half years elapsed between the first Jewish revolt of AD 66 and the fall of Jerusalem in AD 70. See also Dan. 12.12, which contains a blessing on the faithful who persevere for 1,335 days; in *Asc. Isa.* 4.9–13 Jesus is said to rule for that length of time. Similarly, the ministry of Jesus on earth possibly took place over roughly three years (Beale 567). Moffatt (416), less cogently, notes that the figure of 'three and one half' reflects the extent of the Babylonian winter, which lasted three and a half months. The 'three and a half days' of Rev. 11.9, 11, which is the interval between the death and resurrection of the two witnesses, probably includes an allusion to the 'three and a half years' of the time-references in Rev. 11—13, with their Danielic background.

The Two Witnesses (11.3–14)

3 The theme of faithful Christian witness, in the face of oppression and suffering, leads into the content and meaning of the prophetic oracle in 11.3–13(14). The divine voice which was heard in verses 1–2 (and 10.11) continues to speak (note the linking καί [*kai*, 'and'] at the start of verse 3). However, despite the obvious literary and theological connection between verses 1–2 and 3, verse 3 begins a new paragraph, in which the character of the 'two witnesses' is described.

The use of the personal pronoun, in the phrase 'I will permit *my* two witnesses' (δώσω τοῖς δυσὶν μάρτυσίν μου, *dōsō tois dysin martysin mou*, lit. 'I will give to my two witnesses'), suggests that the commission in this context derives from God, or perhaps God in Christ (see verse 8, where a shift in the narrative perspective occurs). This is the only indication in the present scene of the identity of the speaker, since the remainder of Rev. 11 is cast in the third person.

The use of the definite article, in the expression 'my two witnesses' (the Greek is literally '*the* two witnesses of me'), points to the likelihood that this pair would be familiar to John's audience. The witnesses are clearly modelled on the figures of Moses and Elijah, who were expected to return before the end of the world (cf. Deut. 18.18; Mal. 4.5 and Mark 9.11–12). It was also anticipated in the later literature of Judaism that Elijah and Enoch *redivivi* would appear before the coming of the Messiah (see *Apoc. Elijah* 4.7; 5.32; also *1 Enoch* 90.31). However, Enoch does not fit the description of the prophetic witnesses in Rev. 11.5–6; whereas the actions of the witnesses in those two verses reflect closely the portrait of Moses and Elijah in the Old Testament. Like Elijah, they have power to destroy their enemies by fire (2 Kings 1.10–17) and to lock up the heavens so that no rain can fall (1 Kings 17.1). Like Moses, they have the ability to turn the waters into blood (Exod. 7.14–20) and to afflict the land with every kind of plague (Exod. 8.1–17). Moreover, the ascension of the two witnesses into heaven (Rev. 11.12) corresponds to the ascent of Elijah at 2 Kings 2.11–12 and to the tradition behind the pseudepigraphical *Testament (Assumption) of Moses* (see 12.13). Moses and Elijah also appear together with Jesus at his transfiguration (Mark 9.4 par.).

The two witnesses in the context of Rev. 11.3, however, are not two individual figures, whether Jewish or Christian (Stephen, Peter, Paul; cf. Sweet 183). Beckwith (595), for example, identifies them as two great prophets who, in the spirit and power of Elijah and Moses, will 'call Israel to repentance'. Rather, they symbolize the witnessing Church, and not its martyrs alone, at the end-time (for the future tense of verse 3 see below). Despite opposition and suffering (verse 2), and even martyrdom (verses 7–10), the testimony of the faithful to God in Christ continues, and will prevail. For evidence that the two witnesses should be understood in a corporate, and not individual, manner see further Beale 574–75. He notes, for example (ibid. 575), that the powers of both Moses and Elijah are attributed to the two witnesses equally, and not divided among them. They are 'identical prophetic twins'; cf. also Bauckham, *Climax of Prophecy* 275–76. For the basic interpretation adopted here see further (*inter alia*) Beasley-Murray 183–84; Boring 145–46; Wall 143–44; Wilcock 105–106; Mounce 217.

Bousset (317–19) argues that the notion of *two* eschatological, prophetic witnesses cannot stem from a Jewish source, since in early Judaism the return of only a *single* such figure (Elijah) was anticipated. But the teaching of the Qumran community, to go no further, included the expectation of at least two, and in some texts three, Messiahs: priestly, kingly and prophetic; cf. 1QS 9.10–11; 4QTest 1–20; et al.

Aune (610) notes correctly that the term 'witness' (lit. 'martyr'), in the passage 11.3–13, has the meaning of 'prophet'. Thus, the phrase οἱ δύο μάρτυρες (*hoi duo martyres*, 'my two witnesses') exactly parallels 'the two prophets' (οἱ δύο προφῆται, *hoi duo prophētai*) in verse 10. Equally, the verb προφητεύειν (*prophēteuein*, 'to prophesy') and the noun προφητεία (*prophēteia*, 'prophecy') are used to describe the ministry of the witnesses in verses 3 and 6; and μαρτυρία (*martyria*, 'witness', 'testimony') in verse 7 is parallel to προφητεία (*prophēteia*, 'testimony') in verse 6. In a period when it seems that 'the nations' dominate the world (verse 2), 'the people' of God maintain their prophetic witness, even to death, within it (Wilcock 106). The testimony of the Church for all time is to the judgement and reconciliation of God through Christ. He is one with God and one with us, so that he can be the Saviour of the world (John 4.42; 1 John 4.14). For the idea of the rejection and violent death of the prophets, as a background to 11.3–13, see (e.g.) 2 Chron. 36.15–16; Neh. 9.26; *Jub.* 1.12; Matt. 5.11–12 par.; Matt. 23.34–37 par.; Acts 7.52; 1 Thess. 2.15; *Barn.* 5.11.

The two witnesses are 'permitted to prophesy'. The Greek is δώσω . . . καὶ προφητεύσουσιν (*dōsō . . . kai prophēteusousin*, lit. 'I will give . . . and they will prophesy'). God is among his people, and protects them despite their oppression (11.1–2). He allows the Church of Christ to be 'handed over' to the Gentiles (verse 2, using ἐδόθη, *edothē*, lit. 'it has been given') for a while; but he also 'gives' the saints strength to continue in the faith (verse 1; cf. 7.3–4), and to declare a prophecy of judgement against their persecutors. Cf. Beale 572. The believing community thus shares in the prophetic recommissioning of the seer himself (10.11). This includes a suffering and possible death which reflect the ministry of Jesus (Roloff 131). The use of the future tenses of the verbs in verse 3 speak more of divine determination than events which are yet to happen; for the passage 11.1–6 includes the entire period of the Church, past, present and future (Beale 572).

The fact that 'two' witnesses act on behalf of the community of faith is not intended to represent the activity of individuals (see also verse 4). It derives from the Old Testament requirement for at least two witnesses to be involved in judging an offence against the law, so that a valid verdict is guaranteed (cf. Num. 35.30; Deut. 17.6; 19.15). In the New Testament, following the principle of Deut. 19.15, see Matt. 18.16; Luke 10.1; John 8.17; 2 Cor. 13.1; et al. For two angelic witnesses to judgement and truth see 2 Macc. 3.26, 33; *2 Enoch* 1.4–5; Luke 24.4–9; Acts 1.10–11; *Gospel of Peter* 9.35—10.42; 1Q22 = 1QDM col. 1.11–12 (two people with the same ministry). Beale (575) notes that this legal atmosphere is enhanced by the use of μαρτυρία (*martyria*, 'witness', 'testimony', lit. 'martyr') language in this passage (see 11.3, 7; also 1.9; 6.9; 12.11, 17; 20.4).

The period during which the witnesses will be active is described as 'twelve hundred and sixty days'; and this is the same length of time as the 'forty-two months' allocated to the trampling of the holy city in verse 2 (q.v.). The description in days, rather than solar months, is probably no more than a literary variation (Mounce 218). The figure denotes an indefinite but restricted interval of time during which evil as well as prophecy are evident; such an interval also allows for repentance on the part of the unfaithful (11.13). At the same time, however, the rejection of the testimony of the witnesses in the court of this world becomes the basis of judgement on the oppressors in the court of heaven (Beale 575). For the 'sackcloth', worn by these prophetic figures, see on 6.12 (the only other appearance of the term in the Apocalypse). The latter-day prophets are clothed in the rough material of their predecessors (Zech. 13.4); sackcloth was also worn by Elijah (2 Kings 1.8) and his counterpart John the Baptist (Mark 1.6). The witnesses of Rev. 11.3 wear sackcloth to emphasize that they are lamenting the sin and judgement of the unrighteous, and calling for repentance as an outcome of their prophetic message (cf. Matt. 11.21 par.; also *Asc. Isa.* 2.9–11).

4 The divine voice, which has been speaking since 10.11, is silent for the moment. Meanwhile, the seer takes up the descriptive and vivid narrative, and continues it in the third person. The two witnesses, representing the community of faith, are now identified as 'the two olive trees and the two lampstands' which are in attendance on the Lord. For the introductory phrase, οὗτοί εἰσιν (*houtoi eisin*, 'these are'), see 7.14; although in the present context we do not have the response to a question, or indeed the explanation of an apocalyptic guide (Aune 612). For the significance of the numeral 'two' see on verse 3.

Both images, olive trees and lampstands, appear in verse 3 with a definite article (αἱ, *hai*, 'the'); and this suggests that the metaphors and their significance would be well known to John's audience. The background is to be found in Zech. 4 (see verses 2–6, 11–14). In that setting, a single golden lampstand (menorah), a symbol for Yahweh among his people, supports a bowl with seven lamps (Zech 4.2); and these are said to be 'the eyes of the Lord' (verse 10). The menorah is flanked by two olive trees (4.3), which supply the lampstand with golden oil (verse 12). The olive trees symbolize the two heads of Israel: clearly Zerubbabel, the Davidic governor under Darius (4.4–10), and, by implication, Joshua the high priest (cf. the 'anointed ones', lit. 'sons of oil', in verse 14), who features prominently in Zech. 3.1–9. The angelic interpretation of this complex imagery (4.6) is that the new Temple, for which Zerubbabel was responsible (Ezra 3.8–13), will be brought to completion by the Spirit of God, who gives needed support to his chosen leaders.

John interprets this material from Zechariah with great freedom (Charles 1, 283); but he makes the same theological point, by adapting the Old Testament source to his own situation. The one menorah becomes two, and they in turn are presented as synonymous with the two olive trees. In Rev. 1.12–13, 20 (q.v.); 2.1, 5, the seven Johannine churches of Asia appear under the symbol of seven lampstands; and, in that context, the menorahs represent the Church of God in its universality. The community of faith is called to let its light shine before others (Matt. 5.15–16); in other words, its prophetic commission is to bear witness to the judgement and salvation which are from God in Christ (see on 11.3). In the same way, John the Baptist is referred to figuratively as 'a burning and shining lamp' (cf. also 2 Pet. 1.19). Equally, the faithful light-bearers are olive trees, in that they dispense the 'oil' of the Spirit which 'keeps alive the light of life' (Swete 135); cf. Matt. 25.4; Rom. 11.17–18. By these two striking metaphors the seer is reminding the persecuted and divided community of his own day, and of all time, that 'the power and authority for effective witness lie in the Spirit of God' (Mounce 218). This is the last occurrence of the term λυχνία (*lychnia*, 'lampstand') in the Apocalypse; it is also the only time in Revelation when the noun ἐλαία (*elaia*, 'olive tree') is used.

The olive trees and the two lampstands, symbolizing the Church of God, are described as being 'in attendance on the Lord of the earth' (αἱ ἐνώπιον τοῦ κυρίου τῆς γῆς ἑστῶτες, *hai enōpion tou kyriou tēs gēs hestōtes*, lit. 'which stood before the Lord of the earth'). This is a direct allusion to Zech. 4.14 (the two anointed ones 'stand by the Lord of the whole earth'). To be in the presence of God the Creator may indicate the heavenly character of the witnesses; and indeed the members of the Church, according to Rev. 1.6, have a function which derives from the Father of Jesus, and is both royal and priestly (cf. Zerubbabel and Joshua, above; also *Jub.* 30.18). In 4QpPsᵃ (171) col. 3.13–16 the Priest, the Teacher of Righteousness, is chosen to 'stand' before God; and angels are sometimes described as 'standing before God' as an aspect of their priestly function (see on Rev. 8.2; also Job 1.6; Zech. 6.5). Standing before God, in the sense of being 'in attendance' on him, can also include (as in Rev. 11.4) the idea of serving him (cf. Jer. 15.19; Luke 1.19; et al.); and this is part of the Church's ministerial role in heaven and on earth (Rev. 7.15).

The masculine perfect participle ἑστῶτες (*hestōtes*, lit. 'stood') is harsh, after the feminine nouns 'olive trees' and 'lampstands' to which it refers. Grammatically, the participle looks back to the masculine dative noun μάρτυσιν (*martysin*, 'witnesses') in verse 3; and these are understood as 'men' (hence the masculine plural pronoun, οὗτοι [*houtoi*, 'these'] at the start of verse 4). The abruptness of the syntax is softened by the prepositional phrase, 'in attendance on the Lord of the earth', which separates the third feminine article αἱ (*hai*, 'the') from ἑστῶτες (*hestōtes*, 'in attendance'). So Aune 579. See the textual note on verse 4.

5–6   These two verses describe the prophetic ministry of the ecclesial witnesses, as they begin to unfold the judgemental and salvific contents of the 'small scroll' (cf. 10.2–4, 8–11; also the seven seals and six trumpet-calls of 6.1—9.19); although the manner of their prophecy, rather than its actual message, is primarily in view at this point. Concern for the protection of the prophets (verse 5) precedes reference to their activity (verse 6); so God keeps his people safe from physical harm until their testimony is complete (Mounce 218). The introduction to verse 5 is a conditional sentence, in which the protasis εἴ τις αὐτοὺς θέλει ἀδικῆσαι (*ei tis autous thelei adikēsai*, lit. 'if anyone wishes to harm them'), using the particle εἰ (*ei*, 'if') with the present indicative (θέλει, *thelei*, 'tries', lit. 'wishes'), followed in the apodosis on this occasion by indicatives in the present tense (ἐκπορεύεται . . . κατεσθίει, *ekporeuetai . . . katesthiei*, lit. 'comes out' . . . 'eats up'), suggests that the situation is real (BDF 371–72). But see below.

No tradition associates either Moses or Elijah (see on verse 3) directly with fire pouring from the mouth in order to destroy enemies. However, the situation evokes the encounters of Elijah with the messengers of King Ahaziah in 2 Kings 1.9–16, where fire 'came down from heaven' at the prophet's command, and consumed the emissaries (similarly Sir. 48.1). The idea of fire emanating from the mouth was also used in the Old Testament as a metaphor to describe speaking God's word to his people, usually as a rebuke for wrongdoing (Jer. 5.14; cf. 4 Ezra 13.10). God himself is personified in the Old Testament as breathing out devouring fire (2 Sam. 22.9, 13; cf. Leviathan in Job 41.18–21); and in Ps. 18.13 (MT) the voice of God is said to include 'coals of fire' (cf. Ps. 29.7; Rev. 9.17–18). The same ability to dispense judgemental fire is ascribed to angelic beings in *2 Enoch* 1.5; *3 Enoch* 18.25; 22.3–4; see also the offer of the Sons of Thunder to call down fire from heaven on the Samaritans who rejected Jesus (Luke 9.54).

The image of fire as a means and symbol of refining judgement is common in biblical theology (cf. Gen. 19.24–25; Exod. 24.17; Deut. 4.9–14; Josh. 7.15; Isa. 64.1–2; Amos 7.4; Zech. 3.2–5; Mal. 3.2; Matt. 3.11; 1 Cor. 3.12–15; et al.). Beale (580–81) claims that the language of fire and destruction in Rev. 11.5 must be understood figuratively (cf. 1.16; 4 Ezra 13.25–39); in his view, it is best seen as 'the legal pronouncement of the ensuing judgment of the enemies' (Beale 580; also Milligan 178–82; Kiddle 197); similarly Hughes (124), who notes that the word of the witnesses is given to them by the Lord, and that his message either destroys or saves (see John 12.47–48). Alternatively Hendriksen (129–30), followed by Mounce (218–19), interprets the situation in Rev. 11.5–6 literally, in line with the drought and plagues mentioned in verse 6. 'Fire-breathing prophets would not seem strange in the bizarre world of apocalyptic imagery' (Mounce 219). Nevertheless, while the predominant significance of this passage is undoubtedly spiritual, since this is part of the seer's eschatological vision, its literal meaning need not be excluded. The Church of Christ will be protected by God until its mission has been completed, and its testimony delivered (11.1–4); but if its witness is rejected, it has divine authority to deliver God's judgement (if need be, John appears to be saying, in physical terms) on the unfaithful world (11.11; 18.2–24).

The two witnesses possess punitive powers, although it is not stated in this section that they used them (but note that they 'tormented the people of the world', verse 10). The second part of verse 5 forms a parallel to the previous clause. The protasis of the condition in verse 5*b* uses εἰ (*ei*, 'if') with the subjunctive (θελήσῃ, *thelēsē[i]*, lit. 'should wish'). Normally in Revelation such a conditional sentence, which allows for the possibility that the intention can be realized, uses the conjunction ἐάν (*ean*, 'if'); so 2.5; 3.3; 22.18–19; et al. The apodosis here is introduced by the adverb οὕτως (*houtōs*, 'in this way', lit. 'so'); and this clause repeats and intensifies the terrifying nature of the judgement (death by incineration) which the witnesses are capable of inflicting on the enemies of God and his gospel.

Verse 6, like verse 5, consists of two parallel clauses. The two witnesses, representing the community of faith (see on verse 3), have the 'authority' and 'power' (τὴν ἐξουσίαν, *tēn exousian [bis]*) to cause a drought as did Elijah and to plague the earth as did Moses (for the interpretation of these miracles, as both figurative and literal, see on verse 5). The powers of the witnesses are in each case punitive.

For the figures of Moses and Elijah, as a model for the two witnesses, see further Beale 582–85. According to 1 Kings 17.1; 18.1, and as a sign to King Ahab, Elijah stopped the rain for three years. See Luke 4.25; Jas. 5.17, where the length of the drought brought about by the prophet is extended to three years and six months, which coincides with the Jewish symbol for a time of calamity (Dan. 4.32; 7.25; et al.; and see on Rev. 11.2–3; [12.6]). For the idea of shutting up the heaven, as the storehouse of the waters, so that it will not rain see 1 Kings 8.35 = 2 Chron. 6.26; cf. also 1Q22 (1QDM) 2.10, where Moses (this time) enjoins the Israelites, 'Be very careful for your lives, . . . lest the wrath of your God be enkindled and break out against you, and he closes the skies above, which make rain fall upon you'. The precise image of 'locking up the heavens' appears in the Elijah tradition only at Sir. 48.3; Luke 4.25; Rev. 11.6; and the texts in Luke and the Apocalypse share the verb κλείειν (*kleiein*, 'to lock up' or 'shut up'). The desperate importance of rain for the people of Palestine meant that the possibility of drought was a constant threat, and therefore an equally effective incentive to remain faithful. Cf Aune 615.

The two witnesses also have power over the waters, 'to turn them into blood'. This is an allusion to the first plague of the Exodus, during which Moses turned the waters of the River Nile into blood (see Exod. 7.14–21). The Church, in the course of delivering its message of saving judgement, also has the authority to 'afflict the land with every kind of plague' whenever it wishes (cf. 11.3–4). The background to this statement can be found in 1 Sam. 4.8, where the Philistines hear that the ark of the covenant has come into the camp of the Israelites, and say, 'These are the gods who struck the Egyptians with every kind of plague in the wilderness'. The LXX version of that text, οἱ πατάξαντες τὴν Αἴγυπτον ἐν πάσῃ πληγῇ (*hoi pataxantes tēn Aigypton en pasē[i] plēgē[i]*, lit. 'who struck Egypt with every plague'), is very close to the Greek of Rev. 11.6*b*. But, more generally, the reference in verse 6 is to disasters of all kinds suffered by humanity, such as those inflicted on Egypt by Moses at the time of the Exodus (Exod. 7.14—12.39).

Beale (583) suggests that Peter and Paul, together with Elijah and Moses, belong to the prophetic model in Rev. 11.6, since they represented respectively the Church's witness to Jews and to Gentiles (Gal. 2.7–9), and were both martyred in Rome for their witness to Christ (Barker, *The Revelation* 194, puts forward the possibility that John the Baptist and James, Aaronic and Davidic messianic leaders, were the two witnesses). But the links between these New Testament characters and the material in Rev. 11.(5–)6 are tenuous; and the background figures of Elijah and Moses seem to have natural prominence in this passage. Beale (583–84) also argues that the plagues in verse 6, like the imagery in verse 5, must be interpreted in a purely figurative manner; but see the comments on verse 5. The Exodus-like motifs of fire and plague in verses 5–6 have parallels in the sequences of seven trumpets and bowls (cf. Rev. 8.6–11.19; 15.1—16.21); see the tables in Aune 500–501.

The point of the seer's vision in 11.5–6 is to demonstrate that the Church's witness to God's word of judgement, so long as it remains faithful, will be inviolable; and that, in their mission and ministry to an unbelieving and unrighteous world, the servants of the Lord possess gifts and resources which are just as great as those which were available to Moses and Elijah (cf. Mounce 219).

7 The καί (*kai*, lit. 'and') which introduces this sentence is adversative (hence the translation, 'but'). The two witnesses are protected during a symbolic and restricted period of time, during which evil is judged (see on verses 2 and 3). *However*, at the end of that interval, faithful prophecy may be followed by martyrdom ('when they have completed their testimony', the beast will kill them; the verb τελέσωσιν, *telesōsin*, 'have completed', indicates fulfilment rather than just the passage of time). The ultimate measure of a disciple's faithfulness to God is faithfulness unto death (Wall 146). For a verbal parallel to this phrase see Rev. 20.7. Note also the close association between 'witness' (μαρτυρία, *martyria*) here and 'prophecy' in verses 3 and 6.

The image of the 'beast' appears at this point for the first time in Revelation (but see 6.8). The figure is introduced almost casually (Ladd 155), and plays no further part in this scene. The beast represents major opposition to God, the Lamb and the Church at the end-time; and he is θηρίον (*thērion*, a 'wild beast'), rather than ζῷον (*zō[i]on*, a 'living being'), as in Rev. 4.6–9; et al. The demonic derivation and character of the beast are emphasized when the seer describes him as 'ascending from the bottomless pit', which is the haunt of demons (cf. Luke 8.31; Mounce 219). On the 'bottomless pit' (abyss) see 9.1. The adjectival phrase 'ascending from the bottomless pit' is descriptive of the beast's origin; it does not mean that he appeared during the ministry of the two witnesses (cf. 12.9; et al.; Aune 616).

The use of the definite article with the noun (τὸ θηρίον, *to thērion*, 'the beast') suggests that the symbol is familiar to John's audience. The actual identity of the beast is not important to the action of the drama at this moment; although there appear to be strong links between the figure in this passage and both the beast ascending from the sea in Rev. 13.1–10 and the beast of Rev. 17 (note verse 8, where it is described as 'about to ascend from the abyss'). However, in Rev. 13 and 17 (q.v.) the noun θηρίον (*thērion*, 'beast') is used anarthrously, suggesting that the image is *not* well known to John's readers. The probable background in each case is to be found in Dan. 7. There, in Daniel's vision, four beasts came up from the sea (verse 3), and the fourth 'made war with the holy ones and was prevailing over them' (verse 21; see verses 7–22). As the little horn of Dan. 7 (cf. verse 8) attacked the saints, so it must be expected that the beast from the bottomless pit will conquer and kill God's faithful witnesses (cf. Rev. 20.7–10; see Roloff 133; Mounce 220). Beckwith (601; see 393–411) argues correctly that the beast of Dan. 7.7–22 had by now become a familiar representation of Antichrist (cf. Matt. 24.15), which is introduced at Rev. 11.7 incidentally, and described more fully in Chapters 13 and 17.

The language of 'making war' (ποιήσει πόλεμον, *poiēsei polemon*, lit. 'he will make war') against the witnesses suits the interpretation, offered here (see on verse 3), of the 'two witnesses' as a corporate reference to the Church of Christ (cf. the satanic figures making war in 12.17 and 13.7; similarly *T. Job* 4.4; et al.). Too much should not be made of the military metaphor in this context. The significance here is 'conquest by whatever means' (Ladd 157); and this anticipates the spiritual conflict of 12.7–9. The scene is that of 'the last epic struggle', whenever that takes place, between the kingdoms of this earth and the witnessing Christian community (Mounce 220; cf. Swete 137). The three future indicative verbs in the second half of verse 7 (ποιήσει, *poiēsei*, lit. 'he will make' [war]; νικήσει, *nikēsei*, lit. 'he will conquer'; ἀποκτενεῖ, *apoktenei*, lit. 'he will kill') are prophetic. The last two, used with καί (*kai*, 'and'), should be construed with a consecutive meaning ('in order to conquer and kill'); hence the translation.

As Aune (617) notes, like all the battle descriptions in the Apocalypse (cf. 12.7–8; 17.14; 19.19–20; 20.9), the narrative in 11.7 is terse and unspecific. We are not told how the witnesses died, nor how they reacted at the time of their martyrdom (cf. 6.9, 11); but in view of their bold testimony (11.3–6), they presumably faced death fearlessly. On not fearing the terrors of death see Seneca, *Epist. Mor.* 4.3–9; for Christian witness leading to death and then resurrection, preserved in a tradition clearly influenced by Rev. 11.7–11, see *Acts Pil.* 9 (25).

8 The dead bodies of the witnessing martyrs lie unburied. To be deprived of burial was totally undignified in the biblical world (cf. 1 Sam. 17.44; Ps. 79.1–4; Isa. 14.19–20; Jer. 8.1–2; Tobit 2.3–8; *Pss. Sol.* 2.27; *Sib. Or.* 3.643–46; *Jub.* 23.23; et al.). In this context, we are not to understand that the entire Church of God has been eliminated, but that (in an expression which is hyperbolic) the true Church – faced by fierce opposition to its witness to Jesus, and prepared for martyrdom – may seem insignificant, and will be treated with indignity (cf. Beale 590). At all periods of persecution and difficulty, a faithful remnant in Christ continues to endure patiently (verses 11–13; cf. Rev. 1.9; 17.8; 20.7–15). See Hendriksen 130–31.

The bodies of the martyrs are to be found in 'the square of the great city'. The noun ἡ πλατεῖα (*hē plateia*) can mean either 'wide road' or 'public square'; and in the present context it seems to signify the latter (Aune 580). Since the word appears here for the first time in Revelation (otherwise only at 21.21; and 22.2), and with the article, it must refer to a geographical area which was familiar to John's audience; for suggestions see Aune 618–19. Much then depends on the identity of the 'great city'. Some commentators assume that John means Jerusalem; and this proposal largely depends on the assumption that Jerusalem itself is the setting for Rev. 11.1–2, 13, and on the allusion to the site of the crucifixion of Jesus later in the present verse (8). So e.g. Charles 1, 287–88; Aune 619; for Milligan 184–85 and Swete 137–38 the Jerusalem in question is the apostate city, representative of a degenerate Church and an oppressive world.

It is certainly true that Jerusalem is elsewhere designated as a 'great city', albeit mostly in non-biblical sources (cf. Jer. 22.8; *Sib. Or.* 5.154, 226, 413; *Apoc. Elijah* 4.13; et al.). However, on the seven other occasions in the Apocalypse when the metaphorical expression 'the great city' is used (16.19; 17.18; 18.10, 16, 18, 19, 21; see also 18.24), it clearly refers to the authority of Rome, under the figure of Babylon. In 11.8, therefore, it seems best to understand the writer as saying that the faithful witnesses met their death at the hands of the Antichrist, whose universal dominion in John's day was epitomized by the power of Rome, lying at the heart of the ungodly world. Note also the description of Babylon as 'great' in Rev. 14.8; 16.19; 17.5; 18.2. In line with this exegesis Caird, *Apostolic Age* 179–80, points out that Rome, denoting the pagan world order, is depicted in Revelation by three symbols of developing intensity: Sodom and Egypt (11.8); the beast (13.1); and the great harlot (Chapters 17—18). See also Beale 591, who draws attention to the tendency of Old Testament prophets (cf. Dan. 1—6) to speak of Babylon as the region where God's people lived in exile, oppressed by ungodly regimes, and where they were tempted to compromise their faith.

The city is 'prophetically' called 'Sodom and Egypt'. The Greek word translated 'prophetically' is πνευματικῶς (*pneumatikōs*), the root meaning of which is 'spiritually'. This indicates that the 'city' in question is not to be understood in literal terms (see above); rather, the idea should be interpreted figuratively, and through prophetic and spiritual eyes (cf. 1 Cor. 2.14, using the same term; so Beale 592). The metaphor stands for any and every realm on earth, such as Rome, which is held in the grip of the powers of evil, and therefore becomes ready to deny freedom to the faithful. (Mounce [220–21] notes that *Jerusalem* itself is never directly designated in the Old Testament as either Sodom or

Egypt.) That kingdom of unrighteousness is like the infamous Babylon, and therefore subject to divine discrimination. But it is also to be compared to Sodom, the wickedness of which deserves God's judgement (Gen. 19.1–25; Deut. 29.22–28; Isa. 1.9–16; 3.9; Jer. 23.14–15; *Asc. Isa.* 3.10 [Isaiah has called Jerusalem Sodom!]; et al.); and it is like Egypt, the leaders of which enslave and persecute the saints (cf. Exod. 5.1–21; Joel 3.19). For Sodom and Egypt together, as places of persecution and enticement, see Wis. 19.14–17; Ezek. 16.26, 44–58. In Amos 4.10–11 the prophet describes Israel's punishment for unfaithfulness, adding that this is merited because of the nation's likeness to Egypt and Sodom. Inasfar as the world without God shares the same character, John seems to be saying in Rev. 11.8, it is subject to the same fate (cf. further Sweet 187; Hughes 127).

The concluding phrase in verse 8, 'where also their Lord was crucified', should not be taken with the earlier expression, the 'great city', thereby supporting the identification of that area as the geographical Jerusalem; so Moffatt 417–18; Aune 620, both of whom cite Luke 13.33 (Jerusalem as the traditional place for the death of prophets, including Jesus himself). It is more naturally linked with the immediately preceding clause, and should therefore be understood as part of the general description of the 'city', which John has referred to precisely as 'prophetically' figurative (see Caird 137–38). This exegesis is supported by the use of ὅπου (*hopou*, 'where') at the start of the sentence, since that adverb is always used elsewhere in Revelation to introduce symbolic, spiritual realms, either divine (12.6, 14; 14.4) or satanic (2.13; 20.10; cf. 17.3, 9). The reference to the crucifixion of Jesus here illustrates the response of ungodliness to righteousness; the 'great city' of the world is spiritually in tune with Jerusalem, whose ultimate degradation was marked by its responsibility for the death of Christ.

The title κύριος (*kyrios*, 'Lord') is used of Jesus in this verse for the first time in the Apocalypse; and it appears in an absolute form. In other contexts of Revelation the term occurs with a predicate; see Rev. 17.14; 19.16 ('Lord of lords'); and 22.20, 21 ('Lord Jesus'). The seer is surprisingly restrained in his application of the title 'Lord' to Jesus, given the frequency with which it belongs to christological contexts elsewhere in the New Testament. Beale (593) suggests that the plural in the expression ὁ κύριος αὐτῶν (*ho kyrios autōn*, '*their* Lord') refers not just to the members of the witnessing Church, but also to the unbelievers in the world around it; for Jesus is Lord of both communities (cf. Rev. 1.5; 17.14; 19.16).

9–10 For 'three and a half days' the martyred witnesses are viewed in the square. This period of time, repeated in verse 11, corresponds to the temporal references in verses 2–3 (q.v.); see also 13.5. The formula is derived from Dan. 7.25; 12.7; it normally symbolizes a divinely restricted duration, which can involve eschatological tribulation. In the present context it recalls the length of the ministry of Jesus (three and a half years) and of his burial in the tomb (three days). The time during which the witnesses are exposed to shame, three and a half days, ironically evokes the period of their invincibility: three and a half years (verse 3). The victory of antichristian forces is brief and insignificant, when set against the victorious and lasting testimony of the Church of Christ (Michaels 141; Beale 595). In any case, believers will rise again (verses 11–12), and the unrighteous may be converted (verse 13).

Those who gaze at the dead bodies are 'some of the peoples and races, and language groups and nations'. The plural form, βλέπουσιν (*blepousin*, 'gaze', lit. 'they see'), continues the plural antecedent ('their Lord') in the final phrase of the previous verse. Those who stare are members of the unbelieving world, walking the streets of the 'great city', Rome-Babylon or its equivalent (see on verse 8, and cf. the repeated phrase 'the earth's inhabitants' in verse 10). The partitive genitive, ἐκ τῶν λαῶν (*ek tōn laōn*), translated as '*some* of the peoples', should not be pressed (as it is by Aune 621) to mean some but not all people in the world; it probably refers generally to those who represent the whole world of unbelief and wrongdoing (as in 10.11; and 11.10). Note the partitive genitive used collectively as the subject of a sentence in John 16.17. The fourfold formula, 'peoples, races, language groups, nations', is used positively of all the redeemed in Rev. 5.9; 7.9 (cf. Dan. 3.4; et al.), but negatively and universally of the world which rejects God, and therefore deserves his judgement, at 10.11 and subsequently in the Apocalypse (11.9; 13.7; 14.6; 17.15). See further on 10.11.

For the indignity in the Near Eastern world of the 'refusal to allow burial' see on verse 8. The Greek, οὐκ ἀφίουσιν τεθῆναι εἰς μνῆμα (*ouk aphiousin tethēnai eis mnēma*), means lit. 'they do not permit [the dead bodies] to be laid in a tomb'. For the thought in this passage see Ps. 79.2–4. The Greek word for 'dead bodies', τὰ πτώματα (*ta ptōmata*), appears at the end of verse 9 in the plural; whereas in verses 8*a* and 9*a* the same term, 'dead body' (τὸ πτῶμα, *to ptōma*), is used in the singular. The singular form is probably collective (cf. 11.5; also Acts 18.6). The plural then denotes the extent of the witness which is being offered, even to death. Christians belong to one body, but there are many of them (cf. Beale 594; against Swete 138–39, who claims that 'separate treatment' would be needed for the burial of the bodies).

Verse 10 begins and ends with an allusion to the 'earth's inhabitants' ('people of the world') who rejoice over the plight of the martyrs. For this expression see on 3.10. It is a technical term, used throughout the Apocalypse (12 times in all, sometimes with variations in the phraseology) to describe unbelievers who are subject to divine judgement because they persecute God's people (cf. esp. 6.10). The phrase sometimes occurs in the Old Testament with reference to those living in Palestine who are liable to God's imminent judgement (cf. Jer. 6.12; Hos. 4.1; Joel 1.2, 14). Here it draws attention to the universality of the opposition to God (*all* 'earth-dwellers'), symbolized both by the 'great city' (verse 8) and by the representatives of the total world of evil (verse 9, where the 'peoples, races, language groups and nations' form a parallel to the 'earth's inhabitants' in verse 10); cf. Isa. 24.6; 26.21. Beale (595–96) correctly notes that the description 'inhabitants of the earth' appears in Rev. 13—17 exclusively in association with idolatry (13.8; et al.). Thus, the unbelieving persecutors in this passage are also 'people of the world' because they are idolaters, who trust in some aspect of the world and not in God (see 6.17).

The oppressive and pagan inhabitants of the world 'rejoice' over the dead witnesses, and 'celebrate by exchanging gifts'. The earth's inhabitants expressed joy (χαίρουσιν, *chairousin*, 'they are glad') because, as it seemed, the prophetic message of salvation through a crucified and risen Lord (verses 8–9), and God's judgement on oppression and idolatry (10.11; 11.3–7), had been finally silenced. That judgement includes the destruction of the earth in which the unrighteous trust (6.12–17; 21.1; Beale 596); for while the saints are protected for eternity (7.1–17; 11.1–2), unbelievers remain subject to divine discrimination (11.14).

The ideas of 'celebrating' (εὐφραίνονται, *euphrainontai*, 'they celebrate', ESV 'make merry') and 'exchanging gifts' are related. In the Graeco-Roman world gift-exchange, on occasions of joy such as betrothal and marriage, was an important part of public and private life (Homer, *Odyssey* 15.16–18; 20.341–44; cf. Homer, *Iliad* 6.119–236). Exchanging gifts at times of happiness was also a Jewish custom (cf. Esth. 9.22 [at the Feast of Purim]; Matt. 2.11; see also Luke 11.13 par.). As in the parable of the rich man (Luke 12.16–21), the merry-making of the gloaters is to be short lived (verses 11–13).

The term προφῆται (*prophētai*, 'prophets') is used for the first time in this scene, although the ministry of the 'two witnesses' has earlier been described as 'prophecy' (11.3, 6). For the corporate, ecclesial identity of the two prophetic witnesses see on verse 3. The 'torment' (ἐβασάνισαν, *ebasanisan*, lit. 'they tormented') associated with the prophecy arose not so much from its content, which is not specified, as from its judgemental effects. The same language is used in 9.5 (q.v.), of the exquisite pain caused by the sting of a scorpion; and in the present context there may be an allusion to the emotional anguish brought about by the testimony of the two prophets, and the unbearable trials inflicted as part of the series of woes (so Giblin, 'Revelation 11.1–13' 443–44).

11 God restores the believing and witnessing community to himself, after its apparent eschatological conquest by the powers of darkness. For the interval of time, 'after the three and a half days', see on verse 9; and for the anaphoric use of the article (τάς, *tas*, '*the* [three and a half days]') see the textual notes on verse 11. In the present context of exaltation, there may be an allusion to the resurrection of Jesus 'after three days' (Mark 8.31; Matt. 27.63; et al.). Behind the notion of 'a breath of life' (πνεῦμα ζωῆς, *pneuma zōēs*) from God entering the prophetic witnesses, so that they stood upright, lies the passage in Ezek. 37.1–14. There the prophet is commanded by the Lord to bring life into a multitude of dry bones, through a 'breath' entering into them (see esp. verses 5 [LXX has πνεῦμα ζωῆς, *pneuma zōēs*, 'breath of life'], 10), with the result that they 'stood up on their feet'. The phrase 'breath of life' often occurs in Genesis (cf. 1.30; 2.7; 6.17; et al.; see also Job 32.8; 4 Ezra 3.5); while 'standing on one's feet' is a phrase sometimes used to demonstrate that a formerly dead person is really alive (2 Kings 13.21; cf. Ezek. 3.24; Mark 5.40–42 par.; Luke 7.14–15).

Beale (597) suggests that, while the spiritual deliverance in 11.11–12 may be understood as a literal resurrection, the focus in this scene is rather on the vindication of the total community of believers in the face of their oppressors at the end-time; for not all Christian witnesses become martyrs as such. See 20.7–10; also Ezek. 37.10–13 (the dry bones revivified represent 'the whole house of Israel', verse 11).

The 'great terror' (φόβος μέγας, *phobos megas*, lit. 'great fear') which struck the unfaithful bystanders is reminiscent of the collective response of the Egyptians, at the time of the Exodus, to the apparent invincibility of the Israelites (Exod. 15.16; Deut. 11.25; cf. 1 Macc. 3.25). This is not the 'fear of the Lord' experienced by the saints (Rev. 14.7; 15.4; 19.5), but the terror felt by God's 'enemies' (11.12) at the reversal of their fortunes and the disclosure of his handiwork (cf. 18.10, 15). The verb θεωροῦν (*theōroun*, 'to see') appears only twice in the Apocalypse: here, and in verse 12; although it is used often in John's Gospel. The word for 'seeing' in Revelation is usually βλέπειν (*blepein*, 19 times), which occurs 16 times in the Fourth Gospel.

12 The theme of the deliverance of the witnesses is continued in this verse, which includes the record of their ascension to heaven. The scene is a recapitulation of 4.1–2 (q.v.), where the seer is taken up to the throne room of God and the Lamb; note the similar language in 4.1–2 and 11.12, especially in the form of the command, ἀνάβα (ἀνάβατε) ὧδε (*anaba [anabate] hōde*, 'come up [pl.] here!'). Both situations involve a rapture; but in neither context should this be understood literally. Rather, the prophet-seer is 'taken up' spiritually, so that more of a heavenly vision may be disclosed to him (cf. Ezekiel's experience, described in Ezek. 1—3 [see esp. 3.12–15]; also the non-literal 'rapture' language of Rev. 17.1–3; 21.9–10); and the same is true of the two witnesses here (against Aune 625–26). Theologically, there is a connection in the Apocalypse between John's first commissioning as a prophet (1.10–19), his second (4.1–2a) and third (10.1–11). The witnesses, representing the Church of Christ as a whole (see on 11.3), participate in the seer's prophetic task (11.3–7). This accounts for the parallels between the activity of John and the two witnesses in Rev. 10 and 11, as in the 'clouds' of 10.1 and 11.12; the designation of both John and the witnesses as 'prophets' (10.11; 11.3, 10, 18); and their joint and universal message of judgement (10.11; 11.5–10). Cf. Beale 598–99.

The resurrected witnesses, rather than the bystanders (the 'enemies'of verse 12*b*), 'heard a loud, heavenly voice' of command (against Charles 1, 290, who claims that the speaker is audible to everyone). This connects with the unidentified 'voice' of 10.4, which is doubtless in turn the divine voice of 9.13 (q.v.); and, given the associations between 11.12 and 4.1–2 noted above, it could be that the 'loud voice' from heaven in the present verse shares in the character of the 'trumpet-like voice' of 4.1, and therefore begins the sounding of the seventh trumpet mentioned at 11.15 (cf. Beale 599). For 'hearing' in Johannine thought, often associated with sight and understanding, see on 4.1; et al.; also 8.13.

The witnesses 'ascended to (εἰς, *eis*, lit. 'into') heaven in a cloud'; and this points to their vindication, on the basis of faithful Christian testimony and behaviour. The presence of the article with the noun 'cloud' (ἐν τῇ νεφέλῃ, *en tē[i] nephelē[i]*, lit. 'in *the* cloud') suggests that this allusion would be familiar to John's audience; and there is certainly a tradition in Judaism that divine approval was given to loyal witnesses by 'assumption' to heaven in a cloud. Such was true of Enoch (Gen. 5.24), Moses (*Assum. Moses* 10.12; Josephus, *Ant.* 4.320–26; cf. Deut. 34.5–6), Elijah (2 Kings 2.11, where the 'whirlwind' is theophanic; cf. Ezek. 1.4), Ezra (4 Ezra 14.7–9,[50]) and Baruch (*2 Apoc. Bar.* 76.1–5). However, as Aune (625–26) points out, all these figures were taken up into heaven to await the end, at which time it was predicted that they would return. The same directly eschatological dimension does not belong to Rev. 11.12. Nevertheless, there is in the New Testament a 'cloud' tradition, associated with Jesus, which denotes the authentication and approval given to his ministry by the Father. See Mark 13.26; 14.62; Acts 1.9–11; cf. Rev. 14.14–16; *Gospel of Peter* 35–36). It is possible that in Rev. 11.12 the anaphoric article introducing 'cloud' picks up this tradition, as well as referring back to the 'cloud' in 10.1 (cf. Beale 600).

Clouds in Jewish and Christian tradition are often represented as a means of transport between heaven and earth, or between one part of heaven and another; and this applies to divine and angelic beings, as well as to mortals (cf. Deut. 33.26; Ps. 68.4; Acts 1.9; Rev. 1.7; Exod. 14.24; Rev. 10.1; 2 Kings 2.11; *1 Enoch* 39.3; et al.). See Aune 625. The ascension of the witnesses by cloud, in the present context (Rev. 11.12), takes place 'in full view of their enemies'. Ascent narratives sometimes include the fact that bystanders look on, and see what is happening (Judg. 13.20; 2 Kings 2.11–12; Acts 1.9–11; *Jub.* 32.20–21; *2 Enoch* 67.1–3; *T. Job* 52.8–10). In these instances, however, the viewers are friendly; whereas in Rev. 11.12 they are representatives of a hostile and oppressive world, which has rejected the message of the believing and suffering Church. The ascent to heaven of the two witnesses, therefore, becomes not only a divine demonstration of their authority and authenticity but also a judgement on the world's mistaken view of truth and righteousness as these have been revealed in God through Christ.

13   The ascension of the witnesses (verse 12) coincides exactly with the moment when 'a violent earthquake' occurs; this levels part of 'the city', and causes those who do not die to offer homage to the Lord of heaven (note the earthquake which takes place at the time of the resurrection of Jesus, Matt. 27.51). The term ἡ ὥρα (*hē hōra*, 'the moment', lit. 'hour', in the sense of 'point of time' [BDAG 1103*a*]) does not appear frequently in Revelation (only at 3.3, 10; 9.15; 11.13; 14.7, 15; 17.12; 18.10, 17, 19). But in each of these contexts, including the present one, the situation being described is eschatological, and indeed judgemental (cf. Dan. 3.15; 5.5; Matt. 8.13; John 4.53). Earthquakes in Revelation are usually theophanic (as in 6.12; 8.5; 11.19); but at 11.13 (and 16.18) they become specifically an instrument of divine punishment.

The expression 'violent earthquake' (σεισμὸς μέγας, *seismos megas*, lit. 'great shaking') derives from Ezek. 38.19 LXX, where the phenomenon of 'great shaking' describes God's judgement on Gog for trying to destroy the land of Israel (cf. Hag. 2.6–7; Zech. 14.4).

See also Rev. 6.12; 11.19; 16.18. But even if all these contexts speak of final judgement, in the sense of divine discrimination against human rebellion, there is no necessary allusion here to the *last* judgement (against Beale 602; cf. Hughes 130). John, in this passage and elsewhere in the Apocalypse, depicts the last times from different points of view (Beasley-Murray 138); and while the portents he catalogues are eschatological, and share in the character of the end-time ('final judgement'), they do not refer simply to events which are due to take place at the end of history. The present and the future, the temporal and the eternal, are fused in Johannine theology, so that the end is always pressing in. See further on 6.12–14.

As a result of the earthquake, which is mentioned twice in verse 13, a tenth of the city collapsed (ἔπεσεν, *epesen*, lit. 'fell'), and seven thousand people (ὀνόματα ἀνθρώπων, *onomata anthrōpōn*, lit. 'names of men') were killed. This could be to some extent a response to the cry of the martyrs at Rev. 6.9–11 (cf. Beale 595). 'The city' is the 'great' complex mentioned in verse 8 (q.v.), where it symbolizes Rome (= Babylon) as the world of unbelief and oppression. The destruction signalled at this point is partial, because John's vision includes just one aspect of God's ongoing and saving, eschatological judgement. In Jewish thought the figure of one 'tenth' is sometimes used with reference to those who *survive* divine judgement (Isa. 6.13; Amos 5.3; cf. *Jub.* 10.9); and the situation described here would then be a reversal of that conception (Aune 627). If Jerusalem were in mind in this verse (so Aune 627), 'a tenth of the city' could be regarded as roughly 'seven thousand', since the population of Jerusalem in the first century AD was about 70,000; although Josephus (*Cont. Ap.* 1.197), on the authority of Hecataeus, put the figure at 120,000 (cf. Swete 140–41; Sweet 189). Even so, the city of 'Jerusalem' in this context must figuratively represent the whole world (see above). In 1 Kings 19.18 'seven thousand' is the number of Israelites who do not worship Baal; and these are described by Paul in Rom. 11.4–5 as a 'remnant'. Clearly this is the role of the 'survivors' (rather than the victims) of the earthquake (see the last part of verse 13).

The double reaction of the 'survivors' (οἱ λοιποί, *hoi loipoi*, lit. 'the rest, those who were left') is highly significant. They were terrified (the term ἔμφοβοι, *emphoboi*, 'filled with terror', only here in the Apocalypse, is intensive; cf. also verse 11*b*), and they were amazed (ἔδωκαν δόξαν τῷ θεῷ, *edōkan doxan tō[i] theō[i]*, lit. 'they gave glory to God'). These responses regularly follow miracle narratives in the Gospels (see Mark 4.41; Matt. 17.6; Mark 1.27; Luke 2.9); and occasionally, as here, they are combined (Mark 2.12; 16.8). The phrase, 'to glorify God', is frequently used as an acclamation in Luke-Acts, and means just that (cf. Luke 17.18; Acts 4.21; et al.); it can also be a periphrasis for 'telling the truth' (John 9.24). But in Rev. 11.13 the activity of offering homage to the God of heaven signifies a widespread process of conversion; even if this is the only example in the Apocalypse of a spiritual change of heart and mind as the result of a punitive miracle. For 'fearing God and giving him glory', as an idiom for conversion in the face of judgement, see Rev. 14.6–7. At 16.9, after the fourth bowl of God's wrath has been poured out, the unfaithful 'did not repent and glorify God'; and this implies that conversion (offering homage to God) was a possibility, although it was rejected. See further 6.12–17; also other texts in which 'giving glory to God' is a synonym for turning to God in repentance and with faith (Dan. 4.34 LXX, where the conversion of Nebuchadrezzar is signified by the angelic command to 'give glory to the Most High'; 1 Esdras 9.8; Acts 13.48; Hermas, *Sim.* 6.3.6; et al.). See further Aune 628–29. For arguments against the positive interpretation of verse 13 see Beale 603–604; cf. also Kiddle 206; Mounce 224.

Here can be found the centre of the message of Revelation, and the heart of the contents of the (little) scroll (10.2). When the Church is faithful, even to suffering and death, in its task of proclaiming the truth of God's thunder and love, as these have been disclosed in Jesus the Christ, the sovereign rule of God can be brought inclusively to the nations as salvation, rather than judgement. This teaching will be developed later, in Rev. 12—15. See Bauckham 1296a; also Bauckham, *Climax of Prophecy* 273–83. Beale (605) notes that the demise, disgrace and vindication of the witnesses follows the pattern of the final stages of the ministry of Jesus himself (cf. Matt. 28.1–4 and Rev. 11.12–13); and we have already discovered parallels between the activity of Christ and his Church in 11.7–11.

The concluding words of 11.13, '(the survivors offered homage) to the God of heaven' (τῷ θεῷ τοῦ οὐρανοῦ, *tō[i] theō[i] tou ouranou*), reflect the Old Testament use of this phrase to denote (as here) God's sovereignty over the affairs of the earthly world (see Gen. 24.7; 2 Chron 36.23; Ezra 1.2; Neh. 1.4–5; Ps. 136.26; Dan. 2.18–19; 4.37 LXX; Jonah 1.9). For a striking parallel to Rev. 11.11–13 see 4 Ezra 6.23–27.

14 This verse is pivotal and transitional. It may be taken both as the conclusion to the section Rev. 11.3–13, and as the introduction to verses 15–19 and, more particularly, to what follows (see the literary analysis above, 255). The announcement that two woes have already taken place, and that a third disaster will quickly occur, looks back to 9.12 and 8.13 (q.v.). At 9.12 it is recorded (possibly by an editor, as in the present context) that the first woe, following the fifth trumpet, has passed, and that two more are yet to come. The second is described in 9.13–19. It is important now to determine the content of the third 'woe' (οὐαί, *ouai*), and at what point it follows the sounding of the seventh and final trumpet (verse 15).

Some commentators (e.g. Charles 1, 292–93) regard the third woe as the 'divine drama' which is unfolded in the second part of the Apocalypse as a whole (12.1—22.17); and the heavenly songs of 11.15–18 then form an introduction to the 'great themes' of those chapters (Charles 1, 292; cf. Sweet 191–93). Others see Rev. 12—14 as a description of the events leading up to the pouring out of the seven bowls of wrath in Chapter 16, which then detail the content of the seventh trumpet and the third woe mentioned at 11.14–15; so Beckwith (606–608, esp. 608, 669–71). Alternative views take 12.13—13.18 by itself, following the reference to 'woe' in 12.12, as the substance of the third disaster (Sweet 190); or understand this to be merely the resistance of the dragon represented at 12.13–18 (Allo 101). Beale (609–10) claims that the liturgical passage 11.15–19 is the seventh trumpet, and therefore the third woe. See further Vanni, *La struttura letteraria* 131–33.

John's vision, at this stage, is allusively presented; and all the perceptions mentioned here accordingly contain elements of truth. The apocalypse of salvation history is constantly being unfolded, without attention to chronology; and the 'mystery' of God (10.7, q.v.) is always on the point of fulfilment, right up to and beyond the end. As a result, it is sometimes difficult, as here, to relate the seer's imagery to its exact point of explanation; and this is all the more problematic when it appears that the result of the seventh trumpet-blast should be, as in the case of the previous two trumpet-woes, the action which follows immediately. Nevertheless, it seems appropriate in this case to interpret the contents of the third 'disaster', heralded by the seventh trumpet-sound, as the material in Rev. 12.1—15.8 (which, in our dramatic scheme, makes up Scene 4 and its subsequent interval). The following considerations are offered in support of this conclusion.

(a) The closing verse of the section (15.8) looks back to 11.19, and uses similar language (so also Knight 89).
(b) When the angel blows the seventh trumpet (11.15), a final calamity is expected (cf. 8.13). Instead of this, a chorus is heard; and the positive hymns of judgement and victory which are sung in heaven set in relief the account of calamities to follow on earth (12—15), together with the underlying theme in that section of redemption through conflict (cf. a similar interval after the breaking of the seventh seal in 8.1).

(c) It could be argued that 10.7 (q.v.) presupposes such an interval. There the strong angel prophesies that the 'hidden purpose of God' will be fulfilled 'when the moment arrives' (ἐν ταῖς ἡμέραις, en tais hēmerais, lit. 'in the days') for the seventh angel to sound his trumpet. The phrase 'in the days' may refer not to the actual moment of sounding the final trumpet, but to the *period introduced* by the seventh trumpet-woe, namely, the trumpet-visions of Rev. 12—15, which belong to a series of judgements presaging the consummation. Cf. Beckwith 606.

(d) The appearance of the adverb ταχύ (*tachy*, 'soon', 'quickly') in 11.14 does not imply that the third woe is to follow at once, in the action of 11.15–19 (against Beale 610). This word is used six times in the Apocalypse (2.16; 3.11; 11.14; 22.7, 12, 20), but never in the sense of 'immediately' (Beckwith 608). In any case, eternal truths cannot be measured by temporal means.

(e) The bowls of judgement in Rev. 16, on this showing, then recapitulate the ongoing process of divine judgement on inadequate belief and wrong behaviour, and prepare the way for the discrimination of Chapters 17—18, and the salvation through judgement which flows from that situation. Cf. further Beasley-Murray 187–88.

Trumpet 7 (Third Woe): Redemption through Conflict (11.15–19)

15 For the sounding of the trumpet by the seventh angel see on verse 14; cf. also 8.2, 6. Sevens are important for John (see on 1.11). For the formula 'the angel sounded his trumpet', see 8.7, 8, 10, 12; 9.1, 13 (at 8.7 the term ἄγγελος, *angelos*, 'angel', is missing). Before the events take place which the final trumpet-woe introduces, recorded in chapters 12—15 (see above), a heavenly chorus is raised. Instead of the silence in heaven which follows the breaking of the seventh seal (8.1), the seventh trumpet-blast precipitates the sound of 'loud', supernatural voices (ἐγένοντο φωναὶ μεγάλαι, *egenonto phōnai megalai*, lit. 'great voices occurred'). It is unusual in Revelation for the verb γίνομαι (*ginomai*, 'come into being') to appear in contexts of audition or sight; and only here is the plural expression 'loud voices' used in the Apocalypse (contrast the 'loud voice' at verse 12).

The resounding, heavenly voices could be generally 'angelic', or those of the heavenly multitude of saints, as in 7.9–10; 19.1, 6 (Beale 611). Equally, they may belong to the living creatures of the throne-vision in Rev. 4—5 (see 4.8–9; 5.8–10, 14; so Swete 141; Charles 1, 293–94; Beasley-Murray 188; Roloff 137; Prigent 361); while in verse 16 they are distinguished from the voices of the elders (cf. Rev. 4.4). But it is simpler, and probably more accurate, to understand the unidentified voices in verse 15 as no more, and no less, than 'heavenly' (cf. Beckwith 608; Aune 638). The hymnody here, and in verses 16–18, is heard '*in* heaven' (ἐν τῷ οὐρανῷ, *en tō[i] ouranō[i]*). This phrase signifies the seer's heavenly perspective on the events being narrated (cf. 12.10; 19.1); whereas elsewhere (10.4, 8; 11.12; 14.2, 13; 18.4) the expression ἐκ τοῦ οὐρανοῦ (*ek tou ouranou*, '*from* heaven') suggests that the action is taking place on earth, rather than being witnessed in the vicinity of heaven (Aune 638). For the liturgical structure of the praise offered in this section see further above, 255.

The heavenly declaration at this point is a victory chorus, which discloses and summarizes the centre and meaning of John's apocalyptic drama (cf. Knight 89). The pervading theme, from Rev. 11.15 to 15.8, is that of redemption through conflict: the achievement of a new exodus and a new covenant (note 11.19). The first two woes (the fifth and sixth trumpets) also prompt announcements from heaven (see 8.13; 9.13–14). In this case we may have the celebration of an answer to the prayers of God's people (8.4), in the gift of his kingdom (Beasley-Murray 188). The extensive use of the aorist tense in 11.15–19 suggests 'absolute certainty about the events taking place' (Mounce 225), and above all the inevitability of God's sovereignty being established over and within his creation. It is this truth which provides John's audience with the encouragement needed by its members, in the face of external pressures and internal conflicts (cf. Fiorenza, *Book of Revelation* 55–56).

The angelic voices proclaim that rule in absolute terms: 'the kingdom of the world has become the sovereign realm of our Lord and his Messiah'. The final realization of God's universal kingship, through a series of cataclysmic eschatological events, is a regular theme in the teaching of the Old Testament prophets (cf. Dan. 2.44; see 2.31–45; Zech. 14.9. Note also the declaration of God's sovereignty at the time of the Exodus (Exod. 15.1–18, esp. verse 18, 'The Lord will reign for ever and ever'). In the present context, the verb ἐγένετο (*egeneto*, 'has become') is in the aorist; cf. the appearance of the same verb in the same tense to introduce the hymn at 12.10. The use of a past tense here, as in verses 17–18, suggests that God's total sovereignty has already been established (the Greek means lit. 'the kingdom of the world has become [the kingdom] of our Lord'). But the reference is proleptic, and the verb is a 'prophetic perfect' (Aune 638); the seer speaks with prophetic certainty of a future event as if it has even now taken place.

The term κόσμος (*kosmos*, 'world') occurs in Revelation only here, and at 13.8; 17.8. It appears frequently in the Gospel and Letters of John, where it can mean positively the created universe (John 3.16, 'God loved the world'; 1 John 4.17, 'in this world we are even as he is'), or negatively human society, temporarily controlled by the powers of evil, organized in opposition to God (John 16.11, 'the ruler of this world has been condemned'; 1 John 5.19, 'the whole world lies in the power of the evil one'). See Smalley, *1, 2, 3 John* 80–90, esp. 81. It is the latter significance which the word carries at Rev. 11.15. The world, in conflict with the purposes of God, must eventually submit to the demands of his sovereign kingdom. See John 12.31; 2 Cor. 4.4; Eph. 2.2; (6.12); *T. Sol.* 2.8–9; Ignatius, *Magn.* 1.2; *Trall.* 4.2; et al.

During his earthly ministry, Jesus resisted the temptation to surrender the 'kingdoms of the world' to the Satan in exchange for worship (Matt. 4.8–9; cf. John 14.30). Now, because he has successfully completed his messianic ministry, this sovereignty passes to him (Mounce 226); cf. Acts 2.36. For the expression 'our Lord (that is, the Church's God) and his Messiah' (τοῦ χριστοῦ αὐτοῦ, *tou christou autou*, lit. 'of his Christ'), see Ps. 2.2 (the kings of the earth, and the rulers, oppose 'the Lord and his anointed'), which was interpreted messianically by the primitive Church (cf. Acts 4.26–28; also, for the messianic language of 'the Lord's anointed', 1 Sam. 24.6; Luke 2.26; *1 Enoch* 48.10; *Odes Sol.* 29.6). Similar thought and phraseology occurs in the proclamation at Rev. 12.10 (q.v.).

The hymn in progress (verse 15), the first of two anthems of praise in 11.15–18, has the literary form of a distich, the second line of which ('who will reign for ever and ever') is introduced by a linking καί (*kai*, 'and', submerged in the translation). The verb βασιλεύειν (*basileuein*, 'to reign, rule') is used three times in the Apocalypse with God as the subject, on each occasion in liturgical contexts: here, and at 11.17 and 19.6. In 11.17; 19.6 the ruler is clearly God himself. In 11.15 the singular person of the word βασιλεύσει (*basileusei*, lit. 'he will reign') is ambiguous; for it seems at first to refer naturally to Jesus Christ, the 'Messiah', who has just been mentioned. But although, in the Christian scheme, the Son will eventually be subject to the Father (1 Cor. 15.28), nevertheless he shares in eternity the rule of God (Rev. 22.5, 'they will reign for ever and ever'; see also 1.17–18; 5.12–13). The singular verb underlines the unity of this joint sovereignty (Mounce 226). For the liturgical expression 'for ever and ever' see LXX Exod. 15.18; Ps. 144.13; Ezek. 43.7; Wis. 3.8; et al.; also Luke 1.33; Heb. 1.8.

16–18 The 'elders' now join in the victorious worship of heaven. For the 'twenty-four elders', who are angelic counterparts of God's people, see on 4.4. Normally seated (4.4), they here 'prostrate themselves' before God (cf. 4.10; 5.8, 14; 19.4); they last appeared in this posture at 7.11. In the court imagery of Judaism, God is always seated (1 Kings 22.19; Isa. 6.1; Dan. 7.9), while the officials *stand* before him (1 Kings 22.19; Isa. 6.2; Dan. 7.10). For the expression 'in God's presence' (ἐνώπιον τοῦ θεοῦ, *enōpion tou theou*, lit. 'before God'), see on 8.2. Verse 16 links together the two anthems of verses 15 and 17–18 (cf. 4.9–10; 7.11).

For the word λέγοντες (*legontes*, 'singing', lit. 'saying'), introducing the hymn of verses 17–18, and for music generally in the Apocalypse, see Smalley, *Thunder and Love* 115 n. 86; cf. also Rev. 7.12. The collective prayer in verses 17–18 begins with thanksgiving, and then moves on to a declaration of the basis for the gratitude of God's people, who are represented by the worshipping elders (verse 16). It is now claimed that God has assumed his 'full authority', and that he has entered already upon his reign. In verse 18 the eschatological acts of God, upon which his overt kingship is based, are specified.

The liturgical formula, εὐχαριστοῦμέν σοι (*eucharistoumen soi*, 'we thank you'), is found only here in Revelation, as is the verb εὐχαριστέω (*eucharisteō*, 'thank') itself; the noun εὐχαριστία (*eucharistia*, 'thanks[giving]') appears at 4.9; 7.12. For the use of this language in general prayers of thanksgiving see John 11.41; Acts 28.15. Cf. also Mark 8.6; John 6.11, 23; Acts 27.35 (in the context of meals); *Did.* 9.3–4; 10.2–6 (in the course of the eucharist, as such, and using the same formula as in Rev. 11.17); note further Judith 8.25; 3 Macc. 7.16; *T. Abr.* (*A*) 15.4. The literary form, εὐχαριστεῖν (*eucharistein*, 'to give thanks'), followed by a ὅτι- (*hoti-*, 'that', 'because') clause (verse 17*b*), to introduce the reason for returning thanks, is a feature of Paul's epistolary style (cf. 1 Cor. 1.4–5; 2 Thess. 1.3). See the similar formula 'I thank you, Lord, because . . .', in the Hodayoth of the Qumran community (cf. 1QH 2 [10].20; 3 [11].3, 19; et al.); also 2 Macc. 1.11; Luke 18.11; Ignatius, *Smyrn.* 10.1.

The expression 'the Lord God Almighty' (κύριε ὁ θεὸς ὁ παντοκράτωρ, *kyrie ho theos ho pantokratōr*) appears seven times in the Apocalypse (1.8; 4.8; 11.17; 15.3; 16.7; 19.6; 21.22), and twice in the form ὁ θεὸς ὁ παντοκράτωρ (*ho theos ho pantokratōr*, 'God the Almighty'), at 16.14 and 19.15. See further on 1.8. The title, ὁ παντοκράτωρ (*ho pantokratōr*, 'the Almighty'), is confined in the New Testament to Revelation, apart from 2 Cor. 6.18. The phrase 'Lord God Almighty' reflects the Hebrew יהוה צבאות (YHWH *ṣēbā'ôt*, 'Yahweh of Hosts'), which contains evocations of military power (cf. 2 Sam. 5.10; Jer. 15.16; Amos 3.13; 4.13; et al.; see also *T. Abr.* [*A*] 15.12; *3 Apoc. Baruch* 1.3). However, in the present context of Rev. 11.17, as elsewhere in the Apocalypse, the description speaks of God's eternal power and abiding sovereignty, achieved through his victory over the powers of evil in the final conflict. For 'power' in Revelation see on 7.12. The further attestation, 'you were and you are', which also points to the eternal being of God (see on 1.4), is three times in the Apocalypse linked to the full ascription, 'Lord God Almighty' (1.8; 4.8; 11.17).

Thanksgiving is offered in heaven because God has 'assumed his full authority and entered upon his reign'. A background to verses 17 and 18 may be located in Ps. 99.1 (LXX 98.1), 'the Lord reigns, let the peoples be enraged!'; see also Ps. 93.1; 96.10; et al. For the verb βασιλεύειν (*basileuein*, 'to reign, rule') see on 11.15; note also the close parallels in phraseology between this verse (11.17) and 19.6. The perfect tense of the verb, εἴληφας (*eilēphas*, 'you have assumed', lit. 'you have received') is proleptic, and the aorist ἐβασίλευσας (*ebasileusas*, 'you have entered upon your reign', lit. 'you reigned' or 'you began to reign') is ingressive. God is eternal in his being and powerful, creative and recreative activity; his kingdom and might are therefore exercised endlessly, both in heaven and on earth. However, this is not always evident to the 'inhabitants' of the world (11.10, q.v.); although in the end, and through conflict and suffering endured by the Church meanwhile, the sovereignty and reign of God, his judgement and salvation, will become universally apparent (see verses 9–12). In that sense, the abiding truth that the Lord and his Messiah reign for ever (verse 15) is perpetually disclosed, and about to be revealed, to those who believe (verse 18).

The seventh trumpet (11.15) prompts the offering of heavenly worship, rather than immediate portents of judgement (see above, and on 8.7—9.19). The justice involved will be recorded later (Chapters 12—15; and beyond). Nevertheless, the theme of judgement and its salvific outcome belongs to the thanksgiving and proclamation of 11.17–18, as it does to verse 19 (q.v.). So verse 18 begins and ends with a reference to the judgement of the unrighteous; but the emphasis in the middle section is on the 'reward' which is to be given to the faithful. It is important not to interpret verses 15–18 as a chronological account of what is to take place at the end-time (against Charles 1, 295–96, who believes that verse 18 catalogues the order of events after the close of the millennial kingdom). God's being and sovereignty are eternal; so are his judgement and salvation, which may be experienced by sinners and saints at any time up to the end, as well as in the end-time (see also on verse 17).

The rebellious 'nations' of the world, the elders declare, 'became enraged' (ὠργίσθησαν, *ōrgisthēsan*; the aorist is again ingressive); and the anger of the unfaithful is directed against the 'Lord and his anointed' (cf. verses 15*b*, 17; see also Ps. 2.1–12, esp. verse 2; Ps. 98.1 LXX). For the 'nations' in Revelation see on 10.11; 11.2, 9; for the 'excitement' of the nations see Exod. 15.14; *1 Enoch* 55.5–6; 4 Ezra 13.30–31; *Jub.* 23.23; *Sib. Or.* 3.660–68; et al. However (the conjunction καί, *kai*, lit. 'and', is adversative; hence the translation 'but'), in the face of this rage, God's wrath is disclosed. For the term ὀργή (*orgē*, 'wrath') see on 6.16; cf. also 6.17; 14.10; 16.19; 19.15. For 'the day of the Lord's wrath' see Ezek. 7.19; Zeph. 1.18. The word 'wrath' is used theologically in the Apocalypse to describe God's righteous opposition to human wrongdoing at any moment in time, and does not refer simply to 'the final great outpouring of wrath at the end of history' (so Beale 615). Moreover, John's perception of divine wrath is constructive, in that it includes the healing which may result from God's reaction of anger to the unfaithfulness of his creation (cf. 11.4–13).

The fact that 'the moment for judging the dead' has arrived certainly seems to suggest that the seer's vision at this point has taken us forward to the last judgement (Beale 615). However, Johannine eschatology is markedly balanced, since it includes a perpetual tension between time and eternity. In the Apocalypse, as in the Fourth Gospel, immediate events look forward to the future, and the end is wrapped around the present. This tension is evident in the present context. The Greek word here for 'moment' (καιρός, *kairos*) is to be distinguished from χρόνος (*chronos*, '[period of] time'); see further on 1.3. That is to say, the moment for judging the dead (rather than, as may be expected, the 'nations' who are mentioned at the outset of verse 18) may occur at any moment in salvation history; and 'final', eschatological judgement is not confined, in verse 18 or elsewhere, simply to the end of time. See Smalley, *Thunder and Love* 62–63, 174–76.

For the Jewish expectation that, at the end-time, the dead who sleep will awake either to life or to 'contempt' see Dan. 12.2; cf. also Rev. 20.12–13. Judgement of *the living* and the dead in the New Testament and early Christian literature is assigned to God (e.g. 1 Pet. 4.5; *Acts Thom.* 30), or Jesus Christ (so Acts 10.42; 2 Tim. 4.1; Polycarp, *Phil.* 2.1; et al.), or both (*2 Clem.* 1.1); but, apart from Rev. 11.18; 20.12 (cf. also Heb. 12.23), the expression 'judging the dead' (as such) is very rare. The aorist passive infinitive, κριθῆναι (*krithēnai*, lit. 'to be judged'), modifying καιρός (*kairos*, 'moment'), has a consecutive force: 'this is the moment that (as a result of which) the dead should be judged'.

The hymn in verse 18 continues by announcing that the moment has also arrived, positively, for the faithful to be rewarded. The term μισθός (*misthos*, 'reward') appears elsewhere in the Apocalypse only in the saying of the exalted Christ at Rev. 22.12,

'I am coming soon, my reward is with me', where the noun may be understood in both a positive and a negative sense. Here the idea of 'reward' is an inclusive one, pointing to the salvific benefits which God will give to the faithful at the end (cf. Aune 644); cf. *Apoc. Ezra* 1.14. The notion of recompense, without using this language, is present at Rev. 2.23; 20.13. Various metaphors also occur throughout Revelation to express the theme of spiritual reward, such as eating from the tree of life and entering the city (2.7; 22.14); receiving the hidden manna, white stone and new name (2.17; 3.12); being clothed in white garments (3.5; 7.13–14); and sharing the presence of God and the Lamb in their sovereignty (3.21; 7.15–17; 22.3–4). The reward specified in the present hymn may in part reflect an answer to the prayer of the martyr-witnesses recorded at 6.9–11 (Beale 616).

The syntax in this part of verse 18 is not immediately clear, since τοῖς δούλοις σου (*tois doulois sou*, 'your servants') may be taken either with τοῖς προφήταις (*tois prophētais*, 'the prophets'), to mean 'your servants the prophets', or with τοῖς προφήταις καὶ τοῖς ἁγίοις (*tois prophētais kai tois hagiois*, 'the prophets and the saints'), giving the sense, 'your servants, namely, the prophets and saints'. Mounce (227–28) opts for the former interpretation, and distinguishes here between '(your servants) the prophets', whom John holds in high esteem, and other believers (the saints and those who revere God's name, both insignificant and mighty). He does so on the basis of the distinction which he observes in 16.6; 18.24; and 22.9 between 'prophets' and 'saints'. But those passages doubtless contain fuller descriptions of the one Christian community; and since the witnesses in 11.3–12 (q.v.) are representatives of the Church in general, we may regard each of the descriptions in verse 18 (servants, prophets, saints) as equally applicable to all members of the new Israel. Notice also that, in Revelation, prophets and saints are called servants (10.7; 2.20; 7.3; 19.2, 5; 22.3), and saints are equated with prophets (16.6; 18.20, 24); furthermore, the covenant community as a whole is charged with a testimony to Jesus (1.9; 2.13; 6.9–11; 12.11) which is described as 'the spirit of prophecy' (19.10, q.v.). See further Beckwith 609–10; Beale 617.

In the anthem of verse 18, the description of the believing Church continues. It is said to include 'those who revere your name (καὶ τοῖς φοβουμένοις τὸ ὄνομά σου, *kai tois phoboumenois to onoma sou*, lit. "and [to give the reward] to those who fear your name")'. The introductory καί (*kai*, 'and') is epexegetic, giving the sense, 'your servants the prophets and saints, *that is to say* those who revere your name'. The phrase 'one who fears God' (Acts 10.2, 22; et al.) and its equivalent 'one who worships God' (e.g. Acts 16.14; 18.7) may be regarded as near-technical descriptions of proselytes: Gentile converts to Judaism (the actual term προσήλυτος, *prosēlytos*, 'proselyte', appears in the context of [God-]worship at Acts 13.43). Cf. Ps. 2.11; 115.11; 135.20. But there is no need to discover such an allusion in the present context, and identify those who 'revere (fear)' God's name as Christians from a Gentile background; in which case the 'saints' become Jewish believers (so apparently Aune 645); although Caird (143) may well be correct to assume that some pagan converts, who were 'filled with terror (ἔμφοβοι, *emphoboi*)' at the ascension of the witnesses (verse 13), are among all those members of the Church who 'revere' the name of God. In the context of the hymn of praise as a whole in verses 17–18, as in 19.5 (q.v.), it is much more likely that 'reverence of God' at this point is a description of the attitude which should belong to any and all of those who follow Christ (as in *1 Clem.* 21.7); and of these mention has already been made, in a variety of roles, earlier in the verse. See similarly Beckwith 610; Charles 1, 296–97; Mounce 227–28; Beale 617.

For the additional specification of members of the Christian community as 'both the insignificant and the mighty' (τοὺς μικροὺς καὶ τοὺς μεγάλους, *tous mikrous kai tous megalous*, lit. 'the small and the great') see Ps. 115.13 (MT); 113.21 LXX ('he will bless those who fear the Lord, both small and great'). Elsewhere in Revelation the phrase describes the faithful (19.5), as here; the unfaithful (13.16; 19.18); or both (20.12). In the Old Testament and early Jewish literature 'least and greatest' is used as an idiom to denote social inclusivity (e.g. Gen. 19.11; Deut. 1.17; 1 Kings 22.31; Job 3.19; Jer. 6.13; Judith 13.4; Wis. 6.6–7; 1 Macc. 5.45). In the New Testament, apart from the Apocalypse, see similarly Acts 8.10; 26.22; Heb. 8.11 (quoting Jer. 31.34). In the present verse (Rev. 11.18), as at 19.5, the 'insignificant and mighty' represent those in the Christian Church who are at opposite ends of the social and economic spectrum, for such disparities have no meaning within the community of faith to which the saints inclusively belong.

The visionary prayer of thanksgiving returns in the closing line to the theme of judgement, thus forming an inclusion with the opening sentence of verse 18 (q.v.). The moment has arrived not only for rewarding the saints but also for 'destroying those who ruin the earth'. That noun, τὴν γῆν (*tēn gēn*, 'the earth'), is probably metonymy for 'people of the earth' (Aune 645); cf. Isa. 42.5; Rev. 6.4; 9.4; et al. The judgement in this part of the verse reflects Jeremiah's prophecy that the Lord will condemn the historical Babylon for its wrongdoing (Jer. 51.25 [LXX 28.25]). In the thought and theology of the Apocalypse, Babylon (Rome) represents the eschatological world of opposition to God's truth, the 'great city' which will be destroyed at the end (see on 11.8, 13; cf. also 19.2). So the unfaithful, who ruin others, will themselves eventually be destroyed. Cf. *Pss. Sol.* 2.1–35; *Sib. Or.* 1.387–400; also Beale 616. This teaching seems to evoke the Jewish *lex talionis*, the 'law of retaliation'. Cf. Exod. 21.24; Judg. 1.7; 15.11; Ps. 7.14–16; 3 Macc. 5.1–5; Rom. 2.5; 2 Thess. 1.5–10; et al.; and, in Revelation itself, 16.6; 18.4–8; 18.24—19.8.

The phrase, διαφθεῖραι τοὺς διαφθείροντας (*diaphtheirai tous diaphtheirontas*, lit. 'to destroy completely [the form of the verb is intensive] those who ruin the earth'), involves paronomasia; the writer uses a play on words which balances the literal sense of complete destruction with its figurative counterpart of 'to ruin', in the sense of '(morally) deprave' (similarly Rev. 2.2; 14.8; et al.). See BDAG 239*b*. The only other use of the verb διαφθείρω (*diaphtheirō*, 'to destroy') in Revelation is at 8.9 (q.v.). For the clash between human and divine wrath in this verse, and its destructive yet salvific outcome, see further on 6.16.

19 This verse is a response to the prayerful anthem of thanksgiving in 11.17–18. In the literary structure of the present interval, verse 19 is pivotal; since it both concludes the section 11.15–19 and introduces Scene 4 and its interval (12.1—15.8), which are to follow (see above, 255–56). There are three parts to the verse: the opening of the heavenly temple; the disclosure of the covenantal ark within it; and a description of the portents which follow this manifestation. Mounce (228) claims that the ark corresponds to the reward of the faithful (verse 18), and the cosmic disturbances to the outpouring of God's wrath; but, in view of the Exodus motif clearly present in this verse (see below), this seems to be an over-simplification.

'God's heavenly temple' (ὁ ναὸς τοῦ θεοῦ ὁ ἐν τῷ οὐρανῷ, *ho naos tou theou ho en tō[i] ouranō[i]*, lit. 'the temple of God in the heaven') is the sanctuary of God in heaven, which has its counterpart in the Temple at Jerusalem (so 11.1–2), but ultimately symbolizes the presence of God himself (as in Rev. 21.22; see further on 7.15). In imagery drawn mostly from the Jerusalem Temple, the 'heavenly temple' of the Apocalypse is described as the tabernacle, or 'tent of witness' (15.5), and includes both an 'altar' (6.9, q.v.; 8.3, 5; 9.13; 14.18; 16.7) and, as here, the 'ark of the covenant'. It is also the location of God's throne (cf. Exod. 15.17), which is the sign of his sovereignty (Rev. 4—5); and both of these are shared by the Lamb (5.13; 22.3). See further Walker, *Holy City* 243. For the 'opening' of heaven, and by association the doors of its temple, see also Rev. 4.1; 19.11. In figurative biblical language, the 'splitting' of the heavens, as here, is usually the prelude to a crucial divine manifestation (cf. Exod. 20.22; Isa. 64.1; Mark 1.10; John 1.51; Acts 7.56).

In the Old Testament, the ark of the covenant symbolizes the awesome presence of God (note the effect on the Philistines, according to 1 Sam. 4.5–8, when the ark is brought into the Israelite camp; cf. also Num. 10.33; Deut. 10.8; Josh. 3.5–17; et al.). It was presumably destroyed by Nebuzaradan when he attacked Jerusalem and burned the Temple (2 Kings 25.8–10); and its recovery formed an important element of eschatological and messianic expectation in Judaism (2 Macc. 2.4–8, esp. verse 7; see also on Rev. 2.17). In the New Testament, the 'ark of the covenant' is mentioned only here (verse 19) and at Heb. 9.4.

Rev. 11.19 provides the single reference in early Jewish and Christian literature to a *heavenly* ark of the covenant, although 'throne' can serve as a heavenly counterpart to the ark, as in Jer. 17.12 (Aune 677–78). In the phrase, ἡ κιβωτὸς τῆς διαθήκης αὐτοῦ (*hē kibōtos tēs diathēkēs autou*), translated here as 'the ark of his covenant', it is not immediately clear whether the possessive pronoun αὐτοῦ (*autou*, 'his') modifies just the preceding noun, 'covenant', or the whole noun phrase (to give the sense, 'his ark of the covenant'). In view of the Greek word-order, and the regular use of the expression 'his (God's) covenant' in the Old Testament (as at Exod. 2.24; Deut. 4.13; 1 Chron. 16.15; Ps. 25.10; Ezek. 17.14; Dan. 9.4; et al.; see also Luke 1.72; *1 Clem.* 15.4; [*Barn.* 9.6]), it seems most likely that 'the ark of his covenant' is the correct rendering of the text (against Aune 677). See further the textual notes on verse 19.

The heavenly ark of the covenant, in the context of verse 19, is the true sign of God's faithfulness to the abiding relationship which he established with his people Israel (Exod. 24.3–8; 25.22; 34.27–35), and renewed in Christ (Heb. 8.1—9.28, esp. 9.15). This is the only use of the actual term διαθήκη (*diathēkē*, 'covenant') in the Apocalypse; but the idea of God's close and covenant fellowship with the followers of Jesus is every-where apparent (cf. Rev. 3.20; 5.9–10; 7.15–17; 21.3–4; et al.); see Hendriksen 133. Together with the theme of the new exodus (verse 19*b*), the notion of the new cov-enant in Christ importantly concludes an Act which has spoken of salvation through judgement (against Aune 677).

The cosmic portents which accompany the opening of heaven and the sighting of the covenantal ark (lightning, roarings [φωναί, *phōnai*, lit. 'voices'], peals of thunder, earthquake, hailstorm) are epiphanic in significance; like the opening of heaven and the unveiling of the ark, they disclose the imminent judgement, but also the salvation, of God. There is a typical, formulaic character which structures the passages in Revelation, including the present one, which introduce atmospheric and seismic phenomena (see Vanni, *La struttura letteraria* 141–48). Apart from 11.19, such groups of portents appear at 4.5; 8.5; 16.18. In each case they are associated with the throne of God or the heavenly temple, and reveal the divine character. They also occur in more or less the same order (except that no earthquake is mentioned at 4.5; a heavy hailstorm is included at 11.19; while lightning and thunder are reversed in 8.5). See further on 4.5.

Earthquakes also appear in Revelation at 6.12 and 11.13. Bauckham (*Climax of Prophecy* 199–209) draws attention to the theological importance and weight of the earthquake imagery in the Apocalypse. As one of the images of the events of the end-time, earth-quakes speak perhaps more of divine judgement, than salvation (but see below). So in 11.19, as elsewhere in Revelation, John is sharing with the author of Hebrews (see 12.25–29) the expectation that 'the God whose voice shook Sinai will once again shake heaven and earth' (Bauckham, *Climax of Prophecy* 209). In answer to the 'raging of the nations' (verse 18), divine justice is asserted universally. It is typical of Johannine theology and cosmology that an *earth*quake should take place in heaven, even if its repercussions are experienced by God's creation. To the unrepentant the coming of the one who inhabits the heavenly temple, and of the Lamb, can only bring fear (cf. 6.16–17; also 9.20–21).

The 'heavy hailstorm' (χάλαζα μεγάλη, *chalaza megalē*), which brings to a close the first Act of John's drama, is more positive in its theological implications. Hail, with thunder and fire, marked the seventh plague of the Exodus (Exod. 9.22–26). The motif of the Exodus has been present throughout the sequence of the first six trumpets in Scene 3 (Chapters 8 and 9), with their evocations of the ten plagues. Moreover, the heavenly song of judgement and salvation, which follows the sounding of the seventh trumpet (11.15), may well reflect a segment from the Song of Moses in Exod. 15.13–18 (Beale 618–19). The Exodus theme, in the Apocalypse as elsewhere in biblical thought, contains the theological dynamic of salvation through judgement. In the Christian scheme, Jesus is the new Moses, who brings the new Israel into the new promised land of salvific blessing (cf. Exod. 16.1–36 and John 6.26–58; Exod. 17.1–7 and John 7.37–39; also Smalley, *John* 271–72). Rev. 11.19 must be interpreted against this background (see also 11.3–4, 8, 11–13; and esp. 15.2–4); cf. further Bauckham, *Theology* 98–104. In support of this exegesis, Beale (619) argues that the appearance of the ark of the covenant in 11.19, between two earthquakes (verses 13 and 19), calls to mind the fall of Jericho, which signalled the successful conclusion of Israel's entry into the promised land after the wilderness wanderings. For hail elsewhere in Revelation see 8.7; 16.21.

Theology

The prevailing themes of the first main Act of the drama of Revelation are those of salvation through judgement, and redemption through conflict (for the image of redemption in Revelation see Smalley, *Thunder and Love* 81–83). The action moves from a vision of the exalted Son of man, commissioning the prophecy, in Rev. 1, through judgements on Church (2—3) and society (6.1–8, 12–17; Chapters 8—9), to a depiction of the faithful who are sealed (7; 11.1–2) and witnessing (10—11), but also suffering (6.9–11). At the centre, as the fulcrum of the Apocalypse as a whole, is the throne-vision of 4—5 (cf. Beasley-Murray 108–11). The God of creation (4) is also the Lord of redemption (5); and the scroll received by the Lamb (5.8) becomes the means of unfolding the divine purposes of discrimination and life for the whole world. Throughout, the restoration of God's people, who remain faithful to his covenant in belief and behaviour, is in view.

In the interval following Scene 3 (10.1—11.19), the notion of God's sovereignty is paramount; and this includes his promises of love, as well as his justice (Smalley, *Thunder and Love* 77). In Chapters 10—11, also, John's audience is presented with the main content of his prophetic revelation. This is heralded by the angel of 1.1 (cf. 22.16), anticipated in the throne room (5.1–8), and mediated by the strong angel of 10.1–2 (who combines elements of the Godhead; Boring 139). Cf. Bauckham, *Theology* 81–82. The scroll, which the Lamb takes (5.8) and opens (6.1; et al.; see also the 'open scroll' of 10.2), provides a summary of God's plan of salvation; and this process symbolizes Christ's authority over the Father's intentions of judgement and redemption, inaugurated by his own death and resurrection. Equally, the possession of the open scroll by the prophet-seer indicates his participation in that authority, and his identification with it (cf. Beale 548–49). Moreover, the parenthesis of Chapters 10 and 11 is not placed between the sixth (9.13) and seventh (11.15) trumpets in any chronological sense, but to provide in part the theological basis for the judgement which they promote. To some extent the trumpet-plagues are God's answer to the prayers of the saints that, through suffering and even martyrdom (6.9–11), their faith should eventually be vindicated (cf. Beale 520–22).

Time and eternity cohere throughout the Apocalypse (see on 11.17–18). Like the seer himself, we engage with the theological truths and historical events of the drama from the vantage point of the brink of eternity (Mounce 207). The eschatological end is therefore constantly pressing in, but never seems to arrive: even at the end of the play (cf. 22.20). No more time of waiting is promised by the angel; yet, as in 8.1, the consummation is further delayed. John's visions cannot be interpreted solely, or indeed chiefly, in historical and chronological terms; just as the 'delay' in the fulfilment of the hidden and salvific purposes of God (10.6–7) is not governed by the parameters of time. It is true that in Act 2 (Rev. 12—22) the events of the end-time, as contained in the small scroll of God's plan for his creation, appear to be presented more specifically, and with greater finality. But at no point does John say *when*, exactly, the last judgement and the end will take place; he simply reminds his audience, and us, that the task of the waiting Church is meanwhile that of continuing and faithful prophetic witness (10.11; 11.3–13). So when the seventh angel blows the final trumpet, the judgement which follows is, not surprisingly, a hymn of praise offered to the sovereign and saving God of heaven (11.15–18). The intermediate climax, when it happens, has become a time of rejoicing, rather than a day of wrath (Caird 142; cf. Court, *Revelation* 48–49).

The closing verse of this interlude, Rev. 11.19, occupies a strategic place in the movement of the apocalyptic drama. Structurally and theologically, it ties together the end of Chapters 10—11, and leads into Chapters 12—15 (see above). Verse 19 also brings the audience back to the theme of sovereignty which belongs to Rev. 10, where John is recommissioned as God's spokesman, and charged to declare his hidden and ruling purposes of judgement and love. Those purposes are recapitulated in 11.19, as the ark of the covenant is disclosed in heaven amid cosmic portents. God's kingdom has already been celebrated in the anthems of 11.15 and 17–18. Now, in verse 19, the vision of an opened heaven and its divine sanctuary states afresh the abiding truth that God's covenant faithfulness remains unchanged. His promises to his people will be kept in the future, as they have been in the past (cf. Milligan 195); and this truth is emphasized by the fact that 'temple' references both precede and follow the discussion in 11.3–12 about prophetic activity, suffering and exaltation (cf. Smalley, *Thunder and Love* 77–79). Verse 19 is also positive in its affirmation of the hope which exists, for the Johannine community and for the Church, through the risen and redemptive Christ (cf. 11.11–13); for he makes possible the restoration of a new Israel, through a new exodus into a new life (cf. 14.2–5; 15.3–4).

Act 2

SALVATION THROUGH JUDGEMENT, AND NEW CREATION
(12.1—22.17)

SCENE 4
Seven Signs
(12.1—14.20)

Translation

12 [1]And a great sign appeared in heaven: a woman robed with the sun, beneath her feet the[a] moon, and a crown of twelve stars on her head. [2]She was pregnant, and[b] crying out[c] in labour, and in the pain of childbirth.

[3]Then a second heavenly sign became visible: there was a huge, fiery red[d] dragon, with seven heads and ten horns, and a coronet on each of the seven heads. [4]His tail swept a third of the stars away from the sky, and hurled them down to the earth. The dragon then took his place in front of the woman, as she was on the point of giving birth, so that he could devour her child the moment it was born. [5]But when she was delivered of a male[e] child, who is destined to shatter the totality of nations with an iron crook, her son was snatched away, up to God and to his throne. [6]The woman herself escaped to the wilderness, where[f] she had a place prepared for her by[g] God, and where she would be supported[h] for twelve hundred and sixty days.

[7]And war broke out in heaven. Michael and his angels had to battle[i] against the dragon. The dragon and his angels fought back, [8]but did not have the power[j] to keep their place[k] in heaven any longer. [9]The great dragon was thrown out, that ancient serpent who is called Devil and the[l] Satan, the deceiver of the whole world; he was hurled down to the earth, and his angels were cast down with him.

[10]Then I heard a loud, heavenly voice proclaim:

> 'Now the deliverance and the power and the sovereign realm of our God,
>> and the authority of his Messiah, have been established;
> because the accuser[m] of our comrades has been thrown out,
>> who brought charges against them[n] before our God day and night.
> [11]And they have conquered him through the sacrifice of the Lamb,
>> as well as by the word of their testimony;
> for they did not cling to their lives in the face of death.
> [12]So let the[o] heavens rejoice, and those who dwell there!
> But disaster[p] is coming to the earth and the sea,
>> because the Devil, who is filled with anger, has come down to you,
>> knowing that his time is limited.'

[13]And when the dragon realized that he had been hurled down to the earth, he went in pursuit[q] of the woman who had given birth to the male child.[r] [14]But the woman was provided with the two wings of the great eagle, so that she could fly to her place in the desert, out of the serpent's reach, where she can be supported for a time, times and half a time. [15]Then the serpent spewed a flood of water from his mouth after the woman, trying to drown her in its torrent. [16]But the earth[s] came to the woman's rescue, by opening its mouth and swallowing the river which the dragon spewed from its mouth. [17]Furious with[t] the woman, the dragon then went off to wage war against her descendants, who obey God's commands and maintain their witness to Jesus.

[18]He took his stand[u] on the seashore.

13 ¹Then I saw, emerging from the sea, a beast with ten horns and seven heads; on each of its ten horns was a coronet, and on its head were blasphemous titles.ᵛ ²The beast which I saw resembled a leopard; but its feet were like those of a bear, and its mouth was like a lion's. The dragon conferred on it his own power, and his rule and immense authority. ³One of its heads appeared to have received a death-blow, yet its mortal wound had been healed. The whole world marvelled, and followed the beast. ⁴They prostrated themselves before the dragon, because he had conferred authority on the beast; they also worshipped the beast,ʷ chanting, 'Who is like the beast, and who can fight against it?' ⁵The beast was permitted to mouth boastful words, even blasphemies; and it was given authority to do so for forty-twoˣ months. ⁶So it opened its mouth to utter blasphemies against God, to revile his name and his dwelling-place, that is, all who are sheltered in heaven.ʸ ⁷It was also allowed to make war on the saints and vanquish them;ᶻ and it was given power over every race and people, and every language group and nation. ⁸All the earth's inhabitants will worship it, everyone whose name has not been writtenᵃᵃ since the creation of the world in the bookᵇᵇ of life of the sacrificed Lamb.

> ⁹Let anyone with an ear, listen!
> ¹⁰If you are to be taken captive, into captivity you shall go;ᶜᶜ
> If you are to be killedᵈᵈ with the sword, by the sword you must be killed.

Here is a call for the endurance and faithfulness of God's people.

¹¹Then I saw another beast emergingᵉᵉ from the earth; it has two horns, like a ram, but makes a noise like a dragon. ¹²This beast exercises the full authority of the first beast, on its behalf,ᶠᶠ and forces the earth and its inhabitants to worshipᵍᵍ the first beast, whose mortal wound had been healed. ¹³It performs outstanding miracles, even causing fire to fall from heaven to earth in front of people. ¹⁴It leads the earth's inhabitants astray, through the miracles which it is allowed to perform on behalf of the first beast, persuading those who dwell on the earth to fashion an image in honour of the beast which had beenʰʰ wounded by the sword, only to live. ¹⁵And itⁱⁱ is permitted to breathe life into the statue of the beast, so that it can actually speak, and cause any whoʲʲ will not worship the beast's image to be put to death. ¹⁶It compels all people, the insignificant and the mighty, rich and poor, free and slave, to be brandedᵏᵏ on their right hands or on their foreheads; ¹⁷so thatˡˡ no one canᵐᵐ buy or sell who does not have the mark: that is, the name of the beast, or the number of its name. ¹⁸This calls for discernment. Let the one who has the intelligence interpret the number of the beast; for the number is humanly calculable, and its number is six hundred and sixtyⁿⁿ-six.

14 ¹I looked again, and there was theᵒᵒ Lamb, standingᵖᵖ on Mount Zion! With him were a hundred and forty-four thousand who had his name, and his Father's name, written on their foreheads. ²And I heard a sound from heaven, like the roar of the oceans and a peal of loud thunder; and the resonance�qq which I heard seemed like harpists, playing on their harps. ³They were singing (as it were)ʳʳ a new song before the throne, and in front of the four living creatures and the elders; and no one could learn that hymn apart from the one hundred and forty-four thousand who had been redeemed from the world. ⁴These are the ones who have not defiled themselves with women, since they are chaste. They are the ones who follow the Lamb, wherever he would lead.ˢˢ They, of all people, have been ransomed to be first fruits for God and the Lamb. ⁵They speak without deceit, andᵗᵗ are morally blameless.ᵘᵘ

⁶Then I saw another angel,ᵛᵛ flying in midheaven, with an eternal gospel to proclaimʷʷ to the earth's inhabitants,ˣˣ and among every nation and race, and language group and people. ⁷He was calling aloud, 'Fear God, and glorify him, because the moment of his judgement has arrived; and worship the one who created the heaven and the earth, theʸʸ sea and the water-springs!'

⁸And another angel, a second,ᶻᶻ followed him saying, 'Fallen, fallen is Babylon the great, whoᵃᵃᵃ caused the whole world to drinkᵇᵇᵇ the wine of her passionate immorality.'

⁹And another angel, a third, followed them, crying with a loud voice, 'Those who worship the beast and its image, and are branded with its mark on their foreheads or hands, ¹⁰will also

drink some of the wine of God's wrath, poured out undiluted into the cup of his anger. With sulphurous flames they will be tormented[ccc] in the presence of his holy angels and of the Lamb; [11]and the smoke of their torment will ascend for ever. Those who worship the beast and its statue, and anyone who is branded with its name, will have no respite day or night. [12]This means that the perseverance of the saints involves keeping[ddd] God's commands, and remaining faithful to Jesus.

[13]Then I heard a voice from heaven saying, 'Write down this, that those who from now on die in the Lord are fortunate. "Fortunate indeed", the Spirit agrees,[eee] "so that they can rest[fff] from their labours; for their deeds accompany them!"'

[14]Then I looked, and there was a white cloud, and seated on the cloud was one like a son[ggg] of man! He had[hhh] a golden crown on his head, and a sharp sickle in his hand. [15]Then another angel came out of the temple, shouting at the top of his voice to the one sitting on the cloud, 'Wield your sickle and reap, for the moment to harvest has arrived, and the earth's crop is fully ripe.' [16]So the one seated on the cloud[iii] began to swing his sickle over the earth, and the earth was harvested.

[17]Then another angel came out of the heavenly[jjj] sanctuary; and he also carried a sharp sickle. [18]Yet another angel moved from[kkk] the area of the altar, the one with authority over fire; and he called out in a loud voice to the angel with the sharp sickle and said, 'Put in your sharp sickle to gather the clusters from the earth's vineyard; for its grapes are ripe.' [19]So the angel began to swing his sickle towards[lll] the earth; and he gathered the grape harvest of the earth, and threw it into the winepress of God's great[mmm] wrath. [20]And the winepress was trodden outside the city; and blood flowed from the winepress to the height of horses' bridles, for a distance of two hundred miles.[nnn]

Text

[a] Some MSS of Andreas omit the article ἡ (*hē*, 'the'), before the noun σελήνη (*selēnē*, 'moon'). But the articular version of the Greek is firmly attested, and clearly original.

[b] The order, καὶ κράζει (*kai krazei*, lit. 'and cries out'), is followed by major witnesses, including 𝔓47 ℵ C 1006 Oecumenius[2053], et al. The variations, with καί (*kai*, 'and') after κράζει (*krazei*, 'cries out'; so A), or omitted altogether (1611 2351 Andreas Byz, et al.), are doubtless secondary.

[c] The verb κράζει (*krazei*, 'crying out', lit. 'she cries out') appears in this (historic present) form in A 𝔓47 ℵ Andreas, et al.; and such is the *lectio originalis*. Other MSS (such as C Byz 2351) correct the tense to the imperfect ἔκραζεν (*ekrazen*, 'was crying out'), or to the aorist ἔκραξεν (*ekraxen*, 'cried out'; so some MSS of Byz). For the frequent use of the historic present tense in this section see below.

[d] The form of the adjectival description, μέγας πυρρός (*megas pyrros*, 'huge, fiery red'), as in A 025 051 1006[1841] Andreas lat cop[sa], et al., is probably original (see a similar lexical order, μέγαν λευκόν [*megan leukon*, 'great white'], at 20.11). But the variation πυρρὸς μέγας (*pyrros megas*, lit. 'red great') is strongly supported (so 𝔓47 ℵ C 046 2351 Byz Primasius cop syr eth, et al.).

[e] The neuter accusative, ἄρσεν (*arsen*, 'male [son/child]'), is read by A C, et al. (cf. Charles 2, 308); and this form, strongly supported by the MS combination of the witnesses A and C, is presumably original. Beckwith (624, 630) thinks that the virtually redundant, masculine υἱόν (*huion*, 'son') may be a gloss; in which case the use of the neuter gender would have been 'natural'. The subsequent variations, ἄρσενα (*arsena*, 'male', masculine accusative), as in 051 1006 1611 Oecumenius[2053] Andreas Byz, et al., and ἄρρενα (*arrena*, 'male', accusative singular; so 𝔓47 ℵ 2351, et al.) are probably influenced by the use of ἄρσενα (*arsena*, 'male child') at 12.13 (q.v.).

f The original order of the Greek phrase, ἔχει ἐκεῖ (*echei ekei*, lit. 'she has there') is reversed in Hippolytus, because of the visual similarity of these two words; and some MSS (including C 051 1006[1006 1841] lat syr[h] Tyconius Primasius) omit ἐκεῖ (*ekei*, 'there'), as a redundant adverb. Cf. Aune 653.

g Instead of the *lectio originalis*, ἀπὸ (τοῦ θεοῦ), *apo (tou theou)*, lit. 'from (God)', some witnesses, such as 046 1611 2351 Byz, read ὑπό (*hypo*, 'by'); while others, including some MS of Andreas Byz, have παρά (*para*, 'from'). These variants are corrections, stemming from the fact that ἀπό (*apo*, 'from') is very rarely used in the Apocalypse to introduce an agent (only here, and at 9.18).

h The indefinite present subjunctive, τρέφωσιν (*trephōsin*, lit. 'that they might support'), is attested by A 1006 Oecumenius[2053] Andreas, et al. It is replaced in ℵ C 598 2019, et al., by the present indicative plural, τρέφουσιν (*trephousin*, 'they support'); but, if this were an original reading, the verb here would more probably be in the singular (as at 12.14).

i The articular infinitive, τοῦ πολεμῆσαι (*tou polemēsai*, 'to battle') is attested by A C 1006 1611, and some MSS of Andreas Byz. A few witnesses, including 𝔓47 ℵ, omit τοῦ (*tou*, lit. 'of the'). The presence of the article τοῦ (*tou*, 'of the') with the infinitive, only here in Revelation, is difficult; and this fact, together with the strong evidence provided by the agreement of A and C, indicates that τοῦ πολεμῆσαι (*tou polemēsai*, 'to battle') is the earlier reading.

j In place of the third person singular aorist indicative, ἴσχυσε(ν) (*ischyse[n]*, '[the dragon did not] have the power'), as read by A 1611[1854] cop[bo] Byz, et al., some witnesses (including 𝔓47 ℵ 051 1006) have the third person plural aorist, ἴσχυσαν (*ischysan*, '[they did not] have the power'). Others (046 Byz) substitute the third person plural imperfect, with basically the same meaning, ἴσχυον (*ischyon*). The plural forms of the verb appear to be corrections, designed to accommodate the presence of a plural subject ('his angels') alongside the singular form, 'dragon'. The translation has preserved this ambiguity.

k The phrase, τόπος εὑρέθη αὐτῶν (*topos heurethē autōn*, lit. 'their place was [not] found'), with the genitive of the pronoun, is attested in that form by A Andreas. Other MSS substitute a pronominal dative for the genitive. Thus ℵ² 051 2019 syr[ph] have τόπος εὑρέθη αὐτοῖς (*topos heurethē autois*, 'a place was [not] found for them'); while 1006 1611[1854] Oecumenius[2053] Byz cop[bo] Victorinus read τόπος εὑρέθη αὐτῷ (*topos heurethē autō[i]*, 'a place was [not] found for him'). But these variations seem to be attempts at harmonization with the Greek of Dan. 2.35 Theod., which lies behind Rev. 12.8 (see also 20.11). The singular pronoun in the second variant has been influenced by the leading (singular) subject in this sentence, 'dragon' (see the previous note). The reading, τόπος εὑρέθη αὐτῶν (*topos heurethē autōn*, 'their place was [not] found'), therefore, is likely to be original. The primitive nature of this version is supported by the grammatical difficulty which it manifests: namely, that the genitive of possession, αὐτῶν (*autōn*, 'their') is separated from the governing noun by a verb. That is why, in 1006[1841] 1611 Beatus, et al., the lexical order becomes τόπος αὐτῶν εὑρέθη (*topos autōn heurethē*, lit. 'a place of theirs was [not] found').

l 'The Satan' (ὁ Σατανᾶς, *ho Satanas*) is technically a title, demanding the inclusion of an article (ὁ, *ho*, 'the'). This is present in most MSS; but it is omitted by 𝔓47 1611[2329] Byz, et al., presumably because the preceding title, Διάβολος (*Diabolos*, 'Devil') is anarthrous.

ᵐ The form, κατήγωρ (*katēgōr*, 'accuser'), appears as a New Testament hapax legomenon in A alone. All other MSS, including 𝔓47 ℵ C 025 046 051, have the more usual Greek version of the term, with the same meaning, κατήγορος (*katēgoros*). Unless the scribe of A is reflecting the usage of his day (cf. Metzger, *Textual Commentary* 745–46), it is more likely that the unique κατήγωρ (*katēgōr*, 'accuser') would be altered to κατήγορος (*katēgoros*), than the reverse.

ⁿ The accusative, αὐτούς (*autous*, 'them'), attested by 𝔓47 A 051 Andreas, appears as a genitive (αὐτῶν, *autōn*, lit. 'of them') in ℵ C 1006 2351 Byz, et al. The verb κατηγορέω (*katēgoreō*, lit. 'accuse') in the New Testament normally takes the genitive (cf. Mark 3.2 par.; Luke 23.2; John 5.45; Acts 24.8; et al.); and this makes the occurrence of the accusative in 𝔓47, et al., difficult and therefore original. It is easier to understand how the accusative could be altered to the genitive, than the reverse (Aune 655).

ᵒ The article 'the' (οἱ, *hoi*), with 'heavens' (οὐρανοί, *ouranoi*), is present in A Andreas 1006 235, et al.; but it is omitted by other witnesses, including C ℵ 025 Byz. The articular nominative is probably original since, as often in Revelation, it functions as a vocative (cf. also 4.11; 6.10; 15.3; 18.10; 19.5; et al.).

ᵖ The construction, οὐαί (*ouai*, 'woe' or 'disaster'), with the simple accusative, is unusual; and it is therefore most probably original. Normally the interjection is followed by the dative, as (e.g.) in Matt. 11.21 par.; Mark 13.17 par.; Luke 22.22; 1 Cor. 9.16. But see other uses of οὐαί (*ouai*, 'woe') in Revelation: 8.13 (with the accusative); 18.10, 16, 19 (nominative). Subsequent witnesses (so ℵ) add εἰς (*eis*, 'to') before τὴν γῆν (*tēn gēn*, 'the earth'), to soften the syntax, or (𝔓47 2351 Byz, et al.) change the object into the dative, τῇ γῇ (*tē[i] gē[i]*, 'to the earth').

ᑫ The third person singular aorist, ἐδίωξεν (*ediōxen*, lit. 'he pursued' [BDAG 254*a*, 'persecuted']), as read by most MSS, is original. Other witnesses give derivations of the verb in this form. Thus ℵ² has ἐξεδίωξεν (*exediōxen*, 'he drove out'); and 𝔓47 reads ἀπῆλθεν ἐκδιῶξαι (*apēlthen ekdiōxai*, lit. 'he went away to drive out'). The versions ἔδωκεν (*edōken*, 'he *gave*'; so ℵ*) and ἐδίωκε (*ediōke*, 'he was pursuing', imperfect; so Oecumenius²⁰⁵³ 1611¹⁸⁵⁴, et al.) are the result of scribal errors.

ʳ Instead of ἄρσενα (*arsena*, 'male child'), strongly attested by ℵ C 025 051 1006¹⁰⁰⁶ ¹⁸⁴¹ 1611¹⁶¹¹ ¹⁸⁵⁴ Oecumenius²⁰⁵³, et al., A reads ἄρσεναν (*arsenan*, 'male child'). The addition of -ν (-*n*) to the accusative singular of third declension nouns is a stylistic feature of the MS A (cf. Rev. 13.14; 22.2). See Aune 656.

ˢ A number of major witnesses (including 𝔓47 2019 Byzᵍⁱᵍ Primasius Victorinus) omit ἡ γῆ (*hē gē*, 'the earth'); but this emendation is manifestly secondary, since it leaves the opening sentence in verse 16 without a clear subject.

ᵗ The use of ἐπί (*epi*, lit. 'upon') in this sentence is original, since that preposition with the dative, following the verb ὠργίσθη (*ōrgisthē*, lit. '[he] was angry'), indicates the cause of the emotion involved (cf. LXX Gen. 40.2; Num. 31.14; et al.). The rare use of ἐπί (*epi*, 'upon') in this context produced scribal corrections: 𝔓47 C omit the preposition, and 2351 changes ἐπί (*epi*, 'on') to ἐν (*en*, lit. 'in').

ᵘ The reading, καὶ ἐστάθη (*kai estathē*, lit. 'and he [the dragon] stood'), is strongly supported by 𝔓47 ℵ A C 2351 syrʰ eth arm, et al., and is doubtless original. TR, following 025 046 051 syrᵖʰ copˢᵃ,ᵇᵒ, et al., reads Καὶ ἐστάθην (*Kai estathēn*, 'and I [John] stood'), preceded by a full-stop. The variant seems to have occurred when copyists accommodated ἐστάθη (*estathē*, 'he stood') to the first person singular of the following verb, εἶδον (*eidon*, 'I saw'). Cf. Metzger, *Textual Commentary* 746; see also further on 12.18, below.

^v The plural form, ὀνόματα (*onomata*, 'titles', lit. 'names'), is strongly attested by A 046 051 Oecumenius[2053] Byz it[gig], et al.; and, in view of the parallel (ὀνόματα βλασφημίας, *onomata blasphēmias*, 'blasphemous titles') at 17.3, it is probably original. However, some MSS (including 𝔓47 ℵ C 025 1006 Andreas vg[mss] syr[ph] cop arm Primasius) have the singular form, ὄνομα (*onoma*, 'name'). This variant may have occurred because -τα (-*ta*) was accidentally omitted after -μα (-*ma*); but, equally, a change from singular to plural may have been influenced by the preceding plural, τὰς κεφαλάς (*tas kephalas*, 'heads'). See Metzger, *Textual Commentary* 746.

^w In place of the dative, τῷ θηρίῳ (*tō[i] thēriō[i]*, '[they worshipped] the beast'), a few witnesses (such as A 1611[2344]) read the accusative, with the same meaning, τὸ θηρίον (*to thērion*). The weight of MS evidence suggests that the dative form of the noun is original. But it is also true that, elsewhere in the Apocalypse, neuter nouns such as τὸ θηρίον (*to thērion*, 'beast') are usually in the accusative when following the verb προσκυνέω (*proskyneō*, 'worship'); cf. 13.12; 14.11; 20.4 (note, however, the datives at 4.10; 13.15). The dative form in the present text (13.4) may also have been changed from the accusative to the dative under the influence of the preceding datives, τῷ δράκοντι (*tō[i] drakonti*, '[worshipped] the dragon'), and τῷ θηρίῳ (*tō[i] thēriō[i]*, 'the beast'). See Aune 717.

^x Some MSS (including A 1006[1841] 2351) omit the connective καί (*kai*, lit. 'and') between τεσσεράκοντα (*tesserakonta*, 'forty') and δύο (*duo*, 'two'). The use of καί (*kai*, 'and') to link cardinal numbers is very rare in Revelation (only 11.2, v.l., apart from 13.5); and this suggests that the reading with the conjunction is not original. Cf. Rev. 13.18; also John 2.20; 5.5.

^y There is superior external support for the inclusion of the prepositional phrase, τοὺς ἐν τῷ οὐρανῷ σκηνοῦντας (*tous en tō[i] ouranō[i] skēnountas*, lit. 'those dwelling in heaven'), as read by ℵ* A C 1611 Oecumenius[2053], et al. It is also a *lectio difficilior*, since the insertion of such a phrase between an article (here, τούς, *tous*, 'those') and its substantive (σκηνοῦντας, *skēnountas*, 'dwelling') is most unusual in the Apocalypse (cf. 19.9). For these reasons, the presence of the phrase may be regarded as original, and its omission by 𝔓47 Primasius as secondary. The addition of καί (*kai*, 'and') before τούς (*tous*, 'those') is evidently an attempt by copyists to soften the strained syntax at this point in the text. See Metzger, *Textual Commentary* 746.

^z The clause, καὶ ἐδόθη αὐτῷ ποιῆσαι πόλεμον μετὰ τῶν ἁγίων καὶ νικῆσαι αὐτούς (*kai edothē autō[i] poiēsai polemon meta tōn hagiōn kai nikēsai autous*, 'it was also allowed to make war on the saints, and vanquish them'), as in ℵ 046 051 1006, et al., is missing from some MSS (including 𝔓47 A C 025 Oecumenius[2053] syr[h] cop[sa] arm). This is doubtless the result of a transcriptional error, where the scribe has moved from the first occurrence of καὶ ἐδόθη αὐτῷ (*kai edothē autō[i]*, lit. 'and it was given to him') to the second, and omitted the intervening words. Some minuscules (1859 2020 2065 2432) introduce ἐξουσία (*exousia*, 'power') after αὐτῷ (*autō[i]*, lit. 'to him'), bringing it back from the following clause (q.v.); while other secondary witnesses (such as 1611[1854]) change the order of the words in the sentence.

^{aa} The reading, οὗ οὐ γέγραπται τὸ ὄνομα αὐτοῦ (*hou ou gegraptai to onoma autou*, 'whose name has not been written'), supported by C 1611[1854] Oecumenius[2053] Irenaeus[lat], et al., best accounts for its variants, and is doubtless original. Thus, copyists altered οὗ (*hou*, lit. 'of whom', singular) to ὧν (*hōn*, 'whose', plural), as a means of alleviating the incongruence of a singular number in the relative pronoun after the plural πάντες (*pantes*, lit. 'all'); so 𝔓47 ℵ 025 046, et al. Similarly, in 𝔓47 ℵ 025 051, et al., the singular noun τὸ ὄνομα (*to onoma*, lit. 'the name') becomes the plural τὰ ὀνόματα (*ta onomata*, 'the names'), with or without αὐτῶν (*autōn*, lit. 'their').

^{bb} The reading ἐν τῷ βιβλίῳ (*en tō[i] bibliō[i]*, 'in the book') is strongly attested by A C (omit τῷ, *tō[i]*, 'the') 2351 Andreas Byz, and is evidently superior. However, other MSS (𝔓47 ℵ 2084, et al.) witness to the noun-form ἡ βίβλος (*hē biblos*, 'the book'), instead of its strictly diminutive version, τὸ βιβλίον (*to biblion*, 'the [small] book'); and it is the case that, in the phrase 'book of life', John uses these two forms interchangeably (cf. 3.5; 20.15; and 17.8; 20.12; 21.27).

^{cc} The epigrammatic style of the saying in 13.10*a* 'has perplexed the scribes' (Metzger, *Textual Commentary* 747). The reading, εἰς αἰχμαλωσίαν, εἰς αἰχμαλωσίαν ὑπάγει (*eis aichmalōsian, eis aichmalōsian hypagei*, lit. 'into captivity, into captivity he shall go'), as in A vg, et al., accounts best for the variants. The omission of one of the two appearances of the phrase, εἰς αἰχμαλωσίαν (*eis aichmalōsian*, 'into captivity'), as in the witnesses 𝔓47 ℵ C 025 046 1006 1611 Oecumenius²⁰⁵³, et al., is the result of transcriptional error. The lack of a verb in the first clause encouraged scribes to improve the text, by adding either ἀπάγει (*apagei*, 'leads away'), so 616 1828 1854, et al., or συνάγει (*synagei*, 'gathers into'), so 2059 2081 TR; or by altering the construction to αἰχμαλωτίζει (*aichmalōtizei*, '[if any-one] takes captive'), as in 94 104 459 2019. The substitution of ἔχει (*echei*, lit. 'he has') for εἰς (*eis*, 'into'), in the second clause (051, et al.), is a meaningless scribal blunder.

^{dd} The 'least unsatisfactory' (Metzger, *Textual Commentary* 748), among the many vari-ant readings of this text, is ἀποκτανθῆναι, αὐτόν . . . (*apoktanthēnai, auton . . .* , lit. 'to be killed, he . . .'), as supported by A. This version balances the first line of verse 10, and suits the sense of Jer. 15.2, on which the whole saying is built. The variations are scribal attempts to modify an inherently difficult Greek construction. See further Charles 1, 355–57.

^{ee} Major witnesses (including ℵ A C 1006 1611 Oecumenius²⁰⁵³ 2351 Andreas Byz) have the neuter participle, ἀναβαῖνον (*anabainon*, 'emerging'). This is replaced in a few MSS (such as 𝔓47 792 and some hands of Andreas Byz) by the masculine equivalent, with the same meaning, ἀναβαίνων (*anabainōn*). The variant probably results from a tendency in Revelation to treat eschatological, symbolic figures (such as 'beast'), which are described by nouns in the neuter, as masculine beings (cf. 11.7); note the use of a masculine pro-noun, αὐτόν (*auton*, 'it', lit. 'him'), referring to the neuter θηρίον (*thērion*, 'beast'), at 13.8. Just possibly the variant reading, in the masculine, derives from a scribal confusion be-tween the similar letters -o (*-o*) and -ω (*-ō*), in the Greek. See also verse 14.

^{ff} Hippolytus omits ἐνώπιον αὐτοῦ (*enōpion autou*, 'on its behalf'); but this is an example of homoioteleuton, where the copyist has moved from the first occurrence in the sentence of ποιεῖ (*poiei*, 'makes') to the second, and left out the intervening words.

^{gg} The future indicative in the consecutive construction, ἵνα προσκυνήσουσιν (*hina proskynēsousin*, lit. 'that they will worship') is replaced in some versions (such as 051 2351 Andreas Byz Hippolytus) by the aorist subjunctive, ἵνα προσκυνήσωσι (*hina proskynēsōsi*, 'that they should worship'). However, in Revelation ἵνα (*hina*, 'that') is regularly used with the future indicative to express purpose (cf. 3.9; 6.4, 11; et al.); and when, as regu-larly, there are variants from the subjunctive, the future indicative appears to have the strongest MS support (so 8.3; 9.4; et al.). See Aune 720. Despite the translation, the direct use of the infinitive προσκυνεῖν (*proskynein*, 'to worship') is clearly secondary.

^{hh} In the phrase, ὃς ἔχει (*hos echei*, lit. 'who has'), the relative pronoun in the masculine singular is attested by 𝔓47 A C 025 046 051 1611¹⁸⁵⁴ Andreas Primasius it^{gig}. Some wit-nesses, including ℵ 2377 Byz, correct the masculine form of the pronoun to the neuter ὅ (*ho*, 'who'), to agree with the neuter τὸ θηρίον (*to thērion*, 'beast'). However, the masculine singular, modifying the neuter noun in the dative, τῷ θηρίῳ (*tō[i] thēriō[i]*,

'[in honour of] the beast'), is original, since the symbol of the beast is usually treated by John as a male being (see 13.11); although note the neuter relative pronouns, referring to the beast, at 13.2; 17.11.

ⁱⁱ The textual history of verse 15 is immensely complex; and only two variations have been selected for comment. See further Aune 720–21. The substitution in this instance (by A C 025★ ᵛⁱᵈ, et al.) of the meaningless dative feminine αὐτῇ (*autē[i]*, lit. 'to her') for the masculine αὐτῷ (*autō[i]*, 'to him'), present in 𝔓47 ℵ 025ᶜ 046 and all minuscules, is a primary scribal error. Cf. Swete 172.

ʲʲ In A 025 1006 2065, et al., the Greek stands in the order, ποιήσῃ ἵνα ὅσοι (*poiēsē[i] hina hosoi*, lit. 'he should cause that as many'). The inferior external witnesses 051 1 1854 2073 TR place the word ἵνα (*hina*, 'that') before ἀποκτανθῶσιν (*apoktanthōsin*, lit. 'they should be killed'); and this appears to be a scribal attempt to smooth over the awkward use, in close proximity, of the conjunctions ἵνα . . . ἐάν (μή) (*hina . . . ean [mē]*, 'that . . . unless'), followed by two verbs in the subjunctive. The inclusion of ἵνα (*hina*, 'that') is demanded by the syntax of the sentence in verse 15*b*; although the word is accidentally omitted by ℵ 0466 1611 1959, et al. It could be that the omission was brought about by the abrupt change of subject in this passage: from the image speaking, to its causing death.

ᵏᵏ 𝔓47 ℵ★ A C Andreas Hippolytus read ἵνα δῶσιν αὐτοῖς (*hina dōsin autois*, lit. 'that they should give', where the indefinite third person plural is equivalent to a passive, 'be given'); and this well-attested version is clearly original. It gave rise to several secondary variants, including (so Oecumenius²⁰⁵³ Hippolytus) the future indicative reading, ἵνα δώσει αὐτοῖς (*hina dōsei autois*, 'that he will give to them'), which attempts to specify more clearly the subject of the action.

ˡˡ The connective word καί (*kai*, 'and') is omitted by ℵ★ C 1611 syrᵖʰ·ʰ copˢᵃ·ᵇᵒ, et al.; but it is present in 𝔓47 ℵᶜ Aᵛⁱᵈ 025 046 051 1006 1854 vg arm eth, et al. The omission is a secondary modification, caused by copyists who construed the ἵνα μή (*hina mē*, lit. 'that not') clause in verse 17 as dependent on δῶσιν (*dōsin*, 'they should be given') in verse 16, thus rendering superfluous the conjunction at the start of verse 17. However, the subjunctive clause in verse 17 in fact depends on ποιεῖ (*poiei*, 'it compels'), at the beginning of verse 16, and is coordinate with the ἵνα δῶσιν (*hina dōsin*, 'that they should be given') clause in verse 16. Cf. Metzger, *Textual Commentary* 749.

ᵐᵐ The present subjunctive, δύνηται (*dynētai*, 'can', lit. 'should be able') is attested by 𝔓47 ℵ A C 2351 Aretas, et al.; and it is likely to be original because of its difficulty. The construction of ἵνα (*hina*, 'that') with the present subjunctive is very rare in classical Greek, and appears elsewhere in the New Testament with any certainty only at 1 John 5.20. Consequently, but oddly, 051 Andreas Byz correct to the present indicative, δύναται (*dynatai*, 'is able').

ⁿⁿ In place of ἑξήκοντα (*hexēkonta*, 'sixty'), which is strongly supported by 𝔓47 ℵ A 025 046 051 itᵍⁱᵍ vg syrᵖʰ·ʰ copˢᵃ·ᵇᵒ arm, et al., a few witnesses (Irenaeusᵐˢˢ Tyconiusᵖᵗ) have δέκα (*deka*, 'ten' = a total of 616, rather than 666). This is clearly a secondary emendation, which may have resulted from a change in the Greek characters, when used as numerals, from -ξ (-*x* = 60) to -ι (-*i* = 10). Cf. Metzger, *Textual Commentary* 750; Aune 722. See further below, on verse 18.

ᵒᵒ The anaphoric presence of the article, τό (*to*, 'the'), with ἀρνίον (*arnion*, 'Lamb'), is well-attested (ℵ C 046 1006 1611¹⁶¹¹ ²³²⁹ Oecumenius²⁰⁵³, et al.), and undoubtedly original. The term always appears in Revelation with an article, referring back to earlier usage; the exception is 5.6, where it appears for the first time. The omission of τό (*to*, 'the') by 𝔓47 051 1611¹⁸⁵⁴ Andreas TR therefore makes this reading difficult; but the MS evidence favours the inclusion of the article in the text.

ᵖᵖ The perfect participle, ἑστός (*hestos*, 'standing') has that form (nominative or accusative neuter singular) in ℵ A C 025 1611²³⁴⁴ 2019, et al.; and this reading is probably original. The nominative masculine singular, with the same meaning, ἑστώς (*hestōs*), as in 𝔓47 Oecumenius²⁰⁵³ Andreas, may represent a scribal attempt to make the grammar conform at this point to the masculine character of the Lamb (Christ) figure, despite the fact that the noun ἀρνίον (*arnion*, 'Lamb') is neuter. See also on 5.6.

�qq The original version of this sentence, as in all modern critical Greek texts, includes an article, ἡ (*hē*, 'the'), with φωνή (*phōnē*, 'resonance', lit. 'voice'); so ℵ A C 046 051 1611 2020 Byz, et al. A few witnesses (including 𝔓47 Oecumenius²⁰⁵³ and some MSS of Andreas) omit the article. But the anarthrous reading, which then results, wrongly assumes that the 'sound' in verse 2b differs from that (φωνήν, *phōnēn*, without an article) in verse 2a; whereas the anaphoric article here indicates correctly that this is a further description of the same sound.

ʳʳ The weight of external evidence is balanced between the inclusion of ὡς (*hōs*, 'as', 'like'), as in A C 1006 1841 2042 it⁶¹ vg syrᵖʰ, et al., and its omission (as by 𝔓47 ℵ 025 046 1611¹⁸⁵⁴ Oecumenius²⁰⁵³ itᵍⁱᵍ syrʰ copˢᵃ,ᵇᵒ arm eth, et al.). The word may have been introduced by copyists, influenced by its threefold use in verse 2, or dropped either accidentally or in imitation of 5.9, where the phrase, ᾄδουσιν ᾠδὴν καινήν (*a[i]dousin ō[i]dēn kainēn*, lit. 'they sing a new song') reappears without ὡς (*hōs*, 'as'). Following Metzger, *Textual Commentary* 750, the translation reflects the uncertainty of the text by placing brackets round 'as it were' (= ὡς, *hōs*, lit. 'as').

ˢˢ Instead of ὅπου ἂν ὑπάγῃ (*hopou an hypagē[i]*, 'wherever he would lead'), as read by ℵ Andreas Byz, some MSS (such as A C 1611²³²⁹ 2019) have ὅπου ἂν ὑπάγει (*hopou an hypagei*, 'wherever he leads'), with the verb in the indicative rather than the subjunctive. The use of the particle ἄν (*an*, '[where]ever'), with the present indicative, is unknown in the New Testament apart from this variant; and such a difficulty, together with the strong MS combination of A and C, could suggest that the indicative version is superior. On balance, however, the subjunctive mood seems more likely than a unique indicative to be the original form of the verb (cf. Aune 785).

ᵗᵗ Some MSS (including 𝔓47 ℵ 046 1006 1611²³²⁹ 2344 2351 it⁶¹ vgᵐˢˢ) introduce a connective γάρ (*gar*, 'for') at this point in verse 5. It is absent from A C 025 1611¹⁸⁵⁴ Oecumenius²⁰⁵³ itᵍⁱᵍ vg, et al. The conjunction is a natural addition on the part of copyists (note its presence in verse 4), whereas there is no obvious reason for its omission. The reading without γάρ (*gar*, 'for'), appropriate to the author's style, is therefore, despite the translation, undoubtedly original. The introduction of ὅτι (*hoti*, 'for', or 'because') before ἄμωμοι (*amōmoi*, 'blameless''), by 051 2056 2131 2254, is obviously secondary.

ᵘᵘ Some minuscules, including 424 617 1888, add after εἰσιν (*eisin*, 'are') the clause οὗτοί εἰσιν οἱ ἀκολουθοῦντες τῷ ἀρνιῳ (*houtoi eisin hoi akolouthountes tō[i] arniō[i]*, 'these are the ones following the Lamb''). But this is clearly a gloss, derived from verse 4 (Metzger, *Textual Commentary* 751).

ᵛᵛ The reading, ἄλλον ἄγγελον (*allon angelon*, 'another angel'), which is strongly supported by A C 1006 1611 Oecumenius²⁰⁵³ 2344 itᵍⁱᵍ,⁶¹ vg syrᵖʰ,ʰ copᵇᵒ arm Cyprian, et al., is likely to be original. Apart from the weight of the external evidence, it is a *lectio difficilior*, for no previous angel has been mentioned since 11.15. This fact no doubt caused the excision of ἄλλον (*allon*, 'another'); it is less probable that it was brought about by the similarity between the opening letters of the Greek words ἄλλον (*allon*, 'another') and ἄγγελον (*angelon*, 'angel').

ʷʷ The aorist infinitive active, εὐαγγελίσαι (*euangelisai*, 'to proclaim'), as read by most MSS, is original. The active form of the verb εὐαγγελίζειν (*euangelizein*, lit. 'to evangelize') occurs in the New Testament only here and at Rev. 10.7. The aorist infinitive middle form of the verb, in the variant εὐαγγελίσασθαι (*euangelisathsai*, 'to proclaim [for his own sake]'), as witnessed by 𝔓47 ℵ 1611¹⁸⁵⁴ ²³²⁹ 2019, et al., is inappropriate in the context, and manifestly secondary.

ˣˣ The reading, τοὺς καθημένους (*tous kathēmenous*, lit. 'those dwelling'), attested by 𝔓47 ℵ C 024 Byz, et al., is difficult, and likely to be original; for the verb κάθημαι (*kathēmai*, lit. 'to sit') is not used with this meaning elsewhere in the Apocalypse. As a result, A 051 cop^bo TR, et al., correct to the more usual form, with the same meaning, τοὺς κατοικοῦντας (*tous katoikountas*).

ʸʸ Some MSS (including A C 025 1006) omit τήν (*tēn*, 'the') before θάλασσαν (*thalassan*, 'sea'); whereas the article is present in 𝔓47 ℵ 051 2329 Byz, et al. The articular version is probably secondary; and this is strongly suggested by the parallel, anarthrous noun phrase, πεγὰς ὑδάτων (*pegas hydatōn*, 'water-springs'), which follows. The absence of the article constitutes a difficulty, since the use of θάλασσα (*thalassa*, 'sea') in Revelation is normally articular (so 5.13; 7.1–3; 8.8; 12.12; 16.3; 21.1; et al.; but see 4.6; 15.2); and this strengthens the case for the originality of the anarthrous form of the noun at this point.

ᶻᶻ The reading, ἄλλος ἄγγελος δεύτερος (*allos angelos deuteros*, lit. 'another angel, a second'), is supported by ℵᶜ (C has δεύτερον, *deuteron*, 'second', where the neuter is used adverbially) 025 051 1611 Oecumenius²⁰⁵³, et al., and also by the parallel sequence, ἄλλος ἄγγελος τρίτος (*allos angelos tritos*, 'another angel, a third'), in verse 9. The placing of an adjective, in addition to ἄλλος (*allos*, 'another'), after the noun is also consistent with the author's style in Revelation (cf. 6.4; 10.1; 15.1). This reading is likely to be original, and it best explains the form of the variants. Thus, the sequence is altered by A 046 Primasius, et al. (see Charles 2, 325) to ἄλλος δεύτερος ἄγγελος (*allos deuteros angelos*, 'another, second angel'); while 61 69 296 598 2039 it⁶¹ vg eth TR, et al., omit the seemingly tautological δεύτερος (*deuteros*, 'second').

ᵃᵃᵃ The relative pronoun, ἥ (*hē*, '[she] who'), is attested by A C 1006 1611²³⁴⁴ Oecumenius²⁰⁵³, et al.; but it is omitted in 𝔓47 ℵ¹ 051 Andreas Byz it^gig. The latter version is clearly secondary. The presence of the pronoun has strong MS support; while the immediately preceding word, μεγάλη (*megalē*, 'great'), may well have caused the omission of ἥ (*hē*, 'who') by an error of haplography. See Aune 786.

ᵇᵇᵇ The reading, πεπότικε(ν) (*pepotike[n]*, lit. 'she caused to drink', using the third person singular of the perfect indicative active), is firmly attested by A C 025 1611²³²⁹ Oecumenius²⁰⁵³ MSS of Andreas Byz, and it is suited to the sense of the passage. It is therefore likely to be original. This probability is supported by the LXX of Jer. 28.7 (MT 51.7), including the verb ἐπίοσαν (*epiosan*, 'they drank', an aorist indicative from πίνω [*pinō*, 'drink']), which lies behind the Greek of Rev. 14.8; 18.3 (q.v.). The variants, using forms of the verb πίπτω (*piptō*, 'fall'), such as πέπτωκαν, *peptōkan*, 'they fell' (ℵ² Primasius), and πέπτωκεν, *peptōken*, lit. 'he fell' (1611¹⁸⁵⁴ Beatus), are later substitutions, possibly influenced by the double ἔπεσεν ἔπεσεν (*epesen epesen*, 'fallen, fallen') at the start of verse 8.

ccc The third person singular future indicative passive, βασανισθήσεται (*basanisthēsetai*, lit. 'he will be tormented') appears in the witnesses C ℵ Oecumenius[2053] Andreas Byz arm it[gig] Primasius Beatus, et al. (cf. Charles 2, 326). The third person plural future indicative passive of the same verb, βασανισθήσονται (*basanisthēsontai*, 'they will be tormented'), is read by A 1006 2019 vg cop, et al. In the Greek of verses 10 and 11 there is a change of subject, from the singular into the plural. In A, et al., this movement occurs earlier; and this variant could therefore be original. But the superior external evidence, supporting the singular form, points to its originality.

ddd Some MSS (including ℵ 1006[1006 1841] 1611 2019) replace the nominative masculine participle, οἱ τηροῦντες (*hoi tērountes*, lit. 'those keeping'), with the genitive plural, τῶν τήρουντων (*tōn tērountōn*, lit. 'of those keeping'). The nominative form is a *lectio difficilior*, since it is used in apposition to the genitive plural, τῶν ἁγίων (*tōn hagiōn*, 'of the saints'); and it is therefore doubtless original. The variant, in the genitive, is clearly a grammatical correction.

eee The shorter form, λέγει (*legei*, lit. 'says'), as read by 𝔓47 ℵ* 336 1918 cop[bo] eth, et al., could be regarded as the earliest, and ναί, λέγει (*nai, legei*, lit. 'yes, says'; so ℵ[c] A C 025 051 1006 1611 vg syr[ph,h] cop[sa] arm, et al.) as a scribal expansion. But the version with ναί (*nai*, 'indeed') is strongly supported, and in John's style (cf. Rev. 1.7; 16.7; 22.20); and it is therefore probably original. The readings λέγει ναί, *legei nai*, 'says indeed' (046, et al.), καὶ λέγει, *kai legei*, 'and says' (205 2019 2053) and λέγει καί, *legei kai*, 'says also' (218 522) are obviously secondary. See Metzger, *Textual Commentary* 752.

fff The original form of the verb is the future indicative passive (ἵνα [𝔓47 ὅτι]) ἀναπαήσονται (*hina [hoti] anapaēsontai*, lit. '[that] they will rest'), as in A ℵ. The variants are corrections. Thus, 051[c] Oecumenius[2053] Byz, influenced by the presence of ἵνα (*hina*, 'that'), change the verb to the aorist subjunctive middle, ἀναπαύσωνται (*anapausōntai*, 'they may take rest'); while C 046 1611[2329] 2019 2084 792 MSS of Andreas Byz have the future indicative middle, ἀναπαύσονται (*anapausontai*, 'they will take rest').

ggg The reading, υἱόν (*huion*, 'son', accusative), as in A ℵ 046 1611[2329] Byz Beatus, et al., is difficult, since ὅμοιος (*homoios*, 'like') is normally followed by the dative (so 1.15; 4.3; 9.7; et al; but note 1.13). The variant with the dative, υἱῷ (*huiō[i]*, 'son'), which appears in 𝔓47 C 051 1006 1611 Oecumenius[2053] Andreas lat syr, is well-supported; but it evidently represents an attempt to correct a solecism.

hhh The nominative masculine singular present participle, ἔχων (*echōn*, 'having'), as in A 025 046 MSS of Andreas, is difficult, since it modifies the antecedent noun phrase, in the *accusative*, υἱὸν ἀνθρώπου (*huion anthrōpou*, 'son of man'), and should therefore be ἔχοντα (*echonta*, 'having'). Accordingly, the version ἔχων (*echōn*, 'having') is likely to be original (cf. Rev. 1.13, 16), while the variant in the accusative (as in 𝔓47 ℵ* 1006 MSS of Andreas Byz, et al.) may be regarded as a correction. The neuter form, ἔχον (*echon*), with the same meaning, as in ℵ[a] C, et al., probably occurred because of the phonetic similarity between the neuter and masculine forms of the participle.

iii The genitival phrase, ἐπὶ τῆς νεφέλης (*epi tēs nephelēs*, 'on the cloud'), is attested by ℵ A 1611, et al. However, the accusative form, τὴν νεφέλην (*tēn nephelēn*, 'the cloud'), as in C 051 1006[1006 1841] 1611[1854] Oecumenius[2053] Andreas, et al., could well be original. According to the author's grammatical usage, the case following ἐπί (*epi*, 'on') after ὁ καθήμενος (*ho kathēmenos*, 'the one seated'), in the nominative or accusative, is usually (but not always) accusative; whereas, if that participial phrase should occur in the genitive or dative, the case following ἐπί (*epi*, 'on') is normally genitive or dative. Cf. 6.2.; 19.11; against 7.10; 19.4; et al. So Aune 790.

ⁱⁱⁱ The definite article, in the genitive, τοῦ (*tou*, lit. 'of the'), used here relatively, is in 𝔓47 eth replaced by αὐτοῦ (*autou*, 'his'); but this is clearly a transcriptional error.

^{kkk} The MS evidence for the omission or inclusion of the verb, ἐξῆλθεν (*exēlthen*, lit. 'came out'), is evenly balanced. It may be that the word was inserted by scribes, because of its appearance in verse 17, sometimes after ἄγγελος (*angelos*, 'angel'), as in ℵ C 025 046 it^h syr^{ph,h} cop^{sa,bo} arm, et al., and in other MSS (051 1854 2073) after θυσιαστηρίου (*thysiastēriou*, lit. 'altar'). However, repetition is characteristic of John's style (as in 1.14; 3.3; 10.6; 17.14; 18.17; 19.18; 20.12; cf. Beckwith 241–42); and this may point to the originality of the verb's second appearance shortly after its first. In that case, the absence of the verb in verse 18, according to 𝔓47 A 1611 Oecumenius²⁰⁵³, et al., may be the result of accidental omission, or of excision by scribes who regarded its presence as unnecessary, after its use in verse 17. Nevertheless, the syntax and meaning of verse 18 seem to demand the inclusion of a verb at this point; and the originality of ἐξῆλθεν (*exēlthen*, 'moved from'), as part of the text, is therefore supported in the translation.

^{lll} 𝔓47 ℵ 1611, et al., have ἐπί (*epi*, 'over', lit. 'on'), instead of εἰς (*eis*, 'to[ward]'). But this evidently secondary alteration may have been influenced by the consistent use of the preposition ἐπί (*epi*, 'on') earlier in Chapter 14 (see verses 1, 6 [thrice], 9 [*bis*], 16 [*bis*]); and note the phrase ἐπὶ τὴν γῆν (*epi tēn gēn*, 'over the earth') in verse 16.

^{mmm} Instead of τὸν μέγαν (*ton megan*, 'the vast', lit. 'great'), a form which is supported firmly by C 025 046 051 Andreas Primasius, et al., some MSS (including ℵ 1006 1854 Oecumenius²⁰⁵³ TR, et al.) read the feminine τὴν μεγάλην (*tēn megalēn*, 'the great'), to agree with τὴν ληνόν (*tēn lēnon*, 'the winepress'). This is doubtless a scribal correction; for if the feminine form were original it would be difficult to account for the occurrence of a solecism in its place. A few witnesses (such as 𝔓47 1611 2019) have τοῦ μεγάλου (*tou megalou*, 'the great', genitive), which must be a copyist's erroneous assimilation to the proximate genitive, τοῦ θεοῦ (*tou theou*, 'of God'); cf. 19.15. Other MSS (181 424 468, et al.) omit the adjective completely.

ⁿⁿⁿ The numeral, χιλίων ἑξακοσίων (*chiliōn hexakosiōn*, '1,600 [stadia]') is strongly supported by ℵ^c A C 025 046 Andreas, et al. Some inferior witnesses (including 1876 2014 2082 MSS of Andreas) read χιλίων ἑξακοσίων ἕξ (*chiliōn hexakosiōn hex*, '1,606'); while others have χιλίων διακοσίων (*chiliōn diakosiōn*, '1,200'). Metzger, *Textual Commentary* 753, suggests that the last figure, '1,200 (stadia)', arose because that number 'lends itself better to symbolic interpretation'.

Literary Setting

Chapters 12—15 of the Apocalypse mark a major division within the drama and the beginning of its second Act (see the analysis above, 21–22, 287–88). Scene 4 (Rev. 12—14), and its subsequent interval (15), together make up the contents of the third woe (see on 11.14). The stage is thus set for the final conflict between good and evil; and this is described in eschatological, rather than temporal, terms. In Rev. 12—15 the audience is introduced to the actors who play the major roles in that confrontation (Mounce 229), including the woman, her child, Michael and their opponents. The activity of these characters helps to outline and explain the troubles which may beset God's people at any moment in the history of salvation, and provides an assurance that ultimately the messianic community will prevail over the forces of evil (cf. Wall 158).

The broad literary structure of Rev. 12—14 consists of three sub-divisions (12.1–18; 13.1–18; 14.1–20), which are placed between the episodes of the seventh trumpet (11.15–19) and the seven bowls (15.1—16.21). The visions contained within this scene form a roughly continuous narrative of eschatological events (Aune 660), often cast in mythological form. These range from the birth of the male child, with consequent battles in heaven and on earth, to the divine judgements on human injustice which are mediated by God's angels. Rev. 12.18, like 11.19, is pivotal, since it connects with the material which both precedes and follows the verse itself.

The disclosures in Rev. 12—14(15) have been arranged by commentators in various ways, often organized around the number seven. For example, Kiddle (211–18) finds in these chapters seven oracles, which depict a story of supernatural conflict between the forces of light and darkness, good and evil (ibid. 215); cf. similarly Rist 452–77 (two sequences of seven visions). Beale (621–22) is not alone in taking seriously the vision formulas in this scene ('I saw', 'and behold'), which then provide a sevenfold structure to its material; see also Wilcock 114–15 (the divisions begin at 13.1, 11; 14.1, 6, 14; 15.1, 2); Thompson 131.

It is the case that the contents of Rev. 12—14, which are our immediate concern, constitute one vision, which is extended to the interval in Chapter 15 and beyond. It is proposed here that Scene 4 sets before us, within that vision, seven *signs of the end*. They are arranged as follows:

1 The woman (12.1–2)
2 The huge dragon (12.3–6)
3 War in heaven (12.7–9)
    A song of praise in heaven (12.10–12)
4 War on earth (12.13–18)
5 The beast from the sea (13.1–10)
6 The beast from the earth (13.11–18)
    A vision of the redeemed (14.1–5)
7 Angelic judgement (14.6–20).

Four points may be made in connection with this suggested scheme.

(a) The sevenfold literary pattern in Chapters 12—14 is not as clear as it is in the sequences so far presented in Revelation: the seven oracles, seven seals and seven trumpets (for the significance of the pervasive number seven in Johannine literature see on 1.4). Nevertheless, the action in this scene evidently divides into seven episodes, all of which are drawn together by the theme of an eschatological combat between the powers of God and of the Satan. The sound of conflict is offset by the sound of heavenly voices in two interludes: the song of the faithful in 12.10–12, and the hymn which is heard by the redeemed on Mount Zion in 14.1–5.

(b) The sequence of seven signs in Scene 4 is marked by the first use in Revelation of the term σημεῖον (*sēmeion*, 'sign', or 'portent'). The first sign as such is mentioned in 12.1, and the second (ἄλλο σημεῖον, *allo sēmeion*, lit. 'another sign') in 12.3; after this the order is not specified. Note a similar pattern in John's Gospel, where the first two alone of the seven signs of Jesus are numbered ('first', 2.11; 'second', 4.54). The remaining five portents in the Apocalypse are each introduced by καί (*kai*, 'and'), as in 12.7, 13, or καὶ εἶδον (*kai eidon*, 'then I saw'), as in 13.1, 11; 14.6. The conjunction καί (*kai*, 'and') frequently occurs in Rev. 12—14. As with the repeated adverb εὐθύς (*euthys*, 'immediately') in Mark (1.12, 18, 20, et al.), the use of καί (*kai*, 'and') in these chapters helps to move the composition forward by increasing the pace of the action; it also acts as a connective literary feature in the unveiling of the seven signs. For 'signs' in the Apocalypse see further on 12.1.

(c) We have already noticed in Revelation the dramatic technique which the author uses to present the heptads of seals and trumpets. In both cases, the seventh part of the action is carried through the interval into the next scene; and this helps to control and tighten the overall structure of the Apocalypse in these scenes. (See Smalley, *Thunder and Love* 106; Beale 622, whose literary structuring differs somewhat.) Such an interlocking process is also visible in the present sequence of seven signs, where the appearance of 'another sign' (ἄλλο σημεῖον, *allo sēmeion*) picks up the judgemental portents of Rev. 12—14, and moves into the heptad of plagues poured out from the seven bowls (see 15.1; 15.5—16.21; 17.1).

(d) The location of this scene moves between heaven and earth, and the action brings them together. In this way, John's typical theology is reflected in the structure of his composition at this point. The presentation of the seven signs clearly begins in heaven, with the portent of the woman (12.1), and ends on earth with the anticipated and symbolic judgement on Babylon (14.6–7; and note 14.8). But the woman soon flees to the wilderness (12.6), and the discrimination of the final sign is mediated by angelic messengers, the first of which flies in midheaven (14.6). This conjoining of the material and the spiritual characterizes the five intervening signs; it also belongs to the two interludes of 12.10–12 and 14.1–5, which are situated respectively in heaven and earth, but connect with both dimensions. See further the comments below.

Comment

Sign 1: The Woman (12.1–2)

The Sources beneath Revelation 12

The source-analysis of the material in Rev. 12 has been extensive, as it has been complex. For a detailed history of the background to this chapter, and its interpretation, see Prigent, *Apocalypse 12*. Between them, commentators discover a multiplicity of sources which have been used in this section; and these include both pagan and Jewish traditions. Thus (e.g.) Charles (1, 298–314) detects two major derivations, from Judaism and what he calls primitive, 'international' mythology (ibid., 310–13); and Roloff (142–45) finds mythological ideas stemming from Egyptian and Greek, as well as Jewish and Ugaritic, sagas and personalities. See the survey in Aune 667–74; also Mounce 230 n. 4; and Prigent 366–74, esp. 368–73, who refers to a possible cult of Artemis on Patmos (369–70).

It is evident that various forms of a combat myth, harvested from a variety of sources, find an echo in Rev. 12. Nearest to John, as we might expect, are probably Jewish, rather than pagan, ideas, including those from Hellenistic Judaism and Qumran (see on 12.1). In the Old Testament, note the heavenly battle motif in Isa. 14.12–15; Ezek. 28.11–19 (cf. Roloff 143). But these traditions have been creatively adapted by the author of the Apocalypse, in order to describe vividly and dramatically the situation at the end and in the end-time, when satanic power gives place to the sovereign rule of God in Christ (12.9–10), and the Church shares in the victory of faith (12.11).

The audience of this apocalyptic drama, then, is intended to understand the situation in the present scene with imagination, rather than analytical precision (Boring 149). For in Chapter 12, more clearly than anywhere else in Revelation, John has glimpsed the future by depicting it directly in the language of myth. This literary and theological form seeks to provide a narrative portrayal of primordial activity between gods, heroes and demonic powers, and to express in terms of story the origins and essence of the world, and the place of human beings in it (cf. famously Gen. 1—3). Cf. Roloff 142; also Bruce, 'Myth'.

12.1 The great sign of the woman robed with the sun, in this scene, does not include the typical narrative introduction which belongs to other visions in Revelation, normally using the formula 'I saw' or 'I heard' (cf. 1.10; 4.1; 6.1; 7.1; 8.2; 10.1). This leads Prigent (366) to conclude that the new disclosure in 12.1–2 continues the visionary situation of Chapter 11; and he points out (ibid.) that the holy city and the two witnesses of Rev. 11, and the woman of Chapter 12, are all and at the same time persecuted and preserved. In line with this thinking, Aune (660–64) regards 11.19 as the introduction to 12.1–17, as well as the conclusion to 11.15–18; and his literary analysis, unlike mine (see above, 255–56), places 11.19 with the material in Rev. 12 (see esp. Aune 661–62).

It is true that 11.19 is a pivotal verse in this section of the Apocalypse, and that there are theological and literary connections between Rev. 10—11 and 12—14; so that, for example, the contents of the 'third woe' mentioned in Chapter 11 are described in 12.1—15.8 (see on 11.14). However, the language of vision is still present in 12.1 (see below; note also 'I heard' in verse 10); and this text evidently introduces a new situation and scene. As consistently in Revelation, the prophet-seer brings the audience of his drama to the brink of final judgement and salvation (11.19), only to view the end once more from a different perspective (see 6.17; 8.1; 11.14; et al.). Such is the subject of Scene 4 and its interval (12—15); and a fresh start is marked by the novel use of mythic images (see above).

The term σημεῖον (*sēmeion*, 'sign') is used in the LXX to translate the Hebrew אוֹת (*'ôt*); and in the Old Testament it can mean a mark (e.g. Gen. 4.15), a monument (Deut. 6.8) or an omen (2 Kings 19.29). In the New Testament the word is used with reference to a celestial portent which carries a warning for the future (Luke 21.11; cf. Mark 8.11 par. Matt. 16.1; see also Gen. 1.14; *Sib. Or.* 3.796–808); and it can be the description of a miracle which is either false (Mark 13.22 par.; 2 Thess. 2.9–10; cf. *Did.* 16.6), or genuine (Mark 16.20, in the longer ending; 1 Cor. 14.22; cf. Ps. 78.43).

The term σημεῖον (*sēmeion*, 'sign') in Revelation carries the latter sense, of a miracle which is either genuine or false. This noun appears seven times in the Apocalypse; although the idea extends throughout this scene (see above). The word itself is used by John in the singular on three occasions (Rev. 12.1, 3; 15.1), two of which refer to an ultimately propitious omen (12.1; 15.1); while the plural form occurs in four contexts (13.13–14; 16.14; 19.20), each of which describes a false miracle performed by a member of God's opposition. The meaning of the signs in Revelation is close to the significance of the signs in the Fourth Gospel (2.11, onwards), where the miracles of Jesus point beyond themselves to reveal him as the Son through whom God acts in a decisively salvific way. See Prigent 376–77; also Smalley, *John* 129–32, 234–38. There is, however, a fundamental difference in the function of John's eschatological signs in Revelation. They are not performed by Jesus, and at times they are diabolical counterparts of his ministry, even if, as in the Gospel, they provide a constant call to obedient consecration (Prigent 377). Cf. Rev. 13.4, 14; et al.

In John's Gospel the seven signs express what is symbolized, and draw attention to the life which is finally and fully available to the believer since the tabernacling and exaltation of the Word. Similarly, in the present text of Revelation (12.1), as in 15.1, the visions of the woman robed with the sun, and of the angels bearing bowls of a judgement which leads to salvation, do not merely symbolize the activity of the Father through his messianic Son. The salvific purposes of God have actually been fulfilled, on earth as in heaven; so that the divinely sealed faithful can in time, through the life and death and resurrection of Christ, share the blessings of eternity. Equally, the sign of 12.3–6 (the huge dragon) marks the accomplishment of the Church's victory through Jesus over the powers of the Satan; and this theme is projected throughout the present scene.

The 'great sign', in this context, 'appeared in heaven'. The unusual language of vision here, ὤφθη (ōphthē, lit. 'was seen', aorist passive), is used otherwise in Revelation only at 19.11 and 12.3; Aune (679) accordingly sees this as a further literary indication that 11.19 and 12.1–17 belong together (but see above). This form of the verb 'to see' (ὁράω, horaō) is used in the LXX to introduce theophanies (as in Exod. 16.10; Jer. 38.3; et al.; cf. Acts 7.2), angelophanies (Judg. 13.3; Tobit 12.22) and prophetic visions (Dan. 8.1 Theod.). The term οὐρανός (ouranos, 'heaven'), in verse 1, is also used in verse 4 to describe the place from which the dragon's tail swept away a third of the stars; and there the word has the cosmic sense of 'sky', as in the translation. On this basis, Mounce (231 n. 1) argues that the episode in 12.1–2 is also set in the 'sky', rather than in heaven as the place of God's dwelling (similarly Beckwith 621). But clearly, as in 11.19 (q.v.), the sign in verse 1 is located in the spiritual territory of 'heaven', rather than earth; and the events which flow from it in the remaining signs of Chapter 12 are concerned precisely with the conflict between the sovereignty of God, in that realm, and the powers of his opponents in every part of the universe.

The content of the first 'great' (μέγα, mega) sign is now explained as being 'a woman'. The portent is 'great', in the sense that it is eschatologically of major importance. In verse 3 the same adjective is used to describe the 'huge' dragon; but there the word refers to the demon's power (cf. Milligan 201), as well as possibly to his figurative size. This is the first time in the visions of the Apocalypse that an individual woman has appeared; and, like the 'bride' of the new Jerusalem (21.2), she stands in marked contrast to the unfaithful characters of 'Jezebel' (Rev. 2.20–23) and the 'scarlet woman' (17.1–18). However, as Duff (Who Rides the Beast? 85–87) points out, there is also a paradoxically close correspondence in the opposition of the scarlet woman of Rev. 17 to the unnamed woman of Chapter 12. For example, both are matriarchal figures who are sustained in the desert, surrounded by death; both are splendidly attired and associated with a destructive beast who possesses seven heads and ten horns; and in both scenes reference is made to Christian testimony. For the women of Revelation see Duff, Who Rides the Beast? 83–96.

Neither the 'woman' (γυνή, gynē) of verse 1 nor the 'child' (τὸ τέκνον, to teknon) of verse 4 is named, unlike the carefully styled 'dragon' (verse 9); and this is an immediate indication that the woman and her offspring are to be interpreted in symbolic and collective, rather than historical and individual, terms. The background to some of the ideas in Rev. 12 is to be found in Gen. 3.15–16, a text which records a struggle between the serpent and the woman and her offspring; note also the saga of the embattled but fertile Hagar in Gen. 16.1–15. Mythic sea-serpent imagery, present in biblical poetry as the activity of Leviathan or Rahab, may also have informed the composition of this scene (cf. Job 26.12–13; Ps. 74.14; Isa. 27.1; et al.). See Brown, Introduction 790–91.

The woman is radiant: reflecting the sun, the moon and the stars. Her identity has been variously interpreted (see Aune 680–81). In view of the corporate nature of her person, to which attention has already been drawn, it is highly unlikely that this figure should be understood as Mary, the mother of Jesus; although this equation, which has been a part of Marian theology since the medieval period, is still being made (Farrer 141–43; cautiously, Allo 158; Boxall 68–69). We are on more secure ground if we take proper account of the Old Testament representation of the ideal Zion as the mother of God's people, as in Isa. 54.1–3; 66.7–9; 4 Ezra 10.7; cf. Gal. 4.26–27 (Jerusalem is the mother of the Church); Eph. 5.31–32 (the Church as the bride of Christ); 2 John 1, 5 (the Christian community as an 'elect lady'); also Hermas, Vis. 2.4; 4.2 (the Church as an aged lady and a virgin bride). This explains the female imagery in this passage, as well as the collective character of the woman herself; and both are reinforced by the personification of Babylon and the new Jerusalem, later in the drama (Rev. 17—18; 21.2), as women. The woman of 12.1 is therefore best seen as the heavenly counterpart of the true Israel, the community from which the Messiah descends (see also verses 2–5); and for John (as in Rev. 7.1–17; 11.19; 15.5; 21.12–14) this body embraces both the Jewish and Christian Church (not simply, according to Swete [147], the adherents of Judaism). See further Smalley, 'John's Revelation' 555–56; *idem, Thunder and Love* 78. For this section see Beckwith 621–22; Ladd 166–69; Knight 91–92, esp. 91.

It is unlikely that the sign in Isa. 7.14 lies behind the thought of Rev. 12.1, particularly as that Hebrew text, referring to a 'young woman' in the MT, was used as a testimonium in early Christian thought to support the fulfilment of Old Testament prophecy in the virgin birth of Jesus to Mary (Matt. 1.23); and we have seen that the earthly mother of Jesus is not in view here. In the Isaianic context, the reference to a woman 'bearing a son', albeit supernaturally, marks for Ahaz no more than the limits to an immediate period of time, during which the Lord will act (cf. Filson, *Matthew* 55).

The depiction of the crowned 'woman' in verse 1, in association with sun, moon and stars, has a more direct, collective precedent in the literature of Judaism. In Gen. 37.9, for example (cf. *T. Naph.* 5.1–5), the sun, moon and eleven stars in Joseph's dream represent Jacob, his wife and the eleven tribes of Israel submitting to Joseph himself, who stands for the twelfth tribe. Similarly, in *T. Abr. (B)* 7.4–16 Abraham, Sarah and their house are depicted as sun, moon and stars; and in his dream Isaac is crowned (ibid. 7.5). Cf. also Song of Sol. 6.4–10, where Jerusalem is associated with Solomon's Queen, who was 'fair as the moon, bright as the sun'; and Isa. 60.19–20, where the restored Israel is portrayed as a radiant mother-figure (verses 4–5), whose relationship with the Lord includes a 'light' which eclipses that of the sun and the moon (note the close parallel in Rev. 21.23). In this passage, however, the stars are not mentioned. See further Ignatius, *Eph.* 19.1–2, for the combination of sun, moon and stars; although in that passage the subject is the Virgin Mary.

The metaphorical language in verse 1, of the woman surrounded by sun, moon and stars, is somewhat allusive in its precise significance. Being invested with the sun suggests the light of God in which the messianic, covenant community dwells, both in time and in eternity (cf. 3.4–5; 6.11; 7.13–14; 21.23–24; 22.5; also 1 John 1.5–7). That the woman uses the moon as a footstool is indicative of the victory of the faithful, who now belong to the Church of the risen Christ, over the powers of evil. The twelve stars may be equated with the names of the twelve apostles, written on the walls of the holy city (21.14; cf. Mounce 232 n. 5); but, more probably, they represent the twelve tribes of Israel, the names of which are written on the gates of the new Jerusalem (21.12). It is from the old Israel, after all, that the new is descended (7.4–8). *Targ. Neof. I* Gen. 50.19–21 refers to God's people, Israel, as being ultimately destructible, just as the stars are immune from destruction.

The stars also connect with the 'seven stars' of 1.16, 20, and so with the seven churches of the Johannine circle. For the stars are the 'angels' of the churches (1.20), and therefore symbolize the heavenly counterparts of the Asian communities; and in this way the author of the Apocalypse reminds his audience that the life of God's people involves a commitment to Jesus which is to be expressed in time, as well as in eternity. (See further on 1.20.) The significance of the crown on the woman's head may be determined from Revelation itself, where 'crowns' speak of the saints sharing in the kingship of Christ, and of his followers being rewarded for their faithfulness; see 2.10; 3.11; 4.4, 10; 14.14.

Two further points may be made about the overall picture of the radiant, crowned figure in 12.1. First, her appearance may suggest the priestly character of the messianic community (as in 1.6; 5.10). Both Philo (*De Vit. Mos.* 2.111–12, 122–24; *De Spec. Leg.* 1.84–97) and Josephus (*Ant.* 3.162–72, 179–87) use the imagery of the sun, the moon, a crown and the stars to explain the description in Exod. 28 and 39 of the vestments worn by Jewish high priests; and those priests represented the twelve tribes of Israel in the temple service of the Lord. Second, the woman's brightness reflects the warmth and purity of a (sun)light which is divine in character, and belongs to both God and the Lamb (1.16; 10.1; 21.23; 22.5). Her radiance accordingly denotes the heavenly identity and protection of the new Israel, as well as its purity; and these safeguard the Church's ultimate triumph over erroneous belief, compromise, falsehood and unjust opposition (cf. Wis. 7.24–30). For this interpretation, and for this whole section, see Beale 626–27; also further Barker, *The Revelation* 200–11. Prigent (377) notes the paschal typology associated with both the woman and the dragon-figure of Rev. 12, since the Exodus motif is strong in this chapter (see esp. on 12.6, 14; cf. also 15.3–4). McGuckin, 'Orthodox Eschatology' 118–19, claims that extended paschal typology belongs to the 'theodrama' of Revelation as a whole; see also Shepherd, *Paschal Liturgy*, esp. 77–84.

2   In the exegesis of verse 1, above, the image of the radiant woman has been interpreted corporately, as the community of faith from which the Messiah comes; and this symbol therefore refers to the life and witness of the Church in the age of the old Israel, as well as the new. In verse 2 the woman is further described as a 'pregnant' (ἐν γαστρί ἔχουσα, *en gastri echousa*, lit. 'having in the womb') mother, who is suffering the pain of imminent childbirth. The collective understanding of this figure is further suggested by the fact that the metaphor of Israel as a pregnant mother, in agony because she is about to give birth, is prominent in the Old Testament. See Isa. 26.17–18 (where the language of the text in the LXX is very close to the Greek of Rev. 12.2); 51.2; 66.7–9 (also Isa. 54.1–3; 61.9–10; 65.9); Jer. 4.31; Mic. 4.10; cf. 1QH 3 (11).7–12. *Midr. Rab.* Gen. 85.1 and *Midr. Rab.* Lev. 14.9 relate Isa. 66.7 to the messianic offspring (Beale 632). The birth pangs in all these passages denote the rebirth of Israel, the deliverance of God's people from immediate oppression, and the joy of salvation which they will eventually share; and all these themes are transposed and present in the dramatic action of Rev. 12. The agony and struggle in heaven, caused by the birth and kingly rule of the Messiah, will have consequences for the believing community, and its experience of suffering and victory, on earth (see Ladd 167); for the offspring of the 'woman' include the followers of Jesus, and not simply the Messiah himself (see 12.10–17). Cf. the notion of joy after the pain of childbirth, applied to the reaction of the disciples to the death and resurrection of Jesus, in John 16.19–22.

The corporate figure of the woman in verse 1, then, becomes in verse 2 the true Israel in a 'pre-messianic agony of expectancy' (Kiddle 220). She is not simply in labour, but also enduring the acute 'pain of childbirth' (cf. Gen. 3.14–16). The verb βασανιζομένη (*basanizomenē*, lit. 'is tormented') is a present participle; and it is one of several verbs in this section which are cast in the historic present, as a literary and dramatic means of giving immediacy and pace to the action. In this context, the word carries the particular sense of being persecuted and suffering punishment, so that the woman's birth pangs represent the torment endured by the covenant community in the period leading up to the advent of Christ (Beale 629). See the use of this verb similarly in Mark 5.7 par.; 2 Pet. 2.8; et al. In Revelation the term is applied to the pain inflicted by powers which are demonic (9.5) or divine (11.10; 14.10; 20.10); cf. 4 Macc. 8.1–14; et al. Since Jesus is the head of the new Israel, he shares through his death in the suffering brought on the people of God in the Old Testament (Rev. 5.9–10).

Sign 2: The Huge Dragon (12.3–6)

3   The second heavenly manifestation, possibly in the form of a constellation (Aune 682), appears as a huge dragon. In this verse, as in verse 1, οὐρανός (*ouranos*, 'heaven') is the dwelling-place of God; but it also signifies here the cosmic territory in which powers of evil can operate (see verse 4*a*). For the visionary language of σημεῖον (*sēmeion*, 'sign') and ὤφθη (*ōphthē*, 'became visible', lit. 'was seen') see on verse 1. The battle between Michael and the dragon in 12.7–9 takes place between the activity of the dragon in relation to the woman which is described in verses 4–6, and again in 13–17; so that Chapter 12 as a whole broadly contains the literary pattern of an inclusion.

The background to the dragon imagery in this scene is often attributed to ancient Near Eastern mythology; so e.g. Rist 453–54; Collins, *Combat Myth* 57–100; cf. also the surveys in Beasley-Murray 191–97; Bauckham, *Climax of Prophecy* 185–98. It could be that John is tapping pagan, international sources for his mythical ideas, particularly because these would be familiar to the Hellenistic members of his audience. But essentially the author of the Apocalypse is writing as a Christian, who is deeply indebted to the literary and theological world of Judaism; and any non-biblical characterization in his drama, such as the seven-headed monster Tiamat, in the Babylonian myth of creation, would have been coloured accordingly. See further the introduction to verse 1, above.

In line with this argument, the figure of the 'dragon' (δράκων, *drakōn*) lies close to hand in the Old Testament, as a regular symbol for the powers of evil which oppress the people of God. The dragon is, for example, a synonym for the evil sea monster (also known as Leviathan), representing Egypt and its Pharaoh, who is defeated at the time of the Exodus (cf. Ps. 74.13–14; Ezek. 29.3; 32.2–3; Hab. 3.8–15). See also Ps. 87.4; 89.10, where 'Rahab', the female monster of chaos, is another name for Egypt; at Jer. 51.34 (cf. Amos 9.3) Babylon is the subject. Elsewhere in the Old Testament God is depicted as victorious over the dragon, who stands for apostate Egypt and its supporting forces of evil, both at the beginning of history (Job 26.12–13 LXX; 41.1–34; cf. 7.12; 9.13; 40.18 [the powerful beast Behemoth]) and at its end (Isa. 27.1). *Pss. Sol.* 2.25–26 identifies the dragon, in the arrogant person of the vanquished commander Pompey, 'pierced on the mountains of Egypt', with Rome.

Egypt and Rome are also part of the meaning of the dragon imagery in Rev. 12. The dragon is 'huge' (μέγας, *megas*, lit. 'great'); see on this adjective in verse 1, and note also verse 9. It is probably true that mythical monsters are perceived in the collective unconscious as physically vast, thus enhancing their evil character. But a more important allusion here is to the dragon's power, which is great as it is evil. Even more significant is the allusion to the Exodus narrative, which is in view throughout this scene; for in Ezek. 29.3, and only there in the 'dragon' texts of the Old Testament, the Pharaoh is called 'the *great* dragon' (LXX τὸν δράκοντα τὸν μέγαν, *ton drakonta ton megan*). The huge dragon of Rev. 12.3, who plagues the messianic community (12.13), is thus symbolic of the oppressive powers of Rome, the 'Egypt' of the first century, from which the Church will be delivered (15.2–4). But this figure is the further embodiment of all evil kingdoms, and indeed of all evil itself; for the great dragon is to be equated with the devil, Satan himself (12.9; 20.2), the ultimate force opposed to goodness and to God.

The 'seven heads' of the dragon speak of completeness, as with the seven horns of the Lamb in the throne-vision of 5.6 (for 'seven' in John see on 1.4). But now John is referring to the comprehensiveness and universality of the oppressive power of wickedness, wherever it may be found. The fact that the dragon has 'ten horns' is reminiscent of the fourth beast of Dan. 7.7, 24, a figure who also represents an evil empire; and this feature also identifies the dragon with the 'beast' of 13.1 (q.v.), whose home is also in the sea (cf. 17.12). The earthly emissaries of the Satan are 'like him in their destructive power' (Mounce 233). The seven 'coronets' (διαδήματα, *diadēmata*, lit. 'diadems') on the heads of the dragon are not wreaths of victory (στέφανοι, *stephanoi*, 'crowns'), but 'crowns of arrogated authority' (Hendriksen 136). They are indicative of a devilish claim to royal power which parodies the true sovereignty of the 'King of kings', who wears many diadems (19.12, 16).

The designation of the dragon in verse 2 as 'fiery red' (πυρρός, *pyrros*) in colour emphasizes his oppressive nature, as with the warlike character of the red horse ridden in 6.4, and the 'scarlet' whore riding a red beast, who drinks the blood of the saints, in 17.1–6 (cf. 6.9–10; and contrast 7.14). The fiery character of the satanic figure in this verse also symbolizes the nature of the devil, the incarnation of unjust and wicked persecution, as murderous (see John 8.44; 1 John 3.12). See also Homer, *Iliad* 2.308, describing the portent of a dragon, 'with blood-red markings on his back', devouring a brood of young sparrows with their mother. In *Sib. Or.* 8.88 Rome is identified with a purple dragon.

4 The pageant in heaven continues to unfold, as the dragon hurls stars from the sky to earth. For οὐρανός (*ouranos*, 'heaven'), as cosmic territory but also the realm of God, see verses 1 and 3.

The background to this imagery is to be found in Dan. 8.10, where the 'little horn' (8.9), representing the tyrannical and sacrilegious Antiochus Epiphanes, threw down to the earth 'some of the host (of heaven) and some of the stars', and trampled on them. This is a reference to the 'angels' (people, as in Dan. 10.20–21; 12.1) and 'saints' (stars, as in Dan. 12.3; cf. Gen. 15.5; Matt. 13.43) of Israel being persecuted, but eventually delivered from captivity; cf. Dan. 8.22–25; 12.1–3; 2 Macc. 7.1–42 (note esp. 2 Macc. 7.19, where the persecution of faithful Israelites in the Maccabean period is interpreted as 'fighting against God'). See Beale 635–36. In Rev. 12.4 the prophet-seer is thinking not only of unjust and oppressive powers, such as Rome, but also of the satanic forces which they embody, and through which God's people are persecuted at any time. This vision, and its sequence (12.7–12), promises hope after apparent defeat; and the thought of victorious deliverance from suffering and even martyrdom would have been of obvious relevance to John's first-century audience (cf. Moffatt 424).

The catastrophic action of the dragon in this verse is consonant with his huge size and supernatural power, which in this picture is located in his 'tail' (οὐρά, *oura*). Apart from the present context, 'tails' are mentioned in Revelation only at 9.10 and 19, where they refer to the tails of the demonic scorpions and the serpent-like tails of the fiendish horses. In both cases the tails are similar to that of the dragon: they are powerful, and capable of inflicting harm. With his tail, the dragon of 12.4 'swept away a third of the stars away from the sky'. The verb σύρει (*syrei*, lit. 'sweeps away', 'drags') is in the historic present tense, which occurs frequently in this section (see on verse 2). Sweeping away a 'third' (τρίτον, *triton*) of the stars may be simply figurative of a large number (Mounce 233); but this unit also corresponds to the destruction of a third of creation and its people precipitated by the sounding of the seven trumpets (8.7—9.19). The devilish activity in this scene seems to echo the narrative of the descent of Satan and his angels in the traditional saga of the Watchers in *1 Enoch* 6—11 (Aune 686). In *1 Enoch* (18.14–16; 21.3–6; et al.) stars can represent evil angels; cf. Isa. 24.21–22. For stars as 'good' angels see on 1.20; also on 1.1. The dragon's conduct in verse 4 anticipates his attack on God's people and his universe which follows in verses 7–9.

In the second part of verse 4 the setting changes, since the dragon now stands before the pregnant woman, about to give birth (see on verses 1–2), on earth; and this location is confirmed by the subsequent statements that her child is 'snatched away' to God in heaven (verse 5, q.v.), and that the woman herself escaped to the wilderness (verse 6). The verb κατεσθίειν (*katesthiein*, 'to devour', 'eat up') is used negatively of the dragon's intention here, to destroy the woman's child (cf. Jer. 51.34); whereas the cognate term, καταπίνειν (*katapinein*, 'swallow', lit. 'drink down'), describes in verse 16 (q.v.) the positive help given to the woman by the earth, which comes to her rescue.

Up to this point in verse 4, the writer has been depicting the persecution of the covenant community, faithful Israel, in the Old Testament and intertestamental ages leading up to the birth of the Messiah. Attention is now switched to the moment of that arrival, as the dragon waits to 'devour' the royal child, who springs from the true Israel, as soon as he is born (cf. Jer. 4.31). He has taken up his position (ἕστηκεν, *hestēken*, 'took [his] place', lit. 'stood', is in the perfect tense), and now awaits his victim. The situation illustrates the antagonism which will surround Jesus, throughout his earthly ministry: from the hostility of Herod in the infancy narratives (Matt. 2.1–12), to the temptations and dangers which were characteristic of his life (Mark 1.13; 3.6; John 5.18), up to the climax of his passion and crucifixion (John 18.1—19.42). Resurrection will follow, but that is not in view at the moment; rather, this vision concentrates on the suffering of the Messiah, and of his followers to the extent that they abide in him (John 15.18–25).

5 The radiant woman of verse 1, heavily pregnant and about to be delivered (verse 2), but also threatened by the powers of evil (verses 3–4), finally gives birth to a 'male child'. For the grammatical construction, υἱὸν ἄρσεν (*huion arsen*, lit. 'a son, a male child'), see the textual note on verse 5, above. The repetitive phrase is best construed as a Hebraism (cf. Jer. 20.15 MT, lit. 'a son is born to you, a male'). The neuter form, ἄρσεν (*arsen*, 'male'), may universalize the concept of sonship, and suggest in addition the ideas of importance and domination (cf. Aune 687–88). The description of a personified, true Israel, giving birth to the Messiah, seems to be John's own image; but notice the eschatological concept of Zion, labouring to deliver a son and children, in Isa. 66.7–9.

The messianic offspring of the covenant community is 'destined to shatter the totality of the nations with an iron crook'. See the similar prediction by Simeon, at the birth of Jesus, of Christ's activity during his ministry with reference to Israel itself (Luke 2.34–35). The masculine relative pronoun, ὅς (*hos*, 'who'), at the start of this clause, refers to the preceding masculine noun υἱόν (*huion*, lit. 'son'). The allusion in this part of verse 5 is to Ps. 2.9, which receives a messianic interpretation in *Pss. Sol.* 17.23–24; cf. 17.21–22. There are three citations of Ps. 2.9 in the New Testament, all of which occur in Revelation; apart from 12.5, see 2.27 and 19.15. In all three contexts of the Apocalypse the form of the quotation is similar, including the verb ποιμαίνειν (*poimainein*, 'to shatter' or 'rule', lit. 'shepherd'), and the expression ἐν ῥάβδῳ σιδηρᾷ (*en hrabdō[i] sidēra*, 'with an iron crook [rod]'); cf. Ps. 2.9 LXX. However, the present verse (12.5) introduces two variations: the use of the verb μέλλει (*mellei*, 'is destined to', lit. 'about to'), and the inclusion of the phrase πάντα τὰ ἔθνη (*panta ta ethnē*, 'the totality of nations', lit. 'all the nations'). This may suggest that the author is tapping a different traditional source for his quotation at this point.

The Greek verb translated 'to shatter' (ποιμαίνειν, *poimainein*) in verse 5, as in 2.27 and 19.15, means essentially to 'tend', in the sense of looking after sheep. But it can also signify 'shepherding' as an activity of watching out for, or governing, other people (BDAG 842*b*). It carries that positive significance of nurturing at 7.17 (q.v.), which is the only other passage in the Apocalypse where the verb occurs. However, in the three uses of the verb which appear in Revelation as part of a quotation from Ps. 2.9, its meaning is best understood – as it must be in the original Old Testament text – as a judgemental ruling, and a shattering which may lead to destruction; although it has to be said that this connotation does not belong to the verb ποιμαίνειν (*poimainein*) when it is used in the LXX to translate the ambivalent Hebrew in the MT of Ps. 2.9. See further on 2.27; and for this interpretation cf. Charles 1, 75–77. The translation of ῥάβδος (*hrabdos*, lit. 'rod', 'staff') as 'crook' picks up the positive aspects which remain beneath the shepherding imagery; see 7.17, and below.

John is referring in the present context (12.5) to the authority of the Messiah when he acts for purposes of judgement (see also the associations of God's wrath at 19.15), even if that judicial activity leads to the possibility of salvation. As a shepherd defends his flock against beasts of prey, so Jesus the Christ will shatter the 'dragons' which persecute and trouble his followers in the Church (Mounce 234). Potentially, 'all the nations' stand under this judgement, for injustice and unrighteousness are universal. This phrase, translated as 'the totality of nations', is a formula used four times in the Apocalypse, apart from this verse (14.8; 15.4; 18.3, 23); although 'nations' regularly feature as opponents of God and his truth (cf. 2.26; 10.11; 11.2, 9; 13.7; et al.), as well as members of the redeemed community (5.9; 7.9; et al.). For 'all nations' see further Deut. 17.14; Amos 9.9; *T. Benj.* 9.2; *Pss. Sol.* 9.9; Mark 13.10; Acts 14.16; *2 Clem.* 13.2 (= Isa. 52.5); et al.

The second part of verse 5, where the woman's child (son) is 'snatched up to heaven', is apparently a reference to the ascension of Christ. In this case, the life and earthly ministry of Jesus appear in a very truncated form, with a jump in timescale from the birth to the exaltation of the Messiah, and with everything in between (including the passion) omitted. Furthermore, the language of ascension in the New Testament, where it occurs, normally involves the use of the verb ἀναλαμβάνειν (*analambanein*, lit. 'to take up'; cf. Acts 1.2, 11, 22; 1 Tim. 3.16; see also John 20.17, using ἀναβαίνω, *anabainō*, 'go up' or 'ascend'); whereas the verb in this case, as a hapax legomenon in Revelation, is ἁρπάζειν (*harpazein*, 'snatch up'). Swete (151) argues that these terms overlap; but Aune (689) is among those commentators who conclude that the application of the statement in verse 5*b* to the ascension of Jesus is secondary.

Nonetheless, the pace of the drama is accelerated in this figurative passage, precisely to make the point vividly that the evil intentions of the Satan were overthrown by the victorious outcome of Jesus' messianic life and work; for these were triumphantly consummated in his resurrection, ascension and glorification (cf. the 'lifting up' of the exalted Jesus at John 12.32). See Phil. 2.5–11, which includes in verse 6 the cognate noun, unique in biblical Greek, ἁρπαγμός (*harpagmos*, 'something to be snatched'). For other New Testament uses, in spiritual settings, of the verb ἁρπάζω (*harpazō*, 'snatch, catch up') see Acts 8.39; 2 Cor. 12.2, 4; 1 Thess. 4.17. It should be added that although the death of Christ is not explicitly mentioned, in this condensed survey of his ministry, it is implied. For the way for Jesus to enter God's presence, and be crowned as Lord, was not by escaping death; rather, he defeated the powers of evil and sin precisely through his self-giving in love on the cross (cf. 1 John 3.11–16). The significance of such an ultimate victory would not have been lost on John's immediate audience, who 'faced their own decisions about how to deal with the dragon's activity in their midst' (Boring 158). See also the 'suffering' of the Messiah present in verse 4.

The messianic child is snatched away, or exalted, to the realm of 'God's throne'. The Son leaves his mother, and immediately enters the Father's presence; and this action is here described as being caught up 'to God and to his throne' (cf. Ps. 110.1). The family language is not sustained in this part of the narrative; and, indeed, the reference to God as 'Father' in the Apocalypse occurs during an enthronement scene only at 3.21. For 'throne' (θρόνος, *thronos*), as the leading symbol of God's sovereignty, see on 4.2. Apart from 14.3, this is the only use of the noun 'throne' throughout Rev. 12—15; but note the dragon's 'throne' in 13.2. See further Vanni, *La struttura letteraria* 216.

6   Jesus, the Messiah of Israel, disappears from the vision at this point in the narrative, and the interest moves to the woman and her fate in the light of the dragon's activity (cf. Michaels 149); see also verses 13–17. The location of the scene continues to be on earth, as in verses 4*b*–5; and in this setting she 'escaped to the wilderness'. As in verse 14, the woman is the personification of the Christian community, the true Israel of God from whom the Messiah descends (see on verse 1). After the resurrection of Jesus it is this Church, including the Johannine circle, which experienced conflict within and oppression beyond itself (cf. John 21.18–19). The flight of God's people to the refuge of the wilderness, in the face of persecution, is an apocalyptic theme; see Mark 13.14–23; *Asc. Isa.* 4.13. The reference to 'escape' (ἔφυγεν, *ephygen*, lit. 'she fled') in this passage may reflect historically the flight of believers in Palestine to Pella in Perea at the outbreak of the Jewish War in AD 66 (see Eusebius, *HE* 3.5.3); see also 1 Macc. 2.28–29 (the movement of Mattathias and his sons into the desert) and Matt. 2.13–15 (the flight of the Holy Family into Egypt). However, the emphasis in this verse is less on the escape of the Church from trouble and more on the provision which God makes for his people in times of difficulty.

The 'wilderness' (ἔρημον, *erēmon*, lit. 'desert') is an important motif in the literature of Judaism (as in 1QM 1.1–3, where a retreat to the desert is a prelude to the final eschatological conflict between the sons of light and the children of darkness). Here, the 'desert' picks up the leading idea of the Exodus, which is present throughout the Apocalypse and in this scene (see verse 4; also 15.2–4). To the Israelites the wilderness was also a place of divine provision and fellowship, where God nourished and supported his covenant followers for forty years (Exod. 16.4–35; 1 Kings 17.2–6; 19.3–8; Hos. 2.14). The verb τρέφω (*trephō*) means 'feed', in the sense of the care provided by offering nourishment (BDAG 1014*b*); but here it includes the notion of 'support' (hence the translation). It is the verb used in 1 Kings 18.13 LXX of Elijah, in a cave, protecting some of the Lord's prophets from Jezebel. During the wilderness wanderings, also, the presence and guidance of God was as important to his people as the manna he rained upon them from heaven (cf. Exod.13.17–22; Deut. 8.2–18); and in Rev. 12.6 that thought is also present. John is reassuring his audience that God has made ready, in himself and through Christ, a place of spiritual refuge and eventual conquest, which will enable the saints to resist the powers of evil ranged against them in many forms. For them, the 'desert' of their situation is not a realm of isolation but of protection and succour; it is also the setting in which the eschatological deliverance of the Church, in time and in eternity, will eventually be completed (cf. Prigent 386–87). The woman's flight to the wilderness recalls, in this way, the time of restoration at the end, when Israel was expected to return to the Lord, and once more be nourished and protected by him in the desert (Beale 643); cf. Isa. 32.15; 40.3; Jer. 31.2; Ezek. 34.25; et al. Cf. also the death and defence of the two witnesses in Rev. 11.3–13.

In the phrase, ὅπου ἔχει ἐκεῖ (*hopou echei ekei*, lit. 'where she has there'), for which see also the textual notes on verse 6, ἔχει (*echei*, 'she has') is, despite the translation, a historic present; while ἐκεῖ (*ekei*, 'there') is a resumptive adverb, and may be a Semitism (Aune 653). Believers are promised here a spiritual refuge from satanic forces and a 'place' (τόπον, *topon*) of protection which has been divinely 'prepared' (ἡτοιμασμένον, *hētoimasmenon*) for the messianic community in advance. The promise in this vision relates closely to the thought of the Church as made up of faithful members who are sealed, and therefore protected, by God (see on 7.2–8; also 14.1–5). The expression, ἑτοιμάζειν τόπον (*hetoimazein topon*, 'to prepare a place'), appears in the Farewell Discourse of Jesus at John 14.2–3. For 'twelve hundred and sixty days', as a divinely ordered period of time, see on 11.2–3.

At the end of verse 6, the outcome of the woman's encounter with the dragon remains uncertain (Michaels 149); the drama has yet to be completed (12.13–17).

Sign 3: War in Heaven (12.7–9)

John's vision in Rev. 12 embraces heaven and earth (see above). In 12.7–9 the scene moves from earth back to heaven; and the action shifts from the dragon in relation to the woman, to the dragon and his angels in conflict with the archangel Michael and his heavenly host. Mounce (235) believes that the battle in verses 7–9 takes place in heaven itself, the dwelling-place of God, whereas the combat in verses 1–6 is located in the 'sky'. But the term οὐρανός (*ouranos*) can mean both 'sky' and 'heaven'; and theologically there is virtually no distinction between them in these two passages (see on verses 1, 3). For the literary background to the combat myth in 12.7–9 see on verse 1.

The pericope in verses 7–9 may be interpreted as a heavenly counterpart to the earthly events enacted in 12.1–6; for, as Beale (651) maintains, when there is a battle between the saints and the world on earth, 'there is corresponding conflict in the heavenly dimension'. Equally, 12.7–9 has been viewed as a cosmic prelude to the end-time, parallel to the victory of Christ in his death and resurrection (see John 12.31). So Mounce 235; cf. Sweet 199. Both understandings are valid; but they do not, by themselves, explain the abrupt introduction to this scene, or the sudden resumption of the 'dragon versus the woman' saga, after the heavenly anthem recorded in verses 10–12, at verse 13 (see verses 13–17).

It illuminates the structure and meaning of the section 12.7–12, in the context of Chapter 12 (and indeed Rev. 12—14) as a whole, if it is understood as a 'play within a play'. This is a controlling vision, which in one sense undergirds the theological significance of the drama of the Apocalypse in its totality. For it reminds the audience, as the main narrative progresses, of what is always true: that there is a perpetual battle in progress, both supernaturally and on earth, between evil and God, between the forces of wickedness and goodness. But at the end, and in the end, the powers of the Satan will be defeated; and the victory will belong eternally to God in Christ, and to the faithful who are in him (cf. 1 John 5.4–5). Against this background, the cry of the faithful for vengeance (Rev. 6.9–11) may also be interpreted.

The symbolic battle of the angels in heaven, then, and the defeat of the devil in the resurrection of Jesus, provide between them a standing assurance, which would have been welcomed by the Johannine community, that there will always be a new Exodus, and that there is lasting deliverance for God's people. The perpetual truth of the scene in 12.7–9, culminating in a heavenly song of triumph (verses 10–12), is elucidated in the remainder of Chapter 12, and then in the progress of the second Act of the drama (Rev. 12–22). The fall of the Satan and the corresponding victory of Christ help to explain the hostility of the powers of evil (which find their expression, for example, in the Roman authorities) to the Church of John's day, and indeed of any time. Note the final outpouring of wrath, after the battle has been lost, in 12.17; see also 12.18—13.18.

7–8   For the outbreak of warfare in heaven, between Michael and the dragon, see above. There is a grammatical difficulty in the use of the nominative phrase, ὁ Μιχαὴλ καὶ οἱ ἄγγελοι αὐτοῦ (*ho Michaēl kai hoi angeloi autou*, 'Michael and his angels'), with the genitive articular infinitive (unique in Revelation), τοῦ πολεμῆσαι (*tou polemēsai*, 'had to battle', lit. 'should make war'); see further the textual note on verse 7, above. Normally, in this consecutive construction, the subject of the infinitive would take the accusative (cf. Acts 10.25; et al.). Moule, *Idiom Book* 129, puts this down to John's 'barbarous' Greek; but Beale (653–54) prefers to see the nominative construction as an epexegetical infinitive with γίνομαι (*ginomai*, lit. 'to take place'), repeated from the first part of the verse in a personalized, third person plural form. See also LXX Dan. 10.20 Theod. Charles (1, 322), followed by Beale (654), notes also that the Greek construction in verse 7 is the literal reproduction of a Hebrew idiom, in which the subject before a verb with the prefix ל (*le*, *lamed*) is translated in the LXX as a nominative. For the nominative preceding a genitive articular infinitive in the LXX see 1 Chron. 9.25; Ps. 24.14; Hos. 9.13; et al. This

Septuagintal form conveys the notion of necessity, and such a nuance may be present in Rev. 12.7; hence the translation, 'Michael and his angels *had* to battle against the dragon'.

For Michael the archangel see Aune 693–95; and for 'angels' in Revelation see on 1.1. Michael (whose name means 'who is like God?') is mentioned in the Old Testament at Dan. 10.13, 21; 12.1 as a (chief) prince; cf. 1QM 9.15–16; 17.6–8 (where he is a majestic angel); *1 Enoch* 20.5; 24.6 (a chief angel); *2 Enoch (A)* 22.6 (the Lord's 'greatest archangel'); et al. In the New Testament, the only other named archangel is Gabriel (Luke 1.19). In Rev. 12.7 Michael's angelic status is not specified, and he is not even described directly as an angel; but since he is the leader of a host of angels, he is obviously to be regarded as an archangel. As such, he is mentioned in the New Testament otherwise only at Jude 9.

It is Michael, and not the Messiah, who wages a figurative and eschatological war against the dragon in heaven. (For the imagery of the huge, seven-headed and fiery monster, see on verse 3.) The archangel is Christ-like, but not more. Michael is the latter-day deliverer, who shares in the final battle with the Son of man figure as the heavenly representative of Israel (Dan. 7.21; 8.11; 10.20). He is the guardian of God's people, who will defend them from destruction at the end-time (Dan. 12.1; cf. *1 Enoch* 90.13–15); he is also the mediator between God and humanity who will resist the realm of evil (*T. Dan.* 6.2), and the angelic intercessor who struggles with the devil about the body of Moses (Jude 9).

In the present, apocalyptic scene (Rev. 12.7–9), the archangel Michael gathers up all these roles; but his leading task, assisted by the angelic host, is to wage war with the dragon, and to overcome the unrighteousness which the monster represents. Nevertheless, their victory must be understood as a heavenly and symbolic counterpart of the historical achievement of the cross; since the real conquest of evil has by now been achieved in the death and exaltation of Jesus the Christ. See Caird 153–54; also *idem*, 'Deciphering the Book of Revelation' 13–14. Note in addition *Asc. Isa.* 7.9--12 (esp. verse 10, 'as above, so also [is the struggle] on earth'); 11QMelch 9–13; Ignatius, *Eph.* 13.2. For the concept of a host of angels, accompanying Michael in the heavenly battle, see 'the army of the Lord' which assisted the Israelites in their own warfare (Josh 5.14; 2 Kings 6.17; 2 Macc. 2.21; 3 Macc. 6.18–21; et al.; cf. 1QM 9.4–7); see also Matt. 26.53; Luke 2.13; Jude 14–15. The vision of Michael and his angels has a parallel in the 'Son of man with his angels' at Matt. 16.27 par.; 24.31.

The spiritual battle is joined. The 'dragon and his angels' resist the angelic powers of good, and are expelled from heaven. The primordial fall from heaven of Satan, with whom the dragon is identified in 12.9, is an idea which can be derived from Milton's *Paradise Lost*, rather than from biblical tradition; there is also a parallel in the Babylonian account of the fall of Ishtar, goddess of the morning star. However, the expulsion of Satan from God's presence is a widely known legend in the literature of Judaism, and may stem from a midrash on Isa. 14.12–15 (the fall of the Day Star from heaven to the depths of the Pit). According to Enoch, Satan was once an angel who grasped at equality with God; as a result, he and his angels were cast out of heaven, and left to fly in the air continuously (*2 Enoch [J]* 29.4–5). See also Ps. 82.6–7; *1 Enoch* 55.3–56.4; Luke 10.18; Eph. 2.2; 1 Tim. 3.6; 2 Pet. 2.4; and the later use of this tradition, featuring Michael, in the *Life of Adam and Eve [Vita]* 12–16. In *Midr. Rab.* Exod. 9.9, the plagues on the waters which occurred during the Exodus (Exod. 7.16–18) are interpreted as a judgement on heavenly beings hostile to Israel.

The dragon, then, has his own 'angels' (ἄγγελοι, *angeloi*), a term which designates supernatural beings ('messengers'), both good and evil (see on 'angels', at 1.1); cf. *T. Ash.* 6.4; Matt. 25.41. Satan has mobilized his troops for a major rebellion against God and his authority (Hughes 138–39). As the throne and worship of the beast mimic the authority and adoration of the Lamb (13.2—4; 12.10—12), so the satanic dragon-monster parodies the position of the archangel Michael, for he has minions under him, who do his bidding.

In verse 8, the opening καί (*kai*, lit. 'and') is adversative; hence the translation, 'but'. The expression, οὐκ ἴσχυσεν (*ouk ischysen*, 'did not have the power'), includes a verb which may be translated into Latin as *imperium habere*, 'to have imperium (imperial power)'; and this could therefore be a parody of what will happen to the Roman Emperor (so Aune 695). The phrase, οὐδὲ τόπος εὑρέθη (*oude topos heurethē*, lit. 'nor was there found a place [for them]') has a very close parallel at Rev. 20.11 ('no place was found for them'); and this text alludes to LXX Dan. 2.35 Theod. Cf. Dan. 2.28—45; also *1 Clem.* 9.3. To some extent, Satan *had* a place in heaven, and access to God's presence (Job 1.6—9; 2.1—6; Zech 3.1—2); and this may have inspired the expectation of a final celestial battle before the end-time (cf. *Sib. Or.* 3.796—808; 5.512—17; 2 Macc. 5.1—4; Josephus, *Bell. Jud.* 6.33—41). So Mounce 236. But now the power of the demonic forces has been forfeited, and the sovereignty of God in Christ reasserted. There is more in the drama to come, and the kingdom of God has yet to be fully established on earth; but meanwhile, through the salvific conquest of Christ the dragon's sting has been drawn for all time (cf. 1 Cor. 15.54—57). For the historical dimension to the 'legal battle' between Michael and Satan, as played out in the Gospel of John (see John 13—20), note Caird 155.

9   There is no room in heaven for the satanic forces which have been mustered there; and it only remains for Michael, as the representative of God and of Christ, to remove them. For the 'great dragon' see on verse 3; and for the expulsion of the monster 'and his angels' from the dwelling-place of God see on verses 7—8. It is possible to discover in the progress of the Apocalypse that Satan's descent from the heavens takes place in three stages: from heaven to earth (12.9); from earth to the abyss (20.3); and from the pit to the lake of fire (20.10). See Mounce 236 n. 3. However, in apocalyptic visions details of space, like those of time, are not important. The point of the symbolism in 12.7—9 is not how the dragon fell, but that the reign of evil must in the end give place to the sovereign rule of God and the Lamb (22.3—5).

Aune (695) notices a chiastic structure underlying verse 9: the dragon was thrown out/he is known by four titles/the dragon and his followers were cast down. The aorist verb, ἐβλήθη (*eblethē*, 'was thrown out') is used twice in this context; and on both occasions it functions as the passive of divine activity, to avoid the use of the name of God (see on 9.1, 3). The implication is that the dragon was removed from heaven, on account of his hubris, not by Michael and his angels, but ultimately by God himself.

John names neither the woman nor the child of 12.1—5; but he is careful to identify the dragon here by listing his traditional titles. For a similar collection of aliases see 20.2 (omitting 'deceiver'; but note 20.3, 8, 10). The detailed description of the powers of evil at this point suggests that the writer is concerned to clarify the vast extent of the antagonism to God and his people which may be experienced throughout cosmic and human history. There is a parallel in the eschatological, combat imagery of Isa. 27.1, where a 'reptilian trinity' (Aune 698) is mentioned; cf. Justin, *1 Apol.* 28.1.

In Rev. 12.9 can be found the only explicit biblical identification of Satan with the 'ancient serpent' (ὁ ὄφις ὁ ἀρχαῖος, *ho ophis ho archaios*), the tempter of Eve, in Gen. 3.1—7. But there may be allusions to this myth at Luke 10.19; Rom. 16.20 (cf. Gen. 3.15); 2 Cor. 11.3, 14. In *3 Apoc. Bar.* 9.7 Samael (Syriac *Satanael*) assumes the serpent as a garment; while, according to *3 (Slavonic) Apoc. Bar.* 4.6—13, Satanael planted the vine-tree in Eden through which the serpent deceived Eve and Adam (in the same setting, Michael planted the olive). See also *Life of Adam and Eve (Apocalypse)* 16.4—5, where the serpent speaks for the devil.

The serpent-monster is also 'called Devil and the Satan'. The expression which introduces these titles, ὁ καλούμενος (*ho kaloumenos*, lit. 'the one called'), is used elsewhere in Revelation and the New Testament (with different forms of the verb) as a typical formula which provides an alternative, perhaps more familiar, name for a person or place; cf. Rev. 11.8; 16.16; Luke 6.15; Acts 1.12; et al. The description of the dragon as Διάβολος (*Diabolos*, 'Devil') employs a term which is otherwise fairly rare in Revelation (cf. 2.10; 12.12; 20.2, 10). In the Gospel and Letters of John there are occasional references to the devil's role in the primeval history of Gen. 3 (cf. John 8.44; 1 John 3.8; cf. 3.12, referring to Cain); similarly, those who sin, like Judas the betrayer (John 6.70; 13.2), belong to the devil. So the children of God can stand over against the offspring of the devil (1 John 3.10). The term διάβολος (*diabolos*, 'devil') normally appears in the New Testament and early Christian literature with an article (cf. e.g. Matt. 4.1; Eph. 4.27; Heb. 2.14; Ignatius, *Trall.* 8.1; *2 Clem.* 18.2; Hermas, *Mand.* 5.1.3; et al.). The anarthrous form, here and at 20.2, is unusual. For 'the devil' in the Johannine corpus see further Bietenhard, 'Satan, διάβολος, et al.' 472.

The 'Satan' (ὁ Σατανᾶς, *ho Satanas*), meaning 'adversary' or 'accuser', is the description of an office, rather than a proper name. The title occurs in just three books of the Old Testament, where Satan incites David to count the people of Israel (1 Chron. 21.1), and accuses Job (Job 1.6–12, et al.) or Joshua the high priest (Zech. 3.1–2) before God in the heavenly court. 'Satan' gives place to 'Belial' in Qumran (1QM 1.1, 5; et al.); but the title appears occasionally in Second Temple Judaism (*T. Gad* 4.7; *T. Dan.* 5.6; et al.), often in the New Testament (34 times), and three times in the Fathers (*Barn.* 18.1; Ignatius, *Eph.* 13.1; Polycarp, *Phil.* 7.1), always with the article. The Hebrew term שָׂטָן (*śāṭān*, 'Satan') is regularly translated in the LXX by (ὁ) διάβολος (*[ho] diabolos*, '[the] devil'); so Job 2.3; et al.

The fourth and final description of the dragon, in verse 9, involves his activity as 'the deceiver of the whole world'; and this enlarges even further the universal scope of the powers of evil, set out in their present identification. The substantive participle, ὁ πλανῶν (*ho planōn*, lit. 'the one deceiving') is used of the monster-dragon in Revelation only here and at 2.10 (q.v.). It is not technically a title in these contexts; although it becomes such (as 'Deceiver' of the world) in *Did.* 16.4. Satan is also known as the 'Prince' of deceit ('error') in *T. Jud.* 19.4; cf. *T. Sim.* 3.5. In the Apocalypse the notion of evil deception is prominent; and using the verb πλανᾶν (*planan*, 'to deceive') the subjects vary from Jezebel (2.20) and the devil himself (12.9; 20.3, 8, 10) to the beast from the earth (13.14), who is also named the false prophet (19.20) and Babylon (18.23). The theme of idolatry runs through some of these texts (esp. 2.20; 13.14; 19.20); and this was evidently an attitude and a practice which troubled the community which was being addressed by its leader in this apocalyptic drama.

The 'deceiver of the whole world' was 'hurled down to the earth', and his angels (see above) were 'cast down' with him. The verb βάλλω (*ballō*, lit. 'throw'), in different translations, is used twice in this sentence, and three times in verse 9 as a whole. The repetition underlines the finality of the divine victory over Satan; and the same is true of the virtual replication here, from the first clause of the verse, of the phrase 'the great dragon was thrown out'. The dragon-monster is hurled down 'to the earth' (εἰς τὴν γῆν, *eis tēn gēn*), which in first-century thought is the territory located between the sky and the nether regions. The description of Satan as the deceiver of 'the whole world' (τὴν οἰκουμένην ὅλην, *tēn oikoumenēn holēn*) refers to the *inhabitants* of that earth, or society in its completeness. The exact phrase 'the whole world' (using οἰκουμένη, *oikoumenē*) appears in the Apocalypse three times (apart from 12.9, see 3.10; 16.14). In each case, the situation in view is one of suffering endured inclusively by all people as the result of demonic deceit. But in the present context this evil has been proleptically and universally vanquished (verses 7–9). The heavenly chorus, in the hymn which follows (verses 10–12), will celebrate that triumph.

A Song of Praise in Heaven (12.10–12)

10 The expulsion of the dragon from heaven, which demonstrates the abiding victory of God over Satan, and good over evil, leads into a heavenly proclamation. For similar, spontaneous outbursts of celestial praise in Revelation see 4.8, 11; 5.9–14; 7.10–12; 11.15–18; 14.3; 15.3–4; 19.1–8; 21.3–4. In this passage, the hymn is articulated by a 'loud voice' (φωνὴν μεγάλην, *phōnēn megalēn*), issuing from the dwelling-place of God. This voice could be that of one of the twenty-four elders; cf. 4.11; 7.12; 11.17, where (as in verse 10) the 'power' of God is a cause of thanksgiving. More probably, the voice belongs to a supernatural being who is divine or angelic, or both (cf. 10.4). For 'loud' (μεγάλη, *megalē*, lit. 'great') voices in the Apocalypse, belonging to angels with important messages to declare, see 1.10; 5.2; 7.2; 10.3; 14.7, 9, 15, 18; 19.17.

There is no conflict between the singular noun 'voice' and the use of the plural form of ἀδελφός (*adelphos*, lit. 'brother') later in verse 10; for the heavenly voice in this anthem is the representative of others, and speaks for them. Charles 1, 327–28, followed by Aune 701, regards the 'voice' as standing for a group of heavenly, Christian martyrs, who refer to their colleagues on earth, having overcome the dragon by their deaths, as 'comrades' (verse 10*b*; cf. 6.11). But this is an unnecessarily difficult interpretation, particularly as those who have been martyred for their faith on earth already form part of the heavenly company. There is, in fact, no reason in this passage to restrict either the heavenly speaker or 'our comrades' to the martyrs. Rather, the voice from heaven is proclaiming to the world, deceived by the dragon (12.9), God's saving conquest of unjust evil in time and eternity; and this is true for *all* the saints who belong to the Church of Christ, in heaven and on earth, some of whom may have died for their faith (cf. 19.10).

The adverb ἄρτι (*arti*, 'now') and the aorist (perfective) verb ἐγένετο (*egeneto*, 'established', lit. 'occurred') indicate that the deliverance, power and sovereignty ascribed to God, together with the authority of his Christ (verse 10), are understood as directly related to the fall of Satan from heaven. Despite the caution expressed by Aune (700), this event may be understood as the spiritual counterpart of the salvific and historical work of God in Christ which finds its focus in the death and exaltation of Jesus (similarly Beasley-Murray 202–203; Caird 153–54; Sweet 201; Roloff 149).

As normatively in apocalyptic tradition, the overthrow of the devil signals the coming of the kingdom (cf. Matt. 12.28; 2 Thess. 2.8). So the loud, heavenly voice declares that the age of God's redemptive sovereignty has arrived (Beasley-Murray 202). Even if the powers of evil are still active in his creation, God's salvation and power and kingship have been established over them for all time. The Greek term translated 'deliverance' is σωτηρία (*sōtēria*), for which see on 7.10; cf. also 19.1 (only in 12.10 and these texts is this noun used in the Apocalypse). Its primary sense in 12.10, as at 7.10 and 19.1, is that of 'victory'; and this suits the military setting of Rev. 12 (note the imagery of war and conquest in verses 7–8, 11). But the word includes here the notion of deliverance from the attacks of the evil one (12.7, 12) and 'rescue' as a divine means of bringing help to those in trouble (cf. Exod. 14.13; Rev. 12.6, 14). In this way, the concept of salvation includes the ideas of protection and preservation, which are present in Chapter 12, as well as in Rev. 7 and 19; and indeed it is not far from the leading New Testament theme of the salvific healing and wholeness which are brought to the believer through the person and work of Jesus (John 4.22; Rom. 1.16; et al.). The rendering of the term as 'deliverance', in the translation, attempts to subsume all these shades of meaning.

For the concepts of the 'power' (ἡ δύναμις, *hē dynamis*) and 'sovereign realm' or 'king-dom' (ἡ βασιλεία, *hē basileia*) of God, see on 4.11 (also 5.12; 7.12; 11.17; 15.8; 19.1) and 1.6, 9 (also 5.10; 11.15). The phrase 'of our God' (τοῦ θεοῦ ἡμῶν, *tou theou hēmōn*) modifies all three of the preceding nouns, since the sovereignty of God includes his deliverance and his power. The power belonging to God, and the authority by which he delivers and rules, will in the end replace those which have been temporarily del-egated to the forces of evil (13.2; 17.13; also 17.12, 17–18); cf. the liturgical addition to the Lord's Prayer, 'deliver us from the evil one, for the kingdom and the power are yours for ever', at Matt. 6.13. Christ participates in this divine authority (11.15), because he has defeated Satan in his death and resurrection (5.9; 12.11; cf. 1 John 3.4–10); cf. Mounce 238. This is the only occasion in Revelation where the 'authority' (ἐξουσία, *exousia*) of the Messiah is mentioned (but see 2.26); and note the high Christology which is presupposed by the fact that the Father's authority is shared with the Son. Elsewhere, authority is said to be given by God in the same way to a redeemer figure, or to Jesus himself (cf. Dan. 7.13–14; Matt. 28.18; John 5.27; 13.3; 17.2; *1 Enoch* 69.27–29; et al.).

The sovereign realm of God is established now, and proleptically in the future, 'because (ὅτι, *hoti*) the accuser of the faithful' has been thrown out. Satan's deceitful accusation of the saints before God helps to explain his demonic presence in heaven. The Greek term used as the fifth title to describe the dragon in this passage, 'accuser' (κατήγωρ, *katēgōr*), occurs only here in the New Testament (see the textual notes on verse 10). It is a loanword in Rabbinic literature, but neither a Semitism nor a transliteration of the Aramaic (Charles 1, 327; Mounce 238 n. 13). Rather, it may be regarded as a colloquial Greek formation, which arose from the fact that the genitive plural of the cognate κατήγορος (*katēgoros*, 'accuser'), in both the second and third declensions, is κατηγόρων (*katēgorōn*); so BDAG 533*b*; followed by Aune 700–701.

That the dragon should be represented, in the imagery of this passage, as an 'accuser' indicates that the angelic battle in 12.7–9 is more of a forensic, than a military, conflict. The basic setting is that of a courtroom, in which two lawyers put their case, and the loser is excluded (Caird 154–56). Satan's legal role as an accuser of the righteous is frequently described in the literature of Judaism. See Job 1.6–12; 2.1–7; Zech. 3.1–2; *1 Enoch* 40.7; *3 Enoch* 26.12; *Jub.* 1.20; 17.15–16; *Apoc. Zeph.* 6.17; et al. In *T. Levi* 5.6 and *T. Dan.* 6.1–6 Michael plays the part of an advocate, who defends Israel against the accusations of Satan in the heavenly court (Beale 661). In *Jub.* 48.9–19, the binding and imprisonment of Satan, so that he can be prevented from pursuing the children of Israel and accusing them, is said to be essential to the victory of Israel over Egypt at the time of the Exodus; and this motif belongs to Rev. 12 and the present scene of the Apocalypse, generally (see 12. 6, 14; et al.); cf. Beale 662.

The accusations of Satan are continuous (for this meaning of 'day and night' see on 4.8); and they are laid endlessly before 'our God', the Lord of the Church (see 10*a*). But in the end, and because of the salvific exaltation of Jesus the Christ, the charge against God's people cannot prevail (1 John 1.5–9; 3.4–10; Rom. 8.33–34). For the fourth time in this passage we hear, in a song of victory, that the powers of evil have been over-come and 'thrown out' (ἐβλήθη, *eblēthē*) of heaven.

11   Verses 7–12 of Rev. 12, and especially the action in verses 7–9, may be interpreted as a 'play within a play' (see on 12.7), which dramatizes the theological truth belonging to the Apocalypse as a whole. It is eschatologically and always the case that, in the end, God and his people will triumph over evil, even if his kingdom has yet to be fully estab-lished on earth (12.7–9). That truth is celebrated liturgically in the present hymn, verses 10–12, which need then not be regarded as a redactional interpolation (against Charles 1, 328–29; Aune 702–703). The focus of God's salvific activity on behalf of his creation is to be found in the life and death and resurrection of Jesus the Lamb, in whom salvation history is 'divided anew' (cf. Cullmann, *Christ and Time* 81–93, esp. 84). For 'the sacrifice (τὸ αἷμα, *to haima*, lit. "the blood") of the Lamb' see on 5.9; cf. also 1.5.

This self-giving on the part of Christ leads to the conquest of Satan by the saints, as well as by Michael. 'They (the pronoun αὐτοί [*autoi*] is emphatic) have conquered' the dragon 'through' (διά, *dia*) the sacrifice of Christ, which is the ground as well as the means of their victory. The verb, νικᾶν (*nikan*, 'to conquer'), is used 17 times in Revelation. When Christ is the subject of the action (as in 5.5), the achievement of his conquest is related to his death on the cross (cf. 5.9; 17.14; also John 12.31–33). The same is true when the saints conquer Satan. Explicitly here (12.11), and implicitly elsewhere in the Apocalypse (2.7, 11, 17, 26; 3.5, 12, 21 [*bis*]; 15.2; 21.7), the basis of Christian victory is to be found in the passion and exaltation of Jesus. Cf. 1 Cor. 15.54–57; Col. 1.15. In 4 Macc. (3.17–18; 9.6; 16.14; et al.), by contrast, the conquest of oppression and wrong desire is brought about by an endurance which is based on pure reason.

The victory of the saints is assisted 'by the word of their testimony' (διὰ τὸν λόγον τῆς μαρτυρίας αὐτῶν, *dia ton logon tēs martyrias autōn*). The genitive in this phrase is one of apposition, where the 'testimony' of the faithful to Jesus explains the nature of the 'word' which they speak about him (cf. 1.9; 6.9; 20.4). Christian witness is described by Paul as consisting of the 'word of the cross' (1 Cor. 1.18; cf. 1 John 4.14–15). The believers who testify to the gospel of the Lord, and in this way share in his victory, are commended because 'they did not cling to their lives (οὐκ ἠγάπησαν τὴν ψυχὴν αὐτῶν, *ouk ēgapēsan tēn psychēn autōn*, lit. "did not love their life") in the face of death'. Although this is clearly a reference to the martyrs, whose willingness to proclaim a testimony about Jesus overcame their natural fear of death (Mounce 239; cf. 6.9; 11.7), there is no need to assume that Christian martyrdom alone is in view during this heavenly anthem (so Charles 1, 328–29; and see on verse 10). The victory of God in Christ, and of his saints, is being celebrated by *all* those who belong to his Church, some of whom will have suffered as martyrs for their faith. For the concept of 'loving life' and therefore losing it, as opposed to 'hating' it and consequently achieving it, see John 12.25; Mark 8.35 par.; Matt. 10.39 par.; Ignatius, *Eph.* 9.2 ('you love nothing, according to human life, but God alone'); cf. also, for Rev. 12.11, 1 Cor. 2.6–8; Col. 1.15–20. Note further Beasley-Murray 203–204.

12   The last verse of the heavenly anthem connects with the first (verse 10). Rejoicing can take place among the saints *because* (διὰ τοῦτο, *dia touto*, 'so', lit. 'through this') God's kingdom has been eternally established, and his victory over evil ultimately achieved through Christ's glorification. The heavens themselves are called upon to be joyful, now that Satan has been finally thrown out of them. The term οὐρανός (*ouranos*, 'heaven'), in the singular, is frequently used in Revelation (so verses 7, 8, 10); but this is the only place in the book where the noun appears in the plural. 'Those who dwell there' (οἱ ἐν αὐτοῖς σκηνοῦντες, *hoi en autois skēnountes*, lit. 'those dwelling in them [the heavens]') are the angels and saints of God, who live in his presence. Apart from John 1.14, the verb σκηνόω (*skēnoō*, 'dwell', lit. 'tent') occurs in the New Testament only in the Apocalypse, where it always refers to those who live for ever with God, or God with them, in heaven (7.15; 12.12; 13.6; 21.3). In the Fourth Gospel (1.14) the Word made flesh is described as 'tenting' or 'tabernacling' among us (ἐσκήνωσεν ἐν ἡμῖν, *eskēnōsen en hēmin*, 'he lived among us'), which is perhaps an expression of continuity with God's 'tenting' in Israel (BDAG 929*b*). When the 'inhabitants of the earth', who are usually opposed to God, are mentioned in Revelation (6.10; 8.13; 11.10; et al.), the verb κατοικέω (*katoikeō*, 'inhabit') is used.

The triumphant call for the heavens and its occupants to rejoice has a close LXX parallel at Deut. 32.43*a*. Similar commands are heard elsewhere in the Old Testament and the literature of Qumran, although they are regularly coupled with an additional appeal for the earth to rejoice (cf. Aune 703); cf. Ps. 96.11; Isa. 44.23; 49.13; 4QPs^f 10.5–6; 4QTanḥ *frags.* 1–2, 2.4–5; et al. For the cosmology of this verse (Rev. 12.12), with its three-decker arrangement of heaven, earth and sea, see 5.3; 10.6. The joy in heaven and the promised disaster on earth and sea are inclusive in their nature.

For the exclamation, οὐαί (*ouai*, 'disaster', lit. 'woe'), see on 8.13. The word appears 14 times in Revelation, apart from the present context (8.13; 9.12; 11.14; 18.10, 16, 19), and is often repeated for emphasis and dramatic effect. In this verse and 8.13 alone, in the Apocalypse, the interjection is followed by the accusative (note the nominative in 18.10–19, and the dative elsewhere in the New Testament). The term is used consistently to introduce weighty predictions of judgement, as in the teaching of Jesus recorded in the synoptic Gospels (cf. Matt. 11.21; Mark 13.17; Luke 22.22; et al.); and in both contexts the mood recalls that of the Old Testament prophets in their speeches of denunciation (Isa. 5.11–13; Jer. 22.13; Amos 5.18; et al.). The disaster referred to here is not to be interpreted as the 'third woe' of 11.14 (so Sweet 190, 202, against Beckwith 668–71; cf. Allo 101; et al.), since this is best understood as the contents of Rev. 12—15 (see further on 11.14).

For 'the Devil' see verse 9; and for his descent from heaven see verses 8–10. The term 'devil' (διάβολος, *diabolos*) appears four times in Revelation, apart from the present verse (2.10; 12.9; 20.2, 10); for his 'anger' here see further on verse 17. Satan is represented as 'filled with anger' (ἔχων θυμὸν μέγαν, *echōn thymon megan*, lit. 'having great wrath') because of the temporal limitations placed by God upon his demonic activity. He is angry, 'knowing that his time is limited' (εἰδὼς ὅτι ὀλίγον καιρὸν ἔχει, *eidōs hoti oligon kairon echei*, lit. 'knowing that he has a short time'). The word καιρός (*kairos*, 'time', as also in 1.3; 11.18; 22.10) suggests a moment *in* time, rather than a period *of* time (the usual meaning of χρόνος, *chronos*). As Aune (656) points out, the verb ἔχει (*echei*, lit. 'he has') in this sentence is the only example in the Apocalypse of the general present tense being used in reported *thought*, as opposed to reported speech.

The apocalyptic time span involved here is figurative, and no attempt should be made to understand it literally; as Prigent (393) says, 'there is no longer any need to count the days, the months or the years'. Some commentators link the shortness of the devil's time to his final defeat at the end of history (so Hendriksen 141), or to the relatively brief period between his expulsion from heaven and the final judgement (Mounce 239). Others, more pertinently, point to the limitation of Satan's angry hostility, intensified as a result of his overthrow, as a shortening of days for the sake of protected believers (cf. Wall 164; Michaels 152). See Mark 13.20; and note the divinely restricted period of time in view at 12.6, 14, and the 'short time' of the dragon's release after his binding at 20.3. But the devilish anger expressed in 12.12 is provoked by Satan's defeat for *all* time in the death and exaltation of Christ (Milligan 210), just as his ejection from heaven is a sign of his future destruction at *any* time (Knight 93–94). The end will come eventually, and Satan's temporary rule will be replaced. But, as so often in the Apocalypse, the end is both 'soon' and 'not yet' (3.11; 22.20). See on 6.17; 11.14; and note further the theology of this scene below, 378–79.

Sign 4: War on Earth (12.13–18)

13 The drama of the encounter between the woman and the dragon continues, after the intervening account of the perpetual war in heaven (12.7–9, q.v.), from verses 3–6. The resumption of the narrative after a break provides a literary pattern of inclusion in this scene (see on verse 3), just as verses 13–17(18) draw out the significance of verse 6. The satanic monster, defeated in the heavenly conflict and consequently in the capture of the child, pursues the mother with zeal. The faithful people of God share with their Lord the hostility which is increasingly directed against them by a conquered, and therefore wrathful, enemy (verses 12, 17). Cf. John 15.18–21; and, for the identification of Christ with his Church, see Matt. 5.11; 25.45; Acts 9.4–5; 1 Pet. 4.14; also Rev. 1.9; 14.3.

For the fall of Satan (and his angels), from heaven to earth, see on 12.7–9, 10, 12; and for the identity of the child who is born from the woman, as representatives of the Messiah who descends from the true Israel, see on verses 1–2, 4–5. The verb ἐδίωξεν (*ediōxen*, 'went in pursuit'), used only here in Revelation, may be regarded as an ingressive aorist; that is to say, the writer is using a tense which indicates a starting point, even if the verb itself is not one which normally denotes a state or condition (see Moule, *Idiom Book* 10 and n. 1). The word itself can mean either 'pursue' or 'persecute'; and both ideas are involved in this passage. But, in view of the flight of the woman recorded in the next verse (14), the notion of pursuit is uppermost in verse 13. The anaphoric article, with the masculine singular accusative noun, τὸν ἄρσενα (*ton arsena*, 'the male child'), refers back to the anarthrous form of the term (ἄρσεν, *arsen*, 'male child') in verse 5, where it is in the neuter accusative.

The Exodus theme is prominent in the paragraph 12.13–16, as in Chapter 12 generally (see verse 6) and elsewhere in Revelation. The pursuit of the woman by the dragon is reminiscent of the pursuit of the Israelites by the Pharaoh, as they fled from Egypt (cf. Exod. 14.8–10); and Pharaoh is often likened to a dragon in the Old Testament (Ps. 74.13–14; Isa. 51.9–10; Ezek. 29.3; cf. *Pss. Sol.* 2.25–26; et al.; also *T. Sol.* 14.3–4). See further on verse 3, and below.

14   The pursuit of the woman by the angry dragon (see verse 13) takes an unexpected turning, since she is miraculously provided with the wings of an eagle, enabling her to escape to the wilderness. The theme in this and the following verses (15–17) now becomes the protection and preservation of God's people, the Church, through the victory of Christ over Satan (12.10–12); cf. 7.2–17; 14.1. The verb ἐδόθησαν (*edothēsan*, '[the woman] was provided with', lit. 'there were given') is a third person plural aorist passive; and this form is probably an indication that God is the subject of the action in this scene; cf. the use of the passives of divine permission with the verb βάλλω (*ballō*, 'throw [out]') at 12.9, 10, 13, et al. It is God who provides the means for the woman's escape, as well as a place for her support (cf. Beckwith 629).

The use of the two definite articles, in the reference to '*the* great eagle' of deliverance (τοῦ ἀετοῦ τοῦ μεγάλου, *tou aetou tou megalou*), omitted in some MSS, suggests a creature which is well known; although clearly there is no connection here with the eagle of judgement in 8.13 (q.v.). In the classical mythology of Egypt and Greece, both gods and people in danger are transformed into birds and animals; and such a metamorphosis permits escape and rescue (cf. Apollodorus, *Lib.* 1.6.3; 3.14.8; Ovid, *Metam.* 5.321–31; 6.667–74; 7.350–90). See further Aune 704–705. But (against Charles 1, 330) the Judaic tradition of the eagle, in association with God's care for his people, lies closer to John's thought in this passage. See e.g. Exod. 19.4; Deut. 32.10–14 (a text which appropriately includes the motifs of the eagle, the wilderness and divine nourishment); Isa. 40.31; cf. Jer. 48.40; 49.22; Mic. 4.9–10; also 4QDibHam[a] *frag.* 6.6–7 (God lifts his people 'wonderfully' on eagles' wings, and brings the faithful to himself); *1 Enoch* 96.2, where the righteous are assured that their children will be 'made openly visible' (rise) like eagles.

The figurative transformation of the woman into an eagle (verse 14*a*) enables her to fly 'to her place in the desert' (εἰς τὴν ἔρημον εἰς τὸν τόπον αὐτῆς, *eis tēn erēmon eis ton topon autēs*, lit. 'into the wilderness, to her place [there]'). The wilderness is an evocative motif in scriptural writing, and notably in the Exodus narrative (see on verse 6), which underlies this scene. The people of Israel escaped from the bondage of Egypt by fleeing into the desert, where they were protected and guided by God (Deut.1.30–31; Ps. 78.51–52; Jer. 2.2, 6; Hos. 2.14–15; Amos 2.10).

The desert is a place of safety, but not necessarily one of succour. However, in this case, and whenever the faithful need to be rescued from harm, God can provide his people with support of all kinds: protection, food, training and spiritual help (cf. Beckwith 629; Mounce 241). For the verb τρέφω (*trephō*, 'feed' or 'support'), in this context, see on verse 6. Kiddle (238) claims that the 'desert' in John's vision, which is occupied by him as well as the true Church, represents the Christian way of life. It is 'hedged off from the follies and vices of Babylon the great' (ibid.), and becomes an area of necessary spiritual preparation for life in the new Jerusalem. It is possible that the location of the wilderness, as the place of the woman's escape and support, is subtly linked in addition to the eschatological expectation that the Messiah would come from the desert (Isa. 40.3 = 1QS 8.12–14; 9.19–21; Hos. 11.1; Matt. 2.13–15).

As in the previous section of verse 14, the next sentence picks up the contents of verse 6, and connects with the narrative of 12.1–6 after the 'interval' of 12.7–12. The Church is sustained 'for a time, times and half a time'. This typically apocalyptic phrase alludes to Dan. 7.25 (cf. 12.7), where the cryptic formula, 'time, times, half a time' corresponds to 42 months (= 1,260 days), and is the period during which the Jewish community suffered under the tyrannical Antiochus Epiphanes. See further on 11.2. Beale (674) notes that John is also alluding here to the trial of Israel and the Temple in the related text of Dan. 9.26–27; and this brings into view the idea of a spiritual temple, which lies behind the image of the desert, here and in Rev. 12.6, as a place of nourishment and protection. In the present verse, as elsewhere in Revelation (11.2–3; 12.6; 13.5), the length of eschatological time in view is indefinite, but divinely ordered (see also verse 12). The dragon becomes a 'serpent' (ὄφις, *ophis*) here, and in the next verse; and the use of this synonym has been anticipated in verse 9 (q.v.).

The last phrase of this verse, 'out of reach of the serpent', connects with the verb πέτηται (*petētai*, 'she could fly') and completes the clause 'so that she could fly to her place in the desert'. The Greek expression, ἀπὸ προσώπου (*apo prosōpou*, 'out of reach of', lit. 'from the face of [the serpent]'), is based on a Hebrew idiom. The background word מפני (*mip̄nê*) can mean either 'because of' (cf. Charles 1, 330) or 'for fear of' (GT 551*b*; cf. Hos 10.15 LXX; also Rev. 6.16; 20.11). In any case, the idea expressed in this context is that the woman's flight and her eventual safety are initially brought about by the serpent's presence (Beale 671).

15–16 The persecution of the Church by the powers of evil continues. The serpent tries to catch up with the woman who has fled from him into the desert, and pours after her a potentially destructive torrent of water. In Revelation judgement issues from the mouth of Christ (1.16; 3.16; 19.15; et al.), and deceit from the mouths of demons (9.17–18; 16.13). But this is the sole passage in the Apocalypse where John takes up the metaphor of an overflowing river, stemming from the mouth of the serpent-like monster, to suggest a devilish attempt to destroy the righteous community of the redeemed. The Greek word ποταμοφόρητον (*potamophorēton*, lit. 'swept away by a river'), which is formed from the noun ποταμός (*potamos*, 'river'), is found only here in the New Testament.

If an exact parallel to verse 15 is sought in Jewish literature, none is to be found (Charles 1, 331; Mounce 241). Nevertheless, ideas abound in Judaism which relate to the situation here, and to the life of the Johannine audience which is being addressed. First, it is significant that, in the Old Testament, the imagery of torrential floodwaters is used in three particular contexts: in descriptions of military conquest, where flooding often represents divine judgement (Ps. 32.6; Isa. 8.7–8; Jer. 46.8; Dan. 11.10, 40; Hos. 5.10; *Targ. Jer.* 46.7–8; 51.42); in references to the persecution of God's people, who are delivered from their enemies (2 Sam. 22.5; Ps. 46.1–3; Isa. 42.2–3); and in combat texts, when waters and floods themselves are regarded as overwhelmingly evil, and therefore adamantly opposed to a Lord who is sovereign over them (Ps. 18.4; 29.3–4; 93.3–4; Isa. 50.2; 51.10; Nahum 1.4; Hab. 3.8–9). Elements of all three of these metaphorical interpretations of waters in flood belong to the figurative language of verse 15 (and 16). But the prophetseer seems to have in mind especially the second and third: deliverance from persecution and the victory of God in Christ over evil forces.

It is noteworthy, however, as Beale (672) points out, that in the literature of Qumran floodwaters symbolize deception, as well as persecution by satanic forces (1QH 3[11].12–18; 6.22–24; 8.14–15; CD 1.14–15; et al.; cf. Ps. 144.7–8; Song of Sol. 8.7); although it must be said that the theme of lying, in the imagery of these passages, is not markedly evident. On the basis of the use of the floodwaters image in the Old Testament and the literature of Judaism, and the occurrence of 'mouth' metaphors in the Apocalypse, Beale (673) goes on to argue that the picture of a flood spewing from the serpent's mouth in verse 15 represents his attempt to destroy the Church by deception and false teaching. Deceit and false accusation are certainly a natural part of Satan's character and activity in the end-time, according to both Jewish and Christian writing; cf. *1 Enoch* 69.4; *Jub.* 1.20; Matt. 24.24; Luke 22.31; John 13.2, 27; 2 Cor. 2.11; 11.3; 2 Thess. 2.9–11; 1 Tim. 2.14.

This theme is also evident elsewhere in Revelation. The serpent is identified as the 'deceiver of the whole world' in 12.9; and the oracles addressed to the seven churches of Asia in Rev. 2—3 show that the Johannine community had already begun to experience Satan's flood of deception (2.2, 14, 20; cf. 2.13–16, 20–22; 3.15–17), as well as false accusation (2.9; 3.9) and persecution (2.10, 13). The difficulties which beset the churches around John no doubt included, as well, internal conflict caused by differing Christologies (see above, 4–6; also Smalley, *Thunder and Love* 121–37). When such problems are mentioned in Rev. 2—3, the devil's threatening and powerful presence is also described (2.9, 13, 24; 3.9); so Kiddle 239.

The Exodus motif is continued in verses 15–16. For when Israel escaped from the oppression of Egypt, the flight of God's people to the wilderness was threatened by the barrier of the Sea of Reeds, which God overcame for them (Exod. 14.15—15.10; cf. 1.22; also Isa. 42.15; Dan. 9.26–27). The depiction of the Church under pressure in verse 15 is allegorical, and timelessly applicable to the experience of the saints. It is therefore unnecessary to look for a literal and historical basis to John's imagery in this scene; although notice the attempt by the Jewish authorities, led by Saul, to eradicate the early Church (Acts 8.1–3). However, the problems which surrounded the Johannine circle itself, both externally and internally (see above), provide an immediate as well as a lasting setting for the theological and eschatological battle which is being fought in 12.15, and in Chapter 12 and Revelation generally. The second part of the Apocalypse (12—22) demonstrates that, as in 12.15–16, the faithful will be protected from the agents of satanic deception and persecution (13.14; 18.23; 19.20), who will finally be overthrown (12.7–9). The floods of deceit and destruction are then replaced by the river of the water of life, flowing from the heavenly throne (22.1; cf. Mounce 242). See further verse 16; and, for this verse, Beale 671–75.

Verse 16 reflects the situation of conflict between the dragon-serpent and the woman, between evil and good, described in verse 15; but now the situation is reversed, and the Church is rescued from the serpent's pursuit (see above). The action of the earth 'swallowing the river which the dragon spewed from its mouth' is a further direct allusion to the Exodus narrative, and the experience of Israel in the desert. When the Egyptians pursued the Israelites through the waters of the Red Sea, 'the earth swallowed them' (Exod. 15.12). In the wilderness itself, moreover, 'the earth opened its mouth and swallowed' the family of Korah, Dathan and Abiram because they rebelled against Moses

(Num. 16.32; see 16.20–35). Their rebellion was caused by a perception that Moses and Aaron had exalted themselves in taking up positions of leadership (Num. 16.3), although these were instigated by God himself (16.28–30; Exod. 4.14–16). By challenging the leadership of Moses and Aaron, and counselling a return to Egypt (Num. 16.12–14), the members of the tribe of Korah were in effect despising the Lord (16.30) and attempting to obstruct God's redemptive purposes.

In both settings, at the Exodus and in the desert, divine intervention overcame opposition to God and his people. Equally, by recapitulating these scenes in the present verse, John is figuratively declaring that the Christian community will at all times be protected and supported. The floodwaters (ποταμόν, *potamon*, lit., as in the translation, 'river') of compromise in the face of persecution, false teaching and social pressures, which are satanic in origin, will be overcome; and the Church will be guided to a place of support and preservation prepared by God (Rev. 12.6, 14). See Exod. 15.13, 17; Ps. 74.13–14; Isa. 30.7; 51.10; Jer. 51.34–37; also Beale 675–76. Note the balance in this verse between the 'mouth' (τὸ στόμα, *to stoma*) of the evil dragon and the 'mouth' of the divinely controlled and rescuing earth.

17   The monster-dragon is 'furious with the woman' and goes off to 'wage war with the rest of her descendants'. The verb, ὠργίσθη (*ōrgisthē*, lit. 'was angry'), is used only here and at 11.18 in the Apocalypse. The motif of anger on the part of a persecutor is a feature of martyrologies in both Judaism and early Christianity; cf. Dan. 3.13; 11.30; 2 Macc. 7.39; 4 Macc. 8.2; Acts 7.54; *Mart. Pol.* 12.2; et al. So Aune 707–708. However, this passage is not concerned exclusively with martyrdom (see below).

Verse 17 appears to be a repetitive summary of verses 13–16; although the introductory καί (*kai*, 'then', lit. 'and') suggests a sequential movement in the action of the scene. Nevertheless, the exact relationship between verse 17, and the preceding verses 13–16, is not immediately clear. Beckwith (618–20, 624–30), followed somewhat cautiously by Beale (676–78; cf. Sweet 203–205), argues that the woman in verses 6, 13–16 represents the suffering of the 'ideal' Church from a heavenly perspective, while the 'descendants' of verse 17 are the troubled people of God on earth (see esp. Beckwith 619). Beale (676–77) supports this interpretation by drawing attention to the presentation of the woman first in heaven (12.1–2) and then on earth (verse 17), as well as to the corporate understanding of the woman with children in both dimensions (12.1, 13–16; cf. 19.7–9; 21.2; also Isa. 54.1–3; 66.7–10, 22; et al.). On this showing, Rev. 12.17 delineates a contrast between the whole Church in heaven and on earth; although the metaphorical action of verses 13–16, even if viewed from heaven, is clearly played out on earth (see verses 13 and 16).

Beale (678) also suggests, as a viable alternative understanding of this passage, that four temporal stages are revealed in the narrative of Chapter 12: the messianic community before Jesus (verses 1–4); the appearance of Christ in the covenant circle (5); the persecution of the Christian community immediately following the ascension of Jesus (6, 13–16); and the suffering of the Church at the end-time (17). However, it is difficult to measure temporal progress in apocalyptic visions; and Rev. 12 is essentially concerned with the standing, and timeless, eschatological battle between good and evil (see below, 378; also on 12.7–9).

A key to the interpretation of verse 17, and the explanation of its relationship to verses 13–16 and Chapter 12 generally, is to be found in the statement that the dragon departed 'to wage war with the rest of her (the woman's) descendants'. The term used here for 'descendants' is σπέρμα (*sperma*, lit. 'seed'), and it appears in the Apocalypse only in the present text. The offspring of the woman, who is a corporate, ecclesiological figure, have been implicitly in view throughout this chapter; but this is the first time that they are mentioned explicitly. The dragon now engages in furious battle with the *remainder* of the woman's children: that is, members of the Church *in addition* to the son who has just been born to her (verse 5); cf. BDAG 937. These are neither Gentiles (Hughes 142–43) nor martyrs (Kiddle 239–40); they are the members of the true Israel in its totality, including those who belong to the Johannine community.

The woman's descendants, that is to say, are all those who remain on earth, in the present and in the future, as followers of the Lamb (see Beckwith 619). As such, they maintain obedient and faithful testimony to their Lord (verse 17*b*), and are therefore constantly vulnerable to attacks from the evil one; he regularly 'wages war' against them. But they are also one with the Church in heaven; and we have already seen that the line between the material and the spiritual in Rev. 12 is very finely drawn. The 'war' of the ongoing battle in heaven between Michael and the dragon (verses 7–9, q.v.) is continued on earth (verse 17); and this is a timeless conflict which affects the whole Church, wherever it is to be found (cf. Rev. 6.10–11; 19.1–2). But, through the salvific and protective work of God in Christ (12.6, 14; 7.15–17), victory is always possible for his saints (12.10–11; 15.3–4; 19.11–16; cf. Matt. 16.18).

The assertion that the messianic community consists of those who 'obey God's commands and maintain their witness to Jesus' supports this view. The faithful of any background and of any period of history, John is saying, are able to withstand the onslaughts of Satan by loving obedience to God, and consistent witness to Christ before other people. The phrase, τῶν τηρούντων τὰς ἐντολὰς τοῦ θεοῦ (*tōn tērountōn tas entolas tou theou*, lit. 'those who keep the commands of God') reappears in almost exactly the same form at 14.12. It conforms to the author's practice of describing the actors in this apocalyptic drama by using participial phrases (note also 11.7; 12.9; 17.1; 18.9, 15; 19.20; 21.9, 15); cf. Aune 709. The allusion here to obeying God's commands probably refers primarily to the ethical demands of the Decalogue, and then to the need in the Johannine community for its members to obey the love command (Aune 709–12); cf. John 14.15, 21; 15.10; 1 John 2.3–4; 3.22, 24; 5.3; also Sir. 32.23; Matt. 19.17; Rom. 2.25–27; 1 Cor. 7.19; *2 Clem.* 4.5. For the unique New Testament expression in 1 John 5.2, 'doing the commandments' of God (by obeying the love command), see Smalley, *1, 2, 3 John* 268–69.

The second part of the present couplet, now referring to Jesus, is also reflected in Rev. 14.12. For the concept of 'witness' in Revelation see on 1.2. The genitive, in the phrase ἐχόντων τὴν μαρτυρίαν Ἰησοῦ (*echontōn tēn martyrian Iēsou*, lit. 'holding fast to the witness of Jesus'), may be subjective, as in 1.2, meaning the testimony given *by* Jesus himself which the Church is to reproduce (so Sweet 205). But it is more probable that in this context the genitive should be taken as objective, giving the sense of the need for Christians to maintain their witness *to* Jesus (hence the translation). Beale (679) thinks that there may be a deliberate ambiguity in the text: the witness in question is that given to the Church by Christ, and also the witness borne to him by its members.

It is evident that Gen. 3.15, the prophecy addressed to the serpent in the garden of Eden, lies behind the thought of the narrative in Rev. 12; for the promise that 'enmity will be placed between the serpent and the woman' has been fulfilled in this chapter (see esp. verses 4 and 13). The second part of the prophecy, that 'warfare' will occur between the offspring of both the serpent and the woman, is the subject of verse 17. The time has now come for the woman's posterity 'to confront victoriously the hostility of the serpent' (Prigent 395). This situation will be more fully demonstrated in the next chapter. See also Michaels 153–54.

18   For the placing of this pivotal verse in the drama, and its subject, see the textual note on 12.18; also above, 311. In a clearly theatrical movement the dragon, not the prophet-seer, takes his place centre-stage on the 'seashore' (ἐπὶ τὴν ἄμμον τῆς θαλάσσης, *epi tēn ammon tēs thalassēs*, lit. 'upon the sand of the sea'; cf. Gen. 32.12). The tense of ἐστάθη (*estathē*, 'he took his stand', lit. 'he stood') is aorist; and this may indicate that the temporary stance of the dragon, calling up his 'terrible ally' (13.1) on his way to war (Swete 160–61), is to have ongoing implications.

The restless waters of the sea would have been a familiar sight to John on Patmos, and a natural setting for his eschatological visions (Swete 160); and they may even have provided the seer with a picture of the troubled society and suffering Christian communities which surrounded him (Hughes 143). The 'sand' of verse 18, invaded by the powers of evil, also forms a marked contrast to the 'rock' of Zion, occupied by the Lamb and his redeemed followers, at 14.1. Clearly, verse 18 concludes the action of Chapter 12; but it also anticipates firmly the remainder of this scene, and its subsequent interval (13.1—15.8).

Sign 5: The Beast from the Sea (13.1–10)

13.1–2   Rev. 13 continues the apocalyptic narrative of the third woe (see on 11.14) and introduces the fifth sign in the sequence of seven signs belonging to this scene (see above). Elaborate theories about the sources and composition of this chapter (Charles 1, 334–44; Aune 725–30; cf. Prigent 397 n. 1) do little to explain its meaning.

The satanic dragon stands on the seashore (12.18), ready to call up his bestial acolytes from the troubled waters in front of him (13.1–10) and from the earth behind (13.11–18). These are allied powers of evil, who will continue a war of oppression against the saints of God (12.17). The depiction of the two apocalyptic beasts in Rev. 13 may in part be derived from Job 40—41, which is the only place in the Old Testament where two evil characters are represented as opposing God (Beale 682). The text in Job alludes to a primordial defeat of the dragon by God (40.32 lxx); but, because of continued defiance by his enemies (41.33–34), the conflict extends into the future (Job 7.12; 40.24–25 lxx; 41.25 lxx). There are echoes of this passage in the present chapter; although a more immediate background is to be found in Daniel (see below).

For the expression, καὶ εἶδον (*kai eidon*, 'I saw'), which introduces John's vision at this point, and for the importance of sight and audition (cf. 13.9) in Revelation, see on 5.1; 4.1; et al. The first beast seems to emerge from the sea. The dragon was 'thrown down' with his angels (12.9); but the beast 'rises up' (ἀναβαῖνον, *anabainon*, lit. 'rising'), to join him on the shore (cf. Thompson 138). The noun, θηρίον (*thērion*, 'beast'), is anarthrous (note the article in verse 2); and this distinguishes the creature here from the 'beast' (where the noun is articular), rising from the abyss, at 11.7. In Revelation, the sea symbolizes at times a force which is hostile to God (cf. 20.13; 21.1; Prigent 396); and there may be further evocations of the Exodus motif here, given that Pharaoh, King of Egypt, is described in Ezek. 29.3 as the 'great dragon' of the waters (cf. Kiddle 238–39). The waters in this context are the sphere of primaeval chaos; and, as an alternative source of evil to the abyss (11.7), they are a fitting point of departure for the beast who is characteristically violent (Bauckham 1297*a*). There is no need to find in the figurative manifestation of the first beast in Rev. 13 an eyewitness account of the order in which he came up from the sea (horns, head, body, feet; see also verse 11); so Mounce 244, against Hendriksen 144–45.

The 'ten horns and seven heads' of the beast in Rev. 13.1 connect directly with the description of the dragon in 12.3, where the order, 'horns and heads', is reversed; see also the 'beast from the abyss' in 11.7; 17.3–8. The similarity in the description of the two creatures is a reminder that the power and authority of the beast in 13.1, such as they are, derive from the dragon (cf. verses 2–4). It may be argued that this imagery is a recapitulation in part of the Jewish tradition of Leviathan, a female monster in Near Eastern mythology, who was separated from Behemoth on the fifth day of creation and consigned to the sea (cf. Job 40.15; 41.1; Ps. 74.13—14; Isa. 27.1; *1 Enoch* 60.7—9; 4 Ezra 6.47—52; *2 Apoc. Bar.* 29.4; *Odes Sol.* 22.5; et al.). So Aune 732. But the primary source for the representation of the forces of evil in Rev. 13.1—2, as a sea monster with ten horns, seven heads and animal-like features, is clearly the vision of four great beasts emerging from the sea in Dan. 7.2—3, 7. Indeed, Rev. 13.1—7 seems to be a 'creative reworking' of Dan. 7.1—7 (Beale 683—84; cf. Milligan 218—19; Roloff 154—55; Prigent 401—405; also Barker, *The Revelation* 226—36).

The seven heads of the beast in verse 1 are therefore best understood as a composite of the seven heads of the four beasts in Dan. 7; just as other features of the Danielic beasts belong to the monster from the sea, according to verse 2 (see Dan. 7.4—6). Similarly, the ten 'coronets' (διαδήματα, *diadēmata*, lit. 'diadems'), on the ten horns, refer to Daniel's fourth beast (7.24), whose horns are interpreted as ten 'kings'. The symbol of the coronet, denoting authority, and acting as a parody of the kingship of Christ, is worn on the horns of the beast possibly to suggest 'brute force' (Mounce 245). More to the point, however, the fact that coronets are worn on the *heads* of the dragon, according to 12.3, indicates Satan's superior (if false) claim to dominion (cf. Roloff 156). The imagery of the sea monster is regularly used in the Old Testament to describe oppressive and evil kingdoms (see 12.3). Just as the dragon in Rev. 12 depicts the evil forces behind the kingdoms of this world, then, so in this passage Satan's minion, whose seven heads and ten horns suggest a completeness of usurped and unjust authority, symbolizes in an entirely appropriate manner the ultimate enemy of the believing Church (Mounce 245).

The 'blasphemous titles' on the heads of the satanic creature in 13.1 are also a vivid reminder of the arrogant figure who blasphemes in Dan. 7.8—28; and he is associated with the fourth kingdom (cf. Rev. 13.5—6). This phrase 'blasphemous titles' (ὀνόματα βλασφημίας, *onomata blasphēmias*, lit. 'names of blasphemy') is used at Rev. 17.3, to describe one aspect of the scarlet beast, who also has seven heads and ten horns, upon which the great harlot is seated. Names in Revelation also belong, by contrast, to Christ and his followers (2.3, 17; 14.1; 19.12, 16; 21.14; 22.4).

The titles of blasphemy on the seven heads of the beast may allude to the honorific designations given to Roman emperors in the first century AD, in order to support their wish to be venerated as divine within the cult of Caesar. The imperial coinage of the time bore eloquent testimony to this desire; and, at their deaths, Julius Caesar, Augustus, Claudius and Vespasian were declared by the Senate to be 'divine' (*divus*). See further Swete 161—62; Caird 163. That the Emperor Domitian wished to be addressed as *dominus et deus* ('lord and god'), according to Suetonius, *Dom.* 13, is not relevant to this discussion if the Apocalypse can be dated to the reign of Vespasian (see below, on verse 3; cf. Smalley, *Thunder and Love* 40—50; Wilson, 'Domitianic Date'; also Thompson, *Book of Revelation* 95—197). John would no doubt have regarded such arrogance on the part of the imperial rulers as an attempt to rival God, by assuming titles of which he alone is worthy (cf. *Asc. Isa.* 4.2—12; 2 Thess. 2.4, where impious figures similarly demand to be worshipped in place of God); see Prigent 404—405, and also on verse 4.

All this may suggest that the beast of Rev. 13.1 symbolizes the Roman Empire, the unjust oppressor of the Christian Church. He comes from the sea like the Roman troops, when they invaded the eastern Mediterranean; and he also resembles the proconsul, the imperial representative in the province of Asia Minor, who 'emerged from the sea' annually when he landed at Ephesus (Rowland, *Open Heaven* 431). The beast has the authority of the evil one (verses 2, 4); he boastfully takes the name of God in vain (5—6); he makes war victoriously against the saints (7); and he receives the worship of the pagan world (4, 7—8). In the view of van de Water ('Beast from the Sea'), the two beasts of Rev. 13 are to be identified with political messianism in Palestinian and diaspora Judaism, in the time of Domitian, more than with Roman government.

However, while the vision of the prophet-seer in this passage is historically anchored to the situation confronting his own community, its meaning and relevance move beyond it. The problems which beset the Johannine circle in any case involved more than persecution from Rome (see above, 4–6); and the writer is articulating here a truth about the history of salvation which is spiritual and timeless. The beast is a symbol of the perpetual deification of secular authority (Mounce 246). Even more, he represents the powers of evil which lie behind the kingdoms of this world, and which encourage in society, at any moment in history, compromise with the truth and opposition to the justice and mercy of God.

The grotesque appearance of the beast is described with further detail in verse 2. Its features, like those of a leopard, a bear and a lion, bring together in a single figure the characteristics of the four beasts which appear in the vision of Daniel 7 (see above, on verse 1). There, the prophet saw a winged lion, standing upright like a human being (7.4); a bear with tusks in its mouth (verse 5); a four-headed leopard, with wings (6); and a fourth beast, terrifying and very strong, with great iron teeth, powerful feet and ten horns (7–8). For Daniel, these creatures represented four kingdoms on earth, hostile to God's covenant people (7.17, 23); for John, the beast from the sea becomes the figure of Antichrist (see Rev. 13.5–8), who is spiritually opposed to the messianic community, the descendants of the woman (see further on verse 1, and 12.17). The terms, 'leopard' (πάρδαλις, *pardalis*, which may be the 'panther') and 'bear' (ἄρκος, *arkos*), occur in the New Testament only in the present text. For lions in Revelation see also 4.7; 5.5; 9.8, 17; 10.3. For the interpretation of Dan. 7.1–8 in early Christian texts see *Barn.* 4.4–5; cf. also 4 Ezra 11.1—12.39.

The scene in verse 2 is a brief enthronization; it reveals the beast as the agent of the dragon (Roloff 156), and involves a parody of the divine attributes of sovereignty (contrast 4.2; 5.7; 19.4–5; 22.3). For the 'throne' (θρόνος, *thronos*, 'rule') of Satan see 2.13; 16.10; cf. also 1QM 15.2–3; Luke 4.6; *2 Enoch (J)* 29.4; *Life of Adam and Eve* 47.3. The dragon confers on the beast his own power, rule and great authority, although these are ultimately derived from God himself. Satan and his followers, that is to say, are in league with the anti-Christian forces of this world, wherever they may be found; and, in this way, the plans of the devil to deceive and destroy the Church are potentially in the process of fulfilment. However, the beast from the sea, like the dragon himself, must reckon with the endurance and faithfulness of God's people (13.10), and indeed with the ultimate victory of the Father through the Son (14.1–5, 12; 15.3–4).

To the extent that the Roman Empire is in view in verses 1–2, as the enemy of the saints (see above), it is apparent that the injunction elsewhere in the New Testament, that Christians should be obedient to the powers invested in the state (see Rom. 13.1–7; 1 Tim. 2.1–2; 1 Pet. 2.13–17), differs from the thought underlying Rev. 13. But the apocalyptic situation is manifestly different. Rev. 13.1–2 depicts in part a regime which defies the righteousness of God, whereas the submission of a community to civic authority can only be laid upon believers when the delegated powers of their rulers are properly exercised. In any case, civil disobedience forms no part of biblical ethics. See further Caird, *Apostolic Age* 156–80; Mounce 247; Knight 95–96.

3–4 One of the seven heads of the beast from the sea appears to have received a 'death-blow' (ὡς ἐσφαγμένην εἰς θάνατον, *hōs esphagmenēn eis thanaton*, lit. 'as slaughtered to death'), from which 'mortal wound' (ἡ πληγὴ τοῦ θανάτου αὐτοῦ, *hē plēgē tou thanatou autou*, lit. 'the plague of its death') it had been healed. Hughes (146) oddly interprets this phenomenon to mean the expansion of apostolic Christianity in its earliest days, followed by its falling away in times of persecution by the Antichrist. In accordance with the interpretation given to the beasts in Dan. 7 as kingdoms (note esp. 7.17, 23), however, and to the beast from the sea in Rev. 13 as in part the imperial power of Rome (see on verses 1–2), it is best to assume that the image of a bestial 'head' in the present context, decapitated by the sword (verse 14) yet restored, refers in the first place to one of the oppressive Roman emperors.

Aune (736) notes that if the cardinal number, μίαν (*mian*, 'one [of the heads]'), is construed as an ordinal ('the first'), this might allude to Julius Caesar, the 'first' Roman Emperor according to one reckoning (see Smalley, *Thunder and Love* 46), who was assassinated in March 44 BC; but this is improbable, as Caesar did not survive his attack. A more likely candidate is the Emperor Caligula, who was taken seriously ill during his reign and, according to Suetonius (*Calig.* 14), recovered. For arguments against this identification see Peake, *Revelation* 314–15. The most plausible explanation is that which establishes a link between the slaughtered head and the Emperor Nero, who assumed the throne in AD 54 but took his own life in June 68. Shortly after the tyrant's death, and as early as the time of Vespasian (AD 69–79), rumours began to circulate in Asia that Nero had come back to life (the *Nero redivivus* legend); and several pretenders, claiming to be Nero, appeared (Tacitus, *Hist.* 1.78; 2.8; cf. Swete ci–cii). As a variation on this theme, Nero was eventually regarded as truly dead; but it was also expected that, as an Antichrist figure, he would return from the dead to usher in the end-time (Suetonius, *Nero* 57; cf. *Sib. Or.* 4.137–39; 5.28–34).

For this theory, and its application to the beast of Rev. 13.3, see further Frend, *Rise of Christianity* 331 n. 8; Moffatt 429–30; Beckwith 635–36; Roloff 156–57; Aune 737–40; Prigent 405–406. Klauck, 'Do They Never Come Back?', claims that a *Nero redivivus* figure is mythopoetically present in the texts about the beast in Rev. 13.3 and 17.3 (q.v.), but that the historical figure behind the image is in fact Domitian (see esp. 696–98); for arguments against this identification see Beckwith 706. The understanding of the seven heads of the beast in Chapter 17 is a development of the imagery in Rev. 13, and not truly a part of the immediate vision.

If the *Nero redivivus* legend lies behind at least part of the scene in 13.3, this could affect to some extent the dating of Revelation. Since Nero died in AD 68, the Apocalypse must obviously have been written after that date. But there is no need, as a result, to move the period of its composition to a much later date, say to the reign of Domitian (AD 81–96); so Beckwith 197–208, and others. For reports of the Emperor's survival began to circulate in AD 69, the very next year after Nero's death, and early in the reign of Vespasian (Tacitus, *Hist.* 2.8). The view adopted in this commentary is that Revelation was written in AD 70 (see above, 2–3); and such a conclusion accords with the evidence just cited. Cf. Smalley, *Thunder and Love* 40–49; see further on verse 1, and on 17.9–11.

One problem involved in making a connection between Nero, or any imperial individual, and the slaughtered head in verse 3 is that the second possessive pronoun in this sentence, αὐτοῦ (*autou*, 'its'), refers to the beast. In other words, it was not the *head* which was restored from a mortal wound, but the *beast* itself (similarly verse 14). In that case, the text could mean that an individual, like Nero, was fatally injured (in this case, by his own hand), but that later the Roman Empire he represented recovered its life and stability. An exact situation of this kind occurred in AD 68–69. After the death of Nero in June 68, anarchy and bloodshed took hold in the territories; and this continued throughout the time of the rebellious imperial caretakers, Galba, Otho and Vitellius (AD 68–69). But, when he came to the throne in July 69, Vespasian slowly restored the Empire to peace (cf. Moffatt 430).

However, the interpretation of the imagery in 13.3 so far considered assumes that the beast and its slain head must be related in some way to Rome and one of its emperors.

The exegesis of verse 1 (above) has produced a general, rather than specific, understanding of the beast. The imperial and oppressive strength of Rome may be included in its significance; but essentially John is referring to the powers of this world in opposition to the next. The same is true, it may be argued, in verse 3. Here, the vision refers to the forces of evil and unrighteousness in all their forms. From the beginning of history until now, there has been opposition to God and his people; and in the first century that conflict embraced the Johannine community. Whenever paganism has been resisted, injustice has always managed to be reinstated. In the end, and at the end, evil will be conquered (19.1–10; 17.12–14; 22.3–5). Meanwhile, Satan and his followers can all too often be in control; and, perversely, the powers of darkness regularly command the admiration and allegiance of the whole world (verse 3b; cf. 1 Tim. 5.15, where the phrase ὀπίσω τοῦ σατανᾶ, *opisō tou satana*, lit. '[some have turned away] after Satan', balances ὀπίσω τοῦ θηρίου, *opisō tou thēriou*, lit. '[followed] after the beast' in Rev. 13.3). Such an explanation of the thought in verse 3 also fits the theology of verse 4 (q.v.). Cf. Mounce 248–49.

The phrase 'the whole world' (ὅλη ἡ γῆ, *holē hē gē*, lit. 'the whole earth') is a metaphor meaning 'all the *people* of the world', since the inhabitants of the earth are given a brief speaking part in verse 4. See also 17.8; 4 Ezra 12.3. The syntax of the last sentence in verse 3 is elliptical, and requires the addition of a verb, such as to 'follow'. The adverb ὀπίσω (*opisō*, 'behind') can function as a preposition, when used with the genitive, to mean 'after' (BDAG 716a).

The people of the world now worship the dragon, as well as the beast on whom satanic authority has been conferred. For the interpretation of verse 4 see on verse 3; and for the delegation of the dragon's authority to the beast see on verse 2. The deification of secular power is nothing less than the worship of Satan, whose authority is evidently wielded by the beast (Mounce 249), whereas in the tradition of Judaism God alone deserves to be worshipped (Exod. 20.2–7; Deut. 6.13; Esth. 4.17e LXX; Matt. 4.10 par.). For the worship of Satan see *Asc. Isa.* 2.7. In eschatological combat mythology, the antagonist often claims to be God, broadcasting this pretension arrogantly from the temple; and he demands worship on that basis (cf. Dan. 11.36–37; *Asc. Isa.* 4.6; *Sib. Or.* 5.33–34; 2 Thess. 2.4; et al.; see above, on verse 1). These features are notably absent from the scene in Rev. 13.1–4; and this is probably because John has reshaped the myth for his own purposes, in order to focus attention on the arrogance and blasphemy of the beast, which are directed *against* God (see verses 1, 5–6). Cf. Aune 740. For the verb προσκυνέω (*proskyneō*, 'worship' or 'prostrate'), which is used twice in verse 4, and here for the first time in relation to the beast, see on 4.10. For the worship of the beast from the sea, elsewhere in the Apocalypse, see 13.8, 12, 15; 14.9, 11; 16.2; 20.4.

The rhetorical question, 'who is like the beast?', echoes a similar literary form in Old Testament hymns (cf. Ps. 18.31; 89.8; Isa. 44.7; Mic. 7.18; et al.; also 1QH 15.28). But in those contexts the question, 'who is like you?', refers to God; for only about him can such an interrogation rightly be made. Clearly, therefore, the question in relation to the beast, in verse 4, must be a parody of Judaic expressions of praise (Charles 1, 351); and, in particular, the text in the Song of Moses, 'who is like you, O Lord, among the gods?' (Exod. 15.11) seems to be in mind. The parody is ironic. To worship Satan, rather than the true and eternal Lord (Rev. 7.14–17; 22.8–9), is a vain exercise, for the rule of the devil and his agents is about to end (12.12).

The beast, then, exercises its dominion as the viceregent of Satan's powers; and the worship it receives is a parody of that which is due to God alone. But, as Fiorenza (83–84) points out, the image of the beast from the waters in Rev. 13.1–4 is also the parodic mirror image of the *Lamb*. Thus, the monster's blasphemous names (verse 1; cf. verses 5–6) parody the unknown name of the Lamb, who is called the Word of God, King and Lord (19.11–16). One of the beast's heads has received a 'death-blow' (verse 3); and the verb which appears in this context (ἐσφαγμένην, *esphagmenēn*, lit. 'slaughtered') is used in 5.6, 9, 12; 13.8 to describe the death of the Lamb. The monster shares the authority of the dragon (verses 2–3), just as Christ shares the throne of God (5.6–10; 22.3). Furthermore, the followers of the beast, who prostrate themselves in adoration before the beast, come from the 'whole world' (verse 3); and, in the same way, the members of the covenant community of the Lamb derive from every tribe and language, people and nation (5.9).

The second rhetorical question in the chant of verse 4*b*, 'who can fight against it [the beast]?', which balances the first, is an expression of powerlessness and despair in the face of evil (cf. 1 Sam. 4.8; Lam. 5.8; *Apoc. Sed.* 5.4). Such an excuse for compromising with satanic injustice has about it a modern resonance.

5   The beast, the figurative agent of the satanic dragon, is given permission to act in opposition to God, although his antagonism is not manifested until verse 6. The identical phrase, καὶ ἐδόθη αὐτῷ (*kai edothē autō[i]*, lit. 'and it was given to him'), which includes the verb δίδωμι (*didōmi*, 'give') in the aorist passive, is used four times in verses 5–7. In each case the verb may be construed as a passive of divine activity (see on 6.2, 4, et al.). The authority of the beast is temporary and derived, stemming immediately from the dragon (verses 2, 4), but ultimately from God. This is apparent from the closing statement of verse 5, that the beast's power was divinely limited to 'forty-two months'; for this formula, expressing an eschatological period of time decreed by God, see Dan. 7.25; 8.14; 9.27. See further on Rev. 11.2–3; also 12.6, 14. God, not the devil, appoints the times and seasons; and Satan is angry precisely because his time is limited (12.12). Cf. Beasley-Murray 213; Beale 695.

The reference to the 'boastful words, even blasphemies', spoken by the beast, clearly alludes to Dan. 7.8, 20 (note the similarity in the Greek between Rev. 13.5 and Dan. 7.8, 20 LXX Theod.). In the Danielic passage, the 'little horn' is said to have a 'mouth speaking arrogantly'; and this is an indication that the horn symbolizes a person, who is able to speak in this way. However, in the present verse (Rev. 13.5) the beast already has a mouth (verse 2); so that for the creature to be 'permitted to mouth' boastful and blasphemous words (ἐδόθη αὐτῷ στόμα, *edothē autō[i] stoma*, lit. 'it was given a mouth') reflects a Semitic idiom, meaning 'it was given something to say' (cf. Luke 21.15; Aune 742); hence the translation. In the sentence, 'the beast was permitted to mouth boastful words, even blasphemies', the second καί (*kai*, and) is epexegetic. The proud speech of the beast is explained by the following phrase ('*even* blasphemies'), and expanded in verse 6.

The double theme of arrogant pride and blasphemy, on the part of a usurper of divine authority, appears in Dan. 11.36; although the worship received by the dragon and the beast in Rev. 13.4 does not explicitly stem from a claim to take God's place. For blasphemy in association with the beast see on verse 1; and for the derivation of the beast's description from Dan. 7 see on verses 1–2. See also, for the combination of blasphemy and hubris, Ezek. 28.2; 2 Thess. 2.3–5; *Did.* 16.4; et al. Beale (695–96) notes that the characteristic activity of deception is involved in the boastful words of the beast (see on 12.9; also 13.4, 11–15). The 'blasphemy' of the bestial speech in this passage also includes the notion of deceit; for such words can only come from one who wishes to slander, and thereby denigrate, the name of the true God (cf. BDAG 178); cf. Dan. 11.32, 36.

6   The outcome of the beast's haughty and defamatory activity is described in this verse, which again alludes to Dan. 7.25. In both places there is a description of an eschatological and demonic figure, who speaks in opposition to the Most High, attempts to put himself in the place of God and persecutes the saints (cf. Rev. 13.3–8); see also Dan. 8.10,

25; 11.36. For 'opening the mouth' and 'blasphemies' see on verse 5. The expression ἤνοιξεν τὸ στόμα αὐτοῦ (*ēnoixen to stoma autou*, 'it opened its mouth') is used elsewhere in the New Testament to introduce an extended discourse (e.g. Matt. 5.2; Acts 8.35); and this may suggest here that the blasphemies of the beast against God were to be sustained (cf. Mounce 250). The blasphemous aspects of these speeches lies less in the direct slander of God and more in the pretension of trying to occupy God's place and seize his sovereign power (Roloff 157); see on verse 5.

The verb, βλασφημέω (*blasphēmeō*, 'blaspheme'), occurs four times in Revelation: twice with God as the object (16.11, 21), and on two occasions with the divine 'name' as the object (13.6; 16.9). Elsewhere in the New Testament, the verb is used intransitively (e.g. Mark 2.7; John 10.36; Acts 26.11). The 'name' (ὄνομα, *onoma*) of God is the epitome of his being and sovereign power (cf. Roloff 157–58; and see on 2.3, 13). To 'revile the name' of the true deity, by slandering him, therefore involves misleading people; and such an action violates the third commandment by using the name of the Lord God wrongfully (Exod. 20.11 = Deut. 5.11). This theme is echoed not only in Dan. 7.25 and 11.36 (see above), but also in Isa. 52.5 (q.v.).

The beast blasphemes both against the name of God and against his 'dwelling-place'. There is no historical reference in this text, and no allusion to the Jerusalem Temple. The term, σκηνή (*skēnē*, 'tent' or 'dwelling'), always refers to a temporary structure, in contrast to the permanent construction of a building (cf. BDAG 928*a*; note also the 'tent [of witness]' in Acts 7.44, Heb. 9.2, 6; *1 Clem.* 43.2–3; et al.). Charles (1, 352–53) interprets the term 'dwelling-place', as used in verse 6, to mean the Shekinah, the manifested glory of God which in the thought of Judaism was associated with the tabernacle (cf. Exod. 40.34–35; et al.). But a Danielic background, from Dan. 8.10–13, is more immediately present here. In that eschatological passage the 'sanctuary' is described as being desecrated by the tyrannical oppressor, Antiochus IV Epiphanes, who simultaneously attacks the heavenly 'host' of God's people (see esp. verse 13).

These two ideas, sanctuary and host, appear to be synonymous in Dan. 8; and the same is true of Rev. 13.6. Indeed, their juxtaposition in Dan. 8.13 may account for the awkward syntax of the present verse in the Apocalypse, where the 'dwelling-place' of God is immediately qualified by the descriptive, prepositional phrase 'those who are sheltered in heaven' (Beale 697). By definition, that clause cannot describe a third object of the beast's slander, after the name and dwelling of God, for it makes no sense to 'blaspheme' those who dwell in heaven. It is logical, then, to take 'those who are sheltered in heaven' in 13.6 as a further description of God's 'dwelling-place', his covenant people (see 11.1–2; 12.6, 14); and such an understanding is reflected by introducing an epexegetical and connective expression ('that is'), not present in the Greek, into the translation. The equation between God's 'dwelling' and his saints who are 'sheltered' there is also established by the use in verse 6 of both the noun σκηνή (*skēnē*, 'dwelling', 'tabernacle') and the verb σκηνοῦν (*skēnoun*, 'to dwell/tabernacle'). The only other appearance in Revelation of those two terms, in the same order, occurs at 21.3; and there the emphasis is similarly on the presence of God, 'tenting' among his people (cf. 7.15; 21.22). For the composition of Rev. 13.6, and the need to omit the conjunction καί (*kai*, 'and'), before the last clause, see the textual note on this verse.

The faithful on earth are the focus of secular opposition, because they are loyal to their Christian calling; their ultimate citizenship is in heaven (Phil. 3.20; cf. Eph. 2.6; Col. 3.1). Cf. Caird 167. This means that in Rev. 13.6, as in Dan. 8, the powers of evil, symbolized by the blasphemous and warlike beast (verse 7), are antagonistic towards the saints both on earth *and* in heaven (see 12.12). 'Those tabernacling in heaven' (verse 6), accordingly, include those who have died, and are now in the presence of the Lord, as well as believers on earth (cf. Beale 697). According to the Fourth Gospel, there was similar resistance to truth and goodness when God 'dwelt' (ἐσκήνωσεν, *eskēnōsen*) among us in the Word made flesh (John 1.14; 8.40). Cf. Milligan 223–24.

7–8 The beast, as the representative of Satan, has blasphemed the name of God, and slandered his people (verse 6; see verse 5*a*). To do this he is given by God delegated and temporary authority. For the formula ἐδόθη αὐτῷ (*edothē autō[i]*, lit. 'it was given'), used twice in verse 7, see on verse 5. Now the monster is permitted to extend that derived power (verse 5*b*), and to 'make war on the saints and vanquish them', as well as demand their worship. The conflict between good and evil, described by using the imagery of warfare, is a theme carried forward from Chapter 12 (see esp. verses 7 and 17; cf. also 11.7; 16.14; 19.19; 20.8). The battle in the present scene recalls the situation of Dan. 7.8 (LXX), 21, where 'the horn' (Antiochus) 'made war with the holy ones', who needed to defend Jerusalem. In the Old Testament passage, the forces of evil 'prevail over' the saints until the advent of the Ancient One; and then the holy ones gained possession of the kingdom (Dan. 7.21). In Rev. 13.7, however, the saints are conquered, and submit to the authority of the demonic beast. Nevertheless, as the powers of darkness are limited (12.12), so the defeat of the protected saints will not endure; and eventually, through the suffering and exaltation of the Lamb, universal victory will be theirs (15.2; see also 5.9–10; 7.13–17). In the end, God's sovereignty is invincible (19.1–2, 6). For the 'saints' (ἅγιοι, *hagioi*, lit. 'holy ones'), in this passage, see on 5.8.

The authority of the beast, for the moment, is universal. It extends over every 'race and people, and every language group and nation'. For this polysyndetic formula, consisting of four ethnic units, and for its order, see on 5.9. It appears seven times in Revelation (5.9; 7.9; 10.11; 11.9; 13.7; 14.6; 17.15). Cf. further Bauckham, *Climax of Prophecy* 326–37; Aune 361–62. From the four quarters of the world, and indeed from all the inhabitants of the earth, the forces of Satan expect to be worshipped. Such an attitude is the ultimate blasphemy (see also verse 4), since in the Christian scheme worship is due alone to the one true God through his Son (Matt. 4.8–10; 24.24; John 4.23; Eph. 1.11–12; 1 Tim. 2.1–8; Heb. 1.6). It was not simply the Roman Empire, and the imperial wish to be deified, which commanded the devotion of its subjects in John's day; it was any secular power, which vaunted its injustice, and encouraged others to compromise with the truth (see on 13.1–2; also the contrasting reception of universal adoration by the 'son of man' in Dan. 7.14).

For the expression in verse 8, 'all the earth's inhabitants' (πάντες οἱ κατοικοῦντες ἐπὶ τῆς γῆς, *pantes hoi katoikountes epi tēs gēs*, lit. 'all those living on the earth'), see on 3.10. The phrase is a regular and technical term in the Apocalypse, which (as here) refers negatively to unbelievers who are subject to divine judgement, because they oppress the people of God and practise idolatry; see also on 11.10. Only here, however, are 'all' the inhabitants of the world mentioned; such, John implies, is the scope of the beast's influence. The sudden switch from the aorist tense of ἐδόθη (*edothē*, 'was given') in verse 7 to the future indicative here (προσκυνήσουσιν, *proskynēsousin*, 'they will worship') indicates that this part of the vision relates very firmly to the future, and indeed to the end-time (cf. Aune 746). John's roles as seer and prophet are inextricably entwined.

For the 'book of life' in verse 8*b* see on 3.5. The idea of a 'divine register' (Mounce 251) is present in ancient Judaism; and this image is often used in a forensic and judge-mental setting (so Exod. 32.32–33, those who sin will be 'blotted out' of the book which the Lord has written; see also Ps. 69.27–28; Dan. 7.9–10; *1 Enoch* 108.3; *Jub.* 30.22; et al.). For the New Testament use of the 'book of life' figure, meaning those who belong to God in Christ, see Phil. 4.3; and for its use elsewhere in Revelation note (3.5); 17.8; 20.12, 15; 21.27. In 13.8 and 21.27 the book in question is said to be that of the Lamb, as it is through his victorious sacrifice that life for believers becomes possible (5.9–10).

The syntax of this part of verse 8 is not immediately clear, since it apparently allows for two quite different understandings of the Greek. First, given the word order of the text, it seems natural to connect the phrase, ἀπὸ καταβολῆς κόσμου (*apo katabolēs kosmou*, 'since the creation of the world'), with the immediately preceding participial adjective, ἐσφαγμένου (*esphagmenou*, 'sacrificed', lit. 'slaughtered'). In this case, the reference is to Christ, the Lamb, whose redemptive death was 'decreed in the counsels of eternity' (Mounce 252); cf. *T. Mos.* 1.14; Acts 2.23; 1 Pet. 1.18–20. This exegesis is followed, among others, by REB, Wall (170) and Thompson (140). However, it is not easy, logically or theologically, to make sense of the claim that Jesus the Messiah was crucified at the outset of time (cf. Aune 747), even if he was eternally destined to die for the sins of the world.

It is therefore preferable to adopt the alternative interpretation, which is grammatically possible, and take the prepositional phrase 'since the creation of the world' with the verb γέγραπται (*gegraptai*, 'written'); and, despite the separation in that case between the modifier and its antecedent, such a linkage is strongly supported by the close parallel at 17.8 (q.v.). This means that everyone whose name has not been written 'since the beginning', in the Lamb's book of life, worshipped the beast (hence the translation); so NRSV; Beckwith (638); Aune (746–47); et al. If this sounds like human predestination, it is conditional (Caird 49–50); we cannot earn the right to be included in the register of the faithful, but we may forfeit the privilege, and have our names erased. Christian commitment, in any case, demands a steadfast endurance in right belief and behaviour, which marks a response to the faithfulness of God (13.10; 14.1–5); cf. Roloff 158. In this connection, the movement from the plural ('*all* will worship') to the singular ('*the* name of everyone') in verse 8 may indicate the important and individual responsibility involved in the decision to follow wrongdoing, rather than righteousness. A third, but unnecessary, way of solving the difficulty in the exegesis of this passage is to regard the phrase 'of the sacrificed Lamb' as a redactional gloss (Charles 1, 353; Moffatt 431; Aune 747).

However, as Prigent (410–11) notes, there may be no appreciable theological difference between the alternative suggestions mentioned above: either the Lamb was slain from the creation of the world, or from the outset unbelievers are unrecorded in the roll of the life-giving Christ, just as the faithful find their names there (cf. Eph. 1.4–6). Biblically, God's saving purposes for his creation, in eternity, find their focus in the cross of Christ (Rev. 5.9–10); and, at the same time, salvation is from the beginning God's gift to every believer through the salvific work of the Lamb (14.4; cf. John 6.51). The plan of the Creator, initially and ultimately, 'strives towards the Easter event' (Prigent 411; similarly Beale 703).

For the term, ἐσφαγμένου (*esphagmenou*, lit. 'slaughtered'), used in verse 8 with reference to the Lamb, see on Rev. 5.9. In 13.3 (q.v.), the same word is applied in the form of a parody to one of the heads of the beast. The phrase 'the creation of the world', which is a reference to God's establishment of the visible order (Mounce 252), occurs ten times in the New Testament: always without articles. According to John 17.24, for example, Jesus speaks of the love which the Father gave him 'before (πρό, *pro*) the foundation of the world'. The only other appearance of this expression in Revelation is at 17.8.

9 The directive formula in this verse, 'Let anyone with an ear, listen!', is pivotal (cf. 11.19; 12.18); since it begins to conclude the sign of the beast from the sea (13.1–8) and (more especially) introduces the poetic comment which is to follow (verse 10). The expression is a firm part of the literary structure of the oracles to the seven churches of Asia in Rev. 2—3 (see on 2.7; cf. also 2.11, 17, 29; 3.6, 13, 22); and they reflect a similar saying attributed to Jesus in the synoptic Gospels (Mark 4.9; Matt. 11.15; Luke 14.35). The imperative address to the reader in the present verse has parallels at Rev. 13.18; 14.12;

17.9; but the fact that it connects here so strongly with the command to listen to the Spirit, in the seven oracles of Rev. 2—3, suggests that the prophet-seer is making a direct appeal at this point for the members of the Johannine community to heed the significance of the vision as it now unfolds. Jer. 15.2, to which allusion is made in verse 10 (q.v.), begins with a similarly authoritative proclamation, 'Thus says the Lord'. The formula in verse 9 calls immediate attention to the contents of Jer. 15.2, and suggests in that way how Rev. 13.1–8 should be understood. See further on verse 10.

10   The proverbial saying which makes up the body of this verse is terse and allusive; and its relative obscurity, as it is used in the present context, has produced a number of MS variations (see the textual notes). It is essentially a quotation of the epigram at Jer. 15.2 (LXX); and cf. Jer. 43.11 MT (LXX 50.11). Both of these passages speak of the punishments which will result from the sins of the people; whereas in Rev. 13.10 the consequences of captivity and death are seen to be the lot of the faithful (verse 10*b*). Those whose names are written in the Lamb's book of life (contrast those in verse 8 who worship the satanic beast) are likely to suffer the fate of Jesus himself, at the hands of secular and hostile powers (Matt. 26.50–54; John 15.18). John has therefore selected from the lists in Jeremiah (pestilence, sword, famine, captivity [exile]) the two possible experiences (persecution and the sword [= death]) which relate most closely to the life and expectations of the Johannine community (cf. 13.7; see also Esth. 4.16 for a similar literary formula).

The Greek grammar of the quotation from the Old Testament in verse 10 is complex. In the first half the protasis, εἴ τις εἰς αἰχμαλωσίαν (*ei tis eis aichmalōsian*), which literally means 'if anyone into captivity', lacks a verb, such as 'is taken'; hence the translation. In the second part, the repeated verb in the aorist passive infinitive, ἀποκτανθῆναι (*apoktanthēnai*, 'to be killed'), may be construed in various ways. The best rendering seems to be achieved by taking the first infinitive as the object of an implied verb (so 'if you *are to be* killed by the sword', in the translation) and the second as an imperatival infinitive ('you *must* be killed'). See further Charles 1, 355–57; Aune 749–51.

The final statement of verse 10 is again elliptical, and requires a subject such as 'a call'. The quotation from Jer. 15 in this context is framed by the directive formula in verse 9 (q.v.) and by the interpretative formula in this verse, which shows how the earlier part of verse 10 is to be understood (cf. Aune 751). Since suffering is the potential result of being a Christian, steadfast endurance and unwavering faith are required from the believer (Mounce 254); and the occurrence of articles before the nouns meaning 'endurance' and 'faithfulness' may draw attention to the need for these to be exercised by each individual. For ὑπομονή (*hypomonē*, 'endurance', 'patience'), as a quality which was characteristic of Jesus and is binding on his followers, see on 1.9. The term πίστις (*pistis*, 'faith') here implies 'faithfulness' in tribulation, accompanying 'endurance', more than 'belief' as such. For this noun elsewhere in the Apocalypse see 2.2–3, 19; 14.12; for the idea see 2.13. Cf. also Michel, 'πίστις', esp. 599–605. For 'God's people' (τῶν ἁγίων, *tōn hagiōn*, lit. 'of the saints') see on 5.8; also 13.7; et al. For other uses in Revelation of the adverb ὧδε (*hōde*, 'here'), to introduce a comment by the author, see 13.18; 14.12; 17.9.

The beasts in Rev. 13, from the sea and from the earth, are effectively representatives of the Antichrist figure; although in the New Testament that title is confined to the Johannine literature, and indeed to the Letters of John (see 1 John 2.18, 22; 4.3; 2 John 7). See further on 'Antichrist', as the eschatological antagonist, Smalley, *1, 2, 3 John* 98–100; Aune 751–55.

Sign 6: The Beast from the Earth (13.11–18)

11   The second beast, in this scene of Revelation, emerges from the earth; and its primary mission appears to be that of promoting the worship of the first beast. For the visionary formula, καὶ εἶδον (*kai eidon*, 'then I saw'), see on 5.1; cf. also 13.1. The adjective ἄλλος (*allos*, 'another') is regularly used by John to introduce a new scene (so 7.2; 8.3; 10.1; 15.1; 18.1; 20.12). The imagery in this passage involves the reworking of the Leviathan-Behemoth myth (see on 13.1); cf. Aune 755. According to Judaic tradition Behemoth, the male version of the two primeval monsters, was separated from Leviathan on the fifth day of creation, and made to live in the land (4 Ezra 6.47–54; *1 Enoch* 60.7–10; *2 Apoc. Bar.* 29.4; et al.). The beast from the earth, in this section of Rev. 13 (11–18), is given that description (θηρίον, *thērion*, 'beast') in verse 11 alone. Otherwise, the first monster is identified as a 'beast'; and the second is referred to by means of third-person singular verbs (e.g. verses 11, 12, 13), or the pronoun αὐτός (*autos*, 'it', as in verses 14 and 15).

The phrase, ἀναβαῖνον ἐκ τῆς γῆς (*anabainon ek tēs gēs*, 'emerging [lit. "going up"] from the earth'), is intended as a parallel to the description of the first beast, which John saw 'emerging from the sea' (cf. the beast ascending from the abyss in 11.7). One background to this idea can be found in the prophecy of Daniel, which (as we have seen) exercises a constant influence on the prophet-seer. Thus in Dan. 7.3 the four great beasts emerge from the sea (cf. Rev. 13.1), and in Dan. 7.17 the beasts are interpreted as 'kings arising out of the earth'. Nevertheless, John's symbolism at this point is probably more precise. The sea is the residence of demons, as well as lapping the shores of all the provinces in the Roman Empire; while the realm of the second beast is more limited, and suggests the site of human history, initially Asia Minor (Prigent 415). See further below.

Such an interpretation reinforces the subordination of the second beast to the first, as well as to the dragon; and this secondary role is confirmed by the fact that the beast from the earth has 'two horns, like a ram', instead of the 'ten horns' of the first beast (13.1; cf. Dan. 8.3). The beast from the earth, that is to say, speaks with the full authority of the powers of evil vested in the dragon and the first beast, since he is their agent. If this understanding is correct, there is no reason to regard the two horns of the second beast as an antithetical parody of the two witnesses, two lampstands and two olive trees of 11.3–4 (q.v.); against Kiddle 255; Beale 707. The second beast also 'makes a noise (ἐλάλει, *elalei*, lit. "was speaking" [imperfect]) like a dragon'. Although the noun 'dragon' is anarthrous in this context (ὡς δράκων, *hōs drakōn*, 'as a dragon'), the comparison is almost certainly with *the* dragon of 12.3–18, for whom the second beast is a spokesman.

What, then, is the identity of the second beast in 13.11–18? Clearly, it is associated with deceit (13.14) and falsehood (cf. 16.13; 19.20; 20.10, where this creature is designated as a 'false prophet'). On this basis, it is possible to understand the figure as an eschatological antagonist, anticipating the advent of a false prophet at the end. The beast, in this case, could be a representative of the priesthood which assisted Rome in propagating the imperial cult, and even symbolize individual Roman emperors, governors or proconsuls themselves (cf. Beasley-Murray 215–17; Caird 171–72; Sweet 214–15; Mounce 254–56; Aune 756–57). While these themes may be woven into the tapestry of John's visionary thought at this point, the picture is ultimately broader and deeper. It has been suggested that the dragon in Rev. 12 depicts, in general and timeless terms, the evil forces behind the kingdoms of this world. Similarly, the beast from the sea (13.1) is a satanic minion who represents the ultimate enemy of the believing Church. In the same way, it may be argued, the beast from the land is the ideology which informs any human structure, religious or otherwise, which seeks to regulate itself independently of God (Wilcock 126–28). John is speaking of deceit and falsehood at any time and in any place. The second beast appears to be harmless as a ram; but his truly evil nature is evinced when he speaks with the authority of the dragon and with the alluring, deceptive voice of the serpent (Gen. 3.1–7; cf. Rev. 12.9). The first beast speaks loudly and defiantly against God and his people (13.5–7); while the beast from the earth tries to persuade the covenant community that such rebellious speech and unrighteous behaviour may be regarded as acceptable. Here is the source of the type of false teaching in the Church which had already infected the Johannine community (see the Nicolaitans and Jezebel in Rev. 2). Such deception is liable to seduce believers in any age, by encouraging them to slip into doctrinal error, and to compromise with the pressures exerted by a secular society (cf. Matt. 7.15). See further Beale 707–708.

12 In the course of the present vision, the dragon confers its great authority, delegated by God, on the first beast (13.2, q.v.). Now the beast from the land, as a delegate of the powers of evil, 'exercises the full authority' of the beast from the sea. For ἐξουσία (*exousia*, 'authority', 'power') see 12.10; et al. For the identity of both beasts see on 13.1, 11; the description of the second is developed further in verses 12–18. In such terms, the dragon and the two beasts parody the nature and activity of the Godhead; they become a form of satanic anti-trinity (against Prigent, 415 n. 2). In this section of Rev. 13 the author changes from past to present tenses; and this literary feature switches the audience into the action, and speeds up the immediacy and pace of the dramatic narrative. See Smalley, *Thunder and Love* 105.

The action in this scene is also reminiscent, in parodic terms, of the ministry of Elijah. The beast from the earth, looking like a ram but sounding like a dragon, stands before the first beast. Like the prophet waiting for God's command (1 Kings 17.1–5), the second beast stands ready to speak with the authority of the first and 'on its behalf' (Rev. 13.12*a*, where the Greek is ἐνώπιον αὐτοῦ, *enōpion autou*, lit. 'before it', not here 'in its presence'; cf. BDAG 342*b*). As Elijah was concerned about the worship of Israel, and miraculously brought fire from heaven (1 Kings 18.17–39), so the beast from the land forces the earth's inhabitants to engage in false worship, and causes fire to fall from heaven (Rev. 13.12*b*–14). Cf. Wilcock 126.

The phrase, 'the earth and its inhabitants' (τὴν γῆν καὶ τοὺς ἐν αὐτῇ κατοικοῦντας, *tēn gēn kai tous en autē[i] katoikountas*, lit. 'the earth and those living in it'), is a comprehensive expression meaning the totality of the human race, in opposition to God; see on verse 8, also 3.10. This precise formulation, 'the earth and its inhabitants', rather than 'the inhabitants of the earth' (as also in 6.10; 8.13; 11.10; 13.14; 17.2, 8), or 'the whole earth' (3.10; 12.9; 13.3; 16.14), is found only here in Revelation. Note the parallel 'the heavens and those who dwell there', at 12.12; cf. Bauckham, *Climax of Prophecy* 240–41. To command that Satan should be worshipped, rather than the only God, is the ultimate and blasphemous deceit (see on verse 4). For the first beast, 'whose mortal wound had been healed', see on verse 3.

13 For the 'outstanding miracles' (σημεῖα μεγάλα, *sēmeia megala*, lit. 'great signs') and 'fire from heaven', referred to here, see on verse 12; cf. also 12.1, 3. The expression, ποιεῖν σημεῖα (*poiein sēmeia*, 'to perform miracles [lit. "signs"]'), is found elsewhere in the Apocalypse at 13.14; 16.14; 19.20; but it appears often, sometimes with the noun in the singular, in John's Gospel (2.23; 3.2; 4.54; 6.2; et al.). The verb ποιεῖν (*poiein*, lit. 'to do') is used frequently (ten times) in Rev. 13.

Eschatological figures of the end-time were expected to perform wonders and lead people astray (Deut. 13.1–2; Mark 13.21–23 par.; 2 Thess 2.9–10; *Did.* 16.4; *Asc. Isa.* 4.6–11; *Sib. Or.* 2.165–68; *Apoc. Daniel* 13.1–13; *Apoc. Ezra* 4.26–27; *Apoc. Peter* (Akhm.) 2; et al.). The second beast of Rev. 13 is known later in the drama as simply the 'false prophet' (16.13; 19.20; 20.10); so that, by combining miracles with deceit, the satanic agent is fulfilling exactly his role as an eschatological antagonist. Like Elijah, he causes fire to 'fall from heaven to earth in front of people' (cf. 1 Kings 18.38; 2 Kings 1.10; see also Luke 9.54); and, as a false Elijah, he prepares the way for a false Messiah (Mounce 257). Roloff (163) points out that outwardly the second beast is acting in the same way as the two witnesses at 11.5 (q.v.), when harmful fire 'pours from their mouths' to destroy their enemies. But, at the substantive level, the opposite effect results. The witnesses mediate the salvific judgement of God, whereas the beast from the earth tries to 'establish and stabilize power which has already been emptied of power by God and no longer has any future' (ibid.).

14–15 For the language and symbolism of these verses, see on 13.1–13. The beast from the land shares with the dragon and the first beast the satanic power to deceive (12.9; 13.1, 4–8). On behalf of the beast from the sea, he is permitted to lead astray and into idolatry the pagan world (verse 12); he seduces by his signs (verse 13) those whose names are not written in the book of life from the foundation of the world (verse 8). Cf. 2 Thess. 2.9–12.

The ultimate deceit is symbolized by the creation of an 'image' (εἰκόνα, *eikona*) for the first beast; the dative, τῷ θηρίῳ (*tō[i] thēriō[i]*, lit. 'for the beast'), has the force of making an image 'in honour of' the beast: hence the translation. The fashioning of a cultic image, in the beast's honour (verses 14 and 15; cf. also verse 4), recalls the blasphemous golden sculpture set up by King Nebuchadrezzar of Babylon (Dan. 3.3–6); the universal worship of this image was made obligatory, on pain of death (3.6). See one parallel in the idolatrous image of the golden calf set up by Aaron (Exod. 31.18—32.29); also *Asc. Isa.* 4.1–13. This is the first appearance of the term 'image' in Revelation (see also verse 15; 14.9, 11; et al.); and the noun suggests throughout the sculpted likeness of a god, rather than an image stamped on a coin (so Luke 20.24); cf. BDAG 281*b*; Mounce 258. For λέγων (*legōn*, lit. 'saying'), meaning 'telling/commanding', or as in the translation (to fit the practice of deceit) 'persuading', see 10.9, 11; also Acts 21.21.

Beale (710) argues that in the light of Rev. 2—3, and in view of the background to this section of the Apocalypse in Dan. 7—12, the deceit engendered by the beast takes place inside the believing community, as well as beyond it. Both beasts are described by using characteristics which belong to divine and prophetic acts in the Old Testament, and to representations of God, the Lamb and believers elsewhere in Revelation. This is because the beasts attempt to validate their authority in the same way as false prophets in the Church, who are 'deceitful workers', disguising themselves as apostles of Christ (2. Cor. 11.12–15); and this deception includes the performance of miracles (cf. Acts 8.18; 19.11–20). Such an understanding of the work of the satanic agents in Rev. 13 is supported by the MS variant in the opening sentence of verse 14, (lit.) 'it leads astray *mine* (τοὺς ἐμούς, *tous emous*) who dwell in the earth' (so 051 2377; cf. Charles 2, 318). Beale (710–11) also notes that the beast who 'leads astray' in verses 14–15 is an echo of the end-time king who causes deceit to 'prosper under his hand' (Dan. 8.25), and who will 'seduce with intrigue those who violate the covenant' (Dan. 11.32). For any interpretation of Rev. 13, it is important to bear in mind that the beasts are in any case representatives of far more than Roman imperial power (see on verses 1, 11). They symbolize secular authority, ranged against God, wherever this may be located; they speak of injustice and error, falsehood and compromise, inside the Church as well as throughout the society which surrounds it.

The final relative clause of verse 14 links the vision of the beast from the earth with that of the first beast. See on verses 3, 12. But a detail is added: the second beast is now described as one which 'had been wounded by the sword, only to live'. The aorist ἔζησεν (*ezēsen*) is ingressive, meaning 'sprang to life'; or, as in the translation, 'only to live'. In 2.8; 20.4 this verb, in the same tense, refers to the resurrection of Christ and his followers.

The beast from the land 'is permitted to breathe life into the statue of the (first) beast'. For the divine authorization included in the phrase, ἐδόθη αὐτῷ (*edothē autō[i]*, lit. 'it was given to him/it'), see on 6.2; also 13.5, 7, 14. There is a close verbal parallel in the

LXX of Dan. 7.6 (the four-headed beast 'was given' speech); cf. Dan. 7.4. The ability of the second beast to perform 'outstanding miracles' on behalf of the first satanic monster (Rev. 13.13–14), and now its demonic and idolatrous power to 'breathe life' into the image of the beast from the sea (cf. 9.20), are reminiscent of a widespread use of magical phenomena in the courts of Roman emperors and governors at the time when John was writing; and this included a belief that statues could speak and execute signs. See Acts 8.9–24 (Simon Magus; also Ps. Clem. *Recog.* 3.47; Ps. Clem. *Hom.* 2.32); Acts 13.6–8 (Elymas the sorcerer); 16.16 (the slave girl with a spirit of divination); Philostratus, *Life of Apollonius (of Tyana)* 1.2–3; Lucian (of Samosata), *Alexander the False Prophet*, 12—26; Eusebius, *HE* 2.13.1–8. Cf. further Ramsay, *Letters* 98–103; Charles 1, 361; Aune 762–64.

The notion of 'breathing life' (δοῦναι πνεῦμα, *dounai pneuma*, lit. 'to give spirit') into the ikon of the beast is a satanic parody of the gift of God's Spirit to believers; cf. the πνεῦμα ζωῆς (*pneuma zōēs*, 'breath of life') from God, given to the two faithful prophets, at 11.11 (Mounce 258 n. 20). This is a broad and figurative way of depicting the second beast as a king-maker; by magical deception, the beast from the earth is able to convince people that the image of the first beast represents true deity (cf. Wis. 14.18–21). The image in the present context refers not simply to the likeness of an individual Roman emperor, who claimed divine status (see on 13.1), or even to the first-century demand for submission to the imperial powers. The idol in verse 15 represents 'any substitute for the truth of God in any age' (Beale 711).

The setting of Rev. 13.14–15, then, is one of deceptive idolatry. There is once again a background in the prophecy of Daniel. Nebuchadrezzar commanded the universal adoration of his huge self-image (Dan. 3.2–7; cf. 1 Macc. 1.44–60; 2 Macc. 6.1–9; Dan. 7—8), and condemned those who rebelled against him to the fiery furnace; although the three friends were later delivered (Dan. 3.8–30). So here the faithful, who will not worship the beast's image, are liable to be 'put to death'. The syntax of this part of verse 15 is slightly obscure, as it is not immediately clear who is to bring about the execution of the disobedient. The aorist subjunctive verb, ποιήσῃ (*poiēsē[i]*, lit. '[that] it might cause'), is parallel to λαλήσῃ (*lalēsē[i]*, '[that] it can actually speak', lit. 'it might speak'), the subject of which is ἡ εἰκών (*hē eikōn*, 'the statue'). It would be logical, as a result, to understand the statue of the first beast as the subject of the action, meaning that the speaking ikon causes the death of those who will not worship it. However, it is equally possible to take the subject of ποιήσῃ (*poiēsē[i]*, 'cause') as the *second* beast, from the earth, who is acting with the authority of the first beast, and bringing about the executions. See the devolvement of authority, from the dragon and first beast to the second, in verses 11–12; and note then the mirrored activity of the two beasts in verses 7 and 15.

In the end, however, the outcome is the same. Some people will remain true to the faith of Christ, while others will turn away to the Antichrist (cf. 2 Thess. 2.1–17). The narrative in this part of John's vision does not presuppose a situation of universal martyrdom (against Charles 1, 360–61, 369–70). The text does not say either that the beast's commands will in fact be fully implemented, or that all believers will in the end be martyred (cf. Beale 713). The resurrection hope of the parousia in Revelation is such that some believers in Christ are prepared at all times, and at the end, to welcome him in (3.20; 7.13–17; 13.10; 20.12–15; 22.6–7).

16–17 The beast from the land, who is clearly the subject of the action in this verse, compels everyone to be 'branded' (ἵνα δῶσιν αὐτοῖς χάραγμα, *hina dōsin autois charagma*, lit. 'to be given to them a mark') on their right hand, or on their forehead. The rhetorical list of those affected is comprehensive. It begins with 'everyone' (πάντας, *pantas*, lit. 'all'); and the following couplets of antithetical terms (insignificant, mighty; rich, poor; free, slave) then describe the social polarities which make up the totality of human society

(Aune 765; Mounce 259). No one is exempt (verse 17). For the antithetical pairing 'insignificant and mighty' (lit. 'small and great'), elsewhere in Revelation, see 11.18; 19.5, 18 (which includes 'free and slave'); 20.12. Cf. the Semitic idiom, 'from small to great', used to denote groups at opposite ends of the social pyramid in Gen. 19.11; cf. also Deut. 1.17; 2 Kings 23.2; Jer. 6.13; Jonah 3.5; Wis. 6.7; 1 Macc. 5.45; Acts 8.10; Heb. 8.11 (quoting Jer. 31.34); Ignatius, *Philad.* 6.3 ('small or great matters').

The 'branded mark' (χάραγμα, *charagma*) to be received from the second beast is a term which appears five times in Revelation, apart from 13.16–17, and always in association with the idea of worshipful loyalty to the beast; cf. 14.9, 11; 16.2; 19.20; 20.4. Only in the present context is the resulting possibility of buying and selling mentioned (verse 17). The noun itself is used in the New Testament, outside the Apocalypse, solely at Acts 17.29. The beast's 'mark' has been variously explained. It has a traditional basis in the judgemental and protective activity of God, in relation to his people, recorded at Ezek. 9.3–11; cf. *Pss. Sol.* 15.9. The motif is clearly eschatological, in that it is bestowed by an apocalyptic creature. But, less importantly, it may also reflect historical practice, both secular and religious, at the time; although there is no evidence that an edict of the kind envisioned here was ever issued in the establishment of first-century imperial worship (Beckwith 642).

If the background is historical, there are four major ways of understanding this image.

(a) The mark could refer to the Jewish custom of wearing phylacteries (Deut. 6.6–9; cf. Charles 1, 362–63); although these were normally carried on the *left* (not, as here, the right) arm.
(b) There may be an allusion to the branding, or tattooing, of slaves, defeated soldiers or devotees of particular gods; although branding on the forehead was more often a sign of disgrace, than of loyalty (3 Macc. 2.27–30, Jews who rebelled against Ptolemy Philadelphus were to be marked with the ivy-leaf symbol of Dionysus; cf. Gal. 6.17; Schneider, 'métōpon').
(c) A reference to imperial red seals, bearing the name or effigy of an emperor, could be in view (Moffatt 433); although the practice of sealing, in this case, is imperial and not popular (Swete 173).
(d) The mark of the beast may also relate to Roman coins used in commerce; for the one way in which the authorities could make buying and selling impossible (verse 17) was by the coinage for which they held responsibility (Caird 173). However, if the mark in question is visible on the right hand and forehead, this seems to exclude the link with coins. See further Aune 767–68.

None of these explanations is entirely satisfactory by itself. It is therefore preferable to interpret the branded 'mark' of the beast in verses 16–17 as an entirely apocalyptic and eschatological symbol (see above; cf. Beale 716–17). If historical allusions are to be included at all, they are multiple. But it has already been argued in the exegesis of Rev. 13 that the reference to the dragon and his demonic agents, as the representatives of evil opposition to God, is general rather than particular. Even if the imperial powers of Rome are included in this imagery, any secular authority which usurps the place of a true and just God (Rom. 1.20–25) is the subject of John's narrative at this point, and accordingly the object of divine condemnation (cf. Hughes 153). Furthermore, the significance of receiving the mark of the beast in verses 16–17, so that the normal business of daily life can only be maintained by the enemies of God, is to parody the 'sealing' of God's servants in Chapter 7 (see esp. verses 2–4; also 9.4). The saints in Christ are sealed and protected against the divine judgement to come (8.1—9.19); and, in the same way, the followers of Satan escape his anger unleashed against the Church (12.17) by carrying his mark. At the end-time, the ultimate test of spiritual loyalty for the believer is resistance to branding by the Antichrist, and a faithful commitment which turns away from compromise, error and injustice (cf. Mounce 260).

The mark of the beast identifies his followers; in addition (verse 17), it allows them to participate in the normal commercial activity of the market-place. Harassment, rather than death (verse 15), seems to have been the point of the corresponding restriction on the life of the faithful, who did not receive the bestial branding. Judge, 'Mark of the Beast', speculatively suggests how this worked. Those entering the market-place, he claims, after offering sacrifice, would receive a mark in ink on the wrist or forehead, giving them the right to trade (see esp. ibid. 160).

The inability to 'buy or sell' probably describes an imaginary situation, as part of John's vision (see also on verse 16). But if it alludes to a historical interdict, this may have been an otherwise unknown economic boycott against Christians (Ramsay, *Letters* 105–108). Hemer (*Letters* 108–109) speaks alternatively of the trade guilds in Thyatira. These were social groups, with a ritual character which often gave expression to the imperial cult; and, since membership of the guilds inevitably involved participation in such practices as eating food sacrificed to idols, an activity to which John was clearly opposed (Rev. 2.20), to join such an organization would be regarded as the antithesis of Christian faith. Equally, non-participation in these pagan systems could mean commercial ruin for the believer (Hemer, *Letters* 126–27). See further Charles 1, 69–70; Aune 768. For the noun χάραγμα (*charagma*, 'mark') see on verse 16. Here (verse 17) it is identified as the 'name' of the beast, or as the numerical equivalent of that name.

The 'name of the beast' and 'the number of its name' are references to the *first* beast (from the sea), and not to the second. This is clear from 13.11–15, where the beast from the land acts as the subordinate delegate of the beast from the sea; from verses 16–17, where the second beast compels everyone to be branded with the mark of the first creature; and from 15.2, where the parallel phrase, 'the number of its name', doubtless alluding to the first beast, is used (cf. 20.4). So Beale 718. The branded mark is the number of the name; and it is this which is stamped on the beast's followers, to indicate his ownership of them. For τὸν ἀριθμόν (*ton arithmon*, 'the number'), and for the number of the beast from the sea as 666, see on verse 18. On the 153 fish of John 21.11 see Smalley, 'The Sign in John XXI', esp. 284.

18 A redactional explanation is added to verses 11–17 (cf. 13.9–10 in relation to verses 1–8), using a code which would have been familiar to John's audience but has since become obscured. Great care and sensitivity is needed, therefore, in order to understand it. The introductory formula, 'this calls for discernment (σοφία, *sophia*, lit. "wisdom"), let the one who has the intelligence (νοῦν, *noun*, lit. "mind") interpret . . .', has a close parallel at 17.9 (ὧδε ὁ νοῦς ὁ ἔχων σοφίαν, *hōde ho nous ho echōn sophian*, 'this calls for intelligent discernment'). The expression 'to have understanding' (ἔχειν νοῦς, *echein nous*, lit. 'to have a mind'), in verse 18, may reflect the appeal for wise discernment at Dan. 12.10 (see LXX; Theod.). Similar calls for intelligent perception are found in apocalyptic contexts at Mark 13.14; *Barn.* 4.4–6; see also (referring to sayings on marriage) Matt. 19.12; Ignatius, *Smyrn.* 6.1. In Revelation (13.18; 17.9), however, unlike Gen. 40.8; Dan. 1.17; et al., the need for God to help with the understanding of the mystery is not explicitly mentioned. See Aune 769.

It may be relevant to the interpretation of the phrase 'the number of the beast' (τὸν ἀριθμὸν τοῦ θηρίου, *ton arithmon tou thēriou*), that the Greek term θηρίον (*thērion*, 'beast'), when transliterated into Hebrew (תריון, *trywn*), has a numerical value of 666 (so Bauckham, *Climax of Prophecy* 389); but see further, below. The expression, ἀριθμὸς γὰρ ἀνθρώπου ἐστίν (*arithmos gar anthrōpou estin*, lit. 'for it is the number of a man') is ambiguous. It may be understood as referring to a specific individual, and be translated 'the number of a (certain) person' (so most modern translations; also Charles 1, 364–65; Prigent 423; et al.). However, it is more likely that the phrase should be interpreted in a generic sense, to mean (as in the translation) 'the number is humanly calculable'. Two points may be adduced in support of this view.

(a) The noun ἀριθμός (*arithmos*, 'number'), or its cognate verb, is always used elsewhere in Revelation figuratively with reference to an incalculable multitude, where precise numbers are not important (cf. 5.11; 7.4, 9; 9.16; 20.8). There is no reason why the same, general meaning should not be in view in verse 18.

(b) The noun ἀνθρώπου (*anthrōpou*, lit. 'of a man'), in the present context, is anarthrous. The only other time that the genitive ἀνθρώπου (*anthrōpou*, 'human'), without an article, occurs in Revelation is at 21.17 (q.v.), where it denotes a general (not cryptic) system of measuring the heavenly city, and signifies the 'human calculation' which is used by an angel. The parallel at 13.18 may well carry a similar, generic significance. It then refers (as in 21.17) to a number which may be calculated by any members of the fallen human race. See Beale 723–24; also Swete 174–75.

The fact that the number itself, 'six hundred and sixty-six', is in the masculine, cannot be used to support the identification of the beast from the sea as a human individual; for its gender has been attracted to the preceding masculine noun, ἀριθμός (*arithmos*, 'number'); so Aune 770. There have been three main approaches to discovering the meaning of this symbolic number.

(a) *The number 666 and Pythagorean arithmetic.* This involves the use of numbers which are conceived as shapes; and these are triangular (the sum of successive digits), square (the total of sequential odd numbers), and rectangular (the sum of successive even numbers). The relationships between these series makes it easy to calculate the correspondences between the various numbers. Thus, every rectangular number is double its related triangle; so that 1332, the 36th rectangular, is twice 666, the 36th triangle. The number 666 itself is doubly triangular: it is the triangle of 36, while 36 is the triangle of 8. For a clear explanation of this method, and its possible relationship to a Danielic background, see Bauckham, *Climax of Prophecy* 390–404, who concludes that 666 in this context reveals by isopsephism that Nero is the beast. It is hard to imagine that the symbolism in Rev. 13.18 should need such a remote and complicated numerical system for its elucidation, for John was a prophet-seer, and not a mathematician.

(b) *The number 666 and gematria.* This is a more popular way of understanding the identity of the first beast by using numbers. The ancient Jewish technique of gematria (a Hebrew adaptation of the Greek term *geometria*) involves assigning to each letter of the alphabet its own numerical equivalent, as a result of which rabbinical writers interpreted the hidden significance of words and names. This took two forms: an exegetical method, based on the mysterious significance ascribed to numbers in sacred or traditional texts; and the practice of converting independent words or names into corresponding numbers, which then needed to be decoded. Irenaeus, *Adv. Haer.* 5.29.2–30.4, esp. 5.30.3, seems to have been the first theologian to have used this approach in the interpretation of 666 in Rev. 13.18, from which he concluded that the number stood not for Nero but for *Evanthas* (an unidentifiable name) or *Lateinos* (imperial Rome) or *Teitan* (the Greek mythological Titans, who rebelled against the gods). A good example of gematria is to be found in *Sib. Or.* 1.324–30, where the name of Christ (Jesus) is said to be the equivalent of 888 (I[*J*] = 10, H[*Ē*] = 8, Σ[*S*] = 200, O[*O*] = 70, Y[*U*] = 400, Σ[*S*] = 200). One of the problems surrounding this method is the fact that there were insufficient letters in the then current

Greek alphabet, so that potentially confusing letters and signs were introduced into the system.

Many commentators accept that 666 in verse 18 is, in some way, a cryptogram for the Emperor Nero (AD 54–68). But the tortuous method of arriving at this solution is to start with the title 'Caesar Nero'; and, if this form of the imperial name is transliterated into Hebrew from the Greek, it becomes קסר נרון (*qsr nrwn*), the numerical value of which is 666 (ק[*q*] = 100, ס[*s*] = 60, ר[*r*] = 200, נ[*n*] = 50, ר[*r*] = 200, ו[*w*] = 6, נ[*n*] = 50). In this case, the beast of Rev. 13.18 is Nero *redivivus*, the incarnation of the oppressive Roman Empire; and it is true that the term 'beast' (θηρίον, *thērion*) was used as a designation for Nero in the ancient world (cf. *Sib. Or.* 5.343; 8.157; et al.). For proponents of this conclusion see Beckwith 642; Charles 1, 367–68; Sweet 217–19; Aune 770–71; Knight 100–101 (cautiously); Bauckham 1298*a*; et al. For 666 and gematria generally see Aune 771–73.

Two comments should be made about the Neronic significance of the number 666. First, if 13.18 includes a reference to the Emperor Nero, this fits the dating of AD 70 adopted in the present commentary as the year in which Revelation was originally composed (see Smalley, *Thunder and Love* 40–50; also Hengel, *Johannine Question* 51). Second, such an identification by no means exhausts the interpretation and significance of 666, which in any case is broader and deeper (see below). But there are, in any case, difficulties in the way of this solution to the riddle, apart from the complexities and obscurities already noted, and the fact that the numerical approach, in any form, is amenable to the subjective presuppositions and credulous ingenuity of each interpreter (Hughes 154).

1 The identification with Nero assumes a knowledge of the Hebrew language and the Judaic system of gematria, although the Johannine community would have included those from a totally Hellenistic background.
2 There were many possible titles and names for Nero, not 'Nero Caesar' alone.
3 In the transliteration of Greek into Hebrew, there may be considerable freedom in valuing the letters and vowels. See Beale 719–20.

(c) *The number 666 and generic symbolism.* The passage and enumeration at Rev. 13.18 yields much better sense, and is theologically on safer ground, if it is not approached as an esoteric mathematical puzzle. It is important to notice, at the outset, that nowhere else in the Apocalypse are numbers used in a way which requires literal calculation, or indicates a (historical) individual. On the contrary, all numbers for John are generic; they have a figurative significance, and symbolize a general spiritual reality. This is true, for example, of the twenty-four elders, the seven seals, trumpets and bowls, the 144,000, the three and a half years, the two prophets and the ten horns and seven heads of the beast from the sea. The possibility of a generic interpretation in this instance must accordingly be given serious consideration (see also on the 'humanly calculable number' in verse 18). The clue is to be found in the use of the number six, in relation to the general significance of John's favourite number, seven. Six falls short of seven, the perfect and divine number, as humanity's imperfection and failure fall short of God. On this basis, the threefold six may be understood as a generic symbol for a humanistic and indeed idolatrous trinity, parallel to that triune satanic force made up of the dragon (Satan, Rev. 12.9) and his two demonic agents: the beast from the sea (the figure of Antichrist, 13.5–6), and the beast from the land (the false prophet, 13.14).

The repetitive '666', therefore, stands for those human and secular forces, including the Romes of any period, which are oppressive and unjust, and seek to dethrone the

Creator and enthrone the creature. John is not referring here in the first place to individual and historical tyrants; he is speaking of varied *types* of authority which use power wrongly, so as to induce doctrinal error and ethical compromise. In one sense, that is what the Apocalypse is all about (see above, 194–95); and such a scene was certainly true of the first-century situation, in and around John's own church, which the seer needed to address. It is also typical of any period in which the basic human instinct is allowed to exchange the glory of the immortal God for mortal images (Rom. 1.23), and where the god of this world blinds the minds of unbelievers, to keep them from seeing the light of the gospel (2 Cor. 4.4).

For this interpretation see further Hendriksen 150–51; Beasley-Murray 220–21; Hughes 154–55; Michaels 165–67; Beale 720–28.

Rev. 12 and 13 together have set before John's audience the ultimate conflict between good and evil, which is highlighted in the symbolism of the cryptogram 666. Now the stage is set for the final encounter between the forces of right and wrong. The end is not yet, and the battles to come will be real; but victory, in Christ and for his followers, will be achieved, and the sovereign rule of God will be eternally established. The consequent account of salvation through judgement begins in Chapter 14 (see esp. on the 'name' in 14.1).

A Vision of the Redeemed (14.1–5)

14.1   The introduction to the final section of this scene provides a dramatic and encouraging contrast to the situation of conflict presented in Chapter 13. There, the struggle between good and evil is dominated by two satanic delegates, the beasts from the sea and from the earth, who exercise usurped authority and deceive the earth's inhabitants. Now, we are presented with a vision of Jesus Christ as the true Lamb; and it is clearly to him, rather than to the false lamb (ram) of 13.11 or the first beast of 13.1, that believers are invited to become committed.

For the literary and apocalyptic formula which leads into a following vision, καὶ εἶδον, καὶ ἰδού (*kai eidon, kai idou*, 'I looked again, and there . . .', lit. 'and I saw, and behold!'), see on 6.2; also 4.1; et al. Spiritual sight and hearing are paramount ideas in this drama. The term τὸ ἀρνίον (*to arnion*, 'the Lamb') is a typically Johannine title for Christ; it appears 28 times in the Apocalypse, and otherwise in the New Testament only at John 21.15. See on Rev. 5.6, where for the first and only time in Revelation John uses the noun anarthrously. In the phrase, 'there was the Lamb standing on Mount Zion', the verb ἑστός (*hestos*, 'standing') is a perfect participle functioning as a finite verb. The crucified and risen Lamb 'stands' on the sacred rock, unlike the defeated dragon, who 'took his stand' on the sand of the seashore (12.18; cf. Sweet 221). In an area which speaks of divine deliverance (see below), the Lamb 'stands', as he does in the throne-vision of 5.6. His posture suggests vindicating support for the faithful, as with the Son of man at the death of Stephen in Acts 7.56. In Revelation the Lamb always stands, whereas God is often described as 'seated' on his throne (4.2–3; et al.); and although the Lamb shares the throne of God (22.4), this apparently remains true even when they are worshipped together (5.13; 7.10). As 'Son of man', 'Faithful and True' and 'Word of God', however, Jesus is described in the Apocalypse as seated (14.14–16; 19.11, 19, 21).

'Zion' is one of the names in the Old Testament for the true city of God (Ps. 2.6; Isa. 4.5; Joel 2.17; et al.). The equivalent and longer name, 'Jerusalem', is sometimes associated with judgement (as in Jer. 9.11; Zeph. 1.4); whereas in the prophetic literature Zion is essentially the place of God's dwelling and people, the city which he will establish and govern at the end-time (Isa. 52.7; Obad. 17). The full description, 'Mount Zion', occurs in the Old Testament in connection with God's sovereign rule, or the remnant of his people being saved by calling on his name, or both (e.g. 2 Kings 19.31; Ps. 48.2, 9–14; Mic. 4.7–8). In the last days, God will invest his Messiah as King on Mount Zion; and he will then judge the unrighteous and protect those who fear him (Ps. 2.6–12; cf. 4 Ezra 13.25–52; *2 Apoc. Bar.* 40.1–4). Against this background, 'Mount Zion' in Rev. 14.1 is best understood eschatologically as a kingdom of justice and peace: the place where God dwells with his people and offers them security (cf. 2.26–28; 7.15–17; 12.5; also Acts 2.16–21; Heb. 1.1–5). See further Schultz, 'Jerusalem, Zion', esp. 326; also Beale 731–32. The term 'Zion' occurs only here in the Apocalypse. It is rarely used elsewhere in the New Testament and in early Christian literature, and then mostly in quotations from the Old Testament (see John 12.15 par.; also Rom. 9.33; 11.26; Heb. 12.22; 1 Pet. 2.6; *Barn.* 6.2).

The precise location of Mount Zion in Rev. 14.1 is not immediately clear. In the view of some commentators, the setting of this verse is on earth, even if the reality represented is spiritual (Milligan 240–41; Swete 177; Beckwith 647, 651; Charles 2, 4–5; Wilcock 132; Wall 179; Aune 803). Others regard the vision of the Lamb on Zion, with the 144,000, as taking place in heaven (Kiddle 262–65; Hendriksen 151; Walker, *Holy City* 261; Mounce 264–65); cf. 4 Ezra 2.42–48. A third interpretation equates Zion in this context with the new Jerusalem, which 'comes down from heaven' (Rev. 21.2), and becomes part of the new creation after the destruction of the old; so Ladd 189–90, esp. 189; also Beasley-Murray 222, who believes that there is a contrast here between the earthly Jerusalem, which has become a symbol for the godless world (11.8–10), and the Jerusalem from above, where heaven and earth are brought together in a unity (21.16).

There is no doubt that in 14.1 John's imagery weaves together a number of dramatic, and indeed poetic, strands. 'Mount Zion' is accordingly evocative of God's just and protective presence with his people in time, *as well as* in eternity. Heaven and earth are close together in Rev. 14.1–5 (cf. Bauckham, *Climax of Prophecy* 230), as they are generally in Johannine cosmology; and the eschatology of the prophet-seer is such that past, present and future blend as one. Zion, like the temple of God (8.3; 11.1–2), firmly connects the historical with the timeless, and the material with the spiritual. The present vision assures the audience that, despite the onslaught of satanic forces, the true Israel has become a fulfilled reality on earth, and also that God's sovereign kingdom and kingship, through the victorious Lamb, will be finally established for ever (cf. Walker, *Holy City* 261). For 'Mount Zion' in verse 1 see further Fiorenza, *Book of Revelation* 186; Beale 731–33.

The 'hundred and forty-four thousand' who appear victoriously with the triumphant Lamb on Mount Zion are mentioned in the Apocalypse only here, at 14.3 (which has about it the character of an inclusion) and at 7.4 (q.v.). Although this understanding is debatable, it seems clear that the same group is in mind in 14.1, 3 as in 7.4–8; John is referring to the whole body of the faithful redeemed. The number is a symbol for all the followers of Christ, the true Church in its totality, which is also represented from an eternal perspective as the 'vast multitude' of 7.9–17 (see above, 184–88). There is no need to distinguish between Rev. 7 and 14, and identify the 144,000 saints in the present passage as a different and élite company (see the arguments for and against this view in Beckwith 648–51), as martyrs for the faith (Charles 2, 5–7; Caird 178–79), or as the remnant of God's people who survive to the end (Aune 804; cf. Bauckham 1298a). It is true that the number itself, in the Greek of 14.1, is anarthrous, as it is in 7.4. If it should be claimed that this indicates a separate group of the faithful from those in 7.4, it may be argued that, although the group is the same, it is being presented from another point of view. But throughout Revelation images are repeated; and occasionally, in subsequent uses of an idea, the article is also omitted (as in 1.13; 14.14, 'Son of man'; 13.16–17; 14.9, 'mark'; 13.1; 17.3, 'beast'; et al.). An article of retrospective reference is not required in the present passage, as other features in the scene of 14.1–5 point back clearly enough to 7.4–9 (Beale 733–34). The group in 14.1 may include the martyrs; but it is essentially composed of all believers who, through Christ the Lamb and in response to oppressive powers of evil (Chapter 13), live out their faith with endurance in an idolatrous world (cf. Prigent 431; see further Beasley-Murray 222; Wilcock 132; Mounce 265).

The saints of God have the names of the Lamb and the Father written 'on their foreheads' (ἐπὶ τῶν μετώπων αὐτῶν, *epi tōn metōpōn autōn*). This contrasts directly with the statement in 13.16–17 that unbelievers were branded 'on their foreheads' (ἐπὶ τὸ μέτωπον αὐτῶν, *epi to metōpon autōn*) with the mark of the beast. The number of the body of the faithful is represented figuratively as 144,000 (see on 7.4), which denotes the completeness of the true Israel of God; whereas the number of the name of the beast, written on the right hand or forehead of *his* followers, signifies their inability to achieve God's purposes for his creation (cf. Beale 733). The names and numbers in both 14.1 and 13.18 are to be understood generically, and as part of John's apocalyptic imagery, rather than in any literal or primarily historical sense (see on 13.18); and for this very reason there is no point in trying to decide how the two names in verse 1, of God and the Lamb, could have appeared physically on the foreheads of believers (so Aune 805, who suggests that the names must have been abbreviated!).

The 'names' of Christ and God, on the foreheads of the redeemed saints (verses 3–4), may be identified with the 'seal' of the living God which is placed on the foreheads of believers in 7.2–8 (q.v.) as a mark of divine ownership and protection; cf. also 22.4. The symbols of sealing and naming also carry significance in relation to the response of the Christian; for they demonstrate genuine allegiance to the Lamb and his Father, and the spiritual power which makes that faithful testimony possible. As the members of the Johannine community themselves were well aware, to confess Christ is to be identified with his name (2.17; 3.12); and this new relationship releases an ability to overcome false witness (2.13) and endure tribulation (2.3; cf. 7.14). Cf. Mounce 265. For the 'name' in Revelation see further on 2.17.

In the Apocalypse, apart from 14.1, God is referred to as 'Father' four times (1.6; 2.28; 3.5, 21). In all five contexts the intimate title evokes the close relationship between the Son and the Father ('his Father', 'my Father'), and also the Father's protective concern for his victorious children. Cf. *Odes Sol.* 39.7 ('the sign on them is the Lord'); 42.20 (Christ says, 'I placed my name upon their head'). The joint names in verse 1 suggest the strength of the divine protection and preservation which is enjoyed by all believers (cf. 7.14–17), as well as the sovereign power belonging to the Father in the Son. Once more, the Christology in this part of Revelation is very high.

2–3 From vision in verse 1, the dramatic narrative shifts to audition in verses 2–3. For 'hearing' in the Apocalypse, in relation to 'seeing', cf. 4.1. What is seen on Mount Zion is now interpreted, and the refuge and deliverance evoked by the associations of that sacred space are immediately expressed in song (see also 15.2–4). The oppressive power of the beast on earth (13.7–8) is confronted by a new hymn of conquest, achievable through the power of the Lamb, which is sung by the faithful in heaven (cf. Ewing, *Power of the Lamb* 175).

A 'sound' (φωνήν, *phōnēn*, lit 'voice') is heard by John, who appears to be on earth, as coming 'from heaven', although a sharp distinction between the Church on earth and the saints in heaven dissolves in 14.1–5 (see on verse 1). The voice from heaven is not divine (unlike 10.4). It is a communal liturgical utterance (the singular noun is collective), and derives not from Christian martyrs alone (Kiddle 266), nor from the 144,000 on Mount Zion in any restrictive sense (see on verses 1 and 3). The music in God's presence which emanates from heaven belongs to the angels, the whole company of the faithful in all ages, and to a redeemed creation (as in 5.13; 7.9–10; cf. Milligan 241). Because the multitude is so vast, the sound is correspondingly 'loud' (cf. Ezek. 1.24; 43.2).

The seer characterizes the volume of this resonance by using three similes, two natural and one human; and each of these is introduced by the adverb ὡς (*hōs*, 'like', 'as'). The sound is first described as being 'like the roar of the oceans and a peal of loud thunder' (ὡς φωνὴν ὑδάτων πολλῶν καὶ ὡς φωνὴν βροντῆς, *hōs phōnēn hydatōn pollōn kai hōs phōnēn brontēs*, lit. 'as a voice of many waters and as a voice of thunder'). There is an almost exact parallel to this phraseology in the Greek of 19.6 (q.v.), where once again the saints celebrate the sovereignty of God (as in 14.7; 15.3) and the conquest of the beast (14.8) in a voice of many waters and mighty thunderpeals. See also 1.15, the voice of the Son of man sounded 'like the roar of many waters'; and 6.1, one of the living creatures called out 'in a thunderous voice'.

The saints of God create a heavenly resonance which sounded to the seer, more specifically, like 'harpists, playing on their harps' (ὡς κιθαρῳδῶν κιθαριζόντων ἐν ταῖς κιθάραις αὐτῶν, *hōs kitharō[i]dōn kitharizontōn en tais kitharais autōn*, lit. 'as kitharists, harping on their kitharas'). The Greek phrase is alliterative, and the repetition adds little to its meaning. The introductory nominative absolute, with an anaphoric definite article, ἡ φωνή (*hē phōnē*, lit. 'the voice'), refers to the same heavenly 'sound' which was heard at the beginning of verse 2, and further defines it. The simile in this part of the verse is more than an image, however, since it implies (as with the singers of verse 3) the presence of an actual group of harpists. Apart from 1 Cor. 14.7, the language of 'harp-playing' in the New Testament is confined to Revelation.

The members of the Church triumphant were also 'singing a new song' (verse 3). The subject of 'they were singing' (ᾄδουσι[ν], *a[i]dousi[n]*, lit. 'they sing') is a combination of the two 'voices' of verse 2. It is clearly not the 'harpists' of verse 2*b* (against Aune 808, who claims that this is a logical possibility); rather, the singers embrace the faithful in their totality (see on verses 1–2). For the concept of the qualitatively 'new song' see on 5.9. The imagery of harpists and a heavenly host singing a new song together appears elsewhere in the Apocalypse at 5.8–10; and 15.2–4. In those two contexts praise is offered, by the redeemed saints of God, for the conquest of evil through the power of the Lamb (note 5.5; 15.2); and the same theology is implicit at 14.3. Such praise on Mount Zion at the end-time is heralded at Isa. 35.10; although in Johannine thought the end is perpetually pressing in (see on 6.17; et al.).

In the Old Testament a 'new song' is regularly the means of offering praise to God the creator, for his victory over enemies (cf. Ps. 33.2–7; 96.1–6; 149.1–9; Isa. 42.10–13; et al.). Some writers see the idea of the 'new song' as part of Israelite holy war terminology, used to celebrate military victory, and the 144,000 as heavenly warriors who fight on behalf of the Lamb (2 Chron. 20.27–28; 1 Macc. 13.51; 1QM 4.4–5; 11.1–11); so Bauckham, *Climax of Prophecy* 230; Barker, *The Revelation* 245–47. But, as here in 14.2–3, the saints in the Apocalypse are worshippers rather than soldiers (see above, 186); and, as Aune (808) points out, connections between *new* songs and such occasions of rejoicing are rarely made. The worship of the faithful is appropriately offered 'before the throne' (ἐνώπιον τοῦ θρόνου, *enōpion tou thronou*). For this phrase, as a circumlocution for 'in the presence of God', see on 4.10; also 7.9; 8.3. The 'four living creatures and the elders' are included in the liturgical action; for the identity of these heavenly beings see further on 4.4, 6.

The 'new song' of 5.9 is chanted not only by the angelic host of heaven but also by the whole company of the redeemed. The 'one hundred and forty-four thousand', with the anaphoric article αἱ (*hai*, 'the'), refers back to the group mentioned in verse 1; and this is an inclusive community of believers, which is in no sense restricted (see on verses 1–3*a*; also 7, 4, 9). Verse 3 is the only place in Revelation where a song or hymn is referred to, but not quoted (except, possibly, for 4.9); so Aune 809. The 'learning' of the song by the 144,000, to which the prophet-seer alludes, using the verb μανθάνειν (*manthanein*, 'to learn'), may describe the normal process of being instructed. But it is more likely in the present context to mean *understanding* esoteric knowledge 'of a higher kind' (Rengstorf, 'mantháno, et al.' 554; cf. BDAG 615*b*); cf. 2 Cor. 12.4; *T. Adam* 1.4.

The members of the Church in view during this passage, who seem to be in touch with earth as well as heaven, are said to be 'redeemed from the world'. This is not a reference to the 'earth' (γῆ, *gē*) as such (against Aune 809–10). It is true that in 5.9 the verb ἀγοράζειν (*agorazein*, 'to redeem') is applied to the saints of God 'from every tribe and language, people and nation'; but this simply speaks of the potentially universal origin of the faithful. Equally, the phrase in 14.4 (q.v.), οὗτοι ἠγοράσθησαν ἀπὸ τῶν ἀνθρώπων (*houtoi ēgorasthēsan apo tōn anthrōpōn*), means not 'they have been redeemed from humanity', but 'they, of all people, have been ransomed'. If, however, the significance were 'they have been redeemed from those who dwell on the earth', that phraseology is used in Revelation for those who oppose God (as in 3.10; 6.10; et al.), and not of those who geographically inhabit the earth.

It is therefore preferable to construe 'the earth' in verse 3*b* in social, and not terrestrial, terms. The saints are those who have been rescued by the Lamb from the world of unbelief and error, and from the tyranny of compromising behaviour (cf. Mounce 266). This understanding is typically Johannine, where belonging to the 'world' denotes an attitude of opposition to God, and a 'worldliness' which denies the goodness of his creation (cf. John 7.7; 15.18–19; 17.14; 1 John 2.15–17; 3.13). For the language of 'redemption' in the Apocalypse see Smalley, *Thunder and Love* 81–82; see also on 5.9. The verb ἀγοράζειν (*agorazein*, 'to redeem', or 'buy') appears six times in Revelation; although only in 14.3–4 and 5.9 is it used as a metaphor of salvation through judgement (see further 3.18; 13.17; 18.11).

4–5 The redeemed members of the Church of God (see on verses 1–3) are now characterized in further detail. John uses three figures for this purpose; and each description is introduced by the demonstrative pronoun οὗτοι (*houtoi*, lit. 'these'), which connects with οἱ ἠγορασμένοι (*hoi ēgorasmenoi*, lit. 'the redeemed') in verse 3. The 144,000 are chaste, they are followers of the Lamb, and they have been ransomed as first fruits for God and his Christ. Accordingly, they are without deceit, and morally blameless; and their moral rectitude (verse 5) balances their ritual chastity (verse 4). For the 'Lamb' see on verse 1.

There are two main approaches among commentators to the significance of the statements that those who belong to the company of the faithful have not 'defiled (ἐμολύνθησαν, *emolynthēsan*) themselves with women, since they are chaste (παρθένοι, *parthenoi*, lit. "virgins")'. The verb μολύνω (*molynō*, lit. 'stain') is used elsewhere in Revelation only at 3.4 (of soiled clothing), and otherwise in the New Testament solely at 1 Cor. 8.7 (of a 'defiled' conscience). The first view understands this description to be a literal reference to celibacy, on the part of an inner group, as a Christian ideal (cf. Matt. 19.12; see also *Jos. As.* 4.9); so Moffatt 435–36; Kiddle 267–71. But nowhere else in biblical thought are sexual relationships within marriage regarded as sinful; and, on the contrary, the importance of family life is upheld (Eph. 5.21—6.9). Moreover, if 144,00 is a figure representing the entire people of God (see on verse 1), the present passage might suggest that celibacy is demanded from the whole Church; and that situation is unrealistic.

The second approach is accordingly preferable; and this takes the 'chastity' motif as figurative. Caird (179), for example, understands the symbolism of verse 4 as based on the requirement of ceremonial purity from Israelite soldiers before battle (Deut. 23.9–11;

1 Sam. 21.5; 1QM 7.3–6; et al.); while Bauckham (1298*a*) sees those described in verses 4–5 as Christians who are engaged in an ongoing and ironic holy war. Both Caird and Bauckham, however, limit unnecessarily the scope of the faithful to a martyred remnant of the true Church (see further Bauckham, *Climax of Prophecy* 229–32). The best solution, therefore, is to take the lack of defilement and the 'virginity' of the redeemed as a metaphor of *all* the true saints of God who have not compromised with the standards of the world. These have remained loyal to their Lord as a virgin bride to her betrothed (cf. 19.7–8; 21.2; see also 2 Cor. 11.2); so Beale 739. Such a figurative interpretation is supported further by the idea of Jerusalem as a bride in the Old Testament (Isa. 61.10; cf. Rev. 21.2), and the extent to which the notion of 'virginity' is applied there to Zion as God's people (so 2 Kings 19.21; Isa. 37.22; Jer. 14.17; Lam. 2.13; Amos 5.2; et al.).

The noun παρθένοι (*parthenoi*, 'chaste', lit. 'virgins') is in the masculine, to agree with the preceding pronoun οὗτοι (*houtoi*, 'these') and the participial phrase, οἱ ἠγορασμένοι (*hoi ēgorasmenoi*, 'the redeemed'); and these may in turn have been altered from the feminine form of 'the one hundred and forty-four thousand' in verse 3 because the representatives of the twelve tribes of Israel were men (cf. 1Q28a [= 1QSa] 2.11–17); so Beale 739–40, who further suggests that the masculine noun παρθένοι (*parthenoi*, 'chaste') is a picture of those who have abstained from harlotry and idolatry. For the notion of Babylon as a 'harlot' in the Apocalypse, presented against an Old Testament background, see further 14.8; 17.1–18; also Jer. 3.1–10; Ezek. 23.1–21; Hos. 1.2; et al. Israel's idolatry is also described as 'defilement' in Isa. 65.4 (where the LXX uses μεμολυμμένα, *memolymmena*, 'abominable things'); Jer. 23.15 (LXX μολυσμός, *molysmos*, 'ungodliness'); et al. To refrain from such 'immorality', in the sense of commitment to the secular world, is figuratively represented by John as 'virginity'.

The Johannine community itself had already experienced the 'pollution' of idolatry (1 John 5.20). For its own members this involved replacing God with such worldly institutions as false religion, imperial worship and trade guilds (see Rev. 2.9, 13–15, 20–25; 3.4–5). Similarly, in 2.21; 9.21; 14.8; 17.2, 4; 18.3; 19.2, the noun πορνεία (*porneia*, 'fornication') is used as a metaphor to describe believers who are deceived into practising 'spiritual intercourse' with pagan gods (cf. 2.14). Equally, the fact that the group in 14.1–5 stands on Mount Zion over against the followers of the beast in 13.11–18 supports the conclusion that the concept of 'virginity' in this passage is figurative; for the beast-worshippers are less immoral than idolatrous. So Beale 740–41. In contrast to this idolatry, John sees 'chastity' as an essential mark of the faithful Christian disciple (cf. 2 Cor. 11.2–4, 12–15; Ignatius, *Smyrn.* 13.1; Hermas, *Sim.* 9.11–16). For celibacy in antiquity see further Aune 818–22.

The second feature of the saints in their totality is that they 'follow the Lamb, wherever he would lead', rather than pursuing a life of idolatry. The present participial phrase, οἱ ἀκολουθοῦντες (*hoi akolouthountes*, lit. 'the following ones'), suggests an ongoing commitment to the discipleship of Christ. This is in line with the calls for the believer to follow Jesus elsewhere in the New Testament, and especially in the Gospels (cf. Matt. 8.19; 10.38; 19.28 par.; Mark 8.34; Luke 9.57; 1 Pet. 2.21–22). The thought of 'following' Christ is also strongly present in the Fourth Gospel (John 12.26; 13.36; 21.18–19, 21); cf. also Ignatius, *Philad.* 2.1; *Smyrn.* 8.1. For the idea of Jesus as both shepherd and guide see John 10.3–6; Rev. 7.17. All these texts may include the prospect of martyrdom, without being limited to it. Christians are in any case invited to follow the teaching of their Lord, and summoned to be identified with his cross-bearing, as well as imitating his faithfulness in situations of suffering. They are to accompany the exalted Lamb in his humiliation, as well as his exaltation; for they are members of his body and partakers of his Spirit (Milligan 243–44; Beale 741).

The third characteristic of the people of God in Christ is that they 'have been ransomed to be first fruits for God and the Lamb'; and the imagery of 'redemption' in this context, with its background in market-place commerce, forms an inclusion with the end of verse 3. As in Rev. 5.9 and 14.3 (q.v.), the verb ἀγοράζω (*agorazō*, lit. 'buy') is applied to the whole body of the redeemed, who are 'purchased' for God by the blood of the Lamb; and in all three passages the prepositions ἐκ (*ek*, 'from') or ἀπό (*apo*, 'out of') introduce a group which is universal in nature. Here, the saints have been ransomed 'out of all people' (ἀπὸ τῶν ἀνθρώπων, *apo tōn anthrōpōn*, lit. 'out of men'); and this description is parallel to the 144,000, in verse 3, who have been 'redeemed from the world'. The reference is once more social, and not geographical; for John is speaking of believers who have been rescued from a sphere of unbelief (see also below). There is no justification for interpreting either 5.9 or 14.3–4 as allusions to an exclusive martyred remnant, whose deaths will lead to the salvation of the heathen (so Caird 180–81).

The concept of 'first fruits' (ἀπαρχή, *aparchē*) is drawn primarily from the Old Testament, where the cultic offerings of the Israelites, especially at harvest-time, become an image of sacrifice (e.g. Exod. 23.19; Lev. 2.12; Deut. 26.2, 10 LXX; also 1QS 6.5–6); cf. Charles 2, 6–7. In the New Testament, the use of the term ἀπαρχή (*aparchē*, 'first fruits'), which appears only here in the Johannine literature, suggests – particularly in an eschatological context – that there is a promise of more to come. Thus, Paul mentions new converts as the 'first fruits' of further membership of the Church (Rom. 16.5; 1 Cor. 16.15); he describes Christ's resurrection as heralding the future resurrection of Christians (1 Cor. 15. 20, 23); and he sees the Spirit as the first evidence of a fuller redemption to be inherited at the end (Rom. 8.23). According to James (1.18), Christians are the 'first fruits' of the new creation; cf. also *Did.* 13.3; *Barn.* 1.7; *1 Clem.* 29.3.

The theology belonging to the idea of 'first fruits' in the New Testament as a whole, and in Rev. 14.4, is thus inclusive in nature; and this accords with the representation in Jer. 2.2–3 of the whole nation of Israel, redeemed from Egypt, as 'holy to the Lord, the first fruits of his harvest' (cf. Beasley-Murray 223–24; Beale 743; against Bauckham 1298*a*). Israel, as God's people, became distinct from their surrounding world of unbelief and opposition. Similarly, the vision of the prophet-seer, in the present verse, is of Christian believers belonging to any age, who are called out of any pagan situation: such as that of the unbelieving society, which is about to be judged, represented in 14.14–20. Israel's *first* fruits of the harvest were the best, and not the worst; and, correspondingly, the spiritual harvest of the new Israel is a special token of the perfection and fulfilment in Christ which are to come.

Aune (782, 814) construes the noun ἀπαρχή (*aparchē*), in this context, as meaning 'devoted servants'. This translation does not supply the exact nuance of the Greek which John is seeking to express. However, it is true that in Rev. 14 the saints of God are regarded as *belonging* to God, through the person and work of the Lamb (so 7.4, 17); so that, as a result, they can live for him truthfully in a world of hostility and deceit (14.5–7). On 'first fruits' see further Link and Brown, 'ἀπαρχή', esp. 416–17.

As a result of being uncompromising and loyal members of God's consecrated people, followers of the Lamb and harbingers of the true Church in its eschatological fulness, the faithful redeemed take on the attributes of Christ. This may include a suffering, leading to death, which is an imitation of the cross (5.6; 6.9); but verse 5 also declares that the saints 'speak without deceit' (ἐν τῷ στόματι αὐτῶν οὐχ εὑρέθη ψεῦδος, *en tō[i] stomati autōn ouch heurethē pseudos*, lit. 'no falsehood was found in their mouth'). This is a clear allusion to Zeph. 3.13 LXX, 'they shall utter no lies, nor shall a deceitful tongue be found in their mouth'; although the fact that this text describes the remnant of Israel does not mean that John understands the 144,000 to be an exclusive group (see on verses 1–4). The reference in Zephaniah itself may also pick up the description of the messianic Servant of God in Isa. 53, who suffers as a slaughtered lamb (verse 7), and in whose mouth there was 'no deceit' (verse 9); cf. 1 Pet. 2.21–22. Unlike those who deny Christ, and yet claim to be the true people of God (2.9; 3.9), and in stark contrast to the beast from the earth who deceives the earth's inhabitants (13.13–15), the members of the new Israel are evidently truthful.

However, the prophet-seer is not simply saying here that believers always tell the truth, although that may be the case (Prigent 436). The point at issue in this context is the faithful and true *witness* which the faithful bear in their ongoing testimony to God's love shown in Jesus, even to the point of sacrifice (cf. 1.5–6; 2.13). Against the pressure to compromise with idolatrous falsehood (13.18; 14.9–11), the saints are called to maintain with enduring integrity the sharp distinction which exists between truth and error, and between the service of God and the worship of idols (2.6, 15–17, 20–23; 13.10; 14.12; cf. Isa. 44.20 LXX, using ψεῦδος [*pseudos*, 'fraud']; Jer. 13.25; also John 8.44–45; 1 John 2.22). In the Apocalypse, lying and false prophecy are equated (16.13; 19.20; 20.10); while those who practise deceit and idolatry are excluded from the eternal city (21.8, 27; 22.15). By contrast, the consecrated people of God should by nature be undivided in their loyalty to him, and to his Christ. See further Mounce 268; Beale 745–46; Prigent 436.

Continuing the thought of sacrificial service, rather than providing what might seem to be an afterthought, the faithful are also described as 'morally blameless' (ἄμωμοι, *amōmoi*, lit. 'unblemished'). This adjective, which appears only here in Revelation, is used in the LXX of sacrificial victims which are ritually perfect (e.g. Lev. 1.10; 3.1; Num. 6.14; 19.2), and elsewhere in the New Testament of Christians as believers who are holy, and morally irreproachable (Eph. 1.4; Phil. 2.15; Col. 1.22). In Rev. 14.5 the term 'blameless', as applied to the saints of God, certainly goes beyond the thought of ritual purity (see verse 4), to include the sense of that potential moral perfection which is attainable through the Lamb (against Beale 747); hence the translation, and see also BDAG 56a. Cf. Ps. 24.3–6. But the theology underlying verse 5 is deeper still, in that it points to the followers of Christ as *complete* in their truthful commitment to God through him. In imitation of the 'spotless' (ἄμωμος, *amōmos*), sacrificial work of the Lamb (Heb. 9.14; 1 Pet. 1.18–19), Christians are to be innocent of the worldly temptation to treat wrong as if it were right, error as truth, and injustice as the moral norm (cf. John 16.8–11). That challenge is perpetually relevant; but it was of immediate concern to the Johannine community in the first century AD, and should have been heeded by all whose inclination at the time was to oppress the members of that circle, and of the Church in general.

Sign 7: Angelic Judgement (14.6–20)

6–7   The theme of this section is that of God's salvific judgement on the world for its inadequacy and wrong; and this refers not simply to Rome, but inclusively to all that the imperial powers represent (see on 13.18—14.5). Seven episodes belong to the sign which is dramatically presented in 14.6–20: verses 6–7, 8, 9–11(12), 13, 14–16, 17–18, 19–20. For the introductory visionary formula, 'I saw' (καὶ εἶδον, *kai eidon*), see on 5.1.

'Another angel (ἄλλον ἄγγελον, *allon angelon*), flying in midheaven', introduces this scene. On angels generally in the Apocalypse see above, 28–30. Six such 'other' angelic beings appear in 14.6–20 (at verses 6, 8, 9, 15, 17, 18); and the use of the numbering 'second' and 'third', in verses 8 and 9, indicates that the 'angel' of verse 6 is the first in a series. The identity of these angelic beings is not immediately clear. Elsewhere in Revelation the expression 'another angel' is used to refer back to angels which have clearly been mentioned in the same context (three times only, at 7.2; 8.3; 18.1; however, note the ambiguity surrounding 'another strong angel' at 10.1); but that is not the case in the phrase as it is used in Rev. 14.

Beckwith (655) therefore suggests that a contrast is intended between the heavenly beings here and angels in general who have already appeared in the drama; but John's style, while sometimes allusive, is seldom so vague. Alternatively, Beckwith (ibid.) wonders if the 'other angels' of 14.6–18 are distinguished from the 'angel singers' of verses 2–3; but this is unlikely, since the heavenly chanting in those verses (q.v.) emanates from the whole Church, and not from one section of it alone. Charles (2, 12) construes ἄλλον ἄγγελον (*allon angelon*) to mean 'another (that is, not the Lamb of verse 4), an angel'; although, while such a construction is grammatically possible, this exegesis seems to be unnecessarily forced. Accordingly, it is sensible not to stress the force of ἄλλος (*allos*, 'another') in the description of the angels in this passage, and even to regard the adjective as unimportant (cf. Mounce 270, who points out that the seventh angel of 11.15 is too far removed for an intended contrast). John's reference to 'other angels' amounts to little more than a literary variation (cf. 5.5); so that the phrase in verse 6 means in reality 'a new angel' (Prigent 438). The air is on any showing thick with angels in this apocalyptic drama; and that is certainly the case in Chapter 14.

The angel is 'flying in midheaven', so that it could be seen and heard clearly; for the expression see 8.13 (a verse close to 14.6), where an eagle performs the same action. This is the only occasion in Revelation where an angel, as such, is said to be in flight; and Aune (824) claims that this is the earliest reference in Jewish or Christian literature to such a phenomenon. Otherwise, in the Apocalypse, 'flying' is attributed only to living creatures (4.7) or birds (8.13; 19.17); but see 12.14, the woman 'flies' with the wings of the great eagle from the serpent into the wilderness.

Moreover, the angel of verse 6 has 'an eternal gospel (εὐαγγέλιον αἰώνιον, *euangelion aiōnion*) to proclaim'. The noun εὐαγγελιον (*euangelion*, lit. 'good news') is frequently used in the New Testament, but only here in Revelation; while the active form of the cognate verb, 'to evangelize' (εὐαγγελίζω, *euangelizō*, lit. 'to announce good news'), appears in the Apocalypse only in the present context (verse 6) and at 10.7 (q.v). The active voice of the verb is rare, and is found in the New Testament only at Rev. 10.7 and 14.6 (also Acts 16.17 v.l.). This language does not appear in the Johannine corpus outside Revelation. The noun, translated here as 'a gospel', always occurs with a definite article in the New Testament (τὸ εὐαγγέλιον, *to euangelion*, '*the* gospel'), especially in the Pauline literature, when it refers to the proclamation of the good news about the salvific death and exaltation of Jesus the Christ (so Rom. 1.1; 1 Cor. 4.15; et al.). Rev. 14.6, however, is the single occurrence in the New Testament of the anarthrous use of the noun; and this suggests that the prophet-seer is alluding to a different message, unique in form.

Verse 7 provides the content of the angelic gospel: the flying messenger is about to announce not so much the good news of Jesus as the certainty of God's saving judgement, exercised through him (for similar angelic proclamations see Luke 1.19; 2.10; Gal. 1.8–9). The setting of this declaration in verse 6 is thoroughly eschatological. The angel flying at the zenith proclaims to all people for all time the victorious discrimination of God (Rev. 14.6–7); and his fellow-messengers bring in the harvest, as it will be gathered finally by the angels of the Son of man (14.14–20; cf. Mark 13.27). See Jeremias, *New Testament Theology* 237. It is an 'eternal' gospel (the adjective αἰώνιος, *aiōnios*, 'everlasting', occurs only here in Revelation). This expression draws attention to the special character of the message, which is enduring as the Lord who authorizes its announcement (cf. Rom. 16.26; Jude 21, 25). See Aune 826; and note *Sib. Or.* 3.47–48, which speaks of the 'most great kingdom of the immortal king'. The notion of an 'eternal gospel' also implies a contrast between the eternal life available through God's Messiah, which is of lasting significance (John 3.15–16; 1 John 1.2; Rev. 1.17–18; 2.7; 11.11–12; 21.27; 22.17–19; et al.), and the transient cult of Satan and his oppressive followers (12.12).

The angel's proclamation has universal relevance in its significance and application. John uses two parallel phrases to explicate this fact: the gospel is addressed to 'the earth's inhabitants'; and (as an equivalent) it is announced 'among (ἐπί, *epi* with the accusative, lit. "on") every nation and race, and language group and people'. For these two expressions, as negative symbols of the secular world under judgement for its idolatrous opposition to God and his people, see on 3.10; 10.11; et al. For the thought of eschatological judgement following the proclamation of a gospel of the kingdom, in verses 6–7, see Matt. 24.14; cf. Mark 13.10. To make this connection is to understand the heavenly figure in verse 6 as primarily a messenger of wrath, and his invitation in verse 7 as a call to maintain faithful witness to Christ in the face of unjust opposition (cf. Matt. 24.9– 13, 22–28; also Rev. 13.9–10; cf. Beale 749–50). Such an interpretation of Rev. 14.6–7 is justified, provided the concept of judgement in this passage is not perceived in purely negative terms (see on verse 7, below).

The flying angel (verse 7) 'was calling aloud' (λέγων ἐν φωνῇ μεγάλῃ, *legōn en phōnē[i] megalē[i]*, lit. 'saying in a loud voice'). For angelic 'loud voices' see 7.2; 10.3; also, in Chapter 14, verses 9, 15, 18. The high volume of the call, in each case, signals – almost as a stage direction – the crucial importance of the announcement to follow; it also allows the words to be heard universally. The angelic message of divine discrimination, and the necessary human response to it (verse 7), is indeed both solemn and far-reaching. For it contains the 'good news' (verse 6) that God's purposes of salvation through judgement for his creation are marked by the overthrow of the satanic powers of evil, through the work of Christ, and the establishment of his sovereign kingdom (12.7–10; 19.1–8).

The angel calls for an appropriate reaction, which is to 'fear God, and glorify him' (δότε αὐτῷ δόξαν, *dote autō[i] doxan*, lit. 'give him glory') as Judge and Creator. The 'fear' of God means the reverence or respect of which he is worthy. In the Old Testament and elsewhere it refers to the awe which divine authority should elicit, enabling God's people to obey his laws (Gen. 22.12; Ps. 111.10; Prov. 8.13; Jer. 32.40; *T. Reub.* 4.1; *T. Sol.* 17.4; et al.). The biblical imperative, to 'give God glory', is addressed elsewhere to both the unrighteous (LXX Josh. 7.19; 1 Sam. 6.5; Isa. 24.15; Jer. 13.16, all using δόξα [*doxa*, 'glory']; cf. Acts 12.23) and the righteous (LXX Ps. 21.24; Isa. 42.12; John 9.24; cf. Rev. 4.9). For 'glory' in Revelation see on 1.6. The associated ideas of fear, glory, judgement and worship in verse 7 are also found together in 1 Chron. 16.8–36 and Ps. 96.1–13 (Aune 827).

Beale (751–53) interprets the angelic command in verse 7 as a compulsory edict, signifying that earth's antagonistic inhabitants will be coerced into acknowledging God's imminent judgement (cf. 11.13; Phil. 2.9–11; see esp. Beale 751). He justifies this understanding against the background of Dan. 4, a passage using similar language to that in Rev. 14.6–8, where the tyrannical Nebuchadrezzar is forced by the significance of a terrifying dream to bless the Most High (Dan. 4.34–37). The edict in Rev. 14.7, on this showing, precedes and inaugurates the repentance which will be involved in the last judgement itself (cf. 16.9; Beale 752–53). However, the biblical and theological doctrine of human free will suggests that God invites, but never compels, repentance from sin and faith in him (cf. Isa. 9.12; John 3.16–19; Rom. 10.16–21). Moreover, when 'fearing and glorifying God' are mentioned together elsewhere in the Apocalypse (as at 15.4; 19.5), it is the saints who are the subject of the action. Similarly, 'glory' is given to God in Revelation only by those who are members of the Christian community (e.g. 4.11; 5.12); and the 'worship' of God is always offered by true believers or angelic beings (11.1; 19.4; et al.). It is more satisfactory, therefore, to take the command in verse 7 as an appeal to the nations for people to be converted, and come in their own time to faith in Christ; even if, as experience shows and the following verses (14.8–20) demonstrate, that call is not universally heeded. The angel in midheaven is exhorting unbelievers to turn from the idolatrous worship of the beast (13.15; 14.11) to the true worship of the Creator (cf. Acts 14.15, 18).

The motivation lying behind the angelic gospel is that 'the moment of (God's) judgement has arrived'. The noun κρίσις (*krisis*, 'judgement') appears in this context for the first time in Revelation, and is subsequently used in the drama three times (16.7; 18.10; 19.2). The presence of the article with the noun suggests that the reference is to the final and judgemental 'day' of the Lord, which was an important element in both Jewish and Christian eschatological expectation (cf. Isa. 13.6, 9; Ezek. 30.1–3; Joel 1.15; Mal. 3.2; 4.5; 1QpHab 12.14; *Jub.* 24.30; *1 Enoch* 10.12; 4 Ezra 7.102; Matt. 10.15; 2 Pet. 3.7; 1 John 4.17). The expression, 'the moment (ἡ ὥρα, *hē hōra*, lit. "the hour") of his judgement', as in verse 7, is rare; although the final 'hour' of Jesus is a frequent image in John's Gospel (2.4; 13.1; et al.); see Smalley, *John* 268–69.

The announcement that the time of divine judgement has 'arrived' (ἦλθεν, *ēlthen*, aorist) is typical of the seer's thought in the Apocalypse. The aorist tense is the equivalent of a prophetic perfect (as in Rev. 6.17; 11.18; 14.15; 18.10; q.v.). John's eschatology is such that the day of the Lord and the final judgement are always pressing in; for him, the kingdom of God is always at hand (cf. Mark 1.15). This means that the 'moment of God's judgement' in verse 7 describes what is eternally true: that divine criticism of human wrongdoing and injustice persists, while an answering response of repentance and faith on the part of believers remains a perpetual possibility. For John's balanced eschatology in Revelation see further Smalley, *Thunder and Love* 150–52.

All the world is encouraged to worship the true Creator (4.11), rather than his idolatrous shadow (13.15). This is a theme present in Deut. 10.12–15 (cf. Exod. 20.4–6). The designation, 'who created the heaven and the earth', which brings together (as so often in the Apocalypse) the realms of the material and the spiritual (cf. 'midheaven', in 8.13; 14.6), is a common description of God in the Old Testament (cf. Gen. 1.1; 2 Kings 19.15; Ps. 121.2; et al.). The formula also appears occasionally in the New Testament, as a means of characterizing the sovereignty of the Almighty (e.g. Matt. 11.25 par.; Acts 4.24; cf., in the background, Gen 24.3; Ezra 5.11; note also Rev. 5.3, 13; 10.6). A three-decker perception of the universe is in mind in the present passage (heaven, earth, subterranean waters); cf. 10.5–6; et al. The 'sea and the water-springs' make up one sector of the universe, since it was accepted in ancient cosmology that terrestrial waters were supplied by an ocean beneath the earth (cf. Job 38.16); so Aune 828–29.

8   Seven episodes belong to the final sign in the present scene; and verse 8 forms a discrete unit within that literary framework (see above). In it, a second angel announces the impending judgement of God on the misuse of power. For the 'second' angel, distinguished from the first in a series of six, see on verse 6. The fact that this heavenly being 'followed' (ἠκολούθησεν, *ēkolouthēsen*, aorist) the first angel suggests that it was also flying in 'midheaven' (verse 6); and the same is true of the third angel in verse 9, which 'follows' them both.

The declaration (verse 8) that the great Babylon, which caused the nations to drink the wine of her immorality, is fallen, is a clear allusion to Jer. 51.7–8 (LXX 28.7–8). However, the repeated verb, ἔπεσεν ἔπεσεν (*epesen epesen*, 'fallen, fallen') suggests the added influence of Isa. 21.9, where one MS of the LXX (B) doubles the verb πέπτωκεν (*peptōken*, [Babylon] 'has fallen'); cf. Aune 829. The aorist tense in verse 8 of the reduplicated verb ἔπεσεν (*epesen*, 'fallen') is proleptic, using a prophetic perfect, since it describes a future event as if it has already taken place; see 18.2, where exactly the same phrase is used, by an angel with a loud voice, of the fall of Babylon as accomplished. Cf. also on the 'hour of judgement' in verse 7.

This is the first of six occurrences of the name 'Babylon' in Revelation (see also 16.19; 17.5; 18.2, 10, 21); and in each case, including the present context, the description 'great' is associated with the city (cf. Dan. 4.30). Note the phrase 'Babylon, great in appearance', in *Sib. Or.* 4.93. At Rev. 11.8 (q.v.) 'the great city' is a title given to Jerusalem; but elsewhere in the Apocalypse that designation is used of 'Babylon', meaning the powers of systemic evil in their widest application (16.19; 17.18; 18.10, 16, 18, 19, 21); see below, and on 13.18.

'Babylon' in 14.8 is unlikely to be a literal reference to the Mesopotamian city (against Thompson 146); although, as the political and religious capital of a world empire, Babylon was an enemy of God's people, and renowned for its luxury and moral corruption (Mounce 271); cf. Dan. 4.28–31; 5.1–4; Matt. 1.12; *Sib. Or.* 5.434–46; et al. In post-biblical Judaism and early Christianity (*2 Apoc. Bar.* 11.1–2; 67.7; *Sib. Or.* 5.143–44, 159, 434; 1 Pet. 5.13; Eusebius, *HE* 2.15.2) the imperial city of Rome was understood as a contemporary Babylon, which itself had become the epitome of satanic world power (so Isa. 13.1–22; et al.). Babylon and Rome were easily equated, since both were oppressors of the faithful; and just as Babylon had conquered Jerusalem in 587 BC, so Rome was to subjugate the holy city in AD 70. But, while the use of 'Babylon' in Revelation, at 14.8 and elsewhere, may include a reference to the evil exercise of Rome's imperial powers and the self-importance of its rulers (Swete 183), the significance of this image is more extensive. Babylon, in John's visions, symbolizes the secular and unjust spirit of humanity which, in any age, forces others to compromise with the truth, to worship idols rather than the Creator (13.15; 14.7), and to behave as followers of the devil rather than of Christ (13.16–17). Cf. Roloff 175. In Rev. 17—18, however, the focus of the symbol becomes the seductive forces of any imperial systems which are oppressive and unjust. See further on the 'dragon' and 'beasts' in Rev. 12—13.

The final clause of verse 8 uses four types of genitive in the Greek: τοῦ οἴνου (*tou oinou*, lit. 'of the wine'), partitive; τοῦ θυμοῦ (*tou thymou*, lit. 'of the passion'), epexegetical; τῆς πορνείας (*tēs porneias*, lit. 'of the immorality'), descriptive; αὐτῆς (*autēs*, 'of her'), possessive (Aune 831). In this sentence, the writer mixes two evocative images. First, Babylon did not keep her idolatry and consequent immorality to herself, but forced them on others like an intoxicating drink (cf. 17.4). The implications of cooperating with Babylon's enticements could include the promise of economic security (2.9; 13.16–17; 18.3), just as the effects of her 'wine' may symbolize spiritual blindness and idolatry (Isa. 29.9; Hos. 4.11–12); so Beale 756–57. For the verb πεπότικεν (*pepotiken*), meaning 'she caused to drink', see the textual notes on verse 8. Babylon's attentions were universally addressed, as always; for she encouraged 'the whole world' (πάντα τὰ ἔθνη, *panta ta ethnē*, lit. 'all the nations') to drink; and 'the nations', in this context, are doubtless representative of society in opposition to God (cf. 10.11; 11.2; 12.5; 18.23; et al.). Second, the cup offered by Babylon contained 'the wine of her *passionate* immorality' (τοῦ θυμοῦ τῆς πορνείας, *tou thymou tēs porneias*, lit. 'of the intense desire of her fornication'). Her immorality echoes that of Jezebel (2.20–23; cf. 17.1–2); so Thompson 146.

The word θυμός (*thymos*) here means 'passionate longing' (BDAG 461*b*); and it is initially to be distinguished from the use of the same term in verse 10, where the seer speaks of the wine-cup of 'God's wrath' (τοῦ θυμοῦ τοῦ θεοῦ, *tou thymou tou theou*, lit. 'of the wrath of God'); cf. 16.19. But it is also possible that the thought of God's judgemental and saving wrath, with which the noun θυμός (*thymos*, 'intense displeasure') is mostly associated in the Apocalypse (see also 14.10, 19; 15.1, 7; 16.1, 19; 19.15), is brought back – through a play on words – into the teaching of verse 8. The cup offered to the nations in a seductive manner was equally a potion of divine reaction to human wrong-doing, which God gives the disobedient to drink (cf. Ps. 75.7–8; Isa. 51.17; 1QpHab 11.10–15; et al.), and in which Babylon was instrumental. God's wrathful justice at the end-time, that is to say, is already apparent (cf. 14.7). See Roloff 175. For a close parallel to the language and theology of verse 8 see 18.3.

9–11 For the 'third, following angel' of verse 9, and the loudness of its cry, see on verse 8; cf. also Bousset 385. For the imagery in this verse see on 13.4, 8, 12, 15–17. The syntax of the extended conditional clause in verses 9–10 consists of the protasis in verse 9, εἴ τις (*ei tis*, lit. 'if anyone'), hidden in the translation, which includes two verbs: προσκυνεῖ (*proskynei*, lit. 'worships'), and λαμβάνει (*lambanei*, lit. 'receives'). This is followed by the apodosis in verse 10, which is introduced by καί (*kai*, lit. 'and'). The themes of worshipping the beast and his 'image' (εἰκών, *eikōn*) and receiving his 'mark' (χάραγμα, *charagma*) are juxtaposed in verses 9–11, as they are in later texts of the Apocalypse (16.2; 19.20; 20.4); cf. Aune 832.

Verses 9–11 form a 'counter-proclamation' to that of the image in Rev. 13.15–17 (Mounce 272), where it is decreed that those who would not worship the statue of the beast will be put to death, and also that those who lack the beast's mark will suffer economic deprivation. The third angel of 14.9 now proclaims that a worse fate will befall those who *do* reverence the image of the beast and *are* branded with his mark; for they will 'drink some of the wine of God's wrath', and undergo exquisite torment (verses 10–11, q.v.). This dire threat is addressed to the secular world at large (verse 6), and also to those in John's community and the wider Church who are tempted by impending oppression and internal conflict to deny the true faith of Christ. In view of the comments in verses 12–13, which speak of the need for endurance and faithfulness on the part of believers, in addition to the good fortune of those who die in the Lord, Mounce (272) believes that the audience of the present angelic announcement includes apostate Christians as well.

The consequences of worshipping the beast which pretends to be God (13.4–6), rather than God himself, are now explained in verses 10–11. The condition in verse 9 (lit. 'if anyone worships the beast') is completed by the apodosis in verse 10; and this is introduced with the use of the emphatic singular, hidden in the translation, καὶ αὐτός (*kai autos*, lit. 'and he'). Cf. similar occurrences of this expression at 3.20; 14.17; 17.11; et al. The phrase '(some of) the wine of God's wrath' (τοῦ οἴνου τοῦ θυμοῦ [τῆς ὀργῆς] τοῦ θεοῦ, *tou oinou tou thymou [tēs orgēs] tou theou*), or variations of it, appears five times in the Apocalypse after 14.10 (14.19; 15.7; 16.1, 19; 19.15). The metaphor of God's wrath as a draught of wine, or as the 'cup' of his anger, is regularly found in the Old Testament (Job 21.20; 75.8; Isa. 51.17; Jer. 25.16, 27; 49.12; Lam. 4.21; Ezek. 23.31–34; Obad. 16; Hab. 2.15–16; Zech. 12.2; cf. also *Mart. Pol.* 14.2). The noun 'cup' (ποτήριον, *potērion*), by itself (see below), is used in John 18.11 as an image of destiny, which may involve death; see also Ps. 10.6 LXX; Mark 10.38–39 par.; 14.36 par.

For John's use in Revelation of the biblical concept of divine 'wrath' see on 6.16–17. The understanding adopted in this commentary sees God's wrath as constructive. In the face of the idolatrous evil and injustice which are practised by the followers of Satan, who refuse to accept his love in Christ (9.20–21), the Father expresses his righteousness. But, as always in the Apocalypse, God's reaction to such opposition is not to be thought of in human terms, as an unbridled explosion of anger. Rather, it includes a creative and positive outcome. Through God's judgemental anger flows salvation; accordingly, in the present context (14.9–11), the angelic announcement that God's wrath will be poured out on those who are allied with unholy resistance to the Church introduces a call for the endurance of the saints, and a benediction on those who die in the Lord (14.12–13; cf. 15.2–4). See further Smalley, *Thunder and Love* 149. The two Greek words for 'wrath' in verse 10, θυμός (*thymos*) and ὀργή (*orgē*), are used more or less interchangeably in Revelation (see also 16.19; 19.15). But, if there is a distinction, it is between θυμός (*thymos*) as a state of intense displeasure (Swete, 185, calls it 'the white heat of God's anger') and ὀργή (*orgē*) as a more settled indignation, directed at wrong-doing (cf. BDAG 461*b*; 720*b*–721*a*).

The wine of God's wrath is said to be 'poured out undiluted' (τοῦ κεκερασμένου ἀκράτου, *tou kekerasmenou akratou*) into the cup of his anger (for the final image see above). The participle derives from the verb κεράννυμι (*kerannymi*, lit. 'mix', used only here and at Rev. 18.6 in the New Testament), which referred originally to the preliminary process of adding spices to wine before it was dispensed (cf. Ps. 75.8). But this word came to be used, by assuming the initial preparation, in the straightforward sense of 'pouring out'. The adjective ἄκρατος (*akratos*, lit. 'unmixed'), used only here in the New Testament, draws attention figuratively to the strength of the wine, since it was normal in the classical world at this time to dilute wine with water, in a vessel called a κρατήρ (*kratēr*, 'mixing bowl') cf. Prov. 9.2 LXX. For the phraseology of this section of verse 10 see the close parallels in the LXX versions of Ps. 74.9; Jer. 32.15. By combining these two ideas ('poured out' and 'undiluted') in the present clause of Rev. 14.10, therefore, John has created an oxymoron: the wine of God's wrath is both (lit.) 'mixed', so as to increase its strength, and 'unmixed', because its potency is not diluted by water. The third angel is saying that those who consistently reject divine love, by succumbing to the worldly enticements of the idolatrous beast, will experience God's animosity, untempered by his mercy. Having drunk the wine offered by Babylon (verse 8), the unfaithful will quaff the judgemental wine of God's anger; and while the effect of the former will wear off at the end of time, the latter will have force until God's sovereignty is established, and his kingdom is acknowledged. See further BDAG 540*b*; Beckwith 657; Aune 833; Mounce 272–73; Beale 759–60.

The severity of God's judgement is heightened, in the context of verse 10, by the seer's symbolic description of the fate of the wicked in the final sentence: they will be tormented 'with sulphurous flames' (ἐν πυρὶ καὶ θείῳ, *en pyri kai theiō[i]*, lit. 'in fire and sulphur') in the presence of the holy angels and of the Lamb. The combined apocalyptic imagery of fire and brimstone, as a means of torment, appears in three other texts of the Apocalypse (19.20; 20.10; 21.8; cf. 9.17–18). In Rev. 14.10 and elsewhere, the allusion is doubtless to the judgement of Sodom and Gomorrah by sulphur and fire from heaven in Gen. 19.24 (cf. Luke 17.29; *1 Clem.* 11.1). In the Old Testament, 'sulphur and fire', or brimstone alone, are often mentioned in association with divine punishment (Deut. 29.23; Job 18.15; Ps. 11.6; Isa. 30.33; Ezek 38.22; et al.). The people of Qumran, also, expected the unrighteous to be destroyed by fire (1QS 2.8; 4.13; 1QH 17.13; et al.). The character of the 'torment' (βασανισθήσεται, *basanisthēsetai*, lit. 'he will be tormented') involved is spiritual and psychological, rather than physical (Beale 760); similarly 9.5–6; 11.10; 14.11. For the same idea in direct relation to final judgement, and accompanied by grief, see 18.7, 9–10, 15; also 20.10. To say that the judgement of God on wrongdoing is presented figuratively in verses 10–11 is not to deny its fierce reality.

The situation in which the unrighteous are judged in the presence of the righteous is a familiar picture in the literature of Second Temple Judaism (cf. *1 Enoch* 27.2–3; 48.9; 62.12–13; 90.20–36; 4 Ezra 7.36; *2 Apoc. Bar.* 30.1–5). But, as Aune (835) notes, there seems to be no parallel in Jewish or early Christian eschatological scenes for the notion that the wicked are punished in the presence of (ἐνώπιον, *enōpion*, lit. 'before') God's 'holy angels and of the Lamb'. It appears that, in this court of angels and the Godhead, the angels participate in the work of judgement. The expression '*holy* angels' (ἄγγελοι ἅγιοι, *angeloi hagioi*) is used in Revelation only here; but see *1 Enoch* 21.5; 46.1; 74.2; 93.2; 100.5; *Life of Adam and Eve (Apocalypse)* 7.2; Tobit 11.14; Mark 8.38 par.; Acts 10.22; *1 Clem.* 39.7; Hermas, *Vis.* 2.2.7; *Sim.* 5.5.3. An equivalent phrase, 'the holy ones', occurs at Job 5.1 (LXX 'holy angels'); Dan. 4.17; Zech. 14.5; cf. also *Pss. Sol.* 17.43;

1QS 11.7–8; Col. 1.12; Eph. 1.18; 1 Thess. 3.13; 2 Thess 1.10; et al. See further Williams, *Case for Angels* 96–97, who maintains that angels are 'wholly good by the grace of God' (ibid. 96).

At his previous appearance in this scene, the Lamb was standing with the redeemed on Mount Zion (14.1; see 14.1–5). Hendriksen (154) believes that now he not only presides at an eschatological act of judgement against the unfaithful, but also acquiesces in what must be understood as a never-ending chastisement. However, it should not be presupposed that the Lamb, in John's theology, reacts to such a situation with ease, since it does not accord with the salvific purposes of God in his Messiah (cf. Isa. 35.4; Luke 15.4–32; John 3.16–17; 10.11–16; 1 Tim. 2.3–6; 1 John 4.9). In any case, escape from the clutches of the beast must remain a constant possibility (Rev.19.2, 7–8; 22.14–15).

Verse 11 is probably the completion of the proclamation by the third angel; but the speaker here may also be regarded as the prophet-seer, who makes a chorus-like comment on the significance of this scene, and then continues it in verse 12 (q.v.). The solemn announcement in verse 11 itself provides a further warning about the horrific results of human idolatry and wrongdoing (Prigent 444). Verse 11 forms a complementary inclusion with verse 9. Those who worship the beast and its image, and also receive his branding (verse 9), will experience the fierceness of God's wrath (verse 10); and the same group of the unfaithful (verse 11*b*) will undergo lasting suffering (verse 11*a*). For the imagery of worshipping the beast, rather than the Lamb, and of being branded as his, see on verse 9; cf. also 13.11–17. The inclusion at 14.11*b* picks up the additional feature from 13.17–18 that the 'mark' (χάραγμα, *charagma*) of the beast is its name and corresponding number (666; see further on 3.18).

The idea that the torment of God's opponents can be detected by 'ascending smoke' (verse 11) evokes Old Testament images of conquered cities which are visible from a distance by their burning smoke (cf. Gen. 19.28; Josh. 8.19–21; Judg. 20.40; in the Apocalypse see 18.9–10, 17–18). In his song of deliverance from Saul (2 Sam. 22), David refers to the 'smoke' which went up from the nostrils of the avenging Lord (verse 9). A more specific allusion in the present verse (14.11) is to Isa. 34.10 (MT), where it is said of the destruction of Edom by fire that its smoke will not be quenched 'night and day', but will 'go up for ever'. See the close parallels in Rev. 19.3; 20.10. The phrase 'for ever' (εἰς αἰῶνας αἰώνων, *eis aiōnas aiōnōn*, lit. 'to the ages of ages') is found in this anarthrous form only here in the New Testament. It appears 12 times elsewhere in Revelation, with the same meaning and always with two articles (εἰς τοὺς αἰῶνας τῶν αἰώνων, *eis tous aiōnas tōn aiōnōn*); so 1.18; 4.9; 5.13; et al. For the language and idea of 'torment', in verse 11, see on verse 10.

The angel declares that the unfaithful 'will have no respite (ἀνάπαυσιν, *anapausin*, lit. "cessation") day or (καί, *kai*, lit. "and") night' from their suffering. The Greek phraseology here is very close to the description of the four living creatures who, in the throne room, 'day and night do not cease' to chant their praise to the Lord God (Rev. 4.8). But there is an ironic, and dramatic, contrast. While the cherubim offer an unceasing liturgy of worship to the Almighty, those who worship and follow the beast will undergo ceaseless torment (cf. Aune 836). See also 20.10. For the hendiadys 'day and night', meaning 'for twenty-four hours at a time', and therefore 'unceasingly', see on 4.8. The expression includes an earthly measurement of time, but it is one used here with an obviously spiritual reference.

The key theological issue raised by verse 11 is whether John means that those who reject Christ in favour of materialistic values will literally suffer divine judgement *for ever*, although it is the case that literal interpretations of the Apocalypse are always likely to be problematic. Some commentators certainly accept that the writer is speaking here not of the annihilation of unbelievers, but of their suffering throughout eternity (so

Hendriksen 154; Mounce 274–75; Beale 761–63). Such a picture of unremitting punishment by God, however, calls into question both the justice and character of God, and indeed his saving purposes for the world (see above; also Boring 170–72). John is without question a 'prophet who burns with the holy zeal of absolute convictions' (Prigent 444); but his teaching is always balanced, and never separates the judgement and justice of God from his love.

An alternative way of understanding this passage of the Apocalypse, therefore, is to interpret the declarations that the unfaithful will be tormented 'for ever', and that their suffering will be unremitting (continuing 'day and night'), in qualitative terms. These descriptions of the time-span involved in God's judgement, that is to say, do not indicate the duration of a temporal period, but the *kind* of time which is involved. Elsewhere in biblical literature, for example, 'day and night' indicates a period of ceaseless activity (e.g. LXX Ps. 21.3; Isa. 34.10; Jer. 8.23; Lam. 2.18; Mark 5.5; Luke 18.7; Acts 9.24; 1 Thess. 3.10; 2 Tim. 1.3), which is intense while it lasts, but which will not last for ever. In the same way, the angel is saying, the ongoing torment of the wicked, and their lack of respite, will be uninterrupted while their suffering continues; but there will be a conclusion to that period (see Beale 762). Those who knowingly wish to be excluded from God's love in Christ may follow that destructive course of action (cf. 2 Thess. 1.7–10; Rev. 20.14–15); but repentance is a possibility which is as everlasting as divine judgement. For a similar interpretation see further Milligan 249–51; Caird 186–87; Hughes 163–64.

12   This verse belongs structurally with verses 9–11, as an interpretative comment on the action in this part of the scene; and this is all the more true if verse 11 is understood as a chorus-like aside by the author, which helps to explain the significance of the third angel's proclamation, rather than as part of that announcement (see further on verse 11). In that case, verse 12 continues the commentary. It acts as a gathering-point in Chapter 14, and provides a direct challenge to the audience of this apocalyptic drama to persevere through suffering, and remain true to Jesus rather than Satan (cf. Beasley-Murray 226–27; against Charles, who claims that 14.12–13 do not belong in their present context, but originally followed either 13.17–18 [1, 368] or 13.15 [2, 18]).

For ἡ ὑπομονή (*hē hypomonē*, 'perseverance', 'patient endurance'), in the Apocalypse, see on 13.10; also (1.9); 2.2–3, 19; 3.10. For the idea see 2.13. This is the last use of the noun in Revelation. For the title 'saints' (οἱ ἅγιοι, *hoi hagioi*, lit. 'the holy ones'), used as a description of faithful members of God's people, see on 5.8; also 8.3–4; 11.18; 13.7, 10; 19.8; et al. The grammatical construction of this verse is problematic, in that the initial adverb, ὧδε (*hōde*, lit. 'here', 'in this'), introduces a sentence in the Greek which lacks a verb (lit. 'here the patience of the saints'); for this formula see also 13.10, 18; 17.9. However, the meaning of verse 12 becomes clearer if it is understood as an explanation of the quality of 'perseverance', in the participial phrase beginning with οἱ τηροῦντες (*hoi tērountes*, lit. 'those keeping'), rather than as a definition of the character of the saints themselves. John is not saying here simply that the faithful should obey God's commands and keep faith, true as that may be. Rather, he is claiming that Christian *perseverance* involves 'keeping God's commands, and remaining faithful to Jesus' (hence the translation). For this interpretation see NEB (but not REB); also Aune 837. On this showing, the angelic proclamation of judgement with its elaboration, in verses 9–11, calls believers to carry on living in society with commitment and conviction, and with an obedient loyalty to Christ which may well include suffering and even martyrdom (verse 13).

The final section of verse 12 consists of a couplet: perseverance in the Christian life involves both 'keeping God's commands' and 'remaining faithful to Jesus' (cf. the close parallel at 12.17). For the notion of obedience to the commandments of God see on

12.17. The reference here is primarily to the ethical demands of the Torah, and then to the demand for members of the Johannine circle to obey the divine love command (cf. Deut. 6.20–25; 1QpHab 8.1–3; Matt. 19.17; also John 14.15, 21; 15.10, 12, 17; 1 John 2.3–4; 3.22; et al.). See further Aune 710–12. For 'remaining faithful' (καὶ τὴν πίστιν Ἰησοῦ, *kai tēn pistin Iēsou*, lit. 'and [keeping] the faith of Jesus') see also on 12.17. The genitive here, Ἰησοῦ (*Iēsou*, 'of Jesus'), is most probably objective, meaning the testimony which needs to be given by believers *to* Jesus, rather than the doctrine received *from* him (against Beale 766–67, who thinks that both ideas, faith in Jesus and faith from him, are present); cf. 2 Tim. 4.7. Followers of Christ, John is claiming in the present context, need to be consistently loyal in their witness to him, as well as obedient to divine law in their behaviour towards others for his sake.

13 A heavenly voice now confirms the outcome of the angelic judgements announced so far in this section of the seventh sign of Scene 4 (14.6–20), and comments on their significance. For the 'voice from heaven' which John hears in his vision, as a joint declaration from God and the Lamb, see on 10.4 (also 11.12; 14.2; et al.); and for the importance of 'hearing' in Revelation see on 4.1. Heavenly voices are an important element within apocalyptic imagery; and, as so often in the Johannine literature, they bring heaven and earth together. The announcement in verse 13 promises victorious and eternal rest to those who have unjustly endured suffering and oppression, with obedience and faithfulness (verse 12), as well as to all those who 'die in the Lord'. Indeed, the promise seems to provide a spiritual motivation for such behaviour (cf. Kiddle 283; Sweet 228).

The divine command, 'write down this' (γράψον, *grapson*, lit. 'write'), is one of several which occur in the Apocalypse; and in each case it adds authority to the message which is to follow. The injunction is used in the transcription of each of the seven oracles to the Johannine churches of Asia (2.1, 8, 12, 18; 3.1, 7, 14); but, when it appears elsewhere in Revelation (1.11, 19; 19.9; 21.5), the vision of the apocalyptic drama as a whole seems to be in view (Aune 838). The benediction in verse 13, on those who die as Christians (they are 'fortunate', μακάριοι, *makarioi*, lit. 'blessed'), is the second of seven formulations of blessing in the Apocalypse (see elsewhere 1.3; 16.15; 19.9; 20.6; 22.7, 14). Three of these, including 14.13, are in the plural (also 19.9; 22.14; cf. Matt. 5.3–12 par.).

There is some ambiguity in the punctuation of verse 13, and therefore over the identity of the saints who 'die in the Lord', and who are therefore 'fortunate'. This stems from the possibility that the words ἀπ' ἄρτι (*ap' arti*, 'from now on') may be construed either with the preceding clause ('those who die from now on'), or with the following sentence ('from now on they can rest'). A third option, for which there is no MS evidence, is to follow Aune (788) and conjecture that the Greek text should read ἀπαρτὶ (λέγει τὸ πνεῦμα), *aparti (legei to pneuma)*, lit. 'truly (says the Spirit)', although that emphasis is already provided by the emphatic particle ναί (*nai*, lit. 'yes'; but see the textual notes on verse 13). The word order in the Greek seems to recommend that ἀπ' ἄρτι (*ap' arti*, 'from this moment onwards') should depend on the verb 'to die' (ἀποθνῄσκοντες, *apothnē[i]skontes*, lit. 'dying'), giving the sense 'fortunate are those who die after this date'. But that exegesis is exclusive, and suggests that eternal blessing is reserved for those who suffer and die in the oppressive days of injustice after the composition of John's Apocalypse. In that case, it could be argued, what about the Christian saints (like Stephen), and indeed the people of God, who have already been in Christ?

It seems theologically more acceptable, as a result, to connect 'from now on' with the subsequent clause, and to interpret this promise as giving assurance that the faithful of the future 'can rest from their labours'. But that rendering still encounters the difficulty, according to the Christian scheme, that such good fortune awaits only the saints of the time to come; and it fails to include, once more, those who have believed in God in the past. The most secure way of understanding this passage, therefore, is by treating the reference to 'now' as eschatological and spiritual, rather than temporal and material. John is speaking here, in his commentary, of the blessings of the new era inaugurated by the work of Christ (Prigent 446). The time of salvation is in the present (12.10; 14.15; cf. 2 Cor. 6.2); but it is characteristic of Johannine eschatology that every present moment contains both the past and the future (see on 6.17; et al.). The voice from heaven in 14.13 is pronouncing a benediction on *all* believers who, at *any* time, die in Christ; and in John's day these have resisted the pressures to conform to idolatry, while remaining faithful to their Lord (contrast 14.11). But such a blessing cannot exclude, for example, the faithful people of God in the wilderness wanderings, who drank from the rock which was Christ (1 Cor. 10.1–4); nor can the fortunate status of the Christian dead be limited to those who suffer martyrdom (against Kiddle 283; Aune 838–39; Mounce 275–77). The general expression οἱ νεκροί (*hoi nekroi*, 'those who die', lit. 'the dead') may include the unjustly oppressed and the martyrs of any age, but it should not be confined to them; for the emphasis here is on 'the dead' themselves, rather than on the manner of their death (cf. Beale 767).

The formulation, μακάριοι οἱ νεκροί (*makarioi hoi nekroi*, 'those who die are fortunate', lit. 'blessed the dead'), with an implied but unstated part of the verb 'to be' ('blessed *are* the dead'), reflects a Semitic style; it also draws attention to the continuing state of good fortune enjoyed by the Christian dead (Beale 767). The phrase, those who die 'in the Lord' (ἐν κυρίῳ, *en kyriō[i]*) are fortunate, includes a spheric dative (where the death occurs); cf. 1.9; 1 Cor. 15.22. The expression 'in Christ' or 'in the Lord', to denote the Christ–Christian relationship, is typically Pauline (e.g. Eph. 1.1; Col. 3.18–20; cf. Ignatius, *Pol.* 8.3); but it is used in Revelation only here (verse 13).

The benediction in the present verse is authoritatively affirmed by the Spirit; hence the translation of λέγει (*legei*, lit. 'says') as 'agrees'; and this confirmation is intensified by the use of the particle ναί (*nai*, 'yes'), as the equivalent of 'amen' (cf. 1.7; 22.20); cf. also 1 Tim. 4.1. In the course of faithful witness on earth, the Spirit responds to the will of heaven (cf. 22.17). For the person and ministry of the Spirit in the Apocalypse see Smalley, 'Paraclete', esp. 292–96. The content of the blessing, in the remainder of verse 13, is introduced by the consecutive conjunction ἵνα (*hina*, lit. 'that'): '*so that* they can rest from their labours'. For the concept of Christian 'rest' in the Apocalypse see otherwise only 6.11; in both contexts the term signifies everlasting respite from hardship and affliction. The followers of the beast discover temporary relief in this world, but not in the next (14. 8, 11); whereas those belonging to Christ, who endure the 'labours' of the spiritual life (cf. Acts 14.22), find eternal rest in him (cf. Isa. 57.1–2; Wis. 4.7; *2 Apoc. Bar.* 85.9; Heb. 4.10; Rev. 7.14–17; 21.5–7).

In the final clause of verse 13, the Spirit claims of victorious believers that 'their deeds accompany them' (REB, 'the record of their deeds goes with them'). The introductory causal particle γάρ (*gar*, 'for') indicates the logical basis for what has already been declared: that the faithful who have persevered in the face of difficulty with obedient commitment will experience rest in Christ Jesus because of their lasting 'deeds'. The noun ἔργα (*erga*, 'deeds', lit. 'works') is equivalent to the Christian κόποι (*kopoi*, 'labours'), mentioned earlier in the verse (cf. 2.2, 19, 26; 3.8). Both terms refer to the active expression of faith in the Messiah, despite oppressive injustice (see 14.6–12), which will in the end be rewarded by sharing the life of Christ in eternity. Individuals are not saved by 'good works'; but 'good works' are a tangible sign of interior belief, or lack of it, by which the saints and others are judged (2.23; 20.12; 22.12; cf. John 3.19–21; 1 Cor. 4.2–5; Eph. 2.8–10; 1 John 3.18; 3 John 10). For further parallels, in the literature of Judaism, see Dan. 12.13; *1 Enoch* 38.2; 41.1–2; 4 Ezra 7.35, 77, 90–96; 8.33. See further Beale 768–69.

14 Verses 14–16 make up the fifth subdivision of seven within the visions of angelic judgement recorded at 14.6–20 (see on verse 6). John describes here the appearance of a Son of man figure, as well as the harvesting of the earth. For the literary formula, καὶ εἶδον, καὶ ἰδού (*kai eidon, kai idou*, lit. 'and I saw, and behold'), see on 4.1; 5.1; also 14.1. At Rev. 4.2 God's throne is mentioned before the divine figure seated on it; in 14.14, similarly, 'a white cloud' (νεφέλη λευκή, *nephelē leukē*) is seen before we are told who occupies it. In Jewish literature, clouds are regularly associated with heavenly beings (see on 10.1). They become a mode of transport between heaven and earth, or from one area of heaven to another (e.g. 2 Kings 2.11; Ps. 104.3; *1 Enoch* 14.8; *T. Abr. [B]* 12.1; cf. Rev. 1.7; 11.12); clouds are also used figuratively as means of enthronement (Sir. 24.4; Rev. 14.14–16), or in association with theophanies and angelophanies (Exod. 14.24; 2 Macc. 2.8; Mark 9.7 par.; Rev. 10.1). See further Aune 840–41.

'Clouds' form part of the apocalyptic scenery of Revelation only in this passage (14.14–16) and at 1.7; 10.1; and 11.12. Moreover, 14.14 is the sole occasion in the Apocalypse when a cloud is said to be 'white'. This may indicate the positive character of the action which is to follow (verses 15–16); cf. Aune 840. At 20.11 God's throne is white in colour. Seated on the cloud is 'one like a son of man' (ὅμοιον υἱὸν ἀνθρώπου, *homoion huion anthrōpou*). As in 1.13, the accusative noun υἱὸν (*huion*, 'son') after ὅμοιος (*homoios*, 'like'), which normally takes the dative, appears to be a solecism (BDAG 707*a*).

Verse 14, with its presentation of a 'son of man' figure, alludes directly to Dan. 7.13. Apart from Rev. 1.7, 13, this is the only place in the New Testament outside the Gospels when such a reference occurs. The Danielic background to Rev. 14.14, and the fact that the expression 'son of man' is anarthrous in the Greek, suggests that John is describing one who is literally 'like a (son of) man'. However, this figure is clearly exalted and divine; he wears a golden crown on his head, and carries an instrument of eschatological judgement in his hand (verse 14*b*). As at 1.13, the 'son of man' seems to merge with God; he shares in his appearance and participates in his work of judgement and salvation. The heavenly being of 14.14, who is seated on a white cloud, must accordingly be understood in the light of the early Christian tradition of Jesus as *the* messianic Son of man and be identified with the risen Christ who features in Rev. 1.12–20 (against Boring 170). See further on 1.13; also Smalley, 'Johannine Son of Man', esp. (for the background to Son of man Christology) 281–87; Dunn, *Christology* 91.

The figurative representation of one 'like a son of man' *seated* on a cloud, in verse 14, may preserve a combination of Dan. 7.13 with Ps. 110.1 such as that reflected in Mark 14.62 (cf. Matt. 26.64; Luke 22.69; at Acts 7.56, Stephen sees the Son of man *standing* at the right hand of God). In the Marcan passage, the Son of man is predicted as coming 'with' (μετά, *meta*) the clouds of heaven (similarly Rev. 1.7); whereas at Rev. 14.14 and Matt. 24.30 he arrives 'on' (ἐπί, *epi*) a cloud or clouds.

In the section Rev. 14. 6–20, there are seven heavenly beings: six angels (verses 6, 8, 9, 15, 17, 18) and the Son of man figure (verse 14). This has led some commentators to suggest that the one like a son of man in verse 14 is also an angel; since the other beings are called 'angels', as such, and the figure on the cloud (verses 14, 16) undertakes the same judgemental function as the angels of verses 17–19. So Kiddle 276–77; Aune 841–82. However, this interpretation is unlikely, even if Jesus functions as the supreme angel in the Apocalypse (see above, 28) and angelic representatives of Christ at times act for him (cf. 10.1; 12.7–10). See further Beale 770–71.

For the heavenly being of verse 14 is set apart. He has a 'golden crown' on his head and a 'sharp sickle' in his hand. The 'crown of gold' (στέφανον χρυσοῦν, *stephanon chrysoun*) is often taken as a symbol of Christ's victory (so Swete 188; Hendriksen 155). But the image of the golden wreath is used in a variety of contexts in Revelation, and does not always connote divine triumph; thus, crowns of gold are worn by the twenty-four elders (4.4, 10), by the rider of the white horse (6.2, 'a crown'), and by members of the locust-like, fiendish cavalry (9.7). Moreover, the scene here is one of salvific judgement; the harvester is the royal judge, and not a warrior (Beckwith 662), so that the crown in 14.14 is rather the mark of the messianic King (cf. 19.12). The Son of man also wields a 'sharp sickle' (δρέπανον ὀξύ, *drepanon oxy*; apart from Mark 4.29, the noun is used throughout the New Testament only in this chapter of Revelation). Its appearance at 14.14 is anarthrous, which suggests that this is not an apocalyptic symbol familiar to John's audience. The same phrase, 'sharp sickle', is used at verses 17–18 to identify the instrument used to gather the grape harvest; and, in both settings, judgement leading to salvation is in view (see below). At 1.16 and 19.15 Christ bears not a sickle, but the sword; and this, in context, is an appropriate instrument to represent his exalted royalty, rather than the eschatological harvesting which he undertakes here.

15–16 Assuming that the heavenly being in verse 14 (q.v.) is not an angel but the messianic Son of man, a fourth angel, in a sequence of six, emerges from the temple. See on verse 6. For the 'temple' (ναός, *naos*), as an image used in the Apocalypse to symbolize the divine presence, see 3.12; 7.15; 11.19; 14.17; 15.5–6, 8. The angel delivers a message from God's throne room, 'shouting at the top of his voice' (κράζων ἐν φωνῇ μεγάλῃ, *krazōn en phōnē[i] megalē[i]*, lit. 'crying with a loud voice') to the son of man figure seated on the white cloud. The importance of the angelic announcement demands that it should be conveyed in stentorian tones; cf. 5.2; 6.10; 7.2, 10; 8.13; 14.7, 9; 19.1. At 16.1, 17 loud voices are similarly heard from the temple throne of God. Note also John 12.44 (Jesus 'cried aloud' his saving words); 1 Thess. 4.16 (the archangel's call initiates the coming of Christ). For the imagery of the heavenly being on the cloud see on verse 14.

There is an apparent difficulty in verse 15, given that an angel issues a command to the Son of man ('wield your sickle'), which implies that he does not know the time to reap ('the moment to harvest has arrived'). However, the unusual character of this scene may be explained by two relevant considerations. First, the angel from the temple is not strictly giving an instruction to the risen Christ, but rather transmitting an order from God himself. Second, that situation presupposes the functional subordination of Jesus to the Father, which is a regular element in New Testament Christology (cf. John 5.19–30; Phil. 2.5–8). In the tradition of the Gospels, moreover, the 'moment' (here ὥρα, *hōra*, lit. 'hour') of final judgement is hidden from the angels and even the Son, and is known to God alone (Mark 13.32; cf. Acts 1.7). Cf. Beale 772; Prigent 450–51.

A major problem is involved in the interpretation of verses 15–16, in relation to the concluding section, 14.17–20. John's vision includes two metaphors, which describe what is to happen at the end-time: the grain harvest and the vintage ingathering. Both ideas clearly run back to Joel 3.13 (MT and LXX 4.13):

> Put in the sickle, for the harvest is ripe.
> Go in, tread, for the wine press is full.

Commentators have discovered two distinct harvests in the passage 14.15–20. Some understand the first reaping (verses 15–16) as redemptive, the assembling of the righteous, and the second (17–20) as the judgement of the wicked. Such a view is supported by the teaching of Jesus, about a 'dual' harvest, recorded at Matt. 3.12; 13.24–30 (the parable of the good seed and the weeds); cf. 2 Esdras 4.28–35; *2 Apoc. Bar.* 70.2; see also Matt. 24.27–31; *Apoc. Peter (Akhm.)* 6. Swete (190) finds 'delicate beauty' in the distinction between the Son of man who reaps the wheat harvest (Rev. 14.16) and the angelic minister of justice who carries out the work of death (verses 19–20).

Bauckham (*Theology* 94–98; see also 1298*b*–1299*a*) argues cogently in favour of this diverse interpretation, on three main grounds.

(a) Each of the two harvest figures is connected to an image which appears earlier in Rev. 14. The antecedent of the universal grain harvest is to be found in the picture of the 144,000 saints, ransomed as 'first fruits' to God and the Lamb (verse 4; cf. 5.9); just as in Lev. 23.9–14 the first sheaf to be cut was offered to the Lord as a sacrificial pledge of the harvest of the earth still to be reaped. Similarly, the 'winepress' of God's wrath (14.19) is anticipated by the 'wine' of Babylon's passionate immorality, offered to the whole world (14.8), and by the judgemental 'wine of God's wrath', poured out on all who refuse to turn aside from the idolatrous deceit which she typifies (14.10).

(b) Second, while the descriptions of the two harvests in 14.15–16 and 17–20 seem to be parallel, there is a major difference between them. The grain harvest involves the single action of reaping, whereas the harvest of grapes is carried out in two stages: gathering the grapes into the winepress (corresponding to the scene in the Apocalypse where the demonic spirits usher the deceived into Armageddon, 16.12–15), followed by treading out the grapes in the winepress (equivalent to the judgement of the nations at the parousia, 19.15). In biblical imagery, the specific action of reaping is always a positive symbol of bringing people into the Kingdom (Mark 4.29; John 4.35–38); and although 'harvest' by itself can be a figure of judgement (Jer. 51.33*b*; Hos. 6.11), threshing and winnowing (rather than reaping) are more readily used as pictures of divine discrimination (Jer. 51.33*a*; Mic. 4.12–13; Hab. 3.12; Matt. 3.12 par.; cf. Rev. 11.2).

(c) The single action of reaping the grain harvest is carried out by a son of man figure (Rev. 14.14), who – like his counterpart at Dan. 7.13–14 – does not judge the nations, but receives their believing members into his universal kingdom. By contrast, the two actions involved in the vintage are performed by an angel of judgement (14.19), and by one who is eventually revealed as the divine warrior-judge (19.11–16). It is Christ who reaps the grain harvest, and who also treads the winepress; but in the first image he is the bearer of salvation, and in the second he becomes the dispenser of judgement. Bauckham concludes that in Rev. 14.15–20 John depicts the outcome of history by using two contrasting images: one is the positive harvest of the earth and the other connotes the negative vintage of the world (Bauckham, *Theology* 98). See further *idem, Climax of Prophecy* 238–337; also Hughes 165–66; Prigent 450–53. It is possible to take issue with some of Bauckham's claims, such as his insistence that the martyrs occupy a prominent position in the apocalyptic scheme of 14.15–16 (e.g. Bauckham, *Theology* 97); but his basic interpretation is worthy of serious consideration (however, see below). A variation of this general understanding takes the reaping of the grain harvest in 14.14–16 to refer to the wicked, as well as the righteous, since tares as well as wheat are present at harvest time (Matt. 13.30); so Beckwith 661–62.

Other commentators adopt a second way of interpreting the present passage, which is to claim that the two 'harvests' in 14.14–16 and 17–20 are describing precisely the same act of (final) judgement. Such a view is supported by the identical imagery and patterns of action surrounding the heavenly beings in these verses, who emerge from God's presence, command in loud voices that the sickle of reaping should be wielded, and give as the reason for the harvests that the moment of divine judgement has arrived (see the parallels between verses 7 and 15). Furthermore Joel 3.13, which lies behind the thought of Rev. 14.14–20, is the only text in the Old Testament where the images of harvesting with a sickle and treading the winepress occur together; and both, it is suggested, are figures of judgement.

On this showing, the seer's double narration of two identical accounts of the same judgement is perceived not as needless repetition but as a means of emphasizing the severity and unqualified nature of God's punishment of the wicked (so Beale 774–75). For this understanding, of both harvests as metaphors of judgement, see further Hendriksen 154–56; Kiddle 284–95; Rist 474–76; Mounce 277–81; Beale 772–79; Knight 106–107.

The view adopted in this commentary is broadly aligned with that of Bauckham, and finds support in the evidence which he adduces (see above) for interpreting the harvest of the grain as an image of salvation and the harvest of the grapes as a metaphor of judgement. However, salvation and judgement never stand entirely apart in the Apocalypse; and its leading theological theme, indeed, is that of salvation *through* judgement (cf. Smalley, *Thunder and Love* 147–49). Thus, while it is arguable that the ingathering of wheat in 14.14–16 refers primarily to the redemption of the believer, which is made possible through Christ, the controlling text of Joel 3.13 beneath those verses reminds John's audience that reaping the harvest is also a biblical image of divine justice. Equally, if 14.17–20 speaks mostly of the wrath of God expressed in his judgement (19–20), his salvific activity is not excluded from this part of the vision (see further on verses 17–20, below). So that, while the underlying vintage imagery of Joel 3.13*b is* judgemental, it occurs in a setting which ultimately concerns God's discrimination against his enemies, *together with* the possibility of restoration and protection for those who believe in him (cf. esp. verses 16–18). John's theology, here as elsewhere in Revelation, remains balanced.

The term δρέπανον (*drepanon*, 'sickle'), used in verses 15–16, can refer to various types of curved knives, including a scythe (Deut. 16.9 LXX) or a pruning hook (Isa. 2.4 LXX). Joel 3.13 LXX, which stands in the background of Rev. 14.14–20, is the only place in the Old Testament where there is a figurative allusion to harvesting with a sickle. The conjunction ὅτι (*hoti*, 'because', 'for') is used twice in verse 15, and again in verse 18, to introduce the reason for the eschatological reaping to begin ('the moment has arrived, the crop is ripe, the grapes are ready'). The noun ὥρα (*hōra*, 'moment', lit. 'hour') signifies a point in time, rather than an extended period, at which the eschatological harvest becomes mature. In Revelation the word frequently refers to the judgement of the unfaithful (as in 3.3; 11.13; 18.10; et al.). But it also has a more generalized meaning in the Apocalypse (see 3.10); while in the Fourth Gospel it is used of the eschatological moment when God's plan of salvation through Jesus the Messiah is to be inaugurated (so John 2.4; 5.25; 7.30; 13.1; 17.1; et al.). The noun ἡ γῆ (*hē gē*, 'the earth'), occurs three times in verses 15–16, where it stands for the world of human society in its universal totality (so also verses 18–19). The fact that the earth's crop is 'fully ripe' (ἐξηράνθη, *exēranthē*, lit. 'dry, and therefore ready for harvesting', BDAG 685*a*) is an allusion to God's salvific judgement at the end-time; but the reference is proleptic, for (as always in Revelation) the end is constantly imminent, but it has not yet arrived (see on 14.7). The verb ξηραίνω (*xērainō*, lit. 'dry up') is used in Revelation solely at 14.15 with reference to spiritual harvesting; otherwise it appears in the Apocalypse only once (16.12), where it describes the 'drying up' of the waters of the river Euphrates after the sixth angel has poured out his bowl over it.

For the imagery and meaning of verse 16 see on verse 15. The action of the Son of man, who 'began to swing his sickle over the earth', implies a further movement from heaven to earth; and it is clear that the spiritual and material dimensions are close together in this scene of Revelation (14.1, 6, 13); cf. Knight 106. The verb ἔβαλεν (*ebalen*, lit. 'threw [his sickle]', aorist) should not be understood as meaning that Christ's gathering of the faithful was in any way violent; hence the translation, 'began to swing'. The Son of man is given authority by God to execute salvific judgement (John 5.27); so that, while he may use for this purpose the ministry of people (Matt. 9.37–38) or angels (Matt. 13.39, 41), it is he who ultimately wields the sickle (cf. Swete 189). John's vision at this point does not indicate how the ingathering is to take place, or how long the process will last. There appears to be no interval between cause (ἔβαλεν, *ebalen,* 'he began to swing') and effect (ἐθερίσθη, *etheristhē,* '[the earth] was harvested'); but, in any case, time and eternity constantly merge in apocalyptic thought (cf. Smalley, *Thunder and Love* 150–52).

17–18 The penultimate subdivision within the seventh sign in this scene begins with these verses (see on verse 6). Verses 17–18 set out the preparations for the final grape harvest of the earth; and this is a vintage which is judgemental, but which also includes the possibility of redemption (see on verse 15 for the imagery and interpretation of 14.17–20). As in verse 15 'another angel', this time a fifth, comes from God's presence, which is described as the 'heavenly sanctuary' (ἐκ τοῦ ναοῦ τοῦ ἐν τῷ οὐρανῷ, *ek tou naou tou en tō[i] ouranō[i]*, lit. 'from the temple [the one] in heaven'). He too carries a 'sharp' sickle (cf. verse 14), for he is the agent of God and his Christ for the work of ingathering. The second harvest (grapes) follows the first (grain), as for the Israelites the vintage followed the wheat harvest (cf. Deut. 16.9–13).

A sixth angel now moves from the divine presence (verse 18). For 'another angel' (ἄλλος ἄγγελος, *allos angelos*), here and in verse 17, see further on verse 6. Angelic beings abound in this part of the Apocalypse; but that is no reason for Charles (2, 18–19, 21) to reduce their number by regarding 14.15–17 as an interpolation. The further angel of verse 18 emerges from 'the area of the altar' (ἐκ τοῦ θυσιαστηρίου, *ek tou thysiasteriou*). This term occurs seven times elsewhere in Revelation, with reference to the heavenly counterparts of the altar of incense (8.3 [*bis*], 5; 9.13), or the place of burnt offering (6.9; 11.1; 16.7). By extension the word can mean the 'sanctuary' of God, as in verse 18, where it becomes a synonym for ναός (*naos*, 'temple'); cf. Aune 845. Because the heavenly 'altar' appears elsewhere in the Apocalypse in association with the prayers of the righteous (6.9–10; 8.3–5), it is possible that John at this point intends his audience to understand that the intercessions of the saints play some part in the judgement of the unfaithful (cf. Mounce 279). Here is God's final answer to the prayers of his people for the establishment of his sovereign power (Roloff 178).

The angel of verse 18 is distinguished by the addition of the descriptive participial phrase, 'having authority over fire' (ἔχων ἐξουσίαν ἐπὶ τοῦ πυρός, *echōn exousian epi tou pyros*). For this literary feature see also 11.7; 17.1; et al.). Angels of service in intertestamental Judaism were assigned to different elements of nature, such as wind, stars, thunder, rain, sea and frost (*1 Enoch* 60.11–22; cf. Rev. 9.11; 16.5); see further above, 28–29, and on 7.1. This ministry included being in charge of fire; see *T. Abr. (A)* 12.14; 13.11–14. The idea that angels were created from fire was common in Second Temple Jewish literature; and this was based on Ps. 104.4, which is quoted in Heb. 1.7 (cf. *Jub.* 2.2; *2 Apoc. Bar.* 21.6; *Apoc. Abr.* 19.6; *2 Enoch* 29.3; 39.5; see also 1QH 1.10–11, the 'winds' [or spirits] became angels of holiness). In Rev. 14.18 the angel of fire recalls the heavenly being of 8.3–5 (q.v.), who filled a censer with burning coals from the altar, and hurled them down in judgement on the earth. Fire is a regular biblical symbol for divine discrimination (cf. Ps. 18.7–15; Jer. 4.4; Amos 2.2; Zeph. 3.8; Matt. 18.8; Luke 9.54; 2 Thess. 1.7–8 [judgement administered by Christ and his angels of fire]; Heb. 12.29; et al.).

The sixth angel 'called out' (ἐφώνησεν, *ephōnēsen*) in a loud voice to the fifth heavenly being and 'said' (λέγων, *legōn*, lit. 'saying') that his sharp sickle should be wielded. The use of λέγειν (*legein*, 'to say'), after a verb of speaking, is strictly a redundancy; it reproduces a Semitic formula of direct discourse (cf. 6.10; 18.2; et al.); so Beale 780. The command from the angel of fire (verse 18) to the angel with the sharp sickle (verse 17) that the vintage should begin because the 'grapes are ripe' runs closely parallel to the angelic instruction in verse 15 to the Son of man figure. But the setting is now more directly judgemental; and the intensity of the judgement is no doubt symbolized by the repeated description of the weapon of destruction in verse 18 as 'sharp' (ὀξύ, *oxy*); see also 1.16; 2.12; 14.14; 19.15. The reference to the earth's 'vineyard' (ἄμπελος, *ampelos*), from which the grape harvest is to be gleaned, has to do more with the fruit of the vine than with the vine itself. Nevertheless, the positive biblical imagery of the 'vine' as representative of the covenant people of God in Christ must also have been evoked in the minds of John's Jewish-Christian listeners (cf. Ps. 80.8–10; Isa. 5.1–7; Jer. 2.21; Ezek. 19.10–14; John 15.1–7). See Boring 171. The word ἄμπελος (*ampelos*), which is used in Revelation only here and at verse 19, strictly means the 'vine', as such; but in the present passage it may be taking on the broader significance of a 'vineyard' (ἀμπελών, *ampelōn*); see BDAG 54*b*. For the language and interpretation of the remainder of verse 18 see on verse 15.

19–20 In the final subdivision of this scene's seventh sign, recorded at 14.6–20, the seer describes the result of the angelic command in verse 18 to begin the ingathering of the grape harvest. For the metaphors in verses 19–20, and for the interpretation of the eschatological action as judgemental, but also including the possibility of salvation, see on verse 15. The vintage process is twofold: picking the clusters of grapes (verse 19; see 18), and treading them out in the winepress (verse 20). In this context, both are metaphors of divine judgement (see Joel 3.13, as above); and, to this extent, the fifth heavenly being (see on verses 6 and 17–18) becomes an angel of punishment (cf. *1 Enoch* 53.3–5; 56.1). For the first use of the aorist verb, ἔβαλεν (*ebalen*, 'swung', lit. 'threw'), in verse 19*a* see on verse 16. The second occurrence of the same verb in the same tense, in verse 19*b*, implies an action which is more violent; hence the translation ('threw').

The harvested grapes are now cast into 'the vast winepress' of God's wrath. There is a grammatical problem in the Greek at this point in verse 19, since τὸ μέγαν (*to megan*, 'the vast', lit. 'the great'), which is masculine accusative singular, appears to be in apposition to τὴν ληνόν (*tēn lēnon*, 'the winepress'), the gender of which is feminine (accusative singular). However, if the adjective *is* intended to modify the noun, it should have the feminine form, τὴν μεγάλην (*tēn megalēn*, 'the great'). This anomaly accounts for a number of MS variations (see the textual notes on verse 19). Beckwith (664) explains the change of gender by suggesting the possibility that the author has in mind here what is symbolized by the 'winepress', and expressed in the intervening masculine phrase, τοῦ θυμοῦ τοῦ θεοῦ (*tou thymou tou theou*, lit. 'the wrath of God'). Aune (790–91) notes the ambiguous character of ἡ ληνός (*hē lēnos*, 'winepress'), as a second declension feminine noun which (apart from the article) is declined in the masculine; in Gen. 30.38, 41 LXX, for example, ληνός (*lēnos*, 'press') is used in the masculine form. Nevertheless, it is entirely possible that the masculine gender of τὸν μέγαν (*ton megan*, 'the great') is intended to agree with the masculine noun τοῦ θυμοῦ (*tou thymou*, 'wrath'), to which it stands near. In this case, the whole phrase may be translated, 'the winepress of the great wrath of God'; and, by intensifying the severity of God's reaction to unbelief in the present setting, this seems to be the most likely, as well as theologically satisfying, solution to this problem. The term ἡ ληνός (*hē lēnos*, 'the winepress') is used in the Apocalypse only here (verses 19–20 [*bis*]) and at 19.15 (q.v.), and otherwise in the New Testament only at Matt. 21.33.

In the period of the Old Testament grapes were trampled by foot in a trough with a duct; and this led to a basin below, where the juice was collected (Mounce 280). Treading the grapes was a striking figure in Judaism for executing divine wrath on the opponents of God; and such is the theme of Isa. 63.1–6. In this passage, which clearly lies behind Rev. 14.19–20, the Lord who comes as a divine warrior, in robes stained with the blood of his enemies, is likened to one who treads the winepress in garments spattered with red grapejuice (see esp. verses 2–3). Cf. also *Targ.* Isa. 63.3–4. For the 'wrath' (θυμός, *thymos*) of God see on verse 10. The evident fierceness, in this scene, of the divine opposition to those who reject God in favour of impious deceit and unjust oppression, must be balanced by God's ultimately salvific purposes of love for his creation. It is apparent from 19.15 that the Son of man carries out the Father's judgement (see also 14.14), and he is involved in the double harvest of grain and grape (see above). But, according to John 5.19–47 (cf. 10.10; 17.1–3), Christ is commissioned by God to dispense eternal life, as well as searing judgement. See further on verse 20; also Hanson, *Wrath of the Lamb* 159–80, esp. 169–70; Robinson, 'Interpreting' 72; Boring 171–72; Roloff 178.

The final stage of the vintage harvest takes place, as the winepress is 'trodden outside the city' (verse 20). For 'winepress' see on verse 19. The actions of gleaning and treading the grapes, in this image of eschatological judgement, appear to follow each other without an interval; although, in an apocalyptic vision, time is difficult to measure (see on verse 16). The identity of the one who treads the winepress is not disclosed at this point; but at 19.11–16 it is revealed as the exalted Christ, the warrior-rider on the white horse, who comes with his heavenly armies in judgement, to tread out the winepress of God's wrath (19.15). The aorist passive verb ἐπατήθη (*epatēthē*, 'was trodden') is a passive used as a circumlocution for divine activity (cf. 6.2, 4; 9.1; et al.).

The use of the article, with the term 'city' (ἔξωθεν τῆς πόλεως, *exōthen tēs poleōs*, 'outside the city') suggests that the place in question is familiar to the members of John's audience, and therefore the leading city of Jerusalem. This is supported by the Jewish expectation that the final eschatological battle would rage in the area of Jerusalem itself (Joel 3.2, 12–14; Zech. 14.1–5; *1 Enoch* 53.1; *2 Apoc. Bar.* 40.1–2; cf. Rev. 19.17–21; 20.7–9). Vineyards were usually located outside urban centres, including Jerusalem. Here, judgement 'outside the city' is a clear allusion to the saving crucifixion of Jesus 'beyond the gate' (see Matt. 27.33 par.; John 19.20; Heb. 13.11–13). The scene may be understood as depicting an act of poetic justice (Aune 847); those who spurn the truth will suffer an exclusion which reflects that of the dying Christ (cf. also Matt. 27.46).

Treading out the winepress produces vast quantities of flowing blood. The link between blood and wine is common in Judaism and early Christianity; and the (red) juice of grapes is at times described as 'the blood of the grape' (see Gen. 49.11; Deut. 32.14; Sir. 39.26; 1 Macc. 6.34; in Mark 14.23–25 and 1 Cor. 11.25–26 the fruit of the vine is likened to the blood of Jesus). That the blood in this scene is said to reach the height of 'horses' bridles' (χαλινῶν τῶν ἵππων, *chalinōn tōn hippōn*) is probably an allusion to a decisive eschatological battle, such as that portrayed in 19.11–21, where the victorious armies of heaven appear on white horses (Aune 848). In that case, the 'bridles' in verse 20 suggest the accompanying presence of a similar cavalry of Christian conquest (cf. Charles 2, 26; Bornkamm, 'lēnós [vat, press]' 532). Χαλινός (*chalinos*, 'bridle') is used in the New Testament only here and at Jas. 3.3.

For the height of the blood see *1 Enoch* 100.3 (in the final judgement, 'the horse shall walk through the blood of sinners up to his chest'). The distance to which it flows, 1,600 stadia, approximately 'two hundred miles', could be a reference to the length of Palestine. Alternatively, it may be symbolic, in that it squares the number four, which in Revelation is associated with the earth (7.1; 20.8), and multiplies it by the square of ten, the number of completeness (5.11; 20.6); so Mounce 281. Rather than attributing to John such complicated mathematical calculation, which has little place in an apocalyptic vision (despite 13.18), it is preferable to regard the measurement in verse 20 as one element of the seer's hyperbolic imagery in this scene. 'Two hundred miles' of blood simply indicates a 'slaughter of exceptional proportions' (Aune 848). Bauckham (*Climax of Prophecy* 40–48, commenting on Rev. 14.20b) notes that such hyperbole is a frequent motif in ancient literature (see esp. ibid. 40–43). For the theme of vengeance underlying

the action in this scene see above, 160–64. The imagery in 14.17–20 is further
developed in 16.12–14 (Bauckham 1299*a*).

Theology

Scene 4 of the Apocalypse (Rev. 12—14), together with the interval which follows it
(Chapter 15), unfolds the contents of the third woe (see on 11.14). For the sacramental
character of the seven signs in Rev. 12—14 see on 12.1. Theologically, this section of
Revelation sets out strongly the abiding themes in this drama of redemption through
conflict, and salvation through judgement (cf. 14.3–4; 15.3; also 5.9). The prevailing
mood is that of exaltation, following the spiritual warfare depicted in Chapter 11 (see
esp. 12.7–9). But the audience is also presented with what is clearly an ongoing battle
between good and evil (12.17), and an explanation of the causes of this warfare. The
hostility of the powers of evil towards the Church of God is evidently derived not only
from the misuse of power by unjust and oppressive authorities outside the Christian
community but also from the troubles within it, brought about by idolatrous compromise and inadequate belief. Throughout the conflict, the messianic community is
shown to be the recipient of divine protection (7.1–12; 12.5–6; 14.1–5, 13), and the
antagonism of Satan is demonstrated as being limited in its length and scope (12.12, 16;
13.5; 14.8–11).

The scene in Rev. 12—14 is set both in heaven and on earth; and the two dimensions
interact closely, as the characters move easily between them, and earthly judgement is
mediated by heavenly angels (12.10; 14.7, 14–20). The action is played out by representative figures (the woman and child, the dragon, Michael, the beasts, the 144,000,
the angels), who personify the participants in the eschatological conflict almost as if they
were heroes and villains in folkloric literature (cf. Aune 674–76); see on 12.1–3, 7; 13.1–
2, 11–18; 14.1, 6–19. The Lamb (12.11; 13.8; 14.1, 4, 10) and the Son of man (14.14)
preside over the judgemental and salvific process, as final victory is promised to the faithful
and obedient saints of God who are sealed by him (12.13–17; 13.7–8; 14.4, 8, 12–13).
As Boring (150) suggests, moreover, the unit Rev. 12—14 forms a cosmic drama in which
all the characters and actions are exaggerated and larger than life. Chapters 12—13 unveil the transcendent world, to offer a 'behind-the-scenes' view of the powers of evil
at work in the present, while Rev. 14 discloses a similar and proleptic vision of God's
sovereign victory in salvation and judgement.

Chapter 12 controls the theological message of Rev. 12—14. As Beale (622–24) shows,
Rev. 12 begins a new vision, but continues to develop earlier themes in the Apocalypse
by investigating the spiritual conflict between the Church and the world from a deeper
perspective. This has been set out progressively in Chapters 1—11. Now, in Chapters
12—14, and indeed in the remainder of the drama (12—22), the prophet-seer tells the
same story, explaining in greater detail what the earlier sections only imply: that Satan
and his agents are the ultimate source of evil and deceit, just as the final origin of goodness and truth are to be found in God and revealed in the messianic Lamb. Furthermore,
in the same way that John throughout this scene retells the warfare of the earlier chapters from a more profound spiritual perspective, so in Rev. 12 he starts the narrative again
from the viewpoint of time. He begins with the period immediately before the birth of
Christ (12.1), continues through the ministry to the death and resurrection of Jesus (12.2–
5, 7–10), and concludes with the destiny of the protected messianic community in the
age of the Church (12.6, 11–17; cf. 14.1–5; 15.3–4). See Beale 623. The result is an
emphatic chiaroscuro of light and darkness which is strikingly reassembled in the parallel verses at John 1.1–5. (Milligan [199–200] finds close links between the theological
ideas of John 1.1–5 and those of Rev. 12.1–6.)

The heavenly announcement at Rev. 12.11, that the saints have conquered the devil through the sacrifice of the Lamb, as well as by the word of their testimony, is a theological affirmation which is central to the thought of this scene; and it connects with the song of the redeemed at 14.3–4 (cf. also Beasley-Murray 203–204). The triumph of light over darkness is rooted in the death and exaltation of Jesus (cf. 5.9; John 12.31–36); although, as in the Fourth Gospel, the writer does not investigate the mechanics of that salvific process (but cf. 1 John 2.2; 4.10). Cf. Smalley, *John* 252–56. As a result, the sacrificial endurance and faithful testimony of believers become a reality (13.9–10; 14.4, 12), and their eternal life is assured (14.13–16). It remains true, however, that the victory of the saints achieved through the cross of Christ has not been universally embraced by the members of the Johannine community; and Rev.12(—14) does not present the audience with a straightforward situation of the Church in opposition to the world. For, in some cases, followers of the Lamb have joined the beast (see 2.2–6, 13–15, 20–24; 13.7; 14.4); cf. Sweet 221.

Despite the strong theology of salvation *through* judgement which pervades Rev. 12—14, initially it seems that the pictures in this scene of the divine justice which is meted out to the unfaithful of the world are fiercely drawn (note in particular the wrath of God, the torment of those who worship Satan and the fate of the wicked in Chapter 14). Yet there is a balanced and constructive side to the seer's thought in this passage. The history of salvation stands under the good news of God as Creator (14.6–7) and includes his work as Redeemer (13.8; 14.3–4); and those who are true members of the Church, while not escaping the sometimes painful effects of the struggle between good and evil, remain under divine protection (12.1–6, 13–17; 13.5–10; 14.12–13). See further on 14.10.

John never finally separates the thunder of God from his love; and that is why the judgemental images of Rev. 12—14 must be interpreted against their rebirth in 19.13–15 (q.v.). John's theology of power speaks in the end of mercy. The vision in Rev. 19 of God's sovereignty, expressed in Christ, begins with the tableau of a just warrior-ruler, who judges the nations with the winepress of God's fury (19.1–2, 11–12, 13–16). But that scene includes the appearance of the Word of God dressed in a robe dipped in blood (19.13). God speaks with truth and justice; but his word is humble and accessible, with love as its motivation and an inclusive redemption as its purpose (5.9–10; 7.9–10; 21.24–26; cf. John 1.14–18; 3.17–21). So Boring 172; Smalley, *Thunder and Love* 179.

INTERVAL
A New Exodus
(15.1–8)

Translation

15 ¹Then I saw another heavenly sign, great and remarkable: seven angels with seven plagues, which are final; for through them God's wrath has reached completion.

²And I saw what appeared to be a sea of crystal, suffused with fire; and those who were victorious over the beast, that is, over its image and the number which is its name, stood on the lake of glass. They held harps given to them by God,ᵃ ³and they sang the song of Moses, God's servant, even the song of the Lamb, chanting,

> 'How great and amazing are your deeds,
>   Lord God, the Almighty!
> Your ways are just and true,
>   King of theᵇ nations.
> ⁴Lord, who will not revereᶜ
>   and glorifyᵈ your name?
> Because you alone are holy;
> for all the nations will come
> to offer worship in your presence,
> since your acts of saving judgement have been revealed.'

⁵Later, as I watched, the heavenly temple, namely, the tabernacle of witness, was opened; ⁶and from the sanctuary emerged the seven angels whoᵉ carried the seven plagues. They were robed in linen,ᶠ pure and glistening, with golden sashes across their chests. ⁷Then one of the four living creatures gave the seven angels seven golden offering bowls, filled with the wrath of the God who lives for ever and ever. ⁸So the temple was filled with smokeᵍ from the glory and power of God; and it was impossible to enter the temple, until the seven plagues of the seven angels had been completed.

Text

ᵃ The *lectio originalis* is τοῦ θεοῦ (*tou theou*, lit. 'of God'). One MS (ℵ) includes κυρίου (*kyriou*, 'Lord') before τοῦ θεοῦ (*tou theou*, 'God'); but this is clearly an interpolation, influenced by the frequent use of the full title, 'Lord God', in Revelation (see 15.3, nearby; also 1.8; 4.8; 11.17; 18.8; 21.22; et al.).

ᵇ The reading ἐθνῶν (*ethnōn*, 'of the nations'), as witnessed by ℵᵃ A 025 046 051 Byz itᵍⁱᵍ,ʰ copᵇᵒ arm eth Andreas Cyprian Beatus, et al., is replaced in several MSS (including 𝔓47 ℵ⋆ ᶜ C 1006 1611 ¹⁶¹¹ ²³⁴⁴ 1841 2040 itᶜ¹ vg syrᵖʰ,ʰ copˢᵃ, et al.) by αἰώνων (*aiōnōn*, 'of the ages'). The weight of external evidence for both of these versions is virtually the same. However, the second reading (αἰώνων, *aiōnōn*, 'of the ages') may well have been introduced by copyists who remembered 1 Tim. 1.17 ('to the King of the ages be honour and glory'; cf. Jer. 10.10 [מלך עולם, *melek 'ōlām*, 'the everlasting King']; *1 Enoch* 9.4, v.l.; Tobit 13.4); and, moreover, the first version fits the context perfectly (see verse 4).

So Metzger, *Textual Commentary* 753–54; against Aune 853. The reading 'King of the nations' is accordingly to be preferred; hence the translation. TR has ἁγίων (*hagiōn*, 'of the saints'); but this variant has minimal support, and is probably the result of confusion (Metzger, *Textual Commentary* 754).

^c The reading which best explains the origin of the others is οὐ μὴ φοβηθῇ (*ou mē phobēthē[i]*, 'who will not revere, lit. fear [your name]?'); and this version is firmly supported by A C 025 046 1611 Oecumenius²⁰⁵³ it^{gig,h} cop^{bo} arm eth Cyprian. Perceiving the need of an object for the verb 'revere', some copyists (represented by such MSS as 𝔓47 ℵ 1006^{1006 1841} 1611^{1854 2329} 2065) added σε (*se*, 'you') before οὐ (*ou*, 'not'); while others (including 051 94 1828 TR) place the pronoun 'you' after φοβηθῇ (*phobēthē[i]*, 'revere'). A few witnesses (ℵ 1006 2040, et al.) have only οὐ (*ou*, 'not'), or (1854) only μή (*mē*, 'not [at all]'). See Metzger, *Textual Commentary* 754.

^d The third person singular future indicative form of the verb δοξάσει (*doxasei*, '[who] will glorify [your name]?') appears in A C 025 046 051 Oecumenius²⁰⁵³ Andreas, et al.; and this is clearly the original version. The variant δοξάσῃ (*doxasē[i]*, 'would glorify', aorist subjunctive), is an obvious assimilation to the preceding and parallel verb, in the aorist subjunctive, φοβηθῇ (*phobēthē[i]*, lit. 'would revere'). Cf. Aune 853.

^e The inclusion of the article οἱ (*hoi*, 'they, the ones') before ἔχοντες (*echontes*, lit. 'having') is well attested (A C 1006¹⁸⁴¹ 1611^{1611 2329} Andreas, et al.). But the *omission* of the article also receives good support, from 𝔓47 ℵ 025 046 1006¹⁸⁵⁴ 1611²³⁴⁴ Byz, et al. The combinations of A with C on the one hand and 𝔓47 with ℵ on the other provide strong external evidence for either reading. However, the Apocalypse manifests a regular syntactical pattern, that when an articular noun is followed by a dependent adjectival, descriptive phrase, introduced by a substantival participle such as ἔχοντες (*echontes*, 'having'), the article is normally repeated with the participle (cf. 8.6; 9.15; 11.4; 14.13; 17.18; 21.9). Moreover, as Aune (854) notes, the MS ℵ has a tendency to omit the article when it recurs in this way (8.6; 9.15; 11.4; et al.). There is good reason, therefore, to regard the article οἱ (*hoi*, 'they') at this point as part of the original text.

^f There is weighty MS support for the reading λίνον (*linon*, 'linen'); so 025 051 1006 1611 syr^{ph,h} it^c vg^{ww} arm Andreas Byz Primasius Beatus, et al. Some witnesses (including A C 2020^{mg} vg; cf. Charles 2, 331) have the variant λίθον (*lithon*, 'stone'); while others (such as 𝔓47 046 it^{gig}) read λινοῦν (*linoun*, 'made of linen'), and ℵ has the masculine equivalent, λινοῦς (*linous*). With 'translational freedom' (Metzger, *Textual Commentary* 754), a few MSS (cop^{sa} eth Cassiodorus) omit the noun altogether. The variant λίθον (*lithon*, 'stone') is a serious contender for originality, since it is the *lectio difficilior*; and is supported by the strong MS combination of A and C. It would also be easier to change λίθον (*lithon*, 'stone') into λίνον (*linon*, 'linen'), than the reverse. However, despite a superficial parallel with Ezek. 28.13 ('every precious stone was your covering'), being 'clothed with stone' makes no sense in the present context; such an image is also inappropriate with the adjective 'pure', which is correspondingly entirely apposite as a description of linen (but see Beale 804–805). It is thus likely that λίνον (*linon*, 'linen') is the original reading in this passage, and that its singular use in Revelation, with a rare use of the noun to mean 'linen *garment*', has given rise to the variants (including the secondary improvements represented by the forms which denote '[garments] *made of* linen').

^g 𝔓47 Byz insert ἐκ τοῦ (*ek tou*, lit. 'from the') before καπνοῦ (*kapnou*, 'smoke'); but this is presumably a subsequent attempt to provide a more precise grammatical introduction to the noun 'smoke', which otherwise appears abruptly, and one which balances the

following doublet, ἐκ τῆς δόξης τοῦ θεοῦ καὶ ἐκ τῆς δυνάμεως αὐτοῦ (*ek tēs doxēs tou theou kai ek tēs dynameōs autou*, lit. 'from the glory of God and from his power').

Literary Setting

The short interval which is provided by Rev. 15 has the new Exodus as its principal theme. It is structured in three literary units, each of which is introduced by the apocalyptic formula, καὶ εἶδον (*kai eidon*, lit. 'and I saw'); see verses 1, 2, 5; and further on verse 5. The first textual subdivision consists of verse 1, which provides an introductory prologue to the chapter. This section speaks of 'another [heavenly] sign' (ἄλλο σημεῖον, *allo sēmeion*), which is the third to receive specific mention in the Apocalypse after 12.1 and 3 (q.v.); although it is possible to detect seven 'signs' in Chapters 12—14. The third sign as such, however, does not occur until the seven bowls of God's wrath are poured out by the angels in Chapter 16 (Scene 5); and preparation for this action takes place during the interval of Chapter 15, when the seven angels emerge from God's presence to receive the bowls of offering (verses 5–7). In between, a new song of Moses is chanted (15.2–4). It seems, then, that the reference to the next (third) 'sign' in 15.1 is both a literary means of connecting the present chapter with the previous scene (12.1—14.20), and also a way of leading into the dramatic content of all that follows in the Apocalypse (Chapters 16—22).

The second textual unit in the interval of Rev. 15 is made up by the catena of Old Testament quotations which forms the hymn in verses 3–4; and this is introduced by the vision of verse 2. Against Aune (863), there seems to be a clear literary relationship between this offering of praise and the song of Moses (verse 3) celebrating the victory of the Exodus (Exod. 15.1–18; cf. Deut. 31.30—32.43); see further Beasley-Murray 231–34; Prigent 454–56; and the discussion below. The setting of the hymn in this section (verse 2) appears to be that of a throne room, even if the presence of God and his throne are not specifically mentioned.

The structuring of the hymn of celebration in verses 3–4 suggests that it may have derived from the liturgy of the primitive Christian Church (Mounce 286), and possibly formed part of the hymnody of the Johannine community itself. The literary character of the song is marked by a series of short strophes (see the translation), the first four of which provide a good example of synonymous parallelism, characteristic of the psalms and songs of the Old Testament. Verse 4 raises a rhetorical question ('Lord, who will not revere and glorify your name?'), and this is followed by three causal clauses, each introduced by ὅτι (*hoti*, 'because', 'for').

The third literary subdivision of Chapter 15 is found in verses 5–8, which provide the seer with an important means of preparing his audience for the apocalyptic action to follow. It begins with the introductory formula, καὶ μετὰ ταῦτα εἶδον (*kai meta tauta eidon*, 'later, as I watched', lit. 'and after this I saw'); and when this phrase appears elsewhere in Revelation, in more or less exactly this form (4.1; 7.1; 18.1), it is used as a preface to a major textual unit (4.1—5.14; 7.1–17; 18.1–24). Here, 15.5–8 serves as a significant introduction to the immediate, climactic narrative of the seven bowls in 16.1–21.

Comment

Prologue (15.1)

15.1   Rev. 15 concludes the unfolding of the contents of the third woe (see on 11.14). The vision first announces the appearance of 'another heavenly sign, great and remarkable', in language which recalls the two earlier signs, explicitly so designated, at 12.1 and 3. The adjectives μέγα (*mega*, 'great', in the sense of 'important') and θαυμαστόν (*thaumaston*, 'wonderful', or 'remarkable' [BDAG 445*a*]) are used in verse 3 of God's works; and this combination appears only here and at 15.3 in Revelation. Those adjectives are separated in verse 1 from the noun phrase which they modify (ἄλλο σημεῖον, *allo sēmeion*, 'another sign') by the prepositional phrase ἐν τῷ οὐρανῷ (*en tō[i] ouranō[i]*, lit. 'in the heaven'). This syntactical pattern occurs only in this context in the New Testament; elsewhere in Revelation, when ἄλλος (*allos*, 'another') is used with another adjective to modify a noun, the adjective ἄλλος (*allos*, 'another') is placed before the noun, and the second adjective follows it (see 6.4; 10.1; 14.8, 9). Cf. Aune 851–52. The sign in question, introduced at 15.1, helps to disclose the meaning of salvation history, as well as making it possible; see further on 12.1.

The group of 'seven angels' (ἀγγέλους ἑπτά, *angelous hepta*), which more closely defines the nature of the 'sign' appearing in heaven, is mentioned in verse 1 for the first time, and the noun phrase is anarthrous as a result; in verse 6, the article οἱ (*hoi*, 'the') is used with ἑπτὰ ἄγγελοι (*hepta angeloi*, 'seven angels'), since those heavenly beings refer back to the ones introduced here; cf. similarly 15.7–8; 16.1; 17.1; 21.9. The adjectival phrase τὰς ἐσχάτας (*tas eschatas*, 'final', lit. 'the last') includes an article since it modifies the anarthrous noun πληγάς (*plēgas*, 'plagues'). Apart from the phrase 'Babylon the great' (Βαβυλὼν ἡ μεγάλη, *Babylōn hē megalē*), at 14.8; 16.19; 17.5; 18.2, 21 (cf. 18.10), this grammatical form appears only here in the Apocalypse. For the importance and symbolism of the number 'seven' in Johannine literature see on 1.4. For 'angels' in the Apocalypse see further above, 28–30.

The seven judgemental plagues are 'final' because they point towards the end-time, and lead into it. They constitute ultimate divine warnings to an impenitent world (Mounce 284); but they must also include the possibility of repentance and renewal. With the seven bowls, John's vision moves towards its climax (Knight 108), and the wrath of God 'has reached completion' (ἐτελέσθη, *etelesthē*, an aorist passive of divine activity). God's wrath has not ended, in the sense of being 'spent' (against Aune 852), since his resistance to evil will be manifested again (19.20; 20.10, 15). It is 'complete', with perhaps the additional connotation of 'intense', because it is God who concludes history; but that consummation is salvific (21—22), as well as just (18—20). Clearly, the present vision cannot be interpreted in strictly chronological terms (so Milligan 259). For, in the eschatology of the Apocalypse, time is constantly invaded by eternity; and, while the end is always pressing in, it has not yet arrived (see on 6.17; et al.).

The biblical verb τελεῖν (*telein*, 'complete' or 'fulfil') is used of the fulfilment of Old Testament prophecy, or of the word of God (10.7; 17.17; Luke 22.37; Acts 13.29). For the concept of the 'wrath of God' in Revelation see on 14.10; also 14.19; 15.7; 16.1; cf. 19.15. Prigent (459) thinks that the tradition of the seven angels with their seven plagues may be traced back to Lev. 26 (note esp. verses 21 and 24). After the promise of protection and blessings, reserved for those who are obedient to God their Redeemer (7.4–17; 11.1–6; 14.1–5, 12–16) comes 'the announcement of the seven plagues and of the sevenfold curse on those who rebel' (Prigent 459). Beale (787) suggests that the 'seven last plagues' might correspond to the ten plagues which God brought against Egypt. This association suits the theological theme of the new Exodus which belongs to this section (see also below); for, according to Jewish expectation, Exodus-type judgements were to be enacted against the world at the end of history, at which time Israel would again be redeemed (cf. Deut. 4.30; 8.16; 31.29; Mic. 7.10–17; 1QM 11.7–12; 14.1; *Apoc. Abr.* 29.15–16; 30.1–8).

An Exodus Hymn (15.2–4)

2   Verses 2–4, which include a hymn to celebrate the new Exodus (verses 3–4), form an interlocking parenthesis in the present interval. The subdivision looks back to the scenes of eschatological judgement in 14.6–20. The song of Moses and the Lamb in 15.3–4 praises the Lord's justice (verse 3), and asserts the victory of the saints of God over his opponents, and over all the evil and injustice which they represent. This, in turn, leads into the sevenfold sequence of the bowl-plagues, already heralded at 15.1, which recalls the seven trumpet-plagues in Chapters 8—9. In that section, 8.3–5 (q.v.) has an interlocking function parallel to 15.2–4 (Beale 787).

The prophet-seer discerns 'what appeared to be a sea of crystal, suffused with fire'. The particle ὡς (*hōs*, 'like', 'as') is typically used in apocalyptic visions to draw attention to their mysterious content (cf. 5.6; 6.6; 8.8; et al.; also Dan. 7.4; 4 Ezra 11.37). The anarthrous comparative phrase ὡς θάλλασαν ὑαλίνην (*hōs thallasan hyalinēn*, lit. 'like a sea of glass'), although without a reference to fire, has already been used in the Apocalypse in the throne-vision of 4.6 (and otherwise only there in Revelation). Since the appearance of the image in 15.2 is anaphoric, it is difficult to account for the absence of the article at this point; although when the phrase occurs a second time, later in verse 2, the article is present.

The 'sea of crystal, suffused with fire' combines the ideas of a celestial sea, the floor of heaven, above which God's throne is set, and the river(s) of fire flowing from his heavenly presence (see on 4.6); cf. Gen. 1.7; 7.11; Ps. 29.10; *1 Enoch* 54.7; Dan. 7.10; *1 Enoch* 71.2; *3 Enoch* 18.19; 19.4 (= Gen. 2.10–14); et al. For a 'sea' in heaven note also *2 Enoch* 3.3; *T. Levi* 2.7; cf. Ezek. 1.22, 'something like a dome, shining as crystal', was spread out over the heads of the living creatures. It is possible that this imagery alludes to the brazen basin of water in Solomon's Temple, which was known as the 'molten sea' (1 Kings 7.23; 2 Chron. 4.2). But more prominent in the figure is the heavenly analogy to the Sea of Reeds, in association with the new Exodus (Beale 789; cf. Kiddle 300–10); and Jewish exegetical tradition evidently depicted the Red Sea as a sea of glass (cf. Exod. 15.8; *Midr.* Ps. 136.7). The Exodus atmosphere is supported by the 'plagues' of verse 1, which clearly resonate with the plagues of Egypt in Chapter 16, by the counterpart of the song of Moses (Exod. 15) at 15.3–4, and by the reference to the 'tabernacle of witness' in verse 5. See further Caird 197; also on verses 3–5.

The Red Sea in the Old Testament is the dwelling of the evil sea monster (Ps. 74.12–14); so the 'sea' in this passage, as elsewhere in Revelation, denotes cosmic evil (13.1; 21.1). John regards the demonic power of the waters as calmed by the authority of God; for, just as the Pharaoh and his allies were conquered by divine power at the time of the Exodus, so Satan and his allies have now been overthrown through the death and exaltation of Christ (cf. 5.5–14). 'Fire' in the Apocalypse is usually a metaphor of divine judgement, as in 1.14; see 2.18; 4.5; 8.5–8; 10.1; 11.5; 14.10, 18; 16.8; 17.16; 18.8; 19.12, 20; 20.9–10, 14–15; 21.8. Rev. 13.13 (the beast making fire to come down from heaven) seems to be the one exception. This is the meaning in 15.2. The sea is not a sphere for the fiery trials of the saints (Milligan 260–61), but the place where the Lamb has judged the beast (Beale 789). The expression '(the sea) suffused with fire' (μεμιγμένην πυρί, *memigmenēn pyri*) uses an instrumental dative (lit. 'mingled *by* fire').

The participial expression τοὺς νικῶντας (*tous nikōntas*, 'those who were victorious', lit. 'those conquering'), in the next part of verse 2, is defined by the object of the victory in question. Those involved were victorious ἐκ τοῦ θηρίου (*ek tou thēriou*, 'over [lit. from] the beast'; using the genitive, where the accusative would have been appropriate). This assertion is followed by two further dependent, genitival clauses, both using the preposition ἐκ (*ek*, lit. 'from'), which further qualify the character of the beast: 'over its image and the number which is its name'. For the significance of this imagery, and for the 'beast' as the symbol of idolatrous opposition to God, see further on 13.1–18, esp. 14–18. Judging by the subsequent hymn in verses 3–4, which is described as the 'song of Moses . . . even the song of the Lamb', the victors in verse 2 are clearly the saints of God; and they may be identified with the faithful who are mentioned in Chapter 14 (see verses 1–5, and note the 'harps' in 15.2 and 14.2; cf. also 14.14–16).

The Greek expression νικᾶν ἐκ (*nikan ek*, lit. 'victorious from') is difficult, and does not appear in any other Greek text. It may be differently construed (see Aune 871–72), and three meanings are worthy of serious consideration.

(a) The phrase is an ellipsis, which in its fuller form includes the notion of salvation, and suggests that the conquerors have 'kept themselves' or 'delivered themselves' from the beast (14.4–5); cf. Prigent 459 n. 4.
(b) It is a Latinism, although such constructions are very rare in the Apocalypse, yielding the sense 'carrying victory from (the beast)' (using *victoriam ferre ex . . .* , 'to bring victory from . . .'). So Aune 872, against Charles 2, 33.
(c) The most likely interpretation of this expression is the most obvious. The saints of God have 'come victoriously from (the deception of) the beast' (Beckwith 674; Beale 790). They can share in the victory of the Lamb because they have endured faithfully despite persecution from Rome, and because of their refusal to compromise with the world or with inadequate belief (2.7; 3.21; 12.11, 17).

The members of Christ's believing community are further identified with the Lamb, because they 'stood on the lake of glass' (for which image see above). The reference to the posture of the saints may include an allusion to the idea of resurrection; see 5.6 (the slaughtered but risen Lamb was 'standing' in the throne room); 7.9 (the vast multitude of the faithful 'stood' before the throne of God and the Lamb). The verb ἵστημι (*histēmi*, 'stand'), used here with the preposition ἐπί (*epi*, 'on' or 'by'), could signify that the conquerors were standing '*beside* the sea of glass' (so NRSV); cf. 3.20; 7.1. However, this construction can also be translated 'standing *on* the lake of glass', as in the translation; and this is the best way of understanding the picture in verse 2, and one which fits the context (see Beckwith 674; Beale 791; against Aune 872, who translates, 'stood near the sea'). The surface of the sea of crystal is evidently solid, like a bronze laver; so that the saints can stand 'on' it easily, as do the angelic figures of 10.5, 8; cf. 12.18.

This interpretation is also theologically apt. The faithful have been locked into combat with the sea monster (13.1); and this suggests that the waters of conflict are precisely the scene of the battle. Unlike the Israelites, who in their war against the Egyptians stood *beside* the Red Sea to watch the divine victory accomplished for them (Exod. 14.15–31), and who chanted their hymn of victory near its waters (Exod. 15.1–19), the saints have conquered the beast in and *through* the fiery floods of opposition and strife. The faithful witness of Christian believers, in the face of Satan's onslaught (11.3–7) and demonic torrents of deception (12.15–16), will always result in spiritual triumph. See Beale 791.

For the 'harps given (the faithful) by God' (κιθάρας τοῦ θεοῦ, *kitharas tou theou*, lit. 'kitharas of God') see the textual note on verse 2. The genitive is objective, giving the sense, 'harps for playing a celestial litany' (cf. 1 Chron. 16.42 LXX, ὄργανα τῶν ᾠδῶν τοῦ θεοῦ, *organa tōn ō[i]dōn tou theou*, 'instruments for sacred song', lit. 'instruments of the songs of God'; see Mounce 285). They will be used for the Exodus hymn at verses 3–4, just as the Song of Moses at the first Exodus was accompanied by musical instruments (Exod. 15.20–21). The 'sweet harp' is an appropriate instrument with which to praise God (Ps. 81.2).

3–4 The song of celebration in verses 3–4 is one offering of praise to God, which falls into two parts (verse 3 and verse 4). The unity of the hymn is made clear by the epexegetical use of καί (*kai*, lit. 'and') at the start of verse 3: 'they sang the song of Moses,

God's servant, *even* the song of the Lamb' (cf. Beckwith 678). The saints declare the righteous and redemptive activity of the Lord, starting from the time of the covenant with Moses, and culminating in the death and exaltation of the Lamb. The verb ᾄδουσιν (*a[i]dousin*, lit. 'they sing') is in the present tense; but it appears in the translation as if the tense were perfect ('they sang'), to conform with the other verbs in the past at the opening of Chapter 15.

It is not immediately clear how to construe the genitive in 'the song of Moses' (τὴν ᾠδὴν Μωϋσέως, *tēn ō[i]dēn Mōyseōs*). However, it can scarcely be objective ('a song *to or about* Moses'), since what follows is clearly addressed to God. It makes sense, therefore, to understand the genitive as subjective: this is a 'song *by* Moses'. There are two such hymns recorded in the Old Testament: Exod. 15.1–18; and Deut. 31.30—32.43 (Aune [872] includes Ps. 90, a 'prayer of Moses', as a third). In view of the Exodus motif which runs strongly through the theology of Rev. 15, it is likely that the allusion here is to the song of God's victory which Moses recited with the Israelites (Exod. 15.1) after the Exodus. In itself, that event points to the triumphant and new Exodus achieved by the messianic Lamb in his cross and resurrection (14.3–4; cf. John 16.33); see Beale 792.

It is correspondingly less obvious that the hymn of Moses in view is the 'swan-like song ascribed to the dying Lawgiver' (Swete 195; against Beckwith 676–78), used as a Sabbath hymn in the Jewish liturgy, at Deut. 32. As Beale (793) points out, however, the Deuteronomic song may be a part of the liturgy to which reference is made at this point. Redemptive judgement is the theme of Deut. 32, as it is in Exod. 15 and Rev. 15. God's justice, meted out to apostate Israelites because of idolatry, and vengeance taken on enemy persecutors are the focus of Deut. 32 (see verses 19–21, 43); similarly, in Rev. 15.3–4, divine judgement on unfaithful Christians and also on 'the nations' is in view (15.4; cf. 6.9–11; 8.3–5; 14.18–19; 15.7). Moses is described as God's 'servant' in Exod. 14.31, as part of the introduction to the Exodus hymn in Exod. 15; see also Num. 12.7; Deut. 34.5; Josh. 1.1; 14.7; 2 Kings 21.8; Neh. 1.8; Ps. 105.26; Mal. 4.4; Baruch 1.20; *1 Clem.* 4.12; 51.5; et al.

The hymn of the faithful is further described as 'the song of the Lamb' (τὴν ᾠδὴν τοῦ ἀρνίου, *tēn ō[i]dēn tou arniou*); for 'Lamb' see on 5.6. In this phrase, the genitive might be subjective ('the song *by* the Lamb'), as with the preceding parallel genitive just discussed (so Beale 793). But nowhere else is there mention of a hymn sung by the Lamb; and it is much more appropriate to take the genitive here as objective (this is a song '*to or about*' the Lamb), which is exactly what is recorded at 5.9–12 (q.v.). Aune (873) regards the sudden reference to the 'Lamb' at this point as an editorial insertion (cf. 7.9–10; 14.4, 10; 21.22–23; 22.1, 3); and it is true that the song which follows is addressed initially to God and not to Christ. Nevertheless, the Father's salvific purposes were fulfilled in his Son; and the song of 15.3–4 may accordingly be regarded as a hymn to both. In the Apocalypse, they occupy the same throne (5.13; 22.1), and the Lamb is seen as a figure of redemption in the heavenly song at 5.9. The word λέγοντες (*legontes*, 'chanting', lit. 'saying') is strictly redundant after the verb 'sang'. This is a Hebraic formula, used to introduce direct discourse; and the word 'chanting' is included in the translation, at this point, as a logical preface to the song of the faithful.

For the structure of the song in verses 3–4 see the Literary Setting, above. There is no close formal relationship between this hymn of praise and Exod. 15; although that song of Moses is evidently in John's mind, together with the Exodus theme, throughout Rev. 15. Instead, the strophes derive from various passages in the Old Testament which extol the character of God. The first line invokes the 'great and amazing' deeds of God; and these two adjectives are used of the heavenly 'sign' which the seer has already perceived (verse 1).

For the linguistic pattern of a vocative ('Lord God'), followed by two nominative adjectives which function as vocatives ('great and amazing'), see 11.17; 16.7; cf. 16.5; 18.20. The exact Greek expression, μεγάλα καὶ θαυμαστά (*megala kai thaumasta*, 'great and amazing [wonderful]'), used to describe the works of God, is not easy to trace in the Old Testament; although it appears when Job speaks of the 'great and wonderful things' which he has uttered (Job 42.3 LXX). But see Tobit 12.22 LXX; note also the LXX of Deut. 10.21 ('God has done great and awesome things [τὰ μεγάλα καὶ τὰ ἔνδοξα, *ta megala kai ta endoxa*] for you'); Ps. 110.2–3 (God's works are 'great [μεγάλα, *megala*], full of honour and majesty'); (Theod.) Dan. 9.4 (God himself is 'great and wonderful'. *3 Apoc. Bar.* 4.1 ('Lord, you have shown me great and wondrous things') may have been influenced by Rev. 15.1, 3. As Beale (794) notices, however, there is a most appropriate Old Testament parallel for this context to be found at Deut. 28.59–60 LXX, where it is predicted that Israel's future judgement will reflect the Egyptian plagues (the Lord will overwhelm you and your offspring with 'great and amazing plagues', πληγὰς μεγάλας καὶ θαυμαστάς, *plēgas megalas kai thaumastas*).

The 'deeds' (ἔργα, *erga*) of God may include his miracles, as with the 'works' of Jesus in John 5.20, 36; 10.32–33; et al. (so Aune 874). But, although the term 'works' is frequently used in the Apocalypse with reference to the actions of people (2.2; 3.1–2; et al.), it applies to divine 'deeds' only at 15.3; the 'works' which are mentioned at 2.26 are those of Jesus. In the present context, the 'deeds' of God are his good purposes for humanity, seen in creation and salvation (cf. Amos 4.13). The designation 'Almighty' (παντοκράτωρ, *pantokratōr*) is used of God nine times in Revelation (see on 1.8). Here, the full and majestic title 'Lord God, the Almighty' is an appropriate divine ascription in a hymn of victory. God is all-powerful; and, as Sovereign over the universe, he enables his servants to conquer the evil deception of the beast (cf. the song of the elders in 11.17–18).

The remainder of the first part of this song sets out a further reason for praising God. He is not only great in his activity; he is also 'just and true' (δίκαιος καὶ ἀληθινός, *dikaios kai alēthinos*) in his nature. All his redemptive works are amazing, and to be met with awe, not simply because of their scope and extent, but also because of their 'intrinsic righteousness' (Mounce 286). For the assertion that God's ways are just and true see the song of Moses at Deut. 32.4 LXX ('God's works are true, and all his ways are just'); cf. also Ps. 144.17 LXX ('The Lord is righteous in all his ways, and holy in all his works'). The term δίκαιος (*dikaios*, 'just') is descriptive of God's justice, as opposed to human injustice, and of his righteousness in contrast to the evil character and behaviour of his enemies; see Seebass and Brown, 'δικαιοσύνη/δίκαιος' 360–65, esp. 362. For the use of this adjective elsewhere in the Apocalypse see 16.5 ('the Holy One is just'); 16.7; and 19.2 (divine judgements are 'true and just'). Unlike the Pauline literature, the appearance of this word-group in Revelation is restrained (δίκαιος, *dikaios*, 'righteous', occurs five times; δικαιοσύνη, *dikaiosynē*, 'righteousness', twice; see also the single use of δικαιώματα, *dikaiōmata*, to describe God's 'acts of saving judgement', at 15.4). The quality of 'truth' (ἀλήθεια, *alētheia*) is ascribed to Jesus at Rev. 3.7, 14; 19.11, and to God at 6.10 (q.v.); 16.7; and 19.2 ('his judgements are true and just'). At 21.5; 22.6 the words of apocalyptic prophecy are described as 'trustworthy and true' (πιστοὶ καὶ ἀληθινοί, *pistoi kai alēthinoi*).

For the address of praise to God as the 'King of the nations' (ὁ βασιλεὺς τῶν ἐθνῶν, *ho basileus tōn ethnōn*) see the textual note on verse 3. The title reflects Jer. 10.7 ('Who would not fear you, O King of the nations?'). The term 'nations' in Revelation often describes an unbelieving world (as at 10.11; 11.2, 9, 18; 14.8; 15.4; 16.19; 18.3; 19.15). While this connotation may be included in the use of the term here, the reference is ultimately entirely inclusive. Since God is 'Almighty', he is sovereign Lord of the universe, the occupants of which may be faithful, as well as hostile, to him.

The second part of this hymn of praise (verse 4) continues the thought of Jer. 10.7 ('Who would not fear you, King of the nations?'), combining this with a recollection of the song of Moses at Exod. 15.11 ('Who is like you, O Lord, among the gods? Who is like you, majestic in holiness?'). The rhetorical question, 'Lord, who will not revere (using the verb φοβέω, *phobeō*, lit. 'fear') and glorify your name?', is a response to the preceding ascriptions of praise, and provides the basis for the three causes of thanksgiving, each introduced by ὅτι (*hoti*, 'for'), which follow; cf. Mounce 287. Rhetorical questions are common in biblical hymns (so Exod. 15.11; Ps. 6.3; 15.1; Isa. 40.25; Mic. 7.18; et al.; cf. also 1QH 3.23–24). The 'name' (ὄνομα, *onoma*) of God is a symbol for his personal being, which has been fully and finally revealed through Christ in his work of creation and salvation (cf. Bietenhard and Bruce, 'Name', esp. 653–54). For the divine name in the Apocalypse see 3.12; 11.18; 13.6; 14.1; 16.9; 22.4.

The leading attribute of God's nature, which undergirds his 'true and just' ways, is his unique holiness (ὅτι μόνος ὅσιος, *hoti monos hosios*, 'because you alone are holy', where the verb 'to be' has to be supplied). This predication is found only at Rev. 15.4; and the description of God as 'holy' occurs in Revelation only here and at 16.5 (q.v.). The term ὅσιος (*hosios*, 'holy') is rarely used in the context of the holiness of God (cf. LXX Deut. 32.4; Ps. 144.17; also *1 Clem.* 58.1); although the adjective μόνος (*monos*, 'alone') frequently accompanies biblical expressions of his uniqueness and incomparability (so LXX 2 Chron. 6.30; Neh. 9.6; Ps. 82.19; Isa. 2.11; also Rom. 16.27; 1 Tim. 1.17; Jude 25; et al.; cf. Mark 2.7). The 'holiness' of God denotes not his sinlessness, the opposite of which would be a theological impossibility, but the distinction between his nature in its wholeness, as sovereign and powerful, and that of his creation in its incompleteness and injustice (see Beckwith 675; Beale 796–97).

The remaining strophes of the hymn supply the answer to the earlier question, 'Who will revere and glorify (God's) name?' Because of God's innate holiness (the second ὅτι, *hoti*, 'because', in verse 4 is consecutive), 'all the nations will come to offer worship' in his presence. The scene is a metaphorical, rather than temporal, description of the universal recognition of the Lord as the one, true God; and this is a regular theme in biblical thought (cf. Ps. 86.9–10, which underlies the language of Rev. 15.4; also Isa. 45.23 = Phil. 2.9–11; Isa. 60.1–7; Jer. 16.19). Beale (797–98) denies that this prediction is inclusive, and argues that '*all* the nations' (πάντα τὰ ἔθνη, *panta ta ethnē*) in this text is an example of metonymy, whereby the whole of the world is substituted for a part of it, to indicate that *many* (but not all) will worship God (cf. Rev. 5.9; 7.9; 14.3). This is also the understanding elsewhere in Revelation, Beale (798) insists, when πᾶς (*pas*, 'all') occurs with ἔθνος (*ethnos*, 'nation'); cf. 5.9; 7.9; 13.7; 14.8; 18.3, 23.

Rist (479) adopts a similar stance, when he suggests that the line of this hymn, 'all the nations will come to offer worship' to God, is 'thoroughly out of harmony' with the belief in other parts of the Apocalypse that the nations will refuse to repent, but go on their idolatrous, oppressive way to destruction (cf. 9.20–21; 12.13–17; 14.18–20; 16.9, 11). According to Rist (ibid.), this theological anomaly may be explained in three ways: either John used a current Christian hymn, without changing the strophe about the final repentance and conversion of the unfaithful (an idea which is present in 1 Cor. 15.22; Eph. 1.10; 1 Tim. 2.3–4); or he was being inconsistent; or he meant that the 'worship' of the nations included their homage to God's power, without their conversion to him.

However, the apparent contradiction in this passage is superficial. In the liturgy of 15.4, confidence that in the messianic age to come the nations of the world will worship the God of Israel and bring glory to his name (Ps. 86.9; Mal. 1.11; cf. Rom. 15.8–12) is transformed by the seer into an assertion of God's total sovereignty over the beast and his followers at the end-time (Mounce 287; see Rev. 22.2). Not all will repent (22.11, 15), but the universal opportunity will always exist (6.15–17; 7.14; 22.11). In line with this interpretation, it is noteworthy that the evidence which Beale (797–98) adduces to support his view that John is being exclusive, rather than inclusive, in the soteriology of 15.3–4 (see above) is not consistent. For 'all the nations' at 14.8; 18.3, 23 appear in a context of an immediate temptation to *deny* God, rather than of an ultimate and wide-spread possibility of believing in him; and it is true that, in the end, the saints of the Church will derive from *every* nation and people and language-group (cf. 12.5). See further Bengel 338; also on the 'Theology' of Rev. 15, below.

All will come 'to offer worship' (προσκυνήσουσιν, *proskynēsousin*, lit. 'they will worship'; the future tense of the verb functions as if it belongs to a final clause, as in 4.1; et al.). The universal acclaim which belongs to God stems from his holy being and salvific activity. He alone is holy (see above), and therefore worthy to be praised in all the world. Moreover, God deserves the worship of his creation because his 'acts of saving judgement (δικαιώματα, *dikaiōmata*) have been revealed'. The term δικαιώματα (*dikaiōmata*) can mean God's 'righteous ordinances'; and these may include the implication of sentencing the ungodly (cf. lxx Deut. 4.1; 1 Kings 3.28; 2 Chron. 6.35; also Luke 1.6; Rom. 1.32; 5.16); so BDAG 249*b*; Charles 2, 36–37; Prigent 461. But the positive character of the context in Rev. 15.4 suggests that the alternative sense, 'saving acts of judgement', is more appropriate here (hence the translation). God has disclosed himself universally in deeds which are great and amazing, and in ways which are just and true (verse 3); as the holy King of the nations, therefore, he is worthy of universal adoration because he has been 'revealed' through the Lamb in actions which are evidently judge-mental, but also salvific (Baruch 2.17; Rev. 4.8–11; 5.9–10; 7.15–17; 10.11; 11.7–13; 14.6–7; cf. the 'righteous deeds' of the saints at 19.8). See Swete 197; also esv, njb.

The Angelic Commission (15.5–8)

5–6 The previous scene (Rev. 12—14) has been enacted both in heaven and on earth. The present interval (15) seems to take place entirely in heaven; although the seer presumably witnesses the action from a position on earth (14.20), and it involves the salvation of God's people in history. In the following scene (16) the focus of the action returns to earth.

Meanwhile, the vision of the seven judgemental bowls, which was introduced at 15.1, is resumed here; although 'bowls', as such, are not mentioned until verse 7. After a celebration of the new Exodus in Christ (15.2–4), John sees the opening of a heavenly temple (verse 5). For the apocalyptic formula, μετὰ ταῦτα εἶδον (*meta tauta eidon*, 'later, as I watched', lit. 'after this I saw'), see on 4.1; also 7.1; 18.1. For the similar phrase, 'the heavenly temple was opened', see 11.19. The term ναός (*naos*, 'temple') is used in Revelation with four senses: as the Temple at Jerusalem (11.1–2); as a metaphor for the eschatological people of God (3.12); as the heavenly temple of God's presence (7.15; 11.19; 14.15, 17; 15.5, 6, 8; 16.1, 17); and as the appearance of God in the heavenly city (21.22). See Aune 877; also Walker, *Holy City* 243. Here the concept is that of the divine presence, perceived by John in the heavenly realm.

The spiritual temple in verse 5 is described as 'the tabernacle of witness'. In the unusual phrase, ὁ ναός τῆς σκηνῆς τοῦ μαρτυρίου (*ho naos tēs skēnēs tou martyriou*, lit. 'the temple of the tent of witness'), the first genitive is best understood as appositional, and the second as descriptive (Beckwith 678; Beale 801). This yields the sense, as in the trans-lation (also niv), 'the temple, *namely*, the tabernacle of witness'. The background is once more that of the Exodus, thus continuing the theme in this section. During the wilder-ness wanderings, the tabernacle was called 'the tent of the testimony' (σκηνὴ τοῦ μαρτυρίου, *skēnē tou martyriou*), as in lxx Exod. 38.26; 40.34; Num. 10.11; 17.7; et al. It was so designated at this period because it contained the ark, or tablets, of the covenant: that is, the ten commandments which Moses received from God, as a declaration of his nature and just will (see Exod. 34.29; also 16.34; 27.21; 40.24; Acts 7.44).

The 'testimony', to which reference is made in verse 5, may include not only the Law of God but also the 'witness to (or by) Jesus', since he fulfils in himself the covenantal requirements of the Father (1 Cor. 11.25; Eph. 2.12–13; Heb. 8.6–7; et al.); cf. Sweet 241. See on Rev. 12.17; cf. also 1.2, 9; 19.10; 20.4. John's vision is in any case a transposition of the Exodus situation, which demonstrated God's judgement on Egypt, as well as his mercy towards the Israelites (Exod. 15.4–5; 15.16–18). In the same way, the Lamb has secured victory for the new Israel (5.10); but this is not without judgemental action towards the followers of Satan (16.1–21). The drama of the Apocalypse has now reached a moment, which is any case eschatological and therefore ongoing, when God is about to reveal his just will, from the heavenly sanctuary of the new Exodus, by judging those on earth who reject his testimony (Beale 802).

The 'seven angels who carried the seven plagues' now emerge from the heavenly sanctuary. These angelic beings were last mentioned in verse 1 (q.v.); from verse 7 and Chapter 16 it is evident that the judgemental plagues themselves are borne in golden bowls. The fact that the angels come 'out of the temple' (ἐκ τοῦ ναοῦ, *ek tou naou*) may imply that their commission as bearers of judgement is divinely authorized (cf. Mounce 288). The temple is opened in order to allow the angelic procession to emerge, and not to reveal its contents (as in 11.19); so Prigent 462.

Beale (802) notes that the phraseology ἔχοντες τὰς ἑπτὰ πληγάς (*echontes tas hepta plēgas*, 'who carried [lit. having] the seven plagues') could mean that the angels had authority over the plagues which they were about to introduce (see 14.18). He also makes the relevant proposal that Lev. 26, a formative text which underlies the first four seal judgements of Rev. 6.1–8 (Moffatt 442), is part of the background to 15.6 (*idem*, 803). In Lev. 26.18, 21, 24, 28 God promises to judge Israel's unfaithfulness 'sevenfold'; and Lev. 26.21 LXX includes the expression, unusual beyond the Apocalypse, 'seven plagues' ('if you continue hostile to me, I will continue to plague you sevenfold [προσθήσω ὑμῖν πληγὰς ἑπτά, *prosthēsō hymin plēgas hepta*, lit. "bring you seven plagues"] for your sins'). This chapter of Leviticus also deals with the woes which God will send in response to idolatry (26.1, 30, 31), including the promise that repentance will lead to covenant blessing (verses 40–45); and both of these themes belong to the drama of Revelation.

The sevenfold pattern of the bowl-plagues suggests the severity of the judgement involved, rather than a literal sequence of seven plagues in time (cf. Ps. 79.12). As the beast received a 'mortal wound' (13.3, 12, using ἡ πληγὴ τοῦ θανάτου, *hē plēgē tou thanatou*, lit. 'the plague of death'), inflicted by the death and resurrection of Christ (12.10–12), so now the bowl judgements will reveal the decisive effects of the Lamb's defeat of Satan, culminating in final judgement on him and his followers (20.7–10); cf. Beale 803.

The angels in John's vision were 'robed in fine linen, pure and glistening'. For the term λίνον (*linon*, 'linen'), which appears only here in Revelation, and otherwise in the New Testament only at Matt. 12.20, see the textual notes on verse 6. Linen garments are worn in the Old Testament by Jewish priests (Lev. 16.4; 1 Sam. 2.18) and also by angels (e.g. Ezek. 9.2, in a scene which is close to Rev. 15.6; Dan. 10.5; 12.6–7). By wearing linen, the sacred and sacerdotal character of the angels' ministry in this episode is emphasized. But their robes also identify them with the angelic cohorts of Rev. 19.14 and with the faithful, whose white (linen) raiment is a sign of their security and salvation (3.4–5; 6.11; 7.13–14; 19.8); cf. Prigent 462. The 'gold sashes', across the chests of the angels, connect directly with the vision of the exalted Son of man at Rev. 1.13 (q.v.) and symbolize their royal, as well as priestly, functions. They share in the work of God in Christ, that is to say, which is judgemental as well as salvific. Gold is often the colour which is used in association with spiritual realities (cf. Dan. 10.5, the angel has a 'belt of gold'; Heb. 9.4; Rev. 1.20; 4.4; 5.8; 8.3; 9.13; 14.14; 15.7; 21.15).

7 The 'seven golden offering bowls', from which the plagues will be dispensed, are now handed to the seven angels (see verses 1, 6). The action is performed by 'one of the four living creatures', who 'gave' (ἔδωκεν, *edōken*) the bowls to the angels . As in 8.2, where trumpets of judgement were 'given' (ἐδόθησαν, *edothēsan*) to the seven angels, this is part of the divine commissioning of the avenging agents of God. The four living creatures, who guard the throne of God, were last mentioned at 14.3. They appear throughout the Apocalypse (see on 4.6; also 5.6; 6.1; 7.11; 19.4), and are suitable intermediaries between God and the angels of justice (Mounce 288). All members of the heavenly council, up to the highest, share in carrying out the judgement to come (Roloff 185).

Each angel receives a golden 'offering bowl' (see BDAG 1055*a* for this translation). The phrase, ἑπτὰ φιάλας χρυσᾶς (*hepta phialas chrysas*, 'seven golden offering bowls') is anarthrous, since 'seven bowls' are mentioned here for the first time in the Apocalypse; subsequently (16.1; 17.1; 21.9) the expression is articular. The term φιάλη (*phialē*, lit. 'bowl') is used in the New Testament only by the author of Revelation (12 times). It denotes a wide, shallow vessel (not a narrow-necked 'vial', as in AV), from which the contents could be easily poured. Such bowls were cultic objects used by priests, in the worship of Judaism, at the altar in the tabernacle or Temple (see further Aune 879–80). They are connected with service in the tabernacle of witness (Exod. 27.3; 38.3; Num. 4.14–15; 7.13; see Rev. 15.5), and are sometimes described as 'golden' (1 Chron. 28.17; 2 Chron. 4.8; et al.). In the present context, 'angelic priests minister with the bowls at the heavenly altar of the tabernacle of witness' (Beale 806, who points out that the presence of the altar is implied, since it is directly linked to the bowl judgements at 16.7).

The last reference in the Apocalypse to '*golden* bowls', as such, is during the heavenly courtroom scene at 5.8, where the twenty-four elders (angelic beings, who represent the body of the faithful; see on 4.4) hold golden bowls full of incense, described as 'the prayers of God's people'. The fact that the imagery of golden cups is limited to these two passages in Revelation suggests that there is a connection between prayer and justice (see also 6.10; 8.3–5). So in Ezek. 10.7, which may inform the text of Rev. 15.7, one of the cherubim in the house of the Lord gives to an angelic being the fire of judgement; and here, the bowls of worship also contain plagues of justice (Prigent 463). The colour gold is associated in the Apocalypse with abomination (17.4), as well as divine service.

The contents of the bowls are further described; they are 'filled with the wrath (τοῦ θυμοῦ, *tou thymou*)' of the living God. For divine wrath in the Apocalypse, as both judicial and salvific, see on 14.19. A possible background to this scene may exist in Isa. 51, where blessings are promised to God's people, who have previously drunk from the 'bowl of his wrath'; and, it is declared, that cup will be given to Israel's tormentors (see verses 17, 20, 22–23); so Beasley-Murray 231–32. If the song of Moses from Exod. 15 and the sevenfold judgement which offers repentance at Lev. 26 are combined in the setting of Rev. 15 (see on verses 3–6), this draws attention once more to the notion of salvation through judgement as the theme of verse 7. The liturgical formula, 'for ever and ever' (εἰς τοὺς αἰῶνας τῶν αἰώνων, *eis tous aiōnas tōn aiōnōn*, lit. 'to the ages of the ages') accentuates the worshipful nature of this scene (Prigent 463); see also on 4.9.

8 The final verse of this interval dramatically sets the scene for the judgements to come. It also demonstrates that the justice in question derives from God, rather than from the living creatures or the seven angels; and this is true, even if the angels carrying the bowls

of plagues act as agents of divine discrimination. The heavenly temple of God's presence, which was opened to allow the angels to appear (verses 5–6), is now 'filled with
smoke from the glory and power of God'. The 'smoke' (καπνός, *kapnos*) is a theophanic
image, associated with the self-disclosure of God in several Old Testament accounts. An
obvious background is to be located in the Exodus-Sinai tradition of Exod. 19.16–18
('the mountain was wrapped in smoke'); and Exod. 40.34–35 ('the cloud covered the
tent of meeting, and the glory of the Lord filled the tabernacle'); cf. Ps. 18.7–9; 104.32.
See also the cloud which filled the holy place, when incense was burned in front of the
holy of holies, at Lev. 16.12–13, and the cloud of Yahweh's presence which filled the
house of the Lord when the priests ministered before the ark of the covenant after
the Exodus (see 1 Kings 8.9–11). Similarly smoke, or cloud, is part of a Temple theophany
at 2 Chron. 5.13–14; 7.1–2.

Even closer to the text of Rev. 15.8 is the theophany recorded at the time of Isaiah's
prophetic call in Isa. 6.1–4 LXX, when 'the house was filled with smoke' (verse 4, ὁ οἶκος
ἐπλήσθη καπνοῦ, *ho oikos eplēsthē kapnou*); this is the only occasion in the Old Testament
where 'smoke' (not a 'cloud' or 'glory') is said to fill the Temple (Beale 807). Note also the
scene at Ezek. 10.1–5, where the prophet sees an angelic being 'clothed in linen' standing
close to the cherubim in the heavenly temple, and the house was filled with the 'cloud'
(ἡ νεφέλη, *hē nephelē*) of God's glory. In both of those passages, Isa. 6 and Ezek. 10, as in
Rev. 15, the theme of salvific judgement is present (Isa. 6.5–13; Ezek. 10.6–19).

The 'smoke' in verse 8 derives from 'the glory and power of God'. The phrase 'the
glory of God (the Lord)' is often an Old Testament circumlocution for the presence of
God: for example, on Sinai (Exod. 24.16–18), in the tabernacle (Num. 14.10), in the
Temple (Ezek. 11.23) or during prophetic visions (Ezek. 1.28; cf. Acts 7.55). For the
δόξα (*doxa*, 'glory') of God in the Apocalypse see on 4.9; also 11.13; 14.7; 16.9; 19.7;
21.11, 23. For his (just) δύναμις (*dynamis*, 'power') see on 7.12, esp. the Excursus at 194–
95; also 11.17; 12.10. The two nouns are used jointly, in the setting of hymns, at 4.11;
5.12; 7.12; 19.1.

As a result of the holy presence of God, and until the bowl-judgements had been
completed, 'it was impossible to enter the temple' (καὶ οὐδεὶς ἐδύνατο εἰσελθεῖν εἰς τὸν
ναόν, *kai oudeis edynato eiselthein eis ton naon*, lit. 'and no one was able to enter the temple';
the καί, *kai*, 'and', is consecutive). The use of the aorist passive of τελεῖν (*telein*, 'to complete'), in this verse, forms an inclusion with the same form of the verb in verse 1; and
this helps to define 15.1–8 as a literary unit.

It is not immediately clear why entry to the temple is barred on these two counts:
the glory and power of God and the seven plagues yet to come. There are four possible
lines of interpretation.

(a) Because the time of final judgement has arrived, and this is in God's hands, it is too
late for angels or anyone to ask him to save the world, as in 5.8; 8.3 (cf. Charles 2,
40; Caird 200; Mounce 289). Nevertheless, while 'the prayers of the saints' in those
two contexts (q.v.) are evidently petitions for God's judgement on sin (8.6—9.19),
and may include intercessions for divine vengeance (6.9–10; cf. Aune 882), they
are not prayers for humanity, but above all expressions of self-offering and praise on
the part of the faithful; see 19.6–8.

(b) God is for the moment unapproachable because his presence is one of wrathful judgement (Roloff 185). However, despite Rev. 6.17, it is normally God's glory, and not
his wrath, which makes it impossible to stand in his presence.

(c) The full manifestation of God's majesty and power thus becomes, for some commentators, the reason for his remoteness (cf. Exod. 40.35; 1 Kings 8.11; 2 Chron 7.2;
Isa. 6.5; Rev. 5.13–14; cf. Mark 9.2–6). See Beckwith 679; Beasley-Murray 238.

(d) While this third suggestion has much to commend it, more can be said. It is not possible to enjoy uninterrupted fellowship with the Lord, John may be indicating, while meriting his judgemental wrath through sin and unbelief; hence the reactions to the bowl judgements in 16.5–6, 9, 11, 12–21; cf. also 22.14–15. But salvation in response to repentance is still possible (19.1–2); and while the exercise of judgement is a necessary part of salvation history, it cannot exhaust its meaning. God is presented in this part of the Apocalypse as the righteous judge; but in the end he will reveal himself as the saving God, who is with us (21.3); see Prigent 463.

Theology

The divine justice revealed by the seven seals (6.1—8.1), and announced by the seven trumpets (8.6—11.19), is now to be fully implemented by the seven bowls (15.5—16.21). However, the judgement of God which is manifested in these scenes, and forms the content of the bowl-plagues, is ongoing; it is 'final' in the sense of being eschatologically, rather than chronologically, unfolded. From a literary perspective, the bowls expand the meaning of the trumpets, just as the trumpets develop the significance of the seals. But theologically, and together, the three heptads describe God's righteous reaction to human idolatry and injustice. They do so under different sets of images, which illuminate the same situation of divine judgement: in the end-time, and at any time. That is why the song of victory, offered by the saints in this interval (15.3–4), is relevant to any moment of judgemental distress through which the salvation of God's kingdom has appeared (similarly, the hymns at 7.10–12). See further Beasley-Murray 233–34; Mounce 282.

The theme of the Exodus of Israel from Egypt, evident throughout Revelation, has strongly influenced this section of the drama. The conversion of the nations is presented through the imagery of the two prophetic witnesses in Chapter 11, and of the harvest in Chapter 14. In Rev. 15, John's visionary image is that of the Exodus. But now it is a *new* Exodus, made possible through the redemptive work of the Lamb, the new Moses (14.4; 15.3). The language of the song in verses 3–4 clearly alludes to the hymn of deliverance in Exod. 15, even if it does not quote directly from it (Bauckham, *Climax of Prophecy* 297–305; against Fiorenza, *Book of Revelation* 135), while the bowl-plagues of Rev. 16, which in many ways run parallel to the trumpet disasters of 8.7—9.19 (see below), are carefully modelled on the plagues of the Exodus. Both events, the rescuing of the old Israel through the judgement of God's enemies in the Sea of Reeds and the deliverance of the Church of Christ, the new Israel, by enabling its members to triumph over the deceit of the beast, bear witness to the salvation of God revealed through his justice. Here, as elsewhere in the Apocalypse, divine judgement and the saving activity of the Godhead are balanced; and it is important to notice that in Rev. 15—16 that order is reversed, making the salvific work of God feature positively before his judgement (cf. Beasley-Murray 233).

Bauckham, *Climax of Prophecy* 305–307, argues that in the new Exodus theology underlying Rev. 15.1–8, John is preoccupied with the idea of martyrdom. The participation of the redeemed in the sacrifice of Christ (14.4) by means of their martyrdom, he claims, wins the rest of unbelieving humanity for God, as in 11.11–13 (see esp. ibid. 306). There is no need to restrict the reference of the faithful, who are in view throughout this passage, to those who die as martyrs. Nevertheless, Bauckham's general point needs to be taken seriously. In the interval of Rev. 15, and notably in his version of the song of Moses (verses 3–4), John seems to be taking up the most universalistic form of the hope of the Old Testament (see Ezek. 37.27–28; Zech. 2.10–11; cf. Rev. 21.1–4). Ultimately, it will not be Israel alone who will be God's people and dwelling-place, nor even the new Israel of God, redeemed from every nation. Rather, as a result of faithful

Christian testimony in the face of opposition and tribulation, *all* the nations will have the opportunity to worship the true God, and to become his people (Rev. 21.24–26). See further Bauckham, *Theology* 98–104, esp. 104; Bauckham 1299*a*.

The stage is now set for the judgement drama of the golden bowls to begin. The audience has been prepared for its awesomeness by the reminder of God's just and redemptive deeds, opening the way eternally to a new deliverance for all the nations through the risen Christ. Not only are the divine works great and amazing, as they are perceived on earth; God is also holy in himself, just and true in his being. The smoke of his glory and power, issuing from his presence and surrounding the agents of heavenly discrimination, is a dramatic testimony to his nature. But while this cloud keeps those who are persistently unfaithful from him (15.8), potentially it draws all believers to his truth and righteous love (16.7).

SCENE 5
Seven Bowls
(16.1–21)

Translation

16 [1]Then I heard a loud voice[a] from the temple,[b] telling the seven angels, 'Go on your way, and begin to pour out on the earth the seven offering bowls of God's wrath.' [2]So the first angel departed, and emptied his bowl over the earth, with the result that an evil and malignant sore broke out on those who carry the mark of the beast and worship its image. [3]And the second one poured out his bowl over the sea, so that it turned into blood, like that from a dead body; and every living creature in the water perished. [4]Then the third angel emptied his bowl into the rivers and water-springs, and they turned[c] into blood. [5]And I heard the angel of the waters saying,

'You are righteous, the Holy One[d] who is and who was,
   because you have decreed these judgements.
[6]For they poured out the blood of the saints and prophets;
   and you have given them blood to drink,[e]
   as they deserve[f].'
[7]I then heard someone from the altar[g] cry out,
 'Yes, Lord God, the Almighty,
      for your judgements are true and righteous!'

[8]And the fourth angel poured out his offering bowl over the sun, and it was made to scorch people with its flames. [9]They were seared with its intense heat, and cursed the name of the God who held the authority[h] to inflict these plagues; but they refused to repent and pay him homage. [10]The fifth one then emptied his bowl on the throne of the beast, and its empire was plunged into darkness. People bit their tongues in agony; [11]they reviled the God of heaven on account of their sufferings and sores, yet they refused to repent of what they had done. [12]And the sixth angel poured out his bowl over the great river, the Euphrates; and its water dried up, so that the passage of the kings from the east could be prepared. [13]Then I saw three evil spirits, like frogs,[i] emerging from the mouth of the dragon, from the mouth of the beast and of the false prophet. [14]These spirits are demonic, and perform signs; they travel abroad to the kings of the whole world, to rally them for the[j] battle on the great day of the Lord God Almighty. [15]('See, I am coming like a thief! Fortunate is the one who stays awake, fully clothed, not going around naked and exposed[k] to shame.') [16]And they assembled the kings at a place called, in Hebrew, Armageddon.[l]

[17]Then the seventh angel poured out his offering bowl into the air; and a loud voice issued from the sanctuary, namely, from the throne, saying, 'It is over!' [18]Then followed flashes of lightning, roarings and peals of thunder;[m] and a great earthquake occurred, which was so terrifying and violent that nothing like it had ever taken place in human history.[n] [19]The great city was split into three parts, and the cities of the nations collapsed in ruins. And God remembered to give Babylon the great the cup of wine, that is, of his furious wrath; [20]every island vanished, and the mountains disappeared. [21]Then huge hailstones, weighing about one hundred pounds each, dropped from the sky on people until they cursed God for the plague of hail, so extremely fearful was that affliction.

Text

ᵃ Instead of μεγάλης φωνῆς (*megalēs phōnēs*, 'a loud voice'), as read by ℵ 025, et al., some MSS (such as 1611²⁰⁵⁰ ²³²⁹) reverse the order of the adjective and the noun. The sequence in this phrase, of adjective *followed by* noun, is found only here in Revelation (but see 18.2), which suggests the originality of the reading. The normal expression is φωνὴ μεγάλη (*phōnē megalē*, lit. 'voice loud'), with the noun coming first (as in 1.10; 5.12; 6.10; et al.); and this accounts for the secondary correction attested here by 1611.

ᵇ The reading ἐκ τοῦ ναοῦ (*ek tou naou*, 'from the temple') is attested by ℵ A C 025 1611²³²⁹ vg arm Primasius Andreas, et al., and is no doubt original. Some MSS (including 046 94 Arethas Byz) omit the words altogether, perhaps because elsewhere in Revelation the phrase 'I heard a (loud) voice' is followed by a designation of its source as 'heavenly' (ἐκ τοῦ οὐρανοῦ, *ek tou ouranou*, 'from heaven'); so 10.4, 8; 11.12, 15; et al. Cf. Beale 813. For this reason other scribes (42 vgᵐˢˢ copˢᵃ'ᵇᵒ Tyconius Beatus) use οὐρανός (*ouranos*, 'heaven'), rather than ναός (*naos*, 'temple'), in the transcription of this text; although Metzger, *Textual Commentary* 755, thinks that this version arose when ναοῦ (*naou*, 'temple', genitive singular) was taken as the contraction of οὐρανοῦ (*ouranou*, 'heaven'), which is οὐνοῦ (*ounou*).

ᶜ The reading ἐγένετο (*egeneto*, 'turned to', lit. 'became'), with the verb in the singular, is well supported by ℵ C 025 046 051 itᵃʳ vg arm Andreas Beatus, et al.; and, since the subject of the verb ('rivers and water-springs') is plural, this becomes the *lectio difficilior* and could be original. Although the plural variant, ἐγένοντο (*egenonto*, lit. 'they became'), is strongly attested by 𝔓47 A 1006 1611¹⁸⁵⁴ 1773 2019 Oecumenius²⁰⁵³ cop eth syr itᵍⁱᵍ Primasius, et al. (cf. Charles 2, 333), Metzger (*Textual Commentary* 755) suggests that the plural reading has been introduced later by scribes who 'mechanically' conformed the verb to the preceding plural nouns. Aune (856) takes the opposite view and, on the basis of the strength and breadth of the MS testimony, argues cogently that the plural, ἐγένοντο (*egenonto*, 'they became'), is original, and that it has been altered to the singular by copyists who supplied the neuter plural noun, τὰ ὕδατα (*ta hydata*, 'the waters'), before the verb. In this case the singular, ἐγένετο (*egeneto*, 'turned to'), can be grammatically correct. The use of the singular form of γίνομαι (*ginomai*, 'become', 'happen') in verse 3, according to Aune (ibid.), may also have influenced the change into the singular from the plural, which suits exactly the form of the nouns governing the verb in this context.

ᵈ There are slight MS variations of the expression, ὁ ἦν, ὁ ὅσιος (*ho ēn, ho hosios*, lit. 'the one who was, the Holy One'), as read by ℵ 051 copˢᵃ Andreas. Thus, 𝔓47 1611²³²⁹, et al., have ὃς ἦν καὶ ὅσιος (*hos ēn kai hosios*, lit. 'who was and holy'); while 1006¹⁰⁰⁶ ¹⁸⁴¹ Oecumenius²⁰⁵³, et al., read ὁ ἦν καὶ ὁ ὅσιος (*ho ēn kai ho hosios*, lit. 'who was and the Holy One'); and A C 1611¹⁸⁵⁴ support the version, ὁ ἦν ὅσιος (*ho ēn hosios*, 'the one who was holy'). The titular phraseology in this ascription recalls the formula, 'the one who is, and who was, the coming one', at 1.4, 8; 4.8; see also 11.17. At 1.8, ὁ παντοκράτωρ (*ho pantokratōr*, 'the Almighty') follows ὁ ὢν καὶ ὁ ἦν καὶ ὁ ἐρχόμενος (*ho ōn kai ho ēn kai ho erchomenos*, lit. 'the one who is and who was and the coming one'), with an article, but without the use of a conjunction. On this analogy the original reading here, as reflected in the translation, is likely to be ὁ ἦν, ὁ ὅσιος (*ho ēn, ho hosios*, 'the one who was, the Holy One'); cf. Aune 856.

ᵉ There is good MS support (𝔓47 ℵ Andreas Byz) for the spelling of the verb as πιεῖν (*piein*, 'to drink'); and this form appears elsewhere in the New Testament (Mark 10.38; Matt. 27.34; Acts 23.12; Rom. 14.21). It is possible, however, that the non-Attic orthographic form, πεῖν (*pein*, 'drink'), as in A C (cf. Charles 2, 355), is more original (so John 4.7, 9; 1 Cor. 9.4; 10.7).

f The asyndetic construction, ἄξιοι (*axioi*, lit. 'worthy'), as in A Andreas Beatus, is most likely to be original. Its simple form gave rise to the later insertion of transitional language, giving the meaning '*for* they are worthy'. So e.g. Oecumenius[2053 2062] it[gig] (ἄξιοι γάρ, *axioi gar*); 2019 it[c] (ὅτι ἄξιοι, *hoti axioi*); 1611[2329] (ἄρα ἄξιοι, *ara axioi*). Cf. also 3.4; 14.5.

g The reading, τοῦ θυσιαστηρίου (*tou thysiastēriou*, lit. 'of the altar'), is strongly supported by ℵ A C 025 051 Oecumenius[2053] syr cop arm Andreas Beatus, et al. It is also a *lectio difficilior*, because of the ambiguity of the Greek (see further on verse 7), and probably original. Other witnesses have attempted to clarify the meaning of the text with additions before the words τοῦ θυσιαστηρίου (*tou thysiastēriou*, 'the altar'). Thus 046 1611[2311], et al. (ἐκ, *ek*, 'from'); 2019 (φωνὴν ἐκ, *phōnēn ek*, 'a voice from'); and TR (ἄλλου ἐκ, *allou ek*, 'another from').

h There is strong support for including the article, τήν (*tēn*, 'the'), before ἐξουσίαν (*exousian*, 'authority'); so ℵ A 025 051 209 1611[1854 2329] 2019, et al. There is equally good MS evidence for omitting it (C 1006[1006 1841] 1611 Oecumenius[2053] Byz TR, et al.); but the powerful combination of ℵ and A suggests that the article is part of the authentic text, as in the translation (cf. Aune 857).

i The expression, ὡς βάτραχοι (*hōs batrachoi*, 'like frogs'), with the noun in the nominative, appears in A Oecumenius[2053] Andreas. This form is grammatically difficult, since the context demands that ὁ βάτραχος (*ho batrachos*, 'frog'), which qualifies πνεύματα (*pneumata*, 'spirits'), should be in the accusative. The nominative reading may result from an assumption that πνεύματα (*pneumata*, 'spirits') is also in the nominative, which is a possible alternative (cf. 6.2; 7.9; 14.1); but, in any case, this is a *lectio difficilior*, and it is probably original. Other MSS try to ease an apparent solecism; so 𝔓47 ℵ* 94 2019 (ὡσει βατράχους, *hōsei batrachous*, 'as frogs', accusative), and some MSS of Andreas/Byz TR (ὅμοια βατράχοις, *homoia batrachois*, 'like frogs', dative).

j Some witnesses (𝔓47 A 051 1611[1854]) omit the article τόν (*ton*, 'the') before πόλεμον (*polemon*, 'battle'). But the article must be part of the original text, since the reference here is to the final eschatological battle, which would have been familiar to John's audience; and, in this case, an anaphoric τόν (*ton*, 'the') would have been necessary.

k The third person plural present subjunctive, βλέπωσιν (*blepōsin*, lit. 'they should see'), disguised in the translation, is read by ℵ A Byz, et al. Other witnesses (including 𝔓47 051 1611[2329] 2351) have the present indicative, βλέπουσιν (*blepousin*, 'they see'); but this reading is certainly secondary, as nowhere else in the New Testament does ἵνα (*hina*, 'that'), introducing a consecutive clause, occur with the indicative.

l The many MS variations of the Greek name, Ἀρμαγεδών (*Harmagedōn*, usually translated in the English as 'Armageddon'), attested in this form (found only in Rev. 16.16) by ℵ A 051 1006 1611[2329] syr[ph] eth Andreas Beatus, et al., are mostly concerned with spelling (see Metzger, *Textual Commentary* 755). The chief alternative is Μαγεδ(δ)ών (*Maged[d]ōn*, 'Maged[d]on'), as in 1611 Oecumenius[2053] Byz vg[mss] cop[bo], et al. This variant reflects the name of the Palestinian town Megiddo, where battles were often fought in the Old Testament period. See further on verse 16, below.

m The order of the phenomena listed here, ἀστραπαὶ καὶ φωναὶ καὶ βρονταί (*astrapai kai phōnai kai brontai*, 'flashes of lightning, roarings and peals of thunder'), is followed by A 0163 1006 Oecumenius[2053] (cf. Charles 2, 336). It conforms to what appears to be a stereotypical pattern in the Apocalypse (see 4.5; 11.19; but note also 8.5), and is supported by good MS evidence. The major variations, ἀστραπαὶ καὶ βρονταὶ καὶ φωναί (*astrapai kai brontai kai phōnai*, lit. 'lightning and thunders and voices'), as in 𝔓47 051 2329 Byz, et al., and also βρονταὶ καὶ ἀστραπαὶ καὶ φωναὶ καὶ βρονταί (*brontai kai astrapai kai* *phōnai kai brontai,* 'peals of thunder and flashes of lightning and roarings and peals of thunder'), read by א* cop[bo], may therefore be regarded as secondary.

[n] The singular form, ἄνθρωπος ἐγένετο (*anthrōpos egeneto,* lit. 'man appeared'), disguised in the translation, is attested by A 2020 cop[bo], et al. (cf. Charles 2, 336). 𝔓47 has the verb in the plural, ἄνθρωπος ἐγένοντο (*anthrōpos egenonto,* lit. 'man [they] appeared'); while other MSS (including א 051 Oecumenius[2053] latt syr Andreas Byz TR) read the double plural, ἄνθρωποι ἐγένοντο (*anthrōpoi egenonto,* lit. 'men appeared'). The version which best explains the origin of the others, and seems likely to be the *lectio originalis,* is that with both the noun and the verb in the singular (so Metzger, *Textual Commentary* 755–56). The plural forms appear to be attempts to avoid the repetition of the singular ἐγένετο (*egeneto,* lit. 'happened', 'appeared'), which occurs three times in verse 18, and once at the very beginning of verse 19.

Literary Setting

The narrative of Scene 5 (Rev. 16) involves a series of violent, judgemental actions, leading in a crescendo to a climax which anticipates the end. The chapter forms a discrete textual unit, in the course of which the seven bowls of divine criticism are poured out in relentless succession. Unlike the preceding sequences of the seven seals (6.1—8.1), the seven trumpets (8.7—11.18) and the seven signs (12.1—14.20), which introduce an interlude between the penultimate and ultimate events, the sixth and seventh bowls follow each other without delay. See Smalley, *Thunder and Love* 106.

The heptad of bowl-judgements in Rev. 16 shows a marked affinity with the earlier series of trumpet disasters in 8.7—9.19. It is true that there are differences between the two sequences, and that the second is not a mere imitation of the first. For instance, the trumpet-plagues are restricted in the effect they have on the human world (cf. 8.7—12), whereas the bowls dispense a judgement which is universal and final (16.3, 20); the trumpets act as warning calls to repentance, while divine wrath itself is poured out from the bowls; and people are indirectly harmed by the trumpet-calls, but immediately attacked by the wrath in the bowls. Moreover, none of the bowl-plagues exactly duplicates the events in the trumpet series. These are but variations on a common theme; but they lead such a commentator as Beckwith (672–73, 690) to conclude that the two septets are essentially not parallel.

Nevertheless, there are clear literary correspondences between the trumpets and the bowls, not least because in each series there are clear allusions to the Exodus motif, which provides an important background to this part of the Apocalypse. Both the trumpets and the bowls also present the plagues in the same order.

(a) The first trumpet and bowl affect the *earth,* and bring destruction or disease to its inhabitants (cf. Exod. 9.8–11, 22–26).

(b) The second pair of judgements cause the *sea* to turn into blood, so that living creatures in it perish; while

(c) the next portents fall on *rivers* and water-springs, which also become blood-red (Exod. 7.17–21).

(d) The fourth bowl and trumpet afflict the *sun* (moon and stars), and result in darkness or burning (Exod. 10.21–23; 9.22–32).

(e) The fifth trumpet-calls demonic locusts to emerge from *darkness,* to torment the unfaithful; and the fifth bowl darkens the empire of the beast, and brings agony to his followers (Exod. 10.4–15, 21–29).

(f) The sixth bowl is poured on the river *Euphrates,* and evil spirits like frogs rally the kings of the world for the final battle (Exod. 8.2–14); similarly, the penultimate trumpet releases four angels, bound at the Euphrates, whose fiendish cavalry attack humanity.

(g) Following the seventh trumpet and bowl, loud voices announce to the *world* the completion of God's work in Christ, and precipitate cosmic disturbances on an unprecedented scale (Exod. 9.22–26; 19.16–19). See further Beasley-Murray 238–39; Beale 808–10.

The broad, literary and dramatic structure of this scene is clearly drawn. After a prelude (16.1), in which the seven angels are despatched on their mission of judgement, the first three bowls are poured out (verses 2–4); and these consist of natural disasters, which demonstrate God's wrath. The following four bowls (verses 8–21) herald the final, eschatological battle between darkness and light, good and evil. However, the final series of plagues is expanded at three points.

(a) Two judgement doxologies are introduced at verses 5–6 and 7 (cf. 19.1–2).
(b) After the sixth bowl, demonic spirits travel abroad to assemble the leaders of the whole world for the great conflict (verses 13–14).
(c) A comment from the risen Christ, which at first sight seems intrusive, is interpolated at verse 15 (q.v.).

The bowl judgements in 16.1–21 are presented with more stereotypical features in their composition than is true of the earlier heptads of the seals and the bowls.

(a) Each vision, apart from the first, begins with the expression, 'and the (next) one poured out his bowl on/over . . .' (καὶ ὁ [δεύτερος, κτλ.] ἐξέχεεν τὴν φιάλην αὐτοῦ εἰς/ἐπί . . . , *kai ho [deuteros, et al.] execheen tēn phialēn autou eis/epi* . . .). In the case of the first angel a verb of motion, ἀπῆλθεν (*apēlthen*, 'he departed'), is added, to correspond to the command to 'go on your way' (ὑπάγετε, *hypagete*) in verse 1.
(b) The results of pouring out five of the bowls are introduced by the formula, καὶ ἐγένετο (*kai egeneto*, lit. 'and it happened', 'so that'); see verses 2.3, 4, 10, 18 (plural and singular), 19. See also 6.12; 8.1, 7, 8, 11.
(c) Five of the visions record the effects of the plagues on living beings in the troubled area (verses 3, 9, 10, 12, 19).
(d) The negative response of people to the plagues is mentioned in three of the visions (verses 9, 11, 21). See further Aune 868–69.

Aune (867) finds three textual subdivisions in 16.12–16: the effect of the sixth bowl on the great river Euphrates (verse 12); verses 13–14 and 16, the preparations for battle, introduced by the formula, καὶ εἶδον (*kai eidon*, lit. 'and I saw'), which indicates a new textual unit, and using the catchword συνάγειν (*synagein*, lit. 'to assemble') to link verses 14 and 16 (cf. 19.19); the exhortation from Jesus in verse 15.

Comment

Prelude: The Angelic Mission (16.1)

16.1 The dramatic movement in this scene involves a swift and decisive activity of judgement, which is final and eschatological, includes the divine work of salvation, and may be revealed at any time up to and including the end time. Throughout Rev. 16, heaven and earth are once more joined closely together (cf. Chapter 14), as God's salvific discrimination is unleashed by his angelic agents on the world and among its unfaithful inhabitants.

The seer first heard 'a loud voice from the temple', sending the seven angels out on their judgemental mission. For the literary formula in Revelation, 'I heard a loud voice', and the importance of audition as a visionary instrument, see on 1.10; 8.13; 11.12; 12.10; 19.1; 21.3. The order in the Greek here, with the adjective preceding the noun, μεγάλη φωνή (*megalē phonē*, 'loud voice'), occurs only in this text throughout the Apocalypse; although the phrase itself is used many times (cf. 5.2; 6.10; 7.2; 11.15 [plural]; 14.7, 9; et al.). See the textual notes on verse 1. The 'voice' in question is evidently divine, and indeed the voice of God himself (see 15.5–8; also on the unidentified 'heavenly voice' of 10.4). The voice is said to emanate 'from the temple' of God's presence (15.8), rather than 'from heaven' (11.12; et al.), solely in the present context, and at 16.17 (see the textual notes on 16.1). There is a possible, but not strong, connection between the commissioning of the angels in verse 1 and the retributive 'voice (of the Lord) from the temple' at Isa. 66.6.

For the imagery of the seven angelic beings and the seven offering bowls see on 15.1, 5–8; and for God's salvific 'wrath' (θυμός, *thymos*), see on 14.19; 15.1, 7. The command to the angels, 'go on your way, and begin to pour out (the plagues) on the earth', includes two verbs (ὑπάγετε, *hypagete*, lit. 'go away', and ἐκχέετε (*ekcheete*, lit. 'pour out') which have a conative force. The charge relates to the initiation of a process, since a sequence of seven bowls is in view; hence the translation, 'go on your way and *begin* to pour out'. The co-ordinate clause introduced by καί (*kai*, 'and'), καὶ ἐκχέετε (*kai ekcheete*, lit. 'and pour out'), functions as a consecutive ('that you may pour out'), and therefore as the equivalent of ἵνα (*hina*, 'that') with a subjunctive. See Aune 855.

The verb, ἐκχέω (*ekcheō*, 'pour out'), is often used in the LXX with reference to cultic offerings: for instance, libations of water (1 Sam. 7.6) or of wine (Isa. 57.6). Behind the imagery in Rev. 16 of pouring out bowls of judgement may also stand the idea of Jewish priests dispensing sacrificial blood at the altar (LXX Lev. 4.6–7; 8.15; et al.). Cf. Beale 813. In the present context, the use of the verb ἐκχεῖν (*ekchein*, 'to pour out') with φιάλαι (*phialai*, 'offering bowls') clearly suggests cultic practices; but the meaning has been extended figuratively to denote the outpouring of God's wrath. See LXX Ps. 78.3–6; Jer. 7.20; 10.25; Lam. 2.4; 4.11; Ezek. 9.8; 14.19; et al. See further Aune 883.

Bowls 1–3: Natural Disasters of Judgement (16.2–4)

2 The imagery and ideas in this section pick up once more the Exodus motif, as well as symbolism expressed earlier in the drama of Revelation, notably in the septet of trumpet-plagues and in Chapter 13. The first angel 'departed' (ἀπῆλθεν, *apēlthen*) to empty his offering bowl. The verb balances the command in verse 1, ὑπάγετε (*hypagete*, 'go on your way'), and is a literary variation of it.

The first bowl, like the first trumpet (8.7), affects 'the earth'; and this is the only plague in the present sequence which explicitly fulfils the injunction of the heavenly voice in verse 1 to 'pour out on the *earth* (εἰς τὴν γῆν, *eis tēn gēn*) the seven offering bowls of God's wrath'. Unlike the first trumpet-plague, however, the catastrophe is universal, and not partial; although it does not affect those whose names are recorded in the book of life (13.8). They are the conquerors who stand around the Lamb, and who have received the protective seal of God rather than the sign of the beast (14.1); cf. Prigent 465.

The contents of the first bowl are directed against idolatry, since they cause harm to 'those who carry the mark of the beast and worship its image'; for this figurative language, and its significance, see on 13.1–4, 11–18; 14.9–11; cf. also 19.20; 20.4. The followers of Satan are subservient to his temporary power (12.12), and claim his worldly authority as an excuse for turning away from the redemption of God in Christ (5.9; 14.3–4). As a result, the Antichrist and his allies (Rev. 11—13) will experience in a deeper and more spiritual manner the divine judgement which befell Pharaoh and his subjects in Egypt during the time of Moses. Similarly, the unfaithful who have received in their bodies the mark of the beast also suffer a token of punishment in the form of 'an evil and malignant sore (ἕλκος, *helkos*)', reflecting the sixth Egyptian plague (Exod. 9.8–12 LXX; cf. Job 2.7–8; see also Rev. 16.11). See further Beasley-Murray 239–40; Roloff 188; Beale 814.

Swete (201) fancifully notes that a judgemental 'sore', in the plague of boils at the time of the Exodus, attacked even the magicians, the antagonists of Moses (Exod. 9.11); and he concludes that John may have taken this as symbolic of the priest-magicians in his day, who stood under divine criticism for their service not of God but of pagan temples and the imperial cult. The painful sore, inflicted by the angel of the first judgemental bowl, is metaphorical rather than, as in the case of the plagues in Egypt, physical. It corresponds to the spiritual and psychological agony undergone by the unfaithful, who are harmed by the scorpion-like 'torture' (βασανισμός, *basanismos*) of the locusts, after the fifth trumpet-call (9.4–6, 10).

3 There are marked parallels between the results of dispensing the second bowl and sounding the second trumpet (8.8–9). In both cases, the sea becomes blood and living creatures perish. Both passages recall the first Egyptian plague, where Moses turns the Nile into blood, the fish in it die and the polluted water cannot be used (Exod. 7.17–21; cf. also Ps. 78.44; Isa. 15.9; 2 Macc. 12.16). The judgements are similar; but, once more, the effects of the trumpet-plague are partial, whereas the second bowl affects the entire earth. The worldly rule of Babylon, oppressing the faithful and opposed to the reign of God, is the object of this latest judgemental plague (cf. 14.8, 10; 15.7; 16.1, 19).

The supernatural disaster in verse 3 produces unpleasant conditions in the human world; cf. 8.11 (Knight 111). As the fish in the river at the Exodus died because of the blood, so here the waters cannot support life because the blood in them is coagulated and rotting (Mounce 293), like that in a corpse. Beale (815) suggests that this indicates famine conditions and economic deprivation; and he reminds us that the 'mark of the beast' in verse 2 was last mentioned in 13.16–17 (q.v.), where the context is essentially commercial (cf. also the decline of maritime prosperity as a result of the dissolution of the great 'Babylon' in Rev. 18, esp. verses 17–19).

Beale (815) also, and less plausibly, interprets the phrase, πᾶσα ψυχὴ ζωῆς ἀπέθανεν (*pasa psychē zōēs apethanen*, lit. 'every living soul died'), as a reference to the suffering or death of everyone who depended on maritime economy; and he supports this by pointing out that the term ψυχή (*psychē*, 'life-principle' [BDAG 1098*b*]) is mostly used in the Apocalypse in connection with human beings (cf. 6.9; 12.11; 18.13–14; 20.4). He therefore concludes that the sea being turned to blood, in this context, is figurative, at least in part, for 'the demise of the ungodly world's economic life-support system' (ibid.). However, while the scope of this bowl judgement may be potentially wide, in that the (figurative) pollution of the sea will ultimately carry implications for humanity, the primary and immediate application of John's imagery must be (as in 8.9) to all the inhabitants of the *sea*, including the fish; for he states that 'every living creature *in the water* (ἐν τῇ θαλάσσῃ, *en tē[i] thalassē[i]*, lit. "in the sea") perished'. Nevertheless, it remains true that the noun θάλασσα (*thalassa*, 'sea') frequently appears in Revelation as a symbol of sinful humanity, in opposition to God (cf. 12.12, 18; 13.1; 18.17–21; 20.8, 13; 21.1; similarly the 'waters' in 17.1, 15). See further Beale 815–16.

4 The third bowl forms a parallel with the third trumpet (8.10–11). In both cases, the 'rivers and water-springs' turn to blood (cf. 11.6). This action recapitulates the first Egyptian plague (Exod. 7.17–21; cf. Ps. 78.44; 105.29), which in the Apocalypse is distributed between two bowls, the second and third (16.3–4; cf. Mounce 293 n. 13). Once more, the result of pouring out the third bowl has widespread, and indeed universal, judgemental implications; whereas the effects of the third trumpet sounding are restricted.

After the third trumpet-call, the blood bath caused many to die on account of the bitterness of the waters. A similar outcome is not specified when the third bowl is emptied (16.4), but it is implied. In this case the third bowl, like the second, which are both based on the same Exodus plague, may well anticipate a situation of famine and economic disaster such as that described in Rev. 18.10–19.

The 'blood' (αἷμα, *haima*) in the sea and the rivers then becomes a symbol for suffering, which can lead to death. Note the links between 16.6 and 18.20, 24, according to which the unfaithful world will be judged because it has 'poured out the blood of the saints and prophets' (αἷμα ἁγίων καὶ προφητῶν ἐξέχεαν, *haima hagiōn kai prophetōn exechean*); the order, 'saints and prophets', is reversed at 18.24. See also 17.6; 19.2; and cf. Beale 816–17.

Together, the second and third bowls could reflect the situation of economic depression experienced by the church in Smyrna, within the Johannine community (Rev. 2.9–11); for this also included severe suffering, leading to imprisonment and even death (2.10). So Beale 817. In any case, the blood plague of verse 4, as with the second bowl, is seen as God's righteous judgement on a world which has rejected the blood of the Lamb (1.5; 5.9; 7.14; 12.11; 19.13). See Wall 198.

Judgement Doxologies (16.5–7)

5–6   The hymnic interlude in verses 5–6 and 7 provides a theological reflection on the judgemental action in progress, and more immediately on the first three bowls of discrimination poured out by the angels in verses 2–4. Both ascriptions are examples of a 'judgement doxology', or declarative hymn of praise (Aune 864–65, 885–86), in which it is affirmed that the punishment executed by God is both just and appropriate. The literary form, with this significance, can regularly be found in the Old Testament (cf. Neh. 9.33; Ps. 7.11; 9.4; Jer. 46.28; Dan. 9.14; cf. Tobit. 3.2; 3 Macc. 2.3). Aune (865) regards the hymn pieces in 16.5–7 as belonging to a relatively late stage in the composition of the Apocalypse.

The declaration in verses 5–6, which is 'heard' by the seer (cf. verse 1), is made by 'the angel of the waters' (τοῦ ἀγγέλου τῶν ὑδάτων, *tou angelou tōn hydatōn*), who is not to be confused with the angel who poured his bowl into the waters (verse 4); so Wilcock 145. In the thought of Judaism, spiritual powers represented and controlled earthly realities, so that life and the elements of nature could be regarded as controlled by appropriate angels. See *1 Enoch* 40.9; 66.2; *2 Enoch* 19.4–5; *Jub.* 2.2; et al.; Rev. 7.1; 14.18; cf. also Sweet 244; Mounce 294; Thompson 154; and above, 28–29. The bowls were first given to the seven angels by one of the four living creatures, who are angelic beings in touch with creation (15.7); so now nature celebrates the judgemental, but righteous, activity of the Creator (cf. Wilcock 145).

There is a close relationship, in both form and content, between the lyrical utterance of the angel of the waters in 16.5–6 and the new Exodus song of the conquerors at 15.3–4 (q.v.). In both hymns there is a universal acknowledgement that God's salvation is achieved through a judgement which is never arbitrary, as is that of pagan deities, but always 'true and righteous' (verse 7). This remains true because divine criticism derives from one who is himself both 'righteous' (δίκαιος, *dikaios*; for which see on 15.3) and also 'the Holy One' (ὅσιος, *hosios*, lit. 'holy'; see 15.4). Cf. Wall 198. In a moral universe, God must inevitably be opposed to human idolatry and injustice; for he is righteous, and accordingly his judgements are right (Ps. 119.137; cf. Mounce 294).

The declaration in verse 5 includes the liturgical formula, 'the Holy One who is and who was'. This is part of a threefold expression, '(the Lord) who is and who was, and who is coming', which has already appeared at 1.4, 8; 4.8 (where the order is different); cf. 11.17. In the present text (verse 5) 'the Holy One' takes the place of 'the one who is coming', because God's complete and saving activity in history is constantly being revealed in his end-time judgement. The Lord's sovereign holiness, expressed in acts of justice, informs his salvific role as 'the coming one'. See Beale 817–18.

The exact significance of the last phrase in verse 5, ὅτι ταῦτα ἔκρινας (*hoti tauta ekrinas*, lit. 'because you have judged these things'), is not immediately clear. The Greek may be translated as a verbal clause, giving the sense 'for you have judged in this way' (AV, NRSV, NJB; cf. Charles 2, 435), or as a noun clause, meaning '(you are righteous) in these your judgements' (RSV, NIV, REB). As Aune (856) maintains, the causal force of ὅτι (*hoti*, 'for') in this sentence is important; since the text is not affirming *how* God is righteous ('in your judgements'), but *why* he is so ('he has judged'). Since the demonstrative pronoun, ταῦτα (*tauta*, lit. 'these things'), in this context, must refer at least to the preceding three bowl judgements (verses 2–4), and possibly to all seven (including verses 8–21), an adequate translation should also reflect this (see also 'these plagues' in verse 9). The most satisfactory solution, therefore, is to understand the Greek in this instance as a verbal clause, and to render it as, 'because you have decreed these (seven) judgements' (hence the translation; see also ESV; Aune 851). There may be an indication here that the plea for vengeance from the faithful (6.10) is being answered.

The syntactical relationship between verses 5 and 6 is unclear; but it is best to regard verse 6 as beginning a new, if related, sentence. It provides further evidence of God's righteousness in expressing his justice through the bowl-plagues which feature in this scene. For the unfaithful in the world, oppressive followers of the beast and enemies of a just God, have 'poured out the blood of the saints and prophets'. The expression, αἷμα ἐκχεῖν (*haima ekchein*), can be translated either as 'to pour out blood' or 'to shed blood'; and in both cases it means 'to murder' (cf. Gen. 9.6; Deut.19.10; Jer. 7.6; *1 Enoch* 9.1; *T. Zeb.* 2.2; *Pss. Sol.* 8.20; *Sib. Or.* 3.311–13; et al.). In the present context this phrase, which is found only here in Revelation, is best translated as 'they poured out the blood', to balance the 'pouring out' of the bowls of divine wrath in this chapter. When John refers to the blood of 'saints and prophets' (ἁγίων καὶ προφητῶν, *hagiōn kai prophētōn*), he is describing one group and not two: the community of the faithful, within which some believers exercised prophetic gifts. For the use of the conjunction καί (*kai*, 'and') in this clause, to delineate one membership within another, see Mark 16.7; Acts 1.14.

For ἅγιοι (*hagioi*, lit. 'holy ones'), meaning God's people, see on 5.8. Apart from 16.6, the combination of 'saints and prophets (προφῆται, *prophētai*)' appears in the Apocalypse only at 18.20 (where ἀπόστολοι, *apostoloi*, 'apostles' are included) and 18.24 (where the order is reversed, to read 'prophets and saints'), both in a further context of judgement. Prophecy in the early Christian Church involved a ministry of encouragement (1 Cor. 14.3), as well as prediction (Acts 11.28). The rejection and murder of the prophets is a frequent theme in Jewish and Christian literature (so 1 Kings 19.10; Neh. 9.26; *Jub.* 1.12; Matt. 5.11–12 par.; Acts 7.52; 1 Thess. 2.15; *Asc. Isa.* 5.1–16; et al.).

Although the pronoun αὐτοῖς (*autois*, 'them') follows in verse 6 immediately after the reference to the 'saints and prophets', it makes no sense to suggest that they are the (otherwise unidentified) ones who are given 'blood to drink' (cf. Aune 887). The text must mean that the murderers of the faithful, in some way, drink blood as a result of divine judgement (the perfect tense of the verb, δέδωκας, *dedōkas*, 'you have given', suggests that the suffering endured by the world [see verse 2] is more than momentary). There are three possible interpretations of this passage.

(a) 'Drinking blood' may be equated with 'killing', as in Ezek. 39.17–19; Zech. 9.15; Rev. 17.6; et al. In this case, the angel of the waters may be saying that oppressors such as Rome will, during internecine warfare, shed the blood of their former allies, or otherwise slay the Christian martyrs (cf. Charles 2, 123).

(b) The idea of 'giving blood to drink' may be taken, more generally, as a synonym for 'dying' (see Isa. 49.26). The phrase, 'you have given them blood to drink', may then be understood as an expression of the *lex talionis* principle: the punishment of the unfaithful killers will be tailored to fit the crime, and they will also die (Wis. 11.16); see Michaels 186; Mounce 295.

(c) Much more likely than either of these suggestions is the variant explanation of Aune (888), who takes seriously the *setting* of the statement about 'drinking blood'. For it occurs immediately after two plagues which have turned seas, rivers and water-springs into blood (16.3–4); and this action, as we have seen, represents physical suffering as well as economic disaster. That God should give the inhabitants of the earth 'blood to drink' is best understood, therefore, as a figurative description of the punishment experienced by sinful blood-letters. They have murdered the faithful; and they will be forced, in turn, to undergo the spiritual pain symbolized by drinking polluted water. The adjective, ἄξιοι (*axioi*, lit. 'worthy'), in the phrase 'as they deserve', is used ironically (contrast 3.4). For similar occurrences of the term see Luke 12.48; Rom. 1.32.

7   A second voice, from the heavenly altar of burnt offering, affirms the truth and justice of God's judgemental but also salvific activity in this scene (see verse 15). The object of ἤκουσα (*ēkousa*, 'I heard') is the partitive genitive, τοῦ θυσιαστηρίου (*tou thysiastēriou*, 'from the altar'). This means that *someone from* the altar spoke; and this could be one of the martyrs underneath the altar, who appear at 6.9–10, or (less probably) one of the intercessory saints, whose prayers ascend from the altar of incense at 5.8; 8.3 (Hughes 174–75). Accordingly, the antiphon does not ring out from a personified altar (Roloff 189). For the use of θυσιαστήριον (*thysiastērion*, 'altar') in Revelation see on 6.9; also 8.3, 5; 9.13; 11.1; 14.18. Apart from 11.1, the term always appears in the Apocalypse in contexts of judgement, since sacrifice and justice, like prayer and worship, belong together in Revelation (Prigent 467).

The word ναί (*nai*, 'yes', 'indeed') is a synonym for ἀμήν (*amēn*, 'amen'), and is used here to confirm emphatically the judgement doxology of verses 5–6 (cf. 1.7; 14.13; 22.20). For ναὶ κύριε (*nai kyrie*, 'Yes, Lord'), as here, see Matt. 9.28; 15.27. For the Lord God as 'the Almighty' (ὁ παντοκράτωρ, *ho pantokratōr*), in his sovereignty, see on 15.3; also 4.8; 11.17; 21.22. The voice from the altar echoes the song of Moses and of the Lamb at 15.3, where the faithful celebrate the 'just and true' ways of God. Both hymns pick up the notion of God as the righteous judge in such biblical contexts as LXX Deut. 32.4; Ps. 7.12; 18.10; 2 Macc. 12.6; 2 Tim. 4.8; cf. *1 Clem.* 27.1; 60.1. The phrase in verse 7, ἀληθιναὶ καὶ δίκαιαι αἱ κρίσεις σου (*alēthinai kai dikaiai hai kriseis sou*, 'your judgements are true and righteous'), is repeated in almost the same form at 19.2 (q.v.). The divine attributes, 'righteous' (δίκαιος, *dikaios*) and 'true' (ἀληθινός, *alēthinos*), for which see on 15.3, are paired three times in the Apocalypse. They are never predicated of God directly, but describe (in the plural) his 'ways' (15.3) or his 'judgements' (here, and at 19.2).

The last word in the doxologies of 16.5–7 is not spoken by the angel of the waters rejoicing at God's vindication. It is given instead to Christians, who celebrate the perfect truth and righteousness of divine justice (cf. Prigent 467).

Bowls 4–7: The Final Battle Heralded (16.8–21)

8–9   The fourth angel pours out his offering bowl of judgement 'over the sun'. Although the meaning is essentially the same, the first three angelic beings empty their bowls εἰς (*eis*, lit. 'into') the earth, sea and rivers, while the remaining four pour theirs out ἐπί (*epi*, lit. 'upon') the sun, the beast's throne, the river Euphrates and the air. The seer's language, in this vision, continues to be figurative. After the fourth trumpet-blast, a third of the sun, moon and stars were eclipsed. The theme of darkness will be picked up after the fifth bowl; meanwhile, instead of the sun being struck so that its light is diminished, its heat is intensified. It was made to scorch people 'with its flames' (ἐν πυρί, *en pyri*, lit. 'in fire', is an instrumental dative).

The symbolism of the sun in the Old Testament is usually positive (e.g. Ps. 89.36; Eccles. 11.7; Mal. 1.11). Yet the sun's penetrating heat can be dangerous, and shelter is required in such a situation. So the blessings of God, and especially the promises of the messianic age, are metaphorically represented as providing shelter from all danger, including the burning rays of the sun (cf. Ps. 121.6; Isa. 4.6; 49.10). In the Apocalypse (16.8) the scorching heat of the sun becomes a plague for the unfaithful idolaters, whereas those who are protected by God's covenant love are assured that 'neither sun nor burning heat will ever strike them' (7.16). Cf. Prigent 468.

Fire is often associated with judgement in biblical literature (cf. Gen. 19.24; Deut. 4.24 [= Heb. 12.29]; 1 Cor. 3.13; 2 Pet. 3.7). The sovereign control of God over the process of retributive justice is highlighted by the divine passive, ἐδόθη αὐτῷ (*edothē autō[i]*, lit. 'it was given to it'); that is to say, the sun was 'made to scorch people' with its flames. This correctly takes ἥλιον (*hēlion*, 'sun'), rather than ὁ τέταρτος (*ho tetartos*, 'the fourth'), as the antecedent of αὐτῷ (*autō[i]*, lit. 'to it'). See further Mounce 296.

The effect of the fourth bowl, namely, the fact that the sun scorches people with its fire, is repeated for emphasis at the start of verse 9: 'they were seared with its intense heat' (καῦμα μέγα, *kauma mega*, lit. 'great heat', is a cognate accusative of content). The imagery of Rev. 7.16 is reflected in both verses 8 and 9. In the earlier text, the seer's vision depicts a reversal of the physical suffering (hunger and thirst) experienced by the redeemed. Now, in Christ, they will not be afflicted by the sun or its scorching heat. By contrast, the worshippers of the beast are pictured here as tortured by the fierce and burning sun (cf. Deut. 32.24; Isa. 49.10).

As with the sixth trumpet (9.20–21), the fourth bowl-plague produces blasphemy, rather than repentance. Like Pharaoh, at the time of the Exodus, the members of the unbelieving world hardened their hearts. In contrast to the nations, who were 'dazzled into homage and conversion' after the earthquake-judgement in 11.13 (Kiddle 320), the blasphemers 'refused to repent', and 'pay God homage' (δοῦναι αὐτῷ δόξαν, *dounai autō[i] doxan*, lit. 'give glory to him', where δοῦναι, *dounai*, 'to give', is an epexegetical infinitive of consequence). The burning of the sun's 'fire' (πῦρ, *pyr*), in 16.8–9, is a figurative woe which recalls the suffering brought about by the plagues of 'fire (πῦρ, *pyr*), smoke and brimstone' at 9.17–18 (q.v.); cf. also the 'fire' unleashed by the two witnesses against their unfaithful antagonists at 11.5–6, and the fiery judgement of Babylon at 17.16; 18.8.

The 'cursing' of God by the sinful, in verse 9, is the equivalent of defiantly slandering or reviling his name (cf. BDAG 178a; note also the prohibition against using the name of God wrongfully at Exod. 20.7). The 'name' (τὸ ὄνομα, *to onoma*) of the true God denotes his essential being and character, about which the sacrilegious rebels utter falsehoods; for they deny that their afflictions derive from the sovereign judgement of God. Outside Rev. 16 it is only the beast who is said to be 'blasphemous' (cf. 13.1–6; 17.3); and this suggests that, in their impious behaviour, the followers of the beast have become like the false god they worship (Caird 202; cf. Beale 822–23).

The unrepentant would not accept that God held 'the authority to inflict these plagues' (τὴν ἐξουσίαν ἐπὶ τὰς πληγὰς ταύτας, *tēn exousian epi tas plēgas tautas*, lit. 'the power over these plagues'). The use of the plural, 'plagues', seems to imply that the victims of the fourth bowl also suffered from the results of the other six outpourings; cf. 'these judgements', in verse 5. *Targ. Neof. I* Deut. 32.24–25 understands the plague of fire in that context as including a spiritual dimension of punishment, as at Rev. 16.8–9; cf. also the Mosaic plague of fire at Exod. 9.23, which probably informs this passage in the Apocalypse. For the antithesis of the action in Rev. 16.9, where the reprobates 'cursed the name of God, and refused to pay him homage', see *T. Job* 16.7 ('I glorified God and did not blaspheme'); cf. also Job 1.22; 2.10.

10–11 The fifth angel emptied his bowl on 'the throne of the beast'. This description of the beast's sovereignty over his realm is otherwise mentioned in Revelation only at 13.2, where it is said that the dragon conferred on the beast his 'rule' (θρόνον, *thronon*, lit. 'throne') and immense authority. A number of commentators interpret this image as a symbol of Rome, the focus of secular power and oppression in John's day (so Swete 204; Charles 2, 45; Hendriksen 162; Mounce 297). But, while the centre of any antichristian government may be included in this reference, the beast's throne, like Satan himself, must represent all opposition to God, physical and spiritual, however and wherever it is to be discovered (see on 12.18—13.1); cf. Prigent 468 n. 8. The first three bowl-plagues affect the elements of nature, whereas the last four are more political, and directed at the forces of persecution and deception (Sweet 246).

The fifth plague, then, strikes at the diabolical hostility which finds its focus in the kingdom of the beast, the diminished rule of which is pictured by a darkened empire. This 'darkness' echoes the ninth disaster in the Exodus tradition (Exod. 10.21–29), and the fourth trumpet-plague (Rev. 8.12); for references to the significance of darkness in Jewish and Christian literature see Aune 890. The supernatural darkness intensifies the distress of the previous plagues, and adds a terror of its own (Mounce 297). In Exod. 10.22–23 it is recorded that the darkness inflicted on the Egyptians was so dense that they were visually separated from one another. Wis. 17.1—18.4 understands this as a symbol of the separation of the unfaithful from God (note esp. Wis. 17.2, 20–21). At Rev. 16.10, the complete darkness into which the beast's kingdom is plunged has a similarly figurative significance. It indicates the distance between unbelievers and the covenant God, and reminds them that oppression and idolatry are vain (Beale 824).

The darkness of the fifth bowl-plague is symbolic, and not literal (against Mounce 297); cf. Kiddle 321–22; Caird 204–205; Hughes 175. It leads to a spiritual anguish, which is presented in physical terms: 'people bit their tongues in agony'. Aune (890) finds this connection difficult; but, in fact, it is straightforward. As with the Egyptian plague of darkness in Exod. 10, the terrifying and total eclipse in verses 10–11 causes horror and despair to the followers of the beast when they become aware of their isolation from the true God, and their susceptibility to eternal devastation. Their 'agony' (πόνος, *ponos*, lit. 'pain') is comparable to the 'torment' (βασανισμός, *basanismos*), endured by those unprotected by God's seal, when 'darkening' succeeded the fifth trumpet woe (9.5–6); see Charles 2, 45–46. Cf. the use of 'darkness', as a metaphor for the realm where the reprobate will be judged, in 2 Pet. 2.17; Jude 13.

Beale (824) suggests that the demonic locust-scorpions of the fifth trumpet (9.3–11) are the agents of the 'agony' which is poured out from the fifth bowl, and also that the πόνος (*ponos*, 'pain') of 16.10 may be associated with the removal of earthly security, and the awareness of a missing spiritual assurance (cf. 21.4, 'there will be no more pain'). The judgemental action of the fifth angel, despite its figurative and eschatological elements, seems to be expressed in time and space; but it nevertheless anticipates the judgement of the end-time, when weeping and 'gnashing of teeth' await the unbeliever (cf. Matt. 8.12; 22.13; 25.30). For the verb, ἐμασῶντο (*emasōnto*, lit. 'they were biting', imperfect), used only here in the New Testament, see Job 30.4 LXX (MT 30.3, people were 'gnawing the dry ground' from hunger).

The suffering caused by the emptying of the fifth judgemental bowl (verse 10) does not soften the subjects of the beast, but (as in the Exodus saga) causes a hardening of the heart (verse 11); cf. Exod. 7.3; et al. The unfaithful did not repent of their deeds, but 'reviled the God of heaven' on account of their pain. Like the demonic beast, they blaspheme the true and sovereign Lord (13.5–6); and, in protest at their punishment, they vilify God's character (see also on verse 9). The expression, 'the God of heaven' (τὸν θεὸν τοῦ οὐρανοῦ, *ton theon tou ouranou*), may echo Dan. 2.37, 44, in a passage which speaks of God asserting his sovereign and universal rule over the kingdoms of this world (Mounce 297); see also Rev. 11.13. The 'sufferings and sores', experienced by the ungodly (ἐκ τῶν πόνων αὐτῶν καὶ ἐκ τῶν ἑλκῶν αὐτῶν, *ek tōn ponōn autōn kai ek tōn helkōn autōn*, lit. 'from their pains and sores'), include not only 'agony' (πόνος, *ponos*), repeated from verse 10, but also 'sores', repeated from the first bowl-plague (verse 2). This suggests that those affected by the fifth bowl also sustain injury from the previous, and indeed subsequent, plagues (see on 'these judgements' in verse 5, and 'these plagues' in verse 9).

The phrase, 'they refused to repent of what they had done' (οὐ μετενόησαν ἐκ τῶν ἔργων αὐτῶν, *ou metenoēsan ek tōn ergōn autōn*, lit. 'they did not repent from their works'), may mean not only that the unfaithful were unprepared to change their minds about trusting God but also that they would not alter the lifestyle which accords with that attitude (cf. Beale 825). Given the parallel at 9.20–21 (q.v.), such 'works' would have included idolatry, murder, magic arts, immorality and theft; see similarly 2.20–22. It is true that early Jewish tradition understood the lack of repentance on the part of the Egyptians, following the plagues, as the cause of their final condemnation (cf. Wis. 12.26–27). However, and despite the reactions of the unbelievers in 16.9, 11, 21, this need not imply that repentance and faith are ever impossible for those who wish to accept the redeeming work of the Lamb; and passages in the Apocalypse which envisage the ultimate, widespread conversion of the nations cannot be ignored (see on 14.14–20; also 1.7; 11.13; 14.6–7; 15.3–4; 21.24—22.5). So Sweet 243; against Wilcock 144; Beale 825–26.

12 Verses 12–16 form a textual unit, which begins here (see above). Between them, the sixth and seventh bowls of judgement initiate the destruction of 'Babylon'. On Babylon, as the symbolic equivalent of any unjust world system which misuses power and opposes God and his people, see 14.8 and below; also 16.19; 18.2, 10, 21. There is a close relationship between the sixth bowl, in the present passage, and the sixth trumpet (9.13–19), not least because both judgements concern the Euphrates (see below). In the earlier scene, four angels who have been chained up at the river are released, with the result that fiendish cavalry destroy one-third of the human race. The scene in 16.12–16 is different, but provides a variation on the same theme (Prigent 469); for in both cases an object, which has been preventing the approach of a vast army, is removed, and salvific judgement follows.

When the sixth angel dispenses his bowl over 'the great river, the Euphrates', its 'water dried up' (verse 12). The only other reference to this river in the Apocalypse is to be found at 9.14. The Euphrates was called 'great' (μέγας, *megas*) because of its enormous length (nearly 2,000 miles); see also Gen. 15.18; Deut. 1.7; Josh. 1.4. It was one of the great boundaries of the ancient world, and flowed between Israel and her main enemies (Exod. 23.31; 1 Macc. 3.32). As the largest river in south-west Asia, its waters were never known to dry up. The dehydration following the emptying of the sixth bowl, to allow for the passage across it of the 'kings from the east', is accordingly clearly symbolic. It acts in context as an antitype of the Exodus from Egypt, during which the Sea of Reeds dried up and the Israelites under Moses crossed over it (Exod. 14.21–25), and of the later crossing of the Jordan under Joshua (Josh. 3.7–17). When, in the Old Testament, rivers dry up, this is seen as one of the responses of the elements to the advent of God (Aune 891); cf. Isa. 50.2; Hos. 13.15; Nahum 1.4.

There has been much scholarly debate about the identity of the kings 'from the east' (ἀπὸ ἀνατολῆς ἡλίου, *apo anatolēs hēliou*, lit. 'from the rising of the sun'). Several interpretations are possible, and the following deserve serious consideration.

(a) Old Testament prophecy at times foresees the arrival of Israel's enemies from a particular compass point, including the east (see Dan. 11.44). According to Herodotus (1.190–91), the Persian King Cyrus fulfilled such a prediction by diverting the Euphrates, thus allowing his army to cross the river, which ran through the city, and capture the apparently impregnable Babylon (cf. Isa. 41.2, 25 [LXX τὸν ἀφ' ἡλίου, *ton aph' hēliou*, 'one from the rising of the sun']; 44.27–28; 46.11). Cf. Swete 205. The problem with regarding Cyrus as the invading king (singular) from the east is that, according to the Isaianic texts, he was raised up by Yahweh precisely to fulfil the divine purposes for Israel (Isa. 44.28; 45.13). As such, this monarch is presented in a favourable light, and not as a hostile and warring intruder (so Rev. 16.12–16).

(b) A more common view of the 'kings from the east' in verse 12 is to identify them with the Parthian rulers led by Nero *redivivus*. One version of that legend contained the belief that the Emperor Nero would return 'from the east', to cross the river Euphrates at the head of countless armies (*Sib. Or.* 4.119–20, 137–39); cf. Jer. 50.41; 51.11, 28; *1 Enoch* 56.5. So Beckwith 682; Beasley-Murray 243–44; Roloff 190; cf. Bauckham 1299*b*. However, while John was doubtless aware of such myths (see on 13.3), there is nothing to indicate that the advent of a conquering Nero is in mind at this point. The 'kings from the east' are introduced as an indistinct group, and not as a specific individual (so Prigent 469); moreover, the Roman fear of the Parthians at this period was not shared by Palestinian Jews (see Aune 891–94).

(c) Milligan (269–70) makes the unusual suggestion that the 'kings' symbolize the remnant of God's Israel, returning from their places of captivity. To support this view, he points out that the waters of the Exodus were dried up for the safety of Israel, rather than the destruction of the Egyptians; that in 7.2 the angel ascends from the region of the 'rising sun' to seal the people of God, and forces opposed to them would not then arrive from the same quarter; and also that 'preparing the way' (ἵνα ἑτοιμασθῇ ἡ ὁδός, *hina hetoimasthē[i] hē hodos*, lit. 'that the way might be prepared') recalls John the Baptist heralding the coming of Jesus, more than the arrival of enemies. Nevertheless, the martial context of 16.12–16 militates against this interpretation, particularly if the warlike 'kings' who are assembled for battle at verses 14 and 16 (q.v.) are to be associated with the rulers of verse 12 (see also 17.12–13; Bauckham, *Climax of Prophecy* 429–30).

A preferable way of understanding the symbolism in 16.12 is not to interpret it in any way as historical (so Barker, *The Revelation* 271), but to regard it as general and universal; and such an approach accords with John's use of imagery elsewhere in the Apocalypse (as with 'Rome' and 'the beast'). Here Babylon represents unjust world systems, and the dried waters of the Euphrates are a picture of society's religious adherents becoming disenchanted with the deceitful city (17.16–18; 20.8; cf. Beale 827–31). In the same way, the 'kings from the sun's rising' are an emblem of any oppressive and irreligious world forces; they are preparing to attack God's people, without being aware that in the final battle divine judgement will ultimately fall on them. The 'east' may be cited in this passage because it had historical associations in the first century AD. But, in this context, the ideas are more theological than geographical.

13–14 Verses 13–14, together with verse 16, expand the content of verse 12. Throughout this section the theme is preparation for final, eschatological warfare. Verse 12 announces the initiation of divine judgement through the sixth angel, and verses 13–16 specify the earthly agents and purpose of the coming woe. The sentence in verse 13 lacks a verb, such as '(the evil spirits) came from (the mouths)', although it is implied; hence the translation, 'I saw three evil spirits . . . emerging'. For the visionary formula, 'I saw' (καὶ εἶδον, *kai eidon*), see on 5.1; 15.1–2; et al.

The emptying of the sixth bowl releases for demonic action 'three evil spirits'. These derive from the mouths of the dragon, the beast and the false prophet, all of which are mentioned in Chapter 13 (see verses 1, 2, 11). The 'dragon' is doubtless the seven-headed monster of 12.3, who is called serpent, devil, Satan and deceiver (12.9). The 'beast' is the creature from the sea (13.1–8). The 'false prophet', appearing by that name for the first time in Revelation, is the beast from the earth of 13.11 (see also 19.20; 20.10). The wicked triumvirate represent the political and religious forces of evil, which use their power in an idolatrous and unjust manner (cf. Beale 831); they are not to be identified with one imperial rule, such as the Roman, alone (against Swete 206, on the beast).

The term, 'false prophet' (ψευδοπροφήτης, *pseudoprophētēs*), deserves further comment. This is the first time the word appears in the Apocalypse, and it recapitulates the deceptive activity of the second beast in Chapter 13, whose role is to mislead people into worshipping the first beast (13.12). Elsewhere in the New Testament, false prophecy is a description of deceit within the covenant communities of Israel, or of Christ (Matt. 7.15; Mark 13.22 par.; Luke 6.26; Acts 13.6; 2 Pet. 2.1); in 1 John 4.1–3, the spirit of false prophecy in the Johannine circle, especially in producing an unbalanced view of the person of Jesus, is equated with the spirit of Antichrist (see Smalley, *1, 2, 3 John* 217–25). In the view of Beale (831), the fact that false prophecy is characteristic of the Church supports the conclusion that the activity of the second beast in Rev. 13.11–17 takes place among groups of believers, and not exclusively outside them. Such an interpretation is clearly relevant to the understanding of the present context (see 16.14–16).

The seer depicts metaphorically the deceitful nature of the three demonic spirits (verse 14) by saying that they are 'evil' (ἀκάθαρτα, *akatharta*, lit. 'unclean'). This language is also used in 17.4 and 18.2–3, of Babylon's deceptive immorality. See on 14.8; also 21.27; 1 Thess. 2.3. So in verse 13 these spirits also mislead people into the worship of idols; and this accords with the idea of seduction (πορνεία, *porneia*, lit. 'fornication') as idolatry in 2.14, 20; 17.4 (q.v.). Moreover, the evil spirits are 'like frogs' (ὡς βάτραχοι, *hōs batrachoi*), which is an obvious allusion to the plague of frogs at the time of the Exodus (Exod. 8.1–15). As then, so in Rev. 16.14, 16, the frogs are agents of divine destruction (cf. the locusts in 9.3–10); and just as in the Old Testament event frogs belonged to the 'signs' which God worked on behalf of his people (Exod. 8.5–6), so now the frogs 'perform signs' (16.14) under the hand of God (Beale 832). The obvious difference is that John is here applying the plague of frogs symbolically to judgemental spirits of deception, in this way spiritualizing what began life as a historical event (cf. Roloff 190).

The use of the term βάτραχος (*batrachos*, 'frog') in verse 13 is a *hapax legomenon* in the New Testament; and in the LXX it is found solely in accounts of the Exodus plague (LXX Exod. 8.2–11; Ps. 77.45; 104.30; Wis. 19.10). According to Lev. 11.9–12, 41–47, frogs are 'unclean' creatures, from which cleansing is necessary. Their loud and unpleasant croaking is meaningless; and this leads Philo (*De Som.* 2.259–60) to describe the noise of frogs as 'undisciplined speech in which ideas die'. The thrice repeated reference to the 'mouth' (στόμα, *stoma*) of the creatures from which the spirits emerge suggests the 'persuasive and deceptive propaganda' which will drive the secular unfaithful at the end-time to be committed to the cause of evil and isolated from the source of truth (Mounce 299).

The opening clause of verse 14, εἰσὶν γάρ (*eisin gar*, lit. 'for they are'), introduces a further and explicit description of the 'three evil spirits, like frogs' who appear in verse 13: 'these spirits are demonic'. The genitival phrase, πνεύματα δαιμονίων (*pneumata daimoniōn*, lit. 'spirits of demons') is either descriptive ('demonic spirits', as in the translation) or appositional ('spirits which are demons'), although ultimately these two renderings are close together in meaning. Demons are associated elsewhere in Revelation with 'the world's idolatrous system' (Beale 833). So 9.20; 18.2–3; cf. 2.20, 24; 1 Cor. 10.20–21.

The demonic spirits, which emerge from the mouths of their equally devilish fore-bears, are said to 'perform signs (ποιοῦντα σημεῖα, *poiounta sēmeia*, lit. "[they are] doing signs")'. This aligns them with the activity of the beast from the earth (the false prophet) in 13.13 (cf. 19.20), who also 'performed outstanding miracles (σημεῖα, *sēmeia*, lit. "signs")'. In both cases, the agents of Satan try to deceive those who have received the mark of the beast (13.16–17; 16.2); their aim is to lead astray the unfaithful by misleading them about the true nature of secular powers, which is in fact pretentious and idolat-rous. For similar false prophecy see 1 Kings 22.19–23 (a living spirit who, through the mouth of Ahab's prophets, entices the profligate king into battle); also Matt. 24.24 (false prophets using signs to deceive); 2 Thess. 2.10 (Satan's undiluted power to deceive).

The spirits 'travel abroad' to the kings of the world. The verb, ἐκπορεύεται (*ekporeuetai*, lit. 'goes out'), is a third person singular present indicative with the neuter nominative plural noun, 'spirits' (πνεύματα, *pneumata*). Aune (895) tries to limit the reference of this verb to the 'emergence' of the spirits from the mouths of their bearers in verse 13 (where a verb needs to be supplied). They 'came out' of an enclosed space to rally the rulers (cf. Matt. 4.4; Acts 19.12; et al.). But, while that is the starting point, and the verb translated here 'travel abroad' completes the sentence which began in verse 13, John is making the point in verse 14 that the spirits embark on a journey which is world wide, since it is intended to bring a universal gathering of antichristian leaders over to their side. See John 13.30; 1 John 2.19 (false agents of the devil 'go out' to win the allegiance of others).

The 'kings' who are rallied by the three demonic spirits are drawn from 'the whole world' (τῆς οἰκουμένης ὅλης, *tēs oikoumenēs holēs*, lit. 'the entire inhabited earth'; cf. BDAG 699*b*), and not simply from one compass-point, such as the east. The scope of their mission is unlimited and all inclusive (cf. 3.10; 12.9; also 13.3; 1 John 2.2; 5.19). The 'kings' themselves are best understood as equivalent to the 'kings from the east' in verse 12 (q.v.), but now represented from a world-wide perspective (see also the 'ten kings' of 17.12–14). Together they symbolize any idolatrous world forces, political or religious, which use their powers of leadership in ways which are oppressive and un-just. (Cf. Beale 834.) Note also 13.14 and 19.19–20, where both 'the earth's inhabit-ants' and 'the kings of the (whole) earth' are deceived. For the phrase 'rulers of the earth', used in a sense which is predominantly political, cf. further 1.5; 6.15; 17.2, 18; 18.3, 9.

The spirits travel abroad, in their quest for the kings, so as to 'rally (συναγαγεῖν, *syn-agagein*, lit. "to assemble") them for the battle on the great day of God the Almighty'. The rulers of the world are gathered together under the control of demonic, satanic agents. Similar language is used at 19.17, 19; and 20.8 (q.v.), with reference to the dragon-beast rallying the rulers to fight against the Messiah in the final eschatological battle. The present verse (16.14) includes the same thought, of the final confrontation between the forces of the beast and Christ at the end-time (Beale 834–35). All three passages derive from Old Testament texts which predict the gathering together of the nations in Israel for warfare at the climax of history; cf. Ezek. 38—39; Joel 3.2; Zeph. 3.8–10; Zech. 12.3–4; 14.2, 13–14; also 4 Ezra 13.33–36; *1 Enoch* 56.5–8; *T. Jos.* (Arm.) 19.1–12; 1QM 15.2–3. See Knight 112–13. Beale (836) notes that Zech. 13.2 LXX associates 'false prophets and the unclean spirit', the encouragers of idolatry, with the eschatological assembly of the nations.

In verse 14, as at 19.19 and 20.8, the noun τὸν πόλεμον (*ton polemon*, 'the battle', 'the war') is articular, since John is referring to the final conflict between evil and good, Satan and the saints, which would have been familiar to his readers from the prophecies of the Old Testament (e.g. Joel 2.11, 31; Zeph. 1.14). At 11.7 the same noun, in a similar context, is used anarthrously. 'The great day of God', when the climactic battle of the end-time is described as taking place (see also 16.16), is the point at which God manifests his victory over all forms of hostility which are 'directed against him, his plans and his people' (Prigent 472). This means that, while the nations are misled into thinking that they are being rallied to prevail over the helpless faithful, they are in fact being assembled to meet their own judgement at the hands of the Word of God (19.11–21); see Beasley-Murray 244–45. For παντοκράτωρ (*pantokratōr*, 'Almighty'), suggesting the ultimate sovereignty of God and his kingdom, see verse 7; also 1.8; 4.8; 11.17; 15.3; 19.6, 15; 21.22.

15 This verse is an admonition to the faithful, and its parenthetical nature is made clear in the translation by the use of brackets. Some commentators, including Charles (2, 49) and Aune (896), regard this exhortation as an intrusive comment derived from 3.3 (q.v.); on the other side see Caird (207–209). Its occurrence is admittedly abrupt; but, given the context of impending warfare, the thought is entirely appropriate. The exalted Jesus of the seven oracles (Rev. 2—3) breaks into this judgemental scene to warn the faithful of the need for spiritual vigilance, as they await his final appearing (Sweet 249). That is because the coming battle, which will also affect the saints (20.8–9), is due to coincide with 'the great day of God' (verse 14); and, since that 'day' may occur at any hour, it must be unexpected. Therefore believers should remain steadfast in their faith and resist the temptation to compromise in the face of coming judgement (Beale 837). For similar exhortations see 13.9–10; 14.12–13.

The unexpected nature of Christ's return is associated in his teaching with the imagery of a thief suddenly breaking into a house (Matt. 24.42–44 par.); see also 1 Thess. 5.2; 2 Pet. 3.10 ('the day of the Lord will come like a thief'). But the primary background is to be discovered in Rev. 3.2–3 itself, where the risen Lord says to the members of the church at Sardis, 'If you are not vigilant, I will arrive like a thief; and you will not know at what hour I will come upon you.' The blessing which is bestowed on those who are prepared for the coming of Jesus ('fortunate is the one who stays awake') is the third of seven in the Apocalypse (cf. also 1.3; 14.13; 19.9; 20.6; 22.7, 14).

Christ further characterizes the nature of the vigilance to which the faithful are summoned by saying that they should be 'fully clothed, not going around naked and exposed to shame'. This appears to be a development of the thought in Rev. 3.18, where the Laodiceans are counselled to purchase white robes, to keep the shame of their nakedness from being visible; see also Ezek. 16.36–39. The verb τηρέω (*tēreō*, 'keep') in the phrase, τηρῶν τὰ ἱμάτια αὐτοῦ (*tērōn ta himatia autou*, 'fully clothed', lit. 'keeping his garments'), is used metaphorically with the noun 'garments' only here in Revelation. Vigilance and the state of being fully clothed, in the context of Rev. 16, suggest a refusal to 'concede to the idolatrous demands of beast worship in the face of the pressure of the final attack' (Beale 837); cf. 3.4–5. This is all the more urgent, since the members of John's community are themselves susceptible to the deceptions of the beast and the false prophet, who have their agents in the churches (2.14, 20); so Bauckham 1299*b*.

The contrast between being 'fully clothed' and 'going around naked, exposed to shame' is sharp. The idea of nakedness being visible, in verse 15, which is picked up from 3.18, is a metaphor used in the Old Testament to represent God accusing Israel of unfaithful idolatry (cf. Isa. 20.1–6; Ezek. 16.36; 23.29; Nahum 3.4–5). Here, it refers to the need for faithful resistance in the last persecution, 'so that' (ἵνα, *hina*) believers who have been sealed by God will not be shamed, and exposed as idolaters (cf. 17.4–6). 'Nakedness' and 'shame' are commonly associated in Judaism and early Christianity (cf. Gen. 9.20–25; Isa. 47.3; Hos. 2.10; 4QpHos[a] 2.12–13; 1 Cor. 12.23), although, in the creation narrative, the man and his wife are naked but not ashamed (Gen. 2.25). The term, ἀσχημοσύνη (*aschēmosynē*, lit. 'nakedness'), is in the present context a euphemism for the genitalia (BDAG 147*b*). It is possible that one background to the thought of nakedness in verse 15 is the warning to temple guards in *M. Middoth* 1.2 that, if they were caught sleeping while on guard, their clothes would be removed and burned. As Beale (838) agrees, however, although the temple imagery in 15.5—16.7 may support this suggestion, the primary derivation of the imagery in verse 15 is to be discovered in the two parallel exhortations at 3.3 and 18.

Elsewhere in the Apocalypse 'garments' are symbols of the righteous deeds of the saints (3.4–5, 18; 19.8–9), whereas nakedness signifies the absence of right belief and behaviour (Sweet 249). John is concerned that the members of his circle should be prepared for the end-time by being spiritually clothed in the right attire. The relevance of the encouragements in verse 15 to the churches of Asia Minor is obvious from the appeals which derive from two of the oracles in Rev. 3. Each of the letters in Rev. 2—3 is addressed to all seven congregations (2.7; et al.); and this means that everyone in the Johannine community and beyond needs to be prepared for the salvific judgement described in 16.12–16, since it may take place at any time (cf. Beale 837).

16   This verse continues the thought of verse 14 (q.v.), after the relevant exhortation of verse 15. The subject and object of the gathering together in verse 16 are not specified; but the context makes it clear that on this occasion the evil 'spirits' (πνεύματα, *pneumata*, verse 14) 'assembled' (συνήγαγεν, *synēgagen*, aorist singular verb with the neuter plural noun) the kings of the whole world, representatives of the worldly powers, for battle at Armageddon. For the spelling of this place name, which is found only here, see the textual note on verse 16. The use of Hebrew, and the absence of its interpretation, are typical of apocalyptic style (Jeremias, 'Armageddon').

'Armageddon' is a transcription of the Hebrew word, הַר־מְגִדּוֹ (*har-m^egiddô*), which means 'the mount of Megiddo'. This was an ancient city, located on a plain in the southwestern section of the Valley of Jezreel, and the site of several major battles between Israel and her enemies (see Judg. 5.19; 2 Kings 23.29; 1 Chron. 7.29; Zech. 12.11). However, problems arise if any attempt is made to suggest that the final, eschatological battle will take place there. First, Megiddo was nowhere near a 'mountain', nor does any text speak of 'the mount of Megiddo'. Second, that city seems never to have been associated with any apocalyptic tradition (cf. Jeremias, 'Armageddon'; Prigent 474). Boring (177) therefore holds that 'Harmagedon' (the form in NRSV) is the 'mount of assembly' mentioned at Isa. 14.13 (see verses 12–15; but, according to Sweet [250], this interpretation is 'philologically dubious').

A more likely background to the imagery in Rev. 16.16 is to be discovered in Ezek. 38—39. Beckwith (685), for example, suggests that the seer began with Ezekiel's prophecy of an eschatological slaughter of the nations 'on the mountains of Israel' (Ezek. 38.8–21; 39.2, 4, 17), and then defined this general reference by adding the name 'Megiddo', a city where the enemies of God were so often destroyed in Israel's history (Judg. 5.31; et al.). It is certainly true that the hostile nations are called 'Gog and Magog' in Ezek. 38.2, and this connects with their reappearance at Rev. 20.8, and with the 'beloved city' of Jerusalem, where final judgement seems to take place (14.20; 20.9). For alternative proposals about the significance of 'Armageddon' see Mounce 301–302.

These ideas all presuppose that the primary setting for understanding John's language at this point is geographical. Nevertheless, the very difficulties which are involved in making connections between Armageddon and Palestinian locations indicate that the term is a metaphor, and not to be understood literally. It is a cryptic description, like the number of the beast (13.18). The imagery at this point may have been influenced by the Israelite battles associated with Megiddo, and its nearest mountain (Carmel); but, like the 'Euphrates' (9.14; 16.12), 'the east' (16.12) and 'Babylon' (14.8; 16.19; 17.5; 18.2, 10, 21), 'Armageddon' is a symbolic figure for the whole world. It is a basically mythical formulation, which represents the apocalyptic and universal mountain where hostile forces, assembled by the agents of Satan, will come together to wage war at the end against God and his people (cf. Hendriksen 162–64; Aune 898). The victorious outcome of this eschatological battle, for the Lamb and the saints, is predicted at 11.7–11; 17.14; 19.14–21; 20.7–10, since John is writing on this side of the resurrection. Nevertheless, while the consummation of the warfare is likely to take place in history, the conflict between good and evil, justice and injustice, is meantime always to be found in progress. See further Beale 838–41.

17 The battle of Armageddon (verse 16) leads to the ultimate destruction of the corrupt world system (Beale 841); and, as with the sounding of the seventh trumpet (11.15), the outpouring of the seventh bowl points to the consummation of history, even if the end is not yet. The parallels between the last trumpet and the final bowl are striking (cf. Mounce 302–303). In both cases, God's temple is opened and loud voices from heaven proclaim the realization of his rule (11.19, 15, 17; 16.17); while, following the actions of the angels, divine judgement falls on the earth accompanied by theophanic phenomena (11.18–19; 16.18–21).

The statement that the seventh offering bowl was poured out 'into the air' (ἐπὶ τὸν ἀέρα, *epi ton aera*) could be part of the Exodus plague imagery which underlies the scenes in Rev. 8—9 (the trumpets) and 16 (the bowls), and is clearly present in the 'plague of hail' at 16.21 (cf. Exod. 10.21; 9.22–26). In Philo, *De Vit. Mos.* 1.20.114, 119, the Egyptian hail is called a plague of 'heaven and air (ἀήρ, *aēr*)'; cf. ibid. 1.21.120. 'Air' is essentially the atmosphere which surrounds the earth; however, in view of the background to this passage of Revelation (16.17–21), and the fact that the only other use of ἀήρ (*aēr*, 'air') in the Apocalypse (at 9.2) is with reference to demonic spirits, it is likely that the 'air' in 16.17 includes a significance which is judgemental (cf. Eph. 2.2). As with the previous three bowls (16.8–16), the judgement in question falls on the rebellious kingdom presided over by the satanic dragon and his beast (see verse 10).

The 'loud voice' (φωνὴ μεγάλη, *phōnē megalē*), which issues from the sanctuary and from God's throne, is undoubtedly divine; it belongs to God or his Christ, or both (cf. 16.1; also 1.10; 10.3; 11.12; 12.10; 21.3). See the 'voice of the Lord from the temple' at Isa. 66.6. The 'sanctuary' (ναός, *naos*, lit. 'temple') and the 'throne' (θρόνος, *thronos*), which represent the presence and sovereignty of God, are also linked together at 7.15; 8.3 (q.v.); for the use of these terms in Revelation see on 7.15 and 4.2.

The voice utters the one word, γέγονεν (*gegonen*, 'It is over!', lit. 'It has happened!'). The perfect tense contrasts with the use of aorists earlier in this chapter, and it may indicate a climactic end to the series of plagues which God has inflicted on the unbelieving world (Aune 899). Divine judgement is always present in history, not *just* at the end of it; and this affects all nature (the four elements of earth [verse 2], water [verses 3–4, 12], fire [sun, verse 8] and air [verse 17]), as well as all people (verse 21). So the declaration, 'It is over!', is a reminder that, like his salvation, God's justice has become finally and fully active within his creation (15.1; cf. Prigent 475). If it be asked when that occurred, the answer must be in the life and ministry, and death and exaltation of Jesus, whose coming brought decisive judgement and condemnation, as well as life and light, to the whole world (John 1.4–5; 3.16–21; 8.12; 1 John 4.7–16). Despite the last verse of this scene (16.21), repentance in the face of discrimination is always possible (see on verse 9; also 17.14; 21.1–8); for the judgemental cry, 'It is over!', contains within it the triumphant and salvific word of Jesus from the cross, 'It is finished!' (τετέλεσται, *tetelestai*, John 19.30).

18   A typical 'storm-theophany' (Moffatt 449) follows the proclamation made in verse 17; and this, in turn, includes an exceptionally severe earthquake which has devastating consequences (verses 19–20). The imagery is that associated with the end of the cosmos and final judgement (Beale 842; but see below). A background to verse 18 is readily found in the manifestation of God to Moses and the people on Mount Sinai, accompanied by thunder, lightning, cloud, earthquake and a trumpet-blast (Exod. 19.16–18). For the order of the supernatural phenomena in Rev. 16.18 see the textual notes on this verse. Similar lists are present also at 4.5; 8.5; 11.19; and, in each case, the context is one of impending judgement. Cf. Isa. 29.5–6; 30.30.

'Earthquakes' in the Apocalypse always herald the coming of God with justice. See on 8.5; also 6.12; 11.13, 19. At 11.13, as in the present verse (16.18), the word 'earthquake' (σεισμός, *seismos*) is used twice. In both cases the repetition emphasizes the solemn character of the divine intervention which the phenomenon signals. In 16.18 the intensity of the dramatic situation is heightened further by the statement that the great earthquake, which followed the storm, was 'so terrifying and violent that nothing like it had ever taken place in human history (ἀφ' οὗ ἄνθρωπος ἐγένετο ἐπὶ τῆς γῆς, *aph'hou anthrōpos egeneto epi tēs gēs*, lit. "not since man appeared on the earth")' . This seems to be an apocalyptic formula based on Dan. 12.1–2 (cf. LXX), a text which reflects the wording used to describe the hail-judgement in Egypt at Exod. 9.18, 24 ('such heavy hail as had never fallen in all the land of Egypt since it became a nation'). See also the connection with the plague of hail mentioned at Rev. 16.21. For this stereotypical language, denoting eschatological tribulation and suffering, cf. further 1 Macc. 9.27; 1QM 1.11–12; Mark 13.19 par.; Josephus, *Bell. Jud.* 1.4.12; 5.442; 6.428–29; *Sib. Or.* 3.689–92; *Assum. Moses* 8.1.

It appears that in 16.17–21 the seer is referring primarily to God's judgement on a sinful world at the climax of history and the end of the world (cf. 6.12–17). So Hendriksen 164–65; Hughes 178–79; Beale 842. However, it has been argued in the interpretation of verse 17 (above) that the judgement of God, as well as his implicit love and salvation, derive their focus in this scene from the Christ-event. In this case, it must be allowed that verses 18–21 also speak of a process of divine discrimination which is ongoing. The seismic events depicted in the imagery of this passage, that is to say, herald the reaction of God's holiness to false belief, injustice and wrongdoing present in society at *any* moment of human history, up to the consummation and in it (see on verse 19).

19–20   As a result of the catastrophic earthquake described in verse 18, 'the great city was split into three parts' (cf. 11.13). For similar acts of divine judgement see Hag. 2.6–7; Zech. 14.4; Heb. 12.26–27. Earlier commentators have identified 'the great city' (ἡ πόλις ἡ μεγάλη, *hē polis hē megalē*) as Jerusalem (so Rev. 11.8), on the grounds that only in verse 19b does the text say that God remembered 'Babylon the great', which implies that John is there referring to a different metropolis (cf. Milligan 274–76 [the allusion is to Jerusalem *as* Babylon]; see now also Barker, *The Revelation* 279–301). A common later interpretation takes the city as Babylon-Rome, since verse 19 relates to the pagan world ('the cities of the nations'; cf. 10.11; 11.2; et al.), and Babylon was its first city (so Charles 2, 52; Mounce 303; Aune 900–901; Knight 114). Babylon is also repeatedly designated as 'the great' at 17.5, 18; 18.2, 10, 16, 18, 19, 21. As the king of Babylon was judged for his defiance of God (Dan. 4.1–37), the argument runs, so will latter-day Babylon receive divine condemnation (cf. Beale 843).

However, 'Babylon' throughout the Apocalypse represents the secular world, with its focus in the systemic evil ranged against God and his righteousness (see on 14.8; also 17.1–3). More than that, the symbol is theological, and not simply geographical. It stands for all the world's political, economic, sociological and cultural centres (Beale 843; cf. Swete 211), and beyond that again for the whole satanic structure: that is to say, any unbelieving, idolatrous and unjust powers at any time which are hostile to God and his Church. Cf. Kiddle 332–33; Wilcock 150; Hughes 179. The effects of the seventh bowl of God's judgement are devastating, and these will be further catalogued in the interval section Rev. 17—18 (Beasley-Murray 247). Meanwhile, it is said that the great city was 'split into three parts', which implies a complete and universal demolition. The cities of the nations (the antithesis of the city of God, 21.10–27) also 'collapsed in ruins' as a result of the earthquake (verse 18); and this suggests that all the impious structures throughout the world, associated with the image of Babylon (see above), must ultimately be destroyed by God's sovereign power. The term πίπτω (*piptō*, 'fall'), in the phrase, 'the cities of the world collapsed in ruins (lit. "fell")', is also used to describe the destruction of Babylon at 14.8; 18.2 (cf. LXX Isa. 21.9; Jer. 28.8).

Proleptically, the unbelieving world as a whole is judged by God. Although it appears that the judgement of 'Babylon' has already taken place, it is in fact ongoing (see above). The seer expresses the thought of divine discrimination in this context by saying that God 'remembered' Babylon. The Greek construction means literally, 'remembrance was made (ἐμνήσθη, *emnēsthē*, lit. "it was remembered") of Babylon before God'. This passive construction occurs regularly in judicial contexts, where the forensic setting is that of a case tried before the throne of God (LXX Ps. 9.13; Isa. 65.17; Lam. 2.1; Ezek. 3.20; 18.22; 33.16; et al.). Cf. Prigent 476.

For the language of the 'cup of wine' of 'God's furious wrath' see on 6.16–17; 14.8, 10, 19; and for the tautological phrase, 'his furious wrath' (τοῦ θυμοῦ τῆς ὀργῆς αὐτοῦ, *tou thymou tēs orgēs autou*, lit. 'of the anger of his wrath') see 4QapocrMosesᵃ 1.3 ('your God will repent of the fury of his great wrath'). There is a sequence of four genitives in the second sentence of verse 19 (five in 19.15), the last two of which (τῆς ὀργῆς αὐτοῦ, *tēs orgēs autou*, lit. 'of the wrath of him') are best understood as appositional; hence the translation, 'the cup of wine, *that is*, of his furious wrath'. The righteous reaction of a holy God to persistent wrongdoing and unholiness must be terrifying as it is real; but this judgemental process can never be separated from the refining love of God, nor should it ever debar the sinner from repentance, faith and life (22.14); cf. Sweet 251.

The all-embracing and cataclysmic character of the divine judgement released from the seventh bowl (verses 17–19) is vividly illustrated by further disintegration in the cosmos: 'every island vanished (ἔφυγεν, *ephygen*, lit. "fled"), and the mountains disappeared (ὄρη οὐχ εὑρέθησαν, *orē ouch heurethēsan*, lit. "mountains were not found")', verse 20. The earthquake which followed the fraction of the sixth seal produced a similar result (6.12–14; note verse 14, 'every mountain and island was removed from its place'); and it seems that in these two scenes John's audience is proleptically viewing the same, continuous process of divine judgement from different points of view.

Caird (209) finds a possible allusion to Patmos in the author's reference to 'islands'; while Kiddle (335) suggests that the eschatological hostility towards mountains in this verse is coloured by prophetic denunciations of 'high places' as scenes of pagan rites (e.g. Isa. 16.12; Jer. 19.4–6; Ezek. 6.6). However, the reference in this verse is doubtless more general. It is not simply that the seer is describing the devastating outcome of a violent cosmic phenomenon (Mounce 304), but that also, through it, he is depicting the awesomeness of God's judgement disclosed at the end of history (Beasley-Murray 247). For similar language and thought, in addition to 6.14, see 20.11; also *1 Enoch* 1.6; *Sib. Or.* 8.234–35; *Assum. Moses* 10.4. For the formulaic expression, οὐχ εὑρέθησαν (*ouch heurethēsan*, lit. 'were not found'), using a passive verb with a negative particle to mean 'disappear', cf. 18.14, 21, 22. Each of these references is associated with the finality of Babylon's destruction.

21 In the Old Testament, hail is 'part of the accepted arsenal of divine retaliation' (Mounce 304); cf. Josh. 10.11; Job 38.22–23; Isa. 28.17; Ezek. 38.22; Hag. 2.17; *Sib.*

Or. 3.689–92. In the present context, more directly, the fierce hailstorm, which is precipitated by the earthquake (verse 18) and forms part of the subsequent cosmic disjunction (verses 19–21), connects once more with the motif of the Exodus (cf. Exod. 9.13–35 [note verse 24]; also Ps. 78.47; 105.32–33; Josephus, *Ant.* 2.304–306). The intensity of the plague of hail, in verse 21, is underscored by the size of the hailstones themselves, which are described as 'weighing about one hundred pounds each' (ὡς ταλαντιαία, *hōs talantiaia*, lit. 'as weighing a talent'; the word is found only here in the New Testament). A talent was the equivalent of 125 Roman pounds of *c.* 343 gr., or 12 ounces each (BDAG 988*b*). Cf. the 'heavy hailstorm' at 11.19 (q.v.); also, for the weight of the hailstones, Josephus, *Bell. Jud.* 5.270.

The hailstones which 'dropped (καταβαίνει, *katabainei*, lit. "come down") from the sky' at this point in the apocalyptic narrative are reminiscent of the fire which 'descended' (κατέβη, *katebē*) from heaven and consumed the followers of Satan whom he had deceived, at 20.9. The severity of the divine judgement involved in this scene is also picked up in the closing words of verse 21, 'so extremely (σφόδρα, *sphodra*, only here in the Apocalypse) fearful was that affliction'. Nevertheless, the 'plague' (πληγή, *plēgē*; the noun is repeated for literary effect in verse 21*b*) fails to produce an immediate change of heart among unbelievers on the earth. As at 16.9, 11, and in evident agony, they 'cursed God' for his judgement, preferring to remain in thrall to the rule of the angel of the bottomless pit (9.11), rather than submit to the sovereignty of the true and righteous God of heaven (16.5–7). However, repentance from apostasy is never far away (19.1–2); against Beale 845.

One question remains, and that is the *placing* of the hail episode. This appears last in the series of bowl-plagues, but it is not the final Exodus affliction (which, in that saga, is the death of the firstborn; Exod. 12.29–32). Bauckham (*Climax of Prophecy* 199–209, esp. 204–207) has an interesting solution. He draws attention to the fact that in Rev. 16.17–21 the plague of hail (Exod. 9) is combined with the cosmic phenomena surrounding the Sinai theophany (Exod. 19); see verse 18. That plague, together with the Sinai portents, the argument continues, is placed last in the sequence of seven bowls because the associated theophany is a climactic event in the Exodus, and takes place after it. Furthermore, behind verse 21 lies Josh. 10.11 (see above), where huge stones from heaven rain down on the Amorites *following* the Exodus-event; and that chapter of Joshua lays out the climax of God's total plan of deliverance for his people, with its focus on the conquest and settlement of the promised land (note also the Exodus pattern, as typological of end-time events, in Ezek. 38.19–22; *Apoc. Abr.* 30.1–8). The conclusion is that in Rev. 16.17–21, where Exod. 9 and 19 are brought together and influenced by Josh. 10.11, John is thinking of the total history of the Exodus, from the plagues of Egypt to the conquest of Canaan, as one great manifestation of God's redemptive power to judge the nations and deliver his people (Bauckham, *Climax of Prophecy* 205). Cf. further Beale 844–45; Bauckham 1299*b*–1300*a*.

It might be alleged that some of this argumentation is strained; yet the positive interpretation it offers, of a God who judges in order to redeem and deliver, should not easily be set aside. Moreover, while it may seem that this vision of the bowls in this scene (Rev. 16) has brought the judgemental work of God to a close, there is more of his salvific justice to be disclosed. As so often in the Apocalypse, the end is pressing in; but it has not yet arrived (see on 6.17).

Theology

The theology of this scene in Revelation (Chapter 16) is controlled by the crucial thought in verse 17. A divine voice from God's presence has declared that his salvation through judgement has become fully and finally active through the Christ-event; for the triumphant announcement that 'It is over!' includes the victorious Easter cry of 'It is finished!' (see on verse 17). The seven judgemental offering bowls, and all that flows from them (in Rev. 17—18 and beyond), must therefore be construed in the light of this eschatological backcloth of salvific discrimination. It is also important for the audience of this apocalyptic drama to understand that the sequence of bowls in this scene, like the earlier trumpet-plagues (Rev. 8—9; 11.15–18), on the principle of recapitulation, is describing proleptically the same end judgements from a different perspective; and, as always in the Apocalypse, the progression is theological and not chronological (cf. Talbert, *Apocalypse* 76–77). The justice mediated by the bowls, however, is more complete than that involved in the sounding of the trumpets.

The bowls of judgement in Scene 5 are not simply warnings that divine judgement is imminent. Like the Exodus plagues, they are sacramental of God's justice and mediate it; and, as in Egypt, they demonstrate that the unbelieving are punished because of their hardness of heart, expressed in idolatry (16.2), persistent failure to repent (16.9, 11, 21), and persecution of the faithful (16.6). However, these bowls also reveal God's uniqueness and omnipotence, and contain within them, as part of the new Exodus, the seeds of salvation and redemptive deliverance (see on verse 21); cf. Milligan 267. Heaven and earth, God's activity and human response, are close together throughout this scene; but it remains true that the first three bowls contain more directly 'natural' disasters, directed at the followers of the beast; whereas the last four are cosmic and 'supernatural' punishments, concerned with the demolition of the kingdom and city of the powers of Satan (see on verse 12); cf. Sweet 243.

The eschatological imagery of the earthquake and its effects, in Rev. 16 (verses 18–21), is also central to John's thought and theology at this point. The fall of the secular authorities, ranged against God and typified by 'Babylon', is described first in a violent earthquake (16.19), and then at the hands of the armies of the beast (Rev. 17—18). Similarly, instead of the final battle of Armageddon which the penultimate bowl-plague had led the audience to expect (16.16), an earthquake is placed centre stage. As Bauckham (*Climax of Prophecy* 209) points out, this imagery does not disclose all that John has to say about the end, except perhaps to indicate that severe judgement is included. What it does not reveal is that the advent of God which the earthquake heralds is to be a Christophany, the 'manifestation to the world of a Lamb who conquered on the cross (1.7; 19.11–16)' (ibid.).

The seven bowls of judgement together, and the final plague of seismic phenomena in particular, with 'the outpouring of the cup of God's furious wrath' (verse 19), anticipate the more detailed account of the fall of Babylon in the interval which follows (Rev. 17—18); cf. Mounce 292. With this vision, the drama of the Apocalypse might have come to an end (ibid. 305). But the consummation of God's purposes of judgement and love has not yet been achieved, and it will remain in the tension between the present and the future (see 22.20). Meanwhile, the living Christ still breaks in like a thief (16.15). Such an earthed warning, with its promise of hope, is a reminder for those in any age that John's Revelation is not intended to provide speculative information about the future, but to challenge its audience to fashion their faith and life in the present towards the coming eschatological reality (Boring 178).

The Fall of Babylon
(17.1—18.24)

Translation

17 [1]One of the seven angels who held the seven offering bowls came to speak with me, saying, 'Come, I will show you the verdict on the great whore, who is enthroned beside many waters. [2]The kings of the earth have committed fornication with her, and people the world over have become intoxicated with the wine which is her adultery.' [3]Then he carried me away in spirit into a wilderness; and I saw a woman mounted on a scarlet beast, which was covered with blasphemous names,[a] and which possessed seven heads and ten horns. [4]Now the woman was dressed in purple and scarlet, and she glittered with golden jewellery, precious stones and pearls. She held in her hand a gold cup filled with obscenities, that is, the foulness of her[b] sexual immorality. [5]On her forehead was written a title with a secret meaning: 'Babylon the great, the mother of whores[c] and of earth's obscenities.' [6]And I noticed that the woman was drunk with the blood[d] of the saints, even the blood of the witnesses to Jesus. When I saw her, I was completely mystified.

[7]But the angel said to me, 'Why are you perplexed? I will explain to you the secret meaning of the woman, and of the beast with the seven heads and ten horns which is carrying her. [8]The beast which you saw once existed, and now does not, and yet is about to ascend from the bottomless pit and go[e] to its destruction. The earth's inhabitants whose names have not been written in the book of life since the creation of the world will be amazed when they see the beast, because it once existed, now does not, and yet will come.[f] [9]This calls for discernment.

The seven heads are seven mountains, on which the woman is enthroned. They also represent seven rulers, [10]five of whom have already fallen. One is living now, and the other is yet to come; but when he does come, he must stay for only a short time. [11]As for the beast, that was once alive and is living no longer, this one[g] is an eighth ruler who belongs to the seven, and is headed for destruction. [12]And the ten horns which you saw are ten rulers, who have not yet received royal power; but they will receive authority as kings, together with the beast, for a moment. [13]They are of one mind in conferring their power and authority on the beast. [14]They will go to war against the Lamb; and the Lamb will conquer them, because he is Lord of lords and King of kings, and his followers are called and chosen and faithful.'

[15]And the angel continued, 'The waters in your vision, beside which the whore is seated, are peoples and multitudes, and nations and language groups. [16]But the beast and the ten horns which you saw will hate the whore, and make her desolate and naked; they will devour her flesh, and burn her remains with fire. [17]For God had put it into their hearts to carry out his purpose, by agreeing to surrender their authority to the beast until the words of God have been fulfilled.[h] [18]The woman in your vision is the great city, which has dominion over earthly rulers.'

18 [1]After this I saw another angel descending from heaven. He exercised great authority, and the earth was made bright with his glory. [2]He cried out with a mighty voice,[i] saying,

'Fallen, fallen is Babylon the great!
She has become the habitation of demons,
    a haunt for every evil spirit,
    and a preserve for all types of unclean and detestable bird and beast.[j]

[3]All the nations have drunk[k] deeply from the wine which is her passionate adultery;[l]
>   for the kings of the earth have fornicated with her,
>   and worldly merchants have become rich from her excessive wealth.'

[4]Then I heard another voice from heaven, saying,

> 'Come out,[m] my people, away from her,
>   so that you do not share in her sins,
>   or endure any of her plagues.
> [5]For her sins have reached up to heaven,
>   and God has remembered her misdeeds.
> [6]Render to her as she has given to others,
>   and repay her the equivalent of what she has done;
>   mix a double draught for her in the cup which she has mixed.
> [7]As she has glorified herself,[n] and lived luxuriously,
>   so give her a similar measure of torment and grief.
> For in her heart she says,
>   "I rule as a queen;
>   I am not a widow, and I will never experience mourning."
> [8]For this reason her plagues will arrive in a single day,
>   pestilence, and bereavement and famine;
>   and she will be burned with fire,
>   because the Lord God[o] who has judged her is powerful.'

[9]And the earthly rulers, who have fornicated and lived in luxury with her, will weep[p] and wail over her when they see the smoke from her burning. [10]They will stand far off, fearful of her torment, and say,

> 'Woe, woe to the great city,
>   Babylon, the mighty city!
>   For in a single moment[q] your reckoning has arrived.'

[11]And the merchants of the earth weep and mourn for her,[r] since no one buys their goods any more: [12]cargoes of gold, silver, precious stones and pearls, fine linen, purple, silk and scarlet material, every kind of citron wood, all articles made of ivory, all objects made of costly wood, bronze, iron and marble; [13]with cinnamon, spice, incense such as myrrh and frankincense, wine, oil, fine flour, wheat, beasts of burden and sheep, horses and carriages,[s] and slaves, that is, human beings.

> [14]"The ripe fruit for which your soul longed has failed you,
>   and all your luxuries and splendours are lost to you,
>   never to be found again!"[t]

[15]The traders in these wares, who had made a fortune out of her, will stand at a safe distance, fearful of her torment, weeping and mourning aloud, saying,

> [16]"Woe, woe to the great city,
>   clothed in fine linen, in purple and scarlet,
>   adorned with[u] gold, with precious stones and pearls!
> [17]For in a single moment such great wealth has been laid waste!'

And every shipmaster and all sea travellers,[v] sailors and those who make a living from the sea, stood far off, [18]and cried out, as they saw the smoke from her burning,

> 'Has there ever been a city as great as this?'

[19]And they threw dust on their heads and, weeping and mourning aloud, cried out saying,

'Woe, woe to the great city,
    where all who had ships at sea
    grew rich from her prosperity!
For in a single moment she has been made desolate.'

[20]'Rejoice over her, you heavens,
    the saints, apostles and prophets;
for God has given judgement against her for condemning you!'

[21]Then a strong angel picked up a boulder, resembling a huge millstone, and hurled it into the sea saying,

'That is how Babylon, the great city,
    will be violently overthrown,
    and will no longer exist;
[22]and the sound of harpists and musicians,
    and flautists and trumpeters,
    will never be heard in you again;
and an artisan of any trade[w] will be found in you no more,
    and the grinding of the mill will never be heard in you again;
[23]the light of the lamp will never shine in you again,
    nor will the voices of bridegroom and bride ever be heard in you again;
for your merchants were high-ranking people of the world,
    and indeed all the nations were deceived by your sorcery.
[24]And in her the blood of the prophets[x] and saints was to be found,
    and of all who have been slain on the earth.'

Text

[a] The *lectio originalis* appears to be γέμον ὀνόματα (*gemon onomata*, 'covered with [blasphemous] names' lit. 'full of names'), as read by Byz, et al. The chief variation, using the expected genitive (rather than the accusative) after the verb γέμω (*gemō*, 'fill'), γέμον ὀνομάτων (*gemon onomatōn*, 'full of names'), is attested by Andreas Hippolytus TR; but this is clearly a correction, intended to regularize the syntax of the sentence. The verb γέμειν (*gemein*, 'to fill') is used seven times in Revelation, almost always with the genitive of content (4.6, 8; 5.8; 15.7; 21.9), once with the accusative (17.3), and once with the genitive and an accusative (17.4). The accusative form may reflect a Hebraism (Aune 908). Several other versions of the text in 17.3 appear with the accusative, including the variation γέμοντα ὀνόματα (*gemonta onomata*, 'being full of names', a nominative neuter plural present participle, followed by the neuter plural accusative of the noun), as in A ℵ* 025 Oecumenius[2053]; cf. Swete 214–15; Charles 2, 338. NA has γέμον[τα] ὀνόματα (*gemon[ta] onomata*, '[being] full of names').

[b] The best-attested reading is πορνείας αὐτῆς (*porneias autēs*, lit. 'of her fornication'), as in A 1006 1611[2344] vg syr[ph], et al. The substitution of τῆς γῆς (*tēs gēs*, 'of the earth') for αὐτῆς (*autēs*, 'her'), according to 1611[1854, 2329] 2030 Oecumenius[2053] Byz it[gig] Hippolytus, et al., seems to be a copyist's error. The conflation, αὐτῆς καὶ τῆς γῆς (*autēs kai tēs gēs*, 'of her and the earth'), as read by ℵ (cop[sa,bo]), is clearly secondary. See further Metzger, *Textual Commentary* 756.

[c] The reading πορνῶν (*pornōn*, 'of [female] whores'), as given by NA, is doubtless original. But there is strong support for the variant, πόρνων (*pornōn*, 'of [male] prostitutes', from the masculine noun ὁ πόρνος, *ho pornos*, 'male prostitute'); see Aune 909. The further alternative reading, πορνειῶν (*porneiōn*, 'of fornications', Lat. *fornicationum*), attested by

vg Tyconius Primasius Beatus, is a secondary attempt to resolve the ambiguity introduced by an unaccentuated uncial script.

[d] A majority of MSS, including Andreas Hippolytus Byz TR, read ἐκ τοῦ αἵματος (*ek tou haimatos*, 'with [lit. from] the blood [of the saints]'). Some witnesses (such as ℵ[2] 046 025 94 Oecumenius[2053] 2030 Byz) have the simple genitive, τοῦ αἵματος (*tou haimatos*, lit. 'of the blood'), which is a correction influenced by classical Greek usage. A more radical alteration (by ℵ* some MSS of Andreas) is the substitution of the dative of instrument (τῷ αἵματι, *to[i] haimati*, 'with the blood') for the genitive; and this is more characteristic of Hellenistic Greek (cf. Eph. 5.18).

[e] The present indicative, ὑπάγει (*hypagei*, lit. 'he goes'), is attested by A 1611 Oecumenius[2053] Primasius, et al.; cf. Charles 2, 340. It is a *lectio difficilior*, since the verb μέλλει (*mellei*, 'is about to') would normally be followed by the infinitive (as it is with the preceding ἀναβαίνειν, *anabainein*, 'to ascend'). The reading with the infinitive, ὑπάγειν (*hypagein*, 'to go'), as in ℵ 025 046 051 1006 Andreas Byz, et al., should therefore be regarded as a subsequent correction. Metzger, *Textual Commentary* 756, points out that orthographically the difference in the two forms of the verb is minimal, since in Greek MSS a final -ν (*-n*) is often represented simply by a horizontal stroke over the preceding letter.

[f] The major witnesses (including A 025 94 1773 2019 Byz Hippolytus) read καὶ παρέσται (*kai parestai*, 'and yet will come', lit. 'and it will come'); and this is likely to be original. The variants, such as καὶ πάλιν παρέσται (*kai palin parestai*, 'and it will come again') in ℵ*, are clearly later textual emendations.

[g] The pronoun, αὐτός (*autos*, 'he [it]'), is read by A 025 vg Primasius, et al.; whereas ℵ 1006[1006,1841] 2030 Byz syr[h] have the demonstrative οὗτος (*houtos*, 'this one'). Although both pronouns are emphatic, and both are also solecisms, in that the nominative singular form modifies the neuter noun τὸ θηρίον (*to thērion*, 'the beast'), it could be argued that the demonstrative is original. Its MS support is reasonably strong; and the dismissive and slightly contemptuous tone conveyed by the reference to 'this one', who is on the way to destruction, suits the context exactly. The translation reflects this proposal.

[h] Instead of τελεσθήσονται (*telesthēsontai*, lit. 'they will have been fulfilled', third person plural future indicative passive, functioning as a subjunctive after ἄχρι, *achri*, 'until'), attested by the strong combination of ℵ A C 025 051 Oecumenius[2053,2062] 1611[1854] Hippolytus, et al.), some witnesses (including 1006 1611 2030 Byz) read τελεσθῶσιν (*telesthōsin*, 'they had been fulfilled', aorist subjunctive passive). The conjunction, ἄχρι (*achri*, 'until'), is normally followed by an aorist subjunctive (as in 2.25; 7.3; 15.8; 20.3, 5); but the MS evidence in favour of the indicative reading at this point is conclusive.

[i] The MS support for the reading, ἐν ἰσχυρᾷ φωνῇ (*en ischyra[i] phōnē[i]*, 'with [lit. "in"] a loud voice') is superior (so A 025 051 1006 1611 Oecumenius[2053], et al.). However, this expression often occurs in the Apocalypse without the preposition ἐν (*en*, 'in'), as at 5.12; 6.10; 7.2, 10; et al. (but see 5.2; 14.7, 9, 15); and this may account for its secondary absence in ℵ 046 2030, et al. Equally, the omission of the preposition may have arisen as an error of haplography, since the previous word (ἔκραξεν, *ekraxen*, 'he cried out') ends in -εν (*-en*); cf. Aune 965.

[j] For the complicated multiplicity of variant readings in verse 2 see Metzger, *Textual Commentary* 756–57. The major variation is the omission of the phrase, καὶ φυλακὴ παντὸς θηρίου ἀκαθάρτου (*kai phylakē pantos thēriou akathartou*, 'and a haunt [lit. prison] for every unclean beast'), from such witnesses as ℵ 051 vg cop[bo] Byz Andreas Beatus. It is present in A 1611[1611,2329] it[gig] cop[bo], et al. (so also NRSV, ESV, against REB, NJB). While

it is easier to account for the omission of the phrase, because of its similarity to the language of the surrounding text, than its insertion, all three strophes (referring to the preserves of spirits, birds and beasts), given the MS evidence, could have belonged to the original text of Revelation (Metzger, *Textual Commentary* 757; against Aune 965, who regards the phrase in question as a later addition). NA puts the Greek for 'a haunt for every unclean beast' in brackets; the translation in this commentary combines it with the preceding phrase, to give the rendering, 'all types of unclean (and detestable) bird *and beast*'.

k For the plethora of variant readings see Aune 965–66. They divide between those derived from πίπτειν (*piptein*, 'to fall'), from πίνειν (*pinein*, 'to drink'), or from ποτίζειν (*potizein*, 'to give to drink'). The versions, πέπτωκαν (*peptōkan*, 'they fell'), as in A C 69 2031, and πεπτώκασιν (*peptōkasin*, 'they fell / had fallen'), attested by א 046 1611 cop[sa,bo], et al., are well supported, but scarcely make sense in the context; they may have been influenced by the appearance of the verb ἔπεσεν (*epesen*, 'Fallen!') in verse 2. Metzger, *Textual Commentary* 758, adopts the reading πέπωκαν (*pepōkan*, 'they have drunk'), which is supported by 1611[2329] 1828 2321 syr[h] Byz, et al., and suits the thought of the passage.

l The reading which best explains the origin of its variants is τοῦ οἴνου τοῦ θυμοῦ τῆς πορνείας (*tou oinou tou thymou tēs porneias*, lit. 'of the wine of the passion of her adultery'), as attested by א 046 1006 94 1773 cop[bo] Andreas Byz, et al. The complexity of the expression, combined with scribal carelessness, resulted in such stylistic modifications as τοῦ θυμοῦ τοῦ οἴνου τῆς πορνείας (*tou thymou tou oinou tēs porneias*, lit. 'of the passion of the wine of her immorality'), as in 025 051 it[gig] cop[bo] arm Andreas Hippolytus, et al. See further Metzger, *Textual Commentary* 757.

m The command, ἐξέλθατε (*exelthate*, 'come out', second person plural aorist imperative), appears in A א Hippolytus (cf. Andreas). The second person singular aorist imperative with the same meaning, ἔξελθε (*exelthe*), is read by C 046 1611 2030, et al. The plural form is difficult in the context; but it is probably the result of the author treating the subject, ὁ λαός μου (*ho laos mou*, 'my people'), as a collective noun requiring a plural verb. In this case, the singular variant (although well supported) is most probably a later correction.

n The reading, αὐτήν (*autēn*, 'herself'), is strongly supported by א* A C 025 051. The variant, ἑαυτήν (*heautēn*, 'herself', uncontracted reflexive), as read by א[1] 1006 1611[1854] Andreas, et al., is probably secondary, as is the omission of αὐτήν (*autēn*, 'herself') altogether by 046. Swete (230) and Charles (2, 346), supported to some extent by Metzger, *Textual Commentary* 758, have the aspirated form of the reflexive, with the same meaning, αὑτήν (*hautēn*).

o The form, κύριος ὁ θεός (*kyrios ho theos*, 'the Lord God'), is well attested (א[c] C 025 046 051 1611[1854] Andreas Byz it[gig] syr[h] arm Cyprian, et al.), and is doubtless original. There are several variants. The reading, ὁ θεὸς ὁ κύριος, *ho theos ho kyrios*, lit. 'God the Lord' (א*), is an obvious error on the part of a copyist, since that word order occurs nowhere else in the Apocalypse; while the omission of κύριος (*kyrios*, 'Lord') after ἰσχυρός (*ischyros*, 'powerful', 'strong'), as in A 1006[1841] vg eth, et al., seems to be accidental. The insertion of ὁ παντοκράτωρ (*ho pantokratōr*, 'the Almighty'), by 2042 some MSS of Andreas, is a scribal accretion following texts such as 1.8; 4.8; 11.17; et al.

p Several witnesses (including C 025 046 1006 1611[1854] Andreas Byz) read κλαύσουσιν (*klausousin*, 'they will weep', third person plural future indicative); while other MSS (such as A א 1006 Oecumenius[2053] Hippolytus) have the future middle form, κλαύσονται (*klausontai*, lit. 'they will weep [for themselves]'). The latter appears to be a secondary correction of the unusual future active form of the verb (Aune 968).

[q] א C Byz Andreas have μιᾷ ὥρᾳ (*mia[i] hōra[i]*, 'in a single moment', lit. 'in one hour'). The appearance of the identical expression later in Rev. 18 (see verses 17, 19) suggests that this form of the text is original. A 1006 1611 Oecumenius[2053], et al., read μίαν ὥραν (*mian hōran*, lit. 'during one hour'); but this appears to be the later replacement of a dative of time by an accusative of time *length*. The further variant, ἐν μιᾷ ὥρᾳ (*en mia[i] hōra[i]*, lit. 'in one hour'), as in 1611[2329] 1773 TR MSS of Andreas, is a secondary amplification of the dative form (cf. Aune 968).

[r] The weight of external evidence (א C 025 1611 94, et al.) supports the reading, ἐπ' αὐτήν (*ep' autēn*, 'for her', lit. 'over her'). The variants are accidental or deliberate modifications of an earlier text. Hence, *inter alia*, ἐν αὐτῇ (*en autē[i]*, 'in her'), as in A 1611[2329]; ἐπ' αὐτῇ (*ep' autē[i]*, 'over her', with a dative of contiguity after the preposition), as read by 1006 Oecumenius[2053] 1773 Byz, et al.; and ἐφ' ἑαυτούς (*eph' heautous*, 'for themselves'), so Andreas.

[s] The *lectio originalis* appears to be ῥεδῶν (*hredōn*, '[of] carriages'), as in vg[ww]; and this is one genitive form of the Latin loanword ἡ ῥαίδη (*hē hraidē*, 'a horse-drawn carriage'). The normal and expected form, ῥαιδῶν (*hraidōn*, 'carriages'), is a later variant which is attested by a few MSS (including 1006 1611[2329]).

[t] The third person plural future indicative, οὐκέτι οὐ μὴ αὐτὰ εὑρήσουσιν (*ouketi ou mē auta heurēsousin*, 'never to be found again', lit. 'they will not find them again'), is attested by א A MSS of Andreas Byz Hippolytus. There are three significant, but secondary, variations, all of which replace the impersonal third person plural with the second person singular. Thus, 051 it[gig] Andreas Primasius Beatus read οὐ μὴ εὑρήσεις αὐτά (*ou mē heurēseis auta*, 'you will never find them'); MSS of Andreas TR have οὐ μὴ εὑρήσῃς αὐτά (*ou mē heurēsē[i]s auta*, 'that you have not found them', aorist subjunctive); and 1006[1841] 1611[1854, 2329] 2030 94 2019 Byz witness to the version, αὐτὰ οὐ μὴ εὕρῃς (*auta ou mē heurē[i]s*, 'you have not found them', second aorist subjunctive).

[u] Several witnesses (including א C 051 0229 1611 Andreas Hippolytus) include ἐν (*en*, lit. 'in') before χρυσίῳ (*chrysiō[i]*, 'gold'); while others (such as A 025 1006[1841] 1611[1854] 2030 Oecumenius[2053] Byz latt; cf. Charles 2, 349) omit the preposition. As Aune (970) suggests, the insertion of ἐν (*en*, 'in') as a correction is more likely than its deletion; although its deletion may have been an attempt to conform to the absence of the preposition before χρυσίῳ (*chrysiō[i]*, 'gold') at 17.4 (q.v.). NA puts the preposition in brackets.

[v] The reading, ὁ ἐπὶ τόπον πλέων (*ho epi topon pleōn*, 'all sea travellers', lit. 'the one who sails for any part') is strongly supported by A C 1006 1611[1854] it[61] vg, et al. (also א 046 0229, et al., which insert τόν [*ton*, 'the'] before τόπον [*topon*, lit. 'place']). This unusual expression (but see Acts 27.2) encouraged scribal alterations and interpretations. Thus, 025 051, et al. have ἐπὶ τῶν πλοίων πλέων (*epi tōn ploiōn pleōn*, lit. '[everyone] who sails in ships'); 469 582 2254 cop[bo] read ὁ ἐπὶ πόντον πλέων (*ho epi ponton pleōn*, 'the one who sails on the open sea'); syr[ph] has ὁ ἐπὶ τῶν πλοίων ἐπὶ τόπον πλέων (*ho epi tōn ploiōn epi topon pleōn*, 'the one who sails in ships on the high seas'); 2053 2062 witness to the reading, ὁ ἐπὶ τὸν ποταμὸν πλέων (*ho epi ton potamon pleōn*, 'the one who sails on the river'); and ἐπὶ τῶν πλοίων ὁ ὅμιλος (*epi tōn ploiōn ho homilos*, 'the whole throng [of those travelling] on ships') is attested by 1 296 2049 2186 Hippolytus TR. See further Metzger, *Textual Commentary* 759.

[w] The phrase, καὶ πᾶς τεχνίτης πάσης τέχνης (*kai pas technitēs pasēs technēs*, 'and an artisan of any trade'), is adequately supported by C 025 046 051 it[gig] vg syr[h] cop[sa], et al.; it is also in harmony with the seer's style. The omission of the words, πάσης τέχνης (*pasēs technēs*, lit. 'of every trade'), by א A cop[bo] is therefore probably accidental. The addition

in 2053 2138 of καί (*kai*, 'and') before πάσης (*pasēs*, lit. 'every') is doubtless a transcriptional error, influenced by the repeated occurrence of καί (*kai*, 'and') in the first part of verse 22.

ˣ The singular form of the expression, αἷμα προφητῶν (*haima prophētōn*, 'the blood of the prophets') is well attested by א A C Oecumenius²⁰⁵³ 94 2019, et al.; cf. Charles 2, 353. Some MSS (including 046 051 1611¹⁸⁵⁴ Andreas Byz) have the plural, αἵματα προφητῶν (*haimata prophētōn*, lit. 'bloods of the prophets'). The singular version is doubtless original. That reading is supported by superior external evidence; but, in addition, the variant does not accord with the style of the author, who regularly uses the term αἷμα (*haima*, 'blood') in the singular (cf. 1.5; 5.9; 6.10; 16.6; et al.).

Literary Setting

Chapters 17 and 18 of the Apocalypse jointly form an interval which is full of colour, intensity and dramatic interest. As so often in the literary structure of Revelation, the passage provides a commentary on the events of the preceding scene, and leads into the action of the section to follow (notably 19.1–10); cf. Rev. 15. These two chapters (Rev. 17—18) develop the theme of the judgement of Babylon which has been introduced by the pouring out of the sixth and seventh offering bowls by the angels (16.12–21). 'Babylon', in this context, may have a historical, first-century background, located in imperial powers such as Rome. But, more importantly, it is for John a symbol for every focus in any age of institutionalized, secular and unjust opposition to the cause of Christ (see on 14.8; 16.19; 17.1–3). Cf. Morris 198; Mounce 306; Duff, *Who Rides the Beast?* 84–96.

In terms of form and content, Rev. 17 and 18 are closely linked; and the earlier chapter prepares the way for the latter.

(a) The conquered beast of Rev. 17 (esp. verse 14) is related to fallen Babylon in Rev. 18.
(b) The judgement of Babylon, the 'great whore', is predicted in 17.1, 16, but delayed until Chapter 18 (cf. also 19.2), where it becomes the focus of John's literary and theological attention.
(c) There is a distinct parallelism in language and thought between 17.2 and 18.3. Both passages speak of the rulers of the nations being seduced by the 'woman's' superficial blandishments, which turn out to be the source of their own condemnation.
(d) The cognates, πορνεία (*porneia*, 'fornication') in 17.2, 4; 18.3 (cf. 2.21; 14.8; 19.2), and πορνεύειν (*porneuein*, 'to fornicate') in 17.2; 18.3, 9 (cf. 2.14, 20), act as catchwords around which the interval has been composed (cf. Aune 916).

In general terms, Rev. 17 depicts worldly and idolatrous, oppressive powers as a rich and self-indulgent prostitute, enthroned on a beast which ultimately turns on her and brings about her destruction; while Rev. 18 is mostly a threnody (a poetic song of lamentation), in which the fallen 'Babylon' is universally mourned by those who trusted in her falsehood (cf. Mounce 292). The interval as a whole promises an end to satanic injustice and wrongdoing, and the establishment of God's sovereign kingdom (see also 19.1–2, 6–8). Chapter 17 features the only vision in the Apocalypse paired with a detailed interpretation, although this is a common feature in Jewish apocalyptic literature (as in *2 Apoc. Bar.* 36.1—40.4; 53.1—76.5; et al.). Rev. 17 also includes the first narrative appearance in the Apocalypse of an 'interpreting' angel (17.7–18). See 1.1; 21.9—22.9; also above, 29.

The interval of Rev. 17—18 divides into seven sub-sections.

(a) An *Introduction* (17.1–2), which acts as a preface to the whole section. This consists of an invitation for the seer to witness the judgement of the great whore (verse 1) and her twofold indictment (verse 2).
(b) The *Vision* of the Woman, seated on the beast (17.3–6), which is made up of an introduction (verse 3*a*), detailing John's ecstasy; the vision itself (verses 3*b*–6*a*); and a conclusion, noting the reaction of the prophet-seer (verse 6*b*).
(c) The *Interpretation* of the vision (17.7–18), explicating the meaning of the 'woman, and the beast with the seven heads and ten horns'. This is set out in the reverse order, beginning with the beast (verse 8) and ending with the woman (verse 18). The 'beast' plays a subsidiary role in 17.3–6, but becomes the focus of verses 7–17. The allegorical meaning of each major feature in this vision is presented by the use of a stereotypical literary formula, which consists of the appropriate relative pronoun followed by the aorist verb, εἶδες (*eides*, 'you saw'), as in verses 8, 12, 15, 16, 18. The historic present tense of the verb in these contexts might have been expected, rather than the aorist, to make the action of the vision more dramatically immediate; but the very fact that the bowl-angel is interpreting a completed vision presupposes that he is commenting on what has already been disclosed in the past. On this section see Aune 915–17.

Rev. 18 continues the seer's apocalyptic vision at this point, and should be understood in spiritual and eschatological, rather than literal and chronological, terms. The chapter involves three speakers: 'another angel' (18.1–3); 'another voice' (verses 4–20), which relates events before (4–8) and after (9–20) the fall of Babylon; and a 'strong angel' who declares the final downfall of Babylon (verses 21–24).

The sub-divisions of the interval continue as follows.

(d) The *Threnody*, or ritual and poetic lament (18.1–3), which Aune (976) prefers to call a 'prophetic taunt song' (see also Mounce 322); and in formal terms this is an example of angelic speech (see above, 29–30; also the comments below).
(e) The *Summons to Flight* (18.4–8), which interrupts the threnody.
(f) The *Threnody* continued (18.9–20). These are verses carefully arranged to include three laments (without taunting): verses 9–10 (spoken by the rulers); verses 11–17*a* (the merchants); and verses 17*b*–19 (the shipmasters and sea travellers). Each of these subordinate threnodies involves four literary and formulaic elements.

    1 The groups stand at a distance (18.10, 15, 17);
    2 they are all described as 'weeping and mourning' over Babylon (verses 9, 11, 15);
    3 they begin their lament with a double 'woe' (verses 10, 16, 19); and
    4 they end with the expression, 'in a single moment', thus denoting the rapidity of Babylon's fall (verses 10, 17, 19). See further Aune 978–79.

    Rev. 18.20 forms a conclusion to the threnody of verses 9–19, and is a detached call by the voice from heaven (18.4), speaking through the seer, for the Church to rejoice in the judgement and salvation of God.

(g) The seventh and final sub-division in the interval of Rev. 17—18 consists of the ultimate *Destruction of Babylon* (18.21–24). This is a discrete literary text unit, again composed with care. It includes a typically Old Testament act of prophetic symbolism which, like the whole of Rev. 18, is heavily influenced by Jeremiah (see further the comments below). The angelic action of hurling a huge millstone into the sea (18.21*a*) is followed by an interpretation of that sacramental event (verses 21*b*–23); and, in the course of this explanation, the author uses five couplets which include the expression, 'will never be heard (found, seen) in you again'. The entire solemn pronouncement of 18.21–23, at the conclusion of the threnody in this chapter, ends with an angelic statement about Babylon's murderous past (verse 24); and this dictum, through the verb 'be found' (εὑρεθῆναι, *heurethēnai*), forms an inclusion with verse 21.

Aune (919–28) suggests that in Chapter 17 (esp. verses 3*b*–6*a*) John adapts the literary framework of *ekphrasis* ('description [of a work of art]'), a rhetorical form used in the first and second centuries AD, as a framework for his visionary imagery and its interpretation. This insight, although argued at length, does not greatly illuminate the setting and composition of this scene in Revelation, particularly as it refers chiefly to such a short passage. But it is relevant in one respect, since an important feature of the *ekphrasis*, as a narrative digression, is its *static* quality; and it is certainly true that the vision and its interpretation in Rev. 17 are related without movement, and so possess the character of a *tableau*. See esp. Aune 919; note the cautious reception given to this theory by Prigent (56, 90). For the literary and poetic feature in Rev. 18 of repeated sets of threes, see below.

Comment

Introduction (17.1–2)

17.1–2   The scene in Rev. 17—18 is prefaced by the appearance of one of the bowl-angels (cf. 15.1, 7–8), who offers to demonstrate to the seer the judgement on the 'great whore'. Both the sixth and seventh bowls in 16.12–21 foreshadow the downfall of Babylon (note esp. 16.12); but the final judgement in the bowl-sequence refers explicitly to the 'great city' (16.19), so it is likely that the angel of 17.1 is the seventh of 16.17. There are significant parallels between the invitation of the angel here and that of 'one of the seven angels' in 21.9, both of whom say to John, 'Come, I will show you'; and also between 17.3 (the angel 'carried me away in spirit') and 21.10 ('in spirit he carried me away'). The difference lies in the contrast between the subjects. Here it is the whore, seated on the beast; but in Chapter 21 the central character is the bride of Christ in the holy city.

The expression, the angel came 'to speak with me' (ἐλάλησεν μετ'ἐμοῦ, *elalēsen met' emou*, lit. 'he spoke with me'), is a Septuagintalism (cf. 1.12). For the phrase, 'Come, I will show you', in the context of the interpretation of mysteries, see *3 Apoc. Bar.* 2.6. In the sentence, 'I will show you the verdict on the whore' (τὸ κρίμα τῆς πόρνης, *to krima tēs pornēs*, lit. 'the judgement of the whore'), the genitive is objective; hence the translation.

The 'great whore' of verse 1 is identified at 17.5 and beyond as 'Babylon'. For the women in the Apocalypse see Duff, *Who Rides the Beast?* 83–96. However, the identity of the harlot-like Babylon is not immediately apparent to the modern reader, even if the use of the article with '*the* great whore' (ἡ πόρνη ἡ μεγάλη, *hē pornē hē megalē*) suggests that this figure was familiar to John's audience. (The article, now anaphoric, continues to be used later; cf. 17.5, 15, 16; 19.2.) 'Babylon' in the Apocalypse is not the apostate Church nor the world in the Church (so Milligan 289–96); nor is it Jezebel, Cleopatra or (as such) Rome (cf. Caird 212–13; Boxall, *Revelation* 39–42); and it is certainly not Jerusalem (Barker, *The Revelation* 279–301, esp. 279–84). For the prophet-seer, Babylon is in the first place called a prostitute; in other words, this is a symbol for that which 'allures, tempts, seduces and draws people away from God' (Hendriksen 167). The imagery of harlotry was commonly used by the prophets of the Old Testament to denote religious apostasy (cf. Isa. 1.21; Jer. 2.20–28; 13.27; Ezek. 16.15–41; Hos. 2.5). As Mounce (308) points out, the prostitute of the Apocalypse is likened to a 'great city'

(17.18); so that a more immediate background to the symbolism in Rev. 17.1 may be found in Isa. 23.16–17 (Tyre as the forgotten prostitute) and Nahum 3.4 (the whoring Nineveh). However, John's imagery has typically been transposed; for Rev. 17—18 deals not with religious profligacy, but with the prostitution of all that is right for the purposes of misused power. The great whore, Babylon, stands for the ultimately seductive expression of secular wrongdoing (cf. Mounce 308; also on 'Babylon', above). In Rev. 17—18 the focus of the symbol, but not its total significance, becomes that of the state, in its various alluring forms (see on verse 3). For the familiar, and more limited, interpretation see Brown, *Introduction* 793–94.

The harlot-like woman is 'enthroned beside' (καθημένης ἐπί, *kathēmenēs epi*, lit. 'sitting on') many waters. The verb, κάθημαι (*kathēmai*, 'sit, be seated'), is normally used in Revelation of God or Christ or the saints being 'seated' (cf. 4.2; 11.16; 14.14; et al.). It is possible that the author is applying the term to the whore as a deliberate irony. For, like the beast itself, she is attempting to usurp the place and authority of the Godhead; indeed, she imagines that she rules 'as a queen' (18.7). The preposition ἐπί (*epi*) is translated here as 'beside' (as it may be at John 6.19), since enthronement 'on' waters seems to be an impossibility, even for an apocalyptic vision. More importantly, the 'waters' with which the woman is closely associated speak of chaos. They are interpreted in 17.15 (q.v.) as the 'peoples and multitudes, and nations and language groups' which form the opposition to the righteousness of God. Cf. Ps. 144.7; Isa. 17.12–14; Jer. 47.2; by contrast, Ps. 29.10 depicts Yahweh as 'enthroned over the flood'.

Aune (920–23), following Rist (488–89) and others, tries to demonstrate that behind the image of the Babylonian harlot stands the goddess Roma (*Dea Roma*, the personification of the divine State). He does this on the basis of the sestertius, a Roman coin minted during the reign of the Emperor Vespasian (AD 69–79), which depicts on the reverse the goddess Roma in military dress, seated on the seven hills of Rome (see 17.9). The connection is, however, tenuous (so Beale 848). More directly, the condemnation of Babylon in 17.1 and beyond is part of God's answer to the prayer of the martyred faithful for vengeance in 6.9–10 (note the language, in that passage and 17.1–6, of judgement, death and witness). See also Jer. 51.11–13 (LXX 28.11–13); and cf. Beale 848.

The sexual promiscuity which in verse 2 is attributed to the 'great whore' of verse 1 is non-literal. The 'kings of the earth', who have been seduced by the superficial attractions of worldly powers (Babylon/Rome), represent kingdoms which have yielded their allegiance to Satan and his followers (cf. 16.14, 16). For the expression, 'the kings of the earth' (οἱ βασιλεῖς τῆς γῆς, *hoi basileis tēs gēs*), the interpretation of which in Revelation seems to be consistent, see 1.5; 6.15; 16.14; 17.18; 18.3, 9; 19.19; 21.24; see also on the 'ten kings' of 17.12. For the language of 'fornication' and 'adultery' in verse 2, see on verse 1; cf. also 18.3, 9; 19.2. Note further Isa. 23.17 (Tyre will 'prostitute herself with all the kingdoms of the world'); Hos. 4.11–12 ('my people have played the whore, forsaking their God'). The unfaithful relationships in question, between the secular powers and those who have been enticed into the idolatrous worship of the beast, are broadly based. They are best interpreted not in geographical or purely political terms, but with reference to illicit alliances of a social, economic and religious nature, both within and beyond the Johannine community, or the Church in any age. Cf. Aune 931; Mounce 309.

Not only have the rulers of the nations rebelled against God; 'people the world over' have also become 'intoxicated with the wine which is (Babylon's) adultery'. The genitive, τῆς πορνείας αὐτῆς (*tēs porneias autēs*, lit. 'of her fornication'), is epexegetic; hence the translation, '*which is* her adultery'. For the negative expression, 'people the world over' (οἱ κατοικοῦντες τὴν γῆν, *hoi katoikountes tēn gēn*, lit. 'the inhabitants of the earth'), describing those who are opposed to the cause of divine justice, see 3.10; 6.10; 8.13; 11.10; 13.8, 14; 17.8. Only here in Revelation does the phrase appear with the noun in the accusative, and without the preposition ἐπί (*epi*, lit. 'on'). In this passage, the metaphor of sexual proclivity (wrongful liaisons of all kinds) is combined with that of alcoholic intoxication to suggest the widespread and insidious influence which is exercised by the powers of evil. Cf. similarly 14.8; also 17.8. Although Satan's authority is short lived (12.12), his transient rule over the unfaithful is all-encompassing. See further Jer. 51.7 (LXX 28.7); *Pss. Sol.* 8.14; *Odes Sol.* 38.9–14.

Vision of the Woman and the Scarlet Beast (17.3–6)

3 The angel now carries the seer 'away in spirit into a wilderness'. This implies an ecstatic transportation, similar to Paul's experience in 2 Cor. 12.1–4; see also Hermas, *Vis.* 1.1.3; 2.1.1. Being 'carried away in spirit' also indicates that the vision which is to follow, and its significance, are divine in their origin and authority (cf. Ezek. 2.2; 3.12–15; 11.1; 43.5; et al.). Whenever in the Apocalypse John is carried away 'in spirit' (ἐν πνεύματι, *en pneumati*), as here and at 1.10; 4.2; 21.10, there is a deliberate ambiguity in that expression, for it combines the 'spirit' of the writer, who is involved in the ecstasy, with the 'Spirit' of God, who enables the action and informs its meaning. For a similar tension see John 4.23–24.

Beckwith (692) believes that, in the reference to John being caught away in spirit 'into a wilderness' (εἰς ἔρημον, *eis erēmon*), the setting has no particular significance. 'A solitary region was a fitting place for visions' (ibid.), in literature of this kind; so that, in Rev. 17.3, the wilderness is essentially a variation on other locations in Revelation where John receives visions: including earth (1.9–10), sea (10.8), heaven (4.1) and a mountaintop (21.9–10). However, the desert in the Old Testament is likely to provide an immediate background to this scene. There it is a place of testing, as in the Exodus wanderings (Exod. 15.22—16.36; Num. 11.1–35), and during the journey of Elijah (1 Kings 19.4–10); see also the temptations of Jesus in the wilderness (Mark 1.12 par.). In the prophets, and this is relevant to the present context of Revelation (17.3), places of desolation and destruction are also seen as appropriate settings for the doom of Babylon itself (cf. Isa. 13.19–21; 14.22–23; 21.1–10; Jer. 51.24–58). Elsewhere in Revelation, the wilderness is a place of refuge and protection (12.6, 14, q.v., with its counter-echo of the radiant woman); but in 17.3 these positive evocations are evidently mixed with those which are negative and judgemental, while also picking up the significance of the desert in Judaism. The seer is taken to a wilderness precisely to see the judgement on 'Babylon', even if that condemnation cannot be separated from the salvation which is still possible for every believer (19.7–8; note also the parallel and complementary vision of the alternative city of the new Jerusalem, as a result of the ecstasy of the seer, at 21.10). See further Sweet 254; Wall 206; Prigent 486–87.

For the visionary formula in Revelation, καὶ εἶδον (*kai eidon*, 'and I saw'), see on 5.1. Spiritual perception is an important part of John's apocalyptic drama. In this vision, the seer perceives 'a woman mounted on a scarlet beast'. The appearance and identity of the 'woman' (γυναῖκα, *gynaika*) will be elaborated in verses 4–6, 18; see also below. In verse 3 the noun is anarthrous; but clearly this is the 'great whore' (Babylon; cf. verse 5) of verse 1 (q.v.), a symbol of the secular and idolatrous authority which lures people away from God and his justice. The focus, but not the total meaning, of the 'great city' (verse 18) is located here in the state (see further on 14.8; 16.19). The woman is 'mounted' (καθημένην, *kathēmenēn*, lit 'seated') on a beast, just as she is 'enthroned' (using the same verb) beside many waters (verse 1). In both cases, there is an implicit irony; Babylon is a representation of the misuse of power, and of the wrongful desire to usurp the throne of God (4.2).

The reference to '*a* scarlet beast' is also anarthrous. But, once more, this image (without its associated colour) connects directly with the 'beast from the sea' in 13.1 (q.v.). As in Chapter 13, the beast of 17.3 is a symbol of the powers of evil which lie behind the kingdoms of this world, and encourage society in any age to compromise with the truth, and oppose the justice and mercy of God together with the righteousness of his people. As such, the beast acts as a demonic agent of Satan (13.2). The beast in 17.3 is also characterized by impious arrogance, denoted by the 'blasphemous names' (ὀνόματα βλασφημίας, *onomata blasphēmias*; the genitive is one of definition) with which it is covered. These refer to the beast's self-deification and its false claims to be a universal ruler (see 13.1), although such can only be true of God and his Christ (17.14; 19.16). In the present verse the beast is also said to possess 'seven heads and ten horns', the background to which must be located in Dan. 7, and allude to the powers exercised by evil kingdoms in their oppression of the faithful. See further on 12.3; 13.1–2; cf. also 17.9–14, 16–17.

Both the woman and the beast are associated with the colour 'red (scarlet)' (κόκκινος, *kokkinos*; the term is used in Revelation only in Chapters 17—18); see also verse 4. Mounce (310) sees this merely as a way of heightening the terrifying appearance of the beast; but the seer's imagery is likely to be much subtler in its significance. The 'scarlet' colour of the beast refers not to its skin but to a piece of dyed material covering it (Prigent 487). Since red was an expensive pigment, used to dye expensive textiles, the colour of the beast may represent luxurious voluptuousness (Roloff 197). Among the prophets, ostentatious luxury often accompanies human pretension (Isa. 1.18; Jer. 4.30); so that 'scarlet', in this passage, may be a further symbol of worldly arrogance. However, as Beale (853) points out, there is a more obvious interpretation which may be given to the fact that both the beast and the woman in 17.3 are scarlet coloured. 'Red' is also the colour of the 'dragon' in 12.3, and this means that the devil and his agents are presented in the attire of royalty (cf. Matt. 27.28). Both the woman and the beast are supremely pretentious in their idolatrous claims to a kingship which usurps that of God himself. Beale (853) also notes that 'scarlet' suggests the work which both undertake in their persecution of the Christian Church. Contrast the messianic armies, led by the Logos into the final battle against the forces of Satan, who are dressed in 'white' linen, and are mounted on 'white' horses (19.14; cf. Prigent 487). In *Sib. Or.* 8.88 the dragon who 'comes on the waves', probably Nero *redivivus*, is described as being dressed in the royal colour of purple (cf. Mark 15.17–20).

The woman in verse 3 is closely associated with the beast ('mounted' on it), but not equated with it. The distinction is a fine one; but the view adopted in this commentary is that 'Babylon' in the Apocalypse represents the allurement offered by demonic forces in drawing people away from Christian values. This finds a focus in imperial structures (the 'city'; but contrast 21.2, 10), with their anti-Christian pretensions. The beast, in contrast, is that part of the ungodly world which is prepared to submit to the superficial attraction of satanic institutions (Babylon/Rome), with their unrighteous religious, economic and social aspects. (The interpretation of this image in Beale [853] seems to be the reverse.) But, ultimately, 'Babylon' is more than a city; she stands for any organized power group which denies freedom to the individual, and tries to seduce secular society, already rebelling against God, into further doom-laden acts of impious, unjust oppression and wickedness. See further Maurice 252–57 (Babylon is 'idolatry organized into a system', 255); Duff, *Who Rides the Beast?* 62–70, esp. 70 (Babylon is the equivalent of compromising commercialism; note the 'merchants' of Rev. 18). For the reception history of 'Babylon' in Christian tradition see Boxall, 'Many Faces'.

4–5 In his vision, John sees the woman as 'dressed in purple and scarlet'. For the identity of the 'woman' see on verses 1–3, and esp. verse 3. 'Babylon' represents the institutional structures of the secular state, and especially (in the present context) those commercial and economic attractions which seek to draw the demonic forces belonging to society into further idolatrous rebellion against God. This interpretation is supported by the descriptions which follow of the woman's clothing and adornment, and of the golden cup which she holds in her hand.

The colours of the woman's attire, purple and scarlet, do not simply suggest imperial luxury and splendour (cf. Mounce 310), particularly because 'Rome' does not entirely exhaust the meaning of 'Babylon' (17.5; and see above). 'Scarlet' was a colour of magnificence (Nahum 2.3); but, like purple, it also had royal associations (Judg. 8.26; Dan. 5.7; 1 Macc. 10.20; see further on verse 3). As earlier, therefore, the imagery of the 'red' raiment of the great whore ironically indicates her false pretensions to sovereign rule, and her attempted usurpation of the kingship of Christ (see also 17.18; 18.7). 'Red' also speaks in verse 4 of the persecuting activity of the state (cf. 17.6; 18.24), and possibly in addition of the status acquired by wealth (Prov. 31.21–22). 'Purple' (πορφυροῦς, porphyrous), according to Aune (934–35), denotes in antiquity a spectrum of colours, ranging from red to purple to black.

Above all, in the present passage, the woman's adornment symbolizes the prosperous trade of any worldly system; for the language in 17.4, including 'golden jewellery, precious stones and pearls', is reproduced in 18.16 with reference to the clothing of the 'great city', and in 18.12–14 in a list of trade products. Cf. Beale 854. The gaudy appearance of the scarlet woman directly evokes the seductiveness of the harlot Israel (Jer. 4.30; cf. Isa. 1.15–22; Jer. 2.34; Ezek. 16.8–15), and speaks now of a false and rebellious glory (cf. Knight 115). Contrast the image of the great whore (17.1–4), clothed in 'fine linen' (18.16), with that of the bride of the Lamb, who is depicted as a city adorned with 'gold, jewels and pearls' (21.2, 18–21), and clothed in 'pure linen' (19.8). Cf. also the contrast between the scarlet whore of Rev. 17 and the radiant 'woman' of Chapter 12 (q.v.).

When the writer says in verse 4 that the harlot 'glittered with golden jewellery' (κεχρυσωμένη χρυσίῳ, kechrysōmenē chrysiō[i], a pleonasm lit. meaning 'gilded with gold'), this does not mean that she gilded her body (so Swete 216). As the beast is attired in red material (verse 3), so the woman is adorned with gold, as well as other jewels. The nouns which follow (καὶ λίθῳ τιμίῳ καὶ μαργαρίταις, kai lithō[i] timiō[i] kai margaritais, lit. 'and [she glittered with] precious stone and pearls') make this clear. Cf. Ezek. 28.13; 1 Tim. 2.9. In any case, the woman looks the part. This is a 'meretricious display which proclaims her vile trade' (Swete, ibid.).

For the imagery and thought in the last sentence of verse 4 see verse 2; also 14.8; 17.16. The woman holds in her hand a gold cup, which implies that she will blind her subjects not only to her own evil nature but also to the goodness and justice of God. She is dangerous as Circe, the bewitching figure of Greek mythology. An immediate Old Testament background to the 'woman' of verse 4 may be found in Jer. 51.7–9. But there, instead of the woman holding a gold cup, Babylon herself is described as 'a golden cup in the Lord's hand, making all the earth drunken' (Jer. 51.7; LXX 28.7). The whore's cup in Rev. 17.4 promises carnal satisfaction; however, it turns out to be 'filled with obscenities (βδελυγμάτων, bdelygmatōn, lit. "loathsome things")', that is (the καί, kai, lit. 'and', is epexegetic), the foulness (ἀκάθαρτα, akatharta, lit. 'unclean things') of her sexual immorality (τῆς πορνείας αὐτῆς, tēs porneias autēs, lit. 'of her fornication'). All three parts to the contents of the harlot's cup relate to the intoxicating influence which Babylon possesses, in order to deceive her followers into idolatry. The term, βδέλυγμα (bdelygma, 'abomination'), is often used in the LXX with reference to idolatry or idolatrous sacrifice (cf. LXX Lev. 11.10–12; 18.22; Deut. 12.31; Isa. 1.13; Jer. 13.27; Dan. 9.27; et al.; cf. Dan. 12.11 = Mark 13.14). The adjective, ἀκάθαρτος (akathartos, 'unclean'), appears in the Apocalypse in association with demonic and deceptive 'unclean' spirits, which lie behind idols (cf. 16.13–14; 18.2; also 21.27; 1 Thess. 2.3). Equally the noun, πορνεία (*porneia*, 'fornication'), with its cognate verb, are figurative expressions for idolatry elsewhere in Revelation (2.14, 20–21; cf. 9.21). The blandishments of Babylon are designed to tempt the unfaithful into further idolatry, leading to institutional, economic corruption, immorality and disaster (3.17–18; 13.16–17). See further Mounce 310–11; Beale 855–56.

The verb, γέμω (*gemō*, 'fill'), is normally followed by a genitive of content ('filled with . . .'). Here, the writer uses first a genitive (βδελυγμάτων, *bdelygmatōn*, 'obscenities'), which in the Greek is idiomatic, and then an accusative (τὰ ἀκάθαρτα, *ta akatharta*, lit. 'uncleannesses'), which is a Hebraic construction (Aune 909). For a challenge to the androcentric bias embedded in the picture of the whore in Rev. 17, as she perceives it, see Kim, '"Uncovering Her Wickedness"'.

The nature of the harlot Babylon, depicted in verses 1–4, is further revealed by the title (ὄνομα, *onoma*, lit. 'name') written on her forehead (verse 5). In Revelation, if names are written, or a seal is placed, on the forehead, this reveals the true character of those who bear these marks, as well as their relationship to God (7.3; 14.1; 22.4) or Satan (13.16; 14.9; 20.4); cf. Beale 857. So the woman's 'title' discloses her character as both idolatrous and seductive, and indicates once more her close alliance with the beast (verse 3). Although the evidence is not entirely secure, it is possible that the idea of a 'title on the forehead' reflects the practice of prostitutes in Rome, who wore bands across their foreheads with their names written on them (cf. Seneca, *Cont.* 1.2.7; also Juvenal, *Sat.* 6.123). Contrast the names on the foreheads of the faithful, who see the Lord's face in the heavenly city (22.4).

It is not immediately clear whether the word μυστήριον (*mystērion*, lit. 'mystery') should be taken with 'Babylon', as part of the title ('Mystery, Babylon'; so AV, NIV), or as the introduction to it ('a title with a secret meaning', as in the translation; see also NRSV, ESV). It is no doubt better to understand the term 'mystery' here in the sense in which it is used of the harlot and the beast in verse 7 (q.v.): the name of the woman has a secret and mystical, rather than literal, connotation, which needs to be explained. This conclusion is supported by the LXX background to this passage, in Dan. 4.9 (Theod.), where King Nebuchadrezzar tells Daniel the 'mystery' (μυστήριον, *mystērion*) of the dream concerning his pride and coming judgement (4.10–33). In Rev. 17.5 the word 'mystery' includes an eschatological dimension, which also belongs to the other three uses of the Greek term in the Apocalypse (1.20; 17.7; 19.7); for the rare similar use of μυστήριον (*mystērion*, 'mystery') in the LXX see Dan. 2.18–47.

The 'mystery' of the woman and the beast (Rev. 17.7) is explained by the angel in verses 8–18. 'Babylon' represents satanic institutions throughout history which have espoused corrupt religious, moral and economic values. Ultimately these will be destroyed (Chapter 18), and God's sovereignty will be established (19—22). In 17.5 the woman's title is given as 'Babylon the great'; and in Revelation this adjective, 'great' (μεγάλη, *megalē*), is always attached to the city (14.8; 16.19; 17.5; 18.2, 10, 21). The description alludes to Dan. 4.30 (LXX and English versions; 4.27 MT). As the material Babylon reflected the mighty power and glorious majesty of the King, and the self-centred praise for which he was eventually condemned (4.33), so the metaphorical city will unquestionably be judged for its pride and wrongdoing. These are end-time events. But the unveiling of the mystery in the present context also involves the unexpected way in which the kingdom of evil will disintegrate and be defeated (see further on 17.8–17); cf. Beale 858.

The title which John perceives on the forehead of the woman is a 'placard' written from his point of view (Thompson 160). It describes Babylon the great as 'the mother of whores (τῶν πορνῶν, *tōn pornōn*) and of earth's obscenities (τῶν βδελυγμάτων, *tōn bdelygmatōn*)'; and, according to verse 4 (q.v.), these were the two ingredients of her alluring cup of gold. The phrase, 'mother of whores', may be a figurative way of saying that 'Babylon' is the archetype of further disasters to come, or that she is a superlative example of sexual immorality, and 'the most depraved whore' there is (so Aune 937; for Rome and its leaders as a city where horrible and shameful activities of the world 'collect and find a vogue' see Tacitus, *Ann.* 11.12, 26; 15.44; cf. also Juvenal, *Sat.* 10.329–45). But it is much more likely to be a metaphorical reference to false Babylon's progeny, in stark contrast to the descendants of the faithful woman (Rev. 12) and the pure bride of Christ (Chapter 21). The Babylonian whore produces ungodly children, while the 'mother' of Rev. 12 gives birth to faithful offspring. Babylon represents powers and institutions throughout the ages which are demonic and deceitful; whereas the figure of the bride (19.7; 21.2) embodies the Church at every moment of history, and beyond. The woman robed with the sun (Rev. 12.1) gives birth to Christ and his witnesses; while the harlot of Chapter 17, proudly clad in the raiment of worldly magnificence, tries to destroy the Christian community (17.14; cf. 12.15, 17). See further Kiddle 343–44; Beale 858–59. Prigent (489) is cautious about the antithetical parallelism in these contrasts.

6   The seer noticed that the Babylonian woman was 'drunk with the blood of the saints'. For the visionary formula, 'then I noticed' (καὶ εἶδον, *kai eidon*, lit. 'and I saw'), see on verse 3; also 5.1; et al. Evidently persecution of the faithful remains part of the demonic activity of secular powers, and those who follow the beast. For the imagery of being 'drunk with blood' see 17.2; 18.24; 19.2; but the exact expression, 'drunk with blood', occurs only here in Revelation. There is a possible classical background in Suetonius, *Tiber.* 59.1; Pliny, *Nat. Hist.* 14.28.148; but a more direct source in Judaism may be found (e.g.) in Isa. 34.5–7; 49.26; Jer. 46.10; Ezek. 39.18–19.

For the connection between blood and wine see on 14.20. To say that the woman was drunk with the blood of the saints may suggest a shift in the meaning of the cup metaphor. She who held a cup full of abominations and immorality (verse 4), is now herself intoxicated, by the wine of her murdered opponents (so Aune 938). But equally, and more probably, the sense is more straightforward. The harlot's cup of gold was full of idolatrous 'obscenities' (verse 4); and these included a deliberate and impious persecution of the faithful witnesses, leading to martyrdom. That the woman was intoxicated as a result may imply the particular delight taken in such harassment by institutional and unjust power bases. The death of the followers of Jesus becomes, in this case, an extreme and triumphant expression of godlessness (cf. Roloff 197), even if this is not the sole prerogative of the Roman authorities (Prigent 490). See further 6.4, 9–11; 12.11; 16.6.

The persecuted and martyred 'witnesses to Jesus', in the next part of verse 6, do not form a separate group from the faithful people of God (for 'saints' see on 5.8; 8.3–4; 11.18; 13.7, 10; 14.12; 16.6; 18.20, 24; 19.8; 20.9; 22.21). The connective καί (*kai*, 'and') here is epexegetic; hence the translation, 'even the blood of the witnesses'. These are witnesses *to* Jesus, taking the genitive ('Ιησοῦ, *Iēsou*, lit. 'of Jesus') as objective. But the genitive case in this context may be, or may also be, one of possession: Christ's followers are also his witnesses, in the sense that they share the testimony which he bears to the Father (cf. 1.2; 6.9; 12.17; 20.4). The saints, in the present context, are those whose expressed Christian faith has led to martyrdom; they are μάρτυρες (*martyres*, 'witnesses', lit. 'martyrs') indeed. See further Sweet 205, 289.

As a result of his vision of the Babylonian woman, the prophet-seer is 'completely mystified' (καὶ ἐθαύμασα . . . θαῦμα μέγα, *kai ethaumasa . . . thauma mega*, a pleonasm meaning lit. 'and I wondered a great wonder'; the accusative is cognate). The verb, θαυμάζω (*thaumazō*, lit. 'wonder', 'be amazed'), as it is used here and in verse 7, includes a number of overtones. The basic sense is 'astonished perplexity', as at Mark 12.17; Matt. 27.14; Luke 4.22; John 3.7; Acts 2.7; et al.; and, in the present context, the term may include reactions of fear, surprise (Swete 218) and curiosity (picking up the word μυστήριον, *mystērion*, 'mystery', in connection with the woman's title, at verse 5). John marvels that such wickedness as 'Babylon' embodies is allowed by God to exist (Kiddle 344), and is anxious to learn more about the woman's character and fate. Prigent (490) regards the use of the word, θαυμάζειν (*thaumazein*, 'to wonder'), in this context as very Johannine, since it carries the meaning of discerning the truth behind a person or saying with a baffling appearance (cf. John 3.7; 5.28; 1 John 3.13).

Caird (213–14) and Wilcock (160), followed by Beale (861–63), interpret the idea of 'wondering' in verses 6 and 7 to suggest that John was not merely 'mystified' by the vision of the harlot, but also attracted by her in some way; see further Michaels (194); BDAG 444b. Such is the meaning of the verb in verse 8 (cf. 13.3–4), but not here. The possibility that John has to 'steel himself against the intoxicating draughts of the golden cup' held by the Babylonian woman (Caird 214) is ruled out on four counts.

(a) The writer has already been informed that he is to witness 'the verdict' on the great whore (17.1).
(b) The portrait of the woman in verses 2–6 makes it clear that the verdict in question is one of negative judgement, such are her associations with the beast, her seductive appearance, the obscene and immoral contents of her cup of temptation, and her disposition towards the murder of the saints.
(c) The seer's reaction of 'worship' in the presence of an angel (19.10; 22.8) provides no parallel (Beale 862–63), since the figures in those contexts are angelic and good, not demonic and evil.
(d) To propose that John would have been in any way drawn to the prostitute in Rev. 17.1–6 runs counter to everything for which the prophet-seer stood, as a faithful Christian witness, and as a follower of the Lamb and not of the beast.

The Interpretation of the Vision (17.7–18)

7 The seventh angel asks the prophet-seer why he is 'perplexed' (διὰ τί ἐθαύμασας, *dia ti ethaumasas*, lit. 'why did you wonder?'); for the verb see on verse 6. The question is not to be understood as a rebuke, but as an introduction to the following interpretation of the vision. In the Apocalypse, John never asks for the explanation of a mystery; even if, as here, the meaning is volunteered by a supernatural revealer (also 1.20; 7.13–14), or provided by the writer himself (4.5; 11.4; 20.14; et al.). See Aune 919.

For dream-visions and their interpretation in the Old Testament see Gen. 37.2–11 (Joseph); 40.5—41.36 (the officers of Pharaoh, and the Pharaoh himself, revealed by Joseph); Dan. 4.5–27 (King Nebuchadrezzar, interpreted by Daniel). For the 'secret meaning' (μυστήριον, *mystērion*, lit. 'mystery') of the woman and the beast, for which the angel offers an explanation, see on verse 6; and for the 'seven heads and ten horns' of the beast carrying the woman, together with the relationship between those two figures, see on verse 3 (also verses 1–2, and below). The interpreter explains, in the remainder of Chapter 17, one vision, the content of which is set out in verses 3–6. But it consists of two parts, with their subdivisions, and concerns the woman and the beast. In verse 7 the angel promises to disclose the meaning of the two main characters, beginning with the woman; but in verses 8–18 he reverses the order, and deals with the beast (verse 8), the heads (9–11) and horns (12–17) of the beast, and finally the woman (18). See above; also Prigent 490–91. In the end, the angelic interpretation gives greater prominence to the beast than to the harlot.

8   The interpretation, following the vision (verses 3–6), begins. The seer has been promised an explanation of the 'secret meaning' behind the woman and the beast (verse 7); but that order is reversed by the angel in his commentary (verses 8–18), and the identity of the beast, as such, is not disclosed (but see verses 8 and 11; also 13.1–2). Attention is given rather to the symbolic meaning of the creature's heads (verses 9–10) and horns (verse 12). For it is necessary to understand the nature and background of the satanic camp, which has been introduced earlier (Chapters 12—13), in order to appreciate further the relationship to it of 'Babylon' and her followers (cf. Prigent 491).

The phrase, ὃ εἶδες (ho eides, 'which you saw'), is a stereotyped literary expression used five times in this section of Rev. 17 (verses 8, 12, 15, 16, 18). The aorist tense of the verb 'to see' makes it clear that the vision is no longer in progress (cf. Aune 939). Just as there is a deliberate contrast between the scarlet and secular whore of Rev. 17, and the representatives of the Christian community in the radiant woman of Rev. 12 and the bride of Chapter 21, so there is a careful irony in the description of the beast in 17.8 (cf. verse 11). The threefold ascription, 'once existed, now does not, is about to ascend/yet will come', which is repeated at the end of verse 8, parodies the attributes applied to the Godhead ('who is, who was, who is to come') in 1.4, 8; 4.8; 11.17; 16.5; although a negative (καὶ οὐκ ἔστιν, kai ouk estin, 'and now does not [exist]', lit. 'and is not') features in the second statement about the beast. Similarly, the claim that the embodiment of impious and unjust power is 'about to ascend' from the bottomless pit (see 11.7) is clearly a caricature of the death and resurrection of Christ (as in 11.17; cf. 1.18; 2.8; 5.12–13).

For the concept of ascension 'from the bottomless pit' (ἐκ τῆς ἀβύσσου, ek tēs abyssou, lit. 'from the abyss') see on 9.1–2; also 9.11; 11.7; 20.1, 3. The last part of the formula in verse 8, which describes the beast as 'about to ascend from the bottomless pit and go (ὑπάγει, hypagei, lit. "goes", futuristic present) to its destruction', provides an ironic contrast with the divine activity celebrated in the hymn at 11.17, 'now you have assumed your full authority, and entered upon your reign' (cf. 16.5). The eschatological coming of God in Christ results in victory, and judgement on the unfaithful; but the attempt by the beast to assume authority, which rests on a false claim to sovereignty, ends in defeat and its own judgement. For going 'to destruction' (εἰς ἀπώλειαν, eis apōleian) see 9.11 (the angel of the abyss is known as 'Abaddon' ['Destruction'] and 'Apollyon' ['Destroyer']). The idea of 'ascending to be destroyed' reflects Dan. 7.3–26, where the beast of the end-time is depicted as rising on the stage of history, only to be destroyed (verses 3, 11, 26); and in Daniel there is a parallel and ironic contrast between the beast and the Son of man (7.13–14). Cf. Beale 864–65.

When the threefold formula, mocking the pretentious character of the beast, is repeated at the end of verse 8, the last statement is altered from 'yet is about to ascend' to 'yet will come' (καὶ παρέσται, kai parestai, lit. 'and will come'). This is a further and ironic contrast with the 'coming' of Christ at his parousia, promised throughout the Apocalypse ('I am coming', ἔρχομαι, erchomai; cf. 2.5, 16; 3.3, 11; 16.15; 22.7, 12, 20); see Bauckham, Climax of Prophecy 435. The 'advent' of the beast is a feature of salvation history, since the powers of evil are real and indeed fearful (Beasley-Murray 255–56). But the exercise of Satan's authority is also short-lived (12.12; 17.10; 20.1–10); for while demonic agencies and institutions seek to assert their rule throughout history, they will always fail in the end. The kingship of God in his Messiah must prevail in eternity; while the demonic forces of evil (typified by the beast and the woman), consistently opposed to God and all that is just and good, will be revealed in their true light. Cf. Mounce 314.

The inhabitants of the earth, according to the angel, 'will be amazed when they see the beast'. The phrase, οἱ κατοικοῦντες ἐπὶ τῆς γῆς (hoi katoikountes epi tēs gēs, lit. 'those dwelling on the earth'), is often used in the Apocalypse as a literary formula to describe the representatives of the pagan and idolatrous world, who are antagonistic towards God (see also 3.10; 6.10; 8.13; 11.10; 13.8, 12, 14; 17.2). The verb, θαυμασθήσονται (*thaumasthēsontai*, lit. 'they will be amazed'), is in the future tense because the angel is referring to the vision of 17.3–6 as a static tableau which can be viewed, rather than as a narrative description of events in progress. In the present context of verse 8, θαυμάζω (*thaumazō*, 'wonder') implies admiration, rather than (as in verses 6–7, q.v.), astonished perplexity. Indeed, the sense may include worship, since this is the reaction of 'the whole world' to the beast at 13.3 (the only other occurrence of the verb in Revelation); cf. 13.4, 8, 12, 15; 14.9, 11; 16.2; 19.20; 20.4. The secular community is fascinated by a power which will ultimately destroy its members (Wall 207).

The present participle in the genitive plural, βλεπόντων (*blepontōn*, lit. 'seeing'), is difficult, unless it may be understood as an error influenced by the earlier relative pronoun in the genitive, ὧν (*hōn*, lit. 'of whom'); for the subject ('the earth's inhabitants') is in the nominative. However, it is more naturally construed as an absolute genitive, with αὐτῶν (*autōn*, lit. '[of] themselves') being understood (Aune 910). For the ironic formula describing the beast, repeated from the first part of verse 8, see above.

The qualifying phrase, 'whose names have not been written in the book of life since the creation of the world', is repeated from 13.8 (q.v.); see also 3.5; 20.12; 21.27. In 13.8 the formula, to which is added a reference to the 'book' (βιβλίον, *biblion*, as here) as being that of 'the Lamb', further describes the security and protection of the faithful set out in the 'sealing' episode of Chapter 7. As in 17.8, the assurance and preservation of the saints in Christ contrasts markedly with the status and character of the beast, whose deceit and impiety are alluring but short-lived. This Christian security has been available 'since the creation of the world'; but the future of the believer can never be determined apart from human free will. Beale (866) finds a background to this imagery of the protective 'book' of life in Dan. 7.10; 12.1–2; Ps. 69.29.

9–11 The 'call for discernment' at the beginning of verse 9 refers to the riddle of the beast set out in verse 8, rather than to the section of allegorical interpretation which is to follow (verses 9–14). For the phrase itself, ὧδε ὁ νοῦς ὁ ἔχων σοφίαν (*hōde ho nous ho echōn sophian*, lit. 'here [is] the mind having wisdom'), see 13.8 (also Mark 13.14). 'Wisdom' is needed, to prevent the faithful from being deceived by the beast, which may tempt them to submit to its false powers. For the 'biography' of the beast, which is the symbol of all secular rebellion against God, see Aune 941–44.

The 'seven heads' of the beast (see verse 7) are interpreted in two ways: as seven 'mountains' and as seven 'rulers'. The apparently obvious reference of ἑπτὰ ὄρη (*hepta orē*, lit. 'seven hills') is to Rome itself, since classical writers from the mid-first century BC onwards used the phrase 'seven hills' as a symbol for the city (cf. also *Sib. Or.* 2.18; 13.45; 14.108; see Aune 944–45). This is the meaning adopted by several commentators, including Swete (220), Beckwith (707–708), Kiddle (349–51), Caird (216–19), Boring (183–84) and Prigent (492). But, even if the Roman Empire lies behind this image, as the focus of power which is misused, it does not exhaust its meaning. As Beale (868) points out, while ὄρος (*oros*) can mean 'hill', elsewhere in Revelation it always means 'mountain', and is then used as a figure for 'strength' (6.14–16; 8.8; 14.1; 16.20; 21.10). In Jewish literature, moreover, mountains symbolize 'kingdoms' (Isa. 2.2; Jer. 51.25; Ezek. 35.3; Dan. 2.35; *1 Enoch* 52.1–7); and this is the significance of the term in Rev. 8.8; 14.1 (see also Dan. 7.3–7, where the four beasts, or kingdoms, have between them *seven* heads). 'Seven', in the present context (17.9), is not a literal number, nor is it a symbol for the total number of Roman Emperors (e.g. Kiddle 350); it is rather an expression of the quality of completeness (Beale 869), as normatively in the Johannine literature. The 'seven mountains', represented by the 'seven heads' of the beast, like the 'rulers' later in this verse (and verse 10), are therefore best understood as a picture of oppressive, secular government in its totality and at any period of world history, which seeks to challenge the sovereignty of God (cf. 12.3; 13.1–2).

The fact that the woman is 'enthroned' (κάθηται, *kathētai*, lit. 'sits') on the 'mountains' or 'heads' associated with the beast means that 'Babylon', standing for the seductive and demonic forces of the secular state (see on verse 1), is – as always – closely allied with the (limited) powers of Satan (cf. verse 3).

The seven heads of the beast are also interpreted as 'seven rulers'; and their identity is explained in the following two verses (10–11). Two major approaches to the obscure description of the 'rulers' (βασιλεῖς, *basileis*, lit. 'kings') have been adopted in the past.

(a) *Historical.* This solution seeks to align the kings in verses 9–11 with particular first-century AD Roman Emperors, and on that basis to suggest a date for the origin of the Apocalypse. The results differ, depending on whether the count begins with Julius or Augustus Caesar, and whether or not the 'caretaker' rulers Galba, Otho and Vitellius are included in the list. See Swete 220–21; Charles 2, 69–70; Beckwith 704–708; Robinson, *Redating* 242–53; Talbert, *Apocalypse* 80–82; Klauck, 'Do They Never Come Back?', esp. 696–98; Prigent 492–94 (cf. also Aune 946–48).

For a reading of Rev. 17.9–11 which makes sense of the text in historical terms, and also supports a date of AD 70 for the composition of Revelation, see Smalley, *Thunder and Love* 45–48, esp. 47. On this view, the eight Caesars (an 'eighth' is added to the 'seven' rulers at verse 11) are as follows:

1 Augustus (30 BC–AD 14)
2 Tiberius (14–37)
3 Caligula (37–41)
4 Claudius (41–54)
5 Nero (54–68)
6 Vespasian (69–79)
7 Titus (79–81)
8 Domitian (81–96).

The commentary in verses 9–11 now becomes clear. Five Emperors (Augustus to Nero) out of seven (Augustus to Titus) have already died (verse 10). One (Vespasian) is currently reigning ('is living now', verse 10). The next (Titus) has yet to come, but 'he must stay for only a short time' (verse 10); for the reign of Titus lasted for a mere two years, and this is shorthand for the nearness of the end. The eighth Emperor (Domitian), who will eventually be destroyed (verse 11; see also verse 8, he 'goes to destruction'), is one of many Nero *redivivus* figures in his attitude to Church and state. In that sense he harks back to Nero himself, and so 'belongs to the seven' (verse 11; ἐκ τῶν ἑπτά, *ek tōn hepta*, lit. '[one] of the seven', is a partitive genitive), namely, Augustus to Titus, including Nero. The references to Titus in verse 10 and Domitian (the eighth ruler) in verse 11 may indicate a later redaction of the text of Revelation. The formula used in verses 10–11 to describe the beast, who 'was, is not, and is yet to come', reflects the parody of the divine title in verse 8 (q.v.).

(b) *Figurative.* An alternative, and doubtless preferable, means of interpreting the text in verses 9–11 is to regard the number 'seven' in this list as an apocalyptic symbol, representing the totality of Roman imperial power. Seven is not only a typically Johannine numeral, symbolic rather than literal; it is also used frequently in the Revelation to denote the divine arrangement of the world and its history (1.11, 16; 2.1; 5.1; 6.1; 10.3–4; 15.1; 16.1; 21.9; et al.); cf. Aune 948. Furthermore, the imagery of the 'seven heads' of the beast (17.3, 7, 9) derives from the mythic tradition, well known in the ancient world, of the seven-headed dragon (see on 12.3). See further (*inter alios*) Kiddle 350–51; Beasley-Murray 256–57; Caird 218–19; Sweet 257; Talbert, *Apocalypse* 81; Brown, *Introduction* 793–94; Bauckham 1300*b*–1301*a*.

However, the attempt to interpret 17.9–11, either literally or figuratively, in terms which are directly related to the historical situation of the Roman Empire in the first century AD can only be described as misguided. Knowing as we do the way in which the apocalyptist gives significance to his imagery, it is much more likely that the total concept of the 'rulers' in these verses is to be understood in 'transtemporal' terms (so Beale 869). While it is possible that John is writing against a historical background which his audience would have appreciated immediately, it is much more likely that his imagery of the demonic 'rulers' is to be interpreted eschatologically, and in terms which transcend history. Just as 'Babylon' (17.1) represents the idolatrous forces of the state in any period of world history, so the satanic beast symbolizes *any* incarnation of the worldly misuse of power. This regularly manifests itself in the unjust oppression of the innocent, and may be motivated by a corruption which is religious in origin (Milligan 296–99; cf. Dan. 7.3–7). There is an uncanny accuracy in the rise and fall of the secular authorities designated in this passage; for they come and they go on the stage of human progress, and the 'end' is always pressing upon it. Like Satan himself, the time of anti-Christian forces such as Babylon/Rome is limited (12.12); they are bound to be replaced ultimately by the eternal goodness and justice of an all-powerful God (17.17; 18.10, 20; 19.1–2). See further Wilcock 164; Bauckham, *Climax of Prophecy* 406–407; Mounce 315–18.

12–14 These three verses are connected by their allegorical interpretation of the 'ten horns' of the beast (verses 3 and 7). The horns seem to originate from the seventh head of the beast, rather than from all seven, since both the seventh head (verse 9) and the ten horns (verse 12) belong to the timeless future.

An immediate background to the imagery of a beast with ten horns may be found in Dan. 7.7–24; see also *Sib. Or.* 3.388–400; and *Barn.* 4.3–5. The explanation of the 'horns' of the beast as 'ten rulers' (δέκα βασιλεῖς, *deka basileis*, lit. 'ten kings') should be understood in exactly the same light as the earlier imagery of the bestial 'heads' (verses 9–11). The ten rulers cannot represent ten Roman Emperors, because they have 'not yet received royal power' (verse 12; cf. Mounce 319). Neither are they a rounded number of Parthian satraps (so Charles 2, 71–72; Kiddle 351–53), or governors of the ten Roman senatorial provinces (Moffatt 454), or Roman 'client kings' (Aune 951), or forces in the future, arising out of the Empire itself, which will 'turn their arms against Rome and bring about her downfall' (Swete 222).

The 'ten rulers' of 17.12–14 should rather be interpreted in metaphorical, and not historical, terms. They are eschatological figures, denoting the secular self-aggrandizement which seeks to usurp the justice and authority of God in any age and place; and in this passage they represent 'the totality of the powers of all nations on the earth which are to be made subservient to Antichrist' (Beckwith 700; similarly Hendriksen 171; Caird 219–20; Knight 118; Beale 878–79). The number 'ten' is a symbol not only for completeness (Mounce 319), but also for the plenitude of power wielded by demonic forces whenever they exist and are allowed to rule (they 'have not yet' become kings; cf. Beale 878). To this extent, the 'ten horns' of verse 12 may be closely associated with the 'earthly rulers' of 17.18, q.v. (also 16.14; 17.2; 18.3, 9; 19.19); they are allies of the beast, who oppose the Lamb and his followers.

These rulers 'will receive (λαμβάνουσιν, *lambanousin*, lit. "they receive", is a futurist present) authority as kings, together with the beast', in the sense that their authority flows from their close connection with the forces of evil (Hughes 186); cf. Luke 19.12. The kings are those powers which have yielded to the sway of the devil in his varied incarnations, including the impious and unjust deceit and oppression of civic and religious institutions ('Babylon'; cf. 17.1–6). For the relationship between the beast and the harlot see on verse 3; also Milligan 296–302. Such an interpretation, despite 17.17 and the authorization clauses elsewhere in Revelation where God is the implied subject (e.g. 6.2; 7.2; 9.1; 16.8), seems preferable to that of Beale (879), who regards the source of the rulers' authority in verse 12 as divine.

But the control of these idolatrous powers, like that of the Satan himself, is short-lived, and lasts for only 'a moment' (μίαν ὥραν, *mian hōran*, lit. 'one hour'); cf. 12.12; 17.10. Sweet (261) views this expression as an Aramaism, best translated as 'for a moment' (cf. Dan. 4.17a LXX). As in the case of King Nebuchadrezzar, God is sovereign over ungodly rulers who are allied with the beast in order to oppose his Messiah (17.17). The 'hour' strikes repeatedly throughout the threnody of judgement in Chapter 18 (see verses 10, 17, 19). Meanwhile, these rulers 'are of one mind in conferring their power and authority on the beast' (verse 13). The phrase, μίαν γνώμην ἔχουσιν (*mian gnōmēn echousin*, lit. 'they have one mind'), appears to be 'a cliché of local politics' (Sweet 261). The ten rulers collectively have a common purpose, in that they 'confer' (διδόασιν, *didoasin*, lit. 'they give', is another futurist present, replacing διδοῦσιν, *didousin*) on the beast the same powerful authority which they have received from it. They not only reign with Satan but also submit to his rule; for the beast needs to be able to rely on the physical and moral support of his allies (cf. Swete 223). In the end, however, all idolatrous agencies will become self-destructive, and disappear under the judgement of God (17.16; 18.4–8; 19.17–21; 20.7–10).

Inevitably, these earthly rulers will 'go to war against the Lamb' (verse 14; see verses 12–13); for they are in opposition to the Church and everything for which it stands. For 'Lamb' (τὸ ἀρνίον, *to arnion*) see on 5.6; et al. In the final conflict between Antichrist and the Messiah (16.16), however, victory is promised for Christ and the saints. The military phraseology in the opening sentences of verse 14 derives from Dan. 7.21 (Theod.). The Lamb will overcome his opponents (the verb νικήσει, *nikēsei*, lit. 'will conquer', is in the singular) because of his nature. For Jesus is one with God as well as his Church (1.12–18; 5.1–10; 22.1–5); and, as such, he is 'Lord of lords and King of kings'. This superlative expression of sovereignty derives from such Old Testament texts as Deut. 10.17; Ps. 136.3; Dan. 2.47; 4.37 LXX; see also 1QM 14.16; 2 Macc. 13.4; 3 Macc. 5.35; 1 Enoch 9.4; 84.2; 1 Tim. 6.15. The same two titles, in reverse order, occur in 19.16 with reference to the Word of God. The beast and his followers will be conquered, because ultimately everyone will acknowledge the kingdom of God in Christ (cf. Phil. 2.9–11). Slater, ' "King of Kings" ', points out that neither 17.14 nor 19.16 is an exact quotation of Dan. 4.37 LXX, nor indeed of 1 Enoch 9.4, which is based on that text. Rather, the seer has used imagery, concepts and ideas from the Danielic passage to convey John's vision of the end in a new and creative manner. Slater concludes that this gives the Apocalypse 'a sense of continuity and at the same time a sense of spontaneity' (ibid. 160).

The demonstrative pronoun, οὗτοι (*houtoi*, 'they', lit. 'these'), is used here and in verse 13 with reference to the followers of the beast; while at 7.14; 14.4 it occurs in descriptions of the saints of God. The contrast is stark. The beast is the transtemporal power opposing the eternal Lamb, just as the ten rulers span the ages in ceaseless conflicts with the faithful (Beale 878). Similarly, whereas the 144,000 redeemed who have refused to worship the beast accompany the Lamb on Mount Zion, sealed with his name (14.1–5; 7.4–8), now (17.14) they appear with Christ, associated with his victory over the forces of evil (Prigent 495). The defeat of the saints by the beast (Dan. 7.21; Rev. 11.7; 13.7) ironically foreshadows a reversal of the situation; since ultimately the Lamb and his followers overcome the beast and his horned allies (Beale 880).

This assumes that members of the Christian, indeed Johannine, community are to be associated with the Lamb in verse 14; and, although this is not stated, it is implied in this passage that his own adherents participate in the victory over the armies of the beast. (NJB translates the Greek as 'he will defeat them, he and his followers'.) The introduction of the phrase, καὶ οἱ μετ' αὐτοῦ (*kai hoi met' autou*, 'and his followers', lit. 'and those with him [are called, and chosen and faithful]'), immediately after an extended reference to the sovereign and conquering Lamb, supports this view. It also answers the question posed at 13.4, 'who can fight against it (the beast)?' It is those who are 'called, and faithful and chosen' who will go to war with the satanic powers alongside the Lamb, represent the vindication of the persecuted saints (Dan. 7.21; Rev. 6.9–11; 12.10–11; 13.10), and share in the judgement of the unrighteous at the end-time (Dan. 7.22; Wis. 3.8; *1 Enoch* 38.5; 91.12; 96.1–3; 1 Cor. 6.2; et al.). Cf. Bauckham 1301*a*. Bauckham (*Climax of Prophecy* 210–13) notes the prominence of the theme of the holy war in Jewish eschatological expectation, and distinguishes in its apocalyptic presentation between the tradition of a passive role being assigned to the faithful (the victor is God alone, or God accompanied by his heavenly armies) and its active form (the people of God play a strong part in the fight against the Lord's enemies). See also Aune 956.

Of the three adjectives used to describe the members of the Lamb's Church, 'called, and chosen and faithful' (κλητοὶ καὶ ἐκλεκτοὶ καὶ πιστοί, *klētoi kai eklektoi kai pistoi*), the first two appear only here in the Apocalypse. Elsewhere in the New Testament, however, 'called' and 'elect' (the latter in a theologically non-deterministic sense) are regularly used to designate believers (e.g. Rom. 1.6; 1 Cor. 1.24; Jude 1; Col. 3.12; 1 Pet. 1.1; 2 John 1.1, 13); and always the emphasis is on the grace and initiative of God (Prigent 495). The third epithet, 'faithful' (πιστός, *pistos*), is ascribed in Revelation to Christ who died on the cross (1.5; cf. 3.14; 19.11), to his steadfast witness, Antipas (2.13), to the trustworthy nature of the prophetic testimony (21.5; 22.6), and (as here) to the need for the saints of God to keep faith with him (2.10). See further on 1.5; also Michel, 'πίστις', esp. 602–603.

According to Moffatt (454), the success of believers in their holy battle against demonic forces rests not only on their divine election and allegiance to the Lamb but also on their corresponding loyalty to him (cf. 2.13, 19; 13.10; 14.12). Michaels (199) points out that the conditions for the participation of the saints in the Lamb's victory (being called, chosen and faithful) become increasingly specific: first, 'called' (cf. 19.9); then, not only called but also chosen (Matt. 22.14); and finally, not only chosen but also called to be faithful (so 2.10). As in the oracles which are addressed to the Johannine community, and in the drama of the Apocalypse as a whole, the seer's audience itself is being encouraged to remain steadfast in right belief and behaviour, so as to overcome (16.15).

15 The angel 'continued' (λέγει μοι, *legei moi*, lit. 'he says to me', using a historic present) his interpretation of the vision recorded in verses 1–6, by reverting to an explanation of the 'great whore' (verse 1, q.v.) in relation to the beast (see on verses 7–8, where the heavenly messenger promises an understanding of the woman and the beast, and then reverses the order). For the repeated, formulaic phrase, 'in your vision' (ἃ εἶδες, *ha eides*, lit. 'which you saw'), see on verse 8. For the imagery of the harlot 'seated (enthroned) beside the waters' see on verse 1.

Some commentators regard as problematic the fact that, in his earlier vision, John does not 'see' any figurative 'waters' (τὰ ὕδατα, *ta hydata*), as these appear in verse 15; although here they clearly recall the description of the woman in verse 1. A familiar solution of this difficulty is to deem verse 15 as secondary. Thus, Charles (2, 72) encloses the Greek text in brackets, and claims that it is a later gloss on 17.1; and he is followed by Prigent (496). Similarly, Aune (956) sees verse 15 (like verse 14, indeed) as a subsequent insertion into the text. Kiddle (356–57) suggests that this apparent intrusion of water imagery arises from apocalyptic convention. John 'sees' the truth about God and his purposes for creation, and later clothes this in symbolic imagery (such as 'water') which is a familiar part of visionary settings. Less complicated, and more plausible, is the proposal of Mounce (320 n. 61) that John's account of his experience, in 17.1–6, is less complete than the original vision itself. The amplification in verse 15 may then be understood as a developed prophetic insight.

The 'waters' in question, beside which the whore is seated, are identified as 'peoples and multitudes, and nations and language groups'. This fourfold formula, denoting universality, occurs repeatedly in the Apocalypse with reference to the Church (5.9, q.v.; 7.9), and the world in opposition to God (10.11; 11.9; 13.7; 14.6). It derives from Dan. 3—6, where the expression is used of the subjects of the king of Babylon (cf. lxx Dan. 3.2; 4.37a–c; Theod. Dan. 5.19; 6.26). In the same way, this text in Rev. 17.15 declares, the secular world is under the influence of the scarlet woman and captivated by her (see further on verse 18). The '(many) waters' of 17.1, 15 provide an allusion to the system of waterways in and around Babylon (cf. Jer. 51.13 = 28.13 lxx), which provided the city with protection from outside attack, and helped it economically to flourish. In the Old Testament, as here, 'many waters' can symbolize 'many nations' (cf. Isa. 8.7; 17.12–13; 23.3; Jer. 46.7–8; 47.2; Nahum 3.8; see also 1QpNah *frags*. 1.2–4; 3–4 col. 3.8).

16   The fall of Babylon, described in detail at Chapter 18, is now heralded; for the beast and its allies attack the harlot, before they attempt to destroy the Lamb (17.14; 19.19–21). The destruction of the woman in scarlet is portrayed in terms which directly echo the prophecy of God's judgement on unfaithful Israel in Ezek. 23.11–35; cf. Jer. 13.26–27; Ezek. 16.37–41; Hos. 2.3. In the allegory of Ezek. 23, Oholibah lusted after the Assyrians (verse 12), was defiled by the Babylonians (verse 17) and played the whore in Egypt (verse 19). The sister depicted in Ezek. 23.31–34 even holds a cup of drunkenness and sorrow in her hand (cf. Rev. 17.4–6). In the picture of Rev. 17.16, the demonic beast and the ten horns (see verses 7, 12) turn in hatred on the harlot, make her desolate and naked, devour her flesh and burn her remains with fire (cf. Ezek. 23.29a, 26, 29b, 25a, b). The gruesome destruction involved is complete, and is as much spiritual as physical (cf. Ps. 27.2; Mic. 3.1–4).

In the application of Ezekiel's imagery to the figure of Babylon in Rev. 17.16, three metaphors are used: she is exposed like a prostitute, consumed like the victim of a fierce beast and burnt down like a city (cf. the fate of Jezebel at 2 Kings 9.30–37; Lev. 20.14; 21.9); see Mounce 321 and n. 66; Beale 883. Beale (884) also notes the close parallels between Jezebel in the Old Testament and the Babylonian woman in Rev. 17—18, which further links the scarlet whore to the false prophetess 'Jezebel' who belonged to the church at Thyatira (Rev. 2.18–29, esp. 20–23).

The scene unveiled in the present verse (17.16) should not be understood primarily in historical terms. The angel is not referring to the fall of the Roman Empire at the hands of a Nero *redivivus* figure (Swete 224–25; Roloff 200–201; Aune 957); nor is 'Babylon' to be interpreted solely as the apostate Church of the first century (cf. Milligan 289–302), despite the imagery in Ezek. 23 which describes God's judgement on a degenerate Israel (see further on 17.1). The picture is rather that of resentful forces of evil which are likely at any period of history, up to the end and at the end, to attack the very institutional, corrupt structures to which they are attracted, be they political, economic or religious. For all revolutionary and idolatrous power contains within itself the seeds of self-destruction, and evil (symbolized by Babylon) must ultimately yield to evil. Satan will eventually cast out Satan (Mark 3.23–26). See further Boring 184–85; Wilcock 165.

Three further points need to be added to this line of interpretation. First, in this self-destructive process God is perceived as using the powers of wickedness for his own purposes of eschatological judgement (see further on verse 17). Second, although the imagery of 17.16 appears to be impersonal, because of its broad symbolism, it cannot be forgotten either that *people* are involved in rebellion against God or that human attitudes and responses which are unredeemed lead to wrong belief and behaviour (Ps. 14.1–3 = 53.1–3; John 2.24–25; Rom. 3.9–12). Third, such a warning would have been timely for the Johannine community of the first century AD, as it is for the Church of today; it also carries with it implicitly a plea to avoid compromise with any kind of evil system, so as to avoid being judged by it (cf. Sweet 253).

17 The coalition of the beast and its followers will attack the worldly and seductive Babylonian whore (verse 16) because God has prompted them to fulfil what was in origin his judgemental purpose. In the phrase, ὁ γὰρ θεὸς ἔδωκεν εἰς τὰς καρδίας αὐτῶν (*ho gar theos edōken eis tas kardias autōn*, 'for God had put it [lit. "gave"] into their hearts'), the aorist verb translated as 'had put' functions as a Hebrew prophetic perfect; and this signifies the certainty that God's plan will be accomplished. The whole expression is a Semitic idiom (cf. Exod. 35.34; Neh. 2.12; 7.5).

As Aune (957–58) points out, verse 17 provides a commentary on some of the visionary contents of 17.12–16. This explanation is set out in three infinitive clauses, all of which are objects of the verb ἔδωκεν (*edōken*, lit. 'gave'): ποιῆσαι τὴν γνώμην αὐτοῦ (*poiēsai tēn gnōmēn autou*, 'to carry out [lit. "to do"] his purpose'; ποιῆσαι μίαν γνώμην (*poiēsai mian gnōmēn*, 'by agreeing', lit. 'to make one mind' [a technical term in the ancient Greek world for political accord; see verse 13]); and δοῦναι τὴν βασιλείαν αὐτῶν τῷ θηρίῳ (*dounai tēn basileian autōn tō[i] thērio[i]*, 'to surrender their authority [lit. "kingdom"] to the beast'). The first clause is general, whereas the second and third are more specific.

The unanimous decision of the 'ten rulers' to submit their authoritative, royal power to the demonic beast indicates, in this imagery, the way in which the forces of Satan readily come together in order to overthrow other corrupt agencies. The ten horns become allied with the beast in his assault on both the Lamb (17.14) and the whore (verse 16). Thus evil casts out evil, in a process of mutual self-destruction which includes divine judgement (see on verse 16). But this situation is initiated by God himself, who establishes his will through the 'hearts' of the just as well as the unjust (Beale 887). In the end, the powers of evil serve the purposes of the sovereign God, in addition to being condemned by him; and the classic example of this in the Old Testament is the use of King Cyrus of Persia, as a 'messianic' instrument of God, to carry out the divine purposes of judgement on the nations and to achieve the deliverance of Israel (Isa. 44.28; 45.1). In the present context, accordingly, the destruction of the opposition is caused by God, and not merely allowed by him (cf. 6.2; et al.).

The coalition between the beast and his allies, the angel adds, will continue 'until the words of God have been fulfilled'; and this is a reference to the prophecy in Dan. 7, as developed in Rev. 17 and in the Apocalypse generally (see 1.3; 19.9; 21.5; 22.6, 7, 9–10, 18–19; also 10.7), that Antichrist will eventually be defeated, and that God's kingdom will finally prevail.

18 The formula, ἣν εἶδες (*hēn eides*, '[the woman] in your vision', lit. 'whom you saw'), is used here for the fourth time in Rev. 17 (see also verses 8, 12 and 15). The agenda for the angel's interpretation of the vision disclosed in verses 1–6 is set out in verse 7 (for its order, see the comment on that text). The first figure to be seen in John's vision (17.3) is the last to be identified (verse 18).

'The woman' is explicitly and allegorically interpreted in the present verse as 'the great city'. This city should not be aligned directly with the imperial power of Rome (so Aune 959; see on Satan and the beasts in Rev. 12—13, and on 17.3). Nor is 'the great city' to be understood as Jerusalem (so Barker, *The Revelation* 279–87, esp. 284–85). This identification leans heavily on the representation of Jerusalem and its Temple in the Old Testament as an unfaithful harlot (see Isa. 1.21; Ezek. 16.3–52; 23.22–35), and on the disparaging reference to Jerusalem in 11.8 as 'Sodom and Egypt' (ibid. 190–91). In Revelation, however, Jerusalem is generally depicted in a positive light, as 'holy' (11.2; 21.10; 22.19), and as the transformed dwelling of God (3.12; 21.2). It is, of course, possible for any covenant community to become faithless, as well as blessed. Thus in 11.8 Jerusalem is called 'Sodom and Egypt', but is *also* known as the place of Christ's crucifixion; although Barker, *The Revelation* 190, regards the second phrase as a later addition to the text (cf. also 16.19). See Walker, *Holy City* 255–56.

Nevertheless, three pieces of evidence strongly support the conclusion that the 'city' of 17.18 is Babylon.

(a) In the Old Testament, Babylon can be as unfaithful as Jerusalem (cf. Isa. 21.9; Jer. 51.6–10; Dan. 6.28–33; et al.).
(b) The city is named as the harlot 'Babylon' at 17.5.
(c) The phrase, 'great city' is consistently used elsewhere in the Apocalypse to describe Babylon (see 14.8; 16.19; 17.5; 18.2, 10, 16, 18, 19, 21).

'(Babylon) the great city', in this context, may therefore best be regarded as a symbol for the institutionalized prostitution of political, economic and religious ideas in any age and setting, to which satanic forces have surrendered their worldly powers. See further on 11.8; 17.1–5; 20.9; also Swete 226; Hendriksen 172–73; Mounce 321.

The Babylonian woman 'has dominion over earthly rulers' (ἡ ἔχουσα βασιλείαν ἐπὶ τῶν βασιλέων τῆς γῆς, *hē echousa basileian epi tōn basileōn tēs gēs*, lit. '[she] who has rule over the rulers of the earth'; note the play on words). For the relationship between the harlot and the 'kings of the earth', who submit to her superficial attractions (verse 4), see on verses 3, 9–14. For the meaning of 'earthly rulers', as a metaphor for illicit alliances of a socio-political, economic and religious nature, see on 17.2; for the expression itself cf. also 1.5; 6.15; 16.14; 18.3, 9; 19.19. The scarlet woman stands for the powerful allurement of those worldly and unjust principles which may become embodied in corrupt institutional structures. In this respect her appeal is universal, as well as timeless (see also verse 15); for she is the one who deceives 'all the nations of the world' by her sorcery (18.23).

Lament over Babylon and a Call to Rejoice (18.1–20)

For the literary structure and theological content of the threnody in Chapter 18, delivered at the fall of Babylon, see above (425). A special, poetic feature to be observed in this section of the interval is the arrangement of lines in triplets. Thus, Babylon has become a haunt for demons, evil spirits and unclean birds (18.2). Nations have drunk from the adulterous wine of the whore-like city, kings of the earth have fornicated with her, and merchants have prospered from her wealth (verse 3). A voice from heaven prescribes for Babylon an infliction on her of what she has given to others, a double repayment for her own deeds, and a duplicate draught of her own medicine (verse 6). The plagues which await her are those of pestilence, bereavement and famine (verse 8). For John's audience, these strong rhythms would have added dramatic intensity to an already solemn and powerful message. See Mounce 324.

18.1   For the opening, visionary formula in this verse, 'after this, I saw' (μετὰ ταῦτα εἶδον, *meta tauta eidon*), see 4.1; 7.9; 15.5. In the present context, as elsewhere in the Apocalypse, the phrase marks the beginning of a new unit of text, and should not be understood chronologically. In the first part of the disclosure John 'sees' (as well as hearing) an angel from heaven (18.1–3); later he 'hears' the proclamation of a divine voice (verses 4–20). For the importance of spiritual perception and audition in the Johannine corpus see on 4.1.

For angels in Revelation see above, 28–30. Beale (892) suggests that the angel which descends from heaven at this point may be identified with the one which introduced the vision at 17.1. But clearly this is *'another'* angel (ἄλλον ἄγγελον, *allon angelon*), distinguished from the previous, bowl-angel. He is a 'new', 'still another', angelic being (Prigent 502), as in 7.2; 8.3; 10.1; 14.8; et al. Once more, the angel which comes down from heaven connects the spiritual and material dimensions in a typically Johannine manner (see on 10.1); although, as in 10.1, the angelic descent stops short of an actual Christophany (against Beale 892–93, who nevertheless admits that the figure in 18.1 is possibly not Christ, but 'a mere angel reflecting the divine glory' [893]). John observes that this angel 'exercised great authority', which points to the divine origin and therefore importance of the message to be delivered.

The divine authority of the angel is further enforced by the statement that 'the earth was made bright (ἐφωτίσθη, *ephōtisthē*) with his glory'. This is the only place in Revelation where it is said that an angel possesses 'glory', which is otherwise a quality attributed to God or Christ (1.6; 4.9, 11; 5.12–13; 7.12; et al.); but see Ezek. 9.3; 10.4; Sir. 49.8; Heb. 9.5, where angels radiate the glory of God. That the angel of Rev. 18.1 made the earth bright 'with his glory' (ἐκ τῆς δόξης αὐτοῦ, *ek tēs doxēs autou*) is an allusion to Ezek. 43.1–5, which is a prophetic vision of restoration after divine judgement, and the return of God's glorious presence to the rebuilt Temple. The angel is about to proclaim a message of serious judgement; but he is also an angel of the gospel (cf. 14.6), whose purpose is to announce the triumph of God's purposes, and the final liberation of his people (Caird 222; cf. Swete 226). For the imagery of light, in association with the presence of God, see Exod. 34.29–30; Ps. 104.1–2; 1 Tim. 6.16; 1 John 1.5–7.

Sweet (266) connects the allusion to Ezek. 43 behind Rev. 18.1 with the vision beginning in 21.10 (the holy city), which derives from Ezek. 40—48. The destruction of worldly institutions, symbolized by 'Babylon', thus prepares the way for God's everlasting presence to dwell in his new creation (cf. 21.22–23).

2–3   In formal terms, Rev. 18.1–3 is an example of angelic speech (cf. 10.1–7; 14.9–11; 19.17–18; et al.; see also above, 29–30). Here it is recorded that the angel 'cried out with a mighty voice' (ἔκραξεν ἐν ἰσχυρᾷ φωνῇ, *ekraxen en ischyra[i] phōnē[i]*, lit. 'in a strong voice'), which suggests not only the importance of the message he will deliver but also its divine origin and authority (cf. 7.2, 10; 10.3; 14.7, 9, 15; 19.17). Similarly, in the Fourth Gospel, for Jesus to lift his voice indicates that a crucial declaration is to follow (John 7.28, 37; 12.44). Elsewhere in Revelation, the adjective ἰσχυρός (*ischyros*, 'strong', 'mighty') is used of angelic figures who make significant statements (5.2; 10.1; 18.21); but only at 18.2 does it describe the quality of the messenger's voice. The normal word for 'strong' (voice), in such contexts, is μεγάλη (*megalē*), as in all the passages (beginning with 7.2, 10) cited above.

The angel's proclamation, 'Fallen, fallen is Babylon the great!', is a deliberate echo of 14.8; and the repetition ties together the seventh sign of angelic judgement in Scene 4 with the announcement of impending destruction here. There is also an Old Testament background to this threnody in Isa. 21.9 ('Fallen, fallen is Babylon; and all the images of her gods lie shattered on the ground'); see also Dan. 4.30 (LXX, Theod.; MT 4.27). As the first Babylon, with its inherent idolatry, was destroyed, so the secular, institutional powers of any age (the angel promises in verse 2) will become desolate. For the expression, 'Babylon the great', see on 17.5; also 17.1, 18. The imagery in the present context is the same as that in Chapter 17. The repeated verb, ἔπεσεν, ἔπεσεν (*epesen, epesen*, 'fallen, fallen'), in the aorist tense, has the function of a prophetic perfect, for the final judgement of Babylon, with its destructive implications, has yet to be brought about (so 14.8); although here the judgement appears to be more imminent. See the use of the same verb at 11.13; 16.19. As always in John's eschatology, there is a tension between the present and the future, between anticipation and fulfilment (cf. Prigent 502).

In the second half of verse 2, the complete desolation of Babylon, resulting from the judgement on her evil (see also verses 6, 20, 24; 19.2–3), is described in the first of four triplets used in this section (see also verses 3, 6 and 8). The whore-like city will become a dwelling for demons, evil spirits, and unclean and detestable birds and beasts (for the last combination see the textual note on verse 2). This imagery of a city destined for destruction, as potentially a shelter for wild animals and unclean birds (cf. Deut. 14.12–19), features regularly in Old Testament apocalyptic prophecy (see e.g. Isa. 13.21–22; 34.11–15; Jer. 9.11; 50.39; 51.37 [LXX 28.37]; Zeph. 2.14; Baruch 4.35). Some of those texts also mention 'demons' among the wild creatures, as here in Rev. 18.2. Elsewhere in the Apocalypse the demonic realm is associated with idolatry (cf. 2.20, 24; 9.20); so that the demons and evil spirits of this verse become a symbol for Babylon's devilish nature, masked until now behind a deceitful disposition towards idolatry. Cf. further Swete 227; Beale 893–94; Prigent 502.

The term φυλακή (*phylakē*, rendered in the translation as 'haunt' and 'preserve'), used three times in verse 2, basically means a 'prison' (BDAG 1067*b*). In the present setting, the significance is rather that of a 'home' (Mounce 326) or 'lair' (Prigent 502). The location of the unholy assembly is not a place of detention, but an area where they can live undisturbed. On the basis of Hab. 2.1 LXX (cf. Baruch 3.34 LXX), Swete (227) suggests that 'watchtower' or 'stronghold' is the meaning of the noun. In that case, the picture would be one of demonic spirits in a watching post, perched like vultures waiting for their prey. Ultimately, however, the angel at this point in verse 2 is painting a picture of absolute desolation, and a conquest of ungodliness and oppression such as would have encouraged John's immediate audience and his readers at any moment in history. In the final judgement process, the proud achievements of the human race, and the superficial attractions of its secular institutions, will become the demonic preserve of evil and frighteningly unattractive beings who belong to the realms of both spirit and matter.

Verse 3 provides the reasons for the precipitous downfall of Babylon; note the use of the conjunction ὅτι (*hoti*, 'because', 'since'), at the beginning of the first sentence. The first two strophes of the verse run parallel to 14.8 (q.v.), and continue the imagery and thought of that text; see also 14.10, 18–20; 17.1–2. Rev. 18.3 also contains the second formal triplet in this chapter, since it deals with actions performed by the nations, the kings and the merchants. It also speaks of the unholy relationship which exists between 'Babylon' and these three groups, as a means of safeguarding their material, and indeed worldly, security (cf. 2.9; 3.17–19; 13.16–17).

For 'all the nations' (πάντα τὰ ἔθνη, *panta ta ethnē*), as representatives of godless societies, see on 12.5; also 14.8; 15.4; 18.23. In the Apocalypse, 'nations' often feature as opponents of God and his truth in Christ (11.2, 18; 19.15; 20.3, 8; et al.). For 'the wine which is her passionate adultery' (where the genitive, τοῦ θυμοῦ τῆς πορνείας, *tou thymou tēs porneias*, lit. 'of the intense desire of her adultery', is epexegetic) see on 14.8. The reference to alcohol in this setting suggests the insidious influence which is exercised by the powers of evil (cf. 17.1–2). For 'adultery', in this part of verse 3, see on 17.1–5.

The force of καί (*kai*, lit. 'and'), at the beginning of the next line of verse 3, is causal; hence the translation, 'for'. The 'kings of the earth' in this verse are the same as those mentioned in 17.2; see also 17.9–14, 18; 18.9. They represent societies which have yielded their allegiance to Satan and his followers, having been seduced (the kings have 'fornicated') by the superficial attractions of worldly, institutional powers; and the broad reference here is to illicit alliances of a political, economic or religious nature, which may develop at any period in history. According to Beale (895), there is an economic dimension to the imagery in 18.3 ('kings fornicating with Babylon'), which is confirmed by the allusion here to Isa. 23.17: '(Tyre) will prostitute herself with all the kingdoms of the world'. Significantly, the LXX version of Isa. 23.17 reads, 'she will be a market (ἐμπόριον, *emporion*) for all the kingdoms of the earth'; and note the same language in Isa. 23.18 LXX.

The last clause of verse 3 evidently picks up this economic framework to the angel's statement by referring to 'worldly merchants' (οἱ ἔμποροι τῆς γῆς, *hoi emporoi tēs gēs*, lit. 'the merchants of the earth'; the description speaks more of their secular attitude than their geographical location) who have become rich from Babylon's excessive wealth. This picture derives from the judgement on Tyre, which is described in Ezek. 27.12, 18 in terms of nations trading with her in precious cargo (there is repeated reference to such a situation, as set out in Ezek. 26—28, at Rev. 18.9–22). See Beale 895–96. The 'merchants' in the present passage are probably intended to include seafarers (18.17–19), since at the time water was the means of transporting merchandise from east to west in the Empire (so Aune 988). This passage of Revelation (Chapter 18) is the only reference in the New Testament to commercial trade, which remained an important part of Rome's imperialism (Prigent 502); although here the allusion must extend to any abuse of power in worldly realms, and any misuse of economic interests, which involves the acquisition of wealth and leads to idolatry (see below, and on 18.7, 23; against Aune 990).

In the concluding phrase of verse 3, ἐκ τῆς δυνάμεως τοῦ στρήνους (*ek tēs dynameōs tou strēnous*, 'from her excessive wealth', lit. 'from the power of her luxury'), the genitive τοῦ στρήνους (*tou strēnous*, '[from] her wealth') could be descriptive, meaning 'wealthy power'. But it is more likely to be a genitive of source, giving the sense of 'power arising from wealth' (Beale 895–96); for the emphasis in the present context is more on Babylon's ill-gotten wealth than on her power. The term, στρῆνος (*strēnos*, translated by BDAG 949*a* as 'sensuality, luxury'), is found only here in the New Testament; but note the use of the cognate verb at 18.7 and 9 (cf. also 1 Tim. 5.11). Beckwith (713) finds in this language the ideas of excessive luxury and self-indulgence, accompanied by arrogance and a 'wanton exercise of strength'. See the use of the noun, meaning 'arrogance', in 2 Kings 19.28 LXX.

The verb, ἐπλούτησαν (*eploutēsan*, 'have become rich'), is in the aorist, but has the value of a perfect tense. For the thought cf. Ezek. 27.33; also Rev. 18.9, 16–17, 19. Wealth as such does not have a negative connotation in Jewish literature; but see the radical critique of wealth which regularly appears in the teaching of Jesus (Matt. 6.24 par.; Mark 10.23–25 par.; Luke 6.20 par.; et al.); cf. Aune 990. The thrust of verse 3 as a whole is that the judgement to come of secular Babylon has been brought about by her seduction of others, leading groups and individuals into an injustice and impiety which is marked by wrong relationships, ungodly idolatry and worldly greed. Underlying these superficial blandishments is the promise of a false economic security. Cf. Caird 223. Fiorenza (98–101) notes that one important backcloth to the situation dramatically presented in this verse, and in Chapter 18 generally, is the wealth and supposed security of the Roman Empire in the first century AD. However, such prosperity was unevenly distributed, so that a few Asian cities reaped its benefits, while 'the masses of the urban population mostly lived in dire poverty or slavery' (ibid. 100); cf. 18.13. For the much broader interpretation of 'Babylon' adopted in this commentary see on verse 2; also 17.1.

4–5 At this point, the seer heard 'another voice' (ἄλλην φωνὴν, *allēn phōnēn*) from heaven, speaking first to the people of God (verses 4–5), and then to those who will carry out his purposes of salvific judgement (verses 6–20). The reference to a new voice marks the beginning of a fresh subdivision in the text; and it also switches the account of Babylon's destruction from its character of vision to that of audition (Aune 990). As constantly in the Apocalypse, the speaker from heaven in verse 4, like the angel from heaven in verse 1, connects the realms of spirit and matter. The voice in question does not belong to God, despite the reference here to 'my people' (Swete 228; Beckwith 714), since in the following verse 'God' is used in the third person singular. Nor is it necessarily Christ who speaks (Charles 2, 97; Aune 990). As in 10.4 and 14.2, the voice is doubtless that of an angel as such, speaking as the messenger of God (cf. Mounce 327).

The announcement of Babylon's coming destruction serves two purposes. It provides a warning for wavering believers, that they should not participate in systemic and idolatrous compromise; and it also acts as an encouragement to the saints who have avoided such behaviour to continue in their faith and faithfulness (cf. Beale 897). Charles (2, 96–97) regards the exhortation to right belief and praxis in verse 4 as without meaning, since by this stage all the faithful have been put to death (see 13.7–10; 15.2–4). But this is to assume that the chronology of Revelation is literal and linear, whereas it is in fact eschatological and cyclical (see above, 19–20).

The command for the people of God to 'come out' (ἐξέλθατε, *exelthate*; the second person plural aorist imperative is governed by a singular noun group, ὁ λαός [*ho laos*], which is treated as a collective), away from Babylon, closely echoes several prophetic passages in the Old Testament (such as Isa. 48.20 ['go out from Babylon']; 52.11; Jer. 50.8 ['flee from Babylon']; 51.6, 9, 45). The summons to flight is a regular theme in the record of Israel's history, when God's people are urged to escape his coming judgement (cf. Gen. 12.1–3; 19.12–22; Exod. 12.30–32; Num. 16.26–27; *2 Apoc. Bar.* 2.1; also Acts 7.3–4, 7); and it reappears in the New Testament as an exhortation to be separate from the world (2 Cor. 6.14; Eph. 5.11; 1 Tim. 5.22; cf. also Rev. 11.8). It should not be taken here in a literal sense, as in the case of the invitation for those in Judaea to flee to the mountains at the end time (Mark 13.14 par.).

The faithful are exhorted to come away from Babylon, so that they may not 'share in her sins, or endure any of her plagues'. It is likely that Babylon's 'sins', which result in judgemental 'plagues' (πληγαί, *plēgai*), are to be understood here as primarily those of idolatry; for compromise, leading to unfaithfulness and idolatry, is characteristic of the scarlet whore (see 17.1–6; 18.2–3). This view is supported by the background to verse 4 in Isa. 52.11, where the charge to 'depart' is followed by the command to touch nothing 'unclean' (LXX ἀκάθαρτος, *akathartos*), which is a reference to the Babylonian idols; and in Rev. 18.2 (q.v.) Babylon's status as 'unclean', repeated three times, also involves idolatry. Similarly, in Jer. 51.44–52 the summons to flight includes the need to separate from idol worship. See further Beale 898. The 'unclean' city of Babylon contrasts markedly with the 'holy' city of Jerusalem (21.2, 10), into which nothing unclean may enter (21.27; also 22.11–15). Cf. Caird 222–23. The reference to the 'plagues' suffered by Babylon must be an allusion to the bowl-judgements, on all kinds of sinful injustice, which are described in Rev. 16. It is significant, in this case, that the account of Babylon's fall in Rev. 17—18 is introduced by one of the angels with the golden bowls (probably the seventh; see on 17.1).

The faithful are encouraged to separate from Babylon not only to avoid being contaminated by her sinfulness but also to escape her coming judgement. Beale (898) points out that the 'flights' of Abraham and Lot in Genesis, and the withdrawals urged on God's people by the prophets Isaiah and Jeremiah (see above), are both physical and moral in character; whereas the separation mentioned in Rev. 18.4 is spiritual. Nevertheless, in the present passage believers are not being persuaded to retreat from the world itself, where they need to bear faithful testimony to the Lamb, but rather from an attitude of worldliness (cf. Rev. 11.3–7; 12.11; 14.12–13; 16.6, 15; 17.6; John 16.33; 17.14–19; 1 John 2.15–17; 4.14). Cf. Sweet 266.

In the phrase, ἵνα μὴ συγκοινωνήσητε (*hina mē synkoinōnēsēte*, 'so that you do not share [in her sins]'), the unusual verb (which appears in the New Testament only here and at Eph. 5.11; Phil. 4.14) is appropriate; for those who yield to Babylon's seductive attractions will become 'unclean' (κοινός, *koinos*) as she is, and thereby disqualified from entering the holy city (21.27); cf. Beale 899. The final clause, καὶ ἐκ τῶν πληγῶν αὐτῆς ἵνα μὴ λάβητε (*kai ek tōn plēgōn autēs hina mē labēte*, lit. 'and from her plagues that you may not receive'), is untypical of John's grammar in Revelation, since the partitive genitive ('from her plagues') precedes the conjunction ἵνα (*hina*, 'that'). Normally that order is reversed, as in the previous sentence and 2.10; 3.11; et al. Aune (991) notes the chiastic structure of the two strophes which results from the order of the second: lit. 'so that you do not share/in her sins, and from her plagues/that you may not endure'.

The background to the statement in verse 5 that Babylon's 'sins', which caused her to endure judgemental plagues, are so great that they have 'reached up to heaven', is once again to be located in Jer. 51. For this expression of magnitude see Jer. 51.9 ('[Babylon's] judgement has reached up to heaven'); also Gen. 11.4; Deut. 1.28; 2 Chron. 28.9; Dan. 4.11–22. See further Homer, *Odyssey* 15.329. In the literature of Judaism, 'reaching up', or being 'lifted up', is used to denote intense corporate sin which threatens the sovereignty of God himself (cf. Ezra 9.6; Jonah 1.2; 1 Esdras 8.75; 4 Ezra 11.43). The idea that the sins of Babylon have 'reached heaven', so as to provoke from God a judgemental response, may be a deliberate parody of the prayers of the saints rising to heaven in the smoke of angelic incense (8.3–4); cf. Aune 992.

The announcement that God has 'remembered the misdeeds (ἀδικήματα, *adikēmata*, lit. "injustices")' of Babylon suggests that the consequences of her wrongdoing are severe. The verbs in the aorist, in the two halves of verse 5 (ἐκολλήθησαν . . . ἐμνημόνευσεν, *ekollēthēsan . . . emnēmoneusen*, 'reached . . . remembered'), are used as prophetic perfects. Only here in the New Testament does God appear as the subject of a verb meaning 'to remember' (but see Rev. 16.19). In the literature of the Old Testament and Qumran, petitioners ask God to remember them (as in Judg. 16.28; Job 7.7; Ps. 74.2; 89.50; Isa. 38.3; et al.), and God remembers his servants (e.g. Gen. 8.1; 1 Sam. 1.19; cf. *Pss. Sol.* 5.16) or his covenant with them (CD-A 1.4; 6.2). For the general thought of sin being 'remembered', and punished in 'double' measure (so verse 6), see Ps. 109.14–20; Isa. 40.2; Jer. 16.18; Hos. 9.9–17.

6   The plea that Babylon should receive what 'she has given to others' ('paid back in her own coin', REB), and repaid 'the equivalent (τὰ διπλᾶ, *ta dipla*, lit. 'the double') of what she has done', is an allusion to Jer. 50.29 (LXX 27.29): 'Repay her (Babylon) according to her deeds; just as she has done, do to her'. See also Ps. 137.8 (LXX 136.8); Jer. 50.15 (LXX 27.15). The picture of 'repayment' is sometimes used in the New Testament of suffering received in return for suffering inflicted (cf. Rom. 12.17; 1 Thess. 5.15; 1 Pet. 3.9; et al.). The punishment of the historical Babylon foreshadows in Revelation the judgement of God on systemic evil (cf. Beale 901).

For Babylon to be repaid 'double' for her deeds, if that is the strict meaning, appears unjust; since the principle behind the *lex talionis* in the thought of Judaism (Exod. 21.24; Deut. 19.21) is that of 'an eye for an eye'. It also reverses the practice of repaying generously what has been borrowed (cf. *T. Job* 4.7–8; Luke 19.8). In Homer, *Iliad* 13.445–47, the scale of retribution is on the scale of three to one. However, it is more likely that the sense of the line in verse 6 is the one given in the translation: 'repay Babylon the equivalent of what she has done'. For the Hebrew parallel to the uses in the LXX of the verb διπλόω (diploō, lit. 'double', used only here in the New Testament) and the adjective διπλοῦς (diplous, 'double'), namely כָּפַל (kāpal) and כֶּפֶל (kepel), has the meaning of 'to repeat' or 'duplicate', 'equivalent' (e.g. Exod. 36.16 [MT 39.9]; Job 11.6). Repetition and equivalence may also be the significance of the texts at Isa. 40.2 (Jerusalem has received 'double for all her sins') and Jer. 16.18 (the Lord says of the unfaithful, 'I will doubly repay their iniquity and their sin'), which this part of Rev. 18.6 seems to echo; and such is the meaning of the adjective διπλοῦς (diplous) in its two occurrences elsewhere in the New Testament (Matt. 23.15; 1 Tim. 5.17; see also the 'similar measure' of retribution which, according to verse 7, is to be meted out to Babylon). For this interpretation see Beckwith 715; Hendriksen 174 (Babylon will not receive twice as much judgement as she deserves, but 'the exact amount of punishment which she has earned'); Hughes 191; Sweet 269; Beale 901; Bauckham 1301b.

In verse 6, the subject of the imperatives, ἀπόδοτε (apodote, 'render', lit. 'give'), διπλώσατε (diplōsate, 'repay') and κεράσατε (kerasate, 'mix'), is not immediately apparent; see Aune 993–94. It is most unlikely that believers themselves are being urged to take vengeance on Babylon, since this violates the New Testament command that Christians should love their enemies (Matt. 5.44; et al.; cf. Boring 188–89; Prigent 504). Equally, it is not clear that the subject of the action is to be regarded as a group, such as the ten kings of 17.12–14, who are destined to be agents of divine destruction; since the 'kings' are not identified at this point, although they are mentioned at 18.3 and 9 (against Goppelt, 'potērion' 844). The best way of interpreting this passage is to regard the commands to render, repay and mix as being addressed to angels of punishment, who minister God's judgement (see above, on 14.9–11; also Swete 229 ['ministers of Divine justice']; Beckwith 714 ['spirits of vengeance']; Caird 224 ['angelic agents of retribution']).

Nevertheless, as Beale (900) observes, God himself must be included among those who carry out his commands, for ultimately he is the one who dispenses the judgement on Babylon, as on the world. In that case, the imperatives in verse 6 (as in verse 7) become those of entreaty, rather than command (see Luke 17.5). For divine retribution as a positive notion see above, 379; also on 6.9–11. For the idea of retributive justice in general cf. further Judg. 1.7; Ps. 28.4; Prov. 24.12; Isa. 3.11; Sir. 16.12; Pss. Sol. 17.8; Rom. 2.6; 2 Tim. 4.14; 2 Clem. 17.4; et al. If God is involved, then the issue is one of just requital and not divine revenge (Mounce 328). For the imagery and thought of the last strophe in verse 6 ('mix a double draught for her in the cup which she has mixed') see on 14.8; also 17.2, 4; 18.3. In the very cup from which Babylon made corrupt nations and worldly merchants drink the passionate wine of her passionate adultery (verse 3), she must now imbibe the wrath of God (cf. Ps. 75.8; Lam. 4.21; Ezek. 23.31–35; Hab. 2.15–16; 2 Apoc. Bar. 13.8); see Beckwith 714; Mounce 328.

Beale (901) notes that each section of verse 6 contains two forms of the same word or word group: ἀποδίδωμι (apodidōmi, 'give') in the first; διπλο- (diplo-, 'double' cognates, with a third at the end of the line), and κεράννυμι (kerannymi, 'mix') in the third. This literary arrangement ('render . . . given', 'double the double' and 'mix . . . mix double') draws attention to the reality of the matching judgement which is to befall Babylon (ibid.). In the phrase, ᾧ ἐκέρασεν (hō[i] ekerasen, 'which she has mixed'), the relative pronoun in the dative is the only instance in the Apocalypse of a pronoun being attracted to the case of its antecedent (τῷ ποτηρίῳ, tō[i] potērio[i], 'the cup', dative singular). This attraction, by contrast, regularly occurs in other parts of the Johannine literature (John 4.14; 7.39; 1 John 3.24; et al.). See Charles 1, xxix.

7–8 Verse 7 repeats the idea which, it has been argued, belongs to verse 6: that Babylon's judgement should match her wrongdoing. As she has glorified herself, and lived luxuriously, the voice from heaven continues, 'so give her a similar measure of torment and grief'. This is the sense of the Greek, where τοσοῦτον (*tosouton*, 'so much') relates to ὅσα (*hosa*, 'as much'), and gives the meaning '*to the degree that* (she has glorified herself and lived luxuriously), *to the same degree* (give her torment and grief)'. See BDAG 729b. The sin of pride and arrogant self-assertiveness, or *hybris*, is often condemned by biblical writers (cf. 2 Sam. 22.28; Prov. 16.18; 29.23; Isa. 3.16–17; Luke 1.51; 14.11; Jas. 4.6–10), who are clear that 'glory' (δόξα, *doxa*) should be ascribed to the Godhead alone (as in Rev. 1.6; 4.9–11; 5.11–13; 7.12; 15.4; 19.1). Pride, like blasphemy, is appropriately a defining characteristic of the Antichrist (13.5). The verb, ἐστρηνίασεν (*estrēniasen*), found in the New Testament only here and at verse 9, means basically '(she) lived in luxury' (see 17.4). But it can also include the thought of 'living sensually' (BDAG 949a; cf. Aune 963, 994); and this rendering of the term also accords with the nature of the scarlet whore herself (17.1–5).

Babylon's punishment involves 'torment and grief'. For the subject of the imperative, δότε (*dote*, 'give'), as angels of judgement, see on verse 6. 'Torment' (βασανισμός, *basanismos*; as also in verses 10 and 15) means the severe suffering or pain associated with torture. The term is used at 9.5 (*bis*) of the psychological pain experienced by the unfaithful as a result of the plague of locust-scorpions, and at 14.11 of the suffering undergone by the followers of the beast. 'Grief' (πένθος, *penthos*), here and later in verse 7 (also verse 8; otherwise in the New Testament only at Rev. 21.4; Jas. 4.9), signifies the experience or expression of sadness, including that brought about by bereavement (hence the translation of the noun as 'mourning' in verse 7b, and as 'bereavement' in verse 8).

The Babylonian woman now begins a soliloquy ('in her heart'), which provides further basis for her judgement; note the use of ὅτι (*hoti*, 'for' or 'because') here and in verse 5. The short, rhetorical monologue is closely modelled on Isa. 47.7–9 (q.v.); for the literary form see also Ezek. 28.2; *Sib. Or.* 5.168–78, esp. 5.173; Rev. 3.17. For Babylon's claimed status as a 'queen', challenging the nature of God as King, see 4Q179 *frag.* 2.5 (Babylon is called the 'princess' of all the nations, who has become 'desolate like an abandoned woman'). As with the Babylon of history, the eschatological Babylon sees herself as both in control and perpetually surrounded by her equally corrupt offspring ('not a widow', and 'never mourning'). But this self-idolatrous confidence is ill founded, and her apparent social, economic and religious security will be swiftly demolished (see Jer. 50.31–32). As often in this section of the Apocalypse, 'Babylon' becomes typical of the downfall of worldly systems which are self-perpetuating and self-indulgent, up to the end of history and at its climax. Cf. further Caird 223; Beale 903.

The stylistic phrase at the start of verse 8, διὰ τοῦτο (*dia touto*, 'for this reason' or 'therefore'; lit. 'because of this'), refers back to the words following ὅτι (*hoti*, 'for') in verse 7. Babylon will be judged for the pride of her arrogant and idolatrous claims. NRSV inserts a full stop at the end of verse 7a and begins a new sentence with 'Since in her heart she says', which is then carried through to the end of verse 8. But it is probably better to divide verses 7 and 8 into four sentences, as in the translation (also NIV; similarly REV, ESV). An important background to the thought of verse 8 is to be found in Dan. 5, where Belshazzar the Babylonian ruler and his courtiers, drinking wine from the sacred vessels of the Temple and praising gods made with human hands (5.2–4), suddenly see their fate being written on the wall (5.5–6). In the same way Babylon, drunk with the blood of martyrs (17.6; 18.24), will swiftly (ἐν μιᾷ ἡμέρᾳ, *en mia[i] hēmera[i]*, lit. 'in one day'; cf. 18.10, 17, 19, 'in one hour') experience disaster. Cf. Mounce 329.

The judgement of systemic evil, represented by Babylon and including Rome, is symbolized by 'her plagues' (αἱ πληγαί αὐτῆς, *hai plēgai autēs*) of 'pestilence and bereavement and famine'. Charles (2, 100) translates the Greek as 'famine and pestilence and misfortune', and sees this order as chronologically dictated by the anti-Roman activity of the Parthians from the east under the revived Nero. But this interpretation is unnecessarily strained. A more likely connection is to be found in the 'plagues' brought about in the vision of the four horsemen (Rev. 6.1–8), and particularly in the results caused by the opening of the fourth seal (6.7–8). These include 'pestilence' (θάνατος, *thanatos*, lit. 'death'; for this rendering see on 6.8) and 'famine' (λιμός, *limos*; apart from 18.8, the only other occurrence of this term in Revelation appears at 6.8). 'Death' (θάνατος, *thanatos*) is the name of the cavalier who presides over the whole scene in this part of Chapter 6; and this is echoed in the present verse (18.8) through the term 'bereavement' (πένθος, *penthos*), the 'mourning' of verse 7 which can follow physical death.

The thought of Rev. 6.8 as a whole seems to derive from Ezek. 14.21, where the prophet speaks of the fourfold acts of judgement on unfaithful Jerusalem; and three of these are the 'sword' (leading to death), 'famine' and 'pestilence'. Note the reverse of such judgements in 21.4, where the faithful are promised an end to 'death (θάνατος, *thanatos*) and mourning (πένθος, *penthos*; this is the only other use of that noun in Revelation, apart from 18.7–8, but see the appearance of the cognate verb at 18.11, 15, 19)'. In 18.8 the heavenly voice is describing the 'plagues' of the new Exodus (cf. 11.6; 15.3–4; 16.9, 21; 21.9; et al.), heralding further criticism of the injustice and idolatry which may belong to institutional systems. As with the message of the apocalyptic horsemen, opposition to God in any form is seen here to bring its own eschatological judgement; even if, through the process of divine appraisal, it is evident that God can bring to his Church and his world both deliverance and wholeness. See further on 6.8.

Babylon is also to be 'burned with fire'; and, according to 17.16, such an action is carried out by the agents of God's justice, who turn against the scarlet woman. Judgement by fire is a regular biblical image (cf. Isa. 47.14; Jer. 51.25–58; 1 Cor. 3.13), just as the smoke of a burning city is the signal of its destruction (Gen. 19.27–28; et al.). For 'fire', as a metaphor of divine judgement in the Apocalypse, see also 1.14; 8.7–8; 9.17–18; 11.5; 13.13; 14.10; 16.8; 19.20; 20.9–10; 21.8; et al.

The final strophe of verse 8 is best understood as the conclusion to the earlier part of the verse, rather than as a deduction which is to be drawn from 18.4–8 as a whole (Aune 996). The statement answers the question implied in verse 8a. The swift and catastrophic destruction of 'Babylon' is only possible because of the supreme power invested in God himself. The adjective ἰσχυρός (*ischyros*, 'powerful', or 'mighty'), used as an epithet applied directly to God, is found in the New Testament only here (but cf. 1 Cor. 1.25; Eph. 1.19; also Jer. 50.34). For the title 'Lord God' (κύριος ὁ θεός, *kyrios ho theos*), as an ascription of divine sovereignty, see on 1.8; 4.11; 22.5; et al. In the end, John assures his audience, the Christian God of judgement is sovereign in strength; whereas Babylon, even if she has pretensions to 'rule as a queen' (verse 7), is *not*.

9–10 After the summons to flight in 18.4–8, the threnody chanted over Babylon at her judgement continues (verses 9–19). Worldly representatives of opposition to God's goodness and justice, at any level and at any moment, respond to the predicted and final destruction of the city; and their reaction is one of despair, since Babylon's desolation and loss of power point to their own downfall. The section, 18.9–19, consists of three laments, uttered by kings (verses 9–10), merchants (11–17a) and mariners (17b–19). It leads up to a call for the faithful to respond in their own way to the prediction of judgement on systemic evil (verse 20; see on the 'great whore' in 17.1–3). The background to this part of Chapter 18 (verses 9–19) can be located in Ezekiel's lament over Tyre in Ezek. 27. There the same three groups of mourners appear, even if their reactions differ to some extent: the kings are 'horribly afraid' (Ezek. 27.35); the merchants 'hiss' (verse 36), and the mariners 'wail aloud and cry bitterly' (verses 29–31). For this threefold pattern cf. also Ezek. 26.16–18 LXX. See further Mounce 331.

It is possible that the same angelic voice which was heard in verses 4–8 continues to speak in verse 9 (Beale 905); but the narration of the vision at this point may as well be ascribed to the seer himself. Mounce (331) distinguishes between the 'earthly rulers' (βασιλεῖς τῆς γῆς, *basileis tēs gēs*, lit. 'kings of the earth') mentioned here and the group in 17.16, who turn on the woman to bring about her destruction. He regards the 'rulers' of verse 9 as 'the governing heads of all nations', who have entered into illicit commercial dealings with Babylon (ibid.); cf. Beale 906. However, the view adopted in this commentary is that the 'rulers' of 18.9 (also 18.3) *are* to be identified with the 'kings of the earth' at 17.2 (q.v.), and also with the 'ten rulers' of 17.12–17. They represent a totality of worldly realms in general, which have yielded their allegiance to Satan and his followers, and which readily come together in order to overthrow other corrupt agencies. These are eschatological, not historical, figures, denoting the secular self-aggrandizement which attempts to usurp the authority and justice of God in any place at any time (see further on 17.2, 12–14).

In 17.16 the rulers are pictured as trying to destroy the Babylonian harlot; here they do not 'weep and wail over her' in sympathy, but precisely because they are mourning their own downfall, as predicted in hers. The link between the 'kings of the earth' in Rev. 18 and their counterparts in Chapter 17 is further established by the language of 'immorality and luxury', associated with them, which appears here (18.9) and at 17.2; 18.3. Their unfaithfulness, which reveals itself in a promiscuous desire to enter into wrong relationships of all kinds, reflects the idolatry and impurity of the scarlet woman herself (17.1–5; 18.4). The resulting desolation, mirroring that of Babylon, which is feared by the adulterous and therefore idolatrous 'rulers' in 18.9–10 (cf. 9.20–21; 14.8; 17.2), and picked up in the threnodies of the merchants and mariners (verses 11–19), appears to be primarily economic in character; cf. Beale 905–906, who notes the connection in John's day between idolatry and economic prosperity (see on 2.14, 20–22; also 4 Ezra 15.46–63). Nevertheless, while trading on land and sea may be regarded as an important part of the vision in Rev. 18, it should not be understood as the only sphere of wrongdoing which the seer has in mind. The judgement on Babylon which is envisaged involves secular institutions and corrupt systems in general; and if there is lamentation on the part of any of the three representative groups in Rev. 18, this is not so much the result of losing trade as losing status, and therefore power. Even more significantly, the real problem presented by this scene is that throughout the ages people who live without God, or in opposition to him, often remain unaware of the spiritual judgement and deprivation which imminently await them.

The verb, στρηνιάσαντες (*strēniasantes*, 'lived [lit. living] in luxury'), is used only here and at 18.7 in the New Testament; the cognate noun appears at verse 3. Both words may include overtones of sensuality (see on verse 7). For the expression, 'weep and wail (over Babylon)', see Jer. 51.8 ('suddenly Babylon has fallen . . . wail for her!'). The verb, κλαίω (*klaiō*, 'weep', 'cry'), in the context of lamentation, implies a loud expression of sorrow (cf. Luke 8.52; Jas. 4.9; also Rev. 18.11, 15, 19). In the middle voice κόπτω (*koptō*, lit. 'cut') means beating one's breast as a sign of mourning (Mounce 331 n. 32). For 'burning' with fire, as a symbol of divine judgement, see on verse 8; for the combination 'smoke from her burning' see verse 18; also Gen. 19.28; Isa. 34.9–10; Rev. 9.2, 17–18; 14.10–11.

In this account of Babylon's destruction (verse 10), it is said that the earthly rulers 'will stand far off' to continue their lament over the unfaithful city. This evocative stage direction is repeated in verses 15 and 17, with the result that the same symbolic distance is attributed to all three groups of onlookers (rulers, merchants, mariners). John wishes his audience to view the scope of the scene in its totality, through the eyes of those who have formerly gained from Babylon's wealth. 'Passing by' a deserted city is a feature of

Old Testament prophecy (Jer. 18.16; Lam. 2.15; Ezek. 5.14–15; et al.; cf. also 2 Chron. 7.21). Here, the space expresses metaphorically not only the horror felt by the spectators at Babylon's swift and dramatic demise, but also their wish to escape from a judgement which they deserve to share (Aune 997). Note the contrast between this scene and the account of the crucifixion of Jesus in Mark 15.40 par., where the women look on the cross 'from a distance' (also using ἀπὸ μακρόθεν, *apo makrothen*, lit. 'from far away').

The prophetic perfect participle, ἑστηκότες (*hestēkotes*, '[they] will stand', lit. 'were standing'), may be regarded as adverbial, modifying the preceding verb, βλέπωσιν (*blepōsin*, 'they see'). But, as Beale (906) suggests, it is better understood as a temporal modifier of the earlier verbs, κλαύσουσιν καὶ κόψονται (*klausousin kai kopsontai*, '[they] will weep and wail'), in verse 9 (so also the following participle in verse 10, λέγοντες, *legontes*, lit. 'saying'). In that case, two parallel clauses are formed, providing the reasons for the present threnody: the rulers will weep and wail *when* they see the smoke from Babylon's burning, and also *when* they stand far off, fearful of her torment, to continue their lament ('and [they] say . . .'). Here and in verse 15 the genitive, in the expression τὸν φόβον τοῦ βασανισμοῦ αὐτῆς (*ton phobon tou basanismou autēs*, 'fearful of her torment', lit. 'the fear of her torment'), is objective; and this gives the sense, 'the torment which Babylon is about to receive'. The rulers are fearful because the loss of the woman's position, marked by the torture which is to be meted out to her, signals their own sudden downfall (similarly verses 15–17, 19). For 'torment' (βασανισμός, *basanismos*) see on verse 7; cf. also 9.5; 14.11.

The exclamation, 'Woe, woe to the great city!', is repeated by the merchants and the seafarers (verses 16 and 19). The onomatopoeic word 'woe', in Greek (οὐαί, *ouai*) as in English, suggests both the shock and the grief of Babylon's former lovers. That they should identify the scarlet woman as both 'great' (μεγάλη, *megalē*) and 'mighty' (ἰσχυρά, *ischyra*) indicates their own idolatrous nature, as well as that of Babylon herself. For these are epithets properly reserved for God, not least when portraying his judgemental reaction to Babylon and her followers (6.17; 16.14; 18.8; 19.17). The description of Babylon in verse 10, as both 'mighty' (ἰσχυρά, *ischyra*) and caught in a moment of 'reckoning' (κρίσις, *krisis*, lit. 'judgement'), forms an intentional contrast to the presentation of God in verse 8 as 'powerful' (ἰσχυρός, *ischyros*, lit. 'strong') and also as the one who has 'judged' (ὁ κρίνας, *ho krinas*) the plagued city (Beale 907).

Babylon's judgement is dramatically swift: it takes place 'in a single moment' (μιᾷ ὥρᾳ, *mia[i] hōra[i]*, lit. 'in one hour'); for the translation see Black, 'Some Greek Words' 141–42. Note the use of the same formula, with reference to Babylon's destruction by her former allies, at 17.12 (cf. verse 16). It is also used in the other two divisions of the present section (18.9–19), at verses 17 and 19; and in verse 17, as here (verse 10), it introduces an allusion to final judgement (Beale 907). The phrase derives from Dan. 4.17a LXX (see also Dan. 4.19 LXX, Theod.), in the context of the judgement which came upon King Nebuchadrezzar of Babylon, whose prosperity was removed because of his unwillingness to submit to God's sovereignty. The same is true of the 'Babylon' portrayed in Rev. 17—18. The 'reckoning' (κρίσις, *krisis*, lit. 'judgement' or 'condemnation'; cf. BDAG 569a) of secular and systemic wrongdoing, and the punishment for proudly attempting to usurp the Kingship of the Lord, is at least to face economic disaster. But this in itself points to a deeper and more lasting spiritual deprivation, and to a judgement at the end which the earthly rulers now perceive will be shared with Babylon herself. For both, it will be catastrophic, sudden and well deserved. An 'hour' of persecution (17.12–14) is to be balanced by a similar period of retribution (cf. Caird 226).

11–13 These three verses provide a brief prose interlude in what is mostly a threnody in poetic form (but see verses 1, 9, 15, 17*b*, 21). The merchants of the earth and the seafarers, in the remaining two groups of mourners who feature in Rev. 18, like the 'rulers' of verses 9–10, are figurative and indeed eschatological representatives of illicit enterprises which have a primarily economic character. For they are in a close relationship with 'Babylon', and have therefore been engaged in commercial activities which aped the systemic evil of all kinds which she embodies (political, social, religious); as a result, they are subject to her end-time judgement. But the merchants and the maritime traders are more grounded than the rulers in the historical situation of luxury and wealth which belonged to the Mediterranean world of the first century AD. Babylon's worldly 'merchants' (18.23; see also verse 3), engaged in trading with Rome, were mostly provincial citizens of the exporting cities from which the merchandise mentioned here derived (cf. Bauckham, *Climax of Prophecy* 373).

The threnody of the secular merchants, in verses 11–17*a*, is longer than that of the rulers because the song of Ezekiel (Ezek. 27.12–24), which inspired this passage, includes such an extensive catalogue of the wares in which Tyre traded (Beasley-Murray 266–67). For the volume of merchandise involved, and the wealth and luxurious lifestyle of the Empire which it reflects, see Aristides, *In Rom.* 11; Pliny, *Nat. Hist.* 6.26, esp. 101–106; Prigent 505–509; also Rev. 18.3, 9. John's term for 'merchants' (ἔμποροι, *emporoi*) probably includes the independent shipowners who bought and sold their cargoes at the ports; hence the owners are not included in the group of seafarers, who are all their employees, listed at verse 17 (Bauckham, *Climax of Prophecy* 373). The merchants 'weep and mourn' for Babylon, not for her sake but for their own; since (ὅτι, *hoti*, lit. 'because') 'no one buys their goods any more'. Babylon's loss implies their own.

The present tense of the first two verbs in verse 11, κλαίουσιν (*klaiousin*, 'they weep') and πενθοῦσιν (*penthousin*, 'they mourn'), replaces the use of the future tense in the parallel doublet at verse 9, κλαύσουσιν καὶ κόψονται (*klausousin kai kopsontai*, '[they] will weep and wail'); in verses 11, 15 and 19 πενθέω (*pentheō*, 'mourn'), replaces the verb κόπτω (*koptō*, 'wail', lit. 'cut') in verse 9. The future tense accords with the nature of the prophetic description which is in progress here; whereas the present, as often in Revelation (4.4–5; 11.4–6; et al.), is a literary device which helps to switch the audience into the action of the drama, and make the visionary material vivid and immediate (cf. Smalley, *Thunder and Love* 105). It is characteristic for the author, notably in this section of the Apocalypse, to mix past, present and future tenses; see verses 4 (ἤκουσα, *ēkousa*, 'I heard' aorist), 7 (λέγει, *legei*, 'she says', present indicative) and 8 (κατακαυθήσεται, *katakauthēsetai*, 'she will be burned', future); see also verses 15–19 (Beale 909).

The term γόμος (*gomos*, 'goods', 'cargo'), which is used in the New Testament only here and at Acts 21.3, means a load or freight which is carried by a conveyance (BDAG 205*a*). The noun is repeated directly at the start of verse 12, and also by implication before the list of animals and humans towards the end of verse 13, q.v. (note the change of case there from accusative to genitive plural); cf. Bengel 357.

In verses 12–13, the angelic voice (or the seer) lists the items of 'cargo' (γόμον, *gomon*; cf. verse 11) which no longer featured in the corrupt trading systems of 'Babylon'. It is a representative collection, reflecting the economic attractiveness of a systemic evil which seduces rulers and merchants into unfaithful and idolatrous relationships with the scarlet woman (see 17.1–5). The material products of gold, purple and scarlet, which appear at the beginning of the list in verse 12 (also verse 16), pick up the description of the Babylonian whore at 17.4; although in 18.12, 16, and not at 17.4, 'fine linen' is included (cf. Beale 909).

A background to the 'cargo' in verses 12–13 may be found in Ezek. 27.12–24, with its details of the imports sold by the 'merchants' (ἔμποροι, *emporoi*, Ezek. 27.21–23 LXX; as here in Rev. 18.3, 11, 15, 23) who traded with Tyre (cf. Beale, *Use of the Old Testament* 77). Strikingly, 15 of the 29 products which appear in Ezek. 27 are included at Rev. 18.12–13. John's list, like Ezekiel's, echoes the merchandise which was in circulation at the time. But here it is much more than a commercial catalogue; it is theological, rather than historical. In the first place, the items suggest the luxurious and consequently idolatrous style of living adopted by Rome and its imperial followers in the first century AD. Second, while the goods mentioned are not evil in themselves, the wickedness of the whole commercial operation which is taking place is indicated by the injustice and inhumanity of slave trading in human lives with which the list concludes, and by which it is infected (see below). Cf. further Swete 235; Sweet 271; Bauckham, *Climax of Prophecy* 366–68; Prigent 508. Beale (910) comments that the loss of the merchants of the land, as of the sea traders (18.11–19), receives greater attention than that of the rulers (verses 9–10), and concludes that this is meant to act as a warning to those members of the Johannine circle who were attracted to associate themselves with an idolatrous trade system, and compromise dangerously as a result (cf. 2.9, 14, 20–21).

The inventory in verses 12–13 is divided by Mounce (333) into six groups of from four to six items each. Beckwith (715–16) finds seven groups by adding in the 'ripe fruit' of verse 14 (q.v.). But a more natural, and typically Johannine, division into *seven* (*sic*) is possible according to the following structure, which may be determined by considerations of rhetoric (cf. Mounce 333 n. 38):

(a) *metals*, such as gold and silver;
(b) *precious stones*, including pearls;
(c) *cloth*, consisting of linen and rich materials;
(d) *costly articles*, made of wood, ivory, metal and marble;
(e) *food products*, together with spices and aromatic perfumes;
(f) *chattels* of animals, and the provision of horses and chariots;
(g) *humanity*, in the form of slaves.

For the details of the commodities, and their significance, see further Bauckham, *Climax of Prophecy* 350–71; Prigent 506–509.

In verse 12, the reference to 'pearls' (μαργαριτῶν, *margaritōn*), following the metals of gold and silver, is undoubtedly intended to recall the description of the prostitute at 17.4, as 'glittering with (golden jewellery and) pearls'. Babylon and the scarlet whore are one and the same (Prigent 506). The same is true of the inclusion, as one main commodity, of expensive material which is purple and scarlet in colour (see above, and on 17.4). For 'fine linen' (βύσσινος, *byssinos*), an adjective used here in its substantive form, and found only in Revelation in the New Testament, see also 18.16; 19.8, 14. The term, 'silk' (σιρικός, *sirikos*) appears only here in the New Testament, and is not used at all in the Old Testament. Silk came from China, and was so expensive as to be a rare sign of wealth and power. Nevertheless, it was imported in great quantities; and at a celebration of the triumph of Vespasian and his son Titus, according to Josephus (*Bell. Jud.* 7.5.4), they appeared crowned with laurel wreaths and dressed in silk.

The dark and scented 'citron (citrus) wood' (θύϊνον, *thyinon*) was a costly import from North Africa, used to make expensive furniture. The patterns formed by its graining were unusual and ornamental; and its hard nature made it resistant both to decay and staining. As Aune (1000) points out, the latter quality meant that it was an ideal surface on which to serve wine! See further Martial, *Epigrams* 14.3.85; Pliny, *Nat. Hist.* 13.30.96–97. Evidently John is speaking, as in the phrases which follow, about objects of all kinds (πᾶν, *pan*, lit. 'all') made with this precious wood (Prigent 507). The term σκεῦος (*skeuos*), which is used twice in the remaining part of verse 12, refers to a material object used for any purpose at all (BDAG 927*b*); so that, in the phrase καὶ πᾶν σκεῦος (*kai pan skeuos*, lit. 'and every thing'), the translation 'all articles/objects' becomes appropriate. The noun, ἐλεφάντινον (*elephantinon*, 'ivory'), is found only here in the New Testament. Ivory was an expensive decorative product, imported from Africa (cf. Ezek. 27.6, 15); and wealthy Romans were known to eat from ivory plates.

Verse 12 concludes with a group of four costly products: 'wood, bronze, iron and marble'. The corresponding Greek nouns, each in the genitive, follow the preposition ἐκ (*ek*, 'of', 'from'), thus denoting the material from which the articles were made: 'wood' of high value, used for furniture, panelling and sculpture in the homes of the rich; 'bronze', especially associated with Corinth; 'iron', often derived from deposits in Greece, and prized for the fabrication of weapons and statues (cf. Ezek. 27.12–13); and 'marble' (μάρμαρος, *marmaros*, a term found only here in the New Testament), a building material which came from Phrygia, the use of which indicated obvious wealth. The adjective, τιμιωτάτου (*timiōtatou*, 'costly') is one of two superlatives in Revelation (the other is at 21.11), both of which have an elative sense. The meaning is strictly, therefore, 'most precious'. For this section see further Aune 1000–1001.

Verse 13 begins by listing four aromatic spices which were popular throughout the Mediterranean world at the time when the Apocalypse was written. This is to assume, no doubt correctly, that the καί (*kai*, 'such as', lit. 'and') after θυμιάματα (*thymiamata*, 'incense') is epexegetical. The perfumes (Ezek. 27.22) in question are 'cinnamon', or cassia, which was imported from Africa and the Orient, and used as scent or incense, as well as for medicinal purposes and to flavour wine (cf. Prov. 7.17; Song of Sol. 4.14); 'spice' (ἄμωμον, *amōmon*, lit. 'amomum'), a fragrant-smelling shrub from southern India, which helped to scent the hair; with 'myrrh' and 'frankincense', both of which were imported into the Roman world from Arabia and Somalia. Myrrh was an expensive perfume, which could also act as incense and spice, and be used as a deodorant, in medicine or in the embalming process. Frankincense was often used at funerals (Pliny, *Nat. Hist.* 12.41.82–83). Cf. Mounce 333.

The next four products complete the fifth group of cargo no longer bought and sold by the worldly Babylonian merchants. 'Wine, oil, fine flour and wheat' are foodstuffs which at the time were staple goods, rather than luxuries; although this very fact would have made them extremely profitable in trade terms. The one possible exception is 'fine flour' (σεμίδαλις, *semidalis*, another of several words in this section unique to Revelation), which is a high-grade wheat flour of the very best quality (cf. BDAG 919*a*), not available to the general public. It was produced in Italy, and also imported from Egypt (Aune 1002). Wine was available in great quantities from Sicily, Greece and Spain; olive oil came from Italy; while Africa and Egypt supplied Rome with grain for making bread. 'Beasts of burden and sheep' are the first animate creatures to be listed here. Once more they are fairly basic commercial items. The word rendered as 'cattle' in most versions, κτῆνος (*ktēnos*), effectively means (in the plural, as here) domestic 'beasts of burden'; hence the translation (cf. Luke 10.34; Acts 23.24). 'Horses and carriages', by contrast, would have been specially luxurious. The ῥέδη (*hredē*, 'carriage'), a term found only here in the New Testament and usually translated as 'chariot', was a four-wheeled travelling vehicle used by the Roman aristocracy. Bengel (357) rightly points out that γόμον (*gomon*, 'cargo'), from the start of verse 12, needs to be supplied before the genitive plurals (beginning with ἵππων, *hippōn*, 'horses') which at the end of verse 13 suddenly replace the earlier accusatives.

The final phrase of verse 13, καὶ σωμάτων, καὶ ψυχὰς ἀνθρώπων (*kai sōmatōn kai psychas anthrōpōn*, 'and slaves, that is, human beings', lit. 'and of bodies, and the souls of men') is problematic. It is important to recall that first-century Asia Minor was heavily exploited for slaves, with Rome as the greatest of all slave markets (Aune 1003). The word σώματα (*sōmata*, as here), at the time, commonly meant 'slaves'; and a 'slave merchant' was called a σωματέμπερος (*sōmatemperos*); cf. LXX Gen. 36.6; Tobit 10.10; Bel and Dr. 32; 2 Macc.

8.11. This is undoubtedly the significance of the noun at the end of verse 13. The expression, ψυχὰς ἀνθρώπων (*psychas anthrōpōn*, lit. 'souls of men'), is taken from Ezek. 27.13 LXX, where it also alludes to slaves. In view of this evidence, it is possible that the writer has in mind here two kinds of cargo: 'slaves' and 'human lives'. In this case, the reference might be to the regular slave trade on the one hand, and slaves who had to fight for their lives in the Roman amphitheatres on the other (Bauckham, *Climax of Prophecy* 370). But it is much more likely that the connective καί (*kai*, lit. 'and'), after σωμάτων (*sōmatōn*, 'slaves'), is epexegetical, giving the sense captured in the translation: 'slaves, *that is* human beings' (so e.g. Beckwith 717); and this involves the sinister implication that slaves, by definition, are generally regarded as no more than animals, to be bought and sold in the market-place.

Thus, the mention of slaves at the end of a catalogue of luxuries enjoyed by wealthy people, slaves who are exploited by worldly merchants, rather than at the beginning (as in Ezek. 27.13–24), provides the whole list with an important theological statement. John is not simply commenting on the slave trade, and the unjust attitude towards human beings adopted by those who regard them simply as merchandise ('human live-stock', in the phrase of Swete 235). By placing slaves and their unworthy treatment in an emphatic position at the conclusion of his list, the seer is attacking every aspect of the secular traffic of the seas. He is thereby denouncing the 'inhuman brutality, the contempt for human life, on which the whole of Rome's prosperity and luxury rests' (Bauckham, *Climax of Prophecy* 371; cf. Maurice 275–76). Sweet (272) notes that in Rev. 18.13 slaves come at the end of a list which is arranged in *descending* order of value.

Bengel (358) interprets the 'bodies' in this context (verse 13) as 'slaves' used for carrying the merchandise of their owners, and the 'souls of men' as slaves when they are treated as commercial objects. This is somewhat strained; but, as Mounce (334 n. 49) points out, it has the advantage of linking σωμάτων (*sōmatōn*, 'slaves') with the genitives which precede it, as well as allowing the awkward shift to the following accusative ψυχάς (*psychas*, lit. 'souls').

14   At this point the thought of verse 11, which has been interrupted by the list of rejected cargo in verses 12–13, is resumed. The merchants allied with the systemic evil of Babylon lament her vanished luxuries, and their corresponding economic loss. In verses 15–17*a* this threnody will be further articulated. Charles (2, 105–108) regards verse 14 as misplaced, and relocates it after verse 21 as part of the angelic dirge over the adulter-ous city. But this redaction is unnecessary; for even if verse 14 points forward to the speech of final judgement at 18.21–24 (note the echoes of the phrase, 'never to be found again', in verses 21–23), the present verse follows verses 11–13 naturally. The 'ripe fruits' for which Babylon and her allies lusted are exactly those which appear in the catalogue of the two previous verses. See Mounce 334 n. 50; Prigent 509.

The writer does not identify the speaker(s) of the isolated lament in verse 14, which is not introduced by a verb of 'saying' (contrast 18.10, 16, 19, 21). But there is no reason to doubt that these words are uttered by the mourning 'merchants of the earth' (verse 11), who suddenly and directly apostrophize the desolate Babylon (cf. the worldly rulers in verse 10). The failure of the 'ripe fruit', for which the soul of Babylon longed, refers to a cessation of trading in the exotic products listed at verses 12–13. The term, ἡ ὀπώρα (*hē opōra*), which once again is a *hapax legomenon* in the New Testament, is strictly speaking the time when fruit matures, in late summer or early autumn. Hence it comes to mean the 'fruit' itself (BDAG 718*a*). Prigent (509) translates the statement at the opening of verse 14 as, 'the season of your soul's desiring has passed', indicating that the time of Babylon's greedy maturity is over, and the moment to give account before

God is at hand. The Greek expression, τῆς ἐπιθυμίας τῆς ψυχῆς (*tēs epithymias tēs psychēs*, subjective genitive), means lit. 'of the desire of your soul'; but, in the present context, it comes to mean '(the fruit) for which your soul longed' (as in the translation; cf. NRSV, REB). The phrase is based on a Semitic idiom, and regularly appears in the LXX (cf. LXX Deut. 12.20–21; 14.26; Ps. 20.3; Jer. 2.24; 4 Macc. 2.1; also *Pss. Sol.* 2.24; *T. Reub.* 4.9; see further Aune 1003). The merchants' lament turns out to be a condemnation of the self-indulgent attitude of corrupt institutions, which strive for economic wealth and security, rather than the glory of God (cf. Beale 910).

The 'luxuries and splendours' (τὰ λιπαρὰ καὶ τὰ λαμπρά, *ta lipara kai ta lampra*, lit. 'the bright and glistening objects') speak of Babylon's former wealth and supposed glory (REB renders the phrase as '[all] the glitter and glamour are lost'). The poetic, alliterative sentence includes the hendiadys, 'luxuries and splendours', which really means 'luxurious splendours'. These nouns, as used here, are close in meaning; but they could allude respectively to the costly goods and decorative objects already mentioned in verses 12–13. The adjective, λιπαρός (*liparos*, 'luxurious', 'costly'), is found only here in the New Testament. For λαμπρός (*lampros*, 'splendid') see 15.6; 19.8; 22.1, 16). The concluding phrase of verse 14, 'never to be found again!', which summarizes the total void left by the lost causes just cited, forms an inclusion with the final sentence of verse 11 ('no one buys their goods any more'). The negative, οὐκέτι οὐ μή (*ouketi ou mē*, 'never again', lit. 'no longer, certainly not') is intensive (cf. LXX Jer. 38.40; Tobit [BA] 6.8; Odae 11.11).

15–17a For the language and thought of these verses see on 18.9–10; also 17.4. Traders in the market of luxury goods ('of these', τούτων, *toutōn*, verse 15; see verses 12–13) had made their fortune by associating with the corruption of Babylon; and, as a result, they became not only rich but also powerful ('high-ranking people of the world', verse 23). Like the worldly rulers (verse 9), they now 'weep and mourn' over Babylon; and this is not out of sympathy for her, but because the downfall of the city points towards their own judgement (see verse 10). Together with the mariners, the kings and the merchants owe their inclusion in the visionary threnody of Rev. 18 to the prophecy of Ezekiel (see esp. Ezek. 26.17—27.36, lamentation over Tyre). But all three groups should ultimately be understood as symbolic, and part of John's eschatological and apocalyptic apparatus; for in them the seer is really describing the single category of the 'inhabitants of the earth': that is to say, any idolaters of any age, who worship the beast, rather than God in Christ (13.8, q.v.; also 6.10; 8.13; 11.10; 13.12–14; 17.2, 8). See further on 18.9 (the 'rulers') and 18.11 (the 'merchants'); cf. also Prigent 509.

For the stage direction in verse 15, the merchants will stand 'at a safe distance' (ἀπὸ μακρόθεν, *apo makrothen*, lit. 'from afar'), see on verse 10; cf. also verse 17*b*. The traders are horrified by the swift demise of Babylon, but also wish to escape from a judgement which they deserve to share; equally, they fear the 'torment' (βασανισμός, *basanismos*) which is to be meted out to the woman, because it signals their own sudden desolation. This indicates a loss which is total and spiritual, not simply economic and material (against Beale 911–14).

For the poetic lament in verse 16 see the close parallel in 17.4; also 18.12. The glittering adornment of Babylon suggests that she has prostituted herself with those who are seduced by her superficial attractions. Systemic evil in any form and at any time, which seeks the loyalty of others rather than remaining faithful to God and his values, brings judgement upon itself ('Woe, woe to the great city!'; see on verse 9). In the same way, the harlot Israel whom God adorned with splendour was eventually condemned for her idolatrous behaviour (Ezek. 16.8–18). Using triplets, the merchants in verse 16 describe the Babylonian woman as clothed in 'fine linen, in purple and scarlet', and adorned with 'gold, precious stones and pearls'.

Beale (912–13) notes that this description of the impure harlot (the city of Babylon) in verse 16 contrasts markedly with the pure bride of Christ (the holy city of new Jerusalem) in 21.9–21, who is also adorned with gold, precious stones and pearls. The imagery from Exod. 28 and Ezek. 16 which lies behind the portrait of the new Jerusalem in Rev. 21, Beale (913) further proposes, suggests that God's true people (the bride) are set over against not only the economic-religious world of paganism (the whore) but also those members of the Christian Church who have compromised with the entire secular system (cf. the 'synagogue of Satan' in 2.9; 3.9). However, as Beale (913) admits, the imagery in 18.16 concerns not merely religious apostasy of any kind but also pagan systems in general which are oppressive because they are unjust. The 'linen' garment (βύσσινον, *byssinon*, used here as a substantive), which does not feature in the description of the scarlet whore at 17.4, may have been included under the influence of its appearance at 18.12 (cf. Swete 236). 'Adorned with gold' (κεχρυσωμένη [ἐν] χρυσίῳ, *kechrysōmenē [en] chrysiō[i]*, lit. 'gilded with gold'), as at 17.4, is a pleonasm.

The final strophe of the merchants' lament (verse 17*a*) echoes the mournful song of the earthly rulers in verse 10. But there is a significant change of phraseology. For the kings, Babylon is a city of 'power' (ἰσχυρά, *ischyra*, 'mighty', 'powerful'); to the merchants, she is an institution of 'wealth' (πλοῦτος, *ploutos*, a term found elsewhere in the Apocalypse only at Rev. 5.12). Each group views her fall in terms of its own interests (Mounce 335; cf. Swete 236). Note this distinction, in their relationship to each other and to 'Babylon', when the rulers and merchants are paired at 18.3, q.v. ('the kings of the earth have fornicated with her, and worldly merchants have become rich from her excessive wealth'). But, in the final analysis, there is no great difference among unbelievers. Like the scarlet woman, the kings have lost their *power*; while the traders have lost not merely their trade, but also the wealth and therefore the *power* and status which are derived from it. In one sense, it should be added, Revelation is all about the right and wrong use of power (see on 7.12). For the translation of μιᾷ ὥρᾳ (*mia[i] hōra[i]*, lit. 'in one hour') as 'in a single moment' see on verse 10; also verse 19.

17*b*–18   The third group of mourners to lament the destruction of Babylon are the mariners (verses 17*b*–19). In this image maritime agents, who transport the goods of the merchants (verses 11–13), weep more for their own deprivation than for that of the unfaithful city. Their motivation is selfish, and indeed idolatrous, as that of the merchants themselves (cf. Beale 914). This section of Rev. 18 is indebted to Ezek. 27.28–34 (see esp. 29–30), where the prophet is commanded by the Lord to raise a lamentation over Tyre (Ezek. 27.1–2).

Four types of sea-goer are involved in this threnody. First, 'every shipmaster' (πᾶς κυβερνήτης, *pas kybernētēs*), which refers to those who manage or steer ships (the 'captain'), rather than to those who *own* them. Second, 'all sea travellers' (πᾶς ὁ ἐπὶ τόπον πλέων, *pas ho epi topon pleōn*, lit. 'every one who sails to a place'), the meaning of which is not immediately clear (see the textual note on verse 17). Aune (1006; see 1005–1006) translates the phrase as 'all coastal travellers'; but Swete (237) is probably more accurate to understand the expression, one who 'sails for any part', as meaning any merchant with his goods, or chance passenger. The exact phrase does not occur elsewhere in the New Testament; but see Mark 13.8; Acts 27.2; also Strabo, *Geography* 3.1.7. The use of the verb πλέω (*pleō*, 'sail'), with ἐπί (*epi*, 'to') and the accusative, is rare; but see 4 Macc. 7.3; Thucydides, *History* 1.53.2. Third are the 'sailors' (ναῦται, *nautai*), a term which elsewhere in the New Testament is confined to Acts 27.27, 30. Finally, there are 'those who make a living from the sea' (ὅσοι τὴν θάλασσαν ἐργάζονται, *hosoi tēn thalassan ergazontai*, lit. 'those working [on] the sea [for a livelihood]'; cf. BDAG 389*b*). This phrase could mean all mariners in general; but it is better understood literally as a reference to such maritime traders as fishermen and pearl divers (Mounce 335). See Ps. 106.23 LXX.

For the stage direction at the end of verse 17, '(they) stood far off', which is a stance posited of all three groups of mourners in this chapter, see on verses 10 and 15. For the phrase, 'they saw the smoke from her burning', see on verse 9. The question, 'Has there ever been a city as great as this?' (τίς ὁμοία τῇ πόλει τῇ μεγάλῃ;, *tis homoia tē[i] polei tē[i] megalē[i]?*, lit. 'Who is like the great city?'), echoes Ezek. 27.32 ('Who was ever destroyed like Tyre/in the midst of the sea?'). This form of the rhetorical question, which expects a negative response and uses ὅμοιος (*homoios*, 'like') with an interrogative pronoun (τίς, *tis*, 'who'), appears also at 13.4 (q.v.); see also Deut. 33.29; Ps. 34.10 LXX; Sir. 48.4. A more direct variation ('there is no one/nothing like') may be found e.g. at 1 Kings 10.23; 2 Chron. 6.14; Ps. 85.8 LXX, et al. Cf. Aune 1006. Babylon and her allies thought of themselves as incomparable. But the city's greatness is illusory; and, as with all systemic evil, the scarlet woman turns out instead to be on her way to final judgement and permanent demise.

19   The second and final part of the threnody delivered by the sea-goers echoes that of the rulers and merchants (verses 10 and 16–17*a*). But, unlike them, and in a dramatic gesture which accompanies their 'weeping and mourning aloud' (see verse 15), the mariners 'threw dust (χοῦν, *choun*, a term which appears in the New Testament only here and at Mark 6.11) on their heads'. This action is based on the similar sign of lamentation over Tyre made by the wailing and crying seafarers and pilots in Ezek. 27.30 ('they throw dust on their heads and wallow in ashes'). Throwing dust on the head was a Jewish custom, expressing (among other responses) mourning and sorrow (cf. Josh. 7.6; Job 2.12; Lam. 2.10; 1 Macc. 11.71).

For the third time in this part of the interval (Rev. 18) a cry of woe, as uttered by all three groups of mourners, is heard (see on verses 10, 16); cf. Ezek. 27.32. In each case the Greek translated as 'Woe, woe to the great city' is identical. The cause of the lamentation in verse 19 is first attributed to the fact that 'all who had ships at sea grew rich' from Babylon's 'prosperity' (τιμιότης, *timiotēs*, lit. 'costliness', a term found only here in the New Testament). This probably means that trading by sea with any satanic systems such as 'Babylon/Rome' involves the buying and selling of expensive goods (see 18.12–13), as a result of which the seafarers themselves become wealthy (cf. Beckwith 718); and, selfishly, the mariners now regret their added economic loss, which derives from the downfall of the scarlet woman herself (see Ezek. 27.33).

This interpretation is supported by the last sentence of verse 19, where the sea-goers repeat the lament of the other two groups of mourners, and give a second reason for their lamentation: 'for (ὅτι, *hoti*) in a single moment she has been made desolate'. For the translation of μιᾷ ὥρᾳ (*mia[i] hōra[i]*, lit. 'in one hour') as 'in a single moment' see on verses 10, 17*a*. The Greek phraseology is identical in verses 17*a* and 19, but differs to some extent in verse 10, q.v. ('in a single moment your reckoning has arrived'). The swiftness of Babylon's desolation presages the sudden judgement of the mariners; for if all pictured maritime commerce ceases, then those engaged in such trading face bankruptcy. The lamentation in verse 19*b* is thus once more selfishly inspired by the prospect of deprivation. However, the loss involved is not simply economic, although such a dimension is paramount in the imagery of Rev. 18.11–19 (against Beale 914–15). For the symbolism of 'Babylon' and her allies relates to self-centred and secular, idolatrous enterprise of any kind, including that which may corrupt social, economic, religious and political systems in every age (see on 17.1–3).

20   Verse 20 represents a sudden change of mood and thought as, instead of the lamentation over the destruction of Babylon, the people of God are called upon to rejoice
in his justice. To account for this apparent aporia in the text, commentators have re-
sorted to a variety of explanations. For instance, Charles (2, 111–12, 353) 'restores' verse
20 to what he regards as its 'rightful place', after verse 23 and at 'the close of the writer's
dirge over Rome' (*idem* 2, 111). Aune (1006–1007) claims that the 'abrupt interjection'
of verse 20 does not belong to the lament of the sea-goers, and he therefore deems it to
be 'a subsequent addition to the text' (*idem* 1007). Mounce (336) views the swift transposition from threnody to joy as 'in keeping with the free style of the Apocalypse'.

However, neither critical surgery nor desperate devices are needed to justify the
character of verse 20, and its place in Rev. 18. The call to rejoice at this point is *not*
part of the lament by the mariners (verses 17*b*–19), although the punctuation of several
translations makes it appear to be such (see NIV, NRSV, NJB, ESV; but note AV, RV, REB).
The call is issued instead by the 'voice from heaven' (verse 4, q.v.), which speaks again
in verse 20. In Rev. 18.4–20, the vision is narrated by an angelic figure, and it is
mediated through the seer; so that the words of the threnody uttered by the sorrowing
rulers, merchants and mariners belong to a sub-text of which verse 20 does not form
part. This verse, with its call to rejoice, is rather a parenthetical, final comment by the
angel/seer on the dramatic scene which has just been acted out by the mourners; and in
its present, original position after so much that appears negative and without hope, these
words inject into the situation the positive aspect of God's love and life, active through
his judgement (this is underlined in 19.1–4).

The invitation to rejoice in verse 20 is not primarily a call for the saints to be vindictive in the light of 'Babylon's' destruction, although to some extent it may be interpreted
as the climax of the response to the saints' cry for vengeance in 6.10, q.v. (Beale 916).
For the theme of vengeance in the Apocalypse see above, 160–64. Importantly, the
summons in verse 20 is in the first place addressed to 'you heavens' (οὐρανέ, *ourane*, lit.
'O heaven!'); the singular form of the imperative, 'Rejoice!' (εὐφραίνου, *euphrainou*), is
governed by the fact that it precedes a series of subjects, the first of which ('heaven') is
singular, and all of which (including οἱ ἅγιοι καὶ οἱ ἀπόστολοι καὶ οἱ προφῆται, *hoi hagioi
kai hoi apostoloi kai hoi prophētai*, 'the saints, apostles and prophets') may be construed as
being in the vocative case (cf. Aune 1007). Such a call must be interpreted in the light
of 12.12, q.v. ('So let the heavens rejoice, and those who dwell there!'), and its Old
Testament parallel in Jer. 51.48, where the Israelite community as a whole ('the heavens
and the earth') is commanded to 'shout for joy over Babylon'. John picks up Jeremiah's
allusion to 'heaven'; but his reference to 'earth' is replaced by the 'saints, apostles and
prophets'. These three categories need not be distinguished as separate groups of
people, despite the use of three definite articles in the Greek (against Aune 1007),
although they do appear individually in Revelation (for 'saints', meaning the people
of God, see 8.3–4; 13.10; 14.12; et al.; for 'apostles', in the technical sense of those sent
out [or not] by Jesus see 2.2; 18.20; 21.14; for Christian 'prophets' see 11.10, 18; 16.6;
22.9). The combination 'saints and prophets' is used elsewhere in Revelation (16.6;
18.24), but not the trio of 'saints, apostles and prophets' (for which see also Eph. 5.5).

In 18.20, then, the call to rejoice is addressed to believers in general, the Church
glorified in heaven and witnessing on earth, rather than to particular groups in the
Christian community, or indeed to martyrs alone (cf. Beale 916; against Caird 230). In
12.12 the saints were commanded to rejoice because the victory over Satan had been
inaugurated; here they are invited to be joyful because God's triumph over satanic
systems has been consummated (Beale 916).

The last sentence of verse 20 elaborates the reason for celebration among members
of the new Israel: 'for (ὅτι, *hoti*) God has given judgement against her for condemning

you'. This phrase needs to be understood against a forensic background. Babylon has been found guilty of wrongdoing, and of deceiving her followers into the similarly idolatrous behaviour which is the mark of all systemic evil. Secular attitudes inevitably conflict with the ideals shared by God's people; although compromise with the standards of Babylon, on the part of believers, is still possible (Knight 123). Now God has turned back the evidence laid in opposition against the followers of Christ, and has brought judgement on their accusers (cf. verse 6; Isa. 44.23; 49.13); and his just nature has been established as a result. See Mounce 336; also further Caird 228–30; Sweet 274–75. The Greek at this point produces a paronomasia, where ἔκρινεν ὁ θεὸς τὸ κρίμα ὑμῶν (*ekrinen ho theos to krima hymōn*, lit. 'God has judged your judgement') means that God has exacted from Babylon the 'sentence' (κρίμα, *krima*) she passed on the saints (Sweet 275); cf. Deut. 19.16–19. For the literary technique of paronomasia in the Apocalypse see also 2.22; 11.18; 22.18–19; et al.

The lament over Babylon has ended, although the consequences of the city's downfall have yet to be enumerated by the strong angel who takes up the theme in verses 21–24. In this scene, the members of three major sections of society have selfishly mourned the demise of systemic evil, in terms of the loss to themselves. For they have succumbed to the blandishments of the scarlet whore for their own personal gain, and face ruin as a result. Without concern for the justice and love of God in Christ, human nature, in any age, tends to be self-centred and opportunistic, and to lay itself open to divine sentencing as a result. See Mounce 336.

Babylon Destroyed (18.21–24)

21 The threnody at the fall of Babylon (18.2–19) is continued in 18.21–24. These verses pick up and expand the language and thought of 18.14 (q.v.), where the merchants lament the disappearance of the city's wealth, once gained by its trade in exotic commodities. Verses 21–23 also pursue the double theme, enunciated in this section of Rev. 17—18, of the effects of Babylon's judgement both on herself and on her equally secular allies. Potentially, such discrimination could be experienced by compromising and therefore unfaithful members of the Johannine community itself (18.4). Finally, Rev. 18.21–24 provides a further comment on the meaning of verse 20*b* (q.v.). This paragraph forms a single text unit, marked by poetic couplets, in which verses 21 and 24 create an inclusion through the occurrence of the verb, even if used in different senses, 'be found' (see above, 425–26).

In verses 21–24 (esp. 22–23), the collapse of Babylon is witnessed from within the city. Earlier, the three groups of mourners (rulers, merchants, sea-goers) have stood in horror, and 'at a distance' from the city (verses 10, 15, 17*b*), mostly to escape a judgement which they also deserve. From that panoramic and safe vantage point they have looked on at the 'smoke of her burning' (verses 9, 18). Now there is a swift change of scene, and the audience of the drama is moved from the outer stage to the inner, to see for itself the consequences of Babylon's destruction, and to discover that the city is silent and inactive.

The resulting description finds an immediate background in Jer. 51.59–64. In that passage Seraiah the quartermaster was sent to Babylon, in the time of Jeremiah, to proclaim an oracle against the proud city, to tie a stone to the scroll from which the prophecy was read, and to throw it into the river Euphrates with the words, 'Thus shall Babylon sink, to rise no more' (Jer. 51.64). Cf. also Neh. 9.11; Ezek. 26.12, 21; *Sib. Or.* 5.155–61. So here a 'strong angel' picks up a boulder, resembling a huge millstone, and hurls it into the sea accompanied by a prophetic testimony about the imminent fate of Babylon's systemic evil.

As in Jeremiah, and commonly in the Old Testament, the action is an example of prophetic symbolism, through which the prediction is accomplished (cf. 1 Kings 22.11; Isa. 7.10–17; Jer. 28.10–11; Ezek. 5.1–17; et al.). In this case (Rev. 18.21), the hurling of a massive boulder into the sea may be understood as an instance of Johannine sacramentalism, whereby the material conveys the spiritual, and the symbol is transformed into its corresponding reality (see further Smalley, *John* 232–38, esp. 234–37). The divine judgement of Babylon is not merely pictured, but also and proleptically achieved (οὕτως, *houtōs*, 'that is how [Babylon will be thrown down]', lit. 'thus'; cf. Jer. 28.64 LXX). Moreover, the historical judgement of Babylon, like that of Tyre in Jer. 51 (MT), points towards the fall of the final kingdom of the world (Beale 918). Nevertheless, as Aune (982–83, esp. 983) points out, the activity in 18.21 differs from its Jewish counterparts in that first there is no command of Yahweh to launch it, and second the stone is thrown by an angel, and not by a prophet.

This is the third reference in the Apocalypse to 'a strong angel' (εἷς ἄγγελος ἰσχυρός, *heis angelos ischyros*, lit. 'one mighty angel'); see 5.2; 10.1. The inclusion of εἷς (*heis*, lit. 'one') in verse 21 (in 5.2 and 10.1 the noun is anarthrous) distinguishes the angelic figure here from the other two. But all three 'strong angels' intervene at solemn moments in the drama (Prigent 512). The suggestion of Caird (230–31) interprets the role of these heavenly messengers, and relates them to each other, perceptively; for he sees the angel of the great scroll (5.2) as testifying to the redemptive purposes of God, effected in the death of Christ; and the angel of the small scroll (10.1) as unfolding the Church's part in that divine plan. On this basis, the appearance of the strong angel at 18.21, Caird (ibid. 231) argues convincingly, 'must mark the consummation of the contents of both scrolls'. This interpretation is supported by verse 24, where the suffering of the Church at the end is mentioned; furthermore Jer. 51 (LXX 28).63, which is behind Rev. 18.21, mentions a 'scroll', and a scroll (βιβλίον, *biblion*, 'scroll', 'book') accompanies the angels at 5.1–2; 10.8. See further Beale 919.

The reference to the 'strength' of the angel in verse 21 is perhaps additionally appropriate in view of the physical task, of hurling a huge boulder into the sea, which is assigned to him.

The 'boulder' (λίθον, *lithon*, lit. 'stone') used by the strong angel in the imagery of this passage, is said to resemble a huge 'millstone' (μύλινον, *mylinon*). The large grinding stone referred to here is the upper stone of a mill, turned by a mule (so Matt. 18.6 par., μύλος ὀνικός, *mylos onikos*, 'a great millstone'; see also Rev. 18.22), and not the smaller kind pushed by women (Exod. 11.5; Matt. 24.41). The context of Matt. 18.6 (verses 4–7) includes a condemnation by Jesus of the arrogant who deceive (18.7); and this may indicate that the vision of Rev. 18.21–23 similarly involves a warning to those in the Christian community that deceivers will share the judgement of Babylon (see 18.3, 7, 23; also 2.14, 20); see further Beale 919. The 'sea' (θάλασσα, *thalassa*) features often in the visions of the Apocalypse (see on 4.6; also 5.13; 7.1–3; 8.8–9; 10.2; 15.2; 12.12; 16.3; et al.). Sometimes it is referred to as part of God's natural creation, and in other contexts the allusion is figurative. In 15.1–4 the 'sea of glass' is mixed with the fire of judgement against unholiness, and as a means of resisting opposition to God in any form; so that in the vision of the new heaven and earth at 21.1 the sea (to be equated with sin) has disappeared. It is quite possible that judgemental aspects are attached to the appearance of the 'sea' in 18.21, as they are in 13.1, where the beast rises from the sea. If so, the angelic millstone of divine judgement in verse 21, thrown into the waters of discrimination, may be said to represent God's *double* justice, triumphing over Babylon's injustice (cf. verse 6).

For 'Babylon the great city' see on 17.5; also 18.2; et al. The term ὅρμημα (*hormēma*, lit. 'violent rush', or 'onset'; BDAG 724*a*), which is found in the New Testament only here, is used in the LXX to denote anger and impulsion (e.g. LXX Exod. 32.22; Ps. 45.5;

Hos. 5.10). The cognate verb, ὁρμάω (*hormaō*, 'rush [headlong]'), is used in the New Testament only at Mark 5.13 par.; Acts 7.57; 19.29, all of which describe scenes of violence (the Gadarene swine; the stoning of Stephen; people rushing together into the theatre at Ephesus). In the present context of Rev. 18.21, the term seems to combine the ideas of suddenness, and being displaced by divine judgement; and the translation ('violently [overthrown]') tries to capture both senses. Cf. Prigent 512. The two verbs, ἔβαλεν (*ebalen*, 'hurled', lit. 'threw') and βληθήσεται (*blēthēsetai*, 'will be overthrown'), using literal and figurative meanings of the verb 'to throw', produce a further example of paronomasia in Revelation (see on verse 20).

The last phrase of verse 21, 'and will no longer exist' (καὶ οὐ μὴ εὑρεθῇ ἔτι, *kai ou mē heurethē[i] eti*, lit. 'and will never be found again'), is used as a literary basis for the five couplets which follow in verses 22–23 (q.v.), where the verbs 'find' (εὑρίσκω, *heuriskō*) and 'hear' (ἀκούω, *akouō*) virtually alternate (cf. also 'shine' [φαίνω, *phainō*] in verse 23). The effect is that of a tolling funeral bell, which intensifies the dramatic and hauntingly plaintive atmosphere of this scene. For the intensive double negative with the aorist subjunctive, in this clause, which expresses emphatic denial for the future, see Moule, *Idiom Book* 156. The addition each time of ἔτι (*eti*, 'again') strengthens the affirmation in the negative. See Mounce 337 n. 60.

22–23 The theme of these verses is that the punishment of Babylon fits her crime. As she has luxuriated in unfaithfulness, so now the luxury of the city, and indeed the normality of her daily life, will be seen no more. For the literary form of the imagery in verses 22–23 see on verse 21; also above, 425–26. The first line of each of the five couplets here sets out typical features of urban life which have disappeared; while the second uses a plangent chant, including the lament, 'never again!'.

This part of the threnody begins with a declaration that Babylon's judgement means a cessation of music-making. 'The sound (φωνή, *phōnē*, lit. 'voice') of harpists and musicians, and flautists and trumpeters, will never be heard in you again'. For this poetic way of expressing desolation see Isa. 24.8; Ezek. 26.13; 1 Macc. 3.45; *Sib. Or.* 8.114–19. The 'harpist' (κιθαρῳδός, *kitharō[i]dos*, a term found in the New Testament only here and at 14.2) is one who plays the 'kithara', or lyre; and this instrument is regularly associated with the joyful activity of praising the Lord (2 Sam. 6.5; Ps. 150.3, using κιθάρα, *kithara*). The term for 'musician', μουσικός (*mousikos*, used only here in the New Testament), probably includes those who are skilled in both instrumental and vocal music (Swete 239). 'Flutes' were played at funerals (Matt. 9.23), as well as festivals (Isa. 30.29); the noun αὐλητής (*aulētēs*, 'flute player') appears only here and at Matt. 9.23 in the New Testament. The 'trumpeter' (σαλπιστής, *salpistēs*, which is a *hapax legomenon* in the New Testament), would appear at the religious rites of Judaism (e.g. Ps. 81.3; Isa. 27.13), or to provide a rallying call in military campaigns (Josh. 6.4–20; Hos. 5.8). In Rome, the trumpet accompanied events at the games and in the theatre (Juvenal, *Sat.* 6.249–50; 10.213–15).

The angelic lament continues (verse 22*b*) with the assertion that no 'artisan of any trade' will again be visible in Babylon, and that the 'grinding of the mill' will be heard in the city no more. The presence and sound of the working 'artisan' (τεχνίτης, *technitēs*, also 'craftsperson', 'designer' [BDAG 1001*b*]) would have been an essential part of the life and commerce of an ancient city; and their expertise in 'any trade' (πάσης τέχνης, *pasēs technēs*, lit. 'of every trade') would formerly have covered a wide range of skills, from stonemasonry to weaving (see Aune 1009). Note the play on words between τεχνίτης (*technitēs*, 'artisan') and τέχνη (*technē*, 'trade'). Beale (919) suggests that Babylon's economic system would have persecuted Christian communities (cf. 18.24), by excluding from trade guilds those who refused to acknowledge the patron deities of those groups. As believers had been removed from the market-place, and economically destroyed (2.9),

Beale (ibid.) concludes, so now the pursuers of systemic evil will be displaced from the city.

A background to the next three strophes in this poetic threnody (verses 22–23) is to be found in Jer. 25.10, which belongs to the prophecy about the captivity of God's people in Babylon. There, among the sounds to be banished from the land, are listed (in a different order) the grinding of the millstone, the light of the lamp and the voice of the bride and bridegroom. When it is said that the 'mill' (μύλος, mylos) must be silenced, this refers to a handmill, as used in the home by women and slaves to grind the essential staples of meal and flour (contrast the 'millstone' of verse 21). Without such incessant activity there would have been no food, and normal life could not have been sustained. The fact that the author of Revelation speaks of 'the grinding of the mill' (φωνὴ μύλου, phōnē mylou, lit. 'voice of the millstone') in this passage indicates that he is depending directly on the MT of Jer. 25.10; for in the LXX of that verse, the Hebrew phrase 'sound of the handmill' (קוֹל רֵחַיִם, qôl rēḥayim) is wrongly translated ὀσμὴν μύρου (osmēn myrou, 'smell of perfume'). Cf. Aune 1009.

As with the silencing of the artisans and millers, the doleful absence of 'the light of a lamp' (φῶς λύχνου, phōs lychnou, singularly in Jer. 25.10 LXX), to which reference is made at the start of verse 23, means that no one is present and active in the homes of the city. Similarly, the fact that the 'voices of the bridegroom and bride' will never again be heard in Babylon (so Jer. 25.10) means that an important feature of city life has been withdrawn. The biblical metaphor of the bride and groom is regularly used in association with domestic and community joy and celebration (cf. Isa. 62.5; Jer. 7.34; 16.9; 33.11; Joel 2.16; Baruch 2.23; John 3.29; Rev. 21.2; also b. Ketuboth 8a, the blessings of Rabbi Judah, including the sixth, 'Blessed art Thou, O Lord, who maketh the bridegroom to rejoice with the bride').

The angelic prediction of Babylon's devastation (18.21–24) concludes in verses 23 and 24 by setting out three reasons for her judgement. The first two (verse 23), both of which are introduced by the causal particle ὅτι (hoti, 'for', 'since'), are that the city's 'merchants were high-ranking people of the world', and that 'all the nations were deceived' by the woman's 'sorcery'. It is reasonably easy to understand widespread deception as a ground of Babylon's downfall; but why should the status of the merchants be responsible for divine judgement on the city? This apparent problem is solved by commentators in different ways. Charles (2, 112) deems the line about the merchants to be out of place, and needlessly relocates it with verse 11. Swete (240–41) takes the first ὅτι (hoti, 'for') as controlling the whole sentence in verse 23b, and the second clause as explaining the first; while Beckwith (719) understands both clauses as co-ordinate. Apparently Mounce (339) and Aune (1010) have no clear explanation to offer.

The clue is to be found in the allusion to Isa. 23.8 LXX, which lies behind this part of verse 23 (so Beale 921). There, in the context of the oracle against Tyre, the prophet speaks of the city whose merchants were princes and 'whose traders were the honoured of the world' (LXX οἱ ἔμποροι αὐτῆς ἔνδοξοι, ἄρχοντες τῆς γῆς, hoi emporoi autēs endoxoi, archontes tēs gēs, lit. 'her merchants were glorious, princes of the earth'). In Isa. 34.12 LXX, ἄρχοντες (archontes, 'princes') and μεγιστᾶνες (megistanes, 'high-ranking people', 'great ones', the term used at Rev. 18.23) appear in parallel; cf. also Isa. 23.9; Ezek. 28.5, 9. The 'merchants' of Rev. 18.23, who are allies of Babylon ('your merchants'), are to be identified as the group already introduced at verses 11–17a; and in character they have been described as worldly, and selfishly concerned about their own economic wealth and powerful status. Now they are called 'high-ranking'; and, in view of the background just surveyed, this must point to their arrogance and self-glorification (cf. verse 7). Instead of giving the glory to God (4.11; 7.12; 16.9; 19.1; et al.), the secular merchants of any age tend to regard themselves, like Babylon herself, as 'great ones' (cf. 11.17; 15.3;

16.14; against 11.8; 17.1; 18.2; et al.); and such an attitude inevitably provokes the wrathful justice of God (11.18). See further Beckwith 719–10; Bauckham, *Climax of Prophecy* 373.

The second summary reason given in verse 23 for the destruction of all systemic evil ('Babylon') is that 'all the nations' have been deceived by the city's 'sorcery'; and this idea is being used by John figuratively, and not in the literal sense of 'magic'. Behind the thought in this passage lies the phraseology of Isa. 47.9: 'the loss of children and widowhood shall come upon you in full measure in spite of your many sorceries' (LXX ἐν τῇ φαρμακείᾳ, *en tē[i] pharmakeia[i]*, lit. 'in your sorcery'); cf. also Nahum 3.4 = 4QpNah *frags*. 3–4.2.7–9; *Sib. Or.* 5.162–70. The term 'sorcery' (φαρμακία, *pharmakia*) occurs in the New Testament only here and at Gal. 5.20; Rev. 9.21, where it is associated with idolatry and (as in Nahum 3.4) with fornication. In the Apocalypse 'fornication' is a regular metaphor for idolatry and putting self in the place of God (cf. 2.14; 14.8; 17.1–2; et al.; also Isa. 47.8–9). So here, Babylon's judgement in Rev. 18.23 is seen to be the result once more of her self-aggrandizement and of the universal ('*all* the nations') and disastrous effect which her idolatrous and deceitful claim to rule the world (18.7) has wrought upon her followers. See further Boring 186–88, esp. 187; Roloff 208; Michaels 210; Beale 922–23.

For the phrase, 'all the nations' (πάντα τὰ ἔθνη, *panta ta ethnē*), as referring to the opponents of God and his truth, see on 12.5; also 14.8; 15.4; 18.3. The past tenses in this section of the lament, not reflected in the translation, suggest that the seer is speaking as if the prophecy has already been fulfilled (cf. Beckwith 719–20).

24 The strong angel of verse 21 concludes the lament over Babylon by setting out a third reason for her judgement; although the two clauses of verse 24 are introduced by καί (*kai*, 'and'), rather than ὅτι (*hoti*, lit. 'because'), as in verse 23. The scene in the threnody chanted throughout Rev. 18 has been one of total devastation; and in verses 21–23 this is depicted in terms of a complete absence of music, industry, light, love and life (cf. Hughes 195). Nothing could be found in the city. But there is *one* exception: 'the blood of the prophets and saints, and of all who have been slain on earth', was to be 'found' (εὑρέθη, *heurethē*) there. 'Babylon', in the interval of Rev. 17—18, is not Jerusalem (Milligan 310–12; Provan, 'Foul Spirits' 91–97; Barker, *The Revelation* 311), nor is it simply Rome (Beckwith 719–20; Michaels 210; Mounce 339–40). See on 17.1–3. Rather, the eschatological city typifies every secular and oppressive world system, encountered by the Johannine community in the first century AD, and by the members of all churches since then (cf. Hendriksen 178). Provan, 'Foul Spirits' 98–99, believes that the 'Babylonian' world-view in Rev. 18 is shaped more by John's understanding of the Old Testament than by the model of the first-century AD Roman Empire. As a result, it is 'the generalities, rather than the particularities, of the chapter, and indeed the book as a whole, that are important' (ibid. 100).

The apostrophic style of verses 22–23 is suddenly changed, and Babylon is addressed (as in verse 21) in the third person (ἐν αὐτῇ, *en autē[i]*, 'in her . . .'). To the city's crimes of arrogant idolatry and deception (verse 23) is now added that of oppression; and this resulting trio of institutionalized wrongdoing is similarly attributed earlier to the broadly satanic figures of the dragon and the beast (arrogance, 12.13–15; 13.4–8; deception, 12.9; 13.14; oppression, 12.17; 13.15). Elsewhere in this drama the sins of idolatry, deceit and persecution are described as grounds for the fall of Babylon and the judgement of Satan (cf. 6.15–17; 14.8; 16.2–6; 17.1–6; 18.2–3; 19.2).

The final cause of Babylon's destruction is her oppression of humanity in general ('all who have been slain on the earth'), and of the Church in particular ('the prophets and saints'). For 'the blood of the prophets and saints' (αἷμα προφητῶν καὶ ἁγίων, *haima prophētōn kai hagiōn*) see 16.6; also verse 20. This phrase does not refer to two separate groups of believers, but to the body of the Church, within which are to be found Christian 'prophets'. The allusion to the 'blood' of the faithful need not mean that the angel is speaking solely of Christian martyrs (so Caird 232; Mounce 339; Aune 1010–11); for 'blood' may be a figure of speech for all kinds of persecution, including murder (cf. 2.10; 12.10–11; 16.6; 17.6; 19.2; see also Rom. 8.36, 'we are being killed all day long'). Similarly, this imagery need not be interpreted as a reference to persecution in the strict sense of opposition to the saints as practised by Nero, or any other historical imperial ruler (so Mounce 340); it is better understood in terms of all oppressive and unjust behaviour which may issue, in every age, from the wrong use of power in evil world systems (cf. Beale 924).

For the thought in verse 24 see 4 Ezra 1.32; also *Sib. Or.* 3.310–13. Beasley-Murray (269–70) notes the parallel between the judgement on Babylon in this scene and Nahum's oracle against Nineveh (Nahum 3.4); see also on verse 23. In both cases, the ultimate betrayal of the cities is to lead the nations into a false religion, which ends in the worship of Satan and the attempted suppression of those who follow the true Christ (cf. 19.2).

Theology

The interval of Rev. 17—18 looks back to the vision of the seven discriminatory bowl-plagues in Chapter 16 (Scene 5), and onwards to the situation of vindication and final judgement in Scene 6 (19.1—20.15). This section heralds the end of spiritual conflict, and speaks of God's restorative justice being exercised against the worldly powers which oppose him. For the view that revenge, and not merely a concern for justice, played a part in the composition of Rev. 18, see Collins, 'Taunt Song or Dirge?', esp. 204.

'Babylon' throughout, like Babel itself (Gen. 11.1–9), is the archetypal city of confusion; for the scarlet woman symbolizes all human, institutional arrogance which seeks to usurp the sovereignty of God (see on 17.1–3). The imagery surrounding Babylon has more to do with the wrong use of power (see above, 194–95), and of the status conferred by wealth, than with economic prosperity by itself. The luxuriously attired harlot of Chapter 17 becomes the deserted city of Rev. 18 as a result of the divine verdict on secular authorities (social, political, ecclesiastical, economic) which exist solely for themselves, and the inevitable downfall of an idolatrous human arrogance (however, see Provan, 'Foul Spirits' 85–87, who denies that economic exploitation is in mind at this point). Like Sodom, Tyre, Nineveh and Babylon itself, in the Old Testament period, ungodly and self-centred world powers will eventually be overthrown.

John is not describing here one satanic nation, even if Rome lay to hand as a leading candidate, but 'a corporate, depraved worldwide system spanning the ages from the cross to the final parousia' (Beale 924, and see on 17.18; also Wilcock 170; Bauckham, *Climax of Prophecy* 343–50; Boxall 133–37). As Ellul (*Apocalypse* 191–92) notes, 'Babylon' evokes captivity as well as confusion; so that (we may add) her destruction means the deliverance of the believer from both.

Fiorenza (99) compellingly suggests that the scene in Rev. 18 is that of a universal courtroom; and this description could be extended to the whole of the interval, Chapters 17—18. The plaintiffs in the suit are Christians, together with all those killed on earth (18.24); the defendant is 'Babylon', who is charged with murder in the interest of power and idolatry; and the presiding judge is God. But, as the seer's audience has already been informed (14.8), the lawsuit has been lost (14.8); accordingly, Babylon's allies break out into mourning, while the heavenly court and the faithful rejoice over the justice which has been received and the hope which can be shared (17.14; 18.20; cf. 19.1–10).

It is also true to say that this interval, and markedly Rev. 18, is characterized by an eschatological tension between the past, present and future; and this is highlighted by John's use in the section of the past and future tenses in the Greek. Babylon has fallen (18.2); and yet she is still to be thrown down (verses 21–23). The text hesitates between what has been accomplished (using the prophetic past), and what has yet to come; and this creative tension reflects what is constantly true of God's judgemental and salvific purposes: that the victory of Christ transcends human, temporal categories, and divides history anew (cf. Prigent 499). So the end is brought forward; the preliminary condemnation of Babylon is a harbinger of final judgement, while the healing of the nations has already begun (18.2–3; 22.2). Cf. Hughes 195.

Theologically, Rev. 17—18 thus brings its own challenge to the secular and oppressive powers of any age: that God's judgements are true and just (see 19.2), and that in his sovereignty he discriminates against those whose behaviour towards the righteous is sinful and unjust (18.20). Equally, the saints are faced with their own need to maintain a right faith, and to keep it (17.14; 18.4). At the same time, the members of John's audience are individually summoned to identify the spiritual perspective with which they truly sympathize: that of the earth (18.9, 11) and sea (verse 17*b*), or that of heaven (verse 20). So Bauckham 1301*b*. This is further clarified in the heavenly vision and rejoicing of 19.1–10. 'Faced with the competing claims of the Beast and the Lamb, of Babylon and Jerusalem, the Christians of the seven churches of Asia were called upon to discern the appropriate recipient of their reverence'; they were also challenged to consider what activities, cultic or otherwise, 'constituted authentic worship' (Ruiz, 'Praise and Politics' 84). See further on 19.1–5 and 6–10.

SCENE 6

Seven Visions
(19.1—20.15)

Translation

19 ¹After this, I heard what sounded like[a] the loud resonance of a huge crowd in heaven, singing,

'Hallelujah!
Deliverance and glory and power[b] belong to our God,[c]
²because his judgements are fair and just;
for he has condemned the great harlot,
who was corrupting the earth with her immorality,
and he has avenged the death of his servants which she caused.'[d]

³A second time they cried out,[e]

'Hallelujah!
For the smoke from her ascends for ever and ever.'

⁴Then the twenty-four elders and the four living creatures prostrated themselves, and worshipped God who is seated on the throne, saying,

'Amen, Hallelujah!'

⁵And a voice issued from the throne, which said,

'Praise our God, all his servants,
even[f] those, both the least and the greatest, who fear him.'

⁶Then I heard what seemed like the resonance of an extensive crowd, or like the sound of rushing waters, or like the noise of loud thunderclaps, as the cry went up,[g]

'Hallelujah!
For the Lord our[h] God, the Almighty, has begun to reign.
⁷Let us rejoice and exult, and pay[i] homage to him;
since the marriage day of the Lamb has arrived,
and his bride has prepared herself,
⁸given that she was permitted to wear fine linen, shining and clear.'

Now the fine linen stands for the righteous behaviour of God's people.
⁹Next, the angel said to me, 'Write, "Those who have been invited to the wedding feast of the Lamb are fortunate indeed!"' He went on to say to me, 'These are true words[j] from God.' ¹⁰Then I fell down at his feet, in order to worship him. But he said to me, 'See that you do not! I am a servant-companion with you and your colleagues, who are holding to the testimony of Jesus. Worship God! For the witness of Jesus is the spirit of prophecy.'

¹¹And I saw heaven opened, and there was a white horse! Its rider is[k] faithful and true; and he is just in judgement and in war. ¹²His eyes were like[l] a blazing fire; and on his head were many diadems, with a name inscribed[m] on them which no one knows but he himself. ¹³He was robed in a garment soaked[n] in blood; and his name was called, 'The Word of God'. ¹⁴The heavenly[o] armies were following behind him on white horses, wearing fine linen, pure

white. [15]A sharp sword projected from his mouth, with which he can strike down the nations. He himself will rule them with an iron staff, and will personally tread the winepress which is the furious wrath of Almighty God. [16]And he wears on his robe, that is on his thigh, an inscribed name: 'King of kings, and Lord of lords'.

[17]And I saw a certain angel, standing on the sun; and he cried out[p] with a loud voice to all the birds flying in midheaven,

'Come, gather together for the great supper of God, [18]so that you may eat the flesh of rulers, military officers and warriors, the flesh of horses and their riders, and the carrion of all people, free and enslaved, the least and the greatest.'

[19]And I saw the beast and the worldly rulers, with their militia, who had been mustered to wage war against the one mounted on the horse, and against his army. [20]But the beast was caught, and with it[q] the false prophet who has worked miracles in its presence, by which he deceived those who had received the mark of the beast, and those worshipping its image. These two were hurled[r] alive into the fiery lake of burning sulphur. [21]The rest were killed with the sword which projected from the mouth of the rider on the horse; and all the birds were sated with their flesh.

20   [1]And I saw an angel[s] descending from heaven with the key of the abyss, and an enormous chain in his hand. [2]He arrested the dragon, that ancient serpent[t] who is the devil, or the Satan, and chained him up for a thousand years. [3]He hurled him into the abyss, which he locked and sealed over him, to prevent him from deceiving the nations any longer, until the thousand years had come to an end. After that he must be released, but only for a short period.

[4]And I saw thrones; and judgement was given on behalf of those who were seated on them. These were the souls of the ones beheaded on account of their witness to Jesus and to the word of God; others had not worshipped the beast or his image, and had not received his mark on their foreheads or their hands. They all came to life, and reigned with Christ for a thousand years. [5]The remaining dead did not live again until the thousand years had come to an end. (This is the first resurrection.) [6]How happy and holy is the one who shares in the first resurrection! The second death has no hold over such; for they will be priests of God and of Christ, and will reign with him for the[u] thousand years.

[7]And when the thousand years have been completed, Satan will be released from his prison; [8]and he will go out to deceive the nations at the four corners of the earth – Gog and Magog – in order to muster them for the battle. They are countless as the sands on the seashore. [9]They swarmed across the breadth of the land, and surrounded[v] the encampment of God's people, and the beloved city. Then fire descended from heaven,[w] and devoured them. [10]And the devil, who had deceived them, was hurled into the lake of fire and brimstone, where the beast and the false prophet had also been thrown, to be tormented day and night for ever and ever.

[11]And I saw a majestic, white throne, and the one seated on it.[x] Earth and sky fled from his presence,[y] so that no place was found for them. [12]And I saw the dead, the greatest and the least alike, standing in front of the throne,[z] while books were opened.[aa] Then another book was opened, which is the book of life, and the dead were judged according to their deeds, as recorded in these books.[bb] [13]The sea yielded up the dead in it, and Death and Hades gave up the dead in them; then all were judged individually, depending on what they had done.[cc] [14]Death and Hades were hurled into the lake of fire; now the lake of fire is the second death. [15]And anyone whose name could not be found written in the book of life was thrown into the burning lake.

Text

[a]   There is strong MS evidence (including ℵ A C 025 046 1006[1841] Cassiodorus vg) for the inclusion of ὡς (*hōs*, lit. 'as', 'like') with φωνὴν μεγάλην (*phōnēn megalēn*, lit. 'a loud voice'); although it is omitted by 051⋆ 1006[1006] Oecumenius[2053,2062] Andreas Primasius Beatus it[gig]

syr, et al. John normally uses the phrase, 'I heard a voice' (ἤκουσα φωνήν/φωνῆς, *ēkousa phōnēn/phōnēs*), as in 6.7; 11.12; et al., without ὡς (*hōs*, 'as'); so when that word is awkwardly included elsewhere in Revelation (only at 6.6; 19.6) the reading is, as here, open to scribal correction and therefore disputed. This makes the text in 19.1, with ὡς (*hōs*, 'as'), difficult; and, because it is also well supported, it is likely to be original.

ᵇ The version, ἡ δόξα καὶ ἡ δύναμις (*hē doxa kai hē dynamis*, lit. 'the glory and the power'), is well attested by ℵ A C 025 051 1006¹⁰⁰⁶,¹⁸⁴¹ 1611 Oecumenius²⁰⁵³,²⁰⁶² Andreas Apringius copˢᵃ vg, et al., and is doubtless original. Among the variations, the most significant is the inclusion of the ascription to God of 'honour' or 'reverence' (ἡ τιμή, *hē timē*), as in 1611²³²⁹ MSS of Andreas 2019 copᵇᵒ. But this secondary addition is clearly influenced by parallel doxologies in Revelation, such as the ones at 4.11; 5.12; 7.12.

ᶜ The genitive, τοῦ θεοῦ (*tou theou*, lit. 'of God'), appears in ℵ A C 025 046 051 1006¹⁰⁰⁶,¹⁸⁴¹ 1862 1678, et al. The attributes of God in this sentence ('deliverance and glory and power') are in the nominative, so that the slightly awkward predicate in the genitive ('of God') requires a verb such as 'are' or 'belong to'. The normal construction would involve the use of the dative, as at 1.6; 5.13; 7.10; et al.; and this case appears in the later scribal variation, κυρίῳ τῷ θεῷ (*kyriō[i] tō[i] theō[i]*, 'to the Lord [our] God'), as read by MSS of Andreas TR.

ᵈ In the phrase, ἐκ χειρὸς αὐτῆς (*ek cheiros autēs*, 'which she caused', lit. 'from her hand'), some MSS (including 051 Oecumenius²⁰⁵³,²⁰⁶² 1611²³⁴⁴ Andreas) later insert the article τῆς (*tēs*, 'the') before χειρός (*cheiros*, 'hand'). This is probably because parts of the body, such as the hand, normally appear in Greek with an article (so Rev. 6.5; 9.20; 10.2; 14.9; et al.); although there is a tendency in classical and Hellenistic Greek to omit the article in prepositional phrases. In the Old Testament, the term מִיָּד (*miyyad*, 'from the hand') is always anarthrous (as at Gen. 4.11; Job 5.15; Ezek. 33.8; et al.). See Aune 1015.

ᵉ The form εἴρηκαν (*eirēkan*, 'they cried out', lit. 'they said') is attested by ℵ A 1611²³²⁹ Andreas, and is probably original. Some MSS (including 1611¹⁸⁵⁴ ²³⁴⁴ MSS of Andreas 2019 Byz copᵇᵒ) read εἴρηκεν (*eirēken*, lit. 'he [singular] said'). But this is a correction, which derives from taking ὄχλου πολλοῦ (*ochlou pollou*, 'huge [lit. "large"] crowd') in verse 1 as a collective singular; whereas the use of the plural participle, λεγόντων (*legontōn*, 'saying'), in the same verse indicates that the collective noun ὄχλος (*ochlos*, 'crowd') is being understood as a *plural* (cf. similarly 7.9–10; 19.6). A further secondary variation (witnessed by Oecumenius²⁰⁵³ MSS of Andreas) replaces the original third person plural ending of the verb, -αν (*-an*), with the more elaborate termination, -ασιν (*-asin*; cf. otherwise only 8.2), to give the version εἰρήκασιν (*eirēkasin*, 'they said'). Other witnesses correct the verb to εἶπαν (*eipan*, 'they said', as in C), or to εἶπον (*eipon*, 'they said', as in one MS of Andreas).

ᶠ The conjunction καί (*kai*, 'even', lit. 'and') is strongly attested by A 046 051 1006¹⁰⁰⁶,¹⁸⁴¹ 1611¹⁶¹¹,¹⁸⁵⁴,²³²⁹,²³⁴⁴ Oecumenius²⁰⁵³,²⁰⁶² Andreas Byz latt syrᵖʰ copᵇᵒ arm Primasius Beatus; cf. Charles 2, 356. Other witnesses, such as ℵ C 025 copˢᵃ eth, omit the word. It is possible that καί (*kai*, 'and') was added to avoid an asyndetic construction, or omitted in order to avoid any implication that those who 'fear' God are to be distinguished as a group from 'his servants' (so Metzger, *Textual Commentary* 759). But the word, in this context, is epexegetic: God's servants *are* precisely those who fear him (hence the translation 'even'). This interpretation makes sense of the text; and such a conclusion, combined with the weight of the external evidence (against Metzger, *Textual Commentary* 759–60, who regards it as 'evenly balanced'), makes it highly probable that καί (*kai*, 'even'), at this point in verse 5, is original.

g The genitive plural masculine present participle, λεγόντων (*legontōn*, 'as the cry went up', lit. 'saying'), appears in A 025 0229 1006[1006,1841] 1611[1611,2329] Oecumenius[2053,2062] latt; cf. Charles 2, 356. Other MSS (051 Andreas) have the accusative plural participle, λέγοντας (*legontas*, 'saying'); while further witnesses (including 1611[1854] 2030 Byz) read the nominative plural form, λέγοντες (*legontes*, 'saying'). The version in the genitive plural is doubtless original. It is well supported; and it also accords with John's tendency to treat ὄχλος (*ochlos*, 'crowd'), used earlier in the verse in the genitive, as a collective noun in the plural (see also the note on verse 3). Equally, the genitive plural participle, λεγόντων (*legontōn*, 'saying'), is congruent with the two preceding genitive plural forms, ὑδάτων πολλῶν . . . βροντῶν ἰσχυρῶν (*hydatōn pollōn . . . brontōn ischyrōn*, 'of rushing [lit. "many"] waters . . . of loud thunderclaps').

h There is weighty MS evidence (א[2] 025 046 1611 Oecumenius[2053,2062] 1773 2019 Byz it[gig,61] syr vg, et al.) for the inclusion of ἡμῶν (*hēmōn*, 'our') after ὁ θεός (*ho theos*, 'God'). However, the use of such a pronoun is not in accordance with the author's usual style (see 1.8; 4.8; 11.17; 15.3; 16.7; 21.22); and this suggests that the MSS lacking the pronoun (including A 1006[1006,1841] syr[ph] cop[sa,bo] eth arm; cf. Charles 2, 126, 356) may well be witnesses to the original reading. The phrase with the pronoun may have been imported from 19.1, 5. See further Aune 1016.

i Instead of the irregular form of the aorist subjunctive, δώσωμεν (*dōsōmen*, lit. 'let us give'), as read by 025 1611[2329,2344] Andreas, et al. which, although not strongly supported, is probably original, some MSS (including א[2] A Oecumenius[2053] MSS of Andreas, et al.) have the future tense, δώσομεν (*dōsomen*, 'we shall give'). But, after two hortatory subjunctives, this form is intolerable in the Greek, and must be regarded as a scribal blunder (Metzger, *Textual Commentary* 760). The third main version, provided by witnesses such as א⋆ 046 051 94 2030 it[gig] vg syr cop eth Arethas Cyprian Primasius Byz, et al., is the use in this context of the aorist subjunctive δῶμεν (*dōmen*, lit. 'that we should have given'). But if this were original, it is not easy to account for the origin of the alternative readings (Metzger, *Textual Commentary* 760).

j A few witnesses (A, also one MS of Andreas, MSS of Byz) include οἱ (*hoi*, 'the') before the adjective ἀληθινοί (*alēthinoi*, 'true [words]'). There is better MS evidence (א Andreas Byz, et al.) for omitting the article; but its presence is probably original, and it was probably dropped later through the carelessness of copyists. The adjective in this context is in the attributive position; and, following the author's normal style, it should therefore be articular (cf. 2.13; 3.14). In the similar phrases at 21.5; 22.6 the adjective 'true' (ἀληθινοί, *alēthinoi*), there used with πιστοί (*pistoi*, 'faithful'), is predicative and anarthrous. Cf. further Aune 1017.

k There is one major variation in the Greek text of verse 11. Whereas some MSS (including A 025 051 Andreas) have simply πιστὸς καὶ ἀληθινός (*pistos kai alēthinos*, 'faithful and true'), other witnesses (such as 046 1006[1006,1841] 1611[1854,2030] Oecumenius[2053,2062] 1773 Byz Origen Cyprian Primasius Victorinus; cf. Charles 2, 358) add, at the beginning of this phrase, the present participle καλούμενος (*kaloumenos*, 'called'). It is unlikely that 'called' would have been deliberately omitted, in order to avoid the implication that the rider of the white horse was merely *called* 'Faithful and True', without being so (the suggestion of Metzger, *Textual Commentary* 760–61); although it is possible that the omission was accidental, particularly if καλούμενος were placed before καί (*kai*, 'and'), as in א. It is more probable that πιστὸς καὶ ἀληθινός (*pistos kai alēthinos*, 'faithful and true') is the *lectio originalis*, since it is easier to account for the insertion of καλούμενος (*kaloumenos*, 'called') than its omission, and the naming of the rider at this point seems to conflict with the fact that his name is undisclosed at verse 12. The secondary, titular form was probably influenced by 3.14 (q.v.); so Aune 1042.

[1] The word ὡς (*hōs*, 'like'), characteristic of the author of Revelation, is present in A latt syr cop[sa,bo] MSS of Andreas and Byz; cf. Primasius Beatus Cyprian vg, et al. It is omitted by ℵ 025 046 1611[1611,1854] Oecumenius[2053,2062] arm Hippolytus, et al. The addition of the word is easier to explain than its omission, in accordance with the use of ὡς (*hōs*, 'like') and φλόξ (*phlox*, 'fire') together at 1.14; 2.18; and, given its absence in four uncials, this suggests that the presence of the adverbial conjunction is secondary.

[m] Instead of the well-supported phrase, ἔχων ὄνομα γεγραμμένον (*echōn onoma gegrammenon*, 'with a name inscribed', lit. 'having a name written'), some witnesses (including 1006[1006,1841] 1611[1854] 2030 MSS of Andreas Byz) attest to the version, ἔχων ὀνόματα γεγραμμένα καί (*echōn onomata gegrammena kai*, lit. 'having [singular] names written, and . . .'); while 2329 has ἔχοντα ὄνομα γεγραμμένον· καὶ ὄνομα (*echonta onoma gegrammenon· kai onoma*, 'having [plural] a name inscribed; and the name . . .'). These two secondary variations reveal attempts to solve the difficulty presented by the reference to 'many diadems', followed immediately by the mention of *one* name. The first version assumes that the 'names' are inscribed on the rider himself, while the second presupposes that the names are written on the diadems. See further Aune 1042.

[n] The reading, βεβαμμένον (*bebammenon*, 'soaked', lit. 'dipped', perfect passive participle from βάπτειν, *baptein*, 'dip [into]', used only here in the Apocalypse), is well supported by A 046 051 1611[1854] cop[sa] arm syr Arethas Byz, et al. It is the version most likely to have prompted alteration, and is therefore doubtless original. Copyists seem to have felt the verb was inappropriate in the context, which describes the attire of Jesus, the Warrior-King. As a result, a number of clearly secondary variants arose, using the verb ῥαντίζειν (*hrantizein*, 'to sprinkle'), including ῥεραντισμένον (*hrerantismenon*, 'sprinkled', neuter accusative singular perfect passive participle), attested by 025 2019 1611[2329] Hippolytus Origen. See further Metzger, *Textual Commentary* 761–62 and, below, on verse 12.

[o] The article, τά (*ta*, 'the'), before ἐν τῷ οὐρανῷ (*en tō[i] ouranō[i]*, lit. 'in the heaven'), is included by 025 051 1006[1006,1841] 1611[1854] 2030 Byz lat cop[sa] Cyprian (cf. Charles 2, 359); but it is omitted by ℵ A 1611[1611] Oecumenius[2053], et al. The arthrous form is doubtless original, since the author of Revelation tends to repeat the article when an articular noun is followed by an attributive phrase (cf. 1.4; 2.24; 11.16; et al.).

[p] Instead of ἔκραξεν (*ekraxen*, 'he cried out', aorist), as read by ℵ A Andreas Byz, 046 has the imperfect ἔκραζεν (*ekrazen*, lit. 'he was crying out'). The former version is likely to be original, in view of the parallels at 6.10; 10.3; 18.2.

[q] The phrase, μετ᾽ αὐτοῦ ὁ (*met' autou ho*, lit. 'with it [him] the [one]'), as read by ℵ 1773 2019 2329, et al., which is likely to be original, has been replaced with slight alterations in other MSS.

(a) 1006[1006,1841] 2030 94 Byz it[gig], et al. read ὁ μετ᾽ αὐτοῦ (*ho met' autou*, 'the [one] with it');
(b) μετὰ τούτου ὁ (*meta toutou ho*, 'with it the [one]') appears in Andreas;
(c) other witnesses (025, et al.) have ὁ μετ᾽ αὐτοῦ ὁ (*ho met' autou ho*, 'the [one] with it, the [one]'); while
(d) the version in A is οἱ μετ᾽ αὐτοῦ ὁ (*hoi met' autou ho*, lit. 'those with him the').

The last variant (d) supports the form and order of the original reading, except that a scribe has erroneously inserted οἱ (*hoi*, 'the ones') at the beginning of the phrase. Readings (a) and (b) are obvious corrections; and (c) is a conflation of the original and (a). See further Aune 1045.

ʳ Instead of the third person plural aorist indicative passive, ἐβλήθησαν (*eblēthēsan*, 'they were hurled (lit. "thrown")', as in א A Oecumenius²⁰⁵³ 94, et al., Andreas witnesses to the future passive, βληθήσονται (*blēthēsontai*, 'they will be thrown'). Alternatively, 1773 has the aorist passive participle, βληθέντες (*blēthentes*, 'they were being thrown'). The reading in the aorist indicative is best supported, and fits the tenses in the context of verse 20; it is therefore likely to be original.

ˢ Some MSS (including א² 1611²⁰⁵⁰ vgᵐˢ syrᵖʰ copˢᵃᵐˢ Beatus) add ἄλλον (*allon*, 'another') before ἄγγελον (*angelon*, 'angel'). This is clearly a secondary insertion, influenced by the frequent appearance of the expression 'another angel' in Revelation (8.3; 10.1; 14.6; et al.), as well as by the possible need to distinguish the angel of 20.1 from the one who appears at 19.17.

ᵗ The nominative phrase, ὁ ὄφις ὁ ἀρχαῖος (*ho ophis ho archaios*, lit. 'the ancient serpent'), appears in A 1678 1778 2080; cf. Charles 2, 362. In what is obviously a syntactical correction, to bring the Greek into line with the preceding τὸν δράκοντα (*ton drakonta*, 'the dragon', accusative), other witnesses (including א 046 051 Oecumenius²⁰⁵³ Andreas Byz syr TR) have the accusative form, τὸν ὄφιν τὸν ἀρχαῖον (*ton ophin ton archaion*, 'the old serpent'). But, although less well attested, the nominative form is probably original. It is grammatically the *lectio difficilior*; and it conforms to the author's use elsewhere of a nominative in apposition to an oblique case (cf. 1.5; 2.13; also 3.12; 14.12, 14; et al.).

ᵘ The presence of the article τά (*ta*, 'the'), before χίλια ἔτη (*chilia etē*, 'thousand years'), is supported by א 046 1611¹⁶¹¹,²³²⁹ Oecumenius²⁰⁵³,²⁰⁶² 94 copˢᵃ,ᵇᵒ MSS of Byz, et al. It is omitted by A 051 1006 1611¹⁸⁵⁴,²⁰⁵⁰ 2030 arm eth Andreas Arethas, et al. The expression, 'thousand years', is used six times in Revelation, all within Chapter 20 (verses 2–7). In 20.2, where it appears for the first time, it is used (as would be expected) anarthrously; thereafter the phrase would normally occur with the anaphoric article, in which case the inclusion of τά (*ta*, 'the') in verse 6 is likely to be original. At the same time, the external evidence is evenly balanced; and the omission of the article, in view of what has just been noted, constitutes a *lectio difficilior*.

ᵛ The form, ἐκύκλευσαν (*ekykleusan*, 'they surrounded') is attested by A 046 1006¹⁰⁰⁶,¹⁸⁴¹ Byz, et al.; while other MSS (including א 1611¹⁸⁵⁴,²⁰⁵⁰ Oecumenius²⁰⁵³,²⁰⁶² Andreas) read ἐκύκλωσαν (*ekyklōsan*), which has the same meaning. The verb κυκλόω (*kykloō*, 'surround' or 'encircle') is found in four places elsewhere in the New Testament (John 10.24; Luke 21.20; Acts 14.20; Heb. 11.30; cf. *1 Clem.* 22.8; *Barn.* 6.6; Hermas, *Sim.* 9.9.6); whereas the cognate κυκλεύω (*kykleuō*, 'surround') appears only at John 10.24 v.l. (cf. Hermas, *Sim.* 9.9.6). It may be concluded that the original version is ἐκύκλευσαν (*ekykleusan*, 'they surrounded'), and that correctors have opted for the more common verb form.

ʷ The phrase, ἐκ τοῦ οὐρανοῦ (*ek tou ouranou*, 'from heaven'), as read by A vgᵐˢˢ copᵇᵒ ᵐˢˢ MSS of Tyconius and Augustine, has a number of MS variants, mostly involving a modification of the preposition(s), or the rearrangement of clause sequences in expanded versions (cf. Metzger, *Textual Commentary* 762–63). The chief variation, ἐκ τοῦ οὐρανοῦ ἀπὸ τοῦ θεοῦ (*ek tou ouranou apo tou theou*, 'out of heaven from God'), which is attested by 046 Byz itᵍⁱᵍ syrᵖʰ copˢᵃ,ᵇᵒ arm Victorinus, is clearly a secondary expansion, introduced by copyists on the basis of the parallel phrase at 21.2, 10.

ˣ Instead of ἐπ' αὐτόν (*ep' auton*, 'on it', accusative), which is supported by 046 051 1611²⁰⁵⁰ Andreas Byz, some witnesses (including A 1006¹⁰⁰⁶,¹⁸⁴¹ 1611¹⁶¹¹,²³²⁹ Oecumenius²⁰⁵³,²⁰⁶²) attest to the genitive form, with the same meaning, ἐπ' αὐτοῦ (*ep' autou*). א has ἐπάνω αὐτοῦ (*epanō autou*, lit. 'over it'); while a fourth version, provided by 1611[1854] it^gig (*in illa*, lit. 'in it') Irenaeus (*in eo*, 'in it'), uses the dative, ἐπ' αὐτῷ (*ep' autō[i]*, 'on it'). When the phrase, 'the one seated on the throne', is used in Revelation, and the participle ('sitting') is in the nominative or accusative (ὁ καθήμενον, *ho kathēmenon*, as in 20.11), 'throne' is normally in the accusative (τὸν θρόνον, *ton thronon*); cf. 4.2; 11.16; 19.11. This suggests that the accusative form of the pronoun in the context of verse 11, ἐπ' αὐτόν (*ep' auton*, 'on it'), is original. See further Aune 1074.

^y   After οὗ ἀπὸ τοῦ προσώπου (*hou apo tou prosōpou*, 'from his presence', lit. 'from the face of him', or [so AV, RV] 'from whose face'), some witnesses (ℵ 1006 1611[2329] Oecumenius[2053,2062] MSS of Andreas and Byz) add αὐτοῦ (*autou*, 'his'). This reading is rejected by most modern editions of the Greek New Testament, such as NA (cf. Charles 2, 374). However, Aune (1075) argues strongly for its originality, mainly on the basis of the external evidence. Two major witnesses (𝔓 47 and C) have lacunae at this point; and the pronoun is included by two valuable minuscules, Oecumenius[2053] and [2062]. Moreover, whereas προσώπου (*prosōpou*, lit. 'of [the] face') is normally followed in the New Testament by a genitive (e.g. Acts 2.28; 2 Cor. 3.7; Rev. 6.16; 12.14), only at Rev. 20.11 is it *not* so followed. Despite this plea, the presence of αὐτοῦ (*autou*, 'his') after the relative pronoun οὗ (*hou*, 'of whom') is grammatically redundant (but see Aune 1075); and it seems highly unlikely that αὐτοῦ (*autou*, 'his') formed part of the original text of verse 11. See further Kelly, *The Revelation* 58.

^z   In place of ἐνώπιον τοῦ θρόνου (*enōpion tou thronou*, lit. 'before the throne'), as read by all the major witnesses, MSS of Andreas have later substituted in error, τοῦ θεοῦ (*tou theou*, '[before] God'), as distinctively in the AV translation. One MS of Andreas (c) has the expanded version, τοῦ θρόνου θεοῦ (*tou thronou theou*, 'of the throne of God'), which is clearly based on that phrase as it appears elsewhere in the Apocalypse (7.15; 22.1, 3).

^aa   The third person plural aorist indicative passive verb, ἠνοίχθησαν (*ēnoichthēsan*, '[books] were opened'), is attested by 025 1773 MS of Andreas. Other witnesses make minor corrections, mostly involving a change of voice from passive to active, which do not significantly alter the meaning of the Greek sentence in verse 12. The version according to ℵ is the third person *singular* aorist indicative passive, ἠνεῴχθη (*ēneō[i]chthē*, lit. 'was opened'); but this is an obviously secondary attempt to cause the neuter plural subject, βιβλία (*biblia*, 'books'), to be followed by a singular verb, in accordance with Attic and subsequently Hellenistic usage (Aune 1075).

^bb   The majority reading, τοῖς βιβλίοις (*tois bibliois*, '[in] the books'), is replaced in ℵ 94 by ταῖς βίβλοις (*tais biblois*, 'the books'), and in MSS of Byz by τοῖς βίβλοις (*tois biblois*, masculine or neuter dative plural), which has the same meaning. The noun βίβλος (*biblos*, 'book') is usually feminine in gender; and this appears in the first variant. The second alteration may indicate either that the gender of the noun varied, or that βίβλοις (*biblois*, 'books') has simply been shortened from βιβλίοις (*bibliois*, 'books'). Cf. Aune 1075.

^cc   Instead of αὐτῶν (*autōn*, lit. 'their [deeds]'), Byz cop^samss read the singular αὐτοῦ (*autou*, 'of him'). The Greek at this point is ἐκρίθησαν ἕκαστος (*ekrithēsan hekastos*, lit. 'they were judged, each'), where ἕκαστος (*hekastos*, 'each') has a distributive force, amounting to 'all'; so that the plural form of the pronoun, 'their [deeds]', is appropriate, as well as original. Hence the translation, 'all were judged individually'. See further on verse 13.

Literary Setting

Scene 6 (Rev. 19—20) consists of seven visions of the end. In Chapter 19, an introduction is followed by three visions, while in Chapter 20 the seer narrates four more apocalyptic disclosures. Once more, a Johannine predilection for the number seven, denoting completeness, is evident in the structuring of this section of the drama; see on 1.4. The resulting composition of these two chapters is as follows:

Introduction: Rejoicing in Heaven (19.1–5)
Vision 1   The Marriage Feast of the Lamb (19.6–10)
Vision 2   The Warrior-Messiah (19.11–16)
Vision 3   Antichrist Destroyed (19.17–21)
Vision 4   Satan Bound (20.1–3)
Vision 5   A Millennial Reign (20.4–6)
Vision 6   Satan Destroyed (20.7–10)
Vision 7   Final Judgement (20.11–15).

Rev. 19 seems to mark the beginning of a new division in John's material, and of a literary unit which runs through to the end of Chapter 20. Nevertheless, the composition and thought of Rev. 19—20 are continuous to some extent with Chapters 17—18; and this is evident from the later appearance in a few MSS (051 1611[2344] syr[ph] cop[bo] arm eth) of a connective καί (*kai*, 'and') at the start of 19.1. The lament over the desolate city, in 17—18, is succeeded by an episode of joy and judgement in 19—20. More particularly, the heavenly worship and jubilation of 19.1–10 connect with the angelic threnody of 18.21–24, and balance it (note also the injunction to rejoice over Babylon at 18.20); cf. Mounce 341. It is also the case that 19.1–10 forms a discrete sub-unit of text, bounded by 'I heard' (ἤκουσα, *ēkousa*) in 19.1 and 'I saw' (εἶδον, *eidon*) in 19.11. Aune (1019–21) sees 17.1—19.10 as parallel to 21.9—22.9.

Given that 19.1–10 is a literary unit, there is no need to argue that verses 9–10 are a secondary insertion (so Aune 1023); although it is true that the introduction of these verses at the conclusion of the hymns in 19.1–8 appears abrupt, and also that this section has a doublet at 22.6–9. Moreover, 19.1–8 is a coherent unit of material, defined by its hymnic content. This is in fact the longest collection of hymns in Revelation; and it acts as a meditative response to the judgemental descriptions of Chapters 17—18, and as an introduction not so much to 19.11–21, as to the final consummation anticipated in 21.2—22.17.

There are five spontaneous, hymnic units in Rev. 19.1–8, which appear to derive from Christian prophecy as well as from Jewish sources (cf. Prigent 90). As with all liturgies, this one begins with *anamnesis* (verses 1–5), and then unfolds in anticipation (verses 7–8); *idem* 517. The first strophe in this section, 19.1–4, is a two-part poetic celebration, involving a hymn of praise (verses 1–3) and its response (verse 4). The second strophe, 19.5–8, consists of a call to praise (verse 5), followed by a hymnic antiphon (verses 6–8*a*). An editorial comment (verse 8*b*) is added at the conclusion of this section. The second strophe continues the first; but, at the same time, it introduces a new subject, namely, that of the Lamb and the marriage to his bride.

According to Beale (972), Rev. 20 is part of a larger literary unit, 17.1—21.8. Rev. 20.1–15 itself is made up of four sub-divisions, each of which contains a vision of the future.

(a) The temporary binding of Satan (20.1–3), which includes the motifs of imprisoning a malefactor for many days, after which final punishment ensues (cf. Isa. 24; *1 Enoch* 10; and on 20.1–3, below).
(b) The reign of the saints with Christ for a thousand years (20.4–6), a textual unit which is framed by the inclusive reference to the millennium at 20.3 and 7. This section is marked by recapitulatory allusions to the saints of God as suffering for their faith (cf. 1.9; et al.), as sealed by Christ, and not by the beast (14.9; et al.), and as priests of God and his Christ (1.6; et al.).

(c) The eschatological war, which ends with the destruction of Satan (20.7–10). This scene again owes much to the literary and theological background of *1 Enoch* (56, 90, 99; see below), and is also influenced by the Gog and Magog oracle in Ezek. 38— 39. Throughout, the author of Revelation has taken over traditional eschatological scenes, and adapted them creatively, and from a Christian perspective, to describe events at the end-time.

(d) The climactic scene of final judgement (20.11–15). This textual unit may be subdivided into two parts, both introduced by καὶ εἶδον (*kai eidon*, lit. 'and I saw'): a theophanic enthronement, and the reaction of nature to it, in verse 11, which introduces the vision as a whole (verses 11–15); and the focus on opened books of discrimination, and the execution of judgement which follows from that, in verses 12–15.

Comment

Introduction: Rejoicing in Heaven (19.1–5)

19.1–2 The sub-section 19.1–5 is a celebration of divine justice and victory, after the judgement of Babylon (Rev. 17—18). There is a marked contrast, in terms of the dramatic mood which introduces this scene. Whereas three different groups, of rulers, merchants and seafarers, had in their own interests lamented the downfall of the reprobate city, the symbol of systemic evil, now three further groups express liturgically their confidence in God's justice: the huge crowd (19.1–3), the elders and living creatures (verse 4) and a voice from the throne (verse 5). Together they rejoice at the divine victory, which they share, over idolatrous corruption. Cf. Mounce 341. The atmosphere of praise at the outset of this scene finds a parallel in 5.9–14 (Beckwith 720); and the theme of the saints being rewarded after the judgement of their enemies echoes, verbally and theologically, the hymns which are introduced by the seventh trumpet-call at 11.15– 19 (Beale 926). See also 15.3–4.

The expression, 'after this, I heard' (μετὰ ταῦτα ἤκουσα, *meta tauta ēkousa*), is used only here in the Apocalypse; but see the phrase, 'after this, I saw' (μετὰ ταῦτα/τοῦτο εἶδον, *meta tauta/touto eidon*), used as an introduction to John's visions, at 4.1; 7.1, 9; 15.5; 18.1. For the spiritual significance of audition and sight in Johannine thought, and the relation between them, see on 4.1. The 'huge crowd' (ὄχλος πολύς, *ochlos polys*, lit. 'large crowd') has been identified by some commentators as a multitude of angelic, heavenly beings, to which the Church later responds (verse 3); so Swete 242; Beckwith 720–21; Hendriksen 178; Hughes 196; Aune 1024. Beale (926) interprets the assembly as that of the saints, which could include the angels, praising God at the consummation of history. However, it is most likely that this gathering should be regarded as the Church triumphant, in time or eternity; despite the lack of an anaphoric article, this is the same group as the 'vast multitude' (ὄχλος πολύς, *ochlos polys*) which worships God at 7.9–10. Cf. Milligan 319–20; Caird 232; Boring 192; Roloff 210; Mounce 341.

For the saints of God, singing with what sounded like 'a loud resonance' (ὡς φωνὴν μεγάλην, *hōs phōnēn megalēn*, lit. 'as a loud voice'), see 7.10. The genitive masculine plural participle, λεγόντων (*legontōn*, 'singing', lit. 'saying'), following an accusative feminine singular noun phrase ('as a loud voice'), must be construed *ad sensum*; for the genitive ὄχλου (*ochlou*, 'crowd') is treated by the author at this point as collective, and therefore plural (cf. 7.9). See Aune 1014. For music in the Apocalypse see on 11.17; also 7.12; 15.3. Cf. further Smalley, *Thunder and Love* 115 n. 86.

The term, ἀλληλουιά (*hallēlouia*, 'hallelujah'), is a Greek transliteration of the Hebrew formula, used in liturgical texts, הַלְלוּ־יָהּ (*halᵉlû-yāh*), meaning 'praise Yahweh'. It appears in the fourth and fifth books of the Psalms, in the Old Testament, as an introduction (e.g. 106.1), a conclusion (104.35), or both (135.1, 21); and there it is translated as 'Praise the Lord!'. In the LXX it is added to the titles of four hallel psalms (114; 115; 116; 118), which include clear references to the theme of the Exodus. See also LXX Ps. 145.1; Tobit 13.18; 3 Macc. 7.13. The expression is transliterated into Syriac at the end of each of the *Odes of Solomon*.

The exclamation, 'Hallelujah!', appears in the New Testament only in Rev. 19, where it occurs four times (verses 1, 3, 4, 6). Its use in the hymns of this chapter is related to the themes of the Apocalypse, rather than being borrowed directly from the liturgy of the primitive Church (Prigent 520); for it heightens the sense of a new fervour which surrounds the worship of the saints, as they celebrate God's justice and deliverance. It also connects closely the two hymns of 19.1–5 and 19.6–8 (Fiorenza 101), which gather up the adoration of heaven and earth expressed earlier in the Apocalypse, and give it added point in the light of the approaching consummation. Cf. Kiddle 376.

In 19.1, 'Hallelujah!' leads into a judgement doxology (Aune 1024–25) which explains the need to praise God; see the similar ascriptions at 7.10; 11.15; 12.10; and the theme of divine justice at 18.1–3. For he is the sovereign Lord, and a just deliverer (19.1–3). The 'salvation' (ἡ σωτηρία, *hē sōtēria*) of God refers to more than his personal rescue of believers from the devices of Satan; it denotes the totality of his purposes of redemption, prefigured in the Exodus and achieved in Christ (15.3–4). It stands first, in the sequence of divine attributes in this context, because it is fundamental to God's work of corporate and individual healing. The 'glory' (ἡ δόξα, *hē doxa*) and 'power' (ἡ δύναμις, *hē dynamis*) of God follow, because they describe the majesty and might which have been revealed in making so comprehensive a deliverance possible (cf. Mounce 342). See further Knight 125. For 'deliverance' in the Apocalypse see 7.10; 12.10; for 'glory' see on 1.6; 4.11; et al.; and for 'power' see on 4.11; 5.12; et al. At 12.10 'deliverance and power' occur together; while the hymns at 4.11 and 5.12 associate 'glory' and 'power'.

The heavenly chorus continues its hymn of praise by setting out (verse 2) two reasons for ascribing glory and victory to God. Both causes are introduced by ὅτι (*hoti*, 'because', 'for'); and, while the first is general (God's judgements are just), the second is specific (his avenging justice has been directed against Babylon). For the description of divine acts of justice as 'fair and just' (ἀληθιναὶ καὶ δίκαιαι, *alēthinai kai dikaiai*, lit. 'true and just') see 15.3, where the order of the adjectives is reversed, and 16.7, which is exactly parallel to 19.2. For the notion of the Lord's ordinances as righteous and true see Ps. 19.9; also Ps. 51.4; Dan. 3.27 LXX.

For the language and thought of the remainder of verse 2 see 17.1–2, 5, 15–16. The verb, ἔκρινεν (*ekrinen*, 'condemned', lit. 'judged'), is in the aorist tense because the seer is referring to an event in the narrative past (cf. Aune 1025). Babylon and her allies have been condemned for the systemic evil which they represent; and, such is the widespread influence of the scarlet whore, the whole 'earth' has been infected by the seductive immorality and idolatry of the city. The verb, ἔφθειρεν (*ephtheiren*), can mean to 'destroy' physically, as well as to 'corrupt' spiritually (so 11.18); but, in view of the present context, the 'corruption' of human nature seems to be primarily in view at this point (cf. BDAG 1054a). See 14.8; 18.3. However, Beale (927) argues that the meaning of the verb in 19.2 includes the nuance of destruction. In support of this view, he points to the background text in Jer. 28.25 LXX where, in language close to Rev. 19.2, the fall of the historical Babylon is described in terms of God's judgement against the 'destroying mountain which destroys the whole earth'; Beale (ibid.) also notes that the idea of 'destruction' is appropriate at this point in verse 2, since persecution is mentioned in the next phrase. Cf. further Prigent 364. The imperfect tense of the verb φθείρω (*phtheirō*, 'corrupt', 'destroy'; here, 'she was corrupting') is a reminder of the continuous, as well as pernicious, influence of Babylon on the world.

God has also 'avenged the death of his servants', brought about as a result of the evil intent represented by Babylon. The verb, ἐκδικεῖν (ekdikein, 'to avenge'), is rarely used in the New Testament, and occurs only twice in Revelation: here, and at 6.10 (q.v.). Behind this sentence in verse 2 lies a similar, but expanded, text at 2 Kings 9.7, where a young prophet is sent by Elisha to anoint Jehu king, so that the Lord may 'avenge on Jezebel the blood of my servants the prophets'. Although the harlot Jezebel, the idolater, is not mentioned explicitly at Rev. 19.2, John would no doubt have been conscious of her image here, as elsewhere in the Apocalypse (see 2.20–23; 17.16).

The 'blood' of God's servants is the equivalent of their death, and therefore martyrdom (cf. 6.10; 16.6; 17.6; 18.24; see also Deut. 32.43). The theme of the martyrdom of the saints is certainly present in the Apocalypse; and 19.2 is to some extent a response to the cry of the martyrs in 6.10, 'Lord, how long before you administer justice, and avenge our deaths?' But the vision of the saints in glory at 7.9–17 extends far beyond those who have suffered and died for their faith; and the victory of God celebrated by the Church triumphant at 19.1–5 is much more inclusive than 'the victory won by the martyrs' (Caird 232). Here, as elsewhere in the seer's apocalypse, the 'servants' of God are in the end all those who belong to him by faith, some of whom have died for that faith; it is all such who are qualified to enter the heavenly city, and to share in the water of life (22.14, 1). On the theme of vengeance in Revelation see above, 160–64.

The last phrase of verse 2, '(the death of his servants) which she caused' (ἐκ χειρὸς αὐτῆς, ek cheiros autēs, lit. 'from her hand'), is a phraseological Hebraism, found only here in Revelation (Aune 1015). See again 2 Kings 9.7 LXX. It may be construed as meaning 'at her hand' or 'on her'; in other words, Babylon is the object of God's vengeful activity (so NRSV, REB; also Moffatt 462–63). More probably, the expression means that God has taken vengeance on the blood of his servants emanating 'from her hand', denoting that Babylon has been responsible for the death of some of his saints (so NJB; Aune 1013, 1025–26; cf. Ps. 78.10 LXX); hence the translation.

3   The same group of believers, belonging to the Church in glory, expresses God's praise for a second time in an antiphonal response which reinforces the theme of divine judgement belonging to the first hymn (verses 1–2); cf. Prigent 521. John's description of this action as the 'second' (δεύτερον, deuteron) time that worship is offered to God has more than a numerical force, and suggests the intensity of the feelings and hymnody of those who are chanting (Milligan 320). The verb, εἴρηκαν (eirēkan, 'they cried out', lit. 'they said'), is not an aoristic perfect for 'they say', but a vivid and dramatic perfect as such (Mounce 343 n. 7). The repeated shout of 'Hallelujah!' (for which see on verse 1) heightens the tension of the drama at this point; it also draws together the heavenly liturgy which is expressed in the first two sections of this scene (see verses 1, 4, 6). In the present verse (19.3), 'Hallelujah!' is not a conclusion to the hymn in verses 1–2 (cf. Aune 1026), but an introduction to a new section of the same hymn in verse 3.

The use of the second καί (kai, lit. 'and') in verse 3 has a serious purpose in the syntax of the sentence to follow, although several translations (including NIV, NRSV, NJB, ESV) omit it altogether. The word acts here not simply as a conjunction; it is, rather, a Hebraism introducing the next clause, which sets out a further basis for the heavenly rejoicing in progress. The Church, in heaven and on earth, can praise the Lord *because* the smoke from Babylon's judgemental burning 'ascends for ever and ever'; that is to say, God's final judgement on all opposition to his sovereignty, and in particular (since Babylon is front stage in this scene) his criticism of every kind of systemic evil (see on 17.1–6), is disclosed in the city's destruction. Cf. Charles 2, 120.

For the ascending 'smoke' in verse 3, which implies the destruction of the city through burning, see Gen. 19.28 (the incineration of Sodom and Gomorrah); Isa. 34.9–10; also, more immediately, Rev. 14.11; 18.9, 18. The reference to divine judgement in Isa. 34 is more individual than corporate ('no one shall pass through it [the ruined city] for ever and ever'); whereas in Revelation 19 the allusion is more general ('the smoke ascends from *her* [Babylon]'). But a city is made up of individuals; and, in the present scene, the imagery includes those whose faithlessness has precipitated a share in the judgement and downfall of Babylon. The 'smoke' (ὁ καπνός, *ho kapnos*) which ascends to the skies, as a result of the burning of the scarlet woman, contrasts markedly with the smoke of the heavenly incense which rises with the prayers of the saints, according to 5.8; 8.3–4 (Sweet 278). In 19.3 the judgemental fires are not accidental, but deliberate.

The fact that the smoke ascends 'for ever and ever' (εἰς τοὺς αἰῶνας τῶν αἰώνων, *eis tous aiōnas tōn aiōnōn*, lit. 'to the ages of the ages') emphasizes the totality and finality of the city's destruction (as in Isa. 34.10). Note the same hyperbole, of judgemental fire which is unquenchable, at Isa. 66.24; Jer.17.27; Ezek. 20.48; Mark 9.43 par.; 9.48; *Sib. Or.* 1.103. It is possible that Babylon's *eternal* judgement is intended as a partial polemic against the mythical name, *Roma aeterna* ('eternal Rome'), which was one of the designations of the Roman Empire, and appeared on Flavian coins (so Sweet 278; Beale 929). If so, it remains true that 'Babylon' is more than Rome, and that the imagery in this verse is general rather than particular (see on 17.1). For the phrase, 'for ever and ever', which occurs regularly in the Apocalypse, see 1.6; 5.13; 11.15; 22.5; et al.

4 As in 5.14, the twenty-four elders and the four living creatures now share in the heavenly worship of God. For their (angelic) identity see on 4.4, 6. This is their last appearance in Revelation. On the present occasion their adoration is responsive, and marked by the antiphon, 'Amen, Hallelujah!' Such scenes in Revelation are often used as part of the narrative framework surrounding at various points hymns chanted in the heavenly court (cf. 4.10–11; 5.8; 7.11–12; 11.16); so Aune 1026.

The expression, 'fell down and worshipped', appears regularly in association with the heavenly liturgy of the Apocalypse (cf. 4.10; 5.14; 19.10; 22.8; et al.). The verbs, πίπτω (*piptō*, 'prostrate', lit. 'fall down') and προσκυνέω (*proskyneō*, 'worship'), describe two stages belonging to a single act of adoration and are virtually synonymous (Aune 1026–27); cf. the similar pairing at Ps. 72.11; Dan. 3.5; Matt. 2.11; Acts 10.25; 1 Cor. 14.25; *Jos. As.* 28.9; *T. Job* 40.4; et al. 'Falling down' before the Lord is more associated with the elders, than with the living creatures, in the Apocalypse (4.10; 5.14; 11.16; et al.). In verse 4*a* the focus is on the worshippers, while in 4*b* the one who is worshipped is in view; for the sovereign God, as 'seated on the throne', see on 4.2.

For the responsive 'amen' (ἀμήν, *amēn*) in verse 4 see on 1.6–7; also 5.14; 7.12; 22.20–21. The word derives from the Hebrew אָמֵן (*āmēn*, 'amen'), meaning 'so be it'. For the varied but complementary senses of the term in the Apocalypse see on 5.14; also Charles 1, 19–20. At 3.14 it becomes a title of the exalted Jesus. The expression, as it is used in 19.4, has a concluding, affirmative function, where it strengthens what has already been stated about God's judgement on unrighteousness in verses 1–3 (cf. BDAG 53*b*). The combination, 'Amen, Hallelujah!', is found only here in the New Testament. In the Old Testament the couplet is used to conclude the fourth book of the Psalter (Ps. 106.48; cf. Ps. 105.48 LXX), where once more God's people celebrate their deliverance from oppression and wrongdoing (Ps. 106.42–47); see also 1 Chron. 16.36; Neh. 5.13. Beale (930) suggests that the glory offered to God in 19.4 projects into the future the praise which will take place after the final judgement of Babylon has occurred. See further verse 6.

5 A fourth hymn, this time spoken by a solo voice, is heard from the heavenly realm. Whereas the first three chants in Rev. 19 (verses 1–4) are ringing endorsements of God's salvific judgement, and consist of expressions of praise from the community in glory (1–3) and a response from the heavenly court (4), now the Church in the world, which includes John's own community, is invited to share the worship in progress. As so often in the Apocalypse, the boundaries between heavenly and earthly worship grow very thin at this moment (cf. Boring 192).

The expression, 'a voice from the throne' (φωνὴ ἀπὸ τοῦ θρόνου, *phōnē apo tou thronou*), is found in Revelation only here and at 16.17 (q.v.); but see 21.3, using ἐκ (*ek*, 'from', 'out of'). It might be assumed that, because the voice which is heard 'issues from the throne', the seer is referring to the voice of God himself. However, this is impossible, since the exhortation which follows summons all his servants to praise '*our* God'; and this must mean that other beings are involved. The same is true of the equally unlikely suggestion that the voice of *Christ*, representing the saints of God, may be in view (so Beale 930, who notes that in John 20.17 Jesus speaks of ascending 'to my Father and your Father'). Most commentators regard the 'voice from the throne', in this context, as belonging to one of the living creatures or elders, or to another angel (see verse 4); so Beckwith 721; Charles 2, 124; Kiddle 378; Hendriksen 179; Mounce 343. It is doubt-less best to identify the voice in verse 5 as one which emanates from the presence (the 'throne') of God, and therefore speaks with his authority (see on 10.4); cf. Hughes 197. The theme of divine sovereignty, triumphing over evil through the death of the Lamb, is fundamental to the teaching of Revelation generally; and it finds its focus in the hymns of the Apocalypse (15.3–4; et al.), including the present canticle. Cf. Wall 221.

The basis for the injunction to 'praise our God' is provided by the eschatological judgement of Babylon, the representative of systemic evil. This is always in progress, but its imminence is being celebrated in the present scene. The exclamation, 'praise our God' (αἰνεῖτε τῷ θεῷ ἡμῶν, *aineite tō[i] theō[i] hēmōn*), corresponds to the 'Hallelujahs!' of 19.1, 3, 4, 6 (see on verse 1), which mean the same. At Ps. 150.1 LXX (cf. also Ps. 116.1 LXX) the Hebrew expression is translated into the Greek form present at 19.5. The verb, αἰνέω (*aineō*, 'praise'), occurs only here in Revelation. The dative, instead of the accusative, of the direct object (God), following the verb in this sentence reflects a Hebraism, which occurs regularly in the LXX (1 Chron. 16.36; Jer. 20.13; Dan. 2.23; et al). It occurs only here in the New Testament.

The worship which is enjoined is inclusive in its scope, and involves *all* the servants of God, and not simply his martyrs (as Beasley-Murray [273] rightly observes). The 'servants' (δοῦλοι, *douloi*, lit. 'slaves') of God are those who yield him honour and obedience, without being servile, and live in the right fear of him (cf. Moffatt 463; see also Rev. 1.1; 7.3; 19.2; 22.3; et al.). The καί (*kai*, lit. 'and') which introduces this part of verse 5 is epexegetical, and leads into a description of the 'servants'. This group, John says, consists of 'those both small and great who fear him'; hence the translation 'even'. See further the textual note on verse 5.

For the concept of the saints 'fearing' God, as an attitude of awe in the presence of holiness, see 11.18; 14.7; 15.4; cf. also Neh. 5.9; Job 6.14; Ps. 2.11; Prov. 1.7; et al. For the 'small and great' (οἱ μικροὶ καὶ οἱ μεγάλοι, *hoi mikroi kai hoi megaloi*) see 11.18; 13.16; 19.18; 20.12; also Ps. 115.13. The adjectives refer to those of low and high status, mean-ing 'all people, whatever position in life they occupy' (Aune 1028). *Every* believer is called to praise the God of judgement and salvation.

Vision 1: The Marriage Feast of the Lamb (19.6–10)

6 The first main vision of this scene introduces a new image, that of the Lamb's mar-riage supper (see verses 7 and 9). A third heavenly choir is introduced at this point, to sing the praises of God for his saving judgement on all the incarnations of 'Babylon'. In 19.1–3 the rejoicing is led by a 'huge crowd', and this triumphant assembly is joined in verses 4–5 by angelic beings from the divine court who surround God's throne. Now (verses 6–8) an even larger, 'extensive' crowd participates in the worship; and this multitude appears to be human, as well as angelic (see below). Like the 'new song', chanted by the heavenly court at 5.9–14, the fourfold 'Hallelujah!' of 19.1–8 is rendered by both heaven and earth (cf. Fiorenza 101).

For the second time in Rev. 19, the seer 'hears' a voice (see on verse 1). The fact that the noun φωνή (*phōnē*, 'resonance', lit. 'voice') is anarthrous indicates that the 'crowd' in verse 6 is not to be identified precisely with that in verse 1. There is a connection, because the saints are present in both; but the difference is that the multitude in verse 6 (ὄχλος πολύς, *ochlos polys*, lit. 'large crowd') is even more 'extensive'. There is nothing in the text to indicate the exact origin of the members of this latter group; and the reference to the marriage of the Lamb (verse 7) might suggest that the setting remains, as in verses 1–5, heavenly. But already (in verse 5) the saints on earth have been invited to share in the offering of supernatural praise; and this indicates that the multitude in verse 6 is also likely to be human, as well as angelic. This is *not* to say (with Fiorenza 101) that the fourth hymn in this section is sung on earth. Rather, the doubly huge crowd in verse 6 includes the spiritual hosts of 19.1, as well as redeemed humanity itself (7.1–8); it constitutes the Church both militant and triumphant. See Hughes 199.

This point is underscored by the use of the two metaphors which follow: the resonance of the crowd in view sounded like 'rushing waters' (cf. 1.15; also Isa. 17.12; Ezek. 1.24) and 'loud thunderclaps' (cf. 6.1; *3 Apoc. Bar.* 14.1–2). Both metaphors are combined at Rev. 14.2. Normally in Revelation loud speaking or singing is described by the use of the phrase, φωνὴ μεγάλη (*phōnē megalē*, 'a loud voice'); Aune 1028. So the use of the dramatic images of water and thunder here emphasizes the loudness of the sound which is being provided by the vast crowd of worshipping believers in heaven and on earth (cf. the words of the angelic figure at Dan. 10.6, which sounded like 'the roar of a multitude'). For the grammatically awkward participle, in the masculine genitive plural, λεγόντων (*legontōn*, 'the cry went up', lit. 'saying'), see on verse 1. The syntax is unlikely to have been influenced by the preceding genitive plurals, ὑδάτων (*hydatōn*, 'waters', neuter) and βροντῶν (*brontōn*, 'thunders', feminine). The genitive plural participle probably derives from the collective sense of the genitive ὄχλου (*ochlou*, 'crowd'), although this appears much earlier in the verse. See further Beale 932–33.

For the exclamation, 'Hallelujah!', which appears here for the last time in the Apocalypse, see on verse 1. In verse 6 the word functions less as a liturgical formula, and more as a parallel to 'praise our God' (verse 5) and 'Hallelujah!' in verse 1; for, as there, it is followed by the basis for giving thanks to God, introduced once more by ὅτι (*hoti*, 'for'): the Lord has 'begun to reign'. The first three 'Hallelujahs' in Rev. 19 (verses 1, 3, 4) look back to the judgement on Babylon narrated in Chapter 18. In verse 6, the shout points forward in anticipation of the marriage of the Lamb which is to come (Mounce 346). Nevertheless, the thought of God's life-giving sovereignty, established in Christ for all time and over all evil, remains a pervasive theme throughout this scene (see 19.6, 11–16; 20.11–15). The hymn of praise which begins in verse 6, and runs through to verse 8, falls into three parts: an introductory call to worship (verse 6*a*); a thematic sentence (verse 6*b*); and a description of God's activity in Christ which has made the rejoicing possible and necessary (verses 7–8*a*); cf. Aune 1028.

The verb, βασιλεύω (*basileuō*, 'reign'), with God as the subject, occurs in Revelation only here and at 11.15, 17; but see 12.10. The aorist of the verb in verse 6, ἐβασίλευσεν (*ebasileusen*, lit. 'he reigned'), is ingressive, and means (as in the translation) 'he has begun to reign'. That is to say, God is sovereign throughout all time and in eternity. He is always King; but the death and exaltation of the Lamb and the destruction of Babylon make this apparent in history. The hymn of 19.6–8 is therefore prophetic, as well as factual; and the verbs in the past tense (such as 'reigned', 'arrived' and 'prepared') are anticipatory, as well as retrospective. Equally, in the praise of the Church at 19.1–8, which is the antithesis of the lamentation in 18.9–19, temporal sequences are not important. The saints, in heaven and on earth, are perpetually summoned to thank God for his abiding acts of salvific judgement, which belong to the future as much as to the past. To this extent, 19.6 becomes a theological development of the theme of God's kingship in 11.15–17 (q.v.); cf. Beale 931.

For the idea of God's 'reign', elsewhere in biblical literature, see 1 Chron. 16.31; Ps. 93.1; 96.10; 97.1; Isa. 52.7; 1 Cor. 15.25; 1 Tim. 6.15. For the comprehensive divine title, κύριος ὁ θεὸς ὁ παντοκράτωρ (kyrios ho theos ho pantokratōr, 'the Lord, God, the Almighty'), see on 4.8; also 11.17; 15.3; 16.7; 21.22.

7–8 A second reason is now expressed, in the present hymn, for the saints in heaven and on earth to praise God. This has two parts: the Lamb's marriage (feast) has arrived (verse 7), and his bride has prepared herself with fine linen (verses 7–8). A comment on the 'fine linen' of God's people is included by the seer at the end of verse 8. The theme of Christ's wedding banquet is introduced here abruptly; but it prepares the way for its reappearance at 21.2, in much the same way as the imagery of Babylon's fall is mentioned at 14.8, but not developed until Chapters 17—18 (cf. Prigent 525). The pervasive teaching of this passage is that the temptations and oppressions of Babylon are the trials which God uses to refine the faith of the saints, and make them ready for the heavenly city and the consummate communion of God with his people (cf. 2.10–11; Rom. 8.35–39; 1 Pet. 4.12–13); note Charles 2, 126; Beale 934.

Verse 7 begins with the invitation, 'let us rejoice and exult'. The combination of these two verbs, χαίρωμεν καὶ ἀγαλλιῶμεν (chairōmen kai agalliōmen, otherwise 'let us rejoice and be glad') is found elsewhere in the New Testament only at Matt. 5.12; see also Ps. 97.1; 98.4; 118.24; Isa. 61.10a; Joel 2.23. The shift at this point to the use of hortatory subjunctives, in the first person plural, intensifies the eschatological joy which is being expressed by the faithful. The third of these outbursts is, δώσομεν τὴν δόξαν αὐτῷ (dōsomen tēn doxan autō[i], 'pay homage to him', lit. 'let us give him the glory'), for which see Josh. 7.19; 1 Chron. 16.29; Ps. 96.7; Mal. 2.2; et al.; Rev. 1.6; 11.13; 14.7.

The phrase, 'the marriage day of the Lamb' (ὁ γάμος τοῦ ἀρνίου (ho gamos tou arniou, lit. 'the marriage of the Lamb'), occurs in the Apocalypse only here and at verse 9. The covenant imagery derives from two Old Testament ideas. First, some latter prophets conceived Israel as a woman betrothed to Yahweh, whose people were therefore summoned to offer him unconditional loyalty (cf. Isa. 54.6; Ezek. 16.7; Hos. 2.14–23). Unbelief and apostasy, on the part of God's people, were accordingly condemned as harlotry (Ezek. 6.9; Hos. 2.1–7). Second, the notion in Judaism of marriage as a joyful festival becomes in Isaiah (61.10b; 62.5) a picture of the messianic time of salvation. Jesus uses this image to describe the effect of his own ministry (Mark 2.19–20; cf. John 3.29), and the fellowship in God's kingdom which he inaugurated (Matt. 22.1–14). Post-Easter Christianity blended both of these traditions, and interpreted the parousia of Christ at the end as a time of marital joy, when the bridegroom will be united with the Church, the bride who awaits him (cf. 2 Cor. 11.2; Eph. 5.22–33).

In Rev. 19.7–8 John goes a step further. He not only portrays the perfection of believers through the imagery of the Lamb's wedding feast; he also develops this by means of an effective contrast which stems from the negative aspect of the first traditional motif (Israel's wanton unfaithfulness). On the one hand is the city of systemic evil, which seduces the world with ostentation and deceives it with idolatry (14.8; 17.1–6; 18.2–10); on the other is the community of the faithful redeemed, properly clothed in fine linen and waiting obediently to be united with her exalted Lord (3.20; 21.2, 9; 22.17).

For this section see esp. the excursus in Roloff 212. This is the first mention of the 'bride' of Christ, the Lamb, in Revelation (see also 21.9). As Duff (*Who Rides the Beast?* 83–96) notes, this figure is the fourth woman to appear in the Apocalypse; and she is contrasted with the unfaithful whore of Babylon (17—18), just as the woman clothed with the sun (12.1–6) is the opposite of the idolatrous Jezebel (2.20–25). See also Talbert, *Apocalypse* 86–87.

For the wedding clothes of the bride in verses 7–8 see Isa. 61.10; *Targ.* Ps. 45.12–15; Rev. 21.2. Such robes are also associated in the Apocalypse, as here, with the 'white robes' and 'rest' of the faithful (see Rev. 6.10–11; 7.13–15; 14.13). The verb, 'prepare' (ἑτοιμάζω, *hetoimazō*), occurs six times elsewhere in Revelation (8.6; 9.7, 15; 12.6; 16.12; 21.2); and in each context its use indicates that the plan of God, of which the action narrated is a part, must be neither changed nor delayed (Prigent 526). It is probably correct to find a further nuance in the text at 19.7 (so Prigent ibid.); for the Greek, ἡτοίμασεν ἑαυτήν (*hētoimasen heautēn*, lit. 'she has prepared herself', aorist), may include an insistence which means 'she prepared herself *by herself*'. In other words, the Church needs to be actively responsible in preparing for the coming of the Lord. Such faithfulness allows believers to confess the present reality of God's reign, and of his salvation, as well as their future anticipation of these (4.8; 11.15–17; 12.10; 15.3–4; 18.8; 19.6; 21.3). With the 'fine linen' (βύσσινον, *byssinon*), 'shining and clear' (λαμπρὸν καθαρόν, *lampron katharon*, lit. 'bright and pure'), as worn by the bride of Christ (verse 8), contrast the similar material associated with Babylon (18.12) and the scarlet attire of the harlot (17.4; 18.16).

The meaning of the remainder of 19.8 ('she was permitted to wear fine linen . . . [which] stands for the righteous behaviour of God's people') is not immediately clear; but this is no reason to claim that the verse is a later gloss (so Charles 2, 127–28). The key may be found in the interpretation of the term δικαιώματα (*dikaiōmata*, 'righteous behaviour', lit. 'righteous deeds'). This noun, like its cognates in the same word-group, varies in significance; and thus it depends for its exact meaning on the immediate context in Revelation (cf. Beale 934). Here, the sense of 'right behaviour' has to do primarily with believers 'holding faithfully to the testimony concerning Jesus' (verse 10). Before sharing with the Lamb in a close relationship of life within the eternal city (21.22—22.5), Christians are required to complete their preparation for that state by being faithful to their Lord in all that they do. For members of the Church to receive salvific 'white robes' (verse 8; cf. also 3.4–5; 6.11; 7.9, 13–14) may therefore be equated with the task of bearing consistent witness to him; and this, it may be argued, is a proper response by the justified to the call of the heavenly bridegroom (Mounce 348). Cf. further Roloff 212–13. (For ἅγιοι [*hagioi*, 'saints', lit. 'holy ones'], as meaning 'the people of God', see on 5.8; 8.3; et al.)

Such an interpretation presents the exegete with a typical tension in biblical theology, between faith (membership of the bridal community) and good works (the need for righteous behaviour). So, for example, Hughes (200) argues that the 'righteous deeds (plural) of the saints' do not contribute to their justification; rather, their behaviour is required and maintained on the basis of a justified status already achieved in Christ. Paul's thought may help to throw light on the teaching of verses 7–8. Individuals are not saved by good works; but, once saved by grace, the life of faith needs to be accompanied by good works (Rom. 3.21–28, against Eph. 2.8–10; Phil. 2.12–13). The bride of Christ (verse 8) 'was permitted' (ἐδόθη αὐτῇ, *edothē autē[i]*, lit. 'she was given', an aorist passive of divine allowance; cf. 6.2; et al.) to wear fine linen, or to be arrayed in righteous acts; and this involves the Johannine community in particular, and the Church in general, in a life of holiness (cf. the oracles of Rev. 2—3). The unrighteousness of Babylon and her allies contrasts sharply with the ongoing right belief and orthodox praxis to which the servants of God are summoned. Cf. Mounce 348.

Beale (935–38) persuasively adds a further clarification to this analysis. He notes that receiving white robes elsewhere in the Apocalypse (see esp. 7.13–14) conveys the idea of 'purity resulting from a test of persevering faith' (ibid. 936). Accordingly, the wedding garments in this context (19.7–8) may be interpreted as the *reward* of 'righteous behaviour', rather than as the deeds themselves. In this case, the 'fine linen, shining and clear' of verse 8 represents two related ideas: human faithfulness and good works as evidence of a right standing with God; and the vindication or acquittal which God's judgement on the enemy accomplishes for his people (cf. Ps. 58.10–11; Rev. 19.2). Thus the phrase, τὰ δικαιώματα τῶν ἁγίων (*ta dikaiōmata tōn hagiōn*, lit. 'the righteous deeds of the saints'), is ambivalent; it includes the meaning of righteous acts performed *by* believers (where the genitive is subjective), as well as deeds of righteousness carried out by God *for* the saints (objective genitive). For the notion of vindication as belonging to the δικαιόω (*dikaioō*, 'declare righteous') word-group elsewhere in Revelation see 15.3–4; 16.5, 7; 19.2, 11; also Isa. 61.10*b*; *Targ. Zech.* 3.1–5; BDAG 249*b*–250*a*. For the 'protection' of the saints see also *Apoc. Elijah* 5.5–6.

Beale (936–37) also points out that the only other appearance in Revelation of τὰ δικαιώματα (*ta dikaiōmata*, lit. 'righteous deeds'), at 15.4, occurs in a context of divine and just judgement against the oppressors of the saints. Equally, the allusion in verse 7 to Ps. 118.24 and Matt. 5.12 is appropriate, since in both texts the main point is an invitation to praise God for vindicating the faithful. Nevertheless, as Beale (937) agrees, the righteous acts of the saints remain an important part of Christian commitment (verse 7; cf. 22.11). The great supper of God and the marriage feast of the Lamb (19.9) will be finally ready when the Church's total faithfulness to the Lord becomes a proclamation of his sovereignty (Prigent 527).

9   The identity of the being who is heard next is not immediately clear; and, indeed, λέγει (*legei*, lit. 'he says') does not even specify that the status of the speaker is angelic. Hughes (201) thinks that the angel of 14.13 addresses the seer at this point, since the 'rest' promised there to the saints is now being consummated. Most commentators assume that the speaker is the interpreting, bowl-angel of 17.1, who acts as a narrator throughout that chapter (so Beckwith 727; Michaels 212; Aune 1034). Kiddle (380–81) adopts the same stance; but he also notes that the whole of John's apocalypse is mediated from God through 'his angel' (1.1), so that the appearance of an angel at 19.9 need not be regarded as abrupt, but as a natural continuation of an ongoing and intense visionary experience (ibid.). However, following Chapter 17 (in 18.1—19.8) other angelic beings have been introduced; and they have been identified as 'another angel' (18.1–3), 'another voice' (18.4–20) and a 'strong angel' (18.21–24). Since the last voice to be heard before 19.9 is that 'from the throne' (verse 5), it could be argued that this angelic being, with divine authority, speaks here. Yet he is specifically revealed in verse 10 as a visible figure who is recognizable, even in a vision, as a 'servant-companion' of the believing comrades. It seems reasonable, as a result, to connect the speaker in verses 9–10 with the last angel to appear on stage: namely, the 'strong angel' of 18.21, who might easily have commanded sufficient respect to invite 'worship' (verse 10).

The expression, καὶ λέγει μοι (*kai legei moi*, 'next, the angel said to me', lit. 'he says to me'), occurs three times in verses 9–10. The use of the present tense here, in contrast to the past tense of the surrounding verbs, may reflect a moment of immediacy in the seer's narration of his vision (Beale 945–46). The command for John to 'write' applies to the record of his entire apocalypse (1.11), to complete oracles (2.1, 8, et al.), and to brief messages (as here and at 14.13; 21.5). The benediction, 'Those who have been invited to the wedding feast of the Lamb are fortunate indeed!', is the fourth of seven makarisms in Revelation (cf. also 1.3; 14.13; 16.15; 20.6; 22.7, 14). It is very close in form to the wording of 14.13, and consists of an introduction, a command to write, a further introductory formula and a concluding statement (see Aune 1031). In content, however, 19.9 moves from the thought of the saints resting in the Lord after death (14.13) to the possibility of believers actively participating in the eschatological feast, as at Luke 14.15 (cf. Prigent 528).

The syntax of the sentence, 'those who have been invited to the wedding feast of the Lamb are fortunate' is unusual, since it is rare in the Apocalypse for an extensive prepositional phrase (εἰς τὸ δεῖπνον τοῦ γάμου τοῦ ἀρνίου, *eis to deipnon tou gamou tou arniou*, 'to the wedding feast of the Lamb') to be placed between an article (οἱ, *hoi*, 'the [ones]') and a substantival participle, κεκλημένοι (*keklēmenoi*, 'invited', lit. 'called'); note the order in the translation. See Aune 1017, 1032. At Rev. 17.14 the followers of the Lamb who are κλητοί (*klētoi*, 'called') are also described as ἐκλεκτοί (*eklektoi*, 'elect ones'); and this suggests that, in the present context, the idea of 'election' belongs to the invitation ('calling') of the saints to the Lamb's wedding feast (Beale 945).

The imagery of the eschatological wedding 'feast' (δεῖπνον, *deipnon*, 'banquet', lit. 'dinner'), as such, is found only here in Revelation; but it is implied in the marriage theme at 19.7; 21.2. Note the grim balance to verse 9 at 19.17–21, where an angel invites the birds to feast on the remains of the Lamb's enemies (and cf. Prigent 548–49, who points out that the sacrificial meal of Ezek. 39.4–5 becomes the banquet of God and the wedding feast of the Lamb). In the Old Testament (see on verse 7), the 'banquet' motif, with its overtones of intimacy, is used to represent the happiness of the coming messianic kingdom (Isa. 25.6; cf. Matt. 8.11; Luke 14.15–24). Similarly, the 'common meal' of the Qumran sectarians seems to have been a ritual anticipation of the messianic banquet (1QS 6.1–8; cf. 2.19–26). This notion is alluded to at the Last Supper, where Jesus speaks of the meal he is sharing with his disciples as a foretaste of the glory to come, made possible through his death (Matt. 26.27–29 par.; Luke 22.29–30; cf. Rev. 3.20). For the idea of the 'wedding feast' in general see further Matt. 25.10; Luke 12.36; 14.8; 4 Ezra 9.47; *Acts Thom.* 4–5, 7. The eschatological banquet in Rev. 19.9 seems to be viewed as a single event, although in fact it lasts for eternity (Hendriksen 180–81; against Aune 1034); for a similar continuity see Zech. 3.13; *1 Enoch* 62.14; *3 Enoch* 48A.10. See further Smalley, 'Banquet'.

Because the bride of verse 7 represents faithful Christians, who in verse 9 become the wedding guests, Aune (1034) finds the imagery in this passage 'somewhat awkward'. However, Beale (945) must be right to maintain that, whereas both pictures suggest the intimate communion of Christ with believers, the metaphor in each case is viewed from a different perspective. In verse 7 the bride is the Church *corporate*, about to be married to the Lamb; while in verse 9 *individual* Christians are portrayed as guests at the marriage banquet itself. Judging by the universal composition of the Church described elsewhere in John's drama (5.9; 7.9; 14.6; cf. Matt. 8.11), the scope of the invitation to the Lamb's wedding celebrations is by implication inclusive (cf. Hughes 201).

For the expression, 'these are true words (οἱ λόγοι ἀληθινοί, *hoi logoi alēthinoi*) from God', see 21.5; 22.6; although, in those two contexts, the adjective πιστοί (*pistoi*, 'trustworthy', lit. 'faithful') is added to 'true'. See also the 'faithful sayings' at 1 Tim. 1.15; 3.1; 4.9; 2 Tim. 2.11; Titus 3.8; cf. further Moule, *Birth* 283–84. The 'words' in question seem to refer naturally to the beatitude just spoken in verse 9 (Hughes 201; Wall 223). But, equally, this attestation could embrace the song of the heavenly crowd, with its promise of the Lamb's marriage (19.6–8; Mounce 349), and even the vision narrated by the angel from 17.1 onwards (Kiddle 381; Beasley-Murray 275). Roloff (213) claims that the 'true words' are those of the cyclical visions beginning in Chapter 12; while Prigent (529) cautiously argues that the angel's statement authenticates the whole of the book of Revelation. In view of 22.6 (q.v.), this wide-ranging interpretation deserves serious consideration. For the significance of divine 'truth' in the Apocalypse see on Rev. 3.7 (Jesus as true); 6.10 (God); 15.3 (divine activity); also John 1.9; 17.3; 1 John 2.8; 5.20; et al.

10 This verse acts as a conclusion to the sub-section 19.1–10, as well as the introduction to the remainder of the vision, 19.11—20.15 (cf. Beale 946). The beatitude of verse 9 is followed by a dialogue in verse 10, during which the seer's attempt to accord worship to the angel is rejected and redirected towards God. The interlocutor throughout is the strong angel of 18.21 (see on verse 9). For the combination of 'falling down' to 'worship' see verse 4; also on 4.10.

The motif of human obeisance, both involuntary collapse and voluntary prostration, in the presence of angelic or divine revelation, is a fairly common theme in Jewish and Christian literature; and it is at times combined with a rejection of the action by the person so reverenced, because it appears to usurp the rightful worship of God himself (so Rev. 19.10; 22.8–9). See Dan. 2.46; Tobit 12.16–22; *3 Enoch* 1.7; *T. Abr. (A)* 9.1–3; *Asc. Isa.* 7.21; 8.1–5; *Apoc. Zeph.* 6.11–15; Acts 10.25–26; and, in the course of the resurrection narratives, cf. Matt. 28.2–4; Luke 24.5. Sometimes the act of obeisance is no more than a human reaction of great respect (e.g. Gen. 50.18–19, where Joseph rejects his brothers' humility and exclaims, 'Am I in the place of God?'). For this tradition in general see further Moule, *Origin* 175–76; Bauckham, *Climax of Prophecy* 118–49, esp. 133–40.

A repetition of this incident in 19.10 appears at 22.8–9; and a common explanation for the doublet is that John was attempting to oppose a tendency in his community towards the worship of angels (cf. Col. 2.18); although it is by no means clear that a cult of angels existed in Judaism (Aune 1036). So Swete 248, 304; Beckwith 729; Peake, *Revelation* 355 n. 1; Kiddle 382, 449; Sweet 280. Boring (193–94) makes the improbable suggestion that the seer's obeisance to the heavenly messenger is a 'little charade', designed to discourage too high a view of angelic phenomena (cf. 2 Cor. 11.14; Gal. 1.8–9). If angel worship were a serious problem in the churches of Asia addressed in Revelation, it is surprising that no reference to this aberration is made in the oracles of Chapters 2—3 (Caird 237); unless the prophetess 'Jezebel' justified her false teaching (2.20) by an appeal to angelic revelations (Bauckham, *Climax of Prophecy* 133).

The rejection of John's attempt to worship the angel in verse 10 ('See that you do not!'), and the command to 'Worship God' instead, is more likely to be related to one of the main themes of the Apocalypse. The seer is conscious of the insidious danger to Christian witness of idolatry, which has been much in mind during the visions concerning Babylon in Chapters 17 and 18 (see also on 13.3–4; et al.). His concern throughout the present scene (Rev. 19—20) is accordingly to warn the members of his community, and of his audience generally, about the need to maintain faith in a God who is just, and in a Lamb who keeps faith with his Church. A clear choice must be made between 'Babylon' and 'Jerusalem'; and true worship means obedience to the one God, not to those like the beast who claim divine status, or even to God's heavenly agents (Bauckham 1302*a*).

This theological teaching is strengthened by the careful literary design which gives rise to a virtual repetition of 19.10 at 22.8–9, except that the 'strong' angel's claim that he is a servant-companion of those who are 'holding to the testimony of Jesus', which is defined as 'the spirit of prophecy', becomes in 22.9 a differently nuanced but essentially identical statement by the 'interpreting' angel that he is a prophetic colleague of those who 'obey the commands in this book' (see further on 22.9). As Bauckham (*Climax of Prophecy* 133–34) has shown, this is not an example of careless duplication. Rather, the two parallel passages form conclusions to the visions in 17.1—19.10 and the prophecies in 21.9—22.9, which also have openings in tandem (17.1–3; 21.9–10). In Bauckham's view, it was John's intention to mark out these sections of Revelation as 'comparable and complementary' (ibid. 133). Together they portray the two cities of Babylon the harlot and Jerusalem the bride of Christ; and, while one is judged, the other is vindicated.

The seer in verse 10 does not mistake the angel for Christ, but for the impressive, and indeed divine, source of God's true words (verse 9); hence his reaction of obeisance, and the angel's command to worship God alone. Such an attempt at worship is inappropriate because the messenger is a 'servant-companion' (σύνδουλος, *syndoulos*, lit. 'fellow-slave', as at 6.11; 22.9) with John, and with the 'colleagues' (ἀδελφῶν, *adelphōn*, lit. 'brothers') in his own community. As believers and angels are servants of the same Lord (cf. Matt. 18.28–33; Heb. 1.7, 14), and both groups are called to bear witness to him, it follows that they are 'servants' of each other (Mounce 349). In the phrase, τῶν ἐχόντων τὴν μαρτυρίαν Ἰησοῦ (*tōn echontōn tēn martyrian Iēsou*, lit. 'those holding the testimony of Jesus'), the genitive Ἰησοῦ (*Iēsou*, 'of Jesus') is probably subjective: the witness borne *by* Jesus to the truth about God and himself (cf. 1.2, 9; 12.17; so Beasley-Murray 276). But an objective reference may well be included here: the testimony was given by Jesus to believers, who then handed it on to others (so Swete 249; Beckwith 729; Boring 194; Beale 947). A minority opinion takes the genitive as entirely objective ('the testimony which concerns Jesus'; cf. 17.6); so Bruce, 'Spirit' 338.

A similar ambiguity surrounds the two genitival expressions in the final sentence of verse 10: ἡ γὰρ μαρτυρία Ἰησοῦ ἐστιν τὸ πνεῦμα τῆς προφητείας (*hē gar martyria Iēsou estin to pneuma tēs prophēteias*, 'for the witness of Jesus is the spirit of prophecy'). The first ('the witness of Jesus') may be taken as both subjective and objective, as in the preceding clause. If the genitive in the second phrase ('the spirit of prophecy') be understood as objective, this means that Christians are 'prophets' (see 22.9) who bear a testimony to Jesus which is inspired by the Spirit (cf. Caird 238; Smalley, 'Paraclete' 294). However, it is also possible (but less plausible) to take 'the spirit of prophecy' in a subjective sense, meaning that the witness which Jesus gave to himself is the essence of prophetic proclamation (Mounce 351; cf. Beale 947–48). In any case, and this favours an 'objective' exegesis, John's audience would doubtless understand a reference to the 'spirit' of prophecy in terms of the Holy Spirit, the inspirer of all prophecy (1 Pet. 1.10–11; 2 Pet. 1.21). In the context of Rev. 19.10, John is saying that it is ultimately the Spirit of God who moves the faithful to give needed testimony to the truth about the Lamb, as the divine Messiah, which he first disclosed about himself. See further Thompson, *The God* 157–58.

Vision 2: The Warrior-Messiah (19.11–16)

11 This new section contains the second of seven visions in the present scene of Revelation. See the commentary on 19.11–16 in Origen, *Comm. in Joan.* 2.55–59, esp. 55 (on John 1.2); cf. also the literary analysis above, 474–75. Once more, the symbolism of John's apocalyptic thought reaches beyond natural and literal confines to the supernatural dimensions of Christian truth. Mounce (351) regards the appearance in this scene of a white horse, whose rider is to 'wage a holy war', as the figurative means of bringing the present age to a close. But the thought in this part of John's drama continues to be eschatological, and therefore free from chronological limitations; so that the 'end' is not yet. There are further disclosures of God's salvific judgement yet to come, in the remainder of this scene (19.11—20.15) and beyond (21—22).

The new vision is introduced by the now familiar literary formula, καὶ εἶδον (*kai eidon*, 'and I saw'); for this expression, and for the importance of spiritual vision (and audition) in Johannine thought, see on 5.1; cf. also Ezek 1.1 LXX. The phrase, 'I saw', occurs seven times in Scene 6 (Rev.19.11, 17, 19; 20.1, 4, 11, 12). John sees the 'heaven opened' (τὸν οὐρανὸν ἠνεῳγμένον, *ton ouranon ēneō[i]gmenon*). In the Fourth Gospel, as elsewhere in biblical literature, the 'splitting' of the heavens indicates that an important spiritual disclosure is about to be made (John 1.51; cf. Ps. 18.9; Isa. 64.1–3; Matt. 3.16 par.; Acts 7.56); and this notion is undoubtedly present at Rev. 19.11. In 4.1 a 'door' to heaven stands open; at 11.19; 15.5 the heavenly 'temple' is uncovered; but now (19.11) the heavens themselves are torn apart.

The rider of the 'white horse' turns out to be Christ, the sovereign warrior, himself (verses 12–16). A white horse has already appeared in Revelation, at 6.2 (q.v.). But there the cavalier represents a military power which resists the Messiah, rather than Christ himself (against Aune 1053); so that 6.2 becomes a parody of 19.11. The imagery here seems to owe more to the Jewish tradition of the warrior-Messiah than to New Testament teaching about the parousia of Jesus (cf. Exod. 15.3–4; Isa. 63.1–3; Zech. 9.9–10; 2 Apoc. Bar. 72.1–6; Pss. Sol. 17.21–29); so Beckwith 730–31; Mounce 351; and see further Aune 1048–52. However, the portrait of a Messiah ushering in a final conflict against the Antichrist, in the role of a military leader at the head of 'heavenly armies', while unusual, is not at variance with the teaching of the New Testament. See esp. 2 Thess. 1.9–10, where the twin themes of the messianic judgement of the unrighteous and the vindication of Christian hope belong together; cf. also Matt. 25.41; 1 Thess. 4.13–18; 2 Thess. 1.6–8. Note Mounce 351.

It is characteristic of the author's descriptive style in Revelation, as at 19.11, to mention a symbolic object (such as a throne or horse or cloud) and then the individual or group seated on it (cf. 4.2, 4; 6.2–8; 14.14; 20.4); cf. Aune 1052–53. The colour of the horse in verse 11, λευκός (leukos, 'white'), is significant. For in the Apocalypse, here and elsewhere, it suggests not only the purity of Christ (1.14; 14.14; note 20.11; cf. also Mark 9.3 par.), but also the concept of the vindication and preservation of the saints (Rev. 2.17; 3.4–5, 18; 6.11; 7.9, 13; 19.14). See Beale 950.

It is not immediately clear whether the two evocative adjectives which are applied to Jesus the Christ in 19.11, 'faithful and true', should be regarded as descriptive of his nature, or as titular. It seems preferable to understand the epithets as referring to the being of Christ. See the textual note on verse 11, where the reading which adds 'called' at this point is, as in the translation, rejected. The exact combination of terms, 'faithful and true' (πιστὸς καὶ ἀληθινός, pistos kai alēthinos), as applied to the Messiah, is found elsewhere in the Apocalypse only at 3.14; although the same couplet is used to designate the 'words' of revelation at 21.5; 22.6. Cf. also 3 Macc. 2.9–14, esp. 2.11.

For Jesus Christ as 'faithful' see Rev. 1.5; 3.14; the same word occurs as a description of his followers at 17.14. In Hebraic thought, faithfulness and truth are close together in meaning, since 'truth' was virtually synonymous with reliability; cf. Jer. 10.10. The God of truth is faithful to his covenant promises, and will in due course vindicate the faith of all the saints (Mounce 352). The adjective 'true' is applied to God and his activity in the Apocalypse at 6.10; 15.3; 16.7; 19.2, 9. Apart from this verse (19.11) it describes the being of Christ only at 3.7, 14. See also John 1.9; 8.16; 15.1; 1 John 2.8; 5.20; 2 John 3. On the truth of God, as spoken in Jesus, see Kelly and Moloney, Experiencing God 102–105.

The present tenses of the verbs in the final sentence of verse 11, ἐν δικαιοσύνῃ κρίνει καὶ πολεμεῖ (en dikaiosynē[i] krinei kai polemei, 'he is just in judgement and in war', lit. [as in NRSV] 'in righteousness he judges and makes war'), should be taken as gnomic. It is in general the case, the seer is saying, that the Messiah is right in his justice and his judgement. The justness of divine judgement is a prominent theme in Revelation (cf. 15.3–4; 16.5–7; 19.2); see also LXX Ps. 9.9; 10.7; 71.2; 95.13; Isa. 11.4; et al. It is a biblical corollary that human justice should be modelled on its divine source (cf. John 7.24; Rev. 22.11; Barn. 19.11). In the context of Rev. 19.11, the Warrior-Messiah 'makes war' in order to judge the unrighteous, rather than (as in 2.16) to chasten the wayward members of his own community (Aune 1054). Nevertheless, his judgement throughout is salvific; and, like God's, it is designed to rescue his people from evil (Rev. 19.1–10; cf. Isa. 11.1–11; *T. Dan.* 5.13); so Prigent 539–40.

12 This verse provides three further descriptions of the warring and saving Messiah, who was introduced in verse 11; and these details relate to his fiery eyes, his crowned head and his secret name. The conjunction δέ (*de*, lit. 'and', 'but'), hidden in the translation, is found six times elsewhere in Revelation (1.14; 2.5, 16, 24; 10.2; 21.8). Here and at 1.14 it forms an emphatic introduction to a description of the exalted Christ (Aune 1054).

The eyes of the Christ figure are compared to a 'blazing fire' (ὡς φλὸξ πυρός, *hōs phlox pyros*, lit. 'as a flame of fire'; but see the textual notes on verse 12), where the genitive in the Greek is descriptive. This description connects directly with the presentation of the exalted Son of man, whose eyes 'flamed like fire', in 1.14 (q.v.). In that opening vision of the Apocalypse Christ appears as a judge, who also wields a two-edged sword of discrimination (1.16); and it is primarily for the exercise of judgement that the warrior-Messiah is introduced at 19.12 (see also 19.15–21, and note esp. the 'sharp sword' at verse 15). Cf. the ministry of judgement associated with the exalted Jesus, who has eyes of fire, in 2.18–23. The judgemental oracle addressed to Pergamum is also introduced by the one who holds a 'sharp, two-edged sword' (2.12). For an Old Testament background to judgement by fire, and the resulting deliverance of God's people, see Dan. 10.6, 14; 10.16 (Theod.); 11.36–45. In view of the close parallels between Rev. 19.12 and the first two chapters of the Apocalypse, Beale (951–52) suggests that this scene includes apostates from the covenant community, as well as unbelievers beyond it (19.17–21). In any case, the concept of a divine judgement which leads to salvation is constantly in view throughout this scene (see 19.13–14; 20.4–6; et al.).

The Messiah is also said to be wearing 'many diadems' (διαδήματα πολλά, *diadēmata polla*, otherwise, 'many crowns') on his head. The only other figures wearing 'diadems' on their heads in the Apocalypse are false claimants to an authority which is sovereign and universal: namely, the dragon (12.3) and the beast (13.1). The dragon is contrasted with the 'woman robed with the sun' in 12.1 (q.v.), the heavenly counterpart of the true messianic community, who wears a 'crown' of stars on her head. Both dragon and beast are adorned with a limited number of crowns (seven and ten); and they are clearly idolatrous opponents of Christ, whose 'many' diadems speak of a kingship which is cosmic and eternal (see Rev. 1.5; 17.14; 19.16; cf. 1 Macc. 11.13). The crowned Son of man at 14.14 mediates justice (the sharp sickle), but also wholeness (the harvest); see on 14.15–16. The followers of the Lamb are also identified with him by wearing 'crowns', as a reward for their faith (2.10; 3.11; 4.4; cf. 2.26; 3.21).

The final statement about Christ in verse 12 is that he has a 'name inscribed', which no one knows 'but he himself' (εἰ μὴ αὐτός, *ei mē autos*, is emphatic, as in 3.20). A problem of syntax is involved in the use of the masculine singular participle, ἔχων (*echōn*, 'with', lit. 'having'). This form seems to be governed by the masculine singular substantival participle, ὁ καθήμενος (*ho kathēmenos*, lit. 'the one sitting'), in verse 11. As there is no main verb in this part of verse 12, the participle 'having' functions as a finite verb (Aune 1042). A grammatical problem also exists because the plural reference to 'many diadems' here is immediately followed by the mention of *one* 'name' (ὄνομα, *onoma*); and this gave rise to textual variations (see the notes on verse 12). Similarly, it is not clear whether the singular 'name' of the Messiah is written on his 'diadems' or inscribed on the rider himself. Since the phrase, 'on his head were many diadems' immediately precedes the reference to Christ's name, it is likely that the rider's 'name' is to be understood as appearing on his crown; and this view is supported by the fact that the parodic 'blasphemous names' of the beast were written on his diadems (13.1; cf. 17.3, 5). Cf. Beale 955.

An Old Testament background to the image of the Messiah wearing 'many diadems', with a secret name inscribed on them, is to be found in Isa. 62.2–5 (cf. Isa. 65.15), where the 'new name' and 'crown' of Israel (62.2–3) denote the intimate, covenantal relationship with God which his people will share with him at the end-time. At Rev. 19.12 Christ is seen to be fulfilling this prophecy, and enabling the saints to become members of the new Jerusalem (21.2); similarly, at 3.12, believers are promised that the 'name' of God, of the new Jerusalem and of the exalted Jesus himself will be inscribed on them. Rev. 3.12, like 19.12, picks up 2.17, and the pledge that conquerors will be given the 'new name' of Christ, as a demonstration of their close fellowship with him (see also the 'new name' and 'bridal' imagery of Odes Sol. 42.8–9, 20, reminiscent of 19.7–9, 12). See Beale 953.

The name which is 'written' (γεγραμμένον, gegrammenon), but also secret, has been variously identified (see Mounce 353). Rist (513) notes that it could be one of the three names given to the Messiah in the chapter (verses 11 [q.v.], 13 and 16), but thinks that such an association is too obvious. Instead (ibid.), he suggests that the name is the 'name above every name' (Phil. 2.9–11), given to the Lord Jesus in fulfilment of his messianic ministry (also Hughes 203–204). A common interpretation understands the 'secrecy' of the name literally: the meaning of the title expresses the mystery of Christ's being, which finite minds will never grasp (similarly Swete 252; Beasley-Murray 279–80; Bauckham 1302b). Knowledge of a person's name has always meant possessing a degree of power over an individual; and this may account for the refusal of divine visitors in the Old Testament to disclose their identity (Gen. 32.29; Judg. 13.18; cf. 1 Enoch 69.14; Asc. Isa. 9.5; see also the coptic gnostic tractate Gospel Phil. 2.54.5–7 [the secret name of the son is 'the name above all things: the name of the father']; and cf. ibid. 56.3–4). However, as Mounce (353) points out, it is questionable whether the returning Messiah would share such a reluctance.

It is much more likely that the name which is known only to the Messiah himself is a reference to the sacred tetragrammaton, YHWH. This was a name too holy to be pronounced in Judaism, so that these consonants were combined with the vowels of another name for God, Adonai, to give the combination usually represented in English as 'Yahweh' (cf. Wis. 18.24, where the name of God, Yahweh, is written on the 'diadem' of the high priest's head). Cf. Beale 954–55; Prigent 542. This interpretation may be supported by three considerations.

(a) The unknown name of Rev. 19.12 is clearly divine, since the names or attributes assigned to Christ in this section of the Apocalypse (1.11, 13, 16) are also associated with God himself elsewhere in Scripture (cf. 1 Thess. 5.24; Jer. 42.5; Isa. 1.10; John 1.1; Dan. 4.37 lxx). This is doubtless also the way to understand the 'new name' of Jesus, which appears in parallel with 'the name of my God', at Rev. 3.12 (see also the secret 'new name' given to believers at 2.17). God's character will not be fully demonstrated until the end of history, when his justice will have run its full course (19.1–2); and the same is true of Christ's divine nature here (19.12). The fact that the name of Yahweh/Christ is 'unknown' means not that the essence of the Godhead is a mystery to his creation, but that the divine acts of saving judgement have yet to be completed. Meanwhile, as the seer is concerned to point out in this scene, the character and activity of God and his Messiah are to be identified; so that the name of Christ is also the name of God (see Beale 954; Prigent 541–42). John's Christology is consistently high.

(b) The next point follows from the first. In the Old Testament, the name 'Yahweh' is often found in contexts which speak of God's covenant relationship with Israel, and notably in fulfilling his promises to the patriarchs. A good example occurs in Exod.

6.3, where God says to Moses that he appeared to Abraham, Isaac and Jacob as 'El Shaddai (God Almighty)', but not under the name of 'Yahweh'. It was the generation of the Exodus who would experience Yahweh as the fulfiller of his covenant; and it is the people of latter-day Israel, and members of the new Israel, who will come to know the 'name' of Yahweh most completely. That point of consummation will be reached when prophecy is fulfilled, and God's judgemental and salvific purposes are completed in Christ by the restoration of Israel and the final revelation of his character in history (see Exod. 6.7; Isa. 52.6; Ezek. 37.6, 13; Rev. 15.3). So Beale 954–55.

(c) A revealed name of the Messiah in the very next verse (19.13) is the 'Word of God'. Whatever the nuances of this christological title (see below), it manifestly describes the Messiah as the essential expression of God's being (against Cullmann, *Christ and Time* 161–63, who relates this title of Christ to his 'task of preaching the gospel to the world'; ibid. 161).

Such theology, then, seems to undergird the imagery of the 'hidden name' of Jesus the Messiah in 19.12. The symbolic meaning of that name is an affirmation that, in Christ, God's promises and purposes of salvation through judgement have yet to reach their point of final fulfilment. His nature of justice and grace, which he shares with the Father, will be universally revealed when he comes to execute the divine plan in its totality. Then, the Lamb's opponents will experience the full extent of his justice (19.15–21), and his followers will enter into the full disclosure of his grace (2.17; 3.12; 7.15–17; 14.4; 22.3–4). Cf. Beale 954–55.

One problem remains in the exegesis of verse 12. Some commentators (such as Charles 2, 132; Aune 1055) regard it as a difficulty that there appears to be a contradiction between the assertion that Christ's diadems are inscribed with a name which 'no one knows', and the unveiling of that name in verses (11), 13 and 16. But, as Beale (955) rightly points out, a conflict exists only if the phrase in verse 12 ('a name which no one knows but he himself') is understood as an abstract, literal statement. If instead it is properly understood as symbolic, like the other ascriptions in this passage, then the apparent contradiction is removed (so Beasley-Murray 279–80). Cf. the immediate disclosure in 17.5 of the 'mysterious' name of the scarlet woman as 'Babylon the great'. In both instances, the 'hidden' character of the name is discovered in theological, and not literal, terms, and in the light of their historical and redemptive significance (Beale 955).

13   The figure of Christ in 19.11–12 is now said to be 'robed in a garment soaked in blood'. For the word 'soaked' (βεβαμμένον, *bebammenon*, lit. 'dipped') see the textual note on verse 13. The picture is that of a triumphant warrior, rather than a sacrificial victim. The 'blood' associated with the robes of the victorious Messiah, therefore, is not primarily that of the crucified Jesus (Boring 196–97; Wall 231), nor that of the martyred saints (Caird 242–44), but rather a symbol of the death of God's enemies (Beckwith 733; Roloff 218); and this remains true even if the final, eschatological battle has yet to come. For a background to this military imagery, of the warrior-judge winning vengeance and redemption for his people, see Isa. 63.1–4, esp. verse 4; Exod. 15.11–18; Deut. 33.13–17; Judg. 5.1–31; Isa. 59.15–20; Zech. 14.1–21; *Targ. (Pal.)* Gen. 49.11; Isa. 63.1–6. Moreover, the dress worn by embattled Roman field commanders was traditionally red in colour; while, in the imperial period, red or purple was the hue of the garments in which emperors were vested (BDAG 166a; Aune 1057).

Nevertheless, the sacrificial dimension of Christ's 'blood' would not have entirely escaped the Christian sensitivities of the seer and his audience at this point (Swete 252; Aune 1057), particularly in view of the associations between αἷμα (*haima*, 'blood') and the atoning death of Jesus elsewhere in the Apocalypse (1.5; 5.9; 7.14; 12.11). But at 19.13 these links are secondary. Christ is presented here as an avenging judge and triumphant warrior, not as the Redeemer (Kiddle 384–85; and see 19.15); even if the true justice of God (19.2) is finally revealed in the salvific love of his Messiah (19.13).

Revenge produces a revelation in verse 13 (Prigent 544); for now the avenger is named as 'The Word of God'. The Greek phrase, κέκληται τὸ ὄνομα αὐτοῦ (keklētai to onoma autou, 'his name was called'), is awkward, since it includes an apparently unnecessary repetition ('name . . . called'); but cf. Gen. 3.20 LXX; et al. Apart from the present context, the expression, 'the word of God' (ὁ λόγος τοῦ θεοῦ, ho logos tou theou) is found four times in the Apocalypse, at 1.2, 9; 6.9; 20.4. In the plural it occurs at 17.17; 19.9; see also the related 'true (divine) words' of prophecy at 21.5; 22.6. Both the singular and plural forms of the phrase, 'the word of God', refer to the content of the gospel, the good news of salvation through Christ. The genitive, τοῦ θεοῦ (tou theou, 'of God'), may be either subjective or objective: the word from God or about him. In this verse (19.13), it may be construed as both (Beale 957).

Only at 19.13 in Revelation is the term 'Word (of God)' used as a title for Jesus the Christ. It may seem that this christological expression links immediately with the reference to the pre-existent Christ as Logos in John 1.1, and with the 'tabernacling' of the Word at John 1.14. However, the title as used in the Apocalypse is not related, as it is in the Johannine prologue, to the concept of God's self-disclosure in his Son (see also the ambiguous phrase 'the word of life', which suggests both person and proclamation, in 1 John 1.1; cf. Smalley, *1, 2, 3 John* 4–6). In Rev. 19.13 the description has much more to do with God's activity and the fulfilment of his purposes of salvific judgement; and in the immediate context these concern the judgement of the nations (19.15). Cf. the close parallels at Wis. 18.14–16; Heb. 4.12. There is a connection between the high Christology of Revelation and the Fourth Gospel (John 1.1–14); but this is in terms of the theology of the hypostatic 'Voice' (Rev. 1.12), rather than of the 'Word' (19.13). See further Charlesworth, 'Jewish Roots of Christology'; Smalley, 'John's Revelation' 556–57.

Prigent (545) makes an important observation when he points out that 'Logos', in the setting of Rev. 19.13, should not be construed as a proper noun. Rather, the person who is so designated is the full and final expression of God's will. Occurring as it does in a section which emphasizes the common identity of the judging Son and the saving Father, Prigent (ibid.) concludes, the title 'Word of God' as borne by the Messiah looks like 'a confession of faith'.

14   The appearance of the Messiah in verse 13 (q.v.), as the 'Word' of God whose garment is 'soaked in blood', has defined his role in this section as primarily judicial. Soon that judgement is to begin (cf. esp. verses 14–16), even if the final eschatological battle which provides its setting remains proleptic. For such a purpose the Warrior-Judge is surrounded by his followers; and this is so natural a picture that there is no need to regard the mention of the 'heavenly armies' here as intrusive (so Aune 1059). The 'armies' (τὰ στρατεύματα, ta strateumata) evidently take no direct part in the coming battle; although notice that, on their behalf, the Messiah himself eventually smites the enemies of God (19.15, 19–21).

The 'armies of heaven' who accompany the Messiah have been variously identified. It is unlikely that this group should be associated with the force of angels led by Michael, who defeated Satan at 12.7–9 (as suggested by Aune 1059). A common view maintains that those who follow the Lord in this figurative context are angels, who make up the 'host of heaven' (e.g. Beasley-Murray 281; see also Aune 1059); and the notion of angelic armies accompanying Yahweh and Christ for purposes of judgement is certainly a regular part of apocalyptic imagery in both Judaism and Christianity (see Amos 3.13;

Dan. 7.10; Zech. 14.5; *1 Enoch* 102.1–3; *2 Enoch(J)* 17; *T. Levi* 3.3; *Apoc. Elijah* 3.2–4; Matt. 13.40–42; 25.31–32; Mark 8.38 par.; 2 Thess. 1.7; Jude 14–15; et al.; cf. the title 'Lord of hosts', in contexts of blessing, at 2 Sam. 5.10; Isa. 19.24–25; et al.). Mounce (354) adopts a similar interpretation; but he thinks that, on the basis of saints following Christ and remaining faithful unto death at Rev. 17.14, this assembly includes the martyrs.

However, it is much more probable that the 'heavenly armies' referred to in verse 14 should be understood as a figure for all the saints, the company of faithful believers who belong to the Church both militant and triumphant. See Prigent 545–46.

(a) White robes (see later) are a symbol of salvation given to the conquerors, who are with Christ in glory or share the blessings of eternity in time (and may therefore be described as being 'in heaven' already). See 3.4–5; 4.4; 6.11; 7.13–14; et al.
(b) The Lamb's victory over the kings and the beast at 17.14 is won on behalf of the 'called and chosen and faithful'. In other words, as here and at 12.11, the faithful are 'conquerors' on the basis of their participation in the victory of Christ. That is why their 'fine linen' (19.14) remains white, whereas the cloak of the Messiah is red with blood. The link between Rev. 17 and 19 is strengthened by the title, 'King of kings, and Lord of lords', which is given to Christ in both contexts (17.14; 19.16).
(c) The Messiah leads his followers out in order to fulfil the prophecy of Ps. 2.9 (see Rev. 19.15). At 2.26–28 the conquerors receive a promise that they will share in the accomplishment of the same prediction.

So the heavenly army in verse 14 should be regarded as the troop of faithful Christians, conquering saints in heaven and on earth who participate in the victory of Christ, and share in his judgement (20.4; cf. Prigent 546). See further *Asc. Isa.* 4.14–17; *Did.* 16.7. Nevertheless, there is no reason to exclude either angelic beings or martyrs from this company (cf. Charles 2, 135–36; Beale 960).

The heavenly armies are said to be 'following behind' the Messiah on 'white horses' (ἐφ᾽ ἵπποις λευκοῖς, *eph' hippois leukois*). The participle, 'following' (ἠκολούθει, *ēkolouthei*), uses a third person singular verb to follow a neuter plural substantive (στρατεύματα, *strateumata*, 'armies'). But this is a regular grammatical pattern in Revelation (1.19; 14.13; 18.14; et al.); see Charles 1, cxli. According to verse 11 (q.v.), Christ was also mounted on a white steed, which there denoted not only his purity, but also his vindication and preservation of the saints. For the company of the faithful to be riding white horses, therefore, emphasizes their identification with the person of the exalted Jesus, and their participation in his judgemental and salvific work.

In addition, the members of Christ's heavenly army are also said to be 'wearing fine linen, pure white' (ἐνδεδυμένοι βύσσινον λευκὸν καθαρόν, *endedymenoi byssinon leukon katharon*). Apart from the angels of 15.6, only saints in Revelation are attributed with wearing white garments (see above). For the 'fine linen' of the saints, contrasting markedly with the 'linen' of Babylon (18.12, 16), see on 19.8. The white attire of the faithful echoes the purity and truth of Christ (verse 11; cf. Matt. 13.43; Rev. 1.14; 14.14; 19.11); but it may also support the notion that the cause of truth proclaimed by the faithful righteous, and scorned by Babylon (18.4–5), is being vindicated (19.8; 21.5–8); cf. Beale 960. The perfect participle, ἐνδεδυμένοι (*endedymenoi*, 'wearing'), seems to be a syntactical error, since it is masculine nominative plural, but modifies the neuter nominative plural noun, στρατεύματα (*strateumata*, 'armies'). However, the masculine form of the participle probably results from understanding the members of the 'troops' as male riders (Aune 1043).

The 'pure white' robes of the saints in verse 14 may also have a priestly connotation, since the same garments, worn by heavenly beings, are also priestly at 15.6 (cf. Ezek. 9.2; Dan. 10.5; 12.6); and these are similar to the priestly vestments of the exalted Christ at 1.13 (q.v.). See also 7.9, 14–15; 19.8. So Beale 961. However, the white attire in 15.6 is worn by angels, not by saints as such; and the heavenly armies of 19.14 have been identified as saintly, rather than entirely angelic (see above). Nevertheless, the Christian saints of the Apocalypse do possess a priestly character and function (see 1.6; 5.10; 20.6).

15   This part of the second vision in Scene 6 continues the delineation of the character and activity of Jesus the Messiah which began at 19.11–13 (note the repeated καὶ αὐτός, *kai autos*, lit. 'and he [himself]' in verse 15). The seer uses three images for this description: the sword, the staff and the winepress. Aune (1061) claims that these figures are not depictions of Christ, the rider of the white horse, but messianic interpretations of his role. However, that distinction is a very fine one in the present context, since the material within apocalyptic visions is, by its very nature, imaginative and fluid, rather than literal and fixed.

First, the Warrior-Messiah is said to 'strike down the nations' with a sharp sword projecting from his mouth. The 'sharp sword' (ῥομφαία ὀξεῖα, *hromphaia oxeia*) is a symbol for Christ's powerful word of judgement (cf. Prigent 546). For this metaphor, variously expressed in relation to the judgemental activity of the exalted Jesus, see also Rev. 1.16; 2.12, 16; 19.21. The 'sword of the Lord' is regularly mentioned in the Old Testament (Deut. 32.41; 1 Chron. 21.12; Ps. 17.13; Jer. 47.6; Ezek. 30.24; Zech. 13.7; et al.); and this expression is used at times as a symbol of eschatological judgement (Isa. 27.1; 66.16; Jer. 9.16; Ezek. 29.8–9; et al.; cf. 1QM 12.11–12; 4QpIsaᵃ *frags.* 8–10 [col. 3] 22–24). But the exact image of a sword of judgement coming from the mouth of the Messiah occurs nowhere in the literature of Judaism; and this suggests that the idea originated with John himself (but see Heb. 4.12). It may well have been inspired by combining the messianic use of Isa. 11.4 ('he shall strike the earth with the rod [LXX "word"] of his mouth') with an allusion to the servant song of Isa. 49 (verse 2, 'he made my mouth like a sharp sword'); so that Rev. 19.15 not only reaffirms the Isaianic prophecy but also identifies Jesus as the 'servant Israel' (Luke 2.32; Acts 26.23). Cf. Aune 1060–61; Beale 961.

'The nations' (τὰ ἔθνη, *ta ethnē*) is a term used elsewhere in the Apocalypse (10.11; 11.2; 14.8; et al.) for the opponents of God. Their judgement may include that of apostate believers (Beale 961); but, in any case, it marks the vindication of the faithful through the righteous justice of God in Christ.

The second apocalyptic image in this verse, and one which speaks again of messianic judgement, is that of ruling the nations with 'an iron staff'. The verb, ποιμαίνω (*poimainō*, lit. 'tend', 'pasture'), carries at 7.17 the sense of 'shepherding' with gentle care (Mounce 335 n. 22); but elsewhere in Revelation (here, and at 2.27; 12.5, q.v.) it denotes the act of 'shattering' or ruling with stern judgement. The 'sharp sword' (see above) now becomes an 'iron staff', as Jesus fulfils the prophecy of the eventual destruction of God's enemies, and of all that is evil. The phrase as a whole, 'he himself will rule them with an iron staff', alludes to Ps. 2.9 and Isa. 11.4, which are both interpreted messianically. Apart from 19.15 and 2.27; 12.5, Ps. 2.9 is not otherwise quoted in the New Testament. The association of the messianically interpreted texts at Ps. 2.9. and Isa. 11.4, which speak together of the Messiah breaking the nations with a rod and with the breath of his lips, is found elsewhere in Jewish and Christian writing (cf. *Pss. Sol.* 17.24; 4QpIsaᵃ *frags.* 8–10 [col. 3] 15–19; 2 Thess. 2.8); and this suggests that at Rev. 19.15 John is drawing on an existing messianic tradition (cf. Charles 2, 136; Aune 1060).

For the third figure in verse 15, Christ 'will personally tread the winepress which is the furious wrath of Almighty God', see 14.19–20 and 16.19. The Greek of 19.15 and 16.19 is very similar. The phrase, αὐτὸς πατεῖ (*autos patei*, 'he personally will tread', lit. 'he treads'), is important, because it identifies clearly the subject of the one treading the winepress of judgement, which was left enigmatic at 14.20 (q.v.). The immediate back-ground to the imagery of this part of verse 15 is to be discovered in Isa. 63.2–3; Joel 3.13. The two nouns, θυμός (*thymos*, 'anger', 'fury') and ὀργή (*orgē*, 'wrath'), occur 13 times in Rev. 6—19; and this underlines the reality of God's reaction to human in-justice and rebellion against him. The sequence of five genitives in the final sentence of the present verse is exceptional. The second, τοῦ θυμοῦ (*tou thymou*, lit. 'of the fury'), implies a preceding epexegetical καί (*kai*, lit. 'and') following ληνόν (*lēnon*, 'winepress'), to give the sense, 'the winepress, *which is (even)* the furious (wrath of God)'. For the sovereign title of God as 'Almighty' (παντοκράτωρ, *pantokratōr*) see also 1.8; 4.8; 11.17; 15.3; 16.7, 14; 19.6; 21.22.

Mounce (356) speaks of the 'strong and virile realism of the Apocalypse', which draws out the fierceness of God's judgement, and his 'hatred of sin'. While the justice of God in Revelation must be taken seriously, it can never be separated from his love. The sacrificial, and therefore salvific, associations of the 'blood' of the Messiah's garment (verse 13, q.v.) remain in view, even if they are secondary in that context; and the weapon with which Christ finally engages battle is not literally militaristic, but spiritually truthful, and therefore restorative. See Boxall, *Revelation* 78.

16 A further name helps to identify the nature and activity of the Messiah, in addition to the qualities already assigned to him in this scene ('faithful and true', verse 11), and the title 'Word of God' given to him in verse 13. The title at verse 16, 'King of kings and Lord of lords', helps to clarify the ambiguity of the 'hidden name' at verse 12, and is linked directly to it. For it has been argued (see on verse 12, above) that the name which was known to the Messiah alone was the divine name of God himself; and, in the literature of Judaism, the sovereign deity is described precisely as 'Lord of lords and King of kings' (Dan. 4.37 LXX; cf. *1 Enoch* 9.4; also Deut. 10.17; Dan. 2.47; 2 Macc. 13.4; et al.). On this name at Rev. 19.16 see further on 17.14, where it once more appears in a forensic setting, although with the order of titles reversed.

Christ wears this inscribed identification 'on his robe, that is on his thigh'. There are examples in Greek and Roman literature of the names of gods being written on the thighs of their sculptures (cf. Cicero, *Verrine Orations* 4.43); see Aune 1062. More relevantly, in Jewish life the thigh was the usual place for the warrior's sword to be worn (Exod. 32.27; Judg. 3.21; Ps. 45.3; Song of Sol. 3.8), and the symbolic location for the swear-ing of oaths (Gen. 24.2; 47.29). That the name of the Messiah is to be found on his thigh suggests that the Warrior-King will carry out God's promise to judge the nations by his victory over the enemies of righteousness (cf. Beale 963).

Commentators have found difficulty with the fact that, in this vision, the name of the Messiah appears to be written in two places: on his robe and on his thigh. Beasley-Murray (281–82) and Knight (128) think that the name was indeed inscribed on both; similarly Caird (246–47), who maintains that 'thigh' in this context means 'sword'. Charles (2, 137) resorts to textual surgery, and excises altogether the reference to Christ's 'garment' (ἱμάτιον, *himation*). Beale (963) becomes fanciful, and suggests that the name, presumably written on the thigh, was revealed 'as the garment was blown aside or as the rider came into better focus' (ibid.; cf. Prigent 547). The explanation is probably simpler, and involves construing the connective καί (*kai*, lit. 'and') as epexegetic. This gives the sense, as in the translation, the Messiah wears 'on his robe, *that is* on his thigh, an inscribed name'. In other words, Christ's name was written on that part of the robe which fell open across his thigh; and, in the case of a rider, this would be especially con-spicuous (cf. Swete 255; Moffatt 468; Beckwith 733–34; Mounce 356).

The importance of the titular name in verse 16 is not to be gleaned from its precise location, which in an apocalyptic vision is immaterial, but from its theological significance. Yahweh remains truly Lord and King of heaven, in contrast to the attempted usurpation of the Babylonian ruler (Dan. 4.34–37); and equally the Warrior-Christ is manifestly sovereign King and righteous Lord, in contrast to the pretensions to divinity exercised by the followers of Satan (Rev. 17.14), and by Babylon herself (18.7). Even the kingly robe of the Messiah (see also 19.13) differs markedly from the tawdry attire of the scarlet woman (17.4). The final 'name' of the risen Jesus in this passage is once more the name of his Father; for Christ is one with God, as well as one with his Church (John 10.30; 17.23). God demonstrates in Christ his universal sovereignty (King and Lord), which is revealed in the divine purposes of a salvific judgement. Moreover, the lordship and kingship of Christ are manifest in the present (note the tense of the verb ἔχει (*echei*, 'he wears', lit. 'he has'), and not merely in the future (Wilcock 183–84). For this verse see further Slater, ' "King of Kings" '.

Vision 3: Antichrist Destroyed (19.17–21)

17–18   The third vision consists of two related sub-sections, each beginning with καὶ εἶδον (*kai eidon*, 'and I saw'); so verses 17 and 19. The first is a highly dramatic picture of an angel, poised on the sun to issue invitations to God's eschatological feast (19.17–18); while the second (verses 19–21) describes the further outcome of divine judgement. The combination of an angelic appearance and a proclamation formula (he 'called with a loud voice') is found in Revelation only here and at 18.1–2. This serves to tie together the visions of Chapters 18 and 19; and this correlation is further strengthened by the allusions to 'birds' in both (18.2; 19.17). The angel of 18.1 announces the fall of Babylon, and the second messenger gives notice of the defeat of her associates, the beast and the false prophet (19.17–21). The removal of systemic evil (see on 17.1) initiates the final judgement of Antichrist: a world opposed to the righteousness of God (cf. Beale 964–65).

The imagery of this passage, beginning with 19.17, need not be categorized as 'revolting' (Sweet 285) or 'exceedingly crass' (Roloff 220; cf. Mounce 357); although it does draw on the fairly grisly apocalyptic background of Ezek. 38—39, rather than the less graphic depiction of the end-time defeat of evil forces in Dan. 7—12; Zech. 14. The link with the prophecy of Ezekiel, as Beale (966) has shown, stems from the thought in both Ezek. 38—39 and Rev. 19 of the revelation of the divine name. In the defeat of the mythical, eschatological figure 'Gog of Magog' (Ezek. 38.2; cf. Rev. 20.8), God's name is revealed, and his glory is universally recognized (Ezek. 39.7–24). At the same time, his judgement of Gog is an opportunity for restoring the fortunes of Jacob, and making his saving presence known to the house of Israel (39.25–29, esp. verse 29). This twin theme, of judgement and restoration, has emerged dominantly in Rev. 19.11–16; and the allusion to Ezek. 39 gives point to the destruction of God's enemies in Rev. 19.17–21 as the means by which Christ will reveal his 'name' in the deliverance of his people and the judgement of their oppressors (Beale 966). For Ezek. 38—39 as the pretext for Rev. 19.17–21 and 20.7–10 see further Bøe, *Gog and Magog*.

The final combat between good and evil is not described in this passage, but only its outcome in the victory which is won by the Messiah. Nor are his triumphant followers participants in the battle (see on verse 14); note by contrast such Jewish texts as 4 Ezra 13.5–9; 1QM 15.1–10; 18.1–5. A 'certain angel' stands on the sun to invite the birds to God's eschatological feast. The cardinal number, εἷς (*heis*, 'one'), came to be used as a substitute for the indefinite adjective, τις (*tis*, 'a certain'), and it then functioned (so here, in verse 17) as an indefinite article; hence the translation, 'I saw a certain angel'); cf. Aune 1044. See also 8.13.

Angels are at times connected with the sun in the literature of Judaism (cf. *2 Enoch [J]* 11.4–5; *3 Enoch* 14.4; 17.4; *3 Apoc. Bar.* 6.2). But, in the present context (19.17), the angel probably takes up a position on the sun simply in order to be able to address with a supernaturally loud voice the birds who fly at the zenith (Prigent 548); and, as such, the birds are no ordinary creatures, such as predatory vultures (so Beasley-Murray 282). For the imagery of birds flying 'in midheaven' (ἐν μεσουρανήματι, *en mesouranēmati*) see the eagle in flight at the zenith in 8.13. The angelic invitation for a universality of birds ('*all*', πᾶσιν, *pasin*) to gather for the great judgemental supper of God connects in reverse with the faithful being invited to the salvific 'wedding feast of the Lamb' at 19.9, q.v.

There is also a linguistic link between the two banquets of 19.9 and 19.17, since the noun δεῖπνον (*deipnon* 'dinner', 'supper', 'feast') appears in both contexts. But, according to Beale (966), a theological association is also possible; since the meal in verse 9 may be regarded partly as a metaphor for the vindication of the saints, and that in verse 17 is a figure for the judgement which vindicates. The counterpart in verse 17 to the marriage feast at verse 9 involves a further inversion. Ezekiel's prophecy of a sacrificial feast at the end-time, prepared by the Lord on the mountains of Israel (Ezek. 39.17–20), as with the 'great supper' of Rev. 19.17–18, ironically reverses the natural order; so that birds and beasts eat human sacrificial victims, instead of the other way round. The triumph of God's kingdom over the enemies of justice and love is celebrated by a joyful feast for the faithful, but by a nightmarish supper for the waiting birds (cf. Beasley-Murray 282).

The scene of divine judgement on evil of all kinds, in verse 18, is as universal as God's offer of salvation. The audience of this part of the drama is presented here with different aspects of the same judgement, not with a chronological account of stages in that discrimination. The judged 'rulers' (βασιλεῖς, *basileis*, lit. 'kings') are almost certainly to be identified with the generality of resistance to God symbolized by the similar figures at 18.9–10 (q.v.); see also 1.5; 6.15; 16.14; 17.2; 18.3, 9–10; 19.19 (the 'kings of the world') and 17.14; 19.16 (the Lamb is 'King of kings'). For the term, χιλίαρχος (*chiliarchos*, 'military officer', lit. 'chiliarch'), see on 6.15. The word strictly means a military commander of one thousand soldiers. The ἰσχυροί (*ischyroi*, 'warriors', lit. the 'strong', 'powerful') belong with the 'military officers', and may therefore be regarded as those who are 'strong' or 'mighty' in warfare (cf. BDAG 483*b*).

Where Ezekiel speaks of final divine judgement against the mighty, princes, warriors and horses (Ezek. 39.18–20), John extends the list to include the limits of human existence itself: 'the carrion of all people' (σάρκας πάντων, *sarkas pantōn*, lit. 'the flesh of all'), which means the flesh of all *kinds* of people. For the formula, 'free and enslaved, the least and the greatest', in its varied forms, see 6.15; 11.18; 13.16; 19.5; 20.12; also, in the context of the fall of Babylon, 18.13. The cosmic battle at the end is a symbol of worldly humanity as a whole, ranged against the mercy and justice of God, rather than the history of individual leaders and their unrighteous colleagues in crime.

19 For 'and I saw' (καὶ εἶδον, *kai eidon*) see on verse 17. The seer is describing a sequence of visions, and uses a literary formula rather than a chronological marker to link them together (cf. 19.11, 17; 20.1, 4, 11, 12). John has a vision of a final judgement which is, in fact, ongoing (cf. 19.1–3; et al.); and verses 19–21 provide a further aspect of the continuing apocalyptic drama. The conclusive battle of Armageddon (16.16) seems to have arrived; but the end is not yet (cf. 20.1–15; 22.20).

The 'beast' (τὸ θηρίον, *to thērion*), as the representative of the powers of evil, last appeared at 17.16–17; and there he is depicted as the authority behind an assembly of satanic forces which, without knowing it, inaugurate the judgement of God on systemic evil (cf. Prigent 549). The beast is joined for the coming eschatological conflict by 'worldly rulers' (βασιλεῖς τῆς γῆς, *basileis tēs gēs*, lit. 'kings of the earth'); for this expression see on verse 18. At 16.14 (q.v.), these figures were rallied by demonic spirits for the final battle at the last day; and that action is apparently resumed in the narrative of 19.19–21. The 'militia' (τὰ στρατεύματα, *ta strateumata*, lit. 'armies'), a negative parody of the 'heavenly armies' which support the Lamb at verse 14, belong to both the beast and the worldly rulers (against Mounce 358 n. 3), even if the rulers are eventually to be identified with the beast in their unjust and idolatrous character. Hence the plural pronoun, αὐτῶν (*autōn*, 'their'); although a few witnesses (including A sa) have the singular, αὐτοῦ (*autou*, 'his'). The Messiah who makes ready for combat in 19.15 (q.v.) fulfils the prophecy of Ps. 2.9 (he will 'strike down the nations' with a sharp sword). Ps. 2 also refers to the 'kings of the earth' (verses 2, 10), who rebel against God and his Christ. Evidently these same enemies of the truth stand at 19.19 in opposition to the Messiah, who will ultimately annihilate them in the name of his God (cf. Prigent 549).

The concept of God's opponents being 'mustered' (συνηγμένα, *synēgmena*, lit. 'gathered'), mostly by him, to wage war on his people derives from the Old Testament, and Jewish apocalyptic literature (cf. Esth. [Greek] 11.5–9; Ps. 2.1–6; Ezek. 38.14–16; Joel 3.2; Zech. 14.2 [also *Targ.* Zech. 14.2, 14]; *1 Enoch* 90.13–19; *2 Apoc. Bar.* 48.37; *4 Ezra* 13.5; *Jub.* 23.23; *Pss. Sol.* 2.1–2; *T. Jos.* [*Arm.*] 19.b–c; 1QM 1.10–12; cf. Luke 21.20). See further Rev. 17.12–14; 20.8. The passive form of the perfect participle in verse 19, συνηγμένα (*synēgmena*, lit. 'having been gathered together [to wage war]'), is an indicator that the beast and the rulers do not assemble under their own power, but that they are subject to demonic influence (Beale 967). If the thought of God's enemies' carrying out his purposes of saving judgement is brought over to the present context from 17.12–17, where the 'kings' make war on the Lamb and his followers, the passive participle may be a further example of divine permissiveness. The beast and his allies gather under the influence of evil powers, but they are ultimately driven by God. See on 6.2; 13.7; et al.

In the phrase, the beast and the kings were mustered to wage war against 'the one mounted on the horse, and against his army', the articular nouns refer back to the imagery of 19.11, 14. The same is true of the anaphoric reference in verse 19 to '*the* war' (τὸν πόλεμον, *ton polemon*), although the article is hidden in the translation. The final combat, spoken of earlier (16.14; cf. also 11.7; 12.7, 17; 13.7), is directed against the Messiah and all his followers. It prefigures the consummation, which will mark the end of unrighteousness, and the beginning of universal justice and peace (cf. Mounce 358).

20–21   The final conflict of 19.19–21 is proleptic of the judgement of God at the end of time; but, even then, divine discrimination is not separated from divine mercy (cf. 22.10–17). The combat itself is not narrated; as with other battles in the drama of the Apocalypse (17.14; 20.7–10), the audience hears only of the apprehension and defeat of the enemy. The judgement itself is presented in two parts: the capture and destruction of the beast and the false prophet (verse 20), and the execution of their followers (verse 21). The 'beast' represents the incarnation of secular powers in their unjust and idolatrous opposition, at any period of history, to God and his people (see on 13.1, 11). The 'false prophet' is the *alter ego* of the beast, who deceives people by performing miraculous signs, and brands with the mark of the beast everyone who submits to it, rather than to God (see on 13.13–18).

These two personified figures are said to have been 'caught' (ἐπιάσθη, *epiasthē*) by the messianic rider of the white horse (cf. verses 11, 19). The verb πιάζω (*piazō*, 'catch', 'capture'), which carries the sense of 'seizing with intent to overpower' (BDAG 812*b*), is used only here in Revelation, eight times in the Fourth Gospel (7.30, 32, 44; 8.20; 10.39; 11.57; 21.3, 10), and three times in the remainder of the New Testament (Acts 3.7; 12.4; 2 Cor. 11.32). The faithful apparently take no part in the combat, as they do in other eschatological battles in Jewish apocalyptic literature (cf. Bauckham, *Climax of Prophecy* 210–12; Bauckham 1302*b*). For the imagery of this part of verse 20, and its parody of the Christian scheme, see on 13.11–18. John uses a lengthy participial phrase, beginning with ὁ ποιήσας (*ho poiēsas*, 'who had worked [miracles]', lit. 'the one who did'), to describe the false prophet; and this is a common practice in the Apocalypse when the author is referring to leading characters in his dramatic narrative (cf. 11.7; 12.9; 17.1; 18.9; 21.9; et al.). The phrase, ἐνώπιον αὐτοῦ (*enōpion autou*, lit. 'before it' or 'in its presence'), means – as in the translation, and at 13.12 – that the false prophet was working miracles 'on behalf' of the beast and with its authority.

In the judgement scene which follows, the beast and the false prophet are portrayed as being 'hurled alive into the fiery lake of burning sulphur'. The inclusion of the present participle, ζῶντες (*zōntes*, 'alive', lit. 'living'), may be incidental (Beale 969); but see Num. 16.33; Ps. 55.15. In any case, while strictly redundant, the thought of being alive while burning intensifies the fierceness of the punishment which is being represented here; and, in this vision, the seer is depicting more than just the annihilation of the wicked. For the concept of being swallowed up in judgement by Sheol, and perishing by fire, see Num. 16.30–35; also *1 Enoch* 56.8. For this section see further Aune 1065–67.

There is no close literary parallel in Jewish or classical writing to the phrase, 'into the fiery lake of burning sulphur' (εἰς τὴν λίμνην τοῦ πυρὸς τῆς καιομένης ἐν θείῳ (*eis tēn limnēn tou pyros tēs kaiomenēs en theiō[i]*, lit. 'into the lake of fire burning in [with] sulphur'). The image of 'the lake of fire', with or without the mention of 'sulphur', occurs five times elsewhere in Revelation (20.10, 14–15 [thrice]; 21.8; see also 14.10). The article with the noun λίμνη (*limnē*, 'lake') suggests that this apocalyptic symbol would be familiar to John's readers. The element of 'sulphur', which burns easily in air, may be associated with volcanic areas such as the Dead Sea valley (Gen. 19.24; Ezek. 38.22); cf. Mounce 359. A lake of fire and 'burning sulphur' may therefore be regarded as an appropriate location for the judgement of worldly evil and idolatry. Before long, it is predicted, Death and Hades (20.14) and all wrongdoers (21.8) will join Antichrist and the false prophet in this place of restorative torment.

Fire is linked with theophanies in the Old Testament (Exod. 19.18; Ps. 50.3; Ezek. 1.4); and a 'stream of fire' is a metaphor for the throne of God (Dan. 7.9–10; *1 Enoch* 14.18–19). In the thought of Judaism fire is also associated with judgement (4 Ezra 7.36; *1 Enoch* 54.1–2; *Sib. Or.* 3.53–54; 7.118–31; *Apoc. Elijah* 5.22–24, 36–37; et al.). For the concept of underworld conflagration as a means of judgement see Isa. 66.24; also *1 Enoch* 10.4–6; Matt. 5.22; 13.50; Mark 9.43–48; et al. The eschatological image of a critical (and subterranean) 'river of fire' appears in *1 Enoch* 17.5; *2 Enoch* 10.2; and *3 Enoch* 33.4–5; *T. Isaac* 5.21–32; see also *Apoc. Paul* 31, 34–36. The image of a *lake* of fire, when it is used as such in early Christian texts, is evidently derived from this passage in Rev. 19 (see also 15.2); so *Apoc. Peter (Akhm.)* 23; Irenaeus, *Adv. Haer.* 5.30.4 (Antichrist and his followers are sent into the lake of fire at the parousia). Later in Revelation the 'lake of fire' is identified as the 'second death' (20.14, q.v.; see 2.11).

'The rest' (οἱ λοιποί, *hoi loipoi*), who are mentioned at the start of verse 21, may be identified as the supporting armies of the beast and the worldly rulers (verse 19); and they appear in direct contrast to the followers of the Lamb (verse 14; cf. 14.1; et al.). The fate of the two leaders (verse 20) differs from that of their troops; for while the beast and the false prophet were hurled alive into the lake of sulphurous fire, their armies are put to the sword by an avenging Christ (cf. Prigent 550–51). The activity in verses 20–21 differs from such a passage as *Asc. Isa.* 4.14, where Beliar (Antichrist) and his hosts are dragged together into Gehenna. In any case, the destruction of God's enemies signifies the simultaneous vindication of the saints (cf. *1 Enoch* 38.1–6; *2 Apoc. Bar.* 40.1–2; also CD-B 19.5–11). For the metaphor of the judgemental 'sword', issuing from the mouth of the messianic rider on the white horse, see on verse 15 (also 1.16; et al.). The unfaithful are slain by the very words spoken by the Word (verse 13); cf. Heb. 4.12.

The closing statement in verse 21, that 'all the birds were sated (ἐχορτάσθησαν, *echortasthēsan*, lit. "were filled" or "gorged themselves"; the verb is used only here in Revelation)' with the flesh of the unrighteous, forms an inclusion with verse 17 (q.v.; see also verse 18), where the angel invites 'all the birds flying in midheaven' to assemble for God's eschatological supper of judgement. But the 'birds' (ὄρνεα, *ornea*) of verse 21 appear to be more specifically birds of prey, such as vultures (cf. Beasley-Murray 284). The prospect of remaining unburied after death, so that birds and animals could feast on human remains, prompted among the ancients fear, as well as the possibility of taunting or cursing (cf. Deut. 28.26; 1 Sam. 17.44; 1 Kings 14.11; 21.23; Jer. 7.33; et al.; note also Rev. 11.8–10). See Aune 1067–68.

The demise of God's opposition anticipates the downfall of Satan himself, in the next part of the scene (Rev. 20). Meanwhile, it must have been apparent to the members of the Johannine community that the strength of the unjust persecutors and evil idolaters surrounding them, in systemic as well as more general forms (the 'leaders and their armies' of 19.19–21), remained undiminished. Nevertheless, the message of the Apocalypse is that God's vindicating judgement is right, and that his saving power among the nations is ultimately sovereign (Ps. 67.1–2). With God in control, the end must eventually reveal his purposes of love, as well as victory for the Lamb and those who are sealed by him (22.3–4); cf. Mounce 360.

Vision 4: Satan Bound (20.1–3)

20.1   The next vision in this scene describes the beginning of the downfall of Satan and of the total oppression and idolatry in the world which he represents. This section forms part of the literary unit 19.1—20.15 (Scene 6 of Act 2); although Beale (972) sees the segment as extending from 17.1—21.8. Beale (983) also regards the broader context of Rev. 17—22 as chiastic in structure:

A   judgement of the harlot (17.1—19.6)
B   the divine Judge (19.11–16)
C   judgement of the beast and false prophet (19.17–21)
D   Satan bound for one thousand years (20.1–3)
D^1 the millennial reign (20.4–6)
C^1 judgement of Gog and Magog (20.7–10)
B^1 the divine Judge (20.11–15)
A^1 vindication of the bride (21.1—22.5).

On this basis, Beale (983) finds support for his belief that 20.1—22.5 does not chronologically follow 19.11–21 (see further below).

Just as creation involved a triumphant struggle between Yahweh and the water monster of chaos, so the new creation is preceded by two similar victories: the establishment of the millennial Jerusalem and its kingdom, and a terrestrial battle anticipating a new heaven and earth, symbolized by a holy and eternal city (cf. Ford 329, on 20.1–3). For the bearing of the Old Testament on the interpretation of Rev. 20.1–7, including the influence of Ezek. 38—39, see Beale 976–83; also Beale, *Use of the Old Testament* 356–93. For the imagery in this passage see further Isa. 24.21–22; *1 Enoch* 10.4–6.

Prigent (91, 554–55) notes the parallelism between Rev. 20.1–10 and the story of Satan as it is told in Chapters 12—13 and 17; although he admits (ibid. 555) that there are differences as well. The following are examples of correspondence.

(a)   The dragon is cast down to earth, and knows that his time is short (12.9–12), while the beast was and is not, and heads for destruction (17.7–14); in the same way, the defeat of Satan anticipates his end (20.1–10).

(b) Satan's downfall is determined and matched by the reign of the Messiah (12.5; 13.3; 17.8; 20.4).
(c) The period of demonic decline is described in terms which are chronological, but also symbolic (12.6, 14 [cf. 11.3, 9–11]; 13.5; 20.2).
(d) The faithful saints of God triumph with Christ over satanic evil in a way which reflects the experience of the risen Jesus himself (11.11; 12.10–11; 20.4, 6).

In Rev. 19—20, as throughout the Apocalypse, the victory of the exalted Christ is depicted from a variety of viewpoints, rather than being described in chronological succession. The reality of his divine sovereignty and the righteousness of his power and justice are more important than the temporal, and indeed chiliastic, symbolism which is used to portray them (cf. Mounce 360). The rider of the white horse makes war on evil (19.11–21); and, by this means, the lordship and royalty of the Godhead become manifest, and believers are vindicated (11.15–18; 19.13–16; 20.11; 22.3–5).

The symbolism of the sequence of events in this scene is highlighted by the introductory phrase in verse 1, καὶ εἶδον (*kai eidon*), which in the present context means – as in the translation – '*and* I saw', rather than 'then I saw'. This introductory formula is a literary device, used to link together a series of visions in Rev. 19—20 (cf. 19.11, 17, 19; 20.4, 11, 12); it carries no temporal significance, and does not denote a chronological progression from the apocalyptic narrative of 19.17–21, which depicts the destruction of the beast and the false prophet, together with their troops (cf. Swete 259).

John sees 'an angel' (ἄγγελον, *angelon*, lit. 'angel', anarthrous), descending from heaven. Once more, as consistently in Johannine theological thought, heaven and earth are brought together, and the spiritual suffuses the material (cf. Smalley, *Thunder and Love* 58–60, 177–78). The angel appears to be a further, unidentified heavenly messenger (see the textual note on verse 1). He is charged with a special mission, and (as such) is no doubt to be distinguished from the 'other' and 'mighty' angels of 18.1, 21, as well as from the particular being of 19.17 (q.v.). The present angel holds the 'key of the abyss' and 'an enormous chain'. For the key of the bottomless pit, as the location of demonic powers, see on 9.1; see also on verse 3. The deep abyss of 20.1 stands in sharp contrast to the shallow 'lake' of fire (19.20).

The angel also holds in his hand 'an enormous chain' (ἅλυσιν μεγάλην, *halysin megalēn*, lit. 'great manacle'; this is the only use of the term in Revelation). The 'chain' may be distinguished from the lighter πέδη (*pedē*, 'fetter', 'shackle'), as in Mark 5.4 par.; for this angel is charged with restraining a prisoner of exceptional strength (Swete 260). The fact that the manacle is in the angel's 'hand' implies that it is ready for immediate use. In 9.1–2 a fallen angel holds the key to the abyss, and opens up the shaft into it at God's command so that judgement may follow. Now, an angel of God has the key to the pit in his hand, and will himself bind Satan with a chain and hurl him into prison (20.2–3); cf. Prigent 565. For the judicial imagery and apocalyptic motifs in this verse see *1 Enoch* 54.3–5; 88.1; *Prayer of Manasseh* 2–4; *2 Apoc. Bar.* 56.13; *Sib. Or.* 2.286–89; 2 Pet. 2.4; Jude 6.

2 The angel with the key of the pit and the huge chain 'arrested the dragon'. This figure of evil and idolatrous opposition to God appears in the New Testament only in the drama of Revelation. He is introduced at 12.3 (q.v.) as the 'red dragon', and is mentioned thereafter on nine occasions as 'the dragon' (12.4, 7 [*bis*], 9, 13, 16, 17; 13.2, 4), and once as 'the great dragon' (12.9). To make his identity unmistakably clear in the present context (verse 2), the writer adds in parenthesis (as at 12.9, and in the same order) the other titles of the dragon: 'that ancient serpent, who is the devil, or the Satan'. Ὁ Σατανᾶς (*Ho Satanas*, 'the Satan') occurs in the Apocalypse eight times, always with the article;

and this suggests that John is referring to the devil's representative office as the figurative agent of wickedness, more than to his person.

The combination in verse 2 of the two verbs, κρατέω (*krateō*, 'arrest') and δέω (*deō*, 'bind', or 'chain up'), is used of the imprisonment of John the Baptist at Mark 6.17. The metaphor of 'binding' the demonic powers until a time of judgement appears regularly in the literature of Judaism (see Jude 6; *1 Enoch* 10.4–12; 14.5; *2 Enoch* [*J*] 7.1–2; *2 Apoc. Bar.* 56.13; *Jub.* 5.6; et al.). The capture of Satan, by the angel of verse 1, is followed by the statement that the embodiment of evil was chained up for 'a thousand years' (χίλια ἔτη, *chilia etē*). For the apparent limitation in the period of the devil's imprisonment see further on verse 3. The phrase itself, 'a thousand years', demands special attention.

Excursus: The Millennium in Revelation

'Thousand years' is used as a specific, but figurative, unit of time six times in the New Testament, all in Rev. 20 (verses 2, 3, 4, 5, 6, 7). After verse 2, where χίλια ἔτη (*chilia etē*, 'a thousand years') is anarthrous, the expression appears with an anaphoric article, '*the* thousand years' (but there is a MS variation in verse 6; cf. the textual note on that verse).

There are three major ways of interpreting the term, 'a thousand years', in Rev. 20; although wide variations exist within them.

(a) The millennium will occur after the second coming of Christ. This view is traditionally described as 'premillennial'; so, for example, Beasley-Murray 287–92, 314–18. Mealy, *After the Thousand Years*, has his own version of this view. He believes that during the thousand years the saints will reign over a fully recreated earth (ibid. 102–19); that after the millennium Satan will be released in order to deceive the nations again, prompting their second rebellion against God and a repeated judgement for both (120–26); that Rev. 20.11—15 duplicates the earlier judgements of 19.11—20.4 and 20.7–10 (143–89); and that the picture of the new Jerusalem in Rev. 21 recapitulates the parousia, when the saints reign together with God and Christ (190–235). See further Mealy, ibid. 236–43; Beale 974.

(b) The 'postmillennial' stance, which holds that the millennium will occur at the end of the age of the Church, and that at its close the parousia will take place. So, for example, the twelfth-century Abbot Joachim, and the influential Protestant exponent of this understanding, Thomas Brightman (1562–1607).

(c) The millennium was inaugurated at the resurrection of Jesus, and will be concluded at his final coming. This perspective presupposes a symbolic interpretation; it is normally designated as 'amillennial', but is better called 'inaugurated millennianism' (Beale 973). So, for example, Boring 197–98; Hughes 209. For the history of the interpretation of the millennium in Revelation see Bauckham, 'Millennium'; Schwarz, *Eschatology* 322–37; cf. also Smalley, *Thunder and Love* 51 n. 15, 145–47.

Before outlining the understanding of the 'thousand years' of Rev. 20.2–7 which is adopted in this commentary, seven points need to be made.

(a) The scene in Rev. 19—20 consists of seven visions, and includes apocalyptic and eschatological material the character of which is at its most intense. Clearly its imagery, including that of the millennium, cannot be interpreted literally.

(b) The numbers which are used by the seer throughout Revelation have a consistently symbolic significance. This is true, for example, of the figures 'seven' (1.4, 20), 'one thousand, two hundred and sixty days' (12.6, 14; 13.5) and 'six hundred and sixty-six' (13.18). Note the similar symbolism at Ps. 90.4; 2 Pet. 3.8 ('with the Lord, one day is like a thousand years'). Thus, 'a thousand years' in Rev. 20 is not to be thought of in literal and temporal terms. Roloff (226) suggests that behind it lies the idea of a symbolic week of 7 × 1,000 years, so that the present age (6 × 1,000 years) concludes with the seventh day, portrayed as a thousand year sabbath-rest (cf. Gen. 1.31; *2 Enoch [J]* 33 heading and 1–2; *Barn.* 15.3–9). But this is speculative.

(c) There is no specific indication in Rev. 20.1–10 that the reign of the saints with Christ will take place on earth alone, or that it will necessarily precede or follow the second advent of the Lord (cf. Mounce 360). In any case, the parousia of Christ, as such, doe not occupy a large place in John's eschatology compared, say, with Paul's (see Boring 197; also Smalley, *Thunder and Love* 62–63; *idem, John* 265–70); and since, in its classic form, the second coming is missing from this part of the Apocalypse, it should be detached from any discussion of the meaning of the millennium in Rev. 20 (so McKelvey, 'Second Coming' 85–86, 99–100).

(d) The question of a background to the reign of the saints with Christ for a 'thousand years', in Rev. 20.2–7, is intriguing. The notion of an interim kingdom is found outside Revelation only in two Jewish apocalypses. In 4 Ezra 7.26–33 it is anticipated that the Messiah will rule for 400 years, and that his death will be followed after seven days by a resurrection, together with the judgement of the world by the Most High. According to the Syriac *2 Apoc. Bar.* 29–30, the future coming of the Messiah will involve the destruction of the powers of evil, and a time of plenty marked by grapevines which produce thousands of shoots and clusters (29.1–8); this is to be followed by Christ's return to heaven, together with the rising of the righteous and the destruction of the ungodly (30.1–5). However, neither of these passages is very close to the thought in Rev. 20; although both envisage the dawn of a new age, albeit in a primarily earthly setting.

(e) Ford (350–54) notes that John seems to have depended on Jewish, and especially early Rabbinic, tradition for the length of his millennium; but the Rabbis differed in the length of their interim kingdoms, and interpreted them literally. Nearest to the teaching in Rev. 20 (and 21) is the prophecy of Ezek. 37—41, where the restoration of Israel and the reign of the Davidic Messiah (Ezek. 37) are followed by the assault and destruction of the enemy (38.1—39.22), and a vision of the new temple at the end-time (40—41). Nevertheless, as Roloff (225) points out, while the influence of Ezekiel is apparent in this section of the Apocalypse (see esp. 20.8–9), John is not bound by that prophecy. For example, Rev. 20.11–15 is not part of Ezekiel's scheme, which does not in any case mention the 'thousand years' as such.

(f) In terms of the derivation of the Johannine concept of the millennium, it may be concluded that, while the seer's vision may have been coloured by sources in Judaism, there is no reason why this image of Satan being first bound, and then released for a period coinciding with the reign of Christ's followers, and ending in the devil's doom, should not have been new to John (against Beckwith 736).

The prophet-seer appears to have adapted various strands in Jewish tradition, and moved creatively beyond them for his own theological and dramatic purposes. Just as the dragon appeared in the narrative before the two beasts (Rev. 12—13; see 12.3), so his story continues after their destruction (19.17–21). Satan is the ultimate principle of evil, and the beasts are merely his worldly agents. In 12.7–9 he is thrown down from heaven to deceive the nations (12.9; cf. 13.14; 18.23; 19.20; 20.3, 8, 10); now he is imprisoned in the bottomless pit (20.2–3), and prevented from corrupting the world with wicked idolatry for a very long time (Bauckham 1302b–1303a).

(g) Central to the concept of the millennium in Rev. 20 is John's affirmation of God's sovereignty in Christ over heaven *and* earth, both of which are linked by the angel with the key and the chain (verse 1). Thus, the drama of Revelation is played out in those two dimensions at once. As Roloff (225) says, God's salvific purposes through judgement in the Apocalypse cannot be understood as merely otherworldly; they also concern his creation, and are indeed political, because for John 'God is the Lord of the world and of history' (ibid.). That divine relationship, to the Church and society in this life as well as the next, is crucial to the interpretation of the 'thousand years' in this passage. The establishment of a new age is essential to the seer's vision throughout Revelation; in that promise, however, the old world is subsumed into the new, rather than being completely abandoned. For this very reason, the holy city of the new Jerusalem can be 'measured' (21.15–17). Such a balance, it may be argued, is typical of John's theology and cosmology (cf. Smalley, *Thunder and Love* 149–50; also Hendriksen 190).

Conclusion. In view of these considerations, the millennium in Rev. 20 is best interpreted as a symbol for the timeless reign of God in Christ, in heaven and on earth. This figurative period represents 'a long time'. In terms of the age of the Church, it stretches from the event of the Word made flesh to the final parousia of Jesus, and includes his life, ministry, death and exaltation. During that period, which is consummated at the moment of the parousia, evil can be judged and restrained (20.1–10, Satan is bound and released), if not yet contained (22.11–15, the unrighteous remain outside the gates of the heavenly city). In the light of eternity, the 'thousand years' of God's sovereignty are shared by all believers, who endlessly and victoriously experience his salvation as well as his judgement (20.4–6; cf. 1 John 4.1–6). His saving power is known among all nations for ever (Ps. 67.2). There is no need to limit the scope of the millennium to the martyrs of 20.4; against Beckwith 737; McKelvey, 'Second Coming' 97; *idem, Millennium*, esp. 81–84 (who argues that the millennium is integral to the Apocalypse, and symbolizes God's response to those who suffer unjustly for their faith). On the contrary, what happens in the millennial kingdom of Christ on earth has spiritual implications for all time, and into eternity. See further on verse 3; also Beale 972–74; Prigent 552–63.

3   The fourth vision in this scene continues with the statement that the angel 'hurled' (ἔβαλεν, *ebalen*, lit. 'threw') the dragon into the abyss, which he 'locked and sealed over him' (ἔκλεισεν καὶ ἐσφράγισεν ἐπάνω αὐτοῦ, *ekleisen kai esphragisen epanō autou*). As Beale (984) notes, the imagery of the 'key' (κλείς, *kleis*), with which the abyss is locked (see verse 1), is important for understanding the thought in this verse. In Revelation, the keys of 1.18; 3.7; 9.1; and 20.1 are related; whether they are used for opening or locking, or both (3.7–8), they symbolize the sovereignty and judgement of Christ over the realm of Satan, otherwise known as 'Death and Hades' (see 1.18; 6.8). The dragon's imprisonment in 20.3 means that, through the angel of verse 1, the powers of evil are subject to the kingship and authority of Christ, even if they are not banished from the earth entirely (see below). Similarly, the 'sealing' of the bottomless pit may suggest the idea of messianic authority over the dragon (cf. Dan. 6.17; Matt. 27.66). God's sealing of the faithful protects them spiritually, but not physically (Rev. 7.3, 14; 9.4); whereas the sealing of Satan prevents him from harming the salvific security of the true Church, although for a while he may hurt its members physically (12.17; cf. Beale 985–86).

It has been argued above that the millennium of Rev. 20 should be interpreted broadly, as ultimately a symbol for the timeless reign of God in Christ, in heaven and on earth. The figurative expression, 'a thousand years', does not refer to a period of time (Milligan 337), even if the millennium includes a material dimension. In terms of the interim kingdom of God on earth, the focus of the 'thousand years' may be regarded as occurring in the Christ-event: that is to say, between the birth and exaltation of Jesus. Through his death and resurrection, and at his parousia, the consummation of the divine purposes of judgement and salvation achieve their universal fulfilment. Equally, during the age of the Christian Church, Satan is 'bound' (verse 3), in order 'to prevent him from deceiving the nations any longer'. The significance of that phrase demands some attention.

The devil's arrest and incarceration does not mean that the influence of the demonic powers in society comes to an end, as such New Testament texts as 2 Cor. 4.3–4; 2 Tim. 2.26; 1 Pet. 5.8–9 make clear. But Satan's temporary restraint indicates that Jesus is ultimately sovereign over the powers of evil (cf. Matt. 12.29 par.), and that meanwhile the dragon cannot 'deceive the nations' (cf. 9.1–6). He cannot, for example, prevent anyone from being drawn to Christ (John 12.31–32). Nor can he delude and attack the covenant community after the resurrection of Jesus, as he did before it (which is the force of ἔτι, *eti*, 'any longer', lit. 'still'). See 12.7–12; also Gen. 3.1–5; 2 Thess. 2.6–12. Cf. further Beale 985–88. The coming of Christ changes the relationship of unbelievers to him, since they can now be converted. But it also brings about an alteration in the relationship between Satan and the nations, which are no longer in darkness but have seen a great light (Acts 14.16; Isa. 9.1–2; Luke 2.30–32; John 8.12; 9.5). Satan's power over the world has been actually or potentially broken by the power of the gospel (Hughes 209–10). The 'nations' (τὰ ἔθνη, *ta ethnē*) symbolize the opponents of God's Messiah and his truth in any part of the world (as in 2.26; 10.11; 18.3; 19.15; et al.), rather than (as Moffatt 471 suggests) referring geographically to outlying countries on the edge of the Roman Empire who had not entered the battle waged by Antichrist.

After the millennium, verse 3 continues, Satan is to be released from his imprisonment, 'but only for a short period' (μικρὸν χρόνον, *mikron chronon*, lit. 'for a little while', as in NRSV). The abyss is not the place of final perdition for the forces of wickedness; and this prediction is fulfilled at 20.7–10, when Satan emerges once more to undergo what appears to be his final destruction, although this turns out not to be so (20.14; 22.11, 15). The incarnation of evil remains to challenge believers so long as the Church of Christ exists (cf. 1 Pet. 5.8). Cf. Knight 130, who rightly notes that the punishment of the dragon is distinguished in this passage from that of the beast and false prophet in 19.20, since Satan, the opponent of God and the source of the beast's authority (13.4), has yet to be finally vanquished. For the idea of limited time and power in Revelation, which seems to be an image referring consistently to the bounds of the Christian age, see 6.11; 10.6; 12.12; cf. also Milligan 340–41. The use of the verb δεῖ (*dei*, 'must'), at the end of verse 3, suggests divine authority and permission; cf. 1.1; 4.1; 10.11; 11.5; 13.10; 17.10; 22.6.

Vision 5: A Millennial Reign (20.4–6)

4 The fate of Satan, which is described in the previous vision (20.1–3), is now followed by a joyful sight of the saints reigning with Christ. During the age of the Church, and beyond, they share his salvation and participate in his judgement (cf. Ps. 103.6). Maurice (307–309) notes that the millennium, in the passage 20.4–6, involves not the descent of Christ to earth, but rather the ascent of the faithful to reign with him in heaven. However, it has been suggested (see on verse 2) that the 'thousand years' in Rev. 20.1–10 have eternal implications, and embrace what happens in both dimensions, heavenly and earthly. Even less probably, Maurice (ibid.) claims that verses 4–6 refer to the ages during which the gospel was established in different parts of the Roman Empire. For the opening phrase in verse 4, καὶ εἶδον (*kai eidon*, 'and I saw', a literary formula which is non-sequential in character), see on verse 1. Beale (992) draws attention to the parallels between 20.1–6 and 12.7–12.

The prophet-seer does not specify the identity of those who are 'seated on thrones'; nor are the subjects in any part of this scene mentioned by name. But their character and activity make it plain that John is referring broadly to the faithful saints of God. They are the ones who are involved in judgement, and suffer for Christ, and who worship him rather than the beast; these are also priests of God, who rise and reign with Christ for a thousand years and more.

Bauckham (*Theology* 106–108) rightly observes that 'life' and 'rule' are the twin themes of verses 4–6; although he needlessly relates these to the activity of the martyrs alone (ibid. 107; see further below). What is said about the saints in general, it may rather be claimed, contrasts here with the fate of the beast. It is condemned (17.11–14), but they are vindicated (20.4); it is thrown into the lake of fire (19.20), which is the second death (20.14), while they come to life (20.4–5) and the second death has no power over them (20.6); those who ruin the earth are themselves destroyed (11.18), yet Christ's people reign with him (20.4). The millennium thus demonstrates above all the victory of the faithful, including those who suffer for their witness; they will reign in heaven with the Lord to whom they testified on earth, not only for a thousand years, but for the eternity to which the millennium points (cf. 2 Tim. 2.11–12); see Beale 991; Bauckham, *Theology* 107.

It is necessary, however, to define more precisely the character of the 'saints' who occupy thrones, and come to life and rule, in verses 4–6. Rist (520–21), followed by Bauckham (*Theology* 106–107), claims that they are martyrs, who will assist God in the final judgement. Mounce (365) regards them more generally as God's people, who act as members of a heavenly court (so Dan. 7.26–27; and cf. Matt. 19.28 par.; Rev. 2.26–27; 19.14). Beale (996) suggests that the 'court' in this passage consists both of believers and angels (cf. 4.4; 11.16). However, the question of the identity of those who preside in this scene may be answered more straightforwardly. They are 'souls' (τὰς ψυχάς, *tas psychas*) who had been martyred for their Christian testimony, and existed therefore in that spiritual state which obtains between death and the final resurrection (verse 4*a*); and, second, they are faithful witnesses who have testified loyally to Christ, and continue to do so, without being called to seal their faithfulness with martyrdom (verse 4*b*; cf. 13.11–12). So Hughes 211–12, who notes a similar distinction between the 'blood of the saints and the blood of the martyrs' at 17.6. The whole Church is therefore represented as sharing in the millennial reign of the exalted Messiah, in heaven as well as on earth.

Judgement is associated with those who are seated on the thrones of verse 4, following the downfall of Satan. NRSV translates the Greek phrase, κρίμα ἐδόθη αὐτοῖς (*krima edothē autois*, lit. 'judgement was given to them'), as '(they) were given authority to judge'; REB has '(those) to whom judgement was committed'. Thrones in the Apocalypse are places of divine judgement (4.5; 6.16; 8.3–5; 11.16–19; 16.17–18; 19.1–5; 20.11–12; et al.); and in Rev. 20.4–6 the saints appear at first sight to share God's judicial task, even as they reign with Christ (3.21). In that case, the faithful in 20.4–6 are presented as ruling and judging (the unfaithful, perhaps), in a way that anticipates the end of the age (as in Luke 22.30 par.; 1 Cor. 6.2; *1 Enoch* 48.9; et al.).

However, if the background to this forensic activity is to be found in Dan. 7, as seems likely, a more subtle interpretation may be given to the phrase, 'judgement was given' to the saints. In Dan. 7.9 the Ancient One takes his place on the throne, and in 7.22 'judgement was given for the holy ones of the Most High'. In other words, the saints were vindicated; and their triumph, together with the judgement of the evil kingdoms (7.27), becomes a necessary preparation for the Son of man and his followers to reign (7.13–14, 18). So in Rev. 20.4, κρίμα (*krima*) probably means 'judicial vindication' (as in 18.20), and not simply 'judgement' (as in 17.1). Judgement is passed on the devil, 'on behalf of' the saints (as in the translation); that is to say, judgement was given '*for* the faithful' (taking αὐτοῖς, *autois*, as a dative of advantage), rather than *by* them. Accordingly, as in Dan. 7.22, the vindication of the saints, which is the principal concern of this passage, is followed by the possession of the kingdom by the saints (Rev. 20.4–6). For this section see Beale 997; against Caird 252.

The faithful, who reign triumphantly with Christ during the millennium (see above), are described first as 'the souls of the ones beheaded on account of their witness to Jesus and to the word of God'. The word καί (*kai*, 'and'), which introduces this clause, is epexegetic; John 'saw thrones, and those seated on them', *even* the 'souls' (the noun ψυχάς, *psychas*, is in the accusative, following the verb εἶδον, *eidon*, 'I saw') of the martyrs. If it is exegetically correct to interpret the Greek of the first part of verse 4 to mean 'judgement was given on behalf of the saints' (see above), so that they were vindicated, then their millennial and victorious reign with Christ becomes a further answer (see 6.11) to the prayer of the martyrs at 6.9–10 (q.v.), 'Lord, how long will it be before you administer justice, and avenge our deaths?' Cf. Beale 997–98.

The verb, πελεκίζω (*pelekizō*, 'behead'), occurs only here in the New Testament. It includes the idea of beheading with a double-edged axe, and probably refers to the normal Roman method of execution (cf. Mounce 365 n. 6; also BDAG 794*a*); but see Aune (1086–87), who notes that the Roman legal system included more than one form of administering the death penalty. There is no need to dwell on historical detail in such an apocalyptic vision as this; but it is quite possible that Christian martyrs such as Antipas (Rev. 2.13) and others (2.10) were also put to death by decapitation. The martyrs in verse 4 laid down their lives 'on account of their witness to Jesus and to the word of God'; note the close parallels to this phraseology at 6.9. The expression, διὰ τὴν μαρτυρίαν 'Iησοῦ (*dia tēn martyrian 'Iēsou*, lit. 'because of the witness of Jesus'), uses an objective genitive, meaning 'because of their (faithful) testimony *to* their Lord'; hence the translation. The 'word of God' refers to the content of the Christian gospel (as at 1.2; 1.9; 6.9), rather than to Jesus himself (see 19.13). The names of God and Jesus are occasionally linked (directly or indirectly) in other contexts of Revelation, where (as here) the subject is that of the faithfulness of suffering believers (cf. 1.9; 6.9; 12.11, 17; 14.12).

The focus of the fifth vision in this scene, describing the millennial reign of the vindicated saints with their Messiah, now moves to a second group of the faithful. The introductory expression at this point, καὶ οἵτινες (*kai hoitines*, 'and others', lit. 'and whoever'), uses the nominative plural, rather than the accusative which might be expected after the opening verb in verse 4, εἶδον (*eidon*, 'I saw'); cf. the earlier ψυχάς (*psychas*, 'souls'). This suggests that John is referring here to a different assembly of Christians: saints in general, who have received the seal of God (7.2–3; 9.4), rather than the mark of the beast (13.16–18). The seer is not continuing to speak of martyrs alone (see Prigent 569; against Caird 251–54; Mounce 365–66). Even if the beast's image has ordered '*any* who will not worship' him to be killed (13.15), this does not mean that only those who have paid the ultimate sacrifice for their loyal testimony to Christ are left to celebrate the millennium (cf. Mounce 365); such an interpretation presses the details of an apocalyptic vision in an unacceptably literal and specific manner.

It is true that, according to 13.15, believers who refuse to worship the beast and his image risk death, and are in any case subject to economic deprivation and oppression (13.16–17). Nevertheless, they have received the seal of God, and are therefore assured of his protection (7.4–10). As a result, while they are not all martyrs, they *are* all conquerors, who sing in the presence of God a victorious song of Moses and the Lamb (15.2–4). Such are the saints in this section of 20.4, who have survived the great ordeal, and whitened their robes in the blood of the Lamb (7.14). For the imagery of this part of verse 4 see on 13.16–17; cf. also 14.9, 11; 16.2; 19.20. The accusative singular, χεῖρα (*cheira*, lit. 'hand'), is generic; hence the plural ('hands') in the translation. For this section see Prigent 569–70; cf. also Hendriksen 192–93; Roloff 227; Wall 238.

Having spoken of the martyrs, and of believers in general, the seer now gathers up both groups in his vision: 'they (sc. all) came to life, and reigned with Christ'. The aorist, ἔζησαν (*ezēsan*, 'they came to life', lit. 'they lived', as in verse 5), is ingressive, since it describes the beginning of an ongoing process. The vindicated saints of God, who participate in the resurrection of Christ, 'come to life' themselves. This expression, in verses 4 and 5, does not describe an exclusively spiritual resurrection. The aorist indicative active form of the verb, ζάω (*zaō*, 'live'), occurs in two other contexts in the Apocalypse, both of which speak of bodily resurrection: 2.8 (Christ was dead, and 'has come to life'), and 13.14 (the beast was 'wounded by the sword, only to live'). The same verb is similarly used with reference to returning to life at Matt. 9.18 (of the daughter of the leader of the synagogue); Rom. 14.9 (of Christ). In both 20.4 and 5, then, John is primarily discussing the risen life of all believers in and beyond the millennium. See Fiorenza 108; Mounce 366. Nevertheless, the resurrection of Christians during their lifetime, and resulting from their baptism (Rom. 6.3—4), probably forms a further part of John's understanding of 'coming to life' in this context. For him, resurrection is both spiritual (before death) and bodily (after death); see further on verses 5—6.

The faithful 'reigned with Christ for a thousand years'. The term, Χριστός (*Christos*, 'Christ', 'Messiah'), appears in Revelation three times, in conjunction with Ἰησοῦς (*Iēsous*, 'Jesus'): at 1.1, 2, 5 (cf. 22.21 v.l.). On three other occasions apart from 20.4 it is used with the article, on its own (11.15; 12.10; 20.6), to mean 'the Anointed One'. Cf. Aune 1090. For the symbolism of the 'thousand years' see on verse 2. While the millennial reign of Christ and his followers includes a heavenly setting, since martyrs are involved, its location is not necessarily exclusively spiritual (against Hendriksen 191–92). For if the millennium symbolizes the age of the Church, and what takes place timelessly beyond that period, the life and rule of the faithful may also be understood in terms of this world, where God's people already reign as priests (verse 6; cf. 1.6), and the blessings of eternity can be shared in the present (1.20; 5.10 [the saints will 'reign on earth']; cf. John 1.51; 3.6, 16; 1 John 4.17). They share with Christ in eternity (7.14–17); but like all believers, including members of the Johannine community, they are also called to be consistently loyal to the covenant amid the practical and spiritual difficulties which afflict the Church in any age. God in Christ remains sovereign among the nations of the world (11.15; 17.14); but suffering and even martyrdom are still possibilities for his people (3.21). Cf. further Wilcock 192; Michaels 224–25.

5–6   Verse 5 is made up of two parentheses, the second of which follows from the first. John qualifies his reference to an inclusive resurrection (verse 4), by stating what will happen to 'the remaining dead'; and he then subsumes all that he has said about life in the millennium by describing this as 'the first resurrection'. By 'the remaining dead' (οἱ λοιποὶ τῶν νεκρῶν, *hoi loipoi tōn nekrōn*, lit. 'the rest of the dead') the seer apparently means the body of unbelievers, who are distinguished from the assembly of the faithful mentioned in verse 4. However, 'the remaining dead' cannot refer to the unrighteous alone, on the supposition that all the righteous had already come to life in the millennium and for all time. In any case, John is being theological and not chronological at this point. In the broader view, the saints as a total company have yet to enter and enjoy the heavenly city (21.1–7); and the scrutiny of the books at 20.12–15 implies the presence of the righteous, as well as the ungodly, at the general resurrection; cf. Beckwith 740–41. Both groups appear to 'come to life' (for which phrase see on verse 4), to experience the reign of Christ for a 'thousand years' (see on verse 2), and to share in the 'first resurrection' (against Charles 2, 184).

The expression, 'the first resurrection' (ἡ ἀνάστασις ἡ πρώτη, *hē anastasis hē prōtē*), is found in the New Testament only here, at Rev. 20.5–6. To understand this concept, it is important to notice three features which govern the image. First, it cannot involve the martyrs, or indeed the faithful, alone (see above; against Charles 2, 183–86; Caird 254; Mounce 370). Second, although the '*first* resurrection' implies that there is a second coming to life, that is not specified in the remaining part of the drama of the Apocalypse; similarly, a '*second* death' is mentioned (2.11; 20.5, 14), but not a first. Third, 'resurrection' is a Christian concept, which derives from the representative rising of Jesus from the dead (1 Cor. 15.12–26), and moves on from the virtual absence in the Old Testament (but not in post-biblical Judaism) of any belief in life after death, despite such texts as Isa. 11.1–11 (the promise of an earthly paradise) and Dan. 12.2–3 (those who 'sleep in the dust of the earth' will awake to everlasting life or judgement). See Caird 253–54; also Wright, *Resurrection* 85–206, 277–374, et passim. In the New Testament, moreover, the resurrection of believers can be both physical and spiritual (2 Cor. 13.4; Rom 6.3–13; cf. also Rev. 1.18; 3.1; 7.17).

Commentators have made various attempts to interpret the image of the 'first resurrection'.

(a) Improbably, Wall (239) suggests that the phrase refers to the eschatological priority which God affords to the reigning community of Christian overcomers. They are the 'first' to experience the blessings associated with the parousia of Jesus in glory; and this promise becomes an exhortation for 'those in his embattled audience to overcome evil' (ibid.).

(b) Giblin, 'Millennium', takes the 'first resurrection' in 20.5–6 as 'heaven', in accordance with early Christian, non-chiliast views of the martyrs and other blessed. In support of this exegesis, Giblin identifies a convergence of complementary eschatologies in Revelation: first, the millennium brings to a climax a series of images expressing a 'vertical' eschatology (the life of God's witnesses after death); and second, the fulfilment of the Creator's scroll (5.1–8) is viewed 'horizontally', at the very end of time ('it is over', 16.17; 21.6). The heavenly reign of the saints for a thousand years merges with the earthly realization of a new creation (21.1) at the moment they bypass the second death (20.6) and are joined by the rest of the victorious dead (21.6–7). Then all God's sealed worshippers reign as priests not for a thousand years, but for ever (see esp. Giblin, ibid. 568–69). The problem with this well-argued proposal is that it does not accommodate, in the symbolism of the millennium, its earthly relevance (see on verse 2).

(c) Aune (1090–91) finds a background to the idea of a 'first resurrection' in the 'two-stage' coming to life at John 5.28–29, where Jesus speaks of a resurrection to life and to judgement (cf. also 4 Ezra 7.32; *1 Enoch* 51.1–2; *2 Apoc. Bar.* 50.2–4; Acts 24.15; 2 Cor. 5.10). But, as Aune (1091) admits, the reference here is to two aspects of a single general resurrection. Nevertheless, the Pauline concept of a *three*-stage resurrection may well shed light on this subject; since for the apostle the believer 'rises' in baptism (Rom. 6.5), at death ('asleep', 1 Cor. 15.51) and at the consummation ('awake', 1 Cor. 15.52; also 1 Cor. 7.39; 11.30; 15.6, 18, 20; Eph. 5.14). Cf. further Wright, *Resurrection* 356–61.

(d) Beale (1004–1007) notices the close relationship in the New Testament between 'resurrection' and 'life', as well as between physical and spiritual resurrection (cf. John 5.24–29; Rom. 6.4–13; 8.10–11). On this basis Beale (1005) argues that in Rev. 20.4–6 John is speaking of the first physical death of the saints (verse 4) as being followed by their first spiritual resurrection (verses 5–6), just as the second physical resurrection of the ungodly is succeeded by their second spiritual death (verse 6; cf. 20.10, 14–15). This amounts to claiming that the 'first resurrection' of 20.5–6 is the spiritual and eternal condition of the saints after death, which includes salvation from a second eternal, spiritual death.

Such an interpretation as Beale's is persuasive, but it omits any reference to the clear implication in this passage (and, admittedly, it is not stated) that there are *two* resurrections of the faithful. To understand the notion of the 'first resurrection', at Rev. 20.5–6, it is important to begin with the relationship in the New Testament between physical and spiritual rising from the dead (see above). In that case, a simpler explanation of this concept emerges. If spiritual resurrection is possible for the believer, through faith and baptism, *before* death (so Rom. 6.3–11), this involves a transition from spiritual death to spiritual life (against Charles 2, 185, who argues that the context of Rev. 20.5–6 is against taking the words in a spiritual sense). *After* physical death, then, which may include martyrdom, the saints (to use Paul's language) 'sleep' in the Lord (1 Cor. 15.51); and this may be regarded as the 'first' resurrection, which is eventually followed by the 'final' judgement and (second) resurrection ('awake') at the end (Rev. 22.1–5). But one resurrection continually anticipates another. In life, and after death, the faithful participate in the healing and victory of the sovereign Lamb (7.16–17); they reign with him to the end as priests, and throughout are preserved from the 'second death', over which they have authority (20.6). On this section see further Swete (263), who regards the first resurrection as taking place in the present life, in contrast to that which will be introduced by the parousia; also Prigent 571 ('there is but one resurrection'); Beale 1007–1017.

The faithful who share in the first resurrection are described in verse 6 as 'happy and holy'. This is the fifth of seven beatitudes in the Apocalypse (see also 1.3; 14.13; 16.15; 19.9; 22.7, 14). Its unusual double predicate, 'happy *and* holy' (μακάριος καὶ ἅγιος, *makarios kai hagios*, lit. 'blessed and holy'), suggests that John coined the literary phrase himself, and combined it with the equally unique expression, 'the first resurrection' (for which see on verse 5). According to verse 4, the inaugurated judgement of Satan (20.1–3) leads to the vindication of the saints, their resurrection and their reign with Christ. These blessings find their focus in the 'first resurrection', which is now seen to include the protection of the faithful from the 'second death', their 'priesthood' and their kingship. The adjectives, 'happy and holy', appear to be synonymous; but their 'holy' character could relate to their priesthood (Prigent 572). The saints, the 'holy ones' (ἅγιοι, *hagioi*; see on 5.8; 8.3–4; 11.18; 13.7, 10; et al.), are also 'holy' (ἅγιος, *hagios*) in their priestly service.

The 'second death' (for which see on 2.11; 20.14) is a euphemism for the fate of those who refuse to participate in the eternal life which God offers through Christ (Wall 239); the expression embodies an image pointing to a reality that defies verbal expression (Beasley-Murray 299). In this passage John distinguishes between physical and spiritual death, just as he does between spiritual and physical resurrection (see on verse 5). The 'second' death is spiritual, and takes place after death (so 19.20; 20.10, 14–15); and to that extent it is the equivalent of judgement for the unrighteous (as in 20.12–13).

As a result of their authority over the second death, the saints are promised that, unlike those who are separated from God's life for ever (20.10, 14–15; 21.7–8, 27; 22.15), they will be 'priests of God and of Christ, and will reign with him (namely, God in Christ) for the thousand years'. For the millennium see on verses 2 and 3–5. The status of the faithful as priests means that they serve in the presence of God (1.6); while their position as kings denotes their eternal and victorious reign with Christ (5.10). Cf. Beale 1002–1003. In both capacities the saints of God share the life of God, and help to mediate his judgement and salvation in the world. At Rev. 1.6 and 5.10 the saints are described as 'priests serving God'; whereas at 20.6 they become 'priests of God *and* of Christ'. This suggests the unity of nature between God and Jesus; and a similarly high Christology is to be noted elsewhere in the Apocalypse (5.13–14; 7.10; 11.15; 19.6–10; 21.22; 22.1). However, 1.6 and 20.6 are not ultimately too far apart, since the doxology at 1.6 speaks of the redeemed as 'priests to his (αὐτοῦ, *autou*, that is to say the Messiah's) God and Father'.

The background to the notion that the saints act in the dual role of priests and kings is to be found in Exod. 19.6 (the Israelites are assured, through Moses, that they will become a 'priestly kingdom'); Isa. 61.6 (the restoration of God's people at the end-time means that they will be called 'priests of the Lord'; *Targ.* Isa. 61.3–6 adds that they will also be known as 'true princes', wearing diadems); and Zech. 6.13 (the Lord promises the prophet that a Messiah-like figure will 'rule on his throne', accompanied by an understanding priest). Cf. also 1 Pet. 2.5, 9. See further on 1.6; also Beale 1003. Fiorenza, *Book of Revelation* 123–24, argues that the kingship and priesthood of Christians is exercised only in the eschatological future, and not in this world (despite 5.10, the redeemed will 'reign on earth', which she regards as a later interpolation). However, the view of the millennium adopted in this commentary includes a perception of the saints participating in the sovereign and salvific activity of God in Christ eternally, whether in this life or the next (see on verse 2). The claim in 22.5 that the saints will reign 'for ever and ever', that is to say, means that in eternity they continue the kingship (and priesthood) which they began and enjoyed in the age of the Church.

Vision 6: Satan Destroyed (20.7–10)

7–8   The penultimate vision in this scene (20.7–10) describes the release of Satan from his thousand-year imprisonment, and the mustering of the nations for an end-time attack on the people of God. Judgement on evil results in the blessing of life for the saints (verses 4–6). The present section now emphasizes the finality of the dragon's destruction; although this is in fact inaugurated, rather than completed (see 21.8; 22.11, 15), since Satan is set free to act in the world 'for a short period' (20.3). Meanwhile, John's account of the release of Satan and the resumption of the holy war points to the continuing puissance of evil in society, despite the millennial reign of God in Christ, and the resulting human need to depend constantly on divine assistance (cf. McKelvey, 'Second Coming', esp. 98–99). The idea in these verses of God's cosmic judgement on the impious is also present in *Sib. Or.* 3.663–701. For the relationship between Rev. 20.7–10 and 19.11–21 see below.

The conjunction, ὅταν (*hotan*, lit. 'when'), used with the aorist subjunctive τελεσθῇ (*telesthē[i]*, 'have been completed') in an indefinite future clause of time, should strictly be translated 'when*ever* (the thousand years have been completed)'; and such a rendering suits the indefinite, non-literal interpretation of the millennium adopted in this commentary (see on verse 2). Nevertheless, the translation 'when', even in this symbolic setting, remains acceptable (cf. BDAG 730*b*–731*a*). For the statement, 'Satan will be released (λυθήσεται, *lythēsetai*) from his prison' see on verse 3, where the same verb is used. The future passive in this context is one of divine activity and permission, suggesting that *God* will free Satan from his prison (cf. Aune 1093). Evil is still at work in the world, but it is under God's control. Deliverance from the powers of darkness in the present therefore anticipates a perfect expression of that victory for all the saints in the future (cf. Prigent 574). The 'abyss' (ἄβυσσον, *abysson*), into which the ancient serpent is hurled (verse 3), becomes in verse 7 the 'prison' (φυλακή, *phylakē*) from which he is freed. This might imply that the devil's restraint is significant, even if it is not yet total (cf. Beale 1021).

It is possible that there are parallels to the imagery in verse 7 to be discovered in Persian mythology (see Beale 1021 n. 173; cf. Moffatt 473–74; Beasley-Murray 286, 297; Mounce 372). If so, this adds little to our understanding of the present passage; and, in any case, the Old Testament and Jewish apocalyptic are always likely to be more important backgrounds for Johannine thought-patterns.

An essential characteristic of Satan, like the false prophet, in Revelation is the ability to deceive (cf. Rev. 12.9; 13.14; 19.20; 20.3). Once released from captivity, therefore, the devil resumes his seductive activity. He goes out 'to deceive the nations at the four corners of the earth' (verse 8). It is of interest that the verb to 'go out' (ἐξέρχομαι, *exerchomai*), in this context, is the same word used in John 13.30 to describe Judas 'going out' to betray Jesus, and in 2 John 7 to refer to the many deceivers who have 'defected into the world' at the end-time, in order to win over others to their false beliefs; cf. 1 John 2.19 (see Smalley, *1, 2, 3 John* 327–28).

Those who fall prey to satanic deception are said to belong to 'the nations at the four corners of the earth'. 'The nations' (τὰ ἔθνη, *ta ethnē*), in the plural, is a term which in the Apocalypse normally refers to human society in opposition to God and his people (cf. Rev. 2.26; 11.2; 16.19; 18.3; et al.). There can be no suggestion, therefore, that by speaking of the 'nations at the four corners of the earth, Gog and Magog', John is alluding here to demonic powers which exist at the fringes of the underworld (Roloff 228; cf. Sweet 290–91; Mealy, *After the Thousand Years* 127–30). Rather, the imagery in verse 8 is theological and not cosmological; for the writer is claiming that Satan's forthcoming deception will be universal and will affect the whole world (cf. Isa.11.12; Ezek. 7.2; Rev. 7.1); so Mounce 372.

The identity of 'the nations' is also revealed as 'Gog and Magog', a phrase which appears only here in the New Testament. There is a clear background to this identification in Ezek. 38—39, where it is predicted that a hostile nation 'from the remotest parts of the north' (Ezek. 38.6, 15) will attack the people of Palestine who live in safety (38.8–16), but will itself be totally defeated (39.1–6); cf. Jer. 1.13–15; 6.22. In the Old Testament, and the tradition of Judaism, 'Gog and Magog' can be understood in a variety of ways. In Ezek. 38.2–3 (cf. 39.1–16), Gog 'of the land of Magog' is described as the 'chief prince of Meshech and Tubal', who leads the invasion of Israel; and those two East Anatolian groups (the Moschi and the Tibareni) are associated with Magog, a descendant of Japheth, in the table of nations at Gen. 10.2 (cf. 1 Chron. 1.5). 'Gog' is found as a personal name at 1 Chron. 5.4; while in *Jub.* 8.25 Gog is used with a geographical reference.

In Rev. 20.8, however, 'Gog and Magog' are evidently symbolic figures. They are not 'the remaining dead' of Rev. 20.5, who are raised and judged (so Mealy, *After the Thousand Years* 140–42), but hostile nations from across the world which are mustered by the deceptive powers of evil for a final assault on the Church of God (Mounce 372; cf. Beasley-Murray 297). In this way, the seer universalizes the fulfilment of Ezekiel's prophecy (Beale 1022–23). By John's day, moreover, Jewish tradition had transformed 'Gog of Magog' into 'Gog and Magog', and made them into 'the ultimate enemies of God's people to be destroyed in the eschatological battle' (Boring 209); cf. *Sib. Or.* 3.512–13. Indeed, the whole scene in Rev. 20.7–10 moves beyond the dimension of time and space into the realm of myth, although John's mythical presentation of the final battle between good and evil enshrines a deep insight into the reality and resilience of the evil in God's world which is finally to be overcome (verse 10). See Caird 256–57; also Roloff 228, who notes that metaphorical and mythical language, as in this context, ultimately resists translation into the categories of logical and causal thought.

The second infinitive clause in verse 8, συναγαγεῖν αὐτοὺς εἰς τὸν πόλεμον (*synagagein autous eis ton polemon*, 'in order to muster them for battle'), repeated from 16.14, builds on the first (πλανῆσαι τὰ ἔθνη, *planēsai ta ethnē*, 'to deceive the nations'), rather than being parallel to it; hence the consecutive force of the second verb, brought out in the translation. The thought of assembling hostile nations for an attack on Israel, and especially on Jerusalem, is common in Jewish apocalyptic (cf. 1QM 15.2–3; 4 Ezra 13.34–35; *1 Enoch* 90.13–19; *Sib. Or.* 3.663–68). The mustering of enemies for this purpose is occasionally attributed to angels (*1 Enoch* 56.5–8), but more often to God himself (Ezek. 38.14–17; Joel 3.2; Zech. 12.1–9; *Jub.* 23.22–23). In Rev. 20.8, however, this inimical gathering together is inspired by the Satan; and the same is true at 16.14, 16, where demonic spirits rally 'the kings of the whole world' for the eschatological battle (cf. 19.17, 19). See further Aune 1095. In verse 8, the use of the definite article with 'battle' (τὸν πόλεμον, *ton polemon*, '*the* battle'), as at 16.14, indicates a reference to the final conflict between good and evil, the saints and Satan, which would have been familiar to John's audience from Old Testament prophecy (see on 16.14). The articular form is hardly one of previous reference, alluding to the 'final' battle of 11.7 (q.v.); so Beale 1022.

The hostile nations, deceived and mustered as allies by the forces of evil, are said to be 'countless as the sands on the seashore' (ὧν ὁ ἀριθμὸς αὐτῶν ἡ ἄμμος τῆς θαλάσσης, *hōn ho arithmos autōn hē ammos tēs thalassēs*, lit. 'of which their number is as the sand of the sea'). In this phrase αὐτῶν (*autōn*, lit. 'their') is a resumptive pronoun. 'Sand' is a biblical metaphor used to denote great abundance (Gen. 41.49; Ps. 139.18; Hab. 1.9; cf. *Jos. As.* 1.2); and it is particularly associated with the divine promise that Abraham's descendants would be countless as the sand of the sea, or the stars of heaven (Gen. 22.17; *T. Abr. [A]* 1.5; 4.11; Rom. 9.27). The image is also used, as here, to describe a very large army (Josh. 11.4; 1 Sam. 13.5; 1 Macc. 11.1); for this motif, in the setting of a numberless host attacking Israel at the end, see also Ps. 48.1–8; 76.1–12; Ezek. 38—39 (note 38.15); 4 Ezra 13.5. See further Roloff 228; Aune 1095–96.

Aune (1093) finds difficulty with the statement in Rev. 20.8 that hostile nations from every part of the world are mustered for battle against the saints, since at 19.11–21 the enemies of God and his Church are said to be destroyed. This apparent repetition may be explained by the theory of recapitulation in the structure of Revelation, a literary technique which echoes John's Old Testament sources (see McKelvey, *Millennium* 49–50; *idem*, 'Second Coming' 88–97, esp. 88–89; cf. Bauckham, *Climax of Prophecy* 208–209). But if John seems to recapitulate the idea of a final, eschatological combat between the powers of good and evil, mentioned in 16.14–16, both at 19.11–21 and here at 20.7–10, this is not a case of mere repetition. Certainly John presents in all three passages (Chapters 16; 19; and 20) his own version of the same prophecy at Ezekiel 38—39, now fulfilled according to the Christian scheme and narrated in three separate contexts (Beckwith 745; Beale 1023; cf. Bøe, *Gog and Magog*). Yet in each case the thought is subtly developed, rather than being simply restated. In Rev. 16.14 the worldly rulers are mustered for the battle, by demonic spirits, on the Day of the Lord; in 19.19 the beast, with the rulers of the earth and their armies, wages war against the Messiah and his followers; while in 20.8 the Satan himself assembles innumerable and hostile nations from the four corners of the earth, rather than just from the north (as in Ezek. 38.6; et al.), to do battle with God's people on earth and in heaven (20.9, q.v.).

9 The hostile nations, mustered by the forces of evil, attack God's people before they are themselves defeated and destroyed by divine intervention. The scene, including such details as an innumerable multitude being mustered from the four winds of heaven to wage war against the man from the sea, who then causes his enemies to be consumed by fire, is very reminiscent of the passage in 4 Ezra 13.1–11.

The attackers 'swarmed across the breadth of the land'. The aorist verb, ἀνέβησαν (*anebēsan*, lit. 'went up'), may be a loan word from the LXX of Ezek. 38.9, 16 (Gog will 'go up' against Israel). Cf. Prigent 576. Aune (1096–97) points out that the verb ἀναβαίνω (*anabainō*, 'go up') is used in the sense of going 'up' (never 'down') to Jerusalem (as in Ezra 1.5; Ps. 122.4; Isa. 7.1; Obad. 21; John 5.1; Acts 21.15; et al.); and the same idiom is used in the context of nations attacking Jerusalem in the final, eschatological warfare (*1 Enoch* 56.6, 'they will go up and trample upon the land of my elect ones'). The exact meaning of the phrase, 'across the breadth of the land' (ἐπὶ τὸ πλάτος τῆς γῆς, *epi to platos tēs gēs*, lit. 'upon the breadth of the earth'), is slightly obscure; although its general sense is clear, and need not suggest that armies are marching to 'the centre of the earth' (see Ezek. 38.11–12; cf. Aune 1097). BDAG 823*b* notes that the Greek phraseology is based on Dan. 12.2 LXX (which refers to the dead sleeping 'in the breadth of the earth';

cf. Hab. 1.6; Sir. 1.3), and at Rev. 20.9 may be meant to 'provide room for the countless enemies of God' (ibid.). At the same time, 'going up' at this point may be more suited to Satan, who 'ascends' again from the abyss (20.3, 7–8) to deceive the nations (cf. also 11.7–10). In visionary, and even mythical, material such as this, however, geographical detail is not important.

The nations, in this dramatic scene, 'surrounded the encampment of God's people'. The technical term, ἡ παρεμβολή (*hē parembolē*), can mean either an army barracks (cf. Acts 21.34; et al.) or a camp where people temporarily live in tents (e.g. Heb. 13.11) or armed forces themselves (so 1 Macc. 3.27; Heb. 11.34). See Aune 1097–98. In the setting of Rev. 20.9, the noun is not primarily to be understood in the Old Testament, geographical sense of Israelite encampments during the wilderness wanderings (Exod. 14.19–20; Num. 2.2–9; Deut. 23.14; cf. 1QM 3.5; 10.1–2), but more importantly as a description of God's people, the Church, and as a reminder of its spiritual, pilgrim nature (cf. Hughes 217; Mounce 373). For οἱ ἅγιοι (*hoi hagioi*, lit. 'the holy ones'), used to describe Christians as consecrated to God, see on 5.8; also 8.3–4; et al.; BDAG 11*b*.

The conjunction καί (*kai*, 'and'), before τὴν πόλιν τὴν ἠγαπημένην (*tēn polin tēn ēgapēmenēn*, 'the beloved city'), is probably epexegetic and explanatory: 'the camp, *that is* the city'. If 'the beloved city' is a circumlocution for 'Jerusalem', this is a unique description in the Apocalypse. John otherwise refers to Jerusalem as 'the city' (11.13; [14.20]; 21.14–23; 22.14), 'the city of God' (3.12), 'the holy city' (11.2; 21.10; 22.19) or 'the great city' (11.8; 16.19); contrast the 'great city' of Babylon (17.18; 18.10–21). In the present context, however, we have an allusion to the idea of Jerusalem and its special status in the sight of God (cf. Ps. 48.1; Sir. 24.11), without a literal reference to the city (similarly Gal. 4.26; Heb. 12.22). The writer uses language which draws on a rich treasury of biblical thought; and so he describes the community of the people of God, the true Israel, not only as an 'encampment', but also as 'the beloved city' (see Walker, *Holy City* 260–61). Together, the two images of 'camp' and 'city' speak of God's people as both on the move and also as arriving at their destination (ibid. 260).

In view of the parallel between this passage and Rev. 11.7–10, and the reference to the enemies of the Church swarming across 'the breadth of the land' to surround and attack its members (cf. the same phrase in Dan. 12.2 LXX; see above), Beale (1026) suggests that this vision depicts God's people as not only cosmopolitan but also 'scattered throughout the earth'. There is certainly no need to limit the scope of the present passage solely to the life of the Church, besieged but vindicated, in this world and in the earthly Jerusalem (against Aune 1098–99). As Caird (257) says, wherever and whenever God's people are gathered together, 'there is the city of God' (cf. 3.12; 11.2).

'Fire from heaven' is a biblical symbol for divine judgement; cf. 2 Kings 1.9–12 (= 4 Kgdms. 1.10–14 LXX); Ezek. 38.22 (Gog); 39.6 (Magog); Luke 9.51–54. Note the eschatological setting of destruction by fire as an act of God at Zeph. 1.18; 3.8; also 1QM 11.16–18; 4 Ezra 13.8–11; *Sib. Or.* 2.196–205; et al. See further Rev. 11.5. It is an unacceptably literal interpretation of Rev. 20.9 to say with Charles (2, 189) that, since 'Gog and Magog' comprehend all the faithless upon earth, who are totally destroyed by fire from heaven, this means that earth is left without a single inhabitant at the close of the millennial kingdom.

10   The hostile nations, mustered by Satan from throughout the world (verses 7–8), were represented in verse 9 as being destroyed by heavenly fire before they could do more than surround the camp of God's people. Now their leader is said to join the beast and the false prophet to form a satanic triumvirate in 'the lake of fire and brimstone'. The thought and language of verse 10 recapitulate 19.20. For the 'beast' see 11.7; 13.1, 11; and for the 'false prophet' see on 16.13; cf. also Matt. 25.41. If Rev. 20.7–10 repeats

19.17–21 from another perspective, and the seer is in any case presenting visionary material, there is no need to be unduly concerned about the chronology of the events which are described in these two passages (see also below).

The devil is 'tormented' eternally, but not destroyed. Similarly, although Satan apparently 'leaves the stage of history' (Prigent 577), the power of evil remains, and is still able to affect human beings (cf. 21.8, 27; 22.11). For the Judaic background to the apocalyptic imagery of 'fire and brimstone' see on 14.10; and for the 'lake' of fire see 19.20; 20.14–15; 21.8. These are symbols for divine judgement, and are not intended to be taken literally. The same is true of the statement that the devil, the beast and the false prophet were 'tormented (βασανισθήσονται, *basanisthēsontai*) for ever and ever'. See on 14.11; cf. also *T. Jud.* 25.3. However, as Beale (1028–30) points out, even if these three figures are personifications, representing evil and oppressive institutions, a personal element is involved. As with the individual followers of the beast (14.10–11; cf. 20.15), all wickedness evokes God's justice, as well as his mercy (note the fate of Babylon at Rev. 17—18).

There is no verb with the phrase, 'where the beast and the false prophet (sc. had also been thrown)'. But the seer need not be implying that these characters had been hurled into the lake *before* the devil (see 19.20), since he is not sensitive to exact timing in this vision. If necessary, all three members of the triad may be regarded as entering the fire at the same time; cf. Beale 1030. For the hendiadys, 'day and night' (ἡμέρας καὶ νυκτός, *hēmeras kai nyktos*), meaning 'without interruption' or 'ceaselessly', see 4.8.

Vision 7: Final Judgement (20.11–15)

11 The last vision of the septet in Chapters 19—20 introduces a scene of undeniable judgement. Following the apparently definitive destruction of Satan in 20.10, the rest of the dead (20.5, 12) are judged; and the allies of the dragon, the beast and the false prophet now share their fate (verse 15). To say that this action is 'final', however, need not imply that the seer is providing us with a literal description of the way in which God will dispense justice at the end of the world. The unveiling in 20.11–15 does *not* close for ever the era of sin, so that we 'stand ready to enter the eternal state of glory' (Mounce 374; similarly Beale 1032; Prigent 577; on the other side see Wall 240). Nor is this the only possible climax, in a linear and chronological sense, to the judgemental activity which seems to have been in progress throughout the Apocalypse (cf. 6.15–17; 11.19; 14.14–20; 16.20–21; 18.21–24; 19.17–21). Rather, in 20.11–15 John gives his audience once more a figurative and spiritual glimpse into the divine response to human wrongdoing and idolatry, as this is perceived at *any* time in history, up to and at its consummation. At the same time, it is true that Rev. 20.11–15 is the *only* portrayal of the judgement process which John gives, that *everyone* seems to be present for it, and that the justice exercised is *real* (cf. Boring 210–11). For the varied traditions in late Judaism relating to this topic see Glasson, 'Last Judgement' 528–39; at 538 Glasson states that, hermeneutically, such judgement should be regarded as the 'pictorial representation of a transcendent reality'.

'And I saw' (καὶ εἶδον, *kai eidon*), at the start of verse 11 (as at 20.1, 4, 12), is a typical visionary formula in the Apocalypse (see on 5.1; also 6.1; 10.1; et al.). The use of 'and', at the opening of the new vision and in verse 12 (as in the translation), rather than 'then' (as in NRSV), indicates successive revelations, and not their chronological progression (similarly 19.11, 17). John sees 'a majestic, white throne'. For the 'throne' (θρόνον, *thronon*), as a symbol of divine sovereignty, see 4.2; 5.1, 7; et al. The imagery in this passage owes much to the vision in Dan. 7.9–10, where the Ancient of Days, in white clothing, takes his place on the throne, and books of judgement are opened (see verse 12); see also the picture of the Lord's glory at Ezek. 1.26–28. The throne of verse 11 is 'majestic' (μέγαν, *megan*, lit. 'large'). For the symbol of a noble throne of great size, as used in the visionary traditions of Judaism, see Isa. 6.1; 4 Ezra 8.21; Ezekiel the Tragedian, *Exagōgē* 68–72. It is also 'white' (λευκόν, *leukon*) in colour, which in John's thought is normally associated with the heavenly realm. 'White' is the colour belonging to the Godhead (1.14; 14.14; 19.11); to angelic beings (4.4); to the stone given to those who conquer (2.17); and to the dress of the faithful (3.4–5, 18; 6.11; 7.9, 13–14; 19.14). In the present context the colour probably suggests holiness and vindication; although Swete (270–71) opts for 'purity' as its significance, and Charles (2, 192) for the 'equity' of the judgement.

The identity of the Judge is not disclosed, and it is not immediately clear who is 'seated' on the throne. In Revelation 'the one seated on the throne' is normally God (cf. 4.2, 3, 9; 5.1, 7, 13; 6.16; 7.10, 15; 19.4; 21.5); so it could be argued that the one who carries out the judgement of humanity is God the Almighty (cf. 16.14; 19.15). Nevertheless, given that the Lamb shares the throne with God (22.3; cf. 7.17; 14.3; 21.22), that the high Christology of the Apocalypse implies the unity of God and his Messiah (5.11–13; 11.15; 12.10; 22.16; cf. John 5.19; 10.30); and that in Johannine thought saving judgement is committed to the Son, as well as to the Father (1.12–18; 2.26–28; 20.6; cf. 7.10; and esp. John 5.22), it is entirely reasonable to conclude that the judgement in Rev. 20.11–15 is dispensed by God in Christ, and is therefore searching and complete (as in Rom. 2.16; see also *1 Enoch* 45.3; Matt. 25.31–46; Acts 10.42; 2 Tim. 4.1). Cf. Milligan 353; Mounce 375; Prigent 577.

The effect of eschatological justice being administered is that 'earth and sky fled from his (sc. the divine) presence, so that no place was found for them'. For this expression, which is probably a Semitism (as with 21.1), see 12.8; also 6.14; 16.20. Cf. further LXX Dan. 12.2 Theod. The seer is not describing the total destruction of the cosmos (Aune 1101), since a *new* earth and sky are about to appear (21.1–2, q.v.). The apocalyptic scheme in this vision indeed assumes that the boundaries of the old order will disappear (Sweet 294). But, although they are depicted as fleeing in terror from the wrath of God, the manner of their removal (whether by passing away, as here, or by fiery dissolution, as in 2 Pet. 3.10) is not important. For such a theophany, involving the appearance of the deity and the reaction of nature, see 1QH 3.32–36; Judg. 5.4–5; Ps. 68.7–8; Amos 1.2; Sir. 16.18–19; *T. Levi* 3.9; *T. Mos.* 10.3–6; *Sib. Or.* 3.669–84; cf. further Aune 1101.

12 For the visionary formula, 'and I saw', see on verse 11. The company of 'the dead' (τοὺς νεκρούς, *tous nekrous*) appears to be universal, since it contains 'the greatest and the least alike' (τοὺς μεγάλους καὶ τοὺς μικρούς, *tous megalous kai tous mikrous*, lit. 'the great and the small'). This phrase is found in the Old Testament (cf. 2 Chron. 15.13; Ps. 115.13; Jer. 16.6; Jonah 3.5; et al.). It is used elsewhere in Revelation to describe groups which are inclusive in character. See 11.18; 13.16; 19.5, 18, where the reverse order, 'least and greatest', is without significance; as Mounce (376) says, the main point is that no one is so important as to escape judgement, nor anyone so unimportant as to render divine judgement inappropriate.

If the justice which is administered in this scene is final and comprehensive, it must presumably affect the living as well as the dead, and the righteous as well as the unrighteous (see below); cf. Beale 1032; Prigent 579. But it has already been suggested that John's vision in 20.7–15 is 'final' in an eschatological, rather than chronological, sense (see esp. on verse 10). In the same way, the 'first resurrection' (verses 5–6) and the 'last judgement' (verses 11–15) belong in Johannine thought to an ongoing process of salvation through judgement which is experienced by believers and unbelievers at any time up to and including the climax of salvation history. Thus the serious vision of judgement in

Rev. 20.11–15 is salvific, as well as timeless and general in its reference. See on 11.15–18; cf. also Bauckham, *Climax of Prophecy* 18–21; Smalley, *Thunder and Love* 147–49.

There may be a link between the posture of the dead in verse 12, who are depicted as 'standing in front of the throne', and that of the Lamb in the vision of 5.6 (q.v.), who 'stands' victoriously near the symbol of God's sovereignty. If so, resurrection existence could be implied in both scenes (so Beale 1032); and this adds to the salvific content of the judgemental process which is being described at 20.12.

In the statement, 'books were opened' (βιβλία ἠνοίχθησαν, *biblia ēnoichthēsan*), the use of the aorist passive verb suggests that this action was undertaken by God, or by his angels (cf. Aune 1102). The allusion is to Dan. 7.10, when at the end-time 'the court sat in judgement' on the persecutor of God's people, 'and the books were opened' (cf. *1 Enoch* 47.3). The plural form ('books') in Dan. 7.10 and Rev. 20.12 seems to reflect the tradition in Judaism that there were two heavenly books, which recorded respectively the deeds of the righteous and the wicked (cf. Mal. 3.16; Isa. 65.6; also 4 Ezra 6.20; *1 Enoch* 97.6; *2 Enoch* 52.15; *3 Enoch* 30.2; *2 Apoc. Bar.* 24.1; *Asc. Isa.* 9.21–23; *Apoc. Zeph.* 6–9). As Wall (240–41) rightly points out, the act of 'opening the books' does not represent God's oppressive omniscience, so that he publishes at this stage every recorded deed of every individual's life. Rather, the image allows the audience to note with confidence that the divine record is accurate, since God's judgements are 'fair and just' (19.2). The reference here may be collective, as well as personal (see on Theology, below).

A further book, that of 'life', is now opened. For the background and meaning of this expression, which in the Apocalypse always appears in a judicial context, see on 3.5 (also 13.8; 17.8; 20.15; 21.27). The concept of a divine register of the living is an ancient one (Exod. 32.32–33; Isa. 4.3). But the 'book of life' in Revelation has a theological meaning; it is an image of redemption, signifying that those written in it will be given eternal life, while the ones not included will suffer judgement (cf. Dan. 12.1–2; also, elsewhere in the New Testament, Luke 10.20; Phil. 4.3; Heb. 12.23). Such record books are a metaphorical representation of God's unfailing memory (Beale 1033; cf Prigent 579–80).

The dead, according to the seer, were 'judged according to their deeds, as recorded in these books' (cf. 11.18). The quality of people's lives is disclosed, so that it may be assessed. Two theological comments need to be made on the teaching in this part of verse 12. First, divine justice is not arbitrary, but based on the life and activity of society and individuals; and this is a biblical principle (cf. Job 34.11; Ps. 62.12; Prov. 24.12; Jer. 17.10; Rom. 2.6; 1 Pet. 1.17; see Mounce 376). Equally, however, judgement 'according to deeds' (κατὰ τὰ ἔργα, *kata ta erga*) does not imply a legalistic idea of retributive justice, but rather a determination of spiritual loyalty: either to God or to the Satan. The measure in each case is the evidence of personal or corporate behaviour, and whether it is Christian or not; for faith and deeds, as recorded in the books of judgement and life, belong together. Cf. Bauckham 1303*a*. Second, even if judgement is primarily in view in Rev. 20.11–15, redemption is not absent. As in 13.8 and 17.8, the 'book of life' is introduced as a reminder of the possibility of salvation in God and through the Lamb, and as an appeal to embrace it (cf. Beale 1032–33).

13   This verse appears to develop the judgement scene in verse 12 (cf. Swete 272–73; Beckwith 748–49), even if problems of sequence then arise. For example, it may be argued that a reference to the 'sea' (ἡ θάλασσα, *hē thalassa*), yielding up its dead, contradicts the dissolution of 'earth and sky' at verse 11, and the disappearance of the sea mentioned at 21.1. Similarly, the 'final judgement' of the dead occurs in verse 12, although their 'resurrection' seems to take place in the present verse (cf. Aune 1102). Because of these apparent discrepancies Charles (2, 194–98) argues that verse 13 is out of place and originally occurred before verse 12. However, three points in this connection need to be made.

(a) Recapitulation is a feature of the structure and theology of this section of Revelation, and no doubt plays a part in the present passage (see on verse 8). As a result, judgement *and* (implicitly) resurrection are described in both verses, 12 and 13.

(b) If the issue of chronology is to be pressed, it is possible that verses 12 and 13 yield a further instance of John's occasional technique in the Apocalypse of reversing the logical order of events (e.g. 6.4; 10.4, 9); cf. Aune 1102.

(c) Most importantly, the character of the seer's material in these verses needs once more to be appreciated. In an eschatological vision such as this, chronological and doctrinal precision has not been provided, and cannot be expected. The dramatic disclosures of Revelation, here as elsewhere, unfold for its audience not a timetable of salvation history, but a theological account of the ultimate triumph of good over evil. See further Kiddle 405–406; Boxall, *Revelation* 78–79; Prigent 578–79.

In Revelation, 'the sea' frequently carries a neutral connotation, in that it is a part of God's creation (cf. 5.13; 10.6; 14.7; 18.17, 19). But in the present context the significance of this image appears to be more negative (as in 4.6; 13.1; 15.2). It is associated with death, and clearly symbolizes the realm over which the powers of evil have control. From this abode God now forces its demonic leaders to release their captives for judgement (Beale 1034). In Jewish thought, to remain unburied after death was a fate which held terror (see on 11.9; cf. 1 Kings 13.21–22; Jer. 8.1–2; et al.). Among such, an important place would be occupied by those who had drowned at sea, and could not be buried (note *1 Enoch* 61.5). But for the writer of *1 Enoch* there is a promise for all the dead, however they perished: that those destroyed in the desert, devoured by wild beasts or 'eaten by the fish of the sea', would 'all return and find hope in the day of the Elect One' (ibid.); cf. Ps. 68.22; Heb. 9.27; 11.32–40. The same truth is implicit at Rev. 20.13. Those who are forgotten in human memory, and seem to have vanished into an invisible world, are not lost; for God knows them, and 'in his sovereignty calls them back from death' (Prigent 581; cf. Beasley-Murray 302–303; Hughes 219).

Taken together the three figures, 'sea, Death and Hades', represent the demonic realm of death, hostile to the true character of God. The last reference to 'Death and Hades' was in 6.8, where the Lamb uses them, along with other destroyers of the earth (the four horsemen), as instruments of his ultimate purposes of grace. Once that purpose has been achieved, Death and Sheol appear in their real light as enemies of the living God (Caird 260). For the personification, 'Death and Hades', see on 1.18; also 6.8; 20.14. In this pairing, 'Death' is always mentioned first, suggesting that the region of Sheol is under the control of the powers of death, which are themselves nevertheless destined to be destroyed (verse 14; see 1 Cor. 15.26, 54–57); cf. Knight 133. When John says that 'Death and Hades gave up the dead in them', he means that the graves were opened, and all the dead in them were raised; and such language implies a 'second', general resurrection corresponding to the first (verses 5–6, q.v.); cf. Michaels 232. Such an event is not confined to the martyrs (so Mounce 377). All are present for final judgement, and no one escapes the possibilities of God's justice and mercy (cf. Tobit 13.1–6).

John treats 'Death and Hades' as a demonic unity, despite the use of the plural, ἐν αὐτοῖς (*en autois*, '[they gave up the dead] in them'). For the theme of 'giving up the dead', in the apocalyptic traditions of late Judaism and Rabbinic literature, as well as in Rev. 20.13, see Bauckham, *Climax of Prophecy* 56–70. For the final sentence in verse 13, 'all were judged individually (ἕκαστος, *hekastos*, lit. "each one", distributive), depending on what they had done (κατὰ τὰ ἔργα αὐτῶν, *kata ta erga autōn*, lit. "according to their works")', see on verse 12. Despite the visionary nature of the material at this point, the καί (*kai*, lit. 'and') which introduces the final statement may be regarded as having a temporal force; hence the translation ('then').

14–15   For the figurative language and thought in these verses see on 12–13; cf. also 2.11; 19.20; 20.6, 10; 21.8.

The meaning of the phrase, 'Death and Hades were hurled into the lake of fire (εἰς τὴν λίμνην τοῦ πυρός, *eis tēn limnēn tou pyros*)', needs to be considered carefully. A common view, and the most likely, is that ultimately the demonic forces governing the region of death, as the allies of sin, will be defeated and punished for ever; they will suffer the same fate as Satan and his lieutenants (19.20; 20.10). At the same time, the death of death provides spiritual encouragement for the saints (see on verse 13; also 21.4). Cf. Moffatt 477; Beckwith 749; Roloff 232; Mounce 377–78; Prigent 581.

An alternative explanation takes 'Death and Hades' as a metonymy for the sum of their occupants: namely, all the unrepentant dead, who now exchange their temporary bonds for the permanent prison of the burning lake (cf. Luke 16.22–23; 1 Pet. 3.18–20). See Mealy, *After the Thousand Years* 181; Aune 1103; also Sweet 295. One further option, offered by Beale (1034–35), is in effect a subtle variation on this line of thought. It suggests that 'Death and Hades', as the location of those who have suffered the 'first (physical) death', gives way at the end to the 'lake of fire' as the place of those enduring the 'second (spiritual) death' (see on 20.6); so that final perdition supersedes the provisional (cf. 14.10–11). However, these interpretations introduce more problems than they solve. For it has already been proposed that the judgement envisaged in this passage is general, rather than involving just the unrighteous (see on verse 12); and, furthermore, in verse 13 Death and Hades are apparently represented as the powers which preside over the realm of death, and are to that extent precisely distinguished from (all) 'the dead in them'. See further Hendriksen 195–96.

For the 'second death' (verse 14), as a spiritual and not a physical concept, see on 2.11; 20.6; 21.8. God's eschatological purposes do not override human freedom; and those who wish to enter the city of God (21.5–7; 22.14), or to remain outside it (21.8; 22.15), may choose to do so. According to Beasley-Murray (303–304), John's use of the symbolism of the 'burning lake' (verses 14–15), which is equated with 'the second death', shows that the seer views it as the alternative to that city. The lake, here as at 20.10, does not represent annihilation, but rather the tortured existence of those who belong to an evil society which is opposed to life in the community of Christ. God's eschatological judgement, in this passage, like the 'torment' of the unfaithful at 9.5; 14.10–11; 18.7, 10, 15, is not physical. In the vision of the four apocalyptic horsemen (6.1–8, q.v.), the self-induced results of wrong human conduct translate into the causes of military power, war, famine and death; and these are understood as expressions of God's justice experienced in society. In the present context, divine judgement is perceived as spiritual, and not material; and it is administered in heaven, as well as on earth. The image of being 'thrown into the burning lake' may therefore be interpreted as meaning that those individuals who wish are excluded from a relationship with God that is desirable, but rejected.

In verse 15, as in verse 12 (q.v.), the 'book of life' has salvific significance; for it belongs to the Lamb who has been crucified and exalted (13.8; 21.27). At 13.8; 17.8 and here (20.15), inclusion in this heavenly record is expressed negatively: 'anyone, whose name could *not* be found (εἴ τις οὐχ εὑρέθη [*ei tis ouch heurethē*, lit. "if anyone was not found"]) written in the book of life, was thrown into the burning lake'. But the implications are positive (as at 21.27). Those whose names are inscribed in the heavenly roll possess eternal life, and enter a kingdom which is the very opposite of alienation from God's love (2.7, 10; 21.6; 22.1–2, 14, 17, 19).

Theology

The theological content of the seven visions in Scene 6 (Rev. 19—20) looks back to the judgement on Babylon in Chapters 17—18, and prepares the way for the disclosure of the new Jerusalem in Scene 7 (Rev. 21—22). The dramatic and colourful setting for John's teaching in this section of the Apocalypse is clearly forensic, and its main subject is divine judgement. Chapters 17—18, and in particular the depiction of the downfall of Babylon in Rev. 18, have between them demonstrated the integrity of God's justice and of Christian faith (Beale 926). In the present scene there is an enactment of divine judgement on *all* evil: on Babylon, as the representative of systemic wrongdoing in contrast to the true Jerusalem (19.1–2), and on Satan, who symbolizes idolatrous opposition to the truth of the Lord who created the universe (20.7–10). The triumphant Messiah comes (19.11–16), sin and death are conquered (20.13–14) and the loyal saints are vindicated (20.4–6). Cf. Mounce 378.

However, three points need to be made about the nature of God's judgement in these chapters.

(a) Rev. 19—20 provide the first glimpse in the Apocalypse of the actual process of divine judgement, rather than its anticipation (see on 20.11–15). The theme of the reward of believers and the destruction of their enemies has been in view since the sounding of the seventh trumpet at 11.15–19; and, indeed, the theological concept in Revelation of God's purposes of salvation *through* judgement is present from the earlier and pivotal throne-vision in 4—5, and the reception of the scroll by the Lamb at 5.1–14. But now, in 19—20, John sets out what appears to be the final, heavenly judgement. At the same time, the vision moves from the notion of judgement on evil in general, and on systemic corruption in particular, personified by the beast and the harlot, to judgement in more individual and personal terms. Books of justice are opened, and all the dead are judged or rewarded accordingly (20.12–15). Nevertheless, it is also true that individuals belong to collective groups (such as 'Rome' or 'Babylon'), and that societies are made up of people who are capable of a personal response. As a result, God's judgement on individuals must also (as in 17—20) include the world and its corporate bodies; and the consequences of this assessment are spiritual (20.15; see on 20.10), rather than physical.

(b) The response of the individual to the demands of God's justice, and to the offer of healing in Christ, does not involve any kind of predetermined divine plan, despite the possible suggestion in 20.15 (q.v.) that this might be the case ('anyone whose name could not be found written in the book of life was thrown into the burning lake'). Human choice, for or against the gift of God's love and life, is a consistent reality (see 20.15; 22.14–15). Cf. further Michaels 230–31, who tries to balance, in a Pauline manner, the joint ideas of divine election and human free will which might be implicit in this passage (see also on 14.13).

(c) God is the holy Creator (4.8–11) and sovereign Saviour (19.1); and his judgements are therefore true and just (19.2; cf. 6.10; 15.3; 16.7). Truth and righteous judgement are equally characteristic of Christ (19.11). But the vision in Rev. 19 of God as a warrior King (verses 1–5) is transposed into the figure of The Word of God, who is himself a kingly warrior (verses 11–12), but whose robe bears the marks of sacrifice, as well as victory (verse 13). God speaks with truth and judgement; but his word is in the end one of humility and accessibility, having love as its motive, and salvation as its purpose (Smalley, *Thunder and Love* 179). The justice of God is restorative, and cannot be separated from his love. The depiction of the divine assessment of individual and corporate character and action in Rev. 19—20, therefore, is not intended to satisfy the vindictiveness and resentment of the seer or his audience, but to establish the certainty that God opposes his enemies in order to make this earth into a place for his salvific reign (11.18; 19.6; 20.6). Cf. Roloff 220–21; also Ellul, *Apocalypse* 171–213, who refers to God's judgements as demonstrating the 'justice of Love itself' (ibid. 213). Prigent (548–49) notes that salvation and judgement are not two distinct realities but 'two sides of the same act of God' (ibid. 549). See further on 19.1–5, 6–10, 11–16; 20.3, 5–6.

A theology of *power* is also prominent in this scene, notably in the activity of divine judgement in Chapter 20, and the passages which describe the 'restraint' of Satan in this scene (see 19.20; 20.2–3, 7–10). The millennium (20.2–7, q.v.) is a symbol for the final triumph of God's sovereignty through his Christ in time and in eternity. As divine justice reveals itself in terms of unending *love*, so God's true power is ultimately disclosed in his ability to offer eternal *life* to every believer (19.7–9, 14; 20.4, 12). See further on 7.12; also John 1.1–5; 5.24; 1 John 5.10–13. The conquest of the saints over oppression and idolatry, through the victory of the Messiah-Lamb, affirms the truth that the only reality, on earth and in heaven, is the quality of eternal life; although such life needs to be expressed in behaviour which is properly Christian and appropriate for a truly divine order (20.12–13); cf. Prigent 517.

A final point about John's thought in this scene concerns his eschatology; for in the visions of Rev. 19—20, theology is more important than chronology. As always in Johannine teaching, time and eternity are finely balanced; so that past, present and future are fused together (cf. further Smalley, *Thunder and Love* 174–75). It is not essential to debate the temporal relationship of Chapter 20 to Chapter 19, particularly if Rev. 20.11–15 recapitulates 19.11–21; and, equally, the timing of the inauguration and conclusion of the 'thousand years' in Rev. 20 is much less crucial than the theological significance of that image (see on 20.2); cf. Beale 972–73. The 'final judgement' in Rev. 19—20 (as in 17—18) is an eschatological expression of an ongoing and spiritual reality; it depicts God's salvific assessment of the nature and conduct of individuals, churches and societies in *any* age, up to and including the end. In the Apocalypse, moreover, the end never comes (see on 22.20)!

The stage is now set for the remaining interval and last scene in Revelation, and for the presentation of its closing epilogue. The seer is about to inform his audience that a new order is at hand, ready at any moment to replace and transform the old.

INTERVAL
Prelude to the Final Scene
(21.1)

Translation

21 ¹And I saw a new heaven and a new earth; for the first heaven and the first earth disappeared,ᵃ and the sea no longer exists.

Text

ᵃ The *lectio originalis* is evidently the aorist plural, ἀπῆλθαν (*apēlthan*, 'disappeared', lit. 'they went away'), as read by A ℵ 1611²³²⁹. Some witnesses (046 Byz) have the aorist plural version of the verb, with the same meaning, ἀπῆλθον (*apēlthon*); while others have the aorist singular forms, with the meaning 'it went away', ἀπῆλθεν (*apēlthen*, attested by 025 1611¹⁸⁵⁴ 2030) and (as in 051 Andreas) παρῆλθεν (*parēlthen*). These variations chiefly arise as a result of changing the vocalization of the second aorist, from -α (*-a*, Hellenistic) towards -o or -ε (*-o* or *-e*, Attic). See Aune 1110.

Literary Setting

The short interval in 21.1 allows the audience of John's drama to reflect on the activity of divine judgement and salvation which has taken place in the preceding scene (Rev. 19—20). It also introduces the theme of new creation which will dominate the next and concluding chapters of the book (21—22). The final, seventh scene (21.2—22.17) includes seven prophecies; and the first of these (the new covenant, 21.2–4), which introduces a vision of the new Jerusalem, clearly forms a fresh literary unit. The interval thus provides, in a general and not a chronological sense, the opportunity for a significant transition. Instead of worldly Babylon and the Satan, there is a movement towards the new Jerusalem and the Godhead, from an imperfect to a perfected Church (cf. Wilcock 200–203). This presents every reader, including members of the Johannine community, with the challenge to persevere in the face of oppression and the temptation to compromise Christian belief and behaviour, in order to share in the glory to come. See Beale 1039.

The vision of a new heaven and earth, replacing a creation which has 'disappeared', seems to provide a direct literary connection with the flight of earth and sky from the presence of God in the previous scene (20.11); so Beale 1039. But the association is probably not deliberate, particularly since the setting and mood contrast so markedly; for judgemental fear in Rev. 20 gives way to salvific joy in the present chapter. Aune (1113–14) suggests that verse 1 forms part of a chiastic structure, present in 21.1–5. Thus, καινός (*kainos*, 'new'), πρῶτος (*prōtos*, 'first'), ἀπῆλθαν (*apēlthan*, '[they] disappeared') and the phrase οὐκ ἔστιν ἔτι (*ouk estin eti*, 'no longer exists', lit. 'is not still'), in verse 1, occur in reverse order in verses 4–5. However, the correspondence he claims is by no means exact.

Charles (2, 144–54) extensively reconstructs the order of the text in Rev. 20—22, which he sees as 'full of confusion and contradiction' (ibid. 144). Charles speculates that John died once he had completed the Apocalypse up to 20.3, and that a 'faithful but unintelligent disciple' (ibid. 147) completed it by putting together a number of independent documents in a sequence which he mistakenly considered to be correct. This material contains two separate visions of two heavenly cities: the millennial capital of Christ's kingdom, the 'heavenly Jerusalem' occupied by martyrs (21.9—22.2, 14–15, 17, verses which should have followed 20.3); and the eternal city of the 'new Jerusalem' (21.1–5; 22.3–5), in which the saints are to reign for ever. For the suggested reordered text see Charles 2, 153–54.

This proposal by Charles is idiosyncratic, and searches for a consistency which apocalyptic visions rarely exhibit (cf. Sweet 296–97; Mounce 379 n. 2). There is no necessary connection between the millennium and the heavenly Jerusalem; and in any case the holy city in Rev. 21—22, like the end itself, is viewed from three different but complementary perspectives (21.2–8; 21.9–27; 22.1–5). Cf. Prigent 582–88; and see further below. In the literary structure of Revelation adopted in this commentary, moreover, 21.1 forms a discrete textual unit, rather than being an integral part of the vision of the new Jerusalem in 21.2–4 (see above). The material in Chapters 21—22, however, is clearly capable of being analysed in different ways (see on 21.2—22.17, below). Cf. further Bauckham 1303*b*–1305*a*, whose divisions are similar to mine; also Wilcox, 'Tradition and Redaction'.

Comment

The New Creation

21.1 The vision of the prophet-seer in this interval is of the transition to a new order. Typically, the thought in this verse joins together heaven and earth (see on 20.1). In Rev. 17—20 there is a constant movement between these two dimensions of existence; in the interval of 21.1, and the scene which follows (7), heaven and earth seem to merge together (note 21.2, 4, 11, 22; 22.1–2, 7, 16–17, 19, et al.).

For the literary formula, καὶ εἶδον (*kai eidon*, 'and I saw'), introducing a new vision, see on 5.1; and for the translation of καί (*kai*) as 'and', rather than 'then' (as in NRSV) see on 20.1; cf. also 21.2. A verbal shaping of this verse may be involved, notably in its dependence on texts from Isaiah (see below). But (against Aune 1116) this need not imply that the origin of the text in Revelation 21.1 is purely literary and derivative. John's vision of the new creation is real; and, here as elsewhere in the Apocalypse, his perception of God's eternal purposes for the created order is inspired by the Spirit (1.10). As so often, the writer stretches human vocabulary to its limits in order to convey truths which are spiritual and everlasting. Cf. Boring 213–15; Mounce 379–81.

The spontaneity of the vision in 21.1 is emphasized by the language of its expression. The Greek verbs are ἀπῆλθαν (*apēlthan*, 'disappeared'), where the aorist suggests an event which is simultaneous with the time of its narration, and (οὐκ) ἔστιν (*[ouk] estin*, lit. 'is not', present tense). The translation in NRSV masks this immediacy in the dramatic action: the first heaven and earth '*had* passed away', and the sea '*was* no more'. In RV the version is stilted, but more accurate: 'the first heaven and the first earth are passed away; and the sea is no more' (cf. the translation above).

In John's interval vision (21.1), the first heaven and earth are replaced by the new world order. The thought and language of this verse derive from Isa. 65.17 LXX (cf. Isa. 66.22), where Yahweh promises that the time of salvation for the elect community of God's people will be ushered in by a new creation. The rule of God over nature, classically depicted in Gen. 1.1—2.4*a*, is applied here to the new age; and this theme, of the renewal of creation, belongs in varied forms to Jewish apocalyptic literature as well as to the New Testament (cf. 1QH 11.13; *1 Enoch* 45.4–5; 72.1; 91.16; 4 Ezra 7.75; *2 Apoc. Bar.* 32.6; 44.12; *Apoc. Elijah* 5.38 [which depends on Rev. 21.1]; *Jub.* 1.29; *Sib. Or.* 5.211–12; 2 Cor. 5.17; Gal. 6.15; 2 Pet. 3.13). The apocalyptic theme of the destruction of the heavens and earth features occasionally in primitive Christianity (see Heb. 12.26–27; 2 Pet. 3.12; *2 Clem.* 16.3; *Apoc. Peter* 5; cf. 4 Ezra 7.30–31; *Gospel Thom.* 11*a* [Jesus said, 'This heaven will pass away, and the one above it will pass away']). In the synoptic tradition of the New Testament this idea has its counterpart in the preservation of divine law, rather than of creation (cf. Matt. 5.18 = Luke 16.17; Mark 13.31 par.). See Aune 1117–19.

Heaven and earth belong together in biblical thought, so that the renewal of the cosmos involves both (cf. Gen. 1.6–10; Job 37.14–21; Ps. 102.25–26; Isa. 51.6; Matt. 24.35). The antithesis between the 'first' (πρῶτος, *prōtos*) heaven and earth and the new creation in the present context is qualitative, and has nothing to do with temporal considerations. This is clear from the background to verse 1 in Isa. 65.17 (similarly 66.22). Isa. 65.16–18 draws a contrast between the 'former troubles' of captivity in Babylon and the prospect of joy in the 'new heavens and earth' of a restored Jerusalem (cf. Rev. 21.2). The change does not involve temporal novelty, but spiritual renewal. Cf. Minear, 'Cosmology', esp. 27–37; Beale 1041; McKelvey, *Millennium* 85–86.

The terminology in verse 1 throws further light on the nature of the eschatological hope, the anticipation of a 'new heaven and earth', which the seer is offering as an encouragement for his beleaguered audience. In the Greek, there are two words for 'new'. One is νέος (*neos*), which means 'fresh', in the sense of 'renewed'; while the other term is καινός (*kainos*), which signifies a newness hitherto unknown: 'new', in the sense of 'unused'. So Paul assures the Colossian Christians that the 'new (νέος, *neos*) self', with which they have clothed themselves, is 'being renewed' (using ἀνακαινούμενος, *anakainoumenos*) according to the image of its creator (Col. 3.10). At Rev. 21.1 the word for 'new' is καινός (*kainos*). John describes, that is to say, a recreation by which the old is totally transformed into the new (cf. Matt. 19.28). God's activity in the Lamb-Messiah is such that a transfigured dimension is offered to the Church and to the world, as well as to the life and behaviour of their believing inhabitants. Cf. further Smalley, *Thunder and Love* 175; also Caird 265–66; Thompson 181.

Such a transfiguration is marked significantly by the disappearance of the sea, the third level of the cosmos to be mentioned in 21.1 (see on 5.13). But whereas 'the sea' (ἡ θάλασσα, *hē thalassa*) may have a neutral connotation in Revelation, and refer to part of God's creation, the meaning of 'sea' in verse 1 is undoubtedly negative (see on 20.13; also 13.1–8). There may be an allusion here to the dread of the sea felt by the ancients, or to Tiamat, the Babylonian mythological and dragon-like figure of chaos who struggles with Marduk, the god of order (Mounce 381). In such a universe of thought the absence of the sea could represent God's final victory over all the evil it embodied.

It is more likely, however, that John's imagery at this point speaks of the entirely new quality of the new world of existence which God makes possible in Christ. In this realm there is no more chaos, and nothing more to contradict the character of that new world (Swete 275; cf. Isa. 57.20). The removal of the sea does not mean that the physical universe has been completely destroyed (so Aune 1117), but rather that it has been completely transformed, and that there is now no threat from Satan (cf. Bauckham, *Theology* 49–50; Prigent 589–92, esp. 592). However, while God gives the creation a new form of existence, indwelt by his glory and not by the pressures of evil (cf. 21.5), there is also a continuity between the old and the new (see below). Beale (1043) suggests that an important implication in this text would have been relevant for the Johannine community. If the chaos represented by the sea has been removed, there will be no trials over which to weep in the final order of creation (cf. verse 4). This means that there will be no afflictions for God's people such as those which result from idolatry and oppression, and there will be no temptation to compromise with either (see further *idem* 1041–43).

Theology

The concept of the new creation, which dominates Rev. 21.1 and the remainder of the Apocalypse, is figurative and spiritual, not literal and physical. But if we are to understand the real significance of John's theology in this part of the drama, and its contemporary relevance, it is crucial to probe the exact *nature* of that transcendent order, for which creation itself and human history have been prepared. Given that the 'first heaven and the first earth' have disappeared, this seems to involve not simply a universe freed from sin and renewed for rejoicing, as in Isaiah 65 and 66, but rather a completely spiritual and newly formed dimension. The thought and language of the seer, at one level, evidently suggest that the '*new* heaven and earth' *replace* a creation which has ceased to exist (so Beasley-Murray 305–307, esp. 307).

However, Johannine theology consistently associates heaven with earth, and the reverse (see above). The vision in Rev. 21—22 is of a new order which is God himself, dwelling in close relationship with his people (21.3; 22.3–4). The holy city of liberation, the new Jerusalem, replaces the 'great' city of oppression, the fallen Babylon (cf. Fiorenza 92–114). But the connection between earth and heaven remains, and God is at work in both. The new Jerusalem, like its angel, *descends* from heaven; and the eternal temple, which is God and the Lamb (21.22), can be described and even measured (21.10–22).

A close and germane analogy is to be found in the nature of the resurrection body of Christians, since this involves radical renewal, a movement from physical death to spiritual life, without the loss of individual identity (cf. Sweet 297). Resurrection does not mean that believers are disembodied and 'unclothed', but that they become 'further clothed' (2 Cor. 5.1–5, esp. 2–4; 1 Cor. 15.51–54; cf. Rom. 8.18–23). Similarly, in John's language, there is a continuity between the existence of the universe in time and in eternity; and, while heaven and earth disappear in spatial terms, they themselves are transfigured and differently expressed in an entirely new dimension. Yet the divinely given moral and even material values of God's creation, including such abiding qualities as order, beauty, goodness and harmony, are preserved and developed. In it all, the 'new heaven *and new earth*' continues to resonate with the spiritual worship of the saints, and with the joy of God's salvific light (22.3–5). See further, on the relationship between the physical and the spiritual in the resurrection body, Moffatt, *First Epistle to the Corinthians* 260–67; Barrett, *First Epistle to the Corinthians* 380–82; Martin, *2 Corinthians* 105–108; also the extensive discussion in Cullmann, *Christ and Time* 231–42, esp. 241.

Beale (1041) is right to claim that the vision in 21.1 is not a description of the Church prior to the end, since the conditions portrayed in the closing section of Revelation emphasize the absence of all threats, visible and invisible, to the entire redeemed community (see 21.4, 8, 27; 22.3, 5). Rather, John presents in this interval and the following scene not an inaugurated reality of Christian redemption on earth, but the realized hope of an exalted Church; the members of this body share God's life in heaven, while awaiting the final consummation. The eschatology of this passage is dramatically poised between the present and the future, just as its cosmology reveals a characteristic tension between the material and the spiritual.

SCENE 7
Seven Prophecies
(21.2—22.17)

Translation

21 ²And I saw the holy city, the new Jerusalem, descending from God's heaven,ᵃ made ready like a bride finely dressed for her husband. ³And I heard a loud voice, proclaiming from the throne:ᵇ

> 'See, God's dwelling place is with human beings.
> He will make his home among them, and they will be his peoples;ᶜ
> God himself will be with them, as their own God,ᵈ
> ⁴and heᵉ will wipe away every tear from their eyes.
> There will be an end to death,
> and grief and crying and pain will be no more;
> for the old orderᶠ has disappeared!'ᵍ

⁵And the one seated on the throne said, 'See, I am making all creation new!' He also says,ʰ 'Write, for these words are trustworthy and true.' ⁶And he said to me, 'It is complete!ⁱ I amʲ the Alpha and the Omega, the beginning and the end. I will give without cost, to anyone who is thirsty, a drink from the spring of living water. ⁷This is the heritage of those who triumph; for I will be their God, and they will be my children. ⁸But the place for the cowardly and faithless, the detestable and murderers, the immoral, sorcerers, idolaters and liars of every other kind, will be in the lake of burning fire and brimstone, which is the second death.'

⁹And one of the seven angels, who held the seven offering bowls fullᵏ of the seven final plagues, came to speak with me, saying, 'Come, I will make known to you the bride, the wife of the Lamb.'ˡ ¹⁰So, in the spirit, he carried me away to a huge and lofty mountain, and revealed in my presence Jerusalem, the holy city, descending from God's heavenᵐ ¹¹and shining with his glory. Its splendour is like some priceless jewel, similar to a stone of crystalline jasper. ¹²The city is surrounded by a thick, high wall with twelve gates. Twelve angels stand at the gates, on which are inscribed the namesⁿ of the twelve tribes of the children of Israel. ¹³There are three gates to the east, and three to the north, three gates to the south and three to the west.ᵒ ¹⁴The city wall rests on twelve foundation stones, each of which carries the name of one of the Lamb's twelve apostles.

¹⁵And the angel talking to me was carrying a gold measuring rod, with which to describe the city, its gates and its wall. ¹⁶The city lies foursquare, long as it is wide. He measured the city with his rod, and it is twelve thousand stadia; its length, width and height are identical. ¹⁷He also describedᵖ the city wall which, by the human gauge used by the angel, is one hundred and forty-four cubits. ¹⁸The wall is constructed out of jasper, while the city itself is built of pure gold, like transparent glass. ¹⁹The foundations of the city wall have been faced with every type of precious stone. The first base is jasper, the second sapphire, the third chalcedony, the fourth emerald, ²⁰the fifth onyx, the sixth carnelian, the seventh chrysolite, the eighth beryl, the ninth topaz, the tenth chrysoprase, the eleventh jacinth and the twelfth amethyst. ²¹The twelve gates are twelve pearls, with each individual gate made of a single pearl; and the great street of the city is pure gold, like translucent crystal.

²²And I did not see a temple in the city,

> for the Lord God Almighty and the Lamb are themselves its temple.

²³The city has no need of the sun or the moon to shine on it;

> for the glory of God illumines it, and the Lamb is a flaming torch for it.

²⁴The nations will walk by its light,

> and earthly kings will bring their splendour[q] into it.

²⁵The city gates will never be closed by day,

> given that there will be no night time there.

²⁶The glory and the honour of the people will be brought into it;

²⁷however, nothing unclean will enter the city –

> no one,[r] that is, whose behaviour is foul or false –

> but only those whose names are written in the Lamb's book of life.

22 ¹And the angel showed me a river of living water, sparkling like crystal, flowing from the throne of God and of the Lamb ²through the centre of the city's great street. On both banks[s] of the river stand trees of life, each tree producing[t] twelve types of fruit, and yielding[u] its crop month by month; moreover, the leaves of the trees[v] are intended for the healing of the nations. ³The curse of destruction will cease to exist; and the throne of God and of the Lamb will be there, with his servants worshipping him. ⁴They will see his face, and his name will be on their foreheads. ⁵Night time will be no more.[w] So they will need neither lamplight nor sunlight; for the Lord God will shine on them, and they will reign for ever and ever.

⁶Then the angel said to me, 'These words are trustworthy and true; and the[x] Lord, the God of the spirits of the prophets, has sent his angel to reveal to his servants what must soon take place. ⁷See, I am coming soon! Happy is the one who obeys the message of this prophetic document.' ⁸And I, John, am the one hearing and seeing[y] these visions. And when I heard and saw them, I prostrated myself in worship at the feet of the angel revealing them to me. ⁹But he said to me, 'See that you do not! I am a servant-companion with you and your colleagues the prophets, and with those who obey the commands in this book. Worship God alone!'

¹⁰And he continues to say to me, 'Do not secrete the words of this prophetic document, since the time[z] is at hand. ¹¹Meanwhile, let the person who is unjust continue to act unjustly, and the one who is morally defiled, be defiled[aa] more and more; and may the righteous persevere in right behaviour, and the holy still be holy.'

¹²'Look, I am coming soon, and bringing my recompense with me, to repay all people according to their[bb] deeds. ¹³I am the Alpha and the Omega, the first and the last, the beginning and the end'.[cc] ¹⁴Those are blessed who wash their robes clean,[dd] so that they will have access to the tree of life, and may enter the city by its gates. ¹⁵Outside are the unclean and the sorcerers, the fornicators and murderers and idolaters, and everyone who loves and practises falsehood.

¹⁶'I, Jesus, have sent my angel to you with this testimony for the benefit of the churches. I am David's descendant, and from his family, the bright star of dawn.'

¹⁷The Spirit and the bride say, 'Come!'
Let everyone who hears say, 'Come!'
And let everyone who is thirsty, come.
Let anyone who wishes, receive the water of life freely.

Text

^a The phrase, ἐκ τοῦ οὐρανοῦ ἀπὸ τοῦ θεοῦ (*ek tou ouranou apo tou theou*, 'from God's heaven', lit. 'out of heaven from God'), is read by A ℵ 046 1006[1841] 1611 Oecumenius[2053] syr[ph] cop eth, et al. It appears in this form in the textually secure readings at 3.12; 21.10 (cf. 20.9, v.l.), and is doubtless original. In secondary variants, the word order is changed to ἀπὸ τοῦ θεοῦ ἐκ τοῦ οὐρανοῦ (*apo tou theou ek tou ouranou*, 'from God out of heaven', as in 051 Andreas), and ἀπὸ τοῦ θεοῦ (*apo tou theou*, 'from God') is omitted (lat arm[1]).

b In place of the genitive, θρόνου (*thronou*, 'throne'), attested by A ℵ 94 vg Ambrose, et al., some witnesses (including 025 046 051 Oecumenius[2053] Byz it[gig] syr[ph] Beatus) read οὐρανοῦ (*ouranou*, 'heaven'). The context supports the idea of a voice speaking 'from the throne' (see verse 5), while the variation may be explained as a mechanical repetition of the language of descent 'from heaven' in verse 2 (Aune 1110).

c The plural form of the noun, λαοί (*laoi*, lit. 'peoples', as in NRSV and the translation), is well attested (ℵ A 046 2030 1611[2050 2329] it[a] Oecumenius[2053] Andreas, et al.). Some MSS, such as 025 1006[1841] 1611[1854] Byz lat syr, read the singular, λαός (*laos*, 'people', as in ESV). The variant reflects the Old Testament covenantal formula, 'I will be their God, and they shall be my *people*' (Jer. 31.33; Ezek. 37.27; Zech. 8.8, et al.); the plural version is consequently the *lectio difficilior*, and likely to be original.

d It is difficult to establish the original text in the concluding statement of verse 3 (see Metzger, *Textual Commentary* 763–64). There are several MS versions, of which the most strongly supported is, μετ᾽αὐτῶν ἔσται αὐτῶν (ὁ) θεός (*met᾽ autōn estai autōn [ho] theos*, 'he [God] will be with them, as their own God', lit. 'he will be with them as the God of them'), as read by A 2030 1611[2050 2329] 1778[mg] it[c] vg syr[ph,h] eth Oecumenius[2062] Irenaeus MSS of Andreas, et al. Nevertheless, the unemphatic position of the pronoun αὐτῶν (*autōn*, 'their'), preceding θεός (*theos*, 'God'), is uncharacteristic of the author's style (except at 18.5). In 025 051 1006[1854] arm, et al., the order of αὐτῶν θεός (*autōn theos*, 'their God') is reversed; and, despite the poor attestation of the version, this fits the style of the Apocalypse, where the word θεός (*theos*, 'God') is invariably followed by the genitive (cf. 3.12; 4.11; 7.3; 19.1; et al.). However, some major witnesses (including ℵ 1778 2081 94 cop[bo] eth Augustine) omit the words αὐτῶν θεός (*autōn theos*, 'their God') altogether; and the question then arises as to whether this expression was removed as being superfluous in the context, or added as a gloss derived from Isa. 7.14; 8.8 LXX. On balance, it is probably best to follow the reading in A; although the uncertainty involved in this procedure is marked by the fact that NA encloses the words αὐτῶν θεός (*autōn theos*, 'their God') in brackets. There seems to be no justification for the translation in NRSV, which moves the phrase, 'as their (own) God', from the end of verse 3 to the conclusion of the second statement in the speech from the throne (RSV relegates the words to the margin).

e Weighty external evidence, led by ℵ 025 051 1611, supports the use of the verb, ἐξαλείψει (*exaleipsei*, 'he will wipe away'), without a specified subject; and this does not need to be articulated at the beginning of verse 4, especially after the repeated use of θεός (*theos*, 'God') in verse 3. Nonetheless, some witnesses (including A 1006[1841] Tertullian Beatus Apringius vg) add ὁ θεός (*ho theos*, 'God') as the introduction to the sentence; and this secondary version may be an assimilation from (Isa. 25.8) Rev. 7.17.

f Τὰ πρῶτα (*ta prōta*, 'the old order', lit. 'the first things'), by itself, has strong support from A 025 051 1006[1841] 1611[2329] Oecumenius[2053] 2030 Andreas, et al.; cf. Charles 2, 376. This could suggest that the reading is original, and that copyists tried to avoid asyndeton (the omission of conjunctions) by inserting ὅτι (*hoti*, 'for', as in 046 Byz MSS of Andreas, et al.) or γάρ (*gar*, 'for', as in MS of Andreas 94[text]). Equally, the shorter version may have arisen through a transcriptional error, when scribes overlooked ὅτι (*hoti*, 'for') in view of the preceding ἔτι (*eti*, lit. 'yet'). Cf. the absurdity in ℵ*, when copyists produced πρόβατα (*probata*, 'sheep') instead of πρῶτα (*prōta*, 'former things'). Once more, NA voices doubt by enclosing ὅτι (*hoti*, 'for') in brackets.

g Instead of ἀπῆλθαν (*apēlthan*, 'disappeared', 'passed away'), as read by A, other witnesses have secondary variations with the same meaning: ἀπῆλθεν (*apēlthen*, as in ℵ 046 Byz, et al.); ἀπῆλθον (*apēlthon*, 025); and παρῆλθον (*parēlthon*, 1611). The first two variants represent no more than changes in vocalization; see the textual note on the same verb at 21.1.

[h] Although there is good external evidence (A 046 94 Byz) for omitting μοι (*moi*, 'to me'), after λέγει (*legei*, 'he says'), there is some strong support (ℵ 025 051 1006 1611[2050] Andreas it[a] vg syr[ph] cop[sa,bo] arm eth TR) for its inclusion. But the pronoun is more likely to have been added than rejected, and the shorter reading must be regarded as preferable.

[i] The form γέγοναν (*gegonan*, 'It is complete!' or 'It is finished!', lit. 'It has happened!') is unusual, since it is the third person plural perfect tense from the verb γίνεσθαι (*ginesthai*, lit. 'to happen'), with a rare second aorist ending. This reading, supported by A ℵ[1] 1678 1778 Irenaeus[lat] Primasius, et al., is doubtless original, since the uncommon ending of the verb evidently produced a number of subsequent variants in the perfect, with the same meaning: γεγόνασιν (*gegonasin*, as in 254 1006 Oecumenius[2053 2062] it[gig] syr[ph] cop[bo] Tyconius, et al.; cf. the similar correction at Rom. 16:7); γέγονε (*gegone*, 94 vg Primasius; cf. Rev. 16:17); and γέγονα (*gegona*, ℵ* 025 046 051 cop[sa] syr[h] arm Andreas Arethas Beatus). Byz omits the word altogether. Cf. further BDAG 196*b*; see also the next note.

[j] Most of the witnesses having the form γέγονα (*gegona*, 'It has happened!') in the preceding group of variants (see the previous note) lack either εἰμι (*eimi*, 'I am', so ℵ 025 046, et al.; cf. Swete 279), or the intensive form, with the same meaning, ἐγώ εἰμι (*egō eimi*, as in most minuscules). Metzger, *Textual Commentary* 765, voices the difficulty in establishing whether the word εἰμι (*eimi*, 'I am') should be retained (as in Rev. 1.8), or omitted (as at 22.13); accordingly NA encloses the word within brackets.

[k] Instead of τῶν γεμόντων (*tōn gemontōn*, 'full', genitive), as read by ℵ[1] A Andreas, et al., some MSS (including 046 1006 1611 2030 2377) have the accusative form with the same meaning, τὰς γεμούσας (*tas gemousas*). The accusative is linguistically correct, in view of the antecedent φιάλας (*phialas*, 'bowls'), but it is not strongly attested. The genitive receives somewhat firmer support and, since the resulting solecism becomes a *lectio difficilior*, it is likely to be original.

[l] The order, τὴν νύμφην τὴν γυναῖκα τοῦ ἀρνίου (*tēn nymphēn tēn gynaika tou arniou*, 'the bride, the wife of the Lamb'), is supported by ℵ A 025 1006 1611 2030 2377, et al. This seems to be the original and most logical version of the phrase, which is later corrected by 051 Andreas to 'the bride of the Lamb, the wife', and by 94 Byz to 'the wife, the bride of the Lamb'; see the corrections made independently in the Andreas and Byzantine traditions at 3.2; 5.6; 9.14; et al. Cf. Aune 1137.

[m] The form of the phrase in A ℵ Andreas is ἐκ τοῦ οὐρανοῦ ἀπὸ τοῦ θεοῦ (*ek tou ouranou apo tou theou*, 'from God's heaven', lit. 'from heaven from God'), and in view of the parallels at 3.12; 20.9; 21.2 (q.v.) this is likely to be the original reading. Variants, with the same meaning, occur in Oecumenius[2053 2062] (ἀπὸ τοῦ οὐρανοῦ ἐκ τοῦ θεοῦ, *apo tou ouranou ek tou theou*) and Byz (ἐκ τοῦ οὐρανοῦ ἐκ τοῦ θεοῦ, *ek tou ouranou ek tou theou*).

[n] The expression, τὰ ὀνόματα (*ta onomata*, 'the names'), appears in A 1611[2329] 1006[1841] 2030 2377 Oecumenius[2053] it[gig] Primasius Beatus, et al. (cf. Charles 2, 364). Byz drops the article, one MS of Andreas has the article and noun in the singular, and both words are omitted by ℵ 051, et al. There is relatively strong support for the reading, τὰ ὀνόματα (*ta onomata*, 'the names'), which is probably original. The phrase may seem superfluous after the use of the anarthrous ὀνόματα (*onomata*, 'names') just beforehand, and it is easily hidden in the translation. But the repetition of the noun with its article is suitable in the

context, which is defining the specific nature of the 'names' in general already mentioned. NA puts the words in brackets.

° There has been some confusion in transmitting the exact number of the 'twelve gates' in this passage, resulting in a series of inauthentic readings. Thus, ℵ Oecumenius[2053] MSS of Andreas omit ἀπὸ νότου πυλῶνες τρεῖς (*apo notou pylōnes treis*, 'three gates to the south', lit. 'from the south three gates'), but add καὶ ἀπὸ μεσημβρίας πυλῶνες τρεῖς (*kai apo mesēmbrias pylōnes treis*, 'and on the south three gates'). Some MSS of Oecumenius 2037 enumerate *fifteen* gates by including this latter phrase, while omitting no other. Different MSS of Oecumenius mention only *nine* gates, by eliminating the triplet at the west (also missing from ℵ).

ᵖ There is good external support (A ℵ 025 2030, et al.) for the reading ἐμέτρησεν (*emetrēsen*, 'he described', lit. 'measured'), which is doubtless original. The -ν (-*n*) ending in verbs is irregular in its use, and therefore problematic in the textual criticism of the New Testament (see BDF 20). One clearly secondary result of this is the variation, ἐμέτρησε (*emetrēse*, 'measured'), in 1006 1611[1611 2344] Andreas Oecumenius[2053 2062]. A further variant in 1611[2050 2329] is ἐμέτρισεν (*emetrisen*, 'measured'), which involves the simple interchange of η(*ē*) = ι(*i*), and supports the form of the *lectio originalis* (Aune 1138). The verb is awkwardly omitted altogether by 1611[1854] Byz, et al.

ᑫ In place of τὴν δόξαν αὐτῶν (*tēn doxan autōn*, 'their splendour', lit. 'glory'), which is the original reading supported by A ℵ 025 051 1006[1006 1841] 1611[2329] Andreas, some witnesses (such as Oecumenius[2053] 1611[1854 2050]) have τὴν δόξαν καὶ τὴν τιμὴν αὐτῶν (*tēn doxan kai tēn timēn autōn*, 'their splendour and wealth', lit. 'glory and honour'). Others (including 1773 Byz) have αὐτῷ δόξαν καὶ τιμὴν τῶν ἐθνῶν (*autō[i] doxan kai timēn tōn ethnōn*, lit. 'to it the glory and honour of the nations'), or αὐτῇ δόξαν καὶ τιμὴν αὐτῶν (*autē[i] doxan kai timēn autōn*, lit. 'to her their glory and honour'), as in MS of Andreas. These three variants have obviously been shaped by the doublet, 'the glory and the honour of the people', in verse 26.

ʳ A 1006 1611[2050 2329] 2030 2377, et al. omit ὁ (*ho*, lit. 'the') before ποιῶν (*poiōn*, lit. 'doing'). It is present in ℵ⋆ 1611[1854] Byz, et al. The presence of the article is typical of the author's style in the Apocalypse (Aune 1139); but equally it may have been added to ease the difficult construction in verse 27 (q.v.). In either case, the basic sense is clear.

ˢ While A 046 Oecumenius[2053] 1611[1854 2329], et al. read ἐντεῦθεν καὶ ἐκεῖθεν (*enteuthen kai ekeithen*, 'on both banks [of the river]', lit. 'from here and from there'), there is good support (from 051 2030 1611[2050] 2377 syr[ph] Andreas TR) for the version, ἐντεῦθεν καὶ ἐντεῦθεν (*enteuthen kai enteuthen*, lit. 'from here and from here', i.e. 'on each side'). ℵ has ἔνθεν (*enthen*, 'from there', 'from here'). Given the spread of fairly weighty evidence, it is not easy to establish the original reading. The idiom, ἐντεῦθεν καὶ ἐντεῦθεν (*enteuthen kai enteuthen*, 'on one side and on the other'), is found at LXX Dan. 12.5 Theod.; John 19.18; but ἔνθεν καὶ ἔνθεν (*enthen kai enthen*, 'on one side and on the other') is the more common expression (cf. Ezek. 47.12 LXX). It is probably best to adopt the text of A, but in any case the clear meaning is not greatly affected.

ᵗ The *lectio originalis* is ποιοῦν (*poioun*, 'producing', lit. 'making', neuter present participle, following the neuter noun ξύλον [*xylon*, 'tree']), as read by ℵ 046 051. In its place, with the same meaning, A 94 Byz have ποιῶν (*poiōn*, masculine present participle). A uses the masculine ποιῶν (*poiōn*, 'producing') with the following neuter participle, ἀποδιδοῦν (*apodidoun*, 'yielding', lit. 'giving'); so the variant meaning may be the result of merging -ου (*ou*) with -ω (*ō*) in some participles (Aune 1139). See also the next note.

^u The neuter singular present participle ἀποδιδοῦν (*apodidoun*, 'yielding', lit. 'giving'), qualifying the neuter noun ξύλον (*xylon*, 'tree'), appears in A Oecumenius^{2053 2062} MSS of Andreas. This is evidently the original reading, since it is based on the putative verb-form ἀποδιδόω (*apodidoō*, 'give'), rather than on the more usual verb ἀποδίδωμι (*apodidōmi*, 'give'). This form is used by ℵ Byz 94 in the variant, ἀποδιδούς (*apodidous*, 'giving', masculine singular present participle). Unlike the secondary variation, the original reading is also in the correct gender.

^v Most witnesses have the singular form of the article and noun, τοῦ ξύλου (*tou xylou*, 'of the tree'). In ℵ arm¹ this reading is in the plural, τῶν ξυλῶν (*tōn xylōn*, 'of the trees'), which is a scribal correction based on understanding the earlier noun phrase, ξύλον ζωῆς (*xylon zōēs*, lit. 'tree of life'), as a collective plural meaning 'trees of life'; cf. the translation. The plural form fits the sense of the passage.

^w The *lectio originalis* (attested by ℵ A 025, et al.) is ἔτι (*eti*, lit. 'yet', 'still'). Subsequently this becomes ἐκεῖ (*ekei*, 'there', as in 051 syr^{h,ph} cop Andreas, et al.), or the conflate, ἐκεῖ ἔτι (*ekei eti*, 'there still', as in MS of Andreas Irenaeus^{gk}). A few witnesses (including 046 1611^{1611 1854} Byz) omit ἔτι (*eti*, 'still') altogether.

^x There is strong support (in A ℵ 1006¹⁸⁴¹ 1611^{1611 2329} Oecumenius^{2053 2062} 2377 it^{gig} Primasius) for the reading, ὁ κύριος (*ho kyrios*, 'the Lord'). Assimilation to texts such as 1.8; 4.8; 15.3; 16.7; 17.14; 19.16, and especially to the phrase, κύριος ὁ θεός (*kyrios ho theos*, 'the Lord God'), in the immediately preceding verse (22.5), has caused a secondary variant in 051 Andreas Byz, where the article before 'Lord' in verse 6 is omitted.

^y The order, ἀκούων καὶ βλέπων (*akouōn kai blepōn*, 'hearing and seeing'), is present in A 046, et al., and is probably original. It is reversed by ℵ 1006^{1006 1841} 1611²³²⁹ Andreas syr^{ph} cop^{bo} Primasius, et al. The variant may be the result of scribal conviction that John was primarily one who received visions ('seeing'), and only afterwards a listener ('hearing'); so Aune 1141. But these two functions are in any case closely related, and both are important (see on verse 8). The secondary value of the variant is better established by noting that the same two verbs, which follow immediately, are written in the undoubted order, 'heard and saw'.

^z In A ℵ 046 it^{gig} vg arm cop^{bo,sa} the order of this phrase is, ὁ καιρὸς γάρ (*ho kairos gar*, 'since the time', lit. 'the time for'). Three secondary variants seek to correct the unusual position of the conjunction γάρ (*gar*, 'for'), which here occurs as the third word of the sentence. These are ὅτι ὁ καιρός (*hoti ho kairos*, lit. 'because the time'), as in 2377 Andreas Cyprian Tyconius Primasius; ὁ καιρός (*ho kairos*, 'the time', with no particle), as read by 598; and καιρὸς γάρ (*kairos gar*, lit. 'time for', with no article), according to Apringius Beatus, et al. A further variation, ὁ γὰρ καιρός (*ho gar kairos*, 'for the time', with the conjunction in the usual second place), attested by 94 MS of Andreas, is a clear assimilation to the text of Rev. 1.3 (q.v.).

^{aa} The form of the verb which appears in 046 1006^{1006 1841} 1611²³²⁹ Oecumenius²⁰⁵³ Andreas Byz, et al., is ῥυπαρευθήτω (*rhypareuthētō*, lit. 'let that one be defiled'). There are four variants, with the same meaning: ῥυπανθήτω (*rhypanthētō*), attested by ℵ 1611¹⁸⁵⁴ 94 792 Byz MS of Andreas Origen, et al.; ῥυπαρωθήτω (*rhyparōthētō*), as in MSS of Andreas; ῥυπωθήτω (*rhypōthētō*), to which 1773 bears witness; and ῥυπαρυνθήτω (*rhyparynthētō*), read by MS of Andreas. The verb ῥυπαρεύειν (*rhypareuein*, 'to defile') is a *hapax legomenon* in Greek literature as a whole, and its form was possibly coined here by the author of Revelation on the basis of the preceding adjective, ῥυπαρός (*rhyparos*, 'defiled', 'depraved'); so Aune 1197. The more common form of the verb, 'to defile', is ῥυπαίνειν (*rhypainein*; the passive is ῥυπαίνεσθαι, *rhypainesthai*). Two conclusions follow:

(a) The *lectio difficilior* is the very first reading given above, ῥυπαρευθήτω (*rhypareuthētō*, 'be defiled'), because of the extremely rare character of the verb-form just noted. Its uniqueness points clearly to its originality in the present context (Aune 1197); and all the variants can then be identified as secondary attempts by copyists to modify an otherwise unknown form.

(b) As Aune (1197) rightly points out, it is therefore surprising that modern texts tend to follow the version which uses the form derived from ῥυπαίνειν (*rhypainein*, 'defile'), the first variation noted above. So Swete 306; Charles 2, 383; also NA. This reading demonstrates its secondary nature by moving towards the more usual form of the verb; and the support which it receives from external evidence is, in any case, relatively weak.

bb A ℵ give good support to the reading, ἐστὶν αὐτοῦ (*estin autou*, lit. '[as] is his [work]'), which is probably original. Some MSS (046 1006 1611[1854] Oecumenius[2053 2062] Byz) read ἔσται αὐτοῦ (*estai autou*, lit. 'will be his'), and others (1611 Andreas) the reverse ('his will be'), which are secondary attempts to correct the original. The version in 1611[2050], ἐστὶν αὐτῷ (*estin autō[i]*, 'is to him'), is presumably a scribal error, influenced by the preceding dative, ἑκάστῳ (*hekastō[i]*, lit. 'to each').

cc Rev. 22.10 is the only text in the Apocalypse which includes all three titular expressions, 'I am Alpha and Omega, the first and the last, the beginning and the end' (see also 1.8; 21.6). Here, ℵ 046 syr Cyprian Origen Primasius Athanasius support the following form and order of the second and third pair: ὁ πρῶτος καὴ ὁ ἔσχατος, ἡ ἀρχὴ καὶ τὸ τέλος (*ho prōtos kai ho eschatos, hē archē kai to telos*, 'the first and the last, the beginning and the end'); and this reading is probably original. There is some external evidence for minor variations, mostly the omission of the articles; but it is weak. The most significant variant, attested by 2377 arm Andreas Origen Ambrose, reverses the order and reads, ἀρχὴ καὶ τέλος ὁ πρῶτος καὶ ὁ ἔσχατος (*archē kai telos, ho prōtos kai ho eschatos*); but this may well be an attempted assimilation to 21.6.

dd Instead of πλύνοντες τὰς στολὰς αὐτῶν (*plynontes tas stolas autōn*, 'who wash their robes clean', lit. 'washing their robes'), as supported by ℵ A 1006 Oecumenius 2053 2062 MS of Andreas it[61] vg cop[sa], et al., other witnesses (including 046 1611 it[gig] syr[ph,h] cop[bo] Andreas Byz Tertullian TR, et al.) have the similar sounding version, ποιοῦντες τὰς ἐντολὰς αὐτοῦ (*poiountes tas entolas autou*, lit. 'doing his commandments'). The variant appears to be a scribal emendation (Metzger, *Textual Commentary* 765), since elsewhere in Revelation (12.17; 14.12; cf. John 14.15, 21; 15.10; also 1 John 2.3–4; 3.22, 24; 5.3) the author uses the expression, τηρεῖν τὰς ἐντολὰς αὐτοῦ (*tērein tas entolas autou*, '*keeping* his commands'); also, scribes would have been more interested in obeying God's commands than in washing their own robes (cf. Swete 307). However, as Aune (1198) points out, the language of 'doing' (using ποιεῖν, *poiein*, 'to do') the commands of God *does* occur at 1 John 5.2. On balance, the documentary evidence favours the reading, πλύνοντες τὰς στολὰς αὐτῶν (*plynontes tas stolas autōn*, lit. 'washing their robes'; note the similar imagery at Rev. 7.14), and this is the text followed in the translation. On the other side see Goranson, 'Text of Revelation 22.14'.

Literary Setting

The seventh and final scene of the drama of the Apocalypse may be divided into seven text units (for variations in this literary analysis see below). These are 21.2–4; 21.5–8; 21.9–21; 21.22–27; 22.1–5; 22.6–9; 22.10–17. Each of these subdivisions contains a prophetic vision of seven aspects of existence in the new creation of God: new covenant, new life, new Jerusalem, new temple, new relationship, new advent and new testimony. The start of a new proclamation within this scene as a whole is marked by the use of καί (*kai*, 'and'), together with an apocalyptic formula of either vision or speech (usually 'I saw' or 'he said') which is typical of the literary style of the author of Revelation (cf. 21.2; 21.5; 21.9; 21.22; 22.1; 22.6; 22.10; see also on 4.1; 5.1–2; 17.1; et al.). The verse at 22.1 is included, because καὶ ἔδειξέν μοι (*kai edeixen moi*, lit. 'and he showed me') implies a visual disclosure.

The start of Scene 7 (21.2—22.17), in the structural analysis adopted by this commentary, is located at 21.2 rather than at 21.1; see on 21.1. A vision is announced during the interval at 21.1, but its content is not narrated. The seer now receives a series of seven fresh visions, making up one section, which develop and enhance the earlier disclosure of God's new creation (21.1); note the use of καὶ εἶδον (*kai eidon*, 'and I saw') in both 21.1 and 21.2.

Commentators have divided the material which makes up the present scene in a variety of ways, which usually assume that 21.9—22.9 may be regarded as a unity. For example, Bauckham (*Climax of Prophecy* 338–39) sets this passage within the broad structure of the last seven chapters of Revelation (16.1—22.9), and notes the clear parallelism between 17.1—19.10 and 21.9—22.9, describing the contrasting cities of Babylon and Jerusalem. Similarly, Aune (1113) regards 21.1–8 as a final subsection within the unit 19.11—21.8, which is framed by two parallel angelic revelations, containing many verbal equivalents, at 17.1—19.10 and 21.9—22.9 (*idem*, 1144–45); see also Roloff (239–42), who assumes the unity of 21.9—22.5. Prigent (583–88, esp. 583) supports the composite nature of 21.1—22.5, at the least, by pointing out that this section presents the audience of the Apocalypse with three different views of the end (21.1–8; 21.9–27; 22.1–5). Even if 21.1–8 is taken as a discrete section of John's composition, it is nevertheless possible to argue for its close relationship to 21.9—22.5 (9) which, in the view of Beale (1039), both recapitulates 21.1–8 and is anticipated by those verses; cf. also Beasley-Murray 314–15. For arguments against the literary unity of 21.9—22.5 see Wilcox, 'Tradition and Redaction', esp. 206–11.

Revelation 21.2–8

This section consists of two units of text, setting out the first and second prophecies (new covenant and new life). The first sub-unit (verses 2–4) begins with a vision (verse 2), and goes on to report the speech of the interpreting *angel* from the throne (verses 3–4, audition). This oracle divides into seven poetic strophes, which explain the covenantal dimension to life in the new Jerusalem:

> See, God's dwelling place is with human beings,
> he will make his home among them, and they will be his people,
> God will be with them as their God,
> he will wipe away every tear from their eyes,
> there will be an end to death,
> grief and crying and pain will be no more,
> the old order has disappeared!

The second sub-unit (21.5–8) starts with a transitional verse (5), which looks back to verses 2–4, and forward to verses 6–8. Verses 5–8 together record the speech of *God* from his throne (audition); and this proclamation, which further describes the character of life in the heavenly city, in its negative as well as positive aspects, also divides into seven strophic sayings:

God says, I am making all creation new,
these words are trustworthy and true,
it is complete,
I am Alpha and Omega,
I will give living water to the thirsty,
this is the heritage of those who conquer, for I will be their God,
the place for the lying unfaithful will be in the lake of fire.

Revelation 22.6–9

This textual sub-unit, containing the sixth prophecy (the new advent), is transitional. It concludes the section 21.2—22.5, and introduces the prophetic testimony at 22.10–17. There are close verbal parallels between 22.6–9 and 1.1–3 (see further below). Longenecker, ' "Linked like a Chain" ', esp. 110–13, finds careful structuring in these verses, involving ancient transition technique.

Revelation 22.10–17

The view adopted in this commentary is that these verses contain the concluding prophecy of seven which belong to the passage 21.2—22.17. But the literary character of this section, certainly in relation to the preceding material belonging to this scene (21.2—22.9), is by no means coherent. Verses 10–17 include a series of varied statements, which seem to emanate from the interpreting angel, the Godhead and the seer. Because of this, and of the fact that the identity of the speakers is not always clear, the composition of this sub-unit has been analysed in different ways, and rearrangements of the text have been proposed. Cf. Charles 2, 211–13; Aune 1204–205. However, it is possible to argue for the unity of the concluding section of the Apocalypse, particularly when a liturgical influence on the text is perceived; see Vanni, *La struttura letteraria* 107–15, esp. 109–12. For the literary form and structure of 22.10–17, as antiphonal chant, see further below.

Most commentators regard 22.10–20 (or 22.10–21 or 22.6–21) as a distinct textual unit, which forms the concluding part of Revelation. This section is then described in differing ways. See Swete 302 (Epilogue); Beckwith 290–91, 771–72 (Epilogue); Vanni, *La struttura letteraria* 302 (Concluding Liturgical Dialogue); Caird 281–82 (Epilogue); Roloff 248–49 (Conclusion); Smalley, *Thunder and Love* 110, and this commentary (Epilogue, consisting of 22.18–21); Aune 1200–201 (Epilogue); Mounce 402–11 (Epilogue); Beale 1122 (Epilogue; but the term 'Conclusion' is used in the Outline on xvi); Prigent 630–53 (Epilogue). Once more, there are clear verbal parallels between the material in 22.6–17 and 1.1–3 (see below).

Two literary features are noticeable in the final scene, 21.2—22.17. First, as befits a heavenly setting, the style often becomes poetic, even if this is not always apparent; in the translation, see 21.3–4, 22–27; 22.17. Second, notably in Chapter 22, John uses the present tense to heighten the sense of dramatic immediacy (similarly 14.6–14); cf. 22.5, 7, 9–13. When verbs are missing, as in 22.2, the present tense is implied.

Comment

Prophecy 1: New Covenant (21.2–4)

21.2   The seer receives the first of a series of visions, which are in effect prophecies about the nature of the spiritual life of the saints in eternity. The content of 'prophecy', in the present context, has more to do with proclamation than prediction, since John is handing on in this scene various abiding aspects of the 'new heaven and earth', about which he spoke in 21.1. He begins with the basis of Christian faith: the covenant relationship between God and his people, in Christ and by the Spirit, which is perpetually possible for all believers.

The constant use in Chapters 21 and 22 of the conjunction καί (*kai*, 'and'), notably at the start of sub-sections (see above), is typical of John's apocalyptic language. The word is translated 'and' throughout, instead of 'then', as a reminder that the seer's visions in Revelation are sequential, but not in any chronological order conditioned by time. They are received on earth, but ultimately belong to the realm of eternity; for what is 'seen' descends precisely 'from heaven' (see also on 20.1; 21.1). Boring (215) claims that John's portrayal of the new Jerusalem is not 'what he actually saw', but a symbolic, literary composition which is intended to explain his understanding of the nature of God's purposes for this world. Nevertheless, while this visionary record is undoubtedly theological (see below), there is no necessary reason to deny that it is based on a historical and personal revelation (see above, 20, and on 1.9–11). See Mounce 381 n. 6.

For the introductory apocalyptic formula in verse 2, καὶ . . . εἶδον (*kai . . . eidon*, 'and . . . I saw'), see on 21.1. This is the only place in the Apocalypse where the author inserts the object of a vision, in the accusative, between καί (*kai*, 'and') and εἶδον (*eidon*, 'I saw'); cf. 19.11, 17, 19; 20.1; 21.1; et al. The phrase, '(I saw) the holy city (new) Jerusalem, descending from God's heaven' (τὴν πόλιν τὴν ἁγίαν Ἰερουσαλὴμ [καινὴν] εἶδον καταβαίνουσαν ἐκ τοῦ οὐρανοῦ ἀπὸ τοῦ θεοῦ, *tēn polin tēn hagian Ierousalēm kainēn eidon katabainousan ek tou ouranou apo tou theou*), appears again in almost identical form at 21.10, where (in the third prophecy) John explains the nature of the new Jerusalem more fully.

Verse 2 provides a focus to the vision of the new creation depicted in verse 1 by referring to 'the holy city, the new Jerusalem'. For the force of the adjective καινός (*kainos*, 'new'), meaning 'totally transformed', rather than 'renewed', see on verse 1. For the expression, '*holy* city', see 11.2; 21.10; 22.19; at 20.9 (q.v.) the version is 'beloved city'. Walker (*Holy City* 248–50, esp. 248–49) points out that the name 'Jerusalem', in this context, is significant. For in the climactic visions of Rev. 21—22 the seer announces that the purposes of God, who is associated closely with Israel, as with Jerusalem and its Temple, are now being fulfilled. But the Jerusalem of 21.2 is 'new', and has no connection with the earthly city, which stands under judgement (11.2). As such, the new Jerusalem is the 'true fulfilment of the various eschatological prophecies in the Old Testament which had originally been grounded in the physical Jerusalem' (Walker, *Holy City* 249). See further below. The position adopted in this commentary is that John's vision of the new Jerusalem is also and in part intended to encourage his community, the members of which were facing the imminent fall of the earthly city in September AD 70; and such a stance clearly affects the dating of Revelation (see above, 2–6).

The promise that the conqueror will be given the name of the 'new Jerusalem' has been present in Revelation since 3.12 (q.v.). The reference to Jerusalem in the present verse is one of several allusions in 21.1–5 to Isa. 65.17–20 (cf. Aune 1120–21). The background to the actual phrase, 'the holy city, (the new) Jerusalem', may be found in Isa. 52.1; see also Isa. 48.2; LXX Dan. 3.28; Joel 4.17; Tobit 13.10; *Pss. Sol.* 8.4; *T. Dan* 5.12 (using 'new Jerusalem'). For the apocalyptic idea in Rev. 21.2 that the new Jerusalem was pre-existent in heaven, in order to descend to earth in glory at the end, using 'the city' without the name 'Jerusalem', see 4 Ezra 7.26; 10.27; 13.36; *2 Apoc. Bar.* 4.2–6; 32.2–4. For the notion of a 'new Jerusalem' elsewhere in the New Testament see Gal. 4.26; Phil. 3.20; Heb. 11.10; 12.22; 13.14.

The meaning of the symbolism involved in the imagery of the 'new Jerusalem' needs to be carefully established. John is not describing the 'new Israel', the reborn people of God (cf. John 1.47; Gal. 6.16); therefore the heavenly city cannot be equated with the saints, or with a spiritually perfected Church (against Kiddle 410–11; Hughes 222–23; Michaels 235; Mounce 382). In any case, the holy city is compared to a 'finely dressed bride', which at 19.7–8 is an analogy for the saints of God; so the city and the Church in verse 2 must be distinguished. A similar distinction exists at 21.7, where believers 'inherit' the city, and at 21.23–26 (the saints 'enter' the new Jerusalem). See further Aune 1122.

It is much more likely that the figurative language of a 'new Jerusalem' should be understood in terms of a new relationship: as the intimate, covenant fellowship which God shares with his people in his new creation (cf. Beale 1045). The new Jerusalem is not the Church (so Aune 1121), but the new covenant. This new reality is especially characterized by the presence of God himself among the triumphant saints (see Fiorenza 109). Such an interpretation is supported by the fact that, in the present prophecy and the next (21.3–7), the close relationship between the life-giving Lord and his covenant people is the dominant theme, which precisely develops the concept of the 'new Jerusalem' in 21.2. See also Prigent 595.

The phraseology of 'descent from God's heaven' appears elsewhere in the Apocalypse in connection with the new Jerusalem itself (3.12; 21.10), with angelic figures (10.1; 18.1; 20.1), with fire (13.13; 20.9), and with hail (16.21). Because the new Jerusalem is part of God's qualitatively new creation, and involves a relationship between the Lord and his people, John perceives that the new heaven and earth will be merged in eternity (see on 21.1). The new Jerusalem comes down from heaven, but not to 'earth' as such. Its origin is divine, and it will be expressed in a completely new and lasting dimension (cf. verses 3, 7). See further on Theology, below.

The new Jerusalem, in verse 2, is delineated further by the use of wedding imagery. The holy city is said to be 'made ready like a bride finely dressed for her husband'. It is of interest that the noun, νύμφη (*nymphē*, 'bride'), is used of the Church in the Apocalypse only here and at 21.9; 22.17, and nowhere else in early Christian literature (Aune 1121). The same term appears in a neutral and negative sense, with νυμφίος (*nymphios*, 'bridegroom'), at 18.23. In 19.7 the word for the 'bride' of the Lamb (his saints) is γυνή (*gynē*, lit. 'woman', or 'wife'). The verb in verse 2, ἑτοιμάζω (*hetoimazō*, 'make ready', 'prepare'), also occurs at 19.7.

The merging of these two metaphors, city and bride, is natural, since in the Jewish tradition Jerusalem is often depicted as a woman (Isa. 1.8; Jer. 4.31; 4 Ezra 9.38–47; cf. also Gal. 4.22–31; Rev. 12.1). Cf. Roloff 235–36. The simile of Jerusalem being 'finely dressed' (κεκοσμημένην, *kekosmēmenēn*, lit. 'adorned') as the bride of Yahweh, and therefore in close fellowship with him, appears at Isa. 49.18; 61.10. Isa. 52.1–10 promises a time when Jerusalem the holy city, in beautiful garments, will be liberated, and God's people restored from captivity to rejoice in his presence for ever. In Isa. 62.1–5 the prophet speaks of the 'new name' by which Jerusalem is to be called (verse 2); and this is explained (verses 3–5) as meaning the new and personal marriage relationship which Israel is to have with God. The 'new name' which the Christian conquerors are to receive, according to Rev. 3.12 (q.v.), is identified as God's name (that is, his person or nature; see on 3.8), God's city, and the new Jerusalem which descends from heaven. All three names point to the intimate and loving presence of God and Christ with the saints at the end (cf. 22.4). This theme is anticipated by the passages from Isaiah 49—62 quoted above; it is also the special significance of the image of the 'new Jerusalem' itself, and the predominant theme of 21.1–3 (note also 14.1–5). See Beale 1043–44; cf. further on verses 3–4, below.

For this imagery see also Ezek. 16.8–14 (Israel as a finely adorned bride); Isa. 50.1; Hos. 4.5 (Israel as a mother); *Jos. As.* 4.1 (Aseneth adorned as a bride of God); *Pss. Sol.* 2.19–21 (Jerusalem as a woman whose beautiful adornment has been destroyed). Aune

(1121–22) further cites Hermas, *Vis.* 4.2.1 (the Church as a beautifully arrayed, virginal bride); Irenaeus, *Adv. Haer.* 1.13.3 (the bride is to be adorned as one awaiting her spouse); Pliny the Younger, *Ep.* 5.16.7 (the father of a young bride, who died before she could be married, had already set aside money for her clothes and jewels). Aune (1122) also notes that the motif of Jerusalem as a captive woman is repeated on coins minted under Vespasian after the fall of Jerusalem in AD 70.

'The bride' of 21.2 is to be equated with the saints, the inclusive Church of God and the Lamb, already in view at 19.7–8, but not with the new Jerusalem (see above). Babylon the whore (17—18) is to be replaced by the 'bride' of Christ. Believers themselves have been 'prepared' by God for the end-time (cf. 12.1–6); and just as Israel was delivered from its enemies by Yahweh, so the saints who are properly related to God in Christ by their belief and behaviour will be released from Satan's grip (20.10), and enter the heavenly city which is the ultimate dwelling-place of God with his people (cf. 7.15–17; 15.4; 19.8; 22.3–5). See further Beale 1045.

3–4 The introduction to verse 3, 'And I heard a loud voice, proclaiming from the throne' (καὶ ἤκουσα φωνῆς μεγάλης ἐκ τοῦ θρόνου, *kai ēkousa phōnēs megalēs ek tou thronou*), is an apocalyptic and interpretative formula which echoes similar phrases at 16.17 and 19.5. The voice is 'loud', because the words which are to follow are of great, eschatological importance. The seer is reporting what is evidently a proclamation spoken by an angel in the presence of God; thus, God is referred to in the third person in verses 3 and 4. But God is the source of the statement about the finality of judgement at 16.17 (note also the delphic 'It is complete!' there and at 21.6); and it is clear that he is the ultimate origin of the speech from the throne, through an angel, at 21.3–4. Earlier (16.17) the emphasis is on judgement; now (21.3) it falls on the blessing of God's people through that judgement (Beale 1046). God speaks directly from heaven in the following verses, 21.5–8.

For the 'throne', as a symbol of God's sovereign presence, see on 4.1. The entire sentence at the beginning of verse 3, 'And I heard a loud voice, proclaiming from the throne', introduces seven strophes (verses 3–4) which further explain and interpret the 'city' and 'bride' figures in verse 2. The central significance of this imagery is to be located in the intimate covenant relationship between God and his saints, which will be expressed in a new and lasting creation (see on verses 1–2). The angelic and divine proclamation in verses 3–4 looks back to 21.1–2, and on to the vision of 21.9—22.17.

The poetic statements which follow derive from an Old Testament background, but are echoes more than direct quotations. The closest is Ezek. 37.27, quoted in 2 Cor. 6.16 ('My dwelling place shall be with them; and I will be their God, and they shall be my people'). Note also Exod. 29.45; Lev. 26.11–12; Jer. 31.33; Ezek. 37.27; 43.7; Zech. 2.10–11; 8.8; and see further Ps. 46.4 (the 'city of God' is the 'holy habitation of the Most High'); *T. Mos.* 4.2; 11Q19 (= 11QTempleᵃ) 59.13. All these passages bring together the twin themes of the eschatological, covenant promise in Judaism: that God will establish his dwelling place among his followers, and that as he will be their God, so they will be his people (cf. Aune 1123; Prigent 596). For the biblical and theological concept of 'covenant', as a relationship established by the mercy of God and willingly entered into by his people, see on 5.1; see also Guhrt, 'διαθήκη'.

The intimate fellowship between God and his own, which features prominently in verses 3–4, receives a special emphasis through the notion of 'dwelling' in this passage, using the noun σκηνή (*skēnē*, 'tent') and the verb σκηνόω (*skēnoō*, 'take up residence'). In verse 3 the seer is told that 'God's dwelling place (ἡ σκηνὴ τοῦ θεοῦ, *hē skēnē tou thou*, lit. "the tent of God") is with human beings', and that 'he will make his home (σκηνώσει, *skēnōsei*, lit. "dwell") with them'. The source for this imagery is to be found in the Old

Testament picture of God 'tabernacling' with his own, notably in the 'tent of the covenant' during the wilderness wanderings (Num. 10.11; 17.7; cf. Ezek. 37.27; 43.7; LXX Exod. 38.26; 40.34; et al.). The Greek word for 'tabernacle' or 'tent' (σκηνή, *skēnē*) is a close relation of the Hebrew root verb, שׁכן (*šākan*, 'dwell'), which is used to describe God 'making his abode' (משׁכני, *miškānī*) in his sanctuary (Exod. 25.8), or among his people (Exod. 29.45–46; Lev. 26.11). The derivative Hebrew term *Shekinah*, meaning the radiant presence of God in the midst of Israel, is post-biblical.

The language of divine covenant 'dwelling' has been used earlier in the Apocalypse (7.15; 12.12; 13.6; 15.5, q.v.; see also on 19.7–8); elsewhere in the New Testament it appears notably at John 1.14. By now, this imagery and its associated vocabulary has become entirely eschatological, and has lost any reference to the idea of 'tenting' as a temporary wilderness experience. On the contrary, in Johannine thought and elsewhere, the allusion is to a stable and lasting relationship between the Lord and his people (cf. 2 Cor. 5.2–4; Heb. 8.2). A direct link between the text in 21.3 and the Feast of Tabernacles (cf. Zech. 14.16–19) is unlikely, since the future dwelling of God in a tent is not attested in Jewish literature, and rabbinic reference to the wilderness wanderings of the Hebrews is primarily concerned with the divine protection of the children of Israel (cf. *Targ. [Pal.]* Lev. 24.3; 26.11–12; also Rev. 7.15–17). See Prigent 597.

According to Aune (1123), the statement in verse 3 that God's final dwelling place is 'with human beings' (μετὰ τῶν ἀνθρώπων, *meta tōn anthrōpōn*, lit. 'among men') may derive from Ps. 78.60 (Yahweh 'abandoned the tent where he dwelt among mortals'). He also notes (ibid.) that the covenant formula, 'I will dwell among the Israelites, and I will be their God', is found at Exod. 29.45 in association with the establishment of the tabernacle (see 29.44).

John's vision in this passage is that God will ultimately dwell among his saints, and that 'they will be his peoples'. The most secure MS reading at this point (see the second textual note on verse 3) has the plural form, λαοὶ αὐτοῦ (*laoi autou*, lit. 'his peoples'), as in the translation and RV, NRSV (AV, RSV both have the singular). The plural is also theologically apt in the present context. The Church of God in eternity will be universal; for the heavenly city, in relation to its Lord, will embrace a new, covenant community of the redeemed which is inclusive and united. Such a hope stems from Gen. 12.1–3, the promise that in Abram all the families of the earth will be blessed, and is found throughout Scripture (see Deut. 29.12–15; Jer. 11.4–5; Ezek. 47.14; Sir. 44.21–23; Gal. 3.16; et al.; cf. John 3.16; 12.32; Eph. 1.10; 1 John 4.14; Rev. 22.2). Gentiles will form part of the new Israel by following the Lamb, and will be united in Christ with the descendants of Abraham (Rom. 9.6–8; 11.13–18; cf. Rev. 2.17; 7.4–9; 12.5; 22.3–4); and this truth is reinforced during the vision of Rev. 21—22 by the seer's eschatological perception that the divine presence cannot be limited to the bounds of the literal Jerusalem and its Temple (20.6; 21.22–26). See further Beale 1047; Smalley, *Thunder and Love* 176; Walker, *Holy City* 258–59.

The expression in the final strophe of verse 3, αὐτὸς ὁ θεός (*autos ho theos*, 'God himself'), includes a personal pronoun which is intensive. This is the only occasion in Revelation where a pronoun is used in this way with a substantive, and it emphasizes the theme of this passage: the close relationship which God will have with his people in eternity ('as their own God'). Note the parallel at 11Q19.29.7–8 ('They [the Israelites] shall be for me a people, and I will be for them for ever; and I shall dwell with them for ever and always'). The idea of God being 'with' (μετά, *meta*) people is a regular biblical metaphor denoting the judgement or blessings which result from his presence (cf. Exod. 3.12; Deut. 20.1; 1 Chron. 22.18; Ezra 1.3; Isa. 7.14 LXX ['Immanuel']; Isa. 8.8, 10; Ezek. 34.30–31; Zeph. 2.7; Zech. 8.23; et al.; also Matt. 1.23 ['God with us']; John 3.2 [God with Jesus]). See further Aune 1123–24.

The angelic speech from the throne continues in verse 4 with the declaration that, in the new creation (verse 1), the saints who share an uninterrupted fellowship with their Lord and other believers will enjoy perfect peace, and therefore freedom from suffering. The effect of divine indwelling on the life of the saints in eternity is described in negative terms: no tears, no death, no grief, no pain; although elsewhere in the Johannine corpus the eschatological promise is expressed positively: 'we know that when he (Christ) appears we shall be like him, because we shall see him as he really is' (1 John 3.2; for this interpretation of the text see Smalley, *1, 2, 3 John* 145–46). See Swete 278; Mounce (383–84) comments that the new order is more easily pictured in terms of what it replaces, than by attempting to describe what is now impossible to conceive.

The character of eternity represented in this verse is freely adapted from the prophecy of Isa. 25.6–10, which is part of a song of praise for Israel's deliverance from captivity and oppression. This passage also lies behind Rev. 7.17 (note the reference in Isa. 25.8 and Rev. 7.1 to tears being 'wiped away'). For the imagery used in Rev. 21.4 see also Isa. 35.10; 51.11; 4 Ezra 8.53–54; *1 Enoch* 10.22; *2 Enoch* 65.9; *2 Apoc. Bar.* 21.22–25; *T. Dan.* 5.11–13 (the new Jerusalem as the new Eden); 1 Cor. 15.54–55. Beale (1049) draws attention to the significant fact that in Isa. 51.10, just before the promise that (as in Rev. 21.4) 'sorrow and sighing will be no more', the prophet recalls the first Exodus, when the 'sea' was dried up (cf. 21.1, the sea no longer exists in the new creation). As God removed the barrier to Israel's freedom, so he will provide the redeemed with free access to communion with himself and 'unending safety at the consummation' (ibid.).

The blessings of eternity are subsumed in a triumphant cry: all this will be possible because 'the old order has disappeared!'. For 'the old order' (τὰ πρῶτα, *ta prōta*, lit. 'the first things') see on 21.1 ('the first heaven and earth disappeared'). In heaven there is a totally new creation, and a new and abiding covenant relationship of the saints with God's Messiah. Cf. Isa. 43.18–19; 65.17–25; 65.15. Sweet (299) and Prigent (599) compare 2 Cor. 5.17 ('if anyone is in Christ, there is a new creation; everything old has passed away and see, everything has become new!'). However, as Prigent (ibid.) says, while Paul is speaking of the individual's rebirth, John's hope encompasses the world, when a new order will replace an old creation marred by sin (cf. Roloff 236; Mounce 385). It should also be added that the Pauline text refers to the new world experienced by believers in time, as well as in eternity; whereas the Johannine vision is of a new order which implies some degree of continuity with earthly existence, and yet is primarily expressed in heaven (see below).

Prophecy 2: New Life (21.5–8)

5 The first prophecy, about the character of the new Jerusalem as the new covenant between God and his people in eternity (verses 2–4), leads naturally into a further prophetic vision about the life-giving aspects of that relationship (verses 5–8; cf. esp. the theme of 'new life' in verses 6–7). An angelic being has spoken from the throne in verses 3–4; now God himself, 'the one seated on the throne' (see on 4.2; et al.), speaks. This is not the first or only time that the divine voice is heard in the drama of Revelation (against Beasley-Murray 312). See 1.8; also 16.1, 17 (Prigent 599).

God says, 'See, I am making all creation new!' (ἰδοὺ καινὰ ποιῶ πάντα, *idou kaina poiō panta*, lit. 'Behold, I make all things new'). The verb is a prophetic present; although God remains Creator eternally. The new creation, experienced by the saints in heaven, balances the old order which has 'disappeared' (verse 4). For the entirely 'new creation' which is promised see on 21.1; and for the background to this concept see Isa. 43.18–19; also Isa. 66.22. In Rev. 21.1–6 the writer draws extensively on Isaianic texts. At Isa. 43.19, Yahweh declares that he is 'about to do a new thing'; in alluding to this text, however, John adds the inclusive word 'all' ('I am making *all* creation new'). Beale (1052) rightly notes, however, that the reference in 21.5 is to the consummation of the redemptive process, rather than to universal salvation as such. All people, with heaven and earth, will eventually 'be transformed into a new creation' (ibid.). As in verse 4 (q.v.), the thought of 'new creation' in verse 5 is reminiscent of 2 Cor. 5.17 ('in Christ there is a new creation'). But whereas Paul is speaking of the individual Christian, John's vision is cosmic. Moreover, while 2 Cor. 5.16–19 deals with the possibility of reconciliation and renewal through the death and resurrection of Jesus, Rev. 21.6 (as 21.1) suggests that God is the agent of the new creation in its totality; although Father and Son are closely related in the Apocalypse (21.22; 22.1).

The command to 'write' (γράψον, *grapson*), in verse 5, issues from God for the first time in Revelation; although elsewhere a similar directive is given by the exalted Son of man (1.11, 19; and at the start of the seven oracles, in 2.1; et al.), by a divine voice (14.13) or by an angel (19.9). At 10.4 John is told *not* to write. That God himself, near the end of the drama, directs the seer to write down his prophetic vision, and speaks to him in words which are 'valid and trustworthy' (the translation of Beale [1053]), authenticates the truth of divine salvation through judgement which is the basic theological theme of the Apocalypse (see Smalley, *Thunder and Love* 147–49). Throughout this verse the speaker is God, since there is no significance in the stylistic change of tense from the aorist εἶπεν (*eipen*, lit. 'he said') to the more immediate present, λέγει (*legei*, 'he says'), and back again (in verse 6) to the aorist; cf. Mounce 385.

The seer is enjoined to write, '*for* (ὅτι, *hoti*) these words' (of God) are 'trustworthy and true' (πιστοὶ καὶ ἀληθινοί, *pistoi kai alēthinoi*, lit. 'faithful and true'). The conjunction ὅτι (*hoti*, lit. 'that'), at the beginning of this sentence, may be construed as the introduction to a direct statement ('write, these words are trustworthy and true'), or to a substantive clause ('write *that* these words are trustworthy and true'); but it is more likely, in the present context, that the sense is causal ('write *because* these words are trustworthy and true'). See Aune 1111. For the hendiadys itself see also 22.6, where it is repeated verbatim; cf. the background texts, Isa. 65.16 (where God is twice described as 'the God of faithfulness', the Hebrew is אָמֵן ['*āmēn*, lit. 'amen']); 3 Macc. 2.11. God asserts that his salvific purposes will be fulfilled; and the Apocalypse as a whole makes it plain that this promise receives its authentication in his word revealed in Christ, who is himself both 'faithful and true' (3.14; 19.11, q.v.). See Prigent 600.

6   This verse is theophanic (cf. 1.8), as the covenant God of the new Jerusalem further discloses the sovereign nature of his creative being, and the living heritage that awaits his triumphant followers (verses 6–7). The exclamation, γέγοναν (*gegonan*, 'It is complete!', lit. 'It is done!'), echoes a similar cry of the voice from the throne at 16.17, q.v. (γέγονεν, *gegonen* [singular], 'It is over!'); and this suggests a climactic fulfilment of the eschatological judgement promised in the earlier scene. The change from the singular in 16.17 to the plural here may imply that the situation is more inclusive, but equally it may simply be influenced by the plural in the preceding noun, οἱ λόγοι (*hoi logoi*, 'words'), at the end of verse 5. Sweet (299) suggests that in both 16.17 and 21.6 there is an echo of the cry of Jesus from the cross in John 19.30, τετέλεσται (*tetelestai*, 'It is finished'); for in all three contexts the beginning of a new creation is heralded. There is, however, a difference between the announcements at Rev. 16.17 and 21.6 that God's purposes are reaching their consummation. The scene in Rev. 16 is primarily one of *judgement*, as the seventh angel pours out a final bowl of crisis, and the fall of Babylon is foreshadowed (16.17–21, esp. verse 19); whereas in Chapter 21 God's plan of *salvation* for his own in eternity, through his judgement, supplies the main theme (cf. Beale 1054–55). Nevertheless, as throughout Revelation, the salvation and judgement of God belong together (alongside 16.17–19 and 21.6, note 16.15 and 21.8; similarly, the discrimination associated with Christ as 'Alpha and Omega' at 22.12–13 is accompanied by the salvific content of 22.14).

For the second time in the Apocalypse God declares that he is 'the Alpha and the Omega' (τὸ ἄλφα καὶ τὸ ὦ, *to alpha kai to ō*); see on 1.8; but here is added the explanation, 'the beginning and the end'. At 22.13 Jesus calls himself 'Alpha and Omega', adding 'the first and the last' to 'the beginning and the end' (see the textual note on that verse); see also 1.17; 2.8 (Jesus is 'first and last'). In the application of similar titles to God and Christ, John is once more establishing the unity of the Father and the Son (Prigent 601). The figurative title 'Alpha and Omega', using the first and last letters of the Greek alphabet, characterizes the Godhead as the origin and goal of all created and human existence. Moreover, to say that God in Christ is 'beginning and end' means that the one who delivers salvific promises, and keeps them, is Lord of all that takes place between the opposite poles of 'first and last' (Beale 1055); cf. also Isa. 41.4; 44.6; 48.12 (Yahweh is 'first and last').

The promise of salvation to believers, and to all who desire communion with God (the spiritually 'thirsty'), is now specified in terms of the free offer of 'living water'; cf. Beckwith 752. For the imagery of the 'water of life', as a means of quenching spiritual thirst, see on Rev. 7.17; also Ps. 42.1–2; Isa. 55.1; *Odes Sol.* 30.1–7. Rev. 21.6 is very close to the thought of John 4.7–15; note esp. John 4.14; also 6.35. The mention of the 'spring' or 'fountain' (πηγή, *pēgē*) of living water in verse 6, as at 7.17, may imply that the divine resources of eternal life are deep and never-ending. In arid Palestine, flowing water as a means of refreshment and life would have been a very resonant symbol.

The Greek expression, ὕδωρ ζωῆς (*hydōr zōēs*, 'living water', lit. 'water of life'), can mean 'running water', as in a practical, baptismal setting (see *Did.* 7.1–2). But in the present context (21.6), as in John 4.14, the significance is spiritual: living water in the sense of water which gives (eternal) life (taking the genitive as appositional); and this accords precisely with the prophetic theme of new life which is the subject of Rev. 21.5–8. 'Water of life' in the new Jerusalem has its origin in God and the Lamb (22.1, 17) and, like the tree of life (22.14) is reserved for the faithful. Cf. Isa. 49.10, where 'springs of water' for the thirsty become 'the spring of living water' according to Rev. 21.6, and the restoration through the Servant foretold by the prophet is seen to be fulfilled in the life of the Church in the heavenly city. See also Ps. 36.8; Jer. 2.13; John 4.10; 7.38.

The 'spring of living water' (verse 6), it may be concluded, stands for the salvific presence of God through faith in the redeeming Lamb, and the life which results for the saints from eternal fellowship with them (Beale 1056). This is available for all, not just for the martyrs (cf. Beasley-Murray 313), and it is offered 'without cost' (δωρεάν, *dōrean*, lit. 'freely'). The inclusion of this truth, which points directly to the basis of salvation in the love of God, may also be influenced by Isa. 49.10, where the Lord who guides his own to springs of water also 'has pity (LXX uses ἐλεέω [*eleeō*, "have mercy"])' on those he leads. Cf. Beale 1056. Caird (267) finds parallels between the thought of Rev. 21.3–6 and the Beatitudes in Matt. 5.3–10; although it has to be said that only two of those 'blessings', on mourners and those thirsting for righteousness, exist in the passage from Revelation.

7 God's people (verse 3) are now described as inheriting overcomers, as it is declared that 'this is the heritage of those who triumph' (ὁ νικῶν κληρονομήσει ταῦτα, *ho nikōn klēronomēsei tauta*, lit. 'the one conquering will inherit these things'). The language of triumph, or conquest, is found in the oracles to the seven churches of the Johannine community in Rev. 2—3, which seem to be echoed closely in this scene. There, the exalted Christ promises that the overcomers, who remain faithful in the face of opposition, will enjoy the tree of life (2.7), escape the second death (2.13), receive a new name (2.17), assume authority over the nations (2.26), remain in the book of life (3.5), be eternally united with God in the heavenly city (3.12), and share the rule of Christ (3.21). To these blessings of eternity is added, in the present verse (21.7), the gift of life-giving water from a sovereign, and creative, covenant God (see verse 6); although, in verse 7, ταῦτα (*tauta*, 'this', lit. 'these things', plural) may also refer to God's nature as the 'beginning and the end', as well as to his gift of eternal life, and indeed to the blessings of the new creation itself which have been in view since 21.1. See Swete 281.

The spiritual rewards of the saints who enter into the new life of the new Jerusalem are the very opposite of those who compromise, and wish to remain outside its gates (see on verse 8). Moreover, the gifts promised to believers who triumph, according to Rev. 2—3 and 21.1–7, also belong to members of the Church in eternity according to Rev. 21—22 (see 22.2; 21.8; 22.4; 21.24–26; 21.27; 21.22; 22.1; 22.17). This covenant 'heritage', to which the triumphant succeed, is bestowed as a free gift from a loving God. As with the entry into the Promised Land, the blessings of eschatological salvation are received as an act of divine grace, and not as a right; so that the conquerors participate in the very triumph of God himself (Exod. 15.1; Rev. 22.5). Cf. Prigent 602–603, who quotes the 'inheritance' texts at 1 Cor. 15.50; 1 Pet. 1.3–5. All this, as Beale (1057) rightly notes, would have encouraged the members of John's circle to persevere through difficulties, in order to inherit the fulness of eternal life with God and his Messiah in the new Jerusalem.

The formula, 'I will be their God, and they will be my children', includes a metaphor which may be based on ancient adoption law (Aune 1129). It reflects the language of the Davidic covenant tradition in 2 Sam. 7.14 (Yahweh says of Solomon, 'I will be a father to him, and he shall be a son to me'), and thus associates the saints with those in Israel, especially the king, who were in a close and covenant relationship with the Lord (cf. also Lev. 26.12; Ps. 2.7; 89.26–29; Jer. 3.19; Ezek. 11.20; Zech. 8.8; *Jub.* 1.24; 4QFlor *frag.* 1. *col.* 1, 21.2.11). See Thompson 182. The idea of an intimate, Father–child relationship between God and his people recapitulates the main point of 21.2–7 (new life in the new Jerusalem).

The covenant imagery of verse 7 develops the thought of verse 3; but there is a variation, in that while verse 3 refers to the saints collectively as 'peoples', they are mentioned here individually (the singular υἱός, *huios*, 'son', is hidden in the translation). But the reference to the king as 'a son', in 2 Sam. 7.14, includes a corporate dimension; and this becomes clear when the passages associated with that text (see above) apply God's Davidic covenant promise to the Messiah's inheritance of the earth. Since 2 Sam. 7.14, in particular, evidently lies behind Rev. 21.7, it may then be interpreted as a fresh promise that, in the new creation of the heavenly city, all members of the redeemed community (hence 'children', in the translation) will enter into a close relationship with their Father-God. In that setting, they will also inherit what Christ inherits: the privileges of his sonship, including kingship and priesthood (see 1.6; 5.10; 20.6; 22.5; also 2.26–28; 5.12–13; 11.15; 21.22). See further Beale 1058.

8   Rather than being a continuation of the speech of God from the throne (verses 5–7), verse 8 could be an interpolated comment from the seer himself. It contrasts (note the adversative δέ [*de*, 'but']) the offer by God to believers of life-giving salvation (verses 6–7), by describing the character of those who follow the beast, rather than the Lamb, and who wish to exclude themselves from the presence of God in the new Jerusalem. In the process, further light is shed on the nature of the holy city itself, without setting a limit on its final membership. The divine voice does not say that anyone who has ever been guilty of the failings mentioned in verse 8 cannot enter a covenant relationship with God, but rather that such sinful behaviour cannot exist in the new creation (cf. Boring 217–18). John's catalogue of vices has affinities with similar lists to be found elsewhere in Revelation and in the ethical tradition of New Testament Christianity (cf. Rev. 9.21; 22.15; also Mark 7.21–23; Luke 18.11; Rom. 1.28–31; 2 Cor. 12.20; Eph. 5.3–5; Titus 3.3; et al.). But, as Boring (217) points out, the author is doing more in this context than hand on a traditional set of spiritual failings. The fact that the list begins with 'the cowardly', and ends with 'liars of every other kind', suggests that this is not a general statement about cowardice and falsehood, but a definition of those who compromise with truth and righteousness under pressure from doctrinal or imperial sources. Some of the eight vices mentioned, such as murder and immorality, might be more typical of the pagan world beyond the Johannine circle; but any of them, notably idolatry and deceit of all kinds, could apply to apostate believers or lapsed Christians within the community itself. The effect becomes an exhortation to its members to remain faithful to the Lamb in the face of opposition. Cf. also Roloff 238, who notes that the lack of distinction between Christians who are disobedient to their Lord and the practice of pagan cults and vices demonstrates the 'ethical rigour' of Revelation (ibid.).

The failures of 'the cowardly and faithless' (οἱ δειλοὶ καὶ ἄπιστοι, *hoi deiloi kai apistoi*) head the list in verse 8. Both terms occur only here in the Apocalypse, and are found in no other vice lists in the New Testament. Cowards, in this setting, are those who fear the threats of the beast instead of trusting the love of Christ (Beasley-Murray 314); the timidity of such apostates provides a strong contrast to the courage of the 'triumphant' (verse 7). Cf. Sir. 2.12; also 2 Tim. 1.7; Rev. 3.15–16. Cowardice is further marked by a lack of steadfast, true belief, particularly where a balanced Christology is concerned (see above, 4–6). Those who are 'detestable' (dative, ἐβδελυγμένοις, *ebdelygmenois*) may be equated with the 'unclean' (κύνες, *kynes*, lit. 'dogs') of 22.15; see also 17.4. The term implies sexual perversion (Aune 1131), although BDAG (172*b*) suggests that, with cowardice and unbelief, the meaning is related to the abomination of polytheistic worship.

The following three categories, 'murderers, the immoral, sorcerers' (φονεῦσιν καὶ πόρνοις καὶ φαρμάκοις, *phoneusin kai pornois kai pharmakois*, lit. 'for murderers and the immoral and sorcerers'), occur again at 22.15 (cf. 9.21). These are not necessarily examples of compromising behaviour on the part of the unfaithful, and may be understood in a literal sense. However, in Johannine thought Satan is said to be a murderer from the beginning (John 8.44; cf. Rev. 12.9); sexual immorality is closely related to idolatry in the Apocalypse (2.14, 20–22); and 'magic' can mean the seductive attraction of an idolatrous society (18.23). See Prigent 605. The list closes with two terms which sum up apostate conduct, as being essentially the practice of spiritual falsehood and deceit: the 'idolaters, and liars of every other kind' (εἰδωλολάτραις καὶ πᾶσιν τοῖς ψευδέσιν, *eidōlolatrais kai pasin tois pseudesin*, lit. 'for the idolaters and all the lying people'). In view of the behaviour which has been specified earlier on in the list, the true character of idolaters is now apparent; apostate believers do not speak the truth, but more significantly they are enemies of the truth (cf. 14.5). See Prigent 606. By this shift in terminology, the seer makes clear the results of compromising with the beast, rather than receiving that life in the new Jerusalem which is offered by a faithful, covenant God (21.27).

Prigent (606–607) finds an influence on verse 8 from baptismal catechisms and liturgies, with their lists enumerating all that is excluded if a believer is 'in Christ' (cf. Rev. 1.9; also 2 Cor. 6.16–18). But, as Aune (1130) points out, baptismal associations are not clearly discernible in 21.8, even if a baptismal liturgy may lie behind parts of Rev. 22 (see on 22.16–20). Similarly Martin, *2 Corinthians* 201–11, treats 2 Cor. 6.16—7.1 as a passage dealing precisely with the need for holiness, without any reference to baptism (despite the reference to purification at 2 Cor. 6.17). Aune (1131) himself detects allusions to the Ten Commandments in the vice list of Rev. 21.8, in view of the exclusion of idolatry, murder and sexual immorality from the covenant relationship between Yahweh and Israel (Exod. 20.4–5, 13, 14). Nevertheless, the parallels are not numerous; and, even if the prophet-seer is making use of an existing ethical tradition (Christian, no doubt, rather than Jewish), he has subtly applied it to his own, contemporary situation. The primary demand on members of the Johannine community, as on the Church as a whole, is abstention from the threat and contagion of idolatry in all its forms (Prigent 607).

Significantly, each of the eight sins belonging to apostate believers in John's circle, and to those beyond (verse 8), can be balanced by a positive quality possessed by members of the new Jerusalem, and acknowledged already among the churches addressed in the seven oracles of Rev. 2—3 (see also on verse 7); cf. Beale 1059, who gives only one example of this consistent theological feature. Thus:

cowardly	fearless (2.10), conquerors (3.21)
faithless	faithful (2.19)
detestable, murderers, immoral, sorcerers	unsoiled (3.4), persevering (3.8)
idolaters	not denied my name (3.8)
liars	kept my word (3.10); cf. 1 John 2.21–22.

The 'place' (μέρος, *meros*, also 'share') for those who wish to exclude themselves from the new life of the new covenant will be 'in the lake of burning fire and brimstone, which is the second death'. The antithesis between 'first' and 'second', as between 'old' and 'new', suggests a contrast between that which in time is incomplete, and that which is consummate in eternity (cf. 20.5–6; 21.1); so that the 'second death' in verse 8 refers to an everlasting punishment (Beale 1061). For these images, which together portray dramatically the pain of separation from God, see on 2.11; 19.20; 20.6, 10, 14, 15. This is the last time they appear in the Apocalypse.

In the final phrase of verse 8 the relative clause, beginning with ὅ ἐστιν (*ho estin*, 'which is'), the neuter singular pronoun ὅ (*ho*, 'which') may be construed as agreeing with the preceding neuter noun, τὸ μέρος (*to meros*, 'the place'), rather than with the masculine of the following predicate noun, ὁ θάνατος (*ho thanatos*, 'death'). See Aune 1112.

The scene is set for further disclosures about life in the new creation, and the covenant relationship shared in the new Jerusalem between the saints and the Lamb of God. The moment of the wedding feast has arrived, and the Church is prepared for the end (19.7); the new creation is a reality (21.1), all is complete (21.6), and promises of eternal life have been made to the thirsty (21.6–7). However, despite these intimations of immortality, the consummation has yet to arrive (22.17, 20). Meanwhile, the Christian community has been warned about the dire consequences of idolatrous unbelief, and will now be encouraged to participate yet more fully in the blessings of the heavenly city which are available in time, as well as eternity. Cf. Prigent 604.

Prophecy 3: New Jerusalem (21.9–21)

9–10   These two verses include the prophet-seer's technique of recapitulation, a literary feature which is characteristic of the Apocalypse, and becomes evident from the moment the seals of the divine scroll are opened (5.1; 6.1; et al.); cf. McKelvey, *Millennium* 49–50. For the second time, John says that he was introduced to the 'bride' (verse 9) and shown 'Jerusalem, the holy city' (verse 10); cf. 21.2. Simultaneously, the author 'hears' about the bride and 'sees' the city (cf. 5.5–6; for the importance of the audition–vision pattern in Revelation see on 4.1). The significance of the symbols of the bride and heavenly city, mentioned at 21.2 and developed in 21.3–8, will be further explained in 21.11—22.5. See Beale 1063. For the imagery in the present verses see on 3.12; 16.1–21; 17.1; 19.7; 21.2.

Verses 9–10 also repeat closely phraseology which is used at 17.1, 3 (q.v.); although in verse 9 the qualifying clause, 'full of the seven final plagues', is added to the description of the angels holding the seven offering bowls. See the first textual note on verse 9. These are now bowls of salvation ('Jerusalem'), as well as judgement ('Babylon'). See below; also Prigent 609. 'One of the seven angels' may refer to the same angel who appears at 17.1; however, there is nothing in the text to establish that identity. For angels in the Apocalypse see above, 28–30. For the importance in Johannine thought of the number seven, used three times in verse 9, see on 1.4, 11.

Unlike the angel of 17.1, who 'shows' the scarlet woman to the seer in terms of describing at length her character and downfall, the angel of 21.9 'makes known' (δείξω, *deixō*, lit. 'I will show') the bride to John without saying more about the Church under this figure; and there is only one further, brief reference to the 'bride' of Christ in this scene (22.17; cf. Prigent 610). Contrast verse 10, where the same verb, used in relation to 'Jerusalem the holy city' and there translated 'revealed', leads into a full account of the setting for the covenant relationship between God and his people (21.11–21). For the rendering of the verb δείκνυμι (*deiknymi*, usually 'show'), as 'make known', see BDAG 214*b*; cf. also 22.1.

The participial phrases in the genitive, τῶν ἐχόντων (*tōn echontōn*, lit. 'holding') and τῶν γεμόντων (*tōn gemontōn*, 'full'), link this visionary episode with earlier apocalyptic material (as in Chapter 16); cf. 17.1. The recapitulation in 21.9–10 of 17.1, 3 has the dramatic and theological function of providing a stark contrast between the Babylonian whore and the bride of the new Jerusalem. The systemic evil belonging to the religious and economic idolatry of Babylon, in league with the oppression of imperial forces represented by Rome, is replaced by the loyalty and conquest over sin on the part of God's people who trust the Lamb. The redeemed community is like a faithful 'bride and wife' to God, whereas the followers of the beast are immoral and doomed to destruction (cf. Beale 1064). Judgement and salvation, according to Revelation, belong together (Morris 241–42, esp. 241).

The angelic command, 'Come, I will make known to you the bride', includes the Greek adverb δεῦρο (*deuro*, 'come [here]!'), used as an imperative (cf. John 11.43; Acts 7.3). The doublet, 'the bride, the wife (τὴν νύμφην τὴν γυναῖκα, *tēn nymphēn tēn gynaika*) of the Lamb', seems repetitious as a description of God's people; but a distinction may be intended between the virginal purity of the 'bride' of Christ and the intimate, covenant relationship which the Church will enjoy with the Lamb of God in eternity (see on 21.2–4; cf. also Mounce 389). Furthermore, the term γυνή (*gynē*, 'wife'), which can be used to describe any 'adult female', is used of both the 'woman' Babylon (17.3–4, 6–7, 9, 18) and the 'wife' Jerusalem (19.7; 21.9); and this possibly draws attention to the parallels as well as the contrasts which exist between these two representative figures (cf. Aune 1151). The presence of the Lamb himself in the heavenly city becomes more marked from this point onwards; for in the remainder of Scene 7 he is mentioned a further six times (21.14, 22, 23, 27; 22.1, 3).

In verse 10 the seer, 'in the spirit', is 'carried away (ἀπήνεγκέν με, *apēnegken me*, lit. "he carried me away") to a huge and lofty mountain'. The language is again reminiscent of the end-time vision at 17.1–3, where John is 'carried away' by an angel 'in the spirit' (verse 3, using the same verb). On both occasions a prophetic commissioning is implied by the formula of 'lifting up', as with Ezekiel (2.2.; 3.12; 11.1; et al.); and this draws attention to John's own prophet commission and authority (cf. 1.10; 4.2; 17.3). See Beale 1065. Once more, however, there is a marked contrast between the episodes in Rev. 17 and 21. In Chapter 17 the setting is an arid wilderness, and the subject of the disclosure is a 'great whore enthroned beside many waters' (verse 1); while in 21.10 the vision is of a holy mountain, and the central character of the scene is the 'bride of the Lamb'. For the deliberate theological ambiguity included in the expression, 'in the spirit' (ἐν πνεύματι, *en pneumati*, lit. 'in spirit'), which combines the ecstatic state of the writer with the enabling power of the divine Spirit, see on 17.3. The dative at this point, as a result, denotes province ('in the spirit'), as well as instrument ('by the Spirit').

The symbolic style of writing is continued from verse 9, as the prophet-seer is borne away to a mountain which is both 'huge' (μέγα, *mega*, lit. 'great') and 'lofty' (ὑψηλόν, *hypsēlon*, lit. 'high'). In biblical thought mountains are important places of disclosure, notably of a theophanic character (cf. Exod. 19.3–23; Deut. 34.1–4; Matt. 5.1; Mark 9.2–9). That the eschatological mountain in 21.10 is of great significance is emphasized by the use of two adjectives (huge and lofty) which underscore its supernatural size; although the people in this scene, who belong to the heavenly Jerusalem, are more important than the figurative height from which they are observed. Moreover, the parameters of the present vision are neither spatial nor chronological. Lifting the curtain of this apocalyptic drama to reveal a 'mountain' means simply that the reality behind John's presentation of the new Jerusalem will now be viewed from yet another heavenly and eternal perspective (cf. Prigent 610–11). Apocalyptic vision cannot be equated with ordered narrative (Knight 136).

The immediate Old Testament background to the mountainous scenery in Rev. 21.10–11 may be located in Ezek. 40—48, where the prophet receives a vision of the eschatological establishment of God's temple, in which he will dwell with his people for ever. See esp. Ezek. 40.1–2 ('the hand of the Lord brought me to the land of Israel, and set me down on a very high mountain on which was a structure like a city'), and Ezek. 43.5 ('the spirit lifted me up, and brought me into the inner court; and the glory of the Lord filled the temple'). John's visionary account of the future, and of the close, covenant relationship which will exist between the Lord and his people in eternity (21.11 onwards), becomes in effect a Christianized interpretation of Ezekiel's prophecy. See further on this point Beale 1065. For the view that this clear reference to Old Testament ideas was an intentional activity on the part of the seer, rather than an unconscious allusion, see Beale, 'Revelation', esp. 320–21.

The phraseology and symbolism of 'Jerusalem, the holy city, descending from God's heaven' is repeated almost verbatim from verse 2 (q.v.); except that the adjective 'new' (καινή, *kainē*) before 'Jerusalem', at 21.2, is omitted in 21.10. Furthermore, whereas the vision of the holy city at 21.2 is followed immediately by the sight of Christ's adorned bride, the disclosure of Jerusalem at 21.10 introduces a description of God's glory, as he dwells among his people. For the eschatological 'city' in Revelation see also 3.12 ('the city of my God'); 20.9 ('the beloved city'); 21.2, 10; 22.19 ('the holy city'); 21.14–19, 21, 23; 22.14 ('the city').

Aune (1151) notes that fragments of the Qumranic *Description of the New Jerusalem* have parallels with Rev. 21.9–21, including the measurements of the city and the phrase, 'he revealed in my presence' (ἔδειξέν μοι, *edeixen moi*, lit. 'he showed me') in verse 10. Cf. 2Q24 = 2QNJ ar *frag.* 1.3; 4Q554 = 4QNJ[a] ar *frag.* 1, 2.15; 3.20; 5Q15 = 5QNJ ar *frag.* 1, 1.2; 2.6; 11Q18 = 11QNJ ar *frag.* 19.3 ('holy is the temple, and the great glory'), et al.

11 As reflected in the translation, the Greek of this verse continues the descriptive statement which begins in verse 10. Indeed, verses 10–14 together form virtually one, compound sentence. The holy and heavenly city, the new Jerusalem, is said to be 'shining with' (ἔχουσαν, *echousan*, lit. 'having') God's 'glory' (δόξαν, *doxan*); and the reference to this attribute is a further reminder of the main theme of this part of Scene 7

(21.2—22.5): the covenant relationship between God and his people in the dimension of eternity. The four present participles used in the description of the holy city in verses 10–12 heighten the immediacy of the drama which is being enacted.

The tabernacle in the wilderness and the Israelite Temple in Jerusalem were the places which housed the presence, or 'glory', of the Lord (cf. Exod. 40.34–35; Lev. 9.6; 1 Kings 8.11; 2 Chron. 7.1–3; et al.). In the new creation, however, God's presence is unstructured and unlimited; for he will dwell eternally among his people, and they will become the city and the temple in which the divine presence may be found (Rev. 21.2–3, 12–14, 22–26; 22.3). Given John's dependence on Isaiah 40—66 in Rev. 21 and 22 (as at 21.4–5, 23–26; 22.5; et al.), it is likely that the allusion to 'the glory of God' in verse 11 derives from Isa. 58.8 and 60.1–2, 19 (texts which, in the LXX, all use δόξα [*doxa*, 'glory']). See Beale 1066. The genitive, in the phrase τὴν δόξαν τοῦ θεοῦ (*tēn doxan tou theou*, 'his glory', lit. 'the glory of God'), is possessive, since the true nature of the divine being is primarily in view at this point (see also on Rev. 15.8; 21.23).

Beale (1066–67) connects the 'glory' of God in verse 11 with the 'fine dressing' of the bride in verse 2 (q.v.); see also 19.7–8. This association is further established by the references to the jewel-like 'adornment' of the new Jerusalem in 21.11*b*–21. However, it has also been argued that the images of the holy city and the bride need to be distinguished, and that the new Jerusalem speaks first of the covenant *relationship* between God and the Church (the 'bride'). See on 21.2. A more direct linkage is accordingly to be found between the 'glory' of God in verse 11*a* and the Shekinah 'dwelling' of Yahweh with his people in verse 3 (q.v.); cf. Ezek. 43.2–5. The transformation of this fellowship, so that it is now perceived in an eschatological and salvific setting, forms the main subject of the present passage.

The 'splendour' of the city is compared to the brilliance of a priceless jewel. The word φωστήρ (*phōstēr*) strictly means 'a light-giving body', but may also suggest 'radiance' or 'splendour'. The term appears in the New Testament only here and at Phil. 2.15. The rare gem in this passage is described as being 'like some priceless jewel, similar to a stone of crystalline jasper' (ὅμοιος λίθῳ τιμιωτάτῳ ὡς λίθῳ ἰάσπιδι κρυσταλλίζοντι, *homoios lithō[i] timiōtatō[i] hōs lithō[i] iaspidi krystallizonti*, lit. 'like a priceless stone, as a crystal jasper stone'). The choice of 'jasper' in this imagery is significant, since it appears in the description of God sitting on his throne at 4.3; it is also represented as an element in the construction of the wall of the heavenly city at 21.18.

In antiquity, 'jasper' described any opaque but sparkling priceless gem, and in this context may refer to an opal or diamond (cf. BDAG 465*b*; Swete 285; Mounce 390). The 'crystalline' nature of the jasper could describe not only its brilliance as 'rock crystal', but also its ability to shimmer like a sheet of ice (BDAG 571*b*; Mounce 390 n. 11). The simile in its totality is intended to emphasize the radiant, spiritual experience of being constantly and uninterruptedly enjoying God's presence, and seeing him face to face (cf. 1 John 3.2; 4.12; also 1 Cor. 13.12). Note also the projection of this idea in the representation of Jesus as the 'bright star of dawn' at Rev. 22.16 (cf. 2.28).

12–13　　The seer continues to narrate his vision by describing and elaborating the character of the holy city, a subject which was introduced at 21.2 (q.v.), and picked up again at 21.10–11. For the immediacy of the repeated present participle, ἔχουσα (*echousa*, lit. 'having'), see on verse 11. The ramparts surrounding such a leading enclosure as the new Jerusalem are said to be suitably 'thick' (μέγα, *mega*, lit. 'great') and 'high' (ὑψηλόν, *hypsēlon*, the adjective used of the mountain in verse 10). Possibly the two adjectives here may be construed as a hendiadys, meaning 'extremely large' (Aune 1137).

It is true that walls were a conventional feature of cities in the first century AD, so that it would be impossible to imagine an ideal city without them (Swete 285; Prigent

612). However, Johannine thought in the Apocalypse is such that a literal interpretation of the 'wall' (τεῖχος, *teichos*) in verse 12 is most unlikely. Accordingly, the wall around
the heavenly Jerusalem may symbolize spiritual security for God's people in a general
sense, as at Isa. 26.1; Zech. 2.5. More importantly, there is an evident evocation in 21.12
of the concept of the 'sealing' of the saints at 7.2–12 (q.v.). There, and subsequently in
Revelation, the result of being sealed by God is regarded as spiritual protection and
preservation (7.16–17; 9.4; 11.18–19; 14.11–12; 19.1–2; 22.5; et al.). Furthermore,
the description of the sealed Church on earth, at 7.5–8, includes a reminder of its
derivation from Israel; and, according to 21.12 the names of the twelve Israelite tribes
are inscribed on or over the gateways of the city wall.

The association between the 'wall' of the holy city and the eschatological 'sealing' of
the victorious faithful is further established by the threefold reference in 3.12 (q.v.) to
the conquerors receiving the 'name' of God and 'the name of the city of my God – the
new Jerusalem – which descends out of heaven from my God' (see 21.2, 10). If members of the Johannine community, and all the saints, are marked with God's 'name', this
means that they are in an intimate, covenant relationship with him through Christ (see
also 14.1; 22.4); and we have seen that the eternal version of that fellowship is precisely
the theological theme of Rev. 21 so far. The wall of the new Jerusalem therefore stands
not for apartness or exclusion (cf. Mounce 390), but for inclusiveness and the spiritual
safety of the faithful who abide in the Godhead eternally. Cf. Isa. 26.2 ('open the gates,
so that the righteous nation that keeps faith may enter in').

The holy city has 'twelve gates'. The term πυλών (*pylōn*) properly refers to an
entrance containing a gate, and therefore a *gateway*, rather than an actual door or 'gate'
(πύλη, *pylē*); so BDAG 897a–b. Since it would be impossible to inscribe names on an
opening, the πυλῶνας (*pylōnas*) of verse 12 must refer either to the gate within a
gateway or to the tower rising above the city wall and over the gateway itself (Mounce
390 n. 12). According to Roloff (242), the gates of ancient cities were locations of 'communication, deliberation, and administration'.

The 'twelve' gates need not act as a symbol for the twelve signs of the zodiac (cf.
Charles 2, 158–60; Caird 271–72; see also *1 Enoch* 33–36, 72–82), since for the author
of Revelation more immediate and congenial sources lay to hand, not least in the
perceived continuity between the Church of the New Testament and God's people
Israel in the Old Testament (see verse 12; cf. also Isa. 56.1–8; Ezek. 37.1–28; Zeph. 3.20;
Tobit 13.5; *Jub.* 1.15–18; *Pss. Sol.* 17.26–46; Acts 2.16–36; Rom. 9–11; Gal. 6.16; et al.).
Equally, Ezekiel's vision of the restored community includes a city with twelve gates
(Ezek. 40.30–35); although these are seen as exits through which the twelve tribes flow
out to their allotted territory, whereas John regards them as entrances, open to the nations
of the world (21.25); cf. Caird 271. Beasley-Murray (320–21) thinks that the writer has
combined Babylonian and Jewish traditions at this point, in order to emphasize this notion
of the heavenly city as inclusive.

The twelve gates of the new Jerusalem, bearing the names of the twelve tribes
of Israel (one on each gate), are guarded by 'twelve angels'. There is a possible allusion
in this image to Isa. 62.6 ('upon your walls, O Jerusalem, I have posted sentinels'); see
also 2 Chron. 8.14. Cf. Beckwith 758; Sweet 304. Prigent (612) dismisses the Isaianic
reference without discussion. However, Beale (1069) shows that the link is plausible,
since the LXX of Isa. 62.6–9 applies the situation of that passage to the eschatological
Jerusalem, and refers to the 'sentinels', or 'watchmen', as 'guards' (φύλακες, *phylakes*)
who acknowledge God's protection of the city against dangerous strangers; also, *Midr.
Rab.* Exod. 18.5 equates the watchmen of Isa. 62.6 with angels. In the same way, the
new Jerusalem will need guardians who will not only welcome in the faithful through
the open gates but also exclude the unrighteous from the holy city (21.8, 27; 22.15).

For cherubim who act as gatekeepers to Eden and Paradise see Gen. 3.24; Ezek. 28.14; *Life of Adam and Eve* 29.1–2; *2 Enoch* 8.8; *T. Levi* 18.10; et al.; and for the new Jerusalem as the new Eden see Rev. 2.7; 22.1–5. Beale (1068) suggests that there is also a connection between the angels of the gates and the angels of the seven churches (Rev. 2—3), and the twenty-four elders who represent the true Israel (4.4).

In John's vision, the multiple gates of Ezekiel's temple (Ezek. 40.1–49) and the twelve gates of his restored city (48.31–34) become one assembly of twelve gates (Rev. 21.13), arranged around one city-temple (Beale 1068). Ezek. 48 does not mention that, as in Rev. 21.12, one angel is placed at each gate. However, in both descriptions there are four groups of three gates, one group on each side, facing east–north–south–west. This foursquare measurement of the heavenly city suggests perfection and universality (see on 3.12; also below). The order of the points of the compass listed in the present verse (Rev. 21.13) may be influenced by Ezek. 42.15–19 (cf. Kiddle 427). It does not correspond to the sequence in Ezek. 48.30–35 (north–east–south–west), or at Num. 2.3–31 (east–south–west–north). See the textual note on verse 13. Possibly John begins his list with the east, as being the point at which light originates and dawn appears (cf. Rev. 21.23–25; 22.5, 16). Prigent (612) believes that the unusual appearance of the preposition ἀπό (*apo*, 'to', lit. 'from [the east, et al.]') in verse 13 indicates that the gates are destined to admit into the city 'pilgrims *coming from* all directions' (ibid.). Ezek. 48.30–35 LXX uses the more natural πρός (*pros*, 'to' or 'towards').

14 'The city wall rests on twelve foundation stones' (τὸ τεῖχος τῆς πόλεως ἔχων [note again the present participle] θεμελίους δώδεκα, *to teichos tēs poleōs echōn themelious dōdeka*, lit. 'the wall of the city having twelve foundations'). For the 'city wall' see on verse 12. Perhaps there is an allusion here to the construction of Solomon's temple, which included the use of large, costly stones (1 Kings 5.17; 7.10); so Aune 1156. In verse 12 the names of the twelve tribes of the children of Israel were said to be inscribed on the gates of the new Jerusalem; now each foundation stone is described as carrying 'the name of one of the Lamb's twelve apostles'. The gates are marked with the names of the Israelites to indicate that those who enter them, whatever their ethnic origin, are truly God's people; the stones bear the names of the twelve apostles in order to highlight the truth that the members of the holy city belong to the eschatological Israel, newly constituted in Christ (Prigent 613). The meaning of θεμέλιος (*themelios*), in this context, is clearly 'foundation stone', rather than 'foundation' as such (hence the translation). The foundation of the city-temple, the Church in relation to God, is made up of twelve foundation stones. For the architectural metaphor see Matt. 16.18; Eph. 2.20–22; also 4Q164 = 4QpIsaᵈ, a pesher on Isa. 54.11–12.

Beale (1069) notes the importance in this passage of the number twenty-four, the sum of the twelve tribes (verse 12) and the twelve apostles (verse 14). The same number appears in the throne-vision of Rev. 4; and that scene is connected with 21.11–14 through the imagery of God's glory, radiating like jasper, which in 4.4 is said to be shared by the twenty-four elders (see 4.2–4 and 21.11); see also Wilcock 208. Similarly, the figure of twenty-four may be derived from David's organization of the temple servants into twenty-four orders of cultic priests, twenty-four prophetic singers, and the same number of Levitical gatekeepers (1 Chron. 24.3–19; 25.6–31; 26.17–19); cf. Beale 1069. The notion of the new Jerusalem is already merging with the related image of the new temple, as one concept of the city-temple in which God and Christ dwell eternally with the faithful (see on 21.19–22; also 3.12; Ezek. 40—48; 1 Cor. 6.19; 2 Cor. 6.16; 1 Pet. 2.5; et al.); cf. Beale 1070.

The phrase, 'of the Lamb's twelve apostles' (τῶν δώδεκα ἀποστόλων τοῦ ἀρνίου, *tōn dōdeka apostolōn tou arniou*), is of interest. Apart from Rev. 21.14, the exact expression, 'the twelve apostles', is found in the New Testament only at Matt. 10.2, where the evangelist records the 'names of the twelve apostles'; but see the v.l. of Luke 9.1; 22.14. It is also used in the shorter and longer titles of the *Didache*. The parallel phrase, 'the twelve disciples' (οἱ δώδεκα μαθηταί, *hoi dōdeka mathētai*), appears at Matt. 10.1; 11.1 (v.l. 20.17; 26.20). See further Aune 1157–58. The term 'apostle' is derived from the Greek verb ἀποστέλλω (*apostellō*, 'send'), and is regularly used in Christian writings to refer to disciples of Jesus, the one 'sent' by God (Heb. 3.1), who evangelize in his name (Acts 1.2; 1 Cor. 9.5; Gal. 1.17; 1 Thess. 2.7; *1 Clem.* 47.1; Polycarp, *Phil.* 6.3; et al.). In the synoptic Gospels the word describes the original group of those whom Jesus called to be his followers ('the Twelve', Matt. 26.14; Mark 3.16; Luke 8.1; et al.); cf. Mark 3.14; Matt. 10.2; Luke 17.5; et al.; note also John 13.16. 'Apostle' occurs in Revelation only here and at 2.2; 18.20 (q.v.).

In Rev. 21.14, the Lamb's 'twelve apostles' are not named individually, since John is speaking of the 'college' of the apostles collectively; cf. Matt. 19.28; Acts 6.2; 1 Cor. 15.7 (Swete 287). The inclusion of the actual number twelve is no doubt influenced by the mention of the 'twelve Israelite tribes' in verse 12 (q.v.). The Twelve were chosen by Jesus to announce God's salvific purposes for his creation through Christ; this is a plan which has existed from the beginning, and is seen in Rev. 21—22 to be fulfilled in the messianic community of the new Israel, dwelling in the new Jerusalem (21.15—22.5). Cf. Prigent 613. Aune (lxx, 1157) claims that the phrase as a whole, 'the Lamb's twelve apostles' (verse 14), supports a late date for the composition of the Apocalypse, since that expression is not attested before *c.* AD 80, and the 'Lamb' with his followers refers to a historical, rather than exalted, aspect of the ministry of Jesus of Nazareth (cf. the allusions to his death [5.6; 7.14; 13.8; et al.] and resurrection [1.5]). It is possible that some slight redaction has taken place at this point. Nevertheless, (a) 'the Twelve' (apostles) is a pre-Easter title (1 Cor. 15.5; cf. 15.5–9); (b) the 'apostles of the Lamb' are saints in heaven, enjoying the new creation and new covenant life in the new Jerusalem, even if their faith rested and now rests in a risen Lord who was crucified on earth.

15   Just as the first sight of the new Jerusalem at 21.2 is expanded in 21.3–14 by developing its attendant theme of new life within the new covenant, so now the description of the holy city is further amplified in verses 15–27 by recording its measurements and adornments, and adding the explicit imagery of the temple. Were this not an apocalyptic vision, it would be impossible to 'measure' and describe in practical detail the relationship of God in Christ dwelling with his people. Once more, and in a manner which is typical of Johannine thought and theology, heaven and earth are brought together (see below).

'The angel talking' to the seer is the same heavenly speaker, one of the seven angels holding offering bowls full of final plagues, who appears at verse 9 (q.v.). The phrase in this verse, ὁ λαλῶν μετ' ἐμοῦ (*ho lalōn met' emou*, 'the angel talking to me', lit. 'the one speaking with me'), in the present tense, echoes the same expression (in the aorist) at verse 9. But whereas the earlier angel speaks, and interprets the vision of the new Jerusalem for the seer, the angel of verse 15 is silent, and does not explain the further significance of the facts which follow in verses 16–21. There seems to be no apparent justification to claim, with Aune (1158), that the angel of verse 15 is a literary figure, added to make 21.9—22.5 formally balance 17.1–18, since in the vision of Babylon's downfall the angel *does* act as an interpreter. On angels in the Apocalypse see above, 28–30.

At 11.1 the seer is commanded to 'measure' the temple; here the angel describes the heavenly city-temple itself. In both cases the language is metaphorical. In 11.1–2 the imagery denotes the security of God's people, their protection and preservation (cf. the symbolism of 'sealing' at 7.2–10; see also on 21.12). Here, the significance of 'measuring' the new Jerusalem is very similar. It stands for more than 'the enormous size and perfect symmetry of the eternal dwelling place of the faithful' (Mounce 391), although these ideas may well be included (see on verse 13, and below). In verse 15, the 'measuring' is eschatological; echoing 11.1–2, it now demonstrates the truth that in the consummated city-temple God's people will be protected for eternity in every way. So there will be no more death, sorrow or pain (cf. Zech. 2.1–13; Rev. 21.4). Cf. Beale 1072–73.

For the measuring 'rod' (κάλαμος, *kalamos*, also 'reed' or 'staff') see on 11.1 (also verse 16). Cf. Ezek. 40.3–5; 5Q15 = 5QNJ ar *frag.* 1, 1.1–2.15. The fact that it is made of 'gold' (χρυσοῦν, *chrysoun*) suggests the importance of the enclosure which is to be measured; see also 1.12 (golden lampstands); 1.13 (Christ's sash); 4.4 (crowns of the elders); 5.8 (incense bowls); 8.3 (altar); 14.14 (Christ's crown); 15.7 (plague bowls). Cf. Philo, *De Leg. All.* 1.20.66–67 (on Gen. 2.11–12, gold is an image of God's presence). The angel is to 'describe the city, its gates and its walls'; although the eventual order of the measurement is city (verse 16), ramparts (17–20) and gates (21). Aune (1160) refers to cities in Syria-Palestine which because of uneven terrain were surrounded by irregular walls, and those on the plains of Egypt and Babylonia which were enclosed by square or rectangular walls (see verses 13, 16). However, in the account of a figurative and ideal city-temple, such a literal observation is less important than the symbolism belonging to the new Jerusalem: that of a divine–human relationship which is all-embracing.

16–17 The verses which follow in this paragraph (16–20) present a picture of order and beauty within the holy city; and this contrasts markedly with the chaos and ugliness of life under the dragon and his beast-like lieutenants (Boxall, *Revelation* 79–80). For the Satan, the dawning of the new creation and the new covenant means final judgement (16.1–20; 20.10); for the saints, the descent of the new Jerusalem becomes the means of salvation through judgement (22.1–5).

The city is said to lie 'foursquare' (τετράγωνος, *tetragōnos*). This term, which is found only here in the New Testament, means 'four-cornered', in the sense of having four sides with four right angles (BDAG 1000*b*). The city-temple is correspondingly described as being 'long as it is wide'; and, when the angel measures it with his golden rod (see verse 15), the 'length, width and height' of the new Jerusalem are found to be equidistant. The background to this scene may once again be located in Ezek. 40—48, where the complex of the new temple, measured by its length and width, is described as 'square' (τετράγωνος, *tetragōnos*; Ezek. 45.1–2 LXX; cf. also 45.3–5; 48.8–13). Again, at Ezek. 40.5 an angelic figure measures with a reed the height, as well as the thickness, of the temple wall; and for the defence of any city a 'high' wall would be important. 'Height' is added to 'length' and 'width' when the description of the measuring process is repeated in the second part of Rev. 21.16. At the same time, the dimensions of the holy city are suitably increased; so that while Ezekiel's temple is square, the new Jerusalem is cubic (cf. Beale 1073). The thought and language of Zech. 2.6 LXX are also close to verse 16 (and see Zech. 1.16; 5QNJ ar *frag.* 1, 1.1; 11QTª 4.13; 30.6–7; et al.).

The predominant theme suggested by the symbolic action of 'measuring' the holy city, as in 11.1–2, is that of God's protective presence, surrounding his own in the perfection of a new and eternal creation (see also on verse 15). The numerical details which describe the size of the city-temple are part of this imagery and cannot be taken literally. The seer is delineating a heavenly and ideal city, and this means that it must be built on a supernatural scale. He therefore chooses a figure which is appropriately huge: 'twelve thousand stadia' in each direction is the equivalent of about 1,500 miles, or 2,000 km (cf. *Sib. Or.* 5.247–52). In verse 17 the wall of the city is said to be 'one hundred and forty-four cubits', or approximately 72 feet (a 'cubit' [πῆχυς, *pēchys*] was about 18 inches, or 45 cm). If this refers to the breadth, or thickness, of the wall the proportions would be balanced; but if the *height* of the wall is being described, as the immediately preceding τὸ ὕψος (*to hypsos*, lit. 'the height') suggests, the resulting proportions become absurd. Swete (289) thinks that this calculation was deliberate, since the wall was intended not for defence, but for 'delimitation', marking the external form of the city of God with his people. But neither numerical accuracy nor geometric precision are needed in order to interpret the present passage. Human calculations merge here with angelic (verse 17), and the result is the unity of earthly and heavenly realities in a new cosmos. The city-temple is pictured as reaching to the clouds, so that the righteous may see the glory of the invisible God (cf. Kiddle 428–31).

It is possible that the structure outlined in verses 15–17 is to be understood not strictly as a cube but as a pyramid. If so, it could reflect the Babylonian ziggurat, which housed a temple and touched the heavens; and this would introduce a further contrast between the false, doomed institution of the scarlet woman, striving to reach heaven by her own ungodly effort (Gen. 11.4; Rev. 18.4–5), and the true, eternal city-temple, descending from heaven and established by God (Beale 1074–75). According to Herodotus (1.178– 79), however, Babylon was originally designed as an exact square, with gates. Beale (1074) also notes that the size of the new Jerusalem which is specified roughly equates to the area of the then-known Hellenistic world; in which case the concept of the holy city as the inclusive dwelling of all the saints, from Gentile as well as Jewish roots, is reinforced.

Nevertheless, the most natural background to John's thinking in this passage is likely to be his own. The cubic shape of the new Jerusalem is a clear reminder of the holy of holies, also a cube, which stood at the heart of the Temple in the old city of Jerusalem (cf. 1 Kings 6.20; also 2 Chron. 3.8–13). However, only the high priest was qualified to enter that holy space, and then but once a year (Lev. 16; cf. Heb. 9.6–7), whereas the whole redeemed community is found within the cube of heaven (cf. Guthrie, *Relevance* 89–91; Smalley, *Thunder and Love* 176; see also Zech. 9.1 and on Rev. 3.12). Square and cubic measurements, in Hellenic as well as Jewish thought, speak of stability, unity and perfection; see 1QS 8.5–9, esp. 9; Philo, *Quaest. in Exod.* 2.110–11 (on Exod. 28.15– 16, the square shape of the high priest's breastplate of judgement stands for stability); 2.73–74 (on Exod. 25.30, the gold of the temple symbolizes the unity of heaven). The perfect state of existence within the new Jerusalem is further illustrated by the inclusion of the symbolic figures 12, or 12 × 12, in the numerical specification of the city (12,000 stadia, verse 16) and its walls (144 cubits, verse 17); cf. the Church as the new Israel at Rev. 7.4–9; 14.1, 3. In Jewish thought the Temple itself, from the outer court to the holy of holies, was an expression of heaven on earth, and the link between them. The holy city-temple is an eternal dimension where the completeness of God's people, and the accessibility of the divine covenant to all believers, is finally disclosed. See also Moffatt 483–84; Caird 272–73; Prigent 614–15.

The architectural imagery which is used in verse 16, to express the theological significance of the new Jerusalem, is applied in verse 17 to the wall of the holy city. The description of the entire structure is symbolic, and cannot be interpreted literally (see above). John is rather saying that God himself will be both a wall surrounding his own and the glory within the eternal city-temple (verses 10–11; cf. Zech. 2.4–5). The accuracy of this understanding of verses 16–17 is supported by the conclusion of verse 17 in the Greek, μέτρον ἀνθρώπου, ὅ ἐστιν ἀγγέλου (*metron anthrōpou, ho estin angelou*, 'the human gauge used by the angel', lit. 'measure of a man, that is of an angel'), where μέτρον (*metron*, 'measure') may be taken as referring to the preceding πηχῶν (*pēchōn*, 'cubits'). The meaning of this phrase, which appears on the surface to be contradictory, is not immediately clear. Despite the reference to the numeral 'one hundred and forty-four' in verse 17, the 'human number' of 13.18 is evidently not parallel, for no angel plays a part in the calculation of 'six hundred and sixty-six' (see Sweet 305, against Topham, 'Measurement'; Bauckham, *Climax of Prophecy* 397–400; Aune 1163). It may be that 21.17 is influenced by Ezekiel's ideal sanctuary, which is measured by a 'man' who is presumably an 'angel' (Ezek. 40.1–4; et al.). Equally, the close relationship between the human and the angelic in the measurement of the wall of the holy city may arise from the representation of angels in the Apocalypse as 'servant-companions' (σύνδουλοι, *syndouloi*) with human beings (19.10; 22.9); cf. Swete 290.

But the most obvious meaning of 'the human gauge used by the angel' seems to be related to the constant theological pattern in Revelation which brings heaven and earth together. In the new Jerusalem the human and divine worlds merge; so that the seer's vision is experienced on two levels at once, and material symbols such as scrolls or lions or bowls reveal deeper spiritual truths (cf. Beale 1077). Dimensions described by angelic hands are such as are in common use among mortals, so that the heavenly cosmos is never completely detached from the material world (Swete 290). The measurement of the holy city-temple by cubits points in the end to the real character of the cube, which is to shelter a relationship at once human and divine (cf. Kiddle 431; Prigent 615). Beale (1078) points out that the Solomonic Temple, the Second Temple and the sanctuary of Ezekiel 40—48 were divided by a wall into inner and outer courts (cf. Eph. 2.14), and that there were separate courts in the Temple of Herod. By contrast, in the new Jerusalem there is to be only one wall, and that will surround the whole city of God (cf. Boring 221–22).

18–20 These verses describe the materials used in the construction of the holy city, including its walls and foundations. The delineation continues to be figurative, rather than literal, as the seer struggles to represent, in human language, spiritual and eternal truths which defy expression. The imagery of this passage, as in 21.2–17, reveals further aspects of the leading theme in the present scene: that of the redeemed dwelling in a close and living covenant relationship with God's Messiah, protected for eternity by the divine presence and glory (cf. Beale 1079).

The wall is said to be 'constructed out of jasper', while the city itself 'is built of pure gold, like transparent glass'. In both cases this must mean that jasper and gold were used in the construction of the wall and city, so that they sparkled, rather than being the only building materials involved. Thus what is apparently true of the city as whole, according to verse 18 (that it is 'built of pure gold, like transparent glass'), is applied to just one section of it, the 'great street of the city', at verse 21. Such an understanding is supported by the use in 21.18 of the term ἐνδώμησις (*endōmēsis*). Found only here in the New Testament, this noun means 'construction', in the sense of the materials incorporated into a structure, and not the materials themselves (cf. BDAG 334*a*; Swete 290; Prigent 616). The 'jasper'-like quality of the wall is a further reminder of God's glorious presence in the new Jerusalem (see on 4.3; 21.11, 19); the word ἴασπις (*jaspis*) is found in the New Testament only in Revelation.

For the 'gold' of the eternal city see on 21.15. The model for John's depiction of the city appears to be Solomon's Temple, as described in 1 Kings 6—7. At 1 Kings 6.20–22, the 'house' of God's presence is said to be overlaid, inside and out, with gold, so that 'the whole house might be perfect' (6.22); see also Philo, *De Leg. All.* 1.20.66–67 (where gold is, 'there is he whose is the treasure'). For the gold of the heavenly city to be compared at 21.18 to 'transparent glass' (see also 21.21) seems contradictory. But, as Prigent (616) notes, to say that a precious metal is like crystal has more to do with a brilliant and visionary world, which is of great value in every sense, than with plausible logic. It seems that the dimensions of earth and heaven are once again merging in this passage. Interestingly, both gold and glass are associated with divine wisdom at Job 28.17 (cf. 1 Cor. 13.12; see also Prigent 616 n. 25).

The vision of the holy city continues with the statement that 'The foundations of the city wall have been faced with every type of precious stone' (verse 19). Jewels and precious stones are of great value in human terms; so that their use in the construction of a heavenly and metaphorical edifice, which reflects the glory and presence of God, is entirely appropriate. There is an evident connection between the foundations of the new Jerusalem, which have been 'faced' (κεκοσμημένοι, *kekosmēmenoi*, lit. 'adorned') with precious stones, and the 'adornment' of the Lamb's bride, the Church, at 21.2 (the only other text in the Apocalypse where this verb occurs); cf. also 19.7–8 and 4 Ezra 10.25–27; *Jos. As.* 18.6. At Rev. 21.12 the names of Israel's twelve tribes are inscribed on the twelve gates of the city, and at 21.14 the twelve names of the Lamb's apostles, as witnesses to life in the new Israel, appear on the foundations of the new Jerusalem. The thought behind this metaphorical language is continued in 21.19–20, since the combined names of twelve tribes and apostles implicitly appear, with the twelve precious stones, on the foundations of the city wall. But the imagery of a bride adorned for her spouse (the Christian Church) now passes into that of a city (God with his people) built, like Solomon's Temple, on foundations of 'great, costly stones' (1 Kings 5.17). The whole city has become a temple (Rev. 21.16, 22). See Sweet 305–306.

There is no need to follow Charles (2, 167–69), and connect each of the twelve stones of verses 19–20 with one of the twelve signs of the Zodiac, visible on Egyptian and Arabian monuments. As Charles (2, 165) himself admits, a more germane background lies to hand in the similar stones set in gold on the high priest's breastplate of judgement (a pouch, containing the Urim and Thummim) according to Exod. 28.17–20, repeated at Exod. 39.10–13; in Ezek. 28.13 the dress of the King of Tyre has a similar appearance, although in the Hebrew only nine stones are listed, while twelve are mentioned in the LXX. Cf. Philo, *Quaest. in Exod.* 2.110–11. The order of the gems followed by John in Rev. 21.19–20 differs from that in the Exodus texts; but such a detail is not important in the present discussion, and certainly does not mean that the seer was thinking independently of his Old Testament background (so Beale 1080).

In Exod. 28.21 (39.14) the names of the twelve tribes of Israel are recorded as being inscribed on the breastpiece of the high priest, who could in this way 'bear the names of the sons of Israel' when entering the holy place (28.29). Aaron's garments in general spoke of God's tabernacle and the holy of holies (Beale 1081). As therefore the cultic actions within Judaism symbolized the presence of all Israel before God in his tabernacle, so now the foundation stones of the new city-temple surround and embrace a recreated and universal community of God's people, the new Israel. Accordingly, the privilege of sharing the immediate presence and glory of God, previously reserved for the high priest, is in Christ made available for all believers, who share his priesthood (see on 21.12–13; also 1.6; 5.10; 20.6; cf. 1 Pet. 2.5). For the background in the Old Testament and Judaism to the foundations and precious stones of Rev. 21.18–21 see also Isa. 54.11–12; Lam. 4.1–2; Tobit 13.16; 1QM 12.7–15; 4QpIsa[d] *frag.* 1, 1–7; 5QNJ ar *frag.* 1, 2.12–15. For the Old Testament setting of Ezek. 28, and Jewish interpretations of Ezek. 28 (including the jewels of the Garden of Eden in Ezek. 28.13), see further Beale 1087–88.

In the list of the twelve gems of Rev. 21.19–20, a different jewel is allocated to each of the twelve foundations. These precious stones are hard to identify with exactness, because of the variety of colours involved, and a lack of standard terminology in their description at the time when Revelation was written (cf. Mounce 394). For this reason the translation has mostly transliterated the Greek terms, which in each case occur in the New Testament only in the Apocalypse, and mostly as *hapax legomena*.

Jasper (see verses 11, 18; also 4.3) was found in various colours, mostly red, and could designate any translucent or opaque precious stone (BDAG 465*b*). Sapphire was usually blue in colour, and is probably the modern lapis lazuli. The meaning of 'chalcedony' (χαλκηδών, *chalkōdōn*) in this context is uncertain; it may be the equivalent of the modern agate or onyx, but is often taken as a green silicate of copper found near Chalcedon in Asia Minor. The emerald was a green stone; while onyx was a layered stone of various colours, and a version of agate. Carnelian was a reddish stone, often used for engraving (see 4.3), and chrysolite may have been yellow-coloured. The beryl is green, and the topaz is a transparent, bright yellow. The exact significance of 'chrysoprase' (χρυσόπρασος, *chrysoprasos*) is difficult to determine; but it was probably a highly translucent, golden-green gem. Jacinths were similar to the modern sapphire or turquoise (so REB), and blue in colour. The amethyst was a purple variety of transparent, crystalline quartz. See further Hillyer, 'Precious Stones in the Apocalypse'; Marshall, 'Jewels and Precious Stones'.

The picture of the new Jerusalem in its totality is that of a magnificent, brilliantly golden city, surrounded by a wall inlaid with jasper and resting on twelve foundations adorned with precious gems of every colour. Such a figurative enclosure is a fitting spiritual location for the eternal dwelling place of God in Christ with his people (21.3); cf. Mounce 394–95.

21 The detailed description of the construction of the figurative new Jerusalem ends with a further reference to the 'gates' of the holy city, and an allusion to its 'great street'. The seer records that each individual gate is 'made of a single pearl', a picture of opulence which is comprehensible only in spiritual terms. The 'twelve gates' have already been identified with the twelve Israelite tribes (verses 12–13); and the twelve gem stones adorning the twelve foundations of the city wall, together with the names of the Lamb's apostles (verses 14–20), have similar associations (see esp. on verses 14 and 19). The 'twelve gates' (οἱ δώδεκα πυλῶνες, *hoi dōdeka pylōnes*), which are always open (verse 25), accordingly symbolize the security enjoyed by all the redeemed who belong to the new Israel, and their free access to eternal life through the Lamb (7.17; 22.1–2). Cf. Beale 1089. The whole city, in this part of Revelation, shines with the glorious presence of God; since in the eschatological age John anticipates that the barrier between heaven and earth will be removed (Knight 137). For the imagery of twelve gates surrounding the ideal Jerusalem see Ezek. 48.30–34; 5QNJ ar *frag*. 1.1.9–13.

Pearls as such are unknown in the Old Testament, and rarely appear in the Hellenistic world before Alexander (Prigent 621). But see Job 28.18; also the rabbinic prophecy, according to R. Johanan, that God will set up in Jerusalem gateways with vast precious stones and pearls (*[b.] Baba Bathra* 75*a*; *[b.] Sanh*. 100*a*). Elsewhere in the New Testament pearls are regarded as priceless (Matt. 13.45–46), or as a mark of affluence (1 Tim. 2.9); cf. also Matt. 7.6. For the idea of the gates of the eternal city being decorated with precious jewels see Isa. 54.12, which is also cited in the rabbinic texts above. The true beauty belonging to the pearls of the eternal Jerusalem contrasts markedly with the false and tawdry character of doomed Babylon (17.4; 18.12, 16); cf. Sweet 306.

For the second detail belonging to the construction of the holy city according to verse 21, that its 'great street' is 'pure gold, like translucent crystal', see the similar phraseology in verse 18. The heavenly Jerusalem reflects the sea of glass, transparent as crystal, which is before the throne of God (4.6); but it replaces the 'square' of the old city (11.8; see also 22.1–2); cf. Wall 254–55. The meaning of the term, ἡ πλατεῖα (*hē plateia*) is not immediately clear; see Aune 1166. It may be taken in a generic sense, and refer to all the streets in the city; equally, the noun may describe the main 'square' of the new enclosure, which is probably the significance of the word at 11.8 (q.v.). But, in view of the context belonging to 22.2 (q.v.), in which the noun appears again, it is most likely that the seer is speaking here of a broad, central street, running right through the city-temple (see BDAG 823*b*, where the word is translated 'wide road, street').

Like the priests of the Old Testament, whose ministry in the Temple included walking on a floor of gold (1 Kings 6.30), the priestly saints of God share his presence by treading a golden pavement, which reflects his glory. See also Tobit 13.16 (the towers and battlements of Jerusalem will be 'built with pure gold'); 11QT^a 36.10–11 (the timber of the temple framework will be of 'cedar overlaid with pure gold; and its doors will be covered with quality gold'). According to 5QNJ ar *frag.* 1, 1.6–7, the streets of new Jerusalem will be paved with 'white stone, alabaster and onyx'. See also Philo, *De Leg. All.* 1.20.66–67 (gold is a symbol of God's presence). For 'gold' see on verses 15 and 18.

The pure gold of the city's great street is said to be 'like translucent crystal' (ὡς ὕαλος διαυγής, *hōs hyalos diaugēs*). In verse 18, where the parallel phrase is translated 'like transparent glass', the qualifying term is καθαρός (*katharos*, lit. 'pure'; BDAG 489*b* has 'clear'). Both adjectives are virtually synonymous, and suggest the bright and resplendent character of God's presence (Beale 1089). Beale (ibid.) also notes that καθαρός (*katharos*, 'pure') frequently modifies χρυσίον (*chrysion*, 'gold') in descriptions of the high priest's ephod in Exod. 25—39 LXX (e.g. Exod. 28.13–14 LXX). The word διαυγής (*diaugēs*, 'transparent') is a *hapax legomenon* in the New Testament.

Prophecy 4: New Temple (21.22–27)

22 The seven oracular prophecies in the present scene clearly overlap; so that, for example, the verses in this section (21.22–27) amplify the initial sight of the new Jerusalem at 21.2. All the prophecies are concerned with the central theme of 21.2—22.17: the close and eternal covenant relationship which will be established in the new creation, through the Lamb, between God and the redeemed (see 21.1–3). In this broad vision of the new Jerusalem, the figurative idea of the 'new temple' has a brief but important part to play. City and temple have merged in the new fellowship of God and his people in the new creation (see on verse 19); now the seer reveals the unusual character of the temple itself.

The introduction to verse 22, καὶ ναὸν οὐκ εἶδον ἐν αὐτῇ (*kai naon ouk eidon en autē[i]*, lit. 'and I did not see a temple in it'), implies that the seer expected to discover a temple in the new Jerusalem, but did not find one. That is to say, he did not see a *physical* sanctuary, but only (and crucially) a spiritual temple. The expectation of a renewed temple was a regular feature in the eschatology of Judaism (cf. Ezek. 40—48; Hag. 2.9; Zech. 1.16; 6.12–15; *1 Enoch* 90.28–29; et al.), and the lack of one in John's eternal city is therefore surprising, particularly as the new Jerusalem is connected with temple imagery elsewhere in the Apocalypse (3.12; 7.15), and reference is often made to the heavenly temple (11.19; 14.15, 17; 15.5–8; 16.1, 17).

It is not necessary to explain this omission by appealing to anti-temple polemic in Qumran and early Christianity (cf. Aune 1166–67; see 1QS 8.1–10; John 4.21–24; Acts 7.47–51; Heb. 9.1–14; also *Barn.* 16.1–2; et al.), or to the process of redaction (cf. Wilcox, 'Tradition and Redaction' 212–13). The seer himself makes a daring break with tradition, and provides the answer to this lacuna: 'the Lord God Almighty and the Lamb are themselves its temple'. The holy city, in its completeness, is the sanctuary of God (Hughes 229); cf. Jer. 3.14–18; *T. Dan* 5.13. If criticism of the Temple in Jerusalem existed in primitive Christianity, it was based on the experience of the immediate presence of God in the risen Jesus (cf. Mark 13.2 par.; 14.58 par.; 15.29 par.; John 2.18–22; Acts 6.14). Now this theme has been thought through to its logical and theological conclusion, since for John the end-time temple has replaced the original, and is seen to be the final dwelling place of God's presence with his Church. The distinction between the profane and the sacred has disappeared, and the perimeters of the new temple have expanded to enclose the new creation and the new Jerusalem in their entirety. The universe of faith is now one (cf. 1 Cor. 3.16; Eph. 2.19–22; 1 Tim. 3.15). See Ellul, *Apocalypse* 227–29, esp. 227; Caird 278–79; Roloff 241, 245; also McKelvey, *Millennium* 88.

The Christology of verse 22, and in this part of Revelation, is noticeably high. Just as the Lamb shares the throne of God (22.1), so also the presence of God in all his power constitutes the city-temple of the new creation in union with Christ. Cf. also verse 23; 22.13; and see further below. For the sovereign title, ὁ παντοκράτωρ, *ho pantokratōr*, 'Almighty', see on 1.8; also 4.8; 11.17; 15.3; 16.7, 14; 19.6, 15; for ἀρνίον, *arnion*, 'Lamb', see verses 9 and 14. For the central theme, in the Apocalypse, of the right use of power see on 7.11–12.

23–26   The prophet-seer further describes the close and eternal relationship between God and his people; this is a covenant made possible through the exalted Lamb, and symbolized by the city-temple of the consummation (see verse 22). The present passage is heavily indebted to the language and thought of Isa. 60, particularly in terms of the theme of God's presence in glory among his own (see esp. verses 3–19; cf. also Isa. 24.23; Ezek. 43.2–5; 4 Ezra 7.38–42; *1 Enoch* 48.1–7; 50.1–4; *T. Levi* 18.2–7). Verses 22–27, perhaps influenced by Isa. 60, are poetic in form; hence the format of the translation.

It is possible to understand the first sentence of verse 23, 'The city has no need of the sun or the moon to shine on it' (see Isa. 60.19), in a quasi-literal sense. No luminaries, such as the sun or moon of the first Paradise, are needed in the new Jerusalem, 'for (γάρ, *gar*, "because") the glory of God illumines it, and the Lamb is a flaming torch (ὁ λύχνος, *ho lychnos*, lit. "the lamp"; NJB has "lighted torch") for it'; in turn, this may mean that the eternal city is suffused with a divine radiance which originates in God and is revealed by his Messiah (Beale 1093). See John 1.4–5; 8.12; 12.35–36; 1 John 1.5; also Maurice 337. In view of the symbolic nature of the visionary material here and throughout the Apocalypse, however, it is more probable that verse 23 as a whole should be interpreted in a purely figurative manner. The glorious presence of God transcends any physical or spiritual source of illumination, in either the old or new creations (cf. Beale, ibid.); for God and the Lamb are themselves not only the temple of the holy city (verse 22) but also its light (see also 22.5).

The literary expression of verse 23 is closely modelled on Isa. 60.19 (q.v.). However, the last clause of the Isaianic text, 'your God will be your splendour' (using תפארת, *tiperet*, also 'beauty'; LXX has δόξα, *doxa*, 'glory'), is replaced in Rev. 21.23 by 'the Lamb is a flaming torch for it'. Both the glory of God and the lamp of the Lamb together fulfil the prophecy of Isa. 60.19, by being the divine radiance of the heavenly temple-city; and this once more draws attention to John's high Christology, and his balanced view (intended for his own circle) that Jesus is fully divine, as well as fully human.

For 'glory' (δόξα, *doxa*) see on 1.6; 4.9; 21.11. The term is used throughout Revelation in three different contexts.

(a)   In ascriptions of praise to God and the Lamb, mostly liturgical and usually in association with such attributes as power, reverence and thankfulness (1.6; 4.9, 11; 5.12–13; 7.12; 11.13; 14.7; 16.9 [glory *not* given to God]; 19.1, 7). In such settings, the meaning of 'glory' is close to that of 'honour'.

(b)   As a synonym for the Shekinah-like presence of God in Christ, on earth and in heaven, among his people (15.8; 18.1; 21.11, 23). This sense is marked in the later scenes of the Apocalypse.

(c)   To represent the self-offering of kings and nations as members of the holy city (21.24 [the present verse] and 26).

Table 1   Comparison of Isaiah 60 with Revelation 21

Isa. 60.3, 5	Rev. 21.24
Nations shall come to your light, and kings to the brightness of your dawn; . . . the wealth of the nations shall come to you.	The nations will walk by its light, and earthly kings will bring their splendour into it.

Isa. 60.11	Rev. 21.26
Nations shall bring you their wealth, with their kings led in procession.	The glory and the honour of the people will be brought into it.

The form, wording and thought of verses 24 and 26 are very similar, so that these two texts may be considered together. With verse 25, they continue to echo Isa. 60 (see Table 1). See also Isa. 2.2, 5, a prophecy which speaks of 'all the nations' streaming to the mountain of the Lord's house, and of faithful Israelites walking 'in the light of the Lord' (note Rev. 21.24*a*, which connects directly with the theme of 'light' in verse 23). John sees the pilgrimage of the nations to the end-time Jerusalem taking place in the *new* Jerusalem before his own eyes (Beale 1094).

As Beale (1094–95) points out, Isa. 60 (61) does not predict that kings and nations will bring their 'glory' (verse 24) or 'honour' (τιμή, *timē*) to Zion, only that they will bear to the city, for Israel's benefit, their 'strength' or 'power' or 'wealth' (using היל, *ḥayil*, which is never translated by LXX as δόξα [*doxa*, 'glory', 'splendour'] or τιμή [*timē*, 'honour']; see Isa. 60.11 LXX, which has δύναμις, *dynamis*, 'power'). However, the context of Isa. 60 makes it clear that the strength or wealth involved in this action is more than literal; for Isa. 60.6 states that the nations will not only bring 'gold and frankincense' to Jerusalem but also 'proclaim the praise of the Lord' (LXX 'preach the good news of the salvation of the Lord'); similarly Isa. 49.6–8, 23; 60.17; 66.12.

Although BDAG (1005*b*) interprets the nouns δόξα (*doxa*) and τιμή (*timē*) at Rev. 21.26 as 'earthly possessions', it is therefore best to understand the costly gifts of 'splendour (glory)' and 'honour' at Rev. 21.24, 26, brought by nations and leaders into the new Jerusalem, in spiritual rather than literal terms. People will carry into the holy city *themselves*, as those who offer to God at the end-time the worship of their renewed lives. The 'splendour and honour' arises '*from the people*' (τῶν ἐθνῶν, *tōn ethnōn*, lit. 'of the nations', is a genitive of source), rather than being distinguished from them. Note similarly that when the combination of 'glory and honour' occurs elsewhere in the Apocalypse, as at 4.9, 11; 5.12–13, it refers to the praises of God and the Lamb (Beale 1095). There is an obvious contrast in this passage between the true worship (glory, wealth) offered to God by the faithful in the new creation and the false luxury and selfish wealth belonging, as followers of the beast, to Babylon and kings of the earth (18.9, 19). In this connection, Isa. 13.19 is of interest; for there it is promised that 'Babylon, the glory of kingdoms (LXX καλεῖται ἔνδοξος, *kaleitai endoxos*, 'called glorious'), will be like Sodom and Gomorrah when God overthrew them' (see Rev. 18.2; also 11.8). Cf. Bauckham 1304*b* ('the nations offer their own glory to God's glory').

'Nations' and 'earthly kings' in Revelation are often seen as the opponents and oppressors of God and his people (cf. 2.26; 11.2; 17.2, 18; 18.3, 23; 19.15). However, in the light of the background to Isa. 60 which has just been reviewed, it is reasonable to look for a more positive interpretation of the nations and kings at Rev. 21.24, 26. In the Isaianic texts, those who in procession bring material and spiritual gifts to Zion (60.11) recognize God and his people Israel (60.6), unlike the nations and kingdoms which refuse to serve Yahweh (60.12). Cf. *Pss. Sol.* 17.34–35. In the Apocalypse itself, 'nations' some-times refers to the company of the universally redeemed, who are made to reign as kings (5.9–10); while 'kings' include repentant leaders who submit to the rule of Christ and reign with him as priests (1.5–6; 20.4–6; 22.5). It may be concluded that the nations/people and earthly kings of Rev. 21.24, 26 belong to a converted society which has learned to serve the Lord. Those who wish to remain outside the new Jerusalem may do so (verse 27), but those whose names are inscribed in the Lamb's book of life are free to enter (verse 25). Similarly Michaels 245; see also Kiddle 439 (the redeemed belong spiritually, but not ethnically, to Israel).

There is consequently no need to solve the 'problem' that the unregenerate will be present in the new creation by claiming that John has taken over from the prophets conventional imagery which presupposes that Gentiles will remain on earth after the consummation (Beckwith 769–70); see also Rist (539–40), who claims that, in this pas-sage, John has not reconciled Isaiah's vision that Gentiles would convert to Judaism with his severe views about the judgement of the nations. More obviously, the vision of John the Divine is an inclusive one. As Isaiah foresaw the faithful being drawn to the light of the Lord's glory from all points of the figurative compass, so in Rev. 21.24–26 the seer's audience is shown believers from every possible background entering into a final covenant fellowship with God through the Lamb. This relationship is symbolized by an eternal city blazing with the light of the divine presence and adorned with spiritual beauty and lasting truth. A similar theological pattern, demonstrating the comprehensive fulfilment of God's salvific purposes, exists at both ends of the New Testament. At Matt. 2.1–12, wise men from the *east* come to Jerusalem, and to the King of the Jews; while at Rev. 21.24, Jewish *and Gentile* kings of the earth stream into the new Jerusalem. See Prigent 622.

The seer returns to the imagery of gateways as a form of entry to the holy city-temple (see 21.12–13); and he continues to use spatial imagery in this section, although the concepts behind the figurative language are relational and spiritual. Verse 25, with its promise that 'The city gates will never be closed', seems to interrupt the thought of verses 24 and 26, which speak of a universal procession of Christian pilgrims bringing the offering of themselves into the new Jerusalem (Charles 2, 173, predictably regards part of the text as a marginal gloss). But in fact verse 25 ties the two bordering verses together, by speaking of the means by which the nations and earthly kings may enter the eternal city of God.

The purpose of the gateways is not to restrict entry to the city, particularly since, with the demise of evil, 'security measures' are no longer necessary in its precincts (Mounce 397). Nor is their role to defend the saints, who are in any case sealed and protected by God (see on verses 9–14). Ironically, the twelve gates of the eternal city of God do not exist, as is their potential, to be closed at all. Any command for them to be unlocked is unnecessary (cf. Ps. 24.7, 9), since the gates stand open perpetually. Such a scene suggests that any who wish to enter the holy city may do so without hindrance, and implies that the faithful are constantly invited to pass through its gates (cf. John 10.9). The resulting movement is in one direction only: from the outside to the inside (verses 24, 26–27); cf. Boring 222.

The thought of verse 25 is once more dependent on Isa. 60, which has also influ-enced verses 24 and 26. Isa. 60.11*a* reads, 'Your gates shall always be open; day and night they shall not be shut'. John develops this future promise in the direction of the Chris-tian heavenly city, and says that its gates 'will never be closed *by day*' (ἡμέρας, *hēmeras*). He then adds a qualifying clause which is slightly awkward in style, but clear in mean-ing: 'given that (γάρ, *gar*, lit. "for") there will be no night time (νύξ, *nyx*, lit. "night") there'. In the city of God there is no distinction between right and wrong, because evil does not exist; equally, night and day cannot be differentiated, because there is no darkness. There is a similar notion at 7.15 (q.v.), where the redeemed are said to worship God 'day and night within his temple'. John's vision in that context relates to the present as well as the future, while at 21.25 the promise to the saints points towards the end alone. In the new Jerusalem of covenant fellowship there is only light (verse 23), and night is unknown because the sun of the divine presence never sets (Swete 296).

27   The vision of Paradise at the end has implications for everyday life in the present (cf. Prigent 623). The saints, who belong to God through the Lamb, enter into the fellowship which is represented by the new Jerusalem, but the unrighteous consciously exclude themselves from the holy city (see also 21.8; 22.11, 14–15). The seer continues to use the spatial imagery which has marked this scene. 'Entering in' to the life of the new covenant (21.1–3), through the 'gates' of the 'city' (verse 25), are all metaphors which speak of believers sharing a renewed and enduring relationship with the Lord. For the figurative idea of 'entering' the city see the concept of 'entering the kingdom of God/heaven' at Matt. 18.3; Mark 9.47; John 3.5; Acts 14.22, texts which may echo the phraseology of 'admittance to the assembly of the Lord' at Deut. 23.2–3.

The term κοινός (*koinos*, 'unclean'), which occurs in the Apocalypse only here (verse 27), means 'profane' or 'cultically unclean' (cf. Hauck, '*koinós*, et al.' 448); it is broadly a synonym of the adjective, ἀκάθαρτος (*akathartos*, 'foul', lit. 'unclean'), as this is used at 16.13; 17.4; 18.2. Ritual impurity is a centrally important religious category in Judaism (Lev. 10.10; 11.24–28; 4 Macc. 7.6; et al.), and 'being unclean' was a regular description of *people* who were, for various reasons, cultically impure (cf. Num. 5.2–3; Lev. 15.16–18; et al.). Ezekiel commonly linked uncleanness with Israel's idolatrous behaviour (Ezek. 14.6–11, esp. 11; 18.31; 20.7; 37.23; et al.). When the category of ritual impurity was carried over into early Christianity, it became an exclusively moral and personal concern (Matt. 15.11; Mark 7.2; Acts 10.15; Rom. 14.14; Heb. 9.13–14; et al.).

All this shows that the phrase in Rev. 21.27, πᾶν κοινόν (*pan koinon*, lit. 'everything unclean'), must include people, as well as objects; indeed, it is difficult to separate the two (hence the translation, 'nothing unclean . . . no one, that is', taking καί [*kai*, 'and'] as epexegetic). On the other side see Charles (2, 173–74), who finds this phrase problematic because it seems to refer only to objects, whereas the occupants of the heavenly city, whose names are written in the book of life, are clearly individuals. For this section see Aune 1174–75. The group of those 'whose behaviour is foul or false' (ποιῶν βδέλυγμα καὶ ψεῦδος, *poiōn bdelygma kai pseudos*, lit. 'doing something foul or false'), and who therefore merit divine judgement, has already appeared at 21.8 (q.v.); note in that text the cognates, ἐβδελυγμένοις (*ebdelygmenois*, 'detestable') and ψευδέσιν (*pseudesin*, 'liars'). John adds to their number the 'unclean', in order to emphasize that the impurity of all these outcasts is essentially related to idolatry and unfaithfulness to God, conduct which may also be characteristic of apostate Christians. The association spiritually between impurity in general and idolatry in particular is clear from 17.4–5 (q.v.), where both βδέλυγμα (*bdelygma*, 'obscenity') and ἀκαθάρτης (*akathartēs*, 'foulness') refer to idolatry. Those who were cultically unclean could not enter the physical Temple in Jerusalem, and in the same way it will be impossible for the spiritually idolatrous to enter the city-temple of the new Jerusalem. See Beale 1101. For the terminology in verse 27 see further 14.5; 22.15; also 3.9; and 16.13; 19.20; 20.10 (false prophecy).

For the concept of the sanctity of the (city-)temple see Exod. 15.17–18; Isa. 52.1; Ezek. 44.9–10; cf. also Isa. 35.8; 1QH 6.20–21; 4QFlor *frag.* 1, 1.3–4 (on Exod. 15.17–18); 1.16–17 (on Ezek. 44.10); 11QT[a] 47.3–18. In the New Testament see 1 Cor. 6.9–10; 2 Pet. 3.13. In Johannine thought spiritual purity, the opposite of uncleanness, has for the believer a Christological foundation, in that it is linked to the death of Christ (cf. John 13.1–12, esp. 10; 1 John 1.7, 9; see also Rev. 7.13–15; 19.13–14).

In the eternal city of God, accordingly, there is no distinction between the holy and the common, the sacred and the profane (see on verse 22; Zech. 14.20–21; also Caird 278–79; Sweet 310). By definition, no unholy person or object can be part of a covenant relationship which consists solely of the redeemed dwelling in perfect harmony with their God and he with them (21.3). These are the saints 'whose names are written in the Lamb's book of life' (for which see on 13.8, the only other context in which this phrase occurs; cf. also the 'book of life' at 3.5; 17.8; 20.12, 15). Nevertheless, a symbolic place outside the city gates is always available for those who wish to occupy it, since commerce with the harlot Babylon as with the heavenly Jerusalem remains an endless possibility (3.10–13); cf. Sweet 310. According to *b. Baba Bathra* 75*b*, anyone who wishes may go up to the Jerusalem of the world, 'but to that of the world to come only those invited will go'.

John's vision of the new covenant life within the new Jerusalem has reached a climactic point, although he has yet to develop it in terms of the rich blessings belonging to existence in the new cosmos. But the intention of unfolding this dramatic presentation of God's salvation through judgement is not simply to provide information about the future consummation of the divine scheme. It is rather to warn as well as encourage the seer's audience, the members of which consist of the Johannine community and the Church at large, as they undertake their own Christian pilgrimage. See Beale 1102.

Prophecy 5: New Relationship (22.1–5)

22.1–2   The vision of the new Jerusalem, first introduced at 21.2, and expanded in terms of the covenant life which will be available in the eternal city-temple (21.3–27), is now developed further. The focus of the imagery in this scene so far has been a description, mediated by the bowl-angel, of the heavenly city itself, as the place where God dwells in perfect harmony with his redeemed people (verses 9–21). But, on either side of this part of the disclosure (verses 3–8, 22–27), the seer himself has spoken about this relationship (note '*I* saw', verse 2; '*I* did not see', verse 22) with closer reference to the inhabitants of the new Jerusalem themselves, as well as to those who wish to remain outside its gates. In 22.1–5 John's audience is taken through the gateways, to witness more fully the individual and community blessings of eternal life.

The background to 22.1, with its prophetic picture of a 'river of living water' flowing at the end-time out of the city-temple, is to be found at Ezek. 47.1–12 and Zech. 14.8–11, where waters of life (Ezek. 47.9; Zech. 14.8) stream from the latter-day Jerusalem and its temple. See also Isa. 35.5–7; Joel 3.18. But the vision in this passage is also derived, significantly, from the representation of the first Eden in Gen. 2, where a river flows out of the garden (2.10), and gold and precious stones belong to one of its tributaries (verses 11–12); cf. Rev. 21.18–21. Cf. 11QNJ ar *frag*. 10, 1.1–6 ('living water . . . stones overlaid with gold'). In the new Eden of Rev. 22.1–5, which is part of the second creation (21.1), the Lord makes 'the last things as the first' (*Barn*. 6.13), except that the new Paradise surpasses the old in overwhelming measure (Beasley-Murray 330). See Beale 1103. *T. Dan* 5.9–13 brings together a cluster of these images: holy place, eternal peace, new Eden, new Jerusalem (note esp. 5.12, 'the saints shall refresh themselves in Eden; the righteous shall rejoice in the new Jerusalem'); cf. also Talbert, *Apocalypse* 100–103.

As Sweet (311) points out, the juxtaposition of these texts from the Pentateuch and Prophets, in 22.1–5, introduces a number of theologically creative contrasts. Thus, Ezekiel's river flowed from the temple (47.1–5), which in the new Jerusalem is the 'throne of God and of the Lamb' (Rev. 22.1); the water of the river, 'sparkling like crystal', recalls the 'sea of glass, transparent as crystal' in the 'old' heaven at 4.6 (κρύσταλλος, *krystallos*, 'crystal', is used in Revelation only there and at 22.1; but see 21.11); the 'great street' (πλατεῖα, *plateia*) of the city-temple evokes the 'main square' of the earthly Jerusalem, where the dead bodies of the witnesses were exhibited (11.8, q.v.; see also 21.21); and the 'tree of life' in the old Eden (Gen. 2.8–9; cf. 2.16–17; 3.1–24) is replaced by the final life-giving tree (Rev. 22.2). We may add that the mark of Cain (Gen. 4.15) gives way to the name of God and the Lamb on the forehead of the saints (Rev. 22.4).

The prophet-seer is shown 'a river of living water' by the angel who earlier introduced him to the holy city, Jerusalem (21.9, 15). The evocative imagery of 'water' frequently appears in the Johannine corpus. In the phrase, 'water of life' (ὕδατος ζωῆς, *hydatos zōēs*), the second genitive (lit. 'of life') is adjectival, meaning 'living' (hence the translation). The concept of 'living water', denoting the eternal, spiritual vitality which flows from God in Christ and through the Spirit, is used in the New Testament solely by the writers of John's Revelation and Gospel; see Rev. 7.17; 21.6; 22.17; also John 7.38; and for 'water' see Rev. 1.15; 14.2, 7; 16.5; 19.6; John 2.6–10; 3.5; 4.7–15; 13.5; 19.34; 1 John 5.6, 8.

In the words of Jesus at John 7.38–39 the source of the water of life is ambiguous, since the reference in 'from the heart shall flow living water' may be to the believer (so the NRSV translation) or to Christ himself. But in either case the water symbolizes the Spirit (7.39); and, according to the Fourth Gospel, the Spirit is the gift of both Jesus and the Father (John 14.6; 15.26; et al.). The same theology is anticipated by Rev. 22.1, where the living, crystalline water flows from the joint throne of God and the Lamb; and this may well be an early representation of the later Christian, credal confession that the Spirit proceeds from the Father and the Son (see also Rev. 22.17). Cf. Wilcock 212; Beale 1104; also Kruse, *John* 192–93; Smalley, 'Paraclete' 294–95. Sweet (311) notes that the context of John 7.37–39 is the Feast of Tabernacles, the harvest festival of ingathering (Exod. 23.16; cf. Zech. 14.16), and that the themes of this occasion were *water* (Rev. 22.1) and *light* (verse 5). For the high Christology of 22.1, where God and the Lamb share the symbol of sovereignty, see on 21.22–23; and cf. 3.12.

It is not immediately clear how the Greek at the conclusion of verse 1 and the opening of verse 2 should be punctuated. It is possible that verse 2 marks the beginning of a new sentence, in which case 'through the centre of the city's great street' (ἐν μέσῳ τῆς πλατείας αὐτῆς, *en mesō[i] tēs plateias autēs*, lit. 'in the middle of its street') refers prospectively to the location of the 'tree of life' (so NA AV NJB). More probably and less awkwardly, however, the 'centre of the street' relates back to the 'river of living water', which is said to flow 'from the throne, through the city' (as in the translation; see also RV NIV REB NRSV ESV). In the eternal Jerusalem the faithful will live in the closest possible proximity to the life-giving stream which derives from the very presence of God (cf. Mounce 398).

The angel next shows the seer 'trees of life' (ξύλον, *xylon*, lit. 'tree', is a collective singular; cf. Beckwith 765; Charles 2, 176; Swete 299), which stand 'on both banks of the river' (for the phraseology, ἐντεῦθεν καὶ ἐκεῖθεν, *enteuthen kai ekeithen*, lit. 'from here and from there', see John 19.18). The geographical details of the current vision are not important, despite Beasley-Murray (331), who conjectures that the tree is situated in the middle of the river, which at this point diverges into two branches. John continues to use spatial imagery in order to depict the nature of the new relationship which the saints enjoy in the eternal city. The general picture is clear: the writer is thinking of a single, main city-highway, with the river of life flowing along its length and an avenue of trees on either side (see Ps. 46.4); cf. Caird 280.

The 'tree of life' is an idea which occurs three times in the Apocalypse, apart from 22.2 (2.7 [q.v.]; 22.14, 19). Such trees regularly feature in Jewish perceptions of Paradise, where they occasionally become metaphors for the faithful (4 Ezra 8.52; *2 Enoch*

8.3–4; *Pss. Sol.* 14.3; *Odes Sol.* 11.16; see also *The Gospel of Truth* 36.35). More germane to the text of Rev. 22.2 is the observation that, in apocalyptic thought, the end of history and its beginning are often united (Rist 541); and in this passage the two 'Edens', Paradise lost and regained, are evidently present (see above). Indeed, the imagery in verse 2 once more blends *two* biblical traditions, present in Ezekiel as well as Genesis (see also the juxtaposition of the images of trees and water at 1QH 8.5–7). Genesis 2.9; 3.22 associate the tree of life in Eden with immortality. Ezek. 47.12 (see also 47.1–11) offers the promise that healing water will flow from the end-time sanctuary to create a river bordered by trees; and these are said to provide fresh fruit each month and 'leaves for healing'.

Like the water of life, it may be concluded, John is saying that the tree of life represents the close and vital relationship with God which the saints share eternally through Christ. The rich and creative character of this heavenly relationship is emphasized by the statement that each tree produces 'twelve types of fruit', and yields its crop 'month by month'. Abundance and freshness are obvious marks of life in the city of God. The fact that 'twelve' kinds of fruit are harvested from this arboretum may also be a subtle allusion to the nature of the Christian Church as the new Israel (see on 21.12–14, 19–21). Cf. Bauckham 1304*b*.

There remains in verse 2 the slightly perplexing comment that 'the leaves of the trees are intended for the healing of the nations'. Why, it may be asked, is therapy needed in the new Jerusalem, where God dwells with his people in light, and the potential curse of eating one tree of life has been replaced by the actual blessing of sharing the recreative properties of another? The answer is probably to be found in the use by the seer of the term ἔθνη (*ethnē*, 'nations'). This noun occupies a dual role in Revelation, as a description of societies which are opposed to God and his goodness (11.2; et al.), and of those which are converted to him through Christ in time (e.g. 5.9) and in eternity (21.24, 26). The healing of forces hostile to righteousness and justice remains a challenge for the Church militant; but even in the dimension of the new Jerusalem there will be those who choose to remain outside its gates (21.26–27; 22.15), and who will therefore need the opportunity to accept 'leaves of healing' by which to embrace God's universal invitation of love.

Beale (1109–11) considers the worldwide extent of the paradisal city-temple in 22.1–2, and argues plausibly that the Eden imagery introduced at 22.1 is designed to show that the building of the first temple, which in Jewish thought began with Gen. 2, will be 'completed in Christ and his people' (ibid. 1111). However, the further conclusion of Beale (1109) that the city-temple of the new Eden encompasses the new creation of 21.1, and is to be identified with it, may be regarded as less plausible. The vision of the new heaven and earth unveiled at 21.1 *includes* the prospect of an eternally renewed and uninterrupted covenant relationship between God and his people (22.3–5), without disappearing behind it. The new cosmos points *towards* the new Jerusalem; so that the spiritual realities signified by these images are associated, but distinctive.

3–4 The visionary character of the material in 22.1–2 is replaced in verses 3–5 by a more prophetic tone, as the seer describes the covenant relationship between God and his servants which is expected to characterize life in the new Jerusalem (cf. Aune 1178). The introduction to verse 3 continues the thought of 'the healing of the nations', expressed in verse 2 (q.v.).

Verse 3 begins with a negative statement, 'The curse of destruction will cease to exist', followed in verses 3*b*–4 by four positive affirmations about God dwelling with his own: the presence of the divine throne, together with the heavenly worship, spiritual knowledge and enduring mark of the faithful. The term, κατάθεμα (*katathema*, lit. 'that which is accursed'), is a *hapax legomenon* in the LXX and the New Testament. In Zech. 14.11, which lies behind Rev. 22.3 (Jerusalem shall never again be 'doomed to destruction'), the corresponding noun ἀνάθεμα (*anathema*) is used. Both Greek words legitimately render the Hebrew חֵרֶם (*ḥērem*, 'curse'), which is used in the Old Testament of the religious 'ban' of complete destruction, placed on households or individuals because of cultic sin or idolatry (see Exod. 23.31–33; Lev. 27.28–29; Deut. 7.26; Josh. 7.22–26).

The reference in Zech. 14.11 (see also verses 2–10) is to a future age, when a renewed and inhabited Jerusalem, freed from the threat of destruction for her sin, will dwell in security. (Aune [1179] interprets this text to mean that the 'curse of war' will no longer exist.) Rev. 22.3 may also reflect Isa. 34.1–2 where, using the language of חֵרֶם (*ḥērem*, 'curse'), the prophet says that the Lord has 'doomed' all the nations, and later (verse 5) identifies Edom as the people whom Yahweh has 'doomed to judgement' (cf. Bauckham, *Climax of Prophecy* 317–18). In Rev. 22.3 the seer foresees the reversal of such judgemental destruction, in the secure and creative life of the heavenly city which is to be enjoyed by a covenant people. But the backcloth to this scene from the imagery of the two 'Edens', already present in 22.1–2 (q.v.), cannot be excluded from the present verse (3). The 'ban' on the disobedient couple from Paradise (Gen. 3.20–24), and the sentence pronounced against them, will be overturned in the new paradisal city-temple; for in Christ believers from every background will be admitted freely and finally to the place where God dwells among them (cf. Prigent 627). The 'nations' which inhabit the new Eden, healed of their idolatry and injustice by the therapeutic leaves of the tree of life (verse 2), will never again (οὐκ ἔσται ἔτι, *ouk estai eti*, 'will cease to exist', lit. 'will not be again'; see the similar phrase at 21.1) be subject to the spiritual death which is the inevitable result of opposing divine sovereignty (cf. Bauckham 1304*b*).

The Christology in this passage continues to be high; for now it is proclaimed that the *joint* 'throne of God and of the Lamb' will dominate the city-temple (see on 21.22–23; 22.1). The subsequent personal pronouns in verses 3 and 4 are all in the singular ('his', 'him'); but they all refer to the *united* Godhead of Father and Son (cf. Hughes 232). Prigent (627–28) notes that previously in the Apocalypse the vision of God on his throne was the subject of exceptional disclosure, so that (4.1) heaven opened to unveil the Creator-King and his Messiah (4.2—5.14). In Rev. 22.3 God and the Lamb constantly exercise their sovereign rule at the heart of the new Jerusalem, and among their own.

There is no form of destruction in the city-temple, and no ban on the redeemed, because God's 'consummate, ruling presence' will fill the new Jerusalem (Beale 1113). All who pass through its gateways have access to the glory and light of God and the Lamb (21.23). The only possible response to this privilege is for the faithful to become 'servants' (οἱ δοῦλοι, *hoi douloi*, lit. 'slaves') who 'worship' (λατρεύσουσιν, *latreusousin*, lit. 'serve') at the throne. In 7.15 (q.v.), where the thought and language are very similar to 22.3, the saints of all time are said to act as priests in the heavenly temple, by worshipping God day and night before his throne; here they exercise a priestly ministry in the temple of the end-time city (cf. Isa. 61.6, 'you shall be named ministers of our God; you shall enjoy the wealth of the nations' [see also Rev. 21.24–26]). Cf. Beale 1113.

Two further eschatological blessings, which await the covenant members of the new Jerusalem, are specified in verse 4: 'They will see his face, and his name will be on their foreheads'. Both suggest the intimacy of the relationship which they will share with the Lord. Since the glory of God in all his fulness fills the eternal city-temple (22.1–2), access to the divine presence by the saints, serving as priests in the temple (verse 3), becomes immediate; and such a spiritual privilege is represented as 'seeing the face of God'. This hope is clearly expressed in the Old Testament and the thought of Judaism; see Ps. 11.4, 7 (the Lord sees humanity, the upright behold him); 17.15; 27.4; 4 Ezra 7.98; cf. Ps. 42.1–2; *T. Zeb.* 9.8; and it balances the thought of being *unable* to see the face of God because of his holiness (Exod. 33.18–23). The idea of 'seeing God' occurs elsewhere in the Johannine corpus (John 17.24; 1 John 3.2; cf. Rev. 1.7), and in the New Testament (2 Cor. 5.7; Heb. 12.14; 1 Pet. 1.8); it is also a spiritual concept which has deeply influenced the tradition, and in particular the mystical tradition, of the Christian Church (on that point see further Underhill, *Mystic Way* 257). For an exegesis of the notable text at 1 John 3.2 ('we shall be like him, because we shall see him as he really is') see Smalley, *1, 2, 3 John* 146–47. Here 'his face' (τὸ πρόσωπον αὐτοῦ, *to prosōpon autou*, with a singular pronoun) is that of both God and the Lamb (see above).

The second attribute of the faithful who dwell in God's city is that they will bear the divine 'name' on their foreheads, in contrast to the followers of the beast who are marked by him (13.16–18). In the context of 22.1–4 the 'name' of God and the Lamb, inscribed on the 'foreheads' of the saints, picks up the idea of the priestly ministry of the saints in the new Jerusalem (see verse 3); for in Jewish tradition God's name was written on the forehead of the high priest (Exod. 28.36–38). In this case, the metaphor suggests consecration to the service of the Lord (Swete 301). See also the 'new name' of the faithful who belong to the end-time Zion, according to Isa. 62.2; 65.15, with which Yahweh himself is associated (Beale 1114).

However, the idea of the divine name, written on the foreheads of a new people who are in a new relationship, is more directly related to the same image as it appears in the Apocalypse itself; see 7.3; 14.1; also 3.12. At 7.3, marking the foreheads of God's servants with a seal symbolizes their divine possession and protection; and this process, together with the inscription of the new name of God and the Lamb (3.12; 14.1), designates membership of the covenant community, through which the redeemed are empowered to carry out the witness to the nations intended for the true Israel (see further on 7.3). In the new Jerusalem, therefore, the faithful who see God will dwell uninterruptedly in his presence, protected by him and living in fellowship with all the 'nations' which have been healed by his love (verse 2). The figure of the 'name' in verse 4 may include the idea, which is also implied in the earlier imagery of *visio Dei* ('the vision of God'), of the saints being transformed into the *likeness* of God in Christ. Cf. Mounce 400.

5 This verse concludes the fifth prophecy, which concerns the new relationship between God and his people that the saints will enjoy in eternity. It also marks the end of the seer's vision, which began at 21.2, of the New Jerusalem itself. But the present scene does not finish until verse 17, even if the nature of the visionary material changes (see on verse 6).

The character of the heavenly city-temple is such that night time will be unknown to its members. Moreover, there will be no need for artificial or natural light in it, because the joint presence of God and the Lamb in glory will make spiritual darkness impossible, and provide the new Jerusalem with constant illumination. Verse 5 echoes the very similar statements about the city of God at 21.23–25 (q.v.). For the background to this imagery see Isa. 60.19–20; Zech. 14.7; also 4 Ezra 7.38–42 (on the day of judgement there will be no night, sun or brightness, but only 'the splendour of the glory of the Most High, by which all shall see what has been destined'). The phrase, νὺξ οὐκ ἔσται ἔτι (*nyx ouk estai eti*, 'night time will be no more', lit. 'night will not still be'), is repeated almost verbatim from 21.25.

The subject of the next clause ('they will need neither lamplight nor sunlight'), which refers back to verse 3, is δοῦλοι (*douloi*, 'servants'). Beale (1115) suggests that φῶς λύχνου (*phōs lychnou*, 'lamplight', lit. 'light of a lamp') refers to the role of God's people as 'lampstands', witnessing to the light of the divine lamp in a world of darkness (cf. 1.12, 20; 2.1; also 1.4; 4.5; 21.11–26). In the new Jerusalem that role will be finally perfected (ibid.). While this interpretation is plausible, a more obvious reference in this text is to the light of the Godhead, as in 21.23, where the glory of God is the 'light' of the holy city, and the Lamb is a 'flaming torch' (λύχνος, *lychnos*, lit. 'lamp') for it; and this understanding is supported by the parallel statement that 'sunlight' will be unnecessary in the city-temple (so 21.23 again), and by the following description of the Lord God as its 'shining light'. The one divine 'lamp' illuminates the ideal Church, in contrast to the many 'lampstands' of the (seven) churches on earth (Swete 296).

No other light is needed in the new Jerusalem because 'the Lord God will shine' on his people. The doublet, 'Lord God' (κύριος ὁ θεός, *kyrios ho theos*), emphasizes the sovereignty of the Godhead in the new creation, and balances the 'reign' of the faithful mentioned in the next phrase. The 'shining face' of God is a metaphor in the Old Testament for divine favour (see Ps. 4.6; 31.16; 67.1; 119.135; et al.). In the present verse (21.5) the expression most probably echoes the Aaronic blessing at Num. 6.24–26, which includes the prayer, 'the Lord make his face to shine upon you' (6.25). In the heavenly city that hope will be finally realized; for the face of the sovereign Lord God, as seen by the faithful (verse 4), will 'shine on them' (see also Ps. 118.27; 4QTQahat ar 1, 1.1). The priestly blessing of Num. 6 is an appropriate backcloth to the divine 'shining' on the saints in eternity at Rev. 22.5; for their ministry in the new city-temple includes priesthood (1.6; 22.3) and, like Aaron, they bear God's name on their foreheads (verse 4; see also Num. 6.27). Furthermore, preservation and peace are themes in the blessing of Num. 6.23–27; and these resonate with the thought of Rev. 21.2—22.5 (note 21.4, 25; 22.4; et al.). See further Beale 1115–16; also Beasley-Murray 333; Sweet 312.

Although the saints are said to 'reign for ever and ever' in heaven, it is not immediately apparent who will be their subjects; and in this vision such a consideration may not be important. Prigent (628) connects this promise with the millennial rule of the faithful in 20.4–6; but that is unlikely, since the 'reign' of 22.5 is eternal, and not limited to one thousand years. (The formula, 'for ever and ever' [εἰς τοὺς αἰῶνας τῶν αἰώνων, *eis tous aiōnas tōn aiōnōn*, lit. 'to the ages of the ages'], is liturgical in character; see 1.6; et al.) The reign of God's people on earth is referred to at 5.10, and the participation of the faithful in the eternal rule of God is anticipated at Dan. 7.18, 27 (Aune 1181). In an eschatological extension of such a concept, it is probable that the everlasting 'reign' of the saints in the new Jerusalem relates to their share in the divine judgement of the unfaithful (see 2.26–27; 17.14; 19.14–16; also Matt. 19.28; 1 Cor. 6.2–3). As Swete (301) says, there is also a harmonious symmetry between the worship (λατρεύσουσιν, *latreusousin*, 'they will worship') and the rule (βασιλεύσουσιν, *basileusousin*, 'they will reign') of the saints in heaven. 'Perfect service will be accompanied by perfect sovereignty' (ibid.).

Prophecy 6: New Advent (22.6–9)

6–7   The remainder of Scene 7 (22.6–17) includes material which is visionary in character, although the prophetic disclosure of covenant life and relationships in the city-temple of the new Jerusalem has by now been brought to a close. Verses 6–17 look back to 21.2—22.5, and to some extent act as a conclusion to it. But the dialogue between John and the risen Jesus or his angel in this passage also provides important teaching about the nature of the Apocalypse itself, and the authentication of its content, as well as anticipating the final coming of Christ, and the testimony of the faithful to that advent. Those two major themes in 22.6–17, new advent and new testimony, are woven together in a structure that is markedly more fluid than is usual in Revelation.

It may be argued that the epilogue to Revelation as a complete drama does not begin until 22.18 (q.v.), where the seer speaks directly to his audience; even if commentators such as Vanni (*La struttura letteraria* 249) and Roloff (248–49) regard 22.6–21 as the conclusion of the book (see also above). In 22.6–17, the writer picks up a number of major themes which have been highlighted already in this work: for instance, faithfulness (verse 6; cf. 14.12); holiness (verse 11; cf. 11.1–3); new life (verses 14, 17; cf. 3.4–5); and salvation through the work of the Lamb (verses 12–14; cf. 5.9–10; 7.13–14). Beale (1122–56) discovers five exhortations to holiness in the section 22.6–20 (verses 6–7, 8–10, 11–12, 13–17, 18–20).

Verse 6 refers back to the vision so far recorded in this scene, and probably to all that has been disclosed in the Revelation (see below); but it also points forward to the unveiling yet to come in verses 6–17. The speaker in verse 6 is not identified, since εἶπέν μοι (*eipen moi*) means simply 'he said to me'. As it is clearly the exalted Jesus who speaks in verse 7 (note the connective καί, *kai*, 'and', hidden in the translation, which introduces that verse), he may well be the one who refers in verse 6 to 'these words', which are 'trustworthy and true' (cf. Charles 2, 217–18). Equally, the interlocutor in verse 6 could well be the bowl angel who has been addressing and guiding the seer in 21.9, 15; 22.1 (Swete 302). If a heavenly being other than Christ is involved at verse 6, however, that figure is more probably to be associated with the interpreting angel of 1.1 (note the identical phrase at 1.1 and 22.6, ἃ δεῖ γενέσθαι ἐν τάχει, *ha dei genesthai en tachei*, 'what must soon take place', lit. 'the things that will happen soon'); so Aune 1182. In that case, the words of Jesus in verse 7 are spoken through his angelic messenger (cf. Christ's communication through an emissary in Matt. 10.40; John 13.20; 1 Thess. 2.13; et al.). So Beale 1123.

For 'words' which are 'trustworthy and true' (οἱ λόγοι πιστοὶ καὶ ἀληθινοί, *hoi logoi pistoi kai alēthinoi*), see the exact expression at 21.5; cf. also 19.9 'true words (of God)'. The term λόγος (*logos*, 'word'; plural λόγοι, *logoi*, 'words') is used in Revelation in two major ways: to mean the expression of God's nature (in Christ), or the testimony of believers about him (which equates with 'the gospel'), as in 1.2, 9; 3.8, 10; 6.9; 12.11; 17.17; 19.9, 13; 20.4 (cf. John 1.1–14; 4.39; et al.); and with reference to 'the words of (this book of) prophecy' in the Apocalypse itself (1.3; 21.5; 22.6–7, 9–10, 18–19). The fact that the latter meaning occurs only at 1.3, outside the current scene in Chapters 21 and 22, suggests strongly that the 'words' in 22.6 relate to the contents of the Revelation in its totality. The exalted Christ is affirming the truth of the visions concerning God's present and future plans for his creation, as these have been mediated through him by the interpreting angel to his servant John (1.1; cf. the similar attestation, on the human level, at John 21.24). The content of these words, which may be trusted, embraces not only the Apocalypse in its entirety but also the vision of life in the new Jerusalem in particular. Thus 22.6 forms an inclusion with 21.5, where the same phrase appears; and while 21.5 looks back to the drama as a whole, and on to the remainder of the scene, 22.6 concludes the seer's understanding of God's future work of new creation, with its focus in the holy city, and leads into the future itself, with its focus in the advent of the Messiah (22.7–17). Cf. Isa. 65.16–19; also Isa. 43.18–19; 66.22; Dan. 2.45; see also Beale 1123–24.

In the phrase, 'the Lord, the God of the spirits of the prophets' (ὁ κύριος ὁ θεὸς τῶν πνευμάτων τῶν προφητῶν, *ho kyrios ho theos tōn pneumatōn tōn prophētōn*), the expression 'the Lord, the God' is the equivalent of the sovereign title 'Lord God' in verse 5 (but see the textual note on verse 6). The genitive, in the description which follows ('of the spirits', τῶν πνευμάτων, *tōn pneumatōn*), is objective, giving the meaning, 'the Lord God controlling [perhaps inspiring] the spirits'. Note the parallel expression, 'Lord of the Spirits', in *1 Enoch* 37–71 (*The Book of the Similitudes*); e.g. 38.2; 67.8–9. It is then possible to interpret 'the spirits of the prophets' in two ways.

(a) The 'prophets' refers technically and in a restricted sense to those who hold the office of prophet, whether Jewish or Christian, and whose ministry is inspired by the Spirit (in which case 'of the prophets' is also an objective genitive); cf. Knight 140.

(b) More probably, 'prophets' may be understood as a genitive of possession, and mean those who have a spirit which is quickened by the Spirit of God (Swete 303; cf. 2 Pet. 1.21). In that case the reference may well be to prophetic testimony in general, and to the Christian Church as a community of prophecy; although this will include 'prophets' as such. Cf. Smalley, 'Paraclete' 294.

Such an understanding is supported by the evidently parallel allusion in the next part of the sentence in verse 6 to God's 'servants': 'the God of the spirits of the *prophets* has sent his angel to reveal to his *servants* what must soon take place'. The one points to the other; for 'servants' of God, as used by the author of Revelation, is a regular designation for *all* Christians, as for John himself (1.1; 2.20; 7.3; 19.2, 5; 22.3). Note also the combination, in this sense, of God's 'servants, the prophets' at 10.7; 11.18; and the inclusive reference to 'servants, and your colleagues (ἀδελφοί, *adelphoi*, lit 'brothers') the prophets' at 22.9; cf. also on 19.10. On this section see further Beale 1124–26.

The interpreting 'angel' (see above) has been 'sent' (ἀπέστειλεν, *apesteilen*, in the sense of 'commissioned'; cf. 1.1) by God to reveal to his servants 'what must soon take place' (cf. verse 16; also Dan. 2.28–29). See the same phrase at 1.1, and the continuous present tense of the verb in the opening phrase of verse 7, as in verse 12, ἰδοὺ ἔρχομαι ταχύ (*idou erchomai tachy*, 'See, I am coming soon'). John's eschatology in the Apocalypse is balanced (see on 1.1; also above, 12–13, 16–17). For the seer draws together throughout the present and the future, the temporal and the eternal. To him the unveiling of God's salvific purposes for his creation is an ongoing and ever-present reality; while the coming of Christ, and his sovereign rule, are always imminent (1.1, 3; 22.6–7, 12; cf. Mark 13.7). See also on 22.20.

Verse 7 ends with a benediction: happy is 'the one who obeys the message of this prophetic document' (ὁ τηρῶν τοὺς λόγους τῆς προφητείας τοῦ βιβλίου τούτου, *ho tērōn tous logous tēs prophēteias tou bibliou toutou*, lit. 'the one keeping the words of the prophecy of this book'). This is the sixth of the seven makarisms in Revelation (see also 1.3; 14.13; 16.15; 19.9; 20.6; 22.14). For prophetic 'words' in the Apocalypse see on verse 6. The reference in verse 7 is similarly to the drama of Revelation as a whole, the climax of which (in one sense) occurs in this scene. The exhortation to spiritual obedience ('keeping the words' of Christ) evokes the ongoing demands made upon the Johannine community in the seven oracles of Rev. 2—3 (see 3.3, 8, 10; also 2.26); note further 1.3; 12.17; 14.12; 16.15; and see on 22.9. John is concerned that his own circle, and the Church at large, should obey the message of Revelation, with its promise of final salvation through judgement. The Apocalypse is a 'prophecy' to be obeyed, in the sense that it reveals and proclaims the true nature of the conflict between the beast and the Lamb, between Babylon and Jerusalem, and summons its audience to the one victory which can overcome the world (15.2–4; cf. 1 John 5.4). See Caird 283.

8–9 The name 'John' appears at the end of Revelation, as it did at the beginning (see on 1.1, 4, 9). Such an inclusion provides a witness to the apostolic authority of this dramatic work, as well as an authentication of its testimony (cf. Bauckham 1305*a*). The stance adopted in this commentary takes the 'John' in question to be the apostle, the beloved disciple (see above, 2–3). For a similar personal attestation see Dan. 12.5, 9 LXX. The seer identifies himself as 'the one hearing and seeing these visions (ταῦτα, *tauta*, lit. "these things")'. For the close relationship between spiritual audition and sight, and their importance in Johannine thought, see on 4.1; et al.; see also 1 John 1.1–3.

The two verbs in the present tense in verse 8, 'hearing and seeing' (ἀκούων καὶ βλέπων, *akouōn kai blepōn*), which imply the immediacy of John's visions, are repeated at the start of the next sentence in the past tense (ἤκουσα καὶ ἔβλεψα, *ēkousa kai eblepsa*, 'I heard and saw'). There is some textual uncertainty about the reading, ἔβλεψα (*eblepsa*, 'saw', aorist), as supported by NA, Swete 304, since John does not use this form of the aorist of βλέπειν (*blepein*, 'to see') elsewhere, preferring the version εἶδον (*eidon*, 'I saw'). Aune (1141) suggests that the original reading was probably the imperfect, ἔβλεπον (*eblepon*, lit. 'I was seeing'), as read by A and MSS of Oecumenius (see also Charles 2, 384), and that this was corrected to one or other of the aorist forms of the verb to agree with the aorist tense of the accompanying ἤκουσα (*ēkousa*, 'I heard'). In this case, a problem of interpretation arises, since it is not clear why the author should place aorist and imperfect tenses side by side. Aune (ibid.) concludes that the aorist ('heard') refers to John's revelatory experience as a series of events completed in the past, while the imperfect (lit. 'was seeing') is consequential, and anticipates the results of that action (in this case, the seer's obeisance).

The language and thought in the remainder of verses 8–9 echo very closely 19.9–10 (q.v.), even if the angel who speaks to the seer in that context, and receives his reverence, is the 'strong angel' of 18.21, rather than the interpreting angel of 22.6–9. On 'angels' in Revelation see above, 28–30. There is a further difference, in that the statement about those who are 'holding to the testimony of Jesus', at the conclusion of 19.10, is replaced at 22.9 by a reference to those who 'obey the commands (prophetic words) in this book'; although this variation is more apparent than real, since the 'witness of Jesus' is defined at 19.10 precisely as 'the spirit of prophecy' (Prigent 636). See further on 19.9–10. For the combination of prostration and worship in the presence of a heavenly being see the reverence of the elders in the throne-vision at 4.10–11; 5.14. The seer worships at the feet of the angel 'revealing' (δεικνύοντος, *deiknyontos*) the visions to him. The verb, δείκνυμι (*deiknymi*), meaning 'to show' in the sense of revealing or making known, is used in Revelation exclusively of apocalyptic visions in which an angel is the intermediary (cf. BDAG 214*b*; see 1.1; 4.1; 17.1; 21.9–10; 22.1, 6, 8.

The dramatic confrontation between the seer and the angel, and the reaction of the heavenly being to John's 'worship' ('See that you do not!'), appears to be a needless repetition after the identical scene at 19.9–10. Yet this is not an example of the author falling into ways which have already been denounced as erring (Prigent 636), or a case of careless duplication (cf. Bauckham, *Climax of Prophecy* 133). The call to remain obedient to the covenant commands of God, and to direct all worship to him alone, emphasizes the need for members of the Johannine community, and of the Church in general, to reject idolatry of all kinds; and this has been a theme throughout the Apocalypse (see 2.14–29; 9.20; 21.8, 27; 22.15; et al.). The battle against falsehood needs to be fought on more than one front (Caird 283). The synonymous incidents in 19.9–10 and 22.8–9 occur also at the close of scenes which depict the old Babylon and the new Jerusalem; so that this doublet provides not only a structural balance, but also a theological challenge: to choose life, rather than death. For the general reference in verse 9 of 'prophets', as of 'servant' and 'colleagues/brothers', see on 22.6. In Revelation the term, σύνδουλος (*syndoulos*, 'servant-companion', lit. 'fellow-servant'), is used elsewhere only at 6.11 and 19.10.

The authority of the apocalypse in progress in 22.6–9 is not limited to the immediately preceding vision of life in the new Jerusalem (21.2—22.5). Rather, as in verses 6–7, it expands to include the revelation given in the whole document (τοὺς λόγους τοῦ βιβλίου τούτου, *tous logous tou bibliou toutou*, 'the commands in this book', lit. 'the words of this book'). The 'angel' in this episode is the being who 'showed' the seer the whole prophetic vision (1.1; 22.6). Accordingly, the fact that the angel rejects John's reverence at this point indicates that the authority behind the message of Revelation is not angelic but divine, and that to the God of judgement and salvation alone worship is due. Indeed, the purpose of John's Apocalypse is to inspire loyalty and devotion not to the Satan (13.4–15; 14.9–11; 16.2; 19.20; 20.4), but inclusively to the God whose covenant love has been disclosed above all in the exalted Lamb (5.13–14; 7.11–12; 11.15–16; 14.7; 15.4; 19.4, 10). In this connection, note 22.18–19 (God's imprimatur upon the 'book'), and 22.16 (Jesus, not his angelic messenger, speaks directly to the prophet-seer). See further Bauckham, *Climax of Prophecy* 134; Beale 1128–29.

Prophecy 7: New Testimony (22.10–17)

10   The final prophetic oracle in the last scene of Revelation includes the theme of witness. After his vision of the special relationship which will exist between God and his people in eternity, as expressed in the dazzling imagery of the new Jerusalem, the prophet-seer records two divinely inspired testimonies. He is given fresh assurance about the truth of God's salvific life in Christ (verses 14, 17), and also about the authenticity of this disclosure in the Apocalypse itself (verse 16; see also verse 20). Although 22.10–17 may be regarded as a distinct sub-section, its thought is to some extent continued from verses 6–9 (cf. the 'trustworthy and true' words of verses 6–7, 9); moreover, the speaker is still the interpreting angel, who reappeared at verse 6 (see also 1.1; and note the translation of καὶ λέγει μοι, *kai legei moi*, as 'And he continues to say to me'). There are several speakers in this passage (the angel, Christ, John, the Spirit, the Church), and together their sayings provide almost an antiphonal chant (note the strophic form of verses 11 and 17).

The seer is instructed by the angel not to 'secrete the words of this prophetic document' (μὴ σφραγίσῃς τοὺς λόγους τῆς προφητείας τοῦ βιβλίου τούτου, *mē sphragisē[i]s tous logous tēs prophēteias tou bibliou toutou*, lit. 'do not seal up the words of the prophecy of this book'). This command is the opposite of the injunction that John should 'seal up the message of the seven thunderclaps', and not consider writing it down (10.4). The open character of the Apocalypse as a whole is a reminder that its contents are divine in origin (1.10–11, 19; 21.5, the seer is told to record his heavenly vision), and worthy of an obedient response (22.9, 'worship God!'); note also the 'open scroll' of 5.1–9; et al. Cf. *Apoc. Paul* 51 (Syriac), where Paul is said to have been given a revelation to 'make it known'. See Beale 1129. For the 'words of this prophetic document' see on verses 6–7; also 1.3; 17.17; 19.9; 21.5; 22.9, 18–19.

The idea of 'sealing up prophetic words' occurs elsewhere in the Bible only at Dan. 12.4 (see the version in Theod.), where Daniel is told to 'keep the words secret and the book sealed until the time of the end'; but see also Isa. 8.16; Dan. 8.26; 12.9; *1 Enoch* 1.2; 4 Ezra 12.37; 14.5–6. Clearly Dan. 12.4 lies behind Rev. 22.10, but now in reverse. The implications of the Danielic prophecy about the defeat of unrighteous nations, and the establishment of God's eternal reign with his people (Dan. 12.5–13), were not fully understood at the time. But in Christ they have been fulfilled, and the possibilities to which they point have been made available (cf. John 12.37–41; Eph. 3.4–6); and the recorded, unsealed visions of the Apocalypse make this clear.

The remaining clause in verse 10 provides the reason for the injunction to keep the 'prophetic document' unsealed: 'since (γάρ, *gar*, lit. "for", "because") the time is at hand' (cf. 1.1; 22.6). The end-time, of which the prophet spoke in Dan. 12.4, 9, is now imminent. But John's eschatology is balanced, and in his thought the past, present and future are fused together. For him, the parousia of Christ and the consummation of the ages are constantly pressing in, and indeed are always 'at hand' (ἐγγύς, *engus*, lit. 'near', in Rev. 22.10; cf. Mark 1.15, 'the kingdom of God has come near' [ἤγγικεν, *ēngiken*]). This provides no cause for spiritual complacency, but rather a basis for perpetual watchfulness (Mark 13.32–37), and an encouragement for believers, including those in John's own churches, to remain steadfast, obedient and faithful (Rev. 3.3, 11, 20; 14.12; 22.9). See further on 22.12, 20. For Johannine eschatology see above, 12–13, 16–17; also Caird 300–301.

11 The identity of the speakers in the closing stages of the present scene is not always entirely clear. But, since the interpreting angel addresses the prophet-seer in verses 9–10, he presumably continues to speak in verse 11; although these words may be a comment by John himself. In the apocalyptic material of the current sequence, however, precision of this kind is not of major significance, particularly since the origin of the visions in Revelation is in any case ultimately divine. The Greek form of verse 11 is strophic, as the two halves consist of four jussive clauses of the same length, each concluding with ἔτι (*eti*, lit. 'still'). Moreover, the first two imperatives, which are negative ('unjust', 'defiled'), are exactly balanced by the second pair, which are positive ('righteous', 'holy').

The vocabulary in verse 11 is of interest. The verb ἀδικέω (*adikeō*) is used only here in Revelation to mean 'act unjustly' (lit. 'do wrong'); elsewhere (2.11; 6.6; et al.) it signifies 'causing harm'. The second term, ῥυπαίνομαι (*rhypainomai*, 'defile'), occurs only here in the New Testament, while the cognate adjective, ῥυπαρός (*rhyparos*, 'defiled'), is found here alone in the Apocalypse with the sense of moral uncleanness (cf. the literal sense at Jas. 2.2). Similarly, δίκαιος (*dikaios*, 'righteous') and its cognate, δικαιοσύνη (*dikaiosynē*, lit. 'righteousness'), appear only at this point in Revelation with reference to human righteousness; elsewhere these terms describe the character of God or Christ (15.3; 16.5, 7; 19.2, 11). Finally, the adjective ἅγιος (*hagios*, lit. 'holy') is found only here in Revelation in a personal, individual context; otherwise the term is used in a cultic sense ('holy city', 11.2; 21.2, 10; et al.), or as a description of God or Jesus (3.7; 4.8; et al.), of the (Christian) saints (5.8; 8.3–4; et al.), or of angels (14.10). The verb, ἁγιάζω (*hagiazō*, lit. 'keep oneself holy'), occurs only at 22.11 in Revelation.

Because the language of 22.11 is distinctive, although it is still Johannine, and because its thought is slightly complex (see below), Charles (2, 221–22), followed by Prigent (638), regards this verse as a later addition. But there is no need for such a view, particularly if the meaning of verse 11 is carefully considered. The seer is not suggesting that anyone on the outskirts of the new Jerusalem is 'beyond redemption' (so BDAG 20*a*, on 'let the person who is unjust continue to act unjustly'). Rather, he is putting in another way what has been declared already: that, at the consummation, those who wish to remain outside the gates of the holy city, presumably aware of the richness of the relationship within them, have the freedom to do so (see on 21.8; also 21.27; 22.15).

Dan. 12.10 seems to stand directly behind this verse ('many shall be purified . . . but the wicked shall continue to act wickedly; none of the wicked shall understand, but those who are wise shall understand'). Beale (1132–33) also notes the probable link between Rev. 22.11 and the 'hearing' formula present in the seven oracles of Chapters 2—3 (2.7; et al., 'let anyone with an ear listen to what the Spirit is saying to the churches'); and this, in turn, is based on the exhortation to idolatrous Israel in Isa. 6.9–10 (quoted at Matt. 13.9–17; John 12.39–40), where unbelievers are apparently summoned *not* to hear, and believers are called to obey (cf. also Ezek. 3.27, which develops the obduracy motif from Isa. 6; also Jer. 44.25; Ezek. 20.39). But, as Bauckham (1305) says, the notion that in Rev. 22.11 anyone is *commanded* to refuse to hear, or to be unjust and defiled, can only be a figure of speech. The point concerns the inevitable double response which results from any truly prophetic proclamation. Those unwilling to receive the good news increase their evil by refusing to listen, while the righteous develop their faith by heeding the prophecy. Nevertheless, this epigrammatic statement 'does not exclude the two different cases of change from one category to the other' (ibid. 1305*b*). See also Ezek. 3.18–20; 33.12–16.

In all these contexts, therefore, the theme of continuity and consistency does not necessarily imply fixity, or destiny. Note Eusebius, *HE* 5.1.58–61, where the theme of 'persistence' in Rev. 22.11 is applied to the varied and potentially *changeable* situations of the martyrs of Gaul (cf. Prigent 638). Despite the unchanging invitation from a God of covenant love, Israel (old and new) is likely to persist in faithfulness on the one hand, or apostasy and infidelity on the other. However, this does not mean that it is impossible to cross the line, one way or the other, or that new life is denied to those who repent (against Mounce 406; cf. Swete 305; Hendriksen 208; Kiddle 451–52; Wilcock 216; Wall 264–65). To say that 'the time is at hand' (verse 10) need *not* suggest that it is too late to change, as the beatitude at verse 14 shows (Sweet 316); see also verses 16–17. Even if the wicked continue to practise wickedness, the wise will still understand; and, in the face of obduracy, obedience remains a possibility. However, in the end it is still necessary to keep the covenant and be holy, in order to enter the heavenly Jerusalem; and part of John's task is to reveal to his audience that right behaviour, flowing from adequate belief, is enabled by the Lamb himself, who is one with the Father as well as with his Church (Smalley, *Thunder and Love* 180). For a similar interpretation of verse 11 see also Caird 284; Beasley-Murray 337–38; Knight 141.

12–13 These verses provide the basis for the paraenesis in verse 11. The exalted Christ now speaks. For the promise that Jesus is 'coming soon' (ἔρχομαι ταχύ, *erchomai tachy*, 'I am coming soon') see on 2.16; 3.11; 22.7, 20; cf. also 1.1; 3.3; 11.14; 22.6. For John's eschatology in the Apocalypse see above, 12–13, 16–17. The prophet-seer is aware of the imminence of the Lamb's advent, as a focal event within the consummation, without attempting to determine its chronological placing in the scheme of salvation history (cf. BDAG 993*a*). There is an 'inaugurated' dimension to the notion of Christ's coming in 22.12, in the sense that for John the believer's salvation is a possibility before the end (6.9–11; 7.14–17; 14.1–3), and judgement is an ongoing reality in the present (2.22–23; 6.1–8; 12.7–9). Yet, at the same time, it is also true that the emphasis in the vision of Scene 7 is on the future, and indeed on what will happen at the end-time. See further Isa. 47.11; Jer. 6.26; Mal. 3.1; 2 Pet. 3.8–13; also Beale 1134.

The testimony continues with the statement that, at his parousia, Christ will bring with him his 'recompense' (μισθός, *misthos*, lit. 'reward'), and 'repay all people according to their deeds' (ἀποδοῦναι ἑκάστῳ ὡς τὸ ἔργον ἐστὶν αὐτοῦ, *apodounai hekastō[i] hōs to ergon estin autou*, lit. 'to give to each as is his work'). The background to this idea is to be found in Isa. 40.10 (see 62.11; also Jer. 17.10; Matt. 16.27), 'the Lord God comes with might; . . . his reward is with him, and his recompense before him'. The 'reward' given to the faithful, in the context of Isa. 40, is undeserved (verses 6–9), and salvific rather than judgemental (verses 11–31). In Rev. 22.12 this eschatological situation is reinterpreted with reference to universal judgement on the righteous or unrighteous 'deeds' of society (hardly *God's* 'work'; despite Beale 1137); note the association between judgement and human works at 2.23. See also the quotation of Rev. 22.12 at *1 Clem.* 34.3, which includes an allusion to Prov. 24.12 close to the text in the Apocalypse (the Lord will 'repay all according to their deeds'). So Charles 2, 221; although Aune (1218) is cautious about this connection, in view of variations in diction.

The thought of 'repayment for (wrong) deeds' recalls the warning to those in the congregation at Thyatira who are loyal to Jezebel rather than God (2.22–23, 26; cf. also 2.2, 5–6, 19; 3.1–2, 8, 15; 9.20; 16.11; 18.6). At 14.13, by contrast, a benediction is given to the faithful dead who 'die in the Lord', and whose 'deeds accompany them'. For judgement according to works in the Apocalypse see on 20.12–15. It is evident that John is at one with Paul in his teaching about the relationship between faith and deeds in the life of believers. To be in union with Christ, according to both apostles, is to have eternal life (see on 1.9); and from the trust on which this rests should flow the evidence, accountable before God, of good (notably loving) works (see Rev. 2.4, 19; 12.10–12, 17; John 13.34; 15.12, 17 [the Johannine love command]; also 1 John 3.11; 4.7; 2 John 5; Rom. 2.6; 1 Cor. 3.10–15; 2 Cor. 5.10; Eph. 2.8–10; et al.). Christians who are sealed by God (Rev. 7.4) still need to believe and behave properly, even if the judgement on their works is entrusted to one whose coming offers to humanity salvation by grace (1.4–6); cf. Prigent 639. See further Sweet 316; Smalley, 'Christ–Christian Relationship' 96–99.

In verse 13 the risen Christ declares that he is 'the Alpha and the Omega, the first and the last, the beginning and the end'. The title, 'Alpha and Omega', is used of God at 1.8 (q.v.) and 21.6, and of Jesus in 22.13. The equivalent, 'first and last', appears in Revelation solely in association with Christ (1.17; 2.8, where the resurrection is in view; and 22.13); while 'beginning and end' is a description of God at 21.6 and of the Messiah here. Only at 22.13 does the grouping of all three antithetical titles occur (cf. Aune 1219). At 21.6, 'Alpha and Omega' refers to God in a setting of salvation (see 21.2–7), whereas here the title is used of Christ in a judgemental context. However, the two are related in every way, not least because God in his Messiah provides the constant means in the Apocalypse of salvation *through* judgement (see on 19.1–16).

The allocation of the same designations (Alpha and Omega, beginning and end) to both God and Christ points to the high Christology of the prophet-seer (see also the deity of the exalted Lamb implicit at 21.22; 22.1, 3). Father and Son are revealed, in creation and new creation, at both ends of salvation history (cf. John 1.1–14); and, at every point in between, Christ shares the sovereign rule of God. The end is not an event, but a person. Jesus is the firstborn from the dead (1.5), and the origin and goal of God's creation (3.14; 22.13). As such, he stands in sovereign contrast to all false claimants of power and life (13.18). See Sweet 316.

14–15 It is possible that these two verses are spoken by the exalted Christ, who addresses the seer in the flanking passages, 22.12–13 and 22.16–17. But, more probably, the benediction and statement in 22.14–15 form a parenthesis which derives from John the Divine himself. 'Those are blessed who wash their robes clean, so that they will have access to the tree of life' is the final makarism of seven in the Apocalypse (see on 22.7). As at 14.13 and 19.9, the form of the blessing is plural (μακάριοι οἱ, *makarioi hoi*, lit. 'blessed [are] those'). Cf. 4Q525 = 4QBéat *frag*. 2.2.1–4, where three of the five beatitudes are in the plural. The blessing at 22.14 restates in a positive form the fifth benediction in Revelation (20.6, the second death 'has no hold' over the ones who share in the first resurrection). Cf. Beale 1139.

For the imagery of salvation as 'washing robes clean' see on 7.14; cf. also, using the language of a 'robe' or 'garment' (στολή, *stolē*), 6.11; 7.9, 13. At 3.4, a few members of the church in Sardis are commended for *not* 'staining their clothing' (using ἱμάτια, *himatia*, lit. 'garments'), because they have remained faithful to their Christian commitment, and therefore qualify as 'conquerors' (οἱ νικῶντες, *hoi nikōntes*); cf. 2.7; 3.5; et al. But the metaphor of 'washed' robes in 22.14 should be interpreted in line with 7.14, since both passages use the verb πλύνω (*plynō*, 'wash'), which in the earlier text is associated directly and paradoxically with being 'whitened by the blood of the Lamb'. That is to say, the faithful will receive the blessings of eternal life in the new Jerusalem because they have been identified with the sacrificial death of Christ (cf. 19.13), as well as receiving his name on their foreheads (22.4).

However, the metaphor of robes of believers being 'washed clean' through the cross of Jesus includes the thought of responding to God's salvific gifts in Christ by living a holy life which is morally and spiritually renewed (21.5–8; 22.11–13; cf. 16.15; also John 13.5–11). The verb at 7.14, ἔπλυναν (*eplynan*, 'they have washed'), is in the aorist, denoting an action taking place at a particular moment in the past; whereas here, at 22.14, the participle (πλύνοντες, *plynontes*, lit. 'washing'), is present, suggesting a spiritual activity which is immediate and ongoing. See the textual note on verse 14.

The understanding of verse 14 set out above is consonant with the seer's theology elsewhere in Revelation. As a result, there is no need to see in the imagery of cleansing a reference to baptism (so Prigent 640), or limit access to the city of God, in John's thought, to redeemed martyrs alone (Caird 285; followed apparently by Mounce 407 n. 23; see also Rist 546–47). The scope of the divine work of salvation, here as in 7.14 (q.v.), is inclusive. All God's faithful people 'will have access to the tree of life, and may enter the city by its gates'. Like the 'overcomers' of 2.7, they have washed their robes 'so that' (ἵνα, *hina*) they 'may have access to' (ἔσται ἡ ἐξουσία αὐτῶν ἐπί, *estai hē exousia autōn epi*, lit. 'it shall be their authority over') the tree of life.

The phrase, ἐξουσία ἐπί (*exousia epi*, lit. 'authority over'), is used elsewhere in the Apocalypse with verbs of 'giving' and 'having' (see 2.26; 6.8; 11.6; 13.7; 14.18). There is a close parallel to 22.14 at 16.9, where God is described as 'holding the authority to inflict' the bowl-plagues. Similarly, the faithful 'have the right' to enjoy the fruits of the 'tree' of eternal life (for which see on 2.7; 22.2). This corresponds in reverse to Gen. 3.22–24, where sinful man, having tried in the first creation to grasp at equality with God, is banned from Paradise and its tree of life. That sentence of exclusion is now removed, so that all who wish may have access to the life-giving tree in the new creation, through the one who did *not* regard equality with God as something to be exploited (Phil. 2.6). Cf. *1 Enoch* 25.4–5; see also Aune 1221–22; Prigent 640–41. For the twelve 'gates' of the new Jerusalem see 21.12–21. The right to pass through them belongs to those who are faithful members of the *new* Israel.

'Outside' (ἔξω, *exō*) the gates are those who wish to be there (verse 15). For the list of wrongdoers see *Pss. Sol.* 17.21–25, where *all* who 'trample her to destruction' are to be excluded from the eschatological Jerusalem (17.22); cf. the idolatrous behaviour of the surrounding nations which is to be repudiated by God's people, in the land which they are about to enter, according to Deut. 18.9–14. There is also a close parallel to Rev. 22.15 in the extended categorization of those who 'follow the way of death' in *Did.* 5.1–2 (similarly *Barn.* 20.1–2, describing adherents of the 'way of darkness') which, if 'dogs' may be taken as a metaphorical description of the 'wicked', includes all the evils mentioned at Rev. 22.15.

The catalogue of vices in verse 15 corresponds almost exactly to that in 21.8 (q.v.), where the conduct of those whose place is in the lake of fire, which is the second death, is depicted in contrast to the life of the faithful who dwell with God in the new Jerusalem (21.2–7). Five of the six errors in 22.15 appear among others at 21.8, and in the same sequence; except that whereas in verse 15, οἱ φάρμακοι (*hoi pharmakoi*, 'the sorcerers') is followed by οἱ φονεῖς (*hoi phoneis*, 'the murderers'), those two groups are reversed in the earlier list.

'Dogs' (οἱ κύνες, *hoi kynes*) are mentioned in 22.15 alone, and not elsewhere in the Apocalypse. In first-century Palestine and Egypt dogs were regarded as unwelcome scavengers, rather than pets (Brown, 'Animal' 117). 'The wages of a dog', in Deut. 23.18, refers to the income of a male prostitute; while in Prov. 26.11 and Luke 16.21 dogs are associated with habits which are unsavoury. Philonenko, ' "Dehors les Chiens" ', finds a parallel between Rev. 22.15 and 4Q394 = 4QMMT^a *frag.* 8.4.5–10 (see esp. 4.8–9, dogs should not enter the holy camp, Jerusalem, because they might make the temple unclean by eating bones with flesh on them). The term 'dogs' was used by Jews of Gentiles (cf. Mark. 7.27–28 par.; Matt. 7.6) and, elsewhere in early Christian literature, of heretics (Phil. 3.2; 2 Pet. 2.22; Ignatius, *Eph.* 7.1), and of those who are unbaptized and therefore unclean (*Did.* 9.5, quoting Matt. 7.6). See further Aune 1223.

There seems to be sufficient evidence here to suggest that the 'dogs' of Rev. 22.15 is a metaphor not simply for the wicked in general (Aune 1222), but also, as an extension of the idea of ritual purity, for the morally unclean in particular (hence the translation).

In this case, they head the list of wrongdoers appropriately, in contrast to the blessed faithful of verse 14 whose robes are washed '*clean*' by the Lamb. It is also possible that this group provides a parallel to the 'detestable' (ἐβδελυγμένοι, *ebdelygmenoi*) of 21.8 who, like the 'dogs', do not appear elsewhere in Revelation. See also the 'unclean' of 21.27.

'Everyone who loves and practises falsehood' (πᾶς φιλῶν καὶ ποιῶν ψεῦδος, *pas philōn kai poiōn pseudos*, lit. 'all loving and doing a lie'), in verse 15, both explains the preceding term, 'idolaters', and also qualifies the character of all who choose to remain 'outside' the gates of God's city, as specified in verse 15. See also 14.5 (the faithful inside the new Jerusalem do *not* lie), and 21.27 ('liars of every kind' [ὁ ποιῶν ψεῦδος, *ho poiōn pseudos*, lit. 'the one doing falsehood'] are banned from the holy city). The testimony of Revelation has to do with the right use of power, in submission to divine justice and sovereignty (see on 5.12; 7.12), together with an appeal for the members of its audience both to reject idolatrous, satanic worship, and also to remain completely loyal to the God of judgement and salvation (13.5–10; 22.9). This would have been a timely message for the Johannine community around the prophet-seer, and it continues to be an apposite exhortation in the life of the Church of God at large.

16 The exalted Jesus speaks directly through the interpreting angel, who has been 'sent . . . to you with this testimony for the benefit of the churches'. Prigent (643) regards this part of verse 16 as being composed on the model of 22.6, which attributes the inspiration of the Apocalypse to (the Lord) *God*. He therefore finds in 22.16 'a Christocentric correction' (ibid.), which completes what was said earlier by asserting the responsibility of *Jesus* for the visions in Revelation. However, the present verse is in reality another statement of the 'chain' of disclosure in the Apocalypse; see 1.1–2, where it is stated that God 'gave' the complete revelation to Jesus Christ, making it known to the churches through John and by 'his angel' (here '*my* angel', ἄγγελόν μου, *angelon mou*). See 22.6. In any case, God and the Lamb are closely related in this part of Scene 7 (see on 21.22–23; 22.3; also Smalley, *Thunder and Love* 60). Only here in Revelation does the risen Jesus speak of himself directly, using the personal pronoun, ἐγώ (*egō*, 'I'); cf. 'I John' at 1.9; 22.8. The new 'testimony' (verse 16, using μαρτυρέω, *martyreō*, lit. 'witness') to the truth of the message contained in Revelation (cf. 1.5; 21.5; 22.6) derives from the exalted Christ, and is intended for the 'churches' (so also verse 20). At 22.18 (q.v.) the same verb refers to the 'warning' given by the prophet-seer to his hearers.

There is a problem about the exact nature of the angel's audience addressed at 22.16, since this depends on the meaning of the phraseology in this verse, which is not immediately clear. The text runs, 'I have sent my angel to you (ὑμῖν, *hymin*, plural) with this testimony for the benefit of the churches (ταῖς ἐκκλησίαις, *tais ekklēsiais*, also plural)'. Several commentators understand the first dative plural, 'to you', as a reference to the members of the seven churches addressed by John (see 1.4); so e.g. Swete 309; Charles 2, 219; Beasley-Murray 342; Sweet 317; Thompson 188; cf. Roloff 252; Beale 1143–46. But this interpretation imparts a repetitive nature to verse 16 ('sent to the churches for the churches'); and such awkwardness is scarcely improved by taking the first group as the Johannine communities of Asia and the second as 'churches' generally (Swete 309; Beasley-Murray 342), particularly since 'churches' in the plural always refers in the Apocalypse to the seven churches of Asia (1.4, 11, 20; 2.7; et al.). The similar datives at 1.4 do not provide a real parallel to 22.16, as Beale (1145) claims, since at that point John is evidently referring twice over to the same communities ('to the seven churches, grace to you').

It is more probable that two *different*, but perhaps related, groups are mentioned in verse 16. This suggestion is supported by the inclusion of the preposition ἐπί (*epi*, lit. 'for') before ταῖς ἐκκλησίαις (*tais ekklēsiais*, 'the churches'), which implies a separation between the two groups mentioned. The first people to be addressed ('you') are the direct recipients of the testifying action described in the infinitive, μαρτυρῆσαι (*martyrēsai*, 'with this testimony', lit. 'to testify'); whereas the members of the second group are more remote. Such a distinction may exist even if, following BDAG 363, the preposition ἐπί (*epi*) with the dative is taken as a marker of location, meaning 'in' or 'among'. If two circles are indeed involved in the given testimony, this makes natural sense of the Greek, particularly if the preposition is understood as meaning 'for', and the dative case in 'the churches' is construed as one of advantage. Jesus is then saying that his witness, through the angel, comes to 'you' (one group) *for the benefit of* 'the churches' (a second); hence the translation. Cf. Aune 1225.

Given this interpretation, the two sections of John's audience still need to be identified. It is most likely that the 'churches' in verse 16 are the seven Asian congregations of the Johannine community. This is true elsewhere in Revelation, and particularly at its outset (Chapters 1—3), which is evidently being echoed in Chapter 22 (see also above). This leaves the significance of 'you' to be explored. Caird (286) appears to take the words of Jesus throughout verse 16*a* as a reference to the martyrs of the Church; although such a restrictive interpretation of the faithful has been already been regarded as unbalanced (see on 7.14, where martyrs are included among those who have 'survived the great ordeal', but cannot by themselves be equated with that company). A more credible solution is to understand ὑμῖν (*hymin*, 'to you') as a reference to a circle of John's prophetic colleagues, whose task was to transmit the seer's revelatory message to the churches. So Moffatt 491; Beckwith 777; Kiddle 454; Vanni, *La struttura letteraria* 180; Hill, 'Prophecy and Prophets in the Revelation' 411–18; Aune, 'Prophetic Circle'; Aune 1225–26. One problem with this identification, as Aune (1226) admits, is the lack of definition surrounding the term 'prophet' in Revelation (cf. 11.10, 18; 16.6; 18.20, 24; 19.10), and the fact that while the seer can speak of 'prophets' in a general sense, meaning members of the Christian Church as a community of prophecy (see on 22.6, 9), his only reference to a prophetic 'school' in the Apocalypse appears to be the circle around the *false* prophet, Jezebel (2.22–23; cf. also 16.13; 19.20; 20.10).

It so happens that the possibility of a further interpretation exists. There are several recollections in the closing scene and epilogue of Revelation of its prologue and opening scene (cf. 1.1–8, 17–20; 22.6–10, 18–20); and it has just been argued that the 'churches' of 22.16 are precisely the seven Johannine congregations of Chapters 2 and 3. Moreover, the apocalyptic disclosures throughout are mediated by angels, and notably by the interpreting angel who appears at both ends of the drama (1.1; 22.1, 16). Angels are included in the 'chain' of revelation evident in 1.1–2 and 22.8–9, 16, which is initiated by God, and mediated to his people through the risen Jesus and the prophet-seer. Among the heavenly beings involved in the transmission of the Christian testimony are the 'angels' of the seven churches, who are addressed in each case, as 'stars' among lampstands (1.20), by the exalted Son of man figure of 1.12–16 (cf. 2.1; et al.). For the identity of these angels see on 1.20, where it is suggested that they represent on earth the personified, heavenly dimension of the congregations belonging to God through Christ.

It seems perfectly consonant with the content and setting of 22.16, therefore, to conclude that in this verse the risen Christ is addressing primarily *the angels of the seven churches*. The exalted figure who addresses the 'angels' of the seven churches in Rev. 2—3, at the outset of the drama, is once more and inclusively speaking to them as it comes to an end. These angels embody the Church and its prophetic spirit, and are indeed closely related to it. But they are also distinctive beings within the Johannine community, and speak for the people of God at large. In Rev. 2—3 they receive the oracles of the judgemental and salvific Christ, in order to pass on his living testimony to their congregations. At 22.16 the angels of the churches are again in view, since the same Jesus who 'sent' (ἔπεμψα, *epempsa*, aorist) his angel to John and God's servants with a divine testimony now reminds them at the end-time of that message and of its ultimate destiny: *through* the 'angels', *to* the churches of John's community, and beyond that again *to* the Church of God throughout the world. The 'star' (ἀστήρ, *astēr*) of David (verse 16*b*) speaks finally to the 'stars' (ἀστέρες, *asteres*) which are the angels of the seven churches (1.20).

In the concluding section of verse 16 Jesus describes himself (using ἐγώ εἰμι, *egō eimi*, 'I am') as 'David's descendant, and from his family, the bright star of dawn'. This is one of five 'I am' sayings, spoken by God or Christ, in Revelation (see also 1.8, 17; 2.23; 21.6; cf. 22.13). For Jesus to say that he is 'David's descendant, and from his family' (ἡ ῥίζα καὶ τὸ γένος Δαυίδ, *hē rhiza kai to genos Dauid*, lit. 'the root and stock of David') indicates that he is the fulfilment of the promise in Isaiah that the Messiah will come from 'the root of Jesse' (Isa. 11.1, 10; cf. Rom. 1.3; also Rev. 5.5, q.v.). As Beale (1146–47) notes, however, the use of 'root' in the present verse is not a metaphor of origin (so Beasley-Murray 342–43; Wilcock 217–18), but an image of derivation; for the term 'root' is immediately qualified by what is in effect a synonym, 'offspring' or 'family' (in 5.5 only the 'Root of David' is used to describe the Lamb). Cf. Sir. 47.22; also Beckwith 777–78. Jesus did not originate the kingly line of David; but he stands within it, as Messiah, to share God's reign (cf. Isa. 11.10 LXX, 'arising to rule over the Gentiles'; see Rom. 15.12). In that office the exalted Christ can send to the churches the message that in him are gathered up the fulfilment of all known eschatological hopes (cf. Beckwith 778).

Jesus also identifies himself, at the close of verse 16, as 'the bright star of dawn' (ὁ ἀστὴρ ὁ λαμπρὸς ὁ πρωϊνός, *ho astēr ho lampros ho prōinos*, lit. 'the bright morning star'). See 2.28, where the conqueror is promised 'the morning star'. Believers are those who share Christ's authority over opposition and idolatry, highlighted in the oracle to Thyatira (2.18–29), and participate in the messianic status of Christ himself (against Hagner, 'ἀστήρ, κτλ' 736, who is reluctant to identify the morning star directly with Christ). The fourth oracle of Balaam in Num. 24.17 promises that 'a star shall come out of Jacob'; and, while that reference is to David, it is transferred at Rev. 22.16 to his greater descendant (see above; also Mounce 409). Note the similar expectation at *T. Levi* 18.3; *T. Judah* 24.1. It is possible that there is also an allusion in this passage to Isa. 60.1–3 ('nations shall come to your light, and kings to the brightness of your dawn'); and, in this case, Jesus is being presented once more as the source of salvation for the nations (21.22–26); cf. Beale 1147. The final advent of the Messiah, inaugurated in the past, is being accomplished in the present and future. For this reason the invitations of the following verse provide a spirituality which is real and lasting.

17 This verse consists of four invitations in strophic form, linked by the catchword ἔρχεσθαι (*erchesthai*, 'come'). The verb is present in the first three lines, and implied in the fourth. However, in each sentence there is a problem about the identity of the speaker and the audience. Mounce (409) thinks that all four invitations are addressed to the world (similarly Bauckham 1305). The problem with such a view is that the verb, 'come', is used in each half of the verse with different connotations; the first two appeals evidently refer to the advent of Christ at the end, in response to his promise in verse 12 ('I am coming soon'), while the third, and implicitly the fourth (let anyone who 'wishes, [come to] receive' [ὁ θέλων λαβέτω, *ho thelōn labetō*]), are directed towards the spiritually needy of any age. It is therefore preferable to distinguish between the two pairs of invitations, even if they are ultimately related, and to regard the first as addressed to the exalted Jesus (verses 12, 16), and the second as spoken (by the seer) to the world.

In the first strophe of verse 17, 'The Spirit and the bride say, "Come!" ', the 'bride' is clearly the Christian community in its eschatological purity, which in the new Jerusalem shares an eternal covenant relationship with God (see on 21.2, 9–10). But what about the precise identity of 'the Spirit'? Beale (1148) interprets the figure straightforwardly as the Holy Spirit, while Charles (2, 179) takes this as a reference to the Spirit of Christ. But a finer definition, and one closer to the context, is possible. In the Apocalypse, the Spirit is seen as the intermediary of John's visions (1.10; 4.2; 17.3; 21.10), and he is closely associated with prophetic inspiration (see on 19.10). The Spirit is also the one who prompts the oracles addressed by the exalted Christ, through the prophet-seer (1.11), to the angels of the seven Johannine congregations of Asia (2.7, 11, 17, 29; 3.6, 13, 22).

On such a hermeneutical basis, it is possible to interpret 'Spirit and bride' as meaning the spirit of prophecy in the Church, or more precisely as the prophetic spirit of John and his colleagues in the *seven* churches (see on 22.16; also verses 6, 9). In response to Christ's promised advent (verses 7, 12), and as a result of his testimony to the gospel (verses 6–7, 9, 16), the Johannine community (initially) is moved to pray for the final coming of God, through the Lamb, in judgement and salvation (also verse 20). This plea is then echoed through John by the Church at large ('everyone who hears'), the members of which identify themselves with the 'bride', and perhaps also by the nations who are willing to walk by the light of the holy city (21.24–26). Just as the four living creatures cry, 'Come!' (ἔρχου, *erchou*), to the agencies of judgement which herald the Messiah's advent, so the Church cries for her bridegroom (21.9) to come at the end with discrimination and saving love.

For the importance of spiritual audition in the Apocalypse see on 4.1; see also the 'listening' formula at 2.7; et al. Once more, the Spirit draws together heaven and earth. See further on this section Swete 310 ('Spirit and bride' is the equivalent of 'prophets and saints'); Kiddle 455–56; Bruce, 'Spirit' 342–43; Smalley, 'Paraclete' 295–96; Aune 1227–28; Bauckham 1305–1306; Prigent 646–47.

The remaining two invitations in verse 17 are clearly based on Isa. 55.1*a* ('let every-one who thirsts come to the waters'), and both pick up the imagery of the divine gift of living water mentioned at 21.6 (q.v.). See also 7.17; 22.1; John 7.37–38. Those in need anywhere in God's world are offered his spiritual life and fulfilment. The description of the water of life in the present verse as being offered 'freely' (δωρεάν, *dōrean*) is doubt-less an allusion to Isa. 55.1*b*, which affirms that God's eschatological gifts are available 'without money and without price'. Such gifts may be received on earth now, as well as in the new Jerusalem; but their importance and salvific nature are heightened by the imminent return of Christ at the end, in addition to his presence in the life and worship of the Church today (cf. Prigent 647). It is possible, indeed, that a liturgical background has influenced this part of Revelation, and that the eucharist provided an appropriate setting for its public reading (1.3); cf. Bruce, 'Spirit' 344; Robinson, 'Liturgical Sequence', esp. 40. Note the invitation to 'come' to the Lord's Supper, combined with the prayer *Maranatha* ('Our Lord, come!'), at *Did.* 10.6; cf. 14.1; 1 Cor. 11.26; 16.22.

Bauckham (1306) notes that the invitation to receive freely the water of life, in verse 17, combines two major levels of concern in the Apocalypse: that believers should be faithful conquerors (2.10–11; et al.), and that through their steadfast witness the nations should turn to God (9.20–21; 22.1–2; et al.). Christians, imitating Christ (John 4.13–14), are exhorted at 22.17 to be among those who offer living water to anyone who is spiritually thirsty.

Theology

In the seventh and final scene of this apocalyptic drama, the seer has depicted the con-summation of God's plan for his world. In the prophetic proclamations which provide the structural and theological framework of the section, John sets out seven characteristics of life in the new creation (21.1), from new covenant to new testimony. These act as a summary of Revelation as a whole, with its inherent plea that people should reject all that the beast represents and, as members of the new Israel, faithfully follow the Lamb into the salvific relationship that is enshrined in the new Jerusalem. But an even more important theological theme in the Apocalypse, and one which is prominent in Chapters 21—22, is the sovereign glory which God is to receive for accomplishing among the saints his purposes of salvation through judgement (21.11, 23; 22.3–5, 17; cf. 1.6; 5.11–13; 11.17; 19.1–2, 7; et al.). This is a salvific glory which is to be shared with the nations (21.24–26; 22.2, 17). See Beale 1120. For the Old Testament background to the notion of fulfilled prophecy in this scene, using in particular texts from Isaiah and Ezekiel, see Mathewson, *New Heaven* (while Revelation is a fresh composition, 21.1—22.5 shows that the work as a whole resonates with the deeper tones of prior, Jewish texts; see esp. 216–36).

As throughout the Apocalypse, John's eschatology in the final scene is balanced, and draws together the past, present and future (see above, 12–13). After what appears to be the 'final' judgement of Chapters 19—20 (note esp. 19.17–21; 20.10–15), the drama begins again; and, here as elsewhere, the 'end' is always at hand (see 22.6–7, 12–13, 17; also 6.17; 9.20–21; 11.19; 14.20). Moreover, the prophet-seer demonstrates that Christian truths and moral values which characterize the Godhead, and can be exemplified in his Church, belong to time as well as eternity; and this means that what will be true of the saints in eternity, and in the new Eden, may already be experienced by believers on earth. The difference is made by the eschatological perspective which is adopted. In this age the Church, like Jerusalem, stands under judgement; in the age to come the hope of the faithful is to reach perfection by sharing in the divine nature itself (cf. 2 Pet. 1.4). A significant element in the teaching of Revelation is accordingly that our understanding of time, like everything that is earthly and human, needs to be renewed. Cf. Milligan 369–71; Prigent 629.

The focus of the salvific imagery in Rev. 21.2—22.17 is in the concept of the new creation in general (21.1), and of the new Jerusalem in particular; although the reality of divine judgement is not absent from the scene (cf. 21.8, 27; 22.15). The new heaven and earth of John's vision, in line with the nature of his eschatology and cosmology just mentioned, implies a continuity between time and eternity, matter and spirit; and this is a typically Johannine viewpoint (cf. John 1.51). But change is also involved, and the seer expects the boundaries between earth and heaven to be removed in the eschatological age. The 'ultimate future' of the new age and the new Jerusalem has a profound significance for the present; but in the spiritual dimension of eternity it also becomes the setting for a completely renewed covenant relationship with God (see on 21.1–2). Cf. Gilbertson, *God and History* 137; also Knight 134–35. Covenant theology undergirds the thought of this entire section; and it is worth pointing out that any covenant fellowship between God and his own involves *love and unity*, as well as judgement (cf. Deut. 7.6–13; Jer. 31.1–3; Ezek. 16.8; Dan. 9.4; Hos. 11.1–4; Luke 22.14–20; John 15.1–13; 17.20–26; et al.).

The figure of the 'new Jerusalem' has been interpreted in this commentary as the close covenant relationship between God and his people, which will be enjoyed uninterruptedly by the saints in eternity (see on 21.2). The relational aspect of this metaphor needs to be kept in mind throughout the interpretation of 21.10—22.15, despite the 'material' aspects of the holy city as capable of adornment (21.11–14, 18–21) as well as measurement (21.15–17). The precious stones of the eternal enclosure and its foundations are intended to enhance John's description of the special kinship which can exist between God and his own; while the cubic dimensions of the city, with its gateways and walls, speak of its accessibility to all who wish to enter (see on 21.16). The dead, silent streets of Babylon contrast markedly with the life, light and colour of the pathways in the new Jerusalem (Boring 222).

The possible links between the new Jerusalem and the 'thousand years' of 20.2–7 need to be investigated carefully. The millennium has been interpreted as a symbol for the timeless reign of God in Christ, in heaven and on earth (see on 20.2). As with the holy city Jerusalem, this involves a close relationship between God and believers. But in the millennium that sovereignty and fellowship exist *on earth*, as well as in heaven; and this implies that the faithfulness of the saints living in the world can cease, and that their belief and behaviour may be compromised by the idolatrous seduction of Satan.

In contrast, the new Jerusalem represents the perfected indwelling of God with his people in eternity alone (21.2–3). That holy city at the consummation will evidently be inclusive in character (21.3), and its gates will never be closed (21.24–26). However, those who wish to remain outside may do so (21.27; 22.15). This means that they are excluding themselves from God's life, and choosing an annihilation that may, in the end, be described as spiritual euthanasia (cf. 1 John 5.11–12). Thus, in the Christian scheme, human freedom and free will are safeguarded; no one is compelled to share the covenant love of God, even if ultimately such an invitation may be difficult to resist.

In this final scene of the drama, the Father and the exalted Son speak directly to the audience through the interpreting angel or the prophet-seer (see esp. 21.3–8; 22.7, 12–13, 16–17; cf. also 22.20). Such speech patterns are most evident elsewhere in Revelation in the Prologue and the first part of Scene 1 (1.1—3.22). In this way, the beginning and end of the Apocalypse form a literary and theological inclusion, tying together a complete vision of the Godhead, Alpha and Omega, first and last (1.8, 17; 21.6; 22.13), and of the Church living on earth and perfected in heaven (the Johannine community, portrayed in the oracles of 1.11, 20 and Chapters 2—3, reappears at 22.16–17, q.v.).

Central to the dramatic disclosures throughout Revelation is the figure of the exalted Son of man, who speaks to John at both the start and the finish of the action (note 1.10–19; 22.12–13, 16). The Christology of the final scene of the Apocalypse is noticeably high, and this is a reminder that its 'end' is not an event but a person (Sweet 320). The theology of the person of Christ, who shares the throne of God (22.1) and with him illuminates the holy city (21.23), is significantly developed in 21.22 (q.v.) by the use of 'temple' imagery ('the Lord God Almighty and the Lamb are themselves' the temple of the city).

The identification of Jesus with the temple of God is very Johannine. The inauguration of the spiritual temple as the replacement of the physical sanctuary takes place with the first coming and earthly ministry of Christ, who refers to his resurrection as a rebuilding of the temple (John 2.19–22). The writers of the New Testament consequently believe that Jesus himself fulfilled the role of the old Temple as a place of sacrifice, and also as the embodiment of God's presence (e.g. John 1.14; 2.21; Rom. 3.21–25). By extension, his followers are regarded as a spiritual 'temple' (1 Cor. 3.17; 1 Pet. 2.4–5; Rev. 3.12; et al.), with Christ as the 'keystone' (Acts 4.11; Eph. 2.20–21; 1 Pet. 2.6–7). John takes up the implications of this imagery, and portrays the slaughtered but victorious Lamb (5.9–13) as *himself the new temple*, where God finally dwells with his people (21.22–26). See also the heavenly temple scene at 1.12–20, where the risen Son of man is the central character. Cf. further Walker, *Holy City* 302–303. For Jerusalem and the Temple in Judaism and early Christianity see ibid. 296–308; also Aune 1188–91.

Throughout the Apocalypse, the term ναός (*naos*, 'temple' or 'sanctuary'; John does not use the synonym, ἱερόν, *hieron*) refers to the heavenly temple of the present (14.15, 17; 15.5–6, 8; 16.1, 17), or of the consummation (3.12; 11.19; 21.22), or both (7.15); while the same word at 11.1–2 describes the people of God in their heavenly as well as earthly existence. Once again, the material and the spiritual are conjoined in John's theology. The presence of the Father mediated by the Son, glimpsed in time, becomes fully and finally available in eternity to those in Christ who dwell in the holy city-temple, the new Jerusalem. Cf. Beale 1091.

EPILOGUE
The Oracle Is Complete
(22.18–21)

Translation

22 [18]I myself testify to all who hear the words of this prophetic book, that if anyone adds to them, God will add to that person the plagues described in this document; [19]and if anyone removes any part of the message of this prophetic book, God will remove that person's share in the tree of life and the holy city, which are described in this document.

[20]The one who gives this testimony says, 'I am indeed coming soon'. Amen.[a] Come Lord Jesus!

[21]May the love of the Lord Jesus[b] be with you all.[c/d/e]

Text

[a] Some witnesses, including ℵ 1611[2050 2329] 94 it[gig] syr[ph] cop Primasius Beatus, omit Ἀμήν (*Amēn*, 'Amen'). It is possible that the word was added to the text later, particularly if copyists were influenced by its presence in verse 21 (v.l.). But 'Amen' is a regular liturgical response in Revelation, both at the beginning and end of doxologies and prayers (see 1.6–7; 5.14; 7.12; 19.4). Its use at verse 20, in a section which is evidently liturgical in character, therefore appears natural, and is most probably original.

[b] The reading, κυρίου Ἰησοῦ (*kyriou Iēsou*, '[the grace] of the Lord Jesus'), is well supported by ℵ A Oecumenius[2053], et al. It was expanded by 'pious scribes' (Metzger, *Textual Commentary* 766), who added Χριστοῦ (*Christou*, 'Christ') after Ἰησοῦ (*Iēsou*, 'Jesus'; so 046 051 Andreas Byz, et al.), and ἡμῶν (*hēmōn*, 'our') after κυρίου (*kyriou*, 'Lord'; so it[gig,61] vg syr[ph,h] arm, et al.). The whole phrase, ἡ χάρις τοῦ κυρίου Ἰησοῦ (*hē charis tou kyriou Iēsou*, 'the grace of the Lord Jesus'), is omitted by 2329 cop[bo]; but this arose by accident, when the eye of a copyist moved from Ἰησοῦ (*Iēsou*, 'Jesus', genitive), in verse 20, to the same word in verse 21.

[c] The concluding words of the Apocalypse have been transmitted in a variety of forms. The shortest version is μετὰ πάντων (*meta pantōn*, lit. 'with all'), as read by A vg Beatus Tyconius NA, et al.; and there is MS evidence for six variants of this phrase. The chief alternatives are μετὰ τῶν ἁγίων (*meta tōn hagiōn*, 'with the saints'), present in ℵ it[gig], et al.; and μετὰ πάντων τῶν ἁγίων (*meta pantōn tōn hagiōn*, 'with all the saints'), attested by 1006[1006 1841] 1611[1611 1854] syr cop Andreas Byz; cf. Charles 2, 385. The abruptness of the form 'with all' makes it difficult; although it is true that 'saints' is a frequent designation in Revelation for Christian believers (note e.g. 8.3, where John refers to the prayers of '*all* the saints'). However, it is easy to account for all the variations if they are seen as expansions of a brief original, particularly if they have been influenced by the ending of Pauline letters (cf. Gal. 6.18; Phil. 4.21–23; but see 1 Cor. 16.23 ['the grace of the Lord Jesus be with you']); and the weight of external attestation supports 'with (you) all' as the authentic conclusion (so Metzger, *Textual Commentary* 766–67). There seems to be no force in the argument of Aune (1239), that John would have been restrictive in his

final benediction, and directed it to 'saints' in particular, rather than inclusively to any and 'all' who may have wished to 'hear' the testimony of this drama (cf. 22.18).

^d There is good support (from ℵ 046 051 94 1773 MS of Andreas Byz vg syr cop, et al.; cf. Charles 2, 385) for the inclusion of Ἀμήν (*Amēn*, 'Amen') as the final word of verse 21. However, several important witnesses (such as A 1006 2432 it^gig Tyconius) omit the word, making this the *lectio difficilior*; for if the word were original, it is difficult to account for its omission in these MSS (Metzger, *Textual Commentary* 767). The likelihood that 'Amen' was a later addition is further supported by the tendency to conclude New Testament writings, in their original or variant form, with this liturgical response (cf. Rom. 16.27; Gal. 6.18; 2 Pet. 3.18; Jude 25; and v.l. 1 Cor. 16.24; Eph. 6.24; 1 Thess. 5.28; et al.). The conclusion, that 'Amen' is an insertion into the text, is reflected in the translation (NRSV includes, REB also omits). See further Kelly, *The Revelation* 66–67.

^e *The Subscription.* The simplest, and no doubt original, form (as attested by A 1611^1854) is ἀποκάλυψις Ἰωάννου (*apokalypsis Iōannou,* lit. 'The Apocalypse of John'). The variants all appear to be later, scribal expansions. The longest, in MSS of Byz, is ἀποκάλυψις τοῦ ἁγίου Ἰωάννου τοῦ θεολόγου (*apokalypsis tou hagiou Iōannou tou theologou,* 'The Apocalypse of the Holy [or "Saint"] John the Divine' or 'of John the Speaker of Divine Things' [BDAG 449*b*]).

The genitive, Ἰωάννου (*Iōannou,* lit. 'of John'), is one of source or origin, strictly meaning '(The Apocalypse) *by* John' (Aune 1242). However, the ultimate authorship of the Apocalypse is divine, even if the visions of the drama are mediated through (angels and) the apostle (see on 1.1–2). The title of this commentary therefore remains as *The Revelation to John.*

Literary Setting

The structure of the Epilogue is straightforward. It consists of an attestation formula, combined with balanced paraenesis about adding to the words of 'this book', or subtracting from them (22.18–19); a liturgical invocation and response (verse 20); and a final benediction (verse 21). See further Aune 1208–16; Prigent 648–50. The paragraph 22.18–21 is framed by an oath formula, involving a gentle play on words, using the verb μαρτυρέω (*martyreō,* lit. 'witness'): almost antiphonally, John 'testifies' to his hearers, and the risen Jesus 'gives this testimony' as the guarantor of the truth of the revelation in this drama as a whole (see on 22.6–7, 8–9, 16; cf. also John 21.24, where the same language is used with reference to the 'testimony' of the fourth evangelist). The tone of these verses is liturgical, and may well be eucharistically shaped (see below).

For a discussion of the extent and nature of the Epilogue see the 'Literary Setting' of 21.2—22.17. Although the material in 22.6–21 is varied, and commentators divide it differently, a break is evident between 22.17 and 22.18, marking off the final section with its distinctive, forensic and liturgical, content. Although John has spoken previously in the final scene, and is deeply involved in its action (see 22.8, using ἐγώ, *egō,* 'I [myself]', as at 22.18; cf. also verses 14–15), it is noticeable that in verse 18 he articulates directly, for the benefit of his audience, and for almost the first time in Revelation (see 13.9–10), words of solemn warning and exhortation.

Comment

22.18–19   The identification of the speaker in these verses is not immediately clear. Several writers assume that the one who testifies to 'all who hear the words of this prophetic book' is the risen Jesus (so Swete 311; Charles 2, 218–19; Mounce 410; Michaels

257–58; similarly Aune [1229], who on the same page nevertheless appears to take the subject of 'I testify' as the seer). The assumption that Jesus is speaking in verses 18–19 rests chiefly on the (correct) view that the exalted Christ is the interlocutor at verse 20 (he is 'the one who gives this testimony'). But these two balanced acts of witness are to be differentiated, since the first (verse 18) is part of an attestation by the prophet-seer about the consequences of 'hearing the book', whereas the second (verse 20) is an assurance given by the one who is 'coming soon' (clearly Jesus) that he is personally the guarantor of its truth (see above). It is therefore reasonable to conclude that the speaker in verses 18–19 is John himself (so also Caird 287; Sweet 318; Roloff 253; Wall 268; Beale 1154). There is no need to regard these verses as an interpolation by a later redactor, simply because of their distinctive style and content (so Charles 2, 222–23).

The paraenesis of verses 18–19 may be regarded as the obverse side of the blessing pronounced in 1.3 on those who 'listen to the words of the prophecy, and adhere to what is written in it' (cf. Hughes 240). The introductory phrase, μαρτυρῶ ἐγώ (*martyrō egō*, 'I myself testify'), is one of several 'oath formulas' used in the Apocalypse in association with prophetic pronouncements (Aune 1229); see 1.2; 10.5–7; 19.9; 21.5; 22.6; also *1 Enoch* 98.1–6; *2 Enoch (J)* 49.1; *Asc. Isa.* 11.39; *3 Apoc. Bar.* 1.7; *T. Sol.* 1.13; *1 Clem.* 58.2.

The testimony is addressed to 'everyone who hears the words of this prophetic book' (verse 18); and, together with the reference to the reader and audience of Revelation at 1.3, this suggests that the contents of the book were to be read aloud in a (possibly eucharistic) setting of Christian worship. Unlike 1.3, the warnings of 22.18–19 are directed towards 'everyone' (παντί, *panti*) who hears the words, which means that each individual, within the community and beyond, is challenged to hear the truth of God which has been revealed in Christ, and to respond to that gospel with faith and obedience (22.7). For the importance in Johannine thought of spiritual 'hearing', as well as 'sight', see on 4.1. The slightly stilted expression, τοὺς λόγους τῆς προφητείας τοῦ βιβλίου τούτου (*tous logous tēs prophēteias tou bibliou toutou*, 'the words of this prophetic book', lit. 'the words of the prophecy of this book'), is a Semitism (see also 22.7, 10).

Verses 18*b* and 19 consist of two conditional clauses, constructed in parallel, both of which use the particle ἐάν (*ean*, 'if'). The verbs balance one another ('add . . . remove'), involve a play on words ('if anyone adds/removes . . . God will add/remove'), and provide examples of paronomasia, since the first verb of each pair is used literally and the second has a figurative meaning. The protasis in both conditional clauses is made up of 'if' followed by the aorist subjunctives, ἐπιθῇ (*epithē[i]*, 'adds', lit. 'added') and ἀφέλη (*aphelē[i]*, 'removes', 'takes away', lit. 'removed'); while the apodosis in each case has 'if' followed by the future subjunctives, ἐπιθήσει (*epithēsei*, 'will add') and ἀφελεῖ (*aphelei*, 'will remove'). The future tense in such conditional clauses refers to an event which is possible, and even probable (Aune 1230–31). The 'crime and punishment' motif in this passage introduces an instance of eschatological *lex talionis* (Bauckham 1306*b*); cf. 11.18.

It is important to investigate the purpose of John's solemn, and indeed severe, warnings to preserve the integrity of the Apocalypse. Was John really afraid that a scribe would tamper with his script, or was he merely indicating that, since the revelation was now complete, it was also sacred? Aune (1232) lists three reasons why the seer may have feared that someone would have tried to revise his work.

(a) The textual history of Jewish and Christian apocalypses shows that such writings were constantly altered in transmission (cf. Hermas, *Vis.* 2.1.3; 2.4.1–4; note also the 'different gospel' evident in at least one Pauline church, according to Gal.1.6–9).

(b) John belonged to a prophetic community, and was himself a prophet-seer (1.1–3; 22.6–10, 16), opposed by false prophetic circles (2.6, 14–15; 2.20–23). Revelation seems, as a result, to have been written in a situation of prophetic conflict.

(c) There is evidence to suggest that, in early Christianity, prophetic revelations were subject to assessment (cf. 1 Cor. 12.1–3, 10; 14.29; 1 Thess. 5.19–21; 2 Thess. 2.1–2; et al.; 1 John 4.1–3 may be added). See further Roloff 253 (the prohibitions of Rev. 22.18–19 exemplify 'prophetic self-consciousness').

However, a more important reason for John's paraenesis, and one related to the intention of Revelation as a whole, may be found elsewhere. For the idea of adding to sacred texts, or subtracting from them, see particularly *1 Enoch* 104.10–11 (sinners will rewrite Scripture in their own false words); *Letter of Aristeas to Philocrates* 310–11 (there must be no revision of the Septuagintal Pentateuch); also Eusebius, *HE* 5.20.2 (any transcription of Irenaeus' *Ogdoad* is to be accurate). Most significantly, an Old Testament background to the thought in these verses lies in Deut. 4.1–2, which is an exhortation to Israel neither to add to the statutes of Yahweh nor to remove anything from them, but only to 'keep the commandments of the Lord' (verse 2); see also 12.32; 29.19–20. In the same way, the new Israel is receiving a new gospel code which is to be respected and observed (cf. Beale 1150).

But the context of these passages in Deuteronomy is crucial, for it relates specifically to idolatry, and the notion that idol worship was compatible with faith in the God of Israel (see Deut. 4.3 [= Num. 25.1–9, 14–18, reverencing the Baal of Peor], 15–20; 12.29–31; 29.14–18). Leaders who deceive the people in this way are regarded as false prophets (Deut. 13.1–18; note esp. the reference to false prophecy in 13.2–6 LXX, following the prohibition against adding to God's commands, or taking away from them, in 13.1 LXX [= 12.32 MT]). It may be concluded that 'adding and removing', in Rev. 22.18–19, refers not to tampering with God's word, or generally disobeying it, but to following false, idolatrous teaching about the truth which has been disclosed in the Apocalypse: adhering to the beast, rather than to the Lamb (cf. the inclusion of 'false behaviour' in the vice lists of 21.27 and 22.15). Such an interpretation accords well with the situation of the Johannine churches addressed in the oracles of Rev. 2—3, and mentioned again (with their 'angels') at 22.16, since these communities were obviously facing serious threats from overt idolatry (cf. 2.14–15, 20–23). See further Beale 1150–54; Bauckham 1306.

Distorting the message of Revelation, it may be added, and refusing to hear its prophetic truth, means exposure to God's salvific judgement and exclusion from the gifts of his paradise. God will add to idolaters 'the plagues described in this document' (verse 18). This alludes immediately to the seven plagues described in 15.5—16.21, which are symbolic of divine discrimination, but also more generally to the idea of God's judgement present throughout the Apocalypse: including the criticism of Satan, the dragon, the beast and the false prophet (12.7—13.18; 16.12–16; 19.17—20.15; et al.), Jerusalem (11.8; 21.2) and Babylon (17.1—18.24). God will also remove from the idolatrous and unfaithful a share in the blessings of eternity (verse 19), represented by 'the tree of life' (see on 2.7; 22.2, 14) and 'the holy city', the new Jerusalem (cf. 21.2—22.16; note also the 'living water' of 22.17). Cf. Prigent 649.

20 The expression, λέγει ὁ μαρτυρῶν ταῦτα (*legei ho martyrōn tauta*, 'the one who gives this testimony says', lit. 'the one witnessing to these things says'), recalls the formula used at the start of each oracle to the seven churches of John's community in Rev. 2—3 (e.g. 2.1): τάδε λέγει (*tade legei*, 'this is the message [of the one . . .], lit. 'this is what . . . says'). The links between the opening and closing sections of Revelation have already been noted (see on 22.16–17, 19). Forensic language, used by a number of witnesses, is also evident in this part of the drama. Thus, the interpreting angel is sent by the risen and returning Christ with a 'testimony for the benefit of the (angels of the) churches' (22.16);

the Spirit witnesses to the gift of life in the city of God (verse 17; cf. 21.6–7); the seer testifies to the truth of the visions in this book (verses 18–19); and now Jesus himself addresses the audience directly (cf. 22.12–13), in order to authorize the content of the apocalyptic proclamation, and promise his return (verse 20). The role of Jesus, as God's leading 'witness' (μάρτυς, *martys*), has been specifically identified earlier in the Apocalypse (see 1.5; 3.14). The word ταῦτα (*tauta*, lit. 'these things') in verse 20*a* refers to the composition of Revelation as a totality (see also 22.8, 16).

The one giving the testimony says, 'I am indeed coming soon'. In Revelation, the swift 'coming' of Jesus is an important theme, which occurs three times in Rev. 22.7–17 alone (verses 7, 12, 17), and again here; see also 2.16; 3.11(20). However, in Johannine thought this idea relates to the advent of the exalted Christ in the Church and to the world at *any* time, as well as at the end-time. In 22.20, therefore, the reference to the parousia need not be linked exclusively to the consummation, even if it points towards it; and the futurist present tense of the verb, ἔρχομαι (*erchomai*, 'I am coming'), may be construed in a manner which is not strictly chronological (see further below).

The use of the intensive particle, ναί (*nai*, 'indeed', 'yes'), occurs elsewhere in the Apocalypse in contexts which are, as here, both liturgical and antiphonal (see 1.7; 14.13; 16.7). At 22.20, divine affirmation ('I am indeed coming soon') is followed by human response, on the part of John and others ('Amen; come, Lord Jesus!'); cf. 2 Cor. 1.20 (Sweet 319). The invocation, 'come, Lord Jesus!', echoes the Aramaic *marana tha*, meaning 'Our Lord, come!'; and this appears at 1 Cor. 16.22 and in a responsive, eucharistic dialogue at *Did*. 10.6:

> Let grace (Jesus) come, and let this world pass away.
> *Hosanna to the God of David.*
> Let whoever is holy, come; and whoever is not, repent.
> *Marana tha. Amen.*

The advent of the exalted Christ during the eucharist anticipates his final coming as Judge and Saviour (1 Cor. 11.26); so that participation in the Lord's Supper, and in the presence of Jesus, is both a reminder of baptismal dedication (cf. 3.4–5, 20), and a demand for self-examination or 'scrutiny' (1 Cor. 11.27–32).

The ending of 1 Cor. (16.20–24) also includes elements which appear to be liturgical and eucharistic. Cf. Robinson, 'Liturgical Sequence', who suggests that the last words of Paul's letter are the first of the liturgy of the eucharist, and that the closing dialogue of Rev. 22.16–21 repeats the same pattern, ending (verse 21) with the grace (ibid. 40). However Moule ('Reconsideration' 307–10) believes that the invocation, *marana tha*, could be used simply in the context of a curse or ban (see on 22.18–19), although this argument depends on the coincidental use of the term 'anathema' alongside '*marana tha*' at 1 Cor. 16.22. There seems, in conclusion, every reason to suppose that Revelation, which is in the basic literary form of a letter (1.4–11; 22.21), was designed to be read aloud (1.3) on the Lord's Day (1.10) in a setting which was both liturgical and eucharistic (note also the antiphonal use of 'Amen' at 1.6–7; 22.20). In that case, John's hearers are being urged not only to listen carefully to the gospel in Revelation but also to be aware of what is involved in praying that God may come in Christ to save people through his judgement (cf. Mal. 3.1–3). On this section see further Shepherd, *Paschal Liturgy* 77–97; Beasley-Murray 348–49; Vanni, *La struttura letteraria* 107–15; Sweet 319; Prigent 650–53.

21 The Apocalypse comes to a close with an epistolary ending, comparable to the conclusions of letters in other parts of the New Testament: 'the grace of the Lord Jesus be with you all' (note the similar form at 1 Cor. 16.23). The traditional character of the seer's blessing is marked by his use of the theological term, ἡ χάρις (*hē charis*, 'love', 'grace'). This category is found in Revelation only here and at the outset, in the epistolary introduction at 1.4 (q.v.), which indicates once more a close association between the opening and the close of the Apocalypse (see on 22.16, 19–20). Cf. Aune 1240–41. The benediction in verse 21 is pronounced initially on the community of seven Asian churches around John; but it must be intended eventually for any faithful members of his audience, at any time (see the second textual note on this verse).

The epistolary ending of Revelation brings us back to its community dimension, and reminds us why the document was written in the first place. Its immediate purpose has been to encourage its readers in the face of external opposition, and in view of the temptation within the Johannine circle to compromise in matters of belief and behaviour (see above, 5–6). The prophet-seer has set out the purposes of God for his world in terms of a saving judgement, which is brought about through the slaughtered and exalted Lamb (5.9–10). In this way, Old Testament prophecy has been finally fulfilled (1.7). On such a basis the seer can now appeal to the members of his congregations to obey the words of *his* Christian prophecy (22.6–10, 18–19), and also pray for God's gracious 'love' to enable them to remain faithful to their calling (14.1–5, 12). See Beale 1156–57.

Theology

The Epilogue to the Apocalypse marks the conclusion of the drama enacted within it. Although the final verses (22.18–21) display an epistolary character (see esp. verse 21), Revelation as a whole is more than a letter. Similarly, the work is more than a piece of predictive prophecy, explaining what is to happen on earth and in heaven entirely in the future. Revelation is precisely an 'apocalypse' (ἀποκάλυψις, *apocalypsis*, 1.1), a symbolic composition which is designed to unveil divine truths which have hitherto remained hidden. The work is oracular, as well as prophetic, and proclaims God's salvific purposes for his creation in the present, as much as in the future. John, the prophet-seer, was invited at the outset to hand on the visionary contents of the disclosure he was to receive (1.10–11), and his oracle is now complete. See further above, 6–8; also Smalley, *Thunder and Love* 23–24.

But the 'words of this prophetic book' (22.18–19) present a challenge, as well as a disclosure, that is both relevant and timeless. John's community, and the members of the Christian Church beyond, are encouraged to be steadfast in faith and obedience, despite external and internal troubles which may beset them at any moment. They are assured of God's sovereignty and the salvific power of the Lamb (15.3–4; 19.6–7); yet these truths carry with them the responsibility of the saints to avoid all forms of idolatry, and to follow Christ rather than Satan (22.8, 12–14, 16–19). For this task the seer gives his blessing (22.21).

Running through the Apocalypse has been the central motif of the person and work of the exalted Christ, both human and divine, and God's 'coming' to his people through him in judgement and for salvation. It might be thought that the conclusion of Revelation would accordingly include a description of the final parousia of the glorified Lamb, together with an account of the punishment meted out to the unrighteous and of the rewards offered to the faithful. To some extent this 'advent' forms the basis of the narrative in Rev. 21—22, and it is true that the drama concludes with a person rather than a single event. Nevertheless, the end of the Apocalypse is not necessarily synonymous with the end of time. The centre of salvation history lies in the Christ-event, which has taken place already. Thereafter, the Church looks forward to a decisive appearing of Jesus the Messiah; but it also looks back to the moment when history was invaded in a new way by that which is supra-historical.

For John, therefore, theology is more important than chronology (Fiorenza, *Book of Revelation* 35–67). The eschatological climax of Revelation is not at the end of time, or at the end of the drama; its fulcrum is to be found in the vision of God and the Lamb at Rev. 4—5, rather than in the descent of the new Jerusalem and the parousia in Chapters 21—22 (Beasley-Murray 25–26). The crucified and risen Lamb has already accomplished redemption for God's people, and ascended his Father's throne; equally, the sovereignty of God in Christ has already been acknowledged by the heavenly host (5.13–14). However, submission to that life-giving claim by the whole creation, and the consequent subjugation of earth's rebellion, still lies in the future; and the potential achievement of that divine plan is the story of Rev. 6—22. See further Smalley, *Thunder and Love* 150–51.

Perhaps this accounts for the fact that, in Revelation, the end never arrives. The consummation is constantly heralded (6.17; 11.19; 14.17–20; 16.17–21), but the story continues relentlessly. Babylon falls (18.2–24), and Satan and his followers are bound and judged (19.17—20.10), but wrongdoing remains evident (20.11–15; 21.8, 27; 22.15). Idolatry is clearly the mark of the beast, the wicked and the apostate; yet it never seems to be eradicated (9.20). Through it all, God's salvific purposes for his own, in history as in eternity, remain constant; and the message of Revelation is that the divine gift of living water through the redeeming Lamb is always available (21.6; 22.1–2). Meanwhile, in the Spirit (1.10; 22.17) and through the exalted Christ, John has brought his audience from the beginning to the very brink of the end (1.17–18; 22.13). But in the closing scene of the book, as at its outset (2.16; 3.11), the risen Jesus is still heard to promise that he 'is indeed coming soon' (cf. 22.7, 12); and the Church still continues to pray for that advent to take place: 'Amen; come, Lord Jesus!' (21.20). There the prophet-seer leaves us, to react as we will.

The theological dynamic which controls this drama is that God's wrath cannot be separated from his grace, and that ultimately his judgement leads to the salvation of his people. It is perhaps no accident, therefore, that John's last word (verse 21) is not one of discrimination, but of *love*.

Bibliography

Commentaries on Revelation are cited in the text by the name of the author alone

Aalen, S. 'Glory, Honour'. *NIDNTT* 2 (1976) 44–52.

Allo, E.-B. *Saint Jean, L'Apocalypse*, 3rd edn. Paris: Gabalda, 1933.

Aune, D. E. 'The Apocalypse of John and Graeco-Roman Revelatory Magic'. *NTS* 33 (1987) 481–501.

—— 'The Prophetic Circle of John of Patmos and the Exegesis of Revelation 22.16'. *JSNT* 37 (1989) 103–116.

—— 'The Form and Function of the Proclamations to the Seven Churches (Revelation 2—3)'. *NTS* 36 (1990) 182–204.

—— *Revelation 1–5*. WBC 52A. Dallas: Word Books, 1997.

—— *Revelation 6–16*. WBC 52B. Nashville: Thomas Nelson, 1998.

—— *Revelation 17–22*. WBC 52C. Nashville: Thomas Nelson, 1998.

Barker, M. *The Revelation of Jesus Christ. Which God Gave to Him to Show to His Servants What Must Soon Take Place (Revelation 1.1)*. Edinburgh: T. and T. Clark, 2000.

Barr, D. L. 'Waiting for the End that Never Comes: The Narrative Logic of John's Story'. Moyise, (ed.), *Studies in the Book of Revelation*, 101–12.

Barrett, C. K. *A Commentary on the First Epistle to the Corinthians*. BNTC. London: Adam and Charles Black, 1968.

—— 'Gnosis and the Apocalypse of John'. A. H. B. Logan and A. J. M. Wedderburn (eds), *The New Testament and Gnosis: Essays in Honour of Robert McL. Wilson*. Edinburgh: T. and T. Clark, 1983, 125–37.

Bartels, K. H. 'πρωτότοκος'. *NIDNTT* 1 (1975) 667–69.

Bauckham, R. J. 'Millennium'. *NDT* 428–30.

—— *The Climax of Prophecy: Studies on the Book of Revelation*. Edinburgh: T. and T. Clark, 1993.

—— *The Theology of the Book of Revelation*. NTT. Cambridge: Cambridge University Press, 1993.

—— (ed.). *The Gospels for All Christians: Rethinking the Gospel Audiences*. Edinburgh: T. and T. Clark, 1998.

—— 'Revelation'. J. Barton and J. Muddiman (eds), *The Oxford Bible Commentary*. Oxford: Oxford University Press, 2001, 1287–1306.

Beale, G. K. 'Revelation'. D. A. Carson and H. G. M. Williamson (eds), *It Is Written: Scripture Citing Scripture. Essays in Honour of Barnabas Lindars, SSF*. Cambridge: Cambridge University Press, 1988, 318–36.

—— 'The Old Testament Background of Rev 3.14'. *NTS* 42 (1996) 133–52.

—— 'The Hearing Formula and the Visions of John in Revelation'. Bockmuehl and Thompson (eds), *Vision for the Church*, 167–80.

—— *John's Use of the Old Testament in Revelation*. JSNTS 166. Sheffield: Sheffield Academic Press, 1998.

—— *The Book of Revelation: A Commentary on the Greek Text*. NIGTC. Grand Rapids and Cambridge: Eerdmans; and Carlisle: Paternoster Press, 1999.

Beare, W. *The Roman Stage: A Short History of Latin Drama in the Time of the Republic*, 3rd edn. London: Methuen, 1964.

Beasley-Murray, G. R. *The Book of Revelation*. NCB. London: Oliphants, 1974.

Beck, H., and Brown, C. 'Peace'. *NIDNTT* 2 (1976) 776–83.

Beckwith, I. T. *The Apocalypse of John: Studies in Introduction, with a Critical and Exegetical Commentary*. New York: Macmillan, 1919; and Grand Rapids: Baker Book House, 1967.

Behm, J. 'αἷμα'. *TDNT* 1 (1964) 172–76.

Bell, A. A. 'The Date of John's Apocalypse: The Evidence of Some Roman Historians Reconsidered'. *NTS* 25 (1978–79) 93–102.

Bengel, J. A. *Gnomon of the New Testament*, vol. 5, ed. A. R. Fausset. Edinburgh: T. and T. Clark, 1858.

Benson, E. W. *The Apocalypse: An Introductory Study of the Revelation of St John the Divine*. New York and London: Macmillan, 1900.

Bertram, G. 'παιδεύω, κτλ'. *TDNT* 5 (1967) 596–625.

Betz, O. 'δύναμις'. *NIDNTT* 2 (1976) 601–606.

Bietenhard, H. 'ἄγγελος'. *NIDNTT* 1 (1975) 101–103.

—— 'ἀρχή'. *NIDNTT* 1 (1975) 168–69.

—— 'Satan, διάβολος, et al.'. *NIDNTT* 3 (1978) 468–72.

—— and Bruce, F. F. 'Name'. *NIDNTT* 2 (1976) 648–56.

Black, C. C. '"The Words That You Gave to Me I Have Given to Them": The Grandeur of Johannine Rhetoric'. Culpepper and Black (eds), *Exploring the Gospel of John*, 220–39.

Black, M. 'Some Greek Words with "Hebrew" Meanings in the Epistles and Apocalypse'. J. R. McKay and J. F. Miller (eds), *Biblical Studies: Essays in Honour of William Barclay*. London: Collins, 1976, 135–46.

Blount, B. K. 'Reading Revelation Today: Witness as Active Resistance'. *Int* 54 (2000) 398–412.

Bockmuehl, M., and Thompson, M. B. (eds). *A Vision for the Church: Studies in Early Christian Ecclesiology in Honour of J. P. M. Sweet*. Edinburgh: T. and T. Clark, 1997.

Bøe, S. *Gog and Magog: Ezekiel 38—39 as Pre-text for Revelation 19, 17–21 and 20, 7–10*. WUNT 2/135. Tübingen: Mohr Siebeck, 2001.

Boring, M. E. *Revelation*. INT. Louisville: John Knox Press, 1989.

Bornkamm, G. 'lēnós [vat, press]'. *BTDNT* 531–32.

—— 'mystērion'. *BTDNT* 615–19.

—— 'πρέσβυς, κτλ'. *TDNT* 6 (1968) 651–83, esp. 668–70.

Bousset, W. *Die Offenbarung Johannis*, 6th edn. MKNT 16. Göttingen: Vandenhoeck und Ruprecht, 1906.

Bowker, J. *The Targums and Rabbinic Literature: An Introduction to Jewish Interpretations of Scripture*. Cambridge: Cambridge University Press, 1969.

Bowman, J. W. 'The Revelation to John: Its Dramatic Structure and Message'. *Int* 9 (1955) 436–53.

Boxall, I. 'The Many Faces of Babylon the Great: *Wirkungsgeschichte* and the Interpretation of Revelation 17'. Moyise (ed.), *Studies in the Book of Revelation*, 51–68.

—— *Revelation: Vision and Insight*. London: SPCK, 2002.

Braumann, G. 'κράτος'. *NIDNTT* 3 (1978) 716–18.

Brent, A. 'John as Theologos: The Imperial Mysteries and the Apocalypse'. *JSNT* 75 (1999) 87–102.

Brewer, R. R. 'The Influence of Greek Drama on the Apocalypse of John'. *ATR* 18 (1935–36) 74–92.

Brown, C. 'Animal'. *NIDNTT* 1 (1975) 113–19.

Brown, R. E. *The Community of the Beloved Disciple: The Life, Loves, and Hates of an Individual Church in New Testament Times*. London: Geoffrey Chapman, 1983.

—— *An Introduction to the New Testament*. ABRL. New York and London: Doubleday, 1997.

Bruce, F. F. 'The Spirit in the Apocalypse'. B. Lindars and S. S. Smalley (eds), *Christ and Spirit in the New Testament: Studies in Honour of Charles Francis Digby Moule*. Cambridge: Cambridge University Press, 1973, 333–44.

—— 'Myth'. *NIDNTT* 2 (1976) 643–47.

Büchsel, F. 'ἐλέγχω'. *TDNT* 2 (1964) 473–76.

Burkett, D. 'The Nontitular Son of Man: A History and Critique'. *NTS* 40 (1994) 504–21.

Burton, E. de W. *Syntax of the Moods and Tenses in New Testament Greek*. Chicago: University of Chicago Press, 1906.

Caird, G. B. *The Apostolic Age*. ST. London: Duckworth, 1955.

—— 'On Deciphering the Book of Revelation. I. Heaven and Earth'. *ExpTim* 74 (1962–63) 13–15.

—— *The Revelation of St John the Divine*, 2nd edn. BNTC. London: A. and C. Black, 1984.

Carey, G. *Elusive Apocalypse: Reading Authority in the Revelation to John*. Macon: Mercer University Press, 1999.

Carrell, P. R. *Jesus and the Angels: Angelology and the Christology of the Apocalypse of John*. SNTSMS 95. Cambridge: Cambridge University Press, 1997.

Charles, R. H. *A Critical and Exegetical Commentary on the Revelation of St John*, 2 vols. ICC. Edinburgh: T. and T. Clark, 1920.

Charlesworth, J. H. (ed.). *The Old Testament Pseudepigrapha*, 2 vols. ABRL. London: Darton, Longman and Todd, 1983 and 1985.

—— 'The Jewish Roots of Christology: The Discovery of the Hypostatic Voice'. *SJT* 39 (1986) 19–41.

—— 'The Gospel of John: Exclusivism Caused by a Social Setting Different from That of Jesus (John 11:54 and 14:6)'. R. Bieringer, D. Pollefeyt and F. Vandecasteele-Vanneuville (eds), *Anti-Judaism and the Fourth Gospel: Papers of the Leuven Colloquium, 2000*. JCH 1. Assen: Royal Van Gorcum, 2001, 479–513.

Collins, A. Y. *The Combat Myth in the Book of Revelation*. Missoula: Scholars Press, 1976.

—— *The Apocalypse*. NTM 22. Dublin: Veritas Publications, 1979.

—— 'Revelation 18: Taunt Song or Dirge?' J. Lambrecht (ed.), *L'Apocalypse johannique et l'Apocalyptique dans le Nouveau Testament*. BETL 53. Gembloux-Leuven: Leuven University Press, 1980, 185–204.

—— 'The Book of Revelation'. J. J. Collins (ed.), *The Encyclopedia of Apocalypticism*, vol. 1: *The Origins of Apocalypticism in Judaism and Christianity*. New York and London: Continuum, 2000, 384–414.

Conzelmann, H. 'εὐχαριστέω, κτλ'. *TDNT* 9 (1974) 407–15.

Court, J. M. *Myth and History in the Book of Revelation*. London: SPCK, 1979.

—— *Revelation*. NTG. Sheffield: JSOT Press, 1994.

—— 'Reading the Book. 6. The Book of Revelation'. *ExpTim* 108 (1996–97) 164–67.

—— *The Book of Revelation and the Johannine Apocalyptic Tradition*. JSNTS 190. Sheffield: Sheffield Academic Press, 2000.

Cullmann, O. *Christ and Time: The Primitive Conception of Time and History*. London: SCM Press, 1951.

Culpepper, R. A., and Black, C. C. (eds). *Exploring the Gospel of John: In Honor of D. Moody Smith*. Louisville: Westminster John Knox Press, 1996.

Dansk, E. *The Drama of the Apocalypse*. London: T. Fisher Unwin, 1894.

Delling, G. 'Zum gottesdienstlichen Stil der Johannes-apokalypse'. *NovT* 3 (1959) 107–37.

—— 'ἄρχων'. *TDNT* 1 (1964) 488–89.

—— 'καιρός'. *TDNT* 3 (1965) 455–62.

DeSilva, D. A. 'Honor Discourse and the Rhetorical Strategy of the Apocalypse of John'. *JSNT* 71 (1998) 79–110.

Desrosiers, G. *An Introduction to Revelation*. CBS. London and New York: Continuum, 2000.

Dodd, C. H. *The Epistle of Paul to the Romans*. MNTC. London: Hodder and Stoughton, 1932.

—— *The Parables of the Kingdom*. London: Nisbet, 1936.

—— *The Apostolic Preaching and Its Developments*, 3rd edn. London: Hodder and Stoughton, 1963.

Duff, P. B. ' "I Will Give to Each of You as Your Works Deserve": Witchcraft Accusations and the Fiery-Eyed Son of God in Rev 2.18–23'. *NTS* 43 (1997) 116–33.

—— *Who Rides the Beast? Prophetic Rivalry and the Rhetoric of Crisis in the Churches of the Apocalypse*. Oxford: Oxford University Press, 2001.

Dunn, J. D. G. *Christology in the Making: A New Testament Inquiry into the Origins of the Doctrine of the Incarnation*. London: SCM Press, 1980.

Efird, J. M. *Revelation for Today: An Apocalyptic Approach*. Nashville: Abingdon Press, 1989.

Ellul, J. *Apocalypse: The Book of Revelation*. New York: Seabury Press, 1977.

Esser, H.-H. 'εὐχαριστία'. *NIDNTT* 3 (1978) 817–20.

Ewing, W. *The Power of the Lamb: Revelation's Theology of Liberation*. Cambridge: Cowley, 1990.

Farrar, F. W. 'The Beast and His Number (Revelation xiii)'. *Expositor* (second series) 1 (1890) 321–51.

Farrer, A. M. *A Rebirth of Images: The Making of St John's Apocalypse*. Westminster: Dacre Press, 1949.

—— *The Revelation of St John the Divine: Commentary on the English Text*. Oxford: Clarendon Press, 1964.

Fee, G. D. *The First Epistle to the Corinthians*. NICNT. Grand Rapids: Eerdmans, 1987.

Feuillet, A. *The Apocalypse*. Staten Island: Alba House, 1965.

Filho, J. A. 'The Apocalypse of John as an Account of a Visionary Experience: Notes on the Book's Structure'. *JSNT* 25 (2002) 213–34.

Filson, F. V. *A Commentary on the Gospel according to St Matthew*. BNTC. London: A. and C. Black, 1960.

Finkenrath, G. 'ἐπιστολή'. *NIDNTT* 1 (1975) 246–49.

Fiorenza, E. S. *Revelation: Vision of a Just World*. PC. Minneapolis: Fortress Press, 1991.

—— *The Book of Revelation: Justice and Judgment*, 2nd edn. Minneapolis: Fortress Press, 1998.

Foerster, W., and Quell, G. 'κύριος, et al.'. *TDNT* 3 (1965) 1039–98.

Ford, J. M. *Revelation: Introduction, Translation and Commentary*. AB 38. Garden City: Doubleday, 1975.

Frend, W. H. C. *The Rise of Christianity*. London: Darton, Longman and Todd, 1984.

Garrow, A. J. P. *Revelation*. NTR. London and New York: Routledge, 1997.

Giblin, C. H. 'Revelation 11.1–13: Its Form, Function, and Contextual Integration'. *NTS* 30 (1984) 433–59.

—— 'The Millennium (Rev. 20.4–6) as Heaven'. *NTS* 45 (1999) 553–70.

Gilbertson, M. *God and History in the Book of Revelation: New Testament Studies in Dialogue with Pannenberg and Moltmann*. SNTSMS 124. Cambridge: Cambridge University Press, 2003.

Glasson, T. F. *Moses in the Fourth Gospel*. SBT 40. London: SCM Press, 1963.

—— 'The Last Judgment – in Rev. 20 and Related Writings'. *NTS* 28 (1981–82) 528–39.

Goppelt, L. 'potērion'. *BTDNT* 844–45.

Goranson, S. 'The Text of Revelation 22.14'. *NTS* 43 (1997) 154–57.

Grabbe, L. L., and Haak, R. D. (eds). *Knowing the End from the Beginning: The Prophetic, the Apocalyptic and Their Relationship*. JSPS 46. London: T. and T. Clark International, 2004.

Guhrt, J. 'διαθήκη'. *NIDNTT* 1 (1975) 365–72.

Guthrie, D. *The Relevance of John's Apocalypse*. Grand Rapids: Eerdmans; and Exeter: Paternoster Press, 1987.

Hagner, D. A. 'ἀστήρ, κτλ'. *NIDNTT* 3 (1978) 734–37.

Hahn, H.-C. 'Anger, Wrath'. *NIDNTT* 1 (1975) 105–13.

—— 'καιρός'. *NIDNTT* 3 (1978) 833–39.

Hannah, D. D. 'Of Cherubim and the Divine Throne: Rev 5.6 in Context'. *NTS* 49 (2003) 528–42.

Hanson, A. T. *The Wrath of the Lamb*. London: SPCK, 1957.

Hauck, F. 'koinós, et al.'. *BTDNT* 447–50.

Hays, R. B. *The Moral Vision of the New Testament: Community, Cross, New Creation. A Contemporary Introduction to New Testament Ethics*. New York: HarperCollins, 1996.

Hemer, C. J. 'The Sardis Letter and the Croesus Tradition'. *NTS* 19 (1972–73) 94–97.

—— 'Nicolaitan'. *NIDNTT* 2 (1976) 676–78.

—— 'πέντε'. *NIDNTT* 2 (1976) 689–90.

—— *The Letters to the Seven Churches of Asia in Their Local Setting*. JSNTS 11. Sheffield: JSOT Press, 1986.

Hendriksen, W. *More than Conquerors: An Interpretation of the Book of Revelation*. London: Tyndale Press, 1962.

Hengel, M. *The Johannine Question*. London: SCM Press; and Philadelphia: Trinity Press International, 1989.

Hennecke, E. *New Testament Apocrypha*, 2 vols, ed. R. McL. Wilson. London: Lutterworth Press, 1963 and 1965.

Henten, J. W. van 'Anti-Judaism in Revelation? A Response to Peter Tomson'. Bieringer, Pollefeyt and Vandecasteele-Vanneuville (eds), *Anti-Judaism and the Fourth Gospel*, 111–25.

Hill, D. 'Prophecy and Prophets in the Revelation of St John'. *NTS* 18 (1971–72) 401–18.

—— 'On the Evidence for the Creative Rôle of Christian Prophets'. *NTS* 20 (1973–74) 262–74.

Hillyer, N. 'Precious Stones in the Apocalypse'. *NIDNTT* 3 (1978) 395–99.

—— 'Shake'. *NIDNTT* 3 (1978) 556–61.

Hort, F. J. A. *The Apocalypse of St John I—III: The Greek Text*. London: Macmillan, 1908.

Hughes, P. E. *The Book of Revelation: A Commentary*. Leicester: Inter-Varsity Press; and Grand Rapids: Eerdmans, 1990.

Hull, J. M. ' "Sight to the Inly Blind?" Attitudes to Blindness in the Hymnbooks'. *Theology* 105 (2002) 333–41.

Jauhiainen, M. 'Recapitulation and Chronological Progression in John's Apocalypse: Towards a New Perspective'. *NTS* 49 (2003) 543–59.

Jeremias, J. 'ἀρνίον'. *TDNT* 1 (1964) 340–41.

—— *New Testament Theology*, vol. 1. *The Proclamation of Jesus*. NTL. London: SCM Press, 1971.

—— 'Abaddōn'. *BTDNT* 1.

—— 'Armageddon'. *BTDNT* 79.

—— 'poimēn'. *BTDNT* 901–904.

Johnston, G. '*Ecce Homo!* Irony in the Christology of the Fourth Evangelist'. L. D. Hurst and N. T. Wright (eds), *The Glory of Christ in the New Testament: Studies on Christology in Memory of George Bradford Caird*. Oxford: Clarendon Press, 1987, 125–38.

Judge, E. A. 'The Mark of the Beast, Revelation 13:16'. *TynB* 42 (1991) 158–60.

Kelly, A. J., and Moloney, F. J. *Experiencing God in the Gospel of John*. New York / Mahwah: Paulist Press, 2003.

Kelly, W. *The Revelation of John, Edited in Greek*. London: Williams and Norgate, 1860; 2nd edn. London: Chapter Two, 1995.

Kiddle, M. *The Revelation of St John*. MNTC. London: Hodder and Stoughton, 1940.

Kim, J. K. ' "Uncovering Her Wickedness": An Inter(con)textual Reading of Revelation 17 from a Postcolonial Feminist Perspective'. *JSNT* 73 (1999) 61–81.

Kirby, J. T. 'The Rhetorical Situations of Revelation 1—3'. *NTS* 34 (1988) 197–207.

Kitto, H. D. F. *Greek Tragedy: A Literary Study*, 3rd edn. London: Methuen, 1961.

Klauck, H.-J. 'Do They Never Come Back? *Nero Redivivus* and the Apocalypse of John'. *CBQ* 63 (2001) 683–98.

Knight, J. *Revelation*. Readings. Sheffield: Sheffield Academic Press, 1999.

—— 'The Enthroned Christ of Revelation 5:6 and the Development of Christian Theology'. Moyise (ed.), *Studies in the Book of Revelation*, 43–50.

Koester, C. R. 'The Message to Laodicea and the Problem of Its Local Context: A Study of the Imagery in Rev. 3.14–22'. *NTS* 49 (2003) 407–24.

—— *Revelation*. AB. (Forthcoming)

Kruse, C. G. *John*. TNTC. Leicester: Inter-Varsity Press, 2003.

Ladd, G. E. *A Commentary on the Revelation of John*. Grand Rapids: Eerdmans, 1972.

Lambrecht, J. ' "Synagogues of Satan" (Rev. 2:9 and 3:9): Anti-Judaism in the Book of Revelation'. Bieringer, Pollefeyt and Vandecasteele-Vanneuville (eds), *Anti-Judaism and the Fourth Gospel*, 514–30.

Laubach, F. 'Blood'. *NIDNTT* 1 (1975) 220–24.

Läuchli, S. 'Eine Gottesdienststruktur in der Johannesoffenbarung'. *ThZ* 16 (1960) 359–78.

Lieu, J. M. *The Theology of the Johannine Epistles*. NTT. New York and Cambridge: Cambridge University Press, 1991.

Lindars, B. *New Testament Apologetic: The Doctrinal Significance of the Old Testament Quotations*. London: SCM Press, 1961.

—— 'The Place of the Old Testament in the Formation of New Testament Theology: Prolegomena'. *NTS* 23 (1976–77) 59–66.

Link, H.-G. 'Blessing, et al.'. *NIDNTT* 1 (1975) 206–15.

—— and Brown, C. 'ἀπαρχή'. *NIDNTT* 3 (1978) 415–17.

Longenecker, B. W. '"Linked like a Chain": Rev 22.6–9 in Light of Ancient Transition Technique'. *NTS* 47 (2001) 105–17.

Malina, B. *On the Genre and Message of Revelation: Star Visions and Sky Journeys.* Peabody: Hendrickson, 1995.

Marshall, I. H. 'Jewels and Precious Stones'. *IBD* 2 (1980) 781–88.

Martin, R. P. *2 Corinthians.* WBC 40. Waco: Word Books, 1986.

Martínez, F. G., and Tigchelaar, E. J. C. (eds). *The Dead Sea Scrolls. Study Edition*, 2 vols. Leiden: Brill; and Grand Rapids/Cambridge: Eerdmans, 2000.

Mathewson, D. *A New Heaven and a New Earth: The Meaning and Function of the Old Testament in Revelation 21.1—22.5.* JSNTS 238. Sheffield: Sheffield Academic Press, 2003.

Maurice, F. D. *Lectures on the Apocalypse*, 2nd edn. London and New York: Macmillan, 1893.

Mazzaferri, F. D. *The Genre of the Book of Revelation from a Source-Critical Perspective.* BZNW 54. Berlin: Walter de Gruyter, 1989.

McGuckin, J. A. 'The Book of Revelation and Orthodox Eschatology: The Theodrama of Judgment'. C. E. Braaten and R. W. Jenson (eds), *The Last Things: Biblical and Theological Perspectives on Eschatology.* Grand Rapids and Cambridge: Eerdmans, 2002, 113–34.

McKelvey, R. J. *The New Temple.* Oxford: Oxford University Press, 1969.

—— *The Millennium and the Book of Revelation.* Cambridge: Lutterworth Press, 1999.

—— 'The Millennium and the Second Coming'. Moyise (ed.), *Studies in the Book of Revelation*, 85–100.

Mealy, J. W. *After the Thousand Years: Resurrection and Judgment in Revelation 20.* JSNTS 70. Sheffield: Sheffield Academic Press, 1992.

Metzger, B. M. *A Textual Commentary on the Greek New Testament*, corrected edn. London and New York: United Bible Societies, 1975.

Michaelis, W. 'κράτος, κτλ'. *TDNT* 3 (1965) 905–15.

—— 'λευκός'. *TDNT* 4 (1967) 241–50.

Michaels, J. R. *Revelation.* IVPNTC. Downers Grove and Leicester: InterVarsity Press, 1997.

Michel, O. 'σφάζω, κτλ'. *TDNT* 7 (1971) 925–38.

—— 'πίστις'. *NIDNTT* 1 (1975) 593–606.

—— and Marshall, I. H. 'Son'. *NIDNTT* 3 (1978) 607–68.

Millard, A. R., and McKelvey, R. J. 'Temple'. *IDB* 3 (1980) 1522–32.

Milligan, W. *Lectures on the Apocalypse.* New York and London: Macmillan, 1892.

—— *The Book of Revelation*, 3rd edn. EB. London: Hodder and Stoughton, 1893.

Minear, P. S. 'The Cosmology of the Apocalypse'. W. Klassen and G. F. Snyder (eds), *Current Issues in New Testament Interpretation: Essays in Honor of Otto A. Piper.* TPL. London: SCM Press, 1962, 23–37.

Moffatt, J. 'The Revelation of St John the Divine'. *The Expositor's Greek Testament*, vol. 5, ed. W. R. Nicoll. London: Hodder and Stoughton; and New York: George H. Doran Company, 1910, 279–494.

—— *The First Epistle of Paul to the Corinthians.* MNTC. London: Hodder and Stoughton, 1938.

Morris, L. L. *The Cross in the New Testament.* Exeter: Paternoster Press, 1965.

—— *The Book of Revelation*, 2nd edn. TNTC. Grand Rapids: Eerdmans; and Leicester: InterVarsity Press, 1987.

Moule, C. F. D. *An Idiom Book of New Testament Greek.* Cambridge: Cambridge University Press, 1953.

—— 'A Reconsideration of the Context of *Maranatha*'. *NTS* 6 (1959–60) 307–10.

—— *The Origin of Christology.* Cambridge: Cambridge University Press, 1977.

—— *The Birth of the New Testament*, 3rd edn. BNTC. London: A. and C. Black, 1981.

Mounce, R. H. *The Book of Revelation*, revised edn. NICNT. Grand Rapids and Cambridge: Eerdmans, 1998.

Moyise, S. (ed.). *Studies in the Book of Revelation.* Edinburgh: T. and T. Clark, 2001.

—— 'Does the Lion Lie Down with the Lamb?' Moyise (ed.), *Studies in the Book of Revelation*, 181–94.

Müller, H.-P. 'Die himmlische Ratsversammlung: Motivgeschichtliches zu Apc 5: 1–5'. *ZNW* 54 (1963) 254–67.

Murphy, F. J. *Fallen in Babylon: Revelation to John*. NTC. Harrisburg: Trinity Press International; and London: SCM Press, 1998.

O'Rourke, J. J. 'The Hymns of the Apocalypse'. *CBQ* 30 (1968) 399–409.

Pattemore, S. *The People of God in the Apocalypse: Discourse, Structure and Exegesis*. SNTSMS 128. Cambridge and New York: Cambridge University Press, 2004.

Paul, I. 'The Revelation to John'. I. H. Marshall, S. Travis, I. Paul, *Exploring the New Testament*, vol. 2: *The Letters and Revelation*. London: SPCK, 2002, 305–28.

Paulien, J. 'Criteria and the Assessment of Allusions to the Old Testament in the Book of Revelation'. Moyise (ed.), *Studies in the Book of Revelation*, 113–29.

Peake, A. S. *The Revelation of John*. London: Joseph Johnson, 1919.

Philonenko, M. ' "Dehors les Chiens" (Apocalypse 22.15 et 4QMMT B58–62)'. *NTS* 43 (1997) 445–50.

Poirier, J. C. 'The First Rider: A Response to Michael Bachmann'. *NTS* 45 (1999) 257–62.

Poole, M. *Synopsis Criticorum*, vol. 4. London: Carolum Smith, 1676.

Pope, M. H. 'Number, Numbering, Numbers'. *IDB* 3 (1962) 561–67.

Prévost, J.-P. *How to Read the Apocalypse*. London: SCM Press, 1993.

Prigent, P. *Apocalypse 12. Histoire de l'exégèse*. BGBE 2. Tübingen: Mohr, 1959.

—— *Commentary on the Apocalypse of St John*, revised edn. Tübingen: Mohr Siebeck, 2001.

Procksch, O. 'λύτρον'. *TDNT* 4 (1967) 329–31.

Provan, I. W. 'Foul Spirits, Fornication and Finance: Revelation 18 from an Old Testament Perspective'. *JSNT* 64 (1996) 81–100.

Ramsay, W. M. *The Letters to the Seven Churches of Asia: And Their Place in the Plan of the Apocalypse*, 4th edn. London, New York and Toronto: Hodder and Stoughton, 1912.

Rengstorf, K. H. 'manthánō, et al.'. *BTDNT* 552–62.

Resseguie, J. L. *Revelation Unsealed: A Narrative Critical Approach to John's Apocalypse*. BI 32. Leiden: E. J. Brill, 1998.

Rissi, M. 'The Rider on the White Horse: A Study of Revelation 6:1–8'. *Int* 18 (1964) 407–18.

Rist, M. 'The Revelation of St John the Divine: Introduction and Exegesis'. G. A. Buttrick et al. (eds), *The Interpreter's Bible*, vol. 12. New York and Nashville: Abingdon Press, 1957, 345–613.

Robinson, J. A. T. 'Traces of a Liturgical Sequence in 1 Cor. 16.20–24'. *JTS* (ns) 4 (1953) 38–41.

—— *Redating the New Testament*. London: SCM Press, 1976.

—— *Where Three Ways Meet*. London: SCM Press, 1987.

—— 'Interpreting the Book of Revelation'. Robinson, *Where Three Ways Meet*, 35–75.

—— 'What Future for a Unique Christ?'. Robinson, *Where Three Ways Meet*, 9–17.

Robinson, J. M. *The Nag Hammadi Library in English*, 4th edn. Leiden: E. J. Brill, 1996.

Roller, O. 'Das Buch mit sieben Siegeln'. *ZNW* 36 (1937) 98–113.

Roloff, J. *The Revelation of John*. FCC. Minneapolis: Fortress Press, 1993.

Rowland, C. C. *The Open Heaven: A Study of Apocalyptic in Judaism and Early Christianity*. London: SPCK, 1982.

Rudolph, K. *Gnosis: The Nature and History of an Ancient Religion*, ed. R. McL. Wilson. Edinburgh: T. and T. Clark, 1983.

Rudwick, M. J. S., and Green, E. M. B. 'The Laodicean Lukewarmness'. *ExpTim* 69 (1957–58) 176–78.

Ruiz, J.-P. 'Praise and Politics in Revelation 19: 1–10'. Moyise (ed.), *Studies in the Book of Revelation*, 69–84.

Schlier, H. 'ἀμήν'. *TDNT* 1 (1964) 335–36.

—— 'βάθος'. *TDNT* 1 (1964) 517–18.

—— 'θλῖψις'. *TDNT* 3 (1965) 139–48.

Schmitz, E. D., and Brown, C. 'ἑπτά'. *NIDNTT* 2 (1976) 690–92.

Schneider, C. 'métōpon'. *BTDNT* 591.

Schneider, J. 'τιμή, τιμάω'. *TDNT* 8 (1972) 169–80.

—— 'σώζω, σωτηρία'. *NIDNTT* 3 (1978) 205–16.

Scholem, G. G. *Jewish Gnosticism, Merkabah Mysticism, and Talmudic Tradition*, 2nd edn. New York: Jewish Theological Seminary of America, 1965.

Schultz, H. 'Jerusalem, Zion'. *NIDNTT* 2 (1976) 324–30.

Schwarz, H. *Eschatology*. Grand Rapids and Cambridge: Eerdmans, 2000.

Seebass, H., and Brown, C. 'ἅγιος'. *NIDNTT* 2 (1976) 224–32.

—— 'δικαιοσύνη/δίκαιος'. *NIDNTT* 3 (1978) 352–77.

Shepherd, M. H. *The Paschal Liturgy and the Apocalypse*. ESW 6. London: Lutterworth Press, 1960.

Silberman, L. H. 'Farewell to O AMHN: A Note on Rev 3:14'. *JBL* 82 (1963) 213–15.

Slater, T. B. ' "King of Kings and Lord of Lords" Revisited'. *NTS* 39 (1993) 159–60.

—— 'On the Social Setting of the Revelation to John'. *NTS* 44 (1998) 232–56.

—— *Christ and Community: A Socio-Historical Study of the Christology of Revelation*. JSNTS 178. Sheffield: Sheffield Academic Press, 1999.

Smalley, S. S. 'The Johannine Son of Man Sayings'. *NTS* 15 (1968–69) 278–301.

—— 'The Sign in John XXI'. *NTS* 20 (1973–74) 275–88.

—— 'Banquet'. *IBD* 1 (1980) 172.

—— 'Mystery'. *IBD* 2 (1980) 1041–42.

—— 'The Christ-Christian Relationship in Paul and John'. D. A. Hagner and M. J. Harris (eds), *Pauline Studies: Essays Presented to F. F. Bruce on his 70th Birthday*. Exeter: Paternoster Press; and Grand Rapids: Eerdmans, 1980, 95–105.

—— 'Seal, Sealing' (In the New Testament). *IBD* 3 (1980) 1410–11.

—— *1, 2, 3 John*. WBC 51. Waco: Word Books, 1984.

—— 'John's Revelation and John's Community'. *BJRL* 69 (1987) 549–71.

—— *Thunder and Love: John's Revelation and John's Community*. Milton Keynes: Nelson Word, 1994.

—— ' "The Paraclete": Pneumatology in the Johannine Gospel and Apocalypse'. Culpepper and Black (eds), *Exploring the Gospel of John*, 289–300.

—— 'The Johannine Community and the Letters of John'. Bockmuehl and Thompson (eds), *Vision for the Church*, 95–104.

—— *John: Evangelist and Interpreter*, 2nd edn. Carlisle: Paternoster Press, 1998.

Sorg, T. 'καρδία'. *NIDNTT* 2 (1976) 180–84.

Stählin, G. 'Human and Divine Wrath in the NT'. *BTDNT* 722–26.

Stanley, D. M. 'Carmenque Christo quasi Deo dicere . . .'. *CBQ* 20 (1958) 173–91.

Stauffer, E. *Christ and the Caesars: Historical Sketches*. London: SCM Press, 1955.

Sweet, J. P. M. *Revelation*, 2nd edn. TPINTC. Philadelphia: Trinity Press International; and London: SCM Press, 1990.

Swete, H. B. *The Apocalypse of St John*, 3rd edn. London: Macmillan, 1909.

—— *The Holy Spirit in the New Testament: A Study of Primitive Christian Teaching*. London: Macmillan, 1909.

Talbert, C. H. *The Apocalypse: A Reading of the Revelation of John*. Louisville: Westminster John Knox Press, 1994.

Thiselton, A. C. 'Truth'. *NIDNTT* 3 (1978) 874–902.

Thompson, L. L. *The Book of Revelation: Apocalypse and Empire*. New York and Oxford: Oxford University Press, 1990.

—— *Revelation*. ANTC. Nashville: Abingdon Press, 1998.

Thompson, M. M. *The God of the Gospel of John*. Grand Rapids and Cambridge: Eerdmans, 2001.

Topham, M. 'A Human Being's Measurement, Which Is an Angel's'. *ExpTim* 100 (1988–89) 217–18.

—— 'The Dimensions of the New Jerusalem'. *ExpTim* 100 (1988–89) 417–19.

Trites, A. A. 'Μάρτυς and Martyrdom in the Apocalypse: A Semantic Study'. *NovT* 15 (1973) 72–80.

Trudinger, P. 'O AMHN (Rev III.14), and the Case for a Semitic Original of the Apocalypse'. *NovT* 14 (1972) 277–79.

Ulfgard, H. *Feast and Future: Revelation 7: 9–17 and the Feast of Tabernacles*. CB (NT) 22. Stockholm: Almqvist and Wicksell, 1989.

Underhill, E. *The Mystic Way: A Psychological Study in Christian Origins*. London and Toronto: J. M. Dent, 1913.

Vanni, U. *La struttura letteraria dell' Apocalisse*, 2nd edn. Aloisiana 8. Brescia: Morcelliana, 1980.

—— 'Liturgical Dialogue as a Literary Form in the Book of Revelation'. *NTS* 37 (1991) 348–72.

Vaux, R. de *Ancient Israel: Its Life and Institutions*. London: Darton, Longman and Todd, 1961.

Vielhauer, Ph. 'Apocalyptic'. Hennecke (ed.), *New Testament Apocrypha* 2, 582–607.

Walker, N. 'The Origin of the "Thrice-Holy"'. *NTS* 5 (1958–59) 132–33.

Walker, P. W. L. *Jesus and the Holy City: New Testament Perspectives on Jerusalem*. Grand Rapids and Cambridge: Eerdmans, 1996.

Wall, R. W. *Revelation*. NIBC (NT). Carlisle: Paternoster Press; and Peabody: Hendrickson, 1995.

Water, R. van de 'Reconsidering the Beast from the Sea (Rev 13.1)'. *NTS* 46 (2000) 245–61.

Weiss, J. *Die Offenbarung des Johannes. Ein Beitrag zur Literatur- und Religionsgeschichte*. Göttingen: Vandenhoeck & Ruprecht, 1904.

Wilcock, M. *The Message of Revelation: I Saw Heaven Opened*, 2nd edn. BST. Leicester: Inter-Varsity Press, 1991.

Wilcox, M. 'Tradition and Redaction of Rev 21, 9—22, 5'. Lambrecht (ed.), *L'Apocalypse johannique*, 205–15.

Williams, P. S. *The Case for Angels*. Carlisle and Waynesboro: Paternoster Press, 2002.

Williams, R. 'The Touch of God'. R. Williams, *Open to Judgment: Sermons and Addresses*. London: Darton, Longman and Todd, 1994, 112–17.

Wilson, J. C. 'The Problem of the Domitianic Date of Revelation'. *NTS* 39 (1993) 587–605.

Wink, W. *Unmasking the Powers: The Invisible Forces That Determine Human Existence. The Powers*, vol. 2. Philadelphia: Fortress Press, 1986.

Witherington III, B. *Revelation*. New Cambridge Bible Commentary. Cambridge and New York: Cambridge University Press, 2003.

Worth, R. H. Jr *The Seven Cities of the Apocalypse and Roman Culture*. Mahwah: Paulist Press, 1999.

Wright, N. T. *The Resurrection of the Son of God*. Christian Origins and the Question of God, vol. 3. London: SPCK, 2003.

Zahn, T. *Introduction to the New Testament*, 3 vols. Edinburgh: T. and T. Clark, 1909.

Index of Greek Terms

ἄβυσσος 226, 511
ἀγαπᾶν 100
ἄγγελος 28, 58
ἁγιάζω 571
ἅγιοι 135, 368
ἅγιος 88, 159, 571
ἀγοράζω 10
ἀδελφοί 165–66
ἀδικέω 571
ἀετός 224
ᾅδης 56
αἷμα 402
αἰνέω 480
ἀκάθαρτος 430–31
ἄκρατος 366
ἀληθινός 88, 159–60, 404
ἀλληλουιά 476–77
ἀμήν 38, 141, 479
ἄμπελος 376
ἄμωμον 455
ἄμωμος 360
ἀναβαίνω 513
ἀνάθεμα 564
ἀπαρχή 359
ἀποκάλυψις 27
ἀριθμός 351
ἄρκος 337
Ἁρμαγεδών 397
ἀρνίον 131
ἄρσεν 319
ἀρχή 97
αὐλητής 463
Ἄψινθος 205

βασανισμός 449
βασιλεύω 289, 481
βάτραχος 409
βεβαμμένον 472
βιβλαρίδιον 247, 258, 266
βιβλίον 247, 258, 266
βλασφημέω 341
βλέπειν 52
βύσσινον 483
βύσσινος 454, 458

γέμειν 420
γῆ 374
γόμον 453, 455
γόμος 453
γυνή 545

δαιμόνιον 243
δεσπότης 159
διάβολος 325, 329
δίκαιος 387, 404, 571
δικαιώματα 389, 483, 484
δικαιοσύνη 571
διπλόω 448
δισμυριάδες μυριάδων 208
δόξα 36–37, 139, 477, 557, 558
δρέπανον 372, 374
δύναμις 139, 477

ἐγώ εἰμι 56
ἔθνη 563
εἷς 195
ἐκδικεῖν 478
ἐλεφάντινον 455
ἔμποροι 453
ἐν Ἰησοῦ 49–50
ἐν πνεύματι 51, 546
ἐνδώμησις 553
ἐνώπιον τοῦ θεοῦ 214, 216
ἐξέρχομαι 511–12
ἔργα 370, 387
ἔρχεσθαι 577–78
ἑτοιμάζω 483
εὐαγγέλιον 361
εὐλογία 139–40
ἔφθειρεν 477

θάλασσα 401
θαυμάζω 433, 435
θεμέλιος 549
θλῖψις 50, 75
θρόνος 68
θύϊνον 454
θυμίαμα 135, 215
θυμός 170, 364, 365–66, 495
θυσιαστήριον 158, 404

ἶρις 257
ἰσχυροί 497

καὶ εἶδον 126
κοινός 524
καιρός 31, 291, 329
κάλαμος 271
καρδία 76
κατάθεμα 563–64
κεράννυμι 366
κέρας 132

κιθάρα 134
κιθαρῳδός 463
κλαίω 451
κοινός 560
κόποι 370
κόπτω 451
κράτος 140
κρίμα 506
κρίσις 363, 452
κτῆνος 455
κυκλόω 473
κύνες 574
κύριος 282

λαμπρός 457
λατρεύουσιν 198
λευκός 488
ληνός 376
λίβανος 215
λιβανωτός 215
λίμνη 499
λιπαρός 457
λόγος 567
λύσαντι 25

μετρεῖν 272
μισθός 291
μουσικός 463
μυστήριον 265

ναός 389
νέος 524
νεφροί 76

ὄνομα 84, 388
ὀπώρα 456
ὅρασις 239
ὀργή 170–71, 365–66, 495
ὅρμημα 462
ὄρος 435
ὅσιος 388
οὐαί 225, 234–35, 303, 329, 452
οὐρανός 113, 314, 316–17, 322, 328

παράδεισος 64
πάρδαλις 337
παρεμβολή 514
παρθένοι 358
πελεκίζω 507
πένθος 449, 450
πεπληρωμένα 82

πεπότικεν 308, 364
πίστις 344
πιστός 66–67, 439
πλατεῖα 281, 555
πλοῦτος 139
ποιμαίνειν 200, 319
ποιμαίνω 494
πόλεμον 410
πορνεία 244, 358, 409, 424, 431
πορνεύειν 424
πορνῶν 420
ποταμοφόρητον 331
προφήτης 266
πρόσωπον 170
προφητεία 7
πυλών 548
πῶς 82

ῥαίδη 423
ῥέδη 455
ῥομφαία 55, 155
ῥυπαίνομαι 571
ῥυπαρός 571

σαλπιστής 463
Σατανᾶς 325
σεμίδαλις 455
σημαίνειν 27–28
σημεῖον 311, 313
σιρικός 454
σκεῦος 454
σκηνή 341, 537–38
σκηνόω 328, 537
σοφία 139
στέφανον 67
στρηνιάσαντες 451
στρῆνος 445
σύνδουλος 165–66
σφραγίζειν 183
σώματα 455
σωτηρία 10, 192–93, 326, 477

τελεῖν 383
τετράγωνος 551
τιμή 139, 558
τρέφω 321, 331

ὕδατα 439
ὕδωρ ζωῆς 541
ὑπομονή 344, 368

φαρμακία 465
φάρμακον 244
φαρμάκων 209
φιάλας 134
φιάλη 391
φιλεῖν 100
φόνος 244
φρέαρ 226
φυλακή 444

χαλκολιβάνῳ 54
χιλίαρχος 497
Χριστός 508
χρόνος 31, 264, 329

ψευδοπροφήτης 409
ψυχὰς ἀνθρώπων 456
ψυχή 401

ὥρα 363, 374

Index of Scriptural References and Ancient Sources

OLD TESTAMENT

Genesis
1 31, 211
1—3 312
1.1 97, 363
1.1–2.4a 524
1.2 226, 263
1.6–10 524
1.7 119, 384
1.14 313
1.14–19 224
1.26 260
1.30 284
1.30 LXX 155
1.31 18, 503
2 563
2—3 64, 94
2.5 LXX 155
2.7 284
2.8 64, 181
2.8–9 562
2.9 64, 563
2.10 561
2.10–14 384
2.11–12 550, 561
2.15 64
2.16–17 562
2.25 411
3 325
3.1–5 504
3.1–7 324, 345
3.1–15 9
3.1–24 562
3.8 170
3.14–16 316
3.15 324, 334
3.15–16 314
3.20 LXX 492
3.20–24 564
3.22 64, 563
3.22–24 64, 574
3.24 120, 549
4.10 157, 160
4.11 470
4.14 170
4.15 182, 313, 562
5.22 84
5.24 285
6.9 84

6.17 284
7.11 384
8.1 447
9.2 260
9.5–6 164
9.6 403
9.8–17 115
9.20–25 411
10.2 512
11.1–9 466
11.2 175
11.4 447, 552
12.1–3 446, 538
14.19 263
14.22 263
14.22–23 LXX 263
15.5 318
15.5–6 190
15.8 159
15.18 407
16.1–15 314
16.10 190
17.1 84
18.1–16 28
19.1 58
19.1–25 282
19.2 LXX 195
19.11 293, 349
19.12–22 446
19.24 217, 240, 366, 405, 499
19.24–25 278
19.27–28 450
19.28 240, 367, 451, 478
22.11–18 28
22.12 362
22.17 513
24.2 495
24.3 363
24.7 287
24.55 66
30.38 376
30.41 LXX 376
32.12 335
32.29 490
35.22b–26 188
36.6 LXX 455
37.2–11 433
37.9 315

40.2 LXX 303
40.5—41.36 433
40.8 350
41.42 99
41.49 513
44.23 170
46.8–27 188
47.29 495
49.2–28 188
49.9–10 130
49.10 187
49.11 377
50.18–19 486

Exodus
1.2–4 188
1.22 332
2.24 294
3.12 538
3.14–15 32, 123
4.14–16 333
4.24 29, 234
5.1–21 282
6.3 491
6.7 491
7.3 407
7.13 242
7.14—12.39 279
7.14–20 275
7.14–21 279
7.14–24 221–22
7.14–25 219
7.16–18 323
7.17–21 398, 401
7.20 221
7.20–24 221
7.22 242
8—12 9
8.1–15 409
8.1–17 275
8.2–11 LXX 409
8.2–14 398
8.5–6 409
9 416
9.8–11 398
9.8–12 LXX 401
9.11 401
9.13–35 219
9.18 414
9.22–25 219

9.22–26 295, 398–99, 413
9.22–32 398
9.23 406
9.23–24 261
9.23–34 147
9.24 414
9.31–32 LXX 223
10 230
10.1–2 230
10.1–20 227
10.4–15 398
10.(12) 228
10.14–15 227
10.15 228
10.20 230
10.21 413
10.21–23 223, 398
10.21–29 398, 406
10.22–23 406
11.5 462
11.7 229
12 35–36, 182
12.7–28 182
12.12 29, 224, 234
12.12–13 213
12.21–27 64
12.23 234
12.23–27 213
12.29 258
12.29–32 416
12.30–32 446
13.17–22 321
13.21 37
13.21–22 257
14.8–10 330
14.13 193, 326
14.14 212
14.15—15.10 332
14.15–31 385
14.19 28, 257
14.19–20 514
14.21–25 407
14.24 257, 285, 371
14.30 193
14.31 386
15 386, 391
15.1 386, 542
15.1–18 120, 163, 212, 289, 382, 386

15.1–19 385
15.3–4 384, 488
15.4–5 390
15.8 384
15.11 111, 339, 388
15.11–18 491
15.12 332
15.13 139, 333
15.13–18 295
15.14 291
15.16 284
15.16–18 390
15.17 293, 333
15.17–18 560
15.18 LXX 289
15.20–21 385
15.22—16.36 428
15.25 223
16.1–36 295
16.4–35 321
16.10 314
16.32–34 70
16.34 390
17.1–7 295
18.12 117
19.3–23 546
19.4 330
19.5–6 LXX 36
19.6 9, 137, 510
19.9–18 257
19.13–19 214
19.16–18 392, 414
19.16–19 107, 399
19.16–20 167
19.16–24 227
19.16–25 119
19.18 166, 217–18, 416, 499
20.2–7 339
20.4 130
20.4–5 243, 544
20.4–6 363
20.6 185
20.7 405
20.11 130, 140, 260, 263, 341
20.13 544
20.13–15 243
20.14 544

20.22 294
21.24 293, 447
23.16 562
23.19 359
23.20–23 28
23.31 407
23.31–33 564
24.3–8 294
24.9–10 117, 119
24.10 115
24.15–18 257
24.16–18 392
24.17 119, 278
25—39 LXX 556
25.8 538
25.18 120
25.18–22 29
25.22 294
25.29 134
27.2 236
27.3 215, 391
27.21 390
28 315, 458
28.4 54, 85
28.11 LXX 184
28.11–21 184
28.13–14 LXX 556
28.17 115
28.17–20 115
28.17–20 LXX 554
28.20 115
28.21 554
28.29 554
28.36 184
28.36–38 184, 565
29.5 54
29.10–21 197
29.44 538
29.45 537–38
29.45–46 538
30.2 236
30.7–10 215
30.10 36, 236
30.27 158
30.34–37 215
31.18—32.29 347
32.13 190
32.22 LXX 462
32.27 495
32.32–33 85–86, 342, 517
33.7–11 199
33.18–23 565
33.20 170
34.15 74
34.27–35 294
34.29 133, 390
34.29–30 443
35.34 441
36.13 LXX 184
36.16 448
37.16 134
38.3 391
38.26 LXX 389, 538
39 315

39.9 MT 448
39.10–13 554
39.14 554
39.29 54
40.24 390
40.34 LXX 389, 538
40.34–35 341, 392, 547
40.34–38 199
40.35 392

Leviticus
1.10 360
2.1 215
2.12 359
3.1 360
4.5 197
4.6–7 LXX 400
4.7 158
8.15 LXX 400
8.28 158
9.6 547
9.22 263
10.1 LXX 217
10.6 231
10.10 560
11.9–12 409
11.10–12 LXX 430
11.24–28 560
11.41–47 409
13.45 231
15.16–18 560
16 36, 552
16.1–2 214
16.2 257
16.4 85, 390
16.11–13 216
16.12–13 392
16.30 198
17.11 36, 197
18.21 LXX 198
18.22 LXX 430
20.14 440
22.9 440
23.9–14 373
23.40 192
26 391
26.1 390
26.8 229
26.11 538
26.11–12 537
26.12 542
26.14–33 156
26.14–39 261
26.18 390
26.21 383, 390
26.21–26 240
26.24 383, 390
26.25 155
26.26 153
26.28 390
26.30 390
26.31 390
26.40–45 390
27.28–29 564

Numbers
1.1 238
1.2 84
1.2–16 186
1.5–15 188–89
1.20 84
1.20–43 186
1.32 189
1.49 189
2.2–9 514
2.3 188
2.3–31 549
2.33 189
3.14–39 189
3.38 175
4.14–15 391
5.2–3 560
5.18 231
6.14 360
6.23–27 566
6.24–26 566
6.25 170
6.26 32
6.27 566
7.12 188
7.13 391
8.21 198
9.15–17 199
10.9–10 214
10.11 389, 538
10.11–12 257
10.14 188
10.33 294
10.36 138, 185
11.1–35 428
13.2–14 189
13.4–14 188
13.11 189
14.10 392
14.13–14 257
14.22 66
14.44 253
16.3 66, 333
16.6–7 215
16.9 198
16.12–14 333
16.20–35 333
16.26–27 446
16.28–30 333
16.30 333
16.30–35 499
16.32 333
16.33 499
16.40 216
16.46–47 216
17.7 389, 538
19.2 360
19.19 197
20.4 LXX 66
21.29 225
24.17 79, 577
25 9
25.1–2 63
25.1–9 584
25.2 63
25.14–18 584

25.15–20 584
26.1–51 189
26.57–62 189
31.8, 16 70
31.14 303
31.16 9, 63
31.19–20 197
31.24 197
34.19–28 188
35.30 276

Deuteronomy
1.7 407
1.17 293, 349
1.28 447
1.30–31 331
4.1 LXX 389
4.1–2 584
4.3 584
4.9–14 278
4.13 294
4.24 405
4.28 242
4.30 383
5.8 263
5.8–9 243
5.11 341
5.17–19 243
5.24 199
5.26 182
6.6 76
6.6–9 349
6.8 313
6.13 339
6.20–25 369
7.6–13 579
7.9 185
7.26 564
8.2–18 321
8.3 267
8.5 100
8.7 226
8.15 229
8.16 383
8.17 140
10.8 253, 294
10.12–15 363
10.17 438, 495
10.21 LXX 387
10.22 190
11.25 284
12.20–21 LXX 457
12.29–31 584
12.31 430
12.32 584
12.32 MT 584
13.1 LXX 584
13.1–2 346
13.1–18 584
13.2–6 LXX 584
14.12–19 444
14.26 LXX 457
16.9 LXX 374
16.9–13 375
17.6 276
17.14 320

18.9–14 574
18.18 275
19.10 403
19.15 276
19.16–19 461
19.21 447
20.1 538
23.2–3 560
23.9–11 357
23.14 514
23.18 574
24.14 154
26.2 359
26.10 LXX 359
28.25–29 229
28.26 500
28.42 227
28.49 225
28.59–60 LXX 387
29.12–15 538
29.14–18 584
29.17–18 223
29.19–20 584
29.22–23 240
29.22–28 282
29.23 240, 366
31.29 383
31.30—32.43 382, 386
32 386
32.4 LXX 387–88, 404
32.10–14 330
32.14 377
32.16–17 243
32.17 LXX 243
32.19–21, 43 386
32.24 405
32.24–25 406
32.40 LXX 263
32.41 494
32.43 478
32.43a 328
33.1–25 188
33.2–3 111
33.10 135
33.13–17 491
33.29 459
34.1–4 546
34.5 386
34.5–6 285

Joshua
1.1 386
1.4 407
3.5–17 294
3.7–17 407
3.10 56, 182
5.13–15 28
5.14 159, 323
6.1–27 214
6.4–20 463
7.6 459
7.15 278
7.19 482

7.19 LXX 362
7.22–26 564
8.19–21 367
10.11 415–16
11.4 513
14.7 386
21.4–7 188

Judges
1.7 293, 448
2.17 74
3.21 495
5.1–31 491
5.4 218
5.4–5 163, 516
5.5 168
5.19 412
5.20 225
5.31 412
5.31b 55
6.5 231
6.22 258
7.8–22 214
8.26 430
11.5–11 117
13.3 314
13.6 58
13.18 490
13.20 285
15.11 293
16.13–22 232
16.23–25 64
16.28 447
18.2 229
18.30 187
20.27 253
20.40 367

Ruth
4.2–4 117

1 Samuel
1.19 447
2.3 123
2.9–10 212
2.10 119, 139
2.18 390
4.5–8 294
4.8 279, 340
6.5 362
6.20 172
7.6 400
7.10 147, 261
10.25 214
13.5 513
17.5 LXX 232
17.44 281, 500
18.7 185
21.5 358
24.6 289

2 Samuel
3.28–29 161
5.10 290, 493
6.2–21 214
6.5 463

7.7 200
7.14 542
8.2 271
10.4 99
12.14 75
14.25–26 232
18.16 214
22 367
22.5 332
22.8 217
22.9 240, 278
22.10 167
22.13 278

1 Kings
1.32–48 112
1.34 214
1.50–51 236
2.28–29 236
3.8 190
3.28 389
5.12 139
5.17 549, 554
6—7 553
6.20 552
6.20–22 553
6.22 553
6.23 120
6.30 556
6.36 272
7.9–12 272
7.10 549
7.15–22 93
7.23 384
7.23–26 119
7.50 215
8.9–13 392
8.11 392, 547
8.35 279
8.37 227
10.23 459
12.11 229
12.14 229
12.29 187
13.21–22 518
13.30 225
14.11 500
16.31 9, 73
17.1 275, 279
17.1–5 346
17.2–6 321
18.1 279
18.13 LXX 321
18.17–39 346
18.38 346
18.43–45 261
19.1–4 230
19.2–6 321
19.4–10 428
19.10 403
19.11–12 218
19.11–13 163
19.18 286
21.23 73, 500
22 112
22.1–38 112

22.11 271, 462
22.19 114, 116, 138, 290
22.19–22 111
22.19–23 410
22.20 112
22.31 293

1 Kings (3 Kgdms)
5.4 116

2 Kings
1.9–12 514
1.9–16 278
1.10 217, 346
1.10–17 275
1.12 217
1.14 217
2.1–12 111
2.11 285, 371
2.11–12 275, 285
6.17 323
7.1 153
7.18 153
9.7 266, 478
9.7 LXX 478
9.22 243
9.30–37 73, 440
10.1–11 75
11.12(–20) 112
11.14 93
13.21 284
16.14 214
18.18 88
19.4 182
19.15 363
19.16 182
19.21 358
19.22 159
19.28 LXX 445
19.29 313
19.31 354
21.8 386
23.2 349
23.3 93
23.29 412
24.15 LXX 169
25.8–10 294
25.13 119

2 Kings (4 Kgdms)
1.10–14 LXX 514

1 Chronicles
1.5 512
5.4 512
7.29 412
9.25 LXX 322
9.29 LXX 215
12.23–37 188
16.8–36 362
16.15 294
16.27–28 139
16.29 482
16.36 479
16.36 LXX 480

16.42 134
16.42 LXX 385
21.1 325
21.6 189
21.12 494
21.18 258
22.18 538
23.6 116
23.7–24 116
24.3–19 549
24.7–18 116
25.1–31 134
25.6–31 549
26.17–19 549
28.17 391
29.10–13 140
29.11 36
29.11–12 139

2 Chronicles
3.8–13 552
4.2 384
4.8 391
5.13–14 392
6.14 459
6.26 279
6.30 LXX 388
6.35 389
7.1–2 392
7.1–3 199, 547
7.2 392
7.13 228
8.14 548
9.11 134
15.3 160
15.13 516
18.18–21 111
20.17 193
20.27–28 356
24.22 161
28.9 447
32.33 139
34.25 242
36.15–16 276
36.23 287

Ezra
1.2 287
1.3 538
1.5 513
4.15 85
5.11 363
9.5–15 216
9.6 447

Nehemiah
1.4–5 287
1.6 199
1.8 386
2.12 441
4.4–5 161
5.9 480
5.13 479
7.5 441
8.15 192
9.6 140, 263, 388

9.11 461
9.12 257
9.20 201
9.23 190
9.26 276, 403
9.33 402
11.1 273

Esther
4.16 344
4.17e LXX 339
6.1 85
6.6–11 99
6.13 LXX 182
9.22 283
(Greek) *11.5–9* 498

Job
1 66
1.6 28, 111, 116, 135, 277
1.6–9 324
1.6–12 325, 327
1.10 242
1.16 217
1.22 406
2.1 116
2.1–6 324
2.1–7 327
2.3 325
2.7–8 401
2.10 406
2.12 459
3.1–26 230
3.19 293
4.10–11 232
4.16–21 212
5.1 366
5.8 159
5.15 470
5.17–18 100
6.10 159
6.14 480
7.7 447
7.12 335
7.12 LXX 317
7.14–16 230
9.7 182
9.13 LXX 317
11.6 448
11.9 260
12.16 140
14.18 168
15.8 111
16.19 97
18.15 366
21.20 365
21.23 140
26 163
26.6 234
26.12–13 314
26.12–13 LXX 317
28.14 226
28.22 234
28.25 119
30.4 LXX 406

31.12 234
32.8 284
33.22 155
34.11 517
36.16 226
37.1–13 119
37.2–5 147
37.3 179
37.7 182
37.14–21 524
37.18 119
37.22–24 140
38.6–7 28, 225
38.16 363
38.22–23 415
39.19–25 232
40—41 335
40.10 139–40
40.15 336
40.18 LXX 317
40.24–25 LXX 335
40.32 LXX 335
41 240
41.1 336
41.1–34 LXX 317
41.18–21 278
41.25 LXX 335
41.33–34 335
42.3 LXX 387
42.9 25

Psalms
1.2 199
2—8 78
2.1–6 498
2.1–12 291
2.2 289, 498
2.6 353
2.6–12 354
2.7 72, 79, 542
2.8–9 72, 77–78
2.9 79
2.9 78, 271, 319, 493–94, 498
2.10 498
2.11 292, 480
3.8 193
3.9 LXX 193
4.6 566
6.3 388
7.6–9 161
7.9 76
7.11 402
7.12 404
7.14–16 293
8.5 123
9.4 402
9.9 LXX 488
9.13 LXX 415
10.6 LXX 365
10.7 LXX 488
11.4 564
11.6 217, 366
11.7 564
13.1–2 160
14.1–3 441

15.1 388
16.10 157
17.13 494
17.15 564
18.4 332
18.6 158
18.7 168
18.7–9 392
18.7–15 375
18.7–24 119
18.8 217, 240
18.9 167, 488
18.10 122, 180, 404
18.11 257
18.13 278
18.31 339
19 (18) 159
19.7–10 267
20.3 457
21.3 LXX 368
21.24 LXX 362
22.26 76
23.1–3 300
23.2 201
24.3–6 360
24.7 559
24.9 559
24.14 LXX 322
25.10 294
27.4 564
27.8 170
28.1 139
28.2 263
28.4 448
28.8 139
28(29).1 123
29 261
29.1 111
29.3–4 332
29.3–9 147, 163
29.7 278
29.10 384, 427
31.7 212
31.16 566
32.6 331
33.2–7 356
33.3 136
33.5 173
33.17 LXX 170
34.9 135
34.10 LXX 459
36.8 541
36.8–9 200
41.3 74
42.1–2 541, 564
43.4 134
43(42).4 158
45.3 495
45.5 462
46.1–3 332
46.4 537
46.9 150
47.[1–]5 214
48.1 514
48.1–8 513
48.2 354

48.9–14 354
48(49).15–16 155
50.3 499
51.2 25, 198
51.4 477
53.1–3 441
55.4–8 230
55.15 157, 499
57.4 232
58.6 232
58.6–9 161
58.10–11 484
59.12–13 161
61.13 140
62.1 212
62.11 139–40
62.12 517
66.10 99
66.13–15 216
67.1 566
67.1–2 500
67.2 504
67.18 LXX 239
68.7–8 166, 516
68.8 218
68.22 518
69.9 161
69.27–28 342
69.28 85
69.29 435
70(71).22 159
71.2 LXX 488
71.20 226
72.8 260
72.11 479
73.2–20 161
74.2 447
74.9 366
74.9–11 160
74.12–17 163
74.13–14 317, 330, 333, 336
74.14 314
75.5–10 160
75.7–8 364
75.8 365–66, 448
76.1–12 513
76.2 274
76.7 172
77.17–18 261
77.18 218
77.43 313
77.45 409
78.3–6 LXX 400
78.10 LXX 478
78.44 221, 401
78.44 401
78.46 227
78.47 416
78.49 28
78.51–52 331
78.60 538
79.1–4 281
79.2–4 283
79.5–7 161
79.12 390

80.1 120
80.1–2 200
80.8–10 376
80.17 53
81.2 134, 385
81.3 463
82.1 111
82.6 111
82.6–7 323
82.19 388
83.3 LXX 182
84.2 56, 182
84.10 185
85.8 LXX 459
86.9 388
86.9–10 388
86.15 160
87.4 317
87.12 234
88 (89) 159
88.6 (LXX 87.7) 226
88.11 234
88.37 LXX 97
89.6–7 111
89.7 116
89.8 339
89.10 317
89.26 34
89.26–29 542
89.27 34
89.36 405
89.37 34, 97
89.46 160
89.50 447
90 386
90.4 502
90.17 242
91.1–8 163
92.4 242
93.1 290, 482
93.3–4 332
94.12–13 100
95.5 LXX 243
95.13 LXX 488
95(96).7 123
96.1–6 356
96.1–13 362
96.7 482
96.10 290, 482
96.11 329
97.1 482
98.1 LXX 291
98.4 482
98.5 134
99.1 290
101.5 LXX 223
102.25–26 524
103.6 505
103.20 121
103.21 121
104.1–2 115, 443
104.2 85
104.3 119, 371
104.3–4 180
104.4 179, 375
104.30 409

104.32 392
104.35 477
105.26 386
105.29 401
105.32–33 416
105.34–35 227
105.48 LXX 479
106.1 477
106.23 LXX 459
106.42–47 479
106.48 479
108.1 36
108.5 36
109.7–20 161
109.14–20 447
109.17 161
110.1 320
110.2–3 387
111.10 362
112.8 161
113.21 LXX 292
114 477
114.1–8 218
114.7–8 218
115 477
115.4 242
115.4–7 56, 243
115.8 241, 243
115.11 292
115.13 292, 480, 516
115.17 212
116 477
116.1 LXX 480
118 477
118.24 482, 484
118.25 193
118.26–27 192
118.27 566
119.97–104 267
119.135 566
119.137 402
119.154–58 161
121.2 363
121.6 405
122.4 513
125.1–2 168
132.1–9 216
135.1 477
135.7 179
135.15 242
135.15–17 243
135.18 243
135.20 292
135.21 477
136.3 438
136.8 LXX 447
136.26 287
137.8 447
137.8–9 163
139.16 127
139.18 513
141.2 135, 216
144.7 427
144.7–8 332
144.13 289

144.17 388
144.17 LXX 387
145.1 LXX 477
146.5–6 263
146.6 130, 140, 260
148.4 119
149.1–9 356
150.1 LXX 480
150.3 463
150.3–4 134

Proverbs
1.7 480
2.18 155
3.11 101
3.11–12 100
3.12 100
3.18 64
5.3–4 223
7.17 455
8.13 362
8.22 97
8.22 LXX 97
8.29 260
8.30 97
9.2 LXX 366
11.1 153
13.24 100
14.5 97
14.25 97
15.11 234
15.18 98
16.11 153
16.24 267
16.31 54
17.2 159
17.27 98
20.23 153
23.29 225
24.12 448, 517, 572
26.11 574
30.27 233
31.21–22 430

Ecclesiastes
2.5 64
7.24 123
9.8 84
11.7 405

Song of Solomon
3.8 495
3.35–59 140
4.13(12) 64
4.14 455
5.2 101
6.4–10 315
8.6 155
8.7 332

Isaiah
1 197
1.1 LXX 8
1.4 159
1.8 536
1.9–16 282

1.10 63, 490
1.13 430
1.15–22 430
1.16 25
1.18 429
1.21 426, 442
1.25 99
2.2 435, 558
2.4 LXX 374
2.5 558
2.8 242
2.10 169
2.11 388
2.11–12 172
2.13 180
2.17 170
2.19 LXX 170
3.1 159
3.9 225, 282
3.11 448
4.3 85, 517
4.5 353
4.5–6 199
4.6 405
5.1–7 376
5.11–13 329
6 112, 141, 571
6.1 49, 290, 516
6.1–3 122
6.1–4 LXX 392
6.1–13 111–12
6.2 28, 121, 290
6.2–3 28, 120, 135
6.3 123
6.3 LXX 122
6.5 392
6.5–13 392
6.6 217
6.8 112
6.9–10 242–43, 571
6.11 160
6.13 286
7.1 513
7.10–17 462
7.14 528
7.14 LXX 538
8.1–4 271
8.5–8 237
8.7 440
8.7–8 331
8.8 LXX 528
8.8, 10 538
8.16 570
9.1–2 505
9.12 362
10.20 159
10.20 LXX 154
10.22 190
11.1 130, 577
11.1–10 130
11.1–11 489, 509
11.2 33
11.4 55, 494
11.4 LXX 488
11.10 130, 577
11.10 LXX 577

11.12 179, 512
11.13 187
11.14 186
13.6 363
13.6–22 146
13.9 363
13.9–10 167
13.10 224, 227
13.10–13 166
13.19 163, 558
13.19–21 428
13.21–22 444
14.2 186
14.8 180
14.10 LXX 195
14.12 79
14.12–15 222, 312,
    323, 412
14.13 412
14.19–20 281
14.23 428
14.29–31 228
14.30 154
14.31 237
15.9 401
16.12 415
17.7 159
17.12 481
17.12–13 440
17.12–14 427
19—21 169
19.24–25 493
20.1–4 99
20.1–6 411
21.1–10 428
21.9 163, 363,
    442–43
21.9 LXX 415
21.15 150
22.15–25 94
22.20–22 88
22.21 LXX 150
22.23 94
22.25 94
23.2 212
23.3 440
23.8 LXX 464
23.9 464
23.16–17 427
23.17 427, 445
23.18 LXX 445
24 475
24.1–6 166
24.6 283
24.8 463
24.15 362
24.17–23 166
24.18–20 166, 217
24.21 169, 222
24.21–22 318, 500
24.23 557
24.23 LXX 117
25.1 96
25.6 102, 485
25.6–8 64
25.6–10 539

25.6–10a 83
25.7 LXX 201
25.8 177, 201, 528,
    539
25.8 LXX 177
26.1 548
26.2 548
26.16–19 92
26.17–18 316
26.21 283
27.1 152, 314, 317,
    324, 336, 494
27.13 214, 463
28.17 415
29.5–6 414
29.6 14, 147, 163,
    166, 261
29.9 364
29.11 130
29.13 139
29.18 129
30.7 333
30.29 463
30.30 414
30.33 366
31.1–22 364
31.4 260
32.15 321
34 479
34.1–2 564
34.4 167
34.4 LXX 167
34.5–7 432
34.9–10 240, 451,
    478
34.10 368, 479
34.10 MT 367
34.11 271
34.11–15 444
34.12 LXX 464
35.4 76, 169, 367
35.5–7 561
35.8 560
35.10 356, 539
36.3 88
37.4 182
37.17 182
37.22 358
38.3 447
40—66 547
40.2 447
40.3 321, 331
40.7 180
40.10 572
40.11 200
40.12 153
40.24 180
40.25 388
40.31 330
41.1–5 212
41.2 149, 408
41.4 541
41.25 408
42.2–3 332
42.5 293
42.6–7 184

42.10 136, 260
42.10–13 356
42.12 362
42.15 332
43.4 91
43.10–12 97
43.18–19 539, 567
43.19 539
44.6 38, 56, 541
44.7 339
44.20 LXX 360
44.23 113, 329, 461
44.27–28 408
44.28 200, 408, 441
45.1 441
45.13 408
45.14 9, 91
45.23 388
45.24 139
46.6 153
46.11 408
47.3 411
47.5 212
47.7–9 449
47.8–9 465
47.9 465
47.9—48.5 243
47.11 572
47.14 450
48.2 273, 535
48.12 56, 541
48.20 446
49.2 494
49.6–8 558
49.10 199–200, 405,
    541
49.10 LXX 200
49.13 329, 461
49.18 536
49.23 91, 558
49.26 404, 432
50.1 536
50.2 332, 408
50.3 167
50.8 446
51 391
51.2 316
51.6 446, 524
51.9 446
51.9–10 330
51.10 332–33, 539
51.11 539
51.17 364–65
51.45 446
52.1 273, 535, 560
52.1–10 536
52.5 320, 341
52.6 491
52.7 353, 482
52.8 273
52.11 446
53 360
53.7 132
53.7 LXX 136
54.1–3 314, 316,
    333

54.5–8 164
54.6 482
54.8 170
54.10 168
55.1 541
55.1–2 99
55.1–3 102
55.1a 578
55.1b 578
56.1 60
56.1–8 548
57.1–2 370
57.6 400
57.15 263
57.20 524
58.1 214
58.8 547
58.11 201
59.15–20 491
60.1–2 547
60.1–7 388
60.3 558
60.3–19 557
60.5 558
60.6 216, 558–59
60.11 558
60.11 LXX 558
60.11a 559
60.12 559
60.14 91, 94
60.17 558
60.19 547, 557
60.19–20 315, 565
61.3 180
61.6 36, 511, 564
61.8 62
61.9–10 316
61.10 358, 483, 536
61.10a 482
61.10b 482, 484
62.1–5 536
62.2 71, 565
62.2–3 490
62.2–5 490
62.5 464, 482
62.6 548
62.6–9 LXX 548
62.11 572
63.1–3 488
63.1–4 491
63.1–6 198, 376, 491
63.2–3 495
63.9 215
63.17–19 241
63.18 LXX 274
64.1 167, 218, 294
64.1–2 278
64.1–3 488
64.3 218
64.6 197
64.8 242
65—66 525
65.1–2 101
65.6 517
65.9 316

65.15 71, 539, 565
65.15 490
65.15–16 97
65.16 96, 540
65.16–18 524
65.16–19 567
65.17 415, 524
65.17 LXX 523
65.17–20 535
65.17–25 539
65.22 242
66.6 400, 413
66.7 316
66.7–9 314, 316, 319
66.7–10 333
66.12 558
66.16 494
66.18 137
66.20 LXX 273
66.22 333, 523–24, 539, 567
66.24 479

Jeremiah
1.10 8
1.11–13 195
1.13–15 512
2.2 331
2.2–3 359
2.4 63
2.6 331
2.13 541
2.13 LXX 201
2.20–28 426
2.21 376
2.24 457
2.34 430
3.1–10 358
3.14–18 556
3.15 200
3.16 159
3.19 542
4.4 375
4.13 257
4.19 268
4.23–8 166
4.23–26 168
4.27 60
4.29 170
4.30 429–30
4.31 316, 319, 536
5.9 161
5.14 278
6.3 78
6.12 283
6.13 293, 349
6.22 512
6.26 572
7.5–11 243
7.6 403
7.20 400
7.25 248, 266
7.33 500
7.34 464
8.1–2 281, 518

8.3 230
8.13–14 222
8.16–18 233
8.19 222, 233
8.23 368
9.11 353, 444
9.13–14 222
9.15 222
9.16 494
10.7 387–88
10.10 160, 380, 488
10.22 237
10.25 400
11.4–5 538
11.20 76
13.16 362
13.25 360
13.26–27 440
13.27 426, 430
14.17 358
15 344
15.2 305, 344
15.11 159
15.15 161
15.16 267, 290
16.6 516
16.9 464
16.18 447–48
16.19 388
17.10 76, 517, 572
17.12 294
17.27 479
18.1–11 79
18.16 452
19.4–6 415
20.13 LXX 480
20.15 MT 319
21.10 170
22.8 281
22.13 225, 329
22.24 182
23.5 130
23.14–15 282
23.15 222, 358
23.18 111
23.19 180
23.22 111
23.36 182
25.10 464
25.10 LXX 464
25.10 MT 464
25.13 268
25.16 179, 365
25.27 365
27.2–28.16 271
27.15 LXX 447
27.29 LXX 447
28.7 LXX 308, 428, 430
28.7–8 LXX 363
28.8 415
28.10–11 462
28.11–13 LXX 427
28.13 LXX 440
28.25 LXX 477
28.37 LXX 444

28.63 LXX 462
28.64 LXX 462
31.1–3 579
31.2 321
31.10 200
31.16 LXX 201
31.33 528, 537
31.34 293, 349
32.9–15 127
32.15 366
32.24 152
32.30 242
32.30 LXX 268
32.40 362
33.8 198
33.11 464
38.3 314
38.40 LXX 457
42.5 490
43.11 MT 344
44.25 571
46 237
46.7–8 440
46.8 331
46.10 432
46.28 402
47.2 427, 440
47.6 160, 494
48.40 225, 330
49.12 365
49.22 330
49.36 179–80
50.11 LXX 344
50.15 447
50.29 447
50.31–32 449
50.34 450
50.39 444
50.41 408
50.42 150
50.44 172
51 447
51 MT 462
51.6–10 442
51.6–14 163
51.7 428, 430
51.7–8 363
51.7–9 430
51.8 451
51.9 447
51.10 232
51.11 408
51.11–13 427
51.13 440
51.16 179
51.17–18 232
51.24–58 428
51.25 435
51.25 (LXX 28.25) 293
51.25–26 221
51.25–58 450
51.27 221, 231–32
51.28 408
51.33a 373
51.33b 373

51.34 317–18
51.34–37 333
51.37 444
51.44–52 446
51.48 460
51.59–64 461
51.63 462
51.63–64 221

Lamentations
2.1 415
2.4 400
2.8 271
2.10 212, 459
2.13 358
2.15 452
2.18 368
2.21–22 172
3.15 223
3.19 223
4.11 400
4.19 225
4.21 365, 448
5.8 340

Ezekiel
1 59, 111, 122
1—2 112, 126, 141
1—3 257, 284
1.1 53, 167
1.1 LXX 487
1.1–3.11 126
1.4 285, 499
1.4 LXX 113
1.5 LXX 120
1.5–14 28
1.5–28 120
1.6 120–21
1.7 214
1.7 LXX 54
1.8 55
1.10 120–21
1.13 119, 217
1.18 120–22
1.22 119–20, 384
1.24 356, 481
1.26 120
1.26–28 115, 257, 515
1.27 119
1.28 53, 115, 392
1.28—2.1 212
2.2 428
2.8—3.3 8, 267
2.9–10 127, 259, 268
2.10 128, 268
2.10 LXX 108, 235
3.1—7.27 128
3.3 267
3.12 51
3.12–15 428
3.15–16 212
3.16–21 267
3.18–20 571
3.20 160, 415

3.24 284
3.27 571
4.7 268
4.10 153
4.16 153
5.1–4 219
5.1–17 462
5.12 180, 219–20
5.14–15 452
6.6 415
6.9 482
6.11–12 154
7.2 179, 512
7.19 172, 291
7.26 225
7.26 LXX 235
9 9, 182
9.2 390, 493
9.2 LXX 115
9.3 443
9.3–8 229
9.3–11 349
9.4 182, 185
9.4–6 182
9.6 182
9.8 400
9.11 LXX 195
10.1 LXX 115
10.1–5 392
10.2 217
10.4 443
10.6–19 392
10.7 391
10.12 121–22
10.15 120
10.16 122
10.20 120
11.1 114, 428
11.5 114
11.20 542
11.23 392
13.5 172
13.17 268
14.6–11 560
14.12–23 182
14.19 400
14.19–21 155
14.21 156, 181, 450
16 458
16.3–52 442
16.7 482
16.8 579
16.8–14 536
16.8–15 430
16.8–18 457
16.15–41 426
16.23–43 74
16.26 282
16.36 411
16.36–39 411
16.37–41 440
16.44–58 282
17.3 225
17.14 294
17.24 155
18.22 415

18.31 560
19.10 376
20.6 263
20.7 560
20.39 571
20.48 479
21.1–17 152
21.14 152
23.1–21 358
23.11–35 440
23.17 440
23.19 440
23.22–35 442
23.25a 440
23.25b 440
23.26 440
23.29 411
23.29a 440
23.29b 440
23.31–34 365, 440
23.31–35 448
24.3–13 271
25.2 268
26—28 445
26.12 461
26.13 463
26.16–18 LXX 450
26.17—27.36 457
26.18 168
26.21 461
27.1–2 458
27.12 445
27.12–13 455
27.12–24 453
27.13 LXX 456
27.13–24 456
27.15 455
27.18 445
27.22 455
27.28–34 458
27.30 459
27.32 212, 459
27.33 445, 459
27.35 450
28 554
28.2 340, 449
28.5 464
28.9 464
28.11–19 312
28.13 115, 381, 430, 554
28.14 549
29.3 317, 330, 335
29.8–9 494
30.1–3 363
30.2–19 146
30.24 494
32.2–3 317
32.6–8 166
32.7 167
32.7–8 167, 224
33.3–6 214, 219
33.8 470
33.12–16 571
33.16 415
33.27 75

34.4 81
34.11–22 200
34.23–24 200
34.25 321
34.30–31 538
35.3 435
36.7 263
37 503
37—41 503
37.1–14 284
37.1–28 548
37.3 196
37.6 491
37.9 179
37.10–13 284
37.13 491
37.15–23 189
37.16 189
37.19 189
37.23 198, 560
37.26–28 LXX 199
37.27 199, 528, 537–38
37.27–28 393
38—39 234, 241, 410, 412, 476, 496, 500, 512–13
38.1–39.22 503
38.2 412, 496
38.2–3 512
38.6 512–13
38.7–16 241
38.8–16 512
38.8–21 412
38.9 LXX 513
38.11–12 513
38.14–16 498
38.14–17 512
38.15 512–13
38.16 LXX 513
38.19 LXX 285
38.19–22 416
38.19–23 218
38.21 152
38.22 163, 219, 240, 366, 415, 499, 514
39 496
39.1–6 512
39.2 237, 412
39.4 412
39.6 514
39.7 159
39.7–24 496
39.17 412
39.17–19 403
39.17–20 497
39.18–19 432
39.18–20 497
39.24 170
39.25–29 496
39.29 170, 496
40–41.22 503
40—42 271
40—48 195, 443, 546, 549–50, 553, 556

40.1–2 546
40.1–4 553
40.1–6 271
40.1–49 549
40.3 28, 271
40.3 LXX 271
40.3–5 550
40.5 550
40.17–23 271
40.28–37 271
40.30–35 548
42.15–19 549
42.20 271
43.1–5 443
43.2 55, 356
43.2–4 181
43.2–5 547, 557
43.5 428, 546
43.7 289, 537–38
44.9–10 560
44.10 560
44.12 263
45.1–2 LXX 550
45.3–5 550
45.10–11 LXX 153
47.1–5 561
47.1–11 563
47.1–12 561
47.9 561
47.12 563
47.12 LXX 530
47.14 538
48 549
48.8–13 550
48.30–35 549
48.30–35 LXX 549
48.31–34 549
48.35 94
LXX 27.21–23 453

Daniel
1—6 281
1.14 66
1.17 350
2 9
2.18–19 287
2.18–47 LXX 431
2.20 140
2.23 480
2.28 LXX 27
2.28–29 9, 568
2.28–45 324
2.29 LXX 114
2.31–35 243
2.31–45 289
2.35 435
2.35 LXX Theod. 324
2.35 Theod. 302
2.37 139, 407
2.44 289, 407
2.45 9, 567
2.45 LXX 114
2.46 486
2.47 57, 438, 495
3—6 440

3.2 LXX 440
3.2–7 348
3.3–6 347
3.4 137, 283
3.4 LXX 191
3.5 479
3.6 347
3.7 137
3.7 LXX 191
3.8–30 348
3.13 333
3.15 285
3.16 Theod. 195
3.27 LXX 477
3.28 LXX 535
3.96 LXX 191
4.1–37 414
4.5–27 433
4.7a–c LXX 440
4.9 Theod. 431
4.10–33 Theod. 431
4.11–22 447
4.13–14 LXX Theod. 129
4.17 366
4.17a LXX 438, 452
4.19 LXX 452
4.19 Theod. 213
4.23 LXX 129
4.27 431
4.28–31 364
4.30 364, 443
4.30 LXX 431
4.30–33 124
4.32 274, 279
4.33 431
4.34 124
4.34 LXX 286
4.34 Theod. 124
4.34–37 362, 496
4.35 125
4.37 LXX 287, 438, 490, 495
5 449
5.1–4 364
5.2–4 449
5.4 243
5.5 285
5.5–6 449
5.7 430
5.19 137, 191
5.19 Theod. 440
5.23 243
6.17 504
6.20 182
6.25 137, 191
6.26 182
6.26 Theod. 440
6.28–33 442
7 9, 124, 138, 141, 340, 441
7—8 348
7—12 195, 347
7.1–8 337
7.2 179, 237, 496

7.2–3, 7 336
7.3 280, 345
7.3–7 435, 437
7.3–26 434
7.4 337, 348, 384
7.4–6 336
7.6 LXX 348
7.7 132, 239, 317
7.7–22 280
7.7–24 437
7.8 280, 340
7.8–28 336
7.9 54, 85, 191, 290, 506
7.9–10 85, 116, 342, 499, 515
7.9–14 112
7.9–18 195
7.9–28 126
7.10 112, 138, 185, 239, 290, 384, 435, 493, 517
7.10 Theod. 129
7.13 37, 54, 239, 257, 371
7.13–14 53, 112, 133, 257, 327, 373, 434, 506
7.14 137, 191, 342
7.15–27 7
7.17 337–38, 345
7.18 137, 506, 566
7.20 132, 340
7.20 LXX Theod. 340
7.21 323, 342, 438–39
7.21 Theod. 438
7.21–22 135
7.22 439, 506
7.23 337–38
7.24 317
7.25 53, 274, 279, 282, 331, 340–41
7.26–27 506
7.27 137, 506, 566
8 341
8.1 Theod. 314
8.2 239
8.2–3 LXX 113
8.3 132, 345
8.5 132
8.8 179
8.9–14 274
8.10 225, 318, 340
8.11 323
8.13 274, 341
8.15 239
8.17 55
8.22–25 318
8.24 135
8.25 340, 347
8.26 127, 129, 570
9.4 294, 579
9.4 Theod. 387
9.14 402

9.20–23 216
9.21 121, 216
9.24 Theod. 273
9.26–27 331–32
9.27 430
10 59
10.5 113, 390, 493
10.5–6 54
10.6 54, 257, 481, 489
10.12–14 216
10.13 33, 323
10.13–14 58
10.14 489
10.16 195
10.16 Theod. 489
10.20 323
10.20 LXX Theod. 322
10.20–21 58, 318
10.21 323
11—12 264
11.10 331
11.29—12.13 264
11.29–35 196–97
11.30 333
11.30–35 124
11.31 192
11.32 340, 347
11.35 197
11.36 340–41
11.36–37 339
11.36–45 489
11.40 264, 331
11.44 408
12 259, 264
12.1 85, 92, 196–97, 318, 323
12.1–2 435, 517
12.1–2 LXX 414
12.1–3 124, 318
12.2 67, 291
12.2 LXX 513–14
12.2 LXX Theod. 516
12.2–3 509
12.3 55, 318
12.4 146, 570
12.4–9 262
12.5 568
12.5 LXX Theod. 530
12.5–13 570
12.6 493
12.6–7 390
12.7 124, 263–64, 274, 282
12.7 LXX 124
12.8 129
12.9 127, 146, 570
12.9 LXX 568
12.9 Theod. 129
12.10 197, 350, 571
12.11 124, 430
12.12 124, 274
12.13 370
19.6 54

Hosea
1.2 358
1.10 56
2.1 411
2.1–7 482
2.2–13 74
2.3 440
2.5 426
2.14 321
2.14–15 331
2.14–23 482
2.16–23 101
2.18 150
3.1—4.2 243
4.1 63, 283
4.5 536
4.9 161
4.11–12 364, 427
5.8 463
5.9–15 187
5.10 331, 463
6.6 164
6.11 373
9.1 74
9.9–17 447
9.13 LXX 322
10.4 223
10.8 166, 169
10.15 LXX 331
11.1 331
11.1–4 579
11.7–9 101
11.10 260
12.5 123
12.7 153
12.8 99
13.13 92
13.14 233
13.15 408
13.15–16 180

Joel
1—2 230
1.2 283
1.2—2.11 227
1.5–12 230
1.14 283
1.15 363
1.15—2.11 146
1.16–20 230
2.1–2 214, 224
2.1–11 237
2.3 228
2.4–5 231–32
2.4–9 232
2.5 132
2.6 230
2.7 132
2.10 166–67, 227
2.11 172, 410
2.12–14 230
2.15 214, 230
2.16 464
2.17 353
2.18–32 230
2.20–25 237

2.23 482
2.25 230
2.30 219
2.30–31 166, 219
2.31 167, 172, 410
3.2 377, 410, 498, 512
3.12–14 377
3.13 373, 376, 495
3.13 LXX 374
3.13 (MT and LXX) 372
3.13b 374
3.15 166–67
3.16 166, 260
3.16–17 163
3.18 561
3.19 282
4.13 372
4.17 273, 535

Amos
1.1 8
1.2 147, 260, 516
1.6 60
2.2 375
2.10 331
3.7 27, 111, 114, 248, 260, 266
3.7 LXX 8
3.8 260, 268
3.13 290, 492
4.9 227
4.10–11 282
4.13 290, 387
4.13 LXX 123
5.2 358
5.3 286
5.7 223
5.18 224, 329
5.18–20 172
5.24 162
6.12 223
7.1 234
7.4 278
7.7–9 271
7.16 63
7.16–17 161
8.2–3 212
8.5 153
8.8–9 166
8.9 167, 223
8.11–14 231
9.3 317
9.9 320

Obadiah
16 365
17 353
21 513

Jonah
1.2 447
1.9 260, 287
2.10 LXX 193
3.5 349, 516

4.3 159, 230
4.8 230

Micah
1.4 155, 168
4.7–8 354
4.9–10 92, 330
4.10 316
4.12–13 373
5.4 200
5.5 78
5.6–9 186
5.12–15 243
5.13 242
6.11 153
7.10–17 383
7.18 339, 388

Nahum
1.2 161
1.4 332, 408
1.5 155
1.5–6 170
1.6 172
2.3 430
3.4 427, 465–66
3.4–5 411
3.5 123
3.8 440
3.15–17 231
3.17 232
3.18 200

Habakkuk
1.2 160
1.6 514
1.7–8 240
1.8 225
1.9 513
1.12 159
2.1 LXX 444
2.15–16 365, 448
2.18–19 243
2.20 158, 212
3.3 88
3.6 168, 218
3.6–11 166
3.8–9 332
3.8–15 317
3.12 373
3.16 212

Zephaniah
1.4 353
1.7 212
1.14 410
1.14–16 214
1.14–18 172
1.15 167
1.18 291, 514
2.2 172
2.5 225
2.7 538
2.11 168
2.14 444
2.20–22 549

3.8 375, 514
3.8–10 410
3.13 359
3.20 548

Haggai
1.15 238
2.6–7 166, 217, 285, 414
2.9 556
2.17 415
2.21 217
2.21–22 166
2.23 182

Zechariah
1 9
1—6 195
1.7 238
1.8–17 147
1.9 196
1.10 LXX 195
1.12 160
1.16 550, 556
2.1–5 28, 271
2.1–13 550
2.3–5 147
2.4–5 552
2.5 548
2.6 179
2.6 LXX 550
2.6–7 285
2.10–11 199, 393, 537
2.13 212
3.1–2 324–25, 327
3.1–5 84
3.1–9 277
3.2–5 278
3.4 197
3.8–13 277
3.13 485
4 59
4.1–6 58
4.2 277
4.2–6 277
4.2–11 53
4.2b 33
4.4–10 277
4.10 133
4.11–14 277
4.14 277
6 9, 179
6.1 180
6.1–8 147, 179
6.2–6 152
6.3 155
6.5 179–80, 277
6.5–8 237
6.6 155
6.9–14 150
6.12–15 556
6.13 511
8.8 528, 537, 542
8.17 62
8.20–23 91

8.22 137
8.23 538
9.9–10 488
9.10 260
9.14 180, 223
9.14–15 214
9.15 403
10.3 123
12 37
12.1–9 512
12.2 365
12.3 LXX 274
12.3–4 410
12.10 LXX 37
12.11 412
12.12 38
13.4 276
13.7 494
13.8–9 220
14 496
14.1–5 146, 377
14.1–21 491
14.2 410, 498
14.2–10 564
14.4 168, 192
14.5 14, 163, 366, 493
14.7 565
14.8 201, 561
14.8–11 561
14.9 289
14.11 563–64
14.13–14 410
14.13–14 152
14.14 414
14.16 562
14.16–19 192, 538
14.20–21 561

Malachi
1.11 388, 405
2.2 482
2.16 123
3.1 572
3.1–3 585
3.2 172, 278, 363
3.16 517
4.4 386
4.5 172, 363
4.5 275

APOCRYPHA

Tobit
2.3–8 281
3.2 402
3.17 236
5.1–22 116
8.3 236
10.10 455
11.14 366
12.15 33, 135, 213
12.16–22 486
12.20 52
12.22 314

12.22 LXX 387
13.1–6 518
13.4 380
13.5 548
13.10 535
13.16 554, 556
13.18 477
(BA) 6.8 457

Judith
3.8 191
6.16 117
8.25 290
11.17 199
13.4 293
13.18 263
16.17 225

Wisdom of Solomon
2.24—3.6 229
3.8 289, 439
4.7 165, 370
4.8–9 54
6.6–7 293
6.7 349
7.22—11.1 53
7.24–30 316
11.9 229
11.12 229
11.16 404
11.17–18 212
11.18 240
12.3–6 243
12.26–27 407
14.18–21 348
14.27 243
15.1—16.29 224
15.9 243
15.15 243
15.15–17 243
16.1–6 229
16.9 227
16.19 219
16.22 219
17.1—18.4 406
17.1–21 224
17.2 406
17.3–21 227
17.20–21 406
18.1 229
18.3–4 224
18.14 212
18.14–16 492
18.21 212, 216
18.24 490
19.3–21 212
19.4 229
19.10 409

Sirach
1.3 226
2.12 543
16.12 448
16.18 226
16.18–19 516

17.22 182
21.1–3 232
23.10 198
24.4 371
24.11 514
26.7 229
32.23 334
36.18 273–74
39.26 377
39.29–30 228
44.21 190
44.21–23 538
45.16 216
47.22 130
47.23 165
48.1 278
48.3 279
48.4 459
49.8 443

Baruch
1.20 386
2.17 389
2.23 464
3.34 LXX 444
4.35 444

Bel and the Dragon
32 455

1 Maccabees
1.3 212
1.26 117
1.44–60 348
2.7 273
2.28–29 321
3.25 284
3.27 514
3.32 407
3.45 463
4.54 134
4.54–59 192
4.60 274
5.45 293, 349
6.22 160
6.34 377
9.27 414
10.20 430
11.1 513
11.13 489
11.23 117
11.71 459
13.36–37 191
13.51 134, 191–92, 356
14.21 139
14.26–49 94

2 Maccabees
1.11 290
2.2 243
2.4–8 70, 294
2.8 371
2.21 323
3.26 276
3.33 276

5.1–4 324
6.1–9 348
7.1–42 318
7.39 333
8.3 160
8.11 455
10.6–7 192
10.7 191
11.8 84, 191
12.6 404
12.16 401
13.4 438, 495
14.4 191
14.15 273
15.14 195

1 Esdras
6.5 117
6.8 117
6.13 263
8.75 447
9.8 286

3 Maccabees
2.3 402
2.11 97, 540
2.18 274
2.27–30 349
4.16 243
5.1–5 293
5.2 LXX 215
5.35 438
6.5 273
6.18 113
6.18–21 323
7.13 477
7.16 290

2 Esdras
2.33 49
2.38–41 165
4.1 33
4.28–35 372
5.13 130
11.37 130
12.31 130
12.31–32 130
12.37 52
13.39–50 185
15.8 160
16.18–34 154

4 Ezra
1.32 466
2.38 182
2.39–48 165
2.42–48 354
3.5 284
3.7 137
3.16 137
3.17–19 218
4.33–37 160, 165
5.4–8 166
5.5 167
6.5 182
6.17 261

6.20 517
6.22–24 223
6.23 214
6.23–27 287
6.39 211
6.47–52 336
6.47–54 345
7.26 535
7.26–33 503
7.30 211
7.30–31 524
7.32 509
7.36 366, 499
7.38–42 557, 565
7.39 167
7.39–40 166
7.75 524
7.77 370
7.88–101 165
7.90–96 370
7.98 564
7.102 363
8.33 370
8.52 562
8.53 155
8.53–54 539
9.38–47 536
9.47 485
10.7 314
10.27 535
10.29–59 7
11.1—12.39 337
11.7–9 225
11.37 260, 384
11.43 447
12.3 339
12.31–32 260
12.37 570
13.1–11 513
13.5 179, 498
13.5–9 496
13.8–11 514
13.10 278
13.16–19 196
13.25–39 278
13.25–52 354
13.30–31 291
13.33–36 410
13.34–5 512
13.36 535
14.5–6 570
14.7–9, (50) 285
15.46–63 451

4 Maccabees
2.1 457
3.17–18 328
5.1 116
6.29 158
7.3 458
7.6 560
8.1–14 316
8.2 333
9.6 328
16.14 328

NEW TESTAMENT

Matthew
1.12 364
1.23 315, 538
2.1 175, 181
2.1–12 319, 559
2.6 200
2.11 215, 283, 479
2.13–15 321, 331
3.11 129, 278
3.12 372–73
3.16 167, 488
4.1 325
4.4 410
4.5 273
4.8–9 289
4.8–10 342
4.10 339
5.1 546
5.2 341
5.3–10 541
5.3–12 369
5.6 200
5.11 330
5.11–12 276, 403
5.12 482, 484
5.15–16 277
5.18 524
5.22 56, 499
5.23 61
5.29 56
5.30 56
5.34 68
5.44 448
5.48 82
6.10 162
6.13 162, 327
6.24 445
7.6 574
7.15 346, 409
7.17–19 220
7.24–25 79
8.2 124
8.11 485
8.12 224, 406
8.13 285
8.19 358
8.31 243
9.18 508
9.23 463
9.28 404
9.37–38 374
10.1 550
10.2 550
10.5–6 185
10.15 363
10.18 268
10.22 105
10.28 123
10.32 86
10.33 90
10.38 358
10.38–39 157
10.39 328
10.40 567

11.1 550
11.15 63, 343
11.21 276, 303, 329
11.25 363
11.27 139
12.20 390
12.28 326
12.29 505
12.38 195
13.9–17 571
13.24–30 372
13.30 373
13.39 374
13.40–42 493
13.41 374
13.43 257, 318, 493
13.49 236
13.50 499
15.11 560
15.24 200
15.27 404
16.1 313
16.18 334, 549
16.18–19 274
16.19 56, 88
16.27 76, 323, 572
17.1–2 55
17.2 257
17.5 257
17.6 286
17.7 56
17.20 168
18.3 560
18.6 462
18.7 206
18.8 375
18.10 58, 116
18.12–14 200
18.16 276
18.28–33 487
19.12 350, 357
19.17 334, 369
19.21 82
19.28 68, 77, 103, 117, 138, 185, 358, 506, 524, 550, 566
20.2 153
21.33 376
22.13 406
23.5 177
23.15 448
23.18–20 158
23.29–36 157
23.34 66
23.34–37 276
24.9–13 362
24.13 105
24.14 149, 362
24.15 280
24.15–31 91
24.21 196
24.22–28 362
24.24 332, 342, 410
24.27–31 372
24.28 224
24.29 166, 168

24.30 37–38, 371
24.31 179, 214, 323
24.35 524
24.41 462
24.42 81
24.42–44 411
24.43–44 83
25.4 277
25.9–10 99
25.10 485
25.30 406
25.31 68
25.31–32 493
25.31–46 516
25.34 238
25.41 28, 161, 238, 323, 488, 514
25.45 330
26.14 550
26.26 267
26.27–29 485
26.29 102
26.31 200
26.50–54 344
26.53 323
26.63 56
26.64 371
27.14 433
27.28 429
27.33 377
27.34 396
27.46 377
27.51 285
27.51–54 218
27.53 273
27.63 284
27.66 504
28.1–4 287
28.2 218
28.2–4 486
28.10 49
28.18 88, 139, 327

Mark
1.6 227, 276
1.10 167, 294
1.12 311, 428
1.13 319
1.15 31, 363, 570
1.18 311
1.20 311
1.24 88
1.27 286
2.7 341, 388
2.12 286
2.19–20 482
3.2 303
3.5 62, 171
3.6 319
3.14 550
3.16 550
3.22 233
3.23–26 440
4.9 63, 343
4.29 372–73
4.41 286

5.4 501
5.5 368
5.7 316
5.13 463
5.40–42 284
6.11 459
6.17 501
6.39 155, 220, 228
6.50 56
7.2 560
7.21 244
7.21–23 543
7.27–28 574
8.6 290
8.11 313
8.31 117, 284
8.34 358
8.35 328
8.38 366, 493
9.2–6 392
9.2–9 546
9.3 85, 191, 488
9.4 275
9.7 371
9.11–12 275
9.28 101
9.43 479
9.43–48 499
9.47 560
9.48 479
10.23–25 445
10.38 396
10.38–39 365
10.40 103
10.51 195
11.8 192
11.15–17 272
11.25 61
12.14 88
12.17 433
13 7
13.2 556
13.4 265
13.5–27 91
13.7 568
13.7–8 146, 163
13.7–19 196
13.8 92, 153–54, 218, 458
13.9–20 186
13.10 149, 320, 362
13.13 73, 105
13.14 192, 350, 430, 435, 446
13.14–23 321
13.17 206, 303, 329
13.19 75, 414
13.20 262, 329
13.21–23 346
13.22 313, 409
13.24 75, 224
13.24–25 166–68, 227
13.25 167
13.26 37, 257, 285
13.27 179, 361

13.28 167
13.31 524
13.32 372
13.32–37 570
13.35 81
14.22 267
14.23–25 377
14.25 102
14.27 200
14.36 365
14.58 556
14.62 285, 371
14.71 264
15.17–20 429
15.19 271
15.20 99
15.29 556
15.34 82
15.40 452
16.5 85
16.7 403
16.8 286
16.20 313

Luke
1.6 389
1.9–11 216
1.10–11 215
1.19 29, 214, 277, 323, 361
1.32 68
1.33 289
1.35 88
1.52 68
1.68–79 185
1.69 192
1.71 192
1.72 294
1.77 192
2.9 286
2.10 361
2.13 323
2.26 289
2.29 159
2.30–32 505
2.32 494
2.34–35 319
2.37 198
3.33 187
4.6 337
4.22 433
4.25 279
4.29 273
6.15 325
6.20 445
6.24 206
6.26 409
7.14–15 284
7.24 271
7.27 170
8.1 550
8.31 226, 280
8.52 451
9.1 550
9.51–53 170
9.51–54 514

9.54 217, 278, 346, 375
9.57 358
10.1 170, 276
10.18 167, 222, 225, 323
10.18–19 229
10.19 228, 324
10.20 85, 517
10.34 455
11.13 283
11.28 31
11.49 194
11.51 158
12.8 86, 121
12.16–21 99, 283
12.21 65
12.35–38 102
12.36 102, 485
12.36–37 101
12.39–40 83
12.48 404
13.4 273
13.33 282
14.3 195
14.5 226
14.8 485
14.12–24 64
14.15 485
14.15–24 485
14.35 63, 343
15.4–7 200
15.4–32 367
15.10 121
15.17–18 61
16.17 524
16.21 574
16.22 28
16.22–23 519
16.23 157
17.5 448, 550
17.18 286
17.29 366
17.37 224
18.1–8 160
18.7 199, 368
18.11 290, 543
18.20 244
19.8 447
19.9 192
19.12 437
20.24 347
21 146
21.7 265
21.9–36 146
21.11 313
21.15 340
21.20 473, 498
21.22–23 171
21.24 274
21.25–26 220
21.27 37
22.14 550
22.14–20 579
22.22 303, 329
22.28–30 102

22.29–30 185, 485
22.30 102–103, 138, 506
22.31 66, 332
22.37 383
22.61 38
22.69 371
23.2 303
23.27–30 230
23.30 169
23.34 161
24.4–7 28
24.4–9 276
24.5 486

John
1 97
1.1 490, 492
1.1–2 97
1.1–4 56
1.1–5 378, 521
1.1–14 567, 573
1.2 487
1.3 55
1.3–4 97
1.4–5 224, 413, 557
1.5 227
1.6 234
1.9 88, 486, 488
1.14 11, 39, 121, 173, 199, 328, 342, 492, 538, 580
1.14–18 379
1.15 58
1.16 248
1.26 195
1.27 129
1.29 35, 52, 131
1.36 35, 131
1.41 234
1.47 185, 535
1.48 89
1.51 11, 39, 53, 141, 167, 226, 294, 488, 508, 579
2.4 213, 363, 374
2.6 115
2.6–10 562
2.13–22 161
2.17 161
2.18 195
2.18–22 556
2.19–21 273
2.19–22 580
2.20 304
2.21 580
2.23 346
2.24 60
2.24–25 98, 130, 441
2.25 89
3.2 346, 538
3.5 560, 562
3.6 508
3.7 433
3.15–16 361

3.16 10, 82, 164, 289, 508
3.16–17 367
3.16–19 362
3.16–21 76, 413
3.17–21 55, 379
3.19–21 370
3.20 101
3.25 217
3.29 82, 464, 482
3.32 34
4.3 61
4.7 396
4.7–15 562
4.9 396
4.10 541
4.11–12 226
4.13–14 578
4.14 200–201, 448, 541
4.21–24 556
4.22 192, 326
4.23 213, 342
4.23–24 428
4.25 234
4.29 98
4.35–38 373
4.39 567
4.42 4, 16, 82, 113, 193, 276
4.53 285
4.54 346
5.1 513
5.2 234
5.4 179
5.5 304
5.7 195
5.18 319
5.19 516
5.19–30 372
5.19–47 377
5.20 387
5.22 171, 516
5.24 100, 521
5.24–29 509
5.25 169, 374
5.25–29 56
5.26 56
5.27 171, 327, 374
5.28 433
5.28–29 67, 509
5.31 34
5.36 387
5.43 183
5.43–47 185
5.45 303
6.2 346
6.9 229
6.11 290
6.19 427
6.23 290
6.26–58 295
6.27 183
6.35 56, 102, 200–201
6.36 131

6.51 343
6.52–58 102
6.53–56 101
6.57 183
6.64 89
6.69 88, 182
6.70 325
7.3 153
7.7 357
7.18 88
7.24 55, 488
7.28 88, 443
7.30 374, 498
7.32 498
7.37 443
7.37–38 200–201, 578
7.37–39 295, 562
7.38 541, 562
7.38–39 562
7.39 448
7.44 498
8.12 55–56, 224, 413, 505, 557
8.16 488
8.17 276
8.18 34
8.20 273, 498
8.26–29 27
8.40 342
8.44 90, 318, 325, 543
8.44–45 360
8.46 101
8.47 100
8.51–52 89
9.1–3 74
9.4–5 224
9.5 505
9.19 52
9.22 90
9.24 286, 362
9.34 90
9.34–35 273
9.39 100
10.1–16 200
10.3 101
10.3–6 358
10.9 559
10.10 377
10.11 200
10.11–16 367
10.11–18 35, 56
10.12 61
10.16 101
10.20 40
10.23 272
10.24 473
10.25 183
10.30 72, 133, 496, 516
10.32–33 387
10.36 341
10.39 498
11.9–10 224
11.36 100

11.37 153
11.41 290
11.43 545
11.44 55
11.57 498
12.7 73
12.12 176, 191
12.13 191
12.15 354
12.25 328
12.26 358
12.27 213
12.28–29 261
12.31 273, 289, 322
12.31–32 148, 505
12.31–33 328
12.31–39 379
12.32 320
12.33 27
12.35 84
12.35–36 55, 224, 557
12.35–41 52
12.37–41 570
12.39–40 242, 571
12.41 36
12.42 90
12.44 372, 443
12.45 131
12.47 131
12.47–48 278
12.47–50 76
12.49–50 27
13—20 324
13.1 91, 363
13.1–3 34
13.1–12 560
13.2 325, 332
13.3 327
13.5 562
13.7 57
13.16 550
13.20 567
13.27 332
13.30 224, 410, 512
13.34 572
13.34–35 5
13.36 358
14.2–3 157, 321
14.6 34, 56, 88, 562
14.9–10 131
14.10 27
14.10–12 77
14.15 334, 369, 532
14.16 12
14.17 12
14.21 334, 369, 532
14.23 101
14.26 12
14.28 40
14.30 289
15.1 88, 488
15.1–7 376
15.1–13 579
15.3–4 488
15.9 62

15.10 334, 369, 532
15.12 5, 62, 73, 90, 161, 369, 572
15.12–13 77
15.17 5, 369, 572
15.18 344
15.18–19 357
15.18–21 330
15.18–25 319
15.20 89
15.26 562
16.2 90
16.5–7 488
16.8 101, 162
16.8–11 360
16.11 289
16.12 374
16.12–15 77
16.17 66, 283
16.19–22 316
16.24 82
16.27 100
16.28 40, 61, 133
16.33 50, 64, 103, 123, 196, 386, 447
17.1 374
17.1–3 377
17.1–11 133
17.2 327
17.3 10, 160, 486
17.6 89
17.6–26 183
17.11 5
17.12 234
17.12–13 93
17.14 357
17.14–19 447
17.15 91
17.20–26 579
17.22 36
17.23 496
17.24 82, 157, 343, 565
18.1—19.42 319
18.10 234
18.32 27
18.37 34
18.37b 101
19.2 488
19.13 234
19.14–16a 66
19.17 234
19.18 530, 562
19.20 234, 377
19.23 217
19.23–24 99
19.29 115
19.30 413, 540
19.34 37, 562
19.37 37
20.2 100
20.6 234
20.8 131
20.12 85, 191
20.14 52, 131
20.15 177

20.16 131
20.17 82, 320, 480
20.23 61
20.28 38
20.29 52, 100, 113, 131
20.31 30, 56
21.3 498
21.4–11 137
21.9 115
21.10 498
21.11 350
21.15 131, 353
21.17 89
21.18–19 321, 358
21.21 358
21.24 30, 567, 582

Acts
1.2 320, 550
1.7 372
1.9 37, 257, 285
1.9–11 285
1.10 85, 191
1.10–11 276
1.11 320
1.12 325
1.14 403
1.15 84
1.22 320
2.7 433
2.16–21 354
2.16–36 548
2.19–20 166, 219
2.20 167–68
2.23 343
2.28 474
2.33 79
2.36 289
2.47 38
3.6–7 69
3.7 498
3.11 272
3.14 88
4.5 117
4.8 117
4.10–12 68
4.11 580
4.12 90, 192
4.21 286
4.23 117
4.24 159, 263, 363
4.26–28 289
5.8 195
5.12 272
6.2 550
6.3 165
6.14 556
7.2 314
7.3 545
7.3–4 446
7.7 446
7.41 242
7.44 341, 390
7.47–51 556
7.52 276, 403

7.54 333
7.55 392
7.56 167, 294, 353, 371, 488
7.57 463
7.58 273
8.1–3 332
8.10 293, 349
8.18 347
8.35 341
8.39 320
9.4 55
9.4–5 330
9.11–20 347
9.13 135
9.15 268
9.24 368
9.32 135
9.41 135
10.2 292
10.15 560
10.22 292, 366
10.25 479
10.25–26 486
10.42 171, 291, 516
11.3 101
11.28 403
12.4 498
12.11 51
12.15 116
12.23 362
13.6 409
13.6–8 348
13.10–11 161
13.29 383
13.43 292
13.48 286
14.15 56, 182, 363
14.16 320, 505
14.18 363
14.20 473
14.22 50, 196, 560
14.23 117
14.27 89
15.9 198
15.20 243
15.23 49
15.28–29 77
15.29 63, 74
16.6 59
16.14 292
16.14–15 72
16.16 348
16.17 361
17.29 243, 349
18.6 283
18.7 292
18.19–20 59
19.8–10 59
19.10 60
19.12 410
19.23–35 59
19.26 65
19.29 463
20.6 229
20.7 51

20.17 117
20.28 136, 200
20.29–30 61
20.31 82
21.3 453
21.9 73
21.11 271
21.15 513
21.21 347
21.34 514
22.17 51
23.12 396
23.24 455
24.8 303
24.15 509
26.3 57
26.7 199
26.10 71, 135
26.11 341
26.14 233
26.14–23 185
26.22 293
26.23 494
27.2 423, 458
27.27, 30 458
27.34 10
27.35 290
28.15 290

Romans
1.1 361
1.3 577
1.6 439
1.9 96
1.13 49
1.16 192, 326
1.18 170
1.18–27 241
1.20–25 349
1.20–32 243
1.23 353
1.24–29 243
1.25 141
1.28–31 543
1.32 389, 404
2.5 171–72, 293
2.6 76, 448, 517, 572
2.7 123
2.16 171, 516
2.25–27 334
2.29 90
3.5 170
3.9–10 130
3.9–12 441
3.21–25 580
3.21–28 483
3.25 36
5.3 196
5.12–21 64
5.16 389
5.17 138
6.3–4 508
6.3–11 510
6.3–13 509
6.4 84
6.4–13 509

6.5 509
6.22 137
6.23 64
7.24 99
8.3 57
8.9 51
8.10–11 509
8.18–23 525
8.23 359
8.27 135
8.29 165
8.33–34 327
8.36 166, 466
8.39 482
9—11 185, 548
9.6 187
9.6–8 538
9.26 56, 182
9.27 190, 513
9.33 354
10.6–7 130
10.7 226
10.10 10
10.16–21 362
11.1 158
11.3 158
11.4–5 286
11.13–18 538
11.17 49
11.17–18 277
11.22 164
11.25 265
11.26 354
11.33–36 35
12.1 57
12.1–2 157
12.17 447
12.19 161
12.21 157
13.1–7 337
13.4 152
13.8 161
13.9 244
14.9 508
14.10 172
14.14 560
14.21 396
15.8–12 388
15.12 577
15.25 73
16.5 359
16.16 26
16.20 324
16.25–26 265
16.26 361
16.27 25, 388,
     582

1 Corinthians
1.1 53
1.1–3 26
1.3 32
1.4–5 290
1.10 49
1.10–25 16
1.18 328

1.24 194, 439
1.26–29 65
2.6–8 328
2.7 265
2.9–10 77
2.10 76
2.14 281
3.10–15 572
3.12–15 278
3.13 405, 450
3.15 220
3.16 557
3.16–17 270
3.17 580
4.1–5 10
4.2–5 370
4.5 171–72
4.9 28
4.15 361
5.5 172
5.17 49
6.1–2 135
6.2 138, 439, 506
6.2–3 566
6.3 77
6.9–10 560
6.11 25
6.19 273, 549
6.20 136
7.19 334
7.22 188
7.23 136
7.26 196
7.39 509
8.7 357
9.4 396
9.16 206, 303
9.16–17 268
9.23 49
9.24–25 67
9.25 92
10.1–2 257
10.1–4 370
10.7 396
10.14 243
10.18 158
10.19 243
10.20 243
10.20–21 410
11.15 231
11.20 51, 102
11.21 102
11.23–26 64
11.25 102, 390
11.25–26 377
11.26 578, 585
11.27–30 74
11.27–32 585
11.30 509
12.1–3 584
12.10 584
12.28 61
12.33 411
13.2 168
13.9–12 71
13.12 170, 547

14.3 403
14.7 134, 356
14.19 229
14.22 313
14.25 479
14.29 584
15.5 550
15.5–9 550
15.6 509
15.7 61, 550
15.12–26 509
15.12–49 164
15.18 509
15.20 359, 509
15.20–22 56
15.22 370, 388
15.23 359
15.25 482
15.26 518
15.28 289
15.50 542
15.51 265, 509–510
15.51–54 525
15.52 214, 509
15.54–55 539
15.54–57 324, 328,
     518
15.55–56 233
16.9 89
16.15 359
16.20–24 585
16.22 161–62, 578,
     585
16.23 581, 585
16.24 582

2 Corinthians
1.7 49
1.20 585
1.22 184
2.11 332
2.12 89
2.14 84
3.7 474
3.12–18 133
3.18 71
4.4 289, 353
4.12 261
4.17–18 66
5.1 85, 157
5.1–5 164, 525
5.2–4 538
5.4 85
5.7 84, 565
5.8 157
5.10 172, 509, 572
5.16–19 540
5.17 71, 136, 524,
     539–40
6.2 370
6.14 446
6.14–15 224
6.16 270, 273, 537,
     549
6.16—7.1 543
6.16–18 543

6.17 544
6.18 38, 290
7.1 198
8.1–5 65
9.1 73
11.2 358, 482
11.2–4 358
11.3 324, 332
11.12–15 347,
     358
11.13–15 150
11.14 324, 486
11.32 498
12.1–4 428
12.1–10 111
12.2 320
12.4 320, 357
12.7 28
12.11–12 61
12.20 543
13.1 276
13.4 509
15.7 61

Galatians
1.6–9 583
1.8–9 161, 361,
     486
2.7–9 279
2.9 93
3.6–7 190
3.13 136
3.16 538
3.19 28
4.5 136
4.14 28
4.22–31 536
4.26 514, 535
4.26–27 314
5.19–20 243
5.20 209, 465
6.15 524
6.16 90, 187, 535,
     548
6.17 349
6.18 581–82

Ephesians
1.1 370
1.1–2 26
1.4 343, 360
1.10 140, 388
1.11–12 342
1.13 184, 192
1.15 135
1.18 367
1.19 450
1.20 103
2.2 227, 289, 323,
     413
2.6 341
2.8–10 60, 370, 483,
     572
2.12–13 390
2.13 197
2.14 272, 553

2.19–22 270, 557
2.20–21 580
2.20–22 549
2.21 273
3.4–6 570
3.10 194
4.1 84–85
4.11 61
4.27 325
4.30 184
5.2 161, 216
5.3–5 543
5.5 243, 460
5.11 446–47
5.13 101
5.14 509
5.18 421
5.21—6.9 357
5.22–33 482
5.31–32 314
6.1 212
6.12 289
6.24 582

Philippians
1.7 49
1.10 172
1.23 157, 230
2.4–11 68
2.5–8 372
2.5–11 320
2.6 574
2.9–11 362, 388,
     438, 490
2.10 130
2.10–11 37, 140
2.11 35, 38
2.12–13 483
2.15 360, 547
2.16 172
2.17 157–58
3.2 574
3.3 198
3.10 49
3.20 341, 535
3.20–21 164
4.3 342, 517
4.7 230
4.14 447
4.21–23 581

Colossians
1 97
1.2 95
1.7 165
1.10 85
1.11 50
1.12 367
1.13 224
1.15 35, 97, 328
1.15–20 328
1.16 56, 116
1.16–17 97
1.18 97
1.19 133
1.20 140

1.22 360
2.1 95
2.2 265
2.13–15 224
2.15 84
2.18 486
3.1 341
3.4 95
3.5 243
3.6 170
3.10 524
3.12 439
3.18–20 370
4.3 89
4.7 165
4.12 188
4.13 95
4.15 95
4.16 26, 95, 97

1 Thessalonians
1.3 60
1.9 88, 182
1.10 170
2.3 409, 431
2.12 84
2.13 567
2.15 276, 403
3.10 199, 368
3.13 367
4.13–18 488
4.14 157, 164
4.16 29, 372
4.17 157, 320
5.2 83, 172, 411
5.8–9 192
5.15 447
5.19–21 584
5.24 490
5.28 582

2 Thessalonians
1.3 290
1.3–4 60
1.5–10 293
1.6–8 488
1.7 493
1.7–8 375
1.7–10 368
1.9 170
1.9–10 488
1.10 367
2.1–2 584
2.1–17 348
2.2–3 172
2.3 234
2.3–5 340
2.4 336, 339
2.6–12 152, 505
2.7 265
2.8 171, 326, 494
2.9–10 313, 346
2.9–11 332
2.9–12 241, 347
2.10 410
3.5 50

1 Timothy
1.3 59
1.14 73
1.15 485
1.17 139, 380, 388
2.1–2 337
2.1–8 342
2.3–4 137, 388
2.3–6 367
2.6 57
2.9 430
2.14 332
3.1 485
3.6 323
3.15 93, 557
3.16 320
4.1 370
4.9 485
5.11 445
5.15 339
5.17 117, 448
5.19 117
5.22 446
6.1–2 159
6.15 438, 482
6.16 115, 140, 443
6.17–19 65

2 Timothy
1.3 199, 368
1.7 543
1.13–14 82
2.5 67
2.11 485
2.11–12 103, 506
2.12 50, 90
2.19 183
2.21 159
3.12 50, 196
4.1 291, 516
4.2 101
4.6 158
4.7 369
4.8 404
4.14 448

Titus
1.16 90
2.9 159
3.3 543
3.8 485

Hebrews
1.1–5 354
1.2 56
1.3 103
1.3–14 28
1.6 342
1.7 179–80, 375, 487
1.7, 14 487
1.8 289
1.12 167
1.14 121, 192
2.3 192
2.9 139

2.14 325
3.1 49, 550
3.7–19 242
3.12 56
4.10 370
4.12 163, 492, 494, 499
6.10 135
7.7 81
7.13 158
7.14 187–88
8.1–9.28 294
8.2 538
8.6–7 128, 390
8.11 293, 349
9.1–14 556
9.2 341
9.4 70, 294, 391
9.5 443
9.6 341
9.6–7 552
9.11–14 36
9.13 198
9.13–14 560
9.14 197, 360
9.22 197
9.27 518
10.11–18 35
10.22 25
10.30 161
10.34 65
11.7–10 514
11.10 535
11.12 190
11.30 473
11.32–40 518
12.2 103
12.6 100
12.14 565
12.18–21 119
12.22 354, 514, 535
12.23 291, 517
12.26 217
12.26–27 414, 524
12.29 217, 375, 405
12.33 85
13.8 123
13.10 158
13.11 514
13.11–13 377
13.14 535
13.20 200

James
1.1 185
1.2 49
1.18 359
2.1–4 65
2.2 571
2.5 65
2.18–26 60
2.21 158
3.3 377
4.2 70
4.6–10 449
4.8 198

4.9 77, 449, 451
5.14 117
5.17 279

1 Peter
1.1 439
1.2 35
1.3 56
1.3–5 542
1.7 99, 124
1.8 565
1.10–11 487
1.17 517
1.18–19 360
1.18–20 343
1.19 35, 131, 197
1.22 161
1.23 56
2.2 192
2.4–5 580
2.4–10 101
2.5 270, 511, 549
2.6 354
2.6–7 580
2.9 35–36, 118, 137, 511
2.9–10 185
2.12 172
2.13–17 337
2.16 188
2.18 159
2.21–22 358, 360
2.25 200
3.9 447
3.12 170
3.18–20 519
4.3 243
4.5 291
4.11 140
4.12–13 482
4.13 49
4.14 330
5.1 49, 117
5.2 200
5.4 67, 200
5.8 505
5.11 140
5.13 364

2 Peter
1.4 579
1.9 198
1.17 139
1.19 79, 277
1.21 487, 568
2.1 90, 136, 159, 409
2.4 323, 501
2.8 316
2.17 406
2.22 574
3.7 172, 363, 405
3.8 502
3.8–13 572
3.10 83, 167, 172, 220, 411, 516
3.10–12 173

3.12 172, 524
3.13 173, 524, 560
3.15 49
3.18 582

1 John
1.1 492
1.1–3 568
1.1–4 30
1.2 361
1.3 49, 100
1.4 82
1.5 557
1.5–7 224, 315, 443
1.5–9 327
1.6–7 84
1.7 35, 197, 560
1.9 198, 560
2.2 35, 137, 379, 410
2.3–4 334, 369, 532
2.3–5 90
2.5 89
2.6 84
2.8 88, 486, 488
2.11 227
2.13–14 64, 157
2.15–17 357, 447
2.18 149, 344
2.18–26 233
2.19 410, 512
2.20 88
2.21–22 544
2.22 90, 344, 360
2.28–3.10 93
3.2 95, 100, 539, 547, 565
3.4 35
3.4–10 327
3.8 325
3.10 325
3.11 572
3.11–16 320
3.12 132, 318, 325
3.13 357, 433
3.16 164
3.16–24 93
3.18 370
3.22 334, 369, 532
3.23 90, 128
3.24 12, 334, 448, 532
4.1 61
4.1–3 233, 409, 584
4.1–6 504
4.3 344
4.4 64
4.7 572
4.7–14 56
4.7–16 413
4.9 367
4.9–10 35
4.10 379
4.11–12 161
4.12 547
4.14 5, 16, 82, 193, 276, 447

4.14–15 328
4.14–16 164
4.16–21 76
4.17 172, 289, 363, 508
5.2 532
5.3 334, 532
5.4 64, 79, 103, 568
5.4–5 64, 322
5.5 36, 157
5.6 562
5.6–13 72
5.8 562
5.10–13 521
5.11–12 580
5.11–13 56
5.16–20 93
5.17 35
5.19 289, 410
5.20 88, 160, 306, 358, 486, 488
5.20c 88

2 John
1 75, 314, 439
1–3 26
3 488
4 84
5 314, 572
7 5, 344
8 52
12 82
13 439

3 John
1 4
9 4
9–10 5
10 370
12 4
13 271

Jude
1 188, 439, 582
3 135
4 159
6 501–502
7 240
9 29, 323
11 206
12 220
13 167, 225, 406
14–15 323, 493
21, 25 361
25 388, 582

Revelation
1.1 27–28
1.1–3 27–31
1.1–8 25–40
1.2 30
1.3 30–31
1.4 31–34
1.4–8 31–38
1.5 34–36

1.6 36–37
1.7 37–38
1.8 38
1.9 49–51
1.9—3.22 43–105
1.10 51–52
1.11 52
1.12 52–53
1.13 53–54
1.14–15 54–55
1.16 55
1.17–18 55–56
1.19 56–57
1.19–20 56–59
2.1 59–60
2.1—3.22 59–103
2.1–7 59–64
2.2–3 60–61, 81–83
2.4 61
2.5 61–62
2.6 62
2.7 63–64
2.8 64–65
2.8–11 64–67
2.9 65–66
2.10 66–67
2.11 67
2.12 67–68
2.12–17 67–71
2.13 68–69
2.14–15 69–70
2.16 70
2.18 70–73
2.18–29 71–80
2.19 73
2.20–21 73–74
2.22 74–75
2.23 75–76
2.24–25 76–77
2.26–27 77–79
2.28 79
2.29 79–80
3.1 80–81
3.1–6 80–87
3.4 83–85
3.5 85–86
3.6 86
3.7 86–89
3.7–13 86–95
3.8 89–90
3.9 90–91
3.10 91–92
3.11 92–93
3.12 93–95
3.14 95–98
3.14–22 95–103
3.15–16 98
3.17 98–99
3.18 99–100
3.19 100–101
3.20 101–102
3.21 102–103
3.22 103
4.1 113–14
4.1—5.14 106–142

4.2 114–15
4.3 115–16
4.4 116–18
4.5 118–19
4.7 119–21
4.8 121–23
4.9–10 123–24
4.11 124–26
5.1 126–28
5.2 128–29
5.3–4 130
5.5 130–31
5.6 131–33
5.7 133
5.8 134–35
5.9–10 135–38
5.11–12 138–40
5.13 140–41
5.14 141
6.1 146–47
6.1–8 146–56
6.1–17 143–73
6.2 147–51
6.3–4 151–52
6.5–6 152–54
6.7–8 154–56
6.9 156–59
6.9–11 156–66
6.10 159–60
6.11 164–66
6.12–14 166–69
6.12–17 166–73
6.15–16 169–71
6.17 171–73
7.1 178–81
7.1–17 174–202
7.2–3 181–84
7.4 184–88
7.5–8 188–89
7.9 189–92
7.10 192–93
7.11–12 193–94
7.13–14 195–98
7.15–17 198–201
8.1 211–13
8.1—9.21 203–245
8.2 213–14
8.2–6 213–18
8.3–4 214–16
8.5 216–18
8.6 218
8.13 224–25
9.1–12 225–35
9.2 226–27
9.3 227–28
9.4–5 228–29
9.6 229–30
9.7 230–31
9.8 231–32
9.9 232
9.10 232–33
9.11 233–34
9.12 234–35
9.13 240–41
9.13–14 235–37

9.13–21 235–44
9.15 237–38
9.16 238–39
9.17–18 239–40
9.20–21 241–44
10.1 256–58
10.1—11.19 248–96
10.1–11 254, 256–69
10.2 258–60
10.3–4 260–63
10.5–6a 263–64
10.6b–7 264–66
10.8 266–67
10.9–10 267–68
10.11 268–69
11.1-2 269–74
11.1–13 254–55
11.3 275–76
11.3–14 275–88
11.4 276–78
11.5–6 278–80
11.7 280–81
11.8 281–82
11.9–10 282–84
11.11 284
11.12 284–85
11.13 285–87
11.14 255, 287–88
11.15 288–89
11.15–19 255–56, 288–95
11.16–18 289–93
11.19 293–95
12.1 312–16
12.1—14.20 299–379
12.1–2 312–16
12.2 316
12.3 316–18
12.3–6 316–21
12.4 318–19
12.5 319–20
12.6 320–21
12.7–8 322–24
12.7–9 321–26
12.9 324–26
12.10 326–27
12.10–12 326–29
12.11 327–28
12.12 328–29
12.13 329–30
12.13–18 329–35
12.14 330–31
12.15–16 331–33
12.17 333–34
12.18 334–35
13.1–2 335–37
13.1–10 335–44
13.3–4 337–40
13.5 340
13.6 340–42
13.7–8 342–43
13.9 343–44
13.10 344

13.11 344–46
13.11–18 344–53
13.12 346
13.13 346–47
13.14–15 347–48
13.16–17 348–50
13.18 350–53
14.1 353–55
14.1–15 353–60
14.2–3 355–57
14.4–5 357–60
14.6–7 360–63
14.6–20 360–78
14.8 363–65
14.9–11 365–68
14.12 368–69
14.13 369–70
14.14 371–72
14.15–16 372–75
14.17–18 375–76
14.19–20 376–78
15.1 382–83
15.1–8 380–94
15.2–4 383–89
15.3–4 385–89
15.5–6 389–91
15.5–8 389–93
15.7 391
15.8 391–93
16.1 399–400
16.1–21 395–417
16.2 400–402
16.2–4 400–402
16.3 401
16.4 401–402
16.5–6 402–404
16.5–7 402–404
16.8–9 404–406
16.8–21 404–416
16.10–11 406–407
16.12 407–408
16.13–14 408–411
16.15 411–12
16.16 412–13
16.18 414
17.1—18.24 418–67
17.1–2 426–28
17.3 428–29
17.3–6 428–33
17.4–5 429–32
17.6 432–33
17.7 433
17.7–18 433–42
17.8 434–35
17.9–11 435–37
17.12–14 437–39
17.15 439–40
17.16 440–41
17.17 441
17.18 441–42
18.1 443
18.1–20 442–66
18.2–3 443–45
18.4–5 446–47

18.6 447–48
18.7–8 448–50
18.9–10 450–52
18.11–13 452–56
18.14 456–57
18.15–17a 457–58
18.17b–18 458–59
18.19 459
18.20 459–61
18.21 461–63
18.21–24 461–66
18.22–23 463–65
18.24 465–66
19.1—20.15 468–521
19.1–2 476–78
19.1–5 476–80
19.3 478–79
19.4 479
19.5 479–80
19.5–6 508–511
19.6 480–82
19.6–10 480–87
19.7–8 482–84
19.9 484–86
19.10 486–87
19.11 487–89
19.11–16 487–96
19.12 489–91
19.13 491–92
19.14 492–94
19.15 494–95
19.17–18 496–97
19.17–21 496–500
19.19 497–98
19.20–21 498–500
20.1 500–501
20.1–3 500–505
20.2 501–502
20.3 504–505
20.4 505–508
20.4–6 505–511
20.7–8 511–13
20.7–10 511–15
20.9 513–14
20.10 514–15
20.11 515–16
20.11–15 515–19
20.12 516–17
20.13 517–19
20.14–15 519
21.1 522–25
21.2 534–37
21.2—22.17 526–80
21.2–4 534–39
21.2–8 533–34
21.3–4 537–39
21.5 539–40
21.5–8 539–44
21.6 540–41
21.7 541–42
21.8 542–44
21.9–10 544–46
21.9–21 544–56

21.11 546–47
21.12–13 547–49
21.14 549–50
21.15 550–51
21.16–17 551–53
21.18–20 553–55
21.21 555–56
21.22 556–57
21.22–27 556–61
21.23–26 557–60
21.27 560–61
22.1–2 561–63
22.1–5 561–66
22.3–4 563–65
22.5 565–66
22.6–7 566–68
22.6–9 534, 566–70
22.8–9 568–69
22.10 570
22.10–17 534, 570–78
22.11 571–72
22.12–13 572–73
22.14–15 573–75
22.16 575–77
22.17 577–78
22.18–21 581–87
22.20 584–85

DEAD SEA SCROLLS

CD
1.14–15 332
4.6–12 188
9.4 117

CD-A
1.4 447
6.2 447

CD-B
19.5–11 499
19.12 182

1Q22 (1QDM)
2.10 279

1QH
1.10–11 375
2(10).20 290
3(11).3 290
3(11).7–12 316
3(11).12–18 332
3(11).19 290
3.23–24 388
3.32–36 516
6.20–21 560
6.22–24 332
7.11 133
8.5–7 563
8.14–15 332
11.13 524
14.13 213

15.28 339
17.13 366

1QM
1.1 325
1.1–3 321
1.2 189
1.5 325
1.10–12 498
1.11–12 196, 414
2.2 189
2.2–3 186
2.16—3.11 214
3.5 514
4.4–5 356
5.1–2 186
7.3–6 358
7.14 214
8.16 201
9.4–7 323
9.15–16 323
10.1–2 514
11.1–11 356
11.7–12 383
11.16–18 514
12.1–2 85
12.7–15 554
12.11–12 494
12.15 138
13.5–6 224
14.1 383
14.2–3 197
14.16 438
15.1 196
15.1–10 496
15.2–3 337, 410, 512
15.13 263
17.6–8 323
18.1 263
18.1–5 496
18.3 263

1QpHab
2.8–10 266
7.1–5 266
8.1–3 369
12.14 363

1QpNah frags.
1.2–4 440
3—4 col. 3.8 440

1QS
2.2 82
2.8 366
2.19–26 485
4.13 366
6.1–8 485
6.5–6 359
6.8 117
8.1–10 556
8.5–9 552

8.12–14 331
9.10–11 275
9.19–21 331
11.7–8 367

1QSa
2.11–17 358
2.17–21 64

2Q24 = 2QNJ ar frag.
1.3 546

4Q DibHamᵃ (frags. 1–2)
col. 7.8 234

4Q164 = 4QpIsaᵈ
549

4Q179 frag.
2.5 449

4Q242 (4QPrNab ar) frags.
1–3 243
6–8 243

4Q280
1.2 233

4Q394 = 4QMMTᵃ frag.
8.4.5–10 574

4Q403 (4QShirShabbᵈ)
1.23 213

4Q404 (4QShirShabbᵉ) frag.
1.1 213
2.2–10 213

4Q405 (4QShirShabbᶠ) frag.
20 col. 2.2 214

4Q418 frag.
9.16 267

4Q525 = 4QBéat frag.
2.2.1–4 573

4Q554 = 4QNJᵃ ar frag.
1 546
2.15 546
3.20 546

4QapocrMosesᵃ
1.3 415

4QDibHamᵃ frag.
6.6–7 330

4QFlor frag.
1. col. 1 542
1. col. 21.2.11 542
1.3–4 560
1.16–17 560

4QpHosᵃ
2.12–13 411

4QpIsaᵈ frags.
1–7 554

4QpIsaᵃ frags.
8—10 (col. 3) 15–19 494
8—10 (col. 3) 22–24 494

4QpNah frags.
3+4 col. 1.3 274
3–4.2.7–9 465

4QpPsᵃ (171)
col. 3.13–16 277

4QPsᶠ
10.5–6 329

4QTanh frags.
1–2 329
2.4–5 329

4QTest
1—20 275

4QTQahat ar
1 566
1.1 566

5Q15 (= 5QNJ ar) frags.
1.1 551
1.1—2.15 551
1.2 546
1.6–7 556
2.6 546
2.12–15 554

11QMelch
9—13 323

11Q18 (= 11QNJ ar) frags.
1.1–6 561
10 561
19.3 546

11Q19 (= 11QTempleᵃ)
4.13 551
29.7–8 538
30.6–7 551

36.10–11 556
38.1—40.15 272
47.3–18 560
47.14–18 273
59.13 537

PSEUDEPIGRAPHA

1 Enoch
1.2 570
1.6 415
2.12–13 366
5.1 182
6—11 318
9.1 403
9.4 380, 438, 495
10 475
10.4–6 499–500
10.4–12 502
10.6 172
10.12 172, 363
10.21 198
10.22 539
12.3 49
14.5 502
14.8 371
14.9–10 119
14.14 55
14.15 113
14.18–19 499
14.20 191
14.22 138
17.5 499
17.7–8 226
18—21 226
18.1 179
18.2 179
18.11 226
18.13 220, 222
18.14–16 318
18.15 222
18.15–16 225
20.1–7 (8) 213
20.1–8 33
20.2 29, 233
20.5 323
21.3 222
21.3–6 318
21.3–7 220
21.5 366
21.5–10 195
21.6 225
21.7 226
21.86–88 222
22.6–7 196
22.7 195
22.8–9 196
22.9 195
23.3–4 196
24.4—25.7 64
24.6 323
25.4–5 574
27.1–5 7
27.2–3 366
33—36 548

37—71 567
37.2 92
37.5 92
38.1–6 499
38.2 370
38.5 169, 439
39.1–8 157
39.3 285
39.12 122
40 213
40.1 138
40.2 120, 265
40.7 327
40.9 402
41.1–2 370
45.3 103, 516
45.4–5 524
46.1 54, 366
46.2 265
46.5–6 140
47.1–4 157, 165
47.3 85, 127, 138, 517
47.4 160
47.23 116
48.1 200
48.1–7 557
48.5 92
48.9 366, 506
48.10 289
50.1 139
50.1–4 557
51.1–2 509
52.1–7 435
53.1 377
53.3 29, 234
53.3–5 376
54.1–2 499
54.3–5 501
54.6 213
54.7 384
55.3—56.4 323
55.4 169
55.5–6 291
56 476
56.1 376
56.1–4 238
56.5 408
56.5–8 237, 410, 512
56.6 513
56.8 499
59.1 119
60.1 138
60.2 116
60.7–9 336
60.7–10 345
60.11–22 179, 375
61.1–13 181
61.5 518
62.3 169
62.3—63.12 172
62.9 169
62.11 234

62.14 102, 485
62.15–16 164
62.16 85
63.1 169
63.12 169
65.8 179
66.1 238
66.1–2 180
66.2 402
67.8 169
67.8–9 567
67.12 169
69.4 332
69.14 490
69.22 180
69.27–29 327
71.2 384
71.3–4 265
71.7 120–22
71.8 138
71.8–9 213
72—82 548
72.1 524
74.2 366
76.1–14 180
81.1–2 127
84.2 438
86.1 167, 225
86.1–3 58
86.3 167, 225
88.1 225, 501
88.1–3 167
88.2 152
88.3 225
89.36 133
90 476
90.9 132
90.13–15 323
90.13–19 498, 512
90.20 85
90.20–36 366
90.24 167, 225
90.28–29 93, 556
90.31 275
90.37–38 132
91.12 439
91.16 524
92.2 238
93.2 366
96.1–3 439
96.2 330
97.3–5 165
97.6 517
98.1–6 583
99 476
99.1 139
99.6–7 243
100.3 377
100.5 366
102.1–3 493
104.2 55
104.2–3 165
104.5 172

104.10–11 584
108.3 86, 342
108.3–6 220, 226
108.12 103

2 Enoch
1.3 130
1.4–5 276
1.5 55, 257, 278
3.3 119, 384
8.3–4 562
8.8 549
10.2 499
19.4–5 402
21.1 122
22.8 85, 164
29.3 375
39.5 375
52.15 517
65.9 539
67.1–3 285
(A) 22.6 323
(J) 1—2 503
(J) 7.1–2 502
(J) 11.4–5 496
(J) 17 493
(J) 29.4 337
(J) 29.4–5 323
(J) 33 503
(J) 40.10 179
(J) 49.1 583

3 Enoch
1.7 486
1.8 121
2.1 225
7.1 121
14.4 496
16.1–5 214
17.1–3 213
17.4 496
18.19 384
18.25 278
19.4 384
22.3–4 278
25.5–6 121
25.6 122
26.3 225
26.12 327
28.7–10 111
30.2 517
32.1 238
33.4–5 499
35.1–6 111
44.5 225
48a.10 485

2 (Syriac) Apocalypse of Baruch
1.3–4 270
2.1 446
3.7 211
4.2–6 535
6.4 237
6.4–9 180

6.5–9 70
6.7 70
11.1–2 364
13.8 448
21.6 119, 375
21.22–25 539
23.4–7 165
24.1 517
26.1—30.5 163
27.1–15 92, 196
29—30 503
29.1–8 503
29.4 336, 345
30.1–5 366, 503
32.2–4 535
32.6 524
36.1—40.4 424
40.1–2 377, 499
40.1–4 354
44.12 524
48.37 498
50.2–4 509
51.11 120
53.1—76.5 424
56.13 501–502
67.2 274
67.7 364
70.2 372
70.2–10 169
72.1–6 488
76.1–5 285
77.17–26 225
78—87 185
85.9 370

3 (Greek) Apocalypse of Baruch
1.1 130
1.3 290
1.7 583
2.6 426
6.2 496
11.3 147
11.3–4 216
11.4 135
14.1–2 147
16.3 227, 231

3 (Slavonic) Apocalypse of Baruch
4.6–13 324

4 Baruch
4.7–8 270

Apocalypse of Abraham
9.1–4 138
10.3–4 138
19.6 375
27.5–7 270
29.15–16 383
30.1–8 383, 416
31.1 214
31.1–8 223

Apocalypse of Daniel
12.4–5 230
13.1–13 346

Apocalypse of Elijah
1.9–10 183
2.5, 32 230
3.2–4 493
4.7 275
4.11 167
4.11–12 225
4.13 281
5.4–6 183
5.5–6 484
5.22–24 499
5.32 275
5.36–37 499
5.38 524

Apocalypse of Ezra
1.14 292
2.23 159
4.5 159
4.26–27 346

Apocalypse of Sedrach
5.4 340

Apocalypse of Zephaniah
4.4 231
6 327
6—9 517
6.8 231
6.11–15 486
9—12 210
12.1 214
12.6 172

Assumption of Moses
8.1 414
10.4 415
10.12 285

Joseph and Aseneth
1.2 513
4.1 536
4.9 357
15.12 226
16.15–16 267
28.9 479

Jubilees
1.12 276, 403
1.15–18 548
1.20 327, 332
1.24 542
1.27–29 215
1.29 524
2.2 179–80, 213, 226, 375, 402
2.16 226
2.17–22 179
5.6 502
8.25 512

10.7 226
10.9 286
11.4 243
13.20 190
17.15–16 327
18.15 190
23.11–21 196
23.22–23 512
23.23 281, 291, 498
24.30 172, 363
30.18 277
30.22 342
32.20–21 285
33.22 188
48.5 227
48.9–19 327
49.2 213

Letter of Aristeas to Philocrates
310—11 584

Life of Adam and Eve
7.2 366
12—16 323
13.3 172
16.4–5 324
19.2 159
29.1–2 549
33.4 216
33.5 242
37.5 172
38.3 179
47.3 337

Martyrdom and Ascension of Isaiah
2.9–11 276
2.10 130
3.10 282
4.1–13 347
4.2 233
4.2–12 336
4.6 339
4.6–11 346
4.9–13 274
4.13 321
4.14 499
4.14–17 493
4.16–17 164
5.1–16 403
7.9–12 323
7.13–37 116
7.21 486
7.27 116
8.1–5 486
8.9 116
8.10 116
8.14 164
9.5 490
9.9–11 164
9.27–42 135
11.39 583
56.3–4 490

Odes of Solomon
9.6 91
9.11 86
11.11 457
11.16 562
22.5 336
23 111
23.5–22 111
23.13–15 111
23.19–20 111
29.6 289
30.1–7 541
36.1 114
38.9–14 428
39.7 355
42.8–9 490
42.20 355, 490

Prayer of Manasseh
2—4 501

Psalms of Solomon
2.1–2 498
2.1–35 293
2.2 274
2.19–21 536
2.24 457
2.25–26 317, 330
2.27 281
5.16 447
8.4 535
8.12 274
8.14 428
8.20 403
9.9 320
10.1–3 100
10.2 100
10.8 193
11.1 214
12.16 193
14.1 100
14.3 562
15.4–9 229
15.6 182
15.9 182, 349
15.12 172
16.2 155
16.9 242
17 130
17.8 448
17.19 226
17.21–22 319
17.21–25 574
17.21–29 488
17.23–24 77, 319
17.23–26 271
17.24 494
17.26–46 185, 548
17.29 137
17.34–35 559
17.43 366
21—25 130
26—34 130
44—46 130

Questions of Bartholomew
4.31–34 180

Questions of Ezra
11 214

Sibylline Oracles
1.7–8 38
1.103 479
1.324–30 351
1.387–400 293
2.18 435
2.165–68 346
2.170–76 186
2.196–205 514
2.286–289 501
2.307–308 230
3.20–23 263
3.47–48 361
3.53–54 499
3.80–84 167
3.162–64 268
3.272–79 270
3.310–13 466
3.311–13 160, 403
3.388–400 437
3.512–13 512
3.539–44 220
3.544 240
3.556–61 172
3.643–46 281
3.652 181
3.660–68 291
3.663–68 512
3.663–701 511
3.669–84 516
3.675–93 217
3.689–92 414, 416
3.796–808 313, 324
4.93 364
4.119–20 408
4.137–39 338, 408
4.171–77 223
4.171–78 214
5.28–34 338
5.33–34 339
5.77–85 243
5.143–44 364
5.154 281
5.155–61 225, 461
5.158–59 222
5.159 364
5.162–70 465
5.168–78 449
5.173 449
5.211–12 524
5.226 281
5.247–52 550
5.343 352
5.346–85 167
5.377–80 219
5.413 281
5.434 364
5.434–46 364

5.454 227
5.512–14 79
5.512–17 324
5.512–31 220
7.118–31 499
8.88 318, 429
8.114–19 463
8.190 167
8.232–34 167
8.234–35 415
8.248 271
8.341 167
8.353 230
8.412–413 167
13.45 435
14.108 435

Testament of Abraham
(A)
1.5 190, 513
1.7 159
4.6 159
4.11 513
9.1–3 486
12.4 375
12.5 257
13.11–14 375
15.4 290
15.12 290
17.11 182
(B)
7.4–16 315
7.5 315
12.1 371

Testament of Adam
1.1—2.12 117
1.4 357
1.12 212

Testament of Isaac
5.21–32 499

Testament of Job
2.4 263
4.4 280
4.7–8 447
7.9 159
14.1–3 134
16.7 406
23.6 195
38.1 159
40.4 479
52.8–10 285

Testament of Moses
1.14 343
3.1 231
4.2 537
8.1 92, 196
10.3–6 166, 516
10.5 167
12.9 182
12.13 275

Testament of
Solomon
1.6–7 181
1.8–13 181
1.9, 11 147
1.13 583
2.8–9 289
2.9 233
3.1 147
13.1 231
14.3–4 330
17.4 362
20.14–17 225
20.16 167

TESTAMENTS OF THE
TWELVE PATRIARCHS

Testament of Asher
6.4 323

Testament of
Benjamin
9.2 320

Testament of Dan
5.5–6 187
5.6 325
5.9–13 561
5.11–13 539
5.12 535
5.13 489, 556
6.1–6 327
6.2 323

Testament of Gad
4.7 325

Testament of Joseph
3.2 159
19.8 132
(Arm.) 19.1–12
    410
19.b–c 498

Testament of Judah
19.4 325
24.1 577
25.3 515

Testament of Levi
2.7 119, 384
3.3 493
3.4–6 199
3.4–9 111
3.5 213
3.5–6 216
3.8 116, 122
3.9 226, 516
4.1 167
5.1 113, 199
5.6 327
8.2 85, 191, 213
8.10 215
10.3 270

18.2–7 557
18.3 577
18.6 158
18.6–7 199
18.10 549
18.10–14 64

Testament of
Naphtali
5.1–5 315

Testament of Reuben
4.1 362
4.9 457

Testament of Simeon
3.5 325

Testament of Zebulon
2.2 403
9.8 564

RABBINIC MATERIAL

Babylonian
Talmud
Baba Bathra
75b 561
Hagigah
12b 211
Shabbat
152b 158

Midrashim
Psalms
136.7 384

Midrash Rabbah
Genesis
35.3 115
85.1 316
Exodus
9.9 323
18.5 548
Leviticus
14.9 316
Numbers
14.3 115

Mishnah
Middoth
1.2 412
Sanhedrin
113a 56

Targums
(Pal.) Genesis
49.11 491
(Pal.) Leviticus
24.3 538
26.11–12 538
Psalms
45.12–15 483
(Pal.) Isaiah
22.22 88

Isaiah
61.3–6 511
63.3–4 377
Jeremiah
46.7–8 331
51.42 331
Zechariah
3.1–5 484
14.2 498
14.14 498
Neof. 1 406
Neof. 1 Genesis
50.19–21 315

Jerusalem
Genesis
49.11 198

Pseudo-Jonathan
Genesis
11.7 33
Deuteronomy
28.12 56

EARLY CHRISTIAN
LITERATURE

1 Clement
3.4 90
4.12 386
5.7 268
8.4 197
9.3 324
11 165
11.1 366
15.4 294
16.1 200
21.7 292
22.8 473
23.5 88
27.1 404
29.3 359
34.3 572
34.6 138
39.7 366
41.2 158
43.2–3 341
43.6 160
44.3 200
51.5 386
56.4 100
58.1 388
58.2 583
60.1 404
61.1–2 139
64 139
65 139

2 Clement
1.1 291
3.2 86
4.5 334
9.3 270
13.2 320
16.3 172, 524

17.3, 5 117
17.4 448
18.2 325
20.2 182

Acts of Andrew
27 181

Acts of Thomas
4—5 485
7 485
30 291
136—37 138

Andreas
Commentarius in
Apocalypsin
7 54
60—63 15

Apocalypse of
Paul
31 499
34–36 499
43 216
44 215
51 570

Apocalypse of Peter
(Akhmimic)
2 346
5 167, 524
6 372
23 499

Apocryphon of James
14.29–31 136
15.17–22 136

Aristides
Apology
10 71
In Rom.
11 453

Clement of
Alexandria
Paedagogos
1.7 88
Quis dives salvetur
42 50
Stromateis
7.1 97

Didache
5.1–2 574
7.1–2 541
8.2 36
9.3–4 290
9.5 574
10.2–6 290
10.5 36
10.6 578, 585
11 62
13.3 359

14.1 51, 578
15.1–2 117
16.3 172
16.4 325, 340,
    346
16.5 92, 186
16.6 214, 313
16.7 493

Epistle of Barnabas
1.7 359
4.3–5 437
4.4–5 337
4.4–6 350
4.11 270
5.11 276
6.2 354
6.6 473
7.9 172
9.6 294
12.9 172
13.4–6 189
15.3–9 503
15.5 167
16.1–2 556
18.1 325
19.11 488
20.1–2 574

Epistle to Diognetus
8.9 160

Eusebius
Historia Ecclesiastica
2.13.1–8 348
2.15.2 364
3.5.3 321
3.23.1–4 60
3.23.1–19 50
4.15.48 69
4.26.2 51
5.1.58–61 571
5.14 73
5.17.3–4 87
5.20.2 584

The (First)
Apocalypse of
James
28.16–17 84

Gospel of Peter
9.35—10.42 276
35—36 285

Gospel of Philip
2.54.5–7 490

Gospel of Thomas
2 138
11a 524

The Gospel of
Truth
36.35 562

Ignatius
Letter to the
Ephesians
1.1 62
2.1 165
4.1 85
6.2 61
7.1 574
9.1 61, 270
10.3 166
13.1 325
13.2 323
19.1–2 315
Letter to the
Magnesians
1.2 289
2.1 117
7.1 117
9.1 51
12.1 85
Letter to the
Philadelphians
1.1 212
2.1 358
4 165
5 95
6.1 87
6.1–2 90
6.3 349
Letter to Polycarp
8.3 370
Letter to the Romans
2.2 181
Letter to the
Smyrneans
1.2 135
6.1 350
8.1 358
10.1 290
12.1 166
12.1–2 65
13.1 358
Letter to the Trallians
3.1 117
4.2 289
7.2 117
8.1 325

Irenaeus
Adversus Haereses
1.13.3 537
3.11.8 121
4.18, 6 158
5.2.2—30.4 351
5.30.4 499
5.34.2—35.2 15

Justin Martyr
Dialogue with Trypho
61.1 97
62.4 97
81 15
116.1 88
118.2 135
139.4 135

First Apology
28.1 324
31.6 90

The Letter of the
Smyrneans on The
Martyrdom of St
Polycarp
2.4 66
12.2 66, 333
13.1 66
14 165
14.2 365
15.2 215
19.1 87
21 139

Origen
Commentarius in
Evangelium Joannis
1.19 97
2.55 487
2.55–59 487
Contra Celsum
8.17 135
De Principiis
2.11.2–39 15

Polycarp
Letter to the
Philippians
2.1 291
5.1 84
7.1 325

Pseudo-
Clementine
Homilies
2.32 348
Recognitions
3.47 348

Shepherd of
Hermas
Mandates
5.1.3 325
10.3.2–3 158
Similitudes
2.9 85
5.5.3 366
6.2.2 182
6.3.6 286
8.2.5 158
9.9.6 473
9.11–16 358
9.16–17 183
Visions
1.1.3 428
2.1, 4 259
2.1.1 428
2.1.3 583
2.2.7 366
2.2.7–8 196
2.3.1 196
2.3.2 182

2.4 314
2.4.1–4 583
4.1.6 227
4.2 314
4.2.1 537

Tertullian
De Praescriptionem
Haereticorum
36 51
Scorpiace
12 84

Theophilus of
Antioch
Ad Autolychum
2.10 97

ANCIENT WRITERS

Apollodorus
Lib.
1.6.3 330
3.14.8 330

Cicero
Verrine Orations
3.81.188–89
  153
4.43 495

Dio Cassius
Historia Romana
42.27.2 152
57.17.8 87
67.4.3 118

Dio Chrysostom
Discourses
46.5–14 154
Orations
31.84 86

Diodorus (Siculus)
4.49.8 135

Ezekiel the
Tragedian
Exagoge
68–72 516

Herodotus
1.76–84 81
1.178–79 552
1.190–91 408
7.187 153

Hippocrates
Prognostic
2 155

Homer
Iliad
2.308 318
6.119–236 283

7.479 155
9.171 212
13.445–47 447
15.188 155
23.244 155
Odyssey
11.43 155
15.16–18 283
15.329 447
20.341–44 283

Horace
Satires
1.5.30–31 100

Josephus, Flavius
Antiquities of the
Jews
2.304–306 416
3 150
3.143 134
3.162–72 315
3.179–87 315
4.320–26 285
6.332 155
7.356–57 137
11.133–34 185
14.10 69
14.28 153
20.9.2 154
327 85
331 85
Bellum Judaicum
1.4.12 414
5.270 416
5.442 414
6.33–41 324
6.428–29 414
7.5.4 454
Contra Apionem
1.197 286

Juvenal
Satyra
6.123 431
6.249–50 463
10.213–15 463
10.329–45 432

Livy
39.30.4–5 71

Lucian (of
Samosata)
Alexander the False
Prophet
12—26 348

Macarius Magnes
Apocritica
4.7 167

Martial
Epigrams
14.3.85 454

Ovid
Metamorphoses
5.321–31 330
6.667–74 330
7.350–90 330
8.24–37 147
15.41–42 70
Tristia
4.8.23–24 71

Philo of Alexandria
De Decalogo
96—105 31
De Legum Allegoriae
1.20.66–67 550,
  553, 556
De Opificio Mundi
89 31
De Praemiis et Poenis
12.70 67
De Somniis
2.259–60 409
De Specialibus Legibus
1.84–97 315
De Vita Mosis
1.20.114 413
1.20.119 413
1.21.121 413
2.111–12 315
2.122–24 315
Quaestiones et
Solutiones in Exodum
2.73–74 552
2.110–11 554
Quod Deterius Potiori
Insidiari Soleat
145(39) 100
146(40) 100

Philostratus
Life of Apollonius
(of Tyana)
1.2–3 348

Plato
Phaedo
110 115

Pliny (the Elder)
Naturalis Historia
4.12.23 50
5.33(126) 67
6.26 453
12.41.82–83
  455
13.30.96–97
  454
14.28.148 432
36.95–7 59

Pliny (the
Younger)
Epistulae
3.5 128
5.16.7 537

Plutarch
Lives: Anthony
  3.172 152
Moralia, Dinner of the
  Seven Wise Men
  161 F 121

Seneca
Epistulae Morales
4.3–9 281

Seneca (the Elder)
Controversiae
1.2.7 431

Strabo
Geography
3.1.7 458
10.5.13 50
12.3.22 71
12.8.18 87, 89
12.8.20 99
12.16 95
13.4.8 87
13.4.10 87, 89

Suetonius
Lives of the Caesars:
Caligula
14 338

Lives of the Caesars:
Domitian
2.9 4
2.13 4
3.9 4
4.4 118
6.9–11 4
7.2 154
9—10 4
13 125, 336
13.4 4
14.2 154
Lives of the Caesars:
Galba
11 152

Lives of the Caesars:
Nero
45.1 154
57 338
Lives of the Caesars:
Tiberius
59.1 432

Tacitus
Annales
2.47 80
2.47.3–4 87
4.37 68
4.55–56 65, 80
11.12 432
11.26 432
14.27.1 96

15.5 154
15.29 124
15.44 432
Historiarum
1.78 338
2.8 338
3.68 152

Thucydides
History
1.53.2 458
3.33.3 50
6.32.1 212

Xenophon
Hellenica
2.3.51 86

Index of Subjects

Aaron 333, 347
Abaddon (Apollyon) 226, 234
Abiram, destruction 332–33
Abraham 446
abyss (bottomless pit) 226–27, 511;
  angel of the abyss 234–35;
  sealing 504–505
adoption law, of God's relationship
  with believers 542
alcohol, and the insidious influence of
  evil 444
Alexander Philalethes 99
'all the earth's inhabitants' 342
Alpha 26, 38, 541, 573, 580
altars: altar of burnt offering 272;
  heavenly altar 158–59, 215, 235–36,
  375, 404
Amen 141, 479, 540; as Christological
  title 96; as closure of Revelation
  582
amethysts 555
Ammia of Philadelphia 87
Amphisbaena 241
'ancient serpent' 9
angels 11, 28–30; angel of the abyss
  234–35; angel of the waters 402;
  angelic commission 389–93; angelic
  judgement, sign 311; angelic
  mission to proclaim the bowl-
  plagues 399–400; audience of the
  angel during the seventh prophecy
  575–77; and the binding of Satan
  501; censing angel 214–16;
  commands, to other supernatural
  beings 147; distinguished from the
  twenty-four elders 118; dragon's
  angels 323–24; elders' angelic status
  135; flight 361; four angels chained
  at the Euphrates 236–37; four angels
  restrain the elements in defence
  of the Church 178–81, 188; and
  glory 443; guardian angels, possibly
  symbolized by the twenty-four
  elders 116; identity, in the vision of
  angelic judgement 360–61; as link
  between earth and heaven 39; as
  ministers of fire 375; participation
  in the investiture of the Lamb 138;
  participation in the work of
  judgement 366; role with the

Church in heaven 193–94; role in
  the trumpet-plagues 210; sealing of
  the saints 181–83; seven angels 383,
  (and the trumpet-plagues 213–14);
  and the seven churches 58; seventh
  angel 296; speech 181, 443; as
  stars 225–26; and the sun 496–97;
  talking angel at the vision of the new
  Jerusalem 550; twelve guardian
  angels of the gates of the new
  Jerusalem 548–49; voices 362, 446;
  worship, as idolatry 486; see also the
  strong angel
Anna (prophetess), service in the
  Temple 198
Antichrist 149–50, 234; and the beasts
  from the sea and earth 337, 344;
  destruction 496–500; judgement,
  likened to that of Pharaoh 400;
  pride 449
antinomianism 74
Antiochus III the Great 81, 95
Antiochus IV Epiphanes 86, 124, 318,
  341
Antipas (martyr) 13, 34, 46, 69, 73, 507
apocalyptic 7–8, 27, 586; influence
  on Revelation 162–63; Jewish
  apocalyptic, as background to the
  second trumpet-plague 220–21
apocalyptic literature 27
apocalypticism, and symbolism 14–15
apocryphal and pseudepigraphical
  literature 7
Apollo 234
Apollyon (Abaddon) 226, 234
apostles: false apostles 61; twelve
  apostles 549–50
apostolic decree 77
Apsinth (wormwood) 205–206, 222–23
Aquila 59
archangels 29, 323; seven archangels
  213–14
ark of the covenant 19, 294
Armageddon 397, 412–13, 417
armour: fiendish cavalry 239; locusts'
  appearance likened to armour 232
Artemis 59
ascension: beast ascends from the
  bottomless pit 434; as vindication of
  the two witnesses 285

ascent and descent 216–17, 219–20,
  256
Asclepios, worship 68
Asia Minor, social background, and
  importance for Revelation 4
Athene 68
athletics, victors' crowns 231
Attalus I (king of Pergamum) 68
Attalus II Philadelphus 87
Attalus III (king of Pergamum) 68
Augustus Caesar 436
authorship 2–3, 28, 31, 568–69;
  possibility of John's death before
  completion of Revelation
  discounted 523; prophetic
  character 8; Revelation not
  pseudonymous 7; see also John

Babylon 3, 6; capture by Cyrus 407;
  fall see Babylon, fall; as the great city,
  split into three parts 414–15, 417;
  harlotry 358; judgement 221–22;
  judgement as grounds for the praise
  of God 480; persecutes God's
  people 482; replaced by the new
  Jerusalem 525; symbolism 281, 286,
  293, 407, 466
Babylon, fall 15, 19, 47, 363–64,
  418–67, 558; lament over the fall
  442–66; and the praise of God
  478–79; temporal perspective 128
Balaam 9, 62–63, 79; oracle 577;
  teachings, at Pergamum 69–70
banking, at Laodicea 95, 99
barley, price 153
Baruch, ascension 285
the beast 280; mark 183, 187; the
  mount of the woman 425, 429,
  434–38, 441, 445, 451, 497–99;
  symbol, treated as male 306;
  worship 6
the beast from the earth 311; as the
  false prophet 409; judgement on
  those branded with his mark 365,
  400–401; throne 406; vision
  344–53; worshippers of the beast,
  blasphemy and torture 405
the beast from the sea 311, 335–45,
  409; acts as agent of the beast from
  the earth 347; authority 340, 342;

described as the scarlet beast and mount of the woman (Babylon) 429; number of its name 350–53

beatitudes 31; in the opening of the greetings to the seven churches 34

beheading 507

Behemoth 336, 345

Beliar (Antichrist) 499

believers, share in Christ's inheritance 542

Belshazzar 449

beryl 115, 555

birds, banquet 497, 500

bishops, silence 212

blamelessness 360

'blasphemous titles' 336

blasphemy 405, 407; as exercised by the beast from the sea 341

blessings: *eulogia* 139–40; present blessings 369–70

blood: drinking 403–404; symbolism 197, 402; and wine 432; *see also* trumpet-plagues

body, parts 470

'book of life' 85–86, 342, 517, 519

bottomless pit *see* abyss

boulder, thrown into the sea at the fall of Babylon, sacramentalism of the symbol 462

bowl-plagues 383, 389–91, 395–417, 446; *see also* plagues

bowls 19; cultic bowls 134–35

branding: contrasted with the placing of the Lamb's name on the foreheads of the faithful 355; as a mark of the beast from the earth 348–50

'breath of life' 284

'breathing life', as parody of creation 348

bride: and groom, metaphor 464; and the new Jerusalem 536–37, 544–45

Brightman, Thomas 502

brimstone 366

burial, importance 281, 283

'burning lake', symbolism 519

Caesar Augustus 59, 68, 128

Caligula (Roman emperor) 338, 436

'called', used of the members of the Church associated with the Lamb 439

camp, symbolism 514

carnelian 115, 555

Carpocrates 76

carriages, and horses 455

cassia 455

censing 214–15

chalcedony 555

Chares of Lindos 260

chastity 357–58

cherubim 120

child, sign 314, 318–20

Chimaera 239–41

phoenix 153

'chosen', used of the members of the Church associated with the Lamb 439

Christians: as conquerors 64; Hellenistic Christians, as audience for Revelation 4–5; as prophets 487; as saints 581; security, contrasted with the insecurity of the beast 435; as the servants of God 568

Christology 110; balance 11–12, 16; difficulties for the Johannine community 4–6; disputes about 63; unity of God the Father and the Son 56; unity of God and the Lamb 140–41; *see also* Jesus Christ; Lamb of God

chronology 446, 518, 586–87; and eschatology 12–13, 16; and theology 521

chrysolite 555

chrysoprase 555

Church 13, 17–18, 39; assembly in heaven 189–202; as a camp for the people of God, attacked by Satan 514; community, judgement 379; false teaching in, as symbolized by the beast from the sea 344–45; fullness, represented by the one hundred and forty-four thousand 185–88; hope, realization in the final scene 525; as the huge crowd rejoicing in heaven 476; members *see* Church members; militant and triumphant gathered at the marriage feast of the Lamb 481; as the new Israel 187; perfection, as seen in the new Jerusalem 522; persecution *see* Church, persecution of; protection 174–202; represented by the one hundred and forty-four thousand in its totality 354–57; as the royal house of Israel 36; as the Temple and those who worship within it 269–70, 272–73

Church members: associated with the Lamb 358, 438–39; called to rejoice over the fall of Babylon 460–61; characterization 357–60; as descendants of the woman in the desert 334; and their praise of God 292–93; as victors 384–85

Church, persecution of: and fleeing to the wilderness 321; questioned as having taken place under Domitian 142; as symbolized by the pursuit and escape of the woman 330

cinnamon 455

cities 94–95

'city', symbolism 514

Claudius (Roman emperor) 436

clothing: linen clothing 390, 482–84; and nakedness 411–12; red and purple clothing and its symbolism in the Roman world 491; symbolism 84–85; washing, as symbolic of salvation 197, 573–74; *see also* white clothing

clouds 285, 371

codices, use 108

coins: inscriptions, *Dea Roma* 427; possible symbolism in connection with the mark of the beast from the earth 349

Colossae 95

Colossus of Rhodes 260

colours: black 99, 152; purple 430, 491; red 151, 491; scarlet/red, used of the woman mounted on the beast 429–30; white 84–85, 99, 150, 164–65, 191, 197, 488, 516

condemnation, within the oracle to Sardis 81–82

conflict, theme in the oracles 104

conquerors: Christ-like authority 77–79; in the Philadelphian church 93–94

conquest, language, in both the second prophecy and the oracles to the seven churches 541–42

contracts 127–28

coronets: seven coronets of the dragon 317–18; ten coronets 336; *see also* crowns

cosmic catastrophes, and breaking of the sixth seal 166–73

cosmic portents 294

cosmology 11–12, 16–18, 39, 113

cosmos: renewal, involves both heaven and earth 524; three-decker cosmos 226, 263, 363

covenant 294, 579

cowardliness, vice 543

creation: establishment of the new creation 500; Jesus Christ as the origin of God's creation 97; praise of God 140; the result of God's will 125–26; and silence 211–12

Creation narrative, darkness, and the fourth trumpet-plague 224

'creation of the world' 343

Croesus 80–81

crowns: Christ's crowns 489–90; gold crowns 371–72; gold crowns of the twenty-four elders 118; locusts' wreaths 231; symbolism 67; *see also* coronets

crucifixion of Jesus Christ 282, 377; attitudes of the women looking on contrasted with those looking on the judgement of Babylon 452

cups, cup held by the woman mounted on the beast 430–31

curses 563–64

Cybele (Artemis) 80

Cyrus the Great of Persia 80–81, 407, 441

Dan (tribe of Israel) 175, 188–89

Daniel: as background to God's sovereignty 124, 126; as background to the oath of the strong angel 264; as background to the symbolism of the beast from the sea 336–38, 341; as background to the throne room vision 129; as background to the

vision of angelic judgement 362;
as background to the visions of the
beasts 345, 348; expression used to
reflect the universal character of
God's people 137; origins of the
symbolism of the beast 280; and
the son of man figure 371; use in
Revelation 9

darkness: caused by the smoke from the
abyss 227; in the fifth bowl-plague
406; in the fourth trumpet-plague
223–24

Dathan, destruction 332–33

Day of the Lord 171–72

'day and night' 367

Dea Roma 427

dead: Christian dead, blessing 370;
company 516; giving up 518;
judgement 291

Death: as the fourth horseman 155–56,
450; and Hades 518–19; as
punishment of Jezebel's followers
75; second death 67, 510, 519, 544

Death and Hades, keys 47, 56

Dedication, Feast of 192

demonic winds, four 240–41;
associated with the four chained
angels 237–38

demons 410; and idolatry 243

denarii 153

descent and ascent 216–17, 219–20,
256

Devil *see* Satan

Dionysus 68, 87

Diotrephes (3 John 9–10) 5

discipleship, symbolized as walking
84–85

divine healing, as eternal life 10

dogs 574–75

Domitian (Roman emperor) 47, 436;
and the dating of Revelation 2, 4,
50–51, 154; persecution tradition
69, 142, 166; possibly symbolic of
the beast from the sea 338; and the
symbolism of the twenty-four
elders 118; worship 125, 336

doors, imagery 113

doxologies *see* hymns

dragon 316–21, 409, 501–502;
beast from the sea as agent of the
dragon 337; defeat by Michael
322–24; identification 324–25;
imprisonment 504–505; persecution
of the woman's descendants 333–34;
role as deceiver 325; sign 311,
313–14; spokesman, in the beast
from the sea 345

drama: courtroom drama, in the fall
of Babylon 466; intervals 109–110,
177, 209, 253, 522; intervals in the
fall of Babylon 424–26; play within
a play, war in heaven 322; in
Revelation 2, 20–22, 26, 38–39,
109–110; Revelation as 255–56

dramatic dialogues 195

dreams, interpretation 433

dualism 7; ethical dualism 11

Dürer, Albrecht 149

dwelling, concept in relation to the
new covenant 537–39

eagles: eagle of deliverance for the
woman pursued into the desert 330;
voice of the eagle 235; warning
from the eagle 224–25

earth 325; destruction 524; and
heaven 525; inhabitants, negative
imagery 427–28, 434–35; quarters
179; social meaning of the concept
357

'earth and its inhabitants' 346

earthquakes 14, 93, 145, 163, 294–95,
414, 417; and breaking of the sixth
seal 166–73; references in the oracle
to Philadelphia 87, 89; symbolism
217–18; theophanic nature 285

east 181, 408

Ebionites 4

ecclesiology *see* Church

Egypt, plagues: as background to the
locust plague 227–28, 230; as
background to the trumpet-plagues
221–24; and the bowl-plagues
401–402, 406–407; hail plague and
the seventh bowl-plague 416; as
pattern of the trumpet-plagues 219;
and the symbolism of the two
witnesses 279; *see also* plagues

Egypt, symbolism 281–82; and the
symbolism of the dragon 317;
see also Exodus

ekphrasis, John's use 426

elders *see* twenty-four elders

election 485

Elijah: ascension 285; ministry
parodied by the beasts 346; and the
two witnesses 275, 278–80

Elisha 478

emerald 555

emperor worship 68, 336

Enoch: ascension 285; and the two
witnesses 275

Ephesians, works 45

Ephesus 4; importance 52; John's exile
from 50; as place of writing of
Revelation 57; *see also* Ephesus,
church

Ephesus, church: Christ's parousia 83;
contrasted with that at Thyatira 73;
Nicolaitan activities 62–63, 69;
oracle to 59–64

Ephraim (tribe), omission from the
census of the tribes of Israel 188–89

epistolary style, beatitudes within 32

eschatology 12–13, 17, 39–40,
210–11; fall of Babylon 467; history
within 114; nature in Revelation
57; and the new creation 579; and
symbolism 14–15; and time 245;
'time of ordeal' 91–92

eternal life, through divine healing
10

eternity 367–68, 539; and time
212–13

eucharist (Lord's Supper) 102, 109,
585

Eumenes II 86–87

Euphrates river 236–37, 398–99,
407–408

evil, powers, and the sea 518

Exodus: as background to the pursuit
of the woman by the dragon 330;
as background to the trumpet-
judgements 244; as background to
the vision of the heavenly temple
389–90, 392; motif for the
persecution of the Church 330–33;
the new Exodus, prefigured in the
throne room vision 120, 380–94;
and the symbolism of the bowl-
plagues 380–94, 413; and the
symbolism of the dragon 317;
see also Egypt

eye salve 99–100

eyes: Christ's eyes compared to a
blazing fire 489; living creatures
121–22

Ezekiel: as background to the breathing
into the martyrs the breath of life
from God 284; as background to the
eating of the little scroll 267; and the
background to the four horsemen
450; as background for the imagery
of Babylon 440; as background to
the measuring of the temple in the
new Jerusalem 271, 551; as
background to temple imagery 199;
and the lament over Babylon 453;
lament over Tyre 450, 457;
resonances in Revelation 8; sealing
of Israel 182; symbolism of the
living creatures 120–21; and the
trumpet-plagues 220

faith 73

faithfulness: used of the members of the
Church associated with the Lamb
439; used in relation to Christ 488;
within the Ephesian church 61

faithlessness, vice 543

famine 221–22; spiritual famine
230–31; as symbolized by the third
horseman 153–54

fear: fear of God's enemies 284; as
offered to God 362

fiendish cavalry 238–44

fire: angelic ministries of fire 375; and
divine judgement 514; falling fire
as symbol of divine judgement
216–17; fire-breathing monsters
240; and judgement 278, 384, 405;
as the means of judgement over
Babylon 450; as means of
punishment 366; use in the first
three trumpet-plagues 220, 222

first fruits 359

flutes 463

food, sacrificial food 6

fornication 74

four horsemen 9, 145–56; as expressions of God's justice 519; the first (white) horse 147–51; and the four winds 179–80; the fourth (pale-coloured) horse 154–56; plagues 450; red horse, likened to the dragon 318; the second (red) horse 151–52; the third (black) horse 152–54

four living creatures 120–24, 156, 479

'foursquare' 551

frankincense 215, 455

frogs, plague 409

futurism 15

Gabriel (archangel) 29, 33, 213, 258, 323

Gad 175

Galba 152, 338, 436

Galen 68

gardens 94

garments *see* clothing

gematria, and the number six hundred and sixty-six 351–52

generic symbolism, and the number six hundred and sixty-six 352

Genesis, as background to the sign of the woman and child 314

Gentiles, to be part of the new Israel 538

gift-exchange 283

glory 557–58; attributed to an angel 443; as offered to God 139, 362

gnosticism, libertarianism 76

God: as Alpha and Omega 38, 541, 580; attributes 470; authority *see* God, authority of; covenant 128; as creator 363; dwelling place 537–39; fear of God 286, 362, 480; glory 36–37, 477, 565–66; heavenly temple 293; hidden purposes fulfilled 265–66; holiness 388; and Jesus Christ 11–12; judgement *see* God and judgement; kingdom, interim nature and the Millennium 503; as the Living God 182–83; manifestation, and silence 212; name *see* God, name of; nature *see* God, nature of; omnipotence 123; opponents, symbolized by the nations 494; parodied by the dragon and the beasts 346; people, ransom by the Lamb 136–38; people, symbolized by the vine 376; power 194–95, 477; praise *see* God, praise of; presence *see* God, presence of; protection of the saints 199–201; purposes revealed in the opening of the small scroll 258–59; qualities, possibly ascribed to the Lamb in angelic hymns of praise 194; reign 481–82; relationship with the new Israel 13; and remembrance 447; and righteousness 387, 389,

404; salvation 477; seal 182; seeing 564–65; self-disclosure 27; servants, martyrdom 478; servants as term for all Christians 568; service by the saints 198–99; seven spirits of God 33–34, 119; sovereign glory received for salvation through judgement 579; sovereignty *see* God, sovereignty of; Spirit 133; throne *see* God, throne of; truth, revealed through the Lamb 378; unity with Jesus Christ 93, 541; unity with the Lamb 171–72, 200–202; vengeance, for the death of his servants 478; voice *see* God, voice of; word 492; works 387; wrath *see* God, wrath of

God, authority of: and the authority of the strong angel 260; given to angels to protect the Church 183; given to the Son 79; over the locust plague 228–29; shared with the Son 327

God and judgement: on Babylon 448; in the breaking of the sixth seal 169–73; dispensed through Christ 516; and fire 514; and love 520–21; and the seven bowl-plagues 393; on unfaithfulness 145

God, name of 341, 388, 405; as the new name given to Christians 536

God, nature of 39; and benediction upon the Johannine community 32; eternal sovereignty and creativity 263–64; linked with that of Christ 56

God, praise of 477; at the fall of Babylon 478–80

God, presence of 214, 547; at the heavenly altar 236; symbolized by the heavenly temple 372; in union with Christ in the new Temple 557; with Israel (the Church) in persecution 321

God the Son: sovereignty and everlasting nature 65; *see also* Jesus Christ

God, sovereignty of 39, 114–16, 295–96, 521; in administering justice 159–60, 164; announced from heaven 326; in Christ 504; over the beast from the sea and his armies 497–99; over earthly powers 124–26; proclaimed by the heavenly voices in response to the sounding of the seventh trumpet 288–89; proclaimed by the twenty-four elders 289–93; and vengeance 162

God, throne of 216, 537; as symbol of sovereignty 114–15; unity with the Christ, in the new Jerusalem 564

God, voice of 54–55, 261–62, 266, 269; commissions the angel to proclaim the bowl-plagues 400; from the heavenly temple 413; and lion symbolism 260; *see also* voices

God, wrath of 170–71, 391; cup of God's wrath 415; winepress of God's wrath 365–66, 376–77, 379

gods, names 495

Gog 234, 241, 285, 412, 476, 496, 512

'going out', concept 511–12

'going up', concept 513–14

gold 390–91; imagery 551; use in the construction of the new Jerusalem 553, 556

Gomorrah 240, 366, 478, 558

gospel, angelic gospel of God's judgement 361–63

grace, and peace, benediction 32–33

grain harvests, and judgement 373

grape harvests, and judgement 373, 375–77

great city 281–82, 286

'great ordeal' 196

grief 449

groom, and bride, metaphor 464

Hades 56, 155–56; and Death 518–19

Hadrian (Roman emperor) 59

hail, plague 413, 415–16

hailstorms 295

hair, symbolism 231–32

haircloth 167

hallelujah 476–78, 481

harlot, symbol as Babylon 466

harlotry, Old Testament theme 426–27

harps and harpists 134, 385, 463

harvests, and judgement 372–78

hearing, and seeing 113, 131, 147, 224

heart 76

heaven 113, 316–17, 322; armies 492–93; destruction 524; and earth 525; rejoicing in heaven 476–80; silence in 210–13; as the sky 314; splitting 167–68, 487–88; voices, in the vision of the Lamb 355–56

Hebraisms 34, 36, 69–70, 132, 147, 183, 193, 319, 420, 478, 480

Hekate, and witchcraft 72–73

Hellenism: in Philadelphia 87; in Sardis 80

hidden manna 70

historicism 15

history, consummation 264–66

holy, used of God 88, 159–60, 571

holy of holies, as the model for the new Jerusalem 552

holy ones (ἅγιοι) 135

Holy Spirit: summons to the churches 63–64; symbolized by water 562

honour 558

horns: altar horns 236; little horn of Daniel (8.10) 318; symbol 132–33; ten horns of the dragon 317

horsemen *see* four horsemen

horses: and carriages 455; locusts likened to 231

human nature, corruption 477

hymns: angelic hymns with the Church in heaven 194; on the blessing of the saints after their perseverance

198–201; Exodus hymn 383–89; to God's sovereignty and creative power 125; hymn of celebration (15.3–4), structure 382; judgement doxologies 402–404; praise of the Lamb 136–41; song of praise in heaven (12.10–12) 326–29; sung by the Church in heaven 192–93; threnody over the fall of Babylon 425–26, 442–66; trisagion 122–23; use 109–111, 255

'I am' sayings 577
idolatry 587; dangers to Christian witness 486; dangers and the need to preserve the integrity of Revelation 584; and impurity 560; judgement in the first bowl-plague 400; refusal to repent of 242–43, 245; rejection 569; as the sin of Babylon 446; spiritual idolatry 6; as theme of the vision of the beasts 348
Ignatius 18
images, image created by the beast from the sea 347
immorality 243–44, 543
'in Jesus' 58
'in the spirit' 546
incense: and prayer 215–16; as prayers of God's people 135
individuals, response to God's justice 520
'inhabitants of the earth' 92
Irenaeus, on the symbolism of the four living creatures 121
Isaiah 44; as background to the introduction to the final scene 523; prophetic call 392
Israel: and the Church 187; elders within 117; Exodus from Egypt into the desert 330–33; idolatry, described as defilement 358; persecution, symbolized by the activities of the dragon 318; remnant, linked with the kings 'from the east' 408; royal house 36; sealing 182; and the sign of the woman 314–16; tribes *see* Israel, tribes; as Yahweh's betrothed 482; *see also* new Israel
Israel, tribes: census 188–89; listing 175; those who are sealed 184–85
ivory 455

jacinths 555
James, St (apostle) 93, 279
jasper 115, 547, 553, 555
Jehu (king of Israel) 478
Jeremiah 446; as background to the fall of Babylon 425, 461, 464; as background to the second trumpet-plague 221; tradition in connection with 'hidden manna' 70
Jerusalem: fall, and the dating of Revelation 2–3; holiness, compared with Babylon's sin 446; as the holy

city 273–74; possibly 'the beloved city' 514; possibly seen as the great city 281–82; as site of the grape harvest of judgement 377; Solomon's Temple, as model for the new Jerusalem 553–54; symbolic of the world 286
Jerusalem Council 63, 74, 77
Jerusalem Temple 3; desecration by Antiochus IV Epiphanes 341; destruction, and the dating of Revelation 255; housing of God's glory or presence 547; as symbol for heaven on earth 552; symbolized by the measurement of the heavenly temple 269–72; *see also* temples
Jesus Christ: as Alpha and Omega 573; Amen as title 479; ascension 320; authority, given to the conquerors 77–79; blood 36; bride, description compared with that of the harlot 458; bride and the new Jerusalem 536–37, 544–45; clothing, blood-soaked nature and its symbolism 491–92; crowns 489–90; crucifixion 282, 377; death 320; as defender 30; designation in the letters to the churches 33; doxology 35–36; eschatological discourse in the Gospels 146; eyes, compared to a blazing fire 489; faithfulness to 369; faithfulness and truth 488; the four horsemen as his emissaries 148; as God's agent in dispensing judgement 516; and God's glory 36–37; as holy and true, in the oracle to Philadelphia 87–88; Incarnation 413, 417; inheritance, shared with believers 542; inscribed name 489–91; as judge 76; judgement *see* Jesus Christ and judgement; knowledge of the churches 98; knowledge of the Philadelphians 89; lordship, over Sardis 80–81; love of the Laodicean church 100; as Messiah 12, 130–31, 133; millennial reign 505–511; name *see* Jesus Christ, name of; nature *see* Jesus Christ, nature of; as the new Moses 10, 119; person *see* Jesus Christ, person of; proclamation of God's word 27; revelation *see* Jesus Christ, revelation of; as the rider on a white horse 487–88; role as witness 585; as the root of David and the bright star 577; shepherding, as authority of the Messiah 320; as Son of man 53–55, 371; sonship to God contrasted with that of the pagan deities at Thyatira 72–73; sovereignty 58, 105, 289; as the speaker of the epilogue 582–83; speaks of himself directly 575; and the strong angel (10.1) 256–58; as the subject of revelation 27–28; symbolized by the child threatened

by the dragon 318–19; titles in the oracle to Laodicea 96–97; unexpected return of 411; union with 49–50; unity with God the Father 93, 541, 557, 564; victory, to be shared with the martyrs 102–103; voice 101, 113, 261–62, 266, 269; as the Word of God 492; *see also* Christology; crucifixion of Jesus Christ; God the Son; Lamb of God; parousia; Son of man figure
Jesus Christ and judgement 378; as symbolized by the two-edged sword 494; in the treading of the winepress 494–95
Jesus Christ, name of 95, 495–96; indicative of sovereignty 68–69; salvific power 71
Jesus Christ, nature of 39; seen as threefold 34–35; as understood by the Johannine community 4–5
Jesus Christ, person of 580; person, possibly questioned within the Ephesian church 60–61
Jesus Christ, revelation of 8; through signs in John's Gospel 313
Jewish Christians, as audience for Revelation 4–5
Jews: opposition to Christianity, in Smyrna 65–66; synagogues seen as infested by Satan 104
Jezebel 9, 46, 63, 70, 72–77, 84, 440, 572
Joachim of Fiore 502
Joel, imagery of locusts, as background to the locust plague 230
Joḥanan, R. 555
Johannine community 4–6, 16, 37; addressed in the epistolary form of Revelation 27; John's concern for 104; religious backgrounds, at Pergamum 71; as the seven churches 31–32, 52
Johannine literature: and Christology 5; dating, and Revelation 3; and Revelation 4
John 93; brotherhood with the churches 49–50; mystification 432–33; prophetic nature 58–59; as the speaker of the epilogue 583; *see also* authorship
John the Baptist 227, 408; imprisonment 502; witness 279
John, Gospel: Christology 5; pneumatology 12; and Revelation 4; signs as revelation of Christ 313; *see also* Revelation
Joseph, inclusion in the census of the tribes of Israel 188–89
Joshua the high priest 277
Judah (tribe), order in the census of the tribes of Israel 188
Judaism: apocalyptic in 7; influence on Revelation 9; in Laodicea 96; in Philadelphia 87, 90–91; polemic against in the oracle to the church in Philadelphia 94; in Sardis 80

Judas Iscariot 234, 512
judgement 7; angelic judgement, sign 311; associations with fire breathed from the mouth 240; of both righteous and unrighteous 291; by fire, and the fate of Babylon 450; divine judgement 9–11, 360–78; doxologies 402–404; and earthquakes 217–18; and harvests 372–78; imminent nature urged on the Ephesian church 62; natural disasters in the first three bowl-plagues 400–402; and redemption 25; represented by the two-edged sword 55; revelation in the small scroll 262–63; seven seals as symbolic of 145–46; and silence 212; symbolized by fire 216–17, 278; theme in the oracles 104; on those branded with the mark of the beast from the earth 365–66; and the trumpet-plagues 218–19, 244–45; upon Jezebel and her followers 74–76; _see also_ Jesus Christ and judgement; last judgement
Julius Caesar, possibly symbolic of the beast from the sea 338

keys: key of the bottomless pit 226; 'key of David', symbolism 88–89
kings: earthly kings 427, 558–59; kings 'from the east' 407; rallied by the three evil spirits 410
Korah, destruction 332–33

lake of fire 499
Lamb of God 131–34; blood of 197–98; breaking of the seven seals 145–56; bride, clothing 482–84; Christology 28; following of 358; investiture 112, 134–41; and judgement of God's opponents 367, 378; marriage feast 480–87; parodied in the beast from the sea 339–40; as the revelation of God's truth 378; significance 14; song 386; sovereignty 438; unity with God 200–202; vision 353–60; wrath 171; _see also_ Christology; Jesus Christ
lampstands: seven lampstands 57–58; symbolism 53, 55; _see also_ witnesses, two witnesses
Laodice (wife of Antiochus II) 95
Laodicea, church: Christ's parousia 83; oracle to 95–103; spiritual poverty 65
last judgement 515–19; cosmic portents in the breaking of the sixth seal 168
Last Supper 485
'let anyone with an ear listen' 343–44
letters _see_ oracles
Levi, inclusion in the census of the tribes of Israel 189
Leviathan 336, 345

lex talionis 447
lightning and thunder, symbolism, throne room vision 118–19
linen 454, 458; _see also_ clothing
lion, symbolism, used of God's voice 260
literary genre 2, 6–8
literary technique, use of numbers 32
liturgies: Church's liturgy reflected in the hymn of celebration (15.3–4) 382; liturgical formulae 402; prostration during heavenly liturgy 479; Revelation designed to be read in the liturgy 39; _see also_ worship
living creatures (four living creatures) 120–24, 156, 479
locust-demons, possibly seen as male warriors 206
locust-scorpions, as agents of agony 406
locusts: plague 227–34; as symbols of Apollo 234
Lord, applied to Christ 282
Lord's Day 51
Lord's Supper (eucharist) 102, 109, 585
Lot 446
love 100; theme in the oracles 104
love command, made upon the Ephesian church 61–62
lukewarmness, description of the Laodicean church 98
Lydia 72

magic arts 243–44, 348
Magog 234, 412, 476, 512
makarisms 484–85, 568, 573
manacles, the great manacle held by the angel at the binding of Satan 501
Manasseh (tribe) 175, 188–89
manna, representative of the presence of God with Israel 321
marana tha 585
Marduk (Babylonian god of order) 524
marriage, in Judaism 482
martyrologies, associated with Pergamum 69
martyrs 393, 478; cry 156–66; identification with the one hundred and forty-four thousand 186; share in Christ's victory 102–103
Mary Magdalene 52
Masoretic Text 9, 78
meals, sharing 101
measuring, concept 271
measuring rod, gold measuring rod used to measure the new Jerusalem 551
medical schools, Laodicea 96, 99–100
Megiddo 412
Mēn Carus (God of healing, Laodicea) 96
menorah, symbolism, in connection with the two witnesses 277
merchants: mourning over Babylon 452–54, 456–58; responsibility for the fall of Babylon 464

Merkavah ('chariot') mysticism 111
Messiah: authority 327; _see also_ Jesus Christ
metamorphoses, classical mythology 330
Michael (archangel) 29, 33, 213, 216, 258, 323–24; advocacy role on behalf of Israel 327; battle with the dragon 317
might, κράτος 140
millennium, the 502–504, 508, 580
Milton, John 323
Minos 147
miracles, performance by eschatological figures 346–47
modified idealism 16
morning star, symbolism 79
Moses 333; song 386; and the two witnesses 275, 278–80
mountains: blazing mountain of the second trumpet-plague 220–21; symbolism 546; as kingdoms 435
mourners, over Babylon 461
mourning 451
murder 243–44, 543
music: absence in Revelation 136; cessation, at the fall of Babylon 463
myrrh 455
mystery: concept, and the hidden purposes of God 265–66; used of the woman mounted on the beast 431

nakedness, and clothing 411–12
names, use 431
naming, Lamb's name placed on the foreheads of the faithful 355
nations 558–59, 563; concept 387; as God's opponents 494, 512; pilgrimage to the new Jerusalem 558; responsibility for the fall of Babylon 465
Nebuchadnezzar 124
Nebuchadrezzar 347–48, 362; tells Daniel of the mystery of his dream 431
Nero _redivivus_ 338, 408, 429, 436
Nero (Roman emperor) 59, 124, 152, 436; and the dating of Revelation 2–4; famine during the reign of 154; and the number six hundred and sixty-six 352; patron deity Apollo 234; persecution of the saints 166; possibly symbolic of the beast from the sea 338
new advent _see_ parousia
new covenant 533–39; as the new Jerusalem 536; prophecy 522
new creation 539–40; and eschatology 579; introduction 522–25
new Israel: Gentiles' incorporation 538; relationship with God 13
new Jerusalem 6, 17, 94, 522–23, 535–36, 544–56, 579; and the bride of Christ 544–45; construction materials 553–55; entry into 19;

eternal dimension 128; great street 555–56; illumination 557–59, 565–66; measurement 550–51, 579; and the millennium 580; new relationships within 561–66; ordering and beauty of 551–53; replaces Babylon 525; temple 551–52, 580; those outside the gates 574–75, 580; twelve foundation stones 549–50; twelve foundations, gems 554–55; twelve gates 530, 548–49, 554–55, 559; walls 547–48, 552–54

new life 533–34, 539–44

new temple 556–61

New Testament, apocalyptic in 7

new testimony 570–78

Nicolaitans 60–63, 75–76, 79; presence at Pergamum 69–70; presence at Thyatira 74

night, absence in the new Jerusalem 559–60

Nineveh, harlotry 427

non-Christians 30

numbers: number five 229; number four 175, 236; number one hundred and forty-four thousand 184–88, 270, 354–55, 438; number one-tenth 286; number one-third 220; number seven 31, 58, 119, 133, 169, 210, 213, 261, 317, 351, 436–37, 474–75; number six hundred and sixty-six 350–53; number ten 66; number three 32; number twenty-four 116–17, 549; number two hundred million 239; symbolism 14, 31–32, 502

numerical speculation 7

oath-taking, oath of the strong angel 263–64

Oholibah 440

oil 153

Old Testament: angels 28–29; apocalyptic in 7; banquets, theme 485; and the lament over Babylon 443–44; legal requirement of two witnesses 276; 'new song', used of giving praise to God 356; in Revelation 9–10, 163; rhetorical questions in 339; symbolism of the dragon 317; symbolism in relation to apocalypticism 14; testimonies to Jesus Christ's parousia 37; use of images from 36

olive oil 455

olive trees, symbolism, in connection with the two witnesses 277

Omega 26, 38, 541, 573, 580

onyx 555

'open door', symbolism 89–91

Ophitism 77

oracles 7; closing formulae 63–64, 67, 103; introductory formulae 60

Otho 152, 338, 436

pain, as punishment for sin 75

palm fronds, symbolism 191–92

papyrus, as writing material 108

Paradise: and the new Jerusalem 561–63; vision 560–61

Paradise Lost (Milton) 323

parchment 68

parody 181

paronomasia 293

parousia 37–40, 62, 503, 534, 566–70, 572–73, 585–87; a cause for joy in the Thyatiran church 77; likened to the arrival of a thief 82–83; as the new advent 572–73; and the Philadelphian church 92–93; in table fellowship with the Laodiceans 101–102; *see also* Jesus Christ

Parthia: cavalry horses 241; and the kings 'from the east' 408; Roman fear of not shared by Palestinian Jewish-Christians 232; seen as symbolized by the first horseman of the Apocalypse 150–51

Patmos 50–51, 415

Paul, St (apostle): on Christ's sovereignty 68; epistles, closings possibly influence the closing of Revelation 581; evangelistic work at Ephesus 59; and false apostles 61; missionary work at Smyrna 65; on renewal 524; similarities between Christology of Paul and John 97; visions 111; witness 279

pearls 555

Pella, flight to 321

'people of the world' 283

Pergamum 95; altar of Zeus 241; church 60; Christ's parousia 83; faithfulness 45–46; false teaching at 62–63; oracle to 67–71, 489

persecution: as possible theme 2–4; questioned as having taken place under Domitian 142

perseverance 368

Peter (Cephas), St (apostle) 93; on the name of Jesus 68–69; witness 279

Pharaoh: judgement, likened to that of the Antichrist 400; *see also* Exodus

Philadelphia, church: oracle to 86–95; spiritual situation 66

phylacteries 349

pillars, symbolism 93–94

plagues 9, 19; and the judgement of Babylon 449–50; locusts 227–34; *see also* bowl-plagues; Egypt, plagues

pneumatology 12, 26, 39

political power, theology 18

Polycarp of Smyrna 66, 87

Pompey (Roman general) 317

poverty 65

power, δύναμις 139; God's judgement on its misuse proclaimed 363–65; theology 194–95

powers, corrupt powers symbolized as a prostitute 424

prayers: and incense 215–16; thanksgiving 290

pre-gnosticism 4

precious stones, symbolism of God's majesty 115

predestination, conditional predestination 86, 343

pregnant woman, as personification of the Church 318–20

preterism 15

primeval history, Satan's role 324–25, 334

Priscilla 59

prophecy 6, 586; Christians as prophets 487; cognates 254; conflict and assessment 583–84; as proclamation rather than prediction, in the first of the seven prophecies 534; in Revelation 7–8; spirit, within the churches 578; and witness 275–76

prophetic words, sealing 570

prophets 266; the beast from the earth as the false prophet 409; blood, and the fall of Babylon 465–66; Christian prophets, as Christ's servants 27; false prophet, destruction 498–99; as heavenly councillors 111; and saints 292, 403; spirits of 567–68

prostration 124, 134; role in heavenly worship 479

pseudonymity, not found in Revelation 7

Ptolemy Philadelphus 349

Pythagorean arithmetic, and the number six hundred and sixty-six 351

Qumran, banquets, theme 485

Qumran community: association with tribe of Judah 188; elders within 117

Qumran scrolls, apocalyptic in 7

Raguel 33, 213

rainbows, symbolism 115, 257

ransoming 359

Raphael 33, 213

reading, as form of address for Revelation 26

recapitulation 19, 513, 518, 544

Red Sea, Jewish exegetical tradition 384

redeemed, vision of the redeemed 311

redemption 359; through judgement 25

reed of measurement 271

'remaining dead' 508

remembrance 447

Remiel 33, 213

repentance: demanded of the Ephesian church 61–62; lack of 242–45

resurrection: first resurrection 508–510; hope 18–19

Reuben (tribe), order in the census of the tribes of Israel 188

Revelation: as an apocalypse 586; angelology 29–30; Chapter 12, sources 312; dating 2–3, 255, 336; epilogue 581–87; epistolary ending 585–86; epistolary style 46; interpretation 15–16; interpretation of symbolism 14; and John's Gospel, as courtroom drama 30; literary form, as an epistle 26–27; literary style 46; purpose of warnings about preserving the integrity of Revelation 583–84; reading in public worship 583, 585; relevance 16–19; structure 19–20, 26, 47–48; subscription 582; textual considerations 1–2

reverence, τιμή 139

reward 291–92

riches, πλοῦτος 139

rider on the white horse 471–72, 487–88

righteousness 404

ritual impurity 560

rivers: drying up 407–408; floodwaters metaphor 331–33

robes *see* clothing

Roma aeterna 479

Roman authorities, seen as infested by Satan 104

Roman emperors: likened to the seven heads of the beast on which the woman was sitting 436; symbolized as one of the heads of the beast from the sea 337–38

Roman Empire, symbolized as the beast from the sea 336

Rome 3; deification 6; embodiment of opposition to God 66; as the new Babylon 364; possibly symbolized as the throne of the beast from the earth 406; as Satan's residence 68; seven hills, likened to the seven heads of the beast on which the woman was seated 435; symbolism 281, 286, 293; and the symbolism of the dragon 317; symbolized by Babylon 407; trumpet playing at festivals 463; wealth 445

sackcloth 276

sacramentalism, the boulder thrown into the sea at the fall of Babylon 462

sacraments 15

sacred tetragrammaton (YHWH), as the name of Christ 490

saints: blood, and the fall of Babylon 465–66; censing 213–18; character of those who rule with Christ 506–508; clothing, white clothing 493–94; designation for Christians 581; fear of God 480; God's protection of 199–201; as holy ones 368; marking with the divine name 565; number completed 165–66; one hundred and forty-four

thousand saints seen as the worshippers in the heavenly temple 270; persecution 196, 198; perseverance, results in heavenly blessings 198–201; prayers, hearing by God 211; priesthood and kingship 510–11; and prophets 292, 403; reign with Christ 475; righteous deeds 483; sealing 9, 181, 548; victory 328; worship, in the new Jerusalem, as sign of eschatological blessings 564

salvation 10, 326–27; symbolized in the washing of robes 573–74

Samael 324

sand, concept 513

sapphire 555

Saraqa'el 33

Sardis: church *see* Sardis, church; destruction by earthquake 87

Sardis, church 95, 97; commendation for not staining their clothes 573; oracle to 80–87

Sariel 213

Satan 10; as accuser 327; angels of 28–29; anger 329; 'Assembly of', used of Judaism in Philadelphia 90–91; attempted destruction of the Church likened to the spewing forth of floodwaters 332; binding 475, 500–505; classified as a murderer 543; deep things 76; descent, symbolized in the activities of the dragon 318; destruction 476, 511–15; dwelling place 226; dwellings in Rome and Pergamum 68–69; as a fallen star 225; identification as the angel of the abyss questioned 234; persecution of the Church 66; place in heaven and identification with the dragon 324; seen as within the synagogues and Roman power 104; star angel 222; as the ultimate source of evil 378

scales, symbolism 153

scorpions 228–29; used of the description of the locusts 232–33

scrolls: sealed scroll of the throne room vision, as symbolic of God's salvific plan 126–31; the small scroll 247, 258–59, 262–63, 266–67, 295–96; use 108

sea 120, 260, 401; crystal sea 384–85; destruction of one-third of the sea 220–21; drying up 539; removal 524; sea of glass, symbolism 119–20; symbolism 335, 345, 518

Sea of Reeds, drying up 407

seafarers, mourning over Babylon 453–54, 458–59

sealing 355

'sealing of the saints' 9, 181, 548; sealing up of prophetic words 570

seals, breaking 145–73, 209, 211, 244, 431

secular authority, symbolized by the beast from the sea 337

seeing and hearing 113

Seleucus I, foundation of Thyatira 72

Septuagint 9, 78

Seraiah 461

serpent, and the devil 324–25

service, saints' worship of God 198–99

seven churches: angels 29, 47, 58, 575–77; congregations 5; and cosmology 11; designation of Christ in the letters to 33; geographical relationship 52; as the Johannine community 31–32; lampstands 53, 55; oracles *see* seven churches, oracles

seven churches, oracles 46–49, 59–103; language of conquest found also in the second prophecy 541–42; opening formula 584; theological themes 104–105

seven prophecies 522, 526–80

Severus 59

Shekinah 557

shepherding 200–201, 319–20, 494

sickles, as carried by the Son of man figure 372, 374

sickness, as punishment for sin 74

sight, and hearing 131, 147, 224; as introduction to vision narratives 126; and theophanies 314

signs 275–88, 311, 321–26, 329–44, 360–78, 382

silence, in heaven 210–13

silk 454

Simeon 175, 319

sin: emancipation from 35–36; punishment for 74–75

Sinai, theophany 414, 416

sky, heaven as 314

slaves: in the lament over Babylon 455–56; sealing 183

smoke: from the abyss 227; as evidence of judgement 367; symbolism 392, 478–79

Smyrna: church 60, 69; economic depression possibly reflected in the first two bowl-plagues 402; oracle to 64–67, 87

Sodom 240, 366, 478, 558

symbolism 281–82

Son of God, exaltation 53

Son of man figure 12, 53–55, 371, 580; description linked to the oracles to the seven churches 48; involvement in the harvests of judgement 373–75, 377–78; subordination to God 372; *see also* Jesus Christ

sonship, concept 319

sorcery 465, 543

speaking, speaking without deceit 359

'spiralling technique' 110

spirits: seven spirits 32–34, 80–81; three evil spirits, released from the sixth bowl-plague 409–410

stars: falling star associated with the third trumpet plague 221–22; falling stars 167; seven stars 80–81; as supernatural beings or angels 225–26; symbolism 57–58; symbolism for the angels of the churches 53, 55; twelve stars and the sign of the woman 315

steadfastness 50, 104–105

storm-theophanies 414

strong angel 129, 484; oath 263–66; as representative of Christ 256–58, 266–67; throwing a boulder into the sea at the fall of Babylon 462; voice and stature 260–61; *see also* angels

Succoth (Feast of Booths or Tabernacles) 192–93, 199

sulphur 366

sun: and angels 496–97; and the emptying of the fourth bowl-plague 404–405

swords: broad swords, ῥομφαία 155; as symbols of authority 152; two-edged sword 47, 55, 68, 489, 494

symbols and symbolism 13–15, 47, 163

'synagogue of Satan' 66

tabernacle 389–90, 547

Tabernacles, Feast of 562

table fellowship, Christ's parousia in connection with the Laodiceans 101–102

tails, symbolism 318

talents 416

teeth, simile 232

temples: heavenly temple 93–94, 199, 254, 269–74, 293, 372, 389–90, 392; *see also* Jerusalem Temple

testimonies 37; in Revelation 10–13

'testing' 92

theology 2; and chronology 521

thieving 243–44

'thousand years' 473

throne room vision 28–29, 33, 110–11, 113–42, 164

thrones 506, 516; θρόνος 68

thunder, metaphor 147

thunder claps 261–63, 481

Thyatira 54, 95; church *see* Thyatira, church; trade guilds 350

Thyatira, church: false teaching at 62–63; and Jezebel 440, 572; oracle to 71–80, 577; pre-gnostic teaching at 69

Tiamat (Babylonian figure of chaos) 524

Tiberius Caesar 80, 87, 95, 436

time 256, 296; concept of eternity 367–68; and eschatology 245; and eternity 212–13; five months 229; and judgement 31; in relation to the suffering of the saints 274; theology

48; 'time, times and half a time' 331; as time of waiting before the consummation of history 264; and the two witnesses 276; used of restrictive duration in connection with martyrdom 282, 284

'time of ordeal' 91–92

Timothy 59

Tiridates 124

Titus 436; and the fall of Jerusalem 3; wearing of silk 454

topaz 555

torches, seven blazing torches 119

torment 449; everlasting torment of those who worship the beast 366–67, 379

trade, commercial trade 445

trade goods, enumeration in the lament over Babylon 454–56

trampling, concept 274

transfiguration 55–56

tree of life 64, 562–63

trees, targumic interpretation as people 180

'true', used of God 159–60

trumpet-plagues 203–245, 295, 398; symbolism of blood in 219

trumpeters 463

trumpets 19; seventh trumpet 244, 255, 265, 287–88; use in warfare 210, 214

truth, used in relation to Christ 488

twenty-four elders 116–18, 130, 479; and the four living creatures 123–24; holding the harps and bowls for worship 134–35; praise of the Lamb 135–38; proclamation of God's sovereignty 289–93

Tyre: Ezekiel's lament over 450, 457; judgement on 445; as a prostitute 427

uncleanness 430–31

universe, threefold division 130

Uriel 29, 33, 213

vegetation, destruction 220

vengeance 160–64

Vespasian (Roman emperor) 3–4, 152, 436; coinage 427; famine during the reign of 154; wearing of silk 454; will 128

Vesuvius, eruption 220

vices, catalogue 543–44, 574

Victorinus of Pettau 19, 33, 211

victors, as the faithful members of the Church 384–85

vines, symbolic of the people of God 376

Virgin Mary, and the sign of the woman 314–15

visionary experiences, 'being carried away in the spirit' 428

visions 239; interpretation generally lacking in Revelation 7; seven visions 468–521

Vitellius 152, 338, 436

voice, concept 52–53

voices: God's voice commissioning the angel to proclaim the bowl-plagues 400; heavenly voice of the seventh sign 369; heavenly voices as response to the sounding of the seventh trumpet 288–89; heaven's voices, in the vision of the Lamb 355–56; loud voice of the song of praise in heaven (12.10–12) 326; voice from the heavenly altar 235–36, 404; voice of the strong angel 260–62; voice from the throne (19.5) 480; voices of God and Christ 261–62, 266, 269

Vologeses (Parthian general) 150

walking, as symbolism for faithful discipleship 84–85

war: on earth, sign 311, 329–35; in heaven, sign 311, 321–26

warrior-Messiah 487–96

Watchers, saga (*1 Enoch*) 318

water: living water 201, 541; spring waters polluted in the third trumpet-plague 222–23; water of life 562–63, 578

water supplies, Laodicea 96, 98

'waters' 439–40

waters, 'rushing waters', metaphor 481

wealth 445

wedding feasts, eschatological wedding feasts 485

wheat, price 153

wheels, within Merkavah mysticism 111

white clothing 164–65, 191; of the saints 197, 493–94; symbolism 99–100; of the twenty-four elders 118; *see also* clothing

white stone 70–71

'whole world', metaphor 339, 342

whore, scarlet whore likened to the dragon 318

wilderness: concept 321; symbolism 330–31, 428

wills 128

winds: four winds of heaven 179–81; *see also* demonic winds

wine 153, 455; and blood 432

wings, living creatures 122

Wisdom 53; σοφία 139

witness: concept 30; Jesus Christ as the faithful and true witness 96–97

witnesses, two witnesses 254–55, 275–76; symbolism of lampstands 277

woes 225; first woe 225–35; second woe 235–44; third woe 287

woman: as symbol of Babylon 426–27; *see also* woman pursued into the wilderness; woman seated on the beast woman pursued into the wilderness 311–16, 330; descendants 333–34

woman seated on the beast 424–25, 428–33; interpretation of the vision 433–42

women: bride of the Lamb, clothing 482–84; role in the early Church 73

wood, citrus wood 454

wool trade, at Laodicea 95

world 17–18; as opposition to God 289; population, as affected by God's judgement, in the breaking of the sixth seal 169–70

wormwood (Apsinth) 205–206, 222–23

worship: emperor worship 125; human obeisance 486; as offered to God 362; as prostration 124, 134; saints' worship of God described as service 198–99; within the throne room vision 117

wrath 10, 291; wine of God's wrath 365–66

writing, commands to write 540

Xerxes, army, food consumption 153

YHWH (sacred tetragrammaton), as the name of Christ 490

Zechariah: as background to the breaking of the seven seals 146; horsemen imagery 147–48; and the symbolism of the olive trees and lampstands 277; and the trumpet-plagues 220

Zerubbabel 277

Zeus 68

ziggurats 552

Zion 353–54

Zoroastrianism, *fravashis* 58

Index of Modern Authors

Aalen, S. 37, 124, 139
Allo, E.-B. 314, 329
Aune, D. E. 1–2, 9, 19, 30–31, 49–50,
  67, 73, 79–82, 84, 86, 88, 93, 97,
  100–101, 111–13, 116–19, 121–22,
  127–28, 130, 132, 134–35, 138–39,
  141, 145, 147, 149, 151–55, 157,
  159–61, 163, 165–68, 171, 175,
  178, 181–84, 186, 188, 190, 192–94,
  196, 198, 204, 206, 210–18, 220,
  223–25, 229–32, 238–42, 247–55,
  260–64, 266–75, 277–82, 284–86,
  288–89, 292–94, 302–306, 308–
  309, 311–14, 316, 319–21, 323–24,
  326–27, 329–30, 334–36, 338–40,
  342–45, 349–52, 354–59, 361–71,
  375–77, 381–83, 385–87, 389,
  391–92, 396–97, 399–400,
  402–404, 406, 408, 410–11,
  413–14, 420–27, 430–37, 439–42,
  445–47, 449–50, 452, 454–55,
  457–60, 462–64, 466, 470–72,
  474–81, 484–86, 488–89, 491–96,
  499–500, 507–509, 511–14, 516–19,
  522–24, 528–30, 532–38, 540,
  542–47, 549–51, 553, 555–56, 560,
  563–64, 566–67, 569, 572, 574,
  576, 578, 580–83, 586

Barker, M. 20, 133, 264, 279, 316,
  336, 356, 408, 414, 426, 442,
  465
Barr, D. L. 244
Barrett, C. K. 9
Bartels, K. H. 35
Bauckham, R. J. 4, 6, 9, 29, 126, 129,
  131, 133, 156, 165, 186, 189–90,
  197–98, 211, 218, 257, 259, 262,
  266–67, 270, 272–75, 287, 294–95,
  317, 335, 342, 346, 350–52, 354,
  356, 358–59, 372–74, 377–78,
  393–94, 408, 411, 416–17, 434, 437,
  439, 448, 453–54, 456, 465–67,
  486, 490, 498, 502–503, 505–506,
  513, 517–18, 523–24, 533, 553, 558,
  563–64, 568–71, 577–78, 583–84
Beale, G. K. 1, 6, 9–10, 15–16, 19,
  48, 75, 94, 97–98, 102, 107, 112,
  115–16, 118, 124–26, 128–29,
  138–41, 150, 156–58, 166–68, 172,
  179–82, 184, 186, 196, 198–99,
  201, 211–13, 215, 217, 219–20, 222,
  224, 227–28, 230–43, 245, 257–70,
  272–76, 278–79, 281–88, 292–93,
  295, 311–12, 316, 318, 321–22, 327,
  331–36, 340–41, 343, 345–55,
  358–60, 362, 364, 366, 368–72,
  374–75, 378, 381, 383–92, 396,
  399–403, 405–414, 416, 427,
  429–35, 437–38, 440–41, 443–48,
  451–54, 457–60, 462–66, 475–77,
  479–500, 502, 504–507, 509–518,
  520–22, 524–25, 533–34, 536–42,
  544–49, 551–58, 560–68, 570–73,
  575, 577–80, 583–84, 586
Beare, W. 110
Beasley-Murray, G. R. 2, 27, 31–33,
  35, 52–55, 58, 60, 64, 67, 75, 77, 79,
  83, 94, 96, 99, 102–103, 110, 113,
  116–17, 119–20, 125–28, 141, 150,
  155, 164, 168, 179, 181, 188, 190,
  192, 196, 198, 211, 219, 227, 234,
  244, 254, 256, 258, 262, 268, 275,
  286, 288, 295, 317, 326, 328, 340,
  345, 353–55, 359, 368, 379, 382,
  391–93, 399, 401, 408, 411, 415,
  434, 437, 453, 466, 480, 485, 487,
  490–92, 495, 497, 500, 502,
  510–12, 518–19, 525, 533, 539,
  541, 543, 548, 561–62, 566, 572,
  575, 577, 585, 587
Beck, H. 151
Beckwith, I. T. 1–3, 32–33, 45–47,
  51, 55–57, 66, 70–71, 75, 82, 89,
  92, 100, 102, 112–13, 116–18, 120,
  122–24, 126–27, 129–31, 138, 140,
  146, 150–51, 153–54, 158, 160–61,
  165, 167, 186, 190, 214–17, 222,
  225, 229, 237, 239, 241, 254–55,
  258, 265, 269, 272–73, 280, 287–88,
  292, 301, 310, 314–15, 329–31,
  333–34, 338, 343, 349, 352, 354,
  361, 366, 372–73, 376, 385–86,
  388–89, 392, 398, 408, 412, 428,
  435–37, 445–46, 448, 454, 456,
  464–65, 476, 480, 484, 486–88,
  491, 495, 503–504, 508, 513, 517,
  519, 534, 541, 548, 559, 562,
  576–77
Behm, J. 36

Bell, A. A. 234
Bengel, J. A. 15, 69, 119, 155, 271,
  389, 453, 455–56
Benson, E. W. 109
Bertram, G. 101
Betz, O. 125
Bietenhard, H. 30, 35, 90, 135, 325,
  388
Black, C. C. 4
Black, M. 154
Blount, B. K. 157
Bøe, S. 496, 513
Boring, M. E. 2, 14, 30, 36, 49, 56, 63,
  65, 104–105, 114, 133, 149, 151,
  160, 162–63, 178, 185, 198, 215,
  218, 253, 270, 275, 295, 312, 320,
  368, 371, 376–79, 417, 435, 440,
  448, 465, 476, 480, 486–87, 491,
  502–503, 512, 515, 523, 535, 543,
  553, 559, 579
Bornkamm, G. 116, 265, 377
Bousset, W. 275, 365
Bowker, J. 33
Bowman, J. W. 110
Boxall, I. 10, 19, 142, 195, 211, 314,
  426, 429, 466, 495, 518, 551
Braumann, G. 140
Brewer, R. R. 20, 110
Brown, C. 31, 151, 160, 359, 387, 574
Brown, R. E. 4–5, 35, 116–17, 166,
  211, 314, 427, 437
Bruce, F. F. 2, 33, 388, 487, 578
Burton, E. de W. 152
Büschel, F. 101

Caird, G. B. 9, 16, 18, 30–31, 33, 37,
  51, 54, 58, 63, 68, 74, 78–79, 82,
  86, 89, 101–103, 119, 125, 130–31,
  134, 137–38, 141, 148–49, 151,
  161, 164, 179, 185–86, 190, 198,
  211, 216, 222, 227, 237, 241, 259,
  262–64, 270, 281–82, 292, 296,
  323–24, 326–27, 337, 341, 343, 345,
  349, 354, 357–59, 368, 384, 392,
  405–406, 411, 415, 426, 433, 435,
  437, 443, 445–46, 448–49, 452,
  460–62, 466, 476, 486–87, 491,
  495, 506–509, 512, 514, 524, 534,
  548, 552, 557, 560, 562, 568–69,
  572, 574, 576, 583

Carrell, P. R. 28, 30, 54
Charles, R. H. 1, 4, 9, 12, 19, 26–27,
  32, 34, 36, 38, 45, 47–48, 51–52,
  56–58, 61, 63, 68–71, 74, 77–79,
  81, 83, 85, 90, 93, 100, 102–103,
  114–16, 118, 120–21, 124–27, 129,
  133, 141, 146–47, 150, 153–54,
  158–59, 161, 164, 166–69, 171,
  178, 180, 185, 188, 193, 196, 198,
  206–208, 211, 213, 215–16, 222,
  225, 229, 231, 233, 236, 250, 252,
  254, 258, 261, 264–65, 269, 273,
  277, 281, 285, 287–88, 292, 301,
  305, 309, 312, 319, 322, 326–27,
  330–31, 335, 339, 341, 343–44,
  347–52, 354, 359, 361, 368, 375,
  377, 381, 385, 389, 392, 396–98,
  403–404, 406, 411, 414, 420–24,
  436–37, 439, 446, 448–49, 456,
  460, 464, 471, 473, 478–80,
  482–83, 491, 493–95, 508, 510, 514,
  516–17, 522, 523, 528–29, 532,
  534, 548, 554, 559–60, 562, 567,
  569, 571–72, 575, 578, 581–83
Charlesworth, J. 52–53
Collins, A. Y. 11, 163, 317, 466
Conzelmann, H. 124
Court, J. M. 2, 15, 155, 296
Cullmann, O. 264, 328, 491, 525
Culpepper, R. A. 4

Dansk, E. 20
Delling, G. 20, 31, 35
DeSilva, D. A. 31
Dodd, C. H. 83, 160–61, 170
Duff, P. B. 72, 314, 424, 426, 429, 483
Dunn, J. D. G. 54, 371

Efird, J. M. 218
Ellul, J. 15, 47, 148–49, 466, 521, 557
Esser, H.-H. 124
Ewing, W. 355

Farrar, F. W. 15
Farrer, A. M. 314
Fee, G. D. 136
Feuillet, A. 8
Filho, J. A. 20
Filson, F. V. 315
Finkenrath, G. 26
Fiorenza, E. S. 4, 10, 12, 19, 62, 77,
  105, 150, 162, 199, 202, 245, 259,
  289, 339, 354, 393, 445, 466, 477,
  481, 508, 511, 525, 536, 587
Foerster, W. 123
Ford, J. M. 184
Frend, W. H. C. 73, 77, 338

Garrow, A. 2
Giblin, C. H. 254, 284, 509
Gilbertson, M. 579
Glasson, T. F. 10, 515
Goranson, S. 532
Green, E. M. B. 98
Guhrt, J. 128, 537
Guthrie, D. 12, 15, 110, 161, 552

Hagner, D. A. 577
Hahn, H.-C. 31, 171
Hanson, A. T. 170, 377
Hauck, F. 560
Hays, R. B. 161–62
Hemer, C. J. 51–52, 62, 70–71,
  78–81, 83–84, 87, 92–93, 95–96,
  98, 100, 154, 229, 350
Hendriksen, W. 16, 86, 89–90, 115,
  121–22, 134, 149, 186, 215, 233,
  235, 245, 258, 270, 278, 281, 294,
  317, 329, 335, 353–54, 367–68, 371,
  374, 406, 413–14, 426, 437, 442,
  448, 465, 476, 480, 485, 504,
  507–508, 519, 572
Hengel, M. 3, 352
Hennecke, E. 167
Henten, J. W. van 90
Hill, D. 8, 576
Hillyer, N. 218, 555
Hort, F. J. A. 74
Hughes, P. E. 16, 56, 79, 125, 130,
  136, 150–51, 180, 186, 212, 218,
  227, 245, 261–62, 270, 272, 278,
  282, 286, 323, 334–35, 337, 349,
  352–53, 368, 373, 404, 406, 414–15,
  437, 448, 465, 467, 476, 480–81,
  483–85, 490, 502, 505–506, 514,
  518, 536, 556, 564, 583

Jeremias, J. 234
Johnston, G. 37

Kelly, W. 474, 582
Kiddle, M. 2–3, 20, 48, 62, 70, 83, 87,
  93, 102, 116, 120, 133, 150, 154,
  161, 169, 179, 186, 236, 245, 261,
  269, 278, 286, 311, 316, 331–32,
  334–35, 345, 354–55, 357, 369–71,
  374, 384, 405–406, 415, 432–33,
  435, 437, 439, 477, 480, 484, 486,
  492, 518, 536, 549, 552–53, 559,
  572, 576, 578, 2109
Kirby, J. T. 27, 48, 57–58
Kitto, H. D. F. 110
Klauck, H.-J. 338, 436
Knight, J. 2, 16, 115, 118, 122–23,
  137, 161, 184, 197, 223, 287–88,
  315, 329, 337, 352, 374, 383, 401,
  410, 414, 430, 437, 461, 495, 505,
  518, 546, 555, 567, 572
Kruse, C. G. 562

Ladd, G. E. A. 280, 315–16,
  354
Läuchli, S. 20, 109
Lieu, J. M. 110
Lindars, B. 10, 37
Link, H.-G. 359

McGuckin, J. A. 316
McKelvey, R. J. 272, 503–504, 511,
  513, 524, 544, 557
Marshall, I. H. 72, 555
Martin, R. P. 164, 525, 543
Mathewson, D. 10, 579

Maurice, F. D. 59, 150, 429, 456, 505,
  557
Mazzaferri, F. D. 192, 259
Mealy, J. W. 502, 512, 519
Metzger, B. M. 1, 45, 107–108, 144,
  177, 204, 206–209, 248–50, 253,
  303–306, 308–310, 381, 396, 398,
  420–23, 470–72, 528–29, 532,
  581–82
Michaelis, W. 84, 140
Michaels, J. R. 25, 73, 76–77, 123,
  141, 150, 158, 161–62, 171, 180,
  211, 254, 259, 282, 320–21, 329,
  334, 353, 404, 433, 439, 465, 484,
  508, 518, 520, 536, 559, 582
Michel, O. 72, 151, 157, 344, 439
Millard, A. R. 272
Milligan, W. 15, 20, 37, 61, 79, 86,
  124, 148–49, 151, 157, 180, 187,
  189, 192, 198, 213, 215, 245, 258,
  264, 278, 281, 296, 314, 329, 336,
  342, 354, 356, 358, 368, 378,
  383–84, 408, 414, 417, 426, 437–38,
  440, 465, 476, 478, 504–505, 516,
  579
Minear, P. S. 524
Moffatt, J. 2, 114, 116, 119, 124, 136,
  141, 150, 173, 210, 222, 227,
  239–40, 244, 262, 274, 282, 318,
  338, 343, 349, 357, 390, 414, 437,
  439, 478, 480, 495, 505, 511, 519,
  525, 552, 576
Morris, L. L. 33, 35, 54, 69, 73, 79,
  81, 92, 101, 150, 156, 424, 545
Moule, C. F. D. 8, 216, 322, 330, 463,
  485–86, 585
Mounce 6, 19, 32–33, 36, 38, 46, 50,
  54, 56, 64–65, 67–68, 71, 73–74,
  77–79, 82, 84–87, 91–93, 95,
  99–102, 105, 113–14, 116, 120–25,
  128, 132–33, 135, 137, 146, 149,
  151–52, 158–59, 167, 169, 173, 177,
  179, 181, 186, 189–91, 194, 196,
  198, 200–201, 210–12, 215–16,
  219–21, 223–24, 227–29, 231–33,
  235–37, 239, 241, 253, 256,
  258–65, 267–70, 272–78, 280–81,
  286, 288–89, 292–93, 296, 310,
  312, 314–15, 317–18, 320, 322,
  324, 327–29, 331–32, 335–37, 339,
  341–50, 354–55, 357, 360–61,
  363, 365–66, 368, 370, 374–77,
  382–83, 387–88, 390–93, 401–402,
  404–407, 409, 412–15, 417,
  424–27, 429–31, 434, 437, 440, 442,
  444, 446, 448–51, 454–56, 458–61,
  463–66, 475–78, 480–81, 483, 485,
  487–88, 490, 493–96, 498–501,
  503, 506–508, 511–12, 514–20,
  523–24, 534–36, 539–40, 545,
  547–48, 551, 554–55, 559, 562,
  565, 572, 574, 577, 582
Moyise, S. 2, 161
Müller, H.-P. 112, 129

O'Rourke, J. J. 20

Paulien, J. 10
Peake, A. S. 2, 33–34, 51, 76, 186, 189, 486
Poirier, J. C. 150
Poole, M. 78
Pope, M. H. 32
Prévost, J.-P. 20
Prigent, P. 10, 288, 312–13, 316, 321, 329, 334–36, 338, 343, 345–46, 351, 355, 360–61, 367–68, 370, 372–73, 382–83, 385, 389–91, 393, 404–408, 411, 413, 415, 426, 428–29, 432–36, 438–39, 443–45, 448, 453–54, 456–57, 462–63, 467, 475, 477–78, 482–85, 489–90, 492, 494–95, 497–501, 504, 507, 510–11, 513, 515–19, 521, 524, 533–34, 536–37, 539–50, 552–53, 555, 560, 564, 566, 569, 571, 573–75, 578–79, 584–85
Procksch, O. 35
Provan, I. W. 465

Quell, G. 123

Ramsay, W. M. 48, 50, 52, 58–59, 65, 67, 71–72, 74, 80–81, 84, 87, 89, 95–96, 100, 150, 348, 350
Rengstorf, K. H. 357
Resseguie, J. L. 32, 89, 95
Rissi, M. 150
Rist, M. 2, 113, 245, 311, 374, 388, 427, 490, 506, 559, 574
Robinson, J. A. T. 2, 4, 16, 18, 210, 377, 436, 585
Roller, O. 127
Roloff, J. 2, 4, 7, 14, 260–61, 264, 268–69, 276, 280, 288, 312, 326, 336, 338, 341, 343, 346, 363–65, 375, 377, 391–92, 401, 404, 408–409, 429, 432, 440, 465, 476, 483, 485, 491, 496, 503–504, 507, 512–13, 519, 521, 533–34, 536, 539, 543, 548, 566, 575, 583–84
Rowland, C. C. 7, 12, 111, 161
Rudolph, K. 77
Rudwick, M. J. S. 98
Ruiz, J.-P. 467

Schlier, H. 77, 96, 196
Schmitz, E. D. 31

Schneider, J. 139, 183, 193
Scholem, G. G. 111
Schultz, H. 354
Schwarz, H. 502
Seebass, H. 160, 387
Shepherd, M. H. 20, 109, 255, 316, 585
Silberman, L. H. 97
Slater, T. B. 142, 438, 496
Smalley, S. S. 1–5, 8, 11–13, 15, 19–20, 25, 27–28, 31, 34–38, 47, 49, 52–53, 57, 59–64, 66, 69, 75, 77, 79, 82–83, 85, 87–88, 90, 93, 95, 97, 102–103, 109–111, 113, 115, 119, 128, 131, 133, 136–38, 141, 145, 148, 150, 152, 159, 161–64, 169, 173, 182, 185, 190, 195, 197, 202, 210, 212, 230, 239, 245, 255, 263, 265, 271, 290–91, 295–96, 312–13, 315, 332, 334, 338, 344, 346, 350, 352, 357, 363, 365, 370–71, 374–75, 379, 398, 409, 436, 453, 462, 476, 485, 487, 492, 501–504, 512, 517, 520, 524, 534, 538–40, 552, 562, 565, 568, 572–73, 575, 578, 586–87
Stählin, G. 171
Stanley, D. M. 20, 109
Stauffer, E. 128, 147
Sweet, J. P. M. 4, 6, 16, 18, 33–34, 36, 48, 66, 70, 74, 79, 105, 112, 114, 121–22, 131, 145, 149, 161, 184, 192, 211, 218–20, 222, 229, 243, 261, 270, 282, 287, 326, 329, 333–34, 345, 352–53, 369, 379, 402, 406–407, 411–12, 415, 417, 428, 432, 437–38, 441, 443, 447–48, 454, 456, 461, 479, 486, 496, 512, 516, 519, 523, 539–40, 548, 553–55, 560–62, 566, 572–73, 575, 580, 583, 585
Swete, H. B. 1–2, 9, 12, 25, 32–35, 45, 50, 54–56, 58, 61–62, 64–68, 73–74, 78–79, 81–84, 88–89, 95, 98–99, 101–103, 114, 116, 120–24, 127, 133, 136, 143, 147, 150, 156, 158, 167, 169, 184, 188, 190, 201, 206, 211–12, 219–20, 238, 258, 260–62, 264–65, 267, 270, 272, 280–81, 283, 286, 288, 306, 335, 338, 349, 351, 354, 364, 366, 371,

374, 386, 406, 408, 414, 420, 422, 430, 433, 435–38, 440, 442–44, 446, 448, 454, 456, 458, 463–64, 476, 486–87, 490–91, 495, 501, 510, 516–17, 524, 532, 534, 539, 542, 547, 550, 552–53, 560, 562, 565–68, 572, 575, 578, 582

Talbert, C. H. 417, 436–37, 483, 561
Thiselton, A. C. 160
Thompson, L. L. 2, 18, 105, 113, 129, 134, 157, 169–70, 191, 266, 271, 311, 335, 343, 364, 402, 431, 524, 542, 575
Thompson, M. M. 34, 182, 190, 487
Topham, M. 13, 553
Trites, A. A. 157

Ulfgard, H. 192
Underhill, E. 565

Vanni, U. 20, 255, 287, 320, 534, 566, 576, 585
Vaux, R. de 112
Vielhauer, Ph. 8

Walker, N. 123
Walker, P. W. L. 93–94, 159, 199, 211, 274, 293, 354, 389, 442, 514, 535, 538, 580
Wall, R. W. 81, 93, 102, 120, 153, 202, 225, 259, 275, 280, 310, 329, 343, 354, 402, 428, 435, 480, 491, 507, 509–510, 515, 517, 555, 572, 583
Water, R. van de 336
Wilcock, M. 16, 20, 91, 156, 179, 198, 211, 233, 264, 275–76, 311, 345–46, 354–55, 402, 407, 415, 433, 437, 440, 466, 496, 508, 522, 549, 562, 572, 577
Wilcox, M. 523, 533
Williams, P. S. 30, 367
Williams, R. 76
Wilson, J. C. 2, 50
Wink, W. 29
Wright, N. T. 509

Zahn, T. 127